ORANGEBURG LIBRARY
3 2828 00109 3430

D1301275

Weiss Ratings' Guide to Banks and Thrifts

ORANGEBURG
LIBRARY

Weiss Ratings'
Guide to Banks and Thrifts

A Quarterly Compilation of Financial Institutions Ratings and Analyses

Summer 2011

GREY HOUSE PUBLISHING

Weiss Ratings
15430 Endeavour Drive
Jupiter, FL 33478
561-627-3300

Copyright © Weiss Ratings corporate headquarters located at 15430 Endeavour Drive, Jupiter, FL, 33478; telephone 561-627-3300. All rights reserved. This publication contains original and creative work and is fully protected by all applicable copyright laws, as well as by laws covering misappropriation, trade secrets and unfair competition. Additionally, Weiss Ratings has added value to the underlying factual material through one or more of the following efforts: unique and original selection; expression; arrangement; coordination; and classification. None of the content of this publication may be reproduced, stored in a retrieval system, redistributed, or transmitted in any form or by any means (electronic, print, mechanical, photocopying, recording or otherwise) without the prior written permission of Weiss Ratings. "Weiss Ratings" is a trademark protected by all applicable common law and statutory laws.

Published by Grey House Publishing, Inc. located at 4919 Route 22, Amenia, NY, 12501; telephone 518-789-8700. Grey House Publishing neither guarantees the accuracy of the data contained herein nor assumes any responsibility for errors, omissions or discrepancies. Grey House Publishing accepts no payment for listing; inclusion in the publication of any organization, agency, institution, publication, service or individual does not imply endorsement of the publisher.

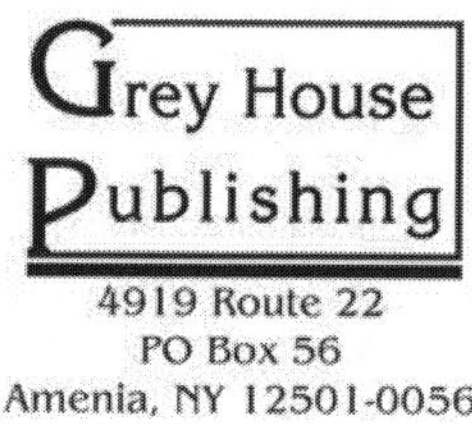

Edition No. 82, Summer 2011

ISBN: 978-1-59237-776-3
ISSN: 2158-5962

Contents

Terms and Conditions

This Document is prepared strictly for the confidential use of our customer(s). It has been provided to you at your specific request. It is not directed to, or intended for distribution to or use by, any person or entity who is a citizen or resident of or located in any locality, state, country or other jurisdiction where such distribution, publication, availability or use would be contrary to law or regulation or which would subject Weiss Ratings or its affiliates to any registration or licensing requirement within such jurisdiction.

No part of the analysts' compensation was, is, or will be, directly or indirectly, related to the specific recommendations or views expressed in this research report.

This Document is not intended for the direct or indirect solicitation of business. Weiss Ratings, LLC and its affiliates disclaims any and all liability to any person or entity for any loss or damage caused, in whole or in part, by any error (negligent or otherwise) or other circumstances involved in, resulting from or relating to the procurement, compilation, analysis, interpretation, editing, transcribing, publishing and/or dissemination or transmittal of any information contained herein.

Weiss Ratings has not taken any steps to ensure that the securities or investment vehicle referred to in this report are suitable for any particular investor. The investment or services contained or referred to in this report may not be suitable for you and it is recommended that you consult an independent investment advisor if you are in doubt about such investments or investment services. Nothing in this report constitutes investment, legal, accounting or tax advice or a representation that any investment or strategy is suitable or appropriate to your individual circumstances or otherwise constitutes a personal recommendation to you.

The ratings and other opinions contained in this Document must be construed solely as statements of opinion from Weiss Ratings LLC., and not statements of fact. Each rating or opinion must be weighed solely as a factor in your choice of an institution and should not be construed as a recommendation to buy, sell or otherwise act with respect to the particular product or company involved.

Past performance should not be taken as an indication or guarantee of future performance, and no representation or warranty, expressed or implied, is made regarding future performance. Information, opinions and estimates contained in this report reflect a judgment at its original date of publication and are subject to change without notice. Weiss Ratings offers a notification service for rating changes on companies you specify. For more information call 1-877-934-7778 or visit www.weissratings.com. The price, value and income from any of the securities or financial instruments mentioned in this report can fall as well as rise.

This Document and the information contained herein is copyrighted by Weiss Ratings, LLC. Any copying, displaying, selling, distributing or otherwise delivering of this information or any part of this Document to any other person, without the express written consent of Weiss Ratings, LLC except by a reviewer or editor who may quote brief passages in connection with a review or a news story, is prohibited.

Date of Data Analyzed: December 31, 2010

Data Source: Call Report and Thrift Financial Report data provided by SNL Financial.

Welcome to Weiss Ratings
Guide to Banks and Thrifts

Most people automatically assume their bank will survive, year after year. However, prudent consumers and professionals realize that in this world of shifting risks, the solvency of financial institutions can't be taken for granted. After all, your bank's failure could have a heavy impact on you in terms of lost time, lost money (in cases of deposits exceeding the federal insurance limit), tied-up deposits, lost credit lines, and the possibility of being shifted to another institution under not-so-friendly terms.

If you are looking for accurate, unbiased ratings and data to help you choose a commercial bank, savings bank, or savings and loan for yourself, your family, your company or your clients, Weiss Ratings' Guide to Banks and Thrifts gives you precisely what you need.

Weiss Ratings' Mission Statement

Weiss Ratings' mission is to empower consumers, professionals, and institutions with high quality advisory information for selecting or monitoring a financial services company or financial investment.

In doing so, Weiss Ratings will adhere to the highest ethical standards by maintaining our independent, unbiased outlook and approach to advising our customers.

Why rely on Weiss Ratings?

Weiss Ratings provides fair, objective ratings to help professionals and consumers alike make educated financial decisions.

At Weiss Ratings, integrity is number one. Weiss Ratings never takes a penny from rated companies for issuing its ratings. And, we publish Weiss Financial Strength Ratings without regard for institutions' preferences. Our analysts review and update Weiss ratings each and every quarter, so you can be sure that the information you receive is accurate and current – providing you with advance warning of financial vulnerability early enough to do something about it.

Other rating agencies focus primarily on a company's current financial solvency and consider only mild economic adversity. Weiss Ratings also considers these issues, but in addition, our analysis covers a company's ability to deal with severe economic adversity in terms of a sharp decline in the value of its investments and a drop in the collectibility of its loans.

Our use of more rigorous standards stems from the viewpoint that a financial institution's obligations to its customers should not depend on favorable business conditions. A bank or thrift must be able to honor its loan and deposit commitments in bad times as well as good.

Weiss's rating scale, from A to F, is easy to understand. Only a few outstanding companies receive an A (Excellent) rating, although there are many to choose from within the B (Good) category. A large group falls into the broad average range which receives C (Fair) ratings. Companies that demonstrate marked vulnerabilities receive either D (Weak) or E (Very Weak) ratings. So, there's no numbering system, star counting, or color-coding to keep track of.

How to Use This Guide

The purpose of the *Guide to Banks and Thrifts* is to provide consumers, businesses, financial institutions, and municipalities with a reliable source of banking industry ratings and analysis on a timely basis. We realize that the financial safety of a bank or thrift is an important factor to consider when establishing a relationship. The ratings and analysis in this Guide can make that evaluation easier when you are considering:

- a checking, merchant banking, or other transaction account
- an investment in a certificate of deposit or savings account
- a line of credit or commercial loan
- counterparty risk

The rating for a particular company indicates our opinion regarding that company's ability to meet its obligations – not only under current economic conditions, but also during a declining economy or in an environment of increased liquidity demands.

To use this Guide most effectively, we recommend you follow the steps outlined below:

Step 1 To ensure you evaluate the correct company, verify the company's exact name as it was given to you. It is also helpful to ascertain the city and state of the company's main office or headquarters since no two banks with the same name can be headquartered in the same city. Many companies have similar names but are not related to one another, so you will want to make sure the company you look up is really the one you are interested in evaluating.

Step 2 Turn to Section I, the Index of Banks and Thrifts, and locate the company you are evaluating. This section contains all federally-insured commercial banks, savings banks, and savings and loans. It is sorted alphabetically by the name of the company and shows the main office city and state following the name for additional verification.
If you have trouble finding a particular institution or determining which is the right one, consider these possible reasons:

- You may have an incorrect or incomplete institution name. There are often several institutions with the same or very similar names. So, make sure you have the exact name and proper spelling, as well as the city in which it is headquartered.
- You may be looking for a *bank holding company*. If so, try to find the exact name of the main bank in the group and look it up under that name.

Step 3 Once you have located your specific company, the first column after the state shows its current Weiss Financial Strength Rating. Turn to *About Weiss Financial Strength Ratings* on page 7 for information about what this rating means. If the rating has changed since the last edition of this Guide, a downgrade will be indicated with a down triangle ▼ to the left of the company name; an upgrade will be indicated with an up triangle ▲.

Step 4 Following the current Weiss Financial Strength Rating are two prior ratings for the company based on year-end data from the two previous years. Use this to discern the longer-term direction of the company's overall financial condition.

Step 5 The remainder of Section I provides insight into the areas our analysts reviewed as the basis for assigning the company's rating. These areas include size, capital adequacy, asset quality, profitability, liquidity, and stability. An index within each of these categories represents a composite evaluation of that particular facet of the company's financial condition. Refer to the table on page 8 for an interpretation of which index values are considered strong, good, fair, or weak. In most cases, lower-rated companies will have a low index value in one or more of the indexes shown. Bear in mind, however, that Weiss Financial Strength Rating is the result of a complex qualitative and quantitative analysis which cannot be reproduced using only the data provided here.

Step 6 If the company you are evaluating is not highly rated and you want to find a bank or thrift with a higher rating, turn to the page in Section II that has your state's name at the top. This section contains Weiss Recommended Companies (rating of A+, A, A- or B+) that have a branch office in your state. If the main office telephone number provided is not a local telephone call or to determine if a branch of the bank or thrift is near you, consult your local telephone Yellow Pages Directory under "Banks," "Savings Banks," or "Savings and Loan Associations." Here you will find a complete list of the institution's branch locations along with their telephone numbers.

Step 7 Once you've identified a Weiss Recommended Company in your local area, you can then refer back to Section I to analyze it.

Step 8 In order to use Weiss Financial Strength Ratings most effectively, we strongly recommend you consult the *Important Warnings and Cautions* listed on page 11. These are more than just "standard disclaimers." They are very important factors you should be aware of before using this Guide. If you have any questions regarding the precise meaning of specific terms used in the Guide, refer to the Glossary beginning on page 373.

Step 9 Make sure you stay up to date with the latest information available since the publication of this Guide. For information on how to set up a rating change notification service, acquire follow-up reports, check ratings online or receive a more in-depth analysis of an individual company, call 1-877-934-7778 or visit www.weissratings.com.

About Weiss Financial Strength Ratings

Weiss Financial Strength Ratings represent a completely independent, unbiased opinion of an institution's financial safety – now, and in the future. The ratings are derived, for the most part, from quarterly financial statements filed with federal regulators. Although we seek to maintain an open line of communication with the companies being rated, we do not grant them the right to influence the ratings or stop their publication.

Weiss Financial Strength Ratings are assigned by our analysts based on a complex analysis of hundreds of factors that are synthesized into five indexes: capitalization, asset quality, profitability, liquidity and stability. These indexes are then used to arrive at a letter grade rating. A good rating requires consistency across all indexes. A weak score on any one index can result in a low rating, as insolvency can be caused by any one of a number of factors, such as inadequate capital, poor underwriting practices, operating losses, or the failure of an affiliated company.

The primary components of Weiss Financial Strength Rating are as follows:

- **Capitalization Index** gauges capital adequacy in terms of each institution's cushion to absorb future operating losses under various potential business and economic scenarios as they may impact the company's net interest margin, securities' values, and the collectibility of its loans.
- **Asset Quality Index** measures the quality of the institution's past underwriting and investment practices, as well as its loss reserve coverage.
- **Profitability Index** measures the soundness of the company's operations and the contribution of profits to the company's financial strength. The profitability index is a composite of five sub-factors: 1) gain or loss on operations; 2) rates of return on assets and equity; 3) management of net interest margin; 4) generation of noninterest-based revenues; and 5) overhead expense management.
- **Liquidity Index** values a company's ability to raise the necessary cash to satisfy creditors and honor depositor withdrawals.
- **Stability Index** integrates a number of sub-factors that affect consistency (or lack thereof) in maintaining financial strength over time. Sub-factors include 1) risk diversification in terms of company size and loan diversification; 2) deterioration of operations as reported in critical asset, liability, income and expense items, such as an increase in loan delinquency rates or a sharp increase in loan originations; 3) years in operation; 4) former problem areas where, despite recent improvement, the company has yet to establish a record of stable performance over a suitable period of time; and 5) relationships with holding companies and affiliates.

Each of these indexes is measured according to the following range of values.

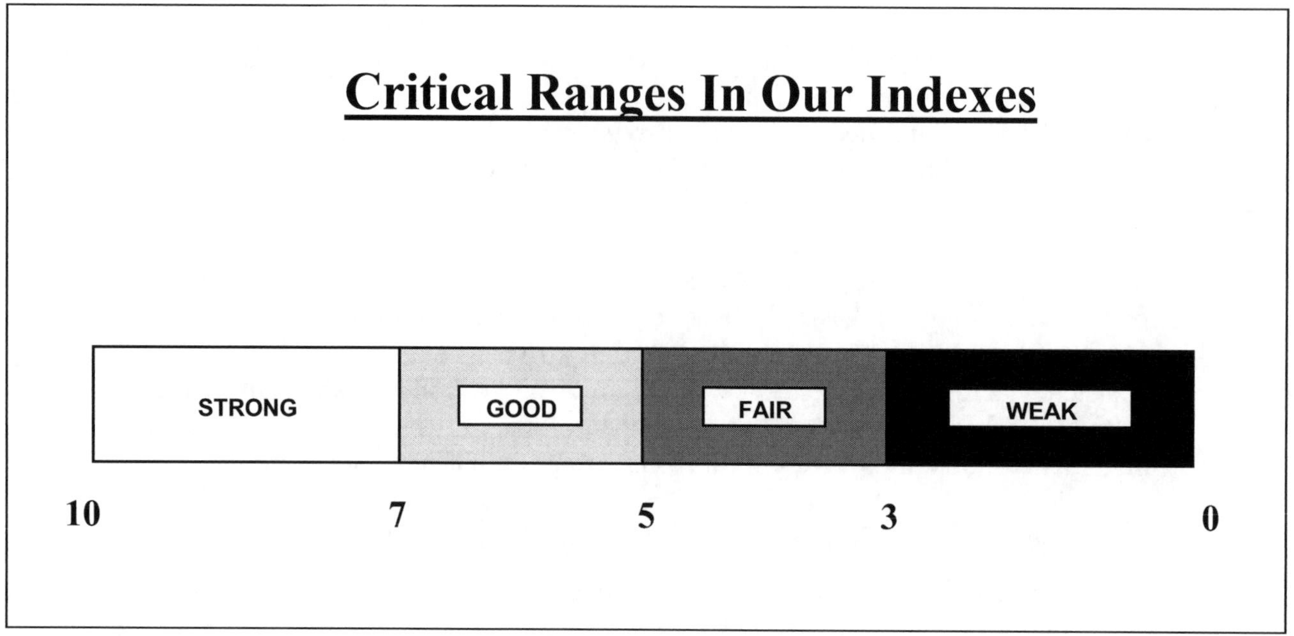

Finally, the indexes are combined to form a composite company rating which is then verified by one of our analysts. The resulting distribution of ratings assigned to all banks and thrifts looks like this:

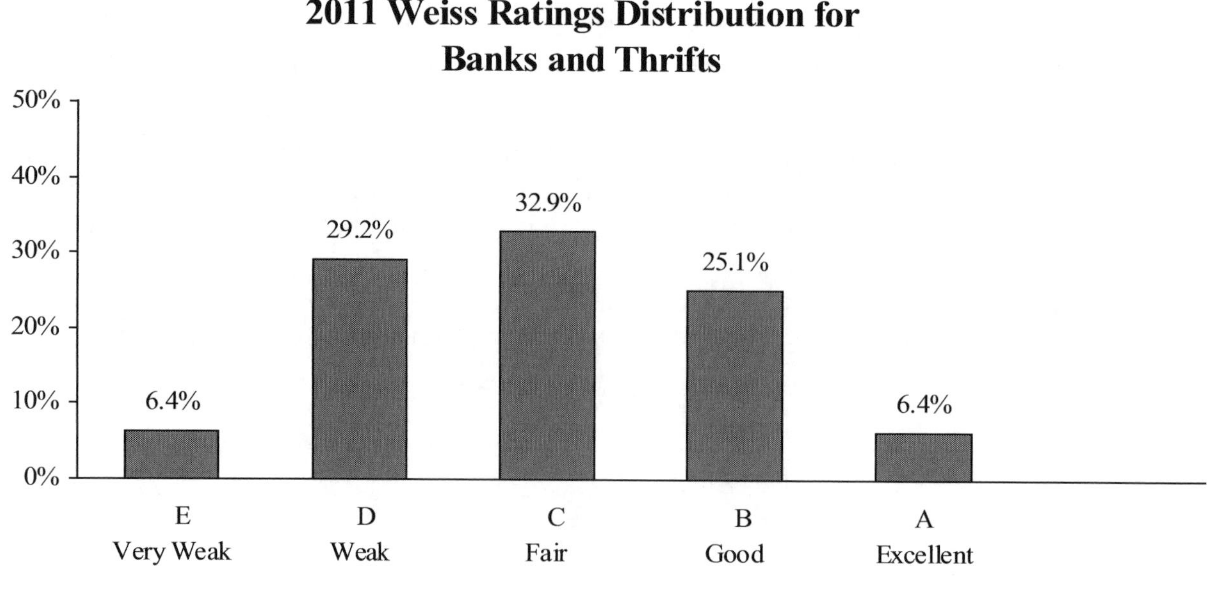

What Our Ratings Mean

A **Excellent.** The institution offers excellent financial security. It has maintained a conservative stance in its business operations as evidenced by its strong equity base, top-notch asset quality, steady earnings, and high liquidity. While the financial position of any institution is subject to change, we believe that this institution has the resources necessary to deal with *severe* economic conditions.

B **Good.** The institution offers good financial security and has the resources to deal with a variety of adverse economic conditions. It comfortably exceeds the minimum levels for all of our rating criteria and is likely to remain healthy for the near future. Nevertheless, in the event of a *severe* recession or major financial crisis, we feel that this assessment should be reviewed to make sure that the institution is still maintaining adequate financial strength.

C **Fair.** The institution offers fair financial security, is currently stable, and will likely remain relatively healthy as long as the economic environment avoids the extremes of inflation or deflation. In a prolonged period of adverse economic or financial conditions, however, we feel this institution may encounter difficulties in maintaining its financial stability.

D **Weak.** The institution currently demonstrates what we consider to be significant weaknesses which could negatively impact depositors or creditors. In an unfavorable economic environment, these weaknesses could be magnified.

E **Very Weak.** The institution currently demonstrates what we consider to be significant weaknesses and has also failed some of the basic tests that we use to identify fiscal stability. Therefore, even in a favorable economic environment, it is our opinion that depositors or creditors could incur significant risks.

F **Failed.** The institution has been placed under the custodianship of regulatory authorities. This implies that it will be either liquidated or taken over by another financial institution.

\+ **The plus sign** is an indication that the institution is at the upper end of the letter grade rating.

\- **The minus sign** is an indication that the institution is at the lower end of the letter grade rating.

U **Unrated Institutions.** The institution is unrated due to insufficient data at the time its rating was updated.

Peer Comparison of Bank/Thrift Financial Strength Ratings

Weiss Ratings	Veribanc	Bauer Financial	IDC Financial	Bankrate.com	Lace Financial
A+, A, A-	Green, Three Stars w/ Blue Ribbon recognition	5 stars, 4 stars	201-300	1, Five stars	A+, A
B+, B, B-	Green, Three Stars w/out Blue Ribbon recognition	3 ½ stars	166-200	2, Four stars	B+
C+, C, C-	Green Two Stars, Yellow Two Stars	3 stars	126-165	3, Three stars	B, C+
D+, D, D-	Green one star, Yellow one star, Green no stars	2 stars	76-125	4, Two stars	C, D
E+, E, E-	Yellow no stars, Red no stars	1 star	1-75	5, One star	E

Important Warnings and Cautions

1. **A rating alone cannot tell the whole story.** Please read the explanatory information contained here, in the section introductions and in the appendix. It is provided in order to give you an understanding of our rating philosophy as well as to paint a more complete picture of how we arrive at our opinion of a company's strengths and weaknesses. In addition, please remember that our financial strength rating is not an end-all measure of an institution's safety. Rather, it should be used as a "flag" of possible troubles, suggesting a need for further research.

2. **Financial strength ratings shown in this directory were current as of the publication date.** In the meantime, the rating may have been updated based on more recent data. Weiss Ratings offers a notification service for ratings changes on companies that you specifiy. For more information call 1-877-934-7778 or visit www.weissratings.com.

3. **When deciding to do business with a financial institution, your decision should be based on a wide variety of factors in addition to Weiss Financial Strength Rating**. These include the institution's pricing of its deposit instruments and loans, the fees you will be charged, the degree to which it can help you meet your long-term planning needs, how these costs/benefits may change over the years, and what other choices are available to you given your current location and financial circumstances.

4. **Weiss Financial Strength Ratings represent our opinion of a company's insolvency risk.** As such, a high rating means we feel that the company has less chance of running into financial difficulties. A high rating is not a guarantee of solvency nor is a low rating a prediction of insolvency. Weiss Financial Strength Ratings are not deemed to be a recommendation concerning the purchase or sale of the securities of any bank or thrift that is publicly owned.

5. **All firms that have the same Weiss Financial Strength Rating should be considered to be essentially equal in safety.** This is true regardless of any differences in the underlying numbers which might appear to indicate greater strengths. Weiss Financial Strength Rating already takes into account a number of lesser factors which, due to space limitations, cannot be included in this publication.

6. **A good rating requires consistency.** If a company is excellent on four indicators and fair on one, the company may receive a fair rating. This requirement is necessary due to the fact that fiscal problems can arise from any *one* of several causes including poor underwriting, inadequate capital resources, or operating losses.

7. **Our rating standards are more conservative than those used by other agencies.** We believe that no one can predict with certainty the economic environment of the near or long-term future. Rather, we assume that various scenarios – from the extremes of double-digit inflation to a severe recession – are within the range of reasonable possibilities over the next one or two decades. To achieve a top rating according to our standards, a company must be adequately prepared for the worst-case reasonable scenario, without impairing its current operations.

8. **We are an independent rating agency and do not depend on the cooperation of the companies we rate**. Our data are derived, for the most part, from quarterly financial statements filed with federal regulators. Although we seek to maintain an open line of communication with the companies being rated, we do not grant them the right to influence the ratings or stop their publication. This policy stems from the fact that this Guide is designed for the protection of our customers.

9. **Inaccuracies in the data issued by the federal regulators could negatively impact the quality of a company's Financial Strength Rating.** While we attempt to find and correct as many data errors as possible, some data errors inevitably slip through. We have no method of intercepting fraudulent or falsified data and must take for granted that all information is reported honestly to the federal regulatory agencies.

10. **Institutions that operate exclusively or primarily as a trust company may have skewed financial information.** Due to the nature of their business, these companies often record high profit levels compared to other more "traditional" banks and thrifts. Trust companies can usually be recognized by the initials "TC" or "& TC" in their names.

11. **This Guide does not cover nonbank affiliates of banking companies.** Although some nonbank companies may be affiliated with the banks and thrifts cited in this Guide, the firms are separate corporations whose financial strength is only partially dependent on the strength of their affiliates.

12. **There are many companies with the same or similar sounding names, despite no affiliation whatsoever.** Therefore, it is important that you have the exact name, city, and state of the institution's headquarters before you begin to research the company in this Guide.

13. **Affiliated companies do not automatically receive the same rating.** We recognize that a troubled institution may expect financial support from its parent or affiliates. Weiss Financial Strength Ratings reflect our opinion of the measure of support that may become available to a subsidiary bank, if the subsidiary were to experience serious financial difficulties. In the case of a strong parent and a weaker subsidiary, the affiliate relationship will generally result in a higher rating for the subsidiary than it would have on a stand-alone basis. Seldom, however, would the rating be brought up to the level of the parent.

    This treatment is appropriate because we do not assume the parent would have either the resources or the will to "bail out" a troubled subsidiary during a severe economic crisis. Even when there is a binding legal obligation for a parent corporation to honor the obligations of its subsidiary banks, the possibility exists that the subsidiary could be sold and lose its parental support. Therefore, it is quite common for one affiliate to have a higher rating than another. This is another reason why it is especially important that you have the precise name of the company you are evaluating.

14. **This publication does not include foreign banking companies, or their U.S. branches.** Therefore, our evaluation of foreign banking companies is limited to those U.S. chartered domestic banks owned by foreign banking companies. In most cases, the U.S. operations of a foreign banking company are relatively small in relation to the overall size of the company, so you may want to consult other sources as well. In any case, do not be confused by a domestic bank with a name which is the same as – or similar to – that of a foreign banking company. Even if there is an affiliation between the two, we have evaluated the U.S. institution based on its own merits.

Section I

Index of Banks and Thrifts

An analysis of all rated

U.S. Commercial Banks, Savings Banks,

and Savings and Loans.

Institutions are listed in alphabetical order.

Section I Contents

This section contains Weiss Financial Strength Ratings, key rating factors, and summary financial data for all U.S. federally-insured commercial banks, savings banks, and savings and loans. Companies are sorted in alphabetical order, first by company name, then by city and state.

Left Pages

1. **Institution Name** — The name under which the institution was chartered. If you cannot find the institution you are interested in, or if you have any doubts regarding the precise name, verify the information with the bank or thrift itself before proceeding. Also, determine the city and state in which the institution is headquartered for confirmation. (See columns 2 and 3.)

2. **City** — The city in which the institution's headquarters or main office is located. With the adoption of intrastate and interstate branching laws, many institutions operating in your area may actually be headquartered elsewhere. So, don't be surprised if the location cited is not in your particular city.

   Also use this column to confirm that you have located the correct institution. It is possible for two unrelated companies to have the same name if they are headquartered in different cities.

3. **State** — The state in which the institution's headquarters or main office is located. With the adoption of interstate branching laws, some institutions operating in your area may actually be headquartered in another state.

4. **Financial Strength Rating** — Weiss rating assigned to the institution at the time of publication. Our ratings are designed to distinguish levels of insolvency risk and are measured on a scale from A to F based upon a wide range of factors. Please see page 9 for specific descriptions of each letter grade.

   Highly rated companies are, in our opinion, less likely to experience financial difficulties than lower rated firms. See *About Weiss Financial Strength Ratings* on page 7 for more information. Also, please be sure to consider the warnings beginning on page 11 regarding the ratings' limitations and the underlying assumptions.

5. **Prior Year Financial Strength Rating** — Weiss rating assigned to the institution based on data from December 31 of the previous year. Compare this rating to the company's current rating to identify any recent changes.

6. **Financial Strength Rating Two Years Prior** — Weiss rating assigned to the institution based on data from December 31 two years ago. Compare this rating to the ratings in the prior columns to identify longer term trends in the company's financial condition.

7. **Total Assets** — The total of all assets listed on the institution's balance sheet, in millions of dollars. This figure primarily consists of loans, investments (such as municipal and treasury bonds), and fixed assets (such as buildings and other real estate).

Overall size is an important factor which affects the company's ability to diversify risk and avoid vulnerability to a single borrower, industry, or geographic area. Larger institutions are usually, although not always, more diversified and thus less susceptible to a downturn in a particular area. Nevertheless, do not be misled by the general public perception that "bigger is better." Larger institutions are known for their inability to quickly adapt to changes in the marketplace and typically underperform their smaller brethren.

8. One Year Asset Growth

The percentage change in total assets over the previous 12 months. Moderate growth is generally a positive since it can reflect the maintenance or expansion of the company's market share, leading to the generation of additional revenues. Excessive growth, however, is generally a sign of trouble as it can indicate a loosening of underwriting practices in order to attract new business.

9. Commercial Loans/ Total Assets

The percentage of the institution's asset base invested in loans to businesses. Commercial loans are the traditional bread and butter of commercial banks, although many thrifts have increased their business lending in recent years.

10. Consumer Loans/ Total Assets

The percentage of the institution's asset base invested in loans to consumers, primarily credit cards. Consumer lending has grown rapidly in recent years due to the high interest rates and fees institutions are able to charge. On the down side, consumer loans usually experience higher delinquency and default rates than other loans, negatively impacting earnings down the road.

11. Home Mortgage Loans/ Total Assets

The percentage of the institution's asset base invested in residential mortgage loans to consumers, excluding home equity loans. Savings banks and savings and loans have traditionally dominated mortgage lending. Indeed, the S&L charter still requires thrifts to invest a minimum percentage of their assets in mortgages and mortgage-backed securities.

This type of loan typically experiences lower default rates. However, the length of the loan's term can be a subject for concern during periods of rising interest rates.

12. Securities/ Total Assets

The percentage of the institution's asset base invested in securities, including U.S. Treasury securities, mortgage-backed securities, and municipal bonds. This does not include securities the institution may be holding on behalf of individual customers.

Although securities are similar to loans in that they represent obligations to pay a debt at some point in the future, they are a more liquid investment than loans and usually present less risk of default. In addition, mortgage-backed securities can present less credit risk than holding mortgage loans themselves due to the diversification of the underlying mortgages.

13. Capitalization Index

An index that measures the adequacy of the institution's capital resources to deal with potentially adverse business and economic situations that could arise. It is based on an evaluation of the company's degree of leverage compared to total assets as well as risk-adjusted assets. See the graph on page 8 for a description of the different critical levels presented in this index.

14. Leverage Ratio

A regulatory ratio defined by the federal banking and thrift regulators as core (tier 1) capital divided by tangible assets. This ratio answers the question: How much does the institution have in stockholders' equity for every dollar of assets? Thus, the Leverage Ratio represents the amount of actual "capital cushion" the institution has to fall back on in times of trouble. We feel that this is the single most important ratio in determining financial strength because it provides the best measure of an institution's ability to withstand losses.

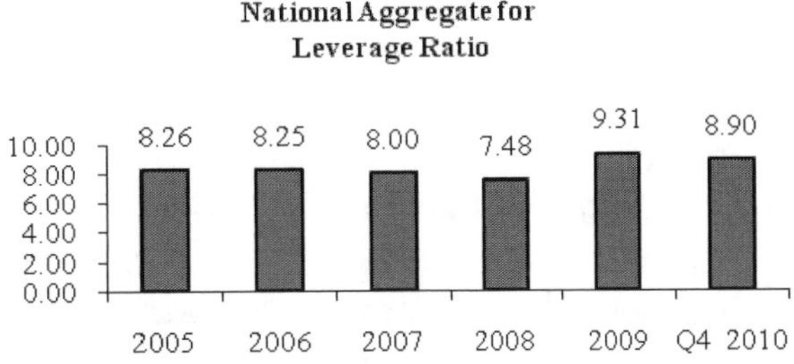

15. Risk-Based Capital Ratio

A regulatory ratio defined by the federal banking and thrift regulators as total (tier 1 + tier 2) capital divided by risk-weighted assets. This ratio addresses the issue that not all assets present the same level of credit risk to an institution. As such, all assets and certain off-balance sheet commitments are assigned to risk categories based on the level of credit risk they pose and then weighted accordingly to arrive at risk-weighted assets.

For instance, assets with virtually no risk, such as cash and U.S. Treasury securities, are risk-weighted at 0% and therefore, not included in the calculation. Assets with low risk, for example, high quality mortgage-backed securities and state and municipal bonds, are partially weighted at 20%.

Those assets possessing moderate risk, such as residential mortgages and state and local revenue bonds, are partially weighted at 50%. And finally, assets considered to possess "normal" or "high" risk, including certain off-balance sheet commitments such as unfunded loans, are risk-weighted at 100%. The summation of these categories of risk-weighted assets results in the figure used in the denominator of this ratio.

Please be aware that not all banks and savings banks are required to report risk-weighted assets as defined by the federal regulators. Consequently, we have estimated this figure when necessary based on estimates used by the regulators themselves.

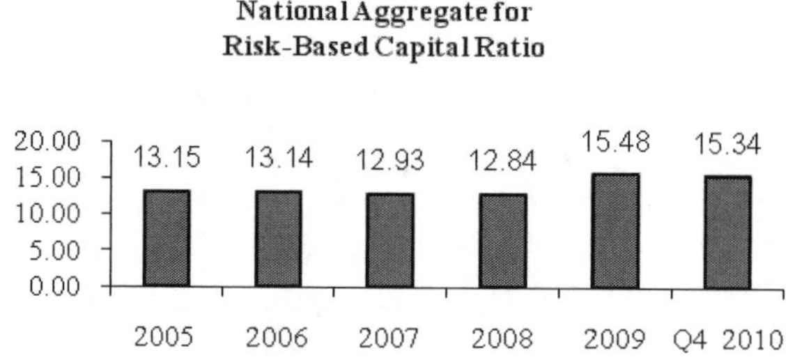

Right Pages

1. Asset Quality Index An index that measures the quality of the institution's past underwriting and investment practices, as well as its loss reserve coverage. See the graph on page 8 for a description of the different critical levels presented in this index.

2. Nonperforming Loans/ Total Loans The percentage of the institution's loan portfolio which is either past due on its payments by 90 days or more, or no longer accruing interest due to doubtful collectibility. This ratio is affected primarily by the quality of the institution's underwriting practices and the prosperity of the local economies where it is doing business. While only a portion of these loans will actually end up in default, a high ratio here will have several negative consequences including increased loan loss provisions, increased loan collection expenses, and decreased interest revenues.

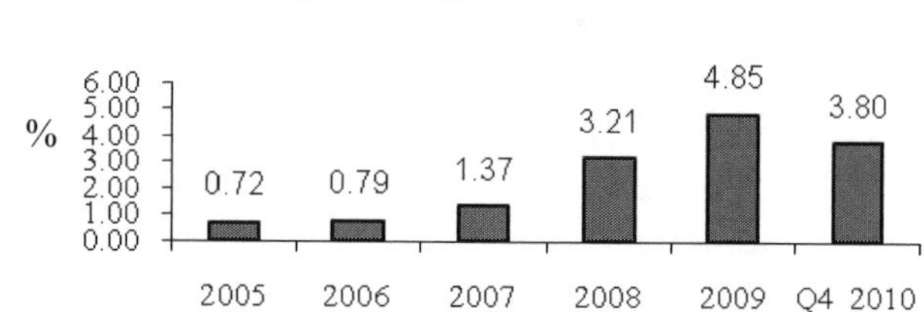

3. Nonperforming Loans/ Capital

The percentage of past due 90 days and nonaccruing loans to the company's core (tier 1) capital plus reserve for loan losses. This ratio answers the question: If all of the bank's significantly past due and nonaccruing loans were to go into default, how much would that eat into capital? A large percentage of nonperforming loans signal imprudent lending practices which are a direct threat to the equity of the institution.

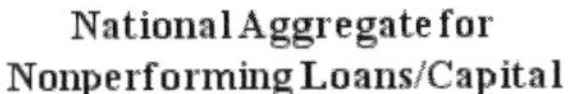

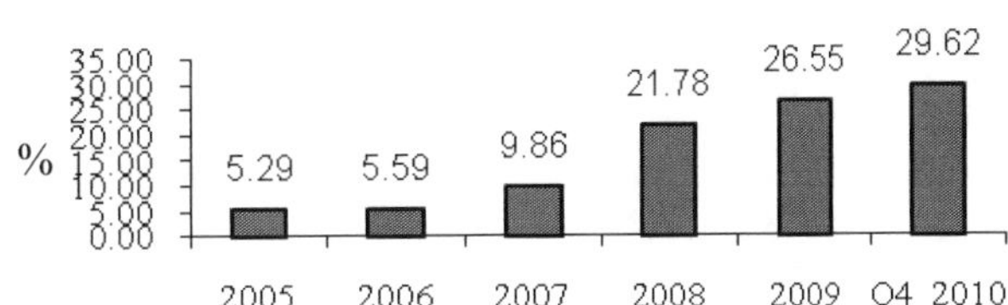

4. Net Charge-offs/ Average Loans

The ratio of foreclosed loans written off the institution's books since the beginning of the year (less previous write-offs that were recovered) as a percentage of average loans for the year. This ratio answers the question: What percentage of the bank's past loans have actually become uncollectible? Past loan charge-off experience is often a very good indication of what can be expected in the future, and high loan charge-off levels are usually an indication of poor underwriting practices.

5. Profitability Index

An index that measures the soundness of the institution's operations and the contribution of profits to the company's financial strength. It is based on five sub-factors: 1) gain or loss on operations; 2) rates of return on assets and equity; 3) management of net interest margin; 4) generation of noninterest-based revenues; and 5) overhead expense management. See the graph on page 8 for a description of the different critical levels presented in this index.

6. Net Income

The year-to-date net profit or loss recorded by the institution, in millions of dollars. This figure includes the company's operating profit (income from lending, investing, and fees less interest and overhead expenses) as well as nonoperating items such as capital gains on the sale of securities, income taxes, and extraordinary items.

7. Return on Assets

The ratio of net income for the year (year-to-date quarterly figures are converted to a 12-month equivalent) as a percentage of average assets for the year. This ratio, known as ROA, is the most commonly used benchmark for bank and thrift profitability since it measures the company's return on investment in a format that is easily comparable with other companies.

Historically speaking, a ratio of 1.0% or greater has been considered good performance. However, this ratio will fluctuate with the prevailing economic times. Also, larger banks tend to have a lower ratio.

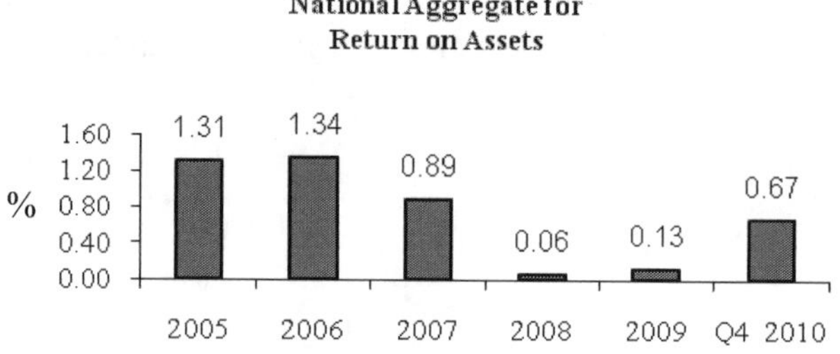

8. Return on Equity

The ratio of net income for the year (year-to-date quarterly figures are converted to a 12-month equivalent) as a percentage of average equity for the year. This ratio, known as ROE, is commonly used by a company's shareholders as a measure of their return on investment. It is not always a good measure of profitability, however, because inadequate equity levels at some institutions can result in unjustly high ROE's.

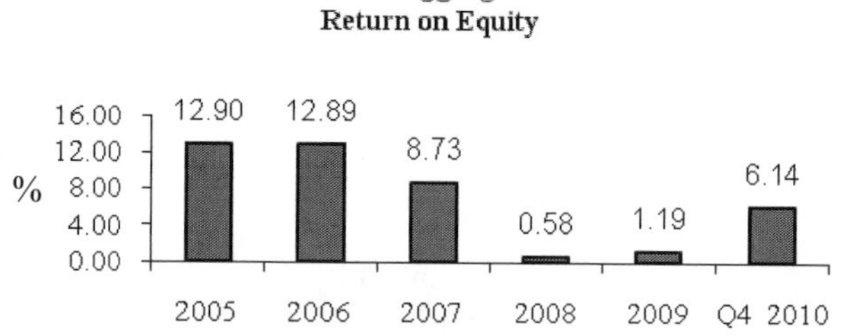

9. Net Interest Spread

The difference between the institution's interest income and interest expense for the year (year-to-date quarterly figures are converted to a 12-month equivalent) as a percentage of its average revenue-generating assets. Since the margin between interest earned and interest paid is generally where the company generates the majority of its income, this figure provides insight into the company's ability to effectively manage interest spreads.

A low Net Interest Spread can be the result of poor loan and deposit pricing, high levels of non-accruing loans, or poor asset/liability management.

10. Overhead Efficiency Ratio

Total overhead expenses as a percentage of total revenues net of interest expense. This is a common measure for evaluating an institution's ability to operate efficiently while keeping a handle on overhead expenses like salaries, rent, and other office expenses. A high ratio suggests that the company's overhead expenses are too high in relation to the amount of revenue they are generating and/or supporting. Conversely, a low ratio means good management of overhead expenses which usually results in a strong Return on Assets as well.

11. Liquidity Index

An index that measures the institution's ability to raise the necessary cash to satisfy creditors and honor depositor withdrawals. It is based on an evaluation of the company's short-term liquidity position, including its existing reliance on less stable deposit sources. See the graph on page 8 for a description of the different critical levels presented in this index.

12. Liquidity Ratio

The ratio of short-term liquid assets to deposits and short-term borrowings. This ratio answers the question: How many cents can the institution easily raise in cash to cover each dollar on deposit plus pay off its short-term debts? Due to the nature of the business, it is rare (and not expected) for an established bank to achieve 100% on this ratio. Nevertheless, it serves as a good measure of an institution's liquidity in relation to the rest of the banking industry.

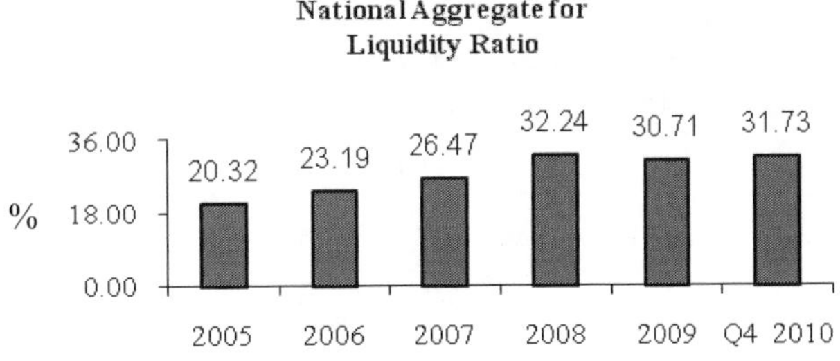

13. Hot Money Ratio

The percentage of the institution's deposit base that is being funded by jumbo CDs and brokered deposits. Jumbo CDs (high-yield certificates of deposit with principal amounts of at least $100,000) and brokered deposits (pooled funds sold by brokers seeking the highest interest rate available) are generally considered less stable (and more costly) and thus less desirable as a source of funds.

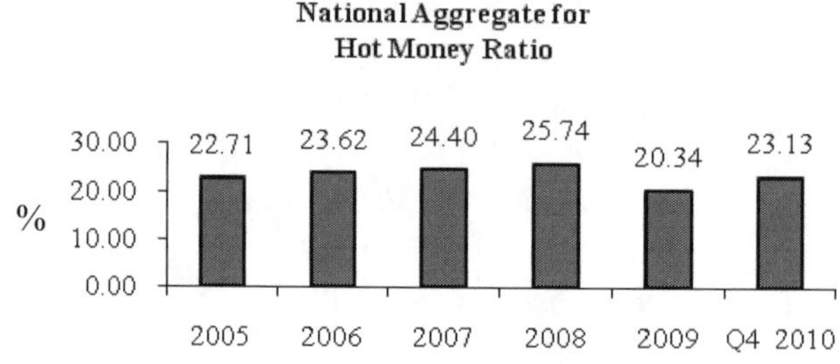

14. Stability Index

An index that integrates a number of factors such as 1) risk diversification in terms of company size and loan diversification; 2) deterioration of operations as reported in critical asset, liability, income and expense items, such as an increase in loan delinquency rates or a sharp increase in loan originations; 3) years in operation; 4) former problem areas where, despite recent improvement, the company has yet to establish a record of stable performance over a suitable period of time; and 5) relationships with holding companies and affiliates. See the graph on page 8 for a description of the different critical levels presented in this index.

ORANGEBURG LIBRARY
20 S. Greenbush Rd.
Orangeburg, NY 10962

Name	City	State	Rating	2008 Rating	2007 Rating	Total Assets ($Mil)	One Year Asset Growth	Asset Mix (As a % of Total Assets) Comm-ercial Loans	Cons-umer Loans	Home Mort-gages	Secur-ities	Capital-ization Index	Leverage Ratio	Risk-based Capital Ratio
1ST ADVANTAGE BANK	SAINT PETERS	MO	E-	D-	C-	93	-16.91	7.2	0.0	9.4	6.8	0.1	3.7	6.1
1ST BANK	SIDNEY	MT	A-	A-	A-	115	11.71	8.9	3.0	3.9	0.9	7.2	9.1	18.7
1ST BANK	EVANSTON	WY	C	C	B	716	9.95	6.1	3.3	8.3	51.6	7.6	9.4	18.9
▼ 1ST BANK & TRUST	BROKEN BOW	OK	B+	A	A	108	-1.61	4.7	10.4	19.0	37.4	6.0	8.0	14.3
1ST BANK OF SEA ISLE CITY	SEA ISLE CITY	NJ	C	C	C+	236	-2.40	0.6	0.4	46.4	5.1	5.6	7.6	12.0
▼ 1ST BANK OF TROY	TROY	KS	D+	C+	C+	23	10.88	4.7	12.3	8.4	30.3	7.1	9.1	14.2
1ST BANK OKLAHOMA	CLAREMORE	OK	B	B	B-	265	9.46	5.6	2.4	13.3	49.3	7.7	9.4	19.1
▼ 1ST BANK YUMA	YUMA	AZ	D+	C	B	134	8.02	13.3	0.6	4.2	12.7	7.4	9.7	12.8
1ST CAMERON STATE BK	CAMERON	MO	C	C	NR	45	-0.22	2.1	2.8	50.0	16.4	8.4	10.0	18.8
▲ 1ST CAPITAL BANK	MONTEREY	CA	C	C-	C-	227	17.96	28.0	0.8	5.4	6.4	10.0	13.9	17.3
▼ 1ST CENTURY BANK NA	LOS ANGELES	CA	D	D	D+	308	13.30	14.8	1.3	8.2	19.0	10.0	12.9	20.2
▼ 1ST COLONIAL NATIONAL BK	COLLINGSWOOD	NJ	D+	C-	C	273	-1.41	7.2	1.4	21.9	29.3	6.0	8.0	13.5
1ST COMMERCE BANK	NORTH LAS VEGAS	NV	E-	E	D+	40	1.62	9.7	0.1	0.0	0.0	0.0	2.5	5.2
1ST COMMONWEALTH BANK	ARLINGTON	VA	D	C	NR	52	-15.54	7.1	0.2	36.3	0.0	10.0	11.8	23.4
1ST COMMUNITY BANK	SHERRARD	IL	C	C+	C+	55	7.96	6.8	5.4	11.9	24.4	6.8	8.8	12.9
1ST CONSTITUTION BANK	CRANBURY	NJ	B-	B	A-	644	-4.80	31.5	0.1	6.6	25.7	7.8	9.5	13.9
1ST ENTERPRISE BANK	LOS ANGELES	CA	C-	C	C	502	30.86	15.0	0.7	2.4	47.4	6.1	8.1	13.4
1ST EQUITY BANK	SKOKIE	IL	B-	B-	A	118	3.20	10.5	0.3	19.1	0.0	10.0	12.6	17.2
1ST EQUITY BANK	BUFFALO GROVE	IL	C+	C-	B	55	0.70	6.6	0.0	19.9	0.0	10.0	15.6	26.5
1ST FINANCIAL BANK USA	DAKOTA DUNES	SD	A-	A-	B+	482	-9.47	0.4	12.7	0.1	45.5	10.0	20.0	38.2
1ST MANATEE BANK	PARRISH	FL	D-	C	C	83	35.31	15.2	0.4	23.7	12.2	6.7	8.7	14.0
1ST NATIONAL BK	LEBANON	OH	C	C-	C-	113	4.54	2.7	1.4	27.0	10.7	10.0	11.4	17.0
1ST NATIONAL BK OF SOUTH	HOMESTEAD	FL	D-	D-	D+	307	8.79	0.9	0.6	17.0	22.7	7.2	9.1	15.4
1ST NATIONAL COMMUNITY	EAST LIVERPOOL	OH	C	C-	C-	121	2.59	5.1	9.6	15.2	34.4	7.2	9.1	17.9
1ST REGENTS BANK	ANDOVER	MN	E-	E-	D-	76	-16.39	21.4	0.6	4.9	13.2	0.3	3.8	6.6
1ST SECURITY BANK OF WA	MOUNTLAKE TERRACE	WA	D-	E+	D+	292	3.72	10.8	46.0	5.1	2.6	5.1	9.1	11.1
1ST SOURCE BANK	SOUTH BEND	IN	B-	B-	B+	4,432	-2.01	36.4	1.3	7.7	21.8	9.0	10.3	15.2
1ST STATE BK	SAGINAW	MI	C-	D+	D+	160	4.07	26.0	1.9	6.8	2.7	6.9	9.2	12.4
1ST STATE BK OF MASON CIT	MASON CITY	IL	B-	B-	B-	25	5.80	2.8	14.2	17.2	30.3	10.0	11.9	22.6
1ST SUMMIT BANK	JOHNSTOWN	PA	B-	B-	B-	668	10.86	6.9	4.1	22.3	39.8	5.1	7.1	13.7
1ST TRUST BANK INC	HAZARD	KY	C	C	C-	124	13.45	26.7	4.3	10.2	13.7	6.4	8.4	12.4
1ST UNITED BANK	BOCA RATON	FL	D+	C-	D	1,263	24.96	9.8	1.1	13.9	8.1	8.4	9.9	20.3
1ST UNITED BANK	FARIBAULT	MN	C+	C	C+	128	-2.15	10.3	2.1	12.5	32.0	6.4	8.4	13.1
21ST CENTURY BANK	LORETTO	MN	C+	C-	D+	362	-6.05	10.8	0.4	8.0	9.2	10.0	12.5	16.2
▲ 5 STAR BANK	COLORADO SPRINGS	CO	B	C-	C-	181	0.99	1.9	0.1	6.0	43.1	10.0	20.5	39.9
A J SMITH FSB	MIDLOTHIAN	IL	C-	D+	C-	250	-0.18	0.0	0.1	38.4	38.5	7.8	9.5	22.1
AB&T NATIONAL BK	ALBANY	GA	D-	E	D-	147	-6.30	7.0	2.5	18.2	19.7	5.9	7.9	12.6
▼ ABACUS FSB	NEW YORK	NY	B+	A-	B-	221	-5.24	0.6	0.2	19.0	38.3	10.0	18.5	33.4
ABBEVILLE B&L ST CHARTERE	ABBEVILLE	LA	B+	B+	A-	41	12.90	0.0	0.5	48.6	2.7	10.0	25.6	34.4
ABBEVILLE SAVINGS & LOAN	ABBEVILLE	SC	D-	D+	D+	82	-6.38	0.1	1.9	38.9	35.6	6.0	8.0	16.7
ABBYBANK	ABBOTSFORD	WI	C	C	B	293	6.84	3.1	1.4	15.1	13.8	7.1	9.0	13.3
ABINGTON BANK	ABINGTON	MA	C-	D+	C-	95	1.55	2.2	0.4	50.8	14.9	7.2	9.1	14.7
ABINGTON SB	JENKINTOWN	PA	C	C-	B-	1,247	0.73	1.3	0.0	31.5	30.2	10.0	13.8	23.9
ACACIA FSB	FALLS CHURCH	VA	D+	D	D+	1,170	-15.70	2.3	0.1	71.3	9.8	9.5	10.7	20.0
ACADEMY BANK NA	COLORADO SPRINGS	CO	D-	D-	C-	335	-31.63	4.5	1.4	8.3	5.7	10.0	11.8	27.6
ACADIA TRUST NA	PORTLAND	ME	U	U	U	14	4.55	0.0	0.0	0.0	0.0	10.0	86.3	227.5
ACB BANK	CHEROKEE	OK	D	D-	D	69	4.07	13.0	3.3	6.5	24.5	6.1	8.1	12.5
▼ ACCESS 1ST CAPITAL BANK	DENTON	TX	E-	D+	C	109	-3.61	10.7	2.7	13.6	4.6	2.9	6.2	9.9
▲ ACCESS BANK	OMAHA	NE	C	C	C	105	26.43	28.9	0.4	2.2	19.5	10.0	14.6	19.1
ACCESS NATIONAL BK	RESTON	VA	B	B	B	831	24.70	11.5	0.4	23.3	15.0	7.3	9.2	14.9
ACKLEY STATE BK	ACKLEY	IA	C+	C+	B-	128	0.69	5.6	1.4	7.8	22.0	7.0	9.0	13.4
ACNB BANK	GETTYSBURG	PA	B-	C+	B-	953	0.70	3.5	1.5	31.2	21.1	6.2	8.2	13.3
ADAMS BANK & TRUST	OGALLALA	NE	C-	C-	C+	513	3.27	14.1	2.9	12.6	0.5	8.9	11.1	14.1
ADAMS CO-OP BANK	ADAMS	MA	D-	D-	D-	192	-2.51	3.9	5.9	58.6	9.7	7.0	9.0	16.1
ADAMS COUNTY BANK	KENESAW	NE	B-	B-	B-	91	2.47	4.1	2.0	8.0	8.0	6.0	8.8	11.7
▼ ADAMS COUNTY BUILDING & L	WEST UNION	OH	D+	C-	C-	26	8.44	0.0	1.6	39.1	2.3	10.0	15.1	33.0
▼ ADAMS DAIRY BANK	BLUE SPRINGS	MO	D	C	C	52	16.65	2.5	1.5	25.1	2.9	10.0	13.9	20.2
▲ ADAMS NATIONAL BK	WASHINGTON	DC	D+	E	D	284	-2.01	5.7	0.1	3.9	20.6	7.1	9.1	16.1
ADAMS STATE BK	ADAMS	NE	B+	B	A-	37	1.90	2.9	4.9	15.2	38.2	10.0	19.7	28.6
ADIRONDACK BANK	UTICA	NY	C	C	C-	529	6.34	14.6	2.7	19.2	34.9	4.9	6.9	14.8

Arrows denote recent upgrades ▲ or downgrades ▼

Asset Quality Index	Non-Performing Loans as a % of Total Loans	Non-Performing Loans as a % of Capital	Net Charge-offs Avg Loans	Profitability Index	Net Income ($Mil)	Return on Assets (R.O.A.)	Return on Equity (R.O.E.)	Net Interest Spread	Overhead Efficiency Ratio	Liquidity Index	Liquidity Ratio	Hot Money Ratio	Stability Index
0.0	15.33	172.2	4.54	**0.0**	-3.7	-3.58	-63.44	2.99	132.9	**0.8**	17.6	43.8	**2.3**
7.7	0.00	0.0	0.02	**5.9**	1.5	1.41	13.33	3.41	62.3	**5.3**	49.7	10.9	**7.6**
3.7	1.30	4.8	0.92	**5.2**	5.7	0.88	5.38	4.28	59.9	**2.6**	29.5	18.6	**6.1**
7.0	0.41	2.3	0.69	**9.8**	2.5	2.29	19.21	5.21	54.9	**3.8**	35.2	14.3	**7.2**
5.4	0.81	8.0	0.00	**2.9**	0.9	0.40	5.36	3.22	72.4	**2.3**	14.1	17.2	**4.0**
6.3	0.00	0.0	1.89	**3.2**	0.1	0.36	3.65	4.04	76.5	**4.4**	37.6	9.6	**3.0**
6.7	0.95	4.1	0.74	**5.3**	3.1	1.25	12.46	3.62	51.1	**3.1**	55.9	30.9	**5.8**
1.5	1.33	9.3	0.91	**4.0**	0.5	0.40	3.66	5.15	71.9	**1.5**	23.9	26.7	**5.8**
9.3	0.00	0.0	0.00	**3.2**	0.2	0.40	3.97	3.93	82.7	**1.6**	10.9	21.2	**4.5**
8.3	0.00	0.0	0.00	**2.4**	1.0	0.51	3.62	4.13	77.7	**1.7**	17.7	22.8	**4.1**
3.7	3.97	15.6	1.72	**0.0**	-1.7	-0.60	-3.92	3.68	90.3	**1.9**	25.8	22.2	**4.7**
3.6	2.82	19.4	1.02	**1.2**	0.3	0.11	1.41	3.34	70.3	**1.6**	7.8	20.4	**4.3**
0.0	18.84	291.5	11.99	**0.0**	-3.3	-7.60	-188.08	2.53	220.1	**1.2**	31.6	66.5	**1.6**
8.9	0.00	0.0	0.00	**0.0**	-2.0	-3.26	-27.56	1.39	150.0	**3.2**	43.3	19.6	**0.0**
4.9	0.78	5.2	0.24	**3.8**	0.5	0.86	9.19	3.36	72.7	**1.5**	32.3	36.2	**5.5**
4.0	2.02	12.5	0.26	**3.9**	4.0	0.60	5.41	3.59	70.6	**2.9**	25.6	15.6	**7.4**
6.7	0.00	0.0	0.00	**2.3**	1.7	0.39	4.24	3.27	77.4	**7.0**	55.0	1.8	**3.1**
2.7	1.29	8.2	0.72	**3.6**	0.9	0.77	5.92	3.57	59.3	**0.8**	16.4	36.8	**5.8**
6.6	1.06	5.0	0.49	**2.5**	0.2	0.39	2.47	3.15	71.1	**0.9**	25.5	51.4	**6.4**
7.5	2.84	1.9	8.79	**8.5**	11.2	2.20	11.39	19.59	81.9	**3.8**	74.9	28.4	**7.1**
0.3	1.69	12.9	0.52	**0.2**	-0.1	-0.14	-1.35	3.88	105.1	**0.9**	19.9	38.8	**1.0**
1.8	4.32	25.7	0.98	**2.6**	0.4	0.41	3.39	4.22	75.4	**1.1**	11.8	29.4	**4.9**
1.9	4.75	27.1	0.99	**0.0**	-1.1	-0.34	-4.41	3.08	107.8	**1.3**	20.7	29.0	**3.8**
4.0	2.05	10.4	0.62	**3.2**	0.7	0.58	6.42	3.97	82.5	**3.7**	21.5	11.1	**4.0**
0.3	3.73	37.2	3.22	**0.0**	-2.7	-3.16	-54.76	2.57	223.5	**0.6**	15.7	65.0	**2.5**
0.0	2.67	20.5	2.05	**2.5**	1.6	0.59	6.64	5.36	69.9	**1.1**	16.0	30.3	**3.0**
3.5	2.33	13.0	0.65	**5.7**	46.4	1.02	7.40	3.79	63.8	**3.4**	20.2	13.3	**8.8**
4.0	0.45	3.4	0.86	**2.4**	0.5	0.32	3.33	3.44	70.5	**1.2**	18.9	29.9	**3.9**
7.4	0.93	3.9	1.67	**3.3**	0.1	0.56	4.67	2.94	63.8	**3.6**	51.0	18.9	**6.1**
6.1	0.52	3.5	0.11	**5.2**	6.5	1.01	13.78	3.43	56.5	**3.9**	38.8	15.0	**5.0**
4.2	2.35	18.9	0.11	**3.1**	0.5	0.43	4.97	3.05	75.9	**0.7**	19.7	55.5	**4.5**
1.9	1.89	13.9	2.00	**2.3**	2.3	0.21	1.74	4.06	68.2	**1.7**	17.2	23.4	**8.0**
3.8	1.21	7.8	0.34	**6.5**	1.9	1.48	16.89	3.98	60.4	**5.5**	40.9	6.7	**6.0**
2.7	0.46	2.8	1.69	**2.6**	1.6	0.42	3.44	4.38	54.9	**1.0**	9.6	29.8	**5.7**
5.2	3.48	6.4	1.43	**6.0**	4.2	2.26	11.20	3.62	72.1	**6.1**	68.9	10.6	**5.6**
3.5	2.51	12.8	0.85	**2.6**	1.5	0.61	6.45	2.91	77.4	**3.7**	45.9	18.0	**3.1**
2.5	2.65	18.6	0.53	**0.0**	-2.0	-1.36	-16.15	3.58	129.4	**2.1**	23.8	19.4	**2.2**
7.6	1.01	2.2	0.05	**3.9**	1.0	0.45	2.50	3.38	86.9	**6.8**	59.3	4.2	**8.0**
4.3	2.70	8.9	0.00	**9.2**	0.9	2.25	8.57	5.18	53.8	**1.8**	6.1	19.3	**9.5**
0.3	7.10	35.1	2.18	**0.3**	-1.5	-1.73	-19.18	3.12	87.3	**2.1**	40.4	33.6	**4.1**
2.6	1.42	10.2	0.28	**5.4**	2.9	1.01	11.02	3.56	58.0	**1.8**	21.9	22.4	**6.2**
4.6	0.38	2.9	1.13	**2.3**	0.3	0.35	3.77	3.71	79.4	**4.0**	20.0	9.6	**5.1**
5.3	1.29	5.1	0.79	**2.6**	7.7	0.61	4.49	2.84	68.2	**1.8**	20.7	23.9	**7.0**
1.8	4.51	30.2	1.55	**1.4**	2.3	0.18	1.87	1.90	59.1	**0.7**	16.2	59.4	**4.7**
0.3	18.61	50.1	4.11	**7.6**	6.5	1.36	14.02	1.24	60.9	**4.0**	48.7	17.3	**5.6**
6.5	0.00	0.0	0.00	**9.5**	0.8	5.91	6.27	-0.08	81.7	**5.0**	392.7	101.0	**6.3**
3.9	0.42	3.2	1.50	**4.2**	0.9	1.27	17.09	4.55	59.2	**0.7**	10.7	34.5	**2.5**
2.0	1.89	17.0	1.48	**0.0**	-3.0	-2.63	-35.15	4.26	116.5	**2.1**	23.1	19.4	**0.5**
8.2	0.40	1.9	0.01	**2.2**	0.6	0.61	3.94	4.10	78.8	**1.1**	25.1	33.1	**3.7**
4.9	1.41	9.3	0.26	**6.9**	8.4	1.09	11.49	3.46	73.1	**0.8**	23.2	57.1	**6.2**
3.8	2.48	14.0	1.59	**1.9**	0.1	0.06	0.57	3.28	83.2	**3.1**	34.0	17.4	**4.2**
3.6	2.34	16.5	0.47	**4.2**	7.7	0.80	9.66	4.09	61.1	**3.8**	14.3	9.9	**5.7**
2.1	1.18	8.1	0.88	**4.9**	3.8	0.76	6.80	4.99	62.7	**1.5**	9.1	22.3	**7.1**
0.3	3.97	31.5	0.53	**0.9**	0.3	0.15	1.65	3.32	89.3	**2.1**	11.2	18.2	**3.3**
3.5	0.90	7.2	0.01	**5.4**	0.9	0.96	10.08	3.64	64.7	**1.6**	8.8	21.1	**6.4**
3.4	6.06	21.9	0.00	**0.7**	-0.1	-0.32	-1.93	3.41	102.8	**3.1**	46.4	22.0	**5.7**
5.8	1.97	9.8	0.33	**1.7**	0.1	0.11	0.68	4.29	82.5	**2.3**	22.1	18.3	**0.6**
0.3	21.78	127.5	0.06	**2.7**	1.2	0.42	3.77	4.31	72.5	**1.6**	19.7	24.9	**5.6**
8.6	0.01	0.0	-0.04	**5.4**	0.5	1.25	6.33	4.26	68.1	**4.0**	46.3	16.1	**7.8**
2.8	2.14	16.6	0.35	**3.5**	3.0	0.58	7.55	4.02	76.6	**3.7**	15.8	10.7	**4.5**

Name	City	State	Rating	2008 Rating	2007 Rating	Total Assets ($Mil)	One Year Asset Growth	Asset Mix (As a % of Total Assets) Commercial Loans	Consumer Loans	Home Mortgages	Securities	Capitalization Index	Leverage Ratio	Risk-based Capital Ratio
ADIRONDACK TRUST CO	SARATOGA SPRINGS	NY	**B**	B-	B-	883	2.95	8.9	4.4	10.9	34.7	**6.4**	8.5	17.9
ADMIRALS BANK	CRANSTON	RI	**D**	D	C-	340	45.88	0.6	38.1	8.3	0.6	**10.0**	13.1	15.5
▼ ADRIAN BANK	ADRIAN	MO	**C**	B-	B-	113	9.99	14.1	5.4	15.4	14.3	**6.2**	8.2	12.0
ADRIAN STATE BK	ADRIAN	MN	**C**	C-	B-	37	7.86	5.9	1.3	6.1	24.0	**7.9**	9.6	15.5
ADVANCE BANK	BALTIMORE	MD	**D-**	D	C-	76	0.17	6.6	1.0	40.6	3.5	**6.1**	8.1	14.2
ADVANTAGE BANK	LOVELAND	CO	**E-**	D-	D	354	-16.39	12.4	0.5	11.4	6.5	**1.8**	5.9	8.8
ADVANTAGE BANK	CAMBRIDGE	OH	**E-**	D-	D-	817	-3.22	3.8	0.4	37.8	4.2	**1.5**	5.6	8.5
ADVANTAGE BANK	SPENCER	OK	**B**	B	B-	50	-1.59	9.1	9.7	27.8	21.1	**10.0**	12.2	19.1
ADVANTAGE COMMUNITY	DORCHESTER	WI	**B-**	B-	C	123	6.05	8.2	2.6	19.0	3.9	**7.8**	9.6	13.1
ADVANTAGE NATIONAL BK	ELK GROVE VILLAGE	IL	**D+**	D	C-	504	11.08	26.2	6.3	2.3	11.9	**6.8**	9.0	12.4
▲ AFFILIATED BANK	ARLINGTON	TX	**C**	C-	C+	199	21.05	3.0	3.1	43.3	3.6	**7.1**	9.1	15.8
AFFINITY BANK	ATLANTA	GA	**E-**	E+	D-	347	-9.24	14.2	0.3	1.9	12.3	**1.2**	5.5	8.2
▼ AFFINITY BANK OF PENNSYLV	WYOMISSING	PA	**D-**	D	D+	170	7.31	6.8	0.2	24.2	42.5	**4.6**	6.6	13.8
AIG FSB	WILMINGTON	DE	**C-**	C-	C-	1,065	-5.63	0.4	0.0	10.5	42.8	**10.0**	12.8	33.8
AIMBANK	LITTLEFIELD	TX	**B**	B	B-	230	21.31	23.7	3.9	15.2	16.3	**6.4**	8.4	12.7
▼ ALABAMA TRUST BANK NA	SYLACAUGA	AL	**E-**	D-	C-	66	-8.53	14.5	4.3	18.9	9.2	**5.1**	7.1	11.1
ALAMERICA BANK	BIRMINGHAM	AL	**C-**	B	A	38	-53.01	16.8	1.1	7.9	21.4	**10.0**	21.1	34.5
ALAMOSA STATE BK	ALAMOSA	CO	**A-**	A-	A-	159	0.86	5.0	8.2	11.9	22.2	**7.2**	9.2	17.0
ALARION BANK	OCALA	FL	**D-**	D+	D+	302	-2.41	6.8	0.6	20.2	16.3	**5.6**	7.6	11.5
▲ ALASKA PACIFIC BANK	JUNEAU	AK	**C-**	D	D+	174	-2.21	11.1	3.6	20.4	1.3	**10.0**	11.2	16.3
ALBANY BANK & TRUST CO NA	CHICAGO	IL	**B-**	B	A	520	-1.12	13.4	0.8	5.1	13.3	**10.0**	13.6	20.2
ALBINA COMMUNITY BANK	PORTLAND	OR	**E-**	E-	D-	145	-28.63	17.6	6.3	6.7	10.9	**0.0**	3.7	6.0
ALDEN STATE BK	STERLING	KS	**C**	C+	C+	19	-9.49	6.4	6.6	20.6	16.5	**8.4**	9.9	19.7
▲ ALDEN STATE BK	ALDEN	MI	**D+**	D	D	169	1.30	5.2	2.6	21.5	17.7	**8.6**	10.1	15.9
ALDEN STATE BK	ALDEN	NY	**B+**	B	B	220	6.06	4.3	2.6	47.2	25.6	**10.0**	13.3	23.4
ALERUS FINANCIAL NA	GRAND FORKS	ND	**B-**	B-	B+	1,112	-0.74	16.9	2.1	11.2	21.8	**5.5**	7.5	13.1
ALGONQUIN STATE BK NA	ALGONQUIN	IL	**C-**	D+	B-	144	7.81	0.2	0.8	15.6	41.6	**10.0**	11.1	25.0
ALIANT BANK	ALEXANDER CITY	AL	**D**	D-	C	905	-7.71	9.5	1.3	13.1	20.2	**6.7**	8.8	13.5
ALL AMERICA BANK	OKLAHOMA CITY	OK	**D+**	B-	C+	129	-3.12	4.6	1.4	6.6	54.5	**6.5**	8.5	12.6
ALL AMERICAN BANK	DES PLAINES	IL	**E-**	E-	D	42	6.92	5.9	1.3	1.5	7.3	**0.8**	5.2	7.5
▲ ALLEGHENY VALLEY BK PITTS	PITTSBURGH	PA	**C**	C	C	409	-0.47	5.3	0.5	26.3	16.9	**5.8**	7.8	14.5
ALLEGIANCE BANK TEXAS	HOUSTON	TX	**C-**	C	C	429	27.09	19.3	1.9	8.8	3.0	**9.6**	10.8	14.9
▼ ALLEGIANCE COMMUNITY	SOUTH ORANGE	NJ	**E-**	E+	D-	121	7.65	2.2	0.2	10.9	24.3	**3.6**	5.6	10.6
ALLENDALE COUNTY BANK	FAIRFAX	SC	**D-**	D	D+	55	-5.65	2.1	33.6	6.7	37.8	**4.1**	6.1	12.0
▼ ALLIANCE BANK	FRANCESVILLE	IN	**C+**	B-	B	274	-1.99	7.4	1.3	9.1	34.9	**6.0**	8.0	13.3
ALLIANCE BANK	TOPEKA	KS	**C+**	C	C+	81	1.55	16.8	2.1	16.3	18.0	**7.8**	9.5	15.5
ALLIANCE BANK	SAINT PAUL	MN	**D-**	D	D	637	-8.06	22.1	5.1	7.8	10.9	**7.1**	9.9	12.5
ALLIANCE BANK	CAPE GIRARDEAU	MO	**C**	C-	D-	130	2.47	7.1	3.6	12.5	12.6	**7.0**	10.1	12.5
ALLIANCE BANK	BROOMALL	PA	**D+**	C-	C-	455	-2.10	1.7	1.6	24.2	17.0	**9.8**	10.8	17.4
ALLIANCE BANK	SULPHUR SPRINGS	TX	**B-**	B-	C+	526	5.54	8.7	4.1	13.2	24.6	**6.6**	8.6	14.3
ALLIANCE BANK	MONDOVI	WI	**C+**	B-	C+	142	3.42	5.9	5.1	21.0	23.7	**8.3**	9.9	15.9
ALLIANCE BANK & TRUST CO	GASTONIA	NC	**D**	D	C-	185	4.80	10.2	0.4	16.8	9.6	**10.0**	11.5	15.1
▼ ALLIANCE BANK CENTRAL TEX	WACO	TX	**D+**	C-	D+	187	33.87	12.7	7.9	33.4	10.0	**3.5**	6.5	10.3
▲ ALLIANCE BANK CORP	CHANTILLY	VA	**D**	D-	D-	537	-6.61	5.1	0.7	14.0	25.3	**5.4**	7.4	12.8
ALLIANCE BANK NA	SYRACUSE	NY	**B-**	B-	B-	1,449	2.79	6.0	13.1	24.3	28.5	**5.7**	7.7	13.8
▲ ALLIANCE BANK OF ARIZONA	PHOENIX	AZ	**D+**	D	C-	1,928	71.66	10.7	0.4	2.7	23.1	**6.3**	8.3	13.7
ALLIANCE BANKING CO	WINCHESTER	KY	**E+**	E+	E+	59	-0.03	8.6	1.9	30.0	4.2	**6.0**	8.1	12.7
▼ ALLIANCE NATIONAL BK	DALTON	GA	**C-**	C	C+	154	1.38	7.0	1.9	10.7	34.1	**7.4**	9.3	15.9
ALLIANT BANK	SEDGWICK	KS	**E-**	D-	E-	14	-6.95	7.3	2.9	16.4	32.6	**0.4**	3.5	7.2
ALLIANT BANK	MADISON	MO	**D+**	C-	C-	119	20.20	6.1	2.8	18.6	22.0	**5.1**	8.2	11.1
ALLIED BANK	MULBERRY	AR	**C+**	C	B	186	6.63	20.0	10.8	23.2	4.1	**5.3**	8.1	11.2
▲ ALLIED FIRST BANK SB	OSWEGO	IL	**D-**	E+	D-	166	0.62	13.7	5.4	30.2	12.2	**5.1**	7.1	11.2
ALLNATIONS BANK	CALUMET	OK	**C+**	C	C	32	37.56	7.7	3.4	2.4	26.5	**10.0**	12.3	24.5
ALLSTATE BANK	NORTHBROOK	IL	**C+**	C-	D+	1,242	2.55	17.7	0.0	0.7	77.0	**7.7**	9.5	17.3
▲ ALLY BANK	MIDVALE	UT	**B-**	D+	B-	70,284	27.09	23.6	26.7	20.2	10.9	**10.0**	15.8	20.5
▲ ALMA BANK	ASTORIA	NY	**C**	C	C-	533	47.82	22.7	0.6	0.2	25.8	**10.0**	13.6	19.8
ALMA EXCHANGE BANK &	ALMA	GA	**D+**	C-	B-	80	-5.22	10.9	5.7	10.0	4.6	**9.4**	10.6	15.4
▲ ALMENA STATE BK	ALMENA	KS	**D**	D	D-	22	9.27	13.4	6.6	10.5	7.4	**3.8**	7.2	10.4
ALPINE BANK	GLENWOOD SPRINGS	CO	**D-**	D-	B-	2,374	-10.97	3.5	1.0	11.0	17.0	**7.6**	9.4	13.2
ALPINE BANK & TRUST CO	ROCKFORD	IL	**C-**	C-	B-	1,009	1.68	12.7	4.7	10.4	25.8	**6.7**	8.7	13.2

Asset Quality Index	Non-Performing Loans as a % of Total Loans	Non-Performing Loans as a % of Capital	Net Charge-offs Avg Loans	Profitability Index	Net Income ($Mil)	Return on Assets (R.O.A.)	Return on Equity (R.O.E.)	Net Interest Spread	Overhead Efficiency Ratio	Liquidity Index	Liquidity Ratio	Hot Money Ratio	Stability Index
4.9	0.83	4.4	0.03	**5.2**	9.3	1.07	9.97	3.80	73.1	**3.8**	25.1	10.8	**8.0**
3.3	1.35	8.4	0.23	**0.6**	-0.2	-0.07	-0.61	6.24	99.3	**0.7**	14.5	48.0	**4.5**
2.3	2.30	19.5	0.30	**6.9**	1.8	1.63	19.15	4.39	57.0	**1.9**	10.0	18.9	**6.2**
4.0	1.95	10.6	0.60	**3.9**	0.3	0.85	8.21	3.94	76.7	**4.4**	31.7	10.3	**4.5**
0.0	6.87	59.0	0.25	**0.5**	-0.5	-0.68	-6.70	4.76	105.5	**3.0**	16.5	14.3	**3.7**
0.0	12.00	109.9	3.32	**0.0**	-10.7	-2.80	-33.97	2.98	178.2	**0.8**	15.7	43.1	**3.5**
0.3	4.91	53.4	2.53	**0.0**	-13.0	-1.53	-23.56	3.56	83.3	**2.2**	6.4	17.3	**2.2**
6.3	0.40	2.1	0.26	**4.9**	0.6	1.30	10.75	5.48	83.4	**5.2**	33.1	5.5	**7.3**
4.8	1.57	11.1	0.77	**3.8**	0.7	0.58	5.73	3.32	61.1	**2.7**	24.2	16.4	**6.0**
2.6	0.91	6.5	0.49	**0.9**	0.9	0.18	1.56	3.09	76.5	**1.2**	17.3	29.6	**4.5**
5.9	0.84	7.1	0.39	**2.9**	0.8	0.41	5.07	4.35	86.9	**1.3**	15.3	27.5	**3.6**
0.0	6.73	68.5	2.66	**0.0**	-10.8	-3.03	-45.53	1.75	340.9	**0.7**	22.5	67.8	**0.7**
2.4	3.98	28.5	0.77	**1.2**	0.3	0.20	2.85	3.15	87.1	**3.7**	20.0	11.0	**2.9**
9.8	1.46	2.1	-1.42	**1.3**	1.3	0.11	1.02	1.35	112.1	**6.0**	90.1	14.9	**6.0**
7.5	0.02	0.2	0.38	**5.9**	3.0	1.51	17.68	4.27	62.3	**0.8**	18.1	37.5	**5.5**
1.1	2.41	19.8	2.64	**0.6**	-0.5	-0.80	-11.10	4.23	90.4	**1.2**	15.2	28.4	**0.0**
2.9	11.30	24.4	11.49	**0.8**	-1.9	-3.84	-19.94	2.26	134.6	**1.4**	19.1	27.9	**8.1**
7.6	0.20	1.1	0.20	**8.6**	2.9	1.84	20.11	3.90	53.7	**2.4**	32.3	21.8	**7.6**
1.7	2.60	21.3	2.45	**0.0**	-2.9	-0.91	-11.03	3.07	83.8	**1.5**	16.3	24.8	**3.8**
5.9	0.29	2.0	-0.06	**2.5**	1.1	0.60	5.82	5.37	83.2	**3.9**	14.8	9.2	**3.5**
3.2	2.45	12.1	0.83	**4.6**	3.4	0.64	4.58	4.19	55.4	**0.9**	21.7	40.0	**7.9**
0.3	4.49	61.1	2.29	**0.0**	-2.8	-1.63	-37.24	4.06	115.1	**1.1**	8.0	29.1	**0.7**
5.5	2.59	12.9	0.04	**2.4**	0.1	0.31	3.10	3.94	92.6	**1.8**	28.8	22.7	**6.2**
1.5	4.51	26.6	1.94	**1.7**	0.5	0.28	2.78	4.46	67.9	**3.8**	27.2	12.0	**4.7**
4.9	3.08	14.7	0.24	**7.0**	2.4	1.14	8.48	4.65	55.8	**3.7**	21.7	11.1	**7.3**
4.6	1.33	9.6	1.39	**5.4**	6.5	0.60	7.16	4.55	80.0	**4.4**	28.8	12.1	**7.3**
5.1	4.62	14.6	0.38	**1.2**	0.4	0.25	2.21	3.44	92.4	**3.6**	43.2	17.9	**3.8**
1.0	4.85	30.9	3.75	**0.0**	-6.2	-0.63	-6.03	3.41	86.4	**1.6**	16.8	23.7	**4.2**
1.7	9.46	42.2	1.53	**2.8**	0.1	0.07	0.85	3.64	78.8	**4.4**	25.5	7.8	**4.7**
0.0	23.44	155.8	4.40	**0.0**	-0.4	-1.09	-22.56	2.66	142.7	**3.1**	29.1	16.1	**0.0**
3.5	2.06	14.8	0.39	**4.1**	3.1	0.75	7.45	3.57	70.2	**4.1**	32.9	12.0	**6.2**
5.6	0.59	3.9	0.29	**2.2**	2.0	0.54	4.83	4.24	77.4	**1.3**	24.7	30.6	**3.0**
0.3	4.97	52.6	0.03	**1.0**	0.4	0.32	5.42	3.38	87.2	**2.6**	11.4	15.6	**0.0**
6.4	0.24	1.6	1.96	**2.1**	0.0	0.03	0.42	5.00	77.6	**2.9**	40.9	21.4	**1.3**
4.3	2.13	13.2	1.45	**4.3**	2.3	0.88	8.50	4.12	62.6	**4.7**	31.8	8.5	**5.2**
5.1	0.62	3.9	1.50	**3.3**	0.4	0.45	4.47	3.78	74.0	**2.1**	31.8	24.7	**6.0**
0.1	3.72	24.3	1.23	**0.7**	-2.9	-0.43	-4.06	4.35	73.6	**1.4**	6.9	23.3	**6.6**
4.9	0.56	3.8	0.47	**3.3**	0.7	0.56	5.58	3.96	71.4	**1.9**	18.1	20.1	**4.4**
1.7	5.50	30.2	0.20	**2.1**	1.1	0.24	2.31	3.24	78.4	**3.1**	32.2	16.7	**5.8**
3.4	1.77	12.4	0.56	**4.6**	4.9	0.96	9.96	4.60	72.1	**3.3**	25.7	14.0	**6.1**
3.9	1.01	6.2	0.50	**4.6**	1.4	0.97	9.73	3.76	66.3	**3.9**	28.3	11.6	**6.5**
0.0	8.18	48.5	0.42	**0.0**	-3.0	-1.74	-12.34	3.57	107.6	**1.1**	16.1	31.4	**4.5**
1.7	0.00	0.0	0.33	**3.4**	0.8	0.48	5.61	4.58	67.3	**1.0**	20.2	33.4	**4.5**
5.5	0.68	4.9	0.61	**0.7**	1.0	0.18	2.29	3.76	94.5	**0.8**	14.7	36.5	**3.0**
4.6	0.90	6.8	0.32	**4.4**	12.3	0.85	8.29	3.64	68.4	**2.4**	3.3	15.8	**8.3**
2.5	1.72	12.2	1.26	**3.6**	12.8	0.86	13.02	4.91	66.9	**1.3**	23.5	36.1	**3.3**
1.7	2.76	21.4	0.69	**0.0**	-0.6	-0.93	-11.65	2.82	128.0	**1.6**	16.0	24.0	**2.8**
5.3	1.22	6.2	0.85	**3.0**	0.9	0.58	6.09	3.84	71.9	**0.9**	24.0	48.8	**4.7**
5.4	0.19	1.5	3.59	**0.0**	-0.6	-3.76	-65.49	3.88	180.3	**1.3**	14.1	26.7	**1.3**
1.8	4.14	27.7	0.31	**4.7**	1.2	1.09	12.42	4.67	70.4	**1.9**	23.9	21.6	**3.1**
3.1	2.92	27.6	1.37	**2.7**	0.7	0.38	4.26	4.44	62.9	**0.5**	4.3	40.4	**6.8**
1.4	4.21	37.7	1.57	**0.3**	0.4	0.25	3.52	2.47	83.4	**0.4**	2.3	51.2	**1.9**
7.0	1.37	4.0	-1.08	**2.8**	0.1	0.50	3.01	3.74	82.3	**5.1**	61.7	13.2	**6.7**
9.6	0.76	1.4	0.19	**3.7**	9.5	0.77	9.04	2.64	45.8	**3.9**	88.3	46.3	**3.9**
5.3	0.81	3.9	0.54	**3.9**	902.4	1.59	10.17	3.03	43.9	**0.7**	14.4	50.7	**6.5**
4.9	1.07	5.1	0.12	**3.0**	2.6	0.55	4.90	4.10	64.7	**1.0**	25.5	44.1	**4.5**
0.9	6.04	34.6	0.90	**1.9**	0.2	0.25	2.36	4.00	73.0	**2.0**	25.5	20.1	**3.9**
5.5	0.22	2.0	0.02	**7.1**	0.3	1.39	20.92	5.84	73.3	**1.6**	17.2	22.4	**3.0**
0.3	6.91	38.7	5.05	**2.0**	-48.2	-1.93	-17.55	4.83	70.4	**1.8**	18.4	21.7	**8.2**
3.9	2.19	13.9	1.83	**2.3**	5.1	0.50	5.61	3.55	69.3	**3.2**	19.8	14.0	**5.9**

Name	City	State	Rating	2008 Rating	2007 Rating	Total Assets ($Mil)	One Year Asset Growth	Asset Mix (As a % of Total Assets) Comm-ercial Loans	Cons-umer Loans	Home Mort-gages	Secur-ities	Capital-ization Index	Leverage Ratio	Risk-based Capital Ratio
▼ ALPINE CAPITAL BANK	NEW YORK	NY	**B+**	A-	A-	227	8.91	4.3	3.6	17.0	16.8	**10.0**	13.6	23.2
ALTA VISTA STATE BK	ALTA VISTA	KS	**C**	C-	D+	19	-2.71	5.2	1.8	10.2	48.4	**10.0**	11.1	24.4
ALTAMAHA BANK & TRUST CO	VIDALIA	GA	**C+**	B-	B-	147	-0.53	9.0	6.0	28.6	11.8	**6.8**	8.9	13.7
▲ ALTAPACIFIC BANK	SANTA ROSA	CA	**B-**	C	C	80	-5.19	15.7	4.6	3.7	12.1	**10.0**	34.0	38.7
ALTERRA BANK	OVERLAND PARK	KS	**D-**	E	D-	121	2.16	17.5	1.4	10.6	0.0	**7.0**	9.0	14.5
ALTON BANK	ALTON	MO	**A-**	A-	A-	51	1.18	3.3	8.9	23.1	23.9	**10.0**	18.2	30.1
ALTOONA FIRST SB	ALTOONA	PA	**B**	B-	B-	201	5.42	4.6	4.1	40.5	2.5	**10.0**	11.3	17.9
ALTURA STATE BK	ALTURA	MN	**A-**	A-	B+	46	-0.90	4.3	2.2	15.4	18.4	**10.0**	13.8	20.9
ALVA STATE BK & TRUST CO	ALVA	OK	**C+**	C-	C	180	-2.49	6.3	4.6	3.3	11.5	**10.0**	17.4	21.9
AMALGAMATED BANK	NEW YORK	NY	**D-**	D-	C-	4,575	-3.82	11.5	0.1	13.9	4.9	**4.0**	6.0	12.3
AMALGAMATED BANK OF	CHICAGO	IL	**D+**	D+	C	921	19.92	5.4	7.5	1.1	15.1	**5.5**	7.5	13.3
AMARILLO NATIONAL BK	AMARILLO	TX	**B-**	B	B	2,785	-0.25	18.9	15.3	6.4	11.4	**8.5**	10.4	13.7
AMBANK	SILVER CITY	NM	**C-**	C	B-	114	10.64	6.0	7.0	12.7	20.9	**8.2**	9.8	16.9
AMBLER SB	AMBLER	PA	**B-**	C	C-	276	9.87	0.3	0.1	50.2	24.4	**7.1**	9.1	16.9
AMBOY BANK	OLD BRIDGE	NJ	**D-**	D-	D-	2,407	-11.92	3.6	0.0	18.7	20.1	**8.3**	11.7	13.6
▲ AMEGY BANK NA	HOUSTON	TX	**D+**	D	B-	11,324	2.12	29.9	1.2	6.8	5.3	**10.0**	13.8	16.9
AMERASIA BANK	FLUSHING	NY	**B-**	B-	A-	228	8.20	3.5	0.0	15.4	2.7	**6.3**	9.8	11.9
AMERIANA BANK	NEW CASTLE	IN	**D+**	D	C-	426	-2.92	5.1	0.9	30.0	9.1	**6.9**	8.9	13.1
AMERICA CALIFORNIA BANK	SAN FRANCISCO	CA	**D-**	D-	B-	128	-7.37	5.4	0.1	8.0	0.5	**9.0**	10.3	16.6
AMERICAN BANK	BETHESDA	MD	**D-**	D	D+	556	9.53	8.9	0.6	34.3	2.7	**6.8**	8.8	15.8
AMERICAN BANK	BOZEMAN	MT	**D-**	D-	D	378	-6.70	9.5	0.6	10.6	1.1	**6.2**	8.2	17.1
▼ AMERICAN BANK	WAGONER	OK	**B-**	B+	B	29	-0.26	1.9	8.5	5.0	32.4	**10.0**	20.2	55.9
▲ AMERICAN BANK	ALLENTOWN	PA	**B**	C+	C+	483	0.72	3.8	0.2	15.4	20.2	**8.6**	10.0	14.2
AMERICAN BANK	FOND DU LAC	WI	**A**	A+	A+	235	0.45	14.2	0.4	10.6	17.9	**10.0**	16.3	28.1
AMERICAN BANK & TRUST	WESSINGTON SPRINGS	SD	**B-**	B	B+	287	7.52	10.5	3.5	2.2	13.6	**7.7**	10.0	13.1
AMERICAN BANK & TRUST CO	COVINGTON	LA	**D**	C	C+	112	4.23	5.8	6.9	17.2	4.1	**6.2**	8.2	13.2
AMERICAN BANK & TRUST CO	OPELOUSAS	LA	**B+**	A-	A-	146	4.09	8.0	5.5	19.2	23.9	**8.4**	9.9	16.6
AMERICAN BANK & TRUST CO	TULSA	OK	**C**	C+	B	172	4.91	25.9	1.4	3.7	34.2	**9.5**	10.6	21.2
AMERICAN BANK & TRUST CO	BOWLING GREEN	KY	**B-**	C+	C	235	7.26	6.7	2.7	33.9	3.0	**6.3**	8.3	12.4
AMERICAN BANK & TRUST CO	DAVENPORT	IA	**D-**	D-	C-	560	-8.35	11.3	0.9	15.8	11.2	**5.7**	7.8	11.5
▲ AMERICAN BANK & TRUST	LIVINGSTON	TN	**D+**	D-	E	123	13.77	8.8	7.5	31.5	6.7	**6.3**	8.3	13.1
AMERICAN BANK & TRUST WI	CUBA CITY	WI	**D**	C-	C-	130	-0.24	13.2	3.5	6.2	6.9	**6.1**	8.1	12.0
AMERICAN BANK CENTER	DICKINSON	ND	**B-**	B-	C+	573	4.45	9.4	11.5	6.0	22.1	**6.7**	8.7	13.1
AMERICAN BANK NA	LE MARS	IA	**B-**	B-	B-	229	0.61	10.2	2.4	5.3	7.9	**7.6**	10.2	13.0
AMERICAN BANK NA	CORPUS CHRISTI	TX	**B-**	C+	B-	949	8.88	17.8	1.4	7.8	23.1	**6.5**	8.5	13.6
AMERICAN BANK NA	DALLAS	TX	**D**	D+	C-	39	30.65	8.9	10.1	1.9	60.6	**10.0**	12.0	19.1
▼ AMERICAN BANK NA	WACO	TX	**B-**	B	A-	352	3.56	13.0	2.4	13.4	23.6	**8.0**	9.7	14.9
▲ AMERICAN BANK OF BAXTER	BAXTER SPRINGS	KS	**D-**	D-	D+	115	-6.81	8.5	1.6	8.9	12.1	**6.9**	9.0	13.4
AMERICAN BANK OF	WOLFFORTH	TX	**C-**	D+	D+	675	-5.28	13.1	1.0	7.4	20.3	**6.0**	8.0	13.0
AMERICAN BANK OF	PROVO	UT	**D+**	C-	B	53	12.26	3.5	2.1	7.2	0.0	**10.0**	16.0	21.3
▼ AMERICAN BANK OF	WELLSVILLE	MO	**D+**	D-	D+	106	0.68	2.2	0.8	37.1	7.7	**9.0**	10.3	15.6
▲ AMERICAN BANK OF	COLLINSVILLE	OK	**C-**	D+	C	132	0.83	15.9	13.5	20.5	0.7	**5.2**	8.8	11.1
AMERICAN BANK OF ST PAUL	SAINT PAUL	MN	**E-**	E	D-	485	-19.92	10.3	0.4	4.5	15.7	**2.1**	5.7	9.1
▲ AMERICAN BANK OF TEXAS	SHERMAN	TX	**D+**	C-	B+	1,106	0.93	12.7	2.7	6.7	10.1	**10.0**	13.3	17.2
▲ AMERICAN BANK OF TEXAS	MARBLE FALLS	TX	**C-**	C-	B+	754	-0.04	4.9	1.4	9.0	15.6	**10.0**	11.1	18.6
AMERICAN BANK OF THE	NASHWAUK	MN	**D**	D	D+	646	-3.70	13.2	2.4	19.3	9.4	**5.0**	7.5	11.0
AMERICAN BUSINESS BANK	LOS ANGELES	CA	**B-**	B-	B-	1,009	11.95	14.2	1.4	0.1	55.0	**4.7**	6.7	15.5
AMERICAN CHARTERED BANK	SCHAUMBURG	IL	**D**	D	C-	2,456	-10.11	18.7	0.1	6.7	25.2	**5.3**	7.3	12.1
AMERICAN CITY BANK	TULLAHOMA	TN	**C+**	C	C+	240	7.13	15.2	7.7	17.9	13.6	**9.5**	10.8	14.6
▲ AMERICAN COMMUNITY BANK	GLEN COVE	NY	**C-**	D	C+	160	1.21	2.5	0.1	3.5	5.5	**8.2**	11.3	13.5
▲ AMERICAN COMMUNITY BANK	WOODSTOCK	IL	**D+**	C-	B-	574	-3.30	4.0	0.3	14.0	2.0	**9.4**	10.6	16.9
▼ AMERICAN CONTINENTAL	CITY OF INDUSTRY	CA	**D**	D	D	129	-5.92	3.7	0.0	14.5	10.0	**10.0**	14.4	19.6
▲ AMERICAN EAGLE BANK	SOUTH ELGIN	IL	**D**	C	C	153	-2.44	2.7	35.5	10.7	3.9	**6.4**	8.7	12.0
▲ AMERICAN EAGLE BANK OF	CHICAGO	IL	**D**	C	C	69	-4.44	0.9	42.7	7.2	0.0	**6.4**	9.4	12.0
AMERICAN EAGLE SAVINGS	UPPER CHICHESTER	PA	**E-**	D	D+	22	-5.06	0.0	0.3	53.5	18.6	**0.4**	3.5	7.1
AMERICAN ENTERPRISE BANK	BUFFALO GROVE	IL	**D-**	E	D	386	10.26	10.5	0.2	4.1	22.1	**7.4**	9.3	14.7
AMERICAN ENTERPRISE BANK	JACKSONVILLE	FL	**D-**	D-	D	221	9.10	19.6	3.7	13.9	10.0	**5.9**	8.3	11.7
▲ AMERICAN EXCHANGE BANK	ELMWOOD	NE	**C+**	D+	C-	37	0.59	9.9	4.4	7.8	21.0	**10.0**	12.0	18.3
AMERICAN EXCHANGE BANK	HENRYETTA	OK	**C+**	C	C+	71	-0.88	5.6	10.0	25.0	24.8	**6.8**	8.8	15.1
▲ AMERICAN EXCHANGE BANK	LINDSAY	OK	**C**	C-	C+	41	4.67	7.9	4.1	10.5	49.8	**8.9**	10.2	18.8

Asset Quality Index	Non-Performing Loans as a % of Total Loans	Non-Performing Loans as a % of Capital	Net Charge-offs Avg Loans	Profitability Index	Net Income ($Mil)	Return on Assets (R.O.A.)	Return on Equity (R.O.E.)	Net Interest Spread	Overhead Efficiency Ratio	Liquidity Index	Liquidity Ratio	Hot Money Ratio	Stability Index
8.5	0.72	2.6	0.00	**3.9**	1.9	0.76	6.24	2.65	62.8	**3.3**	49.2	22.8	**8.5**
7.6	0.81	3.1	-0.26	**4.4**	0.2	0.86	7.83	3.97	65.9	**1.6**	32.2	28.0	**5.1**
2.8	1.86	14.4	0.61	**4.0**	1.0	0.70	7.79	4.71	73.3	**1.2**	18.0	29.6	**5.5**
6.2	0.00	0.0	1.01	**3.5**	0.9	1.10	3.52	6.26	74.7	**2.9**	21.3	15.2	**5.2**
0.8	0.88	6.3	0.13	**0.0**	-0.7	-0.98	-10.04	3.70	101.8	**1.3**	31.2	53.8	**3.6**
6.7	0.43	1.5	0.06	**8.4**	1.1	2.17	12.10	5.18	51.7	**2.2**	23.7	18.6	**8.9**
8.6	0.30	1.9	0.01	**4.1**	1.2	0.63	5.67	4.05	74.4	**2.0**	23.3	20.0	**6.0**
7.8	0.68	3.1	0.01	**8.0**	0.8	1.80	12.91	4.28	54.8	**3.0**	31.4	17.4	**9.5**
2.2	3.38	14.5	0.83	**7.1**	3.1	1.74	9.82	4.08	48.6	**1.4**	18.2	27.1	**8.1**
0.3	6.06	43.0	2.10	**0.8**	-1.2	-0.03	-0.48	1.73	79.2	**4.3**	50.0	18.5	**3.0**
2.0	3.85	23.1	2.04	**2.4**	3.0	0.42	5.58	3.45	82.1	**5.6**	43.9	7.3	**1.9**
4.8	0.55	3.5	0.46	**9.5**	65.0	2.34	23.91	4.14	49.2	**2.8**	13.1	15.0	**9.0**
2.7	2.41	11.1	0.83	**3.4**	1.0	0.95	6.58	5.11	83.7	**4.0**	40.8	15.2	**5.7**
8.1	0.75	5.2	0.02	**4.4**	2.4	0.92	10.45	3.21	56.9	**2.1**	30.8	23.8	**5.2**
0.3	6.92	32.2	0.75	**2.7**	14.1	0.56	6.98	3.06	79.1	**1.9**	17.7	20.9	**6.5**
0.8	4.79	20.4	1.97	**3.3**	57.8	0.50	2.78	4.17	62.2	**5.1**	26.9	7.4	**5.3**
3.7	0.58	4.9	0.07	**8.5**	3.5	1.57	16.60	5.40	43.0	**0.7**	10.5	37.2	**6.4**
1.4	3.55	27.0	0.54	**1.9**	1.3	0.30	3.21	3.75	83.9	**2.5**	9.3	16.1	**5.2**
0.9	3.57	19.2	0.75	**0.2**	-0.9	-0.62	-6.04	2.46	113.0	**1.3**	29.6	40.0	**4.2**
0.0	11.66	78.9	2.05	**2.0**	0.0	0.01	0.06	3.89	66.4	**1.8**	29.8	27.4	**4.8**
0.9	8.20	48.0	1.97	**0.4**	-16.2	-4.13	-40.47	3.11	158.9	**1.1**	19.5	32.6	**6.6**
6.7	0.15	0.2	-0.23	**3.2**	0.2	0.55	2.76	4.09	81.9	**5.8**	79.3	12.0	**7.4**
7.7	0.00	0.0	0.06	**5.1**	4.9	1.00	11.02	2.74	47.3	**3.7**	26.4	11.9	**5.1**
8.4	0.39	1.2	-0.03	**8.3**	3.0	1.30	7.90	3.75	48.8	**3.9**	35.6	14.1	**9.0**
3.3	1.20	8.1	0.27	**6.4**	4.0	1.51	13.44	4.50	58.8	**1.7**	10.5	20.0	**8.2**
0.9	3.22	23.1	0.98	**2.7**	0.3	0.23	3.00	4.94	83.5	**2.3**	27.6	19.5	**4.8**
5.0	1.17	6.6	0.11	**5.2**	1.7	1.23	12.00	4.31	71.8	**3.3**	21.2	13.2	**6.5**
5.6	0.26	1.1	0.05	**2.9**	1.0	0.55	5.03	3.33	87.1	**3.6**	43.1	17.9	**5.3**
5.2	0.57	5.1	0.46	**5.4**	3.2	1.39	17.79	3.97	63.4	**1.4**	14.1	25.2	**5.0**
0.3	7.36	60.9	3.43	**0.0**	-6.0	-1.02	-11.67	3.76	86.8	**1.3**	13.0	26.5	**3.3**
4.1	0.98	8.0	0.04	**2.0**	0.5	0.43	5.39	3.95	84.8	**0.9**	19.9	39.2	**2.6**
0.6	1.45	12.5	0.15	**5.3**	1.6	1.30	12.85	4.03	62.4	**3.0**	17.2	14.5	**5.5**
4.1	0.66	4.7	0.12	**7.4**	7.6	1.38	15.01	5.18	68.8	**3.9**	15.8	9.1	**5.3**
3.6	0.66	4.7	-0.10	**7.2**	4.0	1.80	17.36	3.62	50.7	**2.8**	15.4	14.9	**6.5**
4.4	1.19	8.1	0.26	**5.7**	11.8	1.29	13.11	4.60	75.4	**4.8**	28.5	6.1	**7.7**
8.1	0.00	0.0	2.20	**0.0**	-0.1	-0.23	-1.73	3.56	123.0	**3.1**	81.1	51.9	**3.4**
3.6	2.13	13.5	0.00	**3.7**	1.8	0.51	5.23	3.35	71.0	**1.1**	17.7	31.4	**6.3**
0.2	7.14	37.3	3.38	**0.0**	-4.8	-4.06	-59.32	3.32	86.3	**2.2**	21.9	18.5	**4.3**
2.6	2.56	17.7	0.75	**3.3**	5.4	0.78	9.73	4.01	72.9	**1.7**	25.5	24.9	**4.0**
1.7	6.66	23.6	2.09	**0.7**	-0.2	-0.38	-2.31	4.93	96.0	**2.4**	36.2	25.0	**5.6**
1.6	3.19	21.0	1.39	**1.7**	0.4	0.33	2.34	4.27	80.6	**1.3**	7.0	25.0	**4.6**
4.4	0.14	1.3	0.14	**4.4**	0.8	0.63	7.38	4.61	80.7	**0.7**	8.3	34.8	**3.9**
0.3	4.98	32.6	1.08	**0.0**	-7.6	-1.36	-23.83	3.25	106.1	**2.0**	26.7	22.0	**3.3**
0.0	5.57	28.4	0.64	**4.5**	7.7	0.70	5.31	4.24	63.3	**2.7**	21.1	17.2	**8.0**
3.3	3.71	16.3	1.04	**3.1**	2.6	0.35	2.33	4.28	73.9	**3.5**	28.1	13.5	**6.4**
0.3	5.97	53.8	1.78	**1.0**	-2.3	-0.34	-4.02	3.87	66.0	**3.5**	5.4	10.8	**4.8**
8.7	0.21	1.2	0.06	**4.2**	8.7	0.91	13.70	3.78	67.3	**5.7**	42.2	9.1	**4.8**
1.2	3.92	29.2	1.95	**0.7**	3.3	0.12	1.63	3.40	77.8	**1.7**	20.1	24.1	**4.1**
3.0	1.62	10.9	1.06	**4.4**	2.3	0.97	6.47	4.46	52.7	**0.7**	8.9	36.1	**7.1**
4.1	0.28	1.7	0.16	**4.2**	1.0	0.62	6.62	4.91	62.7	**1.3**	7.2	25.8	**6.5**
1.3	2.61	14.8	1.27	**2.5**	1.6	0.27	2.62	2.90	57.3	**1.2**	29.6	47.1	**5.6**
0.0	9.61	45.1	0.14	**2.4**	0.4	0.33	2.32	3.81	78.6	**0.9**	24.8	43.6	**5.3**
1.7	1.39	11.0	0.54	**5.3**	1.3	0.87	10.12	3.86	56.3	**0.8**	16.6	44.4	**4.3**
0.3	4.90	35.0	0.17	**0.0**	-0.3	-0.43	-4.07	2.49	103.7	**0.5**	9.6	54.4	**2.4**
10.0	0.00	0.0	0.00	**0.0**	-0.6	-2.68	-70.15	3.23	222.2	**5.3**	38.9	4.7	**0.0**
0.3	15.32	78.5	2.08	**0.0**	-9.6	-2.47	-30.20	1.87	145.3	**1.0**	23.6	35.8	**2.6**
0.3	5.19	40.0	0.79	**0.0**	-0.8	-0.38	-4.52	3.49	81.3	**0.9**	20.6	41.9	**3.3**
3.3	1.77	8.4	0.33	**5.9**	0.5	1.37	10.84	4.59	67.4	**4.0**	31.2	11.9	**7.7**
7.9	0.25	1.5	0.28	**4.4**	0.6	0.78	8.40	5.29	78.2	**3.6**	34.9	15.2	**4.8**
2.3	8.74	23.8	0.30	**2.1**	0.1	0.29	2.73	5.33	70.2	**5.9**	62.7	9.3	**4.2**

Name	City	State	Rating	2008 Rating	2007 Rating	Total Assets ($Mil)	One Year Asset Growth	Asset Mix (As a % of Total Assets) Comm-ercial Loans	Cons-umer Loans	Home Mort-gages	Secur-ities	Capital-ization Index	Leverage Ratio	Risk-based Capital Ratio
AMERICAN EXP CENTURION	SALT LAKE CITY	UT	**B**	C	C-	29,947	23.92	0.0	55.3	0.0	13.8	**10.0**	19.4	19.5
AMERICAN EXPRESS BANK	SALT LAKE CITY	UT	**B**	C	C+	34,813	9.48	40.0	30.2	0.0	13.9	**10.0**	16.1	18.8
AMERICAN FEDERAL BANK	FARGO	ND	**C+**	C	C	412	2.87	27.5	1.5	16.7	6.6	**5.6**	7.6	11.8
AMERICAN FIRST NATIONAL B	HOUSTON	TX	**D**	C-	B-	708	-5.58	12.4	0.6	3.6	12.9	**9.1**	10.7	14.2
AMERICAN FOUNDERS BANK	LEXINGTON	KY	**E-**	D-	D-	419	-2.74	10.2	0.7	13.5	22.6	**2.0**	5.9	9.0
AMERICAN FSB	HELENA	MT	**B**	B	B	318	5.95	3.3	3.0	27.7	28.4	**10.0**	13.0	19.6
AMERICAN GATEWAY BANK	BATON ROUGE	LA	**D+**	C-	C-	447	-5.90	5.1	0.7	9.9	25.9	**6.5**	8.5	13.2
AMERICAN HEARTLAND BANK	SUGAR GROVE	IL	**D-**	D-	C-	91	-9.00	8.5	0.1	17.9	11.2	**5.2**	8.1	11.2
AMERICAN HERITAGE BANK	CLOVIS	NM	**C+**	B-	B-	70	11.83	14.6	3.4	9.4	12.4	**9.1**	10.4	14.9
AMERICAN HERITAGE BANK	SAPULPA	OK	**A-**	A-	A-	692	2.14	7.0	4.7	14.4	48.0	**9.4**	10.6	22.7
AMERICAN HERITAGE	LONG PRAIRIE	MN	**B-**	C+	B	213	3.85	6.5	0.5	5.1	13.8	**9.4**	10.6	16.3
▼ AMERICAN HOME BANK	CHICAGO	IL	**D+**	C-	C-	22	-62.79	0.0	0.0	0.0	0.9	**10.0**	94.7	351.3
AMERICAN INTERSTATE BK	ELKHORN	NE	**B**	B-	B-	114	4.81	12.2	1.8	12.9	6.6	**6.0**	8.0	12.3
AMERICAN INVESTORS BANK	EDEN PRAIRIE	MN	**D**	D	D-	72	-5.57	0.1	0.4	37.8	41.8	**5.5**	7.5	14.0
AMERICAN LOAN & SAVINGS A	HANNIBAL	MO	**C-**	C-	C-	6	2.38	0.0	0.2	69.7	0.0	**10.0**	14.4	28.8
▼ AMERICAN METRO BANK	CHICAGO	IL	**E**	E-	E-	95	-4.20	3.0	0.2	16.0	1.3	**3.8**	6.8	10.4
▲ AMERICAN MOMENTUM BANK	TAMPA	FL	**C**	D+	D	664	15.78	13.1	0.5	1.2	14.6	**10.0**	22.5	24.7
AMERICAN NATIONAL BK	DENVER	CO	**C+**	C-	C+	1,716	-4.44	5.0	0.8	5.0	53.4	**9.4**	10.6	22.7
AMERICAN NATIONAL BK	OAKLAND PARK	FL	**C-**	C-	B+	210	16.56	5.9	0.2	1.5	10.4	**10.0**	12.4	18.2
▲ AMERICAN NATIONAL BK	OMAHA	NE	**B-**	C	C	1,688	1.93	8.3	23.2	7.6	22.9	**9.9**	11.0	16.9
AMERICAN NATIONAL BK	ARDMORE	OK	**B+**	B	B	273	42.35	6.4	8.0	9.9	39.9	**6.8**	8.8	15.8
▼ AMERICAN NATIONAL BK	WICHITA FALLS	TX	**C+**	B-	B+	464	-3.25	6.0	3.3	11.9	17.4	**5.9**	7.9	12.6
AMERICAN NATIONAL BK & TR	DANVILLE	VA	**A-**	A-	A	833	3.05	8.9	0.9	14.7	27.8	**10.0**	11.7	17.9
AMERICAN NATIONAL BK OF M	BRAINERD	MN	**D-**	D+	C-	295	-2.28	2.8	1.4	12.5	10.2	**8.2**	9.8	14.0
▲ AMERICAN NATIONAL BK OF S	SIDNEY	NE	**B**	B+	A-	70	-1.56	15.8	6.5	1.2	39.3	**9.3**	10.5	22.0
▲ AMERICAN NATIONAL BK OF T	TERRELL	TX	**C**	C+	B-	2,206	-0.16	6.0	2.2	8.7	26.9	**6.1**	8.1	13.7
AMERICAN NATIONAL TRUST	MUNCIE	IN	**U**	U	U	12	-9.08	0.0	0.0	0.0	33.7	**10.0**	82.8	221.1
AMERICAN NB OF BEAVER	BEAVER DAM	WI	**D+**	D-	D	110	-2.76	5.6	1.3	35.6	19.7	**8.1**	9.8	15.2
AMERICAN NB OF DEKALB	SYCAMORE	IL	**D+**	C-	B	239	-2.99	5.9	7.9	9.1	24.2	**8.4**	9.9	17.1
▼ AMERICAN NB OF MT	MOUNT PLEASANT	TX	**C-**	B	B	100	3.33	4.8	7.2	19.6	32.8	**6.9**	9.0	18.2
AMERICAN NB-FOX CITIES	APPLETON	WI	**D**	C-	C+	240	-1.16	24.7	0.7	5.2	9.0	**9.0**	11.6	14.1
AMERICAN PATRIOT BANK	GREENEVILLE	TN	**E-**	E-	D+	100	-14.50	10.5	1.4	21.7	2.9	**0.0**	3.1	5.3
AMERICAN PERSPECTIVE	SAN LUIS OBISPO	CA	**D+**	C-	C	229	12.77	15.9	3.3	0.0	23.0	**10.0**	17.7	23.8
AMERICAN PLUS BANK NA	ARCADIA	CA	**C-**	C-	C-	159	24.01	2.4	0.0	8.5	0.6	**10.0**	12.9	16.3
▼ AMERICAN PRIDE BANK	MACON	GA	**D**	C	C	106	34.24	3.9	0.5	5.6	19.1	**10.0**	21.7	28.9
AMERICAN RIVER BANK	RANCHO CORDOVA	CA	**D**	D-	C-	577	-2.54	8.0	0.6	5.6	27.9	**10.0**	11.8	19.2
▼ AMERICAN RIVIERA BANK	SANTA BARBARA	CA	**D+**	D	C	140	4.80	17.0	1.3	6.2	11.6	**10.0**	13.3	18.5
AMERICAN SAVINGS BANK	MIDDLETOWN	OH	**C**	C-	D+	39	-1.43	4.1	1.6	60.2	3.1	**10.0**	16.7	26.0
AMERICAN SAVINGS BANK	HONOLULU	HI	**C+**	B-	B-	4,715	-2.92	11.4	1.7	43.4	14.2	**7.3**	9.2	13.9
▼ AMERICAN SAVINGS BANK	PORTSMOUTH	OH	**D+**	B-	C+	231	5.61	4.1	2.7	40.6	17.5	**5.9**	7.9	14.7
AMERICAN SAVINGS FSB	MUNSTER	IN	**D**	D	D+	180	-3.31	4.5	1.1	50.3	3.1	**7.2**	9.1	14.6
AMERICAN SB	TRIPOLI	IA	**A-**	A-	B+	48	4.91	4.4	2.8	12.3	36.8	**10.0**	14.8	24.2
AMERICAN SECURITY BANK	NEWPORT BEACH	CA	**D-**	D	C+	415	-0.65	8.0	0.5	2.7	4.6	**7.5**	9.4	12.9
AMERICAN SECURITY BANK &	HENDERSONVILLE	TN	**D**	D	C-	173	3.59	19.8	1.6	5.7	23.1	**10.0**	11.1	16.0
▲ AMERICAN STATE BK	OSCEOLA	IA	**C+**	C+	B-	118	7.46	18.3	6.5	14.1	17.0	**6.0**	8.0	11.8
AMERICAN STATE BK	SIOUX CENTER	IA	**B-**	B	B-	529	8.84	18.8	1.5	2.6	3.0	**7.1**	10.4	12.5
AMERICAN STATE BK	OLDHAM	SD	**C-**	C-	C+	28	18.07	6.1	2.3	1.3	53.5	**7.5**	9.3	17.3
▼ AMERICAN STATE BK	ARP	TX	**C-**	C-	B-	249	20.77	5.2	5.7	14.8	18.6	**9.0**	10.3	14.9
AMERICAN STATE BK	LUBBOCK	TX	**A-**	A-	A-	2,687	11.76	9.1	1.6	5.3	46.9	**6.6**	8.6	17.2
AMERICAN STATE BK & TRUST	GREAT BEND	KS	**B-**	B-	B-	289	-10.96	6.9	0.9	2.7	38.9	**8.6**	10.0	16.0
AMERICAN STATE BK & TRUST	WILLISTON	ND	**C+**	C+	B-	393	17.48	6.3	7.5	7.6	51.4	**4.8**	6.8	13.7
AMERICAN STATE BK OF ERSK	ERSKINE	MN	**B-**	B-	B	21	2.29	7.2	4.7	14.5	25.9	**10.0**	14.6	27.6
AMERICAN STATE BK OF	GRYGLA	MN	**C**	C-	B-	24	-0.98	11.3	7.3	15.1	15.2	**7.9**	9.6	16.9
AMERICAN STATE BK OF PIER	PIERRE	SD	**A**	A	A	135	7.44	9.9	2.7	2.0	40.6	**8.8**	10.2	18.5
AMERICAN TRUST & SB	DUBUQUE	IA	**D**	D	C-	821	-4.49	21.4	2.4	7.4	10.2	**7.9**	10.2	13.2
▼ AMERICAN TRUST & SB	LOWDEN	IA	**D**	D	D+	29	-1.76	4.0	1.3	2.0	55.1	**10.0**	12.8	17.4
AMERICAN TRUST BANK	KIRKSVILLE	MO	**C-**	C-	C	41	49.69	10.2	1.8	17.1	1.1	**5.5**	7.5	11.4
▼ AMERICAN TRUST BANK OF	KNOXVILLE	TN	**D**	D	D+	134	4.00	10.2	1.0	12.3	28.3	**8.0**	9.7	16.7
AMERICAN UNION SAVINGS &	CHICAGO	IL	**C-**	C	C-	7	-3.27	0.0	1.1	37.5	41.4	**10.0**	11.8	36.9
AMERICANA COMMUNITY	SLEEPY EYE	MN	**E-**	E-	E-	160	-8.04	7.6	2.1	7.4	12.7	**0.0**	2.1	4.2

Asset Quality Index	Non-Performing Loans as a % of Total Loans	Non-Performing Loans as a % of Capital	Net Charge-offs Avg Loans	Profitability Index	Net Income ($Mil)	Return on Assets (R.O.A.)	Return on Equity (R.O.E.)	Net Interest Spread	Overhead Efficiency Ratio	Liquidity Index	Liquidity Ratio	Hot Money Ratio	Stability Index
3.7	2.10	5.3	5.15	**10.0**	1,340.8	4.77	25.88	6.95	52.5	**2.1**	40.7	87.8	**8.4**
4.3	2.01	6.9	5.51	**6.7**	802.2	2.41	15.09	4.98	69.4	**2.0**	30.5	42.9	**8.4**
4.6	0.56	5.7	-0.01	**5.1**	5.0	1.23	16.36	4.07	71.8	**1.0**	9.7	30.7	**4.2**
1.1	2.13	14.2	0.27	**6.2**	8.5	1.16	11.45	4.40	56.1	**0.8**	18.4	36.9	**6.2**
1.3	3.37	30.6	1.60	**0.0**	-4.2	-0.87	-16.19	3.16	118.9	**1.6**	15.8	23.8	**2.2**
5.9	0.92	4.3	0.04	**4.2**	2.6	0.84	7.01	3.64	65.4	**4.2**	34.5	12.3	**6.9**
1.6	3.75	24.9	1.23	**2.7**	1.3	0.30	3.61	3.96	72.5	**1.2**	14.8	29.5	**4.3**
0.0	12.47	96.0	3.38	**0.0**	-2.6	-2.74	-28.01	3.16	95.0	**0.8**	17.1	36.8	**3.4**
3.3	2.49	13.8	0.26	**3.9**	0.4	0.67	5.90	4.02	77.8	**2.3**	34.5	24.8	**6.2**
8.5	0.04	0.2	0.83	**6.1**	9.7	1.43	12.99	3.90	58.5	**2.2**	22.7	18.9	**8.0**
3.5	2.62	15.1	0.12	**3.7**	1.1	0.51	4.76	3.38	64.8	**3.3**	18.1	12.6	**6.2**
7.7	0.00	0.0	6.57	**0.0**	-7.4	-14.58	-19.54	-0.50	-74.0	**5.0**	1,600.2	101.0	**3.9**
6.5	0.31	2.5	0.02	**8.9**	2.5	2.22	27.17	4.36	40.1	**1.4**	16.3	26.2	**6.6**
4.2	2.84	17.6	2.68	**4.4**	1.0	1.36	17.76	4.24	50.4	**5.0**	46.1	10.9	**1.5**
8.0	0.41	2.0	0.00	**0.9**	0.0	-0.35	-2.39	4.08	87.6	**1.7**	21.6	21.7	**4.9**
0.0	19.80	168.8	0.70	**0.0**	-2.2	-2.24	-31.38	2.70	141.2	**0.8**	19.8	49.3	**3.4**
3.3	3.67	13.0	0.14	**2.5**	9.7	1.60	7.03	4.02	75.4	**1.1**	11.2	29.4	**4.8**
3.4	6.83	20.2	1.63	**2.9**	14.4	0.82	7.54	3.47	83.0	**5.5**	46.1	11.4	**7.4**
0.5	3.89	19.7	0.87	**3.9**	1.1	0.55	4.32	4.56	67.2	**3.3**	29.9	15.2	**7.0**
3.6	1.55	8.6	0.54	**7.9**	34.1	2.02	17.54	4.44	58.9	**3.1**	16.0	13.8	**9.8**
8.3	0.02	0.1	0.21	**6.2**	3.5	1.39	14.66	4.52	67.6	**1.9**	38.4	38.4	**6.3**
2.9	2.70	19.3	0.02	**4.0**	2.8	0.57	6.60	3.58	76.3	**1.4**	9.4	24.5	**6.3**
7.2	0.50	2.5	0.24	**6.1**	9.2	1.12	7.73	3.98	61.3	**1.4**	15.3	26.8	**8.6**
0.0	8.83	53.3	1.35	**1.0**	-1.4	-0.46	-4.61	3.97	76.9	**1.2**	17.9	30.1	**6.5**
8.7	0.02	0.1	0.26	**3.9**	0.5	0.67	6.18	3.62	77.0	**4.6**	41.8	12.1	**7.4**
3.6	2.35	14.5	1.75	**2.8**	7.4	0.39	3.81	4.57	74.8	**3.6**	21.6	13.0	**6.1**
10.0	0.00	0.0	0.00	**9.5**	0.5	4.22	6.18	2.01	95.1	**5.0**	231.6	101.0	**5.0**
1.8	4.95	32.0	0.74	**2.2**	0.4	0.40	4.11	4.07	85.4	**4.6**	26.0	6.4	**2.9**
1.7	5.57	30.7	0.42	**4.7**	2.6	1.09	9.89	4.45	65.5	**3.5**	24.3	12.3	**5.0**
4.4	2.72	14.4	1.48	**2.5**	0.0	0.04	0.45	3.50	70.7	**2.2**	33.6	24.9	**5.5**
0.9	0.81	5.1	0.65	**6.5**	3.8	1.58	13.93	4.03	38.8	**0.5**	9.7	54.8	**7.1**
0.0	15.86	199.1	0.31	**0.0**	-1.2	-1.07	-29.67	3.35	114.7	**1.8**	12.2	19.5	**0.2**
5.1	0.00	0.0	0.89	**0.8**	0.5	0.23	1.21	3.73	85.2	**1.0**	6.6	29.7	**2.5**
5.0	1.62	9.2	-0.01	**1.9**	0.5	0.30	2.42	3.53	73.0	**1.0**	18.9	33.1	**3.4**
6.8	1.36	4.2	0.00	**0.3**	-0.1	-0.14	-0.59	4.07	99.1	**0.8**	17.0	44.9	**1.8**
0.2	6.52	30.5	2.11	**3.4**	0.7	0.12	0.83	4.53	65.7	**3.0**	29.6	16.6	**7.7**
1.0	4.91	21.0	0.05	**2.9**	1.0	0.75	5.59	4.64	72.4	**4.3**	38.4	12.8	**3.0**
4.1	3.00	13.3	0.10	**2.5**	0.2	0.40	2.46	4.54	78.1	**3.9**	13.5	8.9	**5.1**
3.8	1.62	12.0	0.59	**4.9**	58.5	1.20	11.67	4.39	56.6	**5.0**	20.6	3.8	**6.9**
1.6	3.54	28.6	0.09	**4.2**	2.0	0.86	10.14	3.74	63.1	**2.4**	24.7	17.7	**5.2**
1.1	3.60	27.1	0.83	**2.1**	0.7	0.37	4.05	3.48	74.3	**1.7**	14.1	21.4	**3.7**
8.0	0.00	0.0	0.46	**6.2**	0.7	1.43	9.09	3.73	48.9	**5.0**	56.0	12.6	**8.9**
0.1	3.68	26.5	0.77	**2.4**	1.8	0.41	3.52	4.37	75.3	**3.5**	16.6	11.8	**5.8**
1.8	3.00	16.2	1.69	**0.0**	-1.9	-1.12	-9.10	2.65	114.1	**0.8**	21.4	47.5	**5.3**
4.4	0.62	5.0	0.22	**7.5**	1.8	1.66	19.86	4.69	64.3	**1.9**	19.5	19.8	**6.1**
4.5	0.32	2.5	0.45	**8.7**	11.1	2.22	22.03	4.17	41.7	**3.3**	10.9	12.1	**7.5**
5.9	2.87	11.3	0.00	**2.0**	0.1	0.42	3.98	3.23	92.4	**5.3**	38.6	7.6	**3.8**
5.6	0.59	3.5	0.02	**0.9**	-0.2	-0.11	-1.08	N/,	141.7	**2.2**	30.5	22.1	**5.0**
7.3	0.83	3.8	0.32	**8.0**	36.7	1.47	15.00	4.06	54.4	**3.0**	28.6	19.3	**7.1**
4.7	0.92	4.5	-0.01	**4.9**	3.2	1.06	9.22	3.62	63.2	**2.2**	29.5	21.7	**6.2**
4.2	1.14	6.6	0.49	**7.6**	7.1	1.97	27.04	4.19	50.6	**5.0**	38.3	9.0	**4.5**
8.6	0.04	0.2	0.01	**4.5**	0.2	1.01	6.89	4.22	75.3	**5.6**	47.7	5.5	**6.8**
3.5	1.84	11.9	0.45	**5.6**	0.3	1.16	11.58	4.41	68.4	**1.7**	26.1	22.9	**8.3**
8.4	0.00	0.0	0.03	**8.2**	1.8	1.36	13.20	4.58	57.8	**2.1**	18.6	18.9	**7.5**
1.6	2.56	17.5	1.06	**4.1**	7.3	0.89	8.83	4.06	67.0	**3.8**	10.0	9.4	**5.4**
3.0	9.82	21.8	0.58	**0.0**	-0.3	-1.00	-5.56	4.15	152.5	**4.4**	60.2	16.4	**5.0**
5.1	0.62	6.0	0.05	**3.7**	0.6	2.01	21.86	4.44	73.2	**1.7**	21.1	22.8	**2.9**
1.7	5.28	27.2	1.75	**0.5**	0.0	0.03	0.32	2.96	80.4	**2.0**	32.5	27.8	**4.8**
10.0	0.00	0.0	0.000	**1.5**	0.0	-0.01	-0.13	4.33	100.0	**4.9**	65.4	13.0	**3.5**
0.3	3.28	44.4	3.31	**0.0**	-6.8	-4.00	-119.55	3.66	136.4	**2.4**	22.0	17.8	**0.0**

Name	City	State	Rating	2008 Rating	2007 Rating	Total Assets ($Mil)	One Year Asset Growth	Asset Mix (As a % of Total Assets) Comm-ercial Loans	Cons-umer Loans	Home Mort-gages	Secur-ities	Capital-ization Index	Leverage Ratio	Risk-based Capital Ratio
AMERICANTRUST FSB	PERU	IN	**D**	D	C-	101	-17.74	16.0	5.2	30.0	4.3	**7.0**	9.0	12.8
▲ AMERICANWEST BANK	SPOKANE	WA	**D**	E-	E	1,624	-1.80	5.0	0.5	4.5	4.5	**7.7**	9.5	14.2
AMERICAS COMMUNITY BANK	BLUE SPRINGS	MO	**D-**	C-	C-	34	-0.60	11.6	0.2	17.5	5.9	**6.3**	8.3	14.6
AMERICAS UNITED BANK	GLENDALE	CA	**D**	D	C-	114	-8.07	15.3	1.8	0.7	0.6	**10.0**	15.0	17.9
AMERICAUNITED BANK &	SCHAUMBURG	IL	**D**	D	C	303	-7.00	10.9	0.9	18.7	9.5	**7.2**	9.1	14.6
▼ AMERIFIRST BANK	UNION SPRINGS	AL	**D+**	C	C+	160	0.46	5.9	5.1	16.9	24.3	**9.5**	10.6	16.0
AMERIPRISE BANK FSB	MINNEAPOLIS	MN	**D+**	D+	D-	3,856	36.79	0.0	5.6	1.4	69.2	**5.7**	7.7	14.8
AMERIS BANK	MOULTRIE	GA	**D**	D	C-	2,971	22.66	4.6	1.6	14.8	10.9	**10.0**	11.1	17.7
AMERISERV FINANCIAL BANK	JOHNSTOWN	PA	**D+**	C-	C+	924	-1.95	8.4	2.1	20.6	17.0	**7.2**	9.1	13.6
AMERISTATE BK	ATOKA	OK	**B-**	B	B+	198	11.95	11.0	7.5	19.1	4.5	**5.8**	7.8	14.8
AMES COMMUNITY BANK	AMES	IA	**D+**	D-	D+	424	11.21	5.0	0.9	14.3	11.3	**7.4**	9.2	13.0
▼ AMFIRST BANK NA	MCCOOK	NE	**D+**	D	C-	253	-2.13	12.7	5.6	6.3	10.6	**5.8**	8.2	11.6
AMG NATIONAL TRUST BANK	ENGLEWOOD	CO	**A-**	B	B+	157	-26.95	3.9	6.4	1.6	38.3	**9.6**	10.8	27.1
AMISTAD BANK	DEL RIO	TX	**A-**	B+	B	20	6.17	6.3	2.7	16.3	0.0	**10.0**	13.9	18.4
AMORY FS&LA	AMORY	MS	**C**	C-	C+	87	18.53	0.0	1.1	69.3	0.0	**7.9**	9.6	21.0
ANADARKO BANK & TRUST CO	ANADARKO	OK	**D**	D	D-	63	7.90	6.2	1.8	9.3	24.1	**8.7**	10.2	15.3
ANAHUAC NATIONAL BK	ANAHUAC	TX	**B-**	B-	B-	69	-3.47	6.1	12.2	18.1	23.1	**7.8**	9.5	15.0
▲ ANCHOR BANK NA	SAINT PAUL	MN	**C**	D+	C+	1,288	-2.79	12.8	0.8	5.9	18.7	**6.6**	8.6	12.8
▼ ANCHOR COMMERCIAL BANK	JUNO BEACH	FL	**E-**	D-	D+	160	-3.81	9.3	2.1	15.1	10.6	**1.8**	5.2	8.8
ANCHOR MUTUAL SB	ABERDEEN	WA	**D-**	D-	D-	496	-15.74	4.1	3.5	27.3	10.1	**6.1**	8.1	12.4
ANCHOR STATE BK	ANCHOR	IL	**D-**	D-	D-	13	0.32	6.3	1.6	6.9	16.7	**8.6**	10.1	18.3
ANCHORBANK FSB	MADISON	WI	**E-**	E-	E	3,588	-19.57	3.0	8.6	24.4	14.9	**1.4**	4.4	8.4
ANDALUSIA COMMUNITY BANK	ANDALUSIA	IL	**B+**	A-	A-	50	41.79	6.2	8.0	21.4	25.1	**10.0**	12.1	22.4
ANDEREN BANK	PALM HARBOR	FL	**D**	C	C	196	31.48	12.5	1.1	3.3	13.3	**10.0**	16.7	21.5
ANDERSON BROTHERS BANK	MULLINS	SC	**D-**	D-	D+	473	1.34	8.5	19.7	17.6	8.8	**3.8**	7.0	10.4
ANDERSON STATE BK	ONEIDA	IL	**B-**	C+	B-	66	3.58	4.7	5.9	8.3	29.1	**10.0**	15.5	27.0
ANDES STATE BK	LAKE ANDES	SD	**D-**	D	D	21	-0.51	6.4	4.5	4.7	21.7	**8.7**	10.1	20.8
ANDOVER BANK	ANDOVER	OH	**B**	B	B	295	5.72	2.9	1.5	30.7	37.3	**6.9**	8.9	17.6
ANDOVER STATE BK	ANDOVER	KS	**D**	D	C-	64	-3.89	3.6	3.1	30.0	14.2	**5.1**	7.1	11.2
ANDREW JOHNSON BANK	GREENEVILLE	TN	**C-**	C+	B-	266	3.92	6.8	3.9	31.9	7.1	**6.3**	8.3	12.3
ANDROSCOGGIN SB	LEWISTON	ME	**C-**	C-	C+	693	2.86	6.3	0.6	33.9	8.5	**6.3**	8.9	12.0
ANGELINA SAVINGS BANK FSB	LUFKIN	TX	**B-**	B	B	52	0.14	2.4	18.5	27.9	1.2	**9.0**	10.4	22.3
ANN ARBOR STATE BK	ANN ARBOR	MI	**C**	C	NR	106	47.76	21.5	0.8	13.1	25.2	**8.9**	10.3	14.9
▼ ANNA STATE BK	ANNA	IL	**B+**	A-	A-	68	9.95	1.9	3.4	24.1	45.2	**10.0**	13.0	27.3
ANNA-JONESBORO NATIONAL	ANNA	IL	**B**	B+	A-	223	6.23	5.4	7.4	28.4	38.8	**10.0**	11.2	22.3
▲ ANNANDALE STATE BK	ANNANDALE	MN	**B-**	C	B	127	5.28	3.0	2.6	23.2	24.1	**10.0**	12.6	16.1
▼ ANSON BANK & TRUST CO	WADESBORO	NC	**D+**	C-	C+	58	4.86	6.7	2.2	33.8	13.5	**6.5**	8.5	13.9
▲ ANTWERP EXCHANGE BANK	ANTWERP	OH	**C+**	C	C+	75	6.70	6.1	3.6	23.9	30.9	**7.1**	9.1	16.4
▼ ANZ GUAM INC	HAGATNA	GU	**C+**	B-	B+	168	-0.01	13.7	1.4	25.6	0.0	**10.0**	11.1	18.0
APOLLO TRUST CO	APOLLO	PA	**B-**	B-	B+	136	15.16	6.2	2.5	11.7	64.9	**10.0**	12.6	27.3
APPLE BANK FOR SAVINGS	NEW YORK	NY	**C+**	C+	B	6,609	-9.36	9.1	0.3	11.4	32.0	**8.6**	10.1	29.1
APPLE CREEK BANKING CO	APPLE CREEK	OH	**C**	C+	C	99	6.91	3.8	1.1	37.6	16.4	**5.5**	7.5	13.6
APPLE RIVER STATE BK	APPLE RIVER	IL	**C+**	C+	B-	260	2.43	13.5	3.6	12.2	27.4	**5.9**	7.9	12.0
APPLIED BANK	WILMINGTON	DE	**A+**	A+	A+	241	-23.08	0.2	0.1	0.5	2.0	**10.0**	15.2	88.3
▼ AQUESTA BANK	CORNELIUS	NC	**D+**	C-	D	196	2.18	11.2	0.1	7.4	22.1	**7.3**	10.4	12.8
▼ ARBOR BANK	NEBRASKA CITY	NE	**D-**	C-	C	154	-5.83	7.0	1.4	14.6	29.2	**6.6**	8.6	13.4
ARCHER BANK	CHICAGO	IL	**D-**	D	D+	583	11.87	0.9	0.3	10.8	11.0	**7.0**	9.0	13.8
AREA BANK	ROSICLARE	IL	**C+**	C	C	53	4.71	7.6	5.9	21.0	41.2	**6.5**	8.5	16.1
ARGENTINE FEDERAL	KANSAS CITY	KS	**C**	C-	C-	58	6.34	0.0	0.6	71.0	5.0	**10.0**	11.2	21.9
ARIZONA BANK & TRUST	PHOENIX	AZ	**C-**	D+	C	224	-13.44	9.9	0.9	6.3	32.6	**7.7**	9.5	15.7
ARKANSAS BANKERS BANK	LITTLE ROCK	AR	**B**	B-	B-	164	-1.58	2.0	0.0	0.9	54.2	**10.0**	13.5	31.7
▲ ARKANSAS COUNTY BANK	DE WITT	AR	**B-**	B-	B-	151	-4.41	5.0	4.4	15.2	21.9	**6.8**	8.8	13.3
ARLINGTON BANK	UPPER ARLINGTON	OH	**D+**	D+	B-	234	2.62	0.7	0.7	45.8	6.7	**9.2**	10.5	17.1
▲ ARLINGTON STATE BK	ARLINGTON	MN	**D+**	D	C+	50	-0.22	5.9	1.9	8.1	30.4	**7.5**	9.3	16.9
ARMED FORCES BANK NA	FORT LEAVENWORTH	KS	**D-**	D-	D	2,009	132.81	8.6	1.0	3.8	11.6	**5.1**	7.1	23.8
▲ ARMED FORCES BANK OF CA	FORT LEAVENWORTH	KS	**C**	C	C-	18	-25.59	0.0	1.9	4.0	18.1	**10.0**	27.4	161.8
▲ ARMSTRONG BANK	MUSKOGEE	OK	**C**	C	C+	555	4.49	5.8	7.2	17.1	19.5	**8.2**	9.8	14.1
ARMSTRONG COUNTY	FORD CITY	PA	**C-**	C	B-	83	3.26	0.0	1.0	45.0	42.3	**10.0**	13.7	29.8
AROOSTOOK COUNTY FS&LA	CARIBOU	ME	**C+**	C+	C+	98	2.18	1.9	2.8	64.5	0.0	**8.2**	9.8	19.5
ARROWHEAD BANK	LLANO	TX	**C+**	B-	A-	123	1.84	6.4	6.0	10.0	9.1	**10.0**	11.0	17.3

Asset Quality Index	Non-Performing Loans as a % of Total Loans	Non-Performing Loans as a % of Capital	Net Charge-offs Avg Loans	Profitability Index	Net Income ($Mil)	Return on Assets (R.O.A.)	Return on Equity (R.O.E.)	Net Interest Spread	Overhead Efficiency Ratio	Liquidity Index	Liquidity Ratio	Hot Money Ratio	Stability Index
0.5	3.20	24.1	0.83	0.5	-0.8	-0.73	-8.59	3.35	92.4	2.4	12.2	16.8	2.4
2.3	3.01	19.0	-0.05	0.5	0.5	0.03	0.66	N/,	75.8	3.9	33.0	16.4	5.6
0.3	0.71	4.8	1.28	0.6	-0.2	-0.61	-7.63	3.59	87.4	2.2	35.0	27.4	4.3
2.9	1.90	9.5	1.90	0.0	-2.5	-2.01	-13.33	4.21	130.3	1.1	15.3	31.0	1.7
0.0	11.99	74.0	2.54	0.3	-1.3	-0.40	-3.91	3.61	74.6	1.3	18.7	28.5	4.0
1.9	4.42	25.0	1.34	2.0	0.4	0.23	2.14	4.21	80.7	1.1	18.8	32.2	4.9
9.7	0.47	1.6	1.29	2.0	10.9	0.32	4.93	2.28	64.5	3.3	77.1	80.7	2.2
1.4	5.29	30.8	2.96	0.5	-2.5	-0.10	-0.91	4.13	63.8	1.6	18.1	24.7	5.5
3.2	1.81	11.9	0.74	2.0	2.5	0.27	2.59	3.92	79.9	2.9	10.3	14.3	5.6
3.7	3.35	25.8	1.10	3.3	1.1	0.53	6.34	4.21	71.5	1.3	22.9	30.5	4.8
1.5	3.67	24.2	2.87	1.3	-1.8	-0.44	-4.89	3.82	80.9	2.3	16.8	17.7	4.8
2.4	1.51	11.8	1.29	1.0	-0.3	-0.13	-1.52	4.48	79.5	1.0	11.9	30.7	4.3
9.2	0.00	0.0	0.00	5.7	1.3	0.90	7.83	1.16	88.9	7.0	50.8	0.3	7.5
7.5	0.02	0.1	-0.03	5.5	0.2	0.96	6.83	6.23	83.1	1.2	9.0	26.7	8.3
2.9	3.10	22.9	0.00	3.3	0.4	0.55	5.25	2.85	63.7	1.1	27.6	46.6	4.7
1.2	7.23	37.2	1.47	2.1	0.2	0.31	2.72	3.90	90.4	3.1	33.7	17.6	4.6
7.7	0.00	0.0	0.20	4.3	0.6	0.89	8.92	5.33	81.0	2.0	29.8	24.3	6.5
2.8	2.73	19.3	1.19	2.7	4.6	0.37	4.24	4.05	72.6	4.3	14.9	7.5	5.1
0.0	9.19	84.6	1.76	0.0	-2.5	-1.43	-23.48	3.31	82.4	1.1	24.3	32.8	3.2
0.3	4.37	32.9	1.16	0.1	-2.2	-0.40	-4.94	3.86	99.3	1.5	13.3	23.4	3.3
1.7	5.85	28.1	0.75	0.4	-0.1	-0.57	-6.05	3.27	101.7	3.6	46.9	16.1	3.3
0.0	12.32	105.5	0.08	0.0	-39.5	-0.97	-23.72	2.53	86.3	1.9	19.3	21.7	3.6
5.5	2.31	9.5	0.15	4.6	0.3	0.67	4.83	4.14	80.1	2.5	43.4	28.9	8.5
3.0	3.82	16.0	1.74	0.0	-2.6	-1.48	-6.87	3.44	103.5	1.0	24.3	38.5	1.5
0.3	8.39	70.3	3.53	0.6	-5.1	-1.06	-14.38	6.20	67.4	0.7	14.2	43.1	3.7
5.5	1.99	6.2	0.63	2.8	0.2	0.37	2.31	3.16	74.4	3.9	47.5	16.6	6.9
5.1	3.41	10.5	0.58	0.1	0.0	-0.15	-1.44	3.68	109.4	2.7	53.7	25.8	3.6
5.5	1.69	9.8	0.18	6.4	3.8	1.34	14.20	4.45	63.4	4.4	30.5	9.5	5.6
7.0	0.13	1.2	1.12	1.6	0.1	0.19	2.65	4.19	88.1	3.7	10.1	9.9	3.0
2.3	1.73	15.9	0.46	4.3	1.4	0.56	6.69	4.81	67.3	2.1	6.4	17.5	5.0
2.1	1.73	14.8	0.28	3.2	3.2	0.46	4.68	3.78	78.1	1.3	7.1	25.1	6.3
7.6	0.14	0.8	0.03	4.4	0.5	0.88	8.41	4.65	74.4	3.3	42.6	18.8	6.1
8.7	0.00	0.0	0.00	2.6	0.8	0.92	7.99	4.17	78.0	2.8	28.0	16.8	3.5
8.1	0.67	2.4	-0.01	4.9	0.5	0.85	6.17	3.80	74.6	3.2	41.0	19.0	7.8
4.0	4.05	19.2	0.51	5.6	2.2	1.03	8.68	4.02	57.6	1.9	28.4	25.7	6.3
4.3	3.23	13.8	0.96	4.1	0.8	0.63	4.80	4.15	73.5	4.6	32.0	8.8	8.2
2.2	3.47	26.6	0.40	1.0	0.1	0.15	1.45	4.38	83.3	1.3	13.6	26.6	4.0
5.8	1.17	7.3	0.05	3.7	0.5	0.71	7.57	3.70	70.3	4.0	25.2	9.9	5.3
6.7	0.44	2.9	0.06	2.4	0.3	0.15	1.34	4.82	97.6	2.7	23.7	16.3	6.4
9.2	0.04	0.1	-0.03	3.6	1.0	0.76	5.99	3.88	80.9	4.8	66.8	16.9	7.1
9.8	0.18	0.8	0.00	3.5	36.5	0.55	5.67	1.97	61.1	5.3	58.8	14.6	6.8
4.0	1.83	15.2	0.38	2.9	0.3	0.32	3.93	4.47	79.7	4.5	24.2	6.8	4.3
4.2	0.84	6.3	0.27	5.5	3.5	1.34	16.36	3.78	59.4	1.8	13.3	20.1	4.9
9.1	0.02	0.0	0.08	9.3	6.5	2.10	8.49	1.96	59.5	8.2	95.1	0.9	8.3
1.8	3.47	20.5	1.55	1.0	0.5	0.25	2.20	3.85	89.6	1.7	28.2	28.2	2.3
2.4	4.24	26.4	0.94	0.3	-1.0	-0.62	-6.82	3.70	96.4	2.2	15.6	18.1	2.9
0.0	14.35	89.3	6.10	0.7	-19.2	-3.05	-32.64	4.43	101.5	1.6	15.6	22.7	4.0
5.9	0.71	3.5	0.16	4.0	0.4	0.81	8.89	4.23	76.4	5.1	39.9	9.5	4.8
8.0	0.38	2.6	0.20	2.5	0.2	0.30	2.66	3.61	81.5	3.1	17.7	13.9	5.2
1.2	7.02	31.5	7.38	0.0	-5.1	-1.99	-23.65	3.62	83.5	4.3	32.3	10.9	4.8
9.7	0.00	0.0	-0.09	5.2	2.4	1.27	10.07	2.84	62.5	7.5	60.3	0.0	7.1
5.0	1.08	7.0	0.21	5.7	2.2	1.45	14.81	4.39	62.5	1.9	26.1	22.6	5.6
1.5	4.58	30.3	0.62	3.9	1.4	0.59	5.74	3.61	66.9	1.7	24.5	23.6	5.1
2.1	4.40	20.9	1.07	1.7	0.2	0.39	3.98	4.01	81.0	4.6	36.6	11.0	4.4
0.0	37.87	91.1	17.34	1.2	-30.0	-1.79	-21.62	2.77	76.8	3.0	34.9	23.7	7.2
7.9	0.00	0.0	3.25	10.0	0.5	2.44	8.26	0.99	78.7	7.2	118.0	8.3	1.7
1.8	2.48	16.1	0.45	8.3	10.6	1.93	19.06	5.02	63.8	1.2	23.5	31.8	6.8
7.4	0.94	3.6	0.02	1.5	-0.1	-0.13	-0.94	1.59	84.2	2.4	51.6	34.8	7.1
5.1	1.26	9.8	0.24	3.4	0.5	0.54	5.64	3.46	66.1	2.6	18.7	16.4	5.2
6.7	0.27	1.4	0.24	2.3	0.3	0.22	1.97	3.31	90.8	4.0	33.2	12.8	5.9

Name	City	State	Rating	2008 Rating	2007 Rating	Total Assets ($Mil)	One Year Asset Growth	Asset Mix (As a % of Total Assets) Comm-ercial Loans	Cons-umer Loans	Home Mort-gages	Secur-ities	Capital-ization Index	Leverage Ratio	Risk-based Capital Ratio
▼ARTHUR STATE BK	UNION	SC	**E**	D+	B-	637	-5.60	8.2	2.2	17.7	6.6	**1.8**	6.5	8.8
ARTISANS BANK	WILMINGTON	DE	**E+**	D	D+	643	-5.35	6.9	0.2	8.5	18.9	**3.0**	7.0	10.0
ARUNDEL FSB	GLEN BURNIE	MD	**C+**	C	C+	492	2.19	0.0	0.1	54.9	36.3	**9.3**	10.5	26.2
ARVEST BANK	FAYETTEVILLE	AR	**D+**	C-	C-	11,527	1.84	9.1	7.0	13.4	14.7	**6.9**	9.0	14.1
ARVEST TRUST CO NA	ROGERS	AR	**U**	U	U	3	0.11	0.0	0.0	0.0	79.5	**10.0**	65.2	178.0
ASHEVILLE SB SSB	ASHEVILLE	NC	**D-**	C-	B-	750	0.09	2.2	6.4	24.4	24.2	**6.7**	8.7	15.0
ASHTON STATE BK	ASHTON	IA	**B+**	B+	B+	34	2.21	8.8	3.8	15.2	21.4	**10.0**	12.2	15.4
ASHTON STATE BK	ASHTON	NE	**C-**	C-	C+	18	22.97	1.9	1.5	0.8	7.2	**7.1**	9.0	16.1
ASIA BANK NA	FLUSHING	NY	**A-**	A-	A	424	-2.24	1.1	0.1	4.9	3.2	**10.0**	14.4	18.4
ASIAN BANK	PHILADELPHIA	PA	**E-**	E-	E-	69	-15.44	2.4	0.1	9.9	10.1	**1.3**	5.0	8.3
ASIAN PACIFIC NATIONAL BK	SAN GABRIEL	CA	**B-**	C	C	52	3.36	1.4	0.1	0.4	31.1	**10.0**	15.4	23.8
▲ASSOCIATED BANK NA	GREEN BAY	WI	**D**	D	C+	21,598	-4.28	11.9	2.9	17.8	28.2	**7.8**	9.6	16.4
ASSOCIATED TRUST CO NA	MILWAUKEE	WI	**U**	U	U	20	9.94	0.0	0.0	0.0	5.1	**10.0**	83.8	159.8
▲ASTORIA FS&LA	NEW HYDE PARK	NY	**D+**	C-	C+	17,862	-10.78	0.1	0.1	60.7	14.3	**5.9**	7.9	14.6
▲ASTRA BANK	SCANDIA	KS	**B+**	B	B	171	-5.60	9.2	2.8	9.3	27.6	**8.0**	9.7	13.4
▼ATASCOSA NATIONAL BK	PLEASANTON	TX	**C**	B-	B	66	28.28	3.1	2.3	4.5	36.4	**7.6**	9.4	28.3
ATHENS FEDERAL	ATHENS	TN	**B-**	C+	C+	277	0.37	4.5	3.6	29.3	15.0	**10.0**	13.5	20.8
ATHENS STATE BK	ATHENS	IL	**A-**	A-	B+	110	23.38	4.1	8.3	28.5	22.2	**7.5**	9.3	16.8
ATHOL SB	ATHOL	MA	**B-**	B-	B	326	2.35	1.4	1.2	37.9	34.9	**10.0**	12.0	25.5
▲ATHOL-CLINTON CO-OP BANK	ATHOL	MA	**D-**	D	C+	85	-10.49	0.0	0.8	75.2	1.6	**6.0**	8.1	11.8
ATKINS SB & TRUST	ATKINS	IA	**B-**	C+	C	62	11.23	6.2	5.0	7.8	40.1	**6.1**	8.1	12.9
ATLANTA NATIONAL BK	ATLANTA	IL	**C+**	B	B-	58	8.98	1.7	5.7	8.1	67.1	**9.0**	10.3	26.3
ATLANTIC BANK & TRUST	CHARLESTON	SC	**E-**	C-	C	239	-11.05	0.9	0.2	25.1	4.7	**0.0**	3.0	6.1
ATLANTIC CAPITAL BANK	ATLANTA	GA	**C-**	C-	C-	842	22.38	26.1	0.1	0.3	10.8	**10.0**	14.4	16.3
▲ATLANTIC CENTRAL BANKERS	CAMP HILL	PA	**C-**	D	D+	724	6.05	0.6	0.0	0.7	12.1	**5.3**	7.3	18.2
ATLANTIC COAST BANK	WAYCROSS	GA	**E-**	D-	D+	829	-8.60	2.7	10.3	40.6	17.9	**3.1**	5.5	10.1
▼ATLANTIC COMMUNITY BANK	BLUFFTON	SC	**E+**	D-	D+	96	3.55	4.0	0.6	18.0	7.9	**5.2**	7.2	12.5
ATLANTIC NATIONAL BK	BRUNSWICK	GA	**D-**	D+	B-	183	-3.03	4.9	0.9	40.5	2.1	**5.0**	7.0	12.5
ATLANTIC SOUTHERN BANK	MACON	GA	**E-**	E-	D	781	-17.64	5.4	0.7	10.4	3.4	**0.0**	2.3	4.3
▲ATLANTIC STEWARDSHIP	MIDLAND PARK	NJ	**D+**	C-	C+	685	4.02	6.5	0.2	15.4	26.8	**6.0**	8.0	12.6
ATLAS BANK	BROOKLYN	NY	**C+**	C+	B-	87	22.17	0.0	0.0	33.2	49.0	**10.0**	19.4	50.5
ATWATER STATE BK	ATWATER	MN	**C+**	C	C+	39	4.87	12.5	5.5	19.0	12.5	**6.6**	8.7	13.8
AUBURN BANKING CO	AUBURN	KY	**B-**	B-	B-	65	2.93	6.5	9.2	27.6	20.2	**6.5**	8.5	14.0
AUBURN SAVINGS BANK FSB	AUBURN	ME	**C-**	C	C-	81	6.95	6.0	1.2	59.2	4.0	**5.4**	7.4	12.1
AUBURN STATE BK	AUBURN	NE	**A-**	A-	A-	84	4.86	6.1	5.0	16.7	31.6	**10.0**	19.2	31.1
AUBURNBANK	AUBURN	AL	**C+**	B-	B-	760	-1.23	6.5	1.4	12.3	41.5	**6.0**	8.0	15.1
AUDUBON SB	AUDUBON	NJ	**E+**	D	D+	214	2.65	2.6	0.1	32.4	30.1	**2.8**	5.7	9.8
AUDUBON STATE BK	AUDUBON	IA	**B**	B	C	86	6.43	9.4	4.5	4.9	18.6	**4.8**	7.6	10.9
▲AURORA BANK FSB	WILMINGTON	DE	**D+**	E+	E-	4,334	-10.64	0.4	0.0	16.2	3.0	**10.0**	19.0	24.6
AUSTIN BANK OF CHICAGO	CHICAGO	IL	**C-**	D+	D+	308	-1.01	3.0	0.6	9.3	16.0	**7.9**	9.7	13.2
AUSTIN BANK TEXAS NA	JACKSONVILLE	TX	**A-**	B+	B+	1,245	19.58	10.5	8.3	24.6	11.8	**7.3**	9.2	14.2
▲AUSTIN COUNTY STATE BK	BELLVILLE	TX	**B-**	C	C-	67	21.56	21.4	6.1	22.3	22.2	**8.6**	10.1	17.0
AUTO CLUB TRUST FSB	DEARBORN	MI	**C-**	C	C+	6	0.30	0.0	0.0	0.0	91.5	**10.0**	91.9	414.3
AVB BANK	BROKEN ARROW	OK	**B-**	C	D-	257	-4.23	13.5	1.4	6.3	28.8	**10.0**	12.9	19.7
AVENUE BANK	NASHVILLE	TN	**D-**	D-	D	589	21.40	20.0	0.6	7.0	24.9	**6.2**	8.2	11.9
AVIDIA BANK	HUDSON	MA	**D+**	D+	D-	994	3.08	6.4	0.7	32.6	23.1	**4.6**	6.6	11.1
AVON CO-OP BANK	AVON	MA	**C+**	C	C-	65	0.12	0.2	0.7	52.2	31.0	**10.0**	12.1	28.8
AVON STATE BK	AVON	MN	**C+**	C	B+	103	-0.56	2.7	3.8	33.9	30.9	**10.0**	11.6	24.4
AZTECAMERICA BANK	BERWYN	IL	**D-**	D-	D-	94	8.20	5.4	0.1	19.4	14.0	**6.3**	8.3	12.4
B&L BANK	LEXINGTON	MO	**D+**	D+	D+	150	2.71	8.4	2.8	33.9	16.2	**7.2**	9.1	16.5
BAC FLORIDA BANK	CORAL GABLES	FL	**D-**	D	C+	1,121	14.97	7.4	0.4	42.6	10.5	**7.7**	9.4	18.4
BADGER BANK	FORT ATKINSON	WI	**D-**	D-	C-	109	-6.59	2.4	2.7	19.6	20.6	**7.5**	9.3	15.4
▼BAILEYVILLE STATE BK	SENECA	KS	**E-**	D	C-	38	7.62	6.6	2.8	11.9	36.2	**4.2**	7.0	10.6
BAKER-BOYER NATIONAL BK	WALLA WALLA	WA	**B-**	B	B	466	3.72	10.9	3.0	18.5	20.7	**6.0**	8.0	12.8
BALBOA THRIFT & LOAN ASSN	CHULA VISTA	CA	**C-**	C-	C-	201	0.89	0.6	79.8	2.3	0.0	**7.4**	10.8	12.9
BALDWIN STATE BK	BALDWIN CITY	KS	**C**	C-	C+	67	7.37	11.2	14.2	12.9	41.6	**7.3**	9.2	20.6
BALLINGER NATIONAL BK	BALLINGER	TX	**B**	B	B	38	-0.71	7.9	7.6	12.9	36.3	**10.0**	11.1	22.0
BALLSTON SPA NATIONAL BK	BALLSTON SPA	NY	**C+**	C+	C+	385	5.41	4.1	8.0	31.2	22.3	**5.4**	7.4	14.8
▼BALLY SB	BALLY	PA	**D+**	C-	C	44	13.57	0.0	0.3	34.9	19.8	**4.9**	6.9	17.2
BALTIC STATE BK	BALTIC	OH	**C+**	C+	C+	41	8.39	1.8	5.3	52.0	14.5	**5.6**	10.9	11.5

Asset Quality Index	Non-Performing Loans as a % of Total Loans	Non-Performing Loans as a % of Capital	Net Charge-offs Avg Loans	Profitability Index	Net Income ($Mil)	Return on Assets (R.O.A.)	Return on Equity (R.O.E.)	Net Interest Spread	Overhead Efficiency Ratio	Liquidity Index	Liquidity Ratio	Hot Money Ratio	Stability Index
1.1	4.09	37.8	2.14	**0.2**	-6.7	-1.02	-13.82	3.43	82.6	**1.5**	10.4	23.7	**3.9**
0.0	5.65	46.1	2.20	**0.0**	-5.5	-0.84	-10.27	3.26	91.9	**1.9**	20.9	20.2	**3.8**
8.0	0.42	2.3	0.02	**3.1**	2.5	0.50	4.80	2.62	67.4	**2.8**	44.2	26.3	**5.7**
0.4	4.05	25.1	1.13	**3.6**	49.6	0.44	4.20	3.78	73.2	**4.4**	22.2	9.1	**7.4**
10.0	0.00	0.0	0.00	**6.3**	0.0	0.59	0.90	2.18	99.7	**3.7**	128.9	101.0	**2.3**
1.1	2.64	17.0	3.32	**0.3**	-9.5	-1.25	-13.32	3.02	78.3	**2.5**	29.5	19.2	**5.3**
6.2	0.78	4.4	0.11	**6.4**	0.5	1.42	11.22	4.11	55.2	**3.5**	21.1	11.9	**8.7**
2.9	1.41	7.2	-0.01	**3.8**	0.1	0.76	8.04	3.39	70.4	**2.3**	45.8	28.0	**5.6**
6.5	0.68	3.7	0.01	**6.7**	4.6	1.03	7.49	4.34	51.0	**1.6**	12.4	22.9	**8.4**
0.3	3.27	35.7	1.05	**0.0**	-1.0	-1.30	-24.31	3.64	101.7	**1.8**	22.5	21.9	**1.4**
7.5	0.72	2.4	0.00	**3.9**	0.4	0.85	5.43	3.63	75.1	**1.8**	39.0	46.4	**7.5**
0.8	4.37	22.4	3.65	**1.2**	23.0	0.10	0.82	3.27	63.8	**4.4**	21.7	8.8	**8.1**
10.0	0.00	0.0	0.00	**8.0**	1.3	6.88	8.40	0.65	94.6	**5.0**	291.4	101.0	**2.3**
1.7	2.77	24.2	0.27	**3.3**	93.6	0.48	6.02	2.53	51.1	**1.9**	16.0	20.6	**5.3**
5.8	0.52	3.2	0.67	**7.1**	2.7	1.53	13.90	4.74	54.6	**3.8**	7.0	9.0	**7.1**
9.7	0.00	0.0	0.03	**2.5**	0.2	0.37	3.34	2.61	90.2	**5.6**	88.7	14.3	**5.1**
5.3	1.02	5.1	0.23	**3.5**	1.7	0.59	4.62	4.06	74.1	**2.1**	23.8	19.3	**6.1**
8.4	0.10	0.7	0.04	**6.1**	1.5	1.46	14.13	4.00	64.5	**2.0**	25.0	19.8	**6.0**
9.1	0.16	0.7	0.44	**3.6**	2.0	0.62	5.05	3.19	75.1	**3.6**	48.4	18.9	**7.3**
0.3	12.34	100.7	1.27	**0.2**	-1.3	-1.43	-14.58	3.55	121.2	**0.9**	7.8	31.4	**4.2**
8.5	0.24	1.3	0.11	**5.7**	0.7	1.20	15.11	4.04	49.8	**4.9**	55.7	13.4	**4.2**
9.0	0.34	0.9	0.00	**3.3**	0.4	0.71	6.06	3.34	79.3	**5.2**	64.4	12.9	**6.7**
0.0	29.25	478.3	0.14	**0.0**	-17.6	-6.55	-110.55	2.49	139.2	**4.1**	29.5	10.8	**0.0**
7.1	0.01	0.1	0.23	**2.9**	12.8	1.66	12.11	2.94	74.3	**2.2**	24.3	19.2	**5.1**
2.0	4.98	23.8	1.48	**2.5**	2.3	0.31	4.27	2.17	65.6	**3.7**	56.5	22.2	**4.3**
0.4	4.33	46.7	2.54	**0.1**	-13.0	-1.46	-24.07	2.86	74.2	**1.7**	20.4	22.9	**0.3**
0.3	4.98	46.2	3.01	**0.0**	-1.3	-1.44	-15.84	4.13	81.7	**1.1**	26.5	38.0	**1.3**
1.7	5.82	44.4	3.28	**0.4**	-5.5	-2.97	-37.31	2.99	70.2	**1.4**	26.1	30.8	**4.7**
0.0	16.76	284.7	2.09	**0.0**	-17.7	-2.00	-54.17	2.07	186.7	**0.6**	9.6	50.6	**1.3**
1.7	4.87	35.4	1.74	**2.3**	1.7	0.25	3.00	3.98	63.3	**2.5**	24.1	17.4	**5.2**
9.0	1.28	2.6	0.00	**2.8**	0.3	0.37	1.75	2.81	83.0	**3.1**	68.5	33.1	**6.8**
2.0	1.91	13.8	0.28	**3.1**	0.2	0.55	6.83	3.95	81.2	**3.5**	17.6	11.5	**4.9**
4.1	1.28	9.9	0.07	**8.7**	1.3	1.94	24.53	4.37	57.6	**1.7**	10.2	20.6	**6.7**
4.9	1.02	10.8	0.01	**2.7**	0.3	0.34	4.60	3.63	73.3	**1.5**	7.9	23.0	**3.7**
7.8	0.35	1.0	0.05	**6.3**	1.0	1.21	6.33	4.20	59.8	**4.2**	37.5	13.2	**8.3**
3.9	3.13	17.1	0.63	**3.8**	5.7	0.73	9.21	2.90	65.3	**1.2**	23.6	31.3	**4.5**
3.3	1.98	19.6	0.00	**1.8**	0.3	0.13	2.23	2.62	90.0	**3.1**	14.1	13.4	**1.0**
4.9	1.10	9.3	0.06	**7.0**	1.4	1.61	18.61	3.97	64.7	**2.0**	9.5	18.2	**6.8**
1.3	14.98	17.1	0.00	**6.0**	149.9	3.27	21.07	-2.67	70.8	**1.6**	32.1	97.7	**7.5**
1.3	1.14	7.9	0.42	**3.4**	2.8	0.91	9.63	4.35	75.2	**0.8**	14.5	36.7	**4.7**
6.4	0.56	4.2	0.32	**7.5**	12.8	1.16	11.28	4.96	64.1	**2.1**	9.2	18.1	**8.6**
7.5	0.00	0.0	0.03	**4.2**	0.6	0.99	9.51	4.62	70.2	**1.8**	34.1	32.0	**5.0**
8.3	0.00	0.0	0.00	**4.1**	0.0	0.35	0.39	3.69	91.5	**5.0**	1,229.0	100.0	**0.2**
4.5	3.66	14.6	0.43	**3.4**	2.1	0.78	5.92	4.20	76.8	**1.4**	12.5	24.7	**6.0**
3.6	1.30	9.4	0.52	**0.2**	0.6	0.12	1.30	2.75	97.1	**1.4**	24.2	29.5	**4.3**
2.2	2.60	24.7	0.34	**2.3**	3.0	0.31	3.96	3.02	78.8	**1.5**	21.3	25.7	**4.6**
7.2	1.99	9.6	0.00	**2.7**	0.3	0.45	3.63	3.52	90.7	**3.3**	39.7	18.2	**6.7**
6.4	1.29	5.5	0.51	**3.3**	0.8	0.83	7.10	3.20	62.9	**4.9**	46.9	12.0	**5.7**
0.0	13.44	93.7	1.23	**0.0**	-1.6	-1.69	-18.84	3.07	120.2	**1.7**	23.9	24.6	**0.8**
1.1	6.57	40.5	0.11	**3.3**	0.7	0.46	4.57	3.02	68.4	**3.6**	36.9	16.1	**6.1**
0.3	4.03	28.4	1.27	**0.8**	0.8	0.08	0.96	2.60	78.1	**1.2**	21.6	34.3	**5.1**
1.4	6.92	35.6	2.60	**0.3**	-0.8	-0.67	-6.50	3.39	89.5	**4.2**	35.8	12.4	**4.3**
2.0	3.05	24.4	2.20	**2.3**	0.1	0.32	4.59	3.96	76.7	**2.5**	27.8	18.3	**0.3**
4.7	1.34	9.2	0.20	**6.4**	5.5	1.16	14.41	4.59	69.1	**4.0**	22.8	9.9	**6.0**
1.9	0.89	6.2	2.80	**5.7**	2.2	1.11	10.91	9.12	49.6	**0.6**	8.0	40.3	**4.8**
3.7	1.84	9.4	0.14	**3.2**	0.4	0.59	5.74	3.16	80.3	**3.9**	29.1	12.0	**5.4**
8.4	0.36	1.6	0.05	**5.5**	0.5	1.36	10.82	4.59	76.1	**3.0**	40.3	19.9	**6.4**
3.1	2.50	17.3	0.17	**4.2**	2.5	0.68	8.64	3.73	72.2	**4.0**	14.9	8.9	**4.6**
3.7	3.41	21.0	0.00	**4.0**	0.3	0.73	9.90	2.18	43.1	**4.8**	57.5	13.8	**3.0**
7.2	0.01	0.0	-0.01	**3.8**	0.3	0.74	6.56	4.18	78.1	**2.8**	25.3	15.9	**6.9**

Name	City	State	Rating	2008 Rating	2007 Rating	Total Assets ($Mil)	One Year Asset Growth	Asset Mix (As a % of Total Assets) Comm-ercial Loans	Cons-umer Loans	Home Mort-gages	Secur-ities	Capital-ization Index	Leverage Ratio	Risk-based Capital Ratio
BALTIMORE COUNTY SAVINGS	BALTIMORE	MD	**C-**	C	C	620	6.49	1.5	0.7	25.9	13.7	**9.9**	10.9	18.3
BANAMEX USA	CENTURY CITY	CA	**C**	C-	C-	1,193	-4.40	22.8	8.6	0.2	10.3	**10.0**	22.3	38.9
BANCFIRST	OKLAHOMA CITY	OK	**B+**	B	A-	4,809	10.06	11.8	5.4	11.4	13.5	**6.4**	8.4	14.4
BANCO BILBAO VIZCAYA	SAN JUAN	PR	**D-**	D-	D	4,832	-12.44	10.9	23.3	20.1	14.1	**5.4**	7.4	14.2
BANCO POPULAR DE PUERTO	SAN JUAN	PR	**D-**	D-	D	28,974	24.51	6.7	9.6	12.3	14.7	**5.1**	7.1	13.2
BANCO POPULAR NORTH	NEW YORK	NY	**D-**	D-	D	8,995	-17.21	14.8	0.8	14.3	11.0	**10.0**	12.9	18.9
BANCO SANTANDER PUERTO	SAN JUAN	PR	**D**	D	D	6,649	0.88	19.3	6.4	34.6	7.7	**9.8**	10.9	16.9
BANCORP BANK	WILMINGTON	DE	**C-**	C	C+	2,392	17.23	11.8	5.4	11.4	10.1	**5.4**	7.4	11.9
BANCORPSOUTH BANK	TUPELO	MS	**C-**	B	B+	13,621	3.48	9.5	2.9	15.3	19.9	**5.8**	7.9	11.6
BANCROFT STATE BK	BANCROFT	WI	**D**	D	C-	67	-6.29	12.6	6.0	28.0	4.8	**6.6**	8.7	12.6
BANDERA BANK	BANDERA	TX	**B+**	B+	B+	43	13.37	4.9	7.4	30.5	8.1	**10.0**	12.0	17.4
▼ BANDERA FIRST STATE BK	BANDERA	TX	**D+**	C	NR	26	52.41	11.2	0.9	7.8	50.1	**10.0**	21.6	46.0
BANGOR SB	BANGOR	ME	**B-**	B-	B-	2,429	2.73	8.3	4.7	23.3	23.1	**8.0**	9.7	15.0
BANK & TRUST CO	LITCHFIELD	IL	**C+**	B-	B-	254	-2.70	19.0	8.3	15.2	27.2	**6.8**	8.8	14.0
BANK & TRUST SSB	DEL RIO	TX	**B**	C+	B+	390	3.96	4.7	2.8	21.9	36.9	**6.5**	8.5	16.9
▼ BANK - OLDHAM COUNTY INC	LA GRANGE	KY	**B-**	B	B+	145	4.88	2.4	2.4	9.0	47.2	**8.8**	10.2	21.0
▼ BANK 1440	PHOENIX	AZ	**D-**	C-	D	100	-2.95	1.9	0.0	10.8	39.2	**6.7**	8.7	14.1
BANK 1ST	ALBUQUERQUE	NM	**E-**	E-	E+	76	-14.28	9.7	0.1	2.9	18.8	**2.1**	4.9	9.1
▲ BANK 2	OKLAHOMA CITY	OK	**A-**	B-	C-	87	-3.02	7.9	2.4	21.1	16.5	**10.0**	14.0	18.9
▼ BANK 21	CARROLLTON	MO	**D+**	B	C+	56	-0.32	20.4	2.1	11.8	32.5	**7.3**	9.2	14.8
▼ BANK 360	BERESFORD	SD	**E-**	C-	C+	46	3.01	11.1	9.4	22.4	13.1	**4.5**	6.5	11.4
▼ BANK 7	OKLAHOMA CITY	OK	**C+**	C+	C-	139	25.18	33.1	1.8	8.1	8.6	**4.1**	8.1	10.6
▼ BANK @LANTEC	VIRGINIA BEACH	VA	**D**	C+	C+	103	-5.51	0.9	1.6	26.9	11.6	**8.0**	9.7	14.7
BANK ARLINGTON	ARLINGTON	TX	**D**	D-	D	41	9.87	14.2	5.5	20.2	13.9	**8.6**	10.1	17.8
BANK AT BROADMOOR	COLORADO SPRINGS	CO	**C+**	B	B	176	4.41	6.7	1.4	7.2	20.6	**6.1**	8.1	14.0
▼ BANK FEDERATED ST	POHNPEI	FM	**B-**	B	B	93	9.30	9.9	16.7	1.5	21.9	**10.0**	17.8	34.6
BANK FIRST NATIONAL	MANITOWOC	WI	**B-**	B-	B-	825	-1.50	14.4	1.5	15.5	16.7	**7.6**	9.4	13.1
BANK FORWARD	HANNAFORD	ND	**D-**	D	D	485	-1.64	10.0	2.4	13.1	14.0	**5.1**	7.1	11.8
BANK INDEPENDENT	SHEFFIELD	AL	**B-**	B	B	989	3.54	4.0	3.2	19.8	4.8	**8.5**	10.0	14.1
BANK IOWA	ALTOONA	IA	**C**	C-	C+	142	-4.11	8.1	0.4	19.0	9.2	**6.8**	8.8	14.6
▲ BANK IOWA	CLARINDA	IA	**B-**	C+	B-	112	5.90	3.8	1.2	6.1	28.2	**6.2**	8.2	13.0
BANK IOWA	DENISON	IA	**B-**	B-	B-	145	2.51	6.4	2.8	8.0	21.0	**6.3**	8.3	12.2
BANK IOWA	HUMBOLDT	IA	**B-**	B-	B-	172	0.80	10.4	1.6	8.0	30.9	**5.9**	7.9	13.1
BANK IOWA	NEW HAMPTON	IA	**C+**	C	B-	206	2.28	11.4	1.8	10.9	20.0	**6.1**	8.1	12.5
▲ BANK IOWA	OSKALOOSA	IA	**C+**	C+	C+	148	0.11	6.4	1.5	16.7	21.7	**6.5**	8.5	13.5
▲ BANK IOWA	RED OAK	IA	**B-**	C+	C+	132	2.28	6.7	2.3	10.3	24.0	**6.1**	8.1	11.9
BANK LEUMI USA	NEW YORK	NY	**C-**	C-	C+	5,212	2.21	47.9	0.0	1.0	17.7	**7.3**	9.2	13.6
BANK MIDWEST	SPIRIT LAKE	IA	**B-**	B-	C+	629	9.23	10.6	2.0	8.5	21.9	**5.4**	7.7	11.3
BANK MIDWEST NA	KANSAS CITY	MO	**C-**	NR	NR	3,365	N/A	3.5	0.8	6.9	27.9	**9.5**	10.7	32.7
▼ BANK MUTUAL	MILWAUKEE	WI	**D**	C+	B-	2,538	-26.19	1.9	1.1	26.6	25.6	**7.2**	9.1	17.9
▼ BANK NA	MCALESTER	OK	**B-**	B	B+	379	-5.01	4.1	3.8	15.3	44.6	**6.5**	8.5	16.3
▲ BANK NORTH	CRIVITZ	WI	**C**	C-	B-	118	-2.47	2.9	2.1	29.2	26.2	**9.7**	10.8	18.4
▲ BANK NORTHWEST	HAMILTON	MO	**B-**	C+	C	103	3.74	14.1	2.8	14.4	10.8	**7.1**	9.1	13.8
BANK OF ABBEVILLE & TRUST	ABBEVILLE	LA	**B-**	B-	B	152	3.26	1.9	4.1	8.6	60.2	**10.0**	16.6	43.3
BANK OF ADVANCE	ADVANCE	MO	**A**	A	A	240	4.34	7.7	8.2	26.2	19.6	**10.0**	14.7	21.6
BANK OF AGRICULTURE &	STOCKTON	CA	**C-**	C	B	473	5.58	10.2	2.0	6.9	12.9	**7.5**	9.4	12.9
BANK OF AKRON	AKRON	NY	**B**	B+	B+	207	11.24	6.3	2.2	13.6	23.1	**8.9**	10.3	16.0
▲ BANK OF ALAMEDA	ALAMEDA	CA	**D**	D-	D	255	3.26	6.3	0.4	9.8	14.3	**9.6**	10.7	17.5
BANK OF ALAPAHA	ALAPAHA	GA	**B**	B+	B+	113	10.92	16.8	11.3	9.8	18.9	**8.4**	11.1	13.6
▲ BANK OF ALMA	ALMA	WI	**C+**	B	A	198	-0.07	3.8	2.4	12.5	20.6	**10.0**	33.5	45.4
BANK OF ALPENA	ALPENA	MI	**D**	D-	D+	69	-21.67	9.6	0.9	16.3	22.4	**7.5**	9.3	15.9
▲ BANK OF AMERICA CALIFORNI	SAN FRANCISCO	CA	**D+**	C	C+	23,163	-1.33	0.0	0.0	96.0	0.0	**6.1**	8.1	15.1
BANK OF AMERICA NA	CHARLOTTE	NC	**D**	D	C+	1,482,278	1.16	10.1	5.1	17.7	21.9	**5.8**	7.8	14.3
BANK OF AMERICA NATIONAL	WILMINGTON	DE	**U**	U	U	3	-6.55	0.0	0.0	0.0	0.0	**10.0**	51.1	219.4
BANK OF AMERICA OREGON	PORTLAND	OR	**D+**	C	C+	13,969	-13.19	0.0	0.0	94.1	0.0	**7.9**	9.6	18.9
BANK OF AMERICA RI NA	PROVIDENCE	RI	**D**	C	C+	20,157	-14.64	0.0	0.0	86.7	0.0	**6.9**	9.0	21.9
BANK OF AMERICAN FORK	AMERICAN FORK	UT	**D**	D-	D-	843	3.94	9.6	1.1	6.0	21.8	**10.0**	11.5	16.1
BANK OF ANDERSON NA	ANDERSON	SC	**D+**	D	D	145	9.53	2.2	0.9	15.5	38.2	**6.3**	8.3	15.5
▲ BANK OF ANGUILLA	ANGUILLA	MS	**C+**	C	B	112	1.53	9.0	7.4	6.4	20.3	**9.1**	10.9	14.2
BANK OF ANN ARBOR	ANN ARBOR	MI	**C-**	C	C	691	27.17	12.4	1.5	19.3	7.7	**4.8**	6.8	11.5

Asset Quality Index	Non-Performing Loans as a % of Total Loans	Non-Performing Loans as a % of Capital	Net Charge-offs Avg Loans	Profitability Index	Net Income ($Mil)	Return on Assets (R.O.A.)	Return on Equity (R.O.E.)	Net Interest Spread	Overhead Efficiency Ratio	Liquidity Index	Liquidity Ratio	Hot Money Ratio	Stability Index
3.0	2.62	14.1	0.17	**2.0**	1.0	0.16	1.50	3.39	77.5	**3.6**	36.1	15.5	**5.4**
8.4	1.07	1.8	2.92	**3.0**	8.0	0.64	2.89	3.02	70.7	**6.3**	66.4	10.3	**6.4**
5.9	0.73	4.6	0.13	**5.4**	42.9	0.94	9.86	3.40	66.6	**5.2**	29.0	8.3	**7.7**
0.0	9.15	62.6	2.66	**1.3**	6.6	0.13	1.21	3.55	60.2	**0.7**	9.4	41.7	**4.4**
0.0	9.45	74.1	4.63	**1.8**	17.0	0.06	0.72	4.62	58.0	**1.5**	9.7	24.4	**5.0**
0.3	9.28	42.9	8.48	**0.0**	-352.3	-3.57	-26.65	3.34	85.1	**1.8**	7.1	19.4	**4.6**
0.3	5.26	35.5	2.11	**1.5**	14.2	0.22	2.07	4.26	62.8	**1.8**	15.3	20.9	**5.4**
4.6	1.08	8.8	0.91	**2.0**	6.1	0.27	3.26	3.37	69.5	**1.9**	31.7	64.7	**5.5**
1.7	3.73	28.5	1.89	**2.9**	32.8	0.25	2.38	3.87	67.0	**2.7**	13.4	15.6	**7.9**
0.3	7.02	59.3	1.24	**1.1**	-0.4	-0.61	-7.02	4.46	76.4	**2.5**	13.6	16.5	**4.5**
6.5	1.53	6.9	0.17	**5.5**	0.5	1.18	9.97	4.60	73.3	**2.8**	43.0	25.2	**7.6**
9.6	0.00	0.0	0.03	**0.0**	-0.6	-2.45	-9.61	1.92	214.7	**3.7**	77.4	26.6	**1.5**
5.2	0.91	6.0	0.28	**4.3**	17.5	0.75	6.82	3.88	71.1	**3.4**	13.9	12.1	**8.2**
2.9	2.26	14.4	1.33	**4.3**	2.0	0.75	8.34	3.90	64.6	**2.1**	27.0	21.0	**5.2**
7.7	0.05	0.3	0.06	**5.5**	5.1	1.39	13.25	4.25	72.6	**2.1**	28.9	22.4	**6.3**
5.3	3.59	12.8	0.31	**3.4**	0.6	0.44	3.83	3.68	84.1	**3.9**	22.5	10.2	**6.4**
1.5	10.18	47.5	5.42	**0.0**	-4.3	-4.24	-32.78	4.21	104.2	**3.5**	47.7	18.5	**1.3**
0.0	2.63	21.5	2.16	**0.0**	-0.6	-0.77	-15.29	3.02	123.4	**2.0**	34.2	29.7	**1.0**
7.6	0.28	1.3	0.25	**8.5**	1.0	1.91	16.18	5.35	74.1	**0.7**	13.6	42.0	**6.2**
5.5	3.16	15.5	0.13	**1.6**	0.1	0.19	2.10	3.61	89.9	**4.4**	47.7	14.5	**3.2**
1.0	4.68	38.5	2.18	**0.2**	-1.7	-3.62	-42.40	4.72	102.2	**5.3**	33.9	5.2	**0.3**
3.7	0.75	7.1	0.70	**6.8**	2.0	1.62	20.41	4.95	55.3	**0.8**	17.1	41.0	**4.6**
2.9	2.50	15.9	0.05	**0.7**	-3.1	-2.98	-22.86	3.18	248.0	**3.2**	28.8	15.3	**5.5**
4.4	0.33	1.8	0.17	**1.3**	0.1	0.33	3.19	4.24	91.6	**2.8**	38.5	21.4	**2.7**
2.9	1.75	10.7	0.55	**3.7**	1.4	0.80	9.52	4.04	73.3	**4.7**	40.6	11.7	**5.7**
3.0	2.66	6.0	-0.13	**7.2**	1.5	1.68	8.88	6.12	71.1	**3.7**	62.2	20.9	**9.0**
4.6	1.10	8.1	1.04	**4.2**	7.5	0.91	8.66	4.02	58.1	**2.9**	9.7	13.9	**6.3**
0.7	3.43	29.4	0.73	**0.4**	-3.2	-0.66	-7.53	3.63	89.1	**1.6**	6.7	20.6	**3.1**
4.6	0.56	3.9	0.77	**5.9**	10.3	1.07	8.61	6.43	67.0	**2.9**	14.9	14.6	**7.7**
1.5	4.95	30.8	3.36	**0.0**	-3.3	-2.24	-26.24	3.19	79.1	**1.9**	28.4	24.9	**4.8**
4.5	1.66	11.2	0.39	**8.2**	1.8	1.76	21.17	4.30	52.5	**5.0**	34.0	7.5	**6.8**
5.7	0.32	2.3	0.12	**5.8**	2.0	1.37	14.45	3.73	56.1	**2.9**	23.4	15.3	**5.7**
8.6	0.12	0.8	0.31	**6.1**	2.5	1.45	18.04	3.42	49.8	**1.8**	26.7	24.6	**5.7**
5.1	0.19	1.4	0.32	**4.9**	2.2	1.10	13.51	3.53	51.5	**4.6**	33.5	9.9	**4.7**
2.9	2.37	15.9	0.96	**3.4**	0.9	0.59	7.03	3.90	65.6	**4.0**	34.2	13.3	**6.0**
4.5	0.95	7.0	0.55	**6.2**	1.9	1.42	17.54	4.23	58.7	**3.1**	31.5	16.8	**6.2**
3.8	2.98	19.8	0.76	**2.2**	15.8	0.31	3.18	2.77	74.3	**1.3**	23.6	45.2	**6.4**
5.2	0.46	3.7	0.18	**4.9**	6.3	1.05	11.23	4.04	69.6	**3.2**	10.4	12.6	**7.0**
8.7	0.00	0.0	0.00	**0.3**	-0.3	-0.01	-0.09	N/,	115.5	**5.8**	77.4	14.5	**3.5**
1.4	8.99	44.5	0.91	**0.9**	-72.2	-2.15	-18.92	1.59	191.5	**4.6**	39.4	14.4	**8.2**
3.8	2.82	14.7	0.53	**5.7**	4.9	1.23	14.44	3.96	66.0	**4.0**	50.6	17.7	**5.8**
3.2	0.66	3.8	0.71	**3.5**	0.6	0.52	4.82	4.44	72.8	**2.5**	33.6	20.5	**6.5**
6.0	0.18	1.3	0.27	**9.6**	2.1	2.26	26.79	5.15	51.4	**3.1**	23.8	14.4	**6.6**
6.6	4.90	7.4	0.75	**3.3**	0.8	0.52	2.98	3.59	77.4	**4.2**	75.6	22.2	**7.2**
7.2	0.51	2.3	0.27	**9.9**	5.5	2.40	15.20	5.16	48.7	**1.8**	15.6	20.3	**9.6**
1.3	1.78	12.7	0.23	**5.8**	5.7	1.22	12.57	5.27	69.1	**3.4**	15.4	11.9	**6.9**
7.1	0.23	1.4	0.08	**4.6**	1.4	0.72	6.48	4.53	76.7	**3.3**	24.1	13.5	**7.5**
1.6	4.45	21.5	2.99	**0.0**	-5.4	-2.13	-21.81	4.19	95.2	**5.0**	32.8	6.9	**4.7**
4.1	2.04	9.8	0.57	**5.1**	1.0	0.90	7.78	4.29	56.9	**2.5**	33.3	20.5	**6.6**
2.6	8.02	16.7	1.40	**10.0**	4.0	2.00	6.16	5.07	19.7	**4.8**	37.3	10.1	**7.5**
1.5	6.05	36.2	1.20	**1.1**	-0.2	-0.24	-2.55	4.80	84.6	**3.8**	17.0	10.0	**3.2**
0.3	5.27	56.9	1.12	**9.1**	326.5	1.36	17.75	4.54	1.2	**0.0**	0.9	100.0	**4.8**
0.5	5.10	27.1	1.80	**3.4**	9,054.8	0.59	5.37	2.71	61.1	**5.6**	34.8	7.5	**6.3**
10.0	0.00	0.0	0.00	**0.0**	-0.1	-3.18	-8.81	-0.30	296.5	**4.9**	193.3	101.0	**3.7**
0.3	5.20	49.9	0.51	**9.4**	344.6	2.43	28.52	4.69	1.3	**0.0**	0.2	100.0	**5.7**
0.3	8.27	69.6	0.76	**9.7**	388.4	1.79	19.47	4.43	8.3	**4.6**	6.6	3.9	**3.4**
0.0	7.86	39.8	2.33	**3.5**	3.4	0.42	3.54	4.82	62.9	**2.9**	23.3	15.3	**7.2**
2.9	3.52	18.9	1.37	**1.4**	0.5	0.33	3.36	4.13	73.3	**2.5**	42.2	29.4	**3.3**
5.0	0.44	2.4	0.21	**4.2**	1.0	0.85	8.46	4.69	72.0	**0.8**	8.8	33.7	**5.0**
2.8	2.05	18.6	0.69	**4.2**	5.3	0.85	12.17	4.40	65.7	**2.4**	19.3	17.5	**2.8**

Name	City	State	Rating	2008 Rating	2007 Rating	Total Assets ($Mil)	One Year Asset Growth	Asset Mix (As a % of Total Assets) Comm-ercial Loans	Cons-umer Loans	Home Mort-gages	Secur-ities	Capital-ization Index	Leverage Ratio	Risk-based Capital Ratio
BANK OF ASH GROVE	ASH GROVE	MO	B	C+	B-	73	-0.59	16.0	1.2	15.5	38.7	10.0	21.6	36.4
▲ BANK OF ATLANTA	ATLANTA	GA	D-	D	D+	205	-29.18	16.3	4.1	4.3	20.4	8.0	9.6	15.3
▲ BANK OF AUGUSTA	AUGUSTA	AR	A	B+	B	59	8.19	7.0	8.2	8.8	38.8	10.0	11.3	19.6
▲ BANK OF BAKER	BAKER	MT	A-	B	B+	112	12.04	16.8	2.5	6.0	29.3	6.3	8.3	13.8
BANK OF BARTLETT	BARTLETT	TN	E-	E-	D+	391	-4.54	6.7	0.5	13.6	26.7	1.4	4.8	8.4
BANK OF BEARDEN	BEARDEN	AR	A-	A-	A-	37	10.03	9.2	6.6	17.9	11.6	10.0	16.7	25.2
▲ BANK OF BEAVER CITY	BEAVER	OK	C-	C	C+	141	9.74	11.6	3.9	14.4	31.2	4.5	6.5	11.8
▼ BANK OF BELLE GLADE	BELLE GLADE	FL	C+	B+	B+	76	13.29	4.9	1.0	16.5	42.9	9.4	10.6	24.2
▲ BANK OF BELLEVILLE	BELLEVILLE	IL	C	C-	C-	70	-1.38	16.7	1.0	18.5	0.0	6.4	8.6	12.1
BANK OF BELTON	BELTON	MO	E-	D-	D-	47	-5.89	23.9	1.7	5.5	12.4	2.3	5.9	9.3
BANK OF BENNINGTON	BENNINGTON	NE	D+	B-	D	61	14.96	20.0	1.1	14.8	8.0	7.2	9.1	14.0
▼ BANK OF BENNINGTON	BENNINGTON	VT	C+	B-	B	291	-6.42	4.5	0.4	55.8	4.6	7.4	9.3	16.0
BANK OF BENOIT	BENOIT	MS	C-	C-	C-	18	5.84	2.3	22.6	1.0	14.8	9.1	10.4	22.4
BANK OF BERTRAND	BERTRAND	NE	B	B	B+	36	17.03	3.3	4.9	2.0	15.0	10.0	15.9	21.9
BANK OF BILLINGS	BILLINGS	MO	B-	B-	B-	52	10.04	5.5	8.8	32.1	12.5	6.6	8.6	14.0
BANK OF BIRCH TREE	BIRCH TREE	MO	B-	B+	B	23	-5.56	25.0	11.2	27.6	16.3	10.0	15.4	23.8
BANK OF BIRMINGHAM	BIRMINGHAM	MI	D+	C-	C	110	19.12	18.8	0.9	3.5	2.9	4.1	8.2	10.6
BANK OF BLOOMSDALE	BLOOMSDALE	MO	C	B	B+	186	3.83	22.0	2.9	17.6	31.3	7.3	9.2	15.2
BANK OF BLUE VALLEY	OVERLAND PARK	KS	D-	D-	D-	721	-6.64	19.2	1.1	6.0	8.8	7.6	9.4	13.2
BANK OF BLUFFS	BLUFFS	IL	B-	B	B	50	2.97	2.5	7.7	18.1	31.3	10.0	16.2	29.3
BANK OF BOLIVAR	BOLIVAR	MO	D+	C-	B	199	1.46	9.1	3.1	22.7	7.7	7.3	9.5	12.8
BANK OF BOLIVAR COUNTY	SHELBY	MS	C	C	C	15	-1.84	3.1	3.4	2.9	58.9	10.0	11.8	43.3
▼ BANK OF BOTETOURT	BUCHANAN	VA	D-	D-	C-	311	0.49	5.2	3.8	22.1	4.9	6.4	8.5	12.0
BANK OF BOURBONNAIS	BOURBONNAIS	IL	B-	C+	B-	75	1.73	2.7	1.5	11.0	19.3	6.6	8.6	15.4
▲ BANK OF BOZEMAN	BOZEMAN	MT	D-	E-	D-	74	-6.38	3.9	0.8	9.8	0.0	6.5	8.5	12.9
BANK OF BRENHAM NA	BRENHAM	TX	B-	B-	B+	85	12.40	7.4	5.7	22.2	42.2	6.1	8.1	17.1
▼ BANK OF BREWTON	BREWTON	AL	B	A-	A-	56	-3.48	10.3	6.6	3.4	50.0	10.0	18.9	36.5
BANK OF BRIDGER NA	BRIDGER	MT	C+	B-	B-	274	5.23	7.6	4.0	9.4	40.0	6.3	8.3	14.7
BANK OF BRODHEAD	BRODHEAD	WI	B	B	B	120	7.12	4.1	3.1	8.2	43.0	10.0	12.5	21.9
BANK OF	BROOKFIELD	MO	B+	B+	A-	76	-1.97	2.5	1.8	9.2	50.6	10.0	11.8	29.5
BANK OF BROOKHAVEN	BROOKHAVEN	MS	B+	B+	A-	119	8.35	8.6	5.4	12.6	32.7	9.6	10.7	18.4
BANK OF BUFFALO	BUFFALO	KY	B	B	B	67	5.97	2.7	6.6	27.5	38.2	6.2	8.2	13.1
BANK OF BURLINGTON	BURLINGTON	CO	C+	C+	C+	50	2.55	1.9	0.9	0.9	75.9	5.8	7.8	27.2
▲ BANK OF CADIZ & TRUST CO	CADIZ	KY	C-	D	D+	99	6.41	4.9	3.8	31.2	19.6	4.6	6.6	11.8
BANK OF CAIRO & MOBERLY	MOBERLY	MO	A	A	A	88	6.41	9.7	3.0	28.7	12.4	10.0	14.3	23.1
BANK OF CALHOUN COUNTY	HARDIN	IL	C-	C	C	63	-1.80	1.0	2.7	31.6	24.1	6.1	8.1	15.6
▲ BANK OF CAMDEN	CAMDEN	TN	C+	C-	C+	179	8.09	6.6	3.9	26.2	16.2	10.0	11.0	17.0
BANK OF CAMILLA	CAMILLA	GA	C-	C	B	112	16.84	8.9	2.2	14.3	14.7	8.8	10.2	15.7
BANK OF CANEYVILLE	CANEYVILLE	KY	C+	C+	C+	44	1.43	2.7	3.9	18.8	56.1	7.2	9.2	20.5
▲ BANK OF CANTON	CANTON	MA	D	D-	D+	661	-8.80	3.4	0.3	37.1	10.5	5.9	7.9	12.7
▲ BANK OF CAPE COD	HYANNIS	MA	C-	C-	C	112	14.21	13.7	0.1	1.1	16.8	9.2	10.5	15.0
BANK OF CARBONDALE	CARBONDALE	IL	B-	C+	C+	189	3.70	11.3	2.8	16.4	22.1	8.3	9.9	14.4
BANK OF CASHTON	CASHTON	WI	C+	D+	D	59	7.60	18.4	2.6	11.0	26.2	7.4	9.2	14.4
BANK OF CASTILE	CASTILE	NY	B-	B-	C+	883	10.89	11.9	1.1	12.7	29.3	5.3	7.3	11.8
▼ BANK OF CATTARAUGUS	CATTARAUGUS	NY	D+	C	C-	15	14.05	2.3	8.4	40.2	21.7	7.1	9.1	19.7
BANK OF CAVE CITY	CAVE CITY	AR	B-	C+	B-	95	-2.65	2.2	5.0	26.9	21.3	8.0	9.7	18.5
BANK OF CENTRAL FLORIDA	LAKELAND	FL	C-	C-	C-	209	13.09	15.5	1.3	7.9	21.0	9.2	10.5	15.0
BANK OF CHARLES TOWN	CHARLES TOWN	WV	C	C-	B	296	-1.93	2.7	2.3	30.9	14.1	7.1	9.1	13.8
BANK OF CHARLOTTE	PHENIX	VA	A-	A-	A	118	0.18	5.4	3.3	34.1	18.4	10.0	13.0	18.7
BANK OF CHEROKEE COUNTY	HULBERT	OK	C	C	C-	96	-1.47	5.2	8.4	21.6	22.4	5.9	7.9	13.8
BANK OF CHESTNUT	CHESTNUT	IL	D+	C-	D	15	3.57	4.8	11.7	27.7	17.2	7.4	9.3	14.5
▼ BANK OF CHICKAMAUGA	CHICKAMAUGA	GA	D	C-	B-	59	-14.61	0.4	2.8	25.5	30.3	6.6	8.6	18.5
▼ BANK OF CHOICE	GREELEY	CO	E-	D-	D-	1,155	-5.72	8.2	0.4	8.9	11.5	0.0	2.3	5.2
BANK OF CLARENDON	MANNING	SC	A-	A	A	189	0.00	6.1	4.1	12.7	26.7	10.0	13.5	25.2
BANK OF CLARKE COUNTY	BERRYVILLE	VA	C+	B	B+	552	4.41	4.4	2.6	31.3	18.8	7.8	9.6	14.6
BANK OF CLARKS	CLARKS	NE	C-	C	D+	37	5.46	4.9	3.0	8.7	5.8	6.5	8.5	12.5
BANK OF CLARKSON	CLARKSON	KY	A-	A-	A-	119	2.78	0.7	4.7	31.8	28.3	9.2	10.4	23.2
BANK OF CLEVELAND	CLEVELAND	TN	B-	B-	B+	253	-0.38	2.9	1.1	21.3	1.6	10.0	12.8	16.8
BANK OF CLOVIS	CLOVIS	NM	B-	B	B	145	21.07	14.6	3.2	6.6	30.9	5.9	7.9	19.1
BANK OF COLORADO	FORT COLLINS	CO	B-	B	B	1,964	3.94	4.1	1.5	10.4	30.7	6.6	8.7	13.9

Asset Quality Index	Non-Performing Loans as a % of Total Loans	Non-Performing Loans as a % of Capital	Net Charge-offs Avg Loans	Profitability Index	Net Income ($Mil)	Return on Assets (R.O.A.)	Return on Equity (R.O.E.)	Net Interest Spread	Overhead Efficiency Ratio	Liquidity Index	Liquidity Ratio	Hot Money Ratio	Stability Index
6.8	2.54	5.2	0.65	4.1	0.7	0.98	4.73	3.36	57.1	3.3	57.4	24.5	6.1
0.3	6.76	38.1	0.26	0.0	-13.9	-5.44	-55.47	2.89	170.6	1.7	35.5	35.4	0.3
8.1	0.26	1.2	0.19	6.1	0.6	1.15	9.31	4.23	64.8	1.4	24.0	28.4	7.7
8.5	0.20	1.2	0.14	9.8	2.5	2.41	27.89	4.07	38.8	5.1	20.6	2.3	7.3
0.3	12.18	108.3	2.05	0.4	1.1	0.27	3.98	3.13	89.3	3.9	19.7	9.8	0.0
8.3	0.28	1.1	0.03	5.9	0.5	1.34	7.87	4.47	64.5	2.1	31.6	24.5	9.2
8.0	0.23	1.9	0.48	4.0	1.5	1.09	16.60	3.42	72.3	1.4	31.8	35.4	2.9
6.1	2.47	8.1	0.18	2.9	0.3	0.44	3.76	3.78	83.5	6.5	63.8	5.0	5.0
7.3	0.00	0.0	0.09	3.2	0.3	0.48	5.14	3.48	80.0	1.6	10.2	22.2	4.0
0.2	11.26	96.8	1.92	0.0	-1.1	-2.37	-26.04	3.94	122.9	5.2	23.0	1.5	2.0
1.7	5.09	33.7	4.18	1.5	-0.9	-1.52	-15.49	4.85	83.6	3.9	21.8	10.1	3.9
3.9	1.22	10.1	0.32	3.9	1.8	0.63	6.95	3.74	68.3	2.7	8.5	14.8	5.0
2.6	4.80	16.2	0.54	2.6	0.1	0.29	2.66	3.68	86.1	2.5	58.7	31.2	4.5
7.0	0.44	1.7	0.15	3.9	0.2	0.61	3.54	3.84	75.8	4.3	34.1	11.3	7.5
6.8	0.05	0.4	0.01	9.3	0.8	1.64	11.17	5.29	48.7	1.5	16.4	25.4	5.0
6.7	0.37	1.6	0.75	5.0	0.2	0.63	4.15	5.56	72.4	1.5	9.7	23.0	8.0
4.5	0.30	2.8	0.36	2.3	0.7	0.62	7.34	4.25	72.6	0.6	6.7	38.7	2.8
3.3	1.89	11.6	0.67	9.8	4.7	2.53	26.35	4.23	40.8	1.0	25.8	42.3	7.2
0.3	5.91	35.4	1.59	0.0	-1.8	-0.23	-2.28	2.32	102.6	1.6	20.4	24.7	4.3
6.8	1.65	5.4	0.12	3.8	0.4	0.79	4.78	3.55	78.3	3.2	36.5	17.8	7.2
1.4	4.29	33.8	0.53	3.4	0.9	0.47	5.02	4.16	71.7	0.7	4.7	33.6	5.2
9.7	0.00	0.0	-0.03	2.0	0.0	0.12	0.92	4.05	98.7	5.4	73.3	11.8	6.3
0.3	5.42	45.3	1.08	2.4	0.5	0.15	1.75	3.87	70.3	1.4	12.4	25.4	4.8
5.8	0.63	3.6	1.56	2.2	0.2	0.27	3.08	3.43	57.2	1.3	31.5	46.2	4.9
0.3	9.34	56.1	5.20	0.0	-5.3	-6.75	-94.04	2.24	207.6	1.2	29.0	45.7	0.7
4.8	1.56	8.6	0.01	5.2	1.0	1.15	13.38	4.33	66.1	2.8	44.7	25.4	5.1
5.7	6.99	12.6	0.97	3.5	0.3	0.53	2.93	4.57	80.0	4.1	65.4	18.9	8.1
3.5	2.52	14.7	0.16	4.8	2.5	0.90	9.94	4.19	63.7	3.2	30.9	16.1	5.7
8.0	0.36	1.4	0.13	4.4	1.0	0.84	6.25	3.86	65.4	3.4	50.5	21.6	7.5
9.4	0.70	1.8	0.02	4.4	0.8	1.02	8.03	3.15	66.5	5.8	60.4	9.1	7.6
8.6	0.01	0.0	0.08	4.8	1.0	0.82	7.37	3.73	70.3	3.2	19.6	13.2	6.3
6.3	0.70	4.4	0.11	10.0	1.9	2.94	31.96	4.91	34.1	2.5	40.9	27.8	7.3
9.8	0.00	0.0	0.00	4.4	0.5	1.02	11.32	3.37	69.5	5.8	81.3	12.5	5.6
5.7	0.23	2.1	0.22	3.3	0.7	0.68	10.05	3.69	82.2	1.5	12.7	23.4	3.1
8.5	0.00	0.0	0.01	9.8	1.4	1.73	11.96	4.59	49.8	3.6	29.0	13.5	9.0
2.9	1.35	8.6	0.38	2.9	0.2	0.34	3.34	3.63	81.5	2.0	21.5	19.6	5.0
3.3	1.30	7.5	0.60	5.7	2.0	1.18	7.12	5.76	56.9	1.4	17.2	26.7	7.0
1.7	7.82	41.1	0.56	3.3	0.4	0.35	2.92	4.80	62.7	0.9	24.3	44.0	5.3
9.2	0.07	0.3	0.22	3.4	0.3	0.67	7.28	3.09	76.3	4.6	63.3	16.0	5.1
1.3	3.46	30.1	0.37	3.2	2.8	0.40	5.46	4.10	82.3	3.0	13.5	13.7	2.9
2.6	2.55	16.4	0.20	2.3	1.9	1.83	18.88	3.31	93.2	1.1	15.6	30.8	3.3
3.6	2.19	13.7	0.26	5.5	1.8	0.98	9.96	3.84	56.4	3.9	13.7	9.5	6.5
5.3	0.60	3.7	-0.03	5.1	0.8	1.37	13.91	4.26	65.0	4.4	37.0	11.8	4.3
4.6	1.10	9.0	0.09	6.3	9.1	1.09	14.32	3.89	57.5	1.8	15.7	20.7	5.3
5.9	1.07	5.7	-0.04	2.1	0.0	0.04	0.52	5.66	99.3	5.2	19.3	0.9	3.9
4.5	1.64	10.4	0.16	3.8	0.3	0.33	3.07	4.30	74.5	1.2	15.1	28.5	5.6
8.6	0.12	0.7	0.00	1.6	0.4	0.23	2.05	3.75	79.3	3.4	33.5	16.0	2.6
4.8	1.02	7.0	1.01	3.2	1.8	0.59	7.12	3.63	70.1	1.6	11.4	21.1	4.1
6.1	0.99	5.0	0.17	6.9	1.5	1.25	9.30	5.03	60.9	3.9	24.4	10.4	8.2
4.4	0.87	6.4	0.13	4.5	0.8	0.78	10.08	4.83	74.3	1.1	12.1	30.2	4.0
3.0	0.92	6.7	1.47	1.5	0.0	0.12	1.24	4.47	86.7	1.6	13.1	22.2	5.0
0.3	4.92	19.7	2.44	0.0	-0.9	-1.32	-13.24	3.63	76.9	3.1	43.7	20.2	3.7
0.2	14.14	157.4	4.88	0.0	-59.5	-4.74	-83.35	2.49	146.0	2.1	31.5	37.2	3.2
5.7	0.37	1.5	0.38	5.6	2.0	1.03	7.50	4.27	67.6	2.1	21.7	19.0	8.3
2.7	2.05	13.9	1.27	4.3	3.6	0.66	6.64	4.47	60.5	2.0	14.6	19.0	6.3
3.7	0.92	6.7	0.55	4.1	0.2	0.61	6.77	4.22	72.6	4.0	22.5	9.9	6.2
6.5	0.74	3.8	0.06	8.8	1.7	1.50	14.20	4.16	50.2	4.7	46.5	13.0	7.9
2.7	1.91	11.5	0.42	9.2	3.5	1.40	11.22	5.26	49.2	1.2	9.2	27.2	8.6
5.5	0.16	0.9	0.12	4.0	1.0	0.74	8.24	3.84	72.0	1.9	33.1	30.2	4.9
4.1	1.61	10.5	0.68	6.0	27.5	1.43	14.10	4.04	57.1	2.7	22.3	17.8	7.6

Name	City	State	Rating	2008 Rating	2007 Rating	Total Assets ($Mil)	One Year Asset Growth	Asset Mix (As a % of Total Assets): Commercial Loans	Consumer Loans	Home Mortgages	Securities	Capitalization Index	Leverage Ratio	Risk-based Capital Ratio
BANK OF COLUMBIA	COLUMBIA	KY	**C+**	C+	B-	130	5.33	17.5	4.7	17.1	13.8	**6.8**	9.1	12.3
BANK OF COMMERCE	SARASOTA	FL	**E-**	E-	D-	297	-12.22	5.9	0.6	7.9	14.6	**0.5**	3.7	8.6
BANK OF COMMERCE	AMMON	ID	**B**	B	A+	777	2.10	12.6	1.6	3.3	18.0	**10.0**	16.4	23.5
BANK OF COMMERCE	WOOD DALE	IL	**E-**	E-	D-	163	-22.28	7.8	0.1	16.8	0.0	**0.0**	0.4	1.0
BANK OF COMMERCE	CHANUTE	KS	**B**	B	B	164	28.61	9.2	3.8	16.2	33.7	**5.7**	7.7	16.6
BANK OF COMMERCE	WHITE CASTLE	LA	**B**	B	B+	59	4.94	11.8	2.7	10.1	16.7	**10.0**	14.0	21.3
BANK OF COMMERCE	GREENWOOD	MS	**B**	B-	B	218	-1.91	8.1	4.0	22.7	27.6	**6.8**	8.8	15.5
▼ BANK OF COMMERCE	CHARLOTTE	NC	**D-**	D-	C	171	-1.35	2.7	0.2	9.6	22.2	**6.0**	8.0	11.8
▲ BANK OF COMMERCE	CHELSEA	OK	**D+**	D	C-	144	-1.13	9.3	6.5	18.3	6.0	**7.8**	9.6	14.4
▲ BANK OF COMMERCE	CHOUTEAU	OK	**D+**	D-	D+	33	-0.89	6.8	10.4	28.8	9.9	**6.8**	8.8	14.7
BANK OF COMMERCE	DUNCAN	OK	**B**	B+	B	135	22.43	19.4	3.8	3.2	18.6	**7.9**	9.7	13.2
BANK OF COMMERCE	STILWELL	OK	**A-**	A-	A	96	2.80	19.9	6.0	11.9	27.9	**8.7**	10.2	14.3
BANK OF COMMERCE	YUKON	OK	**B-**	B	B	159	-2.20	14.2	1.7	14.9	10.1	**6.9**	8.9	12.6
▼ BANK OF COMMERCE	MCLEAN	TX	**B-**	B	B	21	7.36	31.7	0.7	4.6	13.8	**10.0**	12.8	19.3
▼ BANK OF COMMERCE	RAWLINS	WY	**C+**	B+	B	111	4.88	8.7	5.4	7.9	43.9	**8.1**	9.8	20.7
BANK OF COMMERCE &	WELLINGTON	KS	**D-**	D+	D-	49	-0.30	11.9	4.2	15.9	39.4	**5.8**	7.8	16.9
BANK OF COMMERCE &	CROWLEY	LA	**B**	B	B	311	1.61	3.9	3.1	6.5	66.6	**10.0**	11.6	27.8
▼ BANK OF CORAL GABLES	CORAL GABLES	FL	**E+**	D-	C	152	-4.27	3.7	0.2	27.7	16.5	**4.3**	6.3	10.8
▼ BANK OF CORDELL	CORDELL	OK	**D**	D+	C	34	2.88	41.9	1.9	11.5	4.9	**6.1**	8.4	11.8
BANK OF COUSHATTA	COUSHATTA	LA	**C-**	D+	C-	190	37.88	2.3	8.5	11.4	51.8	**4.9**	6.9	15.5
▼ BANK OF CROCKER	WAYNESVILLE	MO	**D**	D+	D+	167	4.87	5.5	4.3	19.6	29.4	**6.6**	8.7	14.6
▼ BANK OF CROCKETT	BELLS	TN	**B**	B+	A-	123	2.88	5.7	2.1	5.1	51.0	**8.3**	9.9	19.1
BANK OF CUSHING & TRUST C	CUSHING	OK	**A-**	A-	A-	91	1.27	13.9	8.0	7.0	44.6	**10.0**	11.7	18.2
▲ BANK OF DADE	TRENTON	GA	**C**	C-	C+	93	-0.50	0.9	4.1	25.0	38.2	**8.0**	9.7	21.2
BANK OF DAWSON	DAWSON	GA	**B+**	A-	B+	106	3.79	4.4	5.6	23.8	28.9	**10.0**	15.4	28.6
BANK OF DEERFIELD	DEERFIELD	WI	**C+**	C+	C	92	0.22	12.2	2.1	35.2	0.6	**9.7**	12.6	14.8
BANK OF DELIGHT	DELIGHT	AR	**A**	A	A	84	-0.95	16.8	8.3	15.2	23.4	**10.0**	20.0	33.0
BANK OF DELMARVA	SEAFORD	DE	**D-**	D	C-	435	1.39	6.9	0.8	20.0	8.4	**7.5**	9.6	12.9
BANK OF DENTON	DENTON	KS	**B-**	B-	B-	13	3.51	3.9	10.5	26.9	34.4	**10.0**	19.6	37.5
▲ BANK OF DENVER	DENVER	CO	**C+**	C	B-	193	-2.05	1.9	7.2	5.8	12.4	**7.6**	9.8	13.0
BANK OF DESOTO NA	DESOTO	TX	**A-**	B+	B+	158	1.69	8.5	15.4	18.9	9.3	**8.4**	9.9	16.3
BANK OF DICKSON	DICKSON	TN	**B+**	B+	A-	188	7.63	2.3	2.9	30.2	34.6	**10.0**	13.3	26.2
BANK OF DIXON COUNTY	PONCA	NE	**C-**	C-	C-	72	9.13	8.0	6.7	14.6	16.0	**8.3**	9.9	16.9
▲ BANK OF DONIPHAN	DONIPHAN	NE	**C+**	C-	D-	81	-3.24	19.4	6.0	16.2	3.7	**6.4**	9.3	12.1
▼ BANK OF DOOLY	VIENNA	GA	**D**	C-	B	125	-0.56	4.8	3.3	12.1	7.7	**10.0**	13.0	18.2
▼ BANK OF DUDLEY	DUBLIN	GA	**D**	C+	A-	186	3.50	6.8	5.9	17.1	19.3	**7.7**	9.4	17.0
BANK OF EARLY	BLAKELY	GA	**D+**	C-	B	84	0.98	8.3	4.3	15.0	10.4	**8.6**	10.1	16.1
BANK OF EAST ASIA (USA) N	NEW YORK	NY	**D**	D+	D-	705	1.67	5.9	0.0	3.3	0.9	**10.0**	16.1	18.8
BANK OF EASTERN OREGON	HEPPNER	OR	**C+**	C-	B-	252	4.81	6.8	1.4	5.9	10.2	**8.8**	10.2	14.0
BANK OF EASTMAN	EASTMAN	GA	**D-**	D	C-	274	-8.28	11.6	6.9	22.6	12.1	**4.0**	6.2	10.5
BANK OF EASTON	NORTH EASTON	MA	**C+**	C	C	100	0.37	0.1	1.2	43.3	25.6	**9.6**	10.8	22.9
BANK OF EDISON	EDISON	GA	**B-**	B	B	41	5.17	2.1	5.2	12.5	40.0	**8.2**	9.8	17.1
BANK OF EDMONSON COUNTY	BROWNSVILLE	KY	**C+**	C+	B+	196	-4.04	3.4	3.8	29.2	25.3	**9.2**	10.4	17.4
BANK OF EDWARDSVILLE	EDWARDSVILLE	IL	**C+**	C+	B-	1,498	5.80	5.6	0.9	10.4	40.0	**6.2**	8.2	13.5
BANK OF ELGIN	ELGIN	NE	**C**	C+	B-	46	13.84	4.4	1.5	1.8	11.5	**6.1**	8.1	11.9
▼ BANK OF ELK RIVER	ELK RIVER	MN	**E-**	D	D	418	-15.39	13.9	4.3	13.8	12.2	**1.1**	5.4	8.1
▲ BANK OF ENGLAND	ENGLAND	AR	**B**	C	C-	214	8.05	10.5	1.8	26.3	12.3	**8.7**	10.1	15.0
BANK OF ERATH	ERATH	LA	**A-**	A-	A-	83	2.79	29.1	4.9	13.5	27.9	**10.0**	14.1	21.7
▼ BANK OF EUFAULA	EUFAULA	OK	**C**	B-	C	89	9.75	11.1	7.4	14.1	45.1	**10.0**	13.5	29.1
BANK OF EVERGREEN	EVERGREEN	AL	**D-**	D+	C	48	-3.19	9.5	8.5	26.6	20.4	**5.6**	7.6	12.4
BANK OF FAIRFIELD	FAIRFIELD	CT	**C**	C	C+	85	22.05	2.8	0.2	35.4	10.1	**10.0**	13.3	17.1
BANK OF FAIRFIELD	FAIRFIELD	WA	**D+**	D+	C+	131	-7.47	3.3	2.9	13.1	5.2	**6.6**	8.6	13.4
BANK OF FAIRPORT	MAYSVILLE	MO	**D-**	C-	D+	24	6.09	1.2	2.6	11.4	48.6	**5.8**	7.8	12.2
BANK OF FARMINGTON	FARMINGTON	IL	**A-**	B+	B	100	12.78	4.9	8.1	16.4	29.2	**10.0**	11.1	17.5
BANK OF FAYETTE COUNTY	MOSCOW	TN	**C-**	C	C+	296	0.35	2.7	6.2	25.3	14.9	**6.6**	8.6	13.2
BANK OF FAYETTEVILLE	FAYETTEVILLE	AR	**D-**	D	D+	436	-8.25	13.7	1.0	8.9	14.3	**6.2**	8.2	12.2
BANK OF FEATHER RIVER	YUBA CITY	CA	**D+**	C	C	39	15.54	9.0	0.5	4.6	0.0	**10.0**	16.1	22.4
BANK OF FINCASTLE	FINCASTLE	VA	**B**	B	B+	176	3.58	11.2	2.1	13.3	8.2	**10.0**	13.8	16.1
BANK OF FLOYD	FLOYD	VA	**D+**	C-	B	240	4.44	3.0	1.2	11.4	23.0	**7.1**	9.1	15.5
BANK OF FOREST	FOREST	MS	**B**	B	A-	140	3.61	3.7	6.6	12.6	35.2	**10.0**	13.8	23.8

Asset Quality Index	Non-Performing Loans as a % of Total Loans	Non-Performing Loans as a % of Capital	Net Charge-offs Avg Loans	Profitability Index	Net Income ($Mil)	Return on Assets (R.O.A.)	Return on Equity (R.O.E.)	Net Interest Spread	Overhead Efficiency Ratio	Liquidity Index	Liquidity Ratio	Hot Money Ratio	Stability Index
3.6	1.45	11.4	0.64	**6.7**	2.0	1.58	16.77	4.55	59.1	**1.6**	9.5	21.0	**5.8**
0.0	9.80	125.3	1.81	**0.0**	-6.9	-2.13	-35.51	3.03	87.4	**2.3**	17.2	17.9	**0.6**
3.7	4.63	16.2	1.69	**6.7**	8.4	1.11	6.62	4.67	51.3	**2.8**	43.3	25.3	**9.1**
0.0	28.31	419.3	3.30	**0.0**	-8.4	-4.57	-159.45	1.82	233.6	**0.6**	11.8	57.9	**0.7**
8.9	0.00	0.0	0.00	**4.0**	1.3	0.80	10.65	3.28	77.3	**3.4**	22.5	12.8	**5.2**
7.4	0.99	3.7	0.02	**4.2**	0.4	0.82	5.69	4.18	81.2	**5.1**	38.5	8.7	**8.3**
5.7	0.56	3.5	0.53	**6.3**	2.6	1.17	12.95	4.58	52.3	**0.9**	14.1	32.8	**5.8**
0.7	2.17	15.3	0.76	**0.0**	-0.8	-0.46	-5.26	3.05	112.4	**0.8**	17.5	39.9	**1.3**
2.3	1.75	11.4	1.08	**1.7**	0.1	0.06	0.62	4.44	89.5	**1.0**	15.9	32.5	**4.6**
2.9	1.17	8.1	0.86	**5.0**	0.3	0.79	9.15	5.96	71.8	**2.4**	15.0	17.0	**6.1**
4.1	1.57	10.2	0.04	**6.9**	2.1	1.69	15.63	4.35	56.9	**1.3**	26.6	31.7	**7.3**
6.4	0.47	2.9	0.25	**5.8**	1.5	1.56	13.16	4.53	72.3	**1.5**	14.4	24.8	**7.4**
4.6	1.15	9.3	0.27	**5.9**	1.4	0.88	9.83	4.62	65.7	**1.4**	13.0	25.0	**5.5**
8.9	0.39	1.6	0.00	**3.3**	0.1	0.57	4.13	3.06	72.5	**1.8**	42.4	32.1	**7.8**
8.4	0.36	1.4	4.54	**2.3**	-0.3	-0.31	-2.74	3.62	71.7	**1.5**	29.9	33.2	**6.4**
5.0	1.46	9.0	0.97	**1.6**	0.1	0.18	2.38	3.72	79.7	**3.5**	29.6	13.8	**2.6**
8.5	1.64	4.0	0.10	**4.3**	2.3	0.75	6.55	2.93	65.1	**2.9**	48.1	27.6	**5.4**
0.3	11.84	92.8	4.04	**0.0**	-5.5	-3.79	-50.31	3.06	116.8	**1.5**	32.8	43.8	**1.3**
2.8	2.22	20.0	0.00	**3.0**	0.3	0.74	9.01	3.08	77.6	**1.2**	16.1	30.0	**2.3**
2.0	7.75	33.5	1.02	**7.4**	2.9	1.81	22.52	4.13	46.9	**2.8**	40.0	22.5	**3.9**
3.6	2.30	15.2	0.80	**0.7**	0.0	0.02	0.17	3.49	86.6	**1.0**	10.5	30.3	**2.7**
8.8	0.43	1.4	0.13	**6.8**	1.6	1.37	11.50	4.19	55.8	**4.9**	54.3	14.1	**6.3**
6.1	0.92	3.2	0.05	**8.8**	1.3	1.41	13.37	5.71	65.9	**3.4**	57.7	23.0	**8.4**
2.7	3.15	15.5	1.59	**6.1**	1.1	1.12	11.65	4.44	57.5	**3.2**	30.5	16.0	**6.9**
5.2	2.66	9.5	0.25	**6.4**	1.2	1.12	6.95	4.54	62.1	**2.0**	35.5	31.1	**7.4**
3.3	2.52	15.8	0.65	**8.6**	1.9	2.03	16.32	4.62	53.2	**0.6**	4.7	38.0	**9.1**
6.5	1.46	4.0	0.47	**6.2**	1.1	1.35	6.85	3.81	56.6	**2.3**	30.1	21.1	**9.2**
0.0	4.34	32.0	1.41	**2.9**	0.7	0.17	1.80	3.68	61.7	**1.6**	12.7	22.4	**4.8**
6.0	2.97	8.3	0.06	**4.1**	0.1	0.73	3.90	3.78	75.1	**5.4**	43.1	5.2	**7.6**
4.3	0.02	0.2	0.16	**6.3**	2.1	1.06	11.06	5.30	66.6	**2.4**	16.7	17.4	**5.6**
6.5	0.32	2.0	0.82	**8.8**	3.3	2.06	21.41	5.78	55.6	**1.3**	28.4	34.3	**7.4**
8.0	0.88	3.5	0.14	**4.7**	1.6	0.87	6.12	3.87	70.2	**3.2**	37.2	18.1	**7.8**
1.9	0.74	4.5	1.16	**3.5**	0.4	0.56	5.66	3.80	63.2	**3.0**	21.5	14.8	**4.1**
3.5	1.07	8.7	0.02	**5.0**	0.8	0.92	8.57	4.92	70.6	**3.2**	8.9	12.4	**5.8**
0.3	6.82	34.5	2.13	**3.5**	0.4	0.34	2.54	4.20	57.6	**1.4**	22.1	27.6	**8.1**
0.3	4.92	30.1	1.60	**1.6**	0.3	0.18	1.70	3.74	79.4	**2.1**	32.0	25.6	**4.9**
1.9	3.33	20.2	0.94	**2.3**	0.1	0.07	0.61	4.42	75.4	**1.2**	15.8	29.7	**6.1**
0.5	3.87	19.2	0.11	**2.9**	4.5	0.65	3.49	4.44	70.7	**1.3**	4.9	24.9	**7.2**
3.1	1.28	8.7	0.93	**4.8**	2.1	0.85	8.13	5.39	68.4	**2.7**	11.6	15.0	**4.5**
0.2	8.61	75.3	4.77	**0.2**	-7.9	-2.66	-35.25	3.72	72.5	**0.8**	14.0	37.6	**3.3**
6.0	1.13	5.8	0.07	**3.4**	0.6	0.65	5.94	3.16	71.9	**4.0**	41.0	15.3	**6.3**
3.3	3.08	15.7	0.09	**4.2**	0.4	0.91	9.03	4.63	83.3	**3.0**	40.5	20.0	**6.1**
3.3	2.17	13.3	0.44	**3.9**	1.5	0.73	6.95	3.64	70.3	**0.9**	19.8	38.7	**5.5**
5.8	2.30	11.7	0.61	**3.1**	9.1	0.62	7.06	3.18	72.6	**3.1**	17.6	14.3	**6.3**
4.6	0.29	2.2	0.00	**4.7**	0.4	1.03	10.11	3.49	67.8	**5.2**	30.0	4.3	**4.3**
0.3	7.53	72.4	3.99	**0.2**	-9.8	-2.14	-25.68	3.76	108.7	**1.2**	13.4	28.8	**3.6**
4.8	0.74	4.7	0.35	**9.7**	4.1	2.02	20.71	4.84	80.0	**0.9**	21.1	39.3	**6.2**
8.4	0.20	0.8	0.07	**5.1**	0.8	0.94	6.27	5.11	73.8	**3.4**	34.4	16.3	**8.0**
6.3	3.46	9.1	0.11	**1.6**	0.1	0.05	0.35	4.67	82.7	**3.5**	43.6	18.4	**6.9**
1.1	2.13	17.6	1.11	**3.8**	0.4	0.74	10.07	4.00	65.3	**1.0**	18.7	33.4	**2.6**
7.9	0.00	0.0	0.00	**0.3**	-0.4	-0.46	-3.54	4.67	104.3	**0.9**	13.9	33.0	**3.6**
1.3	3.03	20.9	3.40	**1.2**	-2.4	-1.82	-19.81	4.64	84.2	**1.6**	19.6	23.7	**5.0**
3.6	5.57	27.2	-0.16	**2.4**	0.1	0.36	4.44	4.18	89.2	**4.4**	28.3	7.4	**1.7**
7.7	0.55	2.9	0.07	**6.1**	1.2	1.26	10.75	4.40	55.1	**2.0**	26.9	21.1	**7.3**
2.2	1.35	10.2	0.45	**2.7**	1.2	0.40	4.74	3.18	73.3	**1.4**	16.2	25.7	**4.1**
2.6	2.16	15.2	2.53	**0.6**	0.2	0.03	0.39	3.25	81.2	**1.6**	23.7	25.8	**3.5**
8.2	0.00	0.0	0.00	**3.1**	0.2	0.51	3.09	5.11	83.7	**1.0**	20.7	34.1	**0.7**
3.2	3.11	16.9	0.32	**4.2**	1.0	0.59	4.18	4.32	67.9	**2.3**	6.2	16.6	**7.9**
1.4	4.41	25.3	0.18	**2.4**	0.9	0.39	4.42	2.93	77.8	**2.3**	36.9	28.0	**5.2**
4.9	1.44	5.1	0.45	**3.7**	1.0	0.72	4.81	3.93	83.1	**2.8**	39.2	22.1	**7.9**

							One	Asset Mix (As a % of Total Assets)						
Name	City	State	Rating	2008 Rating	2007 Rating	Total Assets ($Mil)	Year Asset Growth	Comm-ercial Loans	Cons-umer Loans	Home Mort-gages	Secur-ities	Capital-ization Index	Leverage Ratio	Risk-based Capital Ratio
▼ BANK OF FORT BEND	SUGAR LAND	TX	**E**	C	C	35	12.13	10.7	4.2	12.3	0.0	**10.0**	15.1	20.3
BANK OF FRANKEWING	FRANKEWING	TN	**D+**	D+	B-	203	-6.49	6.7	5.6	20.9	9.0	**7.8**	9.6	14.2
▲ BANK OF FRANKLIN	MEADVILLE	MS	**C-**	D+	B	95	1.02	7.3	6.3	17.6	20.9	**7.8**	9.6	13.3
BANK OF FRANKLIN COUNTY	WASHINGTON	MO	**D**	D	C	218	0.06	7.8	1.3	20.7	13.3	**7.5**	9.3	13.4
▲ BANK OF GALESVILLE	GALESVILLE	WI	**B-**	B-	B-	85	0.08	10.4	4.8	23.8	14.0	**10.0**	13.3	15.9
BANK OF GASSAWAY	GASSAWAY	WV	**B**	B	B+	162	-2.34	2.9	10.8	31.3	28.1	**10.0**	13.0	26.1
BANK OF GENEVA	GENEVA	IN	**A**	A-	A-	142	11.42	3.5	6.1	30.9	8.4	**10.0**	11.8	16.8
BANK OF GEORGE	LAS VEGAS	NV	**D-**	D-	C-	124	3.61	15.4	0.4	2.9	9.5	**6.9**	8.9	13.8
BANK OF GEORGETOWN	WASHINGTON	DC	**C**	C-	C-	468	21.42	10.9	0.2	13.4	27.9	**8.5**	10.0	13.7
BANK OF GEORGIA	PEACHTREE CITY	GA	**E-**	E-	D+	352	-11.87	5.4	1.1	7.5	11.0	**0.8**	4.9	7.6
▼ BANK OF GIBSON CITY	GIBSON CITY	IL	**C-**	B-	C+	69	-6.78	10.1	5.9	8.0	19.7	**6.5**	8.5	15.1
BANK OF GLEASON	GLEASON	TN	**B**	B	C-	115	13.68	2.8	7.5	11.7	51.4	**10.0**	15.7	29.8
BANK OF GLEN BURNIE	GLEN BURNIE	MD	**C-**	B-	B-	347	-1.72	1.3	12.9	26.4	25.2	**5.7**	7.7	12.4
BANK OF GLEN ULLIN	GLEN ULLIN	ND	**B-**	C+	B-	39	0.50	8.0	1.7	0.5	3.8	**4.5**	9.4	10.8
BANK OF GRAIN VALLEY	KANSAS CITY	MO	**A**	A	A	83	-4.94	14.3	1.4	5.0	41.4	**10.0**	18.4	32.6
BANK OF GRANDIN	GRANDIN	MO	**B+**	A	A	153	10.17	12.2	6.4	8.1	45.0	**10.0**	13.6	22.3
BANK OF GRANITE	GRANITE FALLS	NC	**E-**	E-	D-	875	-17.31	7.9	0.4	8.5	29.1	**0.0**	2.7	5.5
BANK OF GRAVETT	GRAVETTE	AR	**C-**	D-	C-	140	-12.83	2.2	3.5	25.3	21.1	**10.0**	12.0	19.7
BANK OF GREELEY	GREELEY	KS	**B**	B	B+	34	0.46	5.3	4.3	17.7	21.1	**10.0**	12.0	21.3
▼ BANK OF GREELEYVILLE	GREELEYVILLE	SC	**D-**	C-	C	76	6.53	11.6	12.6	17.9	7.8	**6.8**	8.8	12.5
▼ BANK OF GREENE COUNTY	CATSKILL	NY	**C+**	B-	C+	531	12.48	3.8	0.8	35.9	34.4	**6.3**	8.3	17.0
BANK OF GREENSBURG	GREENSBURG	LA	**D**	D	D	89	-9.52	4.2	4.0	30.1	8.7	**8.0**	9.7	14.7
BANK OF GROVE	GROVE	OK	**B-**	B-	B-	92	39.43	12.3	3.0	41.8	4.0	**5.5**	7.5	12.3
▼ BANK OF GUAM	HAGATNA	GU	**D**	C-	C+	992	5.54	8.7	11.3	9.9	22.3	**6.5**	8.5	13.9
▼ BANK OF GUEYDAN	GUEYDAN	LA	**B+**	A-	A	82	-4.83	3.8	9.3	3.7	70.0	**10.0**	18.6	46.9
▼ BANK OF HALLS	HALLS	TN	**B**	B+	A-	64	-1.71	5.1	2.0	11.0	53.6	**8.1**	9.7	18.8
▼ BANK OF HAMILTON	HAMILTON	ND	**C+**	B-	B-	17	7.98	3.4	5.8	0.9	11.9	**10.0**	14.4	51.8
BANK OF HAMPTON ROADS	NORFOLK	VA	**D-**	D-	B-	2,579	-2.65	10.9	1.1	9.5	12.2	**4.2**	6.2	11.2
▼ BANK OF HANCOCK COUNTY	SPARTA	GA	**B**	B+	B+	84	1.67	3.8	9.0	25.2	33.4	**10.0**	20.3	35.8
BANK OF HARLAN	HARLAN	KY	**D+**	C-	C-	130	-1.81	5.2	3.4	26.8	32.7	**8.1**	9.7	17.1
BANK OF HARTINGTON	HARTINGTON	NE	**B-**	C+	C+	54	5.31	15.8	3.2	4.9	33.0	**6.5**	8.5	12.1
BANK OF HAWAII	HONOLULU	HI	**B-**	B	B	13,139	6.03	4.6	2.8	15.7	50.8	**4.5**	6.5	17.7
BANK OF HAYS	HAYS	KS	**B-**	B-	C+	181	20.62	15.3	3.0	6.7	39.5	**5.7**	7.7	12.9
BANK OF HAZELTON	HAZELTON	ND	**D**	D+	C-	36	5.60	5.3	1.1	0.3	15.5	**6.2**	8.2	12.9
BANK OF HAZLEHURST	HAZLEHURST	GA	**D-**	D+	C	93	5.24	33.4	6.3	7.0	11.0	**6.4**	8.4	13.1
▲ BANK OF HEMET	RIVERSIDE	CA	**C**	C	C+	445	-4.43	2.8	0.2	1.3	7.0	**9.4**	10.8	14.5
BANK OF HENDERSON INC	HENDERSON	KY	**D-**	D+	C	61	-3.99	12.7	2.5	25.0	10.8	**7.7**	9.5	13.2
BANK OF HERRIN	HERRIN	IL	**C+**	C	B-	239	2.17	7.0	3.5	15.8	34.8	**6.3**	8.4	15.0
▲ BANK OF HILLSBORO	HILLSBORO	MO	**C+**	C+	B-	54	-1.05	2.2	1.5	7.8	45.1	**7.9**	9.6	15.3
▼ BANK OF HINDMAN	HINDMAN	KY	**C+**	B-	A-	168	0.22	6.1	2.1	8.6	63.4	**9.0**	10.3	22.6
BANK OF HOLLAND	HOLLAND	MI	**C+**	C+	C+	618	4.03	29.0	0.5	10.8	9.7	**6.9**	9.5	12.4
BANK OF HOLLAND	HOLLAND	NY	**C-**	C-	C-	67	2.37	2.8	2.3	42.3	12.3	**8.9**	10.2	16.3
BANK OF HOLLY SPRINGS	HOLLY SPRINGS	MS	**B**	B-	B	182	2.50	3.8	14.1	23.0	14.7	**10.0**	12.0	19.4
BANK OF HOLYROOD	HOLYROOD	KS	**B-**	B	B+	48	13.33	12.1	6.6	15.0	10.2	**7.6**	9.4	16.1
BANK OF HOUSTON	HOUSTON	MO	**C-**	C-	C+	45	-3.66	7.6	2.2	13.5	13.5	**10.0**	11.2	16.2
BANK OF HOUSTON	HOUSTON	TX	**C+**	C+	C	600	18.28	26.6	2.4	5.9	9.5	**4.8**	7.8	10.9
BANK OF HYDRO	HYDRO	OK	**B-**	B-	B	108	13.87	6.1	2.8	22.1	0.6	**4.2**	8.1	10.6
▲ BANK OF IBERIA	IBERIA	MO	**C-**	C-	C	55	1.82	4.7	11.9	39.4	7.8	**6.7**	8.7	12.8
▲ BANK OF IDAHO	IDAHO FALLS	ID	**D-**	D+	C-	237	-6.37	16.5	3.4	9.7	10.6	**3.7**	6.6	10.4
▲ BANK OF INDIANA NA	DANA	IN	**C-**	D-	D	102	29.85	20.5	0.6	4.1	26.9	**10.0**	12.2	19.7
▼ BANK OF INTERNET USA	SAN DIEGO	CA	**B-**	B-	C+	1,663	22.88	3.5	2.2	24.6	34.3	**6.1**	8.1	13.9
BANK OF JACKSON	JACKSON	TN	**B**	B	B+	126	-1.69	10.1	2.6	12.8	28.0	**9.9**	10.9	16.8
BANK OF JACKSON COUNTY	GRACEVILLE	FL	**E-**	E+	D-	32	-16.74	7.6	7.8	20.1	7.8	**0.9**	5.2	7.7
▲ BANK OF JACKSON HOLE	JACKSON	WY	**C**	D	B-	551	8.20	4.4	0.3	20.4	1.8	**7.2**	9.2	14.1
BANK OF JAMESTOWN	JAMESTOWN	KY	**C+**	C+	B+	166	5.84	3.0	4.1	12.2	52.7	**8.3**	9.9	16.1
BANK OF JENA	JENA	LA	**C-**	C	C	66	-1.78	8.6	6.4	13.4	36.8	**6.1**	8.1	16.5
BANK OF JONES COUNTY	LAUREL	MS	**A-**	A	A-	208	8.34	7.4	3.3	12.4	50.4	**9.1**	10.4	23.2
BANK OF KAMPSVILLE	KAMPSVILLE	IL	**A-**	A-	A-	98	5.00	3.5	10.8	19.7	29.5	**10.0**	12.8	20.3
▼ BANK OF KANSAS	SOUTH HUTCHINSON	KS	**D-**	D+	C-	337	-7.86	14.0	4.5	8.4	10.2	**7.9**	9.6	16.6
▼ BANK OF KAUKAUNA	KAUKAUNA	WI	**C**	A	A-	109	9.93	19.8	0.7	14.4	2.0	**7.7**	9.5	13.4

Asset Quality Index	Non-Performing Loans as a % of Total Loans	Non-Performing Loans as a % of Capital	Net Charge-offs / Avg Loans	Profitability Index	Net Income ($Mil)	Return on Assets (R.O.A.)	Return on Equity (R.O.E.)	Net Interest Spread	Overhead Efficiency Ratio	Liquidity Index	Liquidity Ratio	Hot Money Ratio	Stability Index
5.0	1.44	7.0	0.04	**0.5**	-0.1	-0.31	-2.13	4.38	93.5	**1.6**	18.1	24.5	**0.0**
1.9	2.92	18.7	1.35	**3.4**	0.8	0.39	4.21	4.30	72.6	**1.0**	18.0	32.7	**4.2**
3.9	0.98	5.1	0.47	**3.0**	0.3	0.33	3.92	4.53	86.8	**2.8**	20.8	15.6	**3.2**
1.7	2.92	18.7	1.08	**0.6**	-0.6	-0.28	-2.93	2.99	83.3	**1.7**	14.2	21.7	**5.1**
2.6	4.06	20.4	0.73	**9.0**	1.7	2.04	15.60	4.67	56.2	**4.1**	21.7	9.2	**9.0**
6.8	1.28	5.0	0.21	**3.8**	0.9	0.56	4.39	4.13	78.4	**3.0**	40.8	20.4	**6.8**
8.3	0.20	1.3	0.20	**7.1**	2.4	1.81	14.96	4.71	62.8	**4.1**	19.1	8.7	**7.2**
0.3	13.81	71.8	2.72	**0.0**	-1.4	-1.10	-14.11	3.51	107.4	**3.3**	30.4	15.2	**1.3**
6.2	0.53	3.3	0.44	**3.0**	2.3	0.55	5.02	3.85	74.8	**0.6**	9.9	52.0	**3.9**
0.0	5.01	51.6	1.13	**0.0**	-2.5	-0.64	-10.30	3.20	102.9	**0.8**	14.6	36.2	**1.4**
1.4	3.45	23.5	0.20	**4.2**	0.5	0.73	6.32	3.27	63.1	**2.6**	16.3	15.9	**5.6**
3.5	4.05	9.2	1.26	**4.6**	1.3	1.17	6.73	4.23	52.3	**3.6**	64.9	27.9	**6.5**
1.8	2.99	23.0	0.52	**4.1**	2.5	0.71	8.61	4.22	71.2	**3.3**	29.7	15.0	**4.2**
3.6	0.77	6.8	0.06	**8.1**	0.7	1.82	15.05	4.92	53.7	**1.1**	2.6	26.9	**8.8**
8.9	0.00	0.0	0.23	**8.0**	1.5	1.78	9.45	3.98	52.5	**4.2**	53.7	16.3	**9.9**
3.1	1.73	5.7	0.97	**7.6**	2.3	1.59	11.71	3.97	45.4	**2.9**	47.1	27.5	**8.7**
0.3	12.23	129.6	4.59	**0.0**	-23.4	-2.37	-70.50	3.41	86.5	**1.9**	28.4	24.9	**1.4**
2.7	4.30	19.1	0.54	**1.4**	0.5	0.31	2.73	4.42	80.0	**1.4**	21.5	28.5	**4.0**
8.7	0.02	0.1	0.03	**4.7**	0.4	1.07	8.61	3.49	66.1	**4.7**	38.7	11.2	**6.6**
0.5	2.15	17.6	0.48	**5.8**	0.9	1.21	13.90	5.06	69.5	**1.0**	15.0	32.0	**5.8**
5.1	2.00	12.3	0.12	**4.8**	5.3	1.07	12.55	4.03	59.7	**5.8**	43.9	6.3	**3.4**
1.4	4.79	33.6	1.54	**1.0**	-0.3	-0.35	-3.54	4.79	74.9	**1.2**	17.5	30.1	**3.1**
8.1	0.06	0.6	0.52	**4.3**	0.8	1.04	12.67	4.48	57.4	**1.1**	12.2	30.0	**4.6**
0.9	4.55	30.0	0.45	**4.0**	7.1	0.72	8.60	5.15	83.8	**1.8**	21.8	22.1	**5.2**
9.1	0.54	0.7	1.60	**3.3**	0.4	0.47	2.53	2.54	70.2	**3.6**	84.2	31.0	**7.5**
6.3	1.36	4.8	0.23	**5.6**	0.7	1.10	9.87	4.08	58.8	**2.8**	46.6	25.6	**7.1**
9.3	0.00	0.0	-0.19	**2.2**	0.0	0.16	0.98	2.48	90.8	**6.0**	94.3	11.8	**6.9**
0.3	13.85	77.3	8.97	**0.0**	-208.9	-7.87	-147.91	2.78	101.6	**1.4**	23.8	34.8	**5.0**
4.4	4.57	11.6	0.64	**3.9**	0.6	0.74	3.59	4.36	72.0	**3.1**	47.9	22.3	**7.1**
5.6	1.27	5.3	0.45	**1.7**	0.5	0.41	4.16	3.74	88.1	**2.3**	40.5	30.8	**4.8**
8.3	0.06	0.4	0.12	**4.7**	0.6	1.08	11.65	4.32	75.5	**4.1**	31.5	11.8	**5.6**
6.8	0.88	4.8	0.94	**7.5**	184.4	1.46	20.85	3.52	55.7	**5.8**	34.0	6.2	**6.5**
4.7	0.35	2.5	0.10	**4.4**	1.3	0.84	11.62	3.54	62.5	**2.7**	36.2	21.1	**3.8**
4.5	1.41	8.4	1.77	**1.8**	0.1	0.35	3.94	3.19	64.6	**3.7**	37.2	15.5	**3.1**
0.3	4.73	29.6	1.67	**1.5**	-0.7	-0.73	-5.49	3.66	75.7	**2.0**	26.7	21.0	**8.1**
1.6	1.62	10.6	0.18	**9.2**	9.7	2.09	20.43	4.64	49.2	**2.7**	12.8	15.3	**8.3**
2.4	2.64	19.3	1.10	**0.3**	-0.6	-1.02	-10.40	3.75	80.8	**1.2**	9.8	27.9	**6.1**
3.9	2.30	13.2	0.39	**4.2**	2.8	1.16	14.89	3.87	74.9	**4.4**	33.2	10.6	**4.3**
6.0	0.00	0.0	0.09	**3.9**	0.4	0.71	8.07	4.01	72.6	**3.6**	47.6	18.1	**4.7**
5.3	1.84	4.7	-0.08	**3.3**	0.8	0.49	3.49	2.76	73.4	**3.1**	59.1	32.3	**7.2**
3.3	2.13	16.6	0.51	**4.7**	6.1	1.03	10.78	3.40	49.6	**0.4**	4.9	55.3	**6.5**
5.1	1.38	8.6	0.71	**2.3**	0.2	0.25	2.48	4.69	84.4	**3.8**	19.9	10.7	**5.1**
4.2	2.07	11.0	0.27	**7.2**	3.0	1.65	12.95	5.57	66.1	**1.0**	10.1	30.9	**8.1**
3.9	1.33	8.2	0.25	**5.6**	0.6	1.29	13.01	3.01	53.7	**2.3**	31.1	22.0	**6.9**
4.6	2.27	13.0	0.23	**0.2**	-0.4	-0.83	-7.11	3.61	114.0	**4.2**	20.3	8.3	**5.1**
4.1	1.47	12.1	0.28	**3.9**	3.6	0.65	7.95	4.30	68.1	**0.9**	20.9	35.0	**4.7**
6.3	0.17	1.8	0.33	**7.5**	1.8	1.74	20.63	3.85	47.2	**1.3**	2.1	24.1	**6.5**
4.1	0.35	3.1	0.62	**3.6**	0.2	0.44	5.11	5.13	78.6	**1.7**	11.7	20.6	**4.6**
0.3	7.76	60.1	2.73	**0.7**	-4.7	-1.92	-24.25	4.67	82.4	**4.1**	16.0	8.4	**3.7**
2.3	4.32	20.3	1.45	**2.8**	0.8	0.97	7.69	4.46	85.0	**1.2**	8.9	27.3	**5.7**
4.0	2.03	14.7	0.48	**5.4**	18.6	1.27	14.54	3.69	32.1	**2.3**	38.2	47.1	**6.1**
2.7	3.59	17.5	0.44	**3.9**	0.8	0.59	5.04	4.00	68.1	**1.9**	31.1	28.1	**6.5**
0.0	12.60	122.3	3.55	**0.0**	-0.8	-2.30	-36.75	4.02	106.0	**3.9**	21.5	10.0	**1.1**
3.8	0.74	5.2	0.45	**3.9**	2.3	0.44	4.76	3.72	59.1	**1.7**	25.5	24.5	**6.3**
5.8	1.38	5.6	0.34	**2.8**	0.8	0.48	5.12	3.15	78.8	**3.0**	41.8	20.8	**4.7**
2.9	3.80	21.3	0.43	**3.3**	0.4	0.56	6.49	4.66	86.6	**3.5**	37.3	16.8	**3.8**
9.2	0.01	0.0	0.09	**7.3**	2.6	1.28	11.90	3.30	44.2	**3.7**	61.5	25.1	**7.8**
8.0	0.12	0.6	0.15	**5.9**	1.0	1.06	7.83	3.82	57.2	**2.9**	33.3	18.5	**7.7**
0.1	3.18	19.7	1.05	**3.9**	1.2	0.33	3.03	4.23	58.8	**1.1**	14.0	30.2	**5.6**
1.7	5.00	34.6	1.86	**2.3**	-1.7	-1.70	-14.69	3.78	70.8	**0.9**	21.6	38.1	**7.9**

Name	City	State	Rating	2008 Rating	2007 Rating	Total Assets ($Mil)	One Year Asset Growth	Asset Mix (As a % of Total Assets) Commercial Loans	Consumer Loans	Home Mortgages	Securities	Capitalization Index	Leverage Ratio	Risk-based Capital Ratio
BANK OF KENTUCKY INC	CRESTVIEW HILLS	KY	**C+**	C	B-	1,664	6.48	13.0	0.9	8.8	17.2	**7.3**	9.2	13.5
BANK OF KEYSTONE	KEYSTONE	NE	**B-**	B-	B-	52	7.23	6.6	3.8	2.7	9.7	**9.2**	11.2	14.3
▼ BANK OF KILMICHAEL	KILMICHAEL	MS	**C-**	C-	C-	88	21.65	23.5	6.3	10.7	16.2	**6.2**	8.2	12.4
BANK OF KIRKSVILLE	KIRKSVILLE	MO	**C+**	C+	C+	448	1.37	10.7	1.5	20.5	39.9	**7.3**	9.2	21.4
BANK OF KREMLIN	KREMLIN	OK	**C+**	C	C	250	18.24	11.0	4.9	4.7	11.4	**5.9**	9.3	11.7
BANK OF LA FAYETTE GEORGI	LAFAYETTE	GA	**B**	B+	A-	210	12.37	1.4	6.4	23.4	44.5	**10.0**	13.6	38.8
BANK OF LAKE MILLS	LAKE MILLS	WI	**D-**	D-	D+	199	10.44	3.3	2.0	28.6	9.5	**6.3**	8.4	12.8
▲ BANK OF LAKE VILLAGE	LAKE VILLAGE	AR	**B-**	D+	C+	56	-2.53	5.5	2.7	4.6	27.7	**9.9**	10.9	23.7
▼ BANK OF LANCASTER	KILMARNOCK	VA	**D+**	C-	C	326	-0.97	3.6	2.7	38.8	10.5	**5.3**	7.3	11.6
BANK OF LANDISBURG	LANDISBURG	PA	**A-**	A-	A	242	5.17	0.0	0.8	46.5	29.5	**10.0**	16.6	32.1
▼ BANK OF LAS COLINAS	IRVING	TX	**E+**	C	C	45	4.10	28.3	5.1	14.8	0.0	**10.0**	12.4	15.7
▼ BANK OF LAS VEGAS	LAS VEGAS	NM	**C-**	B	B	178	-6.17	5.6	1.5	15.4	18.9	**7.9**	9.6	15.8
BANK OF LAS VEGAS	LAS VEGAS	NV	**E-**	NR	NR	376	111.92	6.6	1.1	4.4	0.1	**0.0**	2.1	4.3
BANK OF LAVERNE	LAVERNE	OK	**B+**	B+	B+	55	-0.31	8.3	8.7	3.1	38.7	**10.0**	16.1	29.7
BANK OF LAWRENCE COUNTY	BRIDGEPORT	IL	**C+**	B	B	44	-11.42	9.0	2.3	4.7	8.3	**10.0**	11.7	64.8
▼ BANK OF LEES SUMMIT	LEE'S SUMMIT	MO	**C-**	C	B-	268	5.84	6.6	0.5	8.1	29.8	**10.0**	11.2	20.1
BANK OF LEWELLEN	LEWELLEN	NE	**B-**	C+	C+	21	2.96	5.2	2.7	1.7	20.5	**10.0**	27.9	39.7
▲ BANK OF LEXINGTON INC	LEXINGTON	KY	**C+**	C	C	140	6.25	2.7	0.8	37.1	10.7	**9.6**	10.7	16.2
▲ BANK OF LINCOLN COUNTY	FAYETTEVILLE	TN	**D**	D	D+	139	-14.26	7.5	2.1	16.6	13.1	**9.0**	10.6	14.2
BANK OF LINDSAY	LINDSAY	NE	**D+**	C	D	33	-2.55	19.9	3.5	2.3	1.8	**3.7**	9.7	10.4
▲ BANK OF LITTLE ROCK	LITTLE ROCK	AR	**C-**	D+	C-	167	-13.04	17.9	2.9	21.9	13.3	**7.6**	9.4	14.0
BANK OF LOCUST GROVE	LOCUST GROVE	OK	**C-**	C+	C-	26	0.23	11.0	19.3	16.1	12.1	**8.5**	10.0	15.4
▼ BANK OF LOUISIANA	NEW ORLEANS	LA	**C+**	B-	B	94	1.66	2.9	8.1	21.9	0.0	**10.0**	12.8	19.9
BANK OF LOUISIANA	LOUISIANA	MO	**D**	C-	C-	52	-2.07	5.4	2.0	15.2	28.9	**7.6**	9.4	15.7
BANK OF LUMBER CITY	LUMBER CITY	GA	**C-**	C+	C	21	-3.02	21.3	8.8	16.2	21.9	**10.0**	19.4	21.9
▲ BANK OF LUXEMBURG	LUXEMBURG	WI	**B-**	C+	C+	233	3.06	14.2	2.6	18.7	19.8	**6.5**	9.4	12.2
BANK OF MACKS CREEK	MACKS CREEK	MO	**E-**	E-	E	22	-12.29	4.8	7.4	34.3	9.7	**4.3**	6.3	10.7
BANK OF MADISON	MADISON	GA	**C-**	C-	A-	230	-1.04	3.4	1.2	14.5	19.7	**10.0**	12.0	18.8
▼ BANK OF MAGNOLIA CO	MAGNOLIA	OH	**B-**	B+	B+	68	1.19	4.0	4.0	30.3	42.4	**9.4**	10.6	22.4
BANK OF MANHATTAN NA	EL SEGUNDO	CA	**C-**	C-	C-	151	-0.38	15.2	1.5	3.0	10.2	**10.0**	16.6	22.4
BANK OF MANSFIELD	MANSFIELD	MO	**B+**	B+	B	63	12.99	8.9	4.3	42.1	17.8	**9.0**	10.3	17.0
BANK OF MAPLE PLAIN	MAPLE PLAIN	MN	**C-**	C-	A-	64	7.54	6.4	2.1	22.3	16.0	**10.0**	14.3	26.9
BANK OF MARIN	NOVATO	CA	**B-**	B	B+	1,208	7.70	8.0	2.2	8.3	12.2	**7.2**	9.4	12.7
BANK OF MARINGOUIN	MARINGOUIN	LA	**A-**	A-	B+	49	3.63	6.3	3.6	11.5	34.7	**10.0**	11.7	22.6
BANK OF MARION	MARION	IL	**A-**	A-	B+	327	7.93	4.0	9.8	8.6	38.4	**8.3**	9.9	16.3
BANK OF MARION	MARION	VA	**C+**	C-	B+	348	4.03	3.4	3.6	27.1	17.5	**8.1**	9.7	17.3
BANK OF MARQUETTE	MARQUETTE	NE	**A-**	B+	B+	31	0.74	8.4	5.2	12.1	39.4	**10.0**	19.5	31.9
BANK OF MAUMEE	MAUMEE	OH	**E+**	D-	C-	40	-13.88	17.0	3.1	2.9	0.0	**4.4**	7.3	10.7
▼ BANK OF MAUSTON	MAUSTON	WI	**C+**	C-	C-	237	5.32	3.0	3.1	19.3	24.3	**9.7**	10.8	15.5
BANK OF MAYSVILLE	MAYSVILLE	KY	**A-**	A-	A-	113	1.88	0.5	1.7	32.4	30.9	**10.0**	16.0	32.9
▼ BANK OF MCCREARY COUNTY	WHITLEY CITY	KY	**C-**	B-	A-	138	3.57	4.8	11.9	36.7	16.4	**9.6**	10.7	17.3
▲ BANK OF MCCRORY	MCCRORY	AR	**B**	B	B	74	2.14	3.4	5.2	5.7	39.0	**9.0**	10.4	19.1
BANK OF MCKENNEY	MCKENNEY	VA	**C-**	C-	B	192	4.48	4.7	1.2	23.9	13.8	**8.8**	10.2	14.6
▼ BANK OF MCLOUTH	MCLOUTH	KS	**C+**	B+	B+	39	4.05	8.9	7.5	7.4	19.0	**5.0**	7.0	11.9
BANK OF MEAD	MEAD	NE	**C+**	C+	C+	22	3.75	6.7	6.3	23.1	33.6	**8.8**	10.2	19.0
BANK OF MICHIGAN	FARMINGTON HILLS	MI	**E+**	D	C-	82	-17.63	11.8	0.3	4.5	1.2	**5.7**	7.7	11.6
▼ BANK OF MILAN	MILAN	TN	**C**	C	C+	62	-2.72	7.0	2.8	24.4	33.9	**6.0**	8.0	14.6
▼ BANK OF MILLBROOK	MILLBROOK	NY	**B+**	A	A	184	38.58	2.4	4.1	35.8	21.2	**9.6**	10.7	19.7
▲ BANK OF MILTON	MILTON	WI	**B-**	C+	C+	68	0.52	10.1	4.2	22.4	10.8	**6.7**	8.8	12.5
▲ BANK OF MINDEN	MINDENMINES	MO	**C**	D+	B-	29	1.85	15.2	4.3	19.7	19.0	**10.0**	11.3	20.2
BANK OF MINGO	WILLIAMSON	WV	**C-**	C+	C+	116	0.69	10.3	10.9	25.4	22.2	**10.0**	13.2	24.8
BANK OF MISSOURI	PERRYVILLE	MO	**C+**	C+	C+	825	7.13	7.0	2.8	17.6	19.3	**5.5**	8.6	11.4
BANK OF MODESTO	MODESTO	IL	**C-**	C-	C-	39	1.69	5.0	4.1	6.1	33.6	**6.7**	8.7	14.3
BANK OF MONROE	UNION	WV	**A-**	A-	A-	113	9.75	3.4	5.8	28.1	34.2	**10.0**	13.0	23.8
BANK OF MONTANA	MISSOULA	MT	**C+**	C	C	26	32.53	10.3	1.5	30.2	0.0	**10.0**	14.6	15.1
▲ BANK OF MONTGOMERY	MONTGOMERY	IL	**C**	D+	B-	35	2.03	9.2	2.0	25.2	37.7	**9.1**	10.4	17.2
BANK OF MONTGOMERY	MONTGOMERY	LA	**B**	B-	C+	165	5.76	7.1	9.4	30.4	12.0	**6.2**	8.2	12.5
▼ BANK OF MONTICELLO	MONTICELLO	GA	**D-**	D+	C	99	-1.37	7.6	9.9	29.6	9.9	**5.3**	7.3	12.1
BANK OF MONTICELLO	MONTICELLO	MO	**B-**	B	B+	91	4.06	5.5	5.0	15.9	22.2	**5.8**	9.8	11.6
BANK OF MONTICELLO	MONTICELLO	WI	**D**	D	C-	74	2.64	6.6	3.1	17.6	13.1	**9.0**	10.3	15.1

Asset Quality Index	Non-Performing Loans as a % of Total Loans	Non-Performing Loans as a % of Capital	Net Charge-offs Avg Loans	Profitability Index	Net Income ($Mil)	Return on Assets (R.O.A.)	Return on Equity (R.O.E.)	Net Interest Spread	Overhead Efficiency Ratio	Liquidity Index	Liquidity Ratio	Hot Money Ratio	Stability Index
3.6	1.88	13.1	1.17	**4.6**	12.3	0.79	7.62	3.82	56.3	**3.9**	14.4	9.7	**8.0**
3.9	1.73	10.8	0.20	**5.5**	0.6	1.24	11.50	4.29	65.7	**3.6**	23.8	11.7	**5.8**
3.5	2.32	14.4	0.11	**4.5**	0.5	0.62	6.88	4.17	71.9	**2.4**	39.7	29.3	**4.0**
6.1	0.96	4.8	0.34	**3.8**	5.9	1.33	15.10	2.15	58.9	**1.8**	16.1	20.6	**5.2**
3.7	0.52	4.3	0.40	**7.6**	4.3	1.89	20.10	4.50	48.0	**1.8**	16.8	20.5	**7.1**
3.3	5.90	17.1	0.34	**4.2**	1.6	0.81	5.57	3.76	70.0	**2.3**	31.1	21.5	**7.0**
0.3	6.13	46.0	1.64	**2.1**	0.2	0.08	0.96	3.68	70.0	**2.0**	26.4	20.7	**4.7**
4.2	1.71	7.0	-0.34	**3.5**	0.4	0.73	6.74	4.56	81.4	**4.2**	33.9	12.0	**5.3**
2.4	2.32	21.0	0.50	**1.6**	0.5	0.14	1.77	3.47	92.4	**2.2**	15.7	17.9	**4.0**
6.1	3.18	11.6	0.31	**5.5**	2.4	1.02	6.05	3.37	49.1	**3.1**	30.8	16.3	**8.8**
4.9	2.22	14.4	0.01	**1.4**	0.1	0.24	1.94	4.66	94.4	**1.3**	8.5	24.9	**0.0**
0.7	1.14	8.1	0.73	**7.1**	2.9	1.56	16.79	4.31	55.0	**1.4**	6.0	23.2	**7.0**
0.0	26.36	240.2	5.59	**0.3**	-51.7	-11.18	-296.77	2.50	416.9	**0.8**	20.2	42.9	**3.1**
8.3	0.38	0.9	0.21	**4.8**	0.5	0.96	5.42	4.32	71.5	**4.7**	50.9	13.2	**7.3**
9.5	0.00	0.0	0.00	**2.4**	0.2	0.33	2.86	2.03	82.9	**4.0**	75.2	22.2	**6.7**
3.3	0.61	2.5	1.85	**3.5**	1.2	0.47	2.50	3.69	66.8	**5.0**	41.1	10.2	**6.4**
7.4	0.06	0.1	0.02	**5.1**	0.2	1.05	3.82	4.94	68.6	**2.6**	27.1	16.7	**7.6**
9.1	0.00	0.0	0.03	**3.7**	1.0	0.72	6.87	3.87	71.2	**1.2**	16.6	30.2	**5.0**
1.8	4.45	23.2	1.06	**1.1**	-0.5	-0.35	-3.55	5.06	95.2	**0.9**	20.4	37.5	**3.5**
5.0	0.26	2.4	0.04	**4.4**	0.2	0.58	6.24	4.55	81.8	**2.9**	6.9	13.8	**3.0**
2.1	1.57	10.1	0.69	**2.6**	0.4	0.23	2.74	5.04	85.8	**1.7**	8.0	20.1	**4.0**
3.5	2.03	11.7	0.44	**9.5**	0.4	1.47	14.01	6.06	64.5	**4.5**	21.5	6.4	**2.3**
1.7	6.72	30.0	0.50	**2.9**	0.2	0.26	1.99	7.03	93.1	**4.7**	28.3	6.5	**6.1**
1.7	4.34	24.6	1.21	**0.6**	-0.2	-0.34	-3.51	3.44	77.5	**1.9**	20.9	20.0	**4.6**
4.5	5.02	15.8	2.12	**1.2**	0.0	-0.17	-0.86	5.99	95.9	**2.1**	32.6	21.0	**7.6**
4.6	0.66	4.5	0.64	**4.3**	1.9	0.84	8.37	4.60	72.8	**3.9**	23.5	10.2	**5.7**
1.9	3.12	22.1	0.88	**0.0**	-0.5	-1.94	-27.37	4.54	117.7	**1.4**	11.9	24.2	**1.9**
1.6	5.95	29.3	1.44	**2.1**	0.7	0.31	2.66	3.48	72.5	**1.5**	22.3	26.8	**5.8**
6.7	1.49	6.2	0.15	**3.8**	0.4	0.55	4.75	4.35	81.8	**4.9**	42.8	10.9	**6.8**
8.6	0.00	0.0	0.06	**0.0**	-1.7	-1.30	-7.59	4.31	116.4	**2.5**	39.6	27.3	**5.3**
7.9	0.26	1.7	0.03	**5.7**	0.6	1.07	10.10	5.23	70.8	**1.7**	21.7	23.9	**6.9**
1.7	4.32	15.4	0.44	**4.7**	0.6	0.98	6.41	4.76	67.9	**4.5**	38.4	11.7	**8.5**
3.8	1.37	10.3	0.38	**7.9**	14.0	1.18	12.73	4.99	54.0	**2.8**	16.7	15.5	**8.9**
6.0	3.99	13.3	0.05	**6.0**	0.6	1.28	10.49	4.44	71.4	**5.1**	40.1	9.5	**9.0**
6.2	0.68	3.4	0.01	**7.8**	6.1	1.84	17.59	3.74	52.7	**1.7**	23.2	24.0	**8.0**
3.3	1.71	10.0	0.09	**4.0**	2.2	0.64	6.26	3.63	71.5	**1.9**	25.6	22.0	**5.2**
7.8	1.46	3.9	0.63	**7.1**	0.4	1.41	6.86	4.21	55.6	**3.3**	47.0	19.9	**8.7**
2.4	1.37	10.1	1.07	**0.0**	-1.3	-2.83	-38.72	3.79	119.1	**4.5**	19.4	6.1	**0.0**
2.1	3.43	20.7	0.58	**9.1**	5.7	2.44	22.64	4.36	43.2	**1.5**	11.8	24.0	**7.3**
8.4	0.56	1.8	0.19	**5.7**	1.2	1.06	5.84	4.62	65.9	**2.7**	26.4	17.2	**8.4**
1.8	3.13	19.4	1.17	**5.2**	1.4	1.03	9.31	4.36	63.7	**1.5**	11.8	23.9	**6.0**
4.7	1.85	6.9	0.26	**4.7**	0.7	0.89	8.32	3.88	66.3	**3.8**	48.6	17.4	**5.4**
2.2	1.58	9.8	0.47	**3.8**	1.5	0.79	7.54	4.41	74.8	**1.9**	24.9	20.7	**5.2**
6.4	0.72	5.2	0.10	**4.2**	0.3	0.80	4.49	4.33	59.3	**5.5**	35.9	5.1	**6.1**
7.2	0.12	0.6	0.13	**5.3**	0.2	1.04	9.83	3.95	64.2	**5.1**	36.3	4.7	**5.0**
0.0	3.53	29.2	2.00	**0.9**	-0.3	-0.27	-3.82	3.18	71.0	**0.9**	21.8	45.3	**2.8**
9.2	0.16	1.0	-0.05	**3.2**	0.3	0.45	4.85	3.97	86.5	**3.9**	38.4	15.0	**4.8**
4.5	2.65	13.9	0.07	**4.9**	1.3	0.86	6.36	4.32	73.3	**3.2**	31.0	15.9	**8.2**
5.8	0.31	2.5	0.06	**7.6**	1.2	1.75	20.31	4.68	58.3	**1.7**	15.1	21.5	**5.7**
6.8	0.07	0.4	0.05	**3.0**	0.2	0.81	6.98	4.50	67.7	**2.8**	37.5	21.1	**5.8**
1.4	4.78	18.0	0.81	**4.3**	0.9	0.78	5.79	5.21	72.9	**2.8**	42.3	24.1	**6.9**
4.1	0.66	5.0	0.88	**5.0**	8.0	1.01	11.04	4.42	57.1	**1.0**	6.8	29.0	**5.7**
3.5	1.19	7.1	0.12	**3.7**	0.2	0.58	5.94	3.67	74.6	**4.3**	29.7	10.2	**5.5**
8.7	0.01	0.0	0.09	**6.1**	1.2	1.07	8.27	4.67	66.0	**2.6**	36.0	22.2	**7.3**
8.9	0.00	0.0	0.00	**2.1**	0.1	0.27	1.65	4.22	88.7	**1.3**	30.3	35.8	**3.6**
3.5	3.83	17.6	0.64	**2.8**	0.2	0.51	4.61	4.15	74.8	**4.7**	40.3	11.4	**4.0**
7.8	0.17	1.5	0.23	**9.0**	4.0	2.46	30.48	5.21	56.5	**1.3**	10.5	26.9	**5.0**
1.2	4.92	43.9	2.32	**0.0**	-1.2	-1.17	-13.93	3.54	86.1	**1.2**	13.6	29.1	**2.5**
4.8	0.47	3.1	0.69	**5.4**	1.0	1.20	12.00	3.79	56.2	**1.2**	12.4	27.6	**6.2**
1.1	7.52	42.9	0.47	**2.7**	0.3	0.45	4.14	3.86	82.3	**3.9**	23.9	10.4	**4.5**

Name	City	State	Rating	2008 Rating	2007 Rating	Total Assets ($Mil)	One Year Asset Growth	Asset Mix (As a % of Total Assets) Commercial Loans	Consumer Loans	Home Mortgages	Securities	Capitalization Index	Leverage Ratio	Risk-based Capital Ratio
BANK OF MORTON	MORTON	MS	**A-**	A-	A-	58	8.73	1.3	7.9	32.4	21.7	**10.0**	12.6	19.4
BANK OF MOUNDVILLE	MOUNDVILLE	AL	**C-**	C-	C-	99	-1.44	5.0	2.7	3.2	63.9	**5.7**	7.7	16.3
BANK OF MOUNT HOPE INC	MOUNT HOPE	WV	**A-**	B+	B+	119	0.64	10.1	8.0	18.9	42.7	**8.9**	10.2	23.7
BANK OF NAPA NA	NAPA	CA	**C-**	C-	C	106	25.75	14.5	0.3	3.2	15.1	**10.0**	15.5	21.8
BANK OF NAPLES	NAPLES	FL	**E-**	D-	D+	184	-7.24	2.7	1.4	16.6	16.6	**0.9**	4.2	8.9
BANK OF NEBRASKA	LA VISTA	NE	**C**	B-	C+	119	-12.62	12.6	1.1	14.4	1.7	**8.1**	10.4	13.4
▼ BANK OF NEVADA	LAS VEGAS	NV	**D-**	D	C-	2,772	-0.28	10.1	0.4	9.1	16.9	**7.4**	9.3	12.8
▼ BANK OF NEW CAMBRIA	NEW CAMBRIA	MO	**C-**	C	C	32	9.32	2.1	2.8	7.7	25.2	**8.3**	9.9	16.0
BANK OF NEW CANAAN	NEW CANAAN	CT	**C**	C	C+	310	20.91	2.9	0.2	30.0	16.0	**6.1**	8.2	13.1
BANK OF NEW CASTLE	NEW CASTLE	DE	**C-**	C	B-	16	-1.68	0.0	0.0	0.0	0.9	**10.0**	96.8	467.4
BANK OF NEW ENGLAND	SALEM	NH	**D-**	C	C+	470	-1.19	11.4	0.1	2.8	0.2	**9.2**	11.8	14.4
BANK OF NEW GLARUS	NEW GLARUS	WI	**C-**	B-	B-	193	9.88	8.2	3.1	19.6	17.6	**6.6**	8.6	12.4
BANK OF NEW JERSEY	FORT LEE	NJ	**B-**	C+	C	370	15.85	12.4	0.3	16.3	8.6	**10.0**	13.9	18.0
BANK OF NEW MADRID	NEW MADRID	MO	**C+**	C	C	90	2.61	3.3	2.8	12.4	25.1	**9.0**	10.4	16.1
BANK OF NEW ORLEANS	METAIRIE	LA	**B**	B	B+	319	-0.61	0.2	0.2	32.7	39.2	**10.0**	16.0	34.7
BANK OF NEW YORK MELLON	NEW YORK	NY	**C**	B-	B-	181,855	10.70	1.1	0.0	2.3	34.2	**3.3**	5.3	15.3
▼ BANK OF NEWINGTON	NEWINGTON	GA	**E-**	D-	C+	77	-14.34	8.0	3.1	15.5	1.3	**2.7**	6.5	9.7
BANK OF NEWMAN GROVE	NEWMAN GROVE	NE	**C+**	B-	C+	34	9.91	1.7	3.5	0.4	38.3	**7.1**	9.0	14.1
▼ BANK OF NORTH CAROLINA	HIGH POINT	NC	**C**	C	C+	2,149	31.51	6.4	0.7	14.2	16.7	**5.4**	7.4	13.0
BANK OF NORTH LAS VEGAS	NORTH LAS VEGAS	NV	**D-**	D	C-	82	-13.03	10.0	0.1	2.1	7.3	**6.4**	8.4	12.2
BANK OF NORTHERN	PETOSKEY	MI	**C**	C	C-	362	8.74	19.0	0.5	12.8	14.1	**6.6**	8.7	12.2
BANK OF NY MELLON TRUST N	LOS ANGELES	CA	**B+**	B+	B	2,068	6.13	0.0	0.0	0.0	36.5	**10.0**	52.3	331.7
▼ BANK OF OAK RIDGE	OAK RIDGE	LA	**B-**	B	B-	49	3.65	0.3	3.6	0.0	74.4	**8.0**	9.7	38.8
BANK OF OAK RIDGE	OAK RIDGE	NC	**C-**	C	C	349	3.20	9.9	0.8	16.3	16.0	**6.0**	8.0	11.8
BANK OF OAKFIELD	OAKFIELD	WI	**C-**	C-	C	75	9.45	10.9	1.8	14.0	17.7	**6.7**	8.8	13.0
BANK OF OCEAN CITY	OCEAN CITY	MD	**B+**	B	B-	157	8.87	3.3	1.7	18.0	10.4	**10.0**	12.6	19.5
BANK OF ODESSA	ODESSA	MO	**B-**	B	A-	241	-0.21	3.8	2.4	19.0	50.8	**10.0**	20.0	43.8
BANK OF OFALLON	O'FALLON	IL	**B+**	B+	B+	268	4.08	7.1	2.9	37.7	24.0	**10.0**	13.8	26.0
BANK OF OHIO COUNTY INC	BEAVER DAM	KY	**A-**	B+	A-	93	9.45	11.7	2.3	13.6	34.8	**10.0**	16.1	27.5
BANK OF OKOLONA	OKOLONA	MS	**C**	C-	B	110	18.36	11.6	8.9	12.9	20.3	**6.8**	8.8	14.0
▼ BANK OF OLD MONROE	OLD MONROE	MO	**B**	B+	A-	254	19.86	5.0	1.3	11.2	45.6	**9.3**	10.5	16.7
BANK OF ONTARIO	ONTARIO	WI	**C-**	D+	C-	33	4.93	6.9	8.9	44.8	1.4	**9.2**	10.5	16.7
BANK OF ORCHARD	ORCHARD	NE	**B-**	B-	B-	23	1.19	4.6	4.4	1.4	57.1	**10.0**	12.1	26.1
BANK OF ORRICK	ORRICK	MO	**C-**	C-	B-	35	5.55	9.0	4.0	18.6	16.4	**10.0**	12.0	19.4
BANK OF OSWEGO	LAKE OSWEGO	OR	**C-**	C-	C-	188	55.36	16.5	2.7	19.8	1.6	**4.8**	6.8	12.2
▼ BANK OF PALATINE	PALATINE	IL	**E+**	D-	D	62	-1.90	2.6	1.3	14.8	36.8	**4.9**	6.9	19.3
BANK OF PALMER	PALMER	KS	**C-**	C	C	38	14.24	6.7	3.7	11.6	34.3	**5.8**	7.8	12.7
BANK OF PARSONS	PARSONS	KS	**B**	B	B	12	-0.64	1.1	7.9	44.1	4.6	**4.6**	6.6	14.4
BANK OF PERRY	PERRY	GA	**E-**	D-	C-	121	-5.26	9.4	4.3	12.8	11.8	**2.0**	5.8	9.0
BANK OF PERRY COUNTY	LOBELVILLE	TN	**C**	C-	B-	133	-1.97	6.7	17.7	35.5	6.4	**8.9**	10.3	15.3
BANK OF PINE HILL	PINE HILL	AL	**C-**	C	C+	27	8.67	1.0	1.7	9.5	64.5	**10.0**	12.8	27.2
BANK OF PONTIAC	PONTIAC	IL	**B**	B	A-	365	22.55	11.2	4.2	26.1	25.6	**10.0**	11.8	20.4
BANK OF POYNETTE	POYNETTE	WI	**C-**	C-	C	89	0.64	7.3	0.8	17.9	9.6	**6.2**	8.8	11.9
BANK OF PRAGUE	PRAGUE	NE	**B+**	B	B	19	9.68	5.5	6.1	5.6	23.0	**10.0**	17.3	23.3
BANK OF PRAIRIE DU SAC	PRAIRIE DU SAC	WI	**A-**	A	A	277	3.74	8.6	2.3	7.3	35.5	**10.0**	15.5	24.6
BANK OF PRAIRIE VILLAGE	PRAIRIE VILLAGE	KS	**B**	B	B	92	22.88	21.9	4.1	12.2	24.4	**6.7**	8.7	12.4
BANK OF PRESCOTT	PRESCOTT	AR	**B+**	B+	B+	78	11.38	11.8	5.6	12.5	44.8	**10.0**	12.1	19.0
BANK OF PRINCETON	PRINCETON	NJ	**D+**	C-	C-	489	84.68	5.1	0.4	7.9	33.0	**6.0**	8.0	12.5
BANK OF PROTECTION	PROTECTION	KS	**C+**	C+	C+	51	33.79	3.0	3.6	5.9	41.2	**7.8**	9.5	19.0
BANK OF PUTNAM COUNTY	COOKEVILLE	TN	**B-**	B-	B-	348	4.39	2.7	4.6	23.4	33.7	**5.9**	7.9	19.3
▲ BANK OF QUINCY	QUINCY	IL	**B+**	B-	C+	107	10.50	8.0	2.7	21.8	10.8	**10.0**	11.7	16.4
BANK OF RANTOUL	RANTOUL	IL	**B+**	B	B-	196	7.71	18.4	0.9	6.5	37.5	**6.7**	8.7	14.7
BANK OF RICHMONDVILLE	COBLESKILL	NY	**B+**	B+	A-	114	2.39	5.0	2.8	44.8	22.6	**10.0**	12.0	23.8
BANK OF RINGGOLD	RINGGOLD	LA	**B-**	B-	B	62	8.84	3.2	3.6	10.2	48.9	**10.0**	15.2	42.9
BANK OF RIO VISTA	RIO VISTA	CA	**C-**	B-	B+	176	-1.88	7.6	0.6	0.2	32.8	**10.0**	11.1	18.9
BANK OF RIPLEY	RIPLEY	TN	**B**	B-	B	180	6.05	1.3	7.0	17.4	39.3	**10.0**	15.0	25.5
BANK OF RISON	RISON	AR	**A-**	A-	A-	30	3.39	5.3	21.9	10.7	19.9	**10.0**	17.1	31.2
▲ BANK OF RIVER OAKS	HOUSTON	TX	**B-**	C+	C	253	2.77	26.8	3.7	13.9	23.9	**10.0**	12.6	20.6
BANK OF ROMNEY	ROMNEY	WV	**C-**	B-	B+	231	-0.09	6.0	7.6	46.3	11.6	**9.1**	10.4	16.8
BANK OF RUSTON	RUSTON	LA	**B-**	B-	C+	98	14.22	6.1	5.8	36.9	11.8	**10.0**	14.6	21.4

Asset Quality Index	Non-Performing Loans as a % of Total Loans	Non-Performing Loans as a % of Capital	Net Charge-offs Avg Loans	Profitability Index	Net Income ($Mil)	Return on Assets (R.O.A.)	Return on Equity (R.O.E.)	Net Interest Spread	Overhead Efficiency Ratio	Liquidity Index	Liquidity Ratio	Hot Money Ratio	Stability Index
8.5	0.20	1.0	0.03	**9.5**	1.2	2.02	17.78	5.52	59.0	**1.1**	22.6	33.0	**9.0**
4.6	4.91	14.6	0.75	**2.3**	0.5	0.53	6.81	3.14	85.2	**0.9**	23.0	40.9	**2.8**
8.2	0.35	1.6	0.18	**6.2**	1.2	1.00	9.55	3.55	61.7	**3.0**	41.8	21.1	**7.0**
7.8	1.04	4.5	0.53	**0.9**	0.3	0.26	1.50	4.29	86.4	**1.7**	27.6	26.6	**2.4**
0.3	10.04	58.7	8.20	**0.0**	-25.7	-12.44	-175.84	2.48	149.0	**2.5**	38.2	26.3	**2.9**
0.8	3.42	24.7	0.77	**5.1**	1.6	1.22	12.83	5.08	68.8	**3.8**	13.3	9.9	**6.4**
0.5	4.28	25.3	3.49	**0.0**	-26.4	-0.95	-8.97	4.17	68.9	**1.9**	16.4	20.2	**4.7**
1.7	5.73	28.7	0.59	**2.1**	0.0	0.14	1.38	3.65	91.9	**5.2**	43.9	9.7	**5.9**
3.4	1.04	7.9	0.12	**3.5**	1.2	0.44	5.39	4.10	76.8	**1.4**	25.0	28.7	**4.3**
7.5	0.00	0.0	0.00	**2.0**	0.0	0.04	0.05	0.39	78.7	**3.0**	100.2	100.0	**7.2**
0.5	2.75	17.8	0.79	**5.7**	4.0	0.82	7.11	4.74	65.2	**1.7**	10.2	19.8	**7.2**
2.6	1.38	10.5	0.72	**4.4**	1.4	0.73	7.16	4.14	65.7	**2.6**	18.7	16.3	**6.4**
6.2	0.71	4.0	0.14	**3.9**	2.2	0.62	4.25	3.83	62.5	**0.6**	16.5	58.9	**5.6**
4.6	1.89	9.5	0.65	**4.4**	0.7	0.85	9.62	4.75	74.3	**3.3**	24.6	13.4	**3.3**
9.3	0.38	1.3	0.00	**3.9**	2.3	0.70	4.09	3.10	66.2	**2.9**	49.4	28.3	**8.0**
6.4	1.49	3.4	0.29	**5.6**	1,567.0	0.92	10.89	1.75	72.0	**2.9**	49.5	39.7	**5.9**
0.2	9.34	80.6	1.84	**0.0**	-2.4	-2.87	-35.32	3.29	190.8	**0.8**	16.1	35.8	**2.3**
6.7	0.00	0.0	-0.03	**3.5**	0.2	0.60	5.76	3.52	83.3	**3.9**	33.2	13.1	**6.1**
2.5	2.65	22.1	1.39	**2.7**	8.9	0.44	4.99	3.59	61.3	**0.8**	11.1	35.3	**5.3**
0.0	3.85	20.1	8.18	**0.0**	-3.5	-3.91	-37.59	3.11	205.0	**0.8**	17.4	46.8	**0.5**
2.3	2.20	17.6	0.51	**3.1**	2.2	0.64	7.38	3.29	64.5	**0.5**	5.7	49.3	**4.9**
6.5	0.00	0.0	0.00	**10.0**	201.9	10.27	13.30	0.46	44.8	**9.5**	163.4	0.0	**6.3**
9.8	0.06	0.0	-0.10	**3.8**	0.5	0.94	8.37	2.55	64.1	**3.4**	89.6	43.6	**6.9**
2.8	2.05	16.3	0.67	**2.5**	0.8	0.22	2.60	4.17	81.4	**1.2**	21.9	30.5	**4.0**
2.9	2.35	17.2	0.22	**3.2**	0.4	0.59	6.50	4.53	78.5	**1.5**	23.8	27.0	**4.0**
4.7	0.24	1.3	0.17	**4.8**	1.4	0.86	6.52	4.43	68.8	**2.2**	27.1	19.7	**7.2**
6.6	2.54	5.5	1.67	**3.9**	1.6	0.64	3.22	3.04	44.2	**4.5**	52.1	15.3	**6.6**
8.4	0.79	3.6	0.51	**4.1**	2.5	0.96	6.82	2.92	55.0	**1.5**	10.6	22.5	**8.2**
4.9	3.16	10.3	0.43	**9.3**	2.0	2.22	13.50	5.28	49.5	**3.4**	29.2	14.5	**9.5**
2.7	1.81	12.4	0.83	**6.4**	1.5	1.48	15.50	4.87	57.9	**1.4**	32.6	43.2	**5.8**
5.8	1.02	4.0	1.60	**4.5**	2.4	1.00	9.65	3.88	53.9	**3.8**	38.5	15.7	**5.1**
2.4	2.40	16.4	0.27	**7.6**	0.6	1.76	17.67	5.80	64.8	**1.5**	14.8	23.7	**8.2**
8.9	0.00	0.0	0.11	**4.8**	0.2	1.05	8.74	2.97	61.0	**2.3**	45.1	27.0	**7.8**
3.7	6.28	31.0	0.22	**1.1**	0.0	0.02	0.14	3.94	105.2	**3.5**	27.1	13.2	**6.6**
6.6	0.36	3.2	0.38	**2.5**	0.4	0.25	3.28	3.96	72.4	**3.0**	33.9	18.1	**4.8**
0.3	13.72	56.0	0.27	**0.0**	-1.2	-1.83	-23.46	1.55	183.1	**3.1**	52.5	24.7	**3.2**
5.6	1.34	10.1	0.00	**3.1**	0.2	0.65	7.74	3.26	80.9	**4.2**	32.9	11.8	**4.6**
8.8	0.00	0.0	0.00	**2.7**	0.0	0.34	5.48	3.76	92.6	**2.1**	32.6	20.0	**4.2**
0.3	4.85	47.4	1.32	**0.7**	-0.4	-0.31	-5.38	3.62	92.5	**3.5**	12.0	11.0	**0.0**
2.5	2.11	15.1	0.50	**7.6**	2.6	1.90	18.98	5.30	55.8	**1.2**	12.4	28.8	**6.6**
9.8	0.05	0.1	0.21	**1.2**	0.1	0.26	2.00	2.63	104.2	**3.9**	70.5	21.6	**6.7**
4.5	2.07	10.0	2.33	**4.9**	2.2	0.68	5.53	4.77	49.7	**1.8**	22.9	22.3	**7.1**
2.0	4.41	28.7	1.10	**3.4**	0.4	0.42	4.68	4.00	63.3	**4.5**	33.5	10.5	**4.6**
6.9	0.33	1.2	0.05	**8.6**	0.4	1.85	10.46	4.48	65.2	**4.2**	31.4	9.4	**8.9**
5.5	1.76	5.7	0.32	**9.1**	4.4	1.60	9.98	4.71	41.5	**5.0**	49.9	12.7	**8.9**
8.4	0.00	0.0	0.00	**5.2**	0.8	1.00	10.89	3.67	59.4	**1.5**	32.9	40.1	**5.4**
6.2	1.87	6.7	0.13	**5.8**	0.7	0.96	7.37	3.60	64.0	**2.3**	33.6	24.4	**6.9**
3.6	1.70	11.4	0.79	**1.3**	2.4	0.62	6.73	3.07	75.9	**3.2**	26.0	14.4	**2.1**
6.9	0.82	3.8	0.28	**4.5**	0.4	1.01	10.02	4.05	68.8	**1.9**	24.8	21.7	**4.4**
9.0	0.05	0.3	0.26	**4.6**	4.0	1.17	15.49	2.95	67.7	**3.8**	47.1	17.7	**5.1**
5.2	0.62	3.9	0.11	**6.8**	1.7	1.65	14.45	3.90	60.1	**2.4**	9.9	16.5	**6.9**
5.7	1.50	8.4	0.02	**10.0**	3.8	1.95	22.93	4.90	43.5	**2.7**	6.2	14.8	**5.0**
5.4	2.52	12.4	0.28	**4.7**	1.0	0.81	6.74	4.24	67.1	**3.5**	18.9	12.0	**7.2**
6.9	6.56	10.1	0.08	**2.8**	0.2	0.30	1.95	2.81	85.5	**5.0**	73.7	15.3	**7.6**
0.3	16.43	69.2	3.14	**1.1**	-1.2	-0.67	-5.31	4.10	80.7	**4.0**	36.8	13.8	**6.2**
7.6	1.07	3.1	0.23	**4.2**	1.1	0.63	4.04	4.67	80.7	**2.7**	38.7	23.2	**7.2**
6.3	0.41	1.1	0.42	**8.0**	0.5	1.67	9.15	4.35	54.4	**3.1**	33.5	17.2	**9.8**
8.5	0.00	0.0	0.00	**3.5**	2.0	0.78	6.77	3.75	73.8	**1.7**	15.0	20.9	**5.0**
2.0	3.90	26.1	0.13	**4.6**	1.6	0.69	6.44	4.30	69.1	**1.9**	12.9	19.5	**6.9**
6.2	1.08	5.3	0.01	**3.7**	0.7	0.72	6.25	4.58	76.6	**1.9**	22.9	21.4	**6.6**

Name	City	State	Rating	2008 Rating	2007 Rating	Total Assets ($Mil)	One Year Asset Growth	Asset Mix (As a % of Total Assets) Comm-ercial Loans	Cons-umer Loans	Home Mort-gages	Secur-ities	Capital-ization Index	Leverage Ratio	Risk-based Capital Ratio
BANK OF SACRAMENTO	SACRAMENTO	CA	**D**	D+	C+	369	3.43	10.5	0.6	1.9	27.8	**7.9**	9.6	13.9
▼ BANK OF SALEM	SALEM	AR	**C-**	C	C+	130	0.44	9.7	7.6	28.0	1.7	**8.7**	10.2	14.3
BANK OF SALEM	SALEM	MO	**B-**	B-	B	78	-2.64	3.6	4.8	35.2	27.9	**9.9**	11.0	20.5
BANK OF SAN ANTONIO	SAN ANTONIO	TX	**C+**	C-	C-	187	22.47	26.0	1.7	8.0	29.3	**10.0**	15.3	24.2
▲ BANK OF SAN FRANCISCO	SAN FRANCISCO	CA	**C**	D-	C-	101	14.52	37.2	0.3	2.1	0.0	**7.9**	9.6	13.5
BANK OF SAN JACINTO	COLDSPRING	TX	**B+**	B+	B+	33	-1.77	2.9	8.7	38.1	13.8	**10.0**	12.8	29.1
BANK OF SANTA BARBARA	SANTA BARBARA	CA	**D-**	E+	D+	116	61.06	18.4	0.3	3.4	6.9	**6.1**	8.1	13.6
BANK OF SANTA CLARITA	SANTA CLARITA	CA	**C-**	C	C-	209	20.58	8.2	8.7	1.9	20.7	**8.6**	10.0	15.2
BANK OF SHOREWOOD	SHOREWOOD	IL	**E-**	E	D-	125	-7.15	1.9	4.3	7.7	20.7	**0.0**	3.0	5.6
BANK OF SOPERTON	SOPERTON	GA	**D-**	D-	D-	39	-7.90	4.9	4.1	13.5	25.1	**6.5**	8.5	17.2
▼ BANK OF SOUTH CAROLINA	CHARLESTON	SC	**B+**	A-	A-	281	5.51	18.6	2.1	11.0	14.0	**7.8**	10.3	13.2
▼ BANK OF SOUTH TEXAS	MCALLEN	TX	**E+**	D-	D+	77	-8.99	9.1	3.1	21.6	8.2	**3.3**	6.9	10.2
▼ BANK OF SOUTHERN	SAN DIEGO	CA	**D-**	D	D	180	61.20	16.0	1.7	6.1	4.2	**8.3**	12.4	13.6
BANK OF SOUTHERN	NEW HAVEN	CT	**D-**	D-	C	152	12.75	24.9	0.2	8.1	6.5	**5.3**	8.4	11.2
BANK OF SOUTHSIDE VIRGINI	CARSON	VA	**A**	A	A	504	1.91	3.7	22.0	15.0	20.1	**10.0**	12.5	18.7
BANK OF SPRINGFIELD	SPRINGFIELD	IL	**D+**	C	C-	681	18.21	14.5	1.7	12.1	4.7	**3.3**	7.5	10.2
BANK OF ST AUGUSTINE	SAINT AUGUSTINE	FL	**D+**	D+	B-	181	6.31	4.6	0.7	28.3	10.5	**5.5**	7.5	11.8
BANK OF ST CROIX	CHRISTIANSTED	VI	**B**	B+	A-	110	1.95	2.9	0.2	28.1	42.5	**8.7**	10.1	23.7
BANK OF ST ELIZABETH	SAINT ELIZABETH	MO	**B-**	C+	C+	101	5.92	1.2	5.5	27.1	2.5	**5.4**	7.5	11.3
BANK OF ST FRANCISVILLE	SAINT FRANCISVILLE	LA	**B-**	C+	B	95	-1.65	6.4	7.8	24.9	10.9	**7.9**	9.6	13.4
▼ BANK OF STANLY	ALBEMARLE	NC	**D**	C-	C+	344	8.48	6.8	4.2	22.5	17.0	**6.6**	8.6	12.8
▼ BANK OF STAPLETON	STAPLETON	NE	**D+**	C	D+	20	7.14	23.4	5.6	7.7	10.9	**6.4**	10.6	12.1
BANK OF STAR CITY	STAR CITY	AR	**B+**	A-	A-	101	10.71	8.5	3.1	14.6	33.1	**10.0**	12.2	18.5
BANK OF STAR VALLEY	AFTON	WY	**B**	B+	B+	114	1.84	8.0	7.5	13.1	29.0	**8.3**	9.9	15.3
▼ BANK OF STEINAUER	STEINAUER	NE	**D+**	C	C-	11	15.18	9.2	9.6	21.0	14.8	**6.5**	8.5	15.0
BANK OF STOCKTON	STOCKTON	CA	**B-**	C	B	1,901	-2.39	9.4	8.0	4.1	28.8	**7.3**	9.2	13.5
BANK OF STRONGHURST	STRONGHURST	IL	**B-**	C+	C+	72	-0.68	2.6	2.1	7.9	58.9	**10.0**	16.6	43.5
BANK OF SULLIVAN	SULLIVAN	MO	**C+**	C	C+	266	-5.66	9.4	3.2	37.5	7.0	**7.8**	10.7	13.2
BANK OF SUN PRAIRIE	SUN PRAIRIE	WI	**D**	C-	B	317	-9.10	11.2	1.6	10.3	0.0	**10.0**	12.9	15.2
BANK OF SUNSET & TRUST	SUNSET	LA	**B+**	B+	A-	106	4.30	15.5	1.6	14.0	30.9	**6.9**	8.9	15.1
BANK OF TAMPA	TAMPA	FL	**C-**	C+	B-	969	6.31	16.8	3.5	6.1	21.8	**6.1**	8.1	12.7
BANK OF TENNESSEE	KINGSPORT	TN	**C+**	B-	C+	633	-0.52	6.6	0.9	22.2	12.0	**6.2**	8.2	12.3
BANK OF TERRELL	DAWSON	GA	**C+**	C+	B	146	11.19	7.3	3.8	22.7	7.0	**7.7**	9.5	14.4
BANK OF TESCOTT	TESCOTT	KS	**B+**	A	A	277	9.73	4.5	2.6	26.3	25.7	**8.1**	9.8	15.4
▼ BANK OF TEXAS	AUSTIN	TX	**D+**	C	B-	83	9.23	1.9	3.0	12.4	7.8	**9.7**	10.8	24.5
BANK OF TEXAS	DEVINE	TX	**D-**	C-	C	51	-12.79	8.9	4.2	12.3	6.1	**7.6**	9.4	15.3
▼ BANK OF TEXAS	MIDLAND	TX	**D+**	C	C	97	130.82	33.8	0.7	2.7	3.9	**10.0**	26.1	29.4
BANK OF THAYER	THAYER	MO	**D+**	C	C	77	-0.38	8.2	4.4	23.4	33.0	**6.6**	8.6	15.4
BANK OF THE BLUEGRASS & T	LEXINGTON	KY	**D+**	D-	D-	210	-7.62	1.5	1.4	29.2	21.7	**10.0**	12.7	21.1
▼ BANK OF THE CAROLINAS	MOCKSVILLE	NC	**E+**	D	D	534	-12.38	9.7	0.8	14.7	20.6	**5.5**	8.2	11.4
BANK OF THE CASCADES	BEND	OR	**E-**	E-	D-	1,716	-20.92	9.8	2.8	2.6	6.8	**0.4**	4.2	6.8
▼ BANK OF THE	NORFOLK	VA	**E+**	D-	C-	1,113	-12.78	5.7	0.8	15.1	0.8	**1.5**	5.6	8.5
▼ BANK OF THE EASTERN	CAMBRIDGE	MD	**E-**	D-	B-	205	-10.70	9.6	3.3	22.7	4.3	**1.0**	5.5	8.0
BANK OF THE JAMES	LYNCHBURG	VA	**D+**	D-	C-	419	-4.27	8.6	1.9	22.8	12.7	**5.5**	7.6	11.4
BANK OF THE LAKES NA	OWASSO	OK	**D**	D-	C+	185	-1.93	28.0	6.2	8.0	8.9	**8.1**	9.9	13.5
BANK OF THE MOUNTAINS INC	WEST LIBERTY	KY	**C-**	C+	B-	61	-6.62	9.5	11.9	39.2	8.8	**9.8**	10.9	17.4
BANK OF THE NORTHWEST	BELLEVUE	WA	**E+**	D+	C-	146	286.79	17.6	0.7	5.1	0.0	**8.6**	10.1	14.5
BANK OF THE ORIENT	SAN FRANCISCO	CA	**D-**	D-	D	652	5.08	2.5	0.0	5.9	3.3	**5.7**	7.7	12.5
BANK OF THE OZARKS	LITTLE ROCK	AR	**A-**	A-	A-	3,261	18.36	4.2	1.7	11.2	11.7	**10.0**	11.4	16.8
BANK OF THE PACIFIC	ABERDEEN	WA	**D+**	D	D+	643	-3.63	9.2	1.4	8.5	7.5	**8.2**	9.8	14.6
▼ BANK OF THE PANHANDLE	GUYMON	OK	**B+**	A	A-	117	13.08	10.6	2.3	4.6	41.2	**10.0**	11.4	18.4
BANK OF THE PRAIRIE	OLATHE	KS	**E**	D	C-	97	-14.44	16.6	1.2	16.6	10.2	**4.2**	7.0	10.6
▲ BANK OF THE RIO GRANDE NA	LAS CRUCES	NM	**B**	B-	B+	105	-5.28	10.4	7.7	8.7	12.1	**10.0**	11.8	17.4
BANK OF THE ROCKIES NA	WHITE SULPHUR	MT	**D-**	D+	C+	128	-4.26	2.5	2.0	12.4	19.5	**8.2**	9.8	15.6
BANK OF THE SAN JUANS	DURANGO	CO	**C**	C+	B	230	24.74	3.5	0.5	12.6	12.0	**6.8**	8.8	13.0
BANK OF THE SIERRA	PORTERVILLE	CA	**C-**	C-	B-	1,283	-3.62	7.9	3.6	8.3	25.8	**10.0**	13.1	19.3
BANK OF THE SOUTH	PENSACOLA	FL	**C+**	B-	B-	64	-0.52	0.0	1.1	4.1	64.4	**10.0**	22.7	88.6
BANK OF THE SOUTHWEST	ROSWELL	NM	**B+**	B+	B	151	-1.27	32.4	5.6	16.6	0.7	**6.8**	8.8	13.9
BANK OF THE VALLEY	BELLWOOD	NE	**C+**	C+	C	84	17.44	6.9	2.8	6.9	9.4	**6.3**	8.5	12.0
▲ BANK OF THE WEST	SAN FRANCISCO	CA	**C**	C-	B-	57,653	-3.91	9.0	18.0	15.9	10.6	**9.5**	11.2	14.6

Asset Quality Index	Non-Performing Loans as a % of Total Loans	Non-Performing Loans as a % of Capital	Net Charge-offs Avg Loans	Profitability Index	Net Income ($Mil)	Return on Assets (R.O.A.)	Return on Equity (R.O.E.)	Net Interest Spread	Overhead Efficiency Ratio	Liquidity Index	Liquidity Ratio	Hot Money Ratio	Stability Index
1.0	1.64	9.7	1.51	**1.8**	1.0	0.27	2.85	4.63	77.0	**1.0**	24.4	36.4	**4.8**
2.3	2.66	19.4	0.62	**6.6**	1.3	1.00	9.80	5.22	57.0	**1.3**	7.3	25.7	**5.4**
8.9	0.00	0.0	0.00	**3.6**	0.4	0.47	4.18	4.07	84.0	**2.4**	19.1	17.4	**6.4**
8.6	0.00	0.0	0.00	**3.7**	2.7	1.68	10.55	4.04	84.6	**4.3**	43.0	14.0	**5.2**
7.0	0.26	1.8	0.03	**4.0**	0.7	0.74	8.01	4.77	71.3	**1.9**	24.8	21.3	**4.9**
7.5	0.44	1.7	-0.30	**5.2**	0.4	1.13	8.95	4.80	79.9	**5.3**	50.1	10.2	**8.3**
1.1	4.99	32.8	1.04	**0.0**	-0.8	-0.79	-9.32	2.79	127.2	**6.0**	47.0	5.9	**0.8**
7.9	0.02	0.2	0.05	**1.7**	0.6	0.30	2.83	3.31	95.8	**0.7**	13.8	43.2	**4.9**
0.3	8.94	84.4	2.44	**0.0**	-5.5	-4.21	-94.65	3.36	136.7	**1.0**	22.3	34.2	**0.7**
1.7	4.95	24.0	3.38	**0.0**	-0.3	-0.63	-7.02	3.44	98.8	**2.5**	35.5	23.2	**2.3**
6.6	0.44	3.0	0.36	**7.0**	3.3	1.22	11.53	4.79	62.2	**2.1**	11.6	18.2	**6.7**
1.3	1.58	15.8	0.40	**0.0**	-0.9	-1.13	-9.32	5.02	107.9	**1.3**	13.8	26.7	**5.0**
0.9	3.06	23.0	0.86	**0.0**	-0.7	-0.52	-3.39	4.49	93.8	**2.6**	14.4	16.1	**4.8**
0.0	4.93	39.4	1.67	**0.3**	-1.1	-0.76	-7.85	4.01	85.8	**1.3**	14.8	28.0	**4.1**
6.9	0.53	2.3	0.42	**9.3**	8.1	1.59	12.03	4.94	51.5	**3.8**	32.4	13.7	**10.0**
2.2	1.14	10.3	0.57	**4.1**	3.8	0.57	7.31	3.97	70.1	**2.9**	13.9	14.2	**4.6**
2.6	1.98	18.0	0.33	**1.7**	0.1	0.06	0.80	3.50	73.1	**0.9**	19.2	35.9	**3.1**
6.7	0.79	3.4	0.20	**4.8**	1.1	0.96	8.83	4.05	75.6	**4.4**	40.3	12.9	**7.6**
3.2	1.52	14.0	0.17	**8.3**	1.9	1.91	18.26	4.28	55.4	**3.2**	22.2	13.6	**8.2**
3.5	2.11	14.8	0.70	**4.4**	0.8	0.85	8.83	5.27	75.5	**1.5**	12.1	24.2	**5.9**
0.3	5.86	42.9	0.32	**2.8**	1.5	0.45	4.87	4.20	80.0	**2.7**	13.7	15.4	**4.9**
4.4	1.41	9.1	0.16	**3.4**	0.0	0.12	1.05	5.67	83.7	**4.5**	12.8	5.0	**3.0**
4.3	3.32	15.2	0.87	**5.1**	0.9	0.89	7.06	4.65	62.6	**2.7**	35.6	20.6	**6.8**
4.7	1.24	7.2	0.50	**5.3**	1.2	1.03	10.04	4.84	68.5	**1.3**	16.6	28.1	**7.6**
4.5	0.60	3.9	0.00	**3.5**	0.0	0.40	4.47	4.97	88.4	**4.5**	27.8	6.4	**3.0**
4.2	1.77	9.8	1.12	**4.3**	13.1	0.68	6.54	4.45	65.2	**3.6**	32.6	17.4	**8.1**
9.6	0.00	0.0	-0.01	**3.3**	0.4	0.50	3.12	2.89	76.3	**4.9**	76.0	16.2	**7.5**
4.5	0.74	5.1	0.39	**3.4**	1.2	0.43	3.98	4.21	70.9	**1.7**	2.2	19.3	**4.7**
0.1	2.63	15.5	3.90	**1.3**	-5.9	-1.85	-12.82	4.14	69.5	**2.0**	7.3	18.0	**6.6**
7.5	0.06	0.3	0.08	**5.2**	1.1	1.03	8.68	4.31	67.8	**1.4**	13.5	25.5	**6.4**
1.8	4.34	28.5	1.47	**2.8**	2.1	0.22	2.58	3.79	69.3	**4.4**	29.3	9.5	**5.3**
2.8	1.14	8.8	0.99	**3.6**	5.8	0.90	10.45	4.10	71.1	**2.6**	11.5	15.4	**6.1**
2.9	2.17	14.9	0.50	**4.8**	1.6	1.17	11.82	4.34	60.6	**1.0**	24.7	36.0	**4.2**
4.8	1.31	8.5	0.65	**7.3**	4.2	1.58	15.22	4.12	44.5	**2.1**	20.3	19.2	**9.0**
6.1	1.24	4.5	1.79	**0.3**	-0.7	-0.93	-7.84	3.58	124.6	**6.3**	56.2	5.0	**4.7**
5.5	1.58	8.8	1.13	**0.0**	-1.2	-2.18	-22.25	3.98	137.1	**1.9**	27.3	24.5	**4.4**
8.5	0.00	0.0	0.04	**0.0**	-1.3	-1.96	-5.61	2.29	127.5	**1.2**	30.5	55.8	**4.7**
5.1	0.38	2.4	1.41	**1.6**	0.0	-0.02	-0.25	4.22	86.2	**2.2**	28.7	20.5	**4.6**
1.7	4.51	23.5	0.70	**3.9**	2.9	1.33	11.20	3.88	67.8	**2.5**	26.1	18.1	**4.8**
0.3	6.74	49.2	2.08	**0.0**	-2.4	-0.43	-4.72	3.35	88.1	**0.8**	13.4	35.4	**3.5**
0.0	6.52	66.4	2.61	**0.0**	-7.4	-0.38	-9.15	3.68	92.5	**1.4**	20.0	28.7	**3.6**
0.0	11.78	87.5	1.94	**0.0**	-34.4	-2.82	-37.74	3.02	72.0	**0.6**	11.6	58.8	**5.9**
0.0	15.99	139.1	4.29	**0.1**	-5.7	-2.61	-33.75	2.28	93.6	**0.7**	11.7	39.7	**3.9**
1.6	2.56	22.3	0.49	**3.0**	2.2	0.53	7.16	4.11	70.7	**4.0**	13.7	8.3	**2.6**
1.5	2.78	17.8	0.84	**1.7**	0.5	0.23	2.40	3.50	80.4	**1.6**	19.0	24.7	**4.4**
2.5	3.21	19.4	0.45	**3.9**	0.4	0.60	5.61	5.57	81.6	**1.6**	15.2	22.5	**5.8**
0.0	5.53	34.6	1.23	**0.0**	-1.5	-0.90	-10.16	3.66	112.4	**1.5**	20.1	25.8	**1.7**
0.2	6.66	48.3	0.39	**1.4**	0.8	0.12	1.48	3.92	75.2	**1.1**	22.2	33.2	**3.8**
5.7	0.55	3.3	0.76	**8.5**	65.9	2.21	19.46	5.47	44.6	**1.8**	2.7	19.1	**8.7**
2.5	2.11	13.9	0.84	**1.7**	2.4	0.37	3.29	4.22	83.3	**1.5**	12.9	23.2	**5.9**
6.3	0.66	2.9	0.07	**6.6**	1.8	1.65	13.24	4.27	63.9	**3.4**	32.1	15.3	**8.1**
1.1	3.74	32.3	3.58	**0.2**	-1.2	-1.12	-14.32	3.86	96.9	**1.2**	15.6	28.8	**2.2**
4.4	2.29	10.6	0.86	**6.0**	1.2	1.12	9.97	6.04	72.7	**4.9**	30.8	6.5	**7.7**
0.3	11.29	58.8	0.50	**2.7**	0.3	0.23	2.22	4.51	87.7	**3.1**	26.9	15.1	**6.3**
3.1	2.20	13.6	0.23	**4.8**	1.8	0.93	7.18	4.32	61.7	**1.7**	32.6	31.4	**6.3**
1.8	5.36	22.7	2.26	**3.8**	8.2	0.63	5.00	5.01	66.1	**2.0**	20.6	20.8	**8.5**
10.0	0.00	0.0	0.05	**3.1**	0.2	0.34	1.51	3.10	82.2	**7.2**	96.2	6.3	**6.4**
5.9	0.25	2.1	0.15	**5.6**	1.7	1.14	13.10	5.87	79.0	**3.9**	14.5	9.1	**6.2**
4.4	0.77	6.6	0.01	**5.8**	0.8	1.08	13.11	4.30	61.1	**1.5**	11.2	23.7	**5.5**
1.0	3.51	21.5	1.55	**2.6**	184.6	0.31	1.80	3.55	62.2	**3.4**	5.7	11.4	**6.8**

Name	City	State	Rating	2008 Rating	2007 Rating	Total Assets ($Mil)	One Year Asset Growth	Asset Mix (As a % of Total Assets) Comm-ercial Loans	Cons-umer Loans	Home Mort-gages	Secur-ities	Capital-ization Index	Leverage Ratio	Risk-based Capital Ratio
BANK OF THE WEST	THOMAS	OK	**B-**	B	B	138	-0.74	10.5	1.7	13.3	0.0	**7.4**	9.7	12.9
BANK OF THE WEST	EL PASO	TX	**B**	B	B+	881	7.74	21.7	0.8	5.2	29.1	**6.1**	8.1	12.5
BANK OF THE WEST	GRAPEVINE	TX	**B-**	C-	C	290	4.04	9.2	2.0	6.6	14.6	**7.5**	9.4	14.3
BANK OF THE WICHITAS	SNYDER	OK	**B-**	B	C-	123	0.61	6.6	5.3	8.1	29.3	**5.0**	8.2	11.0
▼BANK OF TIOGA	TIOGA	ND	**B-**	A-	A	89	11.45	4.0	4.1	3.1	30.6	**6.8**	8.8	20.5
BANK OF TRAVELERS REST	TRAVELERS REST	SC	**D**	C+	C+	520	5.06	6.2	5.0	7.6	27.6	**5.0**	7.0	11.9
BANK OF TULLAHOMA	TULLAHOMA	TN	**C+**	C	C	109	23.39	7.7	4.4	16.0	25.1	**10.0**	14.1	20.8
BANK OF TURTLE LAKE	TURTLE LAKE	ND	**B-**	B	B	32	18.28	7.5	2.1	3.0	22.0	**6.1**	8.1	12.7
▼BANK OF TURTLE LAKE	TURTLE LAKE	WI	**C-**	C+	C+	61	-2.78	5.7	5.6	19.9	30.6	**7.1**	9.1	17.9
BANK OF UNION	EL RENO	OK	**B-**	C-	B+	341	10.57	36.0	4.3	9.2	6.6	**6.0**	9.2	11.8
BANK OF UPSON	THOMASTON	GA	**D**	C-	B-	341	8.34	3.4	5.2	12.3	14.0	**6.2**	8.2	15.0
BANK OF URBANA	URBANA	MO	**A-**	A-	A	160	2.98	3.6	3.6	20.0	43.1	**10.0**	14.9	28.8
BANK OF UTAH	OGDEN	UT	**C**	C	B-	747	0.80	7.5	0.3	3.5	18.9	**8.4**	9.9	16.2
BANK OF UTICA	UTICA	NY	**A**	A-	B	849	4.09	2.3	0.7	0.5	90.6	**10.0**	12.3	16.0
BANK OF VERDEN	VERDEN	OK	**B**	B	B	32	7.56	7.7	11.0	9.8	25.3	**10.0**	12.3	18.6
BANK OF VERNON	VERNON	AL	**D-**	D-	C-	180	-3.66	16.8	3.1	15.4	10.8	**10.0**	11.1	15.6
BANK OF VERSAILLES	VERSAILLES	MO	**D-**	C-	B+	320	-9.47	1.1	0.8	39.1	14.0	**6.1**	8.1	14.0
▼BANK OF VICI	VICI	OK	**D**	D+	B-	38	14.56	15.9	19.7	12.9	12.1	**6.7**	8.7	14.1
▲BANK OF VIRGINIA	MIDLOTHIAN	VA	**D-**	D-	D	210	-5.14	16.9	1.2	6.0	16.6	**6.3**	8.3	12.9
BANK OF WALKER COUNTY	JASPER	AL	**C+**	C	B-	84	4.03	10.1	6.8	15.4	19.6	**9.7**	10.8	17.9
BANK OF WALNUT GROVE	WALNUT GROVE	MS	**B+**	B+	B+	48	4.98	3.2	13.6	20.5	10.1	**10.0**	14.0	27.0
▲BANK OF WALTERBORO	WALTERBORO	SC	**C-**	C+	B	156	-5.78	44.7	4.2	7.0	17.5	**10.0**	11.2	16.5
BANK OF WASHINGTON	WASHINGTON	MO	**D**	D+	B+	798	-1.41	19.4	1.1	15.3	6.8	**7.4**	10.5	12.8
BANK OF WASHINGTON	LYNNWOOD	WA	**D-**	E	D	160	-18.15	6.5	3.8	10.5	3.8	**8.5**	10.0	14.2
▼BANK OF WAUSAU	WAUSAU	WI	**E-**	D-	D+	78	-7.80	10.9	0.8	21.1	8.0	**2.0**	6.8	9.0
BANK OF WAYNESBORO	WAYNESBORO	TN	**A-**	A-	B+	148	0.71	3.2	12.5	25.6	9.3	**10.0**	11.5	16.5
▲BANK OF WEDOWEE	WEDOWEE	AL	**C**	C-	C	122	-0.50	3.4	6.2	15.3	26.7	**7.9**	9.6	19.3
BANK OF WESTERN	ELK CITY	OK	**C**	C	C+	205	12.48	14.4	2.2	13.1	7.6	**3.3**	6.9	10.2
▼BANK OF WESTMINSTER	WESTMINSTER	SC	**E+**	D	D+	34	29.64	6.7	12.1	17.1	30.1	**5.4**	7.4	13.1
BANK OF WESTON	WESTON	MO	**C**	C	C	101	7.18	8.8	1.4	15.3	26.6	**6.0**	8.0	12.3
▼BANK OF WHITEWATER	WHITEWATER	KS	**C+**	B-	C+	17	10.87	7.6	14.7	23.3	22.4	**7.1**	9.1	15.8
BANK OF WHITMAN	COLFAX	WA	**E-**	D-	C+	682	-19.51	11.9	0.6	3.9	5.5	**0.0**	3.5	6.1
▼BANK OF WHITTIER NA	WHITTIER	CA	**C**	B	B+	53	-6.47	9.4	1.1	9.3	0.4	**10.0**	15.2	27.2
BANK OF WIGGINS	WIGGINS	MS	**A-**	B+	B-	188	4.17	13.7	9.8	21.0	28.0	**10.0**	13.2	21.1
BANK OF WINNFIELD & TRUST	WINNFIELD	LA	**B+**	A-	B+	126	6.24	12.9	5.4	15.9	20.3	**10.0**	11.7	20.1
▼BANK OF WINONA	WINONA	MS	**C+**	B	C+	102	5.35	3.3	3.8	18.1	34.3	**8.6**	10.0	15.4
BANK OF WISCONSIN DELLS	WISCONSIN DELLS	WI	**D**	C-	B-	384	3.72	10.6	1.4	10.3	14.8	**7.2**	9.1	13.2
▼BANK OF WOLCOTT	WOLCOTT	IN	**B-**	B	B+	105	10.54	6.1	3.3	28.6	17.8	**8.2**	9.8	14.3
BANK OF WRIGHTSVILLE	WRIGHTSVILLE	GA	**D-**	D	C-	56	-8.53	7.2	6.5	14.7	5.8	**7.8**	9.5	18.0
▼BANK OF WYANDOTTE	WYANDOTTE	OK	**D-**	C-	D	15	14.36	10.9	13.2	16.6	23.5	**3.7**	6.2	10.3
BANK OF YATES CITY	YATES CITY	IL	**B-**	C-	B-	51	2.01	6.4	9.0	12.0	44.8	**10.0**	11.1	19.3
BANK OF YAZOO CITY	YAZOO CITY	MS	**C+**	C+	C	203	-4.99	7.8	4.4	20.3	19.6	**7.1**	9.1	13.3
BANK OF YORK	YORK	AL	**B**	B+	B	83	6.52	7.0	4.8	9.3	49.0	**9.6**	10.8	23.9
BANK OF YORK	YORK	SC	**B+**	A-	A	172	-3.61	4.0	3.6	14.8	21.5	**10.0**	13.1	25.1
BANK OF ZACHARY	ZACHARY	LA	**B-**	B-	B-	170	-1.63	2.4	3.0	17.7	50.3	**6.4**	8.4	18.8
▼BANK OF ZUMBROTA	ZUMBROTA	MN	**C-**	B-	B	134	4.86	11.8	3.3	14.1	16.2	**8.8**	10.9	14.0
BANK PLUS	ESTHERVILLE	IA	**C-**	C+	B	89	11.74	5.4	2.6	10.9	11.1	**7.7**	10.2	13.1
BANK REALE	PASCO	WA	**D-**	D-	C-	42	2.78	21.9	0.6	1.6	0.0	**5.5**	8.8	11.4
BANK RHODE ISLAND	PROVIDENCE	RI	**B-**	C+	B-	1,603	0.84	12.3	0.1	18.1	22.5	**6.0**	8.0	12.4
BANK STAR	PACIFIC	MO	**C**	C-	C-	68	-7.93	5.9	2.2	29.7	10.2	**7.5**	10.1	12.9
BANK STAR OF THE	STEELE	MO	**C**	C	C-	89	-0.85	3.8	8.2	32.5	13.5	**6.5**	8.5	13.4
BANK STAR OF THE LEADBELT	PARK HILLS	MO	**C**	C-	D+	113	-7.83	3.6	3.5	40.1	10.1	**6.6**	8.6	13.6
BANK STAR ONE	FULTON	MO	**C**	D+	C-	88	-6.90	4.6	2.3	35.8	11.4	**8.9**	10.3	17.3
BANK TEXAS NA	QUITMAN	TX	**B-**	B-	B-	194	-1.94	5.0	3.1	24.0	28.4	**7.9**	9.6	17.3
▲BANK TOKYO-MITSUBISHI UFJ	NEW YORK	NY	**B-**	C-	C	3,451	-29.62	22.4	0.0	0.0	10.1	**10.0**	22.0	22.5
▼BANK VI	SALINA	KS	**E**	D-	C-	75	-28.75	12.2	0.5	29.6	0.0	**4.2**	7.0	10.6
BANK34	ALAMOGORDO	NM	**C-**	C+	B-	184	5.57	2.2	0.6	36.9	10.8	**10.0**	15.1	22.9
▲BANKANNAPOLIS	ANNAPOLIS	MD	**C-**	D+	B-	432	-2.74	11.7	2.6	12.4	22.3	**7.0**	9.0	14.0
BANKASIANA	PALISADES PARK	NJ	**C**	C	C	150	13.85	40.6	0.1	0.0	9.4	**10.0**	16.3	22.5
BANKATLANTIC	FORT LAUDERDALE	FL	**D-**	D-	D-	4,455	-6.01	5.0	0.4	29.4	9.5	**4.2**	6.2	11.9

Asset Quality Index	Non-Performing Loans as a % of Total Loans	Non-Performing Loans as a % of Capital	Net Charge-offs Avg Loans	Profitability Index	Net Income ($Mil)	Return on Assets (R.O.A.)	Return on Equity (R.O.E.)	Net Interest Spread	Overhead Efficiency Ratio	Liquidity Index	Liquidity Ratio	Hot Money Ratio	Stability Index
4.4	0.31	2.4	0.11	**7.7**	2.6	1.78	18.61	4.41	57.8	**0.7**	13.6	40.8	**8.2**
4.5	1.17	8.9	0.05	**9.5**	19.4	2.28	26.49	4.76	49.7	**1.9**	27.3	23.2	**7.5**
4.0	1.70	10.6	1.16	**4.0**	1.8	0.65	6.34	4.71	82.2	**2.7**	23.7	16.3	**5.6**
3.7	3.21	21.4	0.42	**9.1**	2.6	2.12	22.05	5.43	60.8	**4.1**	34.4	12.5	**6.2**
3.9	3.20	11.1	1.77	**5.2**	0.9	1.09	8.44	3.85	50.9	**5.5**	57.6	10.4	**7.8**
1.3	2.03	15.3	1.83	**2.3**	1.7	0.33	4.63	3.27	71.9	**1.2**	27.8	36.3	**3.9**
7.3	0.89	4.0	0.08	**2.8**	0.9	0.92	6.20	3.30	85.7	**1.7**	22.7	23.2	**4.3**
5.2	0.90	6.1	0.03	**3.6**	0.2	0.48	5.52	3.54	78.3	**3.4**	36.4	16.9	**5.1**
4.5	2.07	11.2	0.43	**2.3**	0.1	0.16	1.50	3.74	86.0	**4.9**	40.3	10.7	**5.3**
3.6	1.96	16.6	0.58	**8.8**	7.5	2.29	25.18	4.91	44.7	**1.0**	14.3	31.7	**4.7**
1.7	7.13	42.1	3.57	**0.9**	-1.1	-0.31	-3.34	3.68	59.2	**1.8**	15.6	20.8	**4.2**
6.4	1.99	6.4	0.45	**5.3**	1.5	0.95	6.45	4.17	65.8	**4.7**	38.4	10.9	**7.8**
3.3	2.41	12.6	0.83	**5.3**	8.7	1.16	10.96	4.35	66.1	**3.8**	25.9	11.4	**7.9**
10.0	0.40	0.2	0.24	**8.1**	13.8	1.63	12.64	3.17	25.2	**6.1**	88.2	13.0	**7.7**
5.1	0.94	4.5	0.61	**4.6**	0.3	1.00	7.66	5.13	73.7	**2.4**	35.6	25.1	**8.0**
0.3	8.40	43.7	1.35	**0.0**	-2.6	-1.43	-13.80	3.41	74.1	**1.0**	17.9	32.6	**5.2**
0.3	11.37	72.6	1.82	**0.5**	-5.4	-1.59	-18.77	3.02	65.8	**1.0**	13.4	31.4	**4.4**
1.0	3.48	22.6	0.58	**4.5**	0.3	0.92	9.74	4.75	76.4	**1.8**	32.8	31.1	**4.8**
0.7	5.54	32.3	3.49	**0.0**	-8.2	-3.75	-51.42	3.10	108.5	**1.3**	29.1	36.3	**3.7**
4.2	0.98	4.8	0.57	**3.1**	0.4	0.43	3.89	3.81	70.7	**1.3**	26.3	31.3	**5.1**
8.0	0.00	0.0	0.15	**4.8**	0.5	1.03	7.24	4.62	70.2	**2.8**	48.0	27.6	**8.2**
1.9	4.56	24.4	1.70	**2.7**	0.5	0.28	2.60	3.77	65.9	**1.1**	23.8	33.5	**5.2**
1.0	5.58	40.1	1.19	**2.5**	3.0	0.39	3.62	3.64	53.7	**1.5**	1.9	20.4	**7.7**
0.0	6.74	38.5	1.24	**0.1**	-0.3	-0.17	-1.99	3.39	98.8	**1.8**	16.6	20.8	**3.5**
0.2	8.58	70.5	1.95	**0.0**	-2.9	-3.63	-39.94	3.29	115.7	**1.0**	8.5	30.0	**2.7**
7.8	0.40	2.3	0.30	**7.1**	1.7	1.14	10.23	4.43	53.7	**1.5**	18.0	25.6	**7.0**
4.6	2.91	11.8	0.21	**3.8**	1.4	1.14	10.45	2.99	69.8	**3.4**	42.2	18.5	**4.8**
5.2	0.62	6.5	0.15	**4.6**	2.0	1.06	12.64	4.39	73.3	**1.2**	15.2	28.7	**4.6**
0.3	11.18	70.9	4.87	**0.0**	-0.8	-2.62	-22.25	4.21	158.3	**3.2**	50.9	21.7	**3.8**
5.6	2.16	15.1	0.04	**2.6**	0.4	0.39	4.80	4.32	87.8	**4.2**	19.5	7.8	**3.9**
3.8	1.61	10.2	0.80	**6.4**	0.2	1.26	13.04	5.16	67.0	**2.6**	26.3	16.8	**7.5**
0.0	6.86	76.9	3.36	**0.1**	-17.5	-2.30	-47.41	3.12	102.1	**0.7**	14.2	47.8	**2.8**
1.7	9.27	26.4	1.82	**3.2**	0.2	0.41	2.83	2.28	72.0	**2.5**	57.3	44.4	**7.5**
6.5	1.01	4.6	0.54	**5.4**	1.6	0.85	7.48	3.69	62.6	**1.3**	28.8	33.6	**7.3**
4.0	4.08	17.9	0.10	**5.8**	1.7	1.40	12.74	4.31	66.9	**2.4**	30.2	19.7	**7.8**
5.6	1.96	8.4	0.10	**3.0**	0.5	0.44	4.40	3.74	85.4	**4.0**	43.4	15.7	**5.3**
0.7	2.57	17.7	1.45	**4.2**	2.4	0.63	6.90	4.21	53.2	**1.1**	13.9	29.5	**4.9**
3.4	2.10	15.1	0.35	**6.9**	1.5	1.62	16.14	4.58	56.5	**2.1**	26.7	20.9	**5.3**
0.3	8.24	39.7	4.44	**0.0**	-1.9	-3.20	-29.59	3.76	133.9	**3.0**	37.6	19.2	**5.1**
4.7	0.63	5.1	0.48	**4.9**	0.2	1.14	16.32	5.81	76.0	**4.4**	31.4	7.5	**0.7**
7.1	0.70	3.1	0.36	**3.6**	0.4	0.80	6.76	3.72	74.9	**4.9**	45.7	11.3	**5.4**
5.3	0.69	4.7	0.13	**3.9**	1.5	0.73	8.49	4.46	74.1	**1.5**	17.2	25.2	**4.1**
8.0	0.83	2.7	-0.28	**4.1**	0.7	0.90	7.04	3.28	75.2	**2.8**	47.1	27.2	**5.9**
6.0	2.14	8.0	0.63	**4.8**	1.4	0.78	5.68	3.95	65.7	**2.5**	34.5	21.3	**7.3**
5.6	1.58	7.4	0.19	**4.5**	1.6	0.93	10.29	3.91	69.3	**3.0**	30.7	17.1	**5.4**
1.7	1.34	8.5	0.43	**5.6**	1.8	1.34	11.87	4.21	63.2	**1.9**	16.5	19.5	**5.9**
2.9	1.53	11.2	0.90	**5.8**	1.0	1.20	11.14	4.92	66.4	**2.7**	5.2	14.3	**5.7**
1.5	3.16	23.4	0.36	**0.0**	-0.6	-1.45	-16.58	3.48	123.4	**0.8**	23.7	51.5	**1.1**
4.9	1.40	11.2	0.42	**4.5**	11.4	0.72	8.27	3.65	62.6	**3.0**	8.9	13.7	**6.4**
3.0	2.62	17.9	2.72	**1.8**	0.0	0.03	0.27	4.54	73.7	**3.3**	7.8	11.5	**4.1**
3.1	0.08	0.6	1.22	**5.5**	0.9	0.93	10.47	4.87	58.8	**0.6**	4.6	34.6	**4.5**
6.9	0.22	1.8	0.53	**4.0**	0.9	0.78	9.23	4.37	71.0	**1.6**	5.9	20.5	**3.9**
2.8	0.11	0.7	0.94	**2.7**	0.4	0.46	4.66	4.57	82.3	**4.0**	22.9	9.5	**3.5**
5.3	1.11	6.1	0.00	**4.6**	1.7	0.89	8.87	4.41	77.5	**3.7**	26.0	12.0	**5.2**
9.0	0.00	0.0	0.15	**5.2**	53.0	1.42	7.71	1.58	85.9	**7.5**	60.5	1.8	**5.9**
1.6	3.60	31.5	2.09	**0.0**	-1.7	-1.84	-26.71	3.05	92.9	**3.3**	7.2	11.7	**2.0**
1.5	5.02	24.0	0.01	**2.3**	0.2	0.12	0.78	3.65	84.4	**1.3**	17.7	28.3	**7.2**
2.3	2.93	17.8	1.16	**3.0**	1.8	0.42	4.64	3.74	70.4	**3.4**	27.4	14.0	**4.2**
5.0	3.52	15.3	0.35	**2.8**	1.3	0.91	6.42	3.99	62.8	**0.9**	22.2	37.1	**4.4**
0.3	9.16	80.4	2.39	**0.0**	-119.1	-2.59	-34.48	3.61	89.6	**4.7**	23.6	7.6	**3.3**

Name	City	State	Rating	2008 Rating	2007 Rating	Total Assets ($Mil)	One Year Asset Growth	Asset Mix (As a % of Total Assets) Commercial Loans	Consumer Loans	Home Mortgages	Securities	Capitalization Index	Leverage Ratio	Risk-based Capital Ratio
▲ BANKCDA	COEUR D'ALENE	ID	**D**	D+	B-	85	-9.06	11.6	1.3	11.1	4.6	**8.4**	10.0	14.6
BANKCHAMPAIGN NA	CHAMPAIGN	IL	**C+**	C	C	203	4.65	15.8	0.4	19.8	22.1	**5.0**	7.0	11.9
BANKCHEROKEE	SAINT PAUL	MN	**E**	E+	D-	235	0.00	11.5	0.6	6.9	22.9	**4.3**	6.3	11.2
BANKEAST	KNOXVILLE	TN	**E-**	D-	D-	282	-12.91	16.2	1.0	7.5	5.6	**0.0**	3.5	5.5
▲ BANKERS BANK	OKLAHOMA CITY	OK	**B+**	C+	C-	193	-1.00	7.8	1.2	1.5	1.0	**10.0**	14.5	19.9
▼ BANKERS BANK	MADISON	WI	**C-**	C+	A-	495	40.00	5.2	0.4	1.6	2.4	**8.3**	9.9	23.1
▲ BANKERS BANK NORTHEAST	GLASTONBURY	CT	**B-**	C-	C	89	-20.70	0.1	0.0	1.4	35.9	**10.0**	12.8	34.5
BANKERS BANK OF KANSAS	WICHITA	KS	**C-**	C+	C+	122	-9.42	11.9	10.2	1.5	1.6	**10.0**	12.7	16.3
BANKERS BANK OF	FRANKFORT	KY	**C+**	C-	B-	60	14.83	2.5	0.0	1.6	0.0	**10.0**	16.7	27.5
BANKERS BANK OF THE WEST	DENVER	CO	**D-**	D	C+	388	-12.95	5.8	0.1	1.7	7.0	**5.4**	7.4	14.9
▼ BANKERS TRUST CO	CEDAR RAPIDS	IA	**C**	C	C-	395	6.42	16.0	1.3	15.2	9.6	**5.6**	8.3	11.5
BANKERS TRUST CO	DES MOINES	IA	**C+**	C	C	2,657	11.25	11.3	0.4	12.6	16.7	**6.2**	8.2	12.6
▼ BANKFINANCIAL FSB	OLYMPIA FIELDS	IL	**D+**	C-	C-	1,504	-2.36	13.4	0.1	12.4	6.1	**10.0**	12.5	18.4
BANKFIRST	WINTER PARK	FL	**D-**	D+	C-	600	-0.66	7.7	0.5	4.5	20.8	**8.8**	10.2	16.5
▲ BANKFIRST	NORFOLK	NE	**C+**	B-	B	266	2.29	15.4	2.4	9.9	20.4	**8.4**	10.0	14.9
▲ BANKFIRST FINANCIAL SERVI	MACON	MS	**C**	D+	C	697	-3.60	7.1	2.4	14.7	15.5	**5.6**	7.6	11.7
▲ BANKFIVE	FALL RIVER	MA	**C+**	C-	C-	709	-0.01	6.2	1.1	26.0	15.4	**6.6**	8.6	14.0
▼ BANKGLOUCESTER	GLOUCESTER	MA	**D+**	D+	C	169	1.70	2.6	0.6	39.0	11.7	**6.1**	8.1	12.6
BANKGREENVILLE	GREENVILLE	SC	**D-**	D-	C-	116	11.95	6.6	0.7	6.4	24.5	**6.8**	8.8	16.5
BANKIOWA OF CEDAR RAPIDS	CEDAR RAPIDS	IA	**B-**	C+	C+	448	6.04	14.5	2.0	13.3	17.9	**5.9**	8.9	11.7
BANKLIBERTY	LIBERTY	MO	**C-**	C+	C-	439	8.75	5.0	1.0	12.4	3.8	**8.8**	10.2	14.9
BANKMERIDIAN NA	COLUMBIA	SC	**E-**	E	D+	257	-8.23	5.3	0.2	17.6	14.7	**0.3**	3.7	6.6
BANKNEWPORT	NEWPORT	RI	**C+**	C	C-	1,081	-2.85	2.9	0.2	43.7	25.0	**7.1**	9.1	15.0
BANKORION	ORION	IL	**C**	C+	B-	318	8.10	7.3	3.1	11.1	36.9	**6.5**	8.5	14.9
BANKPACIFIC LTD	HAGATNA	GU	**B**	B	B+	103	4.76	19.0	19.1	44.8	0.4	**10.0**	12.6	19.8
▼ BANKPLUS	BELZONI	MS	**B**	B+	B+	2,229	3.91	6.6	2.3	16.5	23.5	**7.1**	9.0	13.9
BANKS OF WISCONSIN	KENOSHA	WI	**E-**	E-	C-	210	-12.61	11.7	0.8	17.4	13.8	**3.1**	5.9	10.1
▼ BANKSOUTH	DOTHAN	AL	**C+**	A-	A-	220	-5.20	5.2	1.6	34.7	5.6	**10.0**	13.7	18.9
BANKSOUTH	GREENSBORO	GA	**D+**	D	C-	250	6.58	2.4	2.8	18.4	7.4	**9.9**	10.9	16.7
BANKSTAR FINANCIAL	ELKTON	SD	**D**	D	C	58	12.27	10.4	3.5	12.1	16.9	**5.7**	8.3	11.5
BANKTENNESSEE	COLLIERVILLE	TN	**D+**	D-	D+	253	-7.70	10.4	2.8	19.7	10.7	**6.1**	9.0	11.9
BANKTRUST	MOBILE	AL	**D**	D-	D+	2,156	10.96	13.0	2.6	10.0	19.7	**8.4**	9.9	15.2
▲ BANKUNITED	MIAMI LAKES	FL	**D+**	C	NR	10,811	-2.58	3.0	0.1	25.7	26.9	**9.1**	10.4	41.6
▲ BANKVISTA	SARTELL	MN	**D+**	D	C-	112	9.24	16.1	1.0	11.5	2.0	**6.4**	8.5	12.0
▼ BANKWEST	ROCKFORD	MN	**E-**	D	D+	115	-5.98	11.1	2.3	16.7	6.3	**3.7**	7.1	10.3
BANKWEST INC	PIERRE	SD	**C+**	C-	C-	744	-0.84	10.6	9.8	5.3	11.1	**6.9**	9.0	12.4
▼ BANKWEST OF KANSAS	GOODLAND	KS	**C-**	C	B	97	6.57	4.2	2.1	2.0	28.1	**10.0**	11.3	18.2
BANNER BANK	WALLA WALLA	WA	**D-**	D-	D	4,189	-7.45	12.5	1.8	16.6	6.5	**9.8**	10.8	15.1
▲ BANNER BANKS	BIRNAMWOOD	WI	**C+**	C	C	92	-0.41	3.8	0.9	8.4	28.6	**10.0**	11.3	18.9
▲ BANNER COUNTY BANK INC	HARRISBURG	NE	**B**	B-	C+	58	18.92	9.0	2.0	1.3	8.9	**10.0**	12.9	16.4
BANTERRA BANK	ELDORADO	IL	**C-**	C	B	1,088	1.47	9.8	9.8	11.8	21.3	**6.0**	8.4	11.8
BAR HARBOR BANK & TRUST	BAR HARBOR	ME	**B+**	B	B-	1,117	4.25	3.4	0.4	23.7	32.0	**7.2**	9.1	15.6
BAR HARBOR SAVINGS &	BAR HARBOR	ME	**C+**	C	C+	63	27.43	0.0	0.3	59.6	15.2	**5.7**	7.7	19.7
▲ BARABOO NATIONAL BK	BARABOO	WI	**D**	D-	D-	789	1.93	10.6	3.1	12.6	4.7	**6.7**	8.7	12.6
▲ BARCLAYS BANK DELAWARE	WILMINGTON	DE	**C-**	D	D+	14,345	13.73	1.0	71.4	0.0	1.0	**10.0**	11.0	16.4
▼ BARCLAYS WEALTH	WILMINGTON	DE	**U**	NR	NR	9	N/A	0.0	0.0	0.0	0.0	**10.0**	89.9	341.7
▼ BARRE SB	BARRE	MA	**D-**	C-	C-	143	-4.53	9.0	3.2	45.6	13.6	**6.4**	8.4	14.0
▲ BARRINGTON BANK & TRUST	BARRINGTON	IL	**C-**	D	C-	1,182	14.09	20.3	7.8	33.6	4.9	**7.0**	9.1	12.5
BARTLETT FARMERS BANK	CUTLER	OH	**B+**	B+	B	61	10.98	2.7	3.8	22.0	54.3	**8.1**	9.8	21.2
BARTOW COUNTY BANK	CARTERSVILLE	GA	**E-**	E-	E+	330	-22.71	5.1	1.3	16.7	7.4	**0.0**	0.7	2.2
▼ BARWICK BANKING CO	BARWICK	GA	**E-**	E	D+	13	-6.24	5.9	2.2	8.1	12.8	**4.2**	6.2	19.5
BASILE STATE BK	BASILE	LA	**B-**	B-	C+	50	-0.48	24.6	13.3	33.4	6.2	**7.1**	9.1	14.4
BASIN STATE BK	STANFORD	MT	**A-**	A-	A-	139	7.57	12.4	1.7	5.0	14.0	**7.3**	10.8	12.7
BATH SAVINGS INSTITUTION	BATH	ME	**B**	B	B-	588	10.44	6.3	1.9	32.0	24.1	**8.2**	9.8	17.3
▲ BATH STATE BK	BATH	IN	**C-**	D+	D+	148	-3.67	5.0	2.1	19.3	12.1	**6.7**	8.7	12.5
BATTLE CREEK STATE BK	BATTLE CREEK	NE	**D**	E-	C	25	-5.96	33.7	1.6	3.9	9.7	**6.6**	8.6	14.1
▼ BAXTER STATE BK	BAXTER SPRINGS	KS	**C**	C+	C	27	0.83	3.2	9.7	13.4	22.0	**10.0**	17.4	30.0
BAY BANK	MOBILE	AL	**E-**	D-	C+	89	-0.46	2.8	1.6	13.1	29.5	**1.1**	4.3	8.1
BAY BANK	GREEN BAY	WI	**D**	D-	C	113	-0.40	14.6	2.6	13.9	22.4	**4.9**	6.9	11.3
BAY BANK & TRUST CO	PANAMA CITY	FL	**C-**	C-	B+	236	-0.01	2.6	0.5	11.6	19.0	**10.0**	12.4	23.8

Asset Quality Index	Non-Performing Loans as a % of Total Loans	Non-Performing Loans as a % of Capital	Net Charge-offs / Avg Loans	Profitability Index	Net Income ($Mil)	Return on Assets (R.O.A.)	Return on Equity (R.O.E.)	Net Interest Spread	Overhead Efficiency Ratio	Liquidity Index	Liquidity Ratio	Hot Money Ratio	Stability Index
0.8	0.57	3.7	1.07	**1.7**	0.3	0.34	3.36	4.38	86.9	**1.7**	19.7	22.8	**4.4**
5.4	0.95	8.2	0.04	**4.1**	1.9	0.97	13.18	3.70	77.4	**1.3**	21.1	28.9	**4.3**
0.3	7.59	54.1	1.60	**0.0**	-2.2	-0.93	-13.22	3.32	113.7	**3.7**	30.0	13.1	**1.7**
0.3	9.75	111.6	4.29	**0.0**	-10.9	-3.73	-58.98	3.30	122.5	**1.5**	11.4	23.5	**1.6**
7.3	0.00	0.0	0.13	**7.0**	2.2	1.18	9.15	3.95	73.1	**4.0**	40.1	15.0	**5.3**
1.7	7.65	21.2	1.07	**3.7**	1.8	0.41	3.70	2.25	67.5	**6.7**	69.0	6.9	**5.1**
7.9	0.00	0.0	1.75	**3.9**	0.7	0.73	5.89	3.86	86.4	**6.5**	39.6	0.0	**4.3**
1.1	5.08	25.7	0.78	**5.4**	0.9	0.69	5.65	4.23	74.4	**4.0**	16.8	9.1	**7.4**
2.4	2.76	8.5	0.39	**7.2**	0.7	1.06	6.51	5.02	71.7	**6.6**	43.1	0.0	**7.7**
0.3	12.77	60.0	6.79	**1.0**	-0.1	-0.02	-0.24	2.68	73.9	**2.5**	41.6	28.1	**3.1**
5.6	0.12	1.0	0.58	**3.7**	2.4	0.64	7.46	3.41	56.3	**1.4**	6.3	24.1	**5.1**
4.9	1.31	9.5	0.48	**3.6**	15.4	0.62	7.13	3.24	65.2	**3.6**	17.2	11.8	**5.2**
2.3	3.50	18.6	0.75	**0.9**	-3.9	-0.25	-1.77	3.61	86.1	**4.5**	26.1	10.7	**8.0**
1.2	1.23	6.0	1.51	**0.3**	-1.0	-0.17	-0.79	4.37	90.2	**2.5**	33.1	20.5	**6.7**
3.6	0.99	6.3	0.33	**5.6**	2.6	0.98	8.56	3.92	54.1	**3.6**	15.4	11.2	**5.9**
5.3	0.47	3.9	0.72	**3.0**	4.1	0.55	7.66	3.41	63.0	**1.4**	8.8	23.4	**3.4**
3.9	1.20	8.5	0.15	**3.5**	3.9	0.55	6.10	3.77	80.4	**1.8**	20.6	22.1	**5.5**
1.7	2.68	24.1	0.12	**3.2**	0.7	0.43	5.31	3.44	78.5	**2.4**	15.9	17.0	**4.7**
3.6	2.12	11.2	1.21	**0.3**	0.0	0.01	0.11	2.31	92.5	**2.0**	40.2	37.7	**1.3**
5.2	0.47	3.6	0.44	**4.4**	4.3	0.98	10.06	3.80	69.3	**3.3**	12.8	12.4	**6.2**
1.5	3.80	25.5	0.63	**5.1**	5.1	1.16	11.49	4.47	58.4	**3.3**	11.2	12.2	**6.1**
0.0	18.76	201.9	3.20	**0.0**	-10.7	-3.80	-64.03	2.61	141.9	**1.6**	18.3	24.0	**0.0**
6.7	0.97	6.8	0.14	**3.6**	6.6	0.60	6.46	3.25	77.0	**4.7**	29.0	11.0	**7.2**
3.2	1.42	8.5	0.14	**5.3**	3.2	1.04	10.49	3.88	56.6	**2.6**	28.6	18.4	**5.5**
5.5	1.02	6.9	0.02	**4.6**	1.1	1.05	8.40	6.24	77.8	**2.9**	7.8	13.6	**7.1**
4.8	1.70	11.1	1.02	**4.2**	12.0	0.55	5.93	4.80	69.7	**2.0**	2.9	18.0	**7.3**
0.0	14.67	131.0	2.86	**0.0**	-3.7	-1.61	-23.75	2.90	83.4	**1.4**	21.3	27.5	**1.8**
6.1	0.57	3.2	2.32	**2.0**	-2.9	-1.30	-9.18	3.84	49.1	**0.7**	6.7	34.2	**7.8**
1.7	3.63	20.6	0.39	**5.3**	3.1	1.23	11.46	4.55	57.9	**2.9**	26.0	16.1	**6.1**
1.6	2.72	22.0	1.09	**3.3**	0.3	0.60	6.82	4.01	78.7	**2.1**	17.1	18.8	**3.5**
1.6	2.65	18.6	0.78	**1.6**	1.3	0.48	5.00	3.66	84.5	**2.0**	10.7	18.3	**3.8**
0.9	7.45	39.2	0.72	**1.4**	5.6	0.27	2.54	3.41	77.6	**1.6**	21.7	28.4	**5.8**
1.7	4.24	14.6	0.38	**10.0**	215.4	1.92	18.19	5.23	42.3	**3.5**	36.1	18.9	**2.4**
1.6	1.96	16.4	0.46	**3.5**	0.6	0.59	7.01	3.55	60.0	**1.6**	13.8	22.6	**3.5**
0.9	5.02	42.1	0.91	**0.0**	-1.3	-1.08	-13.96	4.41	97.2	**2.6**	15.9	15.9	**2.7**
4.1	0.91	6.8	0.58	**4.7**	5.6	0.75	9.40	4.51	68.7	**1.3**	14.7	26.7	**4.4**
8.6	0.01	0.0	-0.28	**1.4**	-0.3	-0.28	-2.21	4.69	126.5	**1.7**	35.0	35.8	**6.1**
1.2	4.49	26.0	1.98	**0.0**	-60.4	-1.39	-12.68	3.81	81.7	**1.4**	13.2	25.7	**5.0**
4.3	1.06	4.6	0.60	**4.0**	0.8	0.87	7.47	4.40	62.6	**4.8**	42.4	11.6	**5.9**
6.9	0.22	1.3	0.17	**5.5**	0.5	0.88	6.43	4.55	65.8	**1.2**	16.0	29.5	**6.9**
2.5	2.81	21.3	0.58	**7.1**	18.1	1.68	18.32	4.21	55.5	**2.8**	14.1	15.4	**8.5**
5.7	1.94	12.4	0.24	**5.3**	11.5	1.06	10.95	3.24	54.9	**0.9**	8.8	31.9	**8.0**
9.5	0.00	0.0	0.59	**3.1**	0.3	0.45	5.41	2.37	63.0	**5.2**	32.6	5.6	**4.3**
0.9	4.22	29.9	3.03	**0.8**	-2.5	-0.32	-3.34	3.61	71.1	**1.5**	19.3	25.7	**4.8**
1.7	2.47	11.8	8.96	**2.8**	96.1	0.73	5.53	9.35	45.2	**1.5**	28.1	74.7	**5.8**
10.0	0.00	0.0	0.00	**0.0**	-1.9	-20.34	-22.52	N/,	10,577.4	**5.0**	1,198.6	101.0	**4.4**
1.7	5.39	39.0	1.03	**0.3**	-1.4	-0.92	-9.55	3.51	92.1	**3.7**	16.8	10.5	**5.3**
3.3	1.87	16.8	0.70	**2.9**	3.9	0.37	3.74	3.75	85.6	**1.5**	7.1	22.1	**4.5**
8.5	0.64	2.5	0.00	**5.1**	0.7	1.21	12.58	5.30	75.7	**5.6**	58.5	10.3	**6.0**
0.1	16.21	398.5	4.63	**0.0**	-18.8	-4.84	-116.76	1.89	175.1	**1.2**	15.8	29.9	**0.0**
9.0	0.23	1.3	0.00	**0.0**	-0.1	-1.02	-14.78	1.64	159.5	**3.3**	65.0	22.6	**1.5**
3.6	1.36	10.6	0.41	**8.3**	0.9	1.79	19.65	5.61	64.6	**1.3**	18.7	29.3	**7.3**
7.2	0.03	0.2	0.51	**8.9**	2.5	1.94	17.71	4.62	53.5	**1.8**	22.0	21.5	**8.2**
4.8	1.68	10.3	0.22	**4.9**	5.6	0.99	9.63	3.80	64.3	**1.6**	19.2	24.7	**6.8**
2.4	2.65	19.3	1.24	**2.9**	1.0	0.67	8.17	3.77	62.6	**0.9**	19.2	34.8	**3.3**
2.7	1.89	9.8	0.04	**2.7**	0.1	0.43	5.50	3.73	88.4	**4.4**	34.1	10.9	**2.3**
8.4	0.42	1.1	0.36	**2.4**	0.1	0.41	2.25	4.20	91.9	**4.5**	49.8	14.3	**6.4**
2.1	1.70	15.7	1.66	**0.1**	-1.5	-1.66	-21.46	4.02	146.9	**1.4**	18.2	27.7	**0.0**
1.4	0.86	6.0	3.47	**2.6**	0.4	0.36	4.58	4.03	56.8	**0.6**	7.2	42.0	**3.4**
2.7	5.73	22.9	1.26	**0.8**	0.1	0.03	0.20	3.36	92.1	**3.6**	45.7	18.3	**6.3**

Name	City	State	Rating	2008 Rating	2007 Rating	Total Assets ($Mil)	One Year Asset Growth	Asset Mix (As a % of Total Assets)				Capital-ization Index	Leverage Ratio	Risk-based Capital Ratio
								Comm-ercial Loans	Cons-umer Loans	Home Mort-gages	Secur-ities			
BAY BANK FSB	LUTHERVILLE	MD	**D-**	NR	NR	135	N/A	15.2	1.0	13.8	12.1	**10.0**	20.3	26.4
▼ BAY CITIES BANK	TAMPA	FL	**D-**	D-	D+	622	28.76	6.7	1.0	7.5	25.0	**7.1**	9.1	15.5
BAY COMMERCIAL BANK	WALNUT CREEK	CA	**B-**	C	B-	174	21.31	21.3	0.1	4.8	0.1	**10.0**	20.2	25.0
BAY PORT STATE BK	BAY PORT	MI	**D+**	D+	D+	84	7.40	4.4	3.1	21.8	0.4	**5.4**	7.4	12.7
BAY STATE SB	WORCESTER	MA	**D+**	C	C-	274	-5.18	2.6	3.9	36.1	12.2	**7.5**	9.4	16.1
BAY VIEW FS&LA	MILWAUKEE	WI	**B-**	B-	B+	124	5.54	0.0	0.1	29.7	36.7	**10.0**	13.1	32.5
BAY-VANGUARD FSB	BALTIMORE	MD	**D-**	C-	C-	149	-5.06	0.2	7.4	49.3	14.5	**4.9**	6.9	13.5
BAYBANK	GLADSTONE	MI	**B**	B	B-	81	8.78	9.8	6.3	22.0	27.3	**9.2**	10.5	17.1
BAYLAKE BANK	STURGEON BAY	WI	**D+**	D	D-	1,054	0.82	6.2	1.0	9.0	25.2	**6.1**	8.1	12.5
▼ BAYTREE NATIONAL BK & TRU	LAKE FOREST	IL	**E-**	E-	E-	216	7.34	8.4	0.6	13.1	0.4	**4.9**	8.1	11.0
BB&T FINANCIAL FSB	COLUMBUS	GA	**C-**	C	C+	2,552	8.00	17.0	70.7	0.0	6.8	**10.0**	14.3	16.3
BBU BANK	CORAL GABLES	FL	**D+**	D	D+	402	53.48	4.4	0.1	7.9	40.1	**9.4**	10.6	18.4
▼ BCB COMMUNITY BANK	BAYONNE	NJ	**D-**	B-	B	1,105	75.29	1.6	0.2	32.9	15.2	**7.1**	9.1	15.7
▲ BCBANK INC	PHILIPPI	WV	**D+**	D	C+	112	-11.95	3.8	2.9	9.2	25.8	**7.7**	9.5	14.1
BEACH BUSINESS BANK	MANHATTAN BEACH	CA	**D+**	D	C-	308	20.55	32.6	0.1	6.8	1.6	**10.0**	11.8	15.0
BEACH COMMUNITY BANK	FORT WALTON BEACH	FL	**E-**	D-	D	633	-10.17	5.8	0.2	14.2	9.1	**2.1**	6.0	9.1
BEACON BANK	SHOREWOOD	MN	**C-**	C	B-	306	6.11	20.5	2.1	5.7	28.1	**8.1**	9.8	14.6
BEACON FEDERAL	EAST SYRACUSE	NY	**C**	C-	C-	1,033	-3.22	8.3	16.9	26.5	16.8	**7.8**	9.6	13.4
▲ BEAL BANK NEVADA	LAS VEGAS	NV	**B**	B	B	6,204	17.32	6.5	0.1	13.1	47.8	**10.0**	36.1	42.3
BEAL BANK SSB	PLANO	TX	**C-**	NR	NR	3,779	N/A	0.4	1.1	49.7	2.4	**10.0**	21.2	44.7
BEARDSTOWN SAVINGS SB	BEARDSTOWN	IL	**D-**	D-	D-	45	0.55	1.1	2.9	49.1	28.4	**7.8**	9.5	20.7
BEARTOOTH BANK	BILLINGS	MT	**D-**	D	C-	42	-20.40	14.9	0.8	6.2	0.5	**8.2**	10.8	13.5
BEAUREGARD FSB	DERIDDER	LA	**B+**	B+	B+	52	4.60	2.3	10.5	40.7	23.7	**10.0**	17.2	33.4
▲ BEDFORD FSB	BEDFORD	IN	**D+**	C-	C	127	-3.68	4.2	7.0	54.4	4.0	**5.4**	7.4	11.6
BEDFORD LOAN & DEPOSIT	BEDFORD	KY	**B**	B	B	84	3.27	2.1	6.3	41.5	25.5	**10.0**	12.2	21.8
BELGRADE STATE BK	BELGRADE	MO	**B-**	B	B+	190	4.24	9.7	4.9	30.9	13.4	**9.6**	10.7	16.7
BELLERIVE BANK	PLYMOUTH	IL	**C-**	C-	C	10	-3.59	1.6	1.0	16.3	19.1	**10.0**	13.1	16.3
BELLEVUE STATE BK	BELLEVUE	IA	**B-**	B	B	76	10.87	8.3	7.4	14.4	25.0	**8.4**	10.0	13.7
▲ BELMONT BANK & TRUST CO	CHICAGO	IL	**C-**	D+	D+	157	11.59	8.2	0.3	18.2	21.8	**9.1**	10.4	17.7
BELMONT FS&LA	BELMONT	NC	**C+**	C+	C+	93	1.94	0.0	0.0	55.9	24.2	**10.0**	15.9	37.5
BELMONT SB	BELMONT	MA	**C-**	C	D+	501	-0.79	2.7	1.1	37.7	23.5	**7.3**	9.2	14.7
BELMONT SB	BELLAIRE	OH	**C+**	C+	C+	411	7.98	0.0	3.8	12.4	81.8	**8.1**	9.8	39.2
BELPRE SB	BELPRE	OH	**C+**	C+	C	49	-1.29	0.0	14.5	56.0	0.0	**10.0**	15.6	27.6
BELT VALLEY BANK	BELT	MT	**D-**	C-	B-	66	5.94	8.0	3.8	16.0	22.6	**7.2**	9.1	14.5
▼ BEN FRANKLIN BANK OF ILLI	ARLINGTON HEIGHTS	IL	**D-**	D-	D	116	-2.91	4.5	3.8	32.3	3.4	**5.9**	8.2	11.7
▼ BENCHMARK BANK	GAHANNA	OH	**E+**	D-	C-	126	-15.73	0.5	0.0	41.8	5.7	**5.2**	7.2	12.8
BENCHMARK BANK	PLANO	TX	**B**	C	D	368	3.13	10.4	2.0	51.8	0.6	**7.2**	9.1	15.5
▲ BENCHMARK COMMUNITY	KENBRIDGE	VA	**C**	B	B+	418	8.89	6.5	3.7	36.0	7.4	**6.9**	9.0	14.2
BENDENA STATE BK	BENDENA	KS	**C**	C	C	24	13.23	2.3	4.0	11.2	16.3	**7.0**	9.0	14.0
▼ BENEFICIAL MUTUAL SB	PHILADELPHIA	PA	**D+**	C-	B-	4,922	5.52	2.0	10.1	20.0	33.1	**6.9**	8.9	17.0
▼ BENEFIT BANK	FORT SMITH	AR	**D+**	C	C	227	-1.73	13.4	2.4	32.9	0.0	**6.6**	8.6	12.3
BENNINGTON STATE BK	SALINA	KS	**B+**	A-	B+	403	19.65	12.5	2.8	14.5	24.4	**8.7**	10.1	15.7
BENTON COUNTY STATE BK	BLAIRSTOWN	IA	**A-**	B+	B+	38	4.51	10.9	1.1	13.9	13.1	**10.0**	13.8	17.5
BENTON STATE BK	BENTON	WI	**C-**	C-	C-	50	8.39	5.4	7.1	21.5	5.8	**6.1**	8.4	11.8
▲ BERKSHIRE BANK	PITTSFIELD	MA	**C**	D+	B-	2,845	6.69	9.9	1.5	23.4	12.9	**4.2**	8.0	10.6
BERKSHIRE BANK	NEW YORK	NY	**B-**	C+	C+	836	-6.27	1.3	0.1	12.9	41.6	**10.0**	11.0	21.0
▼ BERKSHIRE BANK	WYOMISSING	PA	**D-**	D-	D-	135	-6.54	4.6	0.4	22.2	1.2	**4.8**	7.6	10.9
BERKSHIRE BANK MUNICIPAL	ALBANY	NY	**B**	B	C+	28	29.03	0.0	0.0	0.0	54.5	**10.0**	48.0	234.6
BESSEMER TRUST CO	WOODBRIDGE	NJ	**B**	B	B+	635	7.93	11.3	34.3	0.0	49.6	**5.2**	7.2	12.9
BESSEMER TRUST CO NA	NEW YORK	NY	**B**	B+	A-	1,393	45.11	2.9	11.1	0.0	32.5	**5.5**	7.5	25.1
BESSEMER TRUST CO OF CA	SAN FRANCISCO	CA	**U**	U	U	6	17.82	0.0	0.0	0.0	81.5	**10.0**	92.9	443.3
BESSEMER TRUST CO OF DE	WILMINGTON	DE	**U**	U	U	11	22.21	0.0	0.0	0.0	77.0	**10.0**	82.0	253.8
BETTER BANKS	PEORIA	IL	**B**	B	B+	195	2.93	3.3	2.3	19.9	42.6	**6.0**	8.0	23.6
BEVERLY BANK & TRUST CO N	CHICAGO	IL	**D+**	D+	C-	356	17.94	25.5	16.0	3.5	10.5	**7.5**	9.6	12.9
BEVERLY CO-OP BANK	BEVERLY	MA	**C**	C-	C-	300	-1.26	5.0	0.2	38.5	6.7	**5.2**	7.2	14.3
BIDDEFORD SB	BIDDEFORD	ME	**C**	C	C-	314	2.01	6.1	1.4	43.3	19.9	**9.0**	10.3	16.6
BIG BEND BANKS NA	MARFA	TX	**A**	A	A	83	10.15	1.9	7.5	7.0	62.7	**10.0**	14.0	35.2
BIG HORN FSB	GREYBULL	WY	**C**	C	C+	197	8.54	5.3	5.0	19.0	11.4	**6.6**	8.6	19.2
▲ BIG SKY WESTERN BANK	BOZEMAN	MT	**C**	C-	B	362	-2.01	4.7	0.9	9.0	23.4	**10.0**	17.4	23.2
▲ BILTMORE BANK OF ARIZONA	PHOENIX	AZ	**D**	D-	D-	258	-2.69	17.2	0.3	4.1	17.7	**7.1**	9.5	12.6

Asset Quality Index	Non-Performing Loans as a % of Total Loans	Non-Performing Loans as a % of Capital	Net Charge-offs / Avg Loans	Profitability Index	Net Income ($Mil)	Return on Assets (R.O.A.)	Return on Equity (R.O.E.)	Net Interest Spread	Overhead Efficiency Ratio	Liquidity Index	Liquidity Ratio	Hot Money Ratio	Stability Index
3.4	5.65	18.1	0.00	**0.0**	**,***.*	**,***.**	**,***.**	N/,	50.0	**1.9**	40.8	57.0	**0.0**
1.7	4.18	22.9	5.21	**0.5**	1.2	0.23	2.20	3.26	61.0	**2.7**	41.9	26.3	**2.9**
4.2	1.42	5.4	0.56	**3.2**	0.6	0.41	2.73	4.41	64.4	**1.0**	25.1	36.1	**7.0**
5.4	0.11	1.1	0.04	**1.4**	0.1	0.06	0.84	3.46	90.6	**1.6**	22.1	25.2	**3.5**
1.6	3.19	22.2	0.42	**2.9**	0.8	0.29	3.03	3.84	82.3	**3.3**	23.8	13.4	**4.8**
4.7	4.40	16.6	1.46	**3.2**	0.5	0.39	2.98	2.45	41.6	**4.3**	53.2	16.6	**7.3**
1.6	3.50	33.3	0.03	**1.6**	0.4	0.22	2.77	3.50	72.1	**2.8**	23.9	15.8	**2.9**
6.5	0.60	3.0	0.24	**4.3**	0.6	0.77	6.88	4.49	75.3	**3.6**	41.6	17.1	**6.2**
2.0	2.59	17.2	0.85	**1.5**	1.9	0.18	1.90	3.71	82.0	**2.9**	22.1	16.5	**5.6**
0.3	11.46	100.7	0.41	**0.0**	-3.7	-0.72	-12.30	3.45	92.0	**0.8**	22.5	53.6	**0.0**
4.0	0.75	3.6	4.39	**10.0**	103.8	4.28	28.22	6.29	32.1	**1.2**	8.6	28.5	**3.0**
3.2	1.20	5.7	0.39	**1.5**	2.0	0.67	6.42	3.57	87.2	**2.8**	51.6	31.3	**2.3**
0.3	5.00	36.4	0.20	**6.7**	13.6	1.53	18.83	3.10	54.0	**1.5**	16.4	26.6	**6.7**
1.9	3.82	21.1	1.45	**2.8**	0.7	0.56	6.45	3.85	78.0	**3.3**	25.3	13.7	**3.1**
1.7	2.63	16.0	1.42	**2.2**	1.6	0.57	4.57	3.90	69.2	**4.0**	18.5	9.0	**4.9**
0.0	19.08	193.9	1.32	**0.0**	-7.6	-1.13	-15.43	2.30	119.8	**0.9**	13.3	32.9	**2.6**
1.3	2.97	17.5	0.57	**2.6**	1.0	0.35	3.45	3.85	72.3	**4.1**	24.4	9.2	**4.8**
3.6	1.31	9.4	0.92	**2.8**	5.4	0.50	5.80	3.13	56.0	**1.6**	19.9	25.6	**5.9**
3.2	21.18	28.1	1.46	**10.0**	520.2	9.53	26.41	12.13	13.0	**1.2**	26.4	92.1	**10.0**
0.3	22.30	63.0	2.15	**7.9**	60.7	1.70	7.89	6.97	53.8	**2.0**	37.7	82.9	**3.7**
4.8	2.24	13.0	0.62	**0.0**	-0.6	-1.29	-12.31	3.05	138.5	**3.7**	34.8	14.9	**3.6**
1.4	2.08	11.3	7.02	**0.0**	-3.3	-6.72	-45.82	3.74	156.4	**1.0**	10.1	29.9	**1.0**
4.6	3.63	13.1	-0.01	**10.0**	1.3	2.62	14.60	5.38	49.6	**2.9**	39.5	20.3	**9.5**
2.7	1.39	14.9	0.06	**2.2**	0.2	0.18	2.42	3.09	89.5	**1.2**	9.4	27.7	**3.8**
3.8	3.02	14.9	0.06	**5.0**	0.7	0.90	7.02	4.83	73.2	**1.5**	20.0	25.7	**7.1**
3.7	1.16	7.4	0.24	**4.7**	1.3	0.65	6.23	4.64	75.1	**1.7**	17.4	22.4	**5.9**
5.4	1.04	3.8	3.29	**0.0**	-0.1	-1.11	-7.02	4.42	91.3	**5.8**	51.8	5.2	**7.0**
5.0	0.68	4.1	0.42	**5.9**	1.1	1.46	13.93	3.76	54.3	**4.8**	36.3	10.0	**6.2**
2.7	1.63	9.6	0.65	**2.8**	0.8	0.52	4.75	3.90	69.9	**1.0**	25.0	41.6	**3.7**
9.1	0.84	3.3	0.00	**3.2**	0.5	0.53	3.36	3.21	71.2	**2.0**	41.4	42.3	**7.5**
7.2	0.50	3.5	0.01	**2.4**	1.7	0.33	3.68	2.96	83.5	**2.3**	19.6	17.8	**5.3**
7.0	3.79	6.4	0.84	**3.5**	2.3	0.58	5.97	2.50	52.7	**2.9**	58.6	34.8	**4.0**
8.0	0.30	1.4	0.30	**3.1**	0.2	0.38	2.50	4.40	76.4	**1.8**	19.3	21.1	**7.4**
0.3	7.63	47.8	1.52	**0.3**	-0.8	-1.22	-12.03	3.66	69.2	**2.4**	33.1	21.5	**4.2**
0.3	6.29	54.5	0.95	**0.4**	-0.8	-0.69	-7.80	3.43	85.2	**2.5**	16.8	16.7	**3.0**
0.3	15.00	107.9	2.61	**0.0**	-4.9	-3.36	-38.45	3.07	113.0	**0.8**	17.7	36.2	**0.5**
4.4	1.25	10.2	0.51	**8.9**	17.4	4.71	50.46	4.34	61.2	**0.5**	5.5	52.7	**5.4**
2.8	2.25	17.2	0.35	**6.2**	4.6	1.12	12.37	4.64	56.6	**2.0**	15.5	18.9	**6.4**
7.3	0.00	0.0	0.00	**4.8**	0.2	1.04	10.87	3.94	70.3	**3.3**	23.4	13.1	**4.3**
2.8	3.45	20.2	2.53	**0.8**	-9.2	-0.19	-1.54	3.40	73.6	**4.5**	16.2	6.1	**8.6**
2.0	2.65	22.7	0.66	**1.0**	-2.9	-1.28	-15.43	4.31	71.6	**0.7**	9.3	37.8	**4.0**
4.8	1.15	6.9	0.62	**6.4**	5.4	1.45	13.44	3.44	53.5	**2.5**	19.9	17.0	**7.6**
8.4	0.08	0.5	0.01	**7.3**	0.5	1.38	9.81	4.62	60.6	**2.6**	17.6	16.3	**8.9**
3.4	1.05	9.2	0.65	**3.4**	0.2	0.44	5.09	4.95	85.3	**1.4**	13.8	25.5	**4.5**
3.6	0.67	5.9	0.42	**2.8**	14.0	0.52	4.05	3.35	72.5	**2.4**	10.6	16.8	**7.1**
5.8	0.55	1.9	0.26	**4.0**	6.3	0.73	6.67	3.53	57.5	**3.0**	49.7	26.7	**5.5**
1.8	2.05	18.5	0.67	**0.0**	-1.2	-0.86	-10.67	3.70	111.2	**3.6**	11.7	10.8	**2.7**
10.0	0.00	0.0	0.00	**4.4**	0.3	0.99	1.92	1.67	32.1	**6.7**	86.4	8.1	**5.6**
6.8	0.00	0.0	0.00	**4.3**	5.7	0.86	11.35	1.73	90.7	**5.1**	3.0	0.0	**6.9**
7.0	0.00	0.0	0.00	**8.9**	32.1	2.88	21.27	0.70	87.2	**7.5**	50.6	0.0	**9.0**
10.0	0.00	0.0	0.00	**10.0**	0.6	10.68	11.62	1.46	51.9	**5.0**	938.3	101.0	**7.0**
10.0	0.00	0.0	0.00	**10.0**	1.8	16.67	20.75	1.78	77.8	**5.0**	535.3	101.0	**7.0**
7.3	0.08	0.4	0.05	**4.0**	1.7	0.90	9.98	2.88	73.8	**5.0**	36.8	8.9	**5.6**
3.2	0.67	4.7	0.90	**0.8**	0.0	0.00	0.01	3.27	75.5	**1.8**	21.7	21.4	**3.8**
3.7	1.56	14.7	0.18	**3.9**	1.6	0.54	7.60	3.62	71.4	**1.8**	16.5	20.6	**3.9**
4.9	1.79	11.9	0.14	**2.8**	1.5	0.47	4.68	3.20	79.2	**3.3**	20.0	13.0	**5.5**
8.8	1.00	1.7	0.13	**7.1**	1.2	1.45	9.01	4.73	69.3	**4.7**	72.1	17.0	**9.7**
4.9	0.66	3.3	-0.01	**3.0**	0.7	0.39	4.27	2.92	83.7	**4.3**	53.7	16.7	**5.1**
2.0	4.03	13.9	1.59	**5.2**	2.7	0.75	4.44	4.49	53.8	**1.5**	13.5	24.4	**7.1**
3.4	0.85	5.3	0.69	**0.7**	0.5	0.17	1.93	3.15	93.0	**0.9**	19.8	35.6	**3.3**

	Name	City	State	Rating	2008 Rating	2007 Rating	Total Assets ($Mil)	One Year Asset Growth	Asset Mix (As a % of Total Assets) Comm-ercial Loans	Cons-umer Loans	Home Mort-gages	Secur-ities	Capital-ization Index	Leverage Ratio	Risk-based Capital Ratio
	BIPPUS STATE BK	HUNTINGTON	IN	**B-**	B-	C+	117	2.21	16.2	2.9	14.0	20.0	**6.7**	8.8	12.9
▼	BISCAYNE BANK	COCONUT GROVE	FL	**E+**	D-	C-	220	-17.48	3.6	0.5	36.5	7.9	**5.1**	7.1	12.1
	BISON STATE BK	BISON	KS	**D+**	C-	D+	10	15.78	4.7	8.7	12.2	47.6	**7.3**	9.2	19.6
▼	BITTERROOT VALLEY BANK	LOLO	MT	**C-**	C	B-	199	-4.45	15.0	4.3	19.0	5.4	**8.4**	9.9	14.2
▲	BK & TRUST BRYAN/COLLEGE	BRYAN	TX	**C**	C-	D+	249	33.15	5.6	2.1	18.7	3.9	**10.0**	11.1	17.6
	BLACK HILLS COMMUNITY BAN	RAPID CITY	SD	**C**	C	C	95	27.57	14.9	1.6	8.8	5.9	**10.0**	13.4	18.4
	BLACK MOUNTAIN SB SSB	BLACK MOUNTAIN	NC	**C+**	C	C	36	-1.72	0.0	0.3	67.7	0.0	**9.9**	11.0	23.3
▲	BLACK RIVER COUNTRY BANK	BLACK RIVER FALLS	WI	**B+**	B+	B+	70	-3.07	5.6	4.2	38.9	10.2	**10.0**	12.5	19.5
	BLACKHAWK BANK & TRUST	MILAN	IL	**C-**	C+	B-	864	1.73	8.0	1.5	11.9	46.4	**6.4**	8.4	14.3
	BLACKHAWK STATE BK	BELOIT	WI	**C-**	C-	C	539	3.05	22.8	1.7	15.7	24.4	**6.4**	8.4	13.6
	BLACKRIDGEBANK	FARGO	ND	**D**	C-	C-	98	15.87	21.6	2.0	10.3	11.2	**5.9**	8.4	11.7
	BLACKROCK INSTITUTIONAL T	SAN FRANCISCO	CA	**U**	U	U	15,786	1.40	0.0	0.0	0.0	3.7	**10.0**	55.1	103.3
	BLAINE STATE BK	BLAINE	MN	**D**	D-	D+	40	9.80	2.6	5.8	42.7	3.2	**5.9**	7.9	12.1
▼	BLANCO NATIONAL BK	BLANCO	TX	**C**	B-	C+	156	1.68	4.5	5.4	18.5	20.7	**7.0**	9.0	14.2
	BLC COMMUNITY BANK	LITTLE CHUTE	WI	**C-**	C+	B+	211	-6.80	10.3	0.7	14.3	8.5	**9.2**	11.0	14.3
▼	BLENCOE STATE BK	BLENCOE	IA	**B-**	B	B-	33	9.26	2.9	5.2	14.5	33.9	**8.9**	10.3	17.4
▼	BLISSFIELD STATE BK	BLISSFIELD	MI	**B-**	B	B+	87	8.08	3.1	2.0	26.8	30.7	**8.6**	10.1	19.6
	BLOOMBURG STATE BK	BLOOMBURG	TX	**C-**	C-	C-	15	-2.33	11.2	6.5	19.6	6.7	**6.7**	8.7	15.7
	BLOOMFIELD STATE BK	BLOOMFIELD	IN	**D-**	D	D+	428	-4.38	6.8	1.2	18.5	18.0	**6.3**	8.3	13.7
	BLUE GRASS FS&LA	PARIS	KY	**B-**	B-	B	41	2.14	0.0	6.0	73.0	1.3	**10.0**	25.9	42.6
	BLUE GRASS SB	BLUE GRASS	IA	**B-**	B-	B	171	-0.23	6.8	1.3	7.5	59.2	**10.0**	13.3	27.5
▼	BLUE GRASS VALLEY BANK	BLUE GRASS	VA	**C-**	C-	B-	36	2.46	6.8	6.6	32.1	7.9	**9.8**	10.9	15.6
	BLUE RIDGE BANK	WALHALLA	SC	**B-**	B-	B+	99	5.16	8.3	3.2	48.8	23.0	**6.3**	8.4	16.0
	BLUE RIDGE BANK & TRUST C	INDEPENDENCE	MO	**D-**	D-	D+	465	-3.28	8.4	10.8	7.6	10.1	**6.1**	8.1	12.6
	BLUE RIDGE SB INC	ASHEVILLE	NC	**E-**	E-	D-	171	-22.40	17.6	0.1	28.2	1.7	**0.7**	4.5	7.4
▼	BLUEGRASS COMMUNITY	DANVILLE	KY	**D**	C	NR	37	21.61	4.6	1.9	25.0	22.9	**10.0**	16.3	25.6
	BLUEHARBOR BANK	MOORESVILLE	NC	**C-**	C	C	130	14.34	9.4	0.9	5.7	12.9	**10.0**	13.3	17.2
▼	BLUERIDGE BANK	FREDERICK	MD	**D-**	C	C	126	42.44	17.6	0.7	9.4	26.0	**8.6**	10.1	16.2
▲	BLUESTEM NATIONAL BK	FAIRBURY	IL	**C**	B	B	88	1.02	2.2	2.8	9.2	42.8	**10.0**	15.0	28.7
	BMW BANK OF NORTH	SALT LAKE CITY	UT	**B-**	B	B-	9,237	28.12	0.0	80.1	0.0	25.4	**3.5**	9.7	10.2
	BNA BANK	NEW ALBANY	MS	**A-**	A	A	401	0.54	2.6	5.6	19.3	33.9	**10.0**	12.2	21.7
	BNB BANK NA	FORT LEE	NJ	**D-**	D-	D-	377	-3.99	3.2	0.0	3.3	14.9	**8.8**	10.2	15.3
	BNC NATIONAL BK	GLENDALE	AZ	**D-**	D	C	745	-14.04	10.4	0.8	7.2	18.4	**5.5**	7.5	12.8
	BNY MELLON NA	PITTSBURGH	PA	**B-**	B-	B-	12,091	23.03	2.7	7.6	10.6	19.0	**6.0**	8.0	14.5
	BNY MELLON TRUST OF	NEWARK	DE	**B**	B	B	289	-23.09	0.0	0.0	30.4	0.0	**10.0**	21.6	53.7
	BODCAW BANK	STAMPS	AR	**B**	B	B	74	2.51	3.5	8.5	14.0	53.1	**9.6**	10.7	20.6
	BOELUS STATE BK	BOELUS	NE	**B-**	B-	B-	14	2.07	1.7	3.9	3.4	2.9	**10.0**	12.8	27.4
	BOGOTA SB	BOGOTA	NJ	**B**	B-	B-	370	-1.18	0.0	0.0	68.4	16.4	**10.0**	11.0	21.0
	BOILING SPRINGS SB	RUTHERFORD	NJ	**C-**	C-	C+	1,344	3.92	0.0	0.1	37.5	19.5	**10.0**	12.2	21.3
	BOKF NA	TULSA	OK	**C+**	C	B-	17,415	5.99	13.4	1.7	8.6	44.5	**3.8**	5.8	13.5
▲	BONANZA VALLEY STATE BK	BROOTEN	MN	**D+**	C-	D+	49	3.87	9.5	3.7	18.3	11.9	**5.3**	8.8	11.2
	BONDUEL STATE BK	BONDUEL	WI	**A-**	A-	A-	50	-1.76	14.5	2.4	7.3	47.1	**10.0**	22.8	56.1
	BONNEVILLE BANK	PROVO	UT	**B-**	B	B+	35	3.31	22.4	5.2	4.9	19.6	**10.0**	17.9	36.2
▲	BOONE BANK & TRUST CO	BOONE	IA	**A-**	B+	B+	105	0.12	8.6	0.5	10.3	47.0	**10.0**	11.7	17.4
	BOONE COUNTY BANK INC	MADISON	WV	**C-**	C-	B-	172	0.89	6.9	2.4	18.9	36.0	**10.0**	11.5	27.7
	BOONE COUNTY NB OF	COLUMBIA	MO	**B-**	B-	B-	1,233	1.55	4.8	5.9	14.6	28.9	**5.7**	7.7	11.9
▼	BOONVILLE FSB	BOONVILLE	IN	**D**	C-	D+	41	-8.11	7.7	9.8	56.6	0.0	**9.5**	10.7	20.1
▲	BORDER CAPITAL BANK NA	MCALLEN	TX	**D+**	D-	C-	170	-4.94	15.8	3.1	11.1	12.2	**10.0**	12.0	17.3
▲	BORDER STATE BK	GREENBUSH	MN	**E+**	D-	D	355	-4.05	15.3	6.1	11.9	12.6	**3.9**	7.7	10.4
	BORDER TRUST CO	AUGUSTA	ME	**E-**	E-	E	55	-30.80	17.1	3.7	37.4	19.4	**3.3**	5.3	10.4
	BOREL PRIVATE BANK & TRUS	SAN MATEO	CA	**C-**	C+	B-	1,637	0.69	3.6	0.7	21.4	6.0	**5.4**	7.4	11.9
	BORREGO SPRINGS BANK NA	LA MESA	CA	**D-**	D+	D	139	34.08	15.9	0.0	0.1	2.7	**6.4**	8.4	13.7
	BOSTON PRIVATE BANK &	BOSTON	MA	**C+**	C	C+	3,449	8.31	6.7	3.0	35.1	16.1	**4.9**	6.9	11.7
	BOSTON TRUST &	BOSTON	MA	**A-**	A-	C-	41	1.20	0.1	0.0	0.0	14.4	**10.0**	64.9	94.6
	BOULEVARD BANK	NEOSHO	MO	**C-**	C	C-	146	-1.16	3.6	25.4	18.3	40.0	**6.1**	8.1	14.5
▼	BOUNDARY WATERS BANK	ELY	MN	**E**	D-	D	119	-9.40	6.7	0.9	9.0	3.4	**2.1**	6.0	9.1
	BPD BANK	NEW YORK	NY	**D+**	C-	D	411	-7.03	18.9	0.6	0.6	18.8	**10.0**	15.6	26.7
	BRADFORD NB OF	GREENVILLE	IL	**B-**	C+	B-	221	11.43	2.2	2.3	21.6	32.8	**5.7**	7.7	14.3
	BRADY NATIONAL BK	BRADY	TX	**B-**	B	B-	85	0.80	5.3	6.1	14.2	25.1	**6.0**	8.0	14.7
▼	BRAINERD S&LA A FEDERAL A	BRAINERD	MN	**D-**	D	D+	67	-2.26	0.3	2.7	54.4	8.8	**5.3**	7.3	11.5

Asset Quality Index	Non-Performing Loans as a % of Total Loans	Non-Performing Loans as a % of Capital	Net Charge-offs Avg Loans	Profitability Index	Net Income ($Mil)	Return on Assets (R.O.A.)	Return on Equity (R.O.E.)	Net Interest Spread	Overhead Efficiency Ratio	Liquidity Index	Liquidity Ratio	Hot Money Ratio	Stability Index
4.8	1.36	9.4	0.36	**4.2**	1.3	1.10	12.11	4.19	64.1	**3.7**	18.9	10.7	**5.5**
0.3	3.49	31.2	1.84	**0.4**	-1.1	-0.44	-6.45	3.40	59.9	**0.7**	18.2	52.6	**0.8**
4.5	1.74	7.1	-0.38	**1.8**	0.0	0.19	1.79	3.29	94.7	**4.2**	50.7	14.0	**6.7**
2.3	1.91	12.9	1.43	**7.4**	3.6	1.73	17.73	4.90	44.3	**3.7**	18.4	10.7	**6.6**
7.3	0.59	3.6	0.36	**2.1**	1.0	0.47	4.72	4.45	84.6	**2.0**	27.0	21.6	**3.6**
8.5	0.00	0.0	0.00	**2.7**	0.4	0.49	3.46	4.03	80.0	**1.4**	23.5	29.0	**4.2**
9.8	0.00	0.0	0.00	**3.4**	0.2	0.50	4.72	3.53	75.8	**1.0**	25.4	35.2	**6.1**
5.4	1.41	8.0	0.13	**7.0**	1.2	1.68	13.71	4.13	56.9	**3.0**	17.8	14.4	**7.3**
2.1	4.53	24.0	0.93	**4.9**	8.9	1.05	12.15	4.27	57.7	**2.0**	18.8	19.4	**4.3**
2.1	1.73	11.0	1.18	**4.1**	3.3	0.62	6.48	4.20	66.5	**3.9**	21.5	10.4	**5.8**
6.1	0.32	2.8	0.00	**2.6**	0.5	0.52	6.00	3.77	72.0	**1.7**	13.7	21.7	**2.1**
6.5	0.00	0.0	0.00	**9.3**	760.2	4.88	6.92	1.81	53.2	**0.4**	14.3	101.0	**7.0**
0.0	9.12	75.4	0.53	**1.8**	0.0	0.02	0.09	5.47	81.1	**1.8**	18.6	21.2	**5.0**
2.5	3.30	20.0	0.31	**3.5**	1.1	0.69	7.63	4.43	83.2	**2.1**	28.1	21.5	**4.8**
2.7	2.18	14.3	0.18	**6.2**	3.4	1.53	13.75	3.88	39.6	**0.6**	7.5	45.2	**7.6**
4.1	2.44	13.0	0.13	**5.3**	0.3	0.90	8.01	4.48	67.1	**4.2**	24.0	8.8	**6.7**
8.9	0.35	1.6	0.75	**3.7**	0.6	0.70	6.21	3.89	72.5	**4.4**	52.0	15.0	**6.4**
8.5	0.00	0.0	0.00	**3.7**	0.1	0.58	6.83	3.89	81.2	**1.3**	32.7	33.0	**3.7**
0.3	3.63	22.1	1.55	**0.0**	-3.7	-0.84	-8.92	4.06	78.2	**1.5**	27.0	30.1	**5.0**
5.5	2.41	8.1	0.63	**3.5**	0.2	0.49	1.90	4.61	72.8	**0.9**	8.5	32.1	**7.0**
5.4	3.52	8.4	2.94	**2.9**	0.9	0.49	3.52	2.54	53.1	**3.8**	65.2	24.6	**7.1**
1.3	4.66	30.0	0.33	**3.3**	0.1	0.40	3.59	3.94	80.6	**3.3**	18.3	12.6	**6.5**
5.5	1.04	7.7	0.04	**3.7**	0.6	0.58	7.10	4.15	73.3	**1.9**	28.5	25.2	**5.3**
0.4	4.00	26.2	0.46	**1.1**	1.0	0.21	2.58	3.54	86.6	**3.0**	20.9	14.6	**2.9**
0.3	9.25	78.0	3.15	**0.0**	-4.3	-2.19	-55.18	2.86	185.7	**1.5**	11.4	24.1	**0.0**
9.0	0.00	0.0	0.01	**0.0**	-0.7	-1.95	-10.82	2.53	167.2	**3.4**	31.7	15.5	**1.5**
5.4	2.38	13.0	1.10	**1.1**	0.2	0.15	1.02	3.57	73.1	**1.6**	19.4	23.8	**2.7**
4.7	1.87	10.7	0.00	**0.0**	-1.2	-1.08	-8.11	2.60	133.6	**2.2**	36.3	28.6	**0.8**
6.6	2.97	7.6	0.86	**2.0**	0.3	0.29	1.87	3.11	83.5	**6.2**	62.6	7.1	**7.9**
5.3	0.22	1.6	0.81	**10.0**	225.7	2.75	29.49	5.13	17.9	**1.4**	28.3	94.6	**7.5**
6.5	1.68	7.0	0.41	**5.9**	4.6	1.15	8.91	4.28	53.2	**2.1**	31.2	25.0	**7.7**
0.0	9.49	59.9	0.65	**0.8**	0.5	0.11	1.08	3.03	84.7	**0.7**	15.9	48.3	**4.9**
0.3	3.93	24.9	1.39	**0.0**	-22.1	-2.80	-33.13	3.35	145.8	**1.7**	25.4	24.2	**3.3**
3.8	1.53	8.7	0.03	**5.2**	88.9	0.82	3.46	1.56	78.0	**2.2**	31.4	33.8	**6.9**
3.9	5.33	9.1	0.12	**9.5**	8.3	2.87	10.63	2.83	55.2	**7.5**	61.5	0.0	**7.9**
8.5	0.36	1.3	0.02	**4.6**	0.7	0.98	8.97	3.46	63.9	**2.9**	64.4	33.7	**7.4**
8.7	0.13	0.4	0.00	**3.8**	0.1	0.64	4.95	2.77	67.3	**5.8**	63.8	8.0	**7.7**
7.6	0.58	4.0	0.02	**4.8**	3.3	0.88	8.40	2.95	48.0	**1.4**	20.0	26.8	**6.8**
1.7	4.70	24.3	0.91	**2.9**	4.6	0.34	2.74	3.60	63.5	**3.0**	27.5	19.0	**7.8**
4.3	2.38	14.0	0.98	**6.8**	218.2	1.28	17.90	3.26	52.4	**5.2**	28.7	8.1	**6.0**
4.0	0.91	7.6	0.38	**5.1**	0.6	1.17	13.63	4.17	63.7	**0.9**	16.4	34.0	**3.7**
9.3	1.00	1.3	0.03	**6.0**	0.6	1.28	5.59	4.28	60.5	**5.9**	85.4	12.2	**8.9**
8.5	0.79	1.8	1.89	**3.2**	0.1	0.30	1.71	4.57	74.4	**3.5**	69.3	27.6	**6.0**
8.5	0.71	2.7	0.11	**8.9**	1.7	1.64	13.29	4.38	50.5	**2.5**	19.3	16.9	**8.0**
2.1	2.31	8.9	0.22	**6.6**	1.6	0.94	6.21	3.73	55.6	**4.4**	30.3	9.4	**7.1**
4.7	1.68	11.4	0.59	**7.0**	15.3	1.29	14.36	4.04	56.4	**4.4**	20.5	7.9	**6.5**
4.9	1.03	6.6	0.54	**0.6**	-0.2	-0.41	-3.96	2.89	89.9	**1.8**	25.1	23.7	**3.9**
0.8	8.71	42.4	0.30	**1.3**	0.4	0.24	1.97	4.02	90.1	**1.4**	9.2	23.6	**4.8**
0.2	4.80	38.5	2.19	**0.2**	-3.2	-0.89	-11.11	3.95	86.0	**0.8**	17.1	38.0	**3.7**
0.3	7.19	80.7	2.60	**0.0**	-0.5	-0.70	-13.21	3.62	98.9	**0.8**	15.3	34.6	**1.0**
0.3	4.70	35.1	3.94	**2.5**	-28.8	-1.73	-21.06	4.24	57.0	**1.1**	15.7	32.5	**6.3**
0.0	3.60	28.4	1.82	**5.0**	2.0	1.47	20.12	4.72	77.0	**0.5**	2.2	44.3	**4.1**
5.9	0.97	9.3	0.15	**4.1**	26.8	0.80	11.29	2.99	60.3	**2.9**	13.3	14.7	**5.6**
6.5	0.00	0.0	0.00	**10.0**	9.8	23.97	26.50	0.95	58.2	**5.0**	270.7	100.0	**10.0**
2.6	1.62	10.4	1.45	**3.4**	0.7	0.48	5.36	5.03	79.0	**5.5**	45.8	8.6	**3.3**
0.0	8.03	59.7	1.74	**0.0**	-4.9	-3.74	-35.78	3.64	157.5	**1.1**	11.6	29.9	**3.6**
1.7	1.35	5.0	2.74	**1.2**	3.8	0.92	6.26	4.56	83.4	**1.4**	17.3	26.7	**4.8**
5.7	0.77	5.1	0.25	**5.5**	2.6	1.23	14.98	3.81	62.2	**3.7**	33.2	14.3	**4.4**
6.6	0.44	2.7	0.04	**5.0**	1.1	1.30	15.51	4.15	69.4	**0.9**	22.7	35.4	**5.7**
3.0	1.79	18.2	0.06	**2.2**	0.1	0.16	2.12	3.11	87.9	**1.6**	15.0	22.6	**2.3**

Name	City	State	Rating	2008 Rating	2007 Rating	Total Assets ($Mil)	One Year Asset Growth	Asset Mix (As a % of Total Assets) Comm-ercial Loans	Cons-umer Loans	Home Mort-gages	Secur-ities	Capital-ization Index	Leverage Ratio	Risk-based Capital Ratio
BRAINTREE CO-OP BANK	BRAINTREE	MA	**C-**	C-	C-	231	5.09	2.6	0.8	45.5	27.2	**5.6**	7.6	13.5
BRANCH BANKING & TRUST	WINSTON-SALEM	NC	**C-**	C-	C+	150,829	-5.54	8.9	5.8	19.8	15.1	**8.4**	9.9	15.5
BRAND BANKING CO	LAWRENCEVILLE	GA	**E**	C-	C+	1,195	6.45	11.1	1.3	15.4	15.1	**1.3**	4.7	8.3
▲ BRANNEN BANK	INVERNESS	FL	**D+**	C-	B-	412	-8.79	0.5	1.1	49.2	26.6	**4.4**	6.4	17.4
BRANSON BANK	BRANSON	MO	**C-**	C+	C+	164	0.22	4.1	2.7	20.6	4.9	**6.2**	8.2	12.0
BRANTLEY BANK & TRUST CO	BRANTLEY	AL	**B**	B+	B+	65	1.51	6.2	7.0	6.2	48.6	**10.0**	14.2	29.5
BRATTLEBORO SAVINGS &	BRATTLEBORO	VT	**C-**	C-	NR	186	-3.04	3.7	2.6	46.7	3.1	**5.2**	7.2	11.3
BRAZOS NATIONAL BK	RICHWOOD	TX	**B-**	B-	B	25	39.75	3.2	5.8	42.4	0.0	**10.0**	13.0	16.2
▼ BRAZOS VALLEY BANK NA	COLLEGE STATION	TX	**D-**	D+	D-	128	-0.56	14.5	1.4	12.8	3.3	**7.3**	9.2	14.4
▼ BREDA SB	BREDA	IA	**B**	B	B	37	11.28	3.8	1.8	9.6	48.3	**10.0**	17.4	32.7
BREMEN BANK & TRUST CO	SAINT LOUIS	MO	**D**	D+	D+	229	-4.91	19.9	0.6	11.1	19.6	**6.9**	9.0	12.4
BREMER BANK NA	ALEXANDRIA	MN	**B-**	B-	B-	612	-0.70	9.1	6.8	7.6	17.9	**7.6**	9.4	13.9
BREMER BANK NA	BRAINERD	MN	**B-**	B-	B-	347	-4.27	10.0	4.7	11.8	25.8	**8.0**	9.7	14.4
BREMER BANK NA	INTERNATIONAL FALLS	MN	**B-**	B-	B-	119	5.11	8.8	4.5	9.0	45.0	**4.8**	6.8	14.5
BREMER BANK NA	MINNEAPOLIS	MN	**B-**	B-	B-	2,856	7.86	10.9	1.1	5.0	17.5	**6.1**	8.1	14.8
BREMER BANK NA	SAINT CLOUD	MN	**B-**	B-	B-	572	-10.62	18.3	2.4	7.1	15.5	**9.3**	11.0	14.4
BREMER BANK NA	WILLMAR	MN	**B**	B-	B-	537	1.41	13.9	6.9	9.0	17.7	**7.3**	9.2	13.1
BREMER BANK NA	FARGO	ND	**B**	B	B-	1,557	5.51	15.1	3.3	6.1	14.7	**6.7**	9.0	12.3
BREMER BANK NA	GRAND FORKS	ND	**B-**	B-	B-	881	5.76	11.8	8.4	5.6	13.7	**5.3**	8.0	11.2
BREMER BANK NA	MENOMONIE	WI	**B-**	B-	B-	657	1.39	5.9	2.2	9.5	33.0	**5.4**	7.4	13.8
BREMER TRUST NA	SAINT CLOUD	MN	**U**	U	U	8	6.83	0.0	0.0	0.0	4.1	**10.0**	87.9	202.7
BRENHAM NATIONAL BK	BRENHAM	TX	**C+**	C	B+	233	-0.29	7.9	2.2	8.6	39.1	**7.1**	9.1	17.4
BRENTWOOD BANK	BETHEL PARK	PA	**C**	C-	C+	427	-5.22	3.9	0.1	27.3	33.1	**7.0**	9.0	12.7
BRICKYARD BANK	LINCOLNWOOD	IL	**D-**	D-	E-	161	-19.65	4.6	0.8	9.8	10.9	**6.3**	8.3	12.8
BRIDGE BANK NA	SAN JOSE	CA	**C**	C-	C	990	17.35	39.3	0.4	1.0	17.9	**10.0**	11.9	15.5
BRIDGE CITY STATE BK	BRIDGE CITY	TX	**B**	B	B-	119	-7.12	4.8	3.9	17.8	36.6	**9.8**	10.9	21.9
BRIDGE COMMUNITY BANK	MOUNT VERNON	IA	**B-**	C+	C+	61	3.23	12.9	7.8	16.9	16.4	**8.0**	9.7	13.4
BRIDGEHAMPTON NATIONAL	BRIDGEHAMPTON	NY	**B-**	B-	B	1,026	14.63	7.5	1.0	7.4	46.0	**5.6**	7.6	13.3
BRIDGEVIEW BANK GROUP	BRIDGEVIEW	IL	**D-**	D-	D+	1,462	-2.42	11.3	0.2	6.8	13.6	**7.6**	9.4	13.0
▼ BRIDGEWATER BANK	BLOOMINGTON	MN	**D+**	C-	D+	351	-3.74	7.5	0.3	24.9	1.3	**7.1**	9.2	12.6
BRIDGEWATER SB	RAYNHAM	MA	**D+**	C	C-	497	23.50	9.3	4.1	14.3	35.9	**7.2**	9.1	17.0
▼ BRIGHTON BANK	BRIGHTON	TN	**E-**	D-	D+	78	10.81	6.3	2.6	16.9	11.7	**3.7**	6.4	10.4
▼ BRIGHTON BANK	SALT LAKE CITY	UT	**C**	B-	A-	143	-3.20	1.3	0.7	2.4	17.1	**10.0**	13.4	23.3
BRIMFIELD BANK	BRIMFIELD	IL	**C**	C+	B-	47	-7.98	7.1	4.7	34.6	25.6	**8.7**	10.2	18.7
BRISTOL COUNTY SB	TAUNTON	MA	**B-**	B-	B-	1,229	5.39	6.6	15.2	21.1	21.8	**10.0**	13.0	18.3
BRITTON & KOONTZ BANK NA	NATCHEZ	MS	**C**	C+	B	375	-4.49	6.0	1.1	10.9	36.8	**9.9**	10.9	16.8
BROADWAY FEDERAL BANK	LOS ANGELES	CA	**D-**	D+	C+	485	-7.08	2.3	0.6	17.0	4.8	**7.0**	9.0	13.3
BROADWAY NATIONAL BK	SAN ANTONIO	TX	**B+**	A-	A+	2,341	6.84	7.9	3.8	7.2	44.6	**8.5**	10.0	17.2
BROOKHAVEN BANK	ATLANTA	GA	**D-**	D	D	169	24.68	22.0	0.6	2.0	17.5	**7.7**	9.4	13.5
BROOKLINE BANK	BROOKLINE	MA	**B**	B	A-	2,636	4.08	13.0	21.1	10.9	11.8	**10.0**	15.4	18.8
▼ BROOKLYN FSB	BROOKLYN	NY	**E+**	D+	A	489	-8.05	0.0	0.1	13.3	14.6	**4.1**	7.8	10.5
BROOKVILLE BUILDING & SAV	BROOKVILLE	OH	**B-**	B-	B-	41	0.64	1.3	1.2	70.5	0.8	**10.0**	16.3	31.2
BROOKVILLE NATIONAL BK	BROOKVILLE	OH	**C-**	C-	C-	96	3.91	4.1	3.0	18.7	43.2	**7.4**	9.2	24.8
BROTHERHOOD BANK &	KANSAS CITY	KS	**D**	D	C	506	-8.97	6.0	0.6	7.7	42.7	**7.1**	9.0	15.5
▼ BROWARD BANK OF	FORT LAUDERDALE	FL	**D+**	C	NR	108	85.78	22.6	0.7	6.4	35.3	**10.0**	11.8	19.6
BROWN BROTHERS	NEW YORK	NY	**U**	U	U	11	-1.57	0.0	0.0	0.0	70.9	**10.0**	67.3	177.3
BROWN BROTHERS	WILMINGTON	DE	**U**	U	NR	7	-1.69	0.0	0.0	0.0	79.6	**10.0**	85.1	296.9
▲ BROWN COUNTY STATE BK	MOUNT STERLING	IL	**B**	C-	C-	87	3.20	6.2	11.6	17.5	10.8	**4.9**	8.1	11.0
BRUNING STATE BK	BRUNING	NE	**B**	B	B+	224	20.08	5.7	1.1	2.5	25.5	**8.8**	10.4	14.0
▼ BRUNSWICK BANK & TRUST	NEW BRUNSWICK	NJ	**D**	C	B+	136	-4.74	3.9	0.3	5.6	1.8	**10.0**	17.4	29.2
BRUNSWICK STATE BK	BRUNSWICK	NE	**B-**	C+	B-	75	7.82	8.2	5.5	1.4	4.4	**6.6**	9.0	12.2
BRUSH COUNTRY BANK	FREER	TX	**C+**	C+	C-	41	20.14	19.3	22.2	19.5	2.1	**3.6**	6.9	10.3
▼ BRYAN BANK & TRUST	RICHMOND HILL	GA	**D-**	C	D+	260	-0.15	6.7	1.1	20.2	8.0	**6.2**	8.2	11.9
▲ BRYANT BANK	TUSCALOOSA	AL	**D+**	D	C+	905	8.88	11.4	1.2	11.0	22.5	**7.5**	9.3	14.6
BRYANT STATE BK	BRYANT	SD	**B**	B	B	22	4.07	6.7	1.8	2.2	29.6	**10.0**	13.4	21.3
BRYN MAWR TRUST CO	BRYN MAWR	PA	**B-**	B	B	1,712	40.06	5.8	0.8	20.9	18.6	**6.6**	8.6	13.5
▼ BTC BANK	BETHANY	MO	**C-**	B-	B-	305	12.11	7.4	2.2	14.8	26.3	**7.8**	9.5	15.4
BUCKEYE COMMUNITY BANK	LORAIN	OH	**D**	D	D+	152	3.31	25.9	0.7	8.8	16.8	**6.7**	8.8	12.8
BUCKHOLTS STATE BK	BUCKHOLTS	TX	**A-**	A-	A-	58	0.62	5.7	7.8	5.9	38.3	**10.0**	14.5	36.7
BUCKLEY STATE BK	BUCKLEY	IL	**B**	B	B+	40	5.50	7.4	2.1	3.5	24.6	**10.0**	12.7	19.4

Asset Quality Index	Non-Performing Loans as a % of Total Loans	Non-Performing Loans as a % of Capital	Net Charge-offs / Avg Loans	Profitability Index	Net Income ($Mil)	Return on Assets (R.O.A.)	Return on Equity (R.O.E.)	Net Interest Spread	Overhead Efficiency Ratio	Liquidity Index	Liquidity Ratio	Hot Money Ratio	Stability Index
3.7	0.56	4.2	-0.02	**2.6**	0.7	0.31	4.29	3.59	84.8	**3.2**	34.6	17.3	**3.8**
0.8	2.83	16.9	2.30	**2.8**	624.9	0.52	4.72	4.01	62.7	**3.3**	5.4	11.5	**7.8**
0.3	16.15	144.8	3.31	**0.0**	-27.2	-2.23	-41.39	2.18	76.6	**1.2**	21.9	34.7	**4.7**
1.7	2.92	23.4	0.88	**4.7**	7.8	1.72	25.80	3.69	68.1	**3.2**	33.7	16.8	**3.2**
2.4	0.82	6.9	0.92	**3.6**	0.7	0.44	5.46	4.36	68.8	**0.7**	10.7	35.2	**4.0**
4.5	4.91	12.3	1.93	**4.4**	0.4	0.68	4.39	4.50	57.9	**4.1**	65.3	18.8	**6.3**
3.4	1.57	16.1	0.48	**2.7**	0.6	0.33	4.77	3.19	83.8	**3.7**	11.8	9.9	**3.9**
6.8	0.00	0.0	0.03	**6.9**	0.5	2.21	12.27	4.48	81.9	**4.6**	39.3	11.8	**6.3**
0.3	2.65	16.9	1.08	**0.8**	-0.2	-0.14	-1.79	4.40	79.9	**1.7**	28.2	27.4	**4.1**
9.1	0.00	0.0	-0.06	**3.5**	0.2	0.52	2.73	3.97	82.4	**6.1**	60.8	7.3	**7.7**
2.0	2.99	20.4	0.83	**1.2**	0.5	0.20	2.21	3.60	74.4	**1.4**	10.6	23.9	**4.2**
3.8	1.59	10.4	0.63	**5.4**	6.3	1.05	10.63	4.26	64.9	**3.9**	15.6	9.6	**5.8**
3.4	1.49	9.3	1.58	**3.3**	2.0	0.56	5.59	4.45	61.4	**3.9**	7.2	8.0	**6.0**
8.9	0.18	1.1	0.18	**5.3**	1.2	1.08	14.90	3.44	61.0	**3.0**	25.6	15.4	**5.3**
3.5	1.60	9.2	1.72	**3.4**	15.0	0.55	5.24	3.50	64.6	**5.9**	43.1	8.6	**6.1**
3.4	1.98	12.9	1.06	**6.7**	7.2	1.20	10.99	4.60	53.8	**4.0**	11.5	8.1	**6.6**
5.2	0.64	4.4	0.47	**7.4**	6.6	1.26	13.03	4.65	56.4	**3.6**	11.6	10.8	**6.7**
6.3	0.45	3.5	0.28	**6.9**	18.6	1.25	13.53	4.14	50.0	**2.4**	8.2	16.5	**6.3**
6.0	0.42	3.9	0.38	**6.5**	10.0	1.20	14.49	4.07	53.6	**2.8**	8.6	14.4	**6.0**
4.1	1.53	11.0	1.05	**4.6**	6.1	0.94	10.62	3.81	64.4	**4.1**	21.7	8.9	**6.3**
9.8	0.00	0.0	0.00	**10.0**	2.2	32.76	39.51	1.16	74.1	**5.0**	382.1	101.0	**5.7**
3.7	1.23	6.0	0.61	**4.2**	2.2	0.93	10.19	3.80	73.9	**4.8**	43.8	12.2	**4.9**
9.0	0.20	1.3	0.02	**3.4**	2.5	0.57	7.78	2.52	70.2	**2.8**	33.5	18.9	**2.9**
0.0	9.19	60.6	2.01	**0.0**	-1.4	-0.74	-9.42	3.36	116.5	**0.8**	16.3	40.7	**3.0**
4.1	2.57	12.8	0.87	**3.0**	4.3	0.47	3.76	5.12	79.1	**5.5**	34.6	4.0	**5.6**
5.9	1.71	7.4	0.10	**5.9**	1.5	1.20	11.23	4.47	71.5	**5.4**	46.2	9.4	**5.7**
6.9	0.13	0.9	0.55	**4.6**	0.5	0.91	9.41	4.43	67.7	**3.7**	17.6	10.5	**5.7**
5.9	1.33	7.8	0.22	**6.0**	10.1	1.05	13.36	4.34	62.3	**4.1**	20.6	10.0	**6.8**
0.0	7.32	49.7	2.25	**0.9**	0.9	0.06	0.61	3.31	68.0	**0.8**	9.7	34.4	**6.6**
1.6	2.46	19.3	1.16	**4.0**	1.7	0.49	5.49	4.26	41.5	**1.3**	12.0	27.1	**2.4**
4.9	1.07	6.2	0.24	**1.8**	0.9	0.17	1.87	3.57	93.8	**3.9**	34.5	13.8	**4.2**
0.3	2.61	21.4	1.56	**0.0**	-1.4	-1.89	-22.74	3.48	120.3	**1.5**	24.5	27.6	**1.8**
0.7	1.26	4.6	0.44	**9.1**	3.1	2.05	14.85	5.52	61.6	**6.4**	39.3	0.5	**9.2**
5.0	1.23	7.3	0.49	**3.5**	0.3	0.52	5.14	3.43	81.9	**1.5**	17.6	25.2	**6.1**
2.9	2.51	13.2	0.48	**3.8**	6.8	0.60	4.34	3.77	71.7	**3.2**	26.6	17.5	**9.6**
2.7	3.69	18.9	1.42	**3.5**	2.1	0.57	5.05	4.00	78.3	**1.7**	9.7	20.2	**5.5**
0.0	9.53	66.9	0.00	**1.2**	-1.4	-0.27	-3.34	4.14	60.4	**0.6**	10.3	46.5	**4.3**
4.5	2.94	13.1	0.36	**5.8**	31.3	1.38	11.66	4.42	66.8	**6.3**	44.4	5.9	**9.4**
6.2	0.92	6.0	0.70	**0.2**	-0.5	-0.30	-2.83	3.65	85.5	**2.3**	30.0	20.0	**1.0**
6.0	0.60	3.1	0.24	**4.7**	26.6	1.03	6.41	3.79	49.3	**1.9**	14.9	19.7	**9.0**
0.0	31.31	184.5	0.02	**1.2**	-41.1	-8.04	-69.79	4.24	266.4	**1.8**	21.9	21.7	**6.3**
7.5	1.24	6.2	0.04	**3.8**	0.3	0.73	4.53	3.82	70.0	**3.4**	14.8	12.2	**7.3**
8.4	0.24	1.0	0.03	**2.3**	0.3	0.32	3.17	3.10	86.3	**5.4**	49.8	9.2	**5.3**
3.5	3.50	16.0	5.46	**0.5**	-1.6	-0.30	-2.87	3.60	86.0	**3.3**	32.4	15.9	**4.2**
8.6	0.00	0.0	0.00	**0.0**	-0.5	-0.59	-4.46	3.61	103.7	**3.0**	48.4	27.0	**1.5**
10.0	0.00	0.0	0.00	**9.5**	0.6	5.83	8.10	2.08	93.2	**5.0**	227.0	101.0	**7.0**
10.0	0.00	0.0	0.00	**0.0**	-0.4	-5.97	-6.98	0.49	112.1	**5.0**	543.9	101.0	**2.0**
3.2	1.30	11.8	0.00	**6.6**	0.9	1.29	13.26	3.90	61.6	**2.7**	12.8	15.3	**7.3**
8.6	0.00	0.0	-0.01	**5.1**	2.0	1.00	9.17	3.66	62.8	**2.9**	14.5	14.3	**7.2**
0.0	11.64	38.2	1.22	**1.4**	-1.5	-0.95	-5.37	3.38	95.5	**2.2**	36.2	27.6	**7.6**
5.7	0.52	3.9	0.06	**9.3**	1.9	2.67	28.70	4.62	45.5	**1.4**	24.0	29.0	**6.3**
6.2	0.06	0.6	0.18	**10.0**	0.9	2.46	25.76	6.30	56.4	**2.5**	32.9	19.9	**5.9**
0.4	2.40	18.5	2.82	**2.8**	-1.1	-0.42	-4.82	4.20	50.0	**1.2**	14.2	29.3	**5.7**
2.1	3.51	20.7	1.11	**1.3**	2.8	0.32	3.43	3.40	68.4	**0.8**	16.3	39.6	**2.8**
8.6	0.00	0.0	0.15	**5.2**	0.2	1.14	8.24	4.06	74.1	**5.4**	48.2	6.5	**9.1**
5.9	0.80	6.0	0.96	**3.9**	8.9	0.61	7.59	3.88	72.7	**3.7**	18.2	11.3	**6.8**
2.3	3.24	19.9	0.21	**7.5**	3.3	1.14	10.94	4.29	45.8	**0.8**	17.7	38.8	**6.7**
1.3	3.23	23.3	1.63	**0.6**	-0.1	-0.06	-0.71	3.48	75.4	**1.6**	18.7	24.5	**4.3**
8.7	0.09	0.2	0.12	**6.1**	0.8	1.38	9.68	3.92	66.8	**4.0**	70.2	20.7	**10.0**
8.6	0.00	0.0	0.64	**4.2**	0.3	0.71	6.12	2.91	67.1	**5.4**	53.1	10.2	**7.0**

								Asset Mix (As a % of Total Assets)						
Name	City	State	Rating	2008 Rating	2007 Rating	Total Assets ($Mil)	One Year Asset Growth	Comm-ercial Loans	Cons-umer Loans	Home Mort-gages	Secur-ities	Capital-ization Index	Leverage Ratio	Risk-based Capital Ratio
▼ BUCKS COUNTY BANK	DOYLESTOWN	PA	**D-**	D-	C-	207	0.70	13.9	0.1	9.1	18.1	**6.0**	8.0	12.6
BUENA VISTA NATIONAL BK	CHESTER	IL	**A**	A-	A-	128	-5.32	6.2	7.2	21.2	37.6	**10.0**	12.7	24.0
BUFFALO FSB	BUFFALO	WY	**D+**	C-	D+	155	2.06	8.5	4.7	15.9	16.7	**6.3**	8.3	13.8
BUFFALO PRAIRIE STATE BK	BUFFALO PRAIRIE	IL	**B**	B	B-	53	7.04	3.1	1.8	1.9	56.0	**10.0**	16.1	34.3
BUFFALO RIDGE BANK	BEARDSLEY	MN	**C+**	C+	C+	38	-2.36	7.6	3.4	6.8	11.7	**5.5**	8.0	11.4
BUFFALO SB	BUFFALO	IA	**D**	D	B-	36	-3.85	9.5	2.2	18.7	15.1	**7.6**	9.4	18.8
▲ BUILDERS BANK	CHICAGO	IL	**E+**	E	D-	306	-37.36	0.0	0.0	1.3	19.0	**5.4**	7.4	12.2
BURKE & HERBERT BK & TRUS	ALEXANDRIA	VA	**A-**	A-	A	2,283	13.42	1.3	0.5	14.8	30.3	**7.7**	10.2	13.1
▲ BURLING BANK	CHICAGO	IL	**C+**	C	B-	114	2.22	11.4	0.2	9.1	59.6	**8.7**	10.2	27.6
BURR RIDGE BANK & TRUST	BURR RIDGE	IL	**C-**	C	NR	151	29.72	21.3	1.2	10.6	3.8	**10.0**	12.0	15.3
▼ BURTON STATE BK	BURTON	TX	**B+**	A-	A-	54	5.17	0.8	6.2	11.0	14.1	**10.0**	11.6	31.3
▲ BUSEY BANK	CHAMPAIGN	IL	**C-**	D	C-	3,590	-5.02	8.1	1.3	14.0	16.4	**7.2**	9.1	14.3
BUSINESS BANK	MINNETONKA	MN	**C-**	D+	C-	156	3.52	13.9	2.1	44.6	7.1	**5.1**	7.1	12.9
BUSINESS BANK	VIENNA	VA	**C+**	C+	C+	275	3.87	7.0	0.7	12.1	7.6	**7.5**	9.3	13.6
BUSINESS BANK	BURLINGTON	WA	**E-**	D-	D	89	-26.39	7.0	0.5	9.6	10.1	**2.8**	6.3	9.8
▲ BUSINESS BANK	APPLETON	WI	**D**	C-	D+	357	-1.51	16.6	0.1	4.1	8.7	**7.2**	9.2	12.8
▼ BUSINESS BANK OF SAINT LO	CLAYTON	MO	**D**	C-	D	565	-1.64	13.2	0.0	8.1	12.9	**7.7**	9.4	13.4
BUSINESS BANK OF TEXAS NA	AUSTIN	TX	**C-**	C	C-	65	7.37	10.0	0.1	0.0	80.6	**10.0**	18.7	63.6
BUSINESS FIRST BANK	BATON ROUGE	LA	**D+**	C	C-	657	-1.44	14.6	0.4	3.8	33.2	**6.9**	8.9	13.5
▲ BUTTE STATE BK	BUTTE	NE	**E+**	D-	C-	44	-5.40	12.6	5.3	5.8	14.9	**5.9**	8.1	11.7
BYRON BANK	BYRON	IL	**C-**	C	C+	216	4.89	7.3	2.5	19.5	25.1	**6.3**	8.4	13.6
BYRON STATE BK	BYRON	NE	**B**	B	B+	36	9.26	9.6	5.5	11.7	3.3	**10.0**	11.7	15.9
C US BANK	CRESCO	IA	**B+**	B	B	336	3.82	12.5	4.4	13.4	16.6	**7.3**	10.2	12.8
C&G SB	ALTOONA	PA	**B-**	B-	B-	128	-3.79	0.0	8.6	64.4	13.6	**10.0**	12.9	24.9
▼ CABARRUS BANK & TRUST CO	CONCORD	NC	**D+**	C-	C+	129	24.65	9.5	1.3	10.2	23.3	**6.9**	8.9	13.4
CABOOL STATE BK	CABOOL	MO	**D**	D+	B-	70	-0.30	3.7	3.4	13.0	12.1	**10.0**	12.2	19.9
CACHE BANK & TRUST	GREELEY	CO	**C-**	C-	C-	166	-4.04	11.4	2.7	10.6	31.6	**6.6**	8.7	15.7
CACHE VALLEY BANK	LOGAN	UT	**A-**	A-	A-	279	7.46	13.8	1.9	8.4	5.3	**10.0**	12.5	15.8
CADENCE BANK NA	STARKVILLE	MS	**E-**	E+	C-	1,581	-13.74	9.0	1.0	8.7	24.6	**3.1**	5.1	10.2
CALDWELL BANK & TRUST CO	COLUMBIA	LA	**D+**	C-	C	99	-1.28	6.0	9.5	24.2	16.6	**5.9**	8.8	11.7
CALDWELL STATE BK IN CALD	CALDWELL	KS	**C-**	C	B+	37	5.03	9.2	3.2	3.5	33.5	**9.3**	10.5	16.2
CALHOUN COUNTY BANK INC	GRANTSVILLE	WV	**C+**	C	B-	113	6.94	20.9	12.1	43.2	8.4	**6.8**	8.9	15.2
▲ CALIFORNIA BANK & TRUST	SAN DIEGO	CA	**D+**	D	C+	10,766	-4.35	13.9	0.8	11.7	3.4	**8.4**	9.9	13.7
▲ CALIFORNIA BANK OF	LAFAYETTE	CA	**D+**	C-	C-	240	23.67	31.1	0.4	3.9	21.0	**6.4**	10.7	12.0
CALIFORNIA BUSINESS BANK	LOS ANGELES	CA	**D-**	D-	D	97	-15.78	25.3	0.1	6.6	0.0	**6.2**	8.2	13.0
CALIFORNIA COMMUNITY	ESCONDIDO	CA	**C-**	C-	C-	222	0.69	9.7	0.8	2.6	11.3	**9.2**	10.4	16.3
CALIFORNIA FIRST NATIONAL	IRVINE	CA	**A**	A	A	323	7.53	26.8	0.0	0.0	12.2	**10.0**	23.5	23.0
▲ CALIFORNIA PACIFIC BANK	SAN FRANCISCO	CA	**B**	B-	A-	97	31.65	20.4	0.0	7.5	0.9	**10.0**	23.7	35.1
CALIFORNIA REPUBLIC BANK	NEWPORT BEACH	CA	**C+**	C	C	313	12.75	18.8	0.0	5.4	0.0	**10.0**	15.3	23.2
▼ CALIFORNIA UNITED BANK	ENCINO	CA	**D**	C	C	756	65.58	22.6	0.7	1.6	12.7	**6.6**	9.6	12.2
▲ CALLAWAY BANK	FULTON	MO	**D+**	C-	C-	274	-3.67	6.1	1.2	21.3	22.6	**8.8**	10.2	16.0
CALUMET COUNTY BANK	BRILLION	WI	**D+**	D+	C+	90	7.61	11.8	1.7	10.9	24.0	**7.8**	9.5	15.6
CALUSA NATIONAL BK	PUNTA GORDA	FL	**D-**	C-	C-	146	25.25	3.1	0.4	32.0	26.4	**5.8**	7.8	14.7
CALVIN B TAYLOR BANKING C	BERLIN	MD	**A**	A-	A+	402	3.49	3.8	0.4	23.5	22.4	**10.0**	16.9	32.1
CAMBRIDGE APPLETON	BOSTON	MA	**U**	U	U	4	9.67	0.0	0.0	0.0	0.0	**10.0**	71.8	284.9
CAMBRIDGE SB	CAMBRIDGE	MA	**C+**	C+	C	2,183	1.01	2.6	0.1	28.8	23.8	**7.7**	9.4	15.3
▼ CAMBRIDGE STATE BK	CAMBRIDGE	MN	**D-**	C+	B-	84	-9.88	10.3	0.7	19.4	15.1	**7.8**	9.5	14.5
▼ CAMBRIDGE STATE BK	CAMBRIDGE	WI	**D+**	C-	C-	91	-16.23	5.0	2.1	23.1	9.4	**8.2**	9.8	14.0
CAMBRIDGE TRUST CO	CAMBRIDGE	MA	**B+**	B	B	1,131	11.00	3.5	0.7	25.9	45.9	**5.4**	7.4	15.5
▲ CAMDEN NATIONAL BK	CAMDEN	AL	**C+**	C+	B-	113	-7.44	11.6	11.1	20.4	15.0	**10.0**	11.7	19.4
CAMDEN NATIONAL BK	CAMDEN	ME	**B**	B-	B-	2,281	3.01	4.1	0.7	30.8	25.9	**5.8**	7.8	13.6
▼ CAMERON STATE BK	LAKE CHARLES	LA	**B+**	A-	A-	706	-10.37	7.4	6.6	9.9	32.0	**9.9**	11.0	17.5
CAMP GROVE STATE BK	CAMP GROVE	IL	**B-**	B-	B-	19	3.22	1.1	6.8	6.2	25.2	**10.0**	16.6	29.3
CAMPBELL & FETTER BANK	KENDALLVILLE	IN	**B**	B	B	265	5.49	4.7	5.5	30.9	42.3	**10.0**	11.2	24.2
CAMPBELL COUNTY BANK	HERREID	SD	**B+**	B+	B	91	-6.45	6.0	0.6	0.0	42.5	**10.0**	11.9	19.6
CAMPUS STATE BK	CAMPUS	IL	**C-**	C-	C-	18	-5.11	0.0	12.6	36.2	17.3	**8.4**	10.0	18.8
CANANDAIGUA NATIONAL BK	CANANDAIGUA	NY	**B-**	B-	B	1,641	6.53	12.9	13.0	15.9	16.6	**6.5**	8.5	12.9
CANANDAIGUA NATIONAL	SARASOTA	FL	**U**	U	NR	4	7.73	0.0	0.0	0.0	12.1	**10.0**	101.3	116.8
CANON NATIONAL BK	CANON CITY	CO	**D+**	D+	C+	228	-9.13	4.0	0.5	9.8	38.3	**8.2**	9.8	17.3
CANTON CO-OP BANK	CANTON	MA	**B-**	C+	C	92	-1.41	0.1	0.2	46.3	18.2	**10.0**	15.5	29.8

Asset Quality Index	Non-Performing Loans		Net Charge-offs	Profitability Index	Net Income ($Mil)	Return on Assets (R.O.A.)	Return on Equity (R.O.E.)	Net Interest Spread	Overhead Efficiency Ratio	Liquidity Index	Liquidity Ratio	Hot Money Ratio	Stability Index
	as a % of Total Loans	as a % of Capital	Avg Loans										
1.7	2.53	17.9	0.91	**0.2**	-0.9	-0.42	-4.95	3.12	101.2	**0.9**	19.4	34.9	**3.0**
7.0	1.24	4.2	0.25	**6.0**	1.5	1.12	8.06	4.53	67.6	**3.4**	33.4	15.9	**7.7**
1.8	3.45	24.6	0.14	**2.2**	0.4	0.22	2.72	4.17	89.4	**1.9**	31.3	28.2	**4.6**
7.6	2.63	5.6	0.04	**3.9**	0.5	0.91	5.52	2.96	50.0	**3.4**	75.4	30.4	**7.0**
3.2	0.99	7.5	0.20	**8.0**	0.7	1.77	21.37	4.83	60.0	**3.5**	30.1	14.0	**7.1**
2.6	3.50	15.8	0.14	**0.7**	0.0	0.02	0.22	3.30	100.0	**4.1**	50.3	16.2	**5.3**
0.0	34.99	229.3	3.26	**0.0**	-7.4	-1.81	-27.86	2.98	120.4	**0.4**	3.9	52.7	**2.4**
6.5	0.89	5.0	0.39	**9.8**	34.2	1.61	16.09	4.65	42.3	**4.1**	31.1	14.6	**9.7**
9.7	0.00	0.0	-0.02	**3.6**	0.7	0.66	6.67	3.09	78.2	**5.7**	66.2	12.2	**5.3**
8.1	0.24	1.4	0.07	**4.9**	1.6	1.13	9.33	3.80	62.6	**0.8**	18.5	42.0	**2.6**
9.1	0.01	0.0	0.01	**4.2**	0.4	0.87	6.73	2.54	66.2	**4.6**	70.8	17.1	**7.7**
2.7	2.74	16.6	2.54	**2.8**	23.1	0.64	6.47	3.70	56.3	**3.4**	19.0	12.9	**5.3**
3.7	1.59	14.8	0.83	**4.3**	1.2	0.76	9.73	4.13	91.4	**0.5**	9.3	64.9	**3.2**
6.0	0.75	5.2	0.12	**3.6**	1.5	0.56	5.44	4.36	76.3	**2.1**	27.0	20.9	**6.2**
0.2	10.33	68.4	2.07	**0.0**	-5.1	-5.04	-88.10	3.08	193.1	**4.3**	21.7	7.4	**0.0**
0.9	2.33	17.0	1.70	**1.2**	-0.2	-0.06	-0.59	3.38	51.2	**0.7**	20.1	54.6	**4.4**
1.5	3.49	22.8	3.86	**0.6**	-3.5	-0.63	-5.97	3.48	54.4	**1.8**	26.3	25.1	**5.9**
10.0	0.00	0.0	0.00	**1.6**	0.7	1.05	5.36	2.59	99.3	**2.5**	31.5	19.5	**3.6**
1.7	3.56	21.5	0.76	**1.3**	1.3	0.19	2.11	3.50	76.6	**1.7**	28.4	28.5	**3.3**
0.2	4.69	33.6	1.44	**0.9**	-0.1	-0.26	-3.24	4.33	62.2	**1.1**	18.3	31.9	**3.4**
2.1	2.69	19.5	0.79	**5.0**	2.5	1.15	13.27	3.70	60.5	**0.9**	8.2	31.2	**5.4**
4.7	0.26	1.6	0.47	**7.0**	0.4	1.16	9.81	3.82	48.8	**1.7**	24.9	24.6	**7.6**
6.0	0.31	2.1	0.15	**6.7**	5.1	1.57	13.35	4.23	57.8	**2.0**	14.9	19.1	**7.6**
5.7	0.87	4.8	0.10	**3.8**	0.8	0.57	4.40	3.62	75.0	**4.0**	21.2	9.3	**7.0**
3.7	3.80	25.4	0.22	**2.5**	0.4	0.31	3.10	4.02	78.6	**1.7**	14.8	21.0	**3.7**
1.3	7.97	35.4	2.50	**0.0**	-0.8	-1.20	-8.91	4.24	88.3	**2.4**	31.1	20.2	**6.7**
5.8	0.43	2.5	0.38	**2.3**	0.6	0.35	4.07	3.64	85.6	**2.6**	39.5	25.8	**4.0**
5.8	0.51	2.7	0.05	**8.6**	4.1	1.52	12.16	5.62	50.8	**0.9**	17.2	34.5	**7.0**
0.3	10.18	75.3	2.35	**0.0**	-32.8	-1.83	-24.42	2.51	103.9	**1.8**	19.8	23.2	**3.8**
1.8	2.48	17.7	0.10	**6.9**	1.6	1.67	18.93	5.35	66.7	**0.8**	17.7	38.5	**4.6**
5.4	0.54	2.9	1.27	**1.7**	0.0	0.12	1.28	3.44	77.0	**2.2**	30.0	22.0	**5.0**
3.0	2.18	16.8	0.23	**4.9**	0.9	0.75	8.70	5.17	73.5	**1.3**	12.5	26.6	**6.1**
0.0	2.30	14.8	1.77	**5.4**	58.8	0.53	4.18	5.01	58.1	**4.4**	12.8	6.0	**5.8**
5.6	1.15	7.1	0.21	**2.1**	3.4	1.56	14.18	3.57	74.5	**1.8**	17.7	21.3	**2.9**
0.7	3.78	26.0	1.28	**0.0**	-3.1	-2.84	-31.29	3.54	118.2	**0.9**	19.5	37.0	**0.5**
2.3	3.44	19.1	0.05	**3.0**	1.7	0.73	6.99	3.78	77.5	**2.9**	34.1	18.6	**6.2**
6.6	0.57	1.9	-0.01	**9.6**	6.1	2.02	8.29	4.34	30.9	**1.0**	25.7	43.4	**9.1**
4.8	2.67	6.0	1.71	**6.4**	0.8	0.94	3.50	4.43	45.8	**2.1**	48.0	55.4	**8.8**
8.8	0.00	0.0	0.00	**2.4**	2.1	0.69	4.35	4.28	74.4	**6.8**	48.2	1.0	**4.1**
3.6	2.26	14.5	0.49	**0.4**	-2.3	-0.42	-3.82	3.49	104.0	**4.6**	33.2	9.8	**1.9**
1.7	4.91	29.4	0.57	**2.2**	1.0	0.35	3.50	4.00	81.1	**3.1**	7.7	13.0	**4.8**
2.0	3.52	20.7	0.80	**1.5**	0.1	0.12	1.26	4.26	81.7	**3.3**	41.5	18.6	**4.7**
3.4	2.93	20.6	1.27	**0.0**	-1.2	-0.88	-10.25	3.65	93.6	**3.2**	33.1	16.5	**0.8**
5.7	2.01	6.8	0.27	**8.3**	5.1	1.28	7.31	4.24	47.7	**4.1**	37.2	13.6	**9.6**
10.0	0.00	0.0	0.00	**8.1**	0.1	5.37	6.41	N/,	93.7	**5.0**	251.3	101.0	**5.7**
7.3	0.65	4.2	0.01	**3.8**	14.4	0.67	7.40	3.26	66.0	**4.1**	31.1	14.8	**6.8**
0.3	7.95	52.1	1.13	**2.0**	0.0	0.01	0.07	4.04	72.0	**2.4**	23.1	17.9	**5.4**
0.3	11.46	47.8	8.45	**0.4**	-3.6	-3.78	-34.08	2.93	115.9	**1.2**	25.5	33.2	**4.1**
9.6	0.20	1.3	0.07	**6.8**	13.3	1.25	15.57	4.22	67.5	**6.2**	46.9	7.8	**7.2**
4.2	1.98	10.1	0.68	**5.9**	1.1	0.97	8.68	4.70	61.5	**1.8**	26.3	25.0	**5.5**
5.1	1.29	9.9	0.28	**6.4**	26.0	1.15	12.01	3.77	51.7	**2.5**	7.5	16.1	**7.8**
5.1	2.24	11.0	0.58	**7.7**	9.3	1.29	12.37	4.82	62.3	**2.6**	20.6	16.4	**7.6**
5.3	5.74	14.4	0.71	**4.1**	0.2	0.98	5.44	3.79	80.5	**2.2**	57.3	41.0	**8.2**
7.2	1.02	4.4	0.01	**4.4**	2.1	0.82	7.29	3.42	65.1	**4.6**	31.1	9.0	**6.2**
6.4	2.25	8.8	0.06	**5.6**	1.7	1.79	15.25	4.37	57.8	**1.0**	22.1	34.6	**7.2**
2.9	2.87	17.9	0.00	**3.3**	0.1	0.46	4.72	3.72	80.7	**3.4**	32.1	13.5	**5.7**
3.7	1.91	14.8	0.40	**6.4**	20.8	1.30	15.62	4.34	61.5	**2.9**	14.7	14.6	**8.0**
10.0	0.00	0.0	0.00	**0.0**	-0.2	-6.03	-6.08	0.23	1,273.3	**5.0**	11,985.7	101.0	**6.4**
2.8	2.88	13.2	1.15	**1.3**	0.5	0.19	1.93	3.94	86.7	**3.4**	31.9	15.2	**4.2**
5.0	2.55	10.5	0.83	**3.3**	0.4	0.43	2.80	3.80	68.1	**3.2**	35.8	17.5	**7.6**

Name	City	State	Rating	2008 Rating	2007 Rating	Total Assets ($Mil)	One Year Asset Growth	Asset Mix (As a % of Total Assets) Commercial Loans	Consumer Loans	Home Mortgages	Securities	Capitalization Index	Leverage Ratio	Risk-based Capital Ratio
CANTON STATE BK	CANTON	MN	**D+**	C-	C-	27	-8.16	11.7	4.1	8.2	16.0	**6.0**	8.0	12.2
CANTON STATE BK	CANTON	MO	**E+**	D-	D+	33	-4.56	3.7	1.4	15.7	24.7	**5.3**	7.3	15.1
CANYON COMMUNITY BANK	TUCSON	AZ	**C-**	C	B-	93	2.43	2.7	0.5	4.9	16.4	**10.0**	11.1	18.8
▲ CAPAHA BANK SB	CAPE GIRARDEAU	MO	**C-**	D+	C-	182	-2.01	7.7	1.5	15.8	9.9	**6.4**	8.4	12.7
CAPE ANN SB	GLOUCESTER	MA	**B-**	B-	B-	421	3.69	0.8	0.5	39.0	29.5	**10.0**	20.4	47.8
CAPE BANK	CAPE MAY COURT	NJ	**D**	D	D+	1,061	-1.08	4.7	0.1	29.4	15.3	**8.4**	10.0	13.9
CAPE COD COOPERATIVE	HYANNIS	MA	**C+**	C-	C+	593	1.59	3.5	0.2	46.1	10.0	**8.1**	9.7	15.0
CAPE COD FIVE CENTS SB	ORLEANS	MA	**C+**	C+	B-	1,974	2.96	4.5	0.1	44.4	19.5	**8.2**	9.8	17.1
CAPITAL BANK	LITTLE ROCK	AR	**D+**	D+	C	167	-6.86	9.1	1.6	10.7	44.5	**8.8**	10.2	18.1
CAPITAL BANK	SAN JUAN CAPISTRANO	CA	**D+**	C	C	94	59.14	13.5	0.1	11.7	1.0	**10.0**	11.1	18.4
CAPITAL BANK	FORT OGLETHORPE	GA	**D**	D	D	131	-2.70	2.6	1.2	18.5	12.8	**5.2**	7.2	11.4
▲ CAPITAL BANK	SAINT PAUL	MN	**B-**	C	C	40	7.28	1.8	1.4	2.9	26.7	**7.1**	9.1	18.2
▼ CAPITAL BANK	RALEIGH	NC	**E+**	C-	B-	1,585	-8.55	9.1	0.5	11.4	13.6	**2.5**	6.4	9.5
CAPITAL BANK	HOUSTON	TX	**B**	B	B-	251	6.83	9.7	2.7	9.4	4.1	**6.1**	8.7	11.8
CAPITAL BANK & TRUST CO	ALBANY	NY	**C**	C	C-	260	-9.16	17.6	0.1	9.6	19.4	**6.3**	8.3	13.0
CAPITAL BANK & TRUST CO F	IRVINE	CA	**B+**	B+	B+	142	-6.00	0.0	0.0	0.0	78.1	**10.0**	57.5	213.0
CAPITAL BANK NA	ROCKVILLE	MD	**D+**	C	C	255	8.43	12.7	0.5	13.1	9.5	**6.3**	8.3	13.7
CAPITAL BANK OF NEW JERSE	VINELAND	NJ	**C-**	C-	C-	203	28.89	10.3	0.3	9.2	27.3	**10.0**	12.0	16.8
CAPITAL BANK OF TEXAS	CARRIZO SPRINGS	TX	**B-**	B	A-	49	23.53	3.0	3.4	12.5	19.9	**10.0**	14.3	35.2
CAPITAL BANK SSB	EL PASO	TX	**D**	D-	C	109	-0.34	0.6	0.2	22.8	5.4	**10.0**	15.9	32.0
CAPITAL CITY BANK	TALLAHASSEE	FL	**D-**	D-	D+	2,596	-3.43	4.8	7.8	14.3	11.5	**8.1**	9.7	14.0
CAPITAL CITY BANK	TOPEKA	KS	**C-**	C	C+	389	-6.92	10.3	2.1	14.2	31.6	**5.8**	7.8	12.7
CAPITAL COMMUNITY BANK	PROVO	UT	**D**	D	D-	106	-13.96	12.7	0.7	5.4	1.2	**10.0**	11.7	17.4
CAPITAL ONE BANK (USA) NA	GLEN ALLEN	VA	**C-**	C+	B-	72,203	90.05	7.1	71.7	0.0	16.4	**6.3**	8.3	23.6
CAPITAL ONE NA	MCLEAN	VA	**D+**	C-	B-	126,901	-0.36	8.6	16.2	9.1	23.4	**6.1**	8.1	12.5
▲ CAPITAL PACIFIC BANK	PORTLAND	OR	**D**	D+	C	170	-13.64	15.2	0.1	3.1	12.1	**7.8**	9.6	13.3
▼ CAPITALBANK	GREENWOOD	SC	**D-**	D-	D	655	-12.50	6.1	1.0	18.9	11.3	**5.6**	7.6	12.0
CAPITALMARK BANK & TRUST	CHATTANOOGA	TN	**C**	C-	C-	464	18.55	20.1	2.1	6.9	24.9	**9.0**	10.5	14.2
▲ CAPITALSOURCE BANK	LOS ANGELES	CA	**D+**	D	C-	6,135	8.06	25.0	0.0	0.0	30.1	**10.0**	13.2	18.1
CAPITOL BANK	MADISON	WI	**C**	C-	C+	253	10.93	7.0	0.6	13.8	26.0	**6.3**	8.3	13.1
CAPITOL CITY BANK & TRUST	ATLANTA	GA	**E-**	E-	D-	295	-6.96	2.7	1.2	6.3	12.5	**0.2**	4.3	6.4
▲ CAPITOL FSB	TOPEKA	KS	**B**	B-	B	9,813	16.93	0.0	0.1	50.0	31.1	**10.0**	13.9	39.0
CAPITOL NATIONAL BK	LANSING	MI	**E-**	E+	D	158	-21.06	17.7	1.0	13.1	0.0	**2.0**	6.1	9.0
CAPMARK BANK	MIDVALE	UT	**D**	D	C	8,819	-16.68	0.0	0.0	0.0	9.0	**10.0**	18.0	26.6
CAPON VALLEY BANK	WARDENSVILLE	WV	**C-**	C-	C+	155	-3.14	1.2	10.5	33.6	3.9	**6.3**	8.3	12.5
CAPSTAR BANK	NASHVILLE	TN	**D**	C	C	514	84.08	25.6	1.4	2.8	20.6	**10.0**	14.3	19.7
CAPSTONE BANK	TUSCALOOSA	AL	**D+**	C-	C-	357	19.38	21.9	3.6	16.1	5.1	**6.3**	9.6	12.0
CAPSTONE BANK	RALEIGH	NC	**B**	C+	C-	197	6.74	5.7	3.4	10.4	13.3	**10.0**	12.7	19.3
▲ CARDINAL BANK	MCLEAN	VA	**B+**	C+	C-	2,062	4.86	12.7	0.1	19.3	16.4	**7.7**	10.3	13.1
▲ CARLINVILLE NATIONAL BK	CARLINVILLE	IL	**D+**	C+	C+	361	20.19	13.1	2.6	8.7	13.3	**3.3**	7.3	10.2
CARLSBAD NATIONAL BK	CARLSBAD	NM	**A-**	B+	A-	205	-3.82	8.4	3.2	17.3	48.5	**8.2**	9.8	19.0
CARMINE STATE BK	CARMINE	TX	**B+**	B+	B+	52	8.50	3.3	12.3	6.6	39.1	**10.0**	12.5	30.2
▼ CARNEY STATE BK	CARNEY	OK	**D-**	D	D-	19	4.73	4.4	9.3	21.8	49.2	**6.1**	8.1	24.1
▼ CAROLINA ALLIANCE BANK	SPARTANBURG	SC	**D**	C	C	225	13.39	14.1	1.4	8.2	17.9	**8.7**	10.1	14.1
CAROLINA BANK	GREENSBORO	NC	**D-**	D+	C-	676	-2.92	10.8	1.0	8.4	6.3	**5.6**	7.6	11.8
CAROLINA BANK & TRUST CO	DARLINGTON	SC	**B+**	B	B+	344	-0.31	6.4	2.8	14.3	12.8	**10.0**	11.7	16.6
CAROLINA FSB	CHARLESTON	SC	**E-**	E+	D-	60	-3.80	2.3	1.4	43.1	0.0	**2.1**	6.2	9.1
CAROLINA PREMIER BANK	CHARLOTTE	NC	**D-**	C-	C-	158	46.68	10.0	0.4	13.4	19.3	**5.1**	8.4	11.1
CAROLINA TRUST BANK	LINCOLNTON	NC	**D**	D-	C+	268	-0.42	10.7	1.8	18.0	10.1	**6.0**	8.3	11.7
CARROLL BANK & TRUST	HUNTINGDON	TN	**C+**	B-	B	249	6.03	3.5	9.1	23.6	24.6	**6.5**	8.5	14.1
CARROLL COMMUNITY BANK	SYKESVILLE	MD	**E+**	NR	NR	96	N/A	0.0	0.2	54.2	19.6	**4.0**	6.0	13.9
CARROLL COUNTY SAVINGS &	CARROLLTON	MO	**C+**	C+	C-	26	0.34	0.0	0.7	38.5	42.0	**10.0**	11.3	36.0
CARROLL COUNTY STATE BK	CARROLL	IA	**C+**	B-	B-	324	0.54	10.5	1.3	13.2	19.9	**5.7**	8.2	11.5
▼ CARROLL COUNTY TC	CARROLLTON	MO	**B+**	A-	A-	115	9.35	5.1	2.5	6.4	46.4	**9.2**	11.5	14.4
▲ CARROLLTON BANK	CARROLLTON	IL	**C**	B-	B-	950	14.49	16.8	2.2	10.3	25.2	**5.2**	7.2	11.7
▼ CARROLLTON BANK	COLUMBIA	MD	**D-**	D+	D	386	-8.57	7.8	0.2	21.3	8.4	**4.7**	9.0	10.8
CARROLLTON FEDERAL BANK	CARROLLTON	KY	**C**	C-	D+	36	4.24	0.6	4.2	46.4	11.3	**10.0**	11.0	20.2
CARSON BANK	MULVANE	KS	**D-**	D	D+	80	0.04	11.7	2.9	16.5	22.7	**6.0**	8.0	13.8
CARSON NATIONAL BK OF	AUBURN	NE	**B-**	C+	B-	62	14.14	6.0	2.3	8.3	43.3	**10.0**	12.2	23.0
CARTER BANK & TRUST	MARTINSVILLE	VA	**C**	C	C-	3,706	9.36	3.1	1.1	4.7	29.5	**4.9**	6.9	11.9

Asset Quality Index	Non-Performing Loans as a % of Total Loans	Non-Performing Loans as a % of Capital	Net Charge-offs Avg Loans	Profitability Index	Net Income ($Mil)	Return on Assets (R.O.A.)	Return on Equity (R.O.E.)	Net Interest Spread	Overhead Efficiency Ratio	Liquidity Index	Liquidity Ratio	Hot Money Ratio	Stability Index
5.9	0.08	0.6	1.52	0.4	-0.1	-0.42	-5.06	3.54	86.0	3.1	27.1	15.1	3.2
1.9	5.07	31.4	4.11	0.0	-0.2	-0.56	-6.65	2.99	80.1	4.4	40.5	13.0	2.7
5.8	1.52	6.1	0.60	0.7	-0.5	-0.48	-4.30	3.82	109.6	5.2	43.1	9.7	5.6
2.5	1.52	11.7	0.96	2.8	0.5	0.29	3.27	4.15	77.0	4.0	16.7	8.6	3.9
6.9	3.28	8.8	0.00	3.0	2.1	0.52	2.21	2.48	76.5	3.0	54.9	30.5	8.2
0.6	5.53	37.6	1.05	2.4	4.1	0.39	3.45	3.76	68.3	2.2	13.2	18.3	5.9
3.5	1.59	12.2	0.36	5.9	6.5	1.12	12.01	3.68	51.8	3.9	12.5	9.2	6.1
6.6	0.97	6.6	0.14	4.0	12.6	0.65	6.67	3.02	68.1	2.4	24.0	20.3	7.9
1.6	4.39	17.2	4.76	1.2	0.6	0.32	3.14	3.34	56.5	1.2	28.8	47.0	3.6
8.4	0.00	0.0	0.00	0.7	0.1	0.11	0.91	3.49	89.7	1.4	31.6	42.3	2.2
3.4	2.13	17.6	1.62	0.4	-0.3	-0.20	-2.62	4.34	80.0	2.9	18.5	14.7	2.5
6.8	3.04	8.7	-0.18	2.5	0.1	0.34	4.02	4.04	89.5	6.0	70.5	10.1	4.5
0.0	5.70	51.1	3.59	0.0	-59.5	-3.52	-39.51	3.34	88.0	0.9	14.5	34.8	4.1
6.5	0.25	2.1	0.13	5.0	2.0	0.81	9.13	4.66	73.0	1.6	16.2	22.6	5.0
3.3	2.60	18.6	0.16	3.1	1.4	0.50	6.34	3.48	61.0	2.0	13.3	19.1	4.1
7.1	0.00	0.0	0.00	10.0	19.2	13.43	19.67	3.30	78.8	9.8	184.1	0.0	4.7
1.1	2.57	22.7	0.33	5.3	2.1	0.84	10.32	4.59	63.8	0.9	12.1	32.8	4.4
8.6	0.38	2.0	0.16	1.9	0.6	0.36	2.73	3.77	79.5	2.1	29.5	22.9	3.4
8.5	0.00	0.0	0.01	3.5	0.2	0.45	2.74	3.63	87.4	6.0	54.7	6.7	7.6
2.0	9.56	31.0	0.91	0.0	-2.3	-2.02	-19.24	2.61	153.5	1.9	34.8	31.4	5.7
0.7	3.75	23.9	1.77	1.7	1.1	0.04	0.37	4.42	85.3	4.5	17.6	6.2	7.6
3.8	0.90	6.1	1.16	2.6	2.0	0.49	6.33	3.35	74.6	1.8	22.7	22.1	3.5
1.6	1.82	8.5	1.91	0.0	-2.3	-2.00	-14.62	3.81	207.5	1.8	29.4	28.0	5.0
1.6	2.31	13.8	8.63	10.0	2,276.9	3.16	41.46	10.60	38.9	0.9	18.7	42.3	7.1
1.1	3.33	21.7	2.23	3.7	732.9	0.83	4.33	5.07	72.6	4.3	24.1	10.8	5.9
1.7	2.02	12.9	0.67	1.8	0.2	0.13	1.35	3.80	92.5	1.2	10.6	27.4	3.6
1.3	5.67	40.3	2.90	0.1	-4.9	-0.68	-7.84	3.21	71.1	3.1	13.1	13.3	3.6
3.7	2.39	14.8	0.14	3.3	3.1	0.75	7.00	4.17	70.0	1.7	18.7	21.8	4.3
0.7	6.35	27.2	4.03	3.2	51.6	0.89	5.86	4.94	39.4	0.9	17.0	37.5	4.0
3.7	1.05	7.4	0.46	5.4	2.2	0.93	11.00	3.94	49.7	1.1	23.9	33.6	5.0
0.0	13.42	157.5	0.10	0.6	0.3	0.08	1.85	2.93	97.3	0.6	8.7	46.3	0.4
9.0	0.54	2.0	0.00	4.0	61.8	0.71	6.64	1.97	45.6	4.0	52.2	20.5	9.0
0.0	9.68	81.6	3.68	0.0	-2.8	-1.46	-24.22	3.96	87.4	2.1	13.1	18.3	2.6
0.0	24.83	72.5	8.24	0.0	-534.8	-5.62	-30.39	0.81	68.7	1.8	35.8	100.0	5.7
1.7	2.05	16.3	0.80	3.2	0.3	0.16	1.90	4.27	73.2	1.3	10.8	25.9	4.5
8.4	0.05	0.2	0.00	0.0	-3.1	-0.79	-4.49	2.47	116.2	2.0	37.6	32.5	1.5
4.4	0.49	3.9	0.46	1.5	0.9	0.28	2.34	3.91	82.2	1.1	8.4	29.2	6.0
5.3	0.40	1.9	0.58	3.7	1.2	0.63	4.72	4.08	57.2	1.0	25.4	39.2	5.7
8.0	0.47	3.2	0.32	5.6	23.2	1.17	10.73	3.77	54.0	1.0	2.4	27.8	8.3
1.7	4.19	38.4	0.10	3.9	1.3	0.40	5.05	3.69	67.8	1.7	8.2	19.6	4.4
8.1	0.05	0.2	0.15	8.5	2.9	1.41	15.62	3.98	59.0	4.2	46.6	15.6	7.4
7.5	1.32	3.0	-0.07	4.5	0.6	1.11	8.60	4.13	67.2	3.3	78.4	33.5	7.4
3.4	4.25	19.6	0.18	1.3	0.1	0.55	6.63	3.39	106.6	3.8	63.0	18.0	3.6
4.1	1.83	11.4	0.62	1.1	0.5	0.25	2.32	3.36	71.1	0.9	21.4	39.9	2.1
0.0	5.84	46.3	2.43	0.6	-2.2	-0.32	-4.16	3.69	68.4	1.4	17.7	26.9	3.7
5.3	1.30	7.5	0.87	4.3	1.7	0.50	4.23	4.67	72.6	1.8	17.1	21.3	6.6
0.0	18.28	213.5	0.86	0.1	-1.0	-1.62	-23.40	3.75	110.8	1.3	6.6	25.6	2.1
3.7	1.82	15.3	0.87	0.3	0.7	0.55	5.53	3.42	104.9	1.8	22.5	22.4	1.1
1.6	2.36	18.4	0.96	0.9	0.2	0.08	0.98	3.86	71.1	1.1	18.7	31.7	3.5
4.0	1.60	10.7	0.48	3.8	1.3	0.54	5.72	4.46	76.0	1.6	25.0	26.3	4.9
0.3	4.74	45.4	0.00	0.1	-0.1	-0.14	-2.31	N/,	104.5	3.6	33.2	14.5	0.8
7.7	2.05	7.5	0.00	2.9	0.1	0.28	2.52	1.74	63.0	5.1	62.5	13.3	5.3
2.4	2.21	16.5	0.64	3.9	1.8	0.56	7.01	4.51	70.0	1.4	17.7	26.2	5.4
5.5	1.84	6.9	0.22	5.3	1.6	1.45	11.28	4.05	67.5	2.3	33.1	23.3	7.7
3.6	0.90	7.6	0.27	4.6	10.3	1.16	16.36	2.90	60.0	1.9	26.6	22.6	5.0
1.9	1.56	12.7	1.25	1.1	-0.9	-0.22	-2.60	3.83	82.7	1.4	5.8	23.1	2.8
5.4	0.51	3.1	0.10	2.4	0.1	0.36	3.14	3.70	84.4	2.5	25.5	17.9	5.4
2.6	1.48	10.0	2.95	0.0	-1.0	-1.21	-14.34	3.98	84.1	2.8	20.8	15.5	3.6
7.6	1.13	3.9	0.00	3.9	0.5	0.89	7.05	3.28	65.0	3.1	27.5	15.1	6.5
5.4	0.90	6.3	0.02	3.2	25.3	0.72	7.93	2.94	71.1	3.0	35.2	24.1	5.9

Name	City	State	Rating	2008 Rating	2007 Rating	Total Assets ($Mil)	One Year Asset Growth	Asset Mix (As a % of Total Assets) Comm-ercial Loans	Cons-umer Loans	Home Mort-gages	Secur-ities	Capital-ization Index	Leverage Ratio	Risk-based Capital Ratio
▼ CARTER COUNTY BK	ELIZABETHTON	TN	**C+**	C-	B-	272	-5.07	5.7	3.2	25.3	19.1	**6.7**	8.7	14.0
CARTHAGE FS&LA	CARTHAGE	NY	**B-**	B-	B-	168	3.95	0.1	4.9	71.6	7.4	**7.7**	9.5	20.0
CARVER FSB	NEW YORK	NY	**D-**	D-	D-	744	-8.35	7.2	0.1	11.2	9.5	**4.4**	6.4	10.8
▲ CARVER STATE BK	SAVANNAH	GA	**D-**	D-	D-	45	9.29	10.4	5.1	29.1	10.1	**5.1**	7.1	11.8
▼ CASCADE BANK	EVERETT	WA	**E**	D-	C-	1,499	-12.11	7.8	0.4	14.3	19.1	**2.6**	5.6	9.6
CASEY COUNTY BANK	LIBERTY	KY	**B+**	A-	A	162	7.96	4.3	8.1	25.9	22.2	**10.0**	11.2	17.4
CASEY STATE BK	CASEY	IL	**B-**	B-	C+	253	5.52	20.1	5.0	18.6	27.7	**6.3**	8.3	12.1
CASHMERE VALLEY BANK	CASHMERE	WA	**B**	B	B	1,095	6.74	6.7	7.9	7.9	39.2	**5.8**	7.8	14.7
CASS COMMERCIAL BANK	BRIDGETON	MO	**B**	B-	B	581	17.06	21.7	0.0	1.2	0.0	**4.4**	8.9	10.7
▲ CASS COUNTY BANK INC	PLATTSMOUTH	NE	**C-**	C-	C+	50	-1.40	11.2	2.5	31.0	5.2	**10.0**	11.2	18.1
▲ CASTLE ROCK BANK	CASTLE ROCK	CO	**D**	D-	D+	104	-7.37	2.4	1.3	21.9	12.7	**7.8**	9.5	14.8
CASTLE ROCK BANK	CASTLE ROCK	MN	**A-**	A-	A	141	6.36	14.1	4.0	10.6	46.6	**10.0**	12.8	23.5
CASTROVILLE STATE BK	CASTROVILLE	TX	**B**	B	B	112	14.67	1.6	7.0	10.8	49.8	**6.5**	8.5	19.5
CATAHOULA-LASALLE BANK	JONESVILLE	LA	**B**	B	A-	98	0.82	12.4	14.3	2.8	14.5	**10.0**	11.1	21.6
▲ CATHAY BANK	EL MONTE	CA	**D+**	D+	C+	10,788	-6.78	13.4	0.1	8.3	26.3	**10.0**	11.0	16.7
CATSKILL HUDSON BANK	ROCK HILL	NY	**C-**	C	C-	322	16.88	13.7	0.7	5.6	42.3	**5.0**	7.0	13.7
▼ CATTARAUGUS COUNTY	LITTLE VALLEY	NY	**C**	C+	C+	174	12.51	9.4	1.4	23.1	25.0	**5.1**	7.1	12.5
▼ CATTLE NATIONAL BK & TRUS	SEWARD	NE	**B**	B+	B	185	5.51	4.6	1.3	17.0	19.6	**9.5**	10.7	15.1
CATTLEMANS NATIONAL BK	ROUND MOUNTAIN	TX	**D**	D	D+	76	2.91	4.5	2.5	7.5	0.3	**6.1**	8.1	13.0
CAYUGA LAKE NATIONAL BK	UNION SPRINGS	NY	**A-**	A-	A-	109	4.42	5.0	4.5	35.3	34.5	**9.4**	10.6	20.0
CB&S BANK	RUSSELLVILLE	AL	**D+**	D	B-	1,231	-9.07	6.7	1.8	11.5	37.9	**8.2**	9.8	17.4
▼ CBANK	CINCINNATI	OH	**C**	C-	C-	71	18.33	32.6	3.7	6.5	9.1	**10.0**	19.5	26.5
CBC BANK	BOWLING GREEN	MO	**C-**	C	C+	33	0.14	7.0	1.9	14.1	9.9	**8.4**	9.9	18.8
CBC NATIONAL BK	FERNANDINA BEACH	FL	**D-**	D-	D+	427	-7.37	2.4	0.5	30.2	9.3	**6.6**	8.6	14.5
▲ CBW BANK	WEIR	KS	**D+**	D+	E+	7	2.61	18.2	4.6	17.4	35.5	**10.0**	13.2	26.4
▼ CCB COMMUNITY BANK	ANDALUSIA	AL	**C-**	B-	B	388	5.14	9.7	3.3	17.2	7.5	**6.0**	8.5	11.7
CECIL BANK	ELKTON	MD	**D-**	D-	D	486	-4.41	2.8	0.8	20.8	2.4	**5.9**	7.9	14.5
▼ CECILIAN BANK	CECILIA	KY	**B-**	B	B	471	15.81	2.7	3.2	20.5	32.2	**6.0**	8.0	13.1
CEDAR HILL NATIONAL BK	CHARLOTTE	NC	**A-**	A-	B+	11	4.71	0.0	3.6	0.0	74.2	**10.0**	87.5	173.6
CEDAR RAPIDS BANK &	CEDAR RAPIDS	IA	**C-**	C	C	548	0.72	20.5	0.9	7.7	21.0	**7.1**	9.0	14.1
▼ CEDAR RAPIDS STATE BK	CEDAR RAPIDS	NE	**D**	D+	D	31	14.99	11.4	2.2	2.1	11.8	**5.1**	9.3	11.0
▼ CEDAR SECURITY BANK	FORDYCE	NE	**B-**	B+	B+	37	16.19	13.3	5.7	7.0	5.8	**8.2**	12.0	13.5
CEDAR VALLEY BANK &	LA PORTE CITY	IA	**D**	D	D+	44	9.99	18.2	4.6	11.5	19.6	**5.7**	7.7	12.2
CEDARSTONE BANK	LEBANON	TN	**D**	D	D-	146	-2.08	13.1	3.4	15.9	17.9	**6.6**	8.6	12.5
CELTIC BANK	SALT LAKE CITY	UT	**D**	D-	C	222	6.06	17.0	0.2	4.9	0.0	**10.0**	12.9	16.2
CENBANK	BUFFALO LAKE	MN	**C+**	C+	B	46	12.08	3.8	4.6	9.4	34.0	**5.1**	7.1	11.7
CENLAR FSB	TRENTON	NJ	**C+**	C	C+	581	10.23	0.0	2.0	8.2	78.9	**6.6**	8.6	22.0
CENTENNIAL BANK	CONWAY	AR	**C-**	C	B-	3,746	40.00	6.1	1.4	13.3	12.5	**9.0**	10.3	15.6
CENTENNIAL BANK	FOUNTAIN VALLEY	CA	**D-**	D-	B	765	-9.78	0.0	0.0	2.0	4.2	**9.2**	11.1	14.3
▼ CENTENNIAL BANK	CENTENNIAL	CO	**D+**	C	B	87	198.67	9.9	1.7	2.9	44.7	**10.0**	11.1	23.3
▼ CENTENNIAL BANK	OMAHA	NE	**D**	C	B-	69	14.33	27.3	2.1	17.8	8.7	**8.3**	11.9	13.6
▼ CENTER BANK	LOS ANGELES	CA	**C-**	C-	B-	2,271	3.69	16.4	1.9	0.3	12.8	**10.0**	12.5	18.5
CENTER NATIONAL BK	LITCHFIELD	MN	**B**	B	B	182	7.07	9.2	6.3	6.5	46.9	**8.4**	9.9	17.1
CENTER POINT BANK & TRUST	CENTER POINT	IA	**B**	B	B	27	-7.80	8.4	3.9	26.0	18.2	**6.3**	8.5	12.0
CENTERA BANK	SUBLETTE	KS	**B**	B	B-	222	7.11	6.2	2.9	5.7	44.0	**5.8**	7.8	13.8
CENTERBANK	MILFORD	OH	**D**	C-	E-	105	1.41	13.6	0.4	14.5	6.9	**6.7**	9.0	12.3
CENTERBANK OF	JACKSONVILLE	FL	**D-**	D-	E	174	-5.97	17.0	0.8	7.7	5.5	**5.1**	7.7	11.1
▲ CENTERPOINTE COMMUNITY	HOOD RIVER	OR	**D+**	C-	C	71	17.09	10.9	0.3	7.4	7.8	**5.8**	8.7	11.6
CENTERSTATE BK OF	WINTER HAVEN	FL	**C**	C	B-	1,838	108.69	5.7	3.0	15.0	26.3	**5.9**	7.9	16.1
▼ CENTIER BANK	MERRILLVILLE	IN	**D**	C-	B	2,001	-0.48	5.3	0.4	23.2	7.9	**5.1**	8.8	11.1
CENTINEL BANK OF TAOS	TAOS	NM	**B+**	B+	B+	165	-4.12	2.2	1.6	20.0	33.2	**6.7**	8.7	18.2
CENTRA BANK INC	MORGANTOWN	WV	**B-**	B-	B-	1,373	6.31	9.9	1.6	19.5	9.4	**8.5**	10.0	14.7
CENTRAL ARIZONA BANK	CASA GRANDE	AZ	**E-**	D-	D+	76	-19.69	9.6	0.5	3.9	0.1	**0.0**	2.2	4.5
▼ CENTRAL BANK	LITTLE ROCK	AR	**D**	C-	B+	84	-0.99	3.0	0.1	5.8	20.6	**10.0**	12.8	18.1
CENTRAL BANK	TAMPA	FL	**D-**	C-	C-	74	11.12	11.6	0.2	1.4	18.0	**7.5**	9.3	13.4
CENTRAL BANK	STORM LAKE	IA	**B-**	B-	C+	432	5.62	30.8	2.0	15.5	4.4	**5.5**	9.8	11.4
CENTRAL BANK	STILLWATER	MN	**C+**	B	C+	777	-9.74	11.2	1.8	10.5	10.9	**5.9**	7.9	15.3
CENTRAL BANK	LEBANON	MO	**C**	D+	B-	254	-2.52	8.9	1.7	21.8	16.9	**9.2**	10.5	14.6
CENTRAL BANK	SAVANNAH	TN	**C+**	C+	B+	167	8.34	6.6	12.2	38.0	6.7	**7.0**	9.1	12.5
CENTRAL BANK	HOUSTON	TX	**C**	C-	D+	395	8.59	11.7	0.8	3.2	32.3	**6.6**	8.6	14.6

Asset Quality Index	Non-Performing Loans as a % of Total Loans	Non-Performing Loans as a % of Capital	Net Charge-offs / Avg Loans	Profitability Index	Net Income ($Mil)	Return on Assets (R.O.A.)	Return on Equity (R.O.E.)	Net Interest Spread	Overhead Efficiency Ratio	Liquidity Index	Liquidity Ratio	Hot Money Ratio	Stability Index
2.6	2.12	14.9	0.86	**4.6**	2.6	0.92	10.87	3.85	63.2	**2.6**	16.2	16.2	**5.5**
6.9	0.28	2.4	0.02	**3.8**	1.3	0.76	8.73	3.46	68.9	**1.7**	15.3	22.2	**5.0**
0.0	14.88	136.8	1.95	**0.4**	-32.3	-4.11	-50.73	3.91	83.4	**1.7**	17.7	22.4	**3.5**
2.4	2.32	18.5	1.27	**3.2**	0.2	0.47	6.61	4.97	79.7	**1.3**	17.1	27.8	**1.7**
0.3	4.85	43.6	5.07	**0.0**	-70.0	-4.25	-62.32	2.51	152.2	**3.2**	13.4	13.2	**3.8**
4.3	0.95	5.5	0.39	**5.0**	1.4	0.88	7.51	4.34	65.6	**1.7**	12.1	21.4	**7.0**
4.4	1.27	9.4	0.17	**7.3**	4.5	1.84	20.56	3.77	48.8	**2.5**	22.0	17.1	**5.0**
4.7	1.19	7.1	1.01	**4.3**	9.8	0.92	10.58	3.35	59.2	**4.2**	37.9	15.9	**6.5**
6.9	0.04	0.3	-0.01	**8.4**	7.1	1.34	14.62	4.51	45.6	**1.3**	12.3	26.7	**6.4**
2.2	1.37	7.9	0.45	**3.5**	0.2	0.43	3.94	4.47	81.2	**1.8**	23.6	22.5	**5.7**
1.1	4.39	24.4	2.00	**1.0**	-0.2	-0.18	-1.85	4.49	73.7	**1.6**	16.7	22.9	**3.9**
6.5	1.67	6.1	0.51	**5.9**	1.8	1.33	10.47	3.75	50.1	**3.9**	48.9	17.6	**8.6**
8.3	0.38	1.6	0.19	**4.8**	1.0	0.94	10.10	3.45	63.9	**2.0**	41.1	37.4	**5.4**
4.6	2.13	7.6	0.35	**5.3**	1.0	1.08	9.10	5.27	72.5	**3.1**	51.0	23.7	**7.3**
1.4	3.63	17.5	1.83	**1.0**	14.8	0.13	1.04	2.83	52.6	**0.8**	15.6	51.6	**7.2**
2.7	1.33	9.0	0.47	**3.7**	1.9	0.62	8.29	4.22	65.7	**1.2**	17.0	29.1	**3.1**
4.0	1.47	10.8	-0.05	**2.7**	0.5	0.28	3.28	4.66	89.5	**4.8**	19.6	4.2	**4.0**
3.2	1.21	7.8	0.26	**5.9**	2.5	1.41	13.03	4.18	61.3	**2.5**	12.3	16.4	**7.2**
5.0	0.92	6.2	0.01	**1.1**	0.0	0.01	0.10	3.89	97.0	**5.0**	35.4	8.2	**3.6**
9.5	0.03	0.2	0.02	**6.6**	1.3	1.24	12.65	4.43	59.8	**1.9**	25.3	22.1	**6.1**
1.5	6.17	27.6	1.73	**2.0**	7.6	0.59	6.05	3.87	78.0	**3.5**	23.5	14.2	**5.0**
8.0	0.17	0.7	1.32	**1.7**	0.2	0.31	1.48	3.88	64.7	**0.9**	23.2	44.5	**3.4**
7.5	0.31	1.5	0.32	**2.2**	0.1	0.19	1.87	3.71	94.3	**5.0**	39.0	9.4	**5.7**
0.3	6.78	51.5	0.89	**0.0**	-1.4	-0.32	-3.51	3.12	95.7	**0.6**	8.0	39.5	**2.3**
8.2	0.70	2.4	0.61	**0.0**	-0.1	-1.10	-7.71	4.32	120.5	**5.4**	49.7	7.2	**4.8**
2.3	1.44	12.2	0.35	**5.9**	5.3	1.40	16.78	4.67	57.9	**0.8**	12.0	34.7	**5.7**
0.0	14.32	102.1	1.10	**2.0**	1.2	0.24	2.82	3.85	62.7	**0.8**	12.2	33.8	**4.5**
4.8	0.78	5.2	0.32	**4.1**	3.3	0.74	7.99	3.63	68.1	**1.8**	20.9	21.5	**4.9**
9.9	0.00	0.0	0.00	**9.5**	0.5	5.35	6.27	0.82	76.1	**10.0**	351.8	0.0	**8.0**
2.4	2.79	17.5	0.88	**3.8**	3.6	0.65	7.19	3.11	56.7	**0.9**	8.6	31.7	**5.2**
4.8	0.00	0.0	0.50	**2.9**	0.1	0.46	4.90	4.20	82.4	**1.6**	8.2	21.1	**2.3**
2.9	2.30	14.3	-0.01	**6.9**	0.4	1.14	9.35	4.63	62.6	**3.9**	19.5	10.1	**7.3**
2.9	0.63	5.0	0.75	**4.2**	0.4	1.01	13.32	4.89	68.4	**4.3**	17.9	6.8	**3.4**
5.8	0.01	0.1	0.07	**1.4**	0.7	0.47	5.45	3.64	79.9	**0.7**	13.3	42.2	**2.4**
0.0	9.20	51.8	3.95	**9.3**	3.8	1.74	14.88	7.09	50.3	**2.6**	11.8	15.5	**7.5**
5.9	0.64	5.0	0.00	**4.0**	0.4	0.95	13.34	4.09	74.0	**3.9**	13.4	9.2	**2.9**
4.3	1.46	1.8	0.45	**8.8**	14.7	2.43	44.97	2.97	82.7	**3.2**	84.6	92.7	**3.6**
2.0	3.10	17.5	2.80	**4.3**	20.8	0.64	5.27	4.32	43.4	**1.2**	13.5	29.7	**8.6**
0.0	11.91	75.2	1.50	**3.4**	3.2	0.39	3.77	3.02	33.6	**0.5**	13.8	67.9	**6.7**
7.0	1.11	3.4	0.03	**0.0**	-1.7	-5.69	-25.76	2.40	347.3	**2.7**	63.3	39.9	**6.8**
1.0	5.03	25.6	0.55	**0.5**	-0.4	-0.64	-4.90	4.22	86.2	**1.6**	18.9	24.2	**6.6**
0.8	2.79	13.6	1.75	**3.4**	24.0	1.08	8.72	3.22	50.0	**1.0**	16.9	33.2	**7.0**
5.7	0.79	3.5	0.44	**5.1**	2.2	1.23	11.58	3.91	63.1	**4.3**	26.0	8.7	**4.8**
7.1	0.00	0.0	0.00	**6.4**	0.3	1.09	13.48	4.52	61.5	**4.0**	17.9	8.9	**5.6**
5.7	0.77	4.6	0.19	**5.5**	2.8	1.33	14.18	4.23	65.8	**2.6**	25.4	17.1	**5.6**
3.6	1.09	8.7	1.52	**1.9**	0.3	0.24	2.74	3.95	64.2	**1.6**	17.9	23.2	**4.0**
0.3	7.93	61.5	2.21	**0.0**	-10.2	-5.73	-52.38	2.53	147.4	**0.8**	21.3	46.2	**2.9**
8.5	0.00	0.0	0.00	**1.6**	0.3	0.44	4.83	5.18	88.8	**2.2**	25.2	19.0	**2.6**
3.7	3.49	20.7	2.13	**2.8**	5.5	0.46	5.33	4.74	85.4	**2.7**	29.4	23.5	**5.9**
0.7	4.43	34.9	0.82	**4.9**	10.2	0.51	6.33	4.31	55.9	**3.0**	13.0	14.0	**6.3**
4.9	0.79	4.2	0.18	**7.1**	3.6	2.05	23.90	4.18	64.4	**4.3**	37.8	12.5	**7.2**
4.4	1.72	11.6	0.47	**4.1**	8.6	0.63	5.86	3.57	66.4	**1.8**	11.1	20.1	**7.8**
0.3	9.64	119.2	5.06	**0.0**	-5.6	-6.61	-172.06	2.91	342.6	**2.2**	28.3	20.8	**2.1**
0.0	5.04	24.2	6.86	**0.2**	-1.5	-1.68	-11.49	3.31	61.6	**1.3**	17.0	28.1	**2.0**
0.0	7.40	42.0	1.87	**0.0**	-1.0	-1.27	-12.15	2.96	85.9	**1.1**	26.8	39.4	**1.0**
4.1	0.96	7.9	0.02	**7.9**	6.0	1.44	14.83	4.49	55.9	**1.2**	7.7	27.4	**6.3**
2.8	0.42	3.1	0.90	**6.9**	11.1	1.35	17.19	5.94	64.2	**1.6**	9.0	21.0	**7.1**
5.1	0.61	3.7	1.24	**3.2**	2.1	0.81	8.08	4.28	73.9	**1.9**	21.3	20.2	**4.7**
3.3	0.89	7.2	0.40	**4.6**	0.7	0.41	4.48	3.94	64.4	**0.6**	9.2	39.4	**5.6**
5.0	0.88	5.2	0.27	**3.5**	3.9	1.02	11.81	4.57	73.8	**1.6**	21.4	24.9	**4.6**

Name	City	State	Rating	2008 Rating	2007 Rating	Total Assets ($Mil)	One Year Asset Growth	Asset Mix (As a % of Total Assets) Comm-ercial Loans	Cons-umer Loans	Home Mort-gages	Secur-ities	Capital-ization Index	Leverage Ratio	Risk-based Capital Ratio
▲ CENTRAL BANK	PROVO	UT	**C-**	D	B-	634	0.97	5.8	1.7	5.4	28.3	**10.0**	15.1	22.0
CENTRAL BANK & TRUST	LANDER	WY	**C**	C	B	156	-0.70	9.9	4.8	19.3	40.7	**9.2**	10.4	20.9
CENTRAL BANK & TRUST CO	HUTCHINSON	KS	**C-**	C-	C	228	3.59	8.8	1.1	11.1	10.1	**7.2**	9.1	13.7
▲ CENTRAL BANK & TRUST CO	LEXINGTON	KY	**D+**	C-	C+	1,760	7.30	11.1	7.8	14.1	5.7	**3.9**	7.5	10.5
CENTRAL BANK ILLINOIS	GENESEO	IL	**D+**	D+	C-	385	0.83	4.6	2.1	12.7	29.3	**6.9**	9.2	12.4
CENTRAL BANK OF GEORGIA	ELLAVILLE	GA	**E-**	D-	C	270	-17.11	4.7	3.4	23.7	6.3	**1.6**	5.1	8.6
CENTRAL BANK OF KANSAS CI	KANSAS CITY	MO	**C-**	C	C	171	-8.21	16.7	1.6	11.8	4.2	**10.0**	12.1	19.2
▼ CENTRAL BANK OF MISSOURI	SEDALIA	MO	**C**	B	B+	81	-2.64	3.9	2.0	35.8	11.3	**7.8**	9.5	14.9
CENTRAL BK LAKE OF THE OZ	OSAGE BEACH	MO	**C**	C+	C+	493	-0.75	5.9	4.5	16.9	12.6	**5.4**	7.9	11.3
CENTRAL BK OF JEFFERSON	LOUISVILLE	KY	**D**	D+	C-	181	-4.15	8.1	3.0	25.7	3.5	**4.7**	8.5	10.9
CENTRAL CO-OP BANK	SOMERVILLE	MA	**C**	C-	D-	512	-8.25	0.5	0.2	36.5	5.5	**7.1**	9.1	16.2
▼ CENTRAL FLORIDA STATE BK	BELLEVIEW	FL	**E+**	D-	D+	83	-15.57	6.3	1.1	13.2	2.8	**3.7**	6.9	10.4
▼ CENTRAL FS&LA	CICERO	IL	**D+**	C-	C+	192	5.86	0.0	0.0	45.9	11.4	**9.0**	10.3	20.7
CENTRAL FS&LA OF CHICAGO	CHICAGO	IL	**B-**	B-	B	102	-3.15	0.0	0.1	25.2	0.0	**10.0**	20.4	26.3
CENTRAL FS&LA OF ROLLA	ROLLA	MO	**B-**	B-	C+	61	2.01	3.2	1.5	53.6	0.0	**10.0**	21.0	37.0
CENTRAL KENTUCKY FSB	DANVILLE	KY	**D+**	D+	C-	129	-0.21	2.1	1.7	61.6	8.4	**7.7**	9.5	17.3
CENTRAL NATIONAL BK	JUNCTION CITY	KS	**D+**	D+	D+	837	0.51	5.2	2.7	14.0	20.8	**9.4**	10.6	17.1
CENTRAL NATIONAL BK	WACO	TX	**B**	B	B-	594	7.74	16.8	2.2	20.4	10.1	**6.0**	8.0	12.8
CENTRAL NATIONAL BK & TRU	ATTICA	IN	**B-**	B	B+	56	0.11	1.4	2.5	17.0	50.3	**10.0**	21.5	37.5
▲ CENTRAL NATIONAL BK & TRU	ENID	OK	**D+**	D	D	504	-1.62	8.9	10.4	16.6	10.9	**6.4**	8.4	12.1
CENTRAL NATIONAL BK OF AL	ALVA	OK	**C**	B	A	253	4.23	6.0	1.9	3.5	48.8	**10.0**	11.7	24.1
CENTRAL NATIONAL BK OF PO	POTEAU	OK	**B+**	B+	A-	207	7.94	6.1	4.4	14.0	36.1	**6.4**	8.4	17.9
CENTRAL PACIFIC BANK	HONOLULU	HI	**E**	D-	D	3,939	-19.06	5.3	2.9	14.8	17.9	**2.5**	4.8	9.7
CENTRAL PROGRESSIVE	LACOMBE	LA	**E-**	E-	E+	422	-0.02	2.8	1.8	8.4	2.2	**2.1**	6.3	9.1
CENTRAL SB	SAULT SAINTE MARIE	MI	**D+**	D+	B-	232	7.82	10.8	3.2	21.6	22.0	**7.7**	9.5	16.8
CENTRAL STATE BK	CALERA	AL	**B+**	B+	A-	148	-3.33	3.2	3.1	14.6	23.3	**10.0**	13.2	21.1
▼ CENTRAL STATE BK	ELKADER	IA	**C+**	A-	A-	158	55.85	10.4	2.6	19.7	10.1	**10.0**	15.1	20.3
CENTRAL STATE BK	MUSCATINE	IA	**C-**	C	B+	288	5.43	6.6	2.4	11.3	35.9	**6.3**	8.3	15.2
▼ CENTRAL STATE BK	STATE CENTER	IA	**C+**	B-	A-	147	16.83	10.9	0.9	5.1	46.7	**10.0**	12.8	18.3
▼ CENTRAL STATE BK	CLAYTON	IL	**C**	C+	C-	87	2.46	13.3	13.8	28.4	4.2	**10.0**	13.8	16.1
CENTRAL STATE BK	BEULAH	MI	**B**	B	B	64	2.52	4.0	1.0	19.4	5.5	**10.0**	12.8	20.4
CENTRAL TRUST BANK	JEFFERSON CITY	MO	**B**	B	B-	1,975	-3.58	4.2	3.9	8.5	42.6	**5.0**	7.0	17.2
▲ CENTRAL VALLEY BANK	TOPPENISH	WA	**C**	C+	B-	163	5.89	10.3	0.6	4.2	5.0	**8.3**	9.9	16.8
CENTRAL VALLEY	FRESNO	CA	**D+**	C-	B-	777	1.58	9.4	1.4	3.9	24.6	**7.5**	9.3	15.2
CENTRAL VIRGINIA BANK	POWHATAN	VA	**E-**	E+	C-	408	-13.55	13.7	1.7	15.7	27.0	**1.2**	4.9	8.2
CENTREBANK	VEEDERSBURG	IN	**D+**	D	D	56	-0.18	14.0	5.8	29.3	8.3	**7.3**	9.2	13.9
CENTREVILLE SB	WEST WARWICK	RI	**C+**	B-	B	992	5.46	0.3	0.5	32.6	52.9	**10.0**	19.6	51.8
CENTRIC BANK	HARRISBURG	PA	**D+**	D-	D	200	24.04	11.2	0.7	16.6	11.8	**7.1**	9.1	13.3
CENTRIX BANK & TRUST	BEDFORD	NH	**C**	C+	C+	684	15.66	16.3	0.2	6.6	26.1	**5.0**	7.0	11.9
CENTRUE BANK	STREATOR	IL	**D-**	D-	B	1,132	-13.44	7.2	0.3	11.2	19.2	**3.2**	6.4	10.1
▼ CENTRUST BANK NA	NORTHBROOK	IL	**E-**	E	D	103	-14.20	23.2	0.2	5.9	7.6	**4.2**	7.8	10.6
CENTURY BANK	LUCEDALE	MS	**B-**	B-	B+	240	-1.70	4.5	16.1	11.7	25.2	**7.8**	9.5	13.9
▼ CENTURY BANK	SANTA FE	NM	**D+**	C+	B	521	4.21	16.7	0.5	8.1	33.2	**9.8**	10.9	16.7
▼ CENTURY BANK	EUGENE	OR	**C-**	C	C+	90	-1.48	24.9	0.9	7.1	0.2	**10.0**	12.3	16.1
▼ CENTURY BANK & TRUST	MILLEDGEVILLE	GA	**C-**	B	A	208	5.56	6.7	2.5	16.8	32.8	**7.6**	9.4	16.5
CENTURY BANK & TRUST	COLDWATER	MI	**C-**	B+	A-	249	2.90	13.1	3.1	17.2	14.8	**10.0**	11.3	16.3
CENTURY BANK & TRUST CO	MEDFORD	MA	**C**	C	C	2,439	8.40	3.4	0.2	10.1	46.9	**4.1**	6.1	13.6
CENTURY BANK OF FLORIDA	TAMPA	FL	**D-**	D-	D+	74	-1.85	13.4	1.2	21.7	8.6	**6.3**	8.3	14.2
CENTURY BANK OF GEORGIA	CARTERSVILLE	GA	**D-**	D-	C	116	1.10	5.8	1.3	15.0	11.8	**9.2**	10.5	16.3
CENTURY BANK OF	LAWRENCEBURG	KY	**D-**	D-	D+	99	-4.88	3.5	2.5	35.9	20.4	**6.8**	8.8	15.0
▲ CENTURY BANK OF	PRYOR	OK	**C**	C	C	63	43.76	14.4	3.7	16.7	0.0	**7.6**	9.6	13.0
CENTURY BANK OF THE	GAINESVILLE	MO	**B-**	B	B	173	-0.28	6.5	4.5	26.2	7.6	**6.4**	8.4	12.9
CENTURY SAVINGS & LOAN	TRINIDAD	CO	**C+**	C+	C+	104	5.85	2.4	1.5	28.3	48.0	**10.0**	11.0	31.6
CENTURY SB	VINELAND	NJ	**C+**	C	C+	318	9.89	3.2	0.1	20.7	54.6	**10.0**	15.3	34.7
CERESCOBANK	CERESCO	NE	**B+**	B+	B	41	4.51	6.8	4.3	22.5	30.9	**10.0**	13.5	20.6
▲ CFBANK	FAIRLAWN	OH	**E+**	D	C+	274	0.73	13.8	0.3	11.1	10.6	**4.8**	6.8	11.0
CFG COMMUNITY BANK	BALTIMORE	MD	**D-**	D	E-	532	113.55	15.1	0.2	6.0	2.7	**6.4**	8.4	12.9
CHAIN BRIDGE BANK NA	MCLEAN	VA	**C+**	C	C-	189	11.85	5.9	0.3	12.7	47.4	**7.7**	9.4	17.0
▼ CHAMBERS BANK	DANVILLE	AR	**D**	B-	C-	743	-2.83	16.2	0.9	12.0	6.9	**8.0**	10.6	13.3
CHAMBERS STATE BK	CHAMBERS	NE	**B+**	B+	A-	36	12.89	4.5	3.6	1.4	4.3	**10.0**	26.1	37.7

Asset Quality Index	Non-Performing Loans as a % of Total Loans	Non-Performing Loans as a % of Capital	Net Charge-offs Avg Loans	Profitability Index	Net Income ($Mil)	Return on Assets (R.O.A.)	Return on Equity (R.O.E.)	Net Interest Spread	Overhead Efficiency Ratio	Liquidity Index	Liquidity Ratio	Hot Money Ratio	Stability Index
2.5	5.79	19.2	1.75	**4.2**	3.8	0.60	3.83	4.69	67.5	**1.8**	17.2	20.3	**8.5**
2.3	3.51	16.0	0.54	**6.9**	2.1	1.35	12.17	4.27	66.9	**1.7**	21.4	23.7	**6.3**
3.9	2.27	13.6	1.77	**3.2**	1.1	0.47	5.07	3.88	66.8	**1.0**	23.7	36.5	**4.8**
2.4	1.46	13.4	0.88	**2.8**	8.6	0.50	6.02	4.12	76.6	**1.4**	11.4	25.3	**5.5**
1.8	2.31	14.1	1.34	**5.3**	4.3	1.14	11.63	4.57	56.4	**3.3**	10.1	12.1	**4.9**
0.1	11.01	112.6	0.71	**0.0**	-4.6	-1.50	-26.05	2.93	130.5	**0.6**	12.6	49.2	**1.4**
1.3	6.04	29.1	1.45	**7.8**	3.0	1.70	13.22	5.14	63.2	**1.7**	27.6	26.6	**7.5**
0.3	4.63	32.5	1.66	**2.9**	0.2	0.23	2.00	3.92	63.6	**2.2**	8.4	17.2	**6.4**
1.0	2.94	24.3	0.61	**9.8**	8.1	1.62	20.14	5.07	51.3	**1.1**	5.5	28.1	**6.7**
0.3	1.95	17.8	1.10	**0.0**	-0.5	-0.25	-2.19	3.37	92.4	**0.7**	2.1	33.5	**4.5**
2.7	2.48	19.9	0.04	**3.6**	2.5	0.48	5.07	3.82	73.8	**2.9**	15.9	14.8	**4.6**
0.0	13.93	87.0	6.54	**0.0**	-4.8	-5.28	-58.54	3.14	117.9	**1.8**	21.9	22.0	**4.0**
3.1	3.43	19.4	-0.01	**1.1**	-0.5	-0.26	-2.33	3.03	85.6	**2.6**	35.6	20.8	**4.7**
4.3	1.86	8.0	0.04	**3.0**	0.4	0.37	1.86	4.09	80.5	**0.7**	10.0	40.7	**7.6**
7.2	1.73	7.1	0.07	**3.0**	0.3	0.41	2.01	3.52	78.0	**1.4**	12.3	24.8	**7.0**
1.8	3.59	28.5	0.40	**2.1**	0.3	0.23	2.28	3.55	71.2	**0.9**	13.8	33.1	**4.9**
1.6	2.75	13.9	1.90	**3.6**	5.7	0.69	6.32	3.83	71.3	**3.9**	17.0	9.3	**6.0**
4.5	1.22	9.7	0.51	**5.9**	7.6	1.31	15.57	3.59	55.8	**1.3**	24.4	30.0	**6.9**
9.2	0.00	0.0	2.22	**2.9**	0.4	0.63	2.89	3.33	66.7	**6.6**	77.1	7.0	**7.1**
1.6	1.79	15.3	1.28	**3.0**	2.6	0.53	6.21	4.15	75.1	**2.6**	18.1	16.2	**3.1**
2.6	8.48	23.5	1.28	**1.8**	0.3	0.10	0.79	4.21	93.0	**3.1**	48.5	25.1	**7.3**
4.7	1.88	11.4	0.07	**9.0**	4.0	2.03	22.16	4.47	58.1	**2.1**	18.2	18.7	**6.7**
0.3	11.34	65.0	6.33	**0.0**	-241.7	-5.54	-91.02	3.04	149.5	**4.2**	23.6	10.7	**4.9**
0.0	13.95	98.8	1.27	**0.0**	-3.3	-0.81	-9.34	3.95	129.4	**1.5**	15.2	25.1	**3.2**
1.8	1.03	5.1	0.82	**4.0**	1.8	0.77	8.01	4.00	73.1	**2.6**	36.3	22.3	**6.9**
5.9	1.37	5.5	1.54	**4.2**	1.3	0.80	6.12	4.82	67.6	**1.6**	26.9	28.4	**7.1**
8.3	0.36	1.7	3.14	**2.3**	-1.3	-1.14	-6.67	6.29	71.8	**1.9**	27.7	23.8	**8.7**
3.2	2.60	13.4	1.22	**3.1**	1.3	0.47	5.62	3.73	73.6	**4.8**	44.4	11.9	**4.9**
2.4	6.24	21.8	1.45	**5.4**	2.2	1.57	12.39	3.53	55.7	**1.8**	38.2	48.9	**6.7**
1.6	6.91	39.7	1.04	**8.5**	1.9	2.15	15.71	5.45	50.8	**1.5**	9.2	23.4	**8.3**
5.4	1.39	6.3	0.58	**3.5**	0.4	0.57	4.42	4.15	76.2	**2.8**	35.8	19.6	**7.1**
6.0	1.38	6.9	0.36	**8.1**	24.9	1.36	15.64	3.21	65.7	**4.5**	24.2	9.3	**6.2**
4.7	1.48	8.8	0.48	**9.0**	2.2	1.38	14.78	5.09	52.5	**3.0**	30.8	16.7	**4.3**
1.2	4.24	22.7	0.66	**4.2**	3.7	0.48	3.68	4.86	75.7	**2.1**	24.0	19.3	**7.0**
0.3	11.76	100.2	2.87	**0.0**	-14.8	-3.31	-55.40	3.13	91.4	**2.8**	30.0	17.7	**1.1**
1.3	2.83	20.4	0.33	**2.2**	0.1	0.16	1.65	4.93	78.4	**1.6**	13.9	23.0	**4.7**
9.4	1.48	3.1	0.04	**2.6**	4.8	0.52	2.37	2.47	80.6	**5.2**	72.3	15.5	**8.6**
4.0	1.39	10.4	0.17	**1.9**	1.0	0.56	6.35	3.14	75.2	**2.0**	12.6	18.9	**2.9**
3.5	1.04	9.3	0.23	**5.0**	5.9	0.93	12.44	3.80	59.1	**0.9**	12.1	32.7	**4.4**
0.0	9.65	70.5	5.45	**0.2**	-33.8	-2.74	-27.23	2.97	86.6	**1.7**	14.3	21.9	**5.5**
0.0	26.20	177.5	2.37	**0.0**	-3.1	-2.84	-30.78	2.01	167.5	**0.5**	5.3	53.2	**0.0**
3.9	1.38	7.7	0.70	**5.9**	1.9	0.78	8.67	5.09	71.5	**2.7**	25.6	16.5	**5.2**
1.6	4.65	23.4	0.81	**2.2**	0.9	0.18	1.61	4.26	85.2	**1.9**	29.8	26.5	**3.6**
0.3	11.14	66.4	1.75	**3.6**	0.5	0.51	4.34	4.46	71.7	**1.5**	21.8	27.3	**6.7**
1.7	1.98	11.0	0.64	**4.3**	1.4	0.66	7.35	3.65	70.5	**2.7**	17.3	15.6	**5.7**
3.7	3.75	19.1	2.01	**1.7**	-0.6	-0.24	-2.21	3.70	73.4	**2.4**	27.6	19.1	**6.4**
6.9	0.90	5.0	0.44	**3.2**	15.1	0.63	10.36	2.60	69.4	**4.6**	38.0	13.9	**4.0**
0.3	8.99	55.4	2.36	**0.0**	-1.0	-1.33	-14.97	3.21	112.3	**4.0**	23.5	9.9	**3.7**
1.6	3.80	19.5	1.07	**0.2**	-0.2	-0.19	-1.83	3.49	92.6	**1.5**	27.5	30.4	**4.5**
0.3	6.54	42.1	1.88	**0.0**	-0.7	-0.65	-6.82	3.84	102.7	**2.2**	18.7	18.2	**3.3**
6.6	0.67	5.1	0.00	**2.9**	0.3	0.52	4.86	4.76	83.2	**1.2**	18.8	30.1	**4.5**
4.6	0.13	1.0	0.46	**7.4**	2.8	1.65	18.96	4.97	59.0	**2.1**	12.9	18.1	**6.1**
4.6	2.97	10.2	0.22	**3.1**	0.4	0.40	3.59	2.70	71.0	**3.0**	63.0	50.9	**6.4**
8.8	1.89	4.1	0.14	**2.7**	1.2	0.39	2.32	3.32	77.0	**5.3**	64.2	14.1	**7.6**
7.1	0.91	3.7	0.28	**5.6**	0.5	1.12	8.19	4.01	67.4	**4.1**	32.1	11.7	**7.7**
1.0	3.68	28.3	1.92	**0.5**	-5.4	-1.92	-25.38	3.23	77.9	**3.0**	24.8	15.1	**2.6**
1.0	1.93	12.5	2.88	**4.3**	4.4	1.14	9.86	3.82	62.8	**1.9**	40.9	58.7	**3.0**
8.6	0.23	0.9	0.07	**3.9**	2.1	1.08	10.89	4.09	66.2	**2.5**	37.5	24.6	**4.9**
0.7	5.03	32.0	4.69	**1.0**	-17.8	-2.34	-20.12	3.73	62.4	**0.9**	8.1	31.9	**9.1**
5.1	1.67	4.1	0.00	**6.0**	0.4	1.03	3.90	3.75	63.9	**2.8**	39.7	23.0	**7.6**

	Name	City	State	Rating	2008 Rating	2007 Rating	Total Assets ($Mil)	One Year Asset Growth	Comm-ercial Loans	Cons-umer Loans	Home Mort-gages	Secur-ities	Capital-ization Index	Leverage Ratio	Risk-based Capital Ratio
									Asset Mix (As a % of Total Assets)						
	CHAMPION BANK	PARKER	CO	**D-**	D-	D-	77	-16.04	0.2	0.3	21.5	4.5	**7.1**	9.1	13.7
	CHAMPLAIN NATIONAL BK	WILLSBORO	NY	**C+**	C+	C+	212	3.87	7.9	3.2	9.2	42.4	**6.1**	8.1	14.6
	CHAPPELL HILL BANK	CHAPPELL HILL	TX	**C-**	C-	C	21	3.44	2.0	4.0	12.0	9.5	**10.0**	16.0	46.7
	CHARLEROI FSB	CHARLEROI	PA	**C+**	C+	C+	564	10.01	1.4	2.5	31.5	34.3	**10.0**	11.6	28.5
	CHARLES RIVER BANK	MEDWAY	MA	**C**	C-	C-	185	0.39	2.7	0.4	45.5	24.4	**5.8**	7.8	14.3
	CHARLES SCHWAB BANK	RENO	NV	**B**	B-	B-	54,907	27.01	0.0	1.0	8.8	73.0	**5.6**	7.6	24.0
	CHARLEVOIX STATE BK	CHARLEVOIX	MI	**C**	C+	B-	146	5.41	3.9	3.0	19.8	8.6	**6.6**	8.6	14.0
	CHARLOTTE STATE BK	PORT CHARLOTTE	FL	**D**	D+	C+	234	-2.35	0.4	0.4	12.3	17.0	**6.1**	8.2	12.5
	CHARTER BANK	JOHNSTON	IA	**B-**	B-	C+	112	8.69	11.9	2.6	14.1	36.3	**6.4**	8.5	15.3
	CHARTER BANK	BILOXI	MS	**D**	C	C	92	31.22	15.9	1.1	19.2	17.0	**10.0**	12.0	16.5
	CHARTER BANK	ALBUQUERQUE	NM	**D**	NR	NR	805	N/A	0.1	0.1	41.5	2.5	**10.0**	26.7	82.6
	CHARTER BANK	CORPUS CHRISTI	TX	**B-**	C	C	159	6.37	19.1	4.9	9.0	38.0	**5.0**	7.0	12.5
▼	CHARTER BANK EAU CLAIRE	EAU CLAIRE	WI	**C**	C	B	535	-0.07	10.5	0.7	19.5	30.3	**10.0**	12.2	18.1
	CHARTER NATIONAL BK & TRU	HOFFMAN ESTATES	IL	**E-**	D-	D+	106	-7.68	6.1	0.3	6.5	13.0	**0.7**	4.7	7.4
	CHARTER PRIVATE BANK	BELLEVUE	WA	**C-**	C-	C-	366	2.04	8.4	0.3	14.5	35.7	**7.6**	9.4	16.2
	CHARTER WEST NATIONAL BK	WEST POINT	NE	**C+**	C	C+	177	-1.26	7.1	3.8	13.8	14.0	**7.5**	9.3	13.0
▼	CHARTERBANK	WEST POINT	GA	**D**	D+	B-	1,058	12.69	4.2	0.5	10.4	14.8	**10.0**	11.5	25.6
	CHASE BANK USA NA	NEWARK	DE	**C**	C-	C+	131,083	43.98	4.6	82.8	0.0	0.1	**9.1**	11.1	14.2
	CHASEWOOD BANK	HOUSTON	TX	**D+**	C-	C-	94	17.62	7.0	0.7	5.0	47.2	**7.2**	9.1	18.3
▼	CHATTAHOOCHEE BANK OF	GAINESVILLE	GA	**D+**	C	D	76	8.26	6.5	0.3	2.0	14.1	**10.0**	21.8	29.5
	CHEAHA BANK	OXFORD	AL	**C+**	C	B-	168	1.50	5.8	6.0	20.8	29.7	**7.1**	9.1	14.9
	CHECKSPRING BANK	BRONX	NY	**D**	C	C	49	57.74	16.0	0.1	8.3	12.8	**10.0**	14.2	20.0
	CHELSEA GROTON BANK	GROTON	CT	**B-**	B-	B	810	7.97	2.2	1.1	42.8	25.6	**10.0**	14.5	24.1
	CHELSEA PROVIDENT CO-OP	CHELSEA	MA	**C-**	C-	C+	49	3.08	0.0	2.0	46.2	7.2	**8.5**	10.0	19.3
▼	CHELSEA SB	BELLE PLAINE	IA	**B+**	A-	A	96	-5.59	11.7	2.2	9.3	45.7	**10.0**	15.5	30.7
	CHELSEA STATE BK	CHELSEA	MI	**C-**	C-	B+	222	2.72	11.7	0.8	12.7	22.8	**9.0**	10.4	16.9
	CHELTEN HILLS SB	ABINGTON	PA	**D-**	D+	C-	38	5.19	0.0	0.0	77.1	1.5	**5.7**	7.7	14.5
	CHEMICAL BANK	MIDLAND	MI	**D**	D+	C	5,238	23.44	10.1	9.0	20.6	14.1	**6.2**	8.2	12.7
	CHEMUNG CANAL TRUST CO	ELMIRA	NY	**B-**	C+	B	957	-1.61	11.7	11.9	23.5	24.2	**6.3**	8.3	13.9
▼	CHEROKEE BANK NA	CANTON	GA	**E-**	D-	D-	181	-10.09	5.7	1.5	14.9	10.1	**3.3**	6.1	10.1
	CHEROKEE STATE BK	CHEROKEE	IA	**B+**	B+	A-	165	1.82	6.8	2.0	6.2	32.8	**10.0**	11.6	15.8
	CHESAPEAKE BANK	KILMARNOCK	VA	**B-**	B	B	603	3.59	12.0	2.5	10.2	26.9	**7.0**	9.0	13.1
▲	CHESAPEAKE BANK & TRUST	CHESTERTOWN	MD	**B+**	B	C	102	18.31	8.4	2.2	30.5	20.5	**8.1**	9.7	16.6
	CHESAPEAKE BANK OF	BALTIMORE	MD	**D+**	D+	D+	198	-2.36	0.3	1.1	44.5	9.6	**8.3**	9.8	17.6
	CHESTER COUNTY BANK	HENDERSON	TN	**C**	B-	B-	52	10.35	5.3	11.2	21.1	28.4	**7.4**	9.3	17.8
	CHESTER NATIONAL BK	CHESTER	IL	**C+**	C+	C+	84	16.09	0.6	0.9	27.0	30.5	**7.2**	9.2	25.7
▼	CHESTERFIELD STATE BK	CHESTERFIELD	IL	**D+**	C	B-	18	12.70	5.6	8.9	17.3	1.4	**6.6**	8.6	16.3
	CHETOPA STATE BK & TRUST	CHETOPA	KS	**B**	B	B	29	-1.93	1.1	4.0	14.2	22.2	**6.2**	8.2	17.0
	CHEVIOT SAVINGS BANK	CHEVIOT	OH	**B-**	C+	B-	355	5.66	0.2	0.1	53.3	26.6	**10.0**	16.2	34.9
	CHEYENNE STATE BK	CHEYENNE	WY	**C**	C	C-	42	0.52	8.9	4.9	11.6	2.8	**10.0**	11.5	15.8
	CHICAGO COMMUNITY BANK	CHICAGO	IL	**D-**	D	D	276	-12.70	4.5	0.4	25.2	1.1	**7.7**	9.5	13.4
	CHICAGO TRUST CO NA	LAKE FOREST	IL	**U**	U	U	8	5.54	0.0	0.0	0.0	1.3	**10.0**	91.6	186.5
	CHICKASHA BANK & TRUST	CHICKASHA	OK	**C+**	C	B-	192	6.75	8.8	2.6	11.2	4.7	**6.8**	8.8	13.8
	CHICOPEE SB	CHICOPEE	MA	**C-**	C	C	573	5.53	12.6	0.6	28.9	10.2	**10.0**	13.2	17.1
	CHILLICOTHE STATE BK	CHILLICOTHE	MO	**B-**	B+	B+	111	5.86	4.7	5.5	28.3	22.0	**7.0**	9.0	16.7
	CHINATOWN FSB	NEW YORK	NY	**C+**	B	A	164	-2.40	0.0	1.4	29.6	0.8	**10.0**	18.1	23.6
	CHINATRUST BANK USA	TORRANCE	CA	**D**	D-	D-	1,374	-39.43	6.8	0.1	6.3	11.7	**10.0**	17.1	29.3
▼	CHINO COMMERCIAL BANK NA	CHINO	CA	**D+**	B-	B+	114	10.01	5.4	0.6	4.5	14.9	**6.8**	8.8	14.5
	CHIPPEWA VALLEY BANK	WINTER	WI	**C**	C	C	235	6.83	4.0	0.7	23.0	1.2	**6.5**	8.5	12.8
▼	CHISHOLM TRAIL STATE BK	WICHITA	KS	**D+**	C+	B-	64	-17.42	3.1	6.4	26.5	25.2	**6.5**	8.5	15.2
▼	CHOICE BANK	OSHKOSH	WI	**D**	D+	C	168	39.15	12.6	0.5	20.8	7.0	**6.8**	8.8	12.3
▲	CHOICE FINANCIAL GROUP	GRAFTON	ND	**D+**	C-	C+	580	6.33	13.3	1.6	3.6	11.7	**4.9**	8.4	11.0
▲	CHOICE FINANCIAL SAVINGS	COMFREY	MN	**D+**	C-	C+	16	-2.94	16.8	1.7	4.0	36.4	**7.1**	9.1	15.8
	CHOICEONE BANK	SPARTA	MI	**D**	D-	D+	478	3.31	10.5	3.4	20.8	19.0	**5.9**	7.9	12.1
	CHURCH POINT BANK &	CHURCH POINT	LA	**C+**	C+	B-	43	-0.16	4.5	7.8	15.5	19.2	**8.2**	9.8	22.1
	CIBM BANK	CHAMPAIGN	IL	**D-**	D-	D	580	-16.69	9.0	0.5	10.4	21.8	**8.1**	10.1	13.4
▲	CINCINNATI FS&LA	CINCINNATI	OH	**D+**	C-	C	109	-3.99	0.1	0.0	39.9	2.0	**7.3**	9.2	13.4
	CINCINNATUS SAVINGS & LOA	CINCINNATI	OH	**C**	C+	C+	90	-6.34	5.5	1.2	57.9	1.0	**10.0**	21.7	30.8
▲	CIRCLE BANK	NOVATO	CA	**C-**	C	C+	301	14.75	5.8	0.1	26.4	0.3	**5.8**	7.8	12.8
	CISSNA PARK STATE BK	CISSNA PARK	IL	**C+**	B-	A	51	-6.30	6.7	1.7	4.7	24.5	**7.3**	9.2	17.2

Asset Quality Index	Non-Performing Loans as a % of Total Loans	Non-Performing Loans as a % of Capital	Net Charge-offs Avg Loans	Profitability Index	Net Income ($Mil)	Return on Assets (R.O.A.)	Return on Equity (R.O.E.)	Net Interest Spread	Overhead Efficiency Ratio	Liquidity Index	Liquidity Ratio	Hot Money Ratio	Stability Index
0.0	17.47	88.1	2.72	**0.0**	-3.5	-3.70	-38.37	1.86	122.1	**0.7**	20.3	57.8	**4.4**
5.7	0.83	4.6	0.38	**4.2**	1.4	0.67	8.79	4.60	78.5	**3.6**	20.6	11.6	**4.4**
9.7	0.67	1.1	0.00	**0.0**	-0.3	-1.25	-7.36	1.83	158.8	**4.4**	82.5	18.5	**6.7**
7.7	0.37	1.3	0.00	**2.4**	1.0	0.18	1.50	1.94	88.4	**3.3**	59.5	30.7	**7.8**
3.4	1.35	11.1	0.04	**3.4**	1.0	0.55	6.87	3.69	81.2	**2.1**	27.9	22.1	**4.5**
9.9	0.55	1.2	0.23	**5.2**	523.6	1.06	14.39	2.13	22.6	**8.5**	89.8	0.0	**5.3**
2.6	1.86	12.8	0.58	**3.6**	1.0	0.73	8.18	4.24	72.0	**4.5**	30.2	9.0	**4.8**
0.0	3.03	20.4	2.38	**0.7**	-0.4	-0.17	-2.19	4.13	68.6	**4.6**	28.0	7.1	**4.2**
6.4	1.00	6.2	0.29	**5.5**	1.4	1.27	15.03	3.69	58.3	**3.9**	45.1	17.0	**5.0**
3.7	0.36	1.9	0.02	**0.0**	-1.3	-1.59	-10.99	3.42	122.6	**0.9**	20.6	35.1	**1.5**
3.8	4.17	10.3	0.00	**0.0**	117.4	**,***.**	**,***.**	N/,	29.4	**0.8**	23.6	51.3	**0.7**
4.2	1.58	11.4	0.28	**10.0**	4.0	2.66	32.39	7.43	62.4	**3.7**	41.9	17.1	**4.8**
1.9	2.91	14.0	1.47	**6.6**	8.8	1.63	13.36	4.90	33.8	**2.5**	35.9	23.6	**6.3**
0.3	9.59	113.4	4.29	**0.0**	-3.5	-3.08	-54.32	3.45	113.8	**3.9**	9.7	8.4	**1.0**
1.7	5.31	27.3	0.21	**0.5**	0.3	0.08	0.79	3.58	129.1	**4.6**	33.7	9.9	**4.9**
3.1	0.43	3.0	0.28	**6.4**	3.2	1.79	17.10	4.22	66.1	**1.2**	8.9	27.3	**5.1**
0.0	9.42	42.7	0.90	**4.4**	9.7	0.85	8.79	2.97	59.2	**2.3**	29.9	30.0	**7.9**
2.6	1.18	6.5	11.04	**7.8**	2,853.6	2.02	11.56	11.05	34.9	**0.1**	2.9	92.2	**6.5**
7.9	0.93	4.0	0.02	**1.1**	0.1	0.07	0.67	3.24	96.5	**2.5**	58.2	52.3	**4.5**
7.6	0.00	0.0	0.00	**0.0**	-0.9	-1.14	-5.05	3.25	137.9	**2.2**	28.5	20.3	**2.0**
5.5	0.49	2.8	0.53	**3.4**	1.3	0.73	8.25	4.25	67.7	**1.2**	20.8	30.7	**4.3**
7.6	0.81	3.6	0.00	**0.0**	-1.7	-4.28	-21.55	5.03	157.6	**1.0**	27.7	63.1	**1.5**
5.4	2.86	11.8	0.84	**3.4**	4.2	0.53	3.57	3.90	77.1	**4.7**	32.8	8.8	**8.5**
2.0	3.75	25.5	0.05	**2.7**	0.2	0.34	3.38	4.29	83.1	**2.5**	22.6	17.3	**5.6**
4.5	6.86	17.2	0.02	**7.3**	2.1	2.13	13.31	3.95	55.7	**6.2**	64.3	7.7	**9.1**
2.1	5.36	26.9	0.84	**4.1**	1.9	0.87	8.28	4.64	64.2	**4.9**	33.2	7.6	**5.9**
0.3	3.25	34.3	0.13	**4.4**	0.3	0.67	8.77	4.14	59.6	**1.2**	13.4	27.8	**4.2**
0.5	2.95	21.5	1.11	**3.6**	26.9	0.56	5.56	3.90	62.1	**3.1**	18.0	14.4	**7.1**
4.1	1.02	7.1	0.27	**5.8**	9.9	1.02	10.93	3.92	69.8	**3.8**	17.1	10.4	**6.4**
0.3	10.18	86.4	3.18	**0.0**	-6.2	-3.18	-40.20	3.32	107.1	**1.6**	17.2	23.4	**1.3**
5.2	1.38	7.2	0.78	**7.2**	2.5	1.55	13.21	4.61	47.2	**3.3**	28.6	14.8	**7.3**
3.6	1.19	7.4	0.44	**6.1**	6.1	1.02	11.79	4.89	67.1	**1.5**	20.6	26.0	**6.6**
7.1	0.21	1.2	0.30	**7.0**	1.7	1.79	16.68	4.33	59.4	**1.2**	8.2	26.2	**6.7**
3.4	1.80	10.8	0.21	**1.6**	0.2	0.08	0.77	3.11	73.4	**2.2**	32.8	24.6	**4.2**
4.3	1.55	8.0	0.18	**6.3**	0.6	1.11	11.30	5.09	68.8	**2.9**	43.3	23.2	**5.3**
10.0	0.05	0.2	-0.01	**3.1**	0.5	0.59	5.92	2.80	80.2	**4.9**	60.6	14.1	**4.9**
2.6	3.11	18.2	0.40	**4.2**	0.1	0.79	8.42	3.06	68.9	**5.3**	49.6	7.7	**5.9**
8.9	0.00	0.0	0.08	**5.2**	0.4	1.19	14.37	3.64	68.1	**2.0**	26.5	22.2	**5.9**
6.8	2.15	8.3	0.10	**3.8**	2.4	0.71	4.33	3.24	64.5	**4.4**	37.9	12.4	**7.6**
3.4	1.68	10.1	0.35	**3.4**	0.3	0.60	5.36	4.48	64.1	**1.2**	19.5	30.3	**5.9**
0.0	13.02	98.9	6.48	**1.5**	-10.4	-3.45	-28.83	4.79	90.4	**2.6**	3.5	15.0	**5.5**
6.8	0.00	0.0	0.00	**8.4**	0.4	5.47	5.93	0.98	89.0	**5.0**	797.3	101.0	**3.7**
2.8	2.33	18.3	0.75	**6.0**	2.3	1.29	13.96	5.43	69.9	**1.8**	23.2	23.2	**5.9**
5.9	1.48	8.2	0.20	**1.3**	0.7	0.13	0.87	3.27	92.2	**1.3**	16.1	27.4	**7.3**
4.6	1.81	10.8	0.00	**8.3**	2.2	2.04	23.35	3.87	48.3	**4.1**	31.1	11.5	**7.1**
1.2	5.04	23.6	0.00	**6.6**	2.7	1.60	9.36	6.24	50.6	**3.5**	12.4	11.0	**9.0**
3.1	1.73	5.1	5.53	**0.0**	-61.8	-3.62	-24.62	2.88	617.2	**2.7**	29.8	24.4	**6.0**
1.7	6.89	36.9	1.00	**3.9**	0.6	0.51	5.94	4.19	70.2	**3.9**	41.4	15.9	**4.8**
2.3	2.94	23.5	0.05	**5.8**	3.0	1.32	15.38	4.56	66.8	**2.1**	23.4	19.6	**6.6**
5.5	0.48	3.2	0.08	**1.9**	0.0	-0.01	-0.19	3.53	95.7	**4.6**	12.8	4.2	**4.7**
3.0	0.18	1.6	1.38	**0.4**	-0.4	-0.30	-2.49	3.65	87.0	**0.9**	9.6	31.9	**1.2**
1.8	2.19	19.4	1.71	**3.5**	4.3	0.77	8.63	3.98	54.7	**0.9**	15.5	33.1	**4.4**
7.1	0.06	0.3	-0.27	**1.6**	0.0	0.12	0.94	3.71	95.1	**2.8**	49.5	22.7	**1.8**
1.4	1.82	14.0	1.12	**3.5**	2.8	0.59	5.13	4.40	68.7	**1.9**	20.6	20.9	**4.8**
8.2	0.23	0.9	0.16	**2.7**	0.1	0.27	2.55	3.88	93.4	**5.0**	53.1	12.4	**6.3**
0.0	8.14	44.5	3.88	**0.0**	-14.9	-2.28	-24.13	3.23	96.5	**2.7**	15.2	15.3	**4.5**
4.8	1.31	11.2	0.00	**1.4**	-0.2	-0.14	-1.54	3.24	92.6	**1.4**	8.0	24.5	**4.5**
4.1	4.39	16.8	0.26	**1.7**	0.0	-0.02	-0.10	4.29	72.6	**1.4**	10.8	24.5	**6.3**
2.5	1.26	11.3	0.10	**5.2**	2.2	0.76	9.98	4.99	67.6	**1.1**	14.7	30.7	**4.8**
2.3	4.44	22.1	0.07	**4.7**	0.5	1.01	10.39	2.91	68.1	**5.1**	46.7	10.5	**6.0**

Name	City	State	Rating	2008 Rating	2007 Rating	Total Assets ($Mil)	One Year Asset Growth	Asset Mix (As a % of Total Assets) Comm-ercial Loans	Cons-umer Loans	Home Mort-gages	Secur-ities	Capital-ization Index	Leverage Ratio	Risk-based Capital Ratio
CIT BANK	SALT LAKE CITY	UT	**B+**	B	B	7,083	-21.04	20.3	53.4	0.0	3.1	**10.0**	24.4	58.1
CITIBANK NA	LAS VEGAS	NV	**C-**	D-	D	1,154,293	-0.61	8.4	7.0	9.3	21.3	**6.9**	8.9	17.1
CITIBANK SOUTH DAKOTA NA	SIOUX FALLS	SD	**C-**	C-	C-	142,350	45.30	5.4	81.9	0.0	0.1	**10.0**	13.0	15.8
▲ CITICORP TRUST BANK FSB	WILMINGTON	DE	**D+**	D	C	13,547	-24.02	0.0	3.5	88.9	0.0	**9.0**	10.3	18.9
CITICORP TRUST NA	PALM BEACH	FL	**U**	U	U	50	2.34	0.0	0.0	0.0	99.2	**10.0**	96.1	516.9
CITIGROUP	NEW CASTLE	DE	**U**	U	U	52	-27.39	0.0	0.0	0.0	2.1	**10.0**	86.0	255.2
▼ CITIZENS & FARMERS BANK	WEST POINT	VA	**B-**	C	C-	901	1.92	3.5	25.0	25.2	14.5	**10.0**	11.4	16.3
CITIZENS & NORTHERN BANK	WELLSBORO	PA	**B+**	B	B	1,306	2.32	4.5	1.2	28.3	33.3	**6.5**	8.5	15.9
CITIZENS 1ST BANK	TYLER	TX	**A+**	A+	A+	729	2.81	1.5	1.4	13.9	64.8	**10.0**	15.8	38.8
▲ CITIZENS ALLIANCE BANK	CLARA CITY	MN	**C+**	C-	C	349	-8.71	13.0	2.4	6.2	18.3	**5.4**	8.6	11.3
CITIZENS B&TC GRAINGER CO	RUTLEDGE	TN	**A**	A-	A-	172	5.53	1.7	3.8	11.9	45.9	**10.0**	17.2	32.2
▲ CITIZENS B&TC OF JACKSON	JACKSON	KY	**C**	D+	D	116	1.11	10.1	8.7	22.1	8.2	**8.8**	10.7	14.0
▼ CITIZENS BANK	ENTERPRISE	AL	**D-**	D+	C	89	-7.08	11.0	1.8	13.2	14.7	**7.6**	9.4	17.1
CITIZENS BANK	GENEVA	AL	**A**	A	A	170	5.07	2.8	6.6	15.1	60.4	**10.0**	15.5	40.5
CITIZENS BANK	GREENSBORO	AL	**A-**	A-	B+	91	5.56	8.4	7.6	8.0	36.6	**8.9**	10.3	18.1
CITIZENS BANK	BATESVILLE	AR	**D+**	C-	B	535	3.88	6.8	5.3	27.3	29.8	**8.0**	9.7	14.3
CITIZENS BANK	CAIRO	GA	**D**	D+	C-	44	-5.49	4.9	4.3	17.9	36.3	**10.0**	12.1	25.9
▼ CITIZENS BANK	NASHVILLE	GA	**D**	D+	C-	289	-1.76	0.9	10.2	29.8	8.2	**8.0**	9.7	14.8
▼ CITIZENS BANK	SAC CITY	IA	**B-**	B	B+	41	16.17	7.3	3.7	7.1	49.8	**6.4**	8.4	14.3
CITIZENS BANK	MOORESVILLE	IN	**D+**	B	B	338	-4.41	3.6	22.5	11.1	20.6	**7.2**	9.1	13.4
CITIZENS BANK	BRODHEAD	KY	**C-**	C	B	132	2.30	3.8	4.7	33.1	11.6	**8.9**	10.3	15.7
CITIZENS BANK	HARTFORD	KY	**C+**	C+	B	23	-4.40	2.3	15.6	26.1	20.4	**10.0**	20.1	43.3
CITIZENS BANK	HICKMAN	KY	**B**	B	B	100	6.51	3.7	5.8	18.4	23.2	**10.0**	12.0	18.1
▲ CITIZENS BANK	MOREHEAD	KY	**C**	C	C+	113	1.30	2.2	3.6	30.7	25.0	**5.6**	7.6	14.5
CITIZENS BANK	VILLE PLATTE	LA	**B**	B	B	225	4.71	6.9	5.4	23.2	29.6	**9.8**	10.8	26.6
CITIZENS BANK	FLINT	MI	**D-**	D-	D+	9,710	-14.34	9.7	9.5	12.2	25.9	**5.3**	7.3	12.8
CITIZENS BANK	AMSTERDAM	MO	**C-**	C	C-	51	13.54	9.2	4.3	44.4	0.3	**5.8**	7.8	11.7
▼ CITIZENS BANK	NEW HAVEN	MO	**D**	D+	C	170	-0.13	8.0	1.7	22.5	5.2	**8.7**	12.0	13.9
▼ CITIZENS BANK	BYHALIA	MS	**B-**	B	B	67	4.61	1.6	10.0	19.2	35.9	**8.9**	10.3	18.2
CITIZENS BANK	COLUMBIA	MS	**B**	B	B	360	4.96	8.2	9.0	25.3	8.5	**7.9**	9.6	14.8
CITIZENS BANK	FARMINGTON	NM	**A-**	A-	B+	580	3.56	6.3	2.6	11.5	51.5	**6.7**	8.7	19.0
CITIZENS BANK	CORVALLIS	OR	**B-**	B+	B+	419	3.86	7.0	1.1	10.3	10.0	**10.0**	12.6	16.0
CITIZENS BANK	OLANTA	SC	**B**	B	B	316	0.93	8.8	7.7	21.3	11.5	**7.2**	9.1	15.1
CITIZENS BANK	CARTHAGE	TN	**A**	A-	A	506	1.63	7.0	3.9	18.2	42.8	**10.0**	16.7	26.1
CITIZENS BANK	ELIZABETHTON	TN	**B-**	C-	B+	593	-1.14	21.9	2.1	7.4	19.3	**10.0**	11.9	21.2
CITIZENS BANK	HARTSVILLE	TN	**C+**	B-	B-	140	1.43	6.3	6.8	26.6	15.6	**6.4**	8.4	12.8
▲ CITIZENS BANK	NEW TAZEWELL	TN	**D**	D	D	155	3.28	14.4	5.7	19.8	17.3	**6.1**	8.1	12.2
CITIZENS BANK	CLAUDE	TX	**B+**	A-	A-	106	10.81	3.5	0.5	1.8	23.8	**8.1**	9.8	15.2
CITIZENS BANK	KILGORE	TX	**D**	C	B	313	10.30	23.4	2.2	7.6	8.2	**8.5**	10.0	16.2
CITIZENS BANK	SLATON	TX	**C+**	C	C	264	9.59	10.9	4.0	10.0	25.2	**5.8**	7.8	12.0
CITIZENS BANK & TRUST	GUNTERSVILLE	AL	**D+**	C-	C+	289	1.92	8.0	5.4	18.9	20.1	**7.5**	9.3	13.4
▼ CITIZENS BANK & TRUST	LAKE WALES	FL	**E-**	D-	D+	466	3.81	4.7	4.6	20.7	22.1	**3.2**	6.0	10.1
CITIZENS BANK & TRUST	ROCK PORT	MO	**B-**	C+	B	82	10.93	10.4	4.1	9.9	44.8	**8.3**	9.9	18.6
CITIZENS BANK & TRUST ARD	ARDMORE	OK	**B**	B+	A-	182	6.48	6.1	4.3	11.4	36.6	**7.8**	9.6	16.2
▲ CITIZENS BANK & TRUST CO	VAN BUREN	AR	**B-**	B-	B	369	7.23	5.4	7.7	22.7	28.9	**7.7**	9.5	15.8
▼ CITIZENS BANK & TRUST CO	EASTMAN	GA	**D-**	C-	C	177	-1.22	5.1	8.5	19.3	6.7	**3.0**	6.2	10.0
CITIZENS BANK & TRUST CO	CAMPBELLSVILLE	KY	**A**	A	A	174	-2.33	7.9	4.4	18.7	38.6	**10.0**	14.6	27.5
CITIZENS BANK & TRUST CO	COVINGTON	LA	**D**	D-	D+	110	-7.32	3.0	1.8	15.3	24.9	**8.6**	10.1	17.2
▼ CITIZENS BANK & TRUST CO	PLAQUEMINE	LA	**C+**	B-	A-	219	9.26	5.1	1.9	17.4	5.0	**9.6**	10.7	15.8
CITIZENS BANK & TRUST CO	SPRINGHILL	LA	**B-**	B-	C+	155	5.98	7.9	6.2	13.5	32.9	**6.1**	8.1	13.0
▼ CITIZENS BANK & TRUST CO	HUTCHINSON	MN	**D-**	C-	C-	184	5.02	11.3	2.6	19.5	27.9	**7.1**	9.1	14.4
CITIZENS BANK & TRUST CO	CHILLICOTHE	MO	**D-**	D-	C-	996	-8.51	7.2	0.4	9.0	37.3	**5.4**	7.4	13.3
CITIZENS BANK & TRUST CO	MARKS	MS	**C-**	C+	C	118	2.67	6.9	5.7	14.0	16.3	**5.9**	10.4	11.7
CITIZENS BANK & TRUST CO	BIG TIMBER	MT	**D+**	C	B-	100	3.90	5.2	3.0	6.2	24.7	**6.6**	8.6	14.7
CITIZENS BANK & TRUST CO	ATWOOD	TN	**D**	D	C-	26	7.77	2.1	17.6	27.6	24.9	**6.2**	8.2	15.4
CITIZENS BANK & TRUST CO	BLACKSTONE	VA	**B-**	B	A-	325	3.20	4.3	3.3	28.5	24.0	**9.4**	10.6	18.9
CITIZENS BANK & TRUST INC	TRENTON	GA	**C**	C	B-	88	4.24	2.4	16.8	38.7	12.7	**8.1**	9.7	16.6
▲ CITIZENS BANK & TRUST ST	SAINT PAUL	NE	**A**	A-	A-	108	7.30	7.0	4.8	5.7	21.2	**7.7**	9.5	13.1
CITIZENS BANK & TRUST VIV	VIVIAN	LA	**C-**	C-	C	144	7.54	7.6	9.1	30.4	27.7	**5.8**	7.8	13.1
CITIZENS BANK CO	BEVERLY	OH	**B+**	B+	B+	90	2.25	5.8	4.3	26.1	38.8	**10.0**	12.5	20.3

Asset Quality Index	Non-Performing Loans as a % of Total Loans	as a % of Capital	Net Charge-offs Avg Loans	Profitability Index	Net Income ($Mil)	Return on Assets (R.O.A.)	Return on Equity (R.O.E.)	Net Interest Spread	Overhead Efficiency Ratio	Liquidity Index	Liquidity Ratio	Hot Money Ratio	Stability Index
5.7	0.11	0.3	0.28	**5.4**	100.9	1.29	5.89	2.60	17.8	**1.1**	26.0	95.4	**7.1**
2.7	3.70	13.7	2.72	**2.4**	7,904.0	0.70	6.76	2.84	60.0	**5.8**	45.5	9.6	**5.7**
2.6	2.25	9.8	10.24	**2.7**	546.2	0.36	2.36	10.34	29.9	**0.5**	3.4	43.1	**7.1**
0.0	9.87	68.8	3.71	**2.3**	63.5	0.39	4.81	4.20	56.1	**2.1**	5.9	17.8	**5.5**
10.0	0.00	0.0	0.00	**9.3**	0.8	1.66	1.69	0.41	47.4	**5.0**	2,352.9	101.0	**4.3**
10.0	0.00	0.0	0.00	**9.5**	1.9	2.86	4.72	0.29	29.0	**5.0**	345.0	101.0	**4.3**
3.3	1.28	6.8	1.48	**5.5**	9.1	1.03	8.38	7.33	68.3	**1.4**	5.8	22.7	**7.3**
5.9	1.51	9.5	0.05	**7.2**	18.5	1.43	13.72	3.88	55.6	**3.1**	7.6	13.0	**6.6**
9.5	1.09	2.3	0.07	**9.4**	17.5	2.46	14.75	3.79	26.8	**2.6**	50.8	34.7	**10.0**
3.2	0.82	5.9	1.50	**3.4**	1.8	0.51	4.99	3.61	55.9	**1.6**	11.8	22.3	**5.6**
5.9	2.74	6.7	0.38	**6.5**	2.1	1.24	7.00	4.70	63.0	**3.5**	46.3	19.1	**8.6**
6.2	0.09	0.6	0.63	**4.8**	1.5	1.32	10.80	4.82	75.0	**1.1**	13.9	29.7	**5.4**
3.0	0.29	1.5	3.46	**0.0**	-1.3	-1.38	-11.11	3.07	118.1	**4.5**	32.1	9.7	**6.6**
8.1	1.40	2.6	0.87	**6.5**	2.0	1.18	7.69	3.67	41.0	**3.9**	73.1	26.8	**8.1**
5.7	0.94	4.4	0.04	**6.9**	1.2	1.36	12.21	3.87	47.2	**2.4**	42.8	30.3	**7.0**
1.9	3.34	19.8	1.24	**3.3**	3.0	0.57	5.92	4.20	65.6	**1.4**	12.3	24.6	**5.7**
3.0	5.88	17.8	3.07	**0.0**	-0.6	-1.23	-9.32	3.33	116.4	**2.4**	42.1	30.7	**4.6**
0.6	3.55	23.4	1.37	**1.7**	0.0	0.01	0.06	3.29	66.6	**0.7**	14.5	46.0	**7.0**
7.1	0.55	2.8	0.01	**6.7**	0.6	1.58	15.39	4.15	66.2	**2.4**	29.3	19.6	**5.0**
1.4	4.75	32.7	2.49	**1.5**	-1.6	-0.44	-4.91	4.32	76.7	**3.2**	11.5	12.7	**6.1**
1.4	3.05	20.7	0.25	**4.8**	1.4	1.09	10.17	4.98	66.7	**1.3**	10.9	26.5	**5.9**
5.3	3.14	7.4	0.50	**4.7**	0.2	0.66	3.46	4.93	73.3	**6.3**	54.0	2.4	**6.7**
4.8	2.15	11.2	0.32	**6.0**	1.1	1.15	9.22	4.55	60.1	**1.1**	24.8	32.8	**6.5**
4.3	0.98	7.3	0.49	**2.8**	0.4	0.40	3.99	4.03	84.8	**1.9**	22.1	20.4	**5.1**
7.5	0.43	1.8	0.00	**4.5**	1.9	0.86	7.79	3.20	59.5	**2.2**	42.4	33.5	**6.7**
1.7	3.46	21.0	6.01	**0.0**	-285.6	-2.67	-31.00	3.42	72.1	**3.5**	24.8	14.9	**5.1**
4.8	0.69	7.0	0.13	**4.7**	0.5	1.00	13.15	5.04	78.2	**4.5**	10.6	4.8	**4.3**
0.4	6.79	36.5	1.22	**2.7**	0.6	0.33	2.75	4.36	65.8	**3.4**	13.2	11.7	**6.3**
5.9	0.60	2.9	0.39	**4.1**	0.4	0.67	6.16	4.46	78.2	**2.8**	43.5	24.4	**6.0**
4.8	1.14	8.1	0.25	**6.8**	5.4	1.53	17.24	4.52	65.5	**1.3**	13.4	27.2	**7.1**
5.9	1.12	4.3	0.26	**9.5**	10.9	1.90	19.23	4.26	52.9	**4.9**	54.4	14.3	**7.7**
3.1	3.71	20.3	0.72	**6.4**	4.1	0.99	7.76	5.31	62.5	**4.4**	11.8	5.5	**7.3**
4.2	1.55	9.9	0.56	**4.4**	2.0	0.64	6.47	4.48	72.4	**2.2**	22.2	18.5	**6.1**
6.4	1.89	5.5	0.54	**10.0**	10.8	2.14	13.44	5.14	32.5	**2.6**	51.1	35.3	**9.7**
3.4	2.37	13.4	0.36	**4.8**	7.1	1.18	9.57	4.46	60.0	**1.9**	16.0	19.6	**7.6**
3.3	0.97	7.8	0.48	**4.4**	0.9	0.65	7.53	4.36	66.6	**0.9**	9.9	32.0	**4.3**
0.7	3.99	31.3	0.25	**1.1**	0.5	0.34	4.01	4.06	97.8	**1.4**	16.7	26.5	**2.2**
7.7	0.00	0.0	0.01	**5.1**	1.3	1.25	11.87	3.26	63.7	**4.4**	40.9	13.2	**6.3**
0.5	8.09	40.6	1.00	**3.0**	0.9	0.32	3.09	4.37	84.8	**2.6**	35.7	21.0	**4.6**
5.1	1.72	13.2	0.19	**5.2**	3.5	1.44	18.83	4.08	66.4	**1.3**	15.6	27.3	**4.2**
1.1	3.28	21.9	0.97	**4.0**	1.8	0.62	7.05	4.03	66.3	**1.3**	16.0	27.9	**3.2**
1.7	1.50	13.6	0.52	**0.9**	0.7	0.15	2.20	3.77	77.2	**1.4**	11.4	24.7	**0.0**
4.3	3.37	14.4	0.54	**5.2**	0.9	1.21	11.38	3.35	66.5	**3.1**	29.9	16.0	**7.1**
8.8	0.06	0.3	0.05	**4.8**	2.0	1.13	11.41	4.03	74.0	**2.5**	31.8	19.6	**6.6**
3.5	2.38	14.6	0.52	**7.9**	4.7	1.31	13.30	4.51	48.6	**0.7**	11.0	38.7	**7.4**
1.6	3.64	28.4	1.98	**1.1**	-2.5	-1.37	-19.44	3.86	90.9	**1.7**	29.4	28.5	**3.5**
8.7	0.22	0.8	0.23	**6.3**	2.0	1.13	7.58	4.10	64.2	**3.6**	37.3	15.8	**8.3**
2.6	3.29	16.9	0.23	**1.1**	0.2	0.15	1.51	4.20	96.8	**3.9**	33.9	13.6	**3.6**
3.3	2.98	17.1	0.59	**5.8**	1.9	0.90	8.45	4.52	64.9	**2.8**	25.3	16.0	**7.3**
6.8	0.62	4.1	0.03	**4.6**	1.6	1.03	12.62	4.58	75.4	**1.7**	22.1	23.3	**5.3**
0.3	2.79	19.0	0.33	**5.4**	2.2	1.23	12.56	4.02	61.2	**4.5**	7.7	4.2	**6.4**
1.7	5.50	30.4	2.72	**0.0**	-3.9	-0.37	-4.16	2.61	98.3	**1.1**	12.6	29.7	**3.6**
4.0	0.85	4.8	1.25	**2.9**	0.4	0.33	3.22	4.10	73.0	**1.5**	20.9	25.6	**6.0**
2.0	3.45	20.1	0.72	**4.2**	0.5	0.53	4.69	4.34	58.3	**2.6**	29.9	18.5	**6.7**
1.8	2.44	15.7	0.35	**3.4**	0.2	0.62	7.46	3.32	76.5	**0.9**	19.9	40.3	**4.7**
4.0	1.95	10.8	0.59	**5.2**	3.1	0.95	9.05	4.07	65.2	**2.0**	24.9	19.9	**7.0**
2.8	1.41	9.5	0.33	**4.7**	0.9	1.02	10.48	5.05	66.1	**2.1**	23.9	19.3	**6.0**
7.3	0.01	0.1	0.18	**8.0**	1.6	1.49	14.86	5.13	59.3	**2.1**	9.4	18.1	**7.8**
2.0	1.75	14.3	0.55	**4.2**	0.9	0.67	7.28	4.53	79.1	**1.6**	18.8	24.2	**5.1**
7.1	0.97	4.6	0.10	**5.1**	0.8	1.00	8.17	4.62	75.0	**4.6**	34.6	10.0	**6.6**

	Name	City	State	Rating	2008 Rating	2007 Rating	Total Assets ($Mil)	One Year Asset Growth	Comm-ercial Loans	Cons-umer Loans	Home Mort-gages	Secur-ities	Capital-ization Index	Leverage Ratio	Risk-based Capital Ratio
									Asset Mix (As a % of Total Assets)						
▼	CITIZENS BANK INC	ROBERTSDALE	AL	**D-**	D	C+	119	6.45	4.4	3.8	13.9	23.4	**6.2**	8.2	13.6
	CITIZENS BANK MINNESOTA	NEW ULM	MN	**B+**	B+	B+	298	9.96	5.6	1.5	15.6	33.0	**7.4**	9.3	14.6
	CITIZENS BANK NA	FORT SCOTT	KS	**D**	C+	C-	278	-4.63	8.3	1.1	10.1	32.6	**8.4**	10.0	15.8
▼	CITIZENS BANK NA	ABILENE	TX	**C+**	B	B-	83	-2.73	15.3	7.6	10.7	13.7	**6.5**	8.5	12.2
	CITIZENS BANK OF ADA	ADA	OK	**B+**	B+	B	169	1.77	19.0	5.8	22.9	17.4	**8.5**	10.0	13.9
	CITIZENS BANK OF AMERICUS	AMERICUS	GA	**D-**	C-	C+	245	7.20	6.4	2.3	13.6	15.2	**6.7**	8.7	14.3
	CITIZENS BANK OF ASHVILLE	ASHVILLE	OH	**D+**	C-	C-	100	-1.00	3.9	1.3	27.6	27.1	**6.5**	8.6	15.7
▼	CITIZENS BANK OF BLOUNT C	MARYVILLE	TN	**C-**	B-	A	319	-7.82	3.0	0.7	4.0	16.3	**10.0**	16.9	23.7
	CITIZENS BANK OF BLYTHEDA	BLYTHEDALE	MO	**C+**	C	C+	32	-0.84	3.0	5.1	20.0	23.0	**8.4**	10.2	13.7
	CITIZENS BANK OF CAPE VIN	CAPE VINCENT	NY	**B**	B-	B	44	7.95	0.9	8.1	46.0	26.1	**10.0**	11.6	25.7
	CITIZENS BANK OF CHARLEST	CHARLESTON	MO	**B**	B	A	104	2.76	8.2	9.6	9.2	9.8	**10.0**	13.8	17.2
▼	CITIZENS BANK OF	CHATSWORTH	IL	**E+**	D-	D+	51	7.59	6.7	4.2	8.5	15.6	**4.7**	7.7	10.8
	CITIZENS BANK OF CLOVIS	CLOVIS	NM	**A**	A	A	281	12.77	4.6	2.0	4.6	48.7	**10.0**	12.1	27.5
	CITIZENS BANK OF COCHRAN	COCHRAN	GA	**D**	C-	B-	65	-5.32	1.6	3.5	13.6	15.4	**10.0**	13.6	19.4
	CITIZENS BANK OF DE GRAFF	DE GRAFF	OH	**C-**	C-	D	28	-0.85	4.6	7.4	16.8	47.2	**10.0**	12.0	20.6
▼	CITIZENS BANK OF EAST TEN	ROGERSVILLE	TN	**E-**	D-	C-	134	-5.95	2.2	2.8	34.2	9.5	**2.3**	5.7	9.3
▲	CITIZENS BANK OF EDINA	EDINA	MO	**B**	B-	C	69	-2.08	11.2	2.7	5.3	7.3	**8.9**	10.3	14.1
	CITIZENS BANK OF EDINBURG	EDINBURG	IL	**C-**	C	C	19	-3.63	10.5	5.3	20.0	10.9	**7.8**	9.5	16.4
	CITIZENS BANK OF EDMOND	EDMOND	OK	**D-**	D-	B-	270	-14.00	3.8	2.0	14.1	26.6	**5.9**	7.9	14.9
	CITIZENS BANK OF ELDON	ELDON	MO	**B+**	B+	A-	113	5.19	3.7	6.4	19.4	39.5	**10.0**	15.1	28.4
	CITIZENS BANK OF FAYETTE	FAYETTE	AL	**D**	C+	B-	188	-1.54	14.6	5.2	8.7	43.7	**10.0**	17.7	32.1
	CITIZENS BANK OF FLORIDA	OVIEDO	FL	**D-**	D	D-	216	-5.21	6.8	1.0	7.4	16.4	**6.3**	8.4	12.2
	CITIZENS BANK OF KANSAS N	KINGMAN	KS	**C-**	C-	B-	216	4.24	5.0	1.4	6.6	55.1	**5.6**	7.6	12.4
	CITIZENS BANK OF LAFAYETT	LAFAYETTE	TN	**B-**	B-	B	419	3.70	4.4	6.8	16.9	40.6	**6.6**	8.6	15.7
▼	CITIZENS BANK OF LAS CRUC	LAS CRUCES	NM	**C+**	B+	B	371	1.63	5.8	2.0	13.5	33.2	**6.8**	8.8	15.7
▼	CITIZENS BANK OF LOGAN	LOGAN	OH	**D**	C	C-	261	2.76	10.6	18.3	21.4	16.1	**5.7**	8.7	11.5
	CITIZENS BANK OF	MUKWONAGO	WI	**D+**	C-	C+	642	0.80	8.2	1.1	12.4	16.6	**9.9**	11.0	17.4
	CITIZENS BANK OF NEWBURG	NEWBURG	MO	**D+**	D+	D	169	-2.45	2.9	4.9	24.8	20.4	**6.6**	8.6	13.2
	CITIZENS BANK OF	NEVADA CITY	CA	**E-**	E	D-	328	-11.48	7.5	1.3	2.1	3.1	**1.1**	5.4	8.1
	CITIZENS BANK OF	NEWPORT	KY	**D+**	D	C-	250	-8.73	4.2	1.2	19.2	16.8	**6.0**	8.0	12.7
	CITIZENS BANK OF	PAWHUSKA	OK	**C+**	B-	B+	148	-2.57	32.7	2.5	10.5	4.5	**8.1**	10.1	13.4
	CITIZENS BANK OF PAGOSA S	PAGOSA SPRINGS	CO	**D-**	D+	C	76	1.24	3.8	0.5	15.5	25.6	**7.4**	9.2	13.7
	CITIZENS BANK OF PENNSYLV	PHILADELPHIA	PA	**D+**	D	C-	32,303	-0.50	11.6	3.0	10.8	19.3	**6.3**	8.3	14.8
	CITIZENS BANK OF PHILADEL	PHILADELPHIA	MS	**C+**	B	B+	818	-2.63	3.5	4.8	16.7	39.1	**6.8**	8.9	16.1
	CITIZENS BANK OF ROGERSVI	ROGERSVILLE	MO	**D**	D-	E+	56	-7.14	8.4	6.5	16.8	19.3	**6.0**	8.0	11.9
	CITIZENS BANK OF SPENCER	SPENCER	TN	**E-**	D+	C	44	3.23	6.0	9.9	39.7	24.1	**0.6**	3.8	8.3
	CITIZENS BANK OF SWAINSBO	SWAINSBORO	GA	**C-**	C	C+	141	1.45	8.5	7.3	25.2	11.8	**6.9**	8.9	12.9
	CITIZENS BANK OF VALLEY H	VALLEY HEAD	AL	**C-**	C-	C-	27	8.52	6.9	12.8	48.3	4.3	**10.0**	12.4	19.6
▼	CITIZENS BANK OF WEST VIR	ELKINS	WV	**D**	C	C-	237	-0.43	9.6	5.2	22.1	18.6	**7.8**	9.5	15.7
	CITIZENS BANK OF WESTON	WESTON	WV	**A-**	A-	A-	169	0.03	13.9	4.6	19.6	35.1	**9.8**	10.8	17.8
	CITIZENS BANK OF WINFIELD	WINFIELD	AL	**A-**	A	A	210	1.92	2.3	4.4	6.3	70.6	**10.0**	17.6	42.7
	CITIZENS BANK WEALTH	FLINT	MI	**U**	U	U	16	20.58	0.0	0.0	0.0	11.1	**10.0**	98.2	342.2
▲	CITIZENS BANKING CO	SANDUSKY	OH	**D+**	D	C-	1,096	-0.34	6.2	1.1	20.3	16.8	**6.1**	8.1	13.4
	CITIZENS BK OF CUMBERLAND	BURKESVILLE	KY	**C**	C+	B-	77	-3.89	5.9	12.6	28.0	5.8	**8.6**	10.0	14.8
	CITIZENS BK OF FORSYTH CO	CUMMING	GA	**D**	C-	C	240	0.76	7.7	2.4	17.7	13.9	**5.7**	7.7	11.8
	CITIZENS BK OF	MORGANTOWN	WV	**B-**	B-	B-	30	0.36	11.5	2.7	38.6	39.9	**10.0**	19.3	42.5
▼	CITIZENS BK OF OREGON MIS	OREGON	MO	**D**	D+	B-	23	-0.39	1.1	0.8	3.8	20.5	**8.1**	9.7	19.5
	CITIZENS BK OF WASHINGTON	SANDERSVILLE	GA	**C**	C	B-	234	0.76	7.1	8.8	28.6	23.2	**6.1**	8.1	13.6
	CITIZENS BUILDING & LOAN	GREER	SC	**C+**	C-	C-	117	13.93	0.0	0.4	47.9	18.8	**10.0**	18.6	30.5
	CITIZENS BUSINESS BANK	ONTARIO	CA	**B-**	B	B+	6,429	-4.49	4.9	0.3	4.2	27.9	**9.3**	10.5	17.8
	CITIZENS COMMERCE	VERSAILLES	KY	**E-**	E-	C+	298	-13.58	4.9	2.3	20.7	16.6	**0.0**	3.0	6.2
	CITIZENS COMMUNITY BANK	HAHIRA	GA	**D+**	C	B+	115	-1.55	5.2	5.5	27.5	16.7	**7.0**	9.0	15.5
	CITIZENS COMMUNITY BANK	POCATELLO	ID	**C+**	B-	B+	290	19.55	9.1	2.1	6.9	32.8	**6.9**	8.9	13.1
	CITIZENS COMMUNITY BANK	MASCOUTAH	IL	**C-**	D+	B-	261	8.71	7.2	2.2	22.5	29.1	**7.1**	9.1	15.9
	CITIZENS COMMUNITY BANK	PILOT GROVE	MO	**D**	D+	C-	104	-11.14	5.4	3.1	20.3	8.4	**5.8**	7.8	12.0
	CITIZENS COMMUNITY BANK	WINCHESTER	TN	**C**	D+	B	167	1.19	14.5	5.6	17.6	10.5	**8.2**	10.0	13.5
	CITIZENS COMMUNITY BANK	SOUTH HILL	VA	**C**	C	C+	165	-4.28	9.7	5.1	23.7	10.7	**10.0**	12.2	16.1
	CITIZENS COMMUNITY BANK O	BERWYN	IL	**D-**	D-	D	210	-8.91	1.0	0.4	15.6	8.2	**7.1**	9.0	12.9
	CITIZENS COMMUNITY	EAU CLAIRE	WI	**D-**	D	C	580	2.42	0.0	32.0	45.4	7.1	**5.7**	9.2	11.5
	CITIZENS DEPOSIT BANK & T	VANCEBURG	KY	**C-**	C-	B-	200	61.99	5.7	3.7	18.3	23.2	**6.2**	8.2	14.0

Asset Quality Index	Non-Performing Loans as a % of Total Loans	Non-Performing Loans as a % of Capital	Net Charge-offs Avg Loans	Profitability Index	Net Income ($Mil)	Return on Assets (R.O.A.)	Return on Equity (R.O.E.)	Net Interest Spread	Overhead Efficiency Ratio	Liquidity Index	Liquidity Ratio	Hot Money Ratio	Stability Index
1.8	3.64	22.3	1.23	**0.0**	-1.2	-0.98	-10.55	3.71	98.7	**1.5**	18.9	24.9	**4.2**
5.9	0.04	0.2	0.30	**4.9**	2.1	0.75	6.93	3.79	69.3	**3.7**	25.3	11.5	**5.7**
1.2	8.07	40.7	1.46	**2.6**	1.3	0.44	4.16	3.71	72.0	**2.7**	13.8	15.4	**5.9**
2.7	0.32	2.5	0.06	**8.4**	1.7	2.00	15.28	5.06	58.6	**1.0**	6.3	29.7	**9.2**
7.4	0.20	1.4	0.06	**5.3**	1.9	1.12	10.75	4.87	79.3	**3.2**	12.4	12.8	**6.1**
1.7	1.85	11.5	2.22	**2.1**	0.1	0.04	0.42	3.84	64.7	**1.0**	22.2	33.6	**3.6**
3.9	0.93	5.6	0.48	**1.4**	0.2	0.15	1.66	3.91	94.0	**4.0**	22.9	10.0	**3.9**
0.7	4.81	17.4	1.91	**3.8**	1.7	0.50	3.18	4.04	54.9	**1.7**	31.0	30.3	**6.7**
3.9	1.79	11.7	0.13	**6.7**	0.5	1.54	15.29	4.71	62.5	**2.2**	25.0	19.0	**5.4**
6.8	1.59	7.8	0.12	**4.0**	0.3	0.69	5.82	4.42	74.6	**4.2**	16.0	7.3	**7.9**
5.0	1.04	5.2	0.20	**6.0**	1.1	1.08	8.00	4.47	50.1	**2.3**	19.1	17.8	**7.0**
1.6	2.62	21.4	0.59	**1.5**	-0.1	-0.16	-1.97	3.89	76.6	**2.7**	24.5	16.3	**1.0**
8.8	0.22	0.8	-0.04	**7.5**	5.2	1.96	15.55	3.92	53.3	**2.7**	40.8	25.3	**9.3**
0.0	15.31	65.3	3.84	**0.0**	-1.1	-1.63	-10.85	3.60	89.7	**1.2**	22.5	31.2	**3.7**
6.0	2.12	6.3	0.32	**0.9**	0.0	0.12	0.99	3.29	98.0	**4.6**	51.2	13.8	**5.8**
0.2	11.60	115.3	1.76	**0.0**	-3.6	-2.59	-33.70	3.40	115.6	**1.2**	7.1	27.0	**2.7**
6.0	0.13	0.9	0.22	**9.3**	1.1	1.53	14.95	4.50	43.7	**2.5**	14.1	16.1	**6.9**
7.0	0.39	2.4	0.05	**3.4**	0.1	0.55	5.80	3.19	76.9	**4.2**	25.4	8.2	**6.0**
1.3	6.81	39.8	2.14	**0.5**	-1.6	-0.54	-7.41	3.85	101.9	**2.5**	31.9	19.6	**2.4**
5.2	2.76	9.3	0.11	**4.8**	0.9	0.83	5.36	3.71	69.6	**4.7**	45.7	13.1	**8.2**
3.5	6.95	15.1	2.39	**0.0**	-0.9	-0.47	-2.54	3.16	61.6	**3.0**	51.9	29.2	**5.9**
0.0	2.02	13.4	1.84	**0.4**	-2.1	-0.93	-10.81	3.85	80.4	**0.6**	4.4	39.9	**4.4**
3.5	3.07	13.5	0.94	**2.5**	1.5	0.74	6.48	3.79	83.4	**4.3**	38.9	13.2	**4.0**
4.7	1.48	8.2	0.52	**4.9**	4.0	0.96	10.57	3.77	62.3	**2.1**	39.2	32.8	**5.5**
3.9	2.16	12.0	0.89	**9.8**	8.4	2.20	23.75	4.67	56.0	**4.0**	25.8	10.4	**7.5**
0.3	8.48	67.9	0.73	**4.0**	2.2	0.82	9.36	4.08	71.9	**1.5**	19.3	25.2	**4.4**
0.3	5.67	31.5	2.66	**1.8**	-1.9	-0.31	-2.82	3.66	60.2	**2.5**	24.7	17.5	**7.0**
2.4	1.71	12.1	0.98	**2.0**	0.5	0.27	3.32	3.91	77.6	**2.1**	12.0	18.1	**3.6**
0.0	13.18	103.5	3.23	**0.0**	-5.3	-1.54	-25.30	4.66	69.4	**3.1**	16.8	13.8	**2.7**
1.7	2.81	21.3	0.48	**2.5**	1.5	0.56	7.05	3.55	77.7	**2.8**	12.5	14.9	**3.9**
5.1	1.09	7.5	0.61	**3.7**	1.0	0.70	7.54	3.75	59.5	**1.1**	26.4	40.2	**4.8**
0.3	8.65	43.3	3.76	**0.0**	-1.9	-2.51	-26.80	4.29	75.4	**4.3**	32.5	10.8	**3.1**
3.1	1.91	14.6	1.25	**1.0**	52.6	0.17	1.18	2.21	79.4	**4.9**	23.7	6.4	**7.6**
3.8	2.83	15.0	0.37	**4.7**	7.3	0.88	9.56	4.12	68.4	**1.7**	13.2	21.5	**6.3**
1.9	3.52	23.5	0.95	**2.3**	0.2	0.39	4.88	4.14	87.9	**3.7**	28.2	12.4	**3.3**
0.3	10.49	97.7	6.19	**0.9**	-1.2	-2.71	-58.65	4.66	67.4	**1.3**	19.6	29.1	**0.0**
1.7	2.28	17.3	1.09	**3.0**	0.3	0.25	2.81	4.32	66.6	**1.5**	12.4	24.2	**4.8**
1.9	4.18	27.6	0.11	**2.6**	0.1	0.43	3.49	6.42	91.5	**3.0**	12.7	13.9	**6.8**
0.3	3.87	24.1	0.82	**2.7**	0.9	0.35	3.70	3.77	77.5	**1.3**	14.7	27.6	**4.8**
6.3	0.68	3.5	0.09	**7.7**	2.4	1.39	12.32	3.96	50.4	**4.2**	27.0	9.3	**7.5**
6.2	5.49	6.1	4.25	**7.3**	3.4	1.60	9.39	4.29	39.4	**2.3**	46.6	36.7	**7.7**
6.8	0.00	0.0	0.00	**10.0**	2.4	15.80	17.26	1.30	77.1	**5.0**	1,003.9	101.0	**1.7**
1.7	3.18	22.1	1.46	**1.7**	1.1	0.18	1.83	4.25	63.2	**2.8**	10.7	14.7	**7.4**
2.4	1.28	9.3	0.62	**5.1**	0.9	1.17	12.17	4.40	59.1	**1.5**	11.4	23.1	**6.2**
2.5	1.45	11.5	1.59	**1.0**	-0.4	-0.15	-1.96	3.57	69.7	**0.9**	19.9	36.1	**3.9**
9.3	0.01	0.0	-0.05	**3.7**	0.2	0.58	2.97	5.23	86.9	**3.2**	37.9	18.5	**7.2**
3.1	4.29	18.6	0.51	**1.4**	0.0	0.22	2.06	3.06	90.9	**5.5**	35.0	1.7	**3.3**
4.3	1.28	9.6	0.70	**2.6**	0.7	0.28	3.52	3.52	78.1	**1.0**	5.7	29.1	**4.0**
3.0	4.31	14.3	0.96	**2.5**	0.2	0.18	0.90	3.17	56.5	**1.4**	31.0	40.5	**6.0**
3.2	4.19	20.0	1.66	**4.9**	68.8	1.02	8.99	4.58	60.6	**1.6**	9.0	22.1	**9.3**
0.0	16.85	199.7	2.74	**0.0**	-6.5	-2.04	-55.78	2.52	120.4	**1.7**	15.7	22.4	**0.2**
3.9	0.91	6.2	2.21	**1.3**	-0.8	-0.65	-6.76	4.03	84.3	**1.7**	26.8	25.9	**5.5**
3.7	2.06	11.7	0.80	**6.9**	3.2	1.21	9.52	4.69	55.3	**1.0**	25.5	42.9	**7.2**
2.5	0.96	6.0	0.03	**3.5**	1.9	0.76	8.24	3.07	59.0	**1.1**	6.4	27.3	**3.8**
1.2	2.95	23.9	2.01	**1.1**	-0.2	-0.19	-2.42	3.69	77.2	**1.7**	15.6	22.1	**2.8**
2.7	1.66	10.6	1.63	**6.3**	1.6	0.92	8.92	5.45	48.3	**1.1**	10.4	29.5	**7.0**
3.9	2.63	14.7	0.64	**2.1**	0.5	0.27	2.10	4.34	73.8	**1.3**	10.8	25.6	**6.3**
0.0	7.91	54.8	1.76	**1.8**	-11.4	-5.10	-37.56	4.90	195.7	**2.0**	9.0	18.4	**5.0**
2.5	1.61	12.6	1.24	**0.1**	-7.3	-1.25	-13.71	4.19	102.9	**1.7**	20.5	23.5	**4.0**
4.1	0.48	3.6	0.17	**7.4**	1.7	1.12	10.64	4.46	63.9	**3.1**	19.6	14.0	**5.7**

Name	City	State	Rating	2008 Rating	2007 Rating	Total Assets ($Mil)	One Year Asset Growth	Asset Mix (As a % of Total Assets) Comm-ercial Loans	Cons-umer Loans	Home Mort-gages	Secur-ities	Capital-ization Index	Leverage Ratio	Risk-based Capital Ratio
CITIZENS DEPOSIT BK ARLIN	ARLINGTON	KY	**A-**	A-	A-	173	6.00	12.1	6.3	22.9	34.6	**9.3**	10.6	17.6
CITIZENS EXCHANGE BANK	PEARSON	GA	**D-**	D+	B	27	2.08	3.5	8.1	17.5	11.2	**9.4**	10.6	22.1
CITIZENS EXCHANGE BANK	FAIRMOUNT	IN	**C+**	C+	C+	58	2.67	2.8	4.6	23.8	29.8	**10.0**	12.0	24.2
CITIZENS FINANCIAL BANK	MUNSTER	IN	**D-**	D-	D	1,123	3.77	7.0	0.1	17.8	19.1	**7.1**	9.1	13.3
▲ CITIZENS FIRST BANK	THE VILLAGES	FL	**C-**	D+	D+	1,202	3.76	0.7	0.7	7.0	58.2	**4.7**	6.7	14.1
CITIZENS FIRST BANK	CLINTON	IA	**C+**	C	C	138	2.79	31.0	3.9	14.1	9.5	**3.2**	9.6	10.1
▲ CITIZENS FIRST BANK	BOWLING GREEN	KY	**C**	D+	C-	349	1.65	15.1	2.8	15.2	11.3	**8.0**	10.0	13.4
▲ CITIZENS FIRST BANK	WARTBURG	TN	**D+**	D	C	156	-3.22	4.5	6.4	32.8	11.3	**6.0**	8.0	12.5
▼ CITIZENS FIRST BANK	VIROQUA	WI	**C**	C+	C+	149	3.61	6.9	5.8	14.8	13.5	**5.7**	9.0	11.5
CITIZENS FIRST NATIONAL B	STORM LAKE	IA	**A**	A	A	194	2.71	7.4	5.7	6.7	40.7	**8.9**	10.3	17.1
CITIZENS FIRST NATIONAL B	PRINCETON	IL	**D-**	D-	D+	1,095	-13.12	4.9	1.2	11.7	23.9	**4.2**	6.6	10.6
CITIZENS FIRST ST BK OF W	WALNUT	IL	**D-**	D	D+	61	0.22	8.8	10.8	26.3	22.3	**5.6**	7.6	14.3
CITIZENS FS&LA	COVINGTON	KY	**B**	B-	B-	29	-2.66	0.0	0.3	63.7	20.7	**10.0**	30.0	61.5
CITIZENS FS&LA OF BELLEFO	BELLEFONTAINE	OH	**C**	C	C	142	6.52	0.0	0.1	57.4	8.8	**6.7**	8.7	16.6
CITIZENS GUARANTY BANK	IRVINE	KY	**C+**	C+	C+	138	8.41	2.8	8.1	31.9	19.0	**5.1**	7.1	12.1
CITIZENS INDEPENDENT BANK	SAINT LOUIS PARK	MN	**D-**	D-	D-	299	-3.16	15.8	11.3	15.0	14.3	**6.0**	8.1	11.8
CITIZENS NATIONAL BK	PUTNAM	CT	**B**	B+	A	291	-1.79	3.5	0.7	11.6	53.9	**10.0**	11.3	22.2
CITIZENS NATIONAL BK	GREENLEAF	KS	**B**	B	B-	175	11.94	3.3	4.2	15.2	54.2	**5.7**	7.7	17.9
CITIZENS NATIONAL BK	ATHENS	TN	**D-**	D-	C-	549	-7.76	7.7	3.0	18.9	11.7	**7.7**	9.5	14.1
CITIZENS NATIONAL BK	SEVIERVILLE	TN	**C-**	C-	B+	851	2.78	2.6	0.6	15.4	16.7	**6.7**	8.8	13.6
CITIZENS NATIONAL BK	CAMERON	TX	**B**	B-	B	305	2.85	6.6	1.5	4.6	49.3	**8.2**	9.8	19.1
CITIZENS NATIONAL BK	CROCKETT	TX	**C+**	C+	B-	83	-8.02	6.6	10.2	7.9	35.3	**6.7**	8.7	18.3
CITIZENS NATIONAL BK	HENDERSON	TX	**B+**	B	B	867	2.13	5.5	4.8	21.3	34.3	**7.9**	9.6	18.8
CITIZENS NATIONAL BK	WINDSOR	VA	**C**	C-	C+	49	3.92	5.4	5.9	22.0	15.7	**10.0**	13.3	19.4
CITIZENS NATIONAL BK NA	BOSSIER CITY	LA	**B**	B	B-	422	14.44	9.4	2.5	15.3	15.9	**7.1**	9.1	13.1
▼ CITIZENS NB AT	BROWNWOOD	TX	**A-**	A	A	188	3.54	14.9	5.9	10.6	14.2	**10.0**	11.4	16.5
▲ CITIZENS NB GREATER ST LO	MAPLEWOOD	MO	**D+**	C	B-	484	0.89	17.5	2.3	7.3	16.9	**6.9**	10.2	12.5
CITIZENS NB OF ALBION	ALBION	IL	**A**	A	A	250	13.37	10.5	3.7	14.1	28.1	**10.0**	15.3	24.4
▼ CITIZENS NB OF BLUFFTON	BLUFFTON	OH	**C-**	C	C+	563	-0.42	9.1	0.6	10.9	22.5	**6.2**	8.3	15.3
CITIZENS NB OF CHEBOYGAN	CHEBOYGAN	MI	**C-**	D+	D+	255	2.37	2.0	2.3	25.9	29.6	**6.5**	8.5	17.2
CITIZENS NB OF CHILLICOTH	CHILLICOTHE	OH	**C-**	D+	C-	144	1.40	9.5	2.3	28.3	12.4	**7.4**	9.3	14.8
CITIZENS NB OF CROSBYTON	CROSBYTON	TX	**A-**	A-	A-	44	2.75	2.7	4.1	4.9	6.3	**10.0**	17.2	34.4
▼ CITIZENS NB OF HAMMOND	HAMMOND	NY	**D**	C-	C-	18	10.71	2.5	6.1	37.6	38.7	**5.9**	7.9	22.4
CITIZENS NB OF HILLSBORO	HILLSBORO	TX	**B**	B	B	169	-2.37	2.6	3.0	4.0	78.2	**9.5**	10.7	29.1
CITIZENS NB OF LEBANON	LEBANON	KY	**B**	B+	A-	116	-4.18	2.5	5.8	12.1	57.8	**7.9**	9.6	18.8
CITIZENS NB OF	MCCONNELSVILLE	OH	**B-**	B-	B+	79	8.63	0.4	5.3	34.0	22.9	**10.0**	12.2	26.7
CITIZENS NB OF MERIDIAN	MERIDIAN	MS	**B**	B	A-	1,176	4.14	8.6	2.6	13.6	24.4	**5.9**	9.8	11.7
CITIZENS NB OF MEYERSDALE	MEYERSDALE	PA	**B-**	B-	B	77	18.80	2.7	3.8	36.6	37.6	**10.0**	13.1	23.9
CITIZENS NB OF PAINTSVILL	PAINTSVILLE	KY	**D**	D+	C	578	-0.64	7.4	9.2	21.9	19.4	**6.4**	8.5	14.2
CITIZENS NB OF PARIS	PARIS	IL	**D**	D-	B-	205	-14.60	13.8	1.5	6.2	24.5	**8.2**	9.8	16.1
▲ CITIZENS NB OF PARK RAPID	PARK RAPIDS	MN	**C+**	C	C	199	2.23	6.1	4.1	29.7	23.7	**6.5**	8.5	13.8
CITIZENS NB OF QUITMAN	QUITMAN	GA	**D**	D+	C	115	5.95	4.5	14.2	17.3	11.9	**6.5**	8.5	13.3
▲ CITIZENS NB OF SOMERSET	SOMERSET	KY	**A-**	B+	B	325	-3.51	5.2	5.1	20.4	40.8	**10.0**	11.7	22.2
CITIZENS NB OF	DAYTON	OH	**C**	C	C-	122	19.38	16.4	7.0	10.0	15.4	**6.4**	8.4	13.3
CITIZENS NB OF TEXAS	WAXAHACHIE	TX	**D-**	C-	C-	514	1.28	6.9	1.8	8.8	0.1	**6.5**	9.7	12.1
CITIZENS NB OF WILLS POIN	WILLS POINT	TX	**A**	A	A-	89	9.61	1.9	8.4	28.2	17.9	**10.0**	11.7	19.5
CITIZENS NB OF WOODSFIELD	WOODSFIELD	OH	**B**	B+	B+	52	0.05	3.7	2.6	36.2	14.4	**10.0**	13.0	25.6
CITIZENS PROGRESSIVE	COLUMBIA	LA	**D**	D	C	67	3.68	13.8	11.1	18.5	10.6	**5.2**	8.4	11.1
CITIZENS SAVINGS & LOAN A	LEAVENWORTH	KS	**B**	B	B+	194	-3.71	0.0	0.9	52.4	35.1	**10.0**	18.2	43.1
CITIZENS SAVINGS BANK	CLARKS SUMMIT	PA	**C**	C+	C+	329	-1.33	0.0	0.2	65.5	22.2	**9.3**	10.5	22.9
CITIZENS SB	ANAMOSA	IA	**B**	B	B-	110	5.08	5.2	1.4	14.1	44.5	**5.5**	7.5	13.4
CITIZENS SB	HAWKEYE	IA	**A-**	A	A-	27	8.32	1.6	4.4	7.5	50.2	**10.0**	13.0	22.1
CITIZENS SB	MARSHALLTOWN	IA	**C**	C	C-	48	-3.40	9.3	2.1	30.0	0.4	**6.1**	8.1	12.0
CITIZENS SB	SPILLVILLE	IA	**A-**	B+	B	60	7.85	5.2	0.7	3.8	34.9	**10.0**	11.7	16.0
CITIZENS SB	BOGALUSA	LA	**D+**	C	C+	234	-0.65	1.5	6.7	44.1	2.0	**6.4**	8.4	14.1
CITIZENS SB	MARTINS FERRY	OH	**C**	C-	C	423	-4.88	10.0	10.9	15.1	24.3	**6.6**	8.6	13.3
▼ CITIZENS SB & TRUST CO	NASHVILLE	TN	**D-**	C	C	87	7.93	2.9	2.7	5.1	13.2	**7.9**	9.6	13.5
CITIZENS SECURITY BANK &	BIXBY	OK	**B-**	C+	B-	635	-0.06	19.4	4.8	17.5	5.1	**5.6**	7.6	11.5
CITIZENS SOUTH BANK	GASTONIA	NC	**D**	C	B-	1,060	33.78	5.1	0.3	16.5	9.3	**8.1**	9.7	16.8
CITIZENS ST BK OF NEW CAS	NEW CASTLE	IN	**C+**	B-	B+	244	-0.23	4.3	7.6	16.8	39.8	**8.1**	9.7	18.9

Asset Quality Index	Non-Performing Loans as a % of Total Loans	Non-Performing Loans as a % of Capital	Net Charge-offs / Avg Loans	Profitability Index	Net Income ($Mil)	Return on Assets (R.O.A.)	Return on Equity (R.O.E.)	Net Interest Spread	Overhead Efficiency Ratio	Liquidity Index	Liquidity Ratio	Hot Money Ratio	Stability Index
6.6	0.74	3.7	0.21	**7.7**	3.2	1.88	16.58	3.78	47.0	**1.2**	30.8	53.6	**8.0**
0.0	15.29	67.5	1.02	**1.8**	0.1	0.24	2.31	3.76	77.2	**3.0**	36.6	19.0	**4.9**
5.6	2.59	9.3	0.29	**2.7**	0.2	0.38	3.01	3.49	84.2	**5.1**	59.1	12.9	**6.5**
0.3	6.76	44.1	0.82	**2.2**	4.3	0.39	3.89	3.80	79.6	**3.9**	27.3	14.2	**5.9**
3.3	5.33	20.7	2.68	**2.2**	4.3	0.37	4.91	3.78	46.4	**6.7**	52.5	5.9	**4.4**
5.7	0.86	6.7	0.63	**5.2**	1.6	1.21	12.93	4.06	64.4	**2.7**	21.2	15.9	**5.3**
5.1	0.47	3.2	0.21	**2.9**	2.8	0.80	7.19	4.15	66.3	**1.4**	7.2	23.0	**4.4**
1.7	5.67	46.2	0.68	**1.9**	0.3	0.20	2.72	3.97	85.4	**1.7**	13.0	20.3	**3.4**
1.9	1.10	8.4	0.29	**5.1**	1.7	1.14	11.03	4.57	64.5	**3.0**	17.2	14.0	**7.0**
8.4	0.16	0.8	0.01	**8.8**	4.1	2.06	18.46	4.13	49.7	**4.8**	46.9	12.5	**8.6**
0.0	11.31	77.4	3.06	**0.0**	-16.4	-1.41	-16.86	3.96	74.8	**2.6**	9.4	15.5	**5.7**
0.7	5.85	41.1	0.63	**0.2**	-0.4	-0.71	-7.86	3.43	106.0	**3.7**	32.9	14.3	**3.9**
9.7	0.49	1.1	0.00	**4.4**	0.3	0.93	3.20	4.10	60.2	**3.0**	35.6	18.6	**7.1**
7.3	0.30	2.6	0.00	**2.8**	0.4	0.28	3.44	2.58	85.2	**1.1**	22.4	32.6	**4.3**
5.2	0.68	5.6	0.26	**4.0**	0.9	0.70	9.09	4.43	81.7	**1.3**	13.2	27.1	**4.8**
0.4	6.11	48.6	1.80	**0.0**	-5.7	-1.82	-22.48	3.45	130.9	**5.2**	14.1	0.3	**3.7**
6.1	1.65	4.4	0.72	**3.4**	1.7	0.55	5.05	3.95	81.7	**3.9**	17.1	9.7	**5.8**
9.0	0.12	0.6	0.09	**5.2**	1.6	0.95	10.91	3.75	69.9	**4.2**	30.9	11.0	**4.7**
0.3	6.55	44.3	1.31	**1.7**	0.1	0.01	0.10	3.62	62.7	**1.1**	11.3	29.0	**5.5**
1.9	1.21	8.3	0.23	**4.2**	7.5	0.87	10.44	3.20	71.7	**0.7**	14.3	43.1	**6.6**
9.2	0.19	0.7	0.25	**4.9**	3.8	1.29	12.52	3.52	62.5	**3.6**	43.5	17.7	**6.4**
8.4	0.00	0.0	1.52	**2.8**	0.3	0.39	4.64	4.00	79.9	**3.2**	36.9	17.8	**3.8**
8.0	0.15	0.7	0.10	**5.7**	11.7	1.35	13.35	3.84	69.1	**2.2**	29.2	20.9	**6.8**
3.2	3.83	19.2	0.40	**1.6**	0.2	0.39	2.86	4.15	93.0	**1.0**	25.7	38.9	**5.2**
7.3	0.15	1.1	0.08	**6.2**	4.1	1.08	11.44	4.99	67.1	**1.5**	13.3	24.1	**5.4**
5.1	1.02	5.5	0.11	**7.4**	2.9	1.60	12.94	4.34	56.3	**3.0**	29.9	16.7	**8.7**
2.2	1.51	10.0	0.64	**5.3**	4.5	0.96	9.31	4.04	52.7	**1.1**	4.1	26.7	**6.5**
8.4	0.29	1.2	0.02	**6.5**	2.8	1.20	7.26	3.81	52.4	**2.6**	31.5	19.0	**8.3**
2.2	2.96	23.9	0.24	**6.7**	9.3	1.69	19.41	4.20	61.2	**2.2**	4.5	16.8	**6.6**
2.0	5.32	29.7	1.60	**2.4**	0.8	0.33	3.97	3.96	80.6	**5.1**	45.3	10.9	**4.6**
2.4	2.08	14.8	0.16	**4.1**	0.9	0.63	6.03	4.63	74.9	**4.3**	13.5	6.7	**5.6**
9.2	0.02	0.1	0.00	**4.1**	0.3	0.75	4.70	2.16	71.4	**3.7**	74.5	26.8	**9.2**
3.8	2.89	15.8	0.17	**3.3**	0.1	0.42	4.72	4.10	85.6	**2.7**	22.9	15.9	**2.3**
9.9	0.43	0.6	0.02	**4.5**	2.9	1.76	13.87	2.77	73.0	**4.3**	57.5	17.7	**7.6**
6.5	1.44	4.6	0.20	**4.8**	1.3	1.12	11.17	3.50	68.8	**3.8**	44.2	16.8	**5.9**
5.7	2.04	9.3	0.11	**3.4**	0.4	0.55	4.46	3.26	76.4	**3.1**	21.8	14.0	**6.9**
4.8	2.32	12.9	0.26	**4.8**	9.9	0.83	9.19	3.55	65.4	**2.1**	22.5	23.0	**8.1**
6.3	1.98	8.8	0.05	**2.8**	0.4	0.54	4.26	3.15	85.5	**2.5**	44.4	30.4	**7.0**
1.2	2.53	17.7	1.28	**2.5**	2.9	0.49	4.35	3.60	81.3	**1.8**	17.1	21.1	**6.0**
1.1	5.68	28.2	3.53	**1.1**	0.6	0.25	2.58	3.08	71.6	**2.5**	21.2	17.3	**3.5**
3.9	1.47	10.7	0.35	**5.9**	2.9	1.49	17.57	4.23	59.9	**1.9**	12.2	19.4	**4.7**
0.9	3.11	22.6	1.55	**3.2**	0.5	0.44	5.41	4.08	58.0	**0.9**	23.1	38.8	**4.4**
6.2	1.63	7.1	0.02	**6.2**	5.5	1.67	15.05	3.91	68.2	**2.3**	20.3	17.9	**6.8**
2.9	1.03	7.0	0.39	**4.1**	0.7	0.63	7.16	3.97	61.8	**3.5**	35.5	16.0	**4.0**
0.0	5.64	45.0	0.28	**6.5**	7.5	1.44	14.16	5.75	66.5	**4.2**	3.5	6.1	**8.9**
8.4	0.09	0.4	0.00	**9.5**	1.9	2.21	19.31	4.62	52.9	**1.8**	25.9	24.0	**8.9**
9.3	0.00	0.0	0.00	**3.9**	0.3	0.51	3.91	4.70	84.5	**5.9**	33.3	1.0	**7.1**
1.0	2.18	17.3	0.14	**6.3**	1.1	1.62	11.35	6.20	71.3	**0.7**	11.9	35.1	**6.5**
8.9	0.26	0.8	0.00	**3.8**	1.4	0.71	4.01	2.88	69.9	**3.3**	47.0	20.8	**7.9**
5.6	0.91	5.8	0.01	**2.5**	0.6	0.18	1.77	3.32	91.8	**3.1**	30.9	16.6	**5.8**
9.1	0.00	0.0	0.00	**7.3**	1.8	1.70	19.63	4.05	52.8	**4.8**	32.1	8.1	**6.4**
7.6	0.00	0.0	0.04	**5.7**	0.3	1.20	8.77	3.84	62.3	**5.8**	54.8	7.8	**8.2**
6.1	0.66	5.8	0.11	**4.6**	0.5	1.09	12.92	4.22	72.1	**4.3**	19.1	7.1	**4.9**
7.0	0.84	4.0	0.04	**7.5**	0.8	1.43	12.89	4.36	50.6	**4.1**	39.1	14.0	**7.6**
1.0	1.62	13.0	0.35	**4.4**	1.6	0.70	8.53	4.92	69.8	**1.4**	13.0	25.0	**4.6**
3.2	1.63	11.4	0.55	**4.7**	3.9	0.87	10.05	4.12	65.5	**3.2**	12.8	12.5	**4.8**
0.0	3.19	22.2	0.19	**4.0**	0.4	0.48	5.03	4.86	76.9	**1.0**	27.3	59.6	**5.3**
4.3	0.77	7.3	0.38	**5.5**	8.6	1.32	17.10	4.97	67.3	**0.7**	7.6	34.4	**5.9**
1.0	5.74	36.6	1.51	**3.6**	10.0	0.95	9.79	3.13	47.9	**2.1**	24.1	24.9	**4.5**
2.6	4.38	19.2	0.64	**3.9**	1.7	0.69	6.68	4.17	71.5	**4.6**	49.8	14.4	**5.3**

Name	City	State	Rating	2008 Rating	2007 Rating	Total Assets ($Mil)	One Year Asset Growth	Asset Mix (As a % of Total Assets) Comm-ercial Loans	Cons-umer Loans	Home Mort-gages	Secur-ities	Capital-ization Index	Leverage Ratio	Risk-based Capital Ratio
▼ CITIZENS ST BK OF TAYLOR	REYNOLDS	GA	**C**	C+	B	44	-2.92	6.6	10.8	16.6	21.3	**10.0**	11.5	20.5
CITIZENS STATE BK	VERNON	AL	**D+**	B-	A-	94	2.61	9.4	5.7	13.8	29.4	**8.7**	10.1	16.8
▼ CITIZENS STATE BK	BALD KNOB	AR	**D**	C-	C	78	-0.64	8.3	3.4	6.7	59.4	**5.3**	7.3	19.0
CITIZENS STATE BK	PERRY	FL	**D-**	C-	C-	98	16.73	33.3	7.9	3.0	9.9	**6.2**	9.9	11.9
▲ CITIZENS STATE BK	KINGSLAND	GA	**D+**	C-	B	73	-11.67	2.9	3.2	19.5	3.2	**4.4**	7.3	10.7
CITIZENS STATE BK	FORT DODGE	IA	**C+**	B-	B-	119	6.33	10.4	2.4	11.2	26.3	**9.2**	10.5	14.8
CITIZENS STATE BK	MONTICELLO	IA	**B+**	B-	B-	302	5.47	8.0	1.4	5.4	24.1	**6.7**	8.7	12.3
▲ CITIZENS STATE BK	SHELDON	IA	**B+**	B-	B	98	2.29	8.3	5.7	16.7	24.1	**8.6**	10.1	15.3
CITIZENS STATE BK	WYOMING	IA	**A**	A	A	85	1.88	6.0	4.7	4.8	48.6	**10.0**	19.1	36.5
CITIZENS STATE BK	LENA	IL	**D+**	C-	D+	204	5.21	13.7	5.6	8.2	21.6	**6.7**	8.7	12.3
CITIZENS STATE BK	GRAINFIELD	KS	**C-**	C	C+	10	8.50	2.9	1.2	2.6	1.2	**5.7**	7.7	20.3
CITIZENS STATE BK	GRIDLEY	KS	**B-**	B-	C+	122	40.36	9.4	6.5	20.8	24.1	**7.2**	9.2	14.2
CITIZENS STATE BK	HUGOTON	KS	**A-**	A-	A	126	-5.31	3.2	1.4	3.0	28.1	**10.0**	11.9	18.6
CITIZENS STATE BK	MARYSVILLE	KS	**D**	C-	B	289	-5.30	16.1	2.0	8.5	17.3	**6.4**	8.5	12.0
CITIZENS STATE BK	MILTONVALE	KS	**C+**	C+	C+	30	-16.48	3.1	2.1	8.5	35.2	**8.5**	10.0	18.7
▲ CITIZENS STATE BK	MORLAND	KS	**B-**	C+	C+	30	6.18	9.5	5.5	8.3	8.9	**7.7**	9.4	15.6
CITIZENS STATE BK	MOUNDRIDGE	KS	**B+**	B+	B	246	7.69	4.5	1.1	5.4	10.9	**6.6**	8.6	13.5
CITIZENS STATE BK	PAOLA	KS	**C-**	C	B-	72	4.48	3.7	1.2	10.3	44.0	**10.0**	12.8	22.1
CITIZENS STATE BK	CARLETON	NE	**D**	C-	C-	15	6.70	8.4	7.2	8.5	0.0	**4.7**	6.7	12.3
▲ CITIZENS STATE BK	WISNER	NE	**C**	C-	C-	240	48.29	7.3	2.6	5.2	8.6	**5.1**	8.4	11.1
CITIZENS STATE BK	MORRISON	OK	**C+**	C	C	76	2.88	11.5	3.3	19.7	19.1	**6.8**	8.8	13.2
CITIZENS STATE BK	OKEMAH	OK	**B**	B-	C	172	11.20	2.6	1.9	82.7	3.9	**6.4**	8.4	16.6
CITIZENS STATE BK	JASPER	TN	**C-**	C-	C	65	-2.08	11.7	9.9	26.9	8.2	**5.9**	8.1	11.7
CITIZENS STATE BK	ANTON	TX	**D**	D+	D+	34	9.96	8.3	4.7	0.0	14.7	**5.7**	7.7	12.7
CITIZENS STATE BK	BUFFALO	TX	**B+**	B	B	405	22.22	3.6	3.4	5.4	67.8	**5.8**	7.8	20.0
▼ CITIZENS STATE BK	GANADO	TX	**D**	C-	C	59	4.39	3.8	2.9	6.5	71.5	**4.3**	6.3	24.1
CITIZENS STATE BK	MILES	TX	**B-**	C+	C+	77	-3.52	10.5	4.9	27.5	3.9	**5.8**	7.8	11.8
CITIZENS STATE BK	PRINCETON	TX	**B-**	B	B+	38	2.76	2.5	2.0	7.4	53.2	**10.0**	15.8	41.4
CITIZENS STATE BK	ROMA	TX	**B+**	B+	A-	71	2.59	4.7	15.7	16.5	47.3	**9.9**	10.9	25.0
▼ CITIZENS STATE BK	SEALY	TX	**B+**	A-	A-	171	-1.53	4.0	2.6	9.5	65.3	**8.7**	10.1	25.4
CITIZENS STATE BK	SOMERVILLE	TX	**C+**	B-	B	363	10.44	7.7	8.2	16.3	32.5	**5.8**	7.8	13.8
CITIZENS STATE BK	TENAHA	TX	**B**	B	B	35	8.36	5.7	28.6	15.5	23.4	**10.0**	12.0	24.1
CITIZENS STATE BK	TYLER	TX	**B**	B	B+	255	2.94	10.4	3.8	11.0	12.8	**7.5**	9.4	14.5
CITIZENS STATE BK	WOODVILLE	TX	**C-**	D	E-	118	1.07	6.0	5.4	42.0	25.9	**6.7**	8.7	15.6
CITIZENS STATE BK	CADOTT	WI	**D**	D-	D+	103	4.31	6.0	1.5	13.8	23.3	**6.1**	8.1	12.4
CITIZENS STATE BK	HUDSON	WI	**E-**	E-	E	145	-15.21	14.7	1.0	14.7	14.8	**0.6**	4.5	7.3
CITIZENS STATE BK & TRUST	ELLSWORTH	KS	**B+**	B+	B-	101	22.38	2.0	3.9	20.9	35.2	**8.7**	10.1	16.7
CITIZENS STATE BK & TRUST	HIAWATHA	KS	**A-**	A	A	71	-0.20	7.1	3.9	8.6	27.4	**10.0**	15.6	24.7
▲ CITIZENS STATE BK & TRUST	WOODBINE	KS	**C-**	D+	C	9	0.13	17.7	3.2	8.9	36.1	**10.0**	14.2	24.7
CITIZENS STATE BK AT MOHA	MOHALL	ND	**B-**	C+	C+	50	7.60	16.0	5.5	9.7	17.6	**4.7**	7.0	10.8
CITIZENS STATE BK CORRIGA	CORRIGAN	TX	**C+**	B	B	102	4.21	9.4	17.1	14.1	31.3	**8.4**	10.0	17.6
CITIZENS STATE BK MIDWEST	CAVALIER	ND	**D-**	D	C-	146	-10.01	6.6	3.6	5.5	14.3	**4.6**	7.3	10.8
CITIZENS STATE BK	NORWOOD	MN	**D+**	D+	C-	90	15.93	14.8	4.2	8.8	2.3	**5.1**	8.5	11.1
CITIZENS STATE BK OF ARLI	ARLINGTON	SD	**B+**	A-	B+	96	8.14	6.9	2.1	5.6	18.6	**10.0**	11.2	16.1
CITIZENS STATE BK OF CHEN	CHENEY	KS	**A-**	A-	A-	46	-1.26	11.7	14.0	17.6	20.6	**10.0**	12.8	19.7
CITIZENS STATE BK OF CHOT	FAIRFIELD	MT	**A**	A	A	183	136.38	7.2	4.2	6.2	15.5	**10.0**	17.7	26.7
▲ CITIZENS STATE BK OF CLAY	CLAYTON	WI	**B-**	C	C-	97	19.51	16.6	1.3	21.8	0.0	**5.3**	8.2	11.2
▲ CITIZENS STATE BK OF CORT	CORTEZ	CO	**E**	D	D	80	-2.78	6.2	3.4	15.8	13.8	**8.9**	10.3	17.1
▼ CITIZENS STATE BK OF FINL	FINLEY	ND	**D+**	B-	C+	115	3.01	13.0	2.6	2.2	17.9	**6.4**	8.4	13.3
▼ CITIZENS STATE BK OF GLEN	GLENVILLE	MN	**B-**	B+	A-	36	7.10	4.3	6.9	8.5	8.9	**7.2**	9.1	25.5
CITIZENS STATE BK OF HAYF	HAYFIELD	MN	**C+**	C+	C+	63	3.99	9.4	4.1	11.8	3.3	**5.2**	7.7	11.1
CITIZENS STATE BK OF LANK	LANKIN	ND	**D**	D	E	37	1.11	4.0	6.6	9.5	8.2	**6.3**	8.5	12.0
▼ CITIZENS STATE BK OF LOYA	LOYAL	WI	**C**	C+	B+	146	5.02	5.7	1.3	14.0	21.0	**8.1**	9.7	14.8
CITIZENS STATE BK OF LULI	LULING	TX	**B-**	C+	B-	54	1.90	11.2	3.8	15.9	11.8	**10.0**	12.3	17.8
CITIZENS STATE BK OF MILF	MILFORD	IL	**D**	D+	C-	47	-13.45	18.3	2.1	2.8	26.9	**3.8**	6.9	10.4
CITIZENS STATE BK OF OLIV	OLIVIA	MN	**D-**	D	D+	26	-1.49	15.1	4.4	1.3	22.7	**6.3**	8.3	14.7
CITIZENS STATE BK OF ONTO	ONTONAGON	MI	**B-**	B	B+	51	-2.61	3.8	6.1	18.7	48.2	**10.0**	15.6	36.6
▼ CITIZENS STATE BK OF OURA	OURAY	CO	**B**	A-	A-	82	1.69	3.2	2.5	9.2	54.3	**8.2**	9.8	21.0
CITIZENS STATE BK OF ROSE	ROSEAU	MN	**A-**	A-	A-	183	2.16	6.0	4.7	3.7	47.2	**10.0**	12.0	21.4
▲ CITIZENS STATE BK OF SHAK	SHAKOPEE	MN	**D+**	D-	D-	22	-19.23	4.7	2.4	13.5	12.7	**4.7**	6.7	18.9

Asset Quality Index	Non-Performing Loans as a % of Total Loans	Non-Performing Loans as a % of Capital	Net Charge-offs Avg Loans	Profitability Index	Net Income ($Mil)	Return on Assets (R.O.A.)	Return on Equity (R.O.E.)	Net Interest Spread	Overhead Efficiency Ratio	Liquidity Index	Liquidity Ratio	Hot Money Ratio	Stability Index
3.5	5.00	19.9	1.44	**0.0**	-0.4	-0.95	-7.64	4.82	109.5	**2.5**	36.0	23.1	**5.4**
1.4	6.77	38.1	1.82	**2.7**	0.3	0.33	3.26	2.68	59.0	**1.2**	29.2	49.7	**5.7**
2.7	8.23	23.0	8.92	**0.3**	-1.0	-1.21	-12.49	3.20	88.6	**3.8**	58.6	19.2	**4.2**
0.3	7.06	50.1	0.51	**0.5**	-0.9	-1.08	-10.81	4.51	82.1	**0.7**	12.7	38.1	**5.6**
0.0	18.05	137.7	2.30	**0.0**	-1.4	-1.79	-21.15	3.17	142.4	**0.7**	14.6	47.8	**3.4**
4.4	0.91	5.4	0.39	**6.7**	1.4	1.21	11.22	4.53	57.9	**3.8**	27.5	11.7	**6.6**
5.8	0.63	4.4	0.19	**7.6**	5.4	1.82	15.50	4.04	52.8	**2.8**	23.6	15.9	**7.5**
6.0	0.50	3.2	0.04	**6.7**	1.6	1.62	14.59	4.14	56.7	**4.8**	28.7	6.1	**7.3**
8.4	0.47	1.0	0.02	**7.8**	1.5	1.77	8.32	4.28	55.6	**4.9**	66.7	14.7	**10.0**
1.6	1.87	13.9	0.47	**5.0**	2.3	1.17	11.70	3.83	60.3	**2.1**	12.5	18.3	**5.3**
8.6	0.00	0.0	0.00	**7.7**	0.2	1.60	22.59	4.53	61.3	**4.2**	45.9	12.8	**4.3**
6.2	0.57	4.1	-0.02	**4.9**	0.6	0.66	7.44	4.58	72.7	**2.6**	12.4	15.7	**4.8**
6.5	1.00	4.6	0.05	**7.7**	1.7	1.35	11.96	4.48	57.2	**2.2**	20.1	18.7	**6.8**
0.8	1.67	13.4	3.39	**2.1**	-1.7	-0.57	-5.93	3.37	41.5	**1.6**	10.3	21.2	**6.4**
8.9	0.04	0.2	0.00	**2.9**	0.2	0.56	6.06	3.59	88.8	**2.1**	33.7	26.7	**5.1**
6.0	0.10	0.7	0.00	**3.9**	0.2	0.77	8.33	4.31	82.8	**2.6**	24.3	17.2	**6.4**
8.1	0.00	0.0	-0.09	**6.2**	2.6	1.09	12.00	3.70	60.5	**3.8**	41.0	16.4	**6.1**
6.3	0.74	2.6	-0.30	**6.0**	0.8	1.08	5.41	4.53	59.1	**2.5**	38.8	25.6	**3.7**
6.8	0.00	0.0	-0.03	**5.0**	0.1	0.86	12.63	4.84	76.7	**1.8**	19.8	21.0	**2.3**
3.9	0.43	3.7	0.24	**6.0**	2.4	1.33	14.00	5.03	65.3	**2.8**	16.4	15.4	**6.5**
5.5	0.34	2.7	0.73	**5.5**	1.0	1.33	15.36	5.00	69.1	**1.5**	20.5	26.8	**4.9**
6.0	0.51	6.3	0.13	**9.4**	3.5	2.31	27.40	3.68	37.6	**0.3**	3.3	70.0	**4.3**
4.1	1.07	9.2	0.26	**3.4**	0.4	0.65	8.33	5.68	89.6	**1.4**	9.3	23.6	**4.4**
8.0	0.00	0.0	0.12	**1.9**	0.1	0.31	3.95	3.23	87.4	**2.4**	53.4	40.7	**2.5**
8.0	0.17	0.5	0.15	**7.2**	6.6	1.80	19.75	4.22	48.4	**2.7**	53.7	35.2	**6.1**
8.6	1.72	3.8	0.03	**2.3**	0.2	0.29	3.69	3.01	87.1	**3.8**	79.0	26.5	**3.0**
8.4	0.00	0.0	0.06	**8.2**	1.6	1.99	26.49	4.82	54.8	**1.0**	18.4	33.7	**5.2**
6.8	0.73	1.2	0.91	**2.4**	0.2	0.57	2.21	2.90	91.9	**4.1**	72.3	19.7	**6.0**
5.5	0.47	1.9	0.36	**4.9**	0.8	1.12	9.28	5.42	72.7	**2.4**	53.0	38.2	**6.9**
8.3	0.03	0.1	0.95	**5.2**	2.5	1.44	13.07	3.96	68.0	**4.3**	71.4	19.8	**7.4**
5.0	0.72	4.7	0.76	**4.4**	2.4	0.68	8.43	4.13	66.8	**3.1**	16.7	13.9	**4.0**
3.8	1.73	7.1	1.57	**8.2**	0.5	1.51	12.79	5.63	47.5	**4.1**	51.9	16.6	**5.9**
7.1	0.00	0.0	0.09	**5.3**	2.6	1.03	11.60	4.03	69.4	**2.4**	29.2	19.4	**4.9**
4.6	1.67	12.0	0.05	**3.0**	0.9	0.76	8.66	5.35	93.5	**4.0**	7.2	7.6	**2.6**
2.1	2.25	15.4	1.18	**0.9**	0.0	0.04	0.41	4.20	86.5	**4.3**	28.0	9.2	**3.0**
0.3	4.99	50.3	2.94	**0.0**	-2.2	-1.37	-25.15	3.77	111.1	**1.3**	14.6	27.4	**1.1**
6.2	0.31	1.7	-0.06	**6.0**	1.2	1.36	14.69	3.69	67.6	**3.0**	26.7	15.6	**6.9**
8.6	0.04	0.1	0.08	**5.0**	0.7	0.96	6.06	3.61	75.7	**5.6**	35.1	4.0	**9.2**
1.5	6.51	22.6	-0.03	**1.3**	0.0	0.14	0.69	4.22	92.8	**4.6**	49.1	11.9	**6.4**
5.5	0.27	2.5	0.72	**3.6**	0.3	0.64	9.01	3.56	65.5	**2.4**	12.5	16.6	**3.9**
3.5	2.00	10.8	0.10	**9.1**	2.2	2.21	20.38	4.81	54.6	**2.2**	29.5	21.4	**7.8**
0.2	9.59	74.3	2.63	**0.1**	-1.9	-1.23	-13.95	3.89	98.3	**2.8**	14.4	14.7	**3.8**
0.3	3.37	28.7	0.93	**3.9**	0.6	0.72	6.04	4.17	68.8	**1.8**	16.6	20.9	**5.6**
4.3	1.89	11.7	0.13	**5.3**	0.8	0.88	7.16	3.88	62.5	**1.9**	23.1	20.8	**7.0**
7.6	0.12	0.6	0.22	**9.9**	1.1	2.23	16.73	5.45	49.5	**1.8**	9.4	19.4	**9.2**
6.1	0.30	0.9	0.44	**9.1**	2.2	1.40	7.62	4.53	49.2	**2.2**	35.8	27.7	**9.0**
6.9	0.04	0.4	0.03	**10.0**	2.6	3.01	39.26	4.79	47.3	**0.6**	7.3	38.8	**5.2**
1.7	4.72	26.9	0.43	**1.4**	0.3	0.29	2.91	3.31	73.3	**1.4**	13.0	24.8	**0.3**
1.7	2.16	15.9	0.59	**4.6**	1.1	0.93	10.52	4.57	68.9	**1.4**	10.9	24.5	**5.0**
5.3	2.17	8.4	0.00	**5.9**	0.4	1.21	13.06	3.65	67.8	**6.6**	63.5	4.5	**7.9**
2.7	1.03	9.5	0.10	**3.5**	0.3	0.42	5.15	4.70	80.7	**2.7**	8.4	14.9	**5.7**
6.9	0.02	0.1	0.03	**2.5**	0.2	0.55	6.54	5.19	86.6	**4.0**	18.0	9.3	**2.6**
2.6	1.99	12.7	0.32	**3.2**	0.5	0.32	3.09	3.68	68.2	**2.8**	19.1	15.6	**6.1**
5.6	0.00	0.0	0.62	**3.7**	0.3	0.56	4.51	4.99	83.5	**3.2**	31.9	16.4	**5.3**
1.8	3.25	25.1	-0.02	**3.7**	0.3	0.72	9.42	4.08	82.4	**2.8**	22.0	15.5	**1.9**
0.9	6.64	33.1	1.45	**0.0**	-0.3	-1.10	-11.90	4.02	118.7	**4.2**	49.5	15.8	**4.1**
3.7	5.26	11.3	0.02	**3.0**	0.2	0.44	2.66	4.08	88.9	**6.4**	72.7	7.6	**7.7**
3.7	0.00	0.0	0.90	**6.9**	0.9	1.16	9.78	5.22	63.8	**4.4**	54.0	15.2	**6.8**
8.8	0.34	1.1	0.20	**5.9**	2.6	1.46	10.77	3.66	58.6	**2.4**	38.1	26.8	**8.7**
1.7	12.12	46.8	0.51	**0.0**	-0.3	-4.55	-52.66	2.11	197.5	**6.4**	51.8	1.3	**3.4**

	Name	City	State	Rating	2008 Rating	2007 Rating	Total Assets ($Mil)	One Year Asset Growth	Comm-ercial Loans	Cons-umer Loans	Home Mort-gages	Secur-ities	Capital-ization Index	Leverage Ratio	Risk-based Capital Ratio
▲	CITIZENS STATE BK OF SHIP	SHIPMAN	IL	**D+**	C+	C+	57	0.99	16.5	4.9	9.3	28.6	**4.5**	6.5	10.9
	CITIZENS STATE BK OF TYLE	TYLER	MN	**D**	C-	C-	17	0.35	11.3	8.2	4.6	41.3	**8.2**	9.8	17.6
	CITIZENS STATE BK OF WAVE	WAVERLY	MN	**B-**	B-	B-	67	13.32	4.9	1.6	16.8	5.4	**6.0**	8.0	14.1
	CITIZENS TRI-COUNTY BANK	DUNLAP	TN	**D**	C-	B	508	1.77	0.0	13.3	23.1	22.1	**6.9**	8.9	14.1
	CITIZENS TRUST BANK	ATLANTA	GA	**D+**	D	D-	388	0.16	4.4	1.9	9.4	33.7	**9.2**	10.4	17.7
	CITIZENS UNION BK SHELBYV	SHELBYVILLE	KY	**D-**	D	C-	641	-10.33	4.1	0.6	18.4	7.5	**6.4**	8.4	12.4
	CITIZENS-FARMERS BK COLE	COLE CAMP	MO	**B+**	B+	A	91	-3.11	5.0	6.2	33.8	15.3	**10.0**	16.4	18.0
	CITIZENS-UNION SB	FALL RIVER	MA	**C**	C-	C-	730	5.23	9.1	0.5	35.0	20.8	**6.0**	8.1	11.8
	CITY BANK	LUBBOCK	TX	**D+**	C	C-	1,944	-4.84	12.2	3.9	9.7	2.8	**7.4**	9.3	13.9
	CITY BANK & TRUST CO	NATCHITOCHES	LA	**B+**	B+	B	242	3.25	2.4	3.7	18.4	53.0	**7.4**	9.3	21.4
	CITY BANK & TRUST CO	LINCOLN	NE	**D-**	D	D+	214	-13.08	13.2	1.2	11.4	6.9	**9.8**	10.8	14.9
	CITY BANK & TRUST CO MOBE	MOBERLY	MO	**C+**	B-	B-	152	2.15	2.8	7.1	4.9	30.5	**6.8**	8.8	13.4
	CITY BANK NEW MEXICO	RUIDOSO	NM	**D+**	C-	C-	108	-9.50	7.1	2.6	15.2	6.8	**7.2**	9.2	14.1
▼	CITY BANK OF HARTFORD	HARTFORD	AL	**C-**	C+	C	60	10.78	4.5	6.9	17.9	18.2	**6.1**	8.1	16.9
▲	CITY FIRST BANK OF DC NA	WASHINGTON	DC	**B-**	C	C	158	0.57	10.5	0.0	4.7	17.6	**10.0**	15.9	23.9
▲	CITY NATIONAL BK	LOS ANGELES	CA	**C+**	C-	B	20,976	1.10	18.3	2.0	17.1	26.9	**6.3**	8.3	15.5
	CITY NATIONAL BK	CORSICANA	TX	**B**	B	B	43	2.49	8.0	9.4	27.6	8.2	**8.3**	9.9	20.0
	CITY NATIONAL BK	COLORADO CITY	TX	**A-**	A	A	91	17.34	4.6	8.1	7.3	53.6	**7.3**	9.2	19.5
	CITY NATIONAL BK OF FLORI	MIAMI	FL	**D-**	D+	A	4,008	-10.02	5.3	0.4	9.5	24.1	**6.8**	8.8	17.7
	CITY NATIONAL BK OF METRO	METROPOLIS	IL	**A-**	B+	B+	278	16.15	4.7	4.3	22.3	47.5	**10.0**	11.7	23.7
▲	CITY NATIONAL BK OF NEW J	NEWARK	NJ	**E**	D	D+	388	-16.86	6.8	0.2	6.8	26.7	**5.7**	7.7	12.8
	CITY NATIONAL BK OF SAN S	SAN SABA	TX	**B+**	A-	A-	54	3.94	2.8	2.4	0.7	47.9	**10.0**	15.6	36.0
	CITY NATIONAL BK OF SHENA	SHENANDOAH	IA	**C**	C+	C+	72	10.89	4.8	3.2	5.9	46.6	**5.5**	7.5	12.7
	CITY NATIONAL BK OF TAYLO	TAYLOR	TX	**C+**	C+	C	184	-17.79	5.2	1.2	13.0	57.9	**7.7**	9.5	28.9
	CITY NATIONAL BK OF WV	CROSS LANES	WV	**A-**	B	B	2,613	0.43	5.5	1.6	32.4	16.1	**7.9**	9.6	13.6
	CITY NB OF SULPHUR SPRING	SULPHUR SPRINGS	TX	**B-**	B-	B-	374	2.95	8.1	7.2	29.7	8.9	**6.5**	8.5	13.3
	CITY NB&TC OF GUYMON	GUYMON	OK	**B-**	B-	B	165	7.52	4.0	4.6	15.0	55.4	**6.5**	8.5	19.9
▼	CITY NB&TC OF LAWTON	LAWTON	OK	**A-**	A	A-	276	-0.46	5.9	5.2	21.7	7.1	**10.0**	12.8	20.4
	CITY SB & TRUST CO	DE RIDDER	LA	**A-**	A	A	187	0.27	7.2	10.0	27.9	8.9	**10.0**	11.9	17.7
	CITY STATE BK	CENTRAL CITY	IA	**D-**	D-	D-	115	14.71	8.2	0.6	14.4	33.4	**7.6**	9.4	14.7
	CITY STATE BK	NORWALK	IA	**B-**	B-	C+	225	10.48	5.1	1.3	13.4	30.4	**6.2**	8.2	13.3
	CITY STATE BK	FORT SCOTT	KS	**B-**	B-	C+	31	-1.69	2.8	3.9	26.6	22.0	**8.2**	9.8	16.3
	CITY STATE BK OF PALACIOS	PALACIOS	TX	**C-**	C	D+	51	8.84	2.4	3.1	11.1	45.2	**8.4**	9.9	25.3
	CITYWIDE BANKS	AURORA	CO	**D**	D-	C-	962	0.21	15.8	0.6	5.3	19.1	**7.7**	9.5	14.2
	CIVIC BANK & TRUST	NASHVILLE	TN	**D-**	D	D+	126	3.95	4.5	1.1	10.4	33.5	**9.9**	10.9	18.4
	CLACKAMAS COUNTY BANK	SANDY	OR	**C-**	C	A-	154	4.86	1.0	1.4	8.2	16.6	**10.0**	15.0	21.9
	CLARE BANK NA	PLATTEVILLE	WI	**B+**	B	B	245	1.75	13.2	3.6	30.6	32.1	**6.6**	8.6	21.1
▲	CLAREMONT SB	CLAREMONT	NH	**C**	C	C	325	0.56	3.7	3.2	55.0	9.7	**10.0**	13.6	21.3
	CLARENCE STATE BK	CLARENCE	MO	**B**	B	B	18	0.59	6.5	4.8	8.4	44.6	**10.0**	21.5	40.3
	CLARION COUNTY	CLARION	PA	**C+**	C+	C-	118	16.40	6.1	3.6	44.1	9.3	**7.0**	9.0	14.5
	CLARKE COUNTY STATE BK	OSCEOLA	IA	**D+**	C-	C-	114	-16.34	6.4	1.0	16.7	18.8	**6.0**	8.0	12.2
	CLARKSON BANK	CLARKSON	NE	**A-**	A-	A-	54	7.10	6.3	1.5	1.6	42.4	**10.0**	11.0	17.4
	CLARKSTON STATE BK	CLARKSTON	MI	**E-**	E-	E-	104	-6.24	7.5	0.9	9.1	8.4	**0.0**	2.3	3.9
	CLASSIC BANK NA	CAMERON	TX	**B-**	C+	C+	217	5.03	6.2	4.1	17.4	27.3	**7.2**	9.1	15.6
	CLATSOP COMMUNITY BANK	SEASIDE	OR	**D**	C	C	42	23.38	9.3	1.7	9.2	13.9	**10.0**	15.7	21.1
	CLAXTON BANK	CLAXTON	GA	**D+**	D-	D	117	17.46	2.1	2.5	11.8	25.9	**7.7**	9.5	15.9
	CLAY CITY BANKING CO	CLAY CITY	IL	**C+**	B	B	82	7.00	7.4	3.6	10.7	31.2	**9.7**	10.8	17.8
	CLAY COUNTY BANK INC	CLAY	WV	**A-**	A-	A-	72	0.22	3.3	12.3	47.4	25.8	**10.0**	12.4	27.0
	CLAY COUNTY SAVINGS BANK	LIBERTY	MO	**C-**	C-	D+	97	-1.51	3.8	0.8	37.8	4.9	**10.0**	11.3	17.1
	CLAY COUNTY STATE BK	LOUISVILLE	IL	**C+**	C+	B-	75	13.27	9.1	6.4	11.7	41.6	**10.0**	12.1	23.2
	CLAYTON BANK & TRUST	KNOXVILLE	TN	**C+**	C-	C	650	8.44	18.7	9.1	11.0	12.4	**10.0**	12.6	15.3
	CLEAR LAKE BANK & TRUST C	CLEAR LAKE	IA	**B**	B-	C+	233	2.51	14.2	6.8	19.0	8.0	**5.6**	8.1	11.5
	CLEAR MOUNTAIN BANK	BRUCETON MILLS	WV	**B**	B	B+	399	3.59	6.2	7.6	39.4	12.7	**7.2**	9.1	15.4
	CLEARFIELD BANK & TRUST C	CLEARFIELD	PA	**C-**	C-	C	370	3.81	9.8	3.1	16.2	22.1	**5.2**	7.2	12.3
	CLEO STATE BK	CLEO SPRINGS	OK	**A**	A	A	68	-1.74	7.3	7.6	1.6	54.7	**10.0**	20.4	36.6
	CLEVELAND BANK	CLEVELAND	OK	**C**	C	C-	55	2.69	6.0	14.5	20.2	28.7	**5.5**	7.5	13.1
	CLEVELAND STATE BK	CLEVELAND	MS	**B+**	B	B-	176	10.37	9.4	7.1	15.5	25.0	**10.0**	11.4	18.5
	CLEVELAND STATE BK	CLEVELAND	WI	**B-**	C+	C+	85	7.84	8.6	4.3	24.3	20.0	**6.3**	8.3	13.4
	CLIFTON SAVINGS BANK	CLIFTON	NJ	**B**	B-	B-	1,122	5.62	0.0	0.1	37.1	53.9	**10.0**	14.4	42.6
	CLINTON BANK	CLINTON	KY	**B+**	B+	B+	50	-1.92	3.0	3.5	8.9	40.0	**10.0**	17.8	29.3

Asset Mix columns (Comm-ercial Loans, Cons-umer Loans, Home Mort-gages, Secur-ities): Asset Mix (As a % of Total Assets)

Asset Quality Index	Non-Performing Loans as a % of Total Loans	Non-Performing Loans as a % of Capital	Net Charge-offs Avg Loans	Profitability Index	Net Income ($Mil)	Return on Assets (R.O.A.)	Return on Equity (R.O.E.)	Net Interest Spread	Overhead Efficiency Ratio	Liquidity Index	Liquidity Ratio	Hot Money Ratio	Stability Index
3.2	3.83	27.1	0.14	2.8	0.2	0.31	3.44	3.83	76.0	4.5	36.8	11.4	4.7
2.5	5.66	20.6	2.94	0.4	-0.1	-0.69	-6.75	3.94	93.2	6.6	56.6	0.7	4.6
7.5	0.56	4.0	1.06	5.7	0.7	1.11	12.88	4.67	62.5	4.1	30.8	11.2	5.7
0.4	4.20	25.3	0.98	5.1	4.6	0.91	8.99	4.91	64.4	1.3	21.9	29.4	7.2
1.7	6.71	29.2	1.19	1.7	0.8	0.20	1.81	4.53	91.2	2.0	33.0	28.1	5.5
0.3	9.69	65.3	1.46	0.0	-5.1	-0.74	-7.89	3.22	104.0	0.8	18.6	44.9	4.1
4.3	3.33	13.5	0.35	5.1	0.8	0.79	4.75	4.04	52.5	2.4	20.2	17.8	7.6
5.9	0.24	2.0	0.12	3.2	3.5	0.50	5.98	3.71	81.4	1.9	23.1	21.3	5.1
1.3	3.07	21.7	1.33	2.6	3.1	0.15	1.63	3.59	76.3	3.8	18.6	10.9	6.0
6.7	1.10	4.4	0.10	6.8	3.3	1.43	14.72	3.86	69.5	4.5	50.7	15.2	6.7
0.0	4.79	29.6	0.65	1.8	0.5	0.22	2.13	3.15	74.5	2.6	10.8	15.5	5.5
4.8	1.20	5.0	0.19	5.7	1.4	0.98	10.91	3.36	62.1	5.0	35.4	7.8	5.5
1.6	4.18	27.6	0.36	2.9	0.3	0.29	3.32	4.12	88.2	2.5	18.0	16.9	4.8
2.2	4.84	27.9	0.32	3.7	0.4	0.77	8.79	3.80	65.2	2.6	45.5	28.6	5.0
4.4	2.83	10.2	0.30	4.1	1.0	0.64	4.43	4.37	77.3	1.1	27.0	45.2	7.0
3.5	2.06	13.2	0.94	4.4	146.1	0.71	7.35	3.94	64.4	5.6	28.5	4.9	7.8
8.4	0.06	0.3	0.09	5.3	0.5	1.15	10.69	4.78	76.2	2.2	31.7	23.6	7.4
7.3	0.50	2.0	0.29	7.0	1.7	2.00	19.35	3.31	65.3	2.6	50.5	32.0	7.6
0.8	3.65	16.5	4.01	0.0	-255.6	-5.66	-22.14	3.34	339.6	4.8	39.3	13.6	8.0
5.4	1.80	7.3	0.25	6.3	3.2	1.26	9.88	3.69	48.6	3.1	33.5	17.4	6.5
0.0	13.94	79.0	2.72	0.0	-7.2	-1.58	-20.60	3.11	102.4	0.7	12.7	36.2	2.6
7.4	5.73	8.0	0.01	4.4	0.4	0.86	5.39	3.95	74.4	5.9	62.1	9.2	8.6
8.8	0.05	0.3	0.01	3.5	0.7	1.06	13.90	3.46	81.2	4.4	39.7	12.8	4.3
5.9	3.08	10.1	0.16	3.1	2.1	1.01	11.34	3.22	87.3	5.1	53.8	13.1	4.4
6.3	0.62	4.4	0.41	9.4	40.8	1.52	15.46	4.09	53.1	3.1	12.3	13.3	9.5
4.3	1.17	9.3	0.41	7.1	6.0	1.64	17.78	5.19	62.3	1.4	17.0	26.4	6.6
7.6	0.59	2.4	0.07	6.9	2.6	1.63	18.47	4.05	60.5	3.3	42.6	19.4	6.2
5.2	2.27	10.7	1.11	9.7	4.1	1.54	10.89	4.54	73.8	4.3	30.2	10.4	8.3
7.5	0.55	3.3	0.17	10.0	4.3	2.30	19.62	6.04	59.3	2.5	14.4	16.5	8.5
4.3	2.40	14.7	0.37	0.6	0.1	0.07	0.71	3.30	96.0	2.4	31.4	20.4	2.9
4.9	0.66	4.6	0.60	4.6	2.4	1.11	12.47	3.79	69.8	3.3	31.5	15.6	5.5
7.2	0.15	0.9	-0.01	4.9	0.3	1.08	10.70	4.46	74.5	2.5	34.6	22.6	6.7
7.7	0.90	3.4	0.41	2.6	0.2	0.45	4.13	4.09	87.6	3.3	52.3	22.0	4.8
0.9	4.91	28.4	0.61	2.9	4.4	0.45	4.61	4.21	79.6	2.0	18.8	19.6	6.5
3.3	4.07	17.5	1.78	0.0	-2.2	-1.77	-16.66	3.24	85.2	1.8	38.7	48.8	0.8
0.7	3.35	13.7	1.46	3.0	0.2	0.10	0.67	4.92	80.2	3.1	28.4	15.6	8.1
7.6	0.25	1.8	0.04	7.3	4.5	1.81	20.01	3.05	42.8	3.6	24.7	12.0	6.7
7.5	1.16	6.3	0.31	2.3	1.2	0.36	2.64	4.01	83.5	2.0	14.6	19.2	7.0
9.1	0.12	0.3	-0.06	5.3	0.2	0.97	4.46	3.63	60.6	5.1	57.0	10.5	8.3
5.3	0.84	6.7	0.08	3.2	0.6	0.49	5.28	3.89	68.6	2.3	16.9	17.7	4.4
0.3	6.35	41.0	4.53	0.0	-3.6	-2.80	-28.08	3.12	119.1	2.2	15.3	18.2	3.8
8.6	0.20	0.9	-0.12	8.4	1.0	1.96	16.01	3.72	52.9	2.6	37.2	22.9	8.0
0.0	3.28	53.5	2.41	0.0	-0.8	-0.76	-30.66	4.25	100.3	2.8	7.0	14.1	0.0
8.5	0.00	0.0	0.24	4.4	2.1	1.01	10.56	4.15	75.9	1.9	21.4	20.7	4.5
6.5	1.08	4.6	0.00	0.0	-1.0	-2.45	-13.99	4.36	141.3	2.2	24.9	18.9	1.5
1.7	3.04	16.1	1.00	1.0	0.2	0.17	1.87	3.83	78.7	2.8	36.0	19.6	2.8
6.6	0.16	0.8	1.45	2.1	0.1	0.10	0.86	3.69	80.0	2.1	26.3	20.4	6.9
6.6	1.04	4.7	0.12	6.8	0.8	1.13	8.83	4.44	64.8	2.8	24.7	15.9	8.4
1.9	4.33	26.7	0.00	1.9	0.1	0.07	0.63	3.24	95.7	2.5	19.2	16.8	5.8
2.4	4.66	17.5	0.16	3.1	0.3	0.39	2.88	3.53	76.3	3.6	24.3	11.8	6.6
2.7	3.13	17.3	1.04	5.0	6.8	1.08	8.90	4.89	38.1	0.5	3.7	41.7	7.2
5.7	0.22	2.0	0.09	7.3	4.1	1.71	20.23	4.45	58.7	2.0	12.3	18.9	6.4
4.3	1.45	11.4	0.71	5.3	3.4	0.87	9.53	4.19	60.4	1.4	14.3	25.8	6.2
1.7	2.50	20.9	0.29	4.2	3.0	0.83	8.21	4.11	72.8	3.8	20.0	10.7	5.3
8.6	0.66	1.1	0.04	9.6	1.6	2.25	10.23	3.69	49.2	4.2	64.4	18.2	9.7
4.1	0.65	4.5	0.27	4.0	0.5	0.90	11.13	4.25	78.8	3.6	32.3	14.3	4.4
8.3	0.02	0.1	0.17	4.6	1.4	0.84	7.05	4.68	74.2	2.3	28.1	19.7	6.4
4.8	1.08	7.8	0.41	6.1	0.8	0.97	11.53	4.08	66.4	2.4	34.7	23.1	4.6
8.7	0.60	1.7	0.00	4.0	8.6	0.78	5.44	2.44	48.3	3.9	65.5	27.2	9.0
6.6	1.71	4.8	0.04	4.8	0.5	0.88	4.98	3.83	68.4	2.5	35.0	23.1	8.3

Name	City	State	Rating	2008 Rating	2007 Rating	Total Assets ($Mil)	One Year Asset Growth	Asset Mix (As a % of Total Assets) Commercial Loans	Consumer Loans	Home Mortgages	Securities	Capitalization Index	Leverage Ratio	Risk-based Capital Ratio
CLINTON NATIONAL BK	CLINTON	IA	C+	C+	B-	351	2.85	7.2	2.6	10.7	34.0	9.5	10.6	18.9
CLINTON SB	CLINTON	MA	D+	D+	D+	492	1.16	3.6	3.3	38.4	18.6	8.2	9.8	17.3
CLINTON STATE BK	CLINTON	MN	A-	A-	A-	68	7.67	6.4	2.3	4.7	24.8	10.0	12.3	17.2
▼CLOVER COMMUNITY BANK	CLOVER	SC	E+	D+	B-	133	-8.01	10.9	2.0	16.8	17.7	4.4	6.4	11.3
CMMNTY BK OAK PARK RIVER	OAK PARK	IL	D-	D-	D	352	-2.46	19.5	0.1	15.1	11.0	5.6	7.9	11.5
▼CMMNTY BK-WHEATON/GLEN	GLEN ELLYN	IL	E-	D	D+	346	1.65	7.4	0.4	8.0	12.5	1.8	5.6	8.8
▼CNB	CENTREVILLE	MD	D+	C+	B-	344	5.98	3.6	1.2	20.8	18.7	7.9	9.6	14.6
CNB BANK	CLEARFIELD	PA	B-	B-	C+	1,393	21.80	15.9	2.6	14.4	35.6	5.8	7.8	13.5
▼CNB BANK INC	BERKELEY SPRINGS	WV	C+	B-	B-	277	-4.29	2.3	5.2	41.1	28.0	7.8	9.5	17.5
CNB COMMUNITY BANK	GREELEY	NE	D	D	D+	20	0.47	3.8	5.6	3.7	27.1	8.3	9.9	21.0
▼CNLBANK	ORLANDO	FL	E+	D-	D	1,453	-11.02	11.3	0.7	9.3	18.7	2.4	6.0	9.4
▼COAST NATIONAL BK	SAN LUIS OBISPO	CA	E	D	D-	141	-8.52	14.6	1.0	4.2	0.0	4.8	6.8	11.0
▼COASTAL BANK	COCOA BEACH	FL	E-	E+	D-	133	-10.61	0.5	0.1	21.4	0.0	0.0	2.9	5.1
COASTAL BANK	SAVANNAH	GA	D-	D-	D	429	-6.07	5.4	0.7	16.8	8.6	6.6	8.8	12.2
▼COASTAL BANK & TRUST	JACKSONVILLE	NC	D+	C	NR	50	23.50	17.4	1.4	7.4	3.9	10.0	14.3	20.3
COASTAL CAROLINA	MYRTLE BEACH	SC	C-	C	NR	71	17.84	1.5	0.5	13.9	40.4	10.0	20.3	52.5
COASTAL COMMERCE BANK	HOUMA	LA	B-	B-	B-	338	0.89	22.3	2.9	17.1	23.3	6.4	8.4	12.3
▼COASTAL COMMUNITY BANK	EVERETT	WA	E-	D-	D	241	-13.72	7.0	0.6	14.1	7.3	3.6	7.2	10.3
COASTALSTATES BANK	HILTON HEAD ISLAND	SC	D-	D-	D	390	-11.16	9.9	0.5	36.0	11.4	4.9	6.9	11.7
COASTWAY COMMUNITY	CRANSTON	RI	D+	C	NR	309	3.82	4.2	2.0	36.0	0.0	6.2	8.3	12.0
COATESVILLE SB	COATESVILLE	PA	E	E+	D+	209	-8.18	8.9	0.3	50.8	15.1	4.6	6.6	11.3
COBIZ BANK	DENVER	CO	D+	D+	B	2,344	-1.37	20.4	0.5	3.8	27.2	5.9	8.4	11.7
▼COCONUT GROVE BANK	MIAMI	FL	E+	D-	C-	602	-11.79	4.7	0.3	11.6	23.4	3.4	5.7	10.2
COFFEE COUNTY BANK	MANCHESTER	TN	D	D-	C	125	-0.59	5.3	8.8	33.0	9.9	7.6	9.4	14.4
COLCHESTER STATE BK	COLCHESTER	IL	B	B-	C	53	8.47	6.3	5.9	12.1	49.0	8.9	10.3	21.6
COLE TAYLOR BANK	ROSEMONT	IL	D-	D-	D	4,479	1.88	26.4	0.1	8.6	28.0	5.3	7.3	12.3
COLEMAN COUNTY STATE BK	COLEMAN	TX	B-	B	B	69	5.40	14.7	3.8	15.9	11.2	6.7	8.7	12.3
COLFAX BANKING CO	COLFAX	LA	B-	C+	B-	79	-3.72	1.1	7.7	25.3	38.0	7.0	9.0	18.8
COLLEGE SB	PRINCETON	NJ	D	D	D-	532	-11.14	0.0	40.1	0.0	54.9	5.0	7.0	26.6
COLLEGIATE PEAKS BANK	BUENA VISTA	CO	C-	C-	B-	196	17.13	13.4	0.9	7.5	9.9	8.1	9.7	14.1
COLLIN BANK	FRISCO	TX	C	C	C	184	19.77	12.1	0.7	10.9	23.3	10.0	15.7	20.6
COLLINS STATE BK	COLLINS	WI	C+	B-	B-	48	20.03	11.3	2.8	23.9	30.1	6.0	8.1	13.5
COLLINSVILLE BUILDING & L	COLLINSVILLE	IL	B-	B-	B-	129	-0.38	0.0	0.1	68.4	22.8	10.0	22.4	61.6
▼COLLINSVILLE SAVINGS SOCI	COLLINSVILLE	CT	D+	C	C	164	4.33	8.1	0.4	32.8	8.9	4.9	6.9	11.8
COLOMBO BANK	ROCKVILLE	MD	E-	E+	C+	166	1.16	4.0	1.1	28.5	21.9	3.1	5.1	10.9
▼COLONIAL AMERICAN BANK	HORSHAM	PA	E-	D-	C-	21	-14.93	0.0	0.3	38.8	0.0	3.6	7.1	10.3
COLONIAL BANK FSB	VINELAND	NJ	C+	C	C	587	3.24	4.0	0.3	28.9	37.8	9.2	10.4	18.4
▼COLONIAL CO-OP BANK	GARDNER	MA	D-	D+	C-	78	6.66	2.8	1.9	59.5	2.9	7.1	9.0	16.9
COLONIAL FSB	QUINCY	MA	B-	B-	C	285	1.00	0.2	0.2	43.2	31.3	8.3	9.9	26.7
▲COLONIAL SAVINGS FA	FORT WORTH	TX	C	C-	C+	1,054	9.25	0.8	0.2	60.3	6.5	10.0	11.6	26.1
COLONIAL VIRGINIA BANK	GLOUCESTER	VA	C-	D+	C-	121	-3.20	10.3	4.9	14.3	21.5	8.4	9.9	14.6
COLONY BANK	FITZGERALD	GA	D	D+	C-	1,273	-2.42	4.2	2.6	15.4	23.9	6.3	8.3	14.4
COLORADO B&TC OF LA	LA JUNTA	CO	D+	C-	C	91	-1.15	9.7	4.1	11.8	30.8	5.8	7.8	14.8
▼COLORADO CAPITAL BANK	CASTLE ROCK	CO	E-	D-	C+	919	8.34	8.8	0.7	12.1	6.1	0.5	3.7	6.9
COLORADO COMMUNITY	YUMA	CO	C+	C-	C	535	8.16	4.7	0.4	13.1	3.0	8.5	10.2	13.8
▲COLORADO EAST BANK &	LAMAR	CO	D	D+	D+	859	0.12	5.7	1.4	4.5	21.3	7.2	9.1	14.1
▲COLORADO FSB	GREENWOOD VILLAGE	CO	B-	C	D-	700	123.87	0.0	0.0	79.1	0.0	9.9	10.9	24.9
COLORADO STATE BK OF	WALSH	CO	B+	B+	B+	38	2.04	0.5	1.2	6.4	36.4	10.0	14.4	25.8
COLORADO VALLEY BANK SSB	LA GRANGE	TX	E-	D	D	28	4.05	1.3	7.3	24.3	0.0	3.7	5.7	12.9
COLUMBIA BANK	LAKE CITY	FL	D-	D	B-	231	-5.45	5.4	0.6	15.4	23.5	6.3	8.3	12.6
COLUMBIA BANK	COLUMBIA	MD	C-	C-	C+	2,101	-5.49	7.1	1.3	11.9	20.7	8.5	10.0	14.7
COLUMBIA BANK	FAIR LAWN	NJ	C+	C+	B+	4,621	1.08	3.2	0.0	41.0	17.3	7.9	9.6	15.9
COLUMBIA COMMUNITY BANK	HILLSBORO	OR	D	D-	D	358	-5.69	21.0	0.3	7.2	17.4	5.3	7.5	11.2
COLUMBIA NATIONAL BK	COLUMBIA	IL	B-	B-	B-	40	4.77	18.5	3.4	29.2	22.2	10.0	12.3	19.0
COLUMBIA SAVINGS & LOAN A	MILWAUKEE	WI	D	D+	D+	23	5.18	0.0	1.1	51.9	0.0	10.0	12.1	18.3
COLUMBIA SB	CINCINNATI	OH	D-	E+	E+	55	-1.11	0.0	0.5	47.8	8.1	6.2	8.3	14.1
COLUMBIA STATE BK	TACOMA	WA	D+	D	D+	4,255	32.96	13.1	1.4	4.4	17.9	9.0	10.3	18.2
COLUMBUS BANK & TRUST CO	COLUMBUS	NE	C+	C+	C+	95	2.20	19.1	3.5	11.0	19.8	6.1	9.3	11.8
COLUMBUS COMMUNITY BANK	COLUMBUS	GA	D-	D	D	93	0.93	3.9	1.0	14.1	11.6	9.4	10.6	14.7
▲COLUMBUS FIRST BANK	WORTHINGTON	OH	B-	C	C-	163	26.77	12.5	0.0	29.6	0.0	7.7	9.5	14.2

Asset Quality Index	Non-Performing Loans as a % of Total Loans	Non-Performing Loans as a % of Capital	Net Charge-offs Avg Loans	Profitability Index	Net Income ($Mil)	Return on Assets (R.O.A.)	Return on Equity (R.O.E.)	Net Interest Spread	Overhead Efficiency Ratio	Liquidity Index	Liquidity Ratio	Hot Money Ratio	Stability Index
5.5	1.06	4.9	0.39	**3.8**	2.4	0.69	5.66	4.02	78.6	**4.8**	38.9	10.6	**6.7**
1.3	5.15	32.8	0.73	**2.0**	1.2	0.24	2.46	3.18	76.4	**2.9**	28.1	16.8	**5.7**
5.8	1.12	6.2	0.00	**9.3**	1.4	2.23	16.84	4.47	45.9	**1.4**	16.6	26.2	**9.1**
0.3	6.07	41.1	3.04	**0.0**	-1.7	-1.19	-15.67	3.96	86.6	**2.1**	26.1	19.9	**3.0**
0.0	8.48	66.8	2.86	**0.0**	-1.7	-0.47	-5.69	3.34	64.5	**0.8**	15.8	38.4	**4.0**
0.3	8.78	80.0	2.40	**0.0**	-3.8	-1.11	-15.56	3.66	95.2	**2.5**	17.7	16.8	**3.1**
2.0	2.61	18.2	0.50	**5.4**	3.0	0.90	8.88	4.13	65.8	**1.7**	15.9	21.9	**5.3**
4.4	1.60	11.2	0.45	**5.0**	11.1	0.88	11.28	3.68	60.7	**3.9**	27.3	14.2	**6.5**
3.2	2.88	16.9	0.53	**3.8**	1.7	0.60	6.44	3.90	70.2	**1.4**	24.1	29.3	**5.8**
5.5	0.81	3.3	0.15	**1.0**	0.0	0.09	0.96	3.07	105.1	**5.2**	54.5	9.5	**5.4**
0.0	2.83	23.5	2.54	**0.0**	-26.2	-1.67	-18.58	3.46	106.9	**2.8**	14.2	15.4	**4.6**
0.7	5.94	44.6	4.14	**0.0**	-4.6	-3.09	-35.99	4.64	97.1	**1.6**	20.7	24.2	**2.4**
0.0	17.66	215.0	0.77	**0.0**	-4.0	-2.73	-43.01	2.66	147.9	**0.9**	20.0	38.2	**1.1**
0.0	9.99	76.5	2.53	**0.1**	-3.3	-0.71	-6.49	3.34	98.4	**1.5**	8.3	22.4	**4.1**
8.7	0.00	0.0	0.00	**0.0**	-1.0	-2.18	-13.01	2.69	164.8	**3.7**	34.4	14.4	**1.5**
9.8	0.59	1.0	1.24	**0.0**	-2.0	-3.08	-13.16	2.00	242.4	**3.3**	72.6	31.0	**1.7**
4.7	0.68	4.5	0.32	**6.1**	4.7	1.34	18.30	3.97	62.8	**1.8**	24.5	22.6	**4.4**
0.0	2.32	18.9	3.48	**0.0**	-3.8	-1.54	-19.56	3.66	120.0	**3.2**	19.3	13.3	**2.7**
0.3	10.78	98.2	3.80	**0.0**	-6.2	-1.46	-16.68	2.92	99.7	**1.5**	11.0	23.8	**2.2**
1.7	3.05	31.5	0.35	**2.5**	0.7	0.24	2.94	3.86	86.2	**3.2**	1.8	11.5	**3.0**
2.5	3.13	32.4	0.11	**0.9**	-1.1	-0.49	-6.79	1.89	96.4	**0.8**	14.5	37.5	**2.2**
3.4	2.43	14.9	2.35	**1.8**	3.5	0.15	1.68	4.52	66.9	**1.9**	19.7	22.0	**6.0**
0.3	9.36	64.8	4.54	**0.0**	-4.6	-0.73	-10.32	3.38	85.1	**1.4**	17.5	26.1	**3.1**
1.0	4.74	32.8	2.27	**3.7**	0.6	0.46	4.92	4.33	53.0	**0.8**	16.4	37.2	**5.8**
8.6	0.07	0.3	0.24	**5.9**	0.6	1.07	9.94	3.88	55.0	**2.6**	42.0	26.7	**5.6**
1.4	4.70	33.0	4.10	**0.0**	-35.1	-0.78	-10.50	3.36	65.9	**0.8**	10.7	36.3	**4.1**
8.2	0.01	0.1	0.10	**6.6**	1.1	1.53	17.82	4.88	69.4	**3.3**	9.4	12.0	**6.3**
6.1	0.65	3.3	0.12	**5.8**	1.2	1.41	14.85	4.76	70.2	**0.9**	20.4	35.1	**5.9**
6.8	0.05	0.3	0.00	**1.0**	-0.1	-0.01	-0.19	0.96	83.0	**1.4**	31.1	36.9	**2.3**
7.2	0.22	1.4	0.04	**1.7**	0.3	0.15	1.13	4.53	90.6	**2.5**	25.0	17.6	**6.7**
4.8	2.70	12.4	0.00	**2.7**	1.2	0.74	4.62	3.55	73.5	**1.4**	33.2	54.9	**4.4**
8.6	0.00	0.0	0.00	**3.7**	0.2	0.50	6.21	4.21	82.9	**2.3**	39.3	30.5	**5.8**
10.0	0.12	0.4	0.03	**3.4**	0.8	0.58	2.63	2.33	58.6	**3.4**	38.6	17.4	**7.8**
0.3	5.36	49.4	0.30	**3.0**	0.6	0.35	4.25	3.64	70.1	**2.7**	27.4	17.3	**4.3**
0.3	10.83	93.3	-0.33	**0.3**	-2.9	-1.74	-29.11	2.87	114.2	**1.8**	41.1	65.3	**0.3**
4.5	1.58	15.3	0.29	**0.0**	-0.7	-2.90	-36.62	4.14	165.1	**3.3**	18.5	12.7	**0.0**
3.6	3.33	16.9	0.11	**4.0**	4.2	0.73	8.07	3.13	60.9	**4.8**	45.5	12.3	**5.7**
3.2	2.94	21.8	0.38	**0.0**	-0.6	-0.76	-7.68	4.42	98.9	**1.7**	18.0	23.0	**4.3**
8.8	0.15	0.7	0.00	**4.0**	2.4	0.83	8.78	2.78	60.3	**4.2**	52.6	17.3	**5.8**
3.2	2.23	10.8	1.15	**6.9**	22.7	2.41	20.54	6.50	69.3	**2.1**	23.2	22.5	**7.9**
5.2	0.30	1.8	0.56	**1.7**	0.4	0.35	3.56	4.26	82.6	**1.8**	22.0	22.2	**4.2**
1.4	3.51	21.7	1.90	**1.0**	1.4	0.11	1.27	3.16	70.8	**1.9**	24.5	28.3	**5.2**
2.2	4.08	21.0	0.11	**3.8**	0.4	0.45	5.39	4.91	76.7	**3.0**	25.8	15.3	**3.8**
0.3	15.78	145.3	2.41	**0.0**	-34.8	-3.90	-56.05	3.41	101.3	**0.8**	24.9	54.0	**2.2**
3.8	1.36	9.2	1.15	**4.3**	2.4	0.46	4.44	4.81	49.7	**0.8**	11.3	34.0	**7.2**
0.3	7.36	45.6	0.92	**3.4**	5.4	0.63	6.12	3.87	72.6	**1.3**	17.3	28.8	**5.8**
5.3	0.73	5.3	0.02	**4.8**	6.9	1.26	11.58	3.02	34.4	**1.7**	17.8	22.9	**5.0**
9.0	0.00	0.0	-0.06	**4.5**	0.3	0.87	5.80	3.97	67.9	**2.9**	51.0	27.7	**7.5**
6.0	0.74	6.2	0.12	**0.0**	-0.8	-3.06	-47.68	3.56	180.7	**2.5**	43.9	29.0	**1.7**
0.0	8.59	59.5	3.39	**0.1**	-3.0	-1.25	-15.26	3.74	70.4	**0.9**	12.9	32.6	**4.3**
1.7	3.67	20.5	2.08	**2.4**	14.1	0.65	4.37	3.93	61.4	**2.0**	20.3	20.5	**5.2**
3.8	2.67	18.3	0.17	**3.3**	21.1	0.46	4.68	2.89	59.8	**4.3**	24.5	10.9	**7.2**
1.3	4.53	32.0	1.55	**0.5**	-0.7	-0.18	-2.29	2.75	90.6	**1.5**	14.3	23.5	**3.6**
2.8	4.46	23.3	0.68	**3.3**	0.2	0.59	4.82	4.03	76.2	**4.5**	31.6	9.8	**6.6**
0.3	9.47	57.0	0.15	**0.5**	-0.1	-0.53	-4.28	4.94	117.7	**1.0**	8.5	29.6	**5.7**
0.3	14.51	106.7	1.14	**0.5**	-0.1	-0.14	-1.74	4.06	83.5	**1.4**	6.1	23.3	**3.0**
1.5	4.56	22.5	1.33	**3.6**	30.9	0.74	5.60	4.76	65.1	**4.3**	22.2	9.4	**6.8**
5.0	0.74	5.1	0.16	**4.6**	1.0	1.06	11.75	4.50	65.5	**3.6**	9.2	10.3	**5.1**
2.5	2.68	13.9	0.95	**0.0**	-0.6	-0.61	-6.42	3.98	96.4	**1.5**	23.4	27.2	**1.3**
8.7	0.04	0.3	0.04	**4.2**	1.2	0.81	8.91	3.90	58.4	**0.9**	18.0	34.2	**5.0**

Name	City	State	Rating	2008 Rating	2007 Rating	Total Assets ($Mil)	One Year Asset Growth	Asset Mix (As a % of Total Assets) Commercial Loans	Consumer Loans	Home Mortgages	Securities	Capitalization Index	Leverage Ratio	Risk-based Capital Ratio
COLUMBUS JUNCTION STATE	COLUMBUS JUNCTION	IA	**D+**	C	C-	54	6.70	11.3	3.1	16.1	36.9	**5.9**	7.9	15.4
COLUMBUS SB	CHICAGO	IL	**C-**	C	C	21	-1.97	0.0	0.0	26.5	67.7	**10.0**	18.3	57.4
COLUMBUS STATE BK	COLUMBUS	TX	**B**	B	B	84	9.32	1.3	0.9	1.5	58.1	**10.0**	14.1	22.3
COMANCHE NATIONAL BK	COMANCHE	TX	**A**	A	A	251	6.16	3.4	5.9	13.6	50.4	**10.0**	11.4	26.6
▲ COMERICA BANK	DALLAS	TX	**C**	C-	B-	53,797	-9.04	39.5	1.0	3.9	14.0	**9.1**	11.4	14.3
▲ COMERICA BANK & TRUST NA	ANN ARBOR	MI	**C+**	C+	B-	18	2.03	0.0	0.0	0.0	0.0	**10.0**	72.3	237.8
COMMENCEMENT BANK	TACOMA	WA	**D**	C	C	112	0.82	27.3	0.4	8.1	6.0	**10.0**	15.8	20.7
COMMERCE BANK	EDINA	MN	**D**	D	D+	217	-8.38	11.4	0.3	12.2	6.4	**10.0**	11.7	16.4
COMMERCE BANK	LAREDO	TX	**A-**	B+	B+	570	20.91	6.2	1.4	5.9	63.7	**10.0**	11.3	31.7
COMMERCE BANK & TRUST	WORCESTER	MA	**B**	B-	B-	1,225	5.65	24.2	3.0	3.5	14.6	**9.4**	10.6	15.1
▲ COMMERCE BANK NA	KANSAS CITY	MO	**B**	B-	B-	18,337	2.11	11.2	9.9	8.6	39.2	**7.0**	9.0	14.0
▼ COMMERCE BANK OF	TUCSON	AZ	**D+**	C-	B-	271	27.75	11.7	0.8	8.1	4.8	**7.1**	9.1	15.1
▼ COMMERCE BANK OF	PORTLAND	OR	**D+**	C-	C+	70	7.62	52.0	0.1	2.3	4.7	**10.0**	17.3	20.0
COMMERCE BANK OF	SEATTLE	WA	**D+**	D+	B-	850	1.82	34.0	2.2	3.1	16.7	**9.0**	10.6	14.2
COMMERCE BANK TEXAS	STOCKDALE	TX	**C-**	C-	B	34	-0.35	15.0	3.6	9.9	29.1	**10.0**	11.4	20.0
COMMERCE BK OF TEMECULA	MURRIETA	CA	**D**	C	C	45	-1.17	18.3	0.2	2.5	0.0	**10.0**	20.2	26.8
COMMERCE NATIONAL BK	NEWPORT BEACH	CA	**D+**	C	C	256	11.87	10.3	4.6	1.0	22.4	**9.1**	10.4	18.3
COMMERCE NATIONAL BK	CORINTH	MS	**A**	A	A-	85	-2.10	13.1	14.0	23.9	24.2	**10.0**	11.4	20.8
▲ COMMERCE NATIONAL BK &	WINTER PARK	FL	**D**	C-	C-	106	-3.31	3.2	0.8	15.7	12.9	**7.3**	9.2	13.6
▼ COMMERCE STATE BK	WEST BEND	WI	**D+**	C-	C-	321	7.28	13.2	0.1	21.4	7.1	**6.4**	9.1	12.1
COMMERCE UNION BANK	SPRINGFIELD	TN	**C**	C	C	187	26.52	5.6	1.1	16.3	26.2	**10.0**	16.5	24.7
▼ COMMERCEFIRST BANK	ANNAPOLIS	MD	**D-**	D	D	203	1.37	25.8	0.0	0.0	0.0	**6.7**	10.3	12.3
COMMERCEWEST BANK NA	IRVINE	CA	**C-**	C	A	303	-13.36	19.7	0.2	1.2	20.6	**10.0**	12.4	21.9
COMMERCIAL & SB OF MILLER	MILLERSBURG	OH	**B**	B+	A-	457	1.42	6.3	1.5	21.6	16.5	**7.9**	9.6	15.7
▼ COMMERCIAL BANK	CRAWFORD	GA	**D-**	D-	C+	103	4.29	0.9	2.0	22.8	35.5	**6.6**	8.6	20.1
COMMERCIAL BANK	PARSONS	KS	**A**	A	A-	233	-7.39	9.0	7.0	11.0	54.3	**10.0**	13.0	27.4
COMMERCIAL BANK	WEST LIBERTY	KY	**C+**	C+	C+	124	-1.68	12.4	4.8	17.4	50.9	**6.9**	8.9	20.6
COMMERCIAL BANK	ALMA	MI	**C-**	C+	B-	402	16.27	8.5	1.8	41.4	5.5	**4.8**	6.8	13.0
COMMERCIAL BANK	SAINT LOUIS	MO	**D**	D	C	173	-1.85	20.1	3.3	16.1	17.9	**6.2**	8.2	12.8
▲ COMMERCIAL BANK	DE KALB	MS	**D**	D	D+	140	-8.49	5.7	15.1	18.6	17.5	**6.3**	8.3	11.9
COMMERCIAL BANK	HONEA PATH	SC	**A**	A	A-	131	10.59	3.8	4.2	17.3	43.4	**10.0**	14.7	32.8
▼ COMMERCIAL BANK	HARROGATE	TN	**D+**	B-	B+	849	8.33	9.6	2.6	24.9	15.5	**6.2**	8.2	12.8
COMMERCIAL BANK	MASON	TX	**C+**	C	C+	28	4.78	7.6	5.0	18.1	33.7	**6.2**	8.2	13.9
▼ COMMERCIAL BANK	WHITEWATER	WI	**C-**	C	C+	96	4.23	0.9	0.7	20.2	23.5	**9.6**	10.8	21.5
▲ COMMERCIAL BANK & TRUST	MONTICELLO	AR	**C**	C-	C-	160	8.11	9.8	13.1	14.8	27.1	**7.5**	9.3	15.1
COMMERCIAL BANK & TRUST	PARIS	TN	**B**	B-	B-	630	3.37	9.1	3.3	19.7	20.1	**7.1**	9.1	13.9
COMMERCIAL BANK & TRUST	LATROBE	PA	**A**	A-	B+	354	-5.92	4.4	0.5	25.0	37.1	**10.0**	11.9	20.7
COMMERCIAL BANK OF	COSTA MESA	CA	**C-**	B-	B+	277	4.48	13.0	0.7	0.0	7.9	**10.0**	11.9	17.6
COMMERCIAL BANK OF	GRAYSON	KY	**B+**	A-	A	164	1.17	4.1	9.0	19.4	46.3	**10.0**	15.6	32.5
▲ COMMERCIAL BANK OF	HERON LAKE	MN	**C-**	C	C+	35	4.07	4.2	0.5	5.5	21.1	**8.2**	9.8	14.5
▼ COMMERCIAL BANK OF MOTT	MOTT	ND	**C**	C+	C+	72	13.91	4.4	2.2	2.5	25.9	**3.4**	7.8	10.2
COMMERCIAL BANK OF	NELSON	NE	**B**	B	B	26	-2.58	9.5	2.8	1.5	31.0	**10.0**	19.6	30.8
COMMERCIAL BANK OF OAK	OAK GROVE	MO	**B-**	B	A-	88	-1.23	3.1	1.8	17.6	49.7	**10.0**	13.5	28.4
COMMERCIAL BANK OF	OZARK	AL	**D-**	C-	C-	73	-10.57	5.7	9.9	25.9	18.6	**6.3**	8.3	14.4
COMMERCIAL BANK OF TEXAS	NACOGDOCHES	TX	**B-**	B	B	409	8.95	3.8	11.4	13.3	43.4	**6.6**	8.6	19.9
COMMERCIAL BANKING CO	VALDOSTA	GA	**C**	C	B-	212	20.55	5.1	2.3	23.5	15.2	**6.6**	8.6	14.5
▲ COMMERCIAL CAPITAL BANK	DELHI	LA	**A-**	B	B+	40	10.27	12.2	2.4	10.4	16.8	**10.0**	11.3	21.9
COMMERCIAL NATIONAL BK	BRADY	TX	**A+**	A	A	113	5.07	6.9	5.7	17.6	40.5	**10.0**	13.0	24.7
COMMERCIAL NB OF	TEXARKANA	TX	**C-**	D+	B-	177	-1.15	11.3	8.3	19.5	25.8	**6.0**	8.0	14.3
COMMERCIAL SB	CARROLL	IA	**B**	B	B	112	3.88	16.0	2.6	19.3	15.7	**6.7**	8.7	13.9
▲ COMMERCIAL SB	UPPER SANDUSKY	OH	**C**	D-	D+	304	3.41	8.6	7.6	14.8	11.1	**5.3**	7.6	11.3
▲ COMMERCIAL ST BK OF EL CA	EL CAMPO	TX	**C-**	D-	D-	114	-14.68	8.2	4.8	8.1	25.5	**8.1**	9.7	20.8
COMMERCIAL STATE BK	DONALSONVILLE	GA	**C+**	C+	B	93	1.21	11.5	7.4	9.3	20.3	**10.0**	13.3	21.2
▼ COMMERCIAL STATE BK	CEDAR BLUFFS	NE	**D**	C	C	23	39.79	2.6	2.2	2.4	23.3	**5.3**	7.3	12.0
COMMERCIAL STATE BK	REPUBLICAN CITY	NE	**A**	A	A-	62	0.00	2.3	1.0	0.0	73.3	**10.0**	19.3	49.8
COMMERCIAL STATE BK	WAUSA	NE	**C-**	C+	B-	71	3.22	20.8	5.6	6.2	7.1	**9.2**	10.8	14.3
▲ COMMERCIAL STATE BK	ANDREWS	TX	**C**	C	C	410	5.09	26.4	4.6	3.9	5.3	**6.4**	8.4	12.5
COMMERCIAL STATE BK	PALMER	TX	**C+**	C	B-	57	5.79	9.7	5.2	8.7	42.9	**5.9**	7.9	15.2
▼ COMMERCIAL STATE BK OF	WAGNER	SD	**C**	C+	A	123	3.34	11.7	5.5	5.2	31.7	**7.6**	9.4	14.6
COMMERCIAL TRUST CO OF	FAYETTE	MO	**B-**	B-	B+	104	-0.96	3.2	4.3	35.3	4.6	**8.5**	10.0	22.1

Asset Quality Index	Non-Performing Loans as a % of Total Loans	Non-Performing Loans as a % of Capital	Net Charge-offs Avg Loans	Profitability Index	Net Income ($Mil)	Return on Assets (R.O.A.)	Return on Equity (R.O.E.)	Net Interest Spread	Overhead Efficiency Ratio	Liquidity Index	Liquidity Ratio	Hot Money Ratio	Stability Index
4.0	2.74	15.5	1.47	**1.7**	-0.2	-0.37	-4.03	4.04	78.9	**4.0**	44.9	15.9	**5.2**
10.0	0.00	0.0	0.00	**1.9**	0.1	0.27	1.38	3.59	97.2	**2.0**	52.3	47.0	**7.8**
10.0	0.00	0.0	0.00	**3.9**	0.5	0.67	4.51	2.98	67.4	**5.7**	96.4	14.9	**7.0**
8.2	0.54	1.8	-0.02	**7.4**	3.1	1.32	9.18	4.51	60.0	**2.5**	44.9	31.9	**8.0**
3.5	2.81	16.2	1.39	**2.8**	329.3	0.56	5.34	3.28	65.0	**4.3**	17.5	7.8	**7.2**
10.0	0.00	0.0	0.00	**10.0**	8.3	38.58	43.46	0.20	52.1	**10.0**	913.5	0.0	**4.3**
2.7	5.32	23.6	1.76	**0.0**	-0.9	-0.78	-4.59	3.99	79.1	**0.7**	16.3	44.8	**2.0**
0.0	5.69	31.1	1.94	**1.0**	-1.6	-0.68	-5.68	3.09	61.3	**0.6**	16.3	63.6	**7.7**
7.0	1.37	3.6	0.60	**8.4**	6.7	1.38	9.42	3.15	41.3	**2.2**	47.2	50.0	**8.2**
5.1	0.81	4.3	0.83	**4.5**	8.9	0.77	6.92	3.43	65.0	**4.2**	27.6	12.8	**8.3**
5.0	1.07	5.7	0.96	**6.7**	219.1	1.22	12.41	3.93	61.2	**4.9**	27.1	8.5	**7.2**
0.7	2.02	14.7	0.83	**6.8**	5.3	2.11	22.14	4.26	45.7	**1.2**	16.6	29.1	**4.7**
7.2	0.17	0.7	1.69	**0.0**	-0.5	-0.80	-3.76	4.32	107.3	**3.3**	15.8	12.4	**3.7**
1.7	3.54	19.2	2.72	**2.7**	-0.5	-0.06	-0.58	3.72	47.6	**4.5**	19.8	6.0	**5.2**
5.2	0.02	0.1	-0.11	**0.3**	-0.3	-0.75	-4.05	4.48	123.7	**2.5**	31.4	19.7	**7.1**
2.7	6.41	20.4	2.59	**0.0**	-1.1	-2.45	-11.49	4.46	120.0	**1.6**	30.8	31.5	**2.0**
2.4	2.86	14.0	0.55	**1.4**	0.1	0.04	0.37	3.73	83.8	**0.8**	23.4	52.8	**5.4**
7.9	0.37	1.8	0.60	**9.1**	1.7	2.02	16.41	4.76	49.8	**3.1**	37.6	18.7	**8.7**
1.3	2.44	18.1	0.78	**1.9**	0.1	0.06	0.66	3.41	83.8	**1.2**	20.6	31.4	**4.4**
2.1	0.94	7.8	0.83	**2.4**	0.8	0.26	2.77	3.29	56.3	**0.5**	8.5	55.0	**3.0**
6.9	1.06	4.0	0.07	**2.5**	0.8	0.45	2.45	3.67	82.6	**1.9**	28.5	25.7	**4.0**
0.0	3.94	30.2	1.04	**4.7**	1.5	0.73	7.44	4.69	50.3	**0.6**	7.5	35.4	**5.6**
2.9	3.18	11.9	1.17	**1.9**	0.6	0.17	1.26	4.34	76.0	**1.8**	28.6	27.1	**5.6**
4.6	1.45	9.7	0.40	**5.0**	3.8	0.86	8.32	3.80	64.6	**2.9**	14.7	14.5	**6.6**
0.3	13.13	60.1	3.99	**0.5**	-1.4	-1.38	-13.07	3.81	83.6	**2.2**	34.9	26.4	**4.9**
8.6	0.29	0.9	0.10	**7.0**	3.8	1.58	12.50	3.71	60.0	**4.1**	62.5	19.7	**7.9**
4.5	1.22	4.8	0.16	**3.5**	1.0	0.80	6.32	3.49	76.8	**3.1**	47.0	23.1	**6.8**
1.7	4.55	46.3	0.78	**4.7**	3.3	0.87	12.13	3.34	56.5	**0.8**	16.0	38.3	**4.1**
1.2	3.84	26.5	2.25	**1.4**	0.7	0.41	4.96	4.19	81.5	**2.4**	24.7	17.9	**2.6**
1.0	3.25	22.6	1.55	**1.2**	-1.0	-0.64	-8.65	4.13	79.4	**1.7**	14.4	21.3	**3.0**
8.8	0.81	2.3	0.26	**5.8**	1.5	1.17	7.25	4.11	65.2	**4.7**	56.8	15.9	**8.0**
1.7	5.61	42.9	0.98	**3.6**	3.9	0.47	4.44	3.65	68.4	**0.6**	7.1	35.5	**6.4**
8.7	0.00	0.0	0.03	**5.4**	0.3	1.07	12.76	4.32	66.6	**2.5**	38.6	26.1	**5.0**
9.3	0.40	1.6	0.00	**2.2**	0.2	0.20	1.80	2.84	90.9	**4.6**	57.8	15.1	**5.7**
2.8	1.68	10.9	0.81	**7.6**	2.9	1.89	19.15	4.97	57.2	**1.4**	16.2	27.0	**4.6**
5.6	0.52	3.5	0.16	**5.6**	7.9	1.28	13.76	3.72	64.7	**2.8**	21.6	15.9	**6.5**
9.4	0.08	0.3	0.02	**8.1**	5.6	1.56	12.37	5.15	62.3	**4.6**	38.3	11.3	**7.7**
3.8	2.21	7.8	1.26	**1.7**	0.5	0.18	1.45	3.32	73.3	**3.5**	53.5	22.2	**6.1**
5.5	3.25	8.7	0.20	**5.0**	1.3	0.81	4.88	4.90	77.8	**5.9**	47.9	6.4	**8.4**
2.9	1.91	11.4	0.69	**4.4**	0.3	0.80	6.92	4.55	78.0	**1.4**	21.1	27.8	**6.0**
7.3	0.01	0.1	-0.01	**6.0**	0.7	1.08	13.79	3.51	52.3	**2.9**	8.4	13.8	**4.5**
8.4	0.85	2.2	-0.13	**4.5**	0.2	0.71	3.53	4.78	71.7	**5.1**	55.8	12.2	**6.9**
2.7	5.55	14.7	3.52	**0.0**	-1.0	-1.17	-7.48	2.46	93.0	**5.1**	49.3	11.2	**5.2**
2.5	2.58	17.8	0.62	**2.4**	0.4	0.50	6.73	4.25	83.7	**3.9**	17.5	9.8	**2.3**
4.8	0.63	3.0	0.18	**5.2**	4.2	1.06	10.78	3.48	66.6	**3.6**	31.7	14.2	**6.3**
5.0	0.59	4.1	0.32	**2.6**	0.5	0.24	2.28	3.13	78.4	**1.4**	31.0	39.2	**4.4**
7.5	1.03	4.9	0.10	**9.0**	0.9	2.29	19.82	5.11	57.5	**2.5**	30.2	19.4	**8.6**
8.4	0.38	1.4	0.14	**8.4**	2.0	1.81	12.24	4.64	62.1	**2.5**	35.8	23.3	**9.9**
4.3	1.18	8.4	0.26	**5.1**	1.8	1.00	12.93	4.52	71.9	**2.8**	17.7	15.3	**3.1**
5.5	1.04	7.9	0.57	**4.9**	1.2	1.17	12.44	4.00	60.7	**4.7**	29.0	7.4	**5.9**
3.7	0.84	7.3	0.41	**4.6**	2.4	0.80	10.43	4.52	68.0	**2.2**	10.2	17.4	**3.7**
3.0	3.14	12.9	-0.68	**3.6**	1.6	1.33	14.08	4.45	77.0	**2.9**	28.5	16.5	**2.4**
3.3	4.61	16.6	1.27	**3.6**	0.5	0.59	3.97	4.24	69.8	**2.4**	32.1	21.3	**6.8**
8.8	0.00	0.0	0.02	**2.4**	0.1	0.36	4.18	3.01	86.5	**3.3**	53.2	19.2	**2.3**
9.5	1.18	1.4	0.74	**9.2**	1.1	1.74	9.15	4.27	36.0	**3.7**	80.2	28.2	**9.0**
1.6	3.13	20.7	0.02	**6.5**	1.0	1.50	14.08	4.37	60.4	**1.8**	11.8	19.5	**7.6**
5.4	0.31	2.2	0.39	**6.4**	5.4	1.37	16.31	4.77	67.0	**1.1**	27.5	40.2	**4.0**
4.9	1.23	6.8	0.07	**6.4**	1.0	1.71	19.90	4.95	71.7	**1.9**	21.7	21.0	**5.1**
2.7	2.52	14.0	0.68	**8.0**	1.9	1.50	14.84	4.98	47.9	**1.9**	9.8	18.8	**7.9**
8.2	0.46	2.3	0.16	**3.9**	0.8	0.75	7.80	2.52	74.6	**5.1**	46.6	11.3	**6.2**

	Name	City	State	Rating	2008 Rating	2007 Rating	Total Assets ($Mil)	One Year Asset Growth	Asset Mix (As a % of Total Assets) Comm-ercial Loans	Cons-umer Loans	Home Mort-gages	Secur-ities	Capital-ization Index	Leverage Ratio	Risk-based Capital Ratio
	COMMODORE BANK	SOMERSET	OH	**C**	C	C	76	9.38	8.9	4.0	21.4	40.6	**6.3**	8.3	16.3
▼	COMMONWEALTH BANK &	LOUISVILLE	KY	**C-**	B-	C+	818	0.40	4.7	2.2	16.8	24.8	**6.5**	8.5	13.3
▲	COMMONWEALTH BANK FSB	MOUNT STERLING	KY	**D+**	C-	C-	21	-4.00	0.0	8.2	67.6	0.0	**10.0**	11.2	17.0
▲	COMMONWEALTH BUSINESS	LOS ANGELES	CA	**C-**	C-	C+	403	19.83	23.8	0.3	0.2	5.2	**10.0**	12.3	15.3
	COMMONWEALTH	HYDE PARK	MA	**C+**	C	C	185	-0.52	0.2	1.6	52.0	9.4	**6.8**	8.8	18.7
	COMMONWEALTH	HARTFORD	KY	**B**	C+	C+	148	-0.93	0.4	3.9	31.9	46.8	**10.0**	11.5	21.6
▼	COMMONWEALTH NATIONAL	MOBILE	AL	**D+**	C-	C-	64	-8.46	7.7	3.6	13.3	20.2	**6.1**	8.1	16.3
▲	COMMUNITY & SOUTHERN	CARROLLTON	GA	**B+**	NR	NR	2,391	N/A	3.4	1.4	12.5	26.7	**10.0**	13.6	66.7
	COMMUNITY 1ST BANK	AUBURN	CA	**D-**	D-	C-	155	0.33	5.2	1.0	1.0	40.3	**8.0**	9.6	19.1
▼	COMMUNITY 1ST BANK	POST FALLS	ID	**C-**	C-	C-	53	13.87	13.5	2.2	5.7	9.0	**10.0**	16.4	23.7
	COMMUNITY 1ST BANK LAS VE	LAS VEGAS	NM	**C**	C+	C+	181	3.98	6.6	2.7	22.3	27.7	**6.4**	8.4	14.6
	COMMUNITY BANK	PASADENA	CA	**D**	C-	B+	2,503	2.60	15.1	0.7	0.4	25.5	**6.8**	8.8	12.5
	COMMUNITY BANK	ALTON	IA	**D+**	D	D	39	1.03	23.1	4.8	11.2	16.7	**7.1**	9.1	13.4
	COMMUNITY BANK	DUNLAP	IA	**B-**	B-	B-	85	14.27	2.8	2.2	9.2	28.7	**8.1**	9.8	16.3
	COMMUNITY BANK	INDIANOLA	IA	**C**	C	C-	133	4.84	13.6	1.3	10.7	24.0	**7.4**	9.2	16.5
▲	COMMUNITY BANK	MUSCATINE	IA	**C**	C+	B	231	1.30	9.3	5.6	18.5	20.9	**5.7**	7.7	12.1
	COMMUNITY BANK	NEVADA	IA	**C+**	B-	B-	119	45.47	6.4	0.6	7.4	6.6	**6.2**	10.3	11.9
▼	COMMUNITY BANK	HOOPESTON	IL	**B-**	B+	B	74	13.66	14.8	3.0	12.4	24.8	**7.7**	9.5	23.3
	COMMUNITY BANK	WINSLOW	IL	**C+**	C+	B-	132	7.57	7.3	1.7	14.7	43.0	**10.0**	12.4	21.5
	COMMUNITY BANK	NOBLESVILLE	IN	**D**	D	D+	248	1.42	5.4	1.4	15.8	9.0	**10.0**	12.4	17.0
	COMMUNITY BANK	LIBERAL	KS	**C-**	B	B+	86	0.08	13.3	4.0	2.1	31.0	**7.9**	9.6	15.6
▲	COMMUNITY BANK	TOPEKA	KS	**C**	C	D+	84	-5.33	14.1	1.4	22.5	7.9	**6.9**	8.9	13.2
▲	COMMUNITY BANK	RACELAND	LA	**C**	C+	C+	419	6.06	19.2	3.1	16.7	13.9	**7.9**	9.6	15.5
	COMMUNITY BANK	ELLISVILLE	MS	**C-**	C	B-	633	0.18	5.0	5.3	23.7	13.3	**7.0**	9.0	13.0
▲	COMMUNITY BANK	ALMA	NE	**C+**	D+	D	44	-3.04	6.9	4.5	8.1	32.1	**10.0**	11.1	17.7
	COMMUNITY BANK	SANTA FE	NM	**D-**	C-	B-	198	2.80	5.8	0.9	13.2	15.6	**7.6**	9.4	14.9
	COMMUNITY BANK	ZANESVILLE	OH	**C**	C	C	241	10.62	7.0	5.1	27.8	21.0	**5.8**	7.8	14.5
	COMMUNITY BANK	ALVA	OK	**B-**	B-	C+	62	-0.67	10.1	9.6	7.9	35.7	**6.4**	8.4	13.2
	COMMUNITY BANK	BRISTOW	OK	**B-**	B	B	68	5.68	6.2	5.1	21.7	17.2	**4.9**	6.9	12.9
▼	COMMUNITY BANK	JOSEPH	OR	**C**	B-	C+	364	2.70	9.0	0.7	5.7	20.9	**6.1**	8.1	13.4
	COMMUNITY BANK	CARMICHAELS	PA	**C+**	C+	C+	497	7.27	6.1	11.1	23.0	26.9	**5.2**	7.2	12.5
	COMMUNITY BANK	AVON	SD	**B**	B-	B-	41	7.57	3.4	4.6	3.0	51.5	**10.0**	16.4	37.1
▼	COMMUNITY BANK	LEXINGTON	TN	**C**	C+	C+	100	12.36	5.8	5.4	25.3	24.0	**6.9**	8.9	13.8
	COMMUNITY BANK	BRIDGEPORT	TX	**D**	C-	C-	44	47.25	13.1	4.0	11.6	15.0	**10.0**	12.2	19.5
	COMMUNITY BANK	FORT WORTH	TX	**B**	B+	A-	503	7.19	8.9	3.5	12.6	17.2	**6.1**	8.1	16.4
	COMMUNITY BANK	LONGVIEW	TX	**B**	B	B-	129	10.68	12.8	7.2	37.1	0.0	**5.2**	7.2	12.2
▼	COMMUNITY BANK	STAUNTON	VA	**D-**	D+	C-	530	-2.31	9.1	7.6	29.0	0.3	**6.3**	9.2	11.9
	COMMUNITY BANK & CO	BRADENTON	FL	**D-**	D-	D-	276	6.36	9.0	1.0	7.2	9.3	**9.8**	11.1	14.8
	COMMUNITY BANK & TRUST	NEOSHO	MO	**B+**	B+	B+	270	-1.18	4.0	2.9	26.0	25.5	**6.2**	8.2	13.6
▼	COMMUNITY BANK & TRUST	ASHLAND CITY	TN	**C+**	C+	C+	217	2.00	9.0	3.3	19.6	22.2	**7.6**	9.4	14.0
	COMMUNITY BANK & TRUST	WACO	TX	**B**	B-	B-	404	2.70	30.3	3.0	21.3	21.1	**8.7**	10.1	14.3
	COMMUNITY BANK & TRUST	SHEBOYGAN	WI	**D**	D+	D	615	-2.67	16.6	1.1	11.9	12.0	**6.1**	8.3	11.8
	COMMUNITY BANK & TRUST -	LAGRANGE	GA	**D-**	D-	E+	100	-11.20	4.0	2.4	24.7	5.6	**5.3**	7.7	11.2
	COMMUNITY BANK & TRUST	OCALA	FL	**D+**	C	C+	537	2.15	5.0	4.6	12.2	29.2	**6.2**	8.2	14.0
	COMMUNITY BANK AUSTIN	AUSTIN	MN	**D-**	D-	D-	35	-28.79	11.4	3.1	28.0	12.6	**4.8**	6.8	11.9
	COMMUNITY BANK CBD	DELAVAN	WI	**C-**	C-	C	252	-5.72	9.3	0.5	20.5	12.4	**8.6**	10.1	14.6
▲	COMMUNITY BANK COAST	BILOXI	MS	**C-**	C+	B-	402	-6.36	4.2	3.9	19.9	8.9	**6.7**	8.7	12.5
▼	COMMUNITY BANK CORP	CHASKA	MN	**D+**	C	B-	194	-0.87	10.8	1.5	4.6	7.7	**4.6**	8.7	10.8
▲	COMMUNITY BANK DELAWARE	LEWES	DE	**D+**	C-	C-	120	18.95	6.2	0.9	17.7	14.3	**7.1**	9.6	12.6
	COMMUNITY BANK DESTIN	MIRAMAR BEACH	FL	**D-**	D	D	77	47.41	4.3	0.4	12.6	12.0	**6.1**	8.1	12.6
▼	COMMUNITY BANK INC	RONAN	MT	**D+**	C-	C-	96	-1.69	13.3	3.3	9.2	8.8	**7.5**	9.4	14.4
	COMMUNITY BANK MANKATO	VERNON CENTER	MN	**C**	C-	C+	174	2.10	8.9	2.5	23.2	5.3	**5.2**	7.4	11.1
▼	COMMUNITY BANK MISSOULA	MISSOULA	MT	**D+**	C+	B	87	-4.98	7.9	0.8	7.1	16.3	**7.9**	9.6	17.8
▼	COMMUNITY BANK NA	MOBILE	AL	**D+**	C	C+	92	37.86	0.7	1.2	19.3	19.0	**6.4**	8.4	14.1
▼	COMMUNITY BANK NA	SUMMERSVILLE	MO	**C+**	B-	B	51	5.14	5.6	7.5	12.5	6.0	**7.5**	9.3	13.8
	COMMUNITY BANK NA	CANTON	NY	**B**	B-	B-	5,420	0.80	5.6	11.7	22.9	31.6	**5.4**	7.4	13.4
	COMMUNITY BANK OF	DANIA BEACH	FL	**D-**	C-	C+	484	4.58	4.2	0.3	0.9	5.4	**6.1**	8.1	12.8
	COMMUNITY BANK OF	CAMERON	WI	**B-**	B-	B-	102	3.60	6.3	1.9	47.2	2.7	**6.2**	8.2	14.3
	COMMUNITY BANK OF	COLBY	WI	**E-**	E	D	119	-16.80	1.5	1.8	15.4	14.2	**0.2**	3.7	6.4
	COMMUNITY BANK OF	DOWNERS GROVE	IL	**D-**	D	D+	63	-1.25	2.6	0.0	19.6	10.9	**7.8**	10.5	13.2

Arrows denote recent upgrades ▲ or downgrades ▼

Asset Quality Index	Non-Performing Loans as a % of Total Loans	Non-Performing Loans as a % of Capital	Net Charge-offs Avg Loans	Profitability Index	Net Income ($Mil)	Return on Assets (R.O.A.)	Return on Equity (R.O.E.)	Net Interest Spread	Overhead Efficiency Ratio	Liquidity Index	Liquidity Ratio	Hot Money Ratio	Stability Index
5.2	1.41	7.8	0.23	**3.2**	0.4	0.60	6.62	4.48	84.5	**4.2**	42.5	14.3	**4.3**
3.0	3.00	21.4	0.85	**2.4**	5.9	0.71	8.56	3.43	78.5	**1.6**	11.9	22.2	**5.0**
6.1	0.61	4.2	0.08	**0.5**	-0.1	-0.53	-4.71	3.89	110.4	**1.4**	10.0	24.3	**4.3**
4.2	1.14	6.7	1.74	**1.1**	0.2	0.06	0.48	3.48	51.3	**1.0**	16.8	32.3	**5.1**
6.5	0.25	1.8	0.00	**3.3**	1.0	0.50	5.50	3.23	75.5	**2.0**	31.6	27.3	**5.2**
8.0	0.55	2.0	0.23	**4.8**	1.6	1.07	9.83	4.30	69.8	**2.9**	44.1	24.3	**6.5**
2.6	4.43	22.7	1.17	**2.3**	0.3	0.42	5.06	4.61	87.9	**2.2**	37.9	29.6	**3.7**
8.4	0.24	0.8	0.00	**9.8**	56.8	2.76	19.51	3.92	36.6	**2.8**	31.9	24.9	**7.0**
1.4	6.72	28.2	3.28	**0.0**	-0.3	-0.20	-1.98	3.45	102.4	**1.6**	12.0	22.0	**1.3**
8.5	0.12	0.5	0.21	**1.6**	0.2	0.35	1.93	3.89	75.1	**1.2**	29.7	49.1	**3.2**
2.8	2.35	16.7	0.40	**4.8**	1.9	1.04	11.44	4.53	67.8	**1.6**	15.8	23.1	**5.4**
0.7	4.17	27.8	0.10	**4.8**	20.7	0.82	8.91	3.71	58.2	**1.8**	19.7	22.5	**7.3**
4.4	0.74	4.6	0.80	**3.0**	0.3	0.84	9.33	4.13	79.7	**5.0**	38.5	9.5	**3.2**
5.7	0.45	2.2	0.04	**4.5**	0.8	1.02	8.10	4.07	70.5	**4.2**	34.6	12.0	**7.0**
4.9	1.87	9.9	-0.03	**3.1**	1.0	0.73	7.93	4.09	77.4	**2.3**	30.5	21.3	**5.0**
3.2	2.07	16.5	0.68	**3.4**	1.2	0.50	4.88	3.67	71.4	**2.6**	20.7	16.4	**5.6**
6.4	0.35	2.9	0.00	**7.0**	1.1	1.07	10.42	3.90	41.5	**0.7**	9.4	36.7	**5.7**
7.3	0.85	3.0	0.00	**4.1**	0.7	0.98	9.94	2.91	68.9	**6.2**	59.6	6.7	**5.6**
2.5	2.86	11.4	1.69	**3.5**	0.9	0.72	5.34	3.43	54.2	**3.7**	41.8	17.2	**6.6**
0.3	6.00	33.2	1.36	**2.6**	0.2	0.08	0.61	3.92	69.6	**4.1**	20.5	8.9	**7.6**
8.3	0.23	1.1	0.39	**2.3**	0.2	0.24	2.40	4.07	69.3	**1.4**	26.4	30.7	**6.5**
4.7	1.49	11.0	0.83	**2.9**	0.3	0.37	4.17	4.18	81.2	**2.3**	14.2	17.2	**4.4**
2.8	2.84	18.0	0.98	**4.8**	2.6	0.64	6.50	3.78	62.6	**4.1**	27.7	10.2	**6.3**
2.1	2.30	17.6	0.58	**5.8**	5.7	0.91	10.56	4.21	62.8	**1.4**	15.9	26.9	**5.4**
4.2	2.69	11.8	1.04	**4.7**	0.6	1.29	11.62	4.11	66.7	**3.5**	30.7	14.4	**5.4**
0.0	4.41	27.4	0.79	**3.5**	0.8	0.42	3.70	4.11	70.8	**1.9**	23.0	21.1	**6.5**
5.3	0.67	5.3	0.38	**3.1**	1.3	0.53	6.35	4.16	77.1	**1.5**	5.8	21.2	**3.9**
7.7	0.23	1.4	0.30	**6.5**	0.9	1.45	15.19	3.73	59.1	**1.0**	26.0	37.8	**5.7**
6.4	0.30	2.6	0.28	**8.9**	1.0	1.38	20.33	4.72	61.2	**4.4**	36.0	11.7	**5.8**
2.5	3.21	23.5	0.55	**4.6**	3.5	0.95	11.00	5.03	68.7	**4.0**	17.8	8.7	**4.8**
5.5	0.61	4.8	0.19	**4.4**	4.2	0.89	11.03	3.89	65.5	**3.3**	10.2	11.8	**4.4**
8.7	0.69	1.4	0.03	**4.6**	0.4	0.93	5.37	4.19	67.1	**5.0**	66.2	14.5	**6.5**
4.7	0.14	1.0	0.04	**4.4**	0.9	0.98	10.54	4.31	71.8	**1.1**	26.6	35.7	**4.9**
8.6	0.05	0.2	0.10	**0.1**	-0.1	-0.25	-1.71	3.35	106.6	**1.7**	36.7	39.6	**1.6**
5.3	0.77	5.0	0.35	**5.6**	6.0	1.20	14.52	4.20	71.8	**5.0**	38.1	9.2	**7.1**
8.3	0.02	0.2	0.02	**9.7**	2.8	2.25	32.13	4.91	56.0	**3.0**	21.0	14.7	**6.1**
0.0	3.82	33.7	0.17	**2.4**	1.5	0.28	3.10	4.36	62.2	**1.9**	1.9	18.2	**5.1**
0.0	4.04	24.8	2.06	**0.0**	-1.3	-0.51	-5.36	2.75	102.3	**1.8**	20.4	21.2	**3.2**
6.6	0.69	4.2	0.06	**7.3**	5.0	1.85	18.58	4.21	71.8	**4.7**	30.9	8.1	**7.2**
4.9	1.02	6.4	0.52	**3.1**	1.1	0.50	4.88	4.14	67.0	**0.9**	14.4	33.0	**4.9**
7.0	0.24	1.6	0.02	**4.9**	3.8	0.97	9.45	4.09	65.5	**1.4**	24.9	28.8	**4.9**
1.7	2.69	19.7	1.44	**0.9**	0.1	0.01	0.11	3.50	71.7	**0.8**	14.2	35.1	**4.5**
0.3	8.35	63.9	2.69	**0.0**	-2.3	-2.15	-27.53	3.34	111.3	**1.6**	14.8	22.2	**1.7**
1.5	3.83	24.8	1.85	**2.4**	1.0	0.19	2.49	3.60	62.0	**2.3**	32.6	22.8	**5.2**
0.8	5.58	47.4	1.53	**0.0**	-0.2	-0.50	-7.56	4.38	101.1	**4.6**	22.9	5.5	**2.1**
2.0	1.19	7.3	0.59	**3.6**	1.0	0.40	4.13	3.71	64.7	**0.7**	13.0	38.1	**4.2**
4.0	1.69	12.8	1.43	**2.6**	0.7	0.16	1.87	3.94	72.6	**0.9**	16.0	33.6	**5.1**
0.3	0.00	0.0	-0.08	**1.8**	0.3	0.14	0.73	4.23	88.5	**1.3**	15.3	27.3	**5.9**
4.9	1.18	9.0	0.74	**1.4**	0.6	0.56	5.89	3.50	74.0	**0.9**	14.7	33.3	**2.4**
7.0	0.00	0.0	0.10	**0.0**	-0.9	-1.32	-11.56	2.91	160.6	**2.1**	27.2	20.4	**0.8**
1.8	3.97	22.8	1.78	**0.8**	-0.9	-0.89	-8.69	5.31	95.4	**3.5**	19.9	11.8	**4.6**
4.1	1.17	11.3	0.91	**4.4**	1.7	1.02	13.42	4.29	62.0	**2.7**	13.7	15.2	**3.8**
2.9	3.67	16.4	2.23	**1.7**	-0.1	-0.14	-1.34	3.59	65.1	**2.5**	46.0	30.7	**5.5**
4.9	0.78	5.5	0.30	**0.0**	-0.4	-0.53	-5.40	2.90	113.3	**2.0**	31.2	26.8	**5.1**
5.9	0.15	1.0	0.17	**6.6**	0.7	1.43	15.48	6.04	74.0	**1.6**	22.0	25.3	**5.7**
5.4	0.58	4.2	0.27	**6.0**	63.0	1.17	9.96	4.14	61.6	**5.0**	22.0	4.7	**9.3**
0.0	7.95	68.4	0.72	**1.9**	0.4	0.09	1.06	4.03	69.7	**1.4**	5.9	23.3	**4.7**
3.4	1.64	14.0	0.19	**6.7**	1.6	1.55	19.71	3.85	56.2	**2.0**	17.1	19.2	**6.4**
0.1	15.25	107.7	1.89	**0.3**	-2.4	-1.75	-24.90	3.65	65.0	**2.0**	25.8	20.6	**0.0**
0.3	11.89	68.1	2.19	**0.0**	-1.3	-2.10	-18.97	4.14	79.5	**0.6**	8.7	41.3	**2.7**

Name	City	State	Rating	2008 Rating	2007 Rating	Total Assets ($Mil)	One Year Asset Growth	Asset Mix (As a % of Total Assets) Comm-ercial Loans	Cons-umer Loans	Home Mort-gages	Secur-ities	Capital-ization Index	Leverage Ratio	Risk-based Capital Ratio
COMMUNITY BANK OF EAST	CLINTON	TN	**D-**	D-	D-	63	-18.96	8.0	1.3	18.6	22.6	**7.0**	9.0	17.5
COMMUNITY BANK OF	EASTON	IL	**B+**	B+	B+	26	6.36	11.3	10.5	9.0	1.9	**10.0**	13.9	26.4
COMMUNITY BANK OF	ELMHURST	IL	**D+**	D+	D+	160	3.76	7.8	0.6	11.2	39.5	**6.1**	8.1	13.7
COMMUNITY BANK OF	HOMESTEAD	FL	**D-**	D-	C	548	-3.64	4.3	1.6	6.7	16.2	**5.8**	8.1	11.6
COMMUNITY BANK OF	BAXLEY	GA	**B**	B	B	63	13.44	20.8	3.6	9.9	8.9	**9.3**	10.5	16.0
COMMUNITY BANK OF LOUISIA	MANSFIELD	LA	**B+**	B+	B-	321	26.92	8.0	4.0	6.9	48.1	**6.0**	8.0	17.1
COMMUNITY BANK OF	MARSHALL	MO	**A-**	A-	A-	103	4.69	4.2	4.0	12.5	39.0	**10.0**	11.9	20.7
COMMUNITY BANK OF	MEMPHIS	MO	**B**	B-	B	39	2.55	1.9	3.5	17.4	36.0	**6.2**	8.2	17.8
▲ COMMUNITY BANK OF MISSISS	FOREST	MS	**C**	C+	C+	628	-2.71	5.1	3.7	13.5	23.6	**7.5**	9.3	14.0
COMMUNITY BANK OF	RICHMOND	MO	**D+**	C-	D+	53	-19.57	7.0	1.5	19.2	6.6	**8.0**	9.7	13.8
▲ COMMUNITY BANK OF	RICE LAKE	WI	**C-**	C	C-	128	11.90	4.8	1.4	26.4	5.3	**6.3**	8.7	12.0
▼ COMMUNITY BANK OF	OELWEIN	IA	**C-**	C	B-	73	27.07	5.1	4.3	7.9	43.8	**5.6**	7.6	13.9
COMMUNITY BANK OF	PARKERSBURG	WV	**A-**	B+	B	225	-0.84	3.9	7.5	42.6	25.3	**8.4**	9.9	18.5
COMMUNITY BANK OF	RAYMORE	MO	**C+**	C	C+	149	19.87	15.2	0.8	4.6	15.3	**5.7**	8.5	11.5
COMMUNITY BANK OF	ROCKMART	GA	**E-**	E	E+	63	-8.32	5.1	2.5	19.2	11.9	**0.0**	2.3	4.6
COMMUNITY BANK OF ROWAN	SALISBURY	NC	**D-**	C-	C-	140	1.84	7.4	1.4	20.2	4.8	**4.8**	6.8	11.3
COMMUNITY BANK OF	RUSSELLVILLE	MO	**B**	B	B-	82	20.89	2.7	5.4	24.0	39.5	**10.0**	11.1	21.8
▼ COMMUNITY BANK OF SAN	STOCKTON	CA	**E+**	D	C+	131	-10.26	13.6	0.4	7.9	24.6	**4.9**	6.9	11.6
COMMUNITY BANK OF SANTA	SANTA MARIA	CA	**D**	C-	B-	152	12.64	18.3	1.7	6.0	10.0	**8.0**	10.2	13.4
COMMUNITY BANK OF SHELL	SHELL KNOB	MO	**E-**	D-	D-	11	-3.12	5.6	4.4	12.6	0.0	**3.8**	7.1	10.4
COMMUNITY BANK OF	SNYDER	TX	**C**	C+	C+	99	-0.17	13.1	5.1	9.3	9.6	**10.0**	11.5	15.4
COMMUNITY BANK OF THE	OAKLAND	CA	**D**	D-	D	116	38.46	37.0	0.6	1.4	7.6	**10.0**	12.1	17.0
COMMUNITY BANK OF THE	GREAT BEND	KS	**B-**	B-	B-	108	5.34	23.6	2.6	7.3	12.9	**5.9**	7.9	15.2
COMMUNITY BANK OF THE	SUNRISE BEACH	MO	**E-**	D	C	60	-8.52	3.7	2.5	17.5	11.4	**2.4**	5.9	9.4
COMMUNITY BANK OF THE	MERRITT ISLAND	FL	**C**	B-	C+	113	0.23	5.3	0.3	4.0	16.6	**7.0**	9.0	14.7
COMMUNITY BANK OF THE	SMYRNA	GA	**E-**	E-	D-	361	-1.80	7.1	0.8	11.3	5.8	**3.1**	6.4	10.0
COMMUNITY BANK OF	TRENTON	IL	**B**	B	B-	72	0.59	8.6	2.6	32.2	22.2	**10.0**	11.5	17.6
COMMUNITY BANK OF	WALDORF	MD	**D+**	C	B	883	8.67	13.9	0.1	15.9	18.3	**7.2**	9.2	12.7
COMMUNITY BANK OF	WICHITA	KS	**C+**	C	C	60	4.48	22.9	6.6	11.7	12.5	**6.8**	9.1	12.4
COMMUNITY BANK	OWATONNA	MN	**C-**	D+	D+	54	0.24	12.5	1.3	11.4	21.8	**6.9**	8.9	13.5
COMMUNITY BANKERS BANK	MIDLOTHIAN	VA	**D+**	D	D+	143	-6.64	0.9	2.0	2.8	20.7	**8.4**	10.0	17.1
COMMUNITY BANKS OF	GREENWOOD VILLAGE	CO	**E-**	D-	D	1,576	-9.60	14.2	3.2	8.1	3.6	**0.0**	3.0	5.3
COMMUNITY BK & TRUST- ALA	UNION SPRINGS	AL	**D-**	E	E+	91	-13.11	9.1	3.9	11.6	28.1	**7.0**	9.0	17.0
COMMUNITY BK A MA CO-OP B	BROCKTON	MA	**E-**	E+	D	332	-4.96	5.5	0.3	32.7	6.3	**2.6**	5.8	9.7
COMMUNITY BK EL DORADO	EL DORADO SPRINGS	MO	**B+**	B+	B+	95	5.69	3.4	3.9	10.4	46.4	**10.0**	11.3	21.3
▲ COMMUNITY BK NORTH	AMORY	MS	**D+**	C-	C+	480	-2.01	4.1	2.7	18.9	20.7	**6.3**	8.3	13.1
COMMUNITY BK OF BERGEN	MAYWOOD	NJ	**D-**	D-	C+	310	2.41	0.4	0.7	39.1	18.2	**6.5**	8.5	13.2
COMMUNITY BK OF PICKENS C	JASPER	GA	**E-**	D-	C-	296	-5.41	5.3	3.9	20.4	13.5	**2.8**	6.5	9.8
COMMUNITY BK OF PLEASANT	PLEASANT HILL	MO	**C+**	C	C+	44	9.14	26.1	1.4	2.1	14.5	**8.2**	10.7	13.5
COMMUNITY BK OF SHELBY	COWDEN	IL	**C-**	C-	C-	48	-1.86	8.4	3.8	10.1	22.2	**9.5**	10.7	22.7
▲ COMMUNITY BK OF THE	SULPHUR	OK	**B-**	C+	C+	83	4.79	7.0	9.4	5.8	36.2	**6.7**	8.7	15.4
▲ COMMUNITY BK OF THE	JAMESTOWN	TN	**D+**	D	E-	132	-7.24	3.7	11.7	16.7	12.8	**10.0**	11.3	16.2
▲ COMMUNITY BKG CO OF FITZG	FITZGERALD	GA	**B-**	C+	B-	102	-1.00	7.2	7.0	21.0	18.3	**10.0**	11.5	18.9
▲ COMMUNITY BUSINESS BANK	WEST SACRAMENTO	CA	**C-**	D	D-	144	15.59	11.2	0.2	10.0	13.1	**10.0**	12.8	17.8
COMMUNITY BUSINESS BANK	CUMMING	GA	**D**	C-	C	102	35.29	5.9	0.7	11.5	19.8	**10.0**	15.4	25.5
▲ COMMUNITY BUSINESS BANK	SAUK CITY	WI	**D+**	D	C	60	-7.93	14.2	1.2	12.0	17.9	**6.0**	8.2	11.8
COMMUNITY CAPITAL BANK	JONESBORO	GA	**E-**	D-	E+	192	-3.29	1.4	0.1	23.5	1.0	**0.0**	2.2	4.4
COMMUNITY CAPITAL BANK	CHRISTIANSBURG	VA	**C+**	C	C	50	101.14	7.1	0.0	3.3	4.0	**10.0**	19.4	30.3
COMMUNITY CENTRAL BANK	MOUNT CLEMENS	MI	**E-**	E-	D-	476	-12.82	8.5	1.5	13.7	8.1	**0.0**	1.7	3.7
COMMUNITY COMMERCE	CLAREMONT	CA	**D-**	D-	D	361	-11.25	0.0	0.0	5.8	0.0	**6.8**	9.2	12.3
▲ COMMUNITY DEVELOPMENT	OGEMA	MN	**D+**	C-	C-	60	50.90	14.2	4.0	15.1	15.8	**6.5**	8.5	15.5
▼ COMMUNITY FINANCIAL BANK	PRENTICE	WI	**D+**	B-	B-	33	5.59	25.6	2.0	20.4	7.5	**9.5**	14.0	14.6
COMMUNITY FINANCIAL SVCS	BENTON	KY	**B**	B+	B+	528	13.66	6.9	10.5	24.5	14.6	**7.1**	9.0	13.0
COMMUNITY FIRST BANK	HARRISON	AR	**D**	C-	C-	540	-3.43	6.8	4.4	22.5	22.1	**7.6**	9.4	14.9
▲ COMMUNITY FIRST BANK	KEOSAUQUA	IA	**B**	B-	A-	135	10.20	10.0	3.4	12.9	23.9	**10.0**	11.5	17.8
▼ COMMUNITY FIRST BANK	FAIRVIEW HEIGHTS	IL	**C+**	B	C+	192	9.88	16.0	0.8	16.8	9.5	**8.2**	9.9	13.5
COMMUNITY FIRST BANK	NEW IBERIA	LA	**B**	B-	B-	232	9.65	8.6	7.0	18.1	29.1	**6.7**	8.7	14.5
COMMUNITY FIRST BANK	PIKESVILLE	MD	**C-**	C	B	58	1.72	3.5	0.2	45.9	0.0	**10.0**	13.1	29.0
COMMUNITY FIRST BANK	BUTLER	MO	**B**	B	B	160	30.33	8.1	2.4	19.4	9.3	**5.9**	7.9	13.7
▼ COMMUNITY FIRST BANK	SOMERSET	NJ	**D**	C	C	48	44.76	3.0	1.9	7.9	1.0	**10.0**	18.0	22.8

Asset Quality Index	Non-Performing Loans as a % of Total Loans	Non-Performing Loans as a % of Capital	Net Charge-offs Avg Loans	Profitability Index	Net Income ($Mil)	Return on Assets (R.O.A.)	Return on Equity (R.O.E.)	Net Interest Spread	Overhead Efficiency Ratio	Liquidity Index	Liquidity Ratio	Hot Money Ratio	Stability Index
1.7	3.98	21.1	4.08	**0.0**	-1.8	-2.52	-25.57	4.01	99.9	**4.3**	31.0	10.3	**2.7**
7.9	0.00	0.0	0.00	**7.5**	0.3	1.30	8.94	3.43	36.8	**4.0**	44.0	15.7	**8.9**
3.7	5.55	33.8	0.11	**1.2**	0.1	0.03	0.35	2.78	88.8	**4.2**	43.1	14.7	**4.3**
0.3	9.09	64.6	2.40	**1.1**	-1.3	-0.22	-2.63	3.78	81.6	**0.9**	9.1	31.1	**5.4**
5.1	2.52	14.2	0.16	**4.8**	0.5	0.83	7.74	4.34	64.2	**1.1**	26.9	37.6	**5.8**
8.9	0.21	1.1	0.13	**8.6**	6.1	2.26	26.46	4.38	55.8	**3.4**	34.6	16.0	**4.9**
8.9	0.51	1.8	0.15	**5.1**	0.9	0.95	7.93	3.47	63.6	**4.9**	38.6	9.9	**7.5**
5.7	1.12	5.9	-0.01	**3.7**	0.2	0.57	5.35	2.87	69.4	**3.8**	47.9	17.3	**6.4**
3.6	0.91	5.9	0.32	**5.0**	5.5	0.87	9.93	4.07	67.6	**1.6**	23.0	24.7	**5.2**
1.7	3.91	26.6	0.49	**2.9**	0.2	0.35	3.86	4.86	72.1	**1.4**	11.2	24.6	**4.9**
2.9	1.81	15.6	0.12	**4.8**	1.5	1.19	15.44	3.85	57.4	**1.1**	7.7	27.8	**4.8**
1.5	4.71	27.0	0.41	**3.9**	0.5	0.83	10.12	3.32	60.6	**2.5**	55.0	39.9	**3.3**
8.1	0.02	0.1	0.13	**7.2**	3.9	1.71	17.78	4.10	62.1	**3.2**	21.8	13.6	**6.7**
5.2	0.00	0.0	0.86	**5.9**	2.1	1.41	15.29	3.69	68.4	**4.0**	14.9	8.9	**5.5**
0.3	12.98	228.6	2.21	**0.0**	-2.1	-3.06	-71.72	3.07	149.7	**0.8**	21.7	54.3	**0.0**
1.7	3.34	29.9	3.00	**0.8**	-1.1	-0.77	-10.57	3.07	69.8	**1.7**	19.2	22.5	**2.2**
8.3	0.43	2.0	0.16	**4.3**	0.9	1.12	9.14	3.58	69.7	**2.7**	43.9	26.4	**7.8**
0.3	11.01	69.5	6.14	**0.0**	-5.6	-4.20	-43.92	3.65	107.1	**1.7**	30.3	30.1	**2.9**
3.6	0.47	3.1	1.71	**1.3**	0.0	0.02	0.17	5.14	79.6	**2.7**	19.8	16.1	**4.9**
4.0	2.17	13.2	0.93	**0.0**	-0.2	-1.30	-16.57	4.13	128.6	**5.3**	43.2	5.9	**2.4**
2.0	4.05	25.3	0.03	**5.4**	1.0	0.98	8.36	4.32	66.8	**1.4**	24.0	28.7	**6.2**
2.2	4.99	24.9	0.25	**0.0**	-0.9	-0.85	-7.38	4.11	100.4	**2.4**	23.1	17.7	**4.0**
7.0	0.25	1.5	0.05	**3.9**	0.6	0.58	6.89	3.66	74.6	**3.2**	36.9	17.9	**4.6**
0.3	11.81	92.9	1.84	**0.0**	-1.6	-2.51	-31.81	3.91	131.9	**1.2**	13.6	28.5	**2.1**
3.0	4.24	21.2	1.91	**2.4**	0.2	0.16	1.76	4.09	78.3	**2.4**	36.7	25.3	**6.1**
0.0	2.55	20.6	1.12	**0.2**	-0.3	-0.08	-1.32	3.11	86.9	**1.2**	21.1	30.9	**2.3**
4.8	2.73	14.9	0.25	**4.5**	0.8	1.04	8.99	3.65	67.1	**3.5**	25.5	12.6	**7.0**
1.2	2.04	15.4	0.60	**4.0**	5.4	0.64	6.79	3.38	59.0	**0.8**	15.1	35.9	**6.2**
7.8	0.11	0.8	0.11	**4.9**	0.5	0.88	9.88	4.96	72.9	**1.7**	17.1	21.7	**5.4**
2.1	2.92	21.4	0.35	**3.3**	0.3	0.47	5.20	3.69	71.5	**1.1**	18.8	32.2	**3.8**
1.8	4.28	18.7	1.51	**1.6**	0.4	0.25	2.60	3.28	77.5	**2.2**	45.5	40.1	**3.5**
0.0	13.23	139.0	3.17	**0.0**	-64.3	-3.73	-70.15	2.42	109.9	**0.9**	15.9	39.9	**3.3**
0.3	13.44	59.1	3.31	**0.1**	-1.4	-1.46	-17.71	3.19	108.1	**2.4**	42.0	30.6	**2.3**
0.3	8.96	94.1	1.09	**0.3**	-1.5	-0.45	-6.64	3.77	106.9	**1.2**	10.4	27.6	**0.0**
5.1	3.46	12.0	0.16	**8.3**	1.7	1.82	15.54	3.27	40.8	**3.8**	47.7	17.3	**9.1**
2.4	2.86	20.0	1.39	**0.9**	-0.1	-0.02	-0.26	3.40	82.5	**1.5**	24.8	28.1	**4.0**
0.3	7.61	57.4	0.46	**3.4**	2.0	0.67	7.79	4.01	75.7	**1.9**	23.5	20.6	**4.5**
0.3	6.23	56.9	3.27	**0.0**	-2.5	-0.82	-11.29	3.12	78.5	**0.7**	14.2	50.7	**2.3**
8.2	0.00	0.0	0.04	**2.2**	0.3	0.72	6.17	3.56	88.7	**3.9**	23.6	10.4	**5.1**
8.9	0.00	0.0	0.05	**1.9**	0.2	0.38	3.67	3.04	88.1	**5.0**	51.9	12.2	**4.9**
5.5	0.39	2.1	0.82	**6.8**	1.4	1.72	20.56	5.23	66.5	**1.9**	27.0	24.1	**4.9**
2.9	1.88	10.1	0.83	**1.9**	0.5	0.33	1.86	5.94	69.1	**1.3**	25.3	30.2	**4.3**
4.8	1.81	9.0	0.15	**4.5**	0.9	0.83	6.71	3.73	69.6	**1.9**	23.2	20.8	**6.4**
2.0	5.35	28.3	0.51	**1.9**	1.0	0.73	5.67	5.24	79.7	**1.0**	23.9	34.9	**3.4**
6.8	0.00	0.0	0.08	**0.1**	-0.1	-0.15	-0.87	3.49	100.4	**2.2**	38.2	30.6	**1.6**
1.9	2.72	19.6	1.03	**0.6**	-0.1	-0.20	-2.20	3.96	88.4	**1.8**	19.1	20.6	**4.2**
0.0	12.05	250.5	4.25	**0.0**	-9.4	-4.63	-80.86	2.78	137.7	**0.8**	16.7	37.8	**2.2**
9.1	0.00	0.0	0.00	**3.1**	0.3	0.87	3.90	2.95	47.1	**2.3**	55.1	55.5	**4.6**
0.0	10.75	144.1	3.95	**0.0**	-26.3	-4.86	-120.06	2.72	106.3	**0.7**	9.1	38.1	**1.2**
0.0	4.06	25.8	0.53	**1.8**	0.3	0.07	0.76	4.42	66.7	**0.7**	15.9	51.5	**5.4**
2.1	2.12	12.8	0.30	**6.2**	0.8	1.53	15.41	3.42	58.2	**2.6**	44.7	29.0	**4.8**
2.2	4.00	18.2	1.41	**0.7**	-0.2	-0.49	-3.35	4.51	96.0	**2.4**	32.7	21.3	**7.3**
4.6	0.73	5.2	0.18	**6.0**	5.5	1.10	11.55	4.09	61.2	**1.2**	12.9	27.7	**6.9**
1.2	3.13	19.9	1.16	**3.6**	3.9	0.69	7.67	3.65	64.8	**1.4**	12.3	24.8	**4.7**
4.0	2.72	13.1	1.32	**5.0**	1.3	1.06	8.94	5.07	64.4	**2.9**	39.1	20.4	**6.4**
5.6	0.76	5.6	0.82	**4.4**	1.8	0.93	9.43	3.63	52.4	**1.7**	13.1	21.0	**7.2**
7.0	0.50	3.2	0.28	**8.1**	4.2	1.92	20.96	4.65	55.3	**1.9**	31.0	28.2	**5.4**
6.8	1.51	6.3	0.33	**0.6**	-0.4	-0.63	-4.59	3.88	99.9	**5.0**	43.2	10.7	**5.9**
4.1	1.67	14.0	0.24	**8.7**	3.2	2.19	25.51	3.83	53.0	**1.7**	15.9	21.4	**5.8**
8.5	0.03	0.1	0.02	**0.0**	-0.5	-1.10	-6.56	3.45	130.1	**1.3**	30.3	36.1	**1.5**

Name	City	State	Rating	2008 Rating	2007 Rating	Total Assets ($Mil)	One Year Asset Growth	Asset Mix (As a % of Total Assets) Comm-ercial Loans	Cons-umer Loans	Home Mort-gages	Secur-ities	Capital-ization Index	Leverage Ratio	Risk-based Capital Ratio
▼COMMUNITY FIRST BANK	REYNOLDSVILLE	PA	**D+**	C-	C-	87	9.33	11.8	6.8	32.3	11.0	**5.5**	7.5	11.4
COMMUNITY FIRST BANK	WALHALLA	SC	**D+**	D+	B-	502	2.65	4.0	5.0	16.5	35.1	**5.9**	7.9	14.2
COMMUNITY FIRST BANK	KENNEWICK	WA	**A-**	B+	B	171	22.51	13.8	1.5	5.5	14.9	**9.1**	10.4	15.6
COMMUNITY FIRST BANK	BOSCOBEL	WI	**D-**	D	D+	243	-2.58	7.2	1.6	18.2	17.7	**6.1**	8.1	13.9
▲COMMUNITY FIRST BANK	ROSHOLT	WI	**D**	D-	D+	66	-1.64	5.9	2.5	13.1	15.8	**7.0**	9.0	12.6
COMMUNITY FIRST BANK & TR	COLUMBIA	TN	**D-**	D-	C-	679	-2.94	7.0	1.4	19.2	9.4	**5.6**	7.6	11.6
COMMUNITY FIRST BANK NA	FOREST	OH	**B-**	B-	C+	47	10.70	5.5	2.6	40.3	7.6	**8.3**	9.9	18.2
COMMUNITY FIRST BANKING C	WEST PLAINS	MO	**B-**	B-	B-	130	-7.60	8.7	4.9	25.8	12.1	**8.8**	10.2	15.1
COMMUNITY FIRST BK	MOUNT VERNON	IL	**B**	B	B	86	12.73	14.4	1.7	15.5	19.2	**5.5**	7.5	12.7
COMMUNITY FIRST BK OF GLE	GLENDIVE	MT	**B-**	B-	B	44	-1.89	1.4	1.9	1.9	24.8	**8.0**	9.7	16.0
COMMUNITY FIRST BK OF IND	KOKOMO	IN	**D+**	C-	B-	185	-8.89	19.5	1.3	10.1	9.6	**7.7**	9.5	13.4
COMMUNITY FIRST NATIONAL	MANHATTAN	KS	**C-**	C	C	137	6.92	16.0	3.3	30.0	0.0	**6.3**	8.6	12.0
▼COMMUNITY FIRSTBANK	CHARLESTON	SC	**D-**	D+	C-	563	-5.61	4.3	0.3	28.7	17.4	**5.6**	7.6	13.0
COMMUNITY FSB	WOODHAVEN	NY	**E-**	E+	D-	52	-19.08	11.7	0.0	1.5	34.5	**4.9**	7.0	11.6
COMMUNITY GUARANTY SB	PLYMOUTH	NH	**C**	C	C	101	3.68	4.9	2.8	35.2	23.1	**5.4**	7.7	11.3
COMMUNITY MUTUAL	WHITE PLAINS	NY	**D+**	C-	D	245	8.16	7.3	0.2	47.2	20.9	**5.7**	7.7	16.2
▲COMMUNITY NATIONAL BK	WATERLOO	IA	**D**	D-	D-	207	-10.98	14.9	1.2	12.2	17.9	**8.0**	9.7	14.6
▲COMMUNITY NATIONAL BK	SENECA	KS	**C**	C	C-	206	3.94	5.4	1.4	12.7	37.6	**8.5**	10.0	16.0
COMMUNITY NATIONAL BK	MONETT	MO	**C+**	C	B	70	-9.43	6.5	3.6	19.1	6.3	**8.6**	10.1	14.9
COMMUNITY NATIONAL BK	GREAT NECK	NY	**C-**	D+	D+	477	18.00	18.1	0.0	26.5	23.3	**10.0**	13.5	21.8
COMMUNITY NATIONAL BK	DAYTON	TN	**C-**	C-	C	213	-6.28	5.7	3.1	18.0	18.3	**8.8**	10.2	17.0
COMMUNITY NATIONAL BK	BELLAIRE	TX	**D**	C-	C-	190	9.19	8.3	5.4	5.4	43.4	**6.1**	8.1	15.3
▼COMMUNITY NATIONAL BK	HONDO	TX	**C+**	B	B	159	40.06	10.9	6.5	14.5	14.7	**5.2**	7.2	13.7
COMMUNITY NATIONAL BK	MIDLAND	TX	**B**	B	B	621	12.27	26.0	2.1	5.0	24.2	**6.2**	8.2	12.3
COMMUNITY NATIONAL BK	DERBY	VT	**C+**	C+	B-	545	8.06	5.5	2.4	34.0	10.8	**5.4**	7.4	12.2
COMMUNITY NATIONAL BK & T	CHANUTE	KS	**C+**	C+	C	719	12.06	8.6	2.7	18.6	18.6	**5.3**	7.3	11.5
▼COMMUNITY NATIONAL BK & T	CORSICANA	TX	**A**	A+	A+	360	8.37	7.7	2.8	12.2	24.9	**10.0**	13.0	20.8
COMMUNITY NATIONAL BK	MONMOUTH	IL	**B+**	B+	B	46	-7.80	4.0	8.7	16.0	38.4	**10.0**	13.4	29.1
COMMUNITY NATIONAL BK OF	ALBION	PA	**A-**	A-	A-	79	3.87	0.5	1.9	40.9	28.5	**10.0**	19.7	54.4
COMMUNITY NATIONAL BK	OKARCHE	OK	**A**	A	A	65	-0.71	6.1	4.8	8.0	50.9	**10.0**	13.4	24.3
COMMUNITY NB OF THE	MORRISTOWN	TN	**D-**	D	D+	109	-12.48	7.4	3.0	25.2	27.4	**8.2**	9.8	17.0
COMMUNITY PRIDE BANK	ISANTI	MN	**D-**	D	D	92	-11.10	18.4	0.7	7.9	4.8	**8.6**	10.3	13.8
COMMUNITY RESOURCE BANK	NORTHFIELD	MN	**D-**	D+	C	241	-1.67	12.5	1.8	7.0	11.5	**4.5**	7.3	10.7
▼COMMUNITY SAVINGS	CALDWELL	OH	**C-**	C+	B-	51	3.67	1.1	2.6	53.8	6.4	**10.0**	12.4	24.2
COMMUNITY SAVINGS BANK	BETHEL	OH	**C**	C-	C-	42	10.89	1.3	0.0	62.0	11.7	**10.0**	12.6	24.3
COMMUNITY SB	EDGEWOOD	IA	**B**	B-	B-	297	-0.16	12.5	2.0	8.3	16.8	**6.9**	9.4	12.5
COMMUNITY SB	CHICAGO	IL	**C-**	C	C	424	2.08	0.0	0.0	39.3	28.3	**10.0**	14.8	38.9
COMMUNITY SHORES BANK	MUSKEGON	MI	**E-**	D-	D+	238	2.62	18.3	1.6	14.5	15.3	**0.5**	4.3	7.1
▼COMMUNITY SOUTH BANK	PARSONS	TN	**E-**	D-	D-	675	2.40	6.1	1.7	8.6	5.3	**0.9**	5.0	7.8
COMMUNITY SOUTHERN BANK	LAKELAND	FL	**D+**	C	C	170	3.81	9.6	1.0	9.2	19.0	**9.0**	10.3	15.4
COMMUNITY SPIRIT BANK	RED BAY	AL	**C**	C	C+	112	-0.55	9.9	6.0	17.4	14.6	**5.7**	7.7	11.7
▼COMMUNITY STATE BK	BRADLEY	AR	**C**	C+	C+	25	24.97	15.1	5.7	14.2	25.4	**9.3**	10.5	18.7
COMMUNITY STATE BK	LAMAR	CO	**C**	C	C	71	22.49	12.3	6.9	11.6	15.3	**10.0**	11.0	17.2
COMMUNITY STATE BK	STARKE	FL	**C-**	B	B+	51	3.84	6.2	3.9	18.8	32.8	**10.0**	15.7	33.2
COMMUNITY STATE BK	PATON	IA	**B+**	B	B	34	0.60	1.5	2.4	4.3	41.3	**10.0**	15.5	24.2
COMMUNITY STATE BK	SPENCER	IA	**B**	B-	B	126	4.39	12.7	2.5	5.5	35.4	**5.6**	7.6	13.5
▲COMMUNITY STATE BK	TIPTON	IA	**C+**	C	B-	98	10.59	7.4	2.9	14.1	15.5	**7.1**	9.1	14.2
COMMUNITY STATE BK	GALVA	IL	**B+**	B-	C+	120	19.24	13.2	2.4	8.7	31.5	**7.5**	9.3	14.2
COMMUNITY STATE BK	AVILLA	IN	**C+**	B-	B-	171	0.53	5.5	2.1	33.6	19.5	**6.8**	8.8	15.3
COMMUNITY STATE BK	BROOK	IN	**B**	B	B	47	-0.17	11.6	4.4	19.9	4.7	**10.0**	15.9	22.6
COMMUNITY STATE BK	ROYAL CENTER	IN	**C+**	C+	C+	93	3.77	3.2	6.8	19.9	18.5	**5.7**	7.7	12.6
COMMUNITY STATE BK	COFFEYVILLE	KS	**B**	B	B-	59	3.55	10.1	2.7	10.0	32.5	**7.4**	9.3	16.0
COMMUNITY STATE BK	SAINT CHARLES	MI	**D**	D	D+	192	4.19	5.3	5.2	22.7	30.6	**5.1**	7.1	12.8
COMMUNITY STATE BK	SHELBINA	MO	**C**	C+	B-	56	-1.55	3.6	9.1	24.6	28.5	**5.6**	7.6	15.1
▲COMMUNITY STATE BK	HENNESSEY	OK	**C+**	C	C	36	7.01	15.9	16.5	11.2	0.3	**6.2**	8.8	11.9
COMMUNITY STATE BK	POTEAU	OK	**B-**	B-	B-	184	5.88	8.7	4.6	21.0	17.5	**6.4**	8.4	12.7
▼COMMUNITY STATE BK	AUSTIN	TX	**E-**	D-	D-	21	-9.23	17.4	3.0	6.3	33.4	**3.4**	5.4	11.4
COMMUNITY STATE BK	NORWALK	WI	**D**	D	C-	27	-6.38	2.2	3.4	32.5	5.2	**6.7**	8.7	14.6
COMMUNITY STATE BK	UNION GROVE	WI	**C**	C	B	265	-5.01	24.1	1.6	14.3	7.4	**9.7**	10.9	14.8
COMMUNITY STATE BK NA	ANKENY	IA	**C-**	D+	D	538	-1.13	11.7	0.5	14.9	14.9	**7.4**	9.3	14.5

Asset Quality Index	Non-Performing Loans as a % of Total Loans	Non-Performing Loans as a % of Capital	Net Charge-offs Avg Loans	Profitability Index	Net Income ($Mil)	Return on Assets (R.O.A.)	Return on Equity (R.O.E.)	Net Interest Spread	Overhead Efficiency Ratio	Liquidity Index	Liquidity Ratio	Hot Money Ratio	Stability Index
2.3	2.21	20.9	-0.01	**2.4**	0.2	0.28	3.61	3.41	90.0	**1.4**	15.2	26.0	**3.9**
1.2	6.36	36.1	1.85	**2.1**	1.2	0.24	3.01	2.75	62.5	**2.1**	36.1	29.2	**4.0**
6.5	0.17	1.0	0.04	**7.8**	2.8	1.79	16.15	4.96	62.2	**4.8**	31.6	7.7	**7.1**
0.3	7.66	52.5	2.39	**0.7**	-1.8	-0.71	-8.50	3.57	71.2	**1.6**	22.1	25.8	**3.2**
0.8	3.52	23.3	1.68	**4.3**	0.5	0.68	7.49	5.29	71.5	**3.0**	28.1	16.1	**5.2**
0.3	5.76	44.3	0.90	**0.3**	-4.2	-0.62	-6.79	3.69	80.5	**0.7**	13.0	36.2	**4.3**
9.0	0.00	0.0	0.00	**3.8**	0.3	0.58	5.56	3.89	77.5	**4.0**	29.1	11.5	**5.8**
4.6	1.13	7.4	0.26	**6.4**	2.0	1.56	15.91	4.27	59.8	**1.6**	11.9	21.6	**5.3**
6.4	0.20	1.7	0.00	**7.5**	1.5	1.91	18.45	4.60	56.6	**1.8**	21.0	21.2	**7.3**
8.5	0.03	0.2	0.00	**4.5**	0.3	0.62	6.15	3.69	73.3	**4.5**	45.3	13.2	**6.2**
1.6	2.70	16.6	0.94	**3.2**	0.8	0.39	4.12	4.11	65.0	**2.6**	23.1	16.9	**4.1**
2.5	1.56	14.3	0.40	**5.3**	1.3	0.97	11.59	4.18	57.8	**1.2**	5.2	26.5	**4.3**
0.3	8.70	69.2	2.17	**2.6**	-0.8	-0.14	-1.90	3.29	68.2	**3.3**	12.4	12.3	**2.6**
0.0	26.39	210.7	0.00	**0.4**	-1.5	-2.53	-33.23	3.24	83.2	**3.3**	41.0	18.6	**0.7**
4.0	1.97	15.6	0.20	**2.9**	0.6	0.56	6.72	4.02	86.3	**3.0**	21.1	14.4	**4.9**
3.8	1.79	16.2	0.00	**1.7**	0.3	0.13	1.72	3.27	90.6	**1.7**	25.8	25.5	**1.0**
1.3	5.08	30.1	0.79	**1.2**	0.5	0.23	2.22	3.73	86.9	**3.8**	15.0	10.2	**3.5**
3.1	3.82	17.0	1.28	**4.1**	2.1	0.99	10.02	3.65	71.9	**4.8**	30.0	7.0	**5.0**
4.6	1.24	8.1	0.13	**4.2**	0.8	1.03	10.21	3.91	74.7	**3.0**	19.8	14.6	**5.7**
5.8	1.27	6.3	0.31	**2.2**	1.5	0.33	2.55	3.39	79.2	**1.1**	8.9	28.0	**3.7**
1.0	5.33	30.9	0.81	**3.6**	0.8	0.38	3.81	4.21	78.6	**2.1**	16.7	18.8	**5.8**
5.9	1.89	10.2	0.15	**0.4**	-0.5	-0.29	-3.26	3.76	105.3	**3.5**	51.5	21.0	**4.4**
3.1	2.46	17.4	0.84	**3.8**	1.2	0.77	8.54	4.89	75.8	**2.3**	36.8	27.4	**5.3**
7.7	0.11	0.8	0.03	**5.4**	5.6	0.96	9.32	4.14	64.9	**5.0**	31.9	6.2	**6.6**
3.9	1.21	10.9	0.19	**4.5**	4.8	0.92	9.60	4.00	71.3	**3.5**	18.0	12.0	**6.6**
4.1	1.04	8.7	0.16	**3.9**	4.5	0.67	8.16	4.13	76.0	**2.9**	14.4	14.5	**5.2**
6.3	0.10	0.4	0.06	**9.4**	5.3	1.57	11.33	5.49	58.2	**2.2**	19.4	18.4	**9.5**
8.6	0.48	1.6	0.82	**4.7**	0.4	0.79	5.78	3.75	72.1	**3.4**	54.4	21.1	**7.3**
10.0	0.28	0.7	0.00	**5.8**	0.8	1.01	5.08	3.38	60.0	**2.2**	25.3	19.3	**8.8**
8.6	0.03	0.1	0.16	**8.4**	1.2	1.82	13.59	3.88	55.0	**1.5**	28.4	30.7	**9.8**
2.2	2.64	15.0	1.47	**0.0**	-0.2	-0.17	-1.63	3.47	95.8	**1.4**	15.6	25.6	**4.3**
1.7	1.80	11.3	1.29	**0.0**	-1.1	-1.12	-10.80	4.36	83.8	**1.7**	17.8	21.9	**4.5**
0.3	7.55	52.1	1.99	**0.0**	-2.6	-1.10	-11.07	4.01	85.9	**2.3**	22.8	18.3	**4.5**
2.1	5.32	28.4	0.01	**1.6**	-0.1	-0.10	-0.78	3.33	100.1	**3.2**	27.1	14.6	**6.4**
8.7	0.60	3.7	0.00	**2.4**	0.2	0.39	3.00	3.55	83.0	**2.7**	21.5	15.9	**6.2**
7.2	0.31	2.2	0.51	**4.1**	2.8	0.96	10.06	3.98	71.6	**1.2**	18.5	30.1	**5.4**
1.7	2.17	8.8	0.17	**1.3**	0.0	-0.01	-0.06	2.60	90.0	**3.0**	40.6	20.2	**7.3**
0.3	4.95	54.8	2.82	**0.0**	-8.2	-3.31	-50.91	3.25	136.6	**1.4**	13.6	26.2	**1.5**
0.0	7.92	89.6	1.01	**0.0**	-21.7	-3.18	-41.58	3.12	163.7	**0.7**	10.3	36.4	**3.9**
6.0	1.10	6.0	0.13	**1.5**	0.8	0.48	5.32	3.45	82.3	**1.4**	31.6	38.3	**2.9**
5.6	0.67	5.5	0.02	**3.9**	0.8	0.68	8.85	4.24	78.5	**1.6**	20.9	25.2	**3.7**
6.3	0.46	2.3	0.41	**5.8**	0.3	1.21	10.70	3.48	61.1	**1.2**	23.3	30.0	**5.0**
8.0	0.30	1.7	0.05	**2.6**	0.4	0.57	4.94	3.57	68.9	**1.2**	29.6	47.9	**4.1**
2.0	11.37	28.5	3.35	**1.0**	-1.0	-1.99	-11.52	5.59	83.6	**5.6**	58.5	10.2	**7.5**
8.6	0.59	1.8	-0.29	**5.0**	0.3	1.00	6.25	3.97	66.2	**5.3**	46.6	9.2	**8.1**
5.4	0.18	1.1	0.02	**6.0**	1.6	1.35	15.85	3.68	66.2	**3.1**	34.2	17.4	**6.2**
6.2	0.00	0.0	1.17	**4.9**	0.8	0.82	9.12	3.97	60.4	**4.8**	28.2	6.4	**5.1**
6.2	0.29	1.8	0.17	**7.8**	2.0	1.80	17.20	5.17	59.5	**1.7**	26.5	25.8	**5.9**
5.7	0.16	1.2	1.16	**3.1**	0.8	0.44	4.90	4.28	71.4	**2.9**	25.7	15.7	**5.5**
5.1	1.35	5.9	0.20	**6.0**	0.5	1.07	6.89	4.95	59.2	**1.3**	31.2	48.9	**6.8**
4.8	0.23	1.9	0.66	**4.4**	0.7	0.75	8.87	4.49	64.6	**3.8**	28.5	12.2	**5.3**
4.3	1.57	8.2	0.01	**7.5**	0.8	1.22	13.10	4.77	61.6	**4.1**	21.8	9.0	**6.7**
0.9	2.64	18.2	0.78	**2.1**	0.4	0.21	2.26	4.48	86.9	**5.6**	42.3	7.2	**4.7**
6.9	0.09	0.6	0.25	**4.6**	0.4	0.75	9.96	2.95	62.7	**4.4**	26.8	7.9	**4.3**
3.4	0.90	7.3	0.63	**7.4**	0.6	1.58	17.56	6.68	74.4	**3.8**	18.2	10.4	**6.8**
5.4	0.43	3.5	0.17	**4.8**	1.7	0.96	11.31	4.89	75.1	**1.8**	21.6	22.6	**4.5**
0.0	8.37	45.9	3.25	**0.0**	-0.5	-2.15	-15.63	4.19	147.4	**3.7**	11.3	9.9	**3.1**
1.7	3.00	21.5	0.82	**0.9**	-0.1	-0.48	-4.68	4.02	95.3	**4.9**	30.2	6.3	**5.1**
1.6	3.95	23.4	0.85	**5.4**	2.7	1.02	9.50	4.90	65.5	**3.5**	21.8	12.0	**7.5**
1.5	2.83	18.3	1.07	**2.1**	2.2	0.40	3.99	3.76	74.4	**4.2**	19.9	8.2	**3.8**

Name	City	State	Rating	2008 Rating	2007 Rating	Total Assets ($Mil)	One Year Asset Growth	Asset Mix (As a % of Total Assets) Commercial Loans	Consumer Loans	Home Mortgages	Securities	Capitalization Index	Leverage Ratio	Risk-based Capital Ratio
COMMUNITY STATE BK OF	CANTON	OK	**D+**	C	B-	34	9.07	7.5	12.5	13.3	13.9	**9.4**	10.9	14.5
COMMUNITY STATE BK OF MIS	BOWLING GREEN	MO	**B+**	B+	A-	207	7.28	6.4	2.1	17.7	36.7	**10.0**	11.5	16.0
COMMUNITY STATE BK	ORBISONIA	PA	**B-**	B-	B	275	10.20	1.3	10.4	62.5	3.0	**6.3**	8.3	13.7
COMMUNITY STATE BK ROCK	ROCK FALLS	IL	**C-**	C-	D+	231	12.85	9.8	3.0	22.9	15.0	**4.7**	6.7	11.3
COMMUNITY TRUST &	OOLTEWAH	TN	**D-**	D-	B-	144	-6.16	13.7	1.4	18.0	4.4	**6.1**	8.1	11.9
COMMUNITY TRUST BANK	IRVINGTON	IL	**B-**	B	B	92	4.42	4.5	1.1	15.2	30.4	**9.2**	10.5	17.9
COMMUNITY TRUST BANK	RUSTON	LA	**C+**	C+	C+	1,882	58.72	24.0	1.8	13.0	13.9	**3.1**	8.0	10.1
COMMUNITY TRUST BANK INC	PIKEVILLE	KY	**C-**	C	C	3,147	2.44	8.4	15.5	22.8	9.8	**7.9**	9.6	13.6
COMMUNITY VALLEY BANK	EL CENTRO	CA	**D**	D	C-	66	52.17	26.3	0.5	8.0	0.8	**10.0**	12.4	16.3
COMMUNITY WEST BANK NA	GOLETA	CA	**D-**	D+	D	667	-2.49	13.5	29.2	4.9	6.1	**7.4**	9.2	12.9
COMMUNITYBANK OF TEXAS	BEAUMONT	TX	**C+**	C	B-	1,453	15.70	23.5	4.2	8.0	6.5	**7.4**	9.3	14.5
COMMUNITYONE BANK NA	ASHEBORO	NC	**E-**	D-	D-	1,918	-8.57	4.4	2.5	12.3	15.9	**0.0**	1.8	4.7
COMMUNITYS BANK	BRIDGEPORT	CT	**D-**	D-	D	40	-13.79	5.5	3.9	9.3	26.9	**5.3**	7.3	13.0
COMPASS BANK	BIRMINGHAM	AL	**D-**	D-	D	63,312	-2.01	14.6	4.0	14.9	12.6	**6.6**	8.7	14.8
COMPASS SB	WILMERDING	PA	**D-**	C-	C-	43	-8.44	0.0	0.5	48.5	42.3	**6.9**	8.9	22.5
COMPUTERSHARE TRUST CO	CANTON	MA	**U**	U	U	21	0.98	0.0	0.0	0.0	59.2	**10.0**	100.5	128.7
▼CONCORD BANK	SAINT LOUIS	MO	**E+**	D+	C-	148	-0.11	16.6	0.9	12.8	7.3	**2.6**	7.3	9.6
CONCORDE BANK	BLOMKEST	MN	**D**	D-	D	52	4.72	6.8	2.7	11.9	13.1	**5.5**	7.5	12.1
CONCORDIA BANK	CONCORDIA	MO	**B-**	B-	B-	50	6.34	6.1	4.4	33.3	11.7	**9.3**	10.5	15.8
CONCORDIA BANK & TRUST	VIDALIA	LA	**A-**	B+	B	496	1.92	4.6	4.1	19.9	26.6	**9.3**	10.5	20.5
CONDON BANK & TRUST	COFFEYVILLE	KS	**C-**	C	C	94	0.87	6.9	4.5	8.2	51.9	**7.7**	9.4	23.5
CONESTOGA BANK	CHESTER SPRINGS	PA	**D+**	D	D-	579	-4.99	6.6	3.3	18.6	25.9	**6.4**	8.9	12.1
CONGAREE STATE BK	CAYCE	SC	**D-**	D	D-	121	-11.98	7.4	1.2	11.7	18.1	**7.2**	9.2	14.1
CONGRESSIONAL BANK	BETHESDA	MD	**C-**	C-	C-	241	10.02	17.0	1.6	17.5	12.4	**8.3**	9.9	14.7
CONNEAUT SB	CONNEAUT	OH	**C**	C	C+	84	4.50	0.0	1.4	60.2	2.4	**6.0**	8.0	17.7
CONNECTICUT BANK & TRUST	HARTFORD	CT	**D+**	C-	D-	274	5.37	22.7	2.0	6.6	12.9	**6.7**	8.9	12.3
▼CONNECTICUT COMMUNITY	WESTPORT	CT	**D-**	C-	C	396	-5.70	15.9	0.8	11.5	4.6	**7.4**	9.3	13.6
CONNECTICUT RIVER BANK	SPRINGFIELD	VT	**C+**	B-	B-	263	7.22	12.0	1.8	19.1	7.2	**5.9**	7.9	13.1
▲CONSOLIDATED BANK &	RICHMOND	VA	**C-**	D	D+	77	-0.33	7.0	0.8	12.3	17.8	**8.5**	10.0	16.4
CONSUMERS NATIONAL BK	MINERVA	OH	**C+**	C+	C+	277	9.01	4.2	2.0	15.0	26.9	**5.7**	7.7	13.8
CONTINENTAL BANK	PLYMOUTH MEETING	PA	**D+**	C	C	515	4.58	12.2	4.6	13.5	19.7	**7.0**	9.0	14.3
▲CONTINENTAL BANK	SALT LAKE CITY	UT	**B+**	B	B	102	-16.02	33.1	0.0	0.0	4.4	**10.0**	20.5	23.1
CONTINENTAL NATIONAL BK M	MIAMI	FL	**D-**	D	C-	267	6.79	4.6	9.1	7.4	19.6	**7.0**	9.0	15.9
CONVERSE COUNTY BANK	DOUGLAS	WY	**A-**	A-	B+	311	13.81	10.3	6.0	7.2	52.6	**7.3**	9.2	19.9
▼CONWAY BANK NA	CONWAY SPRINGS	KS	**D**	D+	C-	77	-0.41	10.3	2.1	15.7	20.7	**10.0**	11.1	18.5
CONWAY NATIONAL BK	CONWAY	SC	**C-**	B	A-	912	-1.09	6.7	4.8	20.3	32.5	**7.3**	9.2	16.6
COOPER STATE BK	DUBLIN	OH	**D-**	D-	C-	94	11.36	0.0	0.5	39.1	4.2	**6.5**	8.5	14.5
COOPERATIVE BANK	ROSLINDALE	MA	**C-**	C-	C-	274	2.43	2.1	0.1	37.6	20.8	**7.6**	9.4	17.9
COPIAH BANK NA	HAZLEHURST	MS	**B-**	B-	B-	149	4.79	6.5	5.8	21.9	10.2	**7.4**	9.3	13.6
▲COPPERMARK BANK	OKLAHOMA CITY	OK	**C**	C+	C+	1,225	7.37	14.8	1.6	6.2	0.2	**6.5**	9.4	12.2
CORDER BANK	CORDER	MO	**B-**	B-	B-	13	-0.05	4.0	5.6	18.5	4.7	**10.0**	12.2	21.9
▼CORE BUSINESS BANK	BELLEVUE	WA	**D+**	C	C	54	10.43	17.1	0.5	1.3	43.8	**10.0**	12.8	28.6
COREFIRST BANK & TRUST	TOPEKA	KS	**D+**	C-	B-	1,194	-6.27	8.7	8.7	9.0	33.5	**6.1**	8.1	13.9
CORN CITY STATE BK	DESHLER	OH	**A-**	A-	A-	52	2.62	0.1	4.5	33.9	35.1	**10.0**	16.8	38.2
CORN GROWERS STATE BK	MURDOCK	NE	**D**	C-	C-	22	8.66	2.0	5.9	12.8	41.2	**5.4**	7.4	15.7
▼CORNER STONE BANK	SOUTH WEST CITY	MO	**D-**	D-	C	129	0.92	13.7	10.9	23.3	21.0	**7.5**	9.3	14.9
CORNERBANK NA	WINFIELD	KS	**C**	D+	C+	242	3.26	4.3	2.4	7.5	44.0	**7.3**	9.2	15.7
CORNERSTONE BANK	EUREKA SPRINGS	AR	**B-**	B+	A-	147	2.36	2.6	3.6	20.3	24.2	**7.6**	9.4	14.9
▲CORNERSTONE BANK	OVERLAND PARK	KS	**D-**	D	C-	209	-15.72	13.7	0.5	23.1	10.9	**5.2**	7.5	11.1
CORNERSTONE BANK	WILSON	NC	**E-**	E	D-	167	-13.48	15.1	2.4	17.6	17.8	**0.0**	2.6	4.9
▲CORNERSTONE BANK	FARGO	ND	**D-**	D-	C-	267	-26.11	14.8	2.5	10.1	7.9	**4.8**	6.8	11.0
CORNERSTONE BANK	YORK	NE	**C+**	B-	B-	940	9.33	15.8	2.7	3.4	20.4	**5.4**	7.8	11.3
CORNERSTONE BANK	MOORESTOWN	NJ	**D**	D-	E+	354	15.69	20.9	0.0	9.9	23.8	**4.9**	6.9	11.2
▼CORNERSTONE BANK	WATONGA	OK	**C+**	B-	B-	117	28.38	9.5	10.4	5.1	37.5	**6.8**	8.8	17.1
CORNERSTONE BANK &	CARROLLTON	IL	**D+**	C+	C+	140	11.13	5.9	1.8	11.8	13.1	**6.0**	8.6	11.7
CORNERSTONE BANK INC	WEST UNION	WV	**B**	B	B+	90	7.33	13.3	2.6	14.9	48.4	**10.0**	14.4	29.0
CORNERSTONE BANK NA	LEXINGTON	VA	**D**	C	NR	64	52.60	6.7	1.9	21.6	8.7	**10.0**	12.6	17.4
CORNERSTONE COMMUNITY	RED BLUFF	CA	**C-**	C	C	76	8.06	7.6	17.2	1.7	21.6	**10.0**	11.9	16.1
CORNERSTONE COMMUNITY	SAINT PETERSBURG	FL	**E+**	E+	D	289	-8.91	1.4	0.6	20.0	11.6	**4.3**	6.8	10.7
CORNERSTONE COMMUNITY	CHATTANOOGA	TN	**E+**	D-	C	443	-16.40	11.2	0.8	11.2	24.5	**4.3**	6.3	10.8

Asset Quality Index	Non-Performing Loans as a % of Total Loans	Non-Performing Loans as a % of Capital	Net Charge-offs / Avg Loans	Profitability Index	Net Income ($Mil)	Return on Assets (R.O.A.)	Return on Equity (R.O.E.)	Net Interest Spread	Overhead Efficiency Ratio	Liquidity Index	Liquidity Ratio	Hot Money Ratio	Stability Index
1.8	3.23	15.6	0.73	**4.9**	0.2	0.65	5.79	5.12	66.2	**2.1**	18.1	18.8	**7.0**
6.0	1.45	6.5	0.51	**5.5**	2.5	1.28	9.85	3.86	65.7	**2.8**	27.0	16.9	**7.5**
4.8	0.32	3.1	0.16	**4.8**	2.2	0.83	10.08	4.27	67.3	**1.1**	5.8	28.5	**4.3**
2.4	1.81	16.6	0.41	**4.2**	1.4	0.67	9.07	3.75	64.9	**3.1**	23.9	14.5	**3.0**
2.1	2.56	19.0	2.92	**0.0**	-3.9	-2.57	-33.71	3.39	83.8	**0.8**	14.9	39.0	**4.8**
4.6	2.31	11.4	0.34	**5.0**	0.9	1.02	9.25	4.57	68.4	**3.3**	35.8	17.3	**6.7**
4.4	1.08	9.6	0.19	**4.0**	11.8	0.75	8.56	4.59	74.1	**2.5**	7.0	15.7	**7.0**
2.2	2.34	17.5	0.59	**6.0**	34.2	1.08	9.23	4.27	57.4	**1.4**	5.3	23.6	**9.0**
4.4	1.84	11.3	0.41	**0.0**	-0.9	-1.61	-11.87	4.83	118.2	**2.6**	22.4	16.6	**1.5**
0.6	2.16	17.0	1.52	**2.9**	2.6	0.38	4.22	4.74	59.6	**0.5**	1.1	34.8	**4.5**
2.8	2.14	13.8	0.50	**3.8**	8.6	0.65	4.68	4.28	68.8	**4.0**	27.3	13.4	**7.9**
0.0	24.57	294.2	5.78	**0.0**	-111.1	-5.46	-101.11	2.97	107.1	**1.0**	14.0	32.2	**3.4**
0.3	9.78	71.7	0.27	**0.0**	-0.5	-1.13	-10.95	3.80	153.9	**1.2**	28.5	40.4	**4.7**
0.3	4.20	28.3	2.37	**0.5**	-318.2	-0.49	-2.53	4.65	83.6	**1.8**	10.2	20.0	**5.7**
8.1	0.79	4.6	0.03	**0.3**	-0.1	-0.21	-2.48	2.01	115.1	**2.9**	47.2	25.6	**1.3**
6.5	0.00	0.0	0.00	**10.0**	1.2	5.74	5.78	1.00	74.6	**5.0**	33,686.5	101.0	**6.7**
0.3	3.59	28.5	1.84	**0.0**	-1.9	-1.27	-13.25	3.21	89.6	**0.8**	18.9	46.3	**5.0**
2.5	2.64	18.4	0.38	**2.4**	0.2	0.33	4.22	4.35	82.1	**4.8**	37.7	10.2	**2.3**
4.0	1.86	12.6	0.07	**4.4**	0.5	0.89	8.59	4.65	73.9	**4.0**	11.8	8.5	**6.1**
6.3	0.68	3.3	0.13	**6.4**	5.5	1.15	10.43	3.90	59.1	**1.4**	25.3	29.3	**6.5**
6.9	1.21	4.0	0.85	**2.6**	0.4	0.40	4.00	3.80	82.1	**5.1**	43.0	10.1	**4.4**
1.7	2.50	15.6	0.95	**1.7**	2.2	0.36	4.65	3.65	83.1	**1.3**	6.8	25.8	**3.8**
3.1	1.57	10.9	0.80	**0.2**	-0.1	-0.05	-0.58	3.36	92.3	**1.9**	21.6	20.3	**1.2**
6.1	1.14	7.6	0.07	**2.5**	1.1	0.48	4.80	3.48	82.6	**1.5**	17.0	24.4	**4.8**
5.0	1.44	11.6	0.09	**2.5**	0.2	0.23	3.00	2.80	87.0	**3.2**	28.4	15.0	**4.6**
1.2	3.51	28.0	0.17	**1.7**	0.6	0.21	2.26	4.12	85.7	**1.2**	6.5	27.1	**4.0**
0.0	9.39	66.1	0.73	**0.0**	-3.2	-0.75	-7.80	3.86	103.5	**1.7**	12.6	20.3	**4.9**
3.9	1.14	8.6	0.49	**3.3**	1.0	0.40	4.96	3.89	81.2	**3.9**	29.3	11.7	**4.6**
0.3	11.86	69.4	-0.05	**5.5**	0.9	1.15	12.28	5.34	63.8	**2.4**	22.6	17.6	**6.0**
4.6	1.02	7.6	0.20	**4.4**	2.2	0.83	10.31	4.34	72.3	**2.7**	19.0	15.7	**4.3**
2.7	2.02	13.2	0.57	**1.8**	1.0	0.19	2.25	3.62	76.6	**3.4**	36.2	16.9	**1.3**
5.0	1.30	4.9	0.78	**10.0**	11.0	10.36	66.53	16.63	20.0	**0.3**	12.4	92.4	**8.2**
2.6	1.99	12.6	0.57	**0.4**	-0.3	-0.12	-1.31	3.90	100.3	**2.1**	32.3	25.4	**3.5**
8.7	0.00	0.0	0.10	**7.3**	4.9	1.72	18.01	3.27	49.4	**1.9**	31.2	28.3	**7.1**
2.5	4.04	19.3	0.78	**0.3**	-0.6	-0.79	-6.13	3.67	110.5	**2.7**	27.4	17.5	**4.8**
2.1	5.01	27.3	1.95	**2.3**	1.2	0.12	1.34	3.50	63.0	**1.2**	16.4	30.1	**5.6**
6.8	0.00	0.0	0.29	**0.0**	-2.0	-2.28	-25.28	4.21	127.0	**4.4**	20.0	6.7	**0.8**
4.4	1.61	10.2	0.21	**2.0**	0.9	0.32	3.29	3.45	89.5	**3.1**	31.5	16.7	**4.9**
4.4	0.56	4.3	0.10	**5.2**	1.0	0.69	7.71	5.42	75.6	**2.3**	12.0	17.3	**5.1**
3.6	1.02	7.5	0.13	**7.2**	13.9	1.16	12.66	4.01	57.7	**2.9**	22.0	16.3	**8.4**
8.5	0.05	0.2	0.01	**3.6**	0.1	0.53	4.30	3.76	80.9	**2.2**	35.7	20.9	**7.4**
3.7	8.22	21.5	2.78	**0.0**	-2.0	-4.18	-25.44	2.72	251.7	**4.5**	67.7	17.3	**1.7**
1.7	4.29	25.4	2.17	**1.1**	-3.3	-0.26	-3.32	3.74	85.7	**2.9**	14.6	14.8	**5.8**
9.4	0.00	0.0	-0.05	**6.9**	0.9	1.70	9.68	3.33	48.1	**3.4**	44.5	18.8	**9.5**
5.7	0.18	1.1	0.20	**3.2**	0.1	0.46	6.41	3.50	80.6	**5.6**	45.3	4.6	**2.3**
0.7	6.35	42.0	0.97	**1.7**	-1.1	-0.83	-7.95	5.03	88.1	**1.4**	17.6	27.1	**5.1**
3.3	2.01	10.0	0.37	**3.2**	1.3	0.57	5.66	4.24	84.7	**1.6**	18.2	23.8	**3.5**
3.7	2.41	14.5	0.51	**4.3**	1.2	0.82	8.97	4.42	74.4	**1.3**	14.3	26.8	**6.4**
0.1	12.59	82.5	3.76	**0.0**	-6.9	-3.13	-36.91	2.86	88.5	**4.1**	14.0	7.9	**3.9**
0.2	11.97	143.1	5.15	**0.0**	-7.7	-4.25	-82.99	2.87	104.8	**0.9**	22.5	39.7	**0.8**
0.3	11.15	75.2	3.28	**0.0**	-12.0	-3.55	-42.47	3.33	96.4	**0.8**	16.3	42.3	**3.1**
3.1	2.13	17.4	0.16	**5.9**	12.8	1.42	17.83	4.29	64.8	**2.7**	12.0	15.4	**6.5**
1.4	4.40	37.6	0.16	**3.2**	2.2	0.66	9.55	3.74	66.5	**3.2**	28.3	15.3	**2.5**
4.4	0.47	2.1	0.37	**2.7**	0.5	0.47	5.22	4.24	85.7	**3.5**	46.7	19.0	**4.8**
0.7	2.66	20.0	0.64	**2.4**	0.3	0.23	1.99	4.21	69.9	**3.0**	12.6	13.6	**5.5**
8.4	1.77	4.3	1.05	**3.3**	0.5	0.59	3.86	3.58	69.7	**2.6**	59.4	45.3	**7.8**
8.8	0.03	0.2	0.01	**0.0**	-0.2	-0.38	-2.70	3.35	96.0	**0.9**	23.0	37.1	**1.5**
7.1	0.32	1.7	0.40	**1.8**	0.3	0.44	3.58	4.45	84.1	**1.6**	4.6	20.2	**3.8**
0.3	9.70	80.9	3.41	**0.0**	-5.0	-1.58	-20.46	3.36	94.2	**1.5**	20.2	25.5	**2.9**
0.3	4.87	40.0	1.30	**1.2**	-0.1	-0.01	-0.18	3.81	84.5	**0.7**	7.5	34.1	**2.0**

Name	City	State	Rating	2008 Rating	2007 Rating	Total Assets ($Mil)	One Year Asset Growth	Asset Mix (As a % of Total Assets) Commercial Loans	Consumer Loans	Home Mortgages	Securities	Capitalization Index	Leverage Ratio	Risk-based Capital Ratio
▲ CORNERSTONE COMMUNITY	GRAFTON	WI	**D+**	C-	C+	126	-1.54	13.4	0.2	10.8	0.1	**5.7**	8.7	11.5
CORNERSTONE NATIONAL BK	EASLEY	SC	**D-**	D-	B	174	-7.92	6.5	0.6	6.9	13.6	**8.1**	9.8	13.8
CORNERSTONE NATIONAL BK	PALATINE	IL	**D**	D	C-	415	4.24	16.6	0.8	7.7	4.9	**7.2**	9.7	12.7
▼ CORNERSTONE STATE BK	MONTGOMERY	MN	**C**	B	B	121	9.50	11.4	3.5	24.6	17.2	**6.8**	9.0	12.4
CORNERSTONEBANK	ATLANTA	GA	**E-**	E-	D-	476	-13.37	7.3	5.7	8.3	13.4	**2.3**	5.0	9.3
CORNHUSKER BANK	LINCOLN	NE	**B-**	B-	B	357	8.59	7.5	1.7	13.7	26.5	**5.9**	7.9	11.8
CORNING SAVINGS & LOAN AS	CORNING	AR	**C-**	D+	D+	34	4.93	13.1	3.2	32.1	3.6	**10.0**	11.5	19.5
CORONADO FIRST BANK	CORONADO	CA	**D-**	D-	C	83	-11.15	10.7	0.5	8.5	8.1	**9.3**	10.5	14.7
▼ CORTEZ COMMUNITY BANK	BROOKSVILLE	FL	**E-**	D	D	71	-12.83	1.4	0.8	19.9	6.6	**0.0**	2.5	5.1
▼ CORTLAND SAVINGS &	CORTLAND	OH	**C**	C+	B-	497	0.60	8.0	1.4	10.5	37.4	**5.9**	7.9	12.7
CORTRUST BANK NA	MITCHELL	SD	**B-**	C-	B+	623	4.60	8.8	7.3	6.0	28.9	**8.4**	10.0	15.5
CORYDON STATE BK	CORYDON	IA	**A**	A	A	73	5.34	9.9	7.4	19.4	17.0	**10.0**	13.4	18.6
▲ COTTAGE SB	CINCINNATI	OH	**B-**	C	C-	42	0.57	2.8	0.0	30.9	0.0	**10.0**	17.2	23.8
▲ COTTONPORT BANK	COTTONPORT	LA	**B-**	C+	C-	308	11.38	3.7	6.6	14.1	25.1	**7.1**	9.1	17.0
COTTONWOOD VALLEY BANK	CEDAR POINT	KS	**C+**	B-	B-	21	4.40	12.1	2.8	1.1	18.5	**9.1**	10.4	17.3
COULEE BANK	LA CROSSE	WI	**B-**	B	A-	266	34.35	15.8	1.5	10.0	31.5	**6.9**	8.9	14.7
COUNTRY BANK	PRESCOTT	AZ	**C**	C-	C+	146	6.19	4.0	0.3	8.7	11.1	**7.2**	9.1	13.6
▼ COUNTRY BANK	ALEDO	IL	**D+**	B-	C	214	1.36	27.5	0.4	1.9	18.2	**7.2**	9.1	12.7
COUNTRY BANK	NEW YORK	NY	**D-**	D	C-	453	-6.08	2.8	0.1	11.2	25.5	**5.5**	7.5	12.7
▲ COUNTRY BANK FOR SAVINGS	WARE	MA	**C+**	B-	B-	1,427	4.42	1.1	0.6	34.0	35.0	**10.0**	11.6	19.5
COUNTRY CLUB BANK	KANSAS CITY	MO	**B**	B	NR	963	2.27	14.0	1.7	10.5	39.6	**5.7**	7.7	14.8
COUNTRY CLUB TRUST CO NA	KANSAS CITY	MO	**U**	U	U	8	22.89	0.0	0.0	0.0	76.7	**10.0**	101.1	317.9
COUNTRY TRUST BANK	BLOOMINGTON	IL	**B+**	B+	B+	29	2.97	0.0	0.0	0.0	83.0	**10.0**	92.9	186.3
COUNTRYSIDE BANK	UNADILLA	NE	**B+**	B+	B+	66	6.92	4.6	5.7	20.9	22.3	**10.0**	13.3	22.8
COUNTY BANK	REHOBOTH BEACH	DE	**D-**	D-	D	379	-9.43	2.7	0.4	17.5	6.8	**5.5**	8.3	11.4
▲ COUNTY BANK	BRUNSWICK	MO	**C**	C	C-	77	-1.03	6.2	5.1	28.9	6.4	**4.3**	7.4	10.7
COUNTY COMMERCE BANK	VENTURA	CA	**B**	B	B+	170	6.44	9.7	0.2	0.6	0.0	**6.4**	8.4	14.4
▼ COUNTY FIRST BANK	LA PLATA	MD	**C+**	B	B+	183	2.28	9.4	0.2	9.0	11.5	**8.5**	11.5	13.7
COUNTY SAVINGS BANK	ESSINGTON	PA	**D**	C-	C-	61	3.99	0.3	0.4	50.3	8.9	**4.9**	6.9	19.2
▼ COUNTYBANK	GREENWOOD	SC	**C-**	C+	B	275	-2.08	5.4	2.3	25.9	22.4	**5.5**	7.5	12.9
COVENANT BANK	LEEDS	AL	**C**	C	D+	112	3.71	13.5	3.8	27.1	8.5	**6.2**	8.2	12.4
▲ COVENANT BANK	CHICAGO	IL	**E**	D-	E+	69	-3.91	0.3	0.7	35.5	7.6	**3.8**	5.8	12.0
COVENANT BANK	CLARKSDALE	MS	**D**	C-	C	247	-6.21	11.9	3.3	12.3	12.6	**6.2**	8.8	11.9
COVENANT BANK & TRUST	ROCK SPRING	GA	**E-**	E-	D-	108	-4.61	5.9	0.5	12.0	11.7	**0.7**	5.1	7.4
COVINGTON COUNTY BANK	COLLINS	MS	**C+**	C+	C+	56	-0.68	4.2	5.1	7.8	37.4	**8.7**	12.0	13.9
COVINGTON SAVINGS & LOAN	COVINGTON	OH	**B-**	B-	B	62	3.79	0.2	0.7	45.4	22.1	**10.0**	14.1	37.0
COWBOY BANK OF TEXAS	MAYPEARL	TX	**B-**	B-	B-	43	3.37	3.2	12.0	30.2	14.4	**7.7**	9.4	19.0
COWBOY STATE BK	RANCHESTER	WY	**D-**	D	C	44	-2.62	14.2	5.0	11.5	11.7	**6.0**	8.0	12.5
▲ CRAWFORD COUNTY TRUST &	DENISON	IA	**C+**	C-	C	114	-0.19	8.0	4.9	8.5	18.4	**6.6**	8.6	13.4
▼ CREDICARD NATIONAL BK	TUCSON	AZ	**E-**	D-	D+	1	-78.39	0.3	81.6	0.0	0.0	**0.0**	2.8	5.4
CREDIT FIRST NA	BROOK PARK	OH	**B+**	B+	B+	23	21.97	0.0	0.0	0.0	0.0	**10.0**	92.5	451.8
CREDIT ONE BANK NA	LAS VEGAS	NV	**A**	A	A	96	-8.55	0.0	2.7	0.0	3.1	**10.0**	73.0	283.5
CREEKSIDE BANK	WOODSTOCK	GA	**E-**	D-	D	101	-13.65	10.0	0.6	3.7	6.9	**0.0**	3.6	6.0
▼ CRESCENT BANK	MYRTLE BEACH	SC	**D-**	D	C-	367	-23.59	5.9	1.0	16.1	15.9	**4.3**	6.4	11.8
▼ CRESCENT BANK & TRUST	NEW ORLEANS	LA	**D**	D+	D+	577	-5.31	5.1	74.2	2.7	3.4	**9.0**	11.4	14.1
CRESCENT STATE BK	CARY	NC	**D-**	C-	C-	975	-5.59	4.9	0.4	10.0	18.9	**6.2**	8.2	12.2
▲ CREST SAVINGS BANK	WILDWOOD	NJ	**C**	C-	C+	371	2.22	1.0	2.3	58.4	7.8	**5.1**	7.1	14.2
CRESTMARK BANK	TROY	MI	**C-**	D+	C	256	41.40	79.2	6.9	0.0	4.3	**6.5**	9.9	12.2
▼ CROCKETT NATIONAL BK	SAN ANGELO	TX	**C+**	B	A-	271	-7.63	4.6	0.6	27.2	4.3	**9.4**	10.6	15.7
▲ CROGHAN COLONIAL BANK	FREMONT	OH	**C**	C	B	489	1.61	3.5	2.7	18.7	28.7	**6.2**	8.2	14.3
CROOKSTON NATIONAL BK	CROOKSTON	MN	**C**	C-	C+	51	-4.65	4.5	3.6	9.4	23.8	**6.1**	8.1	16.3
▲ CROSS COUNTY BANK	WYNNE	AR	**C**	C-	A-	164	-9.24	5.0	1.7	14.9	12.6	**10.0**	12.4	19.4
CROSS COUNTY FSB	MIDDLE VILLAGE	NY	**C-**	C-	C	420	0.53	0.0	0.1	36.2	21.1	**5.8**	7.8	17.1
CROSS KEYS BANK	SAINT JOSEPH	LA	**B-**	B	A-	289	3.24	8.8	2.3	15.2	39.0	**8.6**	10.1	17.0
CROSS RIVER BANK	TEANECK	NJ	**B-**	D+	C	112	25.46	2.8	6.6	15.2	25.5	**10.0**	12.4	16.9
CROSSFIRST BANK	OVERLAND PARK	KS	**D+**	C-	C-	218	60.03	19.3	0.7	2.7	38.0	**9.7**	10.8	15.9
▲ CROSSFIRST BANK LEAWOOD	LEAWOOD	KS	**D+**	D-	D-	81	-1.41	14.5	1.0	8.1	24.1	**7.7**	9.5	13.9
CROSSROADS BANK	EFFINGHAM	IL	**A**	A-	A	130	6.09	10.5	2.1	11.1	14.7	**10.0**	12.0	15.4
CROSSROADS BANK	WABASH	IN	**D-**	C-	C-	325	-4.37	14.4	4.8	26.3	23.8	**7.1**	9.1	13.6
CROW RIVER STATE BK	DELANO	MN	**C+**	C+	B+	79	3.18	6.6	2.6	13.8	55.3	**7.6**	9.4	20.3

Asset Quality Index	Non-Performing Loans as a % of Total Loans	Non-Performing Loans as a % of Capital	Net Charge-offs Avg Loans	Profitability Index	Net Income ($Mil)	Return on Assets (R.O.A.)	Return on Equity (R.O.E.)	Net Interest Spread	Overhead Efficiency Ratio	Liquidity Index	Liquidity Ratio	Hot Money Ratio	Stability Index
2.5	0.70	6.1	0.43	**4.2**	0.8	0.64	7.57	4.06	65.5	**1.2**	9.4	27.2	**4.6**
0.1	8.12	48.1	0.97	**0.4**	-0.5	-0.29	-3.00	3.11	100.7	**1.4**	11.9	25.1	**5.0**
0.7	5.04	36.8	0.94	**2.3**	0.9	0.22	2.22	3.48	68.4	**2.7**	16.9	15.6	**5.5**
2.6	1.84	12.7	0.38	**5.2**	1.1	0.91	9.48	4.58	61.1	**3.0**	13.6	13.9	**5.4**
1.4	2.67	28.5	-0.01	**0.0**	-10.9	-2.13	-37.67	1.82	111.2	**1.4**	32.1	49.5	**0.4**
5.7	0.44	3.4	0.34	**5.0**	4.1	1.19	14.61	4.31	66.6	**3.0**	12.6	13.9	**5.7**
4.0	1.25	7.7	-0.46	**1.9**	0.1	0.21	1.48	3.57	84.4	**2.7**	20.6	16.0	**4.1**
0.0	7.06	42.2	1.06	**0.5**	-0.1	-0.12	-1.18	4.23	96.0	**1.7**	14.9	21.6	**0.5**
0.0	30.67	340.2	9.46	**0.0**	-9.4	-11.67	-110.61	1.76	289.3	**1.1**	18.2	31.6	**3.7**
5.3	0.98	6.5	0.19	**4.6**	3.3	0.69	9.37	3.62	66.1	**2.7**	20.2	16.1	**3.1**
4.6	1.04	5.6	2.02	**7.2**	8.3	1.35	13.04	5.10	64.1	**3.3**	27.7	14.3	**7.3**
5.4	1.37	7.5	0.07	**10.0**	2.6	3.63	22.65	5.39	22.6	**1.6**	21.6	24.3	**9.2**
8.1	0.00	0.0	0.00	**3.7**	0.4	0.98	5.87	2.64	71.2	**1.9**	23.5	20.5	**7.5**
4.1	1.10	6.0	0.39	**5.0**	2.6	0.90	9.24	4.49	73.9	**3.3**	29.9	15.2	**4.8**
5.5	1.48	5.8	-0.15	**2.9**	0.1	0.39	3.57	3.89	90.1	**2.9**	47.5	19.7	**7.0**
6.0	1.18	7.5	0.18	**5.5**	3.0	1.23	13.19	3.57	58.5	**3.3**	22.0	13.1	**5.0**
2.4	0.57	3.7	0.66	**2.7**	0.5	0.33	3.56	4.28	78.9	**4.1**	31.5	11.8	**5.5**
0.3	17.33	97.5	0.45	**1.8**	-2.2	-1.02	-9.39	4.14	53.1	**0.6**	7.0	35.4	**6.0**
0.0	3.41	26.4	0.59	**2.0**	2.6	0.54	6.91	3.35	88.3	**1.3**	26.7	31.6	**4.2**
4.6	1.84	9.0	0.12	**3.3**	8.0	0.57	4.94	3.29	75.1	**2.0**	26.8	29.8	**8.4**
5.3	1.70	9.7	0.30	**4.9**	10.5	1.06	12.78	3.89	80.9	**4.3**	33.5	11.4	**5.9**
10.0	0.00	0.0	0.00	**10.0**	1.4	20.15	20.25	0.73	79.6	**5.0**	3,119.0	101.0	**5.7**
6.7	0.00	0.0	0.00	**10.0**	1.4	4.76	5.14	3.87	91.4	**10.0**	1,105.2	0.0	**3.9**
7.2	0.59	2.4	0.12	**5.7**	0.7	1.15	8.25	3.90	65.9	**5.1**	39.3	9.2	**7.6**
0.0	3.75	30.6	1.08	**1.3**	0.8	0.20	2.23	4.21	77.2	**1.3**	11.4	26.1	**4.5**
5.1	0.39	3.8	0.28	**5.1**	1.0	1.24	16.47	4.20	68.2	**1.5**	5.1	21.0	**5.4**
7.7	0.00	0.0	0.01	**4.7**	1.2	0.73	8.78	4.06	58.6	**2.9**	41.3	22.4	**5.8**
2.0	2.40	15.2	0.14	**4.5**	1.3	0.67	6.02	4.33	69.0	**1.7**	16.0	21.6	**6.4**
5.2	1.51	12.2	0.00	**2.3**	0.2	0.27	3.91	3.57	88.3	**3.6**	38.2	16.4	**3.2**
3.0	2.26	17.7	0.93	**2.4**	0.9	0.32	4.05	4.09	89.4	**4.2**	9.2	6.8	**3.9**
3.9	1.70	14.4	0.78	**2.8**	0.6	0.58	7.17	3.80	80.8	**0.7**	10.6	38.2	**4.2**
0.3	8.25	84.9	0.43	**0.1**	-0.3	-0.45	-7.16	4.19	97.5	**0.6**	12.8	52.9	**2.1**
3.1	2.22	15.6	1.42	**1.0**	-0.2	-0.09	-0.98	3.73	82.6	**0.8**	15.4	37.2	**3.3**
0.0	8.31	100.6	3.20	**0.0**	-2.2	-1.97	-32.86	3.25	88.5	**1.4**	12.2	25.8	**0.0**
4.4	2.71	10.8	0.18	**3.2**	0.2	0.38	3.42	3.95	81.0	**2.9**	44.4	23.4	**5.0**
9.6	0.02	0.1	0.03	**3.0**	0.2	0.38	2.67	3.21	83.4	**5.6**	52.2	8.5	**7.1**
4.9	1.46	9.0	0.07	**9.6**	1.0	2.34	24.46	5.52	60.9	**1.6**	21.9	24.3	**7.8**
4.4	0.74	5.3	0.06	**0.1**	-0.3	-0.65	-7.44	4.19	109.2	**2.1**	22.0	19.4	**3.8**
4.5	0.38	2.6	0.17	**6.7**	1.8	1.58	17.43	3.85	60.5	**4.8**	33.4	8.2	**5.3**
0.0	6.76	58.3	20.69	**0.0**	-0.5	-11.13	794.38	11.81	274.5	**3.9**	3.1	7.5	**3.7**
10.0	0.00	0.0	0.00	**9.5**	10.6	52.96	56.97	0.24	53.5	**5.0**	1,148.2	100.0	**6.5**
6.8	0.00	0.0	0.00	**10.0**	12.6	13.23	17.73	0.41	84.2	**10.0**	251.6	0.0	**9.7**
0.0	24.48	318.9	3.35	**0.0**	-4.5	-4.05	-68.59	1.79	237.2	**1.7**	12.7	21.1	**0.0**
0.0	8.00	69.2	6.56	**0.7**	-12.0	-2.76	-43.84	3.11	77.5	**3.7**	15.8	10.7	**2.6**
0.8	2.31	13.7	2.10	**6.9**	9.9	1.64	15.49	11.30	71.8	**0.7**	11.6	43.6	**7.1**
0.7	4.48	31.0	2.38	**0.0**	-7.2	-0.74	-7.73	3.29	78.5	**0.8**	15.7	42.1	**4.3**
6.5	0.27	3.0	0.01	**3.2**	1.9	0.53	6.95	3.23	74.5	**1.8**	13.9	20.3	**3.2**
2.4	0.80	5.7	0.03	**9.6**	6.3	3.08	25.74	16.23	63.5	**0.4**	12.1	83.1	**7.2**
3.0	1.71	12.0	0.21	**8.3**	5.1	1.78	16.91	4.58	59.0	**0.7**	10.9	39.4	**8.2**
3.1	1.61	10.5	0.38	**4.3**	4.0	0.82	7.73	4.21	68.7	**3.7**	14.4	10.6	**5.8**
6.4	0.00	0.0	0.00	**3.7**	0.4	0.80	9.88	3.24	73.8	**5.5**	42.9	7.5	**5.1**
4.0	1.47	7.5	2.29	**2.2**	0.4	0.23	1.88	4.19	69.5	**2.1**	19.0	18.8	**5.3**
5.2	1.25	9.1	0.00	**2.6**	1.9	0.45	5.92	3.47	72.4	**3.7**	41.6	16.7	**3.6**
4.3	2.65	12.9	0.42	**5.9**	3.3	1.13	10.51	4.66	69.3	**2.2**	32.9	24.5	**7.0**
8.9	0.00	0.0	0.00	**3.9**	1.7	1.71	15.45	5.63	72.5	**2.5**	39.5	26.3	**5.4**
5.5	1.04	4.9	0.88	**1.5**	0.7	0.37	3.76	3.95	71.9	**3.9**	49.4	17.7	**2.7**
5.3	0.00	0.0	0.03	**3.3**	0.6	1.37	15.89	4.85	59.6	**2.3**	41.8	31.3	**3.1**
6.8	0.58	3.5	0.03	**6.7**	1.4	1.12	8.93	3.67	50.9	**2.9**	20.0	15.2	**8.0**
0.3	4.52	29.2	0.45	**3.4**	2.3	0.68	7.80	3.16	64.1	**2.1**	31.2	25.1	**4.8**
6.2	1.50	5.3	0.61	**3.5**	0.7	0.92	9.16	4.18	81.4	**5.4**	40.0	7.2	**4.6**

Name	City	State	Rating	2008 Rating	2007 Rating	Total Assets ($Mil)	One Year Asset Growth	Asset Mix (As a % of Total Assets) Comm-ercial Loans	Cons-umer Loans	Home Mort-gages	Secur-ities	Capital-ization Index	Leverage Ratio	Risk-based Capital Ratio
CROWELL STATE BK	CROWELL	TX	**B-**	B	B+	30	7.25	6.4	9.0	9.5	13.6	**8.5**	10.0	15.2
CROWN BANK	EDINA	MN	**D-**	D	D+	259	-6.28	54.3	1.4	4.0	3.1	**5.1**	8.6	11.1
▲ CROWN BANK	BRICK	NJ	**D+**	D	C	526	-2.73	4.4	0.3	3.0	7.9	**10.0**	12.1	15.4
▲ CRYSTAL LAKE BK & TRUST C	CRYSTAL LAKE	IL	**C-**	C-	C+	692	3.90	18.5	10.0	4.3	13.2	**8.9**	10.4	14.1
CSB BANK	CAPAC	MI	**D**	D	C-	208	-4.77	1.4	1.0	35.0	25.8	**5.7**	7.7	14.8
CSB STATE BK	CYNTHIANA	IN	**B-**	C+	C+	60	8.95	7.2	2.7	17.6	15.4	**8.4**	9.9	15.4
CULBERTSON BANK	CULBERTSON	NE	**C+**	C	C	15	-4.17	6.1	2.1	0.5	47.8	**10.0**	14.5	29.4
▲ CULLMAN SAVINGS BANK	CULLMAN	AL	**B**	C+	B-	223	4.35	3.3	1.8	37.5	10.8	**10.0**	14.7	21.2
▲ CUMBERLAND BANK & TRUST	CLARKSVILLE	TN	**C+**	C-	C-	145	6.23	7.5	1.5	15.1	7.8	**4.6**	8.1	10.8
CUMBERLAND COUNTY BANK	CROSSVILLE	TN	**B-**	B-	B-	264	7.99	2.2	2.0	23.5	30.0	**5.1**	7.1	16.8
CUMBERLAND FEDERAL BANK	CUMBERLAND	WI	**B-**	B-	B-	85	-1.16	6.0	1.7	31.6	35.1	**10.0**	11.2	22.2
CUMBERLAND SECURITY	SOMERSET	KY	**B-**	B-	B	160	-6.02	10.4	4.0	21.6	16.1	**10.0**	11.6	16.9
CUMBERLAND VALLEY NB&TC	LONDON	KY	**C-**	C-	C+	423	0.35	4.8	2.7	15.9	23.6	**9.2**	10.4	18.3
▼ CURRIE STATE BK	CURRIE	MN	**E+**	D-	E-	45	-5.31	12.5	1.9	11.2	3.7	**5.0**	8.7	11.0
CURTIS STATE BK	CURTIS	NE	**C+**	C	B-	30	12.73	11.9	4.5	3.1	22.0	**7.4**	10.0	12.8
▲ CUSTER FS&LA	BROKEN BOW	NE	**D+**	C-	C	66	11.47	14.1	5.7	15.1	31.8	**6.3**	8.3	14.6
▲ CUSTODIAL TRUST CO	JERSEY CITY	NJ	**C+**	B+	A-	308	-21.37	0.0	0.0	0.0	0.0	**10.0**	75.3	411.3
▲ CUSTOMERS BANK	PHOENIXVILLE	PA	**D+**	D-	D-	1,376	293.27	3.4	5.0	37.2	15.0	**6.6**	8.6	17.2
CYPRESS BANK FSB	PITTSBURG	TX	**C**	C+	C+	166	0.64	7.0	10.4	35.3	26.3	**5.5**	7.5	14.5
D L EVANS BANK	BURLEY	ID	**D**	D+	C+	940	5.48	6.5	1.8	5.0	24.0	**6.4**	8.4	14.4
DACOTAH BANK	ABERDEEN	SD	**B-**	B-	B	1,802	9.01	13.5	4.6	7.6	15.1	**5.7**	8.6	11.5
▼ DAIRY STATE BK	RICE LAKE	WI	**D+**	C+	B+	453	2.01	11.8	1.5	12.4	45.8	**6.9**	8.9	17.9
DAIRYLAND STATE BK	BRUCE	WI	**C**	D+	D+	80	-2.38	5.7	3.1	23.1	9.6	**9.7**	10.8	17.6
DAKOTA COMMUNITY BANK	HEBRON	ND	**B-**	B-	B-	467	20.70	12.6	3.7	8.2	16.2	**5.7**	7.7	11.6
DAKOTA HERITAGE BANK OF	HUNTER	ND	**B**	B-	B-	115	3.42	6.7	5.3	2.7	13.6	**6.0**	8.4	11.7
▲ DAKOTA HERITAGE STATE BK	CHANCELLOR	SD	**B-**	C	C+	36	2.57	5.3	4.6	11.1	18.0	**10.0**	11.5	15.3
▼ DAKOTA PRAIRIE BANK	FORT PIERRE	SD	**C-**	B-	B-	56	26.21	15.9	2.9	2.0	14.7	**2.6**	8.4	9.7
DAKOTA STATE BK	BLUNT	SD	**C+**	C	B-	29	-3.62	8.7	0.7	1.0	20.8	**7.9**	9.6	13.5
DAKOTA WESTERN BANK	BOWMAN	ND	**C+**	C	C-	182	1.87	6.7	5.4	3.1	30.9	**6.5**	8.5	13.6
DALHART FS&LA	DALHART	TX	**C**	C-	C	103	-1.12	0.4	2.7	50.1	27.1	**6.6**	8.6	22.9
DAMARISCOTTA BANK &	DAMARISCOTTA	ME	**C**	C-	C	164	3.44	6.0	2.2	25.8	14.1	**8.5**	10.0	16.3
▼ DAMASCUS COMMUNITY BANK	DAMASCUS	MD	**D-**	D+	B	245	6.13	19.8	15.7	10.2	11.4	**5.6**	8.3	11.4
DANVERSBANK	DANVERS	MA	**C+**	C	C	2,833	47.23	14.4	0.1	12.5	30.9	**5.5**	7.5	11.4
DANVILLE STATE SB	NEW LONDON	IA	**A-**	A-	A-	104	1.35	3.5	4.3	18.8	57.1	**10.0**	11.7	25.1
DARIEN ROWAYTON BANK	DARIEN	CT	**D-**	E-	E	137	36.00	3.6	0.3	43.9	10.1	**8.2**	9.8	15.8
DART BANK	MASON	MI	**D+**	D+	C+	260	-7.06	5.1	2.3	19.5	24.1	**6.7**	8.7	14.6
▼ DAVIDSON TRUST CO	GREAT FALLS	MT	**D+**	C	C-	5	-0.18	0.0	0.0	0.0	86.0	**10.0**	80.7	271.2
DAVIS TRUST CO	ELKINS	WV	**C+**	B-	B+	141	1.49	12.9	6.6	23.1	3.4	**10.0**	13.6	17.1
▲ DE WITT BANK & TRUST CO	DE WITT	AR	**B**	B+	A-	132	25.82	7.3	1.3	8.4	31.8	**10.0**	14.4	23.9
▲ DE WITT BANK & TRUST CO	DE WITT	IA	**C-**	C-	C+	120	8.81	8.7	1.9	10.5	23.1	**6.0**	9.2	11.8
▼ DEAN CO-OP BANK	FRANKLIN	MA	**D**	D+	D+	218	-1.53	1.9	0.6	41.8	15.9	**6.0**	8.0	13.4
▼ DEARBORN FSB	DEARBORN	MI	**C-**	C+	B+	262	-3.62	0.0	0.1	66.3	0.0	**10.0**	24.3	42.8
DEARBORN SAVINGS BANK	LAWRENCEBURG	IN	**B-**	B-	B	123	0.71	1.3	0.6	40.8	11.2	**10.0**	12.1	19.2
▼ DECATUR COUNTY BANK	DECATURVILLE	TN	**D-**	D+	B	84	-5.14	9.6	10.0	15.0	26.1	**8.0**	9.7	15.1
DECATUR FIRST BANK	DECATUR	GA	**E-**	E-	D-	198	-15.63	3.9	1.3	5.0	17.2	**0.0**	2.3	4.6
DECATUR STATE BK	DECATUR	AR	**C-**	C	B-	208	-0.41	7.6	11.5	23.2	6.9	**9.9**	10.9	15.3
▲ DECORAH BANK & TRUST CO	DECORAH	IA	**B**	B-	B-	331	1.59	14.8	3.8	10.8	27.3	**7.6**	9.4	13.1
DEDHAM INSTITUTION FOR SA	DEDHAM	MA	**C**	C	C-	1,053	3.70	1.2	0.3	49.0	20.2	**8.3**	9.9	17.3
▼ DEDICATED COMMUNITY	DARLINGTON	SC	**B-**	B	B	41	-3.80	12.9	12.1	8.2	23.4	**10.0**	12.5	19.2
DEFIANCE STATE BK	DEFIANCE	IA	**C**	C-	C-	25	0.37	10.2	6.2	12.0	0.0	**8.3**	9.9	15.1
DEL NORTE FEDERAL BANK	DEL NORTE	CO	**D+**	D+	C-	46	2.25	7.8	3.3	48.1	2.2	**5.7**	7.7	12.2
▲ DELANCO FSB	DELANCO	NJ	**D+**	D-	D-	136	-2.30	1.3	0.8	56.1	11.9	**6.4**	8.4	13.9
DELAWARE COUNTY BK &	LEWIS CENTER	OH	**E-**	D	D	565	-16.26	5.0	2.3	20.7	12.6	**3.5**	6.4	10.3
▼ DELAWARE NATIONAL BK OF	DELHI	NY	**C+**	B	B+	194	7.19	2.3	2.2	18.5	48.8	**8.4**	9.9	23.5
DELAWARE PLACE BANK	CHICAGO	IL	**D-**	D-	D	270	-12.60	11.4	11.0	4.3	21.2	**7.5**	9.4	15.8
DELTA BANK	VIDALIA	LA	**B**	B	B	225	16.29	4.6	3.3	12.5	24.8	**5.4**	7.4	13.8
DELTA BANK NA	MANTECA	CA	**D-**	D	C-	108	-9.72	1.6	0.1	1.0	28.7	**8.6**	10.1	16.8
▼ DELTA NATIONAL BK & TRUST	NEW YORK	NY	**B-**	B+	A	371	-12.43	2.7	1.2	0.0	31.9	**10.0**	12.8	35.4
DELTA TRUST & BANK	PARKDALE	AR	**C+**	C	D+	372	26.43	24.9	2.1	13.6	24.7	**6.3**	8.3	13.1
▼ DEMOTTE STATE BK	DEMOTTE	IN	**C+**	B-	B+	353	3.29	13.2	1.6	19.3	27.6	**10.0**	11.0	17.4

Asset Quality Index	Non-Performing Loans as a % of Total Loans	Non-Performing Loans as a % of Capital	Net Charge-offs Avg Loans	Profitability Index	Net Income ($Mil)	Return on Assets (R.O.A.)	Return on Equity (R.O.E.)	Net Interest Spread	Overhead Efficiency Ratio	Liquidity Index	Liquidity Ratio	Hot Money Ratio	Stability Index
5.7	0.72	4.0	0.70	**4.3**	0.2	0.81	7.92	5.22	76.8	**1.9**	25.0	22.1	**6.9**
0.1	6.42	51.3	1.10	**1.2**	-0.4	-0.14	-1.65	3.85	73.9	**2.3**	11.9	17.0	**3.4**
0.0	9.30	54.9	0.12	**9.3**	17.2	3.21	26.90	5.66	42.2	**1.7**	13.0	21.0	**10.0**
2.4	1.25	7.7	1.47	**2.0**	0.5	0.07	0.75	3.27	70.8	**1.1**	18.9	31.8	**4.8**
2.0	2.97	19.6	1.57	**0.5**	-0.4	-0.16	-1.86	4.10	85.0	**4.3**	20.4	7.1	**3.2**
8.6	0.12	0.8	0.01	**4.1**	0.4	0.74	7.03	3.73	74.6	**2.3**	21.6	18.0	**6.8**
8.8	0.36	0.9	0.05	**2.3**	0.0	0.10	0.68	4.51	95.9	**3.9**	56.2	16.8	**6.4**
8.2	0.12	0.7	0.23	**4.1**	2.1	0.93	6.28	3.97	58.4	**1.2**	14.1	29.4	**7.2**
5.1	0.30	2.8	-0.01	**4.7**	1.3	0.91	11.52	4.35	70.1	**1.7**	12.0	20.7	**4.9**
7.2	0.40	2.6	0.41	**3.7**	1.7	0.66	9.19	3.00	65.4	**4.3**	39.0	13.3	**5.2**
6.0	2.14	10.3	0.00	**4.2**	0.8	0.89	8.14	2.96	57.3	**3.0**	47.3	23.5	**6.4**
3.6	0.90	4.6	0.70	**9.2**	3.5	2.14	17.29	4.88	52.8	**1.8**	21.7	21.4	**8.6**
4.2	1.94	10.1	0.32	**2.4**	1.3	0.31	2.79	3.64	91.8	**2.5**	34.8	21.8	**5.8**
0.0	1.15	10.5	0.15	**3.1**	0.3	0.61	7.30	4.78	78.4	**3.2**	5.2	12.1	**2.5**
4.7	0.00	0.0	1.26	**5.6**	0.4	1.51	13.26	4.98	65.6	**2.0**	25.3	20.0	**5.4**
1.9	2.97	21.4	0.05	**4.2**	0.5	0.86	9.80	3.67	58.9	**3.2**	38.6	18.5	**4.0**
10.0	0.00	0.0	0.00	**2.5**	0.3	0.07	0.09	0.14	48.5	**5.0**	655.6	100.0	**6.9**
2.0	3.56	25.8	0.94	**5.8**	22.4	2.86	30.93	2.59	41.3	**1.6**	26.6	38.6	**3.3**
5.0	0.35	2.9	0.07	**3.3**	0.9	0.52	7.04	3.63	73.6	**1.4**	31.9	38.5	**4.0**
2.8	2.29	14.2	2.00	**0.8**	-2.4	-0.27	-2.89	3.79	72.8	**1.8**	16.4	20.3	**4.2**
3.3	1.29	10.3	0.09	**5.2**	14.7	0.86	9.46	4.13	62.3	**2.5**	12.6	16.5	**7.2**
1.7	2.74	13.6	0.51	**4.1**	3.2	0.71	7.46	3.46	53.2	**3.4**	31.6	15.2	**4.8**
2.5	2.89	16.8	0.60	**2.4**	0.2	0.25	2.16	4.10	83.1	**4.6**	30.7	8.2	**6.1**
6.4	0.26	2.2	0.15	**8.3**	7.9	1.89	24.33	4.71	61.2	**1.7**	21.1	23.6	**5.1**
6.5	0.06	0.5	-0.01	**7.9**	2.1	1.90	19.05	4.68	57.6	**3.4**	14.8	11.8	**6.1**
4.5	0.00	0.0	0.45	**4.5**	0.4	1.03	8.86	3.72	74.2	**1.5**	20.6	26.6	**6.0**
8.2	0.13	0.8	-0.04	**5.5**	0.6	1.17	12.78	4.46	70.1	**2.0**	36.2	31.6	**6.1**
6.0	0.00	0.0	0.09	**6.2**	0.4	1.39	14.13	5.91	71.5	**2.4**	13.4	17.0	**5.7**
3.7	1.79	11.7	0.06	**6.2**	2.7	1.46	17.62	4.15	54.6	**2.5**	14.4	16.6	**4.4**
8.4	0.02	0.1	0.02	**2.4**	0.4	0.39	4.61	3.65	83.5	**1.8**	37.5	43.0	**3.8**
2.6	2.37	15.5	0.29	**3.5**	0.7	0.43	4.31	3.69	78.0	**1.8**	22.8	21.6	**5.8**
0.3	3.58	28.7	1.42	**2.3**	0.7	0.29	3.42	4.20	65.1	**1.2**	23.0	31.6	**4.3**
6.4	0.73	5.9	0.12	**4.0**	20.3	0.81	8.99	4.06	68.5	**2.8**	18.7	16.0	**6.0**
6.1	2.23	7.0	0.28	**6.6**	1.6	1.51	12.76	3.43	55.3	**5.6**	66.1	12.7	**7.6**
3.6	2.12	15.4	-0.11	**0.0**	-2.9	-2.55	-26.78	2.57	204.0	**1.4**	21.2	27.4	**0.8**
2.0	3.00	17.5	1.38	**1.7**	0.5	0.17	1.99	3.76	67.2	**2.2**	25.0	18.8	**4.8**
7.1	0.00	0.0	0.00	**1.4**	0.0	-0.10	-0.12	3.03	99.6	**10.0**	446.6	0.0	**0.0**
3.0	1.14	5.2	0.02	**3.9**	0.7	0.47	3.68	4.54	78.6	**3.3**	19.4	12.9	**7.1**
6.7	2.23	6.0	-0.07	**4.4**	0.6	0.51	3.42	4.05	80.6	**2.5**	42.2	28.8	**7.1**
2.3	2.65	18.3	-0.02	**7.1**	1.6	1.40	14.53	4.05	61.3	**2.4**	22.3	17.9	**6.5**
0.3	4.84	40.3	0.45	**2.8**	0.9	0.42	5.39	3.76	76.3	**2.4**	15.5	17.1	**4.0**
6.3	1.74	5.5	0.00	**0.6**	-2.7	-0.99	-4.04	3.94	62.8	**2.8**	16.0	15.0	**6.4**
5.4	0.57	3.3	-0.02	**3.5**	0.7	0.58	4.88	3.81	59.4	**1.8**	17.9	20.3	**6.6**
8.1	0.19	1.1	1.74	**0.0**	-1.3	-1.54	-16.10	3.32	116.1	**4.0**	27.8	10.7	**2.5**
0.3	8.80	131.2	3.22	**0.0**	-8.0	-3.55	-103.48	2.57	366.9	**1.5**	25.1	27.0	**0.0**
0.3	6.46	39.5	1.55	**3.5**	0.7	0.35	3.10	4.88	59.8	**1.5**	15.3	25.0	**5.5**
4.9	0.63	3.8	0.39	**6.5**	4.9	1.51	12.88	4.35	56.5	**3.6**	30.7	14.1	**7.3**
5.0	2.76	18.2	0.06	**3.1**	6.6	0.64	6.61	3.18	73.0	**3.0**	29.9	19.7	**7.5**
5.4	1.68	7.8	0.45	**4.2**	0.3	0.65	5.27	4.73	80.0	**4.0**	37.1	14.2	**6.6**
4.7	0.88	5.4	0.37	**3.7**	0.2	0.64	6.35	4.32	84.5	**3.1**	41.4	17.5	**5.8**
8.1	0.05	0.6	0.00	**3.7**	0.3	0.70	9.37	4.18	73.5	**0.6**	5.8	37.7	**3.0**
1.7	3.68	31.8	0.02	**2.6**	0.7	0.53	6.38	3.80	74.1	**3.0**	16.6	14.4	**2.2**
0.3	4.33	36.6	2.00	**0.0**	-12.9	-2.03	-28.60	3.68	81.1	**1.1**	6.6	27.8	**2.4**
5.9	1.74	6.8	0.28	**3.8**	1.5	0.79	7.43	3.70	76.5	**4.7**	42.2	11.8	**6.0**
0.3	7.97	39.3	1.75	**0.0**	-3.2	-1.10	-11.59	3.69	92.6	**2.0**	36.1	31.1	**4.8**
6.8	0.30	2.0	0.05	**8.3**	3.6	1.75	22.05	4.51	62.9	**2.5**	38.4	26.2	**5.9**
0.0	27.34	119.1	1.67	**0.0**	-2.5	-2.22	-19.87	3.40	180.2	**2.7**	30.5	18.3	**4.2**
10.0	0.00	0.0	0.02	**3.3**	0.9	0.23	1.81	1.55	91.3	**6.1**	83.7	12.3	**6.5**
5.2	0.82	5.7	0.12	**4.6**	2.9	0.87	9.74	4.27	68.0	**0.9**	21.2	37.6	**3.3**
3.3	2.62	13.6	0.18	**5.2**	2.9	0.84	7.57	4.09	65.6	**3.6**	30.8	14.0	**6.7**

Name	City	State	Rating	2008 Rating	2007 Rating	Total Assets ($Mil)	One Year Asset Growth	Asset Mix (As a % of Total Assets) Comm-ercial Loans	Cons-umer Loans	Home Mort-gages	Secur-ities	Capital-ization Index	Leverage Ratio	Risk-based Capital Ratio
DENALI STATE BK	FAIRBANKS	AK	**C+**	C+	C+	261	6.87	15.0	2.2	13.9	32.3	**5.6**	7.6	13.2
DENISON STATE BK	HOLTON	KS	**B+**	A-	A-	266	9.58	9.1	3.4	21.7	24.1	**9.8**	10.8	16.8
DENMARK STATE BK	DENMARK	WI	**D+**	D+	D+	385	3.71	8.5	2.3	18.5	16.4	**9.5**	10.7	15.1
DENVER SB	DENVER	IA	**C+**	C	B-	105	3.88	2.3	1.8	17.9	52.7	**6.0**	8.0	16.1
DEPARTMENT STORES	SIOUX FALLS	SD	**C**	C-	C-	374	6.76	0.0	24.8	0.0	0.0	**9.6**	10.8	27.2
▼ DEPOSIT BANK OF CARLISLE	CARLISLE	KY	**C+**	B-	A	67	-4.21	1.9	4.3	21.4	36.3	**10.0**	15.8	31.7
DEPOSITORY TRUST CO	NEW YORK	NY	**U**	U	U	3,764	-1.79	0.0	0.0	0.0	5.5	**5.0**	7.0	29.5
▼ DESERT COMMERCIAL BANK	PALM DESERT	CA	**D**	D-	D-	148	4.74	15.5	0.2	8.0	9.7	**9.3**	11.1	14.4
▼ DESJARDINS BANK NA	HALLANDALE	FL	**D-**	D-	C-	167	10.69	1.8	0.9	46.5	7.3	**7.2**	9.2	22.9
▲ DESOTO COUNTY BANK	HORN LAKE	MS	**C+**	C-	D	78	11.44	15.0	1.5	29.0	7.3	**10.0**	13.1	17.0
DEUTSCHE BANK TRUST CO	NEW YORK	NY	**U**	U	U	155	4.01	0.0	0.0	0.0	74.4	**10.0**	88.5	529.9
DEUTSCHE BK NATIONAL	LOS ANGELES	CA	**U**	U	U	167	-0.11	0.0	0.0	0.0	57.9	**10.0**	80.8	333.7
DEUTSCHE BK TRUST CO	NEW YORK	NY	**B+**	B	B-	45,504	-0.81	6.3	2.2	8.8	4.0	**10.0**	19.3	40.7
DEUTSCHE BK TRUST CO	WILMINGTON	DE	**B+**	B+	B+	420	-7.19	6.3	8.6	0.0	8.0	**10.0**	59.8	69.7
DEVON BANK	CHICAGO	IL	**D-**	D-	D-	287	-3.13	2.6	0.3	15.3	23.8	**6.2**	8.2	12.7
DEWEY BANK	DEWEY	IL	**D**	D-	C-	20	-14.88	5.4	1.7	10.8	12.3	**6.6**	8.6	12.3
DEWITT SB	CLINTON	IL	**C+**	B-	C+	91	-1.07	0.0	9.2	27.1	43.7	**9.8**	10.9	23.0
▲ DHANIS STATE BK	HONDO	TX	**C-**	C	C-	51	-8.36	5.3	17.6	25.6	5.3	**8.3**	9.9	16.3
▼ DIAMOND BANK	GLENWOOD	AR	**C+**	B-	B-	461	0.33	3.7	6.8	23.1	28.2	**6.7**	8.7	15.0
DIAMOND BANK FSB	SCHAUMBURG	IL	**D-**	D-	D+	258	-12.17	14.8	1.1	27.3	0.0	**6.6**	8.9	12.2
▲ DICKINSON COUNTY BANK	ENTERPRISE	KS	**D-**	D	C-	9	-36.42	4.7	5.8	23.6	38.1	**9.2**	10.5	21.7
DILLEY STATE BK	DILLEY	TX	**A-**	A-	A-	88	38.69	1.2	3.5	1.0	71.0	**10.0**	19.4	88.0
DIME BANK	NORWICH	CT	**C+**	C+	C	680	7.17	8.0	0.6	33.1	15.8	**8.8**	10.2	14.4
▼ DIME BANK	HONESDALE	PA	**D-**	C-	B-	542	2.16	8.2	2.0	15.1	14.6	**6.2**	8.9	11.9
DIME SAVINGS BANK OF WILL	BROOKLYN	NY	**B-**	B-	B+	3,972	2.28	0.0	0.0	2.7	5.8	**6.2**	8.2	12.0
▲ DISCOVER BANK	NEW CASTLE	DE	**C**	C	C-	62,458	-5.14	0.4	84.9	0.0	9.7	**8.6**	10.1	14.9
DIXON BANK	DIXON	KY	**A-**	A-	B+	78	12.00	5.5	4.4	8.7	60.3	**10.0**	17.8	38.7
DMB COMMUNITY BANK	DE FOREST	WI	**C-**	C+	B-	341	-5.01	3.1	1.4	17.8	5.3	**6.8**	8.8	12.9
▲ DNB FIRST NA	DOWNINGTOWN	PA	**C**	C-	C-	603	-5.08	7.9	1.7	13.1	25.0	**7.3**	9.2	14.2
DNB NATIONAL BK	CLEAR LAKE	SD	**C-**	D+	B-	56	-13.28	3.8	1.6	3.6	54.0	**9.2**	10.5	19.5
DOLLAR BANK FSB	PITTSBURGH	PA	**B-**	B-	C	6,114	3.08	5.9	2.4	53.8	19.6	**8.7**	10.1	18.1
DOLORES STATE BK	DOLORES	CO	**A**	A	A	120	7.37	4.2	8.2	25.7	29.5	**10.0**	12.2	20.7
▼ DONLEY COUNTY STATE BK	CLARENDON	TX	**B**	A-	A-	41	8.54	3.5	3.9	0.2	20.3	**10.0**	17.9	44.8
DOOLIN SECURITY SAVINGS B	NEW MARTINSVILLE	WV	**C-**	C	C-	40	-10.29	1.0	2.5	24.4	41.4	**10.0**	14.1	59.7
DORAL BANK	SAN JUAN	PR	**D-**	D-	D-	7,659	-17.54	7.9	0.7	46.1	19.4	**6.0**	8.0	15.7
▼ DORAL BANK FSB	NEW YORK	NY	**E+**	D-	D	220	102.69	14.4	0.0	5.3	4.7	**4.4**	6.5	11.0
DOUGLAS COUNTY BANK	DOUGLASVILLE	GA	**E-**	E	D-	336	-7.59	1.5	0.5	14.7	7.1	**0.5**	4.8	7.0
DOUGLAS COUNTY BANK	LAWRENCE	KS	**B**	B	B	284	3.14	8.1	1.0	7.3	40.1	**10.0**	11.2	19.4
▲ DOUGLAS NATIONAL BK	DOUGLAS	GA	**C**	C-	C+	160	3.47	7.5	3.4	19.9	7.9	**9.3**	10.5	14.9
DOWNERS GROVE NATIONAL	DOWNERS GROVE	IL	**E-**	D-	C-	219	-13.29	8.0	0.7	18.4	9.2	**0.0**	2.3	5.0
DOWNS NATIONAL BK	DOWNS	KS	**C**	C+	C+	18	3.19	2.8	3.3	4.2	33.9	**7.9**	9.6	24.6
▲ DRAKE BANK	SAINT PAUL	MN	**D+**	D	D+	83	-0.26	27.4	3.6	19.8	6.3	**8.1**	9.7	13.7
DRUMMOND COMMUNITY	CHIEFLAND	FL	**A**	A+	A+	200	14.60	3.2	4.2	16.1	39.4	**10.0**	15.6	29.0
DSRM NATIONAL BK	ALBUQUERQUE	NM	**B**	B	B	3	1.57	0.0	0.0	0.0	92.3	**10.0**	84.4	208.0
▼ DUBLIN NATIONAL BK	DUBLIN	TX	**C+**	B-	B	28	2.78	3.5	5.7	12.6	38.2	**10.0**	13.8	28.4
DUBUQUE BANK & TRUST CO	DUBUQUE	IA	**C+**	C	B-	1,132	-9.41	17.7	0.8	7.5	27.5	**6.3**	8.3	13.3
▼ DUPAGE NATIONAL BK	WEST CHICAGO	IL	**E-**	D+	D	83	-4.35	3.9	1.7	11.5	6.1	**2.9**	6.0	9.9
DUPONT STATE BK	DUPONT	IN	**D**	D+	C-	81	-2.82	4.8	1.9	34.4	5.2	**7.0**	9.0	13.8
DUQUOIN STATE BK	DU QUOIN	IL	**B-**	C+	C+	102	8.97	4.7	2.6	17.9	51.1	**5.1**	7.1	15.1
DURAND STATE BK	DURAND	IL	**D+**	C-	C	87	-2.53	16.2	5.6	17.9	37.3	**6.6**	8.6	14.3
▲ DURDEN BANKING CO INC	TWIN CITY	GA	**C+**	D+	D+	154	1.36	6.7	5.9	32.8	15.5	**10.0**	11.4	20.9
DUTTON STATE BK	DUTTON	MT	**D**	D	C+	29	9.85	4.6	2.6	8.3	26.3	**5.6**	7.6	14.4
DYSART STATE BK	DYSART	IA	**C-**	C-	C+	10	-3.89	2.4	2.3	9.2	5.2	**10.0**	11.4	19.4
▲ E*TRADE BANK	ARLINGTON	VA	**D**	D-	D-	42,325	-1.73	0.2	14.2	21.7	38.6	**5.3**	7.3	15.0
▲ E*TRADE SAVINGS BANK	ARLINGTON	VA	**D**	D	C-	1,350	41.48	24.4	0.0	32.6	43.1	**8.7**	10.1	30.5
E*TRADE UNITED BANK	ARLINGTON	VA	**C-**	C-	D	322	69.42	25.6	0.0	0.0	71.7	**9.7**	10.8	40.5
EAGLE BANK	EVERETT	MA	**C-**	C-	C	429	-4.12	4.5	0.1	17.4	49.3	**7.3**	9.5	12.8
EAGLE BANK	GLENWOOD	MN	**A**	A	A	102	1.71	6.3	4.9	23.4	7.1	**10.0**	14.5	21.0
EAGLE BANK	POLSON	MT	**D+**	C-	C	26	6.94	4.8	9.6	12.6	16.4	**8.8**	10.2	19.1
EAGLE BANK	JARRELL	TX	**D**	C-	D+	22	1.98	3.0	10.2	6.9	48.0	**6.7**	8.7	17.8

Asset Quality Index	Non-Performing Loans as a % of Total Loans	Non-Performing Loans as a % of Capital	Net Charge-offs Avg Loans	Profitability Index	Net Income ($Mil)	Return on Assets (R.O.A.)	Return on Equity (R.O.E.)	Net Interest Spread	Overhead Efficiency Ratio	Liquidity Index	Liquidity Ratio	Hot Money Ratio	Stability Index
4.5	0.19	1.4	0.38	4.5	1.9	0.76	9.49	4.73	72.7	2.6	37.1	22.9	3.7
4.2	1.91	10.9	0.49	6.1	3.3	1.27	10.85	4.39	56.3	3.3	14.1	12.3	8.1
1.6	3.13	19.0	0.22	3.7	2.8	0.77	7.52	4.05	67.1	3.8	26.1	11.5	4.4
7.1	0.01	0.1	0.47	4.1	1.0	0.91	9.90	3.36	60.8	3.1	51.7	27.8	3.9
5.6	1.41	2.5	5.80	3.6	1.5	0.41	3.30	3.29	36.1	2.9	75.4	99.8	6.1
3.7	6.56	20.4	1.25	8.8	1.3	1.84	9.23	4.38	50.2	3.5	34.6	15.9	7.4
10.0	0.00	0.0	0.00	4.4	24.8	0.81	9.13	-0.93	92.8	3.6	98.5	101.0	7.0
0.0	9.54	59.7	1.52	0.9	0.1	0.07	0.65	4.87	88.4	0.8	18.4	38.7	0.8
4.1	0.00	0.0	4.36	0.5	-1.1	-0.72	-7.37	4.17	70.3	5.8	40.1	4.7	2.7
3.9	0.54	3.1	0.17	3.0	0.5	0.68	4.97	4.57	71.5	1.1	10.3	29.4	4.6
10.0	0.00	0.0	0.00	5.3	0.5	0.33	0.36	0.77	96.4	5.0	599.0	101.0	7.0
10.0	0.00	0.0	0.00	0.0	-9.0	-5.49	-6.62	0.73	112.2	5.0	368.6	101.0	6.1
6.5	2.80	4.3	0.38	4.4	529.0	1.22	5.86	1.27	67.1	7.8	70.8	1.3	9.6
7.0	0.07	0.1	0.00	9.5	11.5	2.53	4.30	1.16	31.9	0.6	9.6	47.5	8.5
0.3	10.17	63.2	2.27	0.2	-2.4	-0.82	-9.18	4.19	93.1	3.7	24.6	11.5	4.3
7.6	0.00	0.0	0.24	2.9	0.2	0.81	6.93	3.82	87.9	3.9	22.5	9.7	2.3
7.0	1.48	5.5	0.03	3.7	0.6	0.65	5.91	3.22	75.0	3.2	50.0	21.4	6.4
2.6	1.73	11.3	0.74	2.0	0.0	0.07	0.57	4.52	81.2	1.0	20.9	34.2	6.8
2.6	2.72	17.6	0.31	5.2	6.2	1.30	13.81	3.99	60.6	1.1	21.3	32.0	6.3
1.1	6.20	46.2	3.11	0.0	-9.3	-3.34	-40.97	3.22	90.6	0.6	8.6	49.9	3.0
4.7	3.17	11.0	0.43	0.1	-0.1	-0.66	-7.66	3.36	127.0	5.6	49.1	5.4	4.0
10.0	1.23	0.6	0.37	6.2	0.7	0.99	4.53	3.05	55.6	5.4	104.8	17.4	7.1
3.3	1.71	11.5	0.24	3.5	4.3	0.65	6.85	3.65	78.6	2.9	14.3	14.3	6.2
0.2	4.10	31.0	0.06	5.6	5.3	0.96	11.12	3.51	59.4	0.8	2.3	31.5	6.7
4.1	0.82	8.2	0.17	4.9	44.2	1.09	12.17	3.70	41.6	2.3	8.8	17.0	8.1
1.6	2.19	12.5	7.41	8.5	717.1	1.16	12.97	7.97	33.5	0.6	13.4	59.6	9.7
8.0	1.49	2.6	0.25	6.3	1.1	1.38	7.66	3.87	50.2	3.6	67.7	24.5	7.0
2.2	0.43	3.6	0.38	3.6	2.2	0.63	7.48	3.28	55.4	0.5	6.4	53.7	5.3
4.1	1.82	11.7	0.49	3.0	4.1	0.66	7.53	3.36	74.2	2.8	13.1	14.7	5.0
2.1	5.83	16.3	0.75	1.8	-0.5	-0.74	-8.67	3.47	86.2	3.1	35.6	18.0	4.0
6.4	0.99	7.0	0.33	3.7	39.4	0.67	6.61	3.30	63.2	4.8	23.8	7.2	7.4
7.7	0.63	2.9	0.05	6.8	1.3	1.10	8.52	4.49	61.4	2.2	32.0	24.3	8.1
9.3	0.00	0.0	0.01	3.6	0.4	0.50	2.50	3.01	86.5	3.1	75.0	40.2	7.7
8.7	1.87	3.8	0.00	1.5	0.0	-0.04	-0.26	2.78	101.4	6.8	76.2	5.5	6.3
0.2	9.58	69.6	2.09	0.0	-260.7	-3.04	-39.35	1.85	124.8	0.4	5.8	60.4	4.2
2.0	3.37	25.1	0.00	2.3	0.1	0.05	0.43	2.73	80.1	2.4	50.0	42.5	2.3
0.0	21.12	253.9	3.01	0.0	-8.8	-2.52	-43.53	2.04	151.2	1.3	12.0	26.8	1.7
8.9	0.14	0.6	0.33	3.6	1.8	0.65	5.48	4.17	78.2	4.0	41.8	15.6	7.7
3.2	2.15	14.2	0.93	6.8	2.5	1.55	14.67	4.57	54.1	0.6	11.5	48.1	7.1
0.3	14.31	172.8	5.81	0.0	-11.9	-4.90	-95.41	3.36	94.7	3.6	23.3	11.8	0.9
5.9	0.00	0.0	-0.05	3.2	0.1	0.47	4.63	3.55	86.6	6.1	58.4	4.5	6.2
1.7	2.03	14.9	0.87	3.1	0.6	0.67	6.92	4.56	71.1	1.5	9.0	23.4	4.0
6.2	0.99	2.9	0.86	8.1	3.6	1.92	11.34	6.76	63.4	1.8	23.4	22.8	9.2
10.0	0.00	0.0	0.00	9.2	0.1	1.52	1.81	1.95	86.1	5.0	624.1	100.0	6.2
6.4	1.22	3.8	0.32	2.6	0.1	0.24	1.62	4.35	90.2	4.6	50.7	13.8	6.0
6.2	0.66	4.1	0.17	8.9	17.9	1.52	17.40	4.08	48.2	3.6	20.1	12.0	5.0
0.2	19.90	174.3	0.57	0.0	-1.4	-1.63	-23.15	3.64	134.6	1.5	20.4	26.7	2.9
1.9	2.72	20.2	0.46	3.8	0.3	0.41	4.15	4.54	69.6	0.8	16.5	37.7	4.9
3.8	3.54	18.8	0.03	6.5	1.5	1.52	14.29	4.55	63.4	4.8	37.6	10.3	6.4
2.2	2.74	15.0	1.11	2.7	0.3	0.36	4.19	3.84	68.3	1.8	27.5	25.4	3.6
3.5	2.62	13.6	1.09	5.4	2.0	1.27	11.59	4.64	60.0	1.5	24.7	27.6	6.7
2.6	3.11	18.6	0.18	0.7	-0.1	-0.49	-6.08	3.31	99.1	3.3	41.5	18.8	4.8
9.3	0.00	0.0	0.00	0.6	0.0	-0.23	-2.00	2.88	107.5	6.6	54.0	0.0	5.8
0.3	7.11	38.4	3.46	1.7	150.2	0.34	2.89	3.05	46.0	3.3	50.6	30.5	5.9
1.6	7.41	35.7	0.96	3.5	7.1	0.65	6.73	3.57	37.4	3.6	48.2	24.5	1.7
8.4	0.00	0.0	0.00	0.9	-0.1	-0.04	-0.25	2.69	161.5	7.0	81.9	6.8	5.0
9.0	0.57	2.2	-0.05	2.1	1.2	0.28	2.73	2.86	94.7	4.5	57.1	17.0	5.3
8.2	0.09	0.4	0.36	7.2	1.6	1.58	10.69	4.67	63.5	4.2	16.1	7.2	9.7
7.2	0.87	3.8	0.22	1.6	0.1	0.27	2.67	5.34	89.4	4.7	49.4	13.1	2.9
7.9	0.22	0.9	0.49	3.0	0.4	1.62	19.34	5.67	97.3	3.7	47.8	16.0	3.5

Name	City	State	Rating	2008 Rating	2007 Rating	Total Assets ($Mil)	One Year Asset Growth	Asset Mix (As a % of Total Assets) Comm-ercial Loans	Cons-umer Loans	Home Mort-gages	Secur-ities	Capital-ization Index	Leverage Ratio	Risk-based Capital Ratio
▲ EAGLE BANK & TRUST CO	LITTLE ROCK	AR	**B-**	C+	C-	135	3.61	2.4	2.3	11.3	49.7	**6.6**	8.6	16.1
▼ EAGLE BANK & TRUST CO OF	HILLSBORO	MO	**C-**	B-	B	779	3.00	6.8	1.3	10.4	17.2	**8.0**	9.8	13.3
EAGLE COMMUNITY BANK	MAPLE GROVE	MN	**E-**	E	D-	25	-7.50	9.1	0.6	10.7	5.2	**4.0**	6.7	10.5
▲ EAGLE NATIONAL BK	UPPER DARBY	PA	**C-**	C-	C-	236	-13.80	10.6	0.5	21.8	15.0	**7.4**	9.3	14.3
EAGLE SAVINGS BANK	CINCINNATI	OH	**D+**	D+	C-	107	5.28	2.6	0.2	45.2	1.3	**5.4**	7.4	13.7
EAGLE STATE BK	EAGLE	NE	**D**	C-	C+	16	-2.57	5.7	4.9	14.9	6.2	**7.3**	9.2	25.3
EAGLE VALLEY BANK NA	SAINT CROIX FALLS	WI	**E-**	E-	D-	173	-10.16	11.3	3.8	5.6	31.3	**0.8**	4.1	8.2
EAGLEBANK	BETHESDA	MD	**C**	C	C	2,071	17.11	19.8	0.2	6.8	11.0	**4.6**	8.8	10.8
EAGLEMARK SB	CARSON CITY	NV	**A-**	A-	A-	18	-17.76	0.0	19.7	0.0	74.0	**10.0**	27.7	33.2
EARLHAM SB	WEST DES MOINES	IA	**B**	B-	B	248	6.45	10.2	2.3	12.6	32.8	**10.0**	11.9	19.6
EAST BOSTON SB	EAST BOSTON	MA	**C**	C-	C-	1,810	55.70	1.7	0.3	23.0	18.9	**5.5**	8.5	11.4
EAST CAMBRIDGE SB	CAMBRIDGE	MA	**C+**	C-	C-	799	-0.31	1.5	0.5	42.6	26.9	**8.3**	9.9	18.7
▲ EAST CAROLINA BANK	ENGELHARD	NC	**D+**	C-	C+	920	3.50	6.7	0.7	7.7	29.7	**6.8**	8.8	13.5
EAST COAST COMMUNITY	ORMOND BEACH	FL	**D-**	E+	D+	88	-5.26	11.5	0.8	12.9	7.7	**5.8**	7.8	11.6
▲ EAST DUBUQUE SB	DUBUQUE	IA	**D-**	E	D-	181	-14.23	17.4	5.2	16.1	13.8	**5.5**	7.5	11.7
▲ EAST RIVER BANK	PHILADELPHIA	PA	**D**	C-	C	220	20.33	2.4	0.2	40.4	16.6	**7.9**	9.6	17.8
EAST TEXAS NB OF PALESTIN	PALESTINE	TX	**B-**	B	B	129	2.75	14.8	6.2	9.5	38.1	**4.7**	6.8	15.7
EAST WEST BANK	PASADENA	CA	**C+**	C-	C	20,691	0.64	13.9	3.2	7.8	14.0	**7.4**	9.3	17.4
EAST WISCONSIN SAVINGS BA	KAUKAUNA	WI	**C-**	C-	C-	240	-0.29	0.3	1.1	64.4	19.1	**5.3**	7.3	15.1
EASTBANK NA	NEW YORK	NY	**B**	B-	B-	187	0.91	2.6	0.0	4.6	25.0	**10.0**	12.9	17.9
▼ EASTERN BANK	BOSTON	MA	**C**	B-	B	6,590	0.08	6.0	8.5	11.1	39.5	**6.1**	8.1	14.0
EASTERN COLORADO BANK	CHEYENNE WELLS	CO	**C**	B-	B	215	11.72	6.0	0.8	5.7	27.5	**7.9**	9.6	14.2
▲ EASTERN FEDERAL BANK	NORWICH	CT	**D+**	D-	E+	166	-4.81	2.2	0.3	40.2	1.2	**9.8**	10.9	16.9
EASTERN INTERNATIONAL BK	LOS ANGELES	CA	**B**	B	B	116	13.94	0.0	0.0	0.5	6.9	**10.0**	12.6	17.5
EASTERN MICHIGAN BANK	CROSWELL	MI	**C**	C-	B-	260	3.73	6.3	1.3	16.3	25.5	**6.9**	8.9	16.8
EASTERN NATIONAL BK	MIAMI	FL	**D-**	D-	C	442	-5.00	6.7	0.5	16.9	4.9	**6.2**	8.2	15.2
EASTERN SAVINGS BANK FSB	HUNT VALLEY	MD	**D-**	D-	D	754	-18.04	0.0	0.0	53.6	0.2	**6.0**	8.0	12.6
EASTHAMPTON SB	EASTHAMPTON	MA	**B+**	B	B-	885	7.17	2.6	0.5	49.8	24.7	**10.0**	12.0	22.0
EASTMAN NATIONAL BK OF NE	NEWKIRK	OK	**C+**	C	B-	196	14.02	14.0	3.8	15.6	18.5	**6.6**	8.6	15.5
EASTON BANK & TRUST	EASTON	MD	**D-**	D+	C+	159	0.27	7.4	4.0	26.6	4.5	**6.6**	8.9	12.2
EASTSIDE COMMERCIAL BANK	CONYERS	GA	**E-**	E+	D-	215	-0.19	9.6	0.6	5.3	9.3	**3.1**	6.9	10.0
EASTSIDE COMMERCIAL BANK	BELLEVUE	WA	**E-**	E-	E+	54	-6.61	13.4	1.5	7.8	12.1	**1.5**	5.1	8.5
▲ EASTWOOD BANK	KASSON	MN	**C-**	D+	C-	500	6.19	5.4	4.1	9.5	24.6	**6.0**	8.0	12.0
EATON FSB	CHARLOTTE	MI	**C+**	C+	B	314	-4.88	0.0	0.1	58.1	18.8	**10.0**	13.8	29.5
EATON NATIONAL BK & TRUST	EATON	OH	**D**	D+	C	184	1.28	6.7	4.0	14.1	12.1	**7.3**	9.2	14.7
▲ ECLIPSE BANK INC	LOUISVILLE	KY	**D**	E+	D-	133	16.41	5.3	0.4	15.1	18.2	**7.5**	9.3	14.1
ECONOMY CO-OP BANK	MERRIMAC	MA	**C-**	C-	C-	24	-1.29	0.2	2.1	76.0	6.8	**8.5**	10.0	21.0
EDENS BANK	WILMETTE	IL	**D-**	D-	C-	249	-12.38	3.1	0.4	19.2	0.8	**7.0**	9.0	13.9
▼ EDGAR COUNTY BANK &	PARIS	IL	**C-**	C-	B-	288	-0.36	18.8	1.5	10.7	17.6	**5.1**	8.2	11.0
EDGARTOWN NATIONAL BK	EDGARTOWN	MA	**B-**	C+	C+	132	9.31	2.6	0.2	32.9	14.9	**7.0**	9.0	14.4
EDGEBROOK BANK	CHICAGO	IL	**E**	D-	E+	90	7.25	2.2	0.9	50.2	4.6	**4.2**	6.2	11.3
EDGEWATER BANK	SAINT JOSEPH	MI	**D**	D-	D	149	-9.28	3.3	0.4	43.1	9.6	**5.6**	7.6	12.7
EDISON NATIONAL BK	FORT MYERS	FL	**D**	C-	B-	191	2.94	2.3	2.7	22.1	17.0	**6.3**	8.3	15.9
EDMONTON STATE BK	EDMONTON	KY	**A**	A	A	412	1.90	7.8	7.4	21.5	15.6	**10.0**	12.3	18.4
EDON STATE BK CO OF EDON	EDON	OH	**B+**	B+	B+	61	4.98	4.4	1.1	14.0	51.3	**10.0**	17.4	41.7
EDWARD JONES TRUST CO	SAINT LOUIS	MO	**B**	B	B	38	1.62	0.0	0.0	0.0	77.6	**10.0**	84.5	376.3
▲ EITZEN STATE BK	CALEDONIA	MN	**C**	C	B-	71	17.61	7.7	1.6	6.7	18.5	**6.1**	8.1	12.6
EL DORADO SAVINGS BANK	PLACERVILLE	CA	**B-**	B	A-	1,657	0.07	0.0	0.1	22.5	64.9	**7.8**	9.5	32.8
ELBERFELD STATE BK	ELBERFELD	IN	**B**	B-	C+	57	4.03	3.7	3.0	12.8	34.3	**9.1**	10.4	21.4
ELBERTON FS&LA	ELBERTON	GA	**C-**	C-	C-	21	-1.21	0.0	0.3	43.0	0.1	**10.0**	23.8	55.5
ELDERTON STATE BK	ELDERTON	PA	**C+**	B-	A-	217	25.20	10.0	1.6	12.5	8.1	**7.9**	9.6	15.3
ELGIN STATE BK	ELGIN	IA	**D-**	D	D-	22	-1.05	12.1	3.8	6.6	46.7	**5.8**	7.8	15.7
ELGIN STATE BK	ELGIN	IL	**D-**	D-	B-	294	2.95	6.9	0.8	4.1	9.2	**4.1**	6.1	11.9
▼ ELIZABETHTON FSB	ELIZABETHTON	TN	**B+**	A+	A+	332	-0.07	0.0	1.5	36.8	32.7	**10.0**	28.4	60.0
ELK STATE BK	CLYDE	KS	**C-**	C-	D+	47	0.51	7.7	2.6	14.1	38.6	**6.0**	8.1	15.0
ELKHART STATE BK	ELKHART	TX	**B-**	C+	C+	39	14.09	9.4	21.9	4.9	42.1	**10.0**	14.6	26.6
ELKHORN VALLEY BANK &	NORFOLK	NE	**B**	B	B	463	10.14	9.3	4.3	7.1	38.9	**6.7**	8.7	13.8
ELKTON BANK & TRUST CO	ELKTON	KY	**A-**	A-	A-	119	3.34	5.0	6.5	18.1	42.3	**10.0**	12.7	15.1
▼ ELKVILLE STATE BK	ELKVILLE	IL	**B-**	B	B	23	10.49	1.0	2.7	2.7	72.5	**10.0**	16.1	39.8
▲ ELMIRA SAVINGS BANK FSB	ELMIRA	NY	**B-**	C+	C	487	0.17	6.2	6.7	37.6	26.3	**6.9**	8.9	16.5

Asset Quality Index	Non-Performing Loans as a % of Total Loans	Non-Performing Loans as a % of Capital	Net Charge-offs Avg Loans	Profitability Index	Net Income ($Mil)	Return on Assets (R.O.A.)	Return on Equity (R.O.E.)	Net Interest Spread	Overhead Efficiency Ratio	Liquidity Index	Liquidity Ratio	Hot Money Ratio	Stability Index
4.3	1.58	7.7	0.91	**3.9**	0.9	0.63	6.98	3.97	69.9	**2.6**	45.7	30.9	**5.5**
1.2	1.75	11.8	0.18	**5.1**	7.0	0.91	8.63	3.82	59.4	**2.0**	12.4	18.7	**7.7**
0.0	19.80	159.7	0.10	**0.0**	-0.9	-3.47	-42.41	3.08	236.1	**1.9**	22.9	21.0	**2.5**
3.3	1.83	12.4	0.44	**2.6**	0.8	0.30	3.33	4.10	85.1	**1.4**	6.3	23.9	**4.5**
5.6	0.64	5.5	0.41	**3.1**	0.7	0.63	9.02	3.15	69.5	**3.3**	21.5	13.4	**3.0**
6.0	0.86	2.6	1.01	**0.7**	0.0	-0.24	-2.51	2.88	93.9	**4.0**	67.6	18.0	**5.2**
0.8	4.82	49.2	1.47	**0.0**	-4.2	-2.22	-48.43	2.98	119.2	**1.8**	14.3	20.0	**0.0**
3.3	1.43	12.3	0.34	**5.1**	16.8	0.88	9.87	4.28	58.4	**1.4**	5.2	23.7	**7.2**
8.1	0.00	0.0	0.00	**10.0**	3.1	10.61	44.48	14.88	64.5	**3.8**	113.3	37.9	**9.7**
7.0	0.65	3.1	0.43	**3.6**	1.5	0.63	5.21	3.59	73.4	**4.6**	41.9	12.7	**7.0**
2.7	3.60	26.9	0.19	**3.9**	12.7	0.75	7.85	3.96	69.9	**2.8**	30.1	23.8	**6.0**
9.3	0.22	1.3	0.01	**3.7**	5.4	0.67	6.64	3.43	74.1	**2.4**	34.9	24.3	**6.1**
2.0	2.77	16.8	1.64	**0.4**	0.9	0.09	1.23	3.44	77.4	**2.6**	9.9	15.5	**4.5**
0.0	8.29	62.4	1.40	**1.3**	0.2	0.26	2.95	4.46	62.8	**1.6**	17.7	24.2	**3.7**
0.6	3.61	29.5	1.23	**1.5**	0.8	0.43	6.36	3.31	69.8	**0.7**	8.8	34.9	**2.1**
2.5	2.84	19.4	0.56	**1.1**	0.8	-0.04	-0.56	3.52	77.7	**1.4**	23.7	28.9	**1.9**
8.5	0.00	0.0	0.08	**5.0**	1.3	1.03	13.81	4.20	76.5	**6.0**	46.0	5.5	**5.3**
3.2	1.82	11.9	1.48	**4.6**	169.4	0.84	7.52	5.10	48.7	**1.1**	15.7	31.3	**7.6**
5.7	0.52	5.1	0.41	**2.5**	0.9	0.35	4.85	2.92	75.2	**2.9**	22.8	15.2	**3.1**
7.7	0.00	0.0	0.00	**4.5**	1.6	0.85	6.91	4.34	67.6	**2.8**	40.8	22.9	**7.3**
3.6	1.98	10.1	0.84	**5.3**	68.2	1.03	8.12	3.89	71.7	**6.2**	35.2	4.0	**6.8**
3.0	0.77	4.7	2.03	**2.9**	0.9	0.46	4.02	4.22	60.2	**1.6**	16.3	23.2	**5.3**
2.2	2.00	14.2	0.63	**6.3**	5.6	3.25	39.40	3.30	42.6	**2.0**	10.4	18.8	**4.1**
7.4	0.00	0.0	0.00	**4.6**	0.8	0.71	5.44	4.22	63.1	**1.4**	27.6	31.3	**7.7**
2.6	2.42	14.1	0.99	**3.7**	1.6	0.63	6.84	3.99	69.9	**4.5**	37.0	11.6	**5.0**
0.3	4.36	34.3	1.21	**0.0**	-3.1	-0.69	-8.16	3.06	114.2	**1.3**	12.8	26.5	**2.8**
0.2	47.25	322.2	3.47	**0.2**	-29.9	-3.46	-42.35	2.65	256.0	**0.8**	17.1	45.9	**6.4**
8.5	0.86	4.7	0.02	**5.1**	7.5	0.89	7.33	3.52	61.8	**2.0**	30.4	26.1	**7.6**
4.5	1.16	7.7	0.38	**7.8**	2.5	1.39	15.62	4.65	60.1	**3.2**	24.9	14.1	**3.8**
0.7	4.92	39.8	1.74	**0.2**	-1.4	-0.88	-10.07	3.90	78.7	**1.9**	11.8	19.3	**4.5**
0.0	4.15	33.1	1.84	**0.0**	-4.2	-1.94	-24.61	2.68	124.0	**2.1**	19.0	18.7	**0.0**
0.3	7.31	57.4	2.15	**0.0**	-1.0	-1.81	-34.42	4.01	133.0	**0.7**	16.3	53.3	**2.3**
2.1	1.90	13.9	0.29	**4.8**	5.7	1.17	13.04	4.16	69.6	**2.5**	14.6	16.5	**4.4**
4.5	3.05	14.2	0.71	**3.1**	1.5	0.45	3.36	3.24	61.9	**1.7**	30.0	29.3	**6.6**
0.7	5.36	36.6	0.22	**4.4**	1.5	0.78	8.52	3.98	69.7	**3.0**	21.0	14.5	**4.0**
5.1	0.95	6.6	0.00	**2.1**	2.8	2.24	25.07	3.24	93.7	**1.6**	21.1	25.5	**2.9**
3.9	1.79	13.1	0.43	**2.1**	0.0	0.14	1.38	3.50	87.5	**3.1**	19.9	13.6	**5.8**
0.0	11.21	75.8	2.55	**0.4**	-3.4	-1.27	-13.52	4.04	71.5	**0.8**	16.2	37.9	**4.1**
2.1	1.40	11.5	0.96	**4.6**	3.2	1.13	11.85	4.26	67.4	**1.7**	6.8	19.5	**6.0**
5.5	1.26	9.5	0.07	**4.2**	0.9	0.67	7.19	4.13	73.7	**4.3**	9.9	6.1	**5.3**
0.3	6.51	65.9	0.91	**0.7**	0.0	0.03	0.44	3.65	78.4	**1.1**	14.3	30.6	**0.2**
1.4	3.68	32.3	0.10	**1.2**	0.2	0.12	1.67	3.32	92.6	**3.0**	16.7	14.1	**2.4**
2.8	1.36	8.3	1.90	**0.3**	-1.4	-0.72	-8.59	3.56	81.3	**3.3**	33.0	16.0	**3.6**
8.0	0.22	1.2	0.15	**7.3**	7.0	1.70	14.33	3.86	57.4	**2.3**	14.6	17.5	**8.9**
9.3	0.00	0.0	0.25	**4.7**	0.5	0.79	4.36	3.88	67.9	**6.2**	65.9	8.0	**7.9**
8.0	0.00	0.0	0.00	**7.8**	1.2	3.38	3.97	0.16	90.6	**10.0**	610.4	0.0	**3.7**
3.3	2.56	17.6	0.34	**4.9**	0.7	1.15	12.91	3.19	61.6	**3.0**	34.5	18.0	**6.6**
10.0	0.49	1.2	0.03	**3.7**	10.9	0.65	7.06	2.76	60.1	**5.3**	78.6	16.9	**7.9**
7.8	0.67	2.8	0.07	**4.9**	0.6	0.99	9.17	4.15	70.3	**5.4**	53.7	10.3	**5.9**
9.3	0.66	1.6	0.00	**0.5**	-0.1	-0.51	-2.12	2.71	123.6	**3.9**	55.0	16.1	**5.3**
2.9	1.66	11.0	0.24	**5.6**	1.8	0.98	10.06	3.83	55.1	**4.6**	36.1	10.8	**5.3**
7.8	0.34	1.8	0.00	**1.7**	0.1	0.30	3.74	3.49	92.0	**5.7**	52.7	6.3	**1.7**
0.0	6.03	48.1	2.47	**0.2**	-3.8	-1.25	-16.85	3.42	86.8	**2.8**	22.9	15.8	**3.3**
7.7	1.72	3.3	0.00	**4.5**	3.0	0.91	3.23	3.46	47.2	**3.3**	52.7	25.5	**8.4**
8.4	0.13	0.8	0.00	**3.0**	0.2	0.39	4.61	3.66	87.2	**2.0**	17.8	19.2	**4.4**
4.5	2.83	8.2	1.40	**4.3**	0.4	1.00	6.15	7.10	80.0	**6.6**	42.9	0.0	**6.2**
5.3	1.08	6.3	0.33	**6.3**	5.6	1.27	14.28	3.74	48.0	**5.4**	40.5	7.5	**5.2**
8.1	0.20	0.7	0.38	**6.0**	1.5	1.29	9.62	4.33	60.7	**3.0**	44.7	23.7	**8.0**
9.9	0.00	0.0	0.27	**3.0**	0.1	0.43	2.53	3.01	80.0	**6.5**	97.3	9.5	**7.5**
4.3	0.50	3.4	0.24	**4.4**	4.8	0.97	8.65	3.61	62.1	**3.6**	34.9	15.4	**6.3**

Name	City	State	Rating	2008 Rating	2007 Rating	Total Assets ($Mil)	One Year Asset Growth	Asset Mix (As a % of Total Assets) Commercial Loans	Consumer Loans	Home Mortgages	Securities	Capitalization Index	Leverage Ratio	Risk-based Capital Ratio
ELSA STATE BK & TRUST CO	ELSA	TX	**C+**	C+	C	162	8.07	4.8	13.4	10.9	43.0	**6.2**	8.2	15.1
▼ ELYSIAN BANK	ELYSIAN	MN	**D+**	C-	C-	40	10.48	10.2	8.0	10.2	13.2	**7.7**	9.5	16.9
▲ EMBARCADERO BANK	SAN DIEGO	CA	**C**	C	C	73	59.80	2.1	0.0	15.6	0.0	**10.0**	29.7	37.9
EMBASSY BK FOR LEHIGH VAL	BETHLEHEM	PA	**C+**	C+	C-	514	10.50	5.4	0.3	37.1	17.5	**6.1**	8.1	13.0
▼ EMBASSY NATIONAL BK	LAWRENCEVILLE	GA	**D-**	D	D-	65	9.03	5.8	0.1	2.7	0.3	**8.3**	11.6	13.6
▼ EMERALD BANK	BURDEN	KS	**D**	C	C-	17	19.56	7.1	9.1	42.9	5.3	**5.7**	7.7	13.4
EMERALD BANK	DUBLIN	OH	**D+**	D+	C+	78	8.07	10.4	0.5	26.1	10.5	**7.0**	9.0	14.2
▲ EMIGRANT BANK	NEW YORK	NY	**D+**	D-	C-	8,755	-31.94	6.0	0.1	18.4	34.9	**8.4**	10.0	19.8
▲ EMIGRANT MERCANTILE BANK	NEW YORK	NY	**C-**	C-	C-	4	-2.43	0.0	0.0	0.0	0.0	**10.0**	86.4	390.5
▲ EMIGRANT SB - LONG ISLAND	NEW YORK	NY	**D**	D-	D+	541	2.40	0.0	0.1	49.6	37.0	**5.7**	7.7	20.9
▲ EMIGRANT SB - MANHATTAN	NEW YORK	NY	**D+**	D	C-	1,245	2.95	0.6	0.1	32.7	56.9	**6.4**	8.4	28.4
▲ EMIGRANT	BRONX	NY	**D**	D-	C-	1,042	-0.22	0.0	0.2	32.9	56.1	**5.5**	7.5	24.8
▲ EMIGRANT	BROOKLYN	NY	**D**	D-	D+	799	2.51	0.0	0.1	38.1	52.9	**6.0**	8.0	26.0
EMMET COUNTY STATE BK	ESTHERVILLE	IA	**C+**	C	B-	67	-1.81	1.3	1.4	14.6	13.8	**7.5**	9.3	13.4
EMPIRE BANK	SPRINGFIELD	MO	**C+**	C+	C+	1,066	30.01	8.4	6.4	9.1	18.0	**5.5**	8.5	11.4
EMPIRE NATIONAL BK	ISLANDIA	NY	**D**	C-	C	329	30.58	16.1	0.1	0.1	28.2	**7.7**	9.5	14.6
EMPIRE STATE BK	NEWBURGH	NY	**D**	D-	D-	161	2.44	22.0	0.3	18.8	12.5	**6.0**	8.0	13.0
EMPRISE BANK	WICHITA	KS	**B**	B	B-	1,442	3.26	10.8	2.3	10.2	35.1	**5.6**	7.6	12.7
▼ ENCORE BANK NA	HOUSTON	TX	**D-**	C-	C+	1,461	-10.26	10.1	1.7	32.6	24.7	**5.6**	7.6	13.3
▲ ENCORE NATIONAL BK	NAPLES	FL	**C**	C-	D	238	533.09	1.3	1.4	5.9	1.3	**6.5**	8.6	18.1
ENERBANK USA	SALT LAKE CITY	UT	**C+**	C	C+	410	44.45	0.0	95.2	0.0	1.4	**4.0**	10.0	10.5
ENGLEWOOD BANK	ENGLEWOOD	FL	**D**	D+	C+	184	-3.33	1.1	0.2	24.4	10.6	**6.1**	8.1	12.8
ENLOE STATE BK	COOPER	TX	**B**	B	B	24	9.87	13.9	6.8	25.4	0.1	**10.0**	11.5	15.3
▲ ENNIS STATE BK	ENNIS	TX	**C**	B-	B-	112	5.66	25.9	3.5	15.9	12.6	**8.6**	10.0	15.0
ENTERPRISE BANK	ALLISON PARK	PA	**D-**	C-	E	222	14.72	16.7	0.2	7.2	0.0	**6.1**	8.6	11.8
▲ ENTERPRISE BANK	HOUSTON	TX	**D**	C-	D+	543	-0.25	17.0	1.6	6.5	3.1	**6.0**	8.4	11.8
▲ ENTERPRISE BANK & TRUST	CLAYTON	MO	**C**	C-	C+	2,792	19.29	21.6	0.3	5.9	13.0	**6.6**	8.6	12.7
ENTERPRISE BANK & TRUST C	LOWELL	MA	**D**	C-	B-	1,397	7.15	19.3	0.3	6.7	10.6	**5.6**	8.5	11.4
ENTERPRISE BANK NA	OMAHA	NE	**D**	C	C-	184	0.83	18.7	3.2	21.9	1.4	**7.1**	9.9	12.6
▼ ENTERPRISE BANK OF FLORID	NORTH PALM BEACH	FL	**D**	D-	C-	254	-19.45	6.6	0.8	10.9	19.8	**9.7**	12.2	14.7
▼ ENTERPRISE BANK OF S	EHRHARDT	SC	**D+**	C-	C	420	-2.76	12.2	7.7	10.8	13.8	**10.0**	16.8	22.7
▲ ENTERPRISE NATIONAL BK NJ	KENILWORTH	NJ	**D**	D-	D	113	-1.56	9.4	0.0	5.4	19.7	**10.0**	13.5	18.3
EPHRATA NATIONAL BK	EPHRATA	PA	**B-**	C+	B-	748	2.99	3.7	1.8	20.8	34.7	**8.0**	9.6	17.3
EQUITABLE BANK	GRAND ISLAND	NE	**D-**	D	D	186	-3.87	15.3	2.1	24.1	1.6	**5.5**	8.0	11.4
EQUITABLE BANK SSB	WAUWATOSA	WI	**D-**	D-	D-	458	-6.88	0.0	2.1	40.2	6.1	**6.0**	8.0	13.2
EQUITABLE CO-OP BANK	LYNN	MA	**D**	D+	D	94	-3.00	1.1	0.2	50.4	19.1	**6.8**	8.8	14.2
EQUITABLE SAVINGS & LOAN	STERLING	CO	**B-**	B-	C	178	-2.96	0.0	0.6	87.2	6.5	**10.0**	12.2	25.9
EQUITABLE SAVINGS & LOAN	CADIZ	OH	**C-**	C-	D+	13	-4.62	0.0	0.5	29.5	44.1	**10.0**	21.3	41.5
EQUITY BANK	MINNETONKA	MN	**C**	C	C+	50	-8.12	28.9	0.3	11.2	2.3	**10.0**	13.9	16.2
▲ EQUITY BANK A NA	WICHITA	KS	**C+**	C-	C	486	11.95	14.7	0.7	9.4	33.2	**10.0**	12.2	18.4
▲ ERICSON STATE BK	ERICSON	NE	**D-**	D	D+	48	-7.14	6.2	15.0	3.3	7.1	**4.7**	7.8	10.8
ESB BANK	ELLWOOD CITY	PA	**B-**	C+	C+	1,873	-2.49	0.8	3.4	19.0	55.8	**6.1**	8.1	15.8
ESB FINANCIAL	EMPORIA	KS	**B-**	B-	B-	154	4.83	12.7	8.7	12.1	32.2	**6.7**	8.7	12.9
ESCAMBIA COUNTY BANK	FLOMATON	AL	**D+**	D	C+	96	-0.10	3.2	4.6	7.6	65.2	**8.7**	10.1	24.3
ESPIRITO SANTO BANK	MIAMI	FL	**D**	D-	E-	565	2.79	13.9	2.7	29.2	12.0	**6.2**	8.2	16.8
▼ ESQUIRE BANK	GARDEN CITY	NY	**D**	C-	C	206	10.24	6.2	0.3	9.7	72.8	**6.7**	8.7	28.6
ESSA BANK & TRUST	STROUDSBURG	PA	**B-**	B-	B-	1,076	6.98	2.9	0.2	58.2	23.9	**10.0**	15.0	30.0
ESSEX BANK	TAPPAHANNOCK	VA	**D-**	D-	C-	1,115	-8.98	3.9	0.9	18.7	27.3	**6.0**	8.0	15.5
ESSEX SB	ESSEX	CT	**B+**	B+	A-	291	5.70	3.5	0.1	55.6	2.2	**10.0**	12.7	23.0
▼ EUDORA BANK	EUDORA	AR	**C-**	C+	C+	34	-2.34	10.0	4.9	3.3	56.3	**6.0**	8.0	17.0
EUREKA BANK	PITTSBURGH	PA	**C+**	B-	C-	131	12.87	15.3	0.4	33.1	11.3	**8.5**	10.0	16.6
EUREKA HOMESTEAD	METAIRIE	LA	**C+**	B-	B	97	-1.70	0.0	0.4	48.3	28.7	**10.0**	12.4	24.0
EUREKA SB	LA SALLE	IL	**C+**	C+	B-	398	7.42	0.0	1.2	54.8	33.3	**10.0**	17.2	41.0
EUROBANK	CORAL GABLES	FL	**E-**	D-	D	102	4.95	7.7	1.0	12.9	11.1	**3.4**	5.4	13.2
EVABANK	CULLMAN	AL	**E-**	E-	D	377	-9.18	1.0	6.2	44.6	9.3	**2.9**	5.5	9.9
EVANGELINE BANK & TRUST C	VILLE PLATTE	LA	**B-**	B-	B+	575	1.79	5.9	6.2	24.8	29.1	**10.0**	15.7	27.9
▼ EVANS BANK NA	HAMBURG	NY	**C-**	D+	B-	661	8.70	11.8	0.4	13.0	13.6	**8.1**	9.7	14.0
EVANSVILLE COMMERCE	EVANSVILLE	IN	**E+**	D	C-	53	-6.97	9.8	0.9	17.9	0.0	**6.5**	8.5	13.5
EVB	TAPPAHANNOCK	VA	**D**	C-	C+	1,119	-0.62	6.2	3.2	23.3	22.0	**3.9**	5.9	11.0
▲ EVERBANK	JACKSONVILLE	FL	**D**	C	C	11,982	49.00	4.7	0.1	42.8	17.3	**6.7**	8.7	17.0

Asset Quality Index	Non-Performing Loans as a % of Total Loans	Non-Performing Loans as a % of Capital	Net Charge-offs Avg Loans	Profitability Index	Net Income ($Mil)	Return on Assets (R.O.A.)	Return on Equity (R.O.E.)	Net Interest Spread	Overhead Efficiency Ratio	Liquidity Index	Liquidity Ratio	Hot Money Ratio	Stability Index
4.7	1.31	7.0	0.39	**4.2**	1.6	0.99	11.72	4.49	76.8	**2.3**	41.1	30.8	**4.2**
1.3	7.56	34.1	0.72	**4.8**	0.4	1.11	11.03	4.25	63.9	**5.6**	50.3	8.0	**6.3**
7.1	0.00	0.0	0.00	**2.7**	0.4	0.70	2.02	4.57	73.3	**1.8**	25.8	24.0	**4.2**
4.8	0.77	6.6	0.33	**4.8**	5.0	1.02	12.23	3.99	60.1	**3.7**	12.7	10.0	**5.3**
0.0	7.60	44.7	1.48	**0.0**	-0.7	-1.17	-9.06	5.92	101.2	**1.7**	13.0	21.2	**1.3**
4.2	1.43	12.2	0.01	**3.9**	0.1	0.48	5.87	5.20	82.1	**1.0**	18.9	32.6	**2.3**
0.2	7.53	44.6	1.00	**0.1**	-0.3	-0.39	-3.01	3.31	79.5	**1.6**	28.6	30.3	**4.6**
1.7	11.31	44.4	1.59	**3.2**	74.3	0.67	7.11	2.37	59.0	**6.9**	42.6	1.5	**3.5**
10.0	0.00	0.0	0.00	**0.0**	-0.1	-1.70	-1.96	0.24	1,411.1	**10.0**	707.0	0.0	**4.1**
0.3	19.90	124.1	0.50	**2.5**	1.4	0.27	3.64	2.61	72.9	**5.0**	53.4	13.4	**3.8**
1.7	10.16	39.7	0.41	**2.7**	9.1	0.75	9.93	2.22	78.0	**6.7**	71.7	9.2	**4.1**
0.3	14.80	62.8	0.72	**1.3**	4.2	0.40	5.91	1.83	93.4	**6.7**	70.4	8.6	**3.7**
0.3	18.84	87.8	0.41	**2.4**	6.3	0.80	11.22	2.15	81.5	**6.1**	65.8	10.4	**3.7**
4.1	1.53	8.9	0.13	**3.3**	0.4	0.58	5.62	4.40	82.1	**5.4**	37.4	6.3	**4.9**
3.3	2.60	20.0	1.05	**4.6**	7.5	0.83	9.97	4.39	62.6	**2.3**	15.9	18.0	**6.0**
3.8	1.02	6.3	0.01	**1.2**	2.0	0.64	6.43	3.88	92.0	**1.2**	4.6	25.9	**2.1**
1.2	2.03	17.0	0.37	**0.8**	0.5	0.31	3.99	3.28	88.2	**1.5**	15.2	24.9	**3.7**
5.8	0.87	5.6	0.27	**6.0**	15.7	1.11	12.49	3.79	64.5	**3.9**	25.3	13.3	**7.9**
2.2	3.00	20.0	4.09	**0.0**	-22.6	-1.38	-12.90	3.03	101.0	**2.4**	26.7	24.1	**8.5**
8.2	0.03	0.1	0.60	**5.5**	3.8	4.94	32.32	N/,	36.6	**4.2**	65.2	19.5	**4.6**
4.8	0.15	1.4	1.48	**8.6**	8.8	2.73	29.48	9.62	41.7	**0.1**	4.0	100.0	**4.5**
0.0	5.88	39.2	2.30	**0.0**	-3.7	-1.94	-13.86	4.00	71.6	**4.8**	22.2	4.3	**5.2**
4.9	1.92	11.9	0.04	**6.2**	0.2	0.93	7.39	5.31	68.4	**1.5**	23.7	26.0	**8.3**
3.3	2.34	16.0	0.24	**4.5**	0.7	0.65	6.55	4.73	77.1	**4.1**	15.9	8.1	**5.9**
0.0	1.26	11.9	0.20	**4.4**	1.5	0.73	8.24	4.07	69.4	**0.5**	9.6	55.6	**3.9**
1.8	1.26	10.3	0.98	**2.4**	0.9	0.16	1.33	4.24	69.8	**0.8**	17.5	41.9	**6.4**
4.0	2.03	14.3	1.84	**3.0**	13.8	0.57	6.31	4.08	53.5	**1.2**	18.0	30.7	**5.0**
0.7	1.85	15.3	0.36	**5.0**	12.0	0.88	9.74	4.55	68.0	**3.3**	6.7	12.0	**8.1**
1.3	5.63	42.3	0.98	**3.2**	0.7	0.37	4.29	3.82	62.9	**0.8**	15.9	39.0	**4.7**
0.2	6.82	33.8	2.35	**0.6**	-2.3	-0.78	-7.94	3.80	76.4	**1.0**	21.5	34.2	**4.5**
0.0	12.22	47.1	1.74	**3.5**	1.3	0.30	1.76	3.71	52.7	**1.6**	15.8	22.5	**6.9**
0.8	5.69	28.9	0.18	**1.2**	0.2	0.19	1.75	4.02	87.2	**1.9**	22.8	20.9	**4.9**
5.3	0.97	5.1	0.14	**4.0**	6.5	0.86	8.83	3.58	70.6	**3.7**	32.3	13.8	**6.5**
1.3	3.18	26.0	0.03	**0.6**	-0.9	-0.48	-5.13	3.41	82.9	**2.2**	18.8	18.6	**3.8**
0.3	4.84	42.0	1.58	**0.0**	-3.3	-0.70	-8.34	3.99	109.2	**1.7**	6.1	19.4	**2.0**
8.8	0.00	0.0	1.38	**0.3**	-0.5	-0.49	-5.07	3.70	87.4	**3.5**	25.3	12.7	**3.2**
9.5	0.15	1.1	0.02	**3.7**	1.3	0.69	5.78	3.29	68.0	**2.2**	9.5	17.4	**6.6**
5.5	6.25	12.3	0.00	**0.7**	-0.1	-0.35	-1.65	3.01	109.7	**6.2**	67.4	5.7	**5.3**
5.5	0.70	4.3	0.70	**2.4**	0.1	0.19	1.32	5.11	80.4	**0.5**	3.1	38.3	**7.0**
4.7	1.67	7.8	0.44	**3.1**	1.8	0.41	3.45	3.89	80.1	**2.2**	30.7	22.1	**5.7**
3.9	0.23	2.1	1.26	**3.8**	0.2	0.44	5.99	4.78	54.7	**4.5**	7.4	4.2	**2.3**
6.0	2.03	8.4	0.13	**4.3**	16.0	0.86	7.85	2.88	53.4	**3.0**	30.3	20.1	**7.9**
7.8	0.29	1.8	0.22	**4.1**	1.4	0.93	9.73	4.39	75.3	**3.4**	28.6	14.1	**5.2**
3.7	5.96	15.0	1.67	**1.4**	0.5	0.49	4.45	2.72	86.6	**2.6**	59.1	41.2	**4.0**
1.6	3.08	23.1	0.81	**1.0**	1.4	0.29	4.01	3.18	86.2	**3.2**	26.0	14.4	**2.1**
8.9	1.23	2.6	0.00	**1.0**	0.0	0.01	0.09	2.56	98.4	**3.7**	86.7	34.0	**0.0**
6.3	1.59	7.1	0.08	**3.2**	4.8	0.46	3.02	2.82	74.2	**1.8**	28.8	39.0	**9.2**
1.7	6.07	33.1	2.66	**0.0**	-19.5	-1.63	-16.45	4.19	115.4	**2.7**	29.5	24.4	**5.8**
7.8	1.04	6.1	0.00	**4.8**	2.1	0.73	6.24	3.55	84.5	**3.3**	18.1	12.9	**7.2**
5.8	0.02	0.1	0.25	**2.6**	0.1	0.17	1.92	3.60	94.7	**2.5**	55.2	35.4	**4.6**
7.8	0.04	0.3	0.00	**3.2**	0.7	0.59	5.35	3.63	68.4	**1.8**	21.5	22.1	**6.8**
7.0	0.28	1.2	0.03	**2.4**	0.4	0.36	3.10	2.78	82.7	**2.2**	40.4	32.9	**5.6**
6.0	4.59	15.4	0.20	**2.5**	0.9	0.22	1.25	2.48	73.7	**4.0**	45.3	16.4	**7.7**
0.0	5.67	58.8	1.64	**0.0**	-3.6	-3.47	-54.36	2.83	213.5	**0.7**	18.9	56.5	**1.9**
0.3	3.87	38.9	2.24	**1.7**	0.7	0.18	3.38	4.74	64.3	**0.7**	17.5	52.5	**0.0**
3.8	4.32	15.9	0.78	**5.2**	5.5	0.96	6.08	4.08	59.8	**1.9**	31.5	28.6	**7.8**
1.4	2.18	15.5	0.10	**3.6**	4.1	0.65	7.18	4.32	67.7	**3.5**	6.3	10.5	**4.5**
1.2	4.62	32.6	0.89	**0.2**	-0.3	-0.49	-5.80	3.71	106.4	**1.7**	27.9	26.8	**1.6**
1.2	3.57	31.2	1.89	**0.5**	-10.8	-0.98	-11.27	3.55	79.7	**1.8**	16.3	22.3	**5.6**
0.2	2.68	17.4	1.23	**4.9**	122.7	1.16	12.07	5.39	65.5	**2.5**	29.9	26.7	**5.1**

	Name	City	State	Rating	2008 Rating	2007 Rating	Total Assets ($Mil)	One Year Asset Growth	Asset Mix (As a % of Total Assets) Comm-ercial Loans	Cons-umer Loans	Home Mort-gages	Secur-ities	Capital-ization Index	Leverage Ratio	Risk-based Capital Ratio
	EVERCORE TRUST CO NA	NEW YORK	NY	**U**	U	NR	27	19.88	0.0	0.0	0.0	25.6	**10.0**	79.6	240.2
	EVERENCE TRUST CO	GOSHEN	IN	**D**	C-	C-	5	2.95	0.0	0.0	0.0	70.3	**10.0**	68.6	167.7
▲	EVERETT CO-OP BANK	EVERETT	MA	**B-**	B+	A-	287	6.95	1.0	0.7	46.5	7.9	**10.0**	12.5	20.0
	EVERGREEN BANK GROUP	OAK BROOK	IL	**D+**	C-	C-	389	5.24	1.7	38.5	7.0	18.4	**7.6**	9.4	14.0
	EVERGREEN FS&LA	GRANTS PASS	OR	**C+**	C+	B-	340	8.12	1.4	0.1	22.4	5.7	**9.7**	10.8	16.0
	EVERGREEN NATIONAL BK	EVERGREEN	CO	**D**	D	C	98	12.83	3.6	2.4	10.1	32.8	**7.1**	9.1	18.2
	EVERTRUST BANK	CITY OF INDUSTRY	CA	**D**	D-	B-	492	-11.40	7.0	0.0	0.1	15.1	**10.0**	15.0	20.5
	EVOLVE BANK & TRUST	WEST MEMPHIS	AR	**B-**	C+	C+	160	5.09	8.5	3.4	36.8	18.6	**6.3**	8.3	13.3
▼	EXCEL BANK	SEDALIA	MO	**E+**	D+	C-	274	2.17	17.7	1.5	21.3	4.2	**3.6**	6.7	10.3
	EXCEL NATIONAL BK	BEVERLY HILLS	CA	**E-**	D-	E+	195	-10.05	2.5	0.0	1.0	0.0	**1.0**	5.3	8.0
	EXCHANGE B&TC	NATCHITOCHES	LA	**A-**	B	C	97	-3.98	1.9	3.3	21.9	46.0	**10.0**	11.7	25.8
	EXCHANGE BANK	SANTA ROSA	CA	**D+**	D	D+	1,502	-1.97	9.5	0.9	12.4	21.2	**7.4**	9.2	13.4
▼	EXCHANGE BANK	MILLEDGEVILLE	GA	**D-**	C-	B	226	-2.11	1.7	1.8	17.4	24.6	**7.2**	9.1	13.9
	EXCHANGE BANK	GIBBON	NE	**C+**	C	C-	207	8.89	14.8	1.2	8.2	20.4	**5.6**	9.0	11.5
▼	EXCHANGE BANK	SKIATOOK	OK	**E-**	E+	E	89	-2.25	8.4	5.8	22.3	21.8	**4.6**	6.6	11.4
	EXCHANGE BANK & TRUST CO	PERRY	OK	**B-**	B-	C+	185	8.58	6.3	11.8	22.6	23.7	**6.4**	8.4	13.5
	EXCHANGE BANK OF	ALTOONA	AL	**D**	D	C+	244	-1.11	6.9	3.3	11.0	16.9	**9.2**	10.4	14.5
	EXCHANGE BANK OF	FAYETTE	MO	**D**	D+	C-	68	11.34	2.8	1.3	16.7	14.4	**5.2**	7.3	11.1
	EXCHANGE BANK OF	KAHOKA	MO	**D**	C	C-	136	12.39	2.0	1.6	9.4	41.4	**5.6**	7.6	13.3
	EXCHANGE BANK SOUTH	KINGSTREE	SC	**C+**	C	B+	127	5.60	5.0	8.0	22.7	22.8	**10.0**	16.8	33.6
	EXCHANGE NATIONAL BK & TR	ATCHISON	KS	**B+**	B+	B+	206	0.54	4.2	22.0	15.9	21.4	**6.9**	8.9	13.4
	EXCHANGE NATIONAL BK OF	MOORE	OK	**B-**	B-	B-	158	12.86	3.3	3.4	5.3	38.7	**8.4**	9.9	18.1
▼	EXCHANGE NB COTTONWOOD	COTTONWOOD FALLS	KS	**D-**	C-	C+	36	-0.24	15.3	3.3	5.9	23.9	**7.4**	9.2	17.2
	EXCHANGE STATE BK	ADAIR	IA	**D**	D	D+	52	-11.55	7.5	6.6	19.9	14.7	**5.4**	7.4	12.0
▲	EXCHANGE STATE BK	COLLINS	IA	**C+**	C-	C-	92	-2.12	9.0	1.5	11.6	10.9	**7.2**	9.1	12.7
	EXCHANGE STATE BK	SPRINGVILLE	IA	**B**	B	A-	38	-7.80	2.7	1.4	20.2	25.7	**7.1**	9.1	16.9
▲	EXCHANGE STATE BK	LANARK	IL	**C-**	D+	D+	77	-3.51	5.0	1.3	9.2	49.8	**5.4**	7.4	14.5
▲	EXCHANGE STATE BK	CARSONVILLE	MI	**C+**	B-	B+	125	8.26	5.3	2.4	22.1	15.1	**6.5**	9.9	12.2
	EXCHANGE STATE BK	LUVERNE	MN	**B**	B-	B	122	12.78	3.9	2.6	5.2	17.3	**6.1**	8.1	12.6
	EXCHANGE STATE BK ST	SAINT PAUL	KS	**C-**	C	C-	66	-2.52	10.6	3.3	17.5	38.8	**5.1**	7.1	14.7
	EXECUTIVE NATIONAL BK	MIAMI	FL	**D+**	D-	C	278	5.91	3.3	0.2	6.3	23.7	**6.9**	8.9	14.9
	EXTRACO BANKS NA	TEMPLE	TX	**B+**	B+	B+	1,160	-1.92	4.7	3.9	16.5	29.4	**7.3**	9.2	17.7
	F & C BANK	HOLDEN	MO	**B**	B	B	115	0.63	5.3	4.2	31.3	5.5	**10.0**	12.3	16.2
▼	F & M BANK & TRUST CO	MANCHESTER	GA	**D-**	D+	B-	111	1.89	2.9	3.8	21.2	5.1	**8.4**	9.9	14.1
	F & M BANK MINNESOTA	CLARKFIELD	MN	**B**	B	C+	92	124.32	4.5	0.9	3.0	24.3	**3.1**	8.5	10.0
▲	F & M BANK NA OKLAHOMA CI	YUKON	OK	**C**	D+	D	75	-5.53	8.4	4.4	16.2	20.1	**7.2**	9.1	14.5
	F & M COMMUNITY BANK NA	PRESTON	MN	**B**	B	B	97	9.91	6.9	2.4	9.9	18.3	**9.2**	11.1	14.3
▼	F&M BANK	WASHINGTON	GA	**C**	B-	B+	320	10.29	5.2	3.6	13.0	39.8	**10.0**	12.4	21.1
▲	F&M BANK	WEST POINT	NE	**C+**	C	B-	272	159.85	7.1	1.4	7.3	17.3	**5.9**	8.7	11.7
	F&M BANK	CLARKSVILLE	TN	**C-**	D+	C	790	-0.36	5.4	3.1	17.4	9.7	**6.0**	8.2	11.8
	F&M BANK & TRUST CO	HANNIBAL	MO	**C-**	C-	C	174	-3.99	11.4	1.7	41.2	10.5	**6.2**	8.2	13.7
	F&M BANK & TRUST CO	TULSA	OK	**C+**	C+	C+	1,556	4.11	30.0	1.4	7.2	2.9	**5.3**	8.7	11.3
▼	FAHEY BANKING CO	MARION	OH	**D+**	C+	C+	179	-2.84	2.7	1.2	16.7	14.9	**10.0**	22.7	29.0
▲	FAIRFAX STATE SB	FAIRFAX	IA	**C-**	C	B	138	0.10	8.2	3.5	10.4	48.1	**10.0**	11.0	18.4
▼	FAIRFIELD COUNTY BANK	RIDGEFIELD	CT	**D**	D+	C+	1,557	-0.05	10.6	0.5	28.9	6.5	**6.0**	8.5	11.8
	FAIRFIELD FS&LA	LANCASTER	OH	**D+**	C-	C-	272	1.69	0.1	0.4	73.2	3.3	**6.5**	8.5	15.4
	FAIRFIELD NATIONAL BK	FAIRFIELD	IL	**B-**	C+	B-	357	4.85	22.7	4.4	7.5	39.0	**6.3**	8.3	18.5
	FAIRMOUNT BANK	BALTIMORE	MD	**B-**	B-	B	73	11.90	1.9	4.2	58.6	14.1	**10.0**	12.3	23.4
	FAIRMOUNT STATE BK	FAIRMOUNT	IN	**C+**	C+	B	38	-0.04	0.3	6.6	17.6	35.0	**10.0**	14.5	28.0
	FAIRPORT SAVINGS BANK	FAIRPORT	NY	**C-**	C-	C-	209	-0.96	0.0	0.0	49.2	36.8	**6.0**	8.0	20.2
	FAIRVIEW SAVINGS & LOAN A	FAIRVIEW	OK	**B**	B	B	35	4.46	7.1	3.6	57.9	3.7	**10.0**	13.9	23.0
	FAIRVIEW STATE BANKING CO	FAIRVIEW	IL	**C**	C	C+	24	8.43	7.4	6.4	17.2	46.6	**10.0**	12.1	25.2
	FALCON INTERNATIONAL BK	LAREDO	TX	**D-**	D-	D	870	-4.23	8.6	2.4	11.7	7.8	**7.3**	9.2	14.0
	FALCON NATIONAL BK	FOLEY	MN	**D**	D	C	119	-0.01	12.9	2.0	15.9	11.9	**7.6**	9.4	13.8
▼	FALLS CITY NATIONAL BK	FALLS CITY	TX	**B-**	A-	A	167	15.23	4.8	5.1	17.2	19.4	**9.8**	10.9	21.5
	FAMILY BANK	PELHAM	GA	**D**	C-	C+	86	-1.74	4.2	7.7	44.5	4.8	**6.4**	8.4	14.0
	FAMILY BANK FSB	PAINTSVILLE	KY	**B-**	B-	B-	110	-4.04	0.5	3.8	49.2	20.2	**7.8**	9.5	20.9
	FAMILY FEDERAL SAVINGS FA	FITCHBURG	MA	**D+**	D+	C-	96	2.66	0.0	0.4	59.7	24.8	**9.1**	10.4	24.1
	FAMILYFIRST BANK	WARE	MA	**D-**	D-	D-	58	-3.82	1.1	1.2	36.2	26.1	**5.9**	7.9	16.1
	FANNIN BANK	BONHAM	TX	**C-**	C	C-	60	0.00	8.7	6.9	19.9	27.3	**5.5**	7.5	13.1

Asset Quality Index	Non-Performing Loans as a % of Total Loans	Non-Performing Loans as a % of Capital	Net Charge-offs Avg Loans	Profitability Index	Net Income ($Mil)	Return on Assets (R.O.A.)	Return on Equity (R.O.E.)	Net Interest Spread	Overhead Efficiency Ratio	Liquidity Index	Liquidity Ratio	Hot Money Ratio	Stability Index
6.5	0.00	0.0	0.00	**9.5**	3.1	12.41	14.20	0.56	72.3	**5.0**	278.4	101.0	**6.7**
6.6	0.00	0.0	0.00	**0.1**	-0.4	-8.96	-11.31	3.19	110.0	**5.0**	258.3	100.0	**0.0**
4.1	1.81	11.4	0.13	**7.4**	3.5	1.24	10.23	4.01	47.9	**1.2**	17.1	29.9	**7.4**
1.6	0.83	5.3	2.03	**3.4**	3.4	0.90	9.62	4.33	50.0	**1.3**	31.0	41.3	**3.0**
3.9	2.03	12.7	0.00	**3.0**	1.3	0.39	3.51	4.84	75.6	**4.1**	22.5	9.2	**5.9**
1.4	9.22	36.5	2.12	**0.3**	-0.1	-0.16	-1.76	4.40	119.8	**6.7**	48.8	0.9	**2.9**
0.0	7.17	29.9	0.77	**2.1**	2.4	0.47	2.33	3.56	70.6	**1.1**	25.6	33.5	**5.3**
4.9	0.29	2.3	0.01	**4.8**	1.6	1.07	10.62	4.35	88.7	**0.9**	18.3	34.7	**5.5**
0.3	5.34	49.8	1.62	**2.2**	0.5	0.16	2.19	4.22	50.0	**1.1**	8.5	28.0	**3.9**
0.0	14.64	137.0	3.45	**0.0**	-9.0	-4.17	-54.87	4.21	85.4	**0.5**	9.0	53.8	**2.5**
8.1	0.20	0.7	-0.15	**7.1**	1.8	1.79	12.19	4.39	63.9	**4.6**	30.4	8.4	**7.3**
1.7	3.39	20.7	1.35	**2.9**	10.3	0.67	6.63	5.08	62.7	**3.3**	12.7	12.8	**6.3**
2.0	4.74	27.3	1.54	**0.0**	-1.1	-0.46	-4.56	3.33	93.9	**1.8**	22.4	22.4	**6.0**
4.7	0.83	6.0	0.23	**8.2**	3.4	1.71	20.18	4.39	44.0	**2.0**	13.9	19.0	**5.1**
1.2	4.92	39.6	1.87	**1.1**	0.1	0.15	2.04	4.84	87.9	**2.2**	11.5	17.9	**0.7**
4.2	0.62	4.7	0.31	**6.6**	2.4	1.41	15.73	5.08	62.8	**0.8**	12.2	33.7	**5.5**
1.7	3.83	23.5	3.12	**1.3**	0.0	0.02	0.14	4.16	65.4	**1.7**	13.3	21.7	**4.8**
3.0	1.70	14.2	-0.12	**3.1**	0.4	0.63	5.82	4.04	87.2	**3.0**	21.5	14.6	**2.3**
5.4	1.47	8.6	0.43	**3.0**	0.9	0.66	6.77	3.47	73.1	**4.0**	41.9	15.6	**3.0**
4.7	1.61	5.2	0.24	**5.2**	0.9	0.69	3.76	3.63	72.3	**4.1**	30.5	11.3	**7.5**
6.7	0.22	1.6	0.24	**8.7**	2.7	1.33	14.45	4.07	53.5	**3.6**	17.0	11.1	**7.0**
8.3	0.08	0.2	0.00	**2.8**	0.1	0.06	0.60	N/,	57.8	**2.8**	52.8	33.0	**6.0**
6.2	0.36	1.9	0.67	**0.0**	-0.4	-1.18	-11.99	3.31	114.0	**3.8**	35.6	14.7	**3.1**
1.6	2.03	16.1	0.91	**0.5**	-1.8	-3.19	-29.39	3.45	176.0	**2.7**	27.9	17.2	**4.1**
3.7	0.78	6.5	0.74	**3.8**	0.6	0.69	7.33	3.92	63.8	**1.4**	10.7	24.1	**4.8**
9.1	0.08	0.5	0.00	**2.4**	0.1	0.13	1.52	3.02	84.6	**6.0**	48.8	5.4	**6.9**
7.2	0.22	1.2	0.93	**3.2**	0.9	1.19	14.23	3.38	62.7	**2.9**	38.5	20.2	**2.1**
3.5	2.04	13.9	0.27	**4.6**	1.0	0.86	8.32	4.73	69.9	**4.2**	27.2	10.0	**6.3**
7.2	0.16	1.2	0.13	**5.0**	1.4	1.19	13.60	3.59	62.3	**2.0**	27.4	22.6	**5.4**
3.7	0.13	0.8	0.12	**5.2**	0.7	1.01	15.07	4.41	63.2	**2.7**	38.3	22.7	**2.8**
2.2	1.08	6.1	0.65	**1.6**	0.6	0.21	2.20	4.00	85.4	**3.1**	35.5	18.1	**3.3**
8.5	0.36	1.9	0.30	**5.2**	14.1	1.22	13.38	3.76	71.7	**5.4**	26.1	4.7	**8.7**
4.6	0.73	4.6	0.31	**6.6**	1.8	1.58	13.16	5.77	67.8	**1.8**	5.0	19.2	**7.2**
0.3	7.96	44.1	1.04	**0.0**	-2.8	-2.52	-22.60	3.57	114.8	**0.7**	17.3	54.7	**5.8**
5.7	0.55	4.7	0.00	**4.7**	0.4	0.80	9.90	4.64	78.1	**4.4**	26.1	8.0	**5.6**
6.6	0.13	0.8	0.54	**1.9**	0.3	0.32	3.73	4.44	86.2	**2.5**	13.4	16.3	**3.4**
3.9	2.16	12.0	0.21	**7.5**	1.6	1.71	14.54	5.08	60.1	**2.2**	20.4	18.5	**8.1**
3.4	3.86	14.4	1.52	**1.6**	0.5	0.17	1.33	3.30	74.1	**1.8**	38.1	40.7	**5.5**
5.3	0.59	4.3	1.05	**4.8**	1.9	1.06	14.25	5.10	72.3	**3.0**	24.8	15.1	**3.6**
3.1	1.53	13.6	0.47	**2.8**	5.1	0.64	8.60	3.88	77.1	**0.9**	5.7	31.0	**3.4**
2.9	1.76	15.2	0.17	**3.1**	0.8	0.46	5.26	3.76	83.8	**3.2**	16.4	13.1	**3.6**
3.5	2.46	19.4	0.66	**3.4**	5.9	0.46	5.17	3.72	74.6	**1.5**	23.1	31.5	**5.9**
0.2	8.59	27.9	0.28	**3.8**	1.1	0.62	2.83	4.62	67.5	**1.6**	14.1	22.2	**6.8**
4.8	1.77	6.4	4.94	**0.8**	-0.5	-0.36	-3.10	3.39	63.4	**6.8**	60.6	5.1	**5.9**
0.9	3.29	27.7	0.59	**2.0**	1.1	0.07	0.75	3.79	85.2	**2.5**	8.7	15.9	**6.7**
5.8	0.74	7.5	0.01	**1.7**	0.1	0.03	0.29	3.07	97.3	**2.1**	11.1	18.1	**4.2**
5.9	0.15	0.9	0.57	**4.6**	3.5	1.01	10.28	3.12	56.0	**2.2**	32.8	25.3	**5.7**
5.4	3.23	19.1	0.04	**3.9**	0.5	0.76	6.45	3.70	62.4	**1.4**	22.1	27.6	**5.9**
3.8	6.61	18.6	0.53	**2.1**	0.1	0.14	0.97	4.13	90.4	**5.2**	42.9	9.6	**6.6**
8.7	0.00	0.0	0.00	**1.7**	0.3	0.12	1.48	2.39	94.8	**3.8**	44.0	16.8	**3.8**
8.4	0.00	0.0	0.00	**5.6**	0.4	1.28	9.43	4.34	50.6	**1.5**	9.7	22.9	**7.3**
4.5	3.40	11.2	0.54	**1.9**	0.0	0.13	1.01	4.20	92.3	**2.5**	44.0	23.4	**5.5**
0.0	4.46	29.8	0.16	**5.4**	11.6	1.30	15.23	4.24	69.0	**0.7**	14.6	43.9	**6.2**
1.2	2.62	18.6	1.31	**2.1**	0.5	0.44	4.84	3.93	58.5	**3.8**	18.2	10.4	**3.8**
3.0	5.31	22.1	1.18	**5.5**	1.3	0.84	7.37	3.98	52.0	**2.9**	41.8	23.2	**6.3**
2.6	1.56	13.8	0.63	**2.7**	0.3	0.32	3.76	4.16	77.3	**1.2**	14.9	29.5	**4.6**
7.8	0.35	2.3	0.03	**4.4**	1.0	0.87	9.55	3.29	77.0	**1.9**	33.0	29.8	**5.9**
5.4	1.44	8.5	0.00	**2.0**	0.5	0.51	4.79	3.42	75.1	**3.2**	34.9	17.1	**4.7**
5.5	1.26	8.3	0.48	**0.2**	-0.2	-0.33	-3.61	2.81	112.5	**3.7**	34.3	14.7	**4.8**
5.2	0.45	3.4	0.61	**4.1**	0.6	0.89	11.91	5.12	82.6	**1.9**	14.3	19.4	**4.1**

	Name	City	State	Rating	2008 Rating	2007 Rating	Total Assets ($Mil)	One Year Asset Growth	Asset Mix (As a % of Total Assets) Comm-ercial Loans	Cons-umer Loans	Home Mort-gages	Secur-ities	Capital-ization Index	Leverage Ratio	Risk-based Capital Ratio
▲	FAR EAST NATIONAL BK	LOS ANGELES	CA	**D**	D-	D+	1,651	-20.64	7.3	0.0	2.5	13.8	**10.0**	13.5	21.0
	FARM BUREAU BANK FSB	SPARKS	NV	**C-**	C-	C-	571	-2.99	17.7	69.7	0.9	5.4	**5.2**	8.1	11.1
	FARMER CITY STATE BK	FARMER CITY	IL	**B**	B	C+	64	0.77	1.8	1.1	5.9	53.1	**8.9**	10.2	21.9
	FARMERS & DROVERS BANK	COUNCIL GROVE	KS	**A+**	A+	A+	140	5.59	3.2	9.1	15.5	43.2	**10.0**	28.3	49.5
	FARMERS & MECHANICS	GALESBURG	IL	**C-**	C	B+	213	3.46	14.1	5.0	14.6	30.8	**8.5**	10.0	16.6
	FARMERS & MECHANICS	BLOOMFIELD	IN	**C+**	C+	C-	67	5.30	0.0	0.4	51.3	28.7	**10.0**	17.5	38.5
▼	FARMERS & MERCH BANK	BOSWELL	IN	**B-**	B+	A-	103	6.03	9.3	1.7	12.4	18.2	**9.1**	10.4	18.0
▼	FARMERS & MERCH BANK	UPPERCO	MD	**B-**	B-	B	240	11.97	3.9	0.2	10.8	16.5	**7.8**	9.5	13.4
	FARMERS & MERCH BANK &	BURLINGTON	IA	**D-**	D	D+	199	-4.18	10.5	1.9	20.5	14.8	**5.3**	7.3	11.5
▲	FARMERS & MERCH BANK &	MARINETTE	WI	**C-**	C-	C+	155	1.70	6.0	2.7	23.7	29.4	**7.4**	9.3	14.9
	FARMERS & MERCH BANK	ASHLAND	NE	**B-**	B-	B-	64	-0.59	4.8	1.2	21.0	13.5	**9.5**	10.6	15.7
	FARMERS & MERCH BANK OF	COLBY	KS	**C**	D+	B-	119	10.63	5.6	1.0	6.5	40.0	**8.7**	10.1	17.3
	FARMERS & MERCH BANK OF	HOLLY HILL	SC	**A-**	A-	A-	297	11.69	4.2	5.6	13.5	16.7	**10.0**	15.6	29.8
	FARMERS & MERCH BANK W	KITTANNING	PA	**C**	B-	C-	391	7.07	7.1	3.8	29.9	15.7	**7.5**	9.3	15.4
▼	FARMERS & MERCH BK	LODI	CA	**B+**	A	A-	1,842	3.30	8.9	0.4	6.5	26.8	**8.5**	10.0	13.8
	FARMERS & MERCH BK CRAIG	NEW CASTLE	VA	**A-**	A-	A-	52	0.63	3.8	6.4	40.4	25.5	**10.0**	16.6	32.3
	FARMERS & MERCH BK HILL C	HILL CITY	KS	**B**	B+	B+	40	-7.39	7.0	3.3	3.8	7.0	**10.0**	11.2	16.0
	FARMERS & MERCH BK	HUTSONVILLE	IL	**C+**	B-	B	40	2.03	3.4	6.0	9.5	18.8	**10.0**	14.8	42.6
	FARMERS & MERCH BK LONG	LONG BEACH	CA	**B+**	B+	A-	4,262	7.07	2.3	0.5	5.6	47.4	**10.0**	14.3	26.6
	FARMERS & MERCH BK	MOUND CITY	KS	**D+**	C-	C	37	-9.47	8.2	6.7	18.1	27.8	**4.4**	6.4	12.1
	FARMERS & MERCH BK OF	KENDALL	WI	**C-**	C	C	56	-2.56	2.2	4.5	6.0	0.2	**9.9**	11.4	14.9
	FARMERS & MERCH BK	ORFORDVILLE	WI	**D+**	D+	C+	40	9.45	4.6	6.2	22.8	27.6	**8.4**	9.9	17.1
▲	FARMERS & MERCH BK ST	SAINT CLAIR	MO	**C**	C+	C+	167	-4.99	2.2	2.8	26.6	15.6	**7.7**	9.6	13.0
	FARMERS & MERCH NB	NASHVILLE	IL	**B-**	B-	B-	151	2.59	3.5	2.1	19.0	39.1	**10.0**	12.0	23.3
	FARMERS & MERCH NB OF FAI	FAIRVIEW	OK	**A**	A	A-	81	2.78	7.6	4.9	8.8	47.8	**10.0**	11.1	20.9
▼	FARMERS & MERCH NB OF	HATTON	ND	**E**	D-	E-	30	-12.38	22.8	7.0	15.1	5.5	**5.8**	7.8	13.2
	FARMERS & MERCH SB	LONE TREE	IA	**C-**	C-	C-	113	-1.26	4.2	1.6	11.5	34.8	**10.0**	11.0	19.3
	FARMERS & MERCH STATE BK	NEOLA	IA	**C+**	C+	B-	52	1.78	3.4	3.0	14.7	32.2	**7.5**	9.3	20.0
	FARMERS & MERCH STATE BK	ARGONIA	KS	**D**	C-	D-	26	8.35	11.9	4.9	10.3	16.0	**5.3**	7.3	12.5
	FARMERS & MERCH STATE BK	APPLETON	MN	**B**	B-	B	42	0.01	5.3	2.4	2.8	31.0	**10.0**	12.4	18.4
	FARMERS & MERCH STATE BK	BLOOMING PRAIRIE	MN	**C+**	B-	C+	70	3.88	10.5	3.3	13.9	0.3	**5.9**	7.9	11.7
▲	FARMERS & MERCH STATE BK	PIERZ	MN	**C-**	C	C+	168	-3.04	9.3	2.5	12.7	18.1	**8.0**	9.7	13.7
	FARMERS & MERCH STATE BK	SACRED HEART	MN	**C+**	C+	C	24	0.00	5.1	4.8	3.8	19.2	**10.0**	11.9	18.9
▲	FARMERS & MERCH STATE BK	SPRINGFIELD	MN	**C+**	C-	C	105	-1.42	4.8	2.2	5.3	12.5	**5.4**	8.1	11.3
	FARMERS & MERCH STATE BK	BLOOMFIELD	NE	**C+**	C	C+	103	1.09	4.3	4.3	1.8	14.8	**5.9**	8.7	11.7
▲	FARMERS & MERCH STATE BK	ALPHA	MN	**C-**	C	C-	34	16.01	8.8	3.3	9.8	6.7	**8.8**	10.2	15.7
▼	FARMERS & MERCH TRUST	CHAMBERSBURG	PA	**D+**	C	C+	950	-2.81	8.7	1.8	18.5	12.3	**5.3**	7.7	11.2
	FARMERS & MERCHANTS	LAFAYETTE	AL	**A-**	A-	A-	105	2.88	8.1	5.2	7.5	47.0	**10.0**	13.6	21.4
	FARMERS & MERCHANTS	PIEDMONT	AL	**B**	B	B+	200	0.04	9.1	4.1	18.1	27.5	**9.6**	10.7	17.6
	FARMERS & MERCHANTS	WATERLOO	AL	**A-**	A	A	60	-1.31	4.5	5.3	2.3	75.1	**10.0**	18.4	41.6
▼	FARMERS & MERCHANTS	STUTTGART	AR	**C**	C+	B	608	6.21	7.8	3.6	9.5	29.3	**7.8**	9.6	15.5
	FARMERS & MERCHANTS	MONTICELLO	FL	**D**	D+	B	435	-4.66	6.3	1.8	17.9	19.9	**6.0**	8.0	12.5
	FARMERS & MERCHANTS	EATONTON	GA	**D**	C-	B-	219	0.74	5.4	2.9	17.1	23.9	**9.3**	10.6	16.7
	FARMERS & MERCHANTS	LAKELAND	GA	**E-**	E-	D-	596	-9.05	6.8	5.1	22.9	6.8	**0.1**	3.5	6.2
	FARMERS & MERCHANTS	STATESBORO	GA	**D-**	D-	C-	273	-14.32	6.9	2.9	16.2	5.0	**4.9**	6.9	11.1
	FARMERS & MERCHANTS	SYLVANIA	GA	**C+**	C+	B+	129	0.87	4.9	5.9	10.9	25.5	**10.0**	11.9	16.3
	FARMERS & MERCHANTS	LAOTTO	IN	**B-**	B-	C+	101	11.49	4.7	2.9	30.1	28.3	**5.9**	7.9	14.6
▼	FARMERS & MERCHANTS	BALDWYN	MS	**A-**	A-	A+	193	0.55	2.7	9.9	18.6	24.6	**10.0**	14.5	21.3
	FARMERS & MERCHANTS	GRANITE QUARRY	NC	**D**	D+	D+	657	-4.95	4.6	1.1	20.4	4.0	**10.0**	11.2	15.9
	FARMERS & MERCHANTS	AXTELL	NE	**C-**	C-	C-	6	3.59	2.3	6.0	2.0	63.4	**8.2**	9.8	23.0
	FARMERS & MERCHANTS	MILFORD	NE	**B-**	B-	B-	456	5.15	7.1	22.4	10.5	21.4	**6.6**	9.3	12.2
	FARMERS & MERCHANTS	MILLIGAN	NE	**C+**	C	C	48	10.55	5.0	2.4	4.7	0.0	**5.2**	9.4	11.2
	FARMERS & MERCHANTS	CALDWELL	OH	**C-**	C-	B-	76	5.01	12.5	13.3	35.1	9.2	**10.0**	11.6	18.0
▼	FARMERS & MERCHANTS	MIAMISBURG	OH	**D-**	C-	C+	96	7.93	11.6	1.6	29.7	32.0	**6.0**	8.0	15.5
▼	FARMERS & MERCHANTS	ARNETT	OK	**B+**	A-	A-	46	20.11	8.4	8.9	6.9	27.2	**9.4**	10.6	22.1
	FARMERS & MERCHANTS	CRESCENT	OK	**C**	D+	D+	135	0.36	5.5	4.0	17.0	25.2	**9.0**	10.3	15.9
▼	FARMERS & MERCHANTS	DUKE	OK	**C**	C+	B-	17	12.42	1.4	7.1	1.8	7.9	**9.3**	10.5	23.8
	FARMERS & MERCHANTS	MAYSVILLE	OK	**B**	B	B	19	5.98	12.6	21.5	5.6	4.0	**6.5**	8.5	14.1
▲	FARMERS & MERCHANTS	ADAMSVILLE	TN	**C**	B-	B	30	1.77	1.4	10.1	23.9	28.9	**10.0**	12.5	23.5
	FARMERS & MERCHANTS	DYER	TN	**C**	C+	C+	96	7.67	4.1	4.2	18.1	49.0	**5.9**	8.9	11.7

Asset Quality Index	Non-Performing Loans as a % of Total Loans	Non-Performing Loans as a % of Capital	Net Charge-offs Avg Loans	Profitability Index	Net Income ($Mil)	Return on Assets (R.O.A.)	Return on Equity (R.O.E.)	Net Interest Spread	Overhead Efficiency Ratio	Liquidity Index	Liquidity Ratio	Hot Money Ratio	Stability Index
0.3	11.14	34.7	4.84	**0.0**	-40.4	-2.24	-15.27	2.64	96.8	**2.4**	38.8	39.6	**6.0**
2.0	0.80	7.1	2.92	**2.9**	2.1	0.37	4.42	4.50	53.4	**0.5**	8.3	50.4	**4.3**
8.1	0.31	1.0	0.51	**4.4**	0.6	1.00	8.68	4.41	73.3	**5.5**	52.4	9.3	**5.9**
8.4	0.94	1.5	0.09	**8.6**	1.9	1.44	4.92	4.32	48.9	**3.0**	37.4	19.1	**9.6**
3.1	1.05	5.8	0.86	**8.3**	2.9	1.34	10.50	4.49	56.5	**4.3**	20.3	7.5	**7.1**
9.8	0.34	1.0	0.00	**2.1**	0.0	0.06	0.32	2.99	98.9	**3.8**	52.4	18.0	**7.1**
4.7	1.53	7.7	0.57	**3.8**	0.4	0.37	3.39	4.52	64.5	**2.8**	37.1	20.2	**7.0**
3.9	0.97	6.9	0.10	**5.5**	2.2	0.97	10.04	4.53	63.2	**1.5**	14.5	24.5	**5.4**
0.3	3.88	30.6	1.28	**0.8**	0.2	0.07	0.84	4.22	86.1	**4.2**	14.9	7.7	**3.1**
2.5	3.16	18.4	0.01	**2.6**	0.7	0.43	4.39	3.70	79.7	**3.0**	42.9	22.6	**4.1**
6.2	0.62	3.9	-0.03	**4.6**	0.6	0.86	8.26	4.23	69.5	**4.1**	19.8	8.4	**5.8**
3.4	2.38	11.2	0.74	**5.8**	1.2	1.12	10.32	4.24	53.6	**1.8**	24.5	22.9	**5.2**
6.0	2.15	7.0	0.76	**5.5**	1.8	0.74	4.69	3.70	68.9	**3.5**	44.3	18.4	**7.7**
2.4	3.72	25.8	0.14	**4.0**	2.6	0.68	6.61	3.46	62.8	**4.2**	16.0	7.3	**6.2**
5.0	0.45	2.5	1.04	**7.5**	21.9	1.24	12.10	4.70	47.4	**1.5**	12.6	25.4	**9.5**
8.7	0.35	1.4	0.09	**6.8**	0.6	1.17	7.32	4.67	59.5	**3.3**	20.6	12.9	**8.6**
5.3	0.78	4.3	0.93	**4.0**	0.3	0.64	5.65	4.12	75.4	**3.8**	35.5	14.4	**6.4**
9.1	0.00	0.0	0.00	**2.2**	0.1	0.19	1.25	1.30	85.9	**3.1**	56.2	26.4	**7.3**
4.4	4.81	14.8	1.38	**7.2**	53.0	1.27	8.75	4.28	42.3	**2.6**	28.1	23.6	**8.8**
5.6	1.03	9.0	0.05	**4.4**	0.5	1.14	16.85	3.38	72.2	**1.6**	16.6	23.2	**3.0**
0.6	3.04	21.1	0.63	**10.0**	1.6	2.68	25.14	5.70	38.8	**0.4**	2.7	51.5	**8.6**
1.6	5.09	29.4	0.34	**3.6**	0.2	0.62	6.30	3.77	63.8	**3.8**	31.0	13.0	**5.5**
4.6	0.09	0.6	0.79	**3.1**	0.6	0.33	3.52	4.13	73.8	**2.4**	18.5	17.5	**5.0**
8.8	0.44	1.8	0.00	**3.5**	1.2	0.81	6.15	3.48	78.2	**4.1**	28.2	10.7	**7.4**
8.3	0.89	3.1	0.04	**9.3**	1.6	2.13	16.80	4.92	55.8	**2.9**	35.0	19.1	**8.8**
1.3	2.87	21.2	0.81	**0.2**	-0.2	-0.52	-5.31	3.88	97.9	**1.2**	28.6	44.8	**4.3**
2.5	2.76	11.7	1.57	**1.4**	0.4	0.37	3.32	2.94	78.6	**2.0**	19.5	19.3	**5.7**
7.9	0.30	1.4	0.06	**3.3**	0.3	0.63	6.53	2.85	77.2	**4.4**	60.6	16.4	**5.7**
4.6	1.87	16.1	1.35	**2.9**	0.1	0.40	5.04	4.82	89.4	**1.0**	17.9	32.6	**2.3**
4.2	1.33	6.4	0.11	**8.0**	0.7	1.78	14.12	4.63	58.0	**4.9**	34.8	8.1	**9.6**
6.8	0.06	0.5	0.16	**6.8**	1.1	1.55	19.29	4.92	63.4	**0.6**	9.8	49.4	**5.7**
2.5	2.95	20.7	1.12	**8.4**	3.8	2.19	24.44	4.70	44.1	**1.4**	12.9	25.2	**7.0**
7.3	0.32	1.3	-0.01	**3.2**	0.1	0.55	4.65	3.53	81.9	**2.9**	40.9	18.4	**6.8**
5.0	0.66	5.6	0.04	**3.9**	0.9	0.87	10.75	4.03	76.4	**2.9**	7.3	13.6	**4.3**
4.3	0.39	2.7	0.41	**7.9**	1.3	1.30	13.76	4.54	55.7	**2.3**	24.9	18.4	**4.7**
3.7	1.00	6.0	1.67	**2.7**	0.1	0.19	1.73	3.74	71.7	**2.2**	37.0	29.0	**5.1**
0.8	3.74	34.1	0.45	**5.0**	8.3	0.85	10.68	3.88	64.1	**3.3**	3.5	11.3	**5.7**
8.5	0.46	1.4	0.23	**6.0**	1.5	1.42	10.52	5.06	63.0	**2.3**	30.1	20.9	**7.9**
7.5	0.51	2.4	0.16	**4.4**	1.5	0.79	7.11	4.25	72.7	**2.4**	35.7	25.3	**6.2**
9.2	0.01	0.0	0.33	**3.8**	-0.2	-0.25	-1.34	3.98	100.1	**3.8**	72.9	24.6	**8.7**
2.5	2.61	14.7	0.10	**6.5**	7.4	1.29	10.24	4.23	60.8	**1.0**	14.5	31.9	**9.0**
1.6	4.61	34.5	2.79	**0.4**	-2.9	-0.63	-7.56	4.21	68.5	**1.4**	13.7	25.0	**4.5**
0.3	16.37	90.9	0.36	**2.7**	0.7	0.34	3.33	3.32	74.6	**1.4**	17.4	27.1	**3.7**
0.3	5.52	78.9	1.23	**0.0**	-4.7	-0.75	-19.79	3.27	96.6	**0.5**	8.8	53.1	**0.1**
0.0	12.60	101.1	1.17	**0.0**	-6.1	-2.09	-28.05	2.74	94.0	**0.8**	18.1	38.4	**3.4**
6.3	0.28	1.5	1.57	**2.2**	0.3	0.21	1.81	3.98	72.0	**1.1**	16.2	30.7	**5.2**
9.2	0.00	0.0	0.11	**5.3**	1.2	1.26	15.43	4.32	70.4	**5.3**	42.3	9.0	**4.4**
7.3	1.04	4.2	0.73	**6.9**	2.5	1.25	8.34	5.95	62.8	**1.4**	21.5	27.9	**7.5**
0.3	9.22	56.3	2.01	**3.9**	3.0	0.47	4.10	4.17	56.3	**0.8**	13.5	35.2	**6.7**
8.6	0.00	0.0	0.00	**1.8**	0.0	0.29	2.82	4.19	92.4	**2.9**	73.8	33.2	**6.0**
3.6	0.74	5.1	0.42	**7.4**	4.8	1.07	9.45	4.30	51.7	**1.2**	18.8	30.5	**6.6**
6.5	0.00	0.0	0.19	**8.4**	0.8	1.75	18.96	4.92	54.2	**1.4**	4.3	23.0	**5.0**
1.3	3.73	23.9	1.38	**4.8**	0.6	0.84	7.18	5.45	60.6	**2.5**	14.1	16.2	**6.9**
0.3	3.59	24.2	0.31	**3.8**	0.7	0.76	8.99	4.38	69.8	**5.3**	29.8	3.5	**4.2**
7.2	0.56	2.3	0.16	**5.5**	0.5	1.25	10.49	3.45	62.4	**5.1**	39.8	9.2	**8.5**
4.0	0.48	2.5	0.48	**3.2**	0.9	0.72	7.18	4.09	76.7	**1.8**	21.0	22.1	**3.9**
8.1	0.00	0.0	-0.22	**2.2**	0.1	0.36	3.22	2.10	94.9	**4.3**	72.0	17.2	**6.3**
7.4	0.02	0.1	-0.01	**8.2**	0.3	1.83	20.78	3.85	58.4	**3.7**	48.4	16.3	**6.3**
2.7	4.18	15.6	3.46	**1.7**	0.0	-0.09	-0.69	4.80	74.5	**2.9**	39.1	20.7	**5.3**
5.0	1.73	7.9	0.17	**3.3**	0.9	0.95	9.96	4.17	88.0	**4.1**	34.8	12.6	**4.0**

Name	City	State	Rating	2008 Rating	2007 Rating	Total Assets ($Mil)	One Year Asset Growth	Asset Mix (As a % of Total Assets) Commercial Loans	Consumer Loans	Home Mortgages	Securities	Capitalization Index	Leverage Ratio	Risk-based Capital Ratio
FARMERS & MERCHANTS	TREZEVANT	TN	**C**	C	C+	262	28.41	7.4	6.0	22.2	1.9	**5.0**	8.8	11.0
▼ FARMERS & MERCHANTS	DE LEON	TX	**B+**	A-	A-	58	0.20	2.0	3.0	8.3	43.1	**10.0**	12.2	28.3
▼ FARMERS & MERCHANTS	TIMBERVILLE	VA	**C-**	C	C	536	0.17	3.1	4.1	32.0	2.4	**5.6**	7.6	13.9
▼ FARMERS & MERCHANTS	BERLIN	WI	**B-**	B-	B-	173	2.58	9.4	11.4	28.5	11.4	**9.8**	10.9	15.3
FARMERS & MERCHANTS	RUDOLPH	WI	**C**	C-	C	27	1.66	10.9	4.6	29.3	11.8	**8.4**	9.9	15.1
FARMERS & MERCHANTS	TOMAH	WI	**C-**	C+	C+	205	-7.22	7.3	1.9	14.5	20.1	**7.8**	9.6	13.8
▼ FARMERS & MERCHANTS SB	MANCHESTER	IA	**C+**	B-	B-	308	17.88	32.0	2.0	6.5	8.0	**3.8**	9.0	10.4
FARMERS & MERCHANTS SB	WAUKON	IA	**B-**	B	B	119	11.76	4.6	4.6	12.1	28.1	**6.4**	8.5	13.5
FARMERS & MERCHANTS	WINTERSET	IA	**B+**	B+	B+	173	7.30	4.1	1.2	10.9	27.3	**8.8**	10.2	15.2
FARMERS & MERCHANTS	BUSHNELL	IL	**D+**	D	C-	61	-2.19	2.4	8.8	12.4	13.7	**6.4**	8.4	15.0
FARMERS & MERCHANTS	CAWKER CITY	KS	**C-**	C	C	16	4.52	12.6	3.7	11.7	0.0	**3.8**	8.1	10.4
FARMERS & MERCHANTS	NEW YORK MILLS	MN	**C+**	C	B	51	7.94	10.6	1.8	5.5	36.9	**10.0**	14.4	18.8
FARMERS & MERCHANTS	PAYNESVILLE	MN	**B-**	B-	B	23	-0.99	5.9	4.5	5.9	44.7	**9.5**	10.7	27.7
FARMERS & MERCHANTS	LANGDON	ND	**B+**	B+	A-	65	9.48	5.0	4.0	1.0	25.6	**10.0**	13.0	16.5
▼ FARMERS & MERCHANTS	TOLNA	ND	**B-**	B-	B-	51	-0.70	4.9	4.1	1.6	21.8	**8.5**	10.0	16.9
FARMERS & MERCHANTS	ARCHBOLD	OH	**C**	C-	C	906	6.16	13.0	3.2	7.2	31.7	**6.1**	8.1	14.9
FARMERS & MERCHANTS	PLANKINTON	SD	**B-**	C+	C-	71	-0.13	7.4	6.3	6.5	5.5	**6.2**	9.4	11.9
FARMERS & MERCHANTS	SCOTLAND	SD	**C-**	C-	C-	24	-0.48	6.2	4.1	2.1	34.6	**8.0**	9.6	20.2
FARMERS & MERCHANTS	WATERLOO	WI	**C**	C+	B	136	-1.17	3.2	1.8	13.5	22.3	**10.0**	12.0	16.0
▼ FARMERS & MERCHANTS	COLUMBUS	WI	**D+**	D+	C-	265	-10.33	5.5	1.6	11.9	5.6	**6.7**	8.8	12.2
FARMERS & MINERS BANK	PENNINGTON GAP	VA	**B**	B	B	128	0.01	5.0	11.6	25.7	15.4	**10.0**	11.7	20.4
FARMERS & STOCKMENS	CLAYTON	NM	**C-**	B	B-	81	27.45	17.7	2.2	3.2	14.0	**7.4**	9.3	13.3
▲ FARMERS & TRADERS BK	CAMPTON	KY	**C**	C+	B	42	-6.41	10.1	7.7	27.7	29.8	**6.3**	8.3	15.5
FARMERS & TRADERS SB	BANCROFT	IA	**B-**	C+	B-	53	5.34	4.4	2.7	5.6	33.9	**7.3**	9.2	14.9
FARMERS & TRADERS SB	DOUDS	IA	**C-**	C-	C-	17	0.94	2.3	14.6	39.3	0.0	**8.8**	10.2	18.0
▼ FARMERS & TRADERS STATE	SHABBONA	IL	**D+**	C+	C-	52	24.78	6.8	2.7	16.3	6.2	**8.7**	10.2	15.5
▼ FARMERS BANK	GREENWOOD	AR	**B+**	A	A	187	-2.72	8.2	6.1	22.5	34.1	**10.0**	19.5	34.8
FARMERS BANK	HAMBURG	AR	**C-**	C+	B	40	26.99	4.1	5.8	8.0	33.0	**10.0**	11.8	27.4
FARMERS BANK	AULT	CO	**D-**	D-	C+	270	6.69	5.7	0.6	6.2	4.9	**6.1**	8.1	12.1
▲ FARMERS BANK	FORSYTH	GA	**E**	D-	C-	69	-1.32	6.4	4.0	15.4	9.4	**4.2**	6.3	10.6
FARMERS BANK	GREENSBORO	GA	**D**	C-	B	112	0.02	1.5	0.6	4.8	48.9	**8.7**	10.1	22.1
FARMERS BANK	HARDINSBURG	KY	**A**	A	A-	97	4.83	9.5	4.7	14.7	19.5	**10.0**	20.5	29.1
FARMERS BANK	NICHOLASVILLE	KY	**C**	C-	B	91	4.37	1.9	1.7	29.4	27.0	**10.0**	11.3	20.2
FARMERS BANK	CARNEGIE	OK	**C-**	C-	C-	52	3.68	12.9	13.2	2.5	6.6	**6.5**	9.3	12.2
FARMERS BANK	PARSONS	TN	**C-**	C	C+	38	5.72	5.0	8.0	23.9	18.9	**9.8**	10.9	22.2
FARMERS BANK	PORTLAND	TN	**C-**	D+	B	546	8.62	5.3	1.7	14.2	23.4	**7.4**	9.3	14.3
FARMERS BANK	WINDSOR	VA	**D-**	C-	B-	455	8.25	4.1	1.0	12.0	44.0	**5.7**	7.7	15.1
FARMERS BANK & CAPITAL TC	FRANKFORT	KY	**D+**	D+	C-	750	26.95	2.7	2.1	21.2	26.7	**6.6**	8.6	17.0
FARMERS BANK & SAVINGS	POMEROY	OH	**B-**	C+	B-	252	3.45	3.9	6.1	42.3	16.1	**6.4**	8.4	13.7
▼ FARMERS BANK & TRUST	ATWOOD	KS	**C+**	B-	C+	74	12.54	2.6	1.6	3.3	53.1	**5.3**	7.3	16.3
▼ FARMERS BANK & TRUST CO	BLYTHEVILLE	AR	**D+**	D	D	370	-7.04	13.9	3.2	19.1	5.5	**6.8**	8.8	13.0
▲ FARMERS BANK & TRUST CO	MAGNOLIA	AR	**D**	C-	B-	678	4.66	6.6	3.8	24.3	13.8	**6.7**	8.7	12.6
▲ FARMERS BANK & TRUST CO	MARION	KY	**C+**	C	B-	132	-0.79	4.5	7.8	32.5	15.8	**9.7**	10.8	16.1
FARMERS BANK & TRUST CO	PRINCETON	KY	**A**	A	A	108	4.23	1.7	3.9	19.7	37.1	**10.0**	16.7	29.6
FARMERS BANK & TRUST CO	NEBRASKA CITY	NE	**B-**	B-	B-	42	6.91	1.8	2.2	10.3	40.2	**7.4**	9.2	23.3
FARMERS BANK & TRUST NA	GREAT BEND	KS	**D+**	D+	C+	666	-1.10	3.9	0.7	11.0	45.0	**9.3**	10.5	17.0
▲ FARMERS BANK FRANKFORT	FRANKFORT	IN	**C**	B-	B-	436	1.35	10.6	3.4	8.6	24.4	**7.4**	9.3	14.0
FARMERS BANK OF	APPOMATTOX	VA	**B+**	B+	B+	186	12.35	6.2	12.9	19.8	37.1	**10.0**	11.5	19.1
FARMERS BANK OF COOK	COOK	NE	**C-**	D-	D-	81	-4.80	8.7	3.1	20.7	18.3	**6.2**	8.3	12.9
▼ FARMERS BANK OF GREEN	GREEN CITY	MO	**D+**	D	C+	31	8.30	10.1	2.8	8.8	30.2	**7.7**	9.6	13.0
FARMERS BANK OF LIBERTY	LIBERTY	IL	**C-**	C	C	73	5.21	4.8	6.2	15.9	24.4	**5.8**	7.8	13.0
FARMERS BANK OF LINCOLN	LINCOLN	MO	**B**	B	B	90	2.07	5.7	3.4	37.1	15.2	**7.2**	9.1	15.4
▲ FARMERS BANK OF LOHMAN	LOHMAN	MO	**B**	B-	B	52	4.60	3.0	4.5	9.2	67.7	**10.0**	14.9	43.0
▼ FARMERS BANK OF	LYNCHBURG	TN	**E**	D	B	202	-10.27	12.5	4.3	23.3	5.0	**0.8**	4.5	7.7
FARMERS BANK OF MILTON	MILTON	KY	**A-**	A-	A-	173	12.20	2.7	7.3	30.1	40.1	**10.0**	13.7	24.0
FARMERS BANK OF MT	MOUNT PULASKI	IL	**C+**	C	C	42	0.77	1.1	7.9	28.4	33.4	**10.0**	13.3	29.3
FARMERS BANK OF	UNIONVILLE	MO	**B+**	B-	B	325	2.44	3.1	2.6	11.1	35.6	**8.9**	10.3	18.6
FARMERS BANK OF OSBORNE	OSBORNE	KS	**B-**	C	C+	45	3.12	4.3	3.1	3.7	26.9	**9.6**	10.8	17.0
FARMERS BANK OF WILLARDS	WILLARDS	MD	**D-**	D-	D+	331	-1.10	9.4	4.5	34.1	3.0	**7.3**	9.2	12.8
FARMERS BANK WOODLAND	WOODLAND MILLS	TN	**C-**	C	C+	11	-6.55	4.7	9.2	4.8	41.0	**10.0**	18.5	43.8

Asset Quality Index	Non-Performing Loans as a % of Total Loans	Non-Performing Loans as a % of Capital	Net Charge-offs / Avg Loans	Profitability Index	Net Income ($Mil)	Return on Assets (R.O.A.)	Return on Equity (R.O.E.)	Net Interest Spread	Overhead Efficiency Ratio	Liquidity Index	Liquidity Ratio	Hot Money Ratio	Stability Index
3.3	1.57	14.5	0.66	**3.7**	1.2	0.55	6.25	4.60	66.4	**1.1**	17.3	31.1	**3.7**
9.6	0.04	0.1	0.11	**3.7**	0.3	0.48	3.69	4.12	87.9	**4.6**	47.9	13.2	**7.9**
1.4	3.38	33.6	0.49	**4.3**	4.0	0.74	9.52	3.81	56.5	**1.8**	6.3	19.3	**4.8**
3.8	1.09	7.2	0.63	**6.6**	1.9	1.10	9.95	5.74	60.5	**0.6**	8.1	39.4	**6.6**
4.2	1.83	12.6	0.54	**3.6**	0.3	0.92	9.33	4.51	74.0	**2.2**	22.6	18.7	**3.9**
3.0	2.76	17.9	1.14	**2.3**	0.8	0.37	3.98	3.45	64.2	**1.2**	14.5	28.7	**5.1**
4.1	1.21	10.1	0.42	**6.8**	4.3	1.59	17.62	4.42	53.7	**1.6**	18.2	23.7	**5.7**
4.5	1.21	7.4	0.04	**8.0**	2.2	1.93	21.29	4.11	50.0	**5.4**	39.2	7.2	**6.1**
7.8	0.48	2.8	0.12	**6.2**	1.9	1.18	11.66	3.98	55.8	**4.3**	32.0	11.0	**6.0**
5.3	0.03	0.2	0.35	**1.7**	0.3	0.47	5.48	3.36	86.0	**4.2**	35.3	12.2	**2.4**
6.9	0.00	0.0	0.00	**8.4**	0.3	1.94	23.26	4.56	55.6	**0.5**	1.3	38.0	**3.7**
3.1	4.48	16.4	1.41	**2.2**	0.1	0.22	1.40	3.76	82.8	**2.1**	20.7	18.9	**6.5**
8.8	0.45	1.1	0.17	**4.0**	0.2	0.88	7.49	4.33	78.7	**6.6**	68.1	3.1	**5.8**
4.0	0.49	2.5	-0.03	**7.2**	1.1	1.79	13.93	4.43	57.4	**3.2**	20.7	13.7	**7.6**
5.2	1.69	8.9	-0.01	**3.9**	0.3	0.63	5.56	3.76	77.3	**4.0**	41.6	15.0	**6.2**
3.4	1.12	7.5	1.02	**4.3**	6.8	0.77	8.61	3.59	62.1	**2.0**	17.3	19.0	**5.7**
4.2	0.45	3.7	0.24	**10.0**	1.9	2.71	27.08	5.09	42.7	**1.0**	6.0	29.5	**7.4**
8.3	0.01	0.0	-0.02	**1.9**	0.1	0.26	2.53	4.07	99.7	**3.1**	38.6	16.8	**6.2**
1.8	5.12	25.4	1.08	**2.8**	0.5	0.40	3.21	3.42	70.9	**3.5**	16.6	11.6	**6.4**
1.3	0.78	5.7	0.38	**4.2**	2.0	0.70	8.24	4.13	49.5	**0.7**	10.4	36.7	**5.2**
3.6	3.98	18.6	0.46	**4.4**	0.8	0.64	5.66	5.46	71.6	**2.4**	33.8	23.1	**5.7**
6.1	0.59	4.3	0.26	**2.0**	-0.2	-0.27	-2.45	5.26	95.6	**2.4**	21.5	17.8	**4.2**
1.6	1.81	11.1	1.45	**2.2**	0.1	0.22	2.23	4.36	81.5	**1.8**	25.7	23.0	**4.8**
8.5	0.05	0.3	-0.01	**4.5**	0.5	0.97	9.94	3.76	69.7	**4.2**	39.0	13.8	**6.7**
3.0	2.65	18.0	0.04	**3.0**	0.1	0.35	3.50	3.94	88.3	**2.3**	28.7	18.3	**6.0**
1.2	3.46	21.8	0.16	**4.0**	0.6	1.21	11.31	4.81	72.4	**0.9**	20.3	39.4	**4.9**
6.7	1.66	3.7	0.42	**4.8**	1.2	0.61	3.06	4.97	76.2	**2.4**	30.8	19.9	**7.9**
6.8	1.81	3.9	0.03	**0.9**	0.0	-0.08	-0.57	2.84	108.3	**3.5**	63.9	25.1	**8.5**
0.3	6.16	44.9	4.61	**0.9**	-5.8	-2.17	-26.41	3.55	76.2	**0.9**	18.8	37.6	**6.2**
0.0	11.43	92.6	1.28	**1.5**	0.1	0.15	2.60	3.30	88.3	**1.8**	18.0	20.4	**1.8**
0.3	15.45	52.2	3.77	**0.2**	0.0	0.03	0.29	3.00	92.7	**2.4**	24.7	18.0	**3.2**
8.0	0.34	1.0	0.20	**10.0**	1.9	1.99	9.30	5.41	47.9	**4.3**	29.1	10.1	**9.3**
4.8	0.65	3.3	0.96	**1.7**	0.3	0.33	2.74	4.19	82.2	**3.5**	17.3	11.7	**4.8**
2.0	0.93	7.6	0.23	**9.8**	1.1	2.16	22.61	5.44	60.2	**0.8**	5.4	32.7	**7.5**
7.0	0.32	1.5	1.17	**0.6**	-0.1	-0.17	-1.51	4.22	91.6	**2.2**	36.2	28.8	**5.6**
2.3	2.51	16.6	0.76	**5.2**	4.5	0.87	8.96	4.41	60.7	**1.2**	20.8	30.2	**6.5**
2.6	3.89	20.7	3.79	**0.0**	-2.9	-0.67	-8.05	3.26	65.3	**2.0**	37.6	32.1	**3.9**
1.2	5.96	32.0	1.31	**1.5**	3.6	0.49	5.98	3.43	78.2	**3.0**	24.5	14.8	**3.8**
4.5	0.81	6.5	0.33	**6.1**	2.9	1.17	13.89	4.53	58.6	**1.6**	12.8	22.8	**5.2**
6.8	0.00	0.0	1.17	**5.6**	0.8	1.16	13.63	4.12	63.3	**5.9**	46.4	5.5	**5.0**
1.4	3.02	24.3	0.52	**3.1**	2.8	0.73	8.46	4.07	69.4	**0.7**	8.3	36.6	**3.3**
0.7	1.51	12.1	1.10	**5.2**	7.4	1.12	10.92	4.18	53.9	**0.6**	3.5	35.1	**7.4**
3.6	0.70	4.5	0.28	**6.4**	1.6	1.21	11.66	5.01	58.6	**1.8**	7.8	19.1	**5.5**
9.0	0.19	0.6	0.27	**6.8**	1.7	1.60	9.38	3.97	60.5	**4.8**	36.7	9.9	**8.9**
6.0	1.96	6.3	0.00	**4.2**	0.4	0.85	8.11	3.85	75.8	**6.9**	63.2	2.8	**6.4**
2.8	5.12	19.5	3.28	**2.0**	0.1	0.01	0.07	3.50	72.7	**2.6**	30.3	18.6	**5.5**
2.9	1.92	11.9	0.85	**3.6**	2.6	0.59	6.38	3.98	69.0	**3.5**	24.7	12.3	**5.3**
5.4	1.16	5.6	0.18	**4.7**	1.8	0.98	8.66	4.18	70.3	**2.8**	38.1	20.9	**6.2**
3.1	0.49	3.9	0.70	**2.9**	0.4	0.44	5.20	5.20	74.3	**2.7**	11.3	14.9	**3.6**
3.7	2.04	9.3	0.20	**2.5**	0.1	0.44	4.36	3.69	76.5	**2.4**	34.1	22.5	**3.3**
4.3	1.17	8.5	0.05	**5.9**	0.8	1.13	14.20	4.23	58.4	**2.6**	28.1	18.0	**3.4**
7.8	0.12	0.8	0.09	**5.4**	1.2	1.31	14.32	3.90	64.4	**1.5**	20.7	25.4	**6.9**
9.0	0.50	0.8	0.18	**4.0**	0.4	0.77	4.71	3.37	64.0	**6.5**	85.9	9.5	**7.7**
1.1	1.95	17.9	2.77	**0.1**	-6.6	-3.11	-24.74	3.60	156.3	**1.5**	18.2	25.8	**5.1**
6.1	1.63	6.4	0.09	**5.2**	1.9	1.10	7.58	3.72	57.9	**1.7**	32.2	31.9	**7.7**
6.0	1.99	7.6	-0.20	**2.4**	0.2	0.48	3.55	3.54	87.8	**4.1**	37.9	13.7	**6.4**
7.1	0.76	3.7	0.23	**5.4**	3.2	1.03	8.87	3.99	59.0	**4.1**	30.5	11.3	**6.0**
4.1	1.17	5.5	0.11	**5.0**	0.6	1.38	11.84	4.38	63.7	**3.3**	28.4	14.8	**5.5**
0.3	6.76	54.6	1.66	**2.4**	0.5	0.16	1.74	4.27	52.1	**1.3**	5.9	25.2	**5.6**
4.9	5.48	9.6	0.00	**0.6**	0.0	-0.33	-1.80	3.36	110.2	**6.7**	75.9	4.3	**6.6**

Name	City	State	Rating	2008 Rating	2007 Rating	Total Assets ($Mil)	One Year Asset Growth	Asset Mix (As a % of Total Assets) Commercial Loans	Consumer Loans	Home Mortgages	Securities	Capitalization Index	Leverage Ratio	Risk-based Capital Ratio
FARMERS BUILDING & SB	ROCHESTER	PA	**B+**	B+	B	78	24.41	0.2	0.2	44.6	21.5	**10.0**	16.4	41.2
FARMERS CITIZENS BANK	BUCYRUS	OH	**C**	C	C+	356	9.98	1.7	0.2	8.7	39.4	**6.0**	8.0	14.7
FARMERS DEPOSIT BANK	EMINENCE	KY	**C-**	C-	B-	61	-2.98	6.2	1.5	17.2	13.6	**9.3**	10.5	15.9
▲ FARMERS DEPOSIT BANK	MIDDLEBURG	KY	**C**	D+	D	48	2.09	4.8	9.0	17.4	4.9	**8.2**	9.8	14.7
FARMERS EXCHANGE BANK	LOUISVILLE	AL	**E-**	D-	C-	195	2.17	14.4	5.7	16.4	12.6	**2.7**	6.2	9.8
▲ FARMERS EXCHANGE BANK	CHEROKEE	OK	**C**	C-	D	126	14.61	9.4	2.7	7.7	45.2	**6.0**	8.0	15.2
FARMERS EXCHANGE BANK	NESHKORO	WI	**B-**	C+	C-	54	-0.81	9.2	1.9	25.3	16.7	**8.0**	10.0	13.4
FARMERS NATIONAL BK	PHILLIPSBURG	KS	**A-**	B+	B+	97	6.41	12.4	4.4	8.7	12.8	**10.0**	13.2	22.6
FARMERS NATIONAL BK	STAFFORD	KS	**C**	C-	C	99	4.30	10.3	3.8	8.4	16.2	**5.6**	7.6	12.2
FARMERS NATIONAL BK	WALTON	KY	**C+**	B-	B-	83	-2.41	2.2	1.5	29.7	21.8	**6.9**	8.9	14.7
FARMERS NATIONAL BK CANFI	CANFIELD	OH	**C+**	C	B-	971	-3.06	5.7	13.7	17.1	32.1	**5.4**	7.4	13.4
FARMERS NATIONAL BK	DANVILLE	KY	**D+**	C	B+	490	-0.12	4.7	1.1	28.6	25.9	**7.0**	9.0	15.5
FARMERS NATIONAL BK	EMLENTON	PA	**C+**	C+	C+	480	3.14	6.6	2.8	29.4	25.7	**5.9**	7.9	14.5
▲ FARMERS NATIONAL BK OF	BUHL	ID	**D+**	D-	A	370	-5.07	12.4	2.4	4.3	31.9	**10.0**	11.9	18.1
▲ FARMERS NATIONAL BK OF KA	WALNUT	KS	**B-**	C+	B-	37	5.25	6.6	8.3	27.0	13.4	**8.0**	9.7	14.1
▼ FARMERS NATIONAL BK OF LE	LEBANON	KY	**C-**	C-	B-	95	-2.10	6.5	4.2	10.1	30.0	**8.8**	10.2	16.6
FARMERS NB OF CYNTHIANA	CYNTHIANA	KY	**D+**	D+	A	117	-19.82	12.3	1.8	7.2	40.4	**10.0**	11.5	23.2
FARMERS NB OF	GRIGGSVILLE	IL	**C+**	C	C	51	5.58	1.4	6.4	14.6	13.1	**5.8**	8.9	11.6
FARMERS NB OF NEW CASTLE	NEWCASTLE	TX	**B-**	B-	C+	30	17.96	9.0	8.7	9.0	17.2	**7.3**	9.2	19.0
FARMERS NB OF	PROPHETSTOWN	IL	**B+**	B+	B+	432	4.49	1.8	1.0	5.7	45.9	**10.0**	11.3	18.0
FARMERS NB OF	BOWLING GREEN	KY	**B+**	B+	A	239	8.28	3.1	2.9	20.4	36.5	**10.0**	15.1	24.6
FARMERS SB	COLESBURG	IA	**B**	B-	C+	129	3.21	10.7	4.2	10.1	22.5	**5.6**	8.7	11.5
▲ FARMERS SB	FOSTORIA	IA	**B+**	B-	B	71	23.87	6.1	3.4	13.2	24.9	**10.0**	15.1	20.3
FARMERS SB	FREDERIKA	IA	**B+**	B+	B+	41	0.27	5.5	3.2	11.6	41.5	**10.0**	15.0	28.5
FARMERS SB	KEOTA	IA	**B-**	B	B	74	2.41	2.7	1.1	1.2	47.1	**10.0**	13.6	24.8
FARMERS SB	MARSHALLTOWN	IA	**B-**	C+	C+	119	0.59	11.8	2.7	19.8	15.3	**10.0**	12.2	16.9
▼ FARMERS SB	REMSEN	IA	**C-**	B-	B+	133	7.17	3.3	0.5	4.9	10.8	**8.0**	10.6	13.4
FARMERS SB	VICTOR	IA	**A-**	A-	A-	34	-9.23	12.1	3.3	15.3	15.4	**10.0**	16.4	22.4
FARMERS SB	WALFORD	IA	**D**	D	D	44	-2.02	3.7	1.7	7.6	51.3	**8.6**	10.0	18.4
FARMERS SB	WEVER	IA	**C**	C	C	85	10.33	5.8	5.0	34.7	14.4	**5.3**	7.3	12.2
FARMERS SB	SPENCER	OH	**A-**	A-	A	249	4.65	1.8	0.9	18.7	54.1	**10.0**	21.0	51.1
FARMERS SB	MINERAL POINT	WI	**D+**	C-	C+	222	4.87	8.4	17.6	10.9	23.5	**6.1**	8.1	14.0
FARMERS SB & TRUST	TRAER	IA	**C+**	C	C	146	-1.21	4.6	1.9	15.1	32.9	**4.8**	6.8	13.3
FARMERS SECURITY BANK	WASHBURN	ND	**B-**	B	B	39	12.03	7.1	4.2	7.7	24.7	**6.6**	8.6	13.8
FARMERS STATE BK	DUBLIN	GA	**B+**	A-	A-	120	0.82	46.1	6.6	11.0	22.2	**10.0**	12.0	17.0
FARMERS STATE BK	LINCOLNTON	GA	**C**	C-	B+	120	-1.18	3.9	4.9	23.2	28.3	**10.0**	11.2	20.6
▼ FARMERS STATE BK	LUMPKIN	GA	**E-**	E	D-	50	-8.20	7.6	11.1	13.5	29.8	**4.6**	6.6	11.6
▼ FARMERS STATE BK	ALGONA	IA	**C-**	C+	C+	87	3.70	11.5	2.4	10.2	8.5	**5.5**	8.2	11.4
FARMERS STATE BK	LAKE VIEW	IA	**B-**	B	B	28	-0.15	11.0	6.9	18.0	22.6	**10.0**	11.4	25.0
FARMERS STATE BK	MARCUS	IA	**B+**	B+	A-	68	6.00	5.6	3.4	8.7	31.9	**10.0**	12.2	20.7
▲ FARMERS STATE BK	MARION	IA	**B+**	B-	B+	592	0.17	10.6	1.9	9.5	19.8	**10.0**	11.1	15.2
FARMERS STATE BK	NORTHWOOD	IA	**B**	B-	B-	134	9.48	5.5	3.9	14.8	32.9	**6.8**	8.8	14.7
FARMERS STATE BK	WATERLOO	IA	**C**	C	C-	313	25.97	13.0	4.9	9.9	17.1	**3.3**	7.5	10.2
FARMERS STATE BK	YALE	IA	**C-**	C-	C-	41	1.56	4.0	3.1	9.9	37.9	**5.8**	7.8	13.8
▼ FARMERS STATE BK	ELMWOOD	IL	**D+**	C	C-	51	10.95	2.1	2.9	24.5	37.7	**6.8**	8.8	15.6
FARMERS STATE BK	PITTSFIELD	IL	**C+**	B	B-	230	-1.94	5.2	2.5	10.3	20.0	**8.2**	9.8	13.7
FARMERS STATE BK	BROOKSTON	IN	**C-**	C-	C	65	5.21	5.2	4.2	37.7	26.5	**7.7**	9.5	17.2
FARMERS STATE BK	LAGRANGE	IN	**C**	B-	B-	457	-4.37	4.5	2.2	35.5	12.4	**6.6**	8.6	14.1
FARMERS STATE BK	MENTONE	IN	**C+**	C+	C+	115	1.87	6.1	1.7	23.6	21.5	**8.3**	9.9	16.0
FARMERS STATE BK	SWEETSER	IN	**B-**	B-	B-	17	-5.56	4.0	2.6	13.5	36.9	**10.0**	14.7	36.3
FARMERS STATE BK	ATWOOD	KS	**C-**	C-	C-	22	-0.81	3.7	3.4	6.8	21.0	**6.3**	8.3	16.0
▼ FARMERS STATE BK	DWIGHT	KS	**C+**	B-	C-	16	5.53	2.1	2.8	4.2	42.9	**10.0**	11.6	20.4
FARMERS STATE BK	FAIRVIEW	KS	**D**	C-	D	22	2.77	1.2	6.5	13.2	16.9	**5.1**	7.1	12.1
FARMERS STATE BK	HOLTON	KS	**C**	C-	D+	56	6.04	13.2	2.2	21.7	32.7	**7.5**	9.4	15.8
▲ FARMERS STATE BK	MCPHERSON	KS	**C+**	C	C	83	2.57	8.9	5.6	24.4	31.8	**5.6**	7.6	13.0
▲ FARMERS STATE BK	PHILLIPSBURG	KS	**D+**	C	D+	32	-3.67	11.3	6.6	12.9	31.8	**6.4**	8.4	14.3
▲ FARMERS STATE BK	WATHENA	KS	**B**	B+	A-	62	2.80	12.7	5.6	18.3	37.2	**10.0**	15.2	29.1
▼ FARMERS STATE BK	WESTMORELAND	KS	**C**	B-	A-	125	3.20	9.3	3.5	18.3	18.0	**10.0**	14.1	15.3
▲ FARMERS STATE BK	BOONEVILLE	KY	**C**	C+	B	54	3.37	8.0	7.8	27.0	28.9	**6.6**	8.6	15.3
FARMERS STATE BK	CAMERON	MO	**B-**	B-	B-	168	5.08	1.6	2.0	52.3	5.9	**9.0**	10.3	14.3

Asset Quality Index	Non-Performing Loans as a % of Total Loans	Non-Performing Loans as a % of Capital	Net Charge-offs / Avg Loans	Profitability Index	Net Income ($Mil)	Return on Assets (R.O.A.)	Return on Equity (R.O.E.)	Net Interest Spread	Overhead Efficiency Ratio	Liquidity Index	Liquidity Ratio	Hot Money Ratio	Stability Index
6.5	4.26	11.9	0.00	**4.6**	0.7	0.97	5.64	3.01	57.3	**7.1**	59.2	0.0	**7.7**
6.5	0.44	2.7	0.19	**3.0**	2.0	0.58	6.99	2.80	74.3	**3.9**	37.5	14.9	**3.7**
2.8	0.76	4.3	0.22	**6.9**	0.7	1.11	7.24	4.36	62.5	**1.6**	8.8	20.9	**7.4**
1.4	1.35	8.8	1.14	**1.6**	0.2	0.31	2.47	4.27	91.5	**1.8**	25.3	22.8	**5.4**
0.0	9.29	89.3	2.06	**0.7**	0.1	0.06	1.00	3.51	72.1	**0.7**	15.6	52.9	**0.0**
3.1	2.89	15.0	0.34	**5.2**	1.5	1.26	12.77	4.48	69.1	**2.3**	34.1	25.2	**4.2**
4.0	2.10	11.3	1.34	**5.6**	0.5	1.00	7.90	4.44	61.0	**5.0**	39.1	9.8	**7.0**
8.4	0.32	1.3	0.02	**5.5**	1.0	1.01	7.80	3.72	59.4	**4.2**	41.7	14.1	**7.7**
5.6	0.62	4.3	0.05	**3.6**	0.7	0.72	9.30	4.38	70.7	**2.0**	26.7	21.0	**5.0**
4.8	1.00	6.9	0.20	**3.2**	0.3	0.31	3.45	3.83	84.2	**2.6**	15.6	15.9	**5.5**
3.3	1.51	10.7	1.01	**4.0**	8.8	0.87	11.75	4.11	61.0	**3.3**	18.6	13.1	**5.8**
1.6	4.51	26.6	1.67	**2.5**	1.6	0.31	3.30	3.75	69.7	**1.6**	18.4	24.2	**5.8**
3.5	2.12	16.0	0.13	**3.6**	3.4	0.72	8.17	3.53	74.2	**3.6**	21.5	11.8	**5.1**
0.9	9.97	41.8	2.46	**2.5**	1.4	0.37	2.97	3.88	72.8	**2.3**	31.3	22.4	**6.4**
7.0	0.40	3.0	0.15	**4.6**	0.3	0.77	7.95	4.15	71.3	**0.9**	15.4	33.2	**5.7**
2.6	4.14	21.7	0.06	**1.9**	0.4	0.39	3.56	3.58	97.9	**3.0**	32.8	17.5	**5.6**
0.3	18.00	59.7	3.83	**0.3**	-0.8	-0.60	-5.26	2.62	84.5	**1.9**	32.6	28.4	**4.4**
3.0	2.05	15.5	0.09	**7.2**	0.9	1.71	19.48	4.99	64.5	**3.2**	15.3	13.2	**6.2**
5.1	2.64	13.4	0.60	**5.8**	0.3	1.00	10.39	5.57	68.9	**7.0**	55.1	0.0	**5.0**
6.6	2.04	8.1	0.64	**4.9**	4.9	1.19	10.06	3.64	44.0	**1.6**	31.4	32.0	**7.7**
5.8	1.65	5.7	0.36	**4.1**	1.7	0.76	4.68	3.95	75.1	**2.2**	24.9	19.1	**7.9**
4.6	1.08	8.4	0.23	**8.3**	2.4	1.90	22.97	4.99	47.2	**1.5**	4.7	21.1	**5.9**
5.0	1.25	5.5	-0.11	**6.1**	0.8	1.17	7.34	4.29	59.2	**4.3**	30.8	10.4	**7.0**
7.5	2.04	5.2	0.54	**4.2**	0.3	0.63	4.04	2.60	60.8	**6.2**	66.4	8.2	**8.4**
6.7	1.43	4.2	1.60	**3.8**	0.7	0.95	6.74	3.95	65.0	**6.2**	44.0	2.8	**8.1**
3.9	1.06	5.9	0.92	**3.9**	0.8	0.68	5.57	4.29	66.6	**2.7**	20.1	15.9	**6.1**
1.5	2.85	19.8	0.00	**2.0**	0.0	0.00	0.00	N/,	0.0	**3.2**	32.3	16.4	**5.7**
7.5	0.00	0.0	0.36	**5.2**	0.4	1.13	6.84	3.88	59.3	**4.0**	34.6	13.4	**9.4**
3.7	3.90	13.3	2.37	**0.9**	-0.1	-0.22	-2.10	4.06	89.6	**5.1**	59.6	12.8	**3.1**
4.4	0.55	4.9	0.23	**5.9**	0.9	1.09	15.33	4.40	53.0	**2.8**	20.1	15.3	**4.6**
5.2	7.78	13.2	1.30	**8.0**	4.8	1.95	8.76	4.44	32.1	**3.8**	62.8	23.8	**9.0**
2.0	2.10	15.1	0.54	**5.4**	2.8	1.27	14.89	3.88	52.0	**4.7**	30.2	7.9	**5.6**
4.7	0.50	3.6	0.03	**4.9**	2.3	1.57	20.50	3.36	69.1	**4.6**	36.1	10.8	**4.5**
7.5	0.02	0.1	0.07	**3.4**	0.2	0.45	5.06	3.83	83.5	**4.1**	18.5	8.5	**4.7**
3.1	2.37	12.7	0.60	**5.5**	1.5	1.22	10.00	4.13	67.8	**2.0**	30.4	25.1	**7.8**
2.4	6.46	26.7	0.92	**5.4**	1.5	1.21	10.60	4.52	60.2	**1.5**	31.1	33.1	**6.5**
1.0	7.16	48.9	0.94	**0.0**	-0.6	-1.17	-17.13	3.60	111.0	**1.7**	27.8	27.4	**0.8**
2.1	1.32	11.2	0.32	**6.0**	1.3	1.55	19.37	4.26	58.9	**3.9**	18.0	9.7	**4.7**
7.2	0.39	1.6	1.12	**4.1**	0.2	0.61	5.43	4.14	62.3	**6.0**	55.6	6.5	**6.1**
8.5	0.05	0.2	0.80	**5.0**	0.7	1.20	9.24	3.43	54.0	**5.6**	51.3	8.7	**7.1**
5.6	1.34	7.5	0.53	**6.0**	8.4	1.45	12.51	4.52	60.9	**3.8**	27.7	11.7	**6.4**
5.1	0.99	6.5	0.08	**6.9**	1.7	1.36	14.44	4.54	60.6	**1.7**	26.8	25.8	**5.8**
4.9	0.16	1.6	0.42	**6.1**	4.1	1.45	18.46	4.65	55.1	**2.0**	12.3	18.6	**3.6**
4.6	1.50	8.9	0.06	**4.0**	0.4	0.90	10.41	3.54	74.2	**4.4**	48.1	14.5	**3.7**
4.6	2.78	14.1	0.55	**1.1**	-0.1	-0.24	-2.49	3.71	81.1	**3.1**	42.9	20.7	**5.2**
2.8	2.97	18.9	0.49	**4.9**	2.5	1.05	10.63	4.18	65.3	**3.1**	14.4	13.4	**6.7**
3.2	2.31	14.7	0.62	**1.9**	0.2	0.23	2.39	3.45	87.9	**2.3**	32.8	23.6	**5.0**
2.5	1.77	13.4	0.32	**4.4**	4.0	0.86	9.02	4.01	69.1	**3.9**	17.7	10.0	**6.0**
5.2	1.46	8.8	0.49	**3.2**	0.6	0.57	5.63	4.33	82.7	**3.1**	29.0	15.7	**5.2**
8.0	1.91	4.8	0.30	**3.2**	0.1	0.47	3.06	4.10	86.0	**3.7**	67.5	19.5	**7.1**
8.7	0.00	0.0	0.00	**3.0**	0.1	0.46	5.68	3.19	74.2	**4.4**	32.4	7.9	**5.3**
8.9	0.00	0.0	0.00	**1.5**	0.0	0.02	0.16	3.91	99.5	**5.3**	48.2	7.6	**6.5**
4.6	0.84	6.7	0.05	**3.5**	0.2	0.70	9.81	3.92	76.7	**3.1**	30.9	14.6	**2.3**
4.5	1.29	7.2	0.54	**2.9**	0.3	0.49	5.09	3.82	83.0	**1.6**	24.8	26.2	**4.2**
7.5	0.06	0.4	0.80	**4.7**	0.8	0.97	11.71	4.55	66.5	**3.7**	35.3	15.1	**3.9**
2.3	2.58	16.0	1.80	**3.0**	0.1	0.33	3.76	4.47	65.1	**1.7**	31.1	31.4	**5.7**
4.1	4.99	15.9	1.40	**4.0**	0.4	0.72	4.25	4.40	69.5	**4.5**	41.6	13.0	**7.5**
1.7	8.19	36.5	1.90	**3.7**	0.7	0.53	3.80	3.94	54.5	**1.6**	14.3	23.5	**6.7**
3.2	1.23	7.6	0.74	**5.4**	0.8	1.47	16.77	4.45	68.4	**1.6**	21.5	24.7	**5.6**
4.8	1.30	10.2	0.11	**4.7**	1.3	0.81	7.57	4.36	75.0	**3.1**	11.9	13.4	**6.2**

Name	City	State	Rating	2008 Rating	2007 Rating	Total Assets ($Mil)	One Year Asset Growth	Asset Mix (As a % of Total Assets) Commercial Loans	Consumer Loans	Home Mortgages	Securities	Capitalization Index	Leverage Ratio	Risk-based Capital Ratio
FARMERS STATE BK	VICTOR	MT	**D-**	D	C-	321	-0.03	6.8	3.5	11.2	33.3	**6.6**	8.6	15.2
FARMERS STATE BK	CARROLL	NE	**D+**	C-	D+	23	7.92	2.0	2.0	2.6	43.5	**5.6**	7.6	14.1
FARMERS STATE BK	DODGE	NE	**C-**	C	C-	44	-4.32	8.6	2.0	3.7	26.4	**8.0**	9.6	14.3
FARMERS STATE BK	EWING	NE	**A-**	A-	A-	18	17.50	19.5	2.6	1.4	3.4	**10.0**	23.4	35.3
▼FARMERS STATE BK	HUMPHREY	NE	**B+**	A-	B	34	11.11	3.2	0.9	0.9	36.5	**7.4**	9.3	19.0
▼FARMERS STATE BK	MAYWOOD	NE	**D+**	B-	C	98	9.03	5.0	2.2	9.6	20.8	**6.3**	8.4	12.0
FARMERS STATE BK	WALLACE	NE	**D+**	C-	C+	42	12.97	5.6	2.6	6.9	40.0	**6.5**	8.5	16.5
FARMERS STATE BK	NEW MADISON	OH	**B-**	B-	B	118	4.68	7.9	4.0	25.2	23.4	**9.6**	10.7	18.0
FARMERS STATE BK	WEST SALEM	OH	**C**	B-	B-	81	4.84	2.2	3.6	40.3	19.0	**7.2**	9.2	15.6
FARMERS STATE BK	QUINTON	OK	**C+**	C+	C+	74	10.63	5.2	6.8	18.4	39.0	**6.0**	8.0	15.2
FARMERS STATE BK	FAITH	SD	**D-**	D-	C-	42	-1.03	6.8	2.3	1.9	29.4	**6.7**	8.7	14.5
FARMERS STATE BK	HOSMER	SD	**B**	B+	B	18	0.41	26.5	5.9	0.0	7.7	**10.0**	14.3	17.7
▼FARMERS STATE BK	MARION	SD	**C**	C+	B-	61	-27.68	5.2	3.4	5.8	3.2	**5.0**	7.4	11.0
FARMERS STATE BK	PARKSTON	SD	**A**	A	A	132	1.48	12.2	3.3	0.0	44.0	**10.0**	12.1	21.7
FARMERS STATE BK	STICKNEY	SD	**C-**	NR	NR	102	90.93	7.2	3.4	1.4	19.6	**5.2**	8.8	11.2
FARMERS STATE BK	MOUNTAIN CITY	TN	**D**	C-	B+	133	1.37	1.2	5.9	26.5	22.8	**10.0**	15.2	21.7
FARMERS STATE BK	BERTRAM	TX	**B**	B	B+	35	3.24	2.5	9.7	6.9	55.6	**10.0**	13.1	33.5
FARMERS STATE BK	CENTER	TX	**B+**	A-	B+	325	-0.51	12.0	5.0	8.5	31.1	**8.4**	9.9	15.7
FARMERS STATE BK	GROESBECK	TX	**A-**	B+	B+	116	3.05	3.1	7.4	12.9	30.4	**6.7**	8.7	18.2
FARMERS STATE BK	WINTHROP	WA	**B-**	B-	B-	23	9.66	6.1	2.5	3.8	53.5	**10.0**	14.4	52.7
FARMERS STATE BK	MARKESAN	WI	**C-**	B-	B+	78	-5.45	7.1	2.6	11.0	37.5	**10.0**	12.1	22.8
▼FARMERS STATE BK	PINE BLUFFS	WY	**D**	C+	C+	22	13.02	12.0	9.9	0.0	20.8	**6.3**	8.4	16.3
FARMERS STATE BK & TRUST	JACKSONVILLE	IL	**C+**	C+	B-	175	-1.66	11.8	5.5	15.1	30.8	**10.0**	11.7	17.9
FARMERS STATE BK & TRUST	MOUNT STERLING	IL	**C-**	C	C	77	21.19	15.4	2.9	9.5	15.2	**5.3**	7.8	11.2
FARMERS STATE BK & TRUST	CHURCH POINT	LA	**B**	B	C+	87	7.54	5.9	8.6	16.1	29.9	**6.7**	8.7	15.6
▼FARMERS STATE BK ALLEN	ALLEN	OK	**C+**	C+	C-	39	2.33	8.8	17.0	16.8	17.6	**8.9**	10.3	15.4
▼FARMERS STATE BK ASTORIA	ASTORIA	IL	**B-**	B	B+	18	5.98	2.4	13.5	20.7	22.8	**5.9**	7.9	17.4
FARMERS STATE BK FULTON	LEWISTOWN	IL	**A-**	A-	A-	63	-0.64	4.3	0.8	12.8	29.0	**9.4**	10.6	19.3
▼FARMERS STATE BK	HIGHLAND	KS	**C**	B	B	13	-12.79	5.1	0.7	1.7	18.3	**10.0**	14.4	36.4
FARMERS STATE BK	HILLSBORO	WI	**A**	A	A	92	5.40	2.4	3.6	14.7	40.5	**10.0**	16.0	19.0
FARMERS STATE BK OF	ADAMS	MN	**A-**	B	A-	77	2.49	4.4	1.6	2.1	17.6	**10.0**	11.6	16.7
FARMERS STATE BK OF ALICE	WESTPHALIA	KS	**B-**	B-	B	111	4.32	4.0	2.6	14.0	15.5	**5.2**	7.2	11.8
FARMERS STATE BK OF ALTO	HARRISBURG	IL	**D+**	D	D	183	-24.74	15.1	4.0	21.6	11.6	**7.6**	9.4	13.3
FARMERS STATE BK OF BLUE	BLUE MOUND	KS	**C-**	B	B	39	1.98	3.1	3.1	6.4	9.0	**10.0**	13.4	19.8
FARMERS STATE BK OF	BRUSH	CO	**B+**	B+	A-	90	2.17	2.6	4.3	3.4	31.7	**10.0**	16.2	26.2
FARMERS STATE BK OF	BUCKLIN	KS	**C-**	C-	C-	40	9.72	3.5	1.9	3.6	56.3	**3.8**	5.8	14.7
FARMERS STATE BK OF	CALHAN	CO	**B+**	B+	B+	177	6.69	5.7	3.7	18.3	36.3	**10.0**	11.3	17.3
▲FARMERS STATE BK OF CAMP	CAMP POINT	IL	**B**	B	B	52	10.78	8.4	1.9	4.3	54.9	**7.3**	9.2	19.4
FARMERS STATE BK OF	CANTON	SD	**C+**	C+	C	43	3.25	9.7	7.8	20.6	13.6	**7.5**	9.3	15.0
▼FARMERS STATE BK OF	CROSBY	ND	**B+**	A-	A-	53	9.99	2.5	0.6	0.8	72.0	**10.0**	11.4	24.0
FARMERS STATE BK OF	DANFORTH	IL	**C+**	B+	B	58	7.92	6.1	1.6	6.8	41.6	**5.2**	7.2	16.0
FARMERS STATE BK OF	DARWIN	MN	**B-**	B-	B	31	10.24	11.5	6.4	6.5	33.0	**6.5**	8.5	13.6
▼FARMERS STATE BK OF DENT	DENT	MN	**E+**	D	D	31	2.12	9.7	5.2	12.5	9.2	**5.4**	7.4	12.3
FARMERS STATE BK OF	DENTON	MT	**B-**	B-	C+	18	-5.91	8.0	7.4	0.0	14.2	**10.0**	11.6	16.6
▼FARMERS STATE BK OF	ELKTON	MN	**B-**	B	B	43	2.72	5.7	3.3	6.0	32.0	**9.1**	10.4	16.7
FARMERS STATE BK OF	EMDEN	IL	**B-**	B-	B-	35	1.07	1.9	1.6	2.7	58.7	**10.0**	24.0	54.4
FARMERS STATE BK OF	HAMEL	MN	**C-**	C-	C	84	10.16	6.5	0.5	7.1	33.2	**10.0**	11.5	24.6
▲FARMERS STATE BK OF	HARTLAND	MN	**C-**	D	C-	91	7.05	18.0	1.5	4.4	14.1	**5.8**	8.2	11.6
FARMERS STATE BK OF	HOFFMAN	IL	**A-**	B+	B	124	0.70	3.1	2.8	15.9	43.0	**10.0**	13.2	25.7
FARMERS STATE BK OF	HOFFMAN	MN	**B**	B-	C+	27	-5.35	10.1	4.0	6.8	39.2	**9.5**	10.7	18.4
▼FARMERS STATE BK OF	JETMORE	KS	**C-**	C+	C+	18	2.02	1.2	2.8	3.1	46.3	**10.0**	11.7	32.0
FARMERS STATE BK OF	MADELIA	MN	**B-**	B-	B-	63	8.46	9.4	3.4	11.0	11.0	**8.3**	9.9	17.9
FARMERS STATE BK OF	MEDORA	IL	**B-**	C	C+	18	-6.37	2.1	3.4	3.6	60.8	**10.0**	15.9	40.9
FARMERS STATE BK OF	MUNITH	MI	**D-**	D	D+	61	-1.18	1.1	3.6	45.2	0.9	**6.4**	8.4	15.4
FARMERS STATE BK OF	OAKLEY	KS	**C**	C-	B-	99	7.97	6.6	2.7	6.6	42.3	**10.0**	12.4	22.1
FARMERS STATE BK OF	SHERBURN	MN	**C+**	B-	C+	29	0.82	4.8	3.1	4.6	7.0	**6.2**	8.2	13.6
▲FARMERS STATE BK OF	SUBLETTE	IL	**E+**	D-	C-	50	-13.64	13.8	3.7	9.4	42.4	**6.1**	8.2	16.2
FARMERS STATE BK OF	TRIMONT	MN	**B+**	B	B	53	-5.59	12.0	2.2	3.5	32.3	**10.0**	13.4	18.7
FARMERS STATE BK OF	TURTON	SD	**B-**	B-	B-	21	0.47	2.9	4.5	0.5	15.1	**10.0**	13.1	18.0
FARMERS STATE BK OF	UNDERWOOD	MN	**C+**	C+	C+	44	5.47	6.1	7.5	17.6	13.2	**6.6**	8.6	13.1

Asset Quality Index	Non-Performing Loans as a % of Total Loans	Non-Performing Loans as a % of Capital	Net Charge-offs Avg Loans	Profitability Index	Net Income ($Mil)	Return on Assets (R.O.A.)	Return on Equity (R.O.E.)	Net Interest Spread	Overhead Efficiency Ratio	Liquidity Index	Liquidity Ratio	Hot Money Ratio	Stability Index
0.9	6.26	29.9	3.42	0.2	-0.8	-0.25	-2.65	4.29	79.9	2.6	36.0	21.7	4.7
8.4	0.00	0.0	0.27	3.6	0.1	0.60	8.02	3.62	75.3	3.8	48.7	15.5	3.0
2.8	1.94	12.1	0.19	2.8	0.3	0.57	5.80	3.42	79.5	1.8	19.7	20.6	5.8
7.9	0.78	2.1	0.00	5.0	0.1	0.78	3.18	3.98	72.1	2.5	39.2	20.1	7.6
9.2	0.00	0.0	0.00	4.5	0.3	0.92	9.74	3.09	73.1	6.9	64.9	2.8	7.1
1.7	2.42	17.0	0.13	5.0	0.9	1.00	10.20	4.65	68.3	2.0	23.4	19.6	6.2
5.8	1.87	9.2	0.00	2.5	0.2	0.39	4.56	2.81	76.4	5.1	51.2	11.5	2.9
3.3	0.83	4.6	0.53	4.0	0.8	0.68	6.28	3.99	70.2	1.7	13.1	21.0	6.5
3.8	2.56	17.0	0.29	3.7	0.5	0.58	6.21	4.06	83.2	4.5	24.5	6.5	5.4
5.8	1.01	5.5	0.23	4.1	0.8	1.05	12.64	4.98	90.3	4.8	44.0	11.7	4.3
0.5	3.72	20.1	1.34	2.0	0.1	0.20	2.22	5.03	72.9	1.8	36.5	34.2	4.1
5.1	3.20	15.1	0.91	6.6	0.2	1.09	7.63	5.10	68.3	0.7	16.3	38.3	9.6
4.9	0.37	3.2	0.00	2.2	-0.4	-0.49	-4.88	N/,	58.9	4.8	26.3	5.3	5.1
8.5	0.00	0.0	-0.01	5.9	1.3	1.02	7.87	3.95	59.1	5.5	48.2	9.5	7.9
3.3	1.17	8.6	0.20	8.1	1.0	1.49	18.91	6.31	53.2	2.0	17.8	19.2	3.9
0.3	13.20	52.0	0.23	2.8	0.4	0.32	2.15	4.36	72.9	2.2	14.5	18.0	7.1
8.2	0.61	1.1	0.25	4.1	0.3	0.81	6.14	4.21	75.1	4.3	78.2	19.6	8.1
6.5	0.70	3.4	0.22	5.4	4.1	1.26	11.34	3.93	62.8	2.5	34.2	20.9	7.6
8.6	0.20	0.9	0.07	6.1	1.5	1.28	12.18	4.74	74.5	4.1	39.5	14.2	7.9
8.3	2.88	4.6	0.57	3.0	0.1	0.35	2.18	4.16	87.8	7.7	86.0	0.0	7.3
4.6	3.66	12.6	0.76	1.3	-0.4	-0.51	-3.77	4.86	86.1	5.0	50.8	11.8	6.1
4.6	1.30	6.0	7.89	1.2	-0.9	-4.39	-40.53	4.22	102.6	5.5	52.2	7.5	4.1
5.0	3.02	13.5	0.81	2.0	0.1	0.07	0.55	3.64	84.1	4.4	31.1	10.0	5.9
6.1	0.17	1.5	0.55	4.7	0.6	0.78	9.61	4.26	66.6	1.9	23.8	21.1	4.2
4.6	1.84	9.9	0.23	6.5	1.3	1.52	16.74	5.07	72.8	2.0	30.7	25.4	7.0
2.7	3.17	18.9	0.41	8.3	0.7	1.82	17.50	5.45	63.8	1.7	22.9	23.8	7.1
8.0	0.05	0.3	0.01	4.4	-0.4	0.92	7.71	4.53	79.6	4.7	36.3	7.3	6.1
9.0	0.30	1.5	0.04	7.3	1.1	1.73	16.49	3.54	50.9	4.3	20.6	7.4	8.0
8.9	1.48	2.7	0.00	2.0	0.0	0.08	0.58	2.73	97.0	6.3	58.8	3.2	7.9
6.8	1.25	4.1	0.05	8.0	1.4	1.55	9.86	4.01	47.8	3.4	51.0	20.0	8.9
5.9	0.54	2.9	0.03	9.4	1.7	2.16	17.76	4.73	46.8	2.9	22.9	15.1	8.8
5.6	0.58	5.0	0.02	5.4	1.2	1.10	13.63	3.05	45.7	1.7	19.8	22.7	5.2
1.4	3.65	27.0	2.40	3.8	1.7	0.82	8.88	4.31	68.1	2.2	14.8	17.8	3.8
0.7	1.93	8.4	0.52	3.3	0.3	0.73	5.44	5.02	81.2	2.6	28.0	17.9	7.1
6.5	0.00	0.0	0.01	6.3	1.0	1.12	6.74	4.56	67.8	3.2	23.9	13.8	7.5
8.5	0.09	0.5	0.09	3.6	0.3	0.74	8.73	3.64	80.1	4.4	57.4	16.1	5.2
5.9	1.86	8.5	0.48	5.3	1.2	0.73	7.58	4.96	74.0	2.5	32.3	20.4	5.0
7.0	0.03	0.1	0.01	5.4	0.5	0.97	7.28	3.18	54.9	5.8	47.5	6.4	7.0
4.3	1.54	10.2	0.22	4.5	0.3	0.74	7.59	4.53	77.3	2.7	8.1	14.6	5.0
9.9	0.00	0.0	0.00	4.1	0.4	0.67	5.13	3.18	73.0	7.7	93.7	2.8	8.9
7.3	0.93	4.7	0.74	3.8	0.4	0.66	7.16	4.00	67.4	4.8	51.9	12.8	4.5
4.2	2.78	12.6	0.59	4.2	0.2	0.81	8.92	4.57	76.3	5.3	47.6	9.6	5.4
2.0	2.63	20.9	0.56	1.9	0.1	0.21	2.77	4.55	84.0	4.1	25.7	9.4	1.7
4.0	1.15	6.2	1.33	7.1	0.3	1.58	13.27	6.01	58.3	2.0	25.7	19.4	7.3
3.5	3.57	15.3	0.33	5.3	0.5	1.29	11.06	4.26	55.3	3.9	54.6	18.1	7.1
9.9	0.00	0.0	0.11	2.8	0.2	0.42	1.76	2.52	79.5	3.5	74.5	28.9	6.6
9.7	0.00	0.0	0.69	1.7	0.1	0.16	1.31	3.90	89.6	4.6	54.5	14.2	5.0
2.2	2.13	18.1	0.01	4.9	1.0	1.17	13.25	4.13	68.2	1.0	9.9	30.3	5.3
8.3	1.11	3.6	0.11	5.5	1.3	1.05	7.36	4.03	64.9	5.0	37.6	9.2	8.2
7.3	0.04	0.2	0.04	6.6	0.4	1.48	12.88	4.23	62.4	3.5	46.4	18.8	6.3
9.9	0.40	0.7	-0.11	1.7	0.0	0.04	0.36	3.76	98.7	6.9	63.2	0.0	6.2
5.2	0.95	5.3	0.82	4.3	0.5	0.86	8.26	4.29	68.4	2.6	32.4	19.3	6.6
9.4	0.00	0.0	0.52	3.6	0.1	0.74	4.67	4.26	75.1	5.9	83.6	10.9	7.1
0.3	3.22	23.2	1.41	0.6	-0.1	-0.13	-1.60	4.29	87.4	3.8	24.6	11.1	3.3
5.9	0.50	1.7	1.46	5.6	1.1	1.12	8.37	3.67	55.9	2.9	40.6	21.4	5.0
7.6	0.40	2.5	0.00	3.9	0.2	0.79	9.43	3.90	78.3	4.6	36.6	10.9	6.2
2.2	3.77	19.8	2.07	0.1	0.1	0.10	1.32	2.74	85.4	2.2	30.6	22.4	2.5
5.6	0.93	4.0	0.39	7.3	0.7	1.25	8.92	4.44	55.3	3.1	30.6	16.1	7.7
6.9	0.00	0.0	-0.01	4.5	0.2	0.84	6.38	4.47	71.9	3.4	13.4	11.5	8.1
5.7	0.33	2.4	0.48	5.1	0.5	1.15	12.84	4.01	67.6	1.5	15.8	25.3	5.0

Name	City	State	Rating	2008 Rating	2007 Rating	Total Assets ($Mil)	One Year Asset Growth	Asset Mix (As a % of Total Assets) Commercial Loans	Consumer Loans	Home Mortgages	Securities	Capitalization Index	Leverage Ratio	Risk-based Capital Ratio
▼ FARMERS STATE BK OF W	WEST CONCORD	MN	**D-**	C-	C-	46	-4.65	5.4	4.3	22.6	38.7	**5.9**	7.9	16.0
FARMERS STATE BK OF	WATKINS	MN	**B+**	B+	A-	36	6.55	6.9	4.1	13.4	26.5	**10.0**	13.7	21.2
FARMERS STATE BK OF	WAUPACA	WI	**A-**	A-	A-	186	-0.56	10.5	4.7	27.5	21.0	**10.0**	13.2	19.4
FARMERS STATE BK OF	ALPHA	IL	**A-**	A	A-	119	10.78	4.4	4.0	10.5	22.1	**10.0**	12.1	16.6
FARMERS STATE BK S/B	SCHELL CITY	MO	**C-**	C-	D+	69	-3.93	5.4	2.9	14.6	20.6	**10.0**	15.6	26.4
FARMERS STATE BK	STANBERRY	MO	**A-**	A-	A-	55	4.26	1.2	2.5	8.0	43.6	**10.0**	13.3	23.3
▲ FARMERS TRUST & SB	BUFFALO CENTER	IA	**B**	B	B	169	7.97	6.9	2.1	8.1	4.2	**6.5**	8.7	12.2
▲ FARMERS TRUST & SB	EARLING	IA	**C-**	C	C	80	-1.35	15.8	2.1	8.4	2.7	**6.6**	9.9	12.2
▲ FARMERS TRUST & SB	SPENCER	IA	**D**	D	C-	291	3.15	7.2	1.6	7.7	27.9	**5.9**	7.9	12.8
FARMERS TRUST & SB	WILLIAMSBURG	IA	**A**	A	A	125	18.11	8.4	5.9	18.8	33.3	**10.0**	18.1	28.8
FARMERS-MERCHANTS BANK	BREAUX BRIDGE	LA	**D**	D+	D-	234	-4.74	10.7	3.9	16.3	11.2	**10.0**	11.6	16.1
FARMERS-MERCHANTS	PAXTON	IL	**B**	B+	A-	101	4.01	2.8	2.7	14.3	42.4	**10.0**	11.4	21.0
▼ FARMINGTON BANK	FARMINGTON	CT	**C-**	C-	C+	1,416	12.81	14.3	0.2	33.2	11.8	**3.3**	6.5	10.2
▲ FARMINGTON STATE BK	FARMINGTON	WA	**B-**	C	C+	9	-0.71	6.5	4.3	5.3	2.3	**10.0**	17.0	27.1
FAUQUIER BANK	WARRENTON	VA	**B**	B	B	597	5.13	5.0	1.1	22.8	7.8	**6.1**	8.1	12.4
FAYETTE COUNTY BANK	SAINT ELMO	IL	**C**	C+	B-	28	-1.26	10.3	4.1	4.7	15.9	**7.3**	9.2	18.8
FAYETTE COUNTY NB	FAYETTEVILLE	WV	**B+**	B+	B+	81	5.97	1.5	4.3	36.7	29.4	**9.2**	10.5	21.8
FAYETTE SB SSB	LA GRANGE	TX	**C+**	C+	C+	80	7.68	1.5	2.5	33.4	31.2	**6.0**	8.0	17.1
FAYETTEVILLE BANK	FAYETTEVILLE	TX	**B+**	B	B	234	28.93	3.0	1.9	6.6	67.5	**5.8**	7.8	20.1
FCN BANK NA	BROOKVILLE	IN	**C+**	B-	B+	343	6.97	4.1	1.5	22.7	38.8	**7.3**	9.2	18.3
FDS BANK	MASON	OH	**A**	A	A	126	-1.60	1.8	0.6	0.0	49.6	**10.0**	23.6	60.5
FEDERAL SAVINGS BANK	DOVER	NH	**C-**	C	C+	257	7.33	3.1	0.6	50.9	5.4	**7.8**	9.5	15.6
FEDERAL TRUST BANK	SANFORD	FL	**D-**	E+	E-	349	-35.32	2.0	0.1	38.9	7.3	**10.0**	11.4	19.2
▼ FEDERATED BANK	ONARGA	IL	**D+**	D+	B-	79	-2.00	15.1	5.0	9.8	23.6	**6.8**	8.8	13.9
FEDERATION BANK	WASHINGTON	IA	**C-**	C	C	107	-8.04	9.1	2.7	17.9	27.0	**6.9**	8.9	14.6
▼ FELICIANA BANK & TRUST CO	CLINTON	LA	**B-**	B+	A-	116	7.04	5.9	4.3	26.9	18.1	**10.0**	12.0	17.4
▲ FIA CARD SERVICES NA	WILMINGTON	DE	**C**	C-	C+	196,749	57.34	4.4	78.1	0.0	0.3	**10.0**	13.2	16.9
▼ FIDELITY BANK	ATLANTA	GA	**D-**	D-	D+	1,943	5.23	4.6	37.2	11.8	9.1	**7.5**	9.5	12.9
FIDELITY BANK	WEST DES MOINES	IA	**D**	D	E+	52	-5.50	8.8	1.5	34.3	1.7	**8.1**	11.2	13.4
FIDELITY BANK	WICHITA	KS	**C**	C	C+	1,641	-5.00	3.3	7.8	12.8	26.9	**10.0**	11.6	15.0
FIDELITY BANK	BATON ROUGE	LA	**D-**	D-	D-	157	2.55	11.4	1.3	6.1	6.5	**7.8**	9.5	13.6
FIDELITY BANK	DEARBORN	MI	**E-**	E-	D-	914	-7.18	3.4	0.1	8.6	6.0	**0.1**	4.0	6.2
FIDELITY BANK	EDINA	MN	**B+**	B	C+	374	0.32	24.5	1.8	44.5	7.3	**7.8**	9.5	17.4
FIDELITY BANK	FUQUAY-VARINA	NC	**B-**	B-	A-	1,356	-0.53	4.6	1.3	8.9	10.2	**9.9**	10.9	18.0
FIDELITY BANK	PLANO	TX	**C+**	C	C-	145	-10.27	22.2	6.1	12.4	3.1	**10.0**	12.7	19.3
▲ FIDELITY BANK	WICHITA FALLS	TX	**C+**	C	B-	207	-4.07	17.7	2.9	10.2	3.0	**7.7**	9.4	13.9
FIDELITY BANK & TRUST	DUBUQUE	IA	**C**	C	B-	453	12.33	13.5	1.0	9.8	7.7	**6.7**	9.0	12.3
FIDELITY BANK OF FLORIDA	MERRITT ISLAND	FL	**D-**	D-	D	390	-6.06	2.7	0.1	12.2	2.3	**5.7**	8.2	11.5
▲ FIDELITY BANK OF TEXAS	WACO	TX	**B**	B-	C+	83	4.93	9.6	6.9	38.0	6.2	**9.2**	10.4	17.3
FIDELITY CO-OP BANK	LEOMINSTER	MA	**C**	C-	C-	521	6.09	8.4	0.4	33.9	17.3	**5.5**	7.5	14.3
▼ FIDELITY DEPOSIT & DISCOU	DUNMORE	PA	**C-**	C-	B-	561	1.01	12.0	3.0	20.2	14.8	**6.1**	8.2	11.8
▲ FIDELITY FS&LA	DELAWARE	OH	**B**	B-	B+	100	1.73	0.4	0.1	48.5	23.6	**10.0**	11.4	27.1
FIDELITY HOMESTEAD SB	NEW ORLEANS	LA	**C-**	C+	C	975	7.98	0.4	0.5	35.4	41.3	**10.0**	13.1	32.9
FIDELITY MANAGEMENT	BOSTON	MA	**A-**	A-	A-	92	-12.68	0.0	0.0	0.0	73.2	**10.0**	40.5	42.8
▲ FIDELITY NATIONAL BK	WEST MEMPHIS	AR	**B-**	B+	B	318	4.72	1.9	3.3	8.0	62.9	**6.9**	8.9	22.1
FIDELITY NATIONAL BK	MEDFORD	WI	**D+**	D	D	94	1.00	5.5	3.3	15.1	15.7	**7.9**	9.6	15.2
FIDELITY PERSONAL TRUST C	BOSTON	MA	**B+**	B+	B-	86	151.94	0.0	0.0	0.0	64.9	**10.0**	40.9	41.0
▲ FIDELITY S&LA OF BUCKS CO	BRISTOL	PA	**C**	C-	C-	102	5.09	0.5	0.3	53.0	25.3	**10.0**	11.3	23.1
FIDELITY SB	PITTSBURGH	PA	**D**	D+	C	689	-5.65	3.9	0.5	24.8	35.3	**5.0**	7.0	12.8
FIDELITY STATE BK & TRUST	DODGE CITY	KS	**A**	A	A+	161	5.53	5.0	2.2	4.6	33.5	**10.0**	15.1	37.8
FIDELITY STATE BK & TRUST	TOPEKA	KS	**B+**	B	B-	97	-8.31	23.4	22.3	5.7	26.9	**9.4**	10.6	16.4
FIDUCIARY TRUST CO INTL	NEW YORK	NY	**C**	C	C-	796	2.26	4.1	13.7	0.0	38.3	**10.0**	25.2	60.8
▲ FIELDPOINT PRIVATE BANK &	GREENWICH	CT	**C-**	C	C	464	66.13	1.0	2.6	47.5	31.0	**6.2**	8.3	16.7
FIFE COMMERCIAL BANK	FIFE	WA	**C-**	C-	C+	83	-7.87	9.2	0.8	16.7	2.0	**8.9**	10.2	15.0
FIFTH DISTRICT SAVINGS BA	NEW ORLEANS	LA	**B-**	B-	B	370	-1.62	0.0	0.6	61.3	24.8	**10.0**	15.1	37.6
▲ FIFTH THIRD BANK	CINCINNATI	OH	**C**	C-	C-	108,972	-3.34	21.4	12.2	11.1	13.6	**10.0**	12.1	15.2
FINANCE & THRIFT CO	PORTERVILLE	CA	**C+**	C	C+	121	5.60	0.0	72.3	1.1	10.8	**10.0**	21.8	27.7
FINANCE FACTORS LTD	HONOLULU	HI	**D-**	D-	C	573	-12.31	0.0	0.2	14.2	14.2	**5.4**	7.4	12.6
FINANCIAL FSB	MEMPHIS	TN	**B+**	B+	B+	321	-3.02	5.1	2.6	30.3	0.0	**10.0**	14.4	18.5
FINANCIAL SECURITY BANK	KERKHOVEN	MN	**D**	C	D+	45	20.53	11.4	1.6	10.8	7.7	**8.7**	10.2	14.2

Asset Quality Index	Non-Performing Loans as a % of Total Loans	Non-Performing Loans as a % of Capital	Net Charge-offs Avg Loans	Profitability Index	Net Income ($Mil)	Return on Assets (R.O.A.)	Return on Equity (R.O.E.)	Net Interest Spread	Overhead Efficiency Ratio	Liquidity Index	Liquidity Ratio	Hot Money Ratio	Stability Index
3.8	0.70	3.9	1.62	0.0	-0.4	-0.85	-9.93	4.20	102.4	5.5	40.8	7.1	3.6
5.5	1.35	5.3	1.10	6.3	0.5	1.33	9.21	4.95	63.0	3.6	32.4	14.7	9.9
5.5	1.94	9.1	0.63	6.7	2.4	1.30	9.32	5.15	53.4	2.8	26.4	16.4	7.8
6.4	0.86	4.4	0.38	6.3	1.5	1.40	10.91	4.72	65.4	4.2	27.7	10.1	7.4
8.9	0.25	0.8	0.02	1.2	0.0	0.00	-0.03	3.64	101.2	2.7	29.5	18.0	6.3
8.8	0.12	0.4	-0.01	6.4	0.8	1.52	10.75	3.56	53.3	5.4	49.0	9.3	8.5
5.6	0.31	2.6	0.09	8.3	3.0	1.79	19.25	3.98	52.7	4.2	18.0	7.7	7.8
4.0	0.46	3.7	-0.04	6.8	1.3	1.67	17.45	4.28	60.0	3.2	9.4	12.4	5.0
0.8	4.19	29.7	1.28	4.9	3.1	1.11	13.66	3.91	47.0	1.6	14.0	22.3	5.8
6.4	0.56	1.8	0.19	10.0	2.8	2.49	12.46	4.53	46.6	3.6	34.4	15.2	8.7
0.3	10.21	60.4	1.13	5.6	2.6	1.10	9.80	5.08	63.0	2.4	17.6	17.2	7.9
3.7	8.08	32.4	0.69	5.0	0.9	0.89	7.38	4.11	61.3	2.8	33.2	18.7	7.9
3.1	1.50	15.0	0.21	2.9	5.2	0.37	5.37	3.87	77.8	2.0	2.2	17.5	5.5
8.4	0.00	0.0	0.00	4.5	0.1	0.85	4.85	4.26	73.1	4.7	48.3	10.9	7.3
5.7	0.51	4.3	0.27	4.5	4.2	0.72	8.95	4.17	70.1	1.7	9.3	19.7	5.5
4.6	4.20	17.1	1.55	2.6	0.2	0.58	6.38	3.07	75.9	2.5	53.9	35.9	5.9
6.6	0.73	3.9	0.06	4.9	0.8	1.03	9.14	4.81	70.4	3.6	22.4	11.5	6.9
7.7	0.01	0.0	0.02	4.4	0.6	0.79	9.36	4.02	72.7	5.3	49.5	10.0	5.1
8.0	1.22	3.8	0.67	5.8	3.3	1.60	19.99	3.78	48.8	2.8	57.5	43.0	5.8
3.8	1.88	10.2	0.31	4.1	2.2	0.67	6.33	3.58	61.0	3.9	43.0	16.4	6.3
6.6	0.17	0.0	3.50	10.0	181.8	181.47	624.28	0.74	46.1	8.5	98.8	0.0	8.7
4.4	1.13	9.5	-0.01	2.5	0.8	0.30	3.13	3.81	88.4	2.4	8.5	16.3	4.7
0.0	11.93	66.3	0.00	0.0	-110.7	-24.10	-75.90	6.03	1,654.3	3.1	15.4	13.4	4.8
1.4	3.03	19.3	0.83	2.2	0.3	0.43	3.62	3.72	76.0	3.7	23.9	11.5	4.4
1.7	1.81	11.0	0.64	3.3	0.8	0.74	7.57	3.62	66.5	4.0	33.5	13.0	4.1
2.9	4.26	24.2	0.42	5.9	1.0	0.92	7.33	5.35	68.4	0.9	22.9	40.8	7.7
2.1	2.98	11.8	11.27	4.8	2,241.4	1.15	9.08	9.75	28.2	4.6	17.4	5.6	4.7
0.0	4.36	33.7	1.30	2.8	12.7	0.68	7.01	3.93	69.4	1.8	5.6	19.1	5.7
0.9	3.50	24.4	0.07	3.8	0.5	0.93	7.02	4.95	85.0	2.1	3.5	17.3	5.8
2.9	1.28	5.5	1.43	3.4	10.1	0.60	5.59	3.27	61.5	3.4	41.4	23.3	6.5
0.0	5.57	35.4	0.82	1.6	0.2	0.10	1.02	4.62	81.9	3.2	27.0	14.8	3.7
0.0	9.34	106.8	2.92	0.0	-13.7	-1.44	-31.86	3.77	94.6	0.9	11.8	32.6	2.6
5.6	0.16	1.2	0.15	9.4	9.2	2.55	14.44	4.75	44.9	5.0	2.3	0.1	9.5
4.6	0.94	4.7	0.42	4.0	7.2	0.53	4.43	3.63	75.2	4.3	32.2	14.2	8.2
6.0	1.26	6.6	0.32	2.5	0.3	0.20	1.53	4.49	77.9	1.4	21.2	28.0	6.7
3.4	0.90	6.1	0.50	4.9	1.7	0.81	8.90	3.86	62.1	2.1	24.7	19.7	5.5
2.9	0.72	5.7	1.07	4.5	2.8	0.63	5.65	4.08	57.4	2.2	17.3	18.2	5.5
0.0	16.01	113.2	5.64	1.1	-7.6	-1.87	-19.44	3.67	56.1	1.1	20.2	31.9	5.6
7.7	0.30	2.1	0.23	5.4	0.8	0.96	9.68	4.42	68.4	3.7	19.2	10.9	5.3
3.0	1.28	10.3	0.66	2.8	2.0	0.39	5.19	3.75	74.9	2.4	17.5	17.3	4.4
2.3	2.43	18.1	0.41	3.3	-3.0	-0.52	-6.49	4.05	67.8	3.2	16.0	13.1	5.0
7.8	0.22	1.1	0.33	3.9	0.7	0.74	4.04	4.07	63.4	4.7	39.1	10.9	7.7
7.0	1.67	6.0	0.07	0.6	-5.8	-0.61	-4.38	2.93	118.1	4.1	53.4	18.0	3.3
10.0	0.00	0.0	0.00	10.0	10.0	10.08	26.51	-2.46	94.3	3.8	128.1	100.0	6.7
4.5	3.37	10.9	0.61	6.6	5.2	1.65	15.75	3.82	56.9	1.0	25.8	36.8	7.5
1.9	2.66	17.8	2.04	3.1	0.5	0.54	5.28	4.33	67.7	1.6	18.3	24.0	4.3
7.5	0.00	0.0	0.00	10.0	17.1	36.48	42.99	6.22	54.5	4.4	162.2	100.0	3.4
6.8	1.84	9.6	0.00	2.6	0.4	0.40	3.64	2.77	79.8	3.8	42.0	16.5	6.3
2.2	3.57	24.3	0.41	2.1	0.5	0.07	0.90	2.44	77.6	3.9	21.1	9.9	2.5
9.2	0.15	0.3	0.94	5.5	1.7	1.12	6.75	4.20	62.4	6.3	59.4	7.8	9.1
6.5	0.29	1.6	0.12	5.8	1.4	1.39	12.26	4.42	67.2	3.8	35.7	14.7	6.4
6.8	0.04	0.0	0.00	1.9	3.1	0.38	1.26	1.88	96.1	7.5	59.2	0.0	6.7
9.2	0.00	0.0	0.00	3.6	4.6	1.23	12.40	2.92	88.7	2.0	44.3	68.2	2.5
1.5	1.74	11.6	1.27	6.8	1.3	1.49	15.52	4.73	53.3	1.0	18.1	33.0	7.6
9.2	0.20	0.9	0.00	3.4	2.6	0.70	4.70	3.30	67.5	3.4	34.8	16.1	7.0
1.3	2.79	13.9	2.94	4.1	801.0	0.72	4.85	3.90	58.2	4.4	9.3	5.5	8.9
2.8	1.99	6.2	5.78	7.6	1.9	1.60	7.37	13.11	59.6	1.1	25.3	33.7	6.8
0.3	10.10	59.9	3.86	0.0	-9.5	-1.54	-16.00	2.86	133.0	2.3	30.3	21.0	4.5
7.8	0.50	2.8	0.38	4.5	3.1	0.96	6.70	3.45	51.6	0.3	6.2	75.3	7.9
3.6	0.75	5.2	1.01	1.1	-0.1	-0.25	-2.24	4.64	79.1	2.1	15.9	18.4	6.3

Name	City	State	Rating	2008 Rating	2007 Rating	Total Assets ($Mil)	One Year Asset Growth	Asset Mix (As a % of Total Assets) Comm-ercial Loans	Cons-umer Loans	Home Mort-gages	Secur-ities	Capital-ization Index	Leverage Ratio	Risk-based Capital Ratio
FINEMARK NATIONAL BK & TR	FORT MYERS	FL	**D-**	C-	C-	367	66.26	4.7	3.9	19.5	48.6	**6.1**	8.1	16.1
▲ FIRESIDE BANK	PLEASANTON	CA	**B+**	C	C-	592	-36.88	0.0	64.4	0.0	25.0	**10.0**	37.3	65.9
▼ FIRST & CITIZENS BANK	MONTEREY	VA	**C+**	B-	B-	116	3.80	4.6	5.5	40.5	9.7	**8.8**	10.2	21.1
FIRST & FARMERS BANK	PORTLAND	ND	**E+**	E	E	45	-2.43	13.1	5.8	6.6	7.2	**5.9**	7.9	13.3
FIRST & FARMERS NATIONAL	SOMERSET	KY	**C-**	C-	C	452	0.35	6.3	6.3	21.8	31.5	**6.7**	8.7	14.3
FIRST & PEOPLES BANK & TR	RUSSELL	KY	**C-**	B-	B	191	-2.89	0.7	10.9	20.3	49.4	**10.0**	18.6	39.6
FIRST A NATIONAL BANKING	HATTIESBURG	MS	**C+**	C	C+	502	5.37	9.6	1.9	17.4	20.8	**9.5**	10.7	16.2
FIRST ADVANTAGE BANK	COON RAPIDS	MN	**D-**	D	D-	58	14.64	15.2	1.6	7.5	24.1	**6.2**	8.2	12.2
FIRST ALLIANCE BANK	CORDOVA	TN	**D-**	D	D-	135	-3.00	14.5	2.1	18.3	9.0	**5.8**	7.8	11.7
FIRST AMERICA BANK	BRADENTON	FL	**D-**	D-	C-	256	-7.07	7.4	3.0	29.2	10.1	**7.9**	9.6	15.0
FIRST AMERICAN BANK	FORT DODGE	IA	**D-**	D+	C-	1,549	-7.95	11.5	0.3	6.0	22.5	**4.8**	6.9	11.7
▲ FIRST AMERICAN BANK	ELK GROVE VILLAGE	IL	**D+**	C-	D+	2,782	-2.93	14.9	0.3	6.6	31.4	**7.0**	9.0	13.3
FIRST AMERICAN BANK	ARTESIA	NM	**C-**	C	B-	625	8.22	10.9	1.5	7.4	19.9	**5.9**	7.9	14.7
FIRST AMERICAN BANK	ERICK	OK	**B-**	B-	C+	37	5.87	2.8	4.8	5.0	45.5	**6.6**	8.6	18.8
FIRST AMERICAN BANK	NORMAN	OK	**C-**	C+	C	301	2.06	8.6	3.9	16.8	9.8	**6.0**	8.0	12.3
FIRST AMERICAN BANK	STONEWALL	OK	**B**	B	B-	23	3.79	12.4	16.9	26.1	11.7	**9.6**	10.8	16.4
▼ FIRST AMERICAN BANK & TRU	VACHERIE	LA	**C-**	B-	C+	717	-0.36	2.1	1.8	17.6	21.5	**9.3**	10.6	17.6
FIRST AMERICAN BANK & TRU	ATHENS	GA	**C**	B-	A-	435	1.88	2.4	0.8	15.3	34.7	**7.8**	9.5	17.0
FIRST AMERICAN BANK NA	HUDSON	WI	**D-**	C-	D	75	10.25	4.5	0.4	13.6	11.2	**6.8**	8.8	12.6
FIRST AMERICAN INTL BANK	BROOKLYN	NY	**D-**	D	D+	588	-8.66	2.0	0.1	11.4	4.0	**5.0**	8.8	11.0
FIRST AMERICAN NATIONAL B	IUKA	MS	**B**	B	B	222	2.03	3.6	5.9	21.2	36.2	**9.4**	10.6	15.0
FIRST AMERICAN STATE BK	GREENWOOD VILLAGE	CO	**D-**	D-	D	220	-6.23	5.6	0.2	8.0	16.7	**4.4**	6.4	10.9
▲ FIRST AMERICAN TRUST FSB	SANTA ANA	CA	**C+**	C	B-	1,118	9.06	0.0	0.0	0.0	88.2	**6.8**	8.9	41.5
FIRST ARKANSAS BANK & TRU	JACKSONVILLE	AR	**C+**	C	A-	686	13.79	3.5	3.2	9.2	42.3	**9.4**	10.6	16.1
▼ FIRST ASIAN BANK	LAS VEGAS	NV	**E+**	D	C-	35	-20.15	12.7	0.1	5.6	0.0	**5.9**	7.9	12.4
FIRST ASSOCIATIONS BANK	DALLAS	TX	**B+**	B+	B+	253	9.72	0.0	0.0	0.0	89.3	**10.0**	12.3	54.9
FIRST AVENUE NATIONAL BK	OCALA	FL	**D-**	D	D	108	6.20	4.4	2.0	14.7	14.4	**8.0**	9.7	13.9
▲ FIRST BANK	KETCHIKAN	AK	**B**	B-	C+	460	3.08	5.5	1.2	11.3	37.7	**6.1**	8.1	15.7
FIRST BANK	WADLEY	AL	**C-**	C-	C-	67	-0.46	6.0	2.7	10.5	37.6	**7.7**	9.5	17.7
FIRST BANK	CAMDEN	AR	**C**	B-	A-	247	39.76	7.7	5.6	17.8	24.3	**8.1**	9.7	13.6
▼ FIRST BANK	CLEWISTON	FL	**E+**	D	D+	243	-8.16	4.3	2.0	18.9	6.2	**3.5**	7.0	10.3
FIRST BANK	WEST DES MOINES	IA	**E-**	E-	E-	105	-20.95	11.5	0.7	18.3	18.5	**0.8**	4.5	7.6
FIRST BANK	STERLING	KS	**A-**	A-	B+	111	11.88	9.6	1.5	14.5	41.3	**10.0**	11.6	19.5
FIRST BANK	CREVE COEUR	MO	**D-**	D-	D	7,353	-30.30	13.5	0.4	9.7	20.2	**5.4**	7.4	13.0
▲ FIRST BANK	MCCOMB	MS	**A-**	B+	A-	326	8.31	7.2	3.4	8.6	32.6	**9.1**	10.4	16.0
FIRST BANK	TROY	NC	**D**	D+	B	3,278	-7.64	4.0	2.3	25.7	6.7	**8.0**	9.6	15.6
FIRST BANK	WILLIAMSTOWN	NJ	**D-**	D	C-	212	-3.75	11.9	2.0	5.5	13.0	**8.8**	10.2	14.3
FIRST BANK	LEXINGTON	TN	**D-**	D	D+	2,069	-9.15	10.7	2.0	12.8	16.5	**6.2**	8.2	13.7
▲ FIRST BANK	BURKBURNETT	TX	**B**	B-	C+	237	6.58	21.2	4.2	21.0	3.7	**7.1**	9.1	12.9
▼ FIRST BANK	STRASBURG	VA	**D+**	D+	C-	544	-1.46	6.9	2.4	14.5	11.1	**8.9**	10.4	14.1
FIRST BANK	TOMAH	WI	**D**	D-	D	89	0.22	7.3	2.7	16.5	15.7	**7.2**	9.1	12.8
▼ FIRST BANK & TRUST	EVANSTON	IL	**C+**	B-	B-	601	13.92	24.0	8.2	8.9	16.3	**6.1**	9.3	11.8
FIRST BANK & TRUST	NEW ORLEANS	LA	**E**	D	C-	865	-8.58	11.2	4.8	14.4	11.3	**4.2**	6.2	11.9
FIRST BANK & TRUST	BROOKINGS	SD	**D+**	C-	C+	809	-5.28	11.8	3.0	11.4	13.5	**7.5**	9.6	12.9
FIRST BANK & TRUST	SIOUX FALLS	SD	**C-**	C-	C+	394	2.29	12.9	1.6	10.3	9.2	**5.6**	9.6	11.4
FIRST BANK & TRUST CHILDR	CHILDRESS	TX	**C**	C	C	73	-9.50	40.9	4.2	11.6	9.1	**6.5**	8.5	17.4
FIRST BANK & TRUST CO	COZAD	NE	**D+**	D	D+	209	3.67	15.0	3.3	4.4	30.5	**7.4**	9.5	12.8
FIRST BANK & TRUST CO	MINDEN	NE	**C+**	C+	C+	64	1.93	3.7	2.0	8.5	49.7	**7.5**	9.4	18.0
FIRST BANK & TRUST CO	CLINTON	OK	**B**	B-	B-	50	-8.81	1.6	7.9	23.1	27.3	**7.2**	9.1	25.9
FIRST BANK & TRUST CO	DUNCAN	OK	**C-**	C	B	487	6.75	9.4	8.1	29.4	15.9	**10.0**	11.0	16.7
FIRST BANK & TRUST CO	PERRY	OK	**A**	A	A	113	-6.29	3.2	8.9	13.9	36.9	**10.0**	13.2	24.1
▲ FIRST BANK & TRUST CO	WAGONER	OK	**C**	B-	B-	246	9.88	10.0	7.8	21.9	2.3	**8.4**	10.4	13.7
FIRST BANK & TRUST CO	DAWSON	TX	**D**	C-	D	34	3.42	11.0	7.0	9.8	25.7	**4.8**	6.8	12.8
FIRST BANK & TRUST CO	LUBBOCK	TX	**D-**	C-	C	471	1.29	16.5	3.8	18.6	10.7	**5.9**	8.1	11.6
▼ FIRST BANK & TRUST CO	LEBANON	VA	**C+**	B+	B	1,171	3.65	4.3	3.1	17.0	4.2	**7.5**	9.4	13.6
FIRST BANK & TRUST CO OF	PALATINE	IL	**D-**	D-	E	360	-0.78	6.5	0.0	2.6	0.9	**9.9**	12.5	14.9
FIRST BANK & TRUST EAST T	DIBOLL	TX	**B**	B	B+	774	7.30	11.5	10.5	13.6	24.4	**6.1**	8.1	13.4
FIRST BANK & TRUST FULLER	FULLERTON	NE	**B+**	B+	B	63	10.03	3.8	3.2	2.0	15.0	**10.0**	17.8	25.1
FIRST BANK & TRUST MURPHY	MURPHYSBORO	IL	**C+**	C	C+	64	-2.53	5.7	4.6	19.9	33.1	**9.1**	10.4	14.6
FIRST BANK & TRUST NA	PIPESTONE	MN	**D+**	C	B-	165	1.94	12.3	3.2	4.8	18.1	**8.3**	9.8	13.7

Asset Quality Index	Non-Performing Loans as a % of Total Loans	Non-Performing Loans as a % of Capital	Net Charge-offs Avg Loans	Profitability Index	Net Income ($Mil)	Return on Assets (R.O.A.)	Return on Equity (R.O.E.)	Net Interest Spread	Overhead Efficiency Ratio	Liquidity Index	Liquidity Ratio	Hot Money Ratio	Stability Index
8.7	0.24	1.3	0.31	**0.3**	0.5	0.16	1.62	2.34	104.8	**2.8**	39.1	22.8	**1.1**
5.6	0.11	0.2	4.59	**7.2**	14.1	1.82	5.85	9.06	85.7	**2.7**	65.6	91.8	**6.1**
6.8	0.43	2.6	0.43	**3.1**	0.4	0.32	2.99	3.51	77.9	**3.3**	27.0	14.1	**6.3**
2.9	1.09	8.9	1.44	**1.6**	0.2	0.44	5.47	4.37	83.5	**3.9**	16.1	9.6	**1.8**
2.3	1.78	11.3	1.13	**3.9**	3.1	0.68	5.36	4.38	67.3	**1.8**	25.9	24.3	**5.7**
3.5	7.57	16.5	1.21	**1.4**	0.4	0.20	1.14	4.24	86.6	**4.3**	42.5	14.1	**6.7**
4.3	1.59	9.0	0.34	**3.9**	3.0	0.61	5.60	3.78	73.9	**1.4**	16.8	26.4	**6.4**
0.3	6.89	46.8	0.73	**0.5**	-0.1	-0.21	-1.97	3.78	93.5	**3.4**	26.2	13.4	**5.3**
0.3	4.15	29.5	0.65	**0.0**	-0.8	-0.57	-6.52	3.74	99.0	**1.4**	20.3	27.4	**3.6**
1.2	1.56	10.6	0.35	**0.5**	0.3	0.10	0.94	3.04	86.6	**1.7**	20.1	23.2	**4.4**
1.5	4.18	25.9	2.34	**0.0**	-55.6	-3.45	-37.13	3.24	151.9	**2.2**	26.1	26.1	**5.0**
1.9	5.26	29.2	2.17	**1.4**	1.3	0.04	0.47	3.95	64.3	**2.9**	23.1	17.2	**6.4**
1.7	3.96	23.8	-0.04	**8.7**	13.0	1.95	23.05	4.75	61.9	**3.0**	12.4	13.6	**7.1**
9.3	0.00	0.0	0.07	**6.8**	0.6	1.49	16.70	3.50	61.2	**3.1**	45.0	21.3	**5.7**
2.2	3.34	26.6	0.52	**3.5**	1.4	0.46	5.50	4.68	85.2	**3.3**	19.6	13.0	**4.0**
4.6	0.82	5.3	0.06	**10.0**	0.6	2.65	25.10	5.92	56.0	**1.6**	19.1	23.1	**8.5**
1.7	2.05	11.0	1.79	**4.2**	2.7	0.37	3.29	4.20	58.7	**2.5**	25.3	17.8	**7.2**
2.4	3.53	18.1	0.82	**4.1**	3.2	0.71	7.28	3.11	62.4	**1.9**	10.0	18.8	**6.5**
1.1	3.32	27.8	0.09	**0.2**	-0.2	-0.20	-2.17	4.00	99.9	**0.9**	10.7	32.9	**1.2**
0.0	10.37	71.8	2.40	**1.5**	-7.4	-1.19	-11.94	4.60	67.0	**1.5**	10.4	23.0	**5.6**
5.8	0.58	2.5	0.50	**4.8**	2.2	1.00	8.77	4.17	70.5	**5.1**	43.4	10.5	**6.8**
2.2	1.57	12.7	0.93	**0.5**	-0.9	-0.36	-5.42	3.40	104.7	**1.3**	10.0	26.5	**2.7**
9.6	0.00	0.0	0.00	**3.6**	7.3	0.66	9.64	1.46	66.1	**8.7**	105.2	0.1	**4.2**
3.3	1.88	7.7	0.53	**5.2**	9.4	1.47	9.30	4.43	65.2	**4.7**	34.9	9.5	**8.2**
0.0	15.93	96.9	3.71	**0.0**	-3.0	-7.41	-68.40	2.47	296.4	**1.3**	32.4	55.3	**0.4**
10.0	0.00	0.0	0.00	**6.1**	4.3	1.70	13.77	3.54	51.4	**8.3**	108.1	2.0	**7.0**
1.7	6.02	36.8	0.90	**0.0**	-0.4	-0.36	-3.29	3.38	90.7	**2.5**	17.9	16.8	**1.3**
7.6	0.00	0.0	0.10	**5.7**	6.4	1.42	15.98	4.49	71.7	**2.1**	30.1	23.2	**5.7**
2.1	6.57	28.2	0.59	**6.2**	0.6	0.85	12.56	4.72	69.2	**2.9**	29.9	17.0	**3.6**
3.1	0.90	6.3	1.19	**4.4**	1.1	0.59	5.95	4.14	68.0	**1.7**	17.5	21.5	**5.5**
0.3	5.71	49.8	3.34	**0.0**	-3.1	-1.21	-15.42	3.96	87.6	**1.7**	9.6	20.6	**3.0**
0.3	11.72	105.2	-0.23	**0.9**	0.3	0.28	6.80	3.26	106.3	**1.8**	6.5	19.1	**0.0**
7.5	0.74	3.1	0.03	**5.1**	1.1	1.09	8.80	4.35	68.4	**3.3**	34.4	16.8	**8.0**
0.3	8.83	52.3	4.85	**0.0**	-178.5	-2.13	-26.34	3.08	92.4	**4.6**	33.7	13.2	**4.7**
7.4	0.26	1.3	0.13	**7.0**	5.3	1.63	15.99	3.53	57.8	**3.4**	14.5	11.9	**8.6**
0.9	3.01	21.0	1.66	**5.0**	11.6	0.35	3.00	4.42	54.5	**1.2**	12.3	28.5	**9.4**
2.1	2.73	17.4	1.28	**0.0**	-1.1	-0.51	-5.12	3.02	91.7	**2.1**	27.0	20.3	**1.3**
0.3	6.43	41.4	1.82	**0.1**	-5.1	-0.23	-2.21	3.43	76.6	**1.7**	8.6	19.9	**6.5**
5.0	0.52	3.9	-0.15	**8.1**	4.2	1.82	20.06	5.27	65.4	**2.3**	15.7	17.8	**7.1**
1.0	2.62	15.7	0.63	**1.3**	-3.2	-0.59	-5.06	4.22	75.8	**1.4**	11.8	25.1	**7.3**
1.4	3.15	23.3	1.43	**3.1**	0.8	0.88	9.68	4.15	74.7	**3.1**	16.8	13.9	**3.5**
4.1	1.26	9.1	0.32	**3.9**	2.9	0.51	5.26	3.69	70.9	**2.0**	14.4	18.8	**5.7**
0.3	8.54	65.4	1.51	**0.1**	-5.7	-0.61	-8.68	3.48	112.5	**1.9**	20.8	20.5	**2.4**
0.8	2.23	15.8	0.65	**4.1**	6.2	0.74	7.87	3.78	66.2	**1.8**	14.0	20.0	**4.7**
3.8	0.51	3.9	0.40	**3.5**	2.5	0.67	4.73	4.31	75.5	**2.1**	13.2	18.3	**6.0**
5.4	0.35	3.3	0.00	**4.8**	0.8	1.09	12.95	3.53	69.5	**0.6**	9.6	49.1	**4.5**
1.6	2.94	17.3	1.26	**3.8**	2.2	1.11	10.87	4.44	57.1	**2.4**	29.1	19.3	**4.5**
7.6	0.00	0.0	0.91	**4.0**	0.5	0.85	8.46	3.64	72.2	**4.6**	31.6	9.0	**5.8**
9.0	0.13	0.5	0.15	**5.6**	0.7	1.23	12.50	3.76	72.0	**2.6**	33.6	20.1	**6.3**
2.4	3.84	23.2	0.51	**6.5**	6.9	1.41	12.85	4.30	60.6	**1.5**	21.3	25.8	**8.1**
6.9	0.63	2.4	0.62	**6.8**	1.7	1.41	10.19	4.36	66.5	**3.8**	34.5	14.1	**8.6**
2.4	0.41	3.1	0.28	**8.8**	4.2	1.91	20.28	4.81	50.4	**1.3**	17.3	28.4	**7.7**
3.0	3.66	27.0	0.20	**3.1**	0.2	0.48	7.01	4.52	85.5	**1.9**	37.8	34.8	**2.3**
0.5	1.57	12.9	1.39	**3.0**	3.1	0.64	7.83	4.12	81.6	**0.6**	5.4	37.9	**4.3**
2.5	2.36	17.8	0.41	**6.8**	13.0	1.12	12.31	4.18	48.5	**1.6**	11.9	23.6	**9.0**
0.0	14.05	70.9	-0.08	**0.0**	-4.3	-1.19	-9.08	3.65	132.5	**0.8**	12.1	34.2	**6.3**
4.7	0.75	5.3	0.15	**5.9**	8.1	1.06	11.57	4.44	68.5	**3.4**	21.2	12.7	**6.5**
7.4	0.19	0.6	-0.01	**4.6**	0.5	0.85	4.51	3.77	70.0	**4.3**	38.1	12.7	**8.1**
4.9	0.97	4.8	-0.02	**3.7**	0.6	0.85	8.07	4.71	83.0	**1.9**	25.3	22.1	**6.6**
1.6	1.93	11.9	0.07	**6.9**	2.2	1.39	12.12	4.13	57.0	**2.1**	18.8	18.9	**6.4**

Name	City	State	Rating	2008 Rating	2007 Rating	Total Assets ($Mil)	One Year Asset Growth	Asset Mix (As a % of Total Assets) Comm-ercial Loans	Cons-umer Loans	Home Mort-gages	Secur-ities	Capital-ization Index	Leverage Ratio	Risk-based Capital Ratio
FIRST BANK & TRUST OF MEM	MEMPHIS	TX	**C+**	B-	B-	70	21.42	26.8	0.8	4.3	5.4	**6.6**	9.9	12.2
FIRST BANK & TRUST OF MIL	MILBANK	SD	**D**	D+	C	141	-3.37	8.3	5.4	10.6	12.3	**8.5**	10.5	13.8
▼FIRST BANK & TRUST SB	PARIS	IL	**C-**	C-	C+	405	4.03	6.9	7.6	20.1	15.0	**8.2**	9.8	15.1
FIRST BANK BLUE EARTH	BLUE EARTH	MN	**D+**	D+	D+	162	-2.49	12.8	2.1	4.2	18.7	**7.9**	9.6	14.0
▲FIRST BANK FINANCIAL CENT	OCONOMOWOC	WI	**C**	C-	D	739	10.09	5.3	0.6	12.3	20.5	**6.8**	8.8	13.3
FIRST BANK KANSAS	SALINA	KS	**B**	B	B	234	7.79	4.1	3.9	14.9	48.2	**6.6**	8.6	18.0
▼FIRST BANK OF BALDWIN	BALDWIN	WI	**D+**	C	B	176	0.45	22.2	2.9	11.8	8.9	**6.1**	8.6	11.8
FIRST BANK OF BERNE	BERNE	IN	**B+**	B+	B	426	2.42	1.5	1.4	27.4	17.4	**7.9**	9.6	14.6
FIRST BANK OF BOAZ	BOAZ	AL	**A**	A	A+	173	5.46	4.4	4.4	8.9	65.8	**10.0**	14.5	26.3
FIRST BANK OF CELESTE	CELESTE	TX	**C+**	C+	C+	39	0.30	3.9	9.5	9.8	10.2	**6.8**	8.8	17.5
▼FIRST BANK OF CHANDLER	CHANDLER	OK	**C-**	B-	B+	71	4.14	20.5	6.5	16.9	1.5	**7.9**	10.4	13.3
FIRST BANK OF CHARLESTON	CHARLESTON	WV	**C-**	B	B-	172	5.02	14.7	1.8	19.7	19.2	**9.2**	10.4	15.5
FIRST BANK OF COASTAL GEO	PEMBROKE	GA	**D**	C-	B-	131	-8.31	2.5	1.5	7.5	46.5	**7.8**	9.5	18.9
▲FIRST BANK OF CONROE NA	CONROE	TX	**C+**	C-	C+	263	6.02	10.4	4.6	15.8	10.4	**7.0**	9.0	13.4
▼FIRST BANK OF DALTON	DALTON	GA	**D-**	D-	D+	178	21.56	6.9	2.1	11.4	38.5	**6.2**	8.2	15.4
FIRST BANK OF DELAWARE	WILMINGTON	DE	**A-**	A-	B+	219	56.12	9.8	4.2	6.9	2.4	**10.0**	20.4	33.9
▼FIRST BANK OF FAIRLAND	FAIRLAND	OK	**C-**	C	C+	10	-4.37	2.3	10.4	26.7	13.2	**7.8**	9.6	14.9
▼FIRST BANK OF GEORGIA	AUGUSTA	GA	**D+**	C-	D+	495	2.34	3.9	1.3	16.4	15.5	**7.3**	9.2	12.9
FIRST BANK OF GREENWICH	COS COB	CT	**E-**	E+	C-	52	-3.78	12.3	2.5	15.3	1.5	**3.9**	6.8	10.4
FIRST BANK OF HIGHLAND PA	HIGHLAND PARK	IL	**C-**	C	B-	1,111	-15.49	35.5	0.1	3.9	9.8	**7.6**	10.4	13.0
FIRST BANK OF LINCOLN	LINCOLN	MT	**B**	B+	B+	15	2.08	25.5	8.7	35.1	0.0	**10.0**	12.4	21.1
FIRST BANK OF LINDEN	LINDEN	AL	**B-**	B-	C-	81	1.45	11.8	6.5	12.6	36.3	**10.0**	12.2	20.8
FIRST BANK OF MANHATTAN	MANHATTAN	IL	**D+**	D+	B-	132	-0.09	2.1	1.4	21.9	18.9	**9.1**	10.4	18.8
▼FIRST BANK OF MIAMI	CORAL GABLES	FL	**D-**	C-	C+	259	11.62	2.4	0.8	9.6	23.5	**6.6**	8.6	13.7
FIRST BANK OF MISSOURI	GLADSTONE	MO	**C**	B-	B	496	1.69	12.0	0.7	5.9	17.0	**10.0**	11.7	16.9
FIRST BANK OF MONTANA	LEWISTOWN	MT	**C+**	B	A-	240	10.28	5.7	1.7	3.6	32.3	**7.3**	9.2	15.2
FIRST BANK OF MULESHOE	MULESHOE	TX	**A-**	A-	A-	107	5.88	6.8	2.2	1.7	59.3	**10.0**	12.7	44.4
FIRST BANK OF NEWTON	NEWTON	KS	**C+**	C+	C+	141	2.21	8.9	6.1	29.1	26.7	**5.3**	7.3	12.0
FIRST BANK OF OHIO	TIFFIN	OH	**A**	A-	A	160	4.70	0.0	35.8	0.4	51.4	**10.0**	32.1	60.5
FIRST BANK OF OKARCHE	OKARCHE	OK	**A-**	A	A	57	8.65	8.7	4.2	3.7	23.4	**10.0**	14.1	22.3
▲FIRST BANK OF OWASSO	OWASSO	OK	**B**	B-	B-	216	-2.14	9.0	1.6	9.3	3.6	**6.0**	9.9	11.7
FIRST BANK OF PIKE	MOLENA	GA	**C+**	C-	B	39	1.61	11.9	10.8	30.8	15.1	**10.0**	11.2	19.1
FIRST BANK OF TENNESSEE	SPRING CITY	TN	**D**	C-	B-	222	2.31	7.1	10.0	24.8	7.5	**7.2**	9.1	13.1
FIRST BANK OF THE LAKE	OSAGE BEACH	MO	**D**	D	D	39	-1.86	3.1	1.3	15.9	9.8	**10.0**	14.5	20.6
FIRST BANK OF THE PALM BE	WEST PALM BEACH	FL	**E+**	D-	C-	64	-22.57	15.6	1.1	4.7	1.6	**6.4**	9.4	12.0
▲FIRST BANK OF THE SOUTH	RAINSVILLE	AL	**D**	D	D+	82	0.07	8.6	13.4	26.9	7.0	**5.4**	7.4	11.3
▼FIRST BANK OF UTICA	UTICA	NE	**D**	C-	D+	37	14.68	5.4	3.9	11.9	7.1	**6.3**	9.9	11.9
FIRST BANK OF WHITE	WHITE	SD	**D+**	C-	C+	54	-5.69	8.3	10.7	18.4	8.2	**9.3**	10.9	14.4
FIRST BANK RICHMOND NA	RICHMOND	IN	**D**	D	C-	555	-12.71	14.1	1.0	28.9	8.7	**7.4**	9.3	13.3
FIRST BANK UPPER MICHIGAN	GLADSTONE	MI	**B-**	B-	B-	165	0.43	7.8	10.5	29.2	18.9	**10.0**	15.7	23.4
FIRST BANKERS TRUST CO NA	QUINCY	IL	**B-**	B-	C+	683	10.73	5.5	5.8	7.0	40.3	**6.0**	8.0	13.0
FIRST BETHANY BANK & TRUS	BETHANY	OK	**B-**	B-	B-	156	-1.56	5.0	1.8	9.0	43.9	**6.4**	8.5	14.7
FIRST BEXLEY BANK	BEXLEY	OH	**C**	C	C-	162	24.40	6.8	0.9	25.2	3.2	**6.2**	8.3	13.2
▼FIRST BUSINESS BANK	MADISON	WI	**D-**	C-	C	965	3.68	21.5	0.1	4.3	13.9	**6.0**	9.3	11.7
FIRST BUSINESS BANK-MILWA	BROOKFIELD	WI	**D-**	D+	C	142	-23.58	12.9	0.2	10.9	14.2	**6.3**	8.3	14.6
▼FIRST CAHAWBA BANK	SELMA	AL	**D+**	C	C	72	7.24	10.8	4.4	15.2	19.2	**10.0**	13.5	21.3
FIRST CALIFORNIA BANK	WESTLAKE VILLAGE	CA	**C-**	D+	B-	1,518	4.21	15.1	0.4	7.8	18.0	**9.5**	10.6	16.3
FIRST CAPITAL BANK	MARIANNA	FL	**E-**	E-	C-	45	-13.13	0.8	2.4	14.9	13.6	**1.2**	4.7	8.2
FIRST CAPITAL BANK	GUTHRIE	OK	**E+**	D-	D	122	-3.60	31.9	5.4	11.6	0.0	**2.4**	7.0	9.4
▼FIRST CAPITAL BANK	BENNETTSVILLE	SC	**D**	C-	C-	64	-3.28	6.5	11.2	28.1	0.0	**9.1**	10.6	14.2
FIRST CAPITAL BANK	GERMANTOWN	TN	**D+**	D	D+	175	-5.63	9.3	1.2	11.8	12.0	**10.0**	13.4	17.4
FIRST CAPITAL BANK	GLEN ALLEN	VA	**D-**	C-	C-	536	1.13	9.0	0.7	16.8	16.6	**6.8**	8.8	13.4
▲FIRST CAPITAL BANK OF KEN	LOUISVILLE	KY	**C-**	C-	C	436	-0.41	7.0	0.4	13.1	17.3	**6.8**	8.8	13.2
▼FIRST CAROLINA STATE BK	ROCKY MOUNT	NC	**E-**	D-	D	103	-10.74	7.1	1.4	20.3	7.0	**0.0**	3.1	6.0
FIRST CENTRAL BANK	WARRENSBURG	MO	**C+**	C+	B-	210	2.07	2.8	1.6	16.0	24.9	**9.3**	10.6	17.5
▲FIRST CENTRAL BANK	CAMBRIDGE	NE	**C**	C-	C-	78	5.25	11.2	4.0	5.1	17.4	**7.5**	9.5	12.9
FIRST CENTRAL BANK INC	PHILIPPI	WV	**C-**	C-	B-	132	4.53	10.1	6.6	33.9	3.8	**6.6**	8.6	12.3
▲FIRST CENTRAL BANK	MCCOOK	NE	**C**	C-	C-	82	13.65	15.8	2.5	5.3	9.2	**5.9**	8.9	11.7
FIRST CENTRAL NB OF ST PA	SAINT PARIS	OH	**B**	B	B-	78	3.97	2.8	2.9	18.8	16.6	**10.0**	16.3	27.3
FIRST CENTRAL SB	GLEN COVE	NY	**E-**	E	E	637	-6.82	7.5	1.3	10.5	7.6	**1.1**	5.1	8.1

Asset Quality Index	Non-Performing Loans as a % of Total Loans	Non-Performing Loans as a % of Capital	Net Charge-offs / Avg Loans	Profitability Index	Net Income ($Mil)	Return on Assets (R.O.A.)	Return on Equity (R.O.E.)	Net Interest Spread	Overhead Efficiency Ratio	Liquidity Index	Liquidity Ratio	Hot Money Ratio	Stability Index
8.2	0.17	1.2	0.02	**4.2**	0.6	1.04	10.26	3.05	64.2	**1.8**	33.2	31.4	**5.1**
0.9	2.51	17.0	1.21	**3.9**	0.7	0.49	4.21	4.00	66.1	**2.2**	14.8	18.2	**6.3**
2.3	2.07	14.0	0.65	**3.9**	3.1	0.76	7.54	3.90	62.2	**1.8**	14.0	19.9	**4.3**
2.0	2.27	15.7	0.25	**4.7**	2.3	1.41	15.01	3.78	57.6	**1.6**	7.2	20.8	**5.1**
3.2	2.03	15.3	0.42	**3.8**	4.6	0.71	7.97	3.66	70.2	**1.8**	19.9	21.6	**4.4**
7.1	0.23	1.1	0.18	**5.2**	2.9	1.26	14.09	3.27	69.0	**2.9**	39.3	20.1	**6.2**
0.8	5.68	39.9	0.40	**2.3**	-1.4	-0.77	-6.46	3.86	65.7	**2.7**	11.8	15.2	**8.4**
5.2	0.63	4.3	0.05	**9.4**	10.1	2.45	25.19	4.13	47.1	**3.7**	14.7	10.5	**7.3**
8.0	0.14	0.3	0.40	**8.1**	2.8	1.62	11.32	3.57	43.2	**4.1**	52.6	17.7	**8.8**
8.3	0.00	0.0	0.04	**4.9**	0.4	1.04	11.93	4.07	76.9	**3.1**	44.3	20.9	**6.3**
1.8	2.82	22.0	0.33	**8.9**	1.4	1.92	18.87	4.71	51.0	**1.3**	7.8	26.1	**8.4**
2.4	4.45	29.3	0.79	**6.3**	1.9	1.14	10.79	4.19	41.5	**0.9**	20.2	36.9	**4.7**
0.3	15.78	60.5	3.02	**3.1**	0.5	0.40	4.06	3.83	61.5	**1.8**	15.8	20.1	**3.8**
3.8	0.61	4.7	0.32	**7.5**	4.3	1.66	18.06	5.53	67.7	**1.4**	14.5	25.9	**7.0**
0.3	3.46	19.3	0.44	**2.5**	1.2	0.79	8.85	3.56	69.8	**1.9**	27.7	24.2	**1.9**
6.9	1.14	3.0	3.07	**10.0**	3.4	1.86	8.08	9.75	55.6	**5.6**	47.5	8.3	**7.3**
5.0	0.70	4.9	0.06	**5.0**	0.1	1.04	9.10	4.82	81.2	**3.6**	16.2	10.6	**3.7**
1.4	1.72	12.0	1.48	**2.9**	1.7	0.35	3.83	3.86	67.0	**0.6**	9.6	40.7	**5.2**
0.3	2.85	28.8	1.40	**0.0**	-2.2	-4.04	-71.65	3.83	176.2	**0.9**	16.9	34.5	**0.0**
2.9	1.94	13.5	1.20	**2.1**	1.3	0.10	1.05	2.83	59.1	**0.8**	13.0	44.4	**7.2**
7.1	0.00	0.0	0.02	**4.5**	0.1	0.59	4.54	4.91	80.0	**1.9**	30.0	21.3	**9.1**
6.0	0.51	1.9	0.29	**3.6**	0.7	0.78	6.25	4.45	77.1	**2.1**	46.3	43.1	**6.2**
1.3	5.45	29.2	1.61	**1.7**	0.2	0.13	1.22	4.17	74.0	**2.4**	22.2	17.5	**5.4**
0.3	4.24	25.2	1.14	**1.4**	0.1	0.05	0.58	3.60	94.1	**2.3**	40.2	30.3	**4.9**
3.3	0.55	2.9	0.69	**5.5**	4.8	0.97	8.15	3.75	54.0	**2.5**	23.0	17.2	**6.6**
7.0	0.23	1.1	0.13	**9.4**	3.3	1.57	9.81	4.10	41.0	**3.0**	40.3	20.7	**5.0**
7.7	1.92	3.7	0.18	**5.5**	1.0	1.03	7.80	3.97	68.7	**4.3**	70.0	20.0	**7.9**
5.0	1.26	10.2	0.16	**5.5**	1.9	1.30	18.34	4.27	64.8	**3.3**	8.1	11.7	**4.7**
6.8	0.65	0.7	0.92	**8.2**	2.5	1.56	4.79	4.97	45.8	**3.3**	80.9	59.9	**7.8**
5.0	3.73	14.1	0.37	**9.1**	1.1	2.01	13.24	3.97	47.1	**2.5**	43.8	30.1	**9.9**
6.4	0.27	2.2	0.17	**7.3**	3.8	1.69	17.50	4.61	62.2	**4.3**	3.4	5.3	**8.0**
5.1	2.59	14.1	0.10	**3.3**	0.2	0.51	4.56	5.35	82.7	**2.0**	28.8	24.3	**5.1**
0.9	4.76	37.6	0.42	**5.7**	2.9	1.28	14.67	4.97	61.4	**1.8**	8.6	19.6	**5.8**
0.3	5.96	23.0	2.77	**0.0**	-0.3	-0.89	-6.99	3.67	88.4	**3.0**	39.6	20.2	**4.8**
0.0	9.95	67.5	4.34	**0.0**	-2.7	-3.56	-38.83	4.01	104.4	**0.7**	10.4	35.1	**1.0**
2.7	1.07	9.4	0.65	**1.9**	0.1	0.06	0.85	4.38	85.2	**2.8**	17.5	15.4	**3.5**
0.0	4.02	33.9	0.10	**4.4**	0.2	0.64	6.01	4.72	77.8	**2.0**	4.1	17.9	**6.3**
4.7	0.56	3.9	0.12	**6.3**	0.7	1.24	11.60	3.95	55.1	**0.8**	10.3	33.2	**3.7**
0.3	8.78	63.0	1.69	**1.3**	0.7	0.12	1.32	3.50	69.6	**1.5**	6.3	22.5	**3.6**
3.8	3.09	12.9	0.21	**10.0**	4.1	2.45	15.71	4.90	51.7	**1.4**	23.6	29.2	**9.5**
4.6	1.91	11.0	0.22	**4.9**	6.2	0.97	10.83	3.12	61.4	**1.9**	21.2	20.2	**5.4**
4.4	2.35	12.2	0.64	**5.1**	2.0	1.24	13.64	3.91	65.3	**3.9**	27.6	11.5	**6.5**
3.1	1.75	15.0	0.65	**4.2**	1.2	0.85	9.74	3.74	59.3	**1.3**	25.0	31.2	**3.9**
0.0	4.44	33.3	0.55	**3.9**	5.2	0.55	5.79	3.47	61.9	**0.6**	16.1	61.0	**5.3**
1.7	3.89	25.4	0.74	**0.0**	-2.6	-1.60	-18.11	2.89	122.2	**1.4**	26.5	30.6	**3.7**
5.2	4.24	19.5	0.16	**0.7**	0.0	0.03	0.19	3.64	93.9	**3.1**	30.2	16.1	**2.7**
2.3	1.61	9.4	0.83	**2.1**	3.3	0.23	1.57	3.52	76.9	**2.1**	22.7	22.7	**7.6**
0.3	10.21	88.5	2.33	**0.0**	-1.4	-2.77	-37.08	3.02	153.7	**1.2**	19.8	31.2	**0.0**
0.0	18.87	186.7	1.83	**2.5**	-0.9	-0.73	-10.04	4.79	71.0	**1.5**	2.3	21.2	**4.2**
0.8	4.79	36.4	0.58	**2.9**	0.2	0.35	3.32	5.10	64.0	**0.5**	6.4	50.6	**5.1**
0.7	3.67	19.3	0.48	**1.1**	0.5	0.28	2.15	3.26	77.4	**0.7**	13.5	44.7	**4.4**
2.5	4.55	31.2	0.92	**0.3**	-1.8	-0.34	-3.76	3.23	71.9	**1.1**	23.9	32.5	**5.4**
2.6	1.35	9.6	0.52	**2.2**	1.7	0.37	4.17	2.70	75.1	**2.7**	9.5	15.1	**5.2**
0.1	8.43	111.2	3.57	**0.0**	-8.3	-7.30	-86.44	2.35	255.8	**1.3**	16.6	27.5	**2.5**
3.5	1.02	4.9	0.12	**7.5**	2.6	1.27	7.25	4.44	58.0	**1.9**	25.8	21.9	**7.4**
3.8	0.85	6.0	0.83	**3.7**	0.5	0.69	7.10	4.34	65.9	**1.0**	8.3	29.3	**4.1**
3.5	0.28	2.5	0.12	**7.6**	1.6	1.25	11.94	4.67	55.9	**2.1**	11.2	18.3	**6.5**
2.5	1.86	14.4	0.94	**5.8**	0.8	1.09	12.20	4.65	54.4	**0.8**	18.6	40.9	**4.9**
5.8	2.48	8.9	0.00	**4.6**	0.7	0.92	5.58	4.04	66.3	**4.3**	39.3	13.1	**8.1**
0.0	10.72	100.8	1.52	**0.0**	-5.2	-0.78	-11.65	3.25	62.8	**0.7**	12.6	35.6	**2.7**

								Asset Mix (As a % of Total Assets)						
Name	City	State	Rating	2008 Rating	2007 Rating	Total Assets ($Mil)	One Year Asset Growth	Comm-ercial Loans	Cons-umer Loans	Home Mort-gages	Secur-ities	Capital-ization Index	Leverage Ratio	Risk-based Capital Ratio
FIRST CENTRAL STATE BK	DE WITT	IA	**B**	B	B+	258	4.79	10.7	3.5	13.0	20.9	**7.2**	9.1	13.4
▼ FIRST CENTURY BANK	TAZEWELL	TN	**D-**	D+	D+	257	-2.89	1.7	3.2	19.6	17.3	**7.1**	9.0	14.4
FIRST CENTURY BANK NA	GAINESVILLE	GA	**D+**	D-	E-	72	-5.90	4.1	1.2	31.7	23.3	**6.5**	8.5	16.0
▼ FIRST CENTURY BANK NA	BLUEFIELD	WV	**D+**	C-	C+	407	0.05	5.9	4.5	21.8	24.0	**6.7**	8.7	14.6
FIRST CHATHAM BANK	SAVANNAH	GA	**E-**	D-	C-	600	7.29	13.9	0.5	11.0	12.6	**2.0**	5.7	9.0
FIRST CHEROKEE STATE BK	WOODSTOCK	GA	**E-**	E-	D	248	-9.63	2.4	0.6	9.6	6.7	**0.5**	4.2	7.0
▼ FIRST CHICAGO BANK & TRUS	CHICAGO	IL	**E-**	E+	C-	1,018	-13.51	18.3	0.2	5.5	9.4	**0.1**	3.8	6.2
FIRST CHOICE BANK	CERRITOS	CA	**D**	D	C-	202	36.61	4.9	0.0	1.0	40.2	**6.7**	8.7	16.8
FIRST CHOICE BANK	GENEVA	IL	**E-**	D-	D-	195	2.21	9.5	0.2	20.7	0.5	**0.0**	3.2	5.8
▲ FIRST CHOICE BANK	LAWRENCEVILLE	NJ	**C**	C-	C-	448	67.50	4.9	0.3	28.7	24.7	**10.0**	12.1	19.9
FIRST CHOICE COMMUNITY BA	DALLAS	GA	**E-**	D-	D	309	139.82	3.2	0.5	5.9	5.9	**0.0**	-2.4	-3.0
FIRST CITIZENS BANK	LUVERNE	AL	**D**	C-	B-	223	117.84	4.5	7.9	12.2	21.2	**7.7**	9.4	20.7
FIRST CITIZENS BANK	GLENNVILLE	GA	**D-**	D	D	119	4.63	7.8	3.7	13.1	14.4	**7.0**	9.0	14.0
FIRST CITIZENS BANK	ELIZABETHTOWN	KY	**C-**	B	C	296	-1.92	5.7	1.0	18.7	18.9	**6.5**	8.5	13.5
▲ FIRST CITIZENS BANK & TRU	COLUMBIA	SC	**B-**	B-	B	8,240	-0.43	4.8	6.2	16.2	16.8	**6.1**	8.1	16.1
FIRST CITIZENS BANK OF BU	BUTTE	MT	**C**	B-	B	66	0.59	20.4	2.4	14.3	15.7	**6.8**	8.8	15.8
FIRST CITIZENS BANK OF GE	DAWSONVILLE	GA	**E-**	E-	D-	118	0.99	5.2	1.8	7.5	24.5	**0.0**	3.5	5.8
FIRST CITIZENS BANK OF PO	POLSON	MT	**D-**	D	D	27	-6.66	23.2	7.4	17.2	3.9	**7.6**	9.4	13.8
FIRST CITIZENS NATIONAL B	MASON CITY	IA	**A-**	B+	A-	931	1.47	11.8	1.2	10.4	38.8	**9.6**	10.7	18.5
FIRST CITIZENS NATIONAL B	UPPER SANDUSKY	OH	**B-**	B-	B	219	-4.26	4.3	1.6	25.1	25.8	**10.0**	16.8	32.1
FIRST CITIZENS NATIONAL B	MANSFIELD	PA	**C+**	B-	B-	811	11.26	4.3	1.5	25.5	30.9	**5.7**	7.7	13.9
FIRST CITIZENS NATIONAL B	DYERSBURG	TN	**B-**	B-	B	974	1.86	4.8	3.2	14.9	30.3	**6.9**	8.9	15.3
FIRST CITIZENS STATE BK	WHITEWATER	WI	**A**	A-	A	231	2.14	4.7	1.1	22.4	15.1	**10.0**	15.5	22.9
FIRST CITIZENS TRUST CO N	MASON CITY	IA	**U**	U	U	5	14.42	0.0	0.0	0.0	77.1	**10.0**	95.5	207.7
FIRST CITRUS BANK	TAMPA	FL	**D-**	D-	D	247	4.27	3.2	0.4	6.8	4.4	**6.4**	8.5	13.3
FIRST CITY BANK	COLUMBUS	OH	**D**	C-	C-	64	1.79	0.9	0.0	18.4	8.0	**6.6**	8.6	15.3
FIRST CITY BANK OF FLORID	FORT WALTON BEACH	FL	**E-**	E-	D-	284	-3.17	8.6	0.5	17.9	13.1	**0.0**	2.9	5.4
▼ FIRST CLOVER LEAF BANK FS	EDWARDSVILLE	IL	**D+**	C-	B	562	-1.69	8.0	0.9	24.4	13.7	**9.3**	10.5	16.2
FIRST CMNWLTH BK	PRESTONSBURG	KY	**A-**	A	A	192	5.96	4.4	3.1	30.3	41.3	**7.8**	9.5	17.2
FIRST COLEBROOK BANK	COLEBROOK	NH	**C-**	D+	D+	225	5.56	13.1	1.0	17.4	9.9	**4.4**	7.3	10.7
▼ FIRST COLLINSVILLE BANK	COLLINSVILLE	IL	**C+**	B-	C+	613	6.46	0.8	1.9	52.8	9.5	**6.1**	8.1	16.0
FIRST COLONY BANK OF FLOR	MAITLAND	FL	**C-**	C	C	117	17.44	5.4	0.0	1.6	5.7	**10.0**	11.6	20.1
FIRST COLORADO NATIONAL	PAONIA	CO	**D-**	D	D	57	15.60	9.0	1.6	4.3	6.3	**6.7**	8.7	12.7
FIRST COLUMBIA BANK & TRU	BLOOMSBURG	PA	**B**	B	C	612	1.91	5.1	1.2	23.4	33.5	**7.6**	9.4	17.6
▼ FIRST COMMAND BANK	FORT WORTH	TX	**B+**	B	B	623	1.14	9.7	31.8	0.1	49.8	**6.1**	8.1	16.2
FIRST COMMERCE BANK	MARYSVILLE	KS	**A-**	A-	A-	45	7.49	8.7	5.3	34.3	2.6	**10.0**	11.7	17.0
FIRST COMMERCE BANK	LEWISBURG	TN	**C+**	C	B-	238	2.13	9.5	3.3	14.5	24.7	**6.4**	8.4	14.0
FIRST COMMERCIAL BANK	CHICAGO	IL	**D-**	D-	D	269	-14.80	3.2	0.2	16.1	2.0	**7.9**	9.6	13.2
FIRST COMMERCIAL BANK	BLOOMINGTON	MN	**E-**	D-	D	292	-18.44	11.7	0.1	19.3	7.9	**1.7**	5.3	8.7
FIRST COMMERCIAL BANK	DEXTER	MO	**D-**	D-	C+	209	-7.73	18.2	1.1	5.9	18.8	**6.7**	8.7	12.6
FIRST COMMERCIAL BANK	JACKSON	MS	**B-**	B-	B-	275	7.79	20.4	1.7	12.1	7.8	**7.5**	9.9	13.0
FIRST COMMERCIAL BANK	EDMOND	OK	**C+**	C	C+	281	5.06	18.9	2.5	14.8	13.5	**8.0**	9.6	14.0
FIRST COMMERCIAL BANK (US	ALHAMBRA	CA	**C+**	C-	B	451	-1.24	8.8	0.0	0.8	4.9	**10.0**	19.1	24.7
FIRST COMMERCIAL BANK NA	SEGUIN	TX	**C+**	B-	B-	107	-1.44	8.9	2.2	22.8	7.6	**6.9**	8.9	14.1
FIRST COMMERCIAL BANK OF	TAMPA	FL	**E-**	E	D-	103	-27.41	6.4	0.6	10.3	12.6	**0.0**	2.2	4.3
▼ FIRST COMMONS BANK NA	NEWTON CENTER	MA	**D+**	C	NR	111	72.91	3.9	0.1	35.8	24.1	**10.0**	12.6	20.7
▲ FIRST COMMONWEALTH BANK	INDIANA	PA	**C-**	D+	B-	5,750	-9.99	13.9	9.8	12.1	16.5	**8.2**	10.9	13.5
FIRST COMMUNITY BANK	CHATOM	AL	**C+**	C+	C+	320	-2.84	12.2	3.1	13.2	15.1	**7.9**	9.6	13.8
FIRST COMMUNITY BANK	BATESVILLE	AR	**C+**	C+	C	712	13.39	12.0	5.8	21.8	15.2	**6.4**	8.4	12.7
FIRST COMMUNITY BANK	SANTA ROSA	CA	**D-**	D-	D+	759	0.95	7.8	0.3	13.6	1.3	**8.5**	10.0	14.5
FIRST COMMUNITY BANK	KEOKUK	IA	**C-**	C-	C	116	-4.79	9.5	1.4	9.6	40.7	**6.9**	8.9	16.1
FIRST COMMUNITY BANK	NEWELL	IA	**B+**	B+	B+	58	-1.64	0.7	1.9	7.7	20.7	**9.0**	10.3	14.3
FIRST COMMUNITY BANK	SIDNEY	IA	**D-**	C-	D+	52	-11.40	15.2	3.5	16.0	23.8	**6.4**	8.4	13.0
FIRST COMMUNITY BANK	ELGIN	IL	**D-**	D-	C	163	-1.17	3.4	0.2	6.1	15.8	**9.9**	11.0	15.4
FIRST COMMUNITY BANK	EMPORIA	KS	**D**	D	C	55	-4.77	8.3	1.9	11.4	10.5	**5.4**	7.4	16.0
FIRST COMMUNITY BANK	HAMMOND	LA	**D-**	D-	C	115	-11.29	4.9	2.1	20.3	5.3	**9.8**	10.9	16.2
▲ FIRST COMMUNITY BANK	HARBOR SPRINGS	MI	**D+**	D	D	194	-5.51	3.6	0.8	19.6	6.5	**10.0**	11.0	16.0
FIRST COMMUNITY BANK	LESTER PRAIRIE	MN	**C-**	D+	C-	28	-4.57	9.1	5.3	13.0	28.5	**6.0**	8.1	12.7
▼ FIRST COMMUNITY BANK	LEE'S SUMMIT	MO	**D-**	C-	C-	614	2.32	5.5	2.4	22.6	4.9	**6.3**	8.3	13.6
FIRST COMMUNITY BANK	GLASGOW	MT	**D+**	C	B-	217	0.09	5.7	3.0	9.5	24.2	**6.2**	8.2	13.2

Asset Quality Index	Non-Performing Loans as a % of Total Loans	Non-Performing Loans as a % of Capital	Net Charge-offs / Avg Loans	Profitability Index	Net Income ($Mil)	Return on Assets (R.O.A.)	Return on Equity (R.O.E.)	Net Interest Spread	Overhead Efficiency Ratio	Liquidity Index	Liquidity Ratio	Hot Money Ratio	Stability Index
4.3	1.41	10.4	0.30	5.9	2.6	1.02	11.14	3.62	58.6	2.5	21.2	17.0	6.6
2.9	2.95	16.3	1.93	0.0	-2.4	-0.87	-8.24	4.09	96.3	2.3	23.3	18.4	5.1
3.7	3.28	22.1	1.51	3.9	0.8	1.11	14.61	4.62	84.1	1.1	11.7	30.0	1.8
0.7	6.70	41.0	0.14	3.7	2.2	0.53	5.73	3.73	73.5	2.9	24.9	15.3	4.6
0.3	7.16	69.8	1.35	0.7	-3.4	-0.29	-4.76	2.43	76.7	1.3	10.1	26.0	0.0
0.0	11.30	121.4	3.04	0.0	-5.4	-2.11	-47.60	2.85	158.4	0.8	16.2	35.1	0.4
0.0	13.33	146.6	7.74	0.0	-69.4	-6.25	-91.34	2.75	130.4	0.6	9.8	49.4	4.1
3.8	2.06	10.4	0.54	1.3	1.0	0.58	6.19	3.03	77.9	2.5	52.0	44.8	2.1
0.3	9.04	116.6	2.33	0.0	-8.9	-4.69	-85.38	3.53	126.2	0.8	17.5	39.1	1.6
5.3	1.42	7.8	0.62	2.7	1.6	0.46	4.63	2.87	81.3	1.9	30.4	27.3	4.2
0.0	30.36	862.2	7.98	0.0	-42.4	-12.23	-273.94	3.05	198.2	1.0	14.7	31.6	0.0
1.3	3.24	17.1	0.43	8.3	7.5	3.81	35.36	4.16	37.3	1.8	30.7	28.7	3.9
2.0	1.73	9.8	2.35	0.0	-0.2	-0.21	-2.16	3.13	72.1	1.3	21.9	30.2	4.1
6.1	0.00	0.0	0.03	7.0	6.3	2.05	23.32	3.21	54.1	2.7	13.1	15.4	3.7
3.3	2.54	16.7	1.24	6.0	75.9	0.90	9.66	3.52	58.5	4.1	17.8	9.1	8.3
3.8	2.15	13.1	-0.28	3.9	0.4	0.66	7.03	4.39	71.6	3.0	23.5	15.0	6.2
0.0	12.41	136.5	2.16	0.0	-3.4	-2.94	-50.28	3.30	160.2	1.7	19.9	22.9	0.0
0.0	17.07	85.9	0.98	0.0	-0.7	-2.54	-24.79	4.41	125.3	1.4	18.3	26.7	5.0
7.1	0.40	1.9	0.16	7.6	17.5	1.89	16.07	3.88	49.6	2.7	22.8	16.3	8.6
7.2	0.97	3.0	0.25	3.6	1.4	0.60	3.57	3.92	80.0	3.9	27.9	11.3	7.5
3.0	2.46	17.4	0.05	8.1	11.9	1.55	17.36	4.29	51.7	2.1	17.8	18.8	6.5
4.6	0.85	5.0	1.35	4.7	9.2	0.97	9.36	4.32	62.5	1.4	17.5	27.4	6.5
8.6	0.00	0.0	0.42	7.6	3.1	1.38	9.25	4.55	54.5	1.6	26.7	27.4	8.2
10.0	0.00	0.0	0.00	9.5	0.7	13.70	14.38	2.90	71.5	5.0	2,713.6	101.0	7.0
0.0	2.59	18.1	0.75	1.2	0.5	0.19	2.17	3.33	73.2	2.5	25.4	17.5	4.0
0.9	3.44	28.2	0.59	3.6	0.4	0.68	8.07	3.82	74.3	4.3	21.3	7.2	4.8
0.3	10.28	143.9	2.08	0.0	-6.8	-2.20	-64.51	1.96	144.4	1.4	14.8	26.1	0.9
1.5	3.17	19.7	0.45	3.1	4.1	0.71	5.71	3.09	53.4	2.4	29.3	19.5	6.2
9.2	0.19	0.9	0.10	7.1	3.3	1.69	15.18	4.37	62.8	2.4	31.0	20.2	8.3
4.7	0.94	8.8	0.51	2.7	0.9	0.42	5.21	4.08	84.0	2.6	13.6	15.7	3.9
3.2	0.87	7.2	0.56	3.8	3.7	0.61	7.23	3.42	57.0	3.2	14.4	13.1	4.8
6.1	0.87	4.3	0.00	1.9	0.5	0.49	3.91	3.36	74.6	5.0	42.8	10.7	3.6
0.0	1.24	9.6	1.73	1.4	0.0	0.02	0.14	3.51	78.8	3.1	16.8	13.5	5.4
5.0	1.12	6.3	0.28	5.6	6.5	1.07	9.61	3.73	60.4	2.7	25.4	16.8	6.4
6.7	0.13	0.7	1.13	8.7	13.5	2.23	24.50	3.59	53.8	7.0	60.8	3.6	6.2
8.2	0.11	0.8	0.08	8.6	0.8	1.87	16.15	4.03	52.7	2.6	11.0	15.6	8.0
4.6	0.38	2.5	0.17	4.0	2.0	0.81	9.41	3.81	63.3	0.7	14.2	40.4	3.9
0.0	12.71	94.1	8.05	0.0	-15.0	-5.19	-60.07	4.22	113.1	1.0	2.7	28.0	3.4
0.2	9.51	94.0	4.67	0.0	-13.0	-3.87	-53.55	2.54	106.7	2.7	17.0	15.8	1.8
0.3	7.97	50.7	0.21	3.2	1.0	0.43	4.80	3.12	66.0	1.6	13.8	22.6	5.4
8.2	0.06	0.4	0.04	3.9	1.9	0.73	7.29	3.15	63.2	0.7	15.8	43.3	5.9
4.2	1.44	9.4	0.20	3.9	1.6	0.57	5.36	4.79	74.3	1.2	22.1	30.8	5.5
2.8	3.02	12.6	0.34	4.4	3.6	0.80	4.76	3.60	50.1	0.5	8.5	54.1	7.0
4.6	0.89	6.3	0.66	3.6	0.8	0.74	8.32	5.44	74.1	3.5	19.4	11.7	5.0
0.0	15.44	167.9	6.21	0.0	-5.6	-4.56	-62.35	2.57	135.7	1.1	18.1	30.8	1.0
9.5	0.00	0.0	0.00	0.0	-2.1	-2.21	-14.34	1.90	218.1	2.0	39.9	37.9	1.5
1.8	3.03	18.6	1.61	3.9	34.9	0.57	5.46	3.93	58.3	3.9	7.2	8.4	6.8
4.0	1.66	11.6	0.74	3.3	1.9	0.60	6.42	4.59	76.1	2.5	19.3	16.8	4.8
3.7	1.67	13.6	0.40	5.2	6.3	0.94	11.30	4.02	59.6	0.8	12.4	33.7	5.1
0.0	4.78	29.8	1.77	0.6	-1.2	-0.16	-1.63	3.67	55.1	2.1	25.4	19.7	3.7
2.5	3.81	19.5	1.88	1.3	0.1	0.07	0.74	3.56	68.5	5.4	41.4	7.7	4.5
7.1	0.00	0.0	0.00	6.9	1.0	1.63	13.53	4.04	56.9	4.0	30.6	12.0	8.3
2.5	2.43	18.5	0.59	0.3	-0.6	-1.04	-12.57	3.45	100.7	1.6	28.7	29.9	2.6
0.0	9.03	49.8	1.25	3.1	0.6	0.39	3.54	4.19	61.1	2.0	16.0	18.9	5.9
1.7	2.08	13.1	1.19	0.6	-0.2	-0.28	-3.64	2.98	93.2	4.6	46.1	13.2	3.7
1.9	3.22	19.4	1.68	0.3	-0.8	-0.65	-6.47	3.49	99.4	1.6	22.4	24.6	4.0
0.1	5.07	31.2	1.82	5.2	2.3	1.13	10.52	5.04	57.9	2.2	17.4	18.2	5.0
1.5	4.47	27.5	1.22	3.6	0.2	0.69	8.68	4.81	81.4	3.4	22.8	12.6	4.1
0.3	2.53	19.9	0.52	1.6	1.7	0.28	3.30	3.87	81.2	1.4	15.6	26.8	3.5
1.1	4.52	29.7	0.88	4.4	1.7	0.77	9.04	4.39	62.8	2.6	23.1	17.0	4.8

	Name	City	State	Rating	2008 Rating	2007 Rating	Total Assets ($Mil)	One Year Asset Growth	Asset Mix (As a % of Total Assets) Comm-ercial Loans	Cons-umer Loans	Home Mort-gages	Secur-ities	Capital-ization Index	Leverage Ratio	Risk-based Capital Ratio
	FIRST COMMUNITY BANK	BEEMER	NE	**B-**	C	C	107	5.67	6.7	2.5	1.9	23.0	**6.2**	8.2	12.9
	FIRST COMMUNITY BANK	COLUMBUS	OH	**D**	D	C-	115	-0.55	0.6	0.1	25.0	15.5	**8.0**	9.7	14.5
	FIRST COMMUNITY BANK	CORPUS CHRISTI	TX	**B-**	B-	B-	272	13.55	13.9	9.5	17.3	9.3	**6.1**	8.1	12.4
	FIRST COMMUNITY BANK	MILTON	WI	**C+**	C+	B-	80	-2.25	5.5	2.0	21.6	21.1	**7.2**	9.1	12.7
▼	FIRST COMMUNITY BANK & TR	BEECHER	IL	**D**	C-	B	150	-5.86	3.4	1.5	24.3	22.0	**6.7**	8.7	17.1
	FIRST COMMUNITY BANK MISS	POPLAR BLUFF	MO	**C+**	C+	C	241	4.11	13.5	3.1	13.0	29.5	**5.9**	7.9	13.1
	FIRST COMMUNITY BANK NA	LEXINGTON	SC	**C-**	C-	C+	598	-1.05	3.4	1.0	15.0	31.4	**6.5**	8.5	14.5
	FIRST COMMUNITY BANK NA	SAN BENITO	TX	**D**	C+	C+	197	1.20	14.1	3.8	10.7	13.0	**7.3**	9.2	13.9
	FIRST COMMUNITY BANK NA	SUGAR LAND	TX	**D-**	E+	D-	668	-16.97	9.3	2.4	11.1	6.3	**8.8**	10.2	16.5
	FIRST COMMUNITY BANK NA	BLUEFIELD	VA	**C+**	C-	B	2,228	-0.87	4.3	2.9	24.6	21.3	**6.7**	8.7	14.2
	FIRST COMMUNITY BANK OF A	PINELLAS PARK	FL	**E-**	D-	D+	471	-14.33	3.8	8.3	19.9	9.8	**2.6**	5.8	9.7
	FIRST COMMUNITY BANK OF E	MARION	AR	**C**	C+	C+	105	6.98	4.5	2.6	16.9	5.3	**8.5**	10.0	17.0
	FIRST COMMUNITY BANK OF J	JOLIET	IL	**D**	D	D+	573	5.30	18.7	0.7	3.8	8.9	**3.8**	8.2	10.4
	FIRST COMMUNITY BANK OF S	FORT MYERS	FL	**E-**	E-	D-	305	-1.59	5.1	0.6	14.1	9.8	**0.0**	3.5	6.0
	FIRST COMMUNITY BK	WETUMPKA	AL	**B-**	B-	B-	272	6.68	9.4	4.4	15.3	20.3	**5.7**	7.7	11.7
	FIRST COMMUNITY BK HILLSB	HILLSBORO	IL	**C+**	C+	C	70	6.13	9.7	5.1	21.9	11.6	**7.0**	9.0	16.5
	FIRST COMMUNITY BK HOMER	HOMER GLEN	IL	**D**	C	C	95	1.35	13.3	0.4	18.5	3.2	**7.1**	9.1	14.0
	FIRST COMMUNITY BK LEWIS	VANCEBURG	KY	**C-**	C	C+	27	11.50	4.7	8.8	24.5	23.2	**10.0**	11.1	17.3
	FIRST COMMUNITY BK OF BED	SHELBYVILLE	TN	**A-**	B+	A-	318	13.86	5.3	2.2	29.7	19.6	**10.0**	11.3	17.0
▼	FIRST COMMUNITY BK OF CRA	VAN BUREN	AR	**D+**	C-	C-	96	11.76	8.6	5.0	30.5	5.7	**5.6**	7.9	11.4
▲	FIRST COMMUNITY BK OF EAS	ROGERSVILLE	TN	**D+**	C-	C	219	-6.09	3.3	0.7	12.1	11.0	**10.0**	11.3	16.2
	FIRST COMMUNITY BK OF W K	CLINTON	KY	**A-**	B+	B+	77	5.72	6.9	7.3	9.9	18.3	**10.0**	12.3	15.6
	FIRST COMMUNITY BK PLAINF	PLAINFIELD	IL	**D**	C	C	115	9.64	28.5	0.5	5.6	1.8	**9.4**	11.6	14.5
▲	FIRST COMMUNITY BK SILVER	SILVER LAKE	MN	**C**	C-	C-	24	-9.71	0.7	1.1	4.8	51.3	**7.3**	9.2	18.0
▼	FIRST COMMUNITY BK THE OZ	BRANSON	MO	**E**	D-	C-	103	5.65	6.0	1.2	10.6	16.9	**2.8**	6.7	9.8
	FIRST COMMUNITY BK XENIA-	XENIA	IL	**B**	B	B	33	-1.84	4.3	8.7	23.7	23.1	**8.3**	12.8	13.6
▼	FIRST COMMUNITY NATIONAL	CUBA	MO	**B**	B+	B+	236	6.71	2.2	2.9	30.6	16.3	**5.8**	7.8	14.2
	FIRST COMMUNITY STATE BK	STAUNTON	IL	**C**	C	D	55	8.56	16.6	3.1	8.7	12.6	**6.7**	9.0	12.3
	FIRST COMMUNITY TRUST NA	DUBUQUE	IA	**U**	U	U	6	18.43	0.0	0.0	0.0	68.0	**10.0**	98.4	174.4
	FIRST CORNERSTONE BANK	KING OF PRUSSIA	PA	**E-**	E-	E-	187	-15.93	3.7	1.3	23.2	10.3	**4.6**	6.6	11.3
▲	FIRST COUNTY BANK	STAMFORD	CT	**D**	D+	B-	1,305	0.83	4.3	0.3	37.8	28.5	**6.9**	9.0	14.4
▼	FIRST COUNTY BANK	NEW BADEN	IL	**C+**	B-	C+	396	7.09	1.3	2.5	53.5	8.4	**6.3**	8.3	15.6
	FIRST COVENANT BANK	COMMERCE	GA	**E-**	E-	E+	154	-7.48	4.0	1.3	8.2	6.1	**1.3**	6.0	8.3
▲	FIRST CREDIT BANK	LOS ANGELES	CA	**C-**	D	B	482	-2.48	0.5	0.0	7.8	5.8	**10.0**	23.4	31.0
	FIRST DAKOTA NATIONAL BK	YANKTON	SD	**C-**	C-	C+	788	4.40	8.4	1.8	4.5	14.0	**7.1**	9.1	12.8
	FIRST DELTA BANK	MARKED TREE	AR	**C+**	C+	C+	51	-1.71	4.5	2.2	8.2	44.2	**7.5**	9.4	19.9
	FIRST EAGLE BANK	HANOVER PARK	IL	**B**	C-	C+	332	2.22	1.0	0.3	7.0	27.1	**10.0**	12.7	17.3
	FIRST EAST SIDE SAVINGS B	SUNRISE	FL	**D-**	D-	C-	85	-18.34	0.9	0.2	34.4	17.9	**7.0**	9.0	15.8
▲	FIRST ELECTRONIC BANK	SANDY	UT	**C+**	B-	B	8	-53.61	0.1	0.0	0.0	3.3	**10.0**	82.4	292.9
▼	FIRST ENTERPRISE BANK	OKLAHOMA CITY	OK	**D-**	B	B	163	1.21	15.6	2.3	13.3	0.0	**5.6**	8.5	11.5
	FIRST EXCHANGE BANK	MANNINGTON	WV	**D**	D+	C+	203	1.87	3.5	15.6	39.0	2.6	**6.1**	8.1	12.0
	FIRST FARMBANK	GREELEY	CO	**C+**	C	C-	74	20.54	7.2	0.6	2.9	24.4	**8.8**	10.2	14.8
▼	FIRST FARMERS & MERCH	BROWNSDALE	MN	**B**	B+	B+	80	3.41	8.9	3.0	6.9	32.1	**10.0**	11.8	16.9
▼	FIRST FARMERS & MERCH	GRAND MEADOW	MN	**B**	B+	B+	41	15.25	6.4	0.5	3.5	16.7	**10.0**	12.8	18.0
	FIRST FARMERS &	COLUMBIA	TN	**C**	C	B+	938	0.68	6.0	1.8	17.6	29.1	**8.6**	10.1	15.8
	FIRST FARMERS &	FAIRMONT	MN	**B+**	B+	B+	84	3.29	17.9	5.3	15.8	10.2	**10.0**	12.5	15.4
▼	FIRST FARMERS &	LE SUEUR	MN	**B**	B+	B+	113	14.12	8.5	1.8	9.5	24.1	**7.7**	9.5	13.1
▼	FIRST FARMERS &	LUVERNE	MN	**B+**	A-	A-	145	4.35	14.2	3.2	3.0	17.8	**10.0**	11.4	15.2
	FIRST FARMERS BANK & TRUS	CONVERSE	IN	**C+**	B-	B-	847	9.37	7.0	0.9	7.5	15.9	**6.3**	9.1	12.0
	FIRST FARMERS BANK & TRUS	OWENTON	KY	**D**	C	C-	117	6.34	4.4	2.1	28.0	4.7	**9.0**	10.3	14.7
	FIRST FARMERS NB OF WAURI	WAURIKA	OK	**A-**	A-	B+	43	0.46	5.3	4.2	6.1	48.9	**10.0**	18.4	45.1
	FIRST FARMERS STATE BK	MINIER	IL	**B-**	C	C	139	2.55	7.8	0.9	11.9	34.3	**8.8**	10.2	16.9
	FIRST FEDERAL BANK	FORT PAYNE	AL	**D**	C-	C+	89	1.55	11.2	2.9	26.4	19.6	**5.6**	7.6	16.7
	FIRST FEDERAL BANK	HARRISON	AR	**D-**	D-	D	600	-17.98	1.5	1.9	38.0	13.9	**4.4**	6.4	10.7
	FIRST FEDERAL BANK	LEXINGTON	KY	**D**	D+	D+	140	-1.67	3.3	0.1	30.4	0.4	**10.0**	13.6	19.6
	FIRST FEDERAL BANK	DUNN	NC	**C-**	C-	C	173	-1.52	1.1	2.5	32.5	6.6	**10.0**	11.4	19.0
	FIRST FEDERAL BANK	DICKSON	TN	**C+**	C+	C+	451	2.29	6.4	5.0	25.5	31.4	**6.1**	8.1	15.2
▲	FIRST FEDERAL BANK A FSB	TUSCALOOSA	AL	**D+**	D+	C	176	11.66	0.1	1.2	68.9	0.1	**5.7**	7.7	13.1
	FIRST FEDERAL BANK FSB	KANSAS CITY	MO	**C**	C	C+	386	-0.36	0.0	0.2	54.9	12.6	**10.0**	15.0	26.3
▲	FIRST FEDERAL BANK LITTLE	LITTLEFIELD	TX	**B-**	C+	B	44	-2.25	1.5	6.3	18.9	15.7	**10.0**	16.3	27.6

Asset Quality Index	Non-Performing Loans as a % of Total Loans	Non-Performing Loans as a % of Capital	Net Charge-offs Avg Loans	Profitability Index	Net Income ($Mil)	Return on Assets (R.O.A.)	Return on Equity (R.O.E.)	Net Interest Spread	Overhead Efficiency Ratio	Liquidity Index	Liquidity Ratio	Hot Money Ratio	Stability Index
5.2	0.22	1.5	-0.10	4.3	0.9	0.84	8.71	4.19	73.5	2.2	33.3	25.6	5.8
0.7	4.12	27.8	0.62	1.3	0.1	0.04	0.41	3.76	71.8	1.8	18.5	21.0	4.8
5.2	0.50	4.1	0.47	5.0	2.8	1.09	12.95	5.27	76.4	1.1	18.1	30.9	5.3
2.3	2.61	16.6	0.68	6.4	1.1	1.42	15.48	4.46	59.9	4.2	31.7	11.4	5.6
0.3	7.14	34.8	5.81	0.7	-1.6	-1.05	-10.69	4.86	63.9	3.6	18.9	11.3	4.3
5.1	1.85	12.4	0.85	3.7	1.9	0.79	9.28	4.26	73.9	1.7	21.5	23.0	3.7
3.5	1.90	11.2	0.54	2.5	2.3	0.37	4.16	3.40	75.7	2.6	30.7	18.7	4.2
0.9	3.83	25.3	0.46	3.3	1.0	0.54	6.83	4.42	81.1	1.9	18.6	20.2	5.2
0.9	8.88	47.6	3.44	0.0	-20.8	-2.77	-25.89	3.10	164.5	1.0	25.6	38.2	3.8
3.5	1.39	9.0	0.90	3.8	22.3	0.99	9.01	3.93	63.1	1.8	13.8	20.7	7.2
0.0	10.33	88.7	2.90	0.0	-18.2	-3.48	-50.18	2.94	81.8	1.8	21.7	22.4	2.2
3.0	3.43	18.7	0.21	4.7	0.8	0.73	6.82	4.33	72.1	1.2	21.5	30.2	7.2
0.0	2.76	22.4	3.26	0.2	-10.1	-1.78	-18.35	3.65	45.6	0.6	5.1	37.8	3.7
0.0	3.86	50.5	2.68	0.0	-6.6	-2.03	-39.28	2.76	99.2	0.7	9.8	34.9	2.3
5.2	1.89	15.0	0.27	6.6	4.3	1.59	20.45	4.25	54.1	1.3	20.5	28.5	5.3
5.4	0.80	5.0	0.26	4.2	0.7	0.97	10.55	3.28	71.3	3.2	32.3	16.6	5.1
1.7	7.10	41.3	4.72	0.0	-6.3	-6.34	-59.77	3.19	98.3	1.0	26.0	37.7	2.7
4.5	1.62	7.3	0.81	1.2	-0.3	-0.99	-6.79	5.13	115.7	1.7	24.6	23.8	6.7
6.1	1.21	6.5	1.20	8.8	5.2	1.77	14.67	3.96	62.4	1.0	24.9	39.1	6.6
1.3	2.89	25.0	0.08	1.4	0.1	0.11	0.93	4.21	74.9	0.7	11.0	42.4	3.9
1.6	2.51	13.4	1.32	2.7	0.6	0.25	2.31	3.63	66.3	1.4	13.3	25.8	5.6
6.5	0.72	4.0	0.11	6.7	1.0	1.29	9.86	4.98	63.9	1.1	14.9	30.3	7.8
2.7	3.38	20.8	3.15	0.0	-2.4	-2.15	-19.87	3.61	68.8	0.9	13.7	33.7	2.6
6.5	0.86	3.5	1.07	4.0	0.5	1.81	21.39	4.28	87.5	5.1	53.3	10.3	4.0
0.3	7.11	57.6	0.69	0.4	-0.7	-0.67	-9.17	3.91	99.9	1.5	6.1	22.6	4.1
6.3	0.63	3.3	0.06	6.5	0.5	1.56	12.09	4.24	64.7	4.1	22.6	9.2	8.7
6.5	0.47	3.4	0.13	5.8	2.8	1.25	14.86	4.57	64.1	1.1	14.7	30.1	6.3
5.1	1.85	13.2	0.00	3.1	0.2	0.50	5.59	3.84	86.4	3.3	28.6	14.8	4.6
10.0	0.00	0.0	0.00	10.0	0.6	11.65	12.32	4.57	74.0	5.0	2,354.0	101.0	6.0
0.0	14.69	129.6	0.84	0.0	-2.1	-0.97	-15.65	2.60	134.9	1.5	18.9	25.1	1.4
1.7	3.27	20.8	0.47	1.7	2.6	0.20	2.51	3.30	81.7	2.4	26.2	23.1	5.2
3.5	0.90	8.1	0.07	6.6	4.6	1.17	13.49	3.43	52.3	2.8	6.9	14.4	5.4
0.0	11.11	108.9	3.28	0.0	-1.3	-0.74	-13.73	3.81	96.5	2.7	14.4	15.4	0.0
1.3	5.33	13.8	-1.15	10.0	24.7	5.05	22.45	6.84	14.5	1.0	27.9	63.7	9.2
1.9	2.84	21.1	0.17	7.4	9.8	1.29	13.34	4.88	61.7	3.6	19.1	11.3	6.7
7.2	0.46	1.7	0.07	4.4	0.4	0.72	7.02	4.35	70.0	4.5	57.1	15.2	5.2
4.4	1.57	7.2	0.45	6.0	6.3	1.94	14.81	4.44	45.7	1.5	24.9	27.3	6.0
0.0	29.39	163.6	0.44	0.0	-3.8	-4.00	-39.49	1.61	299.8	1.5	33.9	42.9	3.4
10.0	0.00	0.0	0.00	7.2	0.3	3.16	6.31	0.26	94.3	5.1	446.6	90.6	5.7
0.0	6.55	59.5	0.57	5.2	1.5	0.88	9.97	4.57	71.3	1.1	10.0	29.7	5.8
0.6	3.77	36.4	0.90	5.3	2.2	1.08	14.45	4.26	58.4	1.8	8.9	19.6	4.9
8.3	0.00	0.0	0.00	4.0	0.8	1.21	11.75	4.31	66.8	0.8	18.7	40.0	4.9
5.6	2.31	11.8	0.71	4.5	0.9	1.18	7.88	4.22	64.7	1.8	19.7	21.0	7.5
4.7	1.23	5.7	1.37	2.9	0.3	0.76	5.52	4.61	70.1	2.1	27.7	20.9	5.0
2.9	1.47	7.9	0.24	3.9	7.2	0.77	6.88	4.15	79.0	3.1	15.5	13.4	8.0
5.5	1.30	8.2	0.20	6.4	1.2	1.54	12.05	4.29	62.0	1.1	14.8	30.5	7.3
3.7	2.02	13.1	0.00	4.5	1.2	1.19	9.12	4.40	71.4	2.2	28.6	20.3	5.9
6.2	1.01	5.9	0.23	8.6	2.7	1.95	14.21	4.76	63.7	3.3	10.1	11.8	7.8
3.9	1.26	9.9	0.63	6.7	9.4	1.16	11.61	4.34	56.0	1.8	12.1	19.9	7.0
3.2	2.01	14.7	0.09	7.8	1.5	1.31	9.81	4.62	54.4	1.1	9.0	28.6	2.3
7.5	1.33	3.0	0.48	9.6	0.9	2.09	9.90	5.39	57.4	1.9	32.4	29.1	9.3
6.3	0.52	2.6	0.03	4.9	1.3	0.96	9.56	3.97	69.1	2.8	31.3	18.3	4.8
1.5	4.84	29.3	-0.04	1.8	0.0	-0.04	-0.52	2.90	93.5	3.0	47.2	23.9	3.5
0.0	12.76	80.5	0.40	0.7	-3.7	-0.56	-8.99	3.40	90.3	1.8	21.4	21.3	3.0
1.1	5.40	25.2	0.12	0.0	-3.4	-2.39	-16.07	3.17	128.4	1.2	14.8	28.4	5.7
4.3	2.13	12.2	0.35	0.9	-0.3	-0.15	-1.40	3.35	98.6	1.5	27.2	29.7	4.5
4.2	1.35	8.3	0.88	5.0	4.8	1.06	12.42	4.23	55.0	2.3	38.2	28.6	4.6
1.8	1.77	18.2	0.68	3.6	1.2	0.70	9.56	3.17	76.5	0.3	1.1	63.6	3.9
4.5	1.89	8.3	0.00	2.2	1.3	0.34	2.46	2.81	87.2	3.3	28.5	14.5	5.7
8.6	0.78	2.3	0.02	3.5	0.2	0.49	2.93	3.55	79.8	1.8	37.8	35.1	5.5

								Asset Mix (As a % of Total Assets)						
Name	City	State	Rating	2008 Rating	2007 Rating	Total Assets ($Mil)	One Year Asset Growth	Comm-ercial Loans	Cons-umer Loans	Home Mort-gages	Secur-ities	Capital-ization Index	Leverage Ratio	Risk-based Capital Ratio
FIRST FEDERAL BANK OF FLO	LAKE CITY	FL	C	A	A	933	12.03	4.3	2.0	17.0	33.9	8.5	10.0	18.9
FIRST FEDERAL BANK OF LOU	LAKE CHARLES	LA	B-	B	B	713	9.40	1.8	1.7	28.3	30.9	10.0	12.3	25.5
▼ FIRST FEDERAL BANK OF OHI	GALION	OH	C-	C+	B	252	5.08	6.3	5.2	22.5	12.9	10.0	16.3	29.6
FIRST FEDERAL BANK OF THE	DEFIANCE	OH	C+	C+	B	1,974	-1.06	18.2	1.1	11.6	8.2	8.9	10.8	14.1
▼ FIRST FEDERAL BANK OF WIS	WAUKESHA	WI	D+	C-	C+	128	11.19	7.2	1.0	36.9	3.2	7.9	9.6	14.1
FIRST FEDERAL BANK TEXAS	TYLER	TX	D-	C-	C-	219	-9.29	4.9	1.5	46.0	11.5	6.6	8.7	13.8
FIRST FEDERAL COMMUNITY	DOVER	OH	C+	C+	B+	209	5.82	9.0	3.0	23.8	2.9	5.4	9.0	11.3
FIRST FEDERAL COMMUNITY	PARIS	TX	D+	C	C+	357	-1.12	6.7	5.7	54.2	6.4	6.6	8.6	13.5
FIRST FEDERAL COMMUNITY	BUCYRUS	OH	D+	D	C	125	-1.38	5.9	4.6	46.9	6.2	9.2	10.5	17.3
FIRST FEDERAL OF	ALPENA	MI	D	D-	D-	215	-7.54	4.1	1.0	33.9	17.6	8.4	10.0	15.8
FIRST FEDERAL OF SOUTH CA	WALTERBORO	SC	D-	D	C	106	-11.30	1.2	2.6	36.5	12.2	6.2	8.2	14.3
FIRST FEDERAL SAVINGS OF	MIDDLETOWN	NY	C+	B	A-	184	1.88	0.5	0.0	2.7	41.3	10.0	28.9	83.9
▼ FIRST FEDERAL SB ELIZABET	ELIZABETHTOWN	KY	D	D	C-	1,328	9.90	3.3	3.1	16.7	14.8	5.8	7.8	12.1
FIRST FIDELITY BANK	BURKE	SD	A	A	A+	291	9.26	4.3	3.2	1.6	36.5	10.0	11.0	18.1
▼ FIRST FIDELITY BANK NA	OKLAHOMA CITY	OK	D-	D	C+	1,123	5.57	6.0	12.9	7.0	31.7	5.9	7.9	12.8
▼ FIRST FINANCIAL BANK	BESSEMER	AL	E-	D-	D+	205	-8.25	3.4	2.9	19.9	21.8	3.4	6.3	10.2
▼ FIRST FINANCIAL BANK	EL DORADO	AR	C-	C	C+	727	14.08	4.2	2.8	5.0	2.5	6.5	8.5	15.8
FIRST FINANCIAL BANK	TWIN VALLEY	MN	C+	C+	B-	17	3.60	2.7	2.7	8.9	38.9	10.0	11.2	31.7
FIRST FINANCIAL BANK	HEREFORD	TX	B+	B+	B+	176	19.05	16.1	3.5	5.4	21.3	7.5	9.3	13.3
▼ FIRST FINANCIAL BANK	HUNTSVILLE	TX	B+	A	A-	181	19.53	8.9	3.0	12.2	33.2	5.4	7.4	12.8
FIRST FINANCIAL BANK & TR	PLAQUEMINE	LA	A-	A-	B+	80	4.32	0.2	2.5	15.0	40.6	10.0	15.5	28.8
FIRST FINANCIAL BANK IN W	WINNEBAGO	MN	A-	A-	B+	41	7.63	10.1	3.7	5.6	15.9	10.0	14.4	19.7
FIRST FINANCIAL BANK NA	TERRE HAUTE	IN	B+	B+	A	2,364	-2.93	17.4	11.1	14.5	23.6	10.0	12.4	17.3
FIRST FINANCIAL BANK NA	HAMILTON	OH	B-	B	B+	6,237	-6.18	13.2	1.3	11.0	15.0	6.7	8.8	16.4
FIRST FINANCIAL BANK NA	ABILENE	TX	A-	B+	B+	1,267	16.55	10.4	6.7	5.7	46.7	6.2	8.2	15.7
FIRST FINANCIAL BANK NA	CLEBURNE	TX	B+	A-	A-	278	1.60	8.8	6.1	6.9	37.3	6.7	8.7	15.1
FIRST FINANCIAL BANK NA	EASTLAND	TX	A-	A-	B+	164	-1.89	6.4	4.9	12.8	38.3	5.3	7.3	15.3
▼ FIRST FINANCIAL BANK NA	MINERAL WELLS	TX	B+	A-	A-	197	17.79	4.0	4.9	26.6	30.9	4.9	6.9	12.6
FIRST FINANCIAL BANK NA	SAN ANGELO	TX	A-	A-	A-	384	9.66	9.4	2.5	6.6	51.0	8.2	9.8	19.0
FIRST FINANCIAL BANK NA	SOUTHLAKE	TX	B	B	B+	289	9.27	10.4	3.9	13.2	27.2	8.8	10.2	16.5
FIRST FINANCIAL BANK NA	STEPHENVILLE	TX	B	B+	B+	336	-4.07	8.2	6.0	14.2	30.0	6.9	8.9	15.4
FIRST FINANCIAL BANK NA	SWEETWATER	TX	B+	A-	A-	155	16.12	6.9	5.4	10.8	43.0	6.6	8.6	15.7
FIRST FINANCIAL BANK NA	WEATHERFORD	TX	B	B+	B+	366	2.86	6.4	2.2	9.9	47.7	6.5	8.5	16.4
FIRST FINANCIAL TRUST & A	ABILENE	TX	U	U	U	4	9.10	0.0	0.0	0.0	5.3	10.0	89.6	291.5
FIRST FINANCIAL TRUST NA	NEWTON	MA	U	U	U	8	-5.16	0.0	0.0	0.0	20.7	10.0	103.4	177.1
FIRST FLORIDA BANK	DESTIN	FL	D	D-	C-	163	63.45	7.2	1.3	11.6	32.7	10.0	13.9	24.2
FIRST FOUNDATION BANK FSB	IRVINE	CA	C	C	C	406	71.50	7.9	1.6	9.9	2.5	6.5	8.5	14.1
▼ FIRST FREEDOM BANK	LEBANON	TN	D+	D-	D	231	0.83	15.5	1.6	13.5	11.3	10.0	12.2	15.7
FIRST FS&LA	HAZARD	KY	B	B-	B	103	-1.94	0.0	2.1	63.8	18.3	10.0	18.7	40.2
▼ FIRST FS&LA	MOREHEAD	KY	C+	B-	B-	40	6.29	0.6	2.0	61.9	2.4	10.0	22.9	40.6
FIRST FS&LA	ABERDEEN	MS	B	B-	C+	30	7.25	0.0	3.2	54.5	24.8	10.0	19.3	51.8
FIRST FS&LA	PASCAGOULA	MS	C-	C	C-	263	-3.12	0.0	0.6	74.9	8.8	5.7	7.7	16.3
FIRST FS&LA	DELTA	OH	B-	B	A-	154	4.69	1.1	0.8	55.1	0.0	10.0	11.9	27.5
FIRST FS&LA	NEWARK	OH	C	C+	B-	185	-2.65	0.0	0.3	55.2	4.7	10.0	17.5	28.5
FIRST FS&LA OF BATH	BATH	ME	B-	C+	B	111	1.83	0.9	0.8	74.1	0.5	10.0	15.3	25.3
FIRST FS&LA OF BUCKS COUN	BRISTOL	PA	C	C	D+	610	0.93	1.2	0.1	48.3	25.2	9.5	10.7	19.0
FIRST FS&LA OF	CENTERBURG	OH	C+	C	C	26	6.53	0.0	0.2	65.5	15.3	10.0	15.0	33.1
FIRST FS&LA OF CENTRAL IL	SHELBYVILLE	IL	C	C	C-	88	9.33	0.5	7.4	27.2	48.0	6.8	8.8	23.3
FIRST FS&LA OF	NORTH CHARLESTON	SC	D-	D+	C+	3,246	-5.04	2.3	12.1	33.6	12.1	6.6	8.6	12.7
FIRST FS&LA OF CULLMAN	CULLMAN	AL	C	C-	B-	69	-1.84	1.5	2.2	47.9	4.5	8.7	10.1	18.4
FIRST FS&LA OF GREENE COU	WAYNESBURG	PA	B-	B-	B-	792	12.24	0.0	2.2	63.7	20.5	10.0	13.1	28.6
FIRST FS&LA OF	GREENSBURG	IN	B-	C+	B-	108	2.64	1.6	3.7	54.1	0.6	9.5	10.6	17.1
FIRST FS&LA OF HAMMOND	HAMMOND	IN	E-	D-	C	52	3.46	0.0	0.3	74.5	5.0	3.5	5.5	11.9
FIRST FS&LA OF INDEPENDEN	INDEPENDENCE	KS	D	D	C-	181	-9.91	0.0	8.1	49.4	7.5	6.7	8.7	14.8
FIRST FS&LA OF KEWANEE	KEWANEE	IL	D+	D	C-	77	-1.36	0.0	0.3	47.1	40.6	10.0	11.2	28.0
▲ FIRST FS&LA OF LAKEWOOD	LAKEWOOD	OH	C	C-	C	1,327	7.17	1.5	1.7	56.0	10.1	8.2	9.8	17.2
FIRST FS&LA OF LORAIN	LORAIN	OH	C	C	C-	467	6.89	0.0	0.4	68.5	2.3	10.0	12.7	21.9
FIRST FS&LA OF MATTOON	MATTOON	IL	B	B	B+	92	0.69	0.0	1.3	23.7	43.7	10.0	25.3	77.5
▲ FIRST FS&LA OF MCMINNVILL	MCMINNVILLE	OR	B	C+	A-	343	1.24	0.0	0.3	54.3	3.8	10.0	15.6	25.9
▼ FIRST FS&LA OF OLATHE	OLATHE	KS	C-	C-	B+	65	-0.84	0.0	0.0	75.5	0.0	10.0	13.6	22.2

Asset Quality Index	Non-Performing Loans		Net Charge-offs	Profitability Index	Net Income ($Mil)	Return on Assets (R.O.A.)	Return on Equity (R.O.E.)	Net Interest Spread	Overhead Efficiency Ratio	Liquidity Index	Liquidity Ratio	Hot Money Ratio	Stability Index
	as a % of Total Loans	as a % of Capital	Avg Loans										
3.7	3.37	14.9	0.06	**4.7**	9.5	1.03	10.70	3.81	61.9	**3.6**	44.9	18.0	**7.6**
6.9	1.36	6.0	0.08	**3.8**	4.7	0.68	5.22	3.73	74.8	**2.8**	44.7	27.2	**7.9**
2.7	5.27	15.5	0.63	**0.9**	-4.2	-1.70	-10.49	3.07	374.0	**4.2**	50.2	16.6	**7.2**
3.0	2.42	14.7	0.55	**3.2**	9.1	0.44	3.41	3.91	60.1	**3.0**	19.1	15.1	**8.2**
5.9	0.18	1.3	1.06	**0.6**	-0.5	-0.40	-3.90	2.83	98.7	**4.3**	27.7	9.5	**4.5**
3.4	1.48	11.9	-0.01	**1.0**	-1.0	-0.43	-4.80	3.13	75.7	**1.2**	14.8	29.6	**4.1**
5.5	0.33	3.0	0.04	**4.1**	1.6	0.76	8.49	3.97	63.6	**1.8**	10.1	19.3	**4.8**
4.0	0.53	5.0	0.18	**1.7**	-0.3	-0.09	-1.10	4.25	90.9	**1.0**	9.8	30.2	**4.0**
1.9	4.09	26.3	0.56	**3.1**	0.8	0.60	5.90	4.20	71.7	**3.1**	20.3	14.2	**4.4**
1.3	4.20	28.0	1.16	**2.2**	0.9	0.38	3.83	3.92	82.1	**2.5**	20.7	17.2	**3.8**
1.5	3.81	27.3	1.13	**0.3**	-1.0	-0.90	-11.62	3.26	115.8	**3.1**	29.3	15.8	**2.4**
8.7	0.00	0.0	0.00	**3.1**	1.1	0.60	2.02	2.50	68.0	**6.2**	121.2	15.8	**7.8**
1.3	4.74	35.0	1.27	**1.2**	-0.6	-0.05	-0.59	3.23	71.6	**1.7**	23.9	29.7	**5.9**
8.7	0.66	2.3	0.14	**9.0**	5.3	1.88	17.47	3.93	53.9	**4.7**	51.8	14.6	**6.7**
0.0	4.42	28.6	2.02	**1.9**	2.2	0.19	1.93	4.27	68.3	**3.8**	26.3	14.0	**5.4**
0.3	6.70	49.4	1.25	**0.0**	-4.7	-2.17	-24.83	3.27	146.1	**2.3**	14.9	17.6	**1.8**
2.2	0.93	8.7	0.30	**10.0**	17.1	2.57	28.02	4.59	54.2	**0.6**	5.2	38.8	**7.8**
9.4	0.36	0.9	0.11	**2.1**	0.1	0.35	3.00	3.04	93.6	**6.3**	62.8	4.2	**5.1**
5.6	1.44	8.6	0.23	**9.4**	2.4	1.56	17.62	4.76	48.7	**3.0**	39.3	19.8	**6.8**
7.8	0.00	0.0	-0.01	**5.2**	0.3	0.99	9.36	4.26	64.0	**3.0**	48.1	26.5	**8.4**
6.1	1.71	4.6	0.00	**4.6**	0.5	0.64	4.55	3.17	77.7	**3.9**	62.3	19.4	**8.5**
7.0	0.37	1.7	0.15	**8.1**	0.7	1.86	11.91	4.56	59.5	**4.3**	16.9	7.0	**9.8**
3.9	2.12	10.5	0.44	**6.8**	27.2	1.12	9.18	4.21	56.1	**3.8**	17.2	10.8	**9.4**
3.6	2.59	18.1	1.82	**6.6**	64.0	1.00	11.19	4.91	53.1	**2.9**	9.6	14.0	**8.1**
8.4	0.37	1.7	0.09	**10.0**	21.0	1.88	19.36	4.63	47.6	**5.4**	38.2	9.9	**7.7**
6.9	0.59	3.1	1.72	**6.3**	2.6	0.96	10.46	4.75	59.8	**3.6**	22.5	11.6	**7.5**
7.5	0.16	0.9	0.24	**9.9**	2.7	1.73	15.14	4.79	50.1	**4.8**	41.7	11.7	**8.4**
4.7	0.74	5.7	0.19	**10.0**	3.8	2.15	17.68	5.53	41.7	**1.7**	19.3	22.9	**8.6**
7.2	0.46	1.8	0.21	**10.0**	7.0	1.99	14.41	5.06	46.9	**3.5**	50.4	19.9	**8.6**
2.1	2.88	14.7	0.24	**6.3**	4.6	1.23	8.54	5.00	62.9	**2.1**	13.9	18.6	**8.0**
4.1	0.80	4.6	0.35	**9.3**	5.4	1.62	12.08	5.08	54.1	**2.9**	26.1	15.7	**8.3**
7.8	0.01	0.0	0.18	**10.0**	2.5	1.79	18.42	4.83	54.0	**2.2**	35.4	27.8	**7.5**
3.0	3.65	16.9	0.44	**9.0**	5.5	1.60	15.63	4.64	55.5	**4.4**	33.5	10.8	**7.7**
10.0	0.00	0.0	0.00	**10.0**	3.3	75.66	90.69	1.00	54.7	**5.0**	745.7	101.0	**7.0**
6.5	0.00	0.0	0.00	**0.0**	-0.4	-4.92	-4.85	4.19	118.5	**5.0**	3,718.7	101.0	**1.7**
3.0	1.31	4.3	2.94	**0.5**	0.1	0.10	0.73	3.15	90.1	**2.7**	52.1	33.3	**2.0**
7.2	0.00	0.0	0.00	**2.9**	2.7	0.86	9.17	3.95	65.8	**0.6**	17.8	61.6	**1.8**
4.7	1.61	9.3	0.66	**0.7**	0.6	0.28	2.18	3.51	75.2	**0.6**	9.8	43.4	**2.7**
5.0	3.99	15.7	0.12	**3.7**	0.7	0.63	3.54	3.09	66.3	**1.6**	26.4	27.0	**7.4**
4.2	4.92	17.3	0.00	**2.7**	0.1	0.24	1.02	3.86	76.8	**3.0**	16.4	14.3	**6.2**
9.4	0.05	0.1	0.00	**4.1**	0.2	0.81	4.00	3.39	59.1	**2.9**	50.1	27.0	**7.4**
4.8	1.21	12.0	0.31	**1.7**	0.0	0.00	0.02	2.80	81.0	**0.7**	14.8	43.4	**3.0**
7.8	0.70	3.4	0.11	**2.7**	0.4	0.26	1.60	3.39	90.5	**5.3**	39.5	7.7	**7.7**
5.6	1.71	7.6	0.26	**2.0**	0.2	0.11	0.65	2.88	91.5	**1.0**	17.0	32.9	**6.5**
4.8	2.66	15.3	0.04	**3.2**	0.6	0.50	3.19	4.64	81.9	**3.3**	5.5	11.4	**7.8**
5.3	1.29	7.5	-0.01	**3.1**	3.8	0.63	6.03	3.16	70.5	**3.0**	31.7	17.1	**6.8**
7.2	0.45	1.9	0.00	**3.0**	0.1	0.42	2.74	2.81	78.9	**1.9**	31.9	27.7	**7.0**
4.7	2.56	11.6	0.21	**4.1**	1.0	1.14	13.68	2.75	61.4	**3.6**	61.4	22.3	**4.3**
0.0	6.25	44.8	3.68	**0.7**	-29.3	-0.89	-10.48	4.22	62.0	**1.1**	15.1	31.1	**6.1**
8.3	0.07	0.4	0.03	**2.7**	0.2	0.31	2.98	3.46	88.8	**1.2**	28.1	35.7	**4.7**
7.5	0.73	3.8	0.02	**3.1**	2.8	0.37	2.64	2.46	78.9	**2.0**	31.7	27.0	**8.2**
5.0	1.44	11.1	0.10	**3.6**	0.7	0.67	6.19	4.05	72.1	**4.5**	12.2	5.3	**5.6**
1.7	4.65	49.5	2.30	**0.0**	-1.2	-2.36	-37.33	3.68	68.6	**0.6**	7.6	45.4	**1.6**
0.8	4.63	33.2	0.29	**1.1**	-1.6	-0.84	-9.61	3.82	61.8	**1.6**	20.5	24.7	**3.7**
3.4	5.92	24.7	0.00	**0.6**	-0.2	-0.24	-2.10	2.88	86.6	**5.0**	52.1	11.8	**5.2**
4.3	2.00	15.0	0.01	**2.7**	3.3	0.27	2.64	2.44	71.1	**2.1**	17.6	19.3	**7.1**
2.6	3.75	22.7	0.02	**2.3**	1.2	0.27	2.11	3.87	70.1	**1.9**	13.1	19.1	**6.4**
8.7	0.00	0.0	0.00	**3.8**	0.5	0.58	2.23	3.11	72.0	**5.6**	88.0	14.4	**8.1**
6.0	1.59	7.9	0.11	**4.0**	2.5	0.72	4.75	4.69	60.3	**2.7**	16.6	15.7	**6.6**
1.7	7.25	38.5	-0.15	**5.0**	0.8	1.17	9.25	3.75	43.8	**0.8**	21.1	49.3	**8.3**

Name	City	State	Rating	2008 Rating	2007 Rating	Total Assets ($Mil)	One Year Asset Growth	Asset Mix (As a % of Total Assets) Comm-ercial Loans	Cons-umer Loans	Home Mort-gages	Secur-ities	Capital-ization Index	Leverage Ratio	Risk-based Capital Ratio
FIRST FS&LA OF PEKIN	PEKIN	IL	**E-**	D-	D-	29	-2.27	1.2	3.4	65.4	3.1	**4.8**	6.8	13.5
FIRST FS&LA OF PORT ANGEL	PORT ANGELES	WA	**D+**	C-	C	750	0.79	1.0	2.1	35.1	30.8	**8.4**	9.9	20.2
FIRST FS&LA OF	RAVENSWOOD	WV	**D+**	C	C-	12	33.58	0.0	0.1	59.0	0.7	**7.1**	9.0	20.0
FIRST FS&LA OF SAN RAFAEL	SAN RAFAEL	CA	**B-**	B	B+	176	-0.13	0.0	0.0	9.4	0.0	**10.0**	19.5	28.2
FIRST FS&LA OF VALDOSTA	VALDOSTA	GA	**C+**	C+	B-	168	2.39	1.7	3.6	65.5	0.3	**10.0**	16.4	26.4
FIRST FS&LA OF VAN WERT	VAN WERT	OH	**B-**	B-	B+	118	1.10	0.0	0.3	33.5	44.8	**10.0**	12.4	32.9
FIRST FS&LA OF WAKEENEY	WAKEENEY	KS	**C-**	C+	C+	32	-4.56	0.2	3.2	23.8	42.8	**10.0**	11.5	31.5
FIRST FSB	OTTAWA	IL	**D**	C-	C	413	-0.30	0.1	0.3	54.4	6.4	**7.3**	9.2	17.4
FIRST FSB	EVANSVILLE	IN	**C**	C	C+	334	-1.94	5.6	11.8	18.3	34.5	**7.7**	9.4	15.2
FIRST FSB	HUNTINGTON	IN	**D**	C	C-	256	1.44	11.1	5.2	28.2	16.6	**7.2**	9.1	14.3
FIRST FSB	ROCHESTER	IN	**B-**	C+	B-	360	-11.74	0.0	0.3	65.2	0.0	**10.0**	11.2	17.7
FIRST FSB	MONESSEN	PA	**C**	C-	C-	342	-2.98	3.2	0.6	49.9	23.0	**10.0**	13.0	25.4
▲ FIRST FSB	CLARKSVILLE	TN	**C+**	C-	C-	345	0.30	8.9	1.0	14.4	21.6	**10.0**	13.9	19.2
FIRST FSB	SISTERSVILLE	WV	**B-**	B-	B	49	-1.15	0.0	0.6	48.4	23.5	**10.0**	15.3	37.1
FIRST FSB	SHERIDAN	WY	**C+**	C	B+	221	2.31	3.1	1.4	19.5	36.8	**10.0**	16.7	31.7
FIRST FSB OF ANGOLA	ANGOLA	IN	**B-**	B-	B	139	4.00	0.7	3.4	55.2	0.0	**10.0**	14.0	32.8
FIRST FSB OF BOSTON	BOSTON	MA	**B-**	C+	D	114	60.57	0.0	0.1	74.0	0.0	**10.0**	11.4	24.3
FIRST FSB OF CHAMPAIGN-UR	CHAMPAIGN	IL	**B**	B	B+	159	7.22	5.2	4.0	30.4	0.5	**6.5**	8.5	17.2
FIRST FSB OF CRESTON FSB	CRESTON	IA	**B**	B	B	66	16.88	11.0	5.5	21.8	30.9	**10.0**	11.0	17.5
FIRST FSB OF FRANKFORT	FRANKFORT	KY	**C+**	C+	B-	125	2.60	0.0	0.1	66.7	0.2	**10.0**	14.5	26.7
FIRST FSB OF IOWA	FORT DODGE	IA	**C-**	C	C-	452	-0.58	0.5	3.7	39.3	10.7	**8.9**	10.2	16.5
▲ FIRST FSB OF LINCOLNTON	LINCOLNTON	NC	**C+**	C-	C-	297	5.18	0.6	0.5	55.7	16.3	**10.0**	14.1	26.9
▲ FIRST FSB OF MASCOUTAH	MASCOUTAH	IL	**C+**	C-	C+	134	11.11	0.1	2.5	27.3	56.8	**6.5**	8.6	23.5
FIRST FSB OF TWIN FALLS	TWIN FALLS	ID	**B-**	B-	B	457	3.36	6.4	2.4	37.7	2.1	**9.4**	10.6	17.2
FIRST FSB OF WASHINGTON	WASHINGTON	IN	**C+**	C	C	79	3.19	5.7	3.2	58.3	9.2	**8.3**	9.9	21.1
FIRST GENERAL BANK	ROWLAND HEIGHTS	CA	**B-**	B-	C+	217	14.77	8.1	0.0	5.8	2.3	**10.0**	12.0	17.2
FIRST GEORGIA BANKING CO	FRANKLIN	GA	**E-**	E-	D-	780	-1.53	4.2	1.7	17.8	7.4	**0.0**	2.4	4.9
▼ FIRST GREEN BANK	EUSTIS	FL	**D**	C	NR	120	53.04	7.9	1.0	7.0	20.4	**10.0**	12.2	16.1
FIRST GUARANTY BANK	MARTIN	KY	**A-**	A	A	61	1.00	7.8	6.6	17.0	44.0	**10.0**	16.6	40.8
▼ FIRST GUARANTY BANK	HAMMOND	LA	**D+**	C-	C	1,133	21.69	6.8	1.3	5.0	42.1	**6.1**	8.1	12.1
FIRST GUARANTY BANK & TRU	JACKSONVILLE	FL	**E-**	D-	D-	440	1.42	2.3	0.5	15.3	8.3	**0.0**	2.8	5.1
FIRST HARRISON BANK	CORYDON	IN	**C**	C	B-	447	-0.69	5.3	5.8	30.2	22.1	**7.5**	9.3	15.5
FIRST HAWAIIAN BANK	HONOLULU	HI	**B-**	B-	B+	15,195	10.87	12.0	6.1	14.3	25.0	**10.0**	11.9	19.8
FIRST HERITAGE BANK	SNOHOMISH	WA	**E-**	E	D	179	-16.92	3.3	0.6	19.6	6.7	**0.0**	2.2	4.5
FIRST HOME BANK	SEMINOLE	FL	**E-**	D-	C	82	-15.27	3.7	2.0	32.6	2.6	**0.0**	3.4	6.0
FIRST HOME SAVINGS BANK	MOUNTAIN GROVE	MO	**D-**	D	C-	203	-2.50	1.9	1.2	28.4	35.7	**7.4**	9.3	19.5
FIRST HOPE BANK A NATL BK	HOPE	NJ	**B-**	C+	B-	426	-1.46	2.4	0.4	17.7	20.3	**5.8**	7.8	12.2
▼ FIRST ILLINOIS BANK	EAST SAINT LOUIS	IL	**B-**	B+	A	53	4.00	5.4	2.7	5.5	73.2	**6.5**	8.5	60.0
▼ FIRST INDEPENDENCE BANK	DETROIT	MI	**D**	D	C-	184	15.44	30.7	0.2	14.4	9.5	**6.1**	8.1	15.5
FIRST INDEPENDENT BANK	RUSSELL	MN	**C+**	C	C-	156	0.92	6.3	6.1	10.0	16.7	**7.2**	9.2	12.7
▲ FIRST INDEPENDENT BANK	AURORA	MO	**C-**	D+	C+	91	-2.40	6.3	7.7	24.0	26.8	**7.4**	9.3	16.1
FIRST INDEPENDENT BANK	VANCOUVER	WA	**D-**	D-	D	841	-7.97	9.5	0.5	3.4	29.8	**8.2**	9.8	14.6
FIRST INTERCONTINENTAL BA	DORAVILLE	GA	**D-**	D+	D	285	2.46	16.6	0.4	0.0	4.8	**6.6**	8.6	15.6
▼ FIRST INTERNATIONAL BK	PLANO	TX	**E-**	D-	D+	343	-19.52	6.9	0.5	2.8	0.0	**0.0**	2.8	5.0
FIRST INTERNATIONAL BK &	WATFORD CITY	ND	**D+**	C	C+	979	-1.17	13.9	5.5	8.5	16.4	**6.6**	8.6	12.3
▼ FIRST INTERNET BANK OF IN	INDIANAPOLIS	IN	**D**	D	C	502	-0.31	1.0	34.9	20.9	27.3	**6.2**	9.1	11.9
FIRST INTERSTATE BK	BILLINGS	MT	**D**	C-	C+	7,473	5.06	9.1	8.6	8.1	25.9	**5.7**	7.7	12.8
▼ FIRST INVESTORS FSB	EDISON	NJ	**B+**	A	A	42	-6.90	0.0	0.0	1.1	62.0	**10.0**	22.2	126.5
FIRST IOWA STATE BK	ALBIA	IA	**B**	B+	B+	146	2.92	15.4	2.3	13.1	24.6	**10.0**	13.0	19.2
FIRST JACKSON BANK	STEVENSON	AL	**D**	D+	B+	207	8.33	3.5	8.6	15.7	26.3	**6.5**	8.5	12.6
FIRST KANSAS BANK	HOISINGTON	KS	**B-**	B-	B-	89	14.00	3.2	2.3	4.3	72.1	**5.5**	7.5	20.8
FIRST KENTUCKY BANK INC	MAYFIELD	KY	**B**	B-	B-	363	0.56	4.2	8.6	32.5	15.9	**7.0**	9.0	14.0
FIRST KEYSTONE COMMUNITY	BERWICK	PA	**B**	B	B	804	4.98	3.6	1.1	18.1	38.4	**6.0**	8.0	12.5
FIRST LANDMARK BANK	MARIETTA	GA	**D**	C	C	148	30.50	16.2	1.2	2.3	22.4	**10.0**	12.0	16.0
▲ FIRST LIBERTY BANK	OKLAHOMA CITY	OK	**B-**	C	C-	167	41.21	17.9	0.6	4.3	12.4	**9.3**	12.5	14.4
FIRST LIBERTY NATIONAL BK	LIBERTY	TX	**A-**	A	A	291	23.47	7.1	12.0	8.4	48.4	**9.0**	10.3	28.8
FIRST LOUISIANA NATIONAL	BREAUX BRIDGE	LA	**B+**	A-	A-	111	-3.05	4.2	9.3	19.0	33.9	**8.9**	10.3	22.6
FIRST MADISON BANK & TRUS	ATHENS	GA	**B-**	B-	B-	136	7.56	10.8	2.3	14.4	4.1	**7.4**	9.3	12.8
FIRST MADISON VALLEY BANK	ENNIS	MT	**C-**	B-	B	131	5.25	16.9	6.5	14.4	7.8	**6.0**	8.0	12.6
FIRST MARINER BANK	BALTIMORE	MD	**E-**	E-	E-	1,312	-4.91	6.0	2.2	23.5	2.1	**1.1**	4.8	8.1

Arrows denote recent upgrades ▲ or downgrades ▼

Asset Quality Index	Non-Performing Loans as a % of Total Loans	Non-Performing Loans as a % of Capital	Net Charge-offs Avg Loans	Profitability Index	Net Income ($Mil)	Return on Assets (R.O.A.)	Return on Equity (R.O.E.)	Net Interest Spread	Overhead Efficiency Ratio	Liquidity Index	Liquidity Ratio	Hot Money Ratio	Stability Index
4.5	0.33	3.9	0.03	**1.8**	0.1	0.22	3.28	3.88	86.0	**1.6**	11.5	21.6	**0.3**
2.5	3.03	17.4	0.18	**3.2**	4.5	0.61	6.19	3.27	71.4	**4.2**	37.1	13.0	**4.8**
9.1	0.00	0.0	0.00	**3.6**	0.1	0.72	6.47	3.07	69.5	**1.2**	30.0	32.2	**3.0**
7.1	0.00	0.0	0.00	**3.9**	1.4	0.80	4.23	4.42	69.2	**0.7**	14.5	40.4	**8.1**
3.1	3.03	15.3	0.16	**2.5**	0.4	0.22	1.39	3.39	91.5	**2.1**	10.1	18.2	**7.5**
8.3	0.00	0.0	0.00	**3.6**	0.8	0.66	4.60	3.07	71.3	**4.2**	60.7	19.1	**8.0**
8.6	0.58	1.9	0.00	**0.7**	-0.1	-0.41	-3.57	2.66	102.4	**6.2**	66.6	7.6	**4.5**
0.6	3.91	29.2	0.34	**2.0**	0.0	0.01	0.09	3.06	81.1	**2.4**	16.8	17.1	**4.9**
3.6	1.38	6.5	-0.07	**3.2**	1.4	0.42	4.00	2.96	81.5	**5.7**	48.1	8.3	**5.0**
1.1	3.47	25.5	0.70	**3.9**	2.1	0.82	8.83	3.68	58.8	**2.1**	23.5	19.4	**5.0**
5.2	0.64	4.4	1.00	**3.6**	2.3	0.63	5.71	3.03	66.6	**2.8**	6.9	14.1	**4.8**
7.4	0.53	2.6	0.23	**2.1**	0.7	0.19	1.62	3.10	83.7	**3.9**	29.7	11.9	**5.9**
6.2	1.15	5.5	0.20	**2.7**	1.7	0.51	3.56	3.79	72.7	**3.3**	29.1	14.9	**6.8**
7.9	1.23	4.3	0.00	**3.4**	0.2	0.45	2.78	4.06	85.5	**5.1**	44.5	10.4	**7.2**
4.9	4.16	11.0	0.10	**2.9**	1.1	0.49	2.93	3.09	72.5	**4.1**	59.0	19.3	**6.5**
8.6	0.56	2.4	0.20	**3.6**	0.9	0.62	4.56	2.69	65.4	**2.2**	37.9	29.9	**7.6**
4.0	0.76	5.5	-0.04	**5.2**	0.9	0.97	6.49	3.69	94.5	**0.4**	2.8	59.1	**6.7**
6.3	0.47	3.4	0.01	**4.5**	1.5	0.95	10.28	3.98	73.8	**4.8**	31.6	7.7	**5.9**
8.1	0.57	2.9	0.00	**3.5**	0.3	0.55	4.56	3.54	82.8	**5.5**	42.0	6.9	**6.6**
3.0	2.27	13.8	0.00	**3.7**	0.9	0.63	2.68	3.21	67.5	**1.9**	4.3	18.3	**7.2**
1.6	3.15	20.9	0.24	**2.6**	1.8	0.39	3.82	3.51	71.4	**4.2**	20.3	8.2	**5.2**
6.9	0.73	3.9	0.01	**3.0**	1.7	0.58	4.07	3.71	66.3	**0.9**	22.7	40.8	**7.2**
4.8	3.23	13.8	0.00	**3.4**	0.6	0.47	4.95	2.12	65.7	**5.7**	66.3	12.2	**4.4**
4.6	1.27	8.6	0.19	**3.7**	2.8	0.61	5.73	3.73	75.1	**4.6**	21.1	5.5	**6.2**
6.5	0.37	2.6	0.03	**3.7**	0.5	0.69	7.16	3.32	62.5	**1.1**	29.0	52.3	**5.1**
4.9	0.61	3.4	0.16	**3.6**	1.0	0.50	4.11	3.20	69.1	**1.0**	26.2	48.2	**5.1**
0.3	9.41	152.5	2.61	**0.0**	-15.5	-1.91	-54.84	3.26	108.7	**1.0**	23.5	36.1	**1.0**
7.3	0.00	0.0	0.00	**0.2**	-0.2	-0.23	-1.46	3.93	94.5	**1.5**	20.7	25.8	**1.7**
6.4	2.27	6.1	0.01	**5.4**	0.6	1.09	6.35	3.63	64.2	**5.1**	42.6	10.0	**9.8**
1.7	5.23	31.4	0.88	**5.3**	10.6	1.04	11.40	4.02	57.1	**1.4**	24.9	42.0	**6.3**
0.0	26.84	284.3	1.28	**0.0**	-15.7	-3.49	-72.32	2.03	163.4	**0.9**	21.0	42.7	**1.9**
3.1	1.81	12.5	0.21	**4.3**	4.0	0.87	8.47	3.82	61.8	**4.5**	30.4	9.2	**4.6**
5.6	0.58	2.7	0.73	**9.1**	212.6	1.46	8.22	4.02	43.7	**2.5**	17.5	16.9	**5.0**
0.0	13.56	218.9	5.08	**0.0**	-11.3	-5.49	-100.56	3.57	132.2	**3.4**	16.1	12.1	**1.8**
0.0	7.04	102.4	5.81	**0.0**	-5.0	-5.31	-89.61	3.56	104.1	**2.1**	11.4	18.2	**2.0**
5.4	1.76	9.0	-0.14	**0.0**	-2.8	-1.30	-12.76	3.22	108.8	**4.6**	48.4	14.4	**3.2**
5.8	1.92	15.0	0.02	**3.8**	2.7	0.63	8.24	4.15	83.5	**3.9**	17.9	9.7	**4.6**
10.0	0.09	0.2	0.86	**7.6**	0.8	1.62	16.28	4.51	64.7	**4.5**	25.4	6.8	**5.0**
2.3	1.89	11.5	1.67	**0.5**	-0.3	-0.16	-1.89	4.31	89.0	**3.4**	31.1	14.9	**2.3**
3.8	1.31	9.6	0.28	**4.5**	1.1	0.73	7.26	4.06	67.3	**2.3**	18.3	17.9	**4.7**
2.7	3.09	18.3	0.21	**2.3**	0.3	0.33	3.58	3.32	80.5	**2.1**	32.2	25.9	**4.5**
1.0	5.59	28.1	6.36	**0.0**	-32.0	-3.57	-34.96	4.01	93.2	**3.9**	6.1	8.2	**4.1**
0.0	1.94	11.3	0.80	**1.7**	0.1	0.04	0.42	3.67	76.4	**0.9**	22.1	41.2	**5.1**
0.0	16.26	172.0	4.51	**0.0**	-25.7	-6.58	-104.11	3.29	123.2	**2.6**	18.9	16.2	**4.1**
1.7	0.55	4.0	0.76	**4.9**	10.5	1.08	12.28	4.89	66.1	**2.2**	8.3	17.1	**4.7**
0.9	3.08	18.6	1.35	**3.9**	5.1	1.03	10.90	3.34	53.9	**1.5**	27.0	29.7	**3.2**
0.9	4.50	29.0	1.11	**4.6**	47.7	0.66	6.57	4.02	59.1	**2.2**	15.3	18.3	**8.4**
9.9	3.87	0.2	0.00	**5.9**	0.4	0.97	4.51	1.71	78.3	**8.8**	126.1	0.0	**7.8**
6.1	1.24	5.8	1.51	**4.5**	1.5	1.01	7.74	4.66	44.8	**2.3**	28.0	19.7	**6.8**
1.6	3.62	22.8	1.94	**2.9**	0.6	0.31	3.88	3.77	71.5	**0.9**	22.0	44.0	**3.0**
9.5	0.00	0.0	0.00	**3.9**	0.7	0.79	9.11	2.91	72.8	**4.9**	44.3	11.5	**5.1**
5.2	0.72	5.6	0.47	**5.0**	4.4	1.19	12.23	4.28	67.3	**1.9**	20.1	20.0	**6.4**
5.1	1.04	6.1	0.54	**5.3**	9.0	1.11	10.57	3.67	55.4	**3.4**	17.7	12.2	**7.5**
4.6	0.20	1.0	0.17	**0.0**	-0.9	-0.68	-5.09	3.56	106.3	**1.8**	23.6	22.1	**1.5**
6.0	0.50	3.0	0.06	**5.0**	1.2	0.88	9.11	4.52	53.3	**1.3**	28.6	33.6	**6.3**
8.1	0.24	0.8	0.19	**6.1**	3.8	1.43	12.50	3.39	64.4	**5.3**	47.0	10.5	**7.0**
8.0	0.21	0.9	0.07	**5.0**	1.2	1.07	10.60	3.64	76.1	**3.8**	53.0	19.1	**7.3**
4.5	0.77	5.4	0.07	**4.4**	1.0	0.73	7.81	4.19	52.0	**1.8**	18.7	21.8	**6.2**
1.6	6.34	48.4	0.51	**4.3**	0.5	0.40	4.87	4.91	78.4	**1.7**	23.9	23.9	**6.9**
0.3	5.73	69.8	1.54	**0.0**	-49.5	-3.64	-52.39	2.75	112.6	**0.9**	17.9	42.7	**1.5**

Name	City	State	Rating	2008 Rating	2007 Rating	Total Assets ($Mil)	One Year Asset Growth	Asset Mix (As a % of Total Assets) Comm-ercial Loans	Cons-umer Loans	Home Mort-gages	Secur-ities	Capital-ization Index	Leverage Ratio	Risk-based Capital Ratio
FIRST MERCHANTS BANK NA	MUNCIE	IN	**D+**	D	C-	4,148	-6.78	12.8	2.8	14.4	19.8	**8.7**	10.1	14.9
FIRST METRO BANK	MUSCLE SHOALS	AL	**A-**	A-	A-	425	1.31	9.7	4.5	18.1	29.7	**8.7**	10.1	17.3
FIRST MICHIGAN BANK	TROY	MI	**B**	C	C-	1,691	1750.61	7.3	2.0	10.9	17.6	**10.0**	21.1	51.5
FIRST MID-ILLINOIS BK & T	MATTOON	IL	**B**	B+	B+	1,463	34.51	8.6	1.3	9.7	23.4	**5.1**	7.1	12.3
FIRST MIDWEST BANK	ITASCA	IL	**C-**	D	B-	7,983	4.21	12.3	0.7	6.1	14.3	**8.3**	9.9	13.9
FIRST MIDWEST BANK	CENTERVILLE	SD	**E-**	E-	C	110	-22.40	14.1	3.3	9.2	4.4	**0.0**	3.1	5.7
FIRST MIDWEST BANK OF DEX	DEXTER	MO	**C+**	C+	C+	241	0.82	12.9	2.9	12.0	21.1	**6.6**	8.6	12.9
FIRST MIDWEST BK OF THE O	PIEDMONT	MO	**C+**	B-	B-	113	2.07	10.0	3.8	12.9	24.1	**6.2**	8.2	13.7
FIRST MIDWEST BK POPLAR B	POPLAR BLUFF	MO	**B-**	B-	C+	258	3.48	15.5	6.3	17.6	13.0	**6.7**	8.7	12.9
FIRST MINNESOTA BANK	MINNETONKA	MN	**C+**	C+	B-	376	3.45	4.2	1.2	7.1	58.3	**10.0**	12.0	24.5
▼ FIRST MINNETONKA CITY BAN	MINNETONKA	MN	**C+**	B	B+	176	1.46	11.3	1.9	16.7	25.2	**7.8**	9.6	15.2
▲ FIRST MISSOURI NATIONAL B	BROOKFIELD	MO	**C**	C-	C+	111	-0.79	6.7	6.6	25.6	11.9	**8.7**	10.2	15.8
FIRST MISSOURI STATE BK	POPLAR BLUFF	MO	**B-**	B-	B+	149	0.44	8.8	4.9	27.1	7.4	**7.5**	9.3	13.8
FIRST MO STATE BK OF CAPE	CAPE GIRARDEAU	MO	**B-**	B-	B-	105	-2.41	8.7	3.0	23.4	7.7	**6.9**	8.9	13.3
FIRST MONTANA BANK INC	MISSOULA	MT	**C-**	C-	B-	305	6.58	11.2	5.4	9.4	28.3	**6.0**	8.0	13.3
FIRST MOUNTAIN BANK	BIG BEAR LAKE	CA	**D-**	D-	C	144	4.37	5.9	1.1	5.7	5.4	**8.0**	9.7	13.3
▲ FIRST NATIONAL B&T ELK CI	ELK CITY	OK	**B**	C-	B	262	6.50	8.3	2.2	18.6	36.0	**8.2**	9.8	18.1
FIRST NATIONAL BANKERS BA	BATON ROUGE	LA	**B**	B-	B-	323	-10.01	9.2	0.0	0.3	4.4	**10.0**	13.4	21.6
FIRST NATIONAL BANKERS BA	BIRMINGHAM	AL	**C+**	C	C+	224	-43.89	5.8	0.6	1.1	0.0	**10.0**	14.5	24.1
FIRST NATIONAL BANKING CO	ASH FLAT	AR	**C-**	C-	C+	363	-5.05	6.3	4.7	25.7	23.0	**8.3**	9.9	14.9
FIRST NATIONAL BK	HAMILTON	AL	**A-**	A-	A-	272	0.10	12.2	7.8	12.5	48.3	**10.0**	11.9	22.6
▼ FIRST NATIONAL BK	HOPE	AR	**C**	C	C	305	6.51	12.9	4.9	25.2	3.6	**8.4**	9.9	13.8
FIRST NATIONAL BK	HOT SPRINGS	AR	**B+**	A-	A	653	-5.93	6.0	3.5	13.8	21.2	**9.7**	10.8	18.3
FIRST NATIONAL BK	PARAGOULD	AR	**A**	A-	A-	645	1.84	6.4	4.6	26.2	16.7	**9.8**	10.9	15.9
▼ FIRST NATIONAL BK	DAVENPORT	IA	**C+**	B-	B-	70	-3.07	7.0	1.1	7.9	29.2	**10.0**	11.8	24.3
FIRST NATIONAL BK	FONTANELLE	IA	**D**	C-	C-	179	9.20	8.7	1.4	5.4	19.2	**7.1**	9.1	12.6
FIRST NATIONAL BK	SIOUX CENTER	IA	**C-**	C-	C	244	-6.58	10.1	2.2	9.3	20.6	**7.3**	9.2	14.5
FIRST NATIONAL BK	WAVERLY	IA	**C-**	C+	B-	272	4.80	14.3	1.3	11.0	14.6	**8.8**	10.2	15.1
FIRST NATIONAL BK	MATTOON	IL	**B**	B-	C-	62	8.09	15.7	5.2	10.6	26.4	**10.0**	11.2	18.2
FIRST NATIONAL BK	VANDALIA	IL	**B**	B	A-	267	6.18	7.2	2.7	17.1	28.8	**6.7**	8.7	14.5
FIRST NATIONAL BK	CLOVERDALE	IN	**C+**	B-	B-	234	0.65	5.9	1.9	28.9	2.5	**7.3**	9.2	16.2
▼ FIRST NATIONAL BK	GOODLAND	KS	**E-**	E+	D-	240	-16.66	4.5	1.7	4.1	27.3	**3.5**	5.5	10.4
FIRST NATIONAL BK	HAYS	KS	**D-**	D	C-	87	-4.79	7.8	1.4	26.0	13.3	**8.2**	9.8	16.5
FIRST NATIONAL BK	ARCADIA	LA	**B-**	C	C+	180	-4.16	5.2	6.0	26.9	5.4	**6.1**	8.1	11.9
FIRST NATIONAL BK	HAWLEY	MN	**C**	C	C	89	-5.30	9.7	5.1	9.9	20.6	**6.9**	9.1	12.4
FIRST NATIONAL BK	SLAYTON	MN	**D+**	C+	B	178	0.24	8.3	2.9	2.8	18.4	**6.8**	8.9	13.1
FIRST NATIONAL BK	CAMDENTON	MO	**B**	A+	A+	300	1.35	1.6	3.2	11.4	32.5	**10.0**	17.2	30.0
FIRST NATIONAL BK	MALDEN	MO	**C+**	C+	B-	144	-3.00	6.1	3.7	29.4	4.2	**6.0**	8.0	13.3
FIRST NATIONAL BK	MILNOR	ND	**A-**	A-	A-	62	-0.92	10.9	4.2	4.2	37.5	**10.0**	13.8	22.0
▲ FIRST NATIONAL BK	NORTH PLATTE	NE	**C**	C-	C-	413	-7.29	6.7	4.8	9.9	15.5	**5.7**	7.7	13.5
FIRST NATIONAL BK	SCHUYLER	NE	**B-**	B	B-	108	1.27	9.9	3.5	7.4	25.3	**5.5**	7.5	13.3
FIRST NATIONAL BK	ORRVILLE	OH	**C**	C+	B-	372	0.41	6.1	2.7	12.7	37.2	**5.5**	7.5	13.6
FIRST NATIONAL BK	HEAVENER	OK	**B-**	B-	B	81	-9.19	2.7	5.0	16.7	0.3	**6.4**	8.4	15.9
FIRST NATIONAL BK	IDABEL	OK	**B+**	A-	A-	82	1.61	2.5	2.2	7.5	33.5	**9.1**	10.4	18.4
FIRST NATIONAL BK	MIDWEST CITY	OK	**B+**	B+	B+	411	3.61	4.3	6.0	11.4	49.2	**8.7**	10.1	20.5
FIRST NATIONAL BK	FORT PIERRE	SD	**B+**	B+	B+	653	4.70	11.7	10.7	7.3	16.8	**10.0**	18.7	27.4
FIRST NATIONAL BK	LENOIR CITY	TN	**D+**	D-	C-	398	-4.24	7.1	1.8	12.5	26.4	**8.0**	9.7	16.1
FIRST NATIONAL BK	EDINBURG	TX	**D-**	D	D+	3,826	-0.59	7.5	1.3	11.0	15.6	**7.2**	9.1	13.3
▲ FIRST NATIONAL BK	FABENS	TX	**B-**	B-	B	307	3.36	9.2	0.6	4.7	25.3	**5.9**	7.9	12.7
FIRST NATIONAL BK	GEORGE WEST	TX	**B-**	B-	B	194	15.34	6.8	4.9	14.4	24.2	**8.8**	10.2	15.6
FIRST NATIONAL BK	GROESBECK	TX	**C-**	C	C+	52	7.20	1.7	16.3	29.6	17.2	**6.8**	8.8	17.8
FIRST NATIONAL BK	ROTAN	TX	**B**	B-	B	59	1.77	6.4	5.1	2.3	37.5	**7.5**	9.4	16.4
FIRST NATIONAL BK	SPEARMAN	TX	**B-**	B-	C+	155	20.07	11.1	2.0	3.5	36.4	**6.4**	8.5	14.1
FIRST NATIONAL BK	WICHITA FALLS	TX	**B-**	B-	B-	298	15.05	9.6	6.1	25.7	14.9	**6.6**	8.6	13.2
FIRST NATIONAL BK	WAUPACA	WI	**C-**	C-	C-	748	6.03	6.7	2.8	18.6	5.0	**6.6**	9.4	12.2
FIRST NATIONAL BK	RONCEVERTE	WV	**C-**	C-	B	261	1.33	5.1	3.8	22.5	28.9	**7.8**	9.5	16.3
FIRST NATIONAL BK & TRUST	ATMORE	AL	**C-**	C	B-	157	-0.15	2.3	5.3	17.4	18.5	**9.0**	10.4	16.2
▼ FIRST NATIONAL BK & TRUST	PHILLIPSBURG	KS	**A-**	A	A	159	7.23	4.5	5.1	7.5	41.1	**10.0**	14.6	21.0
▼ FIRST NATIONAL BK & TRUST	LONDON	KY	**D+**	D+	C-	225	0.63	4.5	3.9	17.8	35.1	**7.4**	9.3	16.8
▲ FIRST NATIONAL BK & TRUST	BARRON	WI	**E+**	D-	D	45	3.88	3.6	1.9	26.0	24.1	**6.1**	8.1	14.6

Asset Quality Index	Non-Performing Loans as a % of Total Loans	Non-Performing Loans as a % of Capital	Net Charge-offs Avg Loans	Profitability Index	Net Income ($Mil)	Return on Assets (R.O.A.)	Return on Equity (R.O.E.)	Net Interest Spread	Overhead Efficiency Ratio	Liquidity Index	Liquidity Ratio	Hot Money Ratio	Stability Index
1.9	3.14	18.1	1.82	**2.8**	18.4	0.43	3.39	4.15	64.5	**3.1**	18.8	14.3	**6.1**
7.8	0.31	1.9	0.20	**8.6**	6.1	1.40	13.92	4.03	45.9	**1.6**	18.6	23.4	**7.1**
6.8	1.90	6.8	1.71	**6.6**	48.0	5.33	36.54	6.39	27.4	**4.2**	28.9	13.6	**7.0**
4.8	1.13	8.1	0.39	**5.6**	10.2	0.84	7.96	3.70	62.6	**5.0**	25.7	7.3	**7.3**
1.9	2.74	16.1	2.24	**2.0**	31.5	0.40	3.08	4.40	61.8	**3.7**	13.0	10.4	**7.5**
0.6	3.80	44.8	2.72	**0.0**	-5.2	-4.13	-92.19	3.69	188.1	**1.7**	21.9	23.8	**0.6**
2.7	2.17	15.6	0.41	**4.9**	2.2	0.90	10.29	3.54	58.7	**1.3**	25.0	29.8	**5.0**
4.2	1.71	11.7	0.11	**4.1**	0.8	0.74	8.76	3.39	69.4	**1.9**	27.0	24.0	**4.9**
3.7	1.46	11.9	0.14	**6.4**	4.0	1.57	18.62	4.17	59.1	**1.0**	9.1	30.1	**6.3**
3.7	5.14	11.5	1.26	**2.4**	1.4	0.38	3.04	3.35	77.7	**2.5**	30.0	19.1	**5.1**
8.4	0.25	1.5	1.52	**3.7**	1.7	0.98	10.28	3.88	62.1	**3.7**	33.3	14.1	**6.8**
3.0	1.20	8.2	0.71	**3.2**	0.4	0.38	3.77	3.96	77.3	**1.3**	17.6	28.9	**5.0**
3.9	1.54	11.8	-0.03	**6.2**	1.6	1.05	10.89	3.90	50.2	**1.3**	10.2	26.5	**6.2**
3.3	0.94	8.0	0.14	**5.7**	1.1	0.99	11.15	4.26	56.4	**0.7**	7.5	33.6	**5.0**
2.1	2.33	15.9	0.08	**4.3**	2.0	0.66	7.58	4.48	71.5	**2.4**	21.1	17.6	**5.2**
0.0	7.11	43.6	1.15	**1.3**	0.1	0.06	0.59	4.85	97.7	**1.9**	22.9	20.4	**4.3**
5.4	0.33	1.8	0.19	**7.7**	4.8	1.89	18.04	4.03	51.3	**1.2**	25.6	32.2	**7.8**
5.0	2.80	10.7	1.02	**5.1**	3.0	0.85	6.42	3.19	77.5	**5.8**	29.6	0.0	**7.0**
3.9	3.31	12.3	3.04	**1.6**	0.1	0.02	0.13	2.60	48.2	**6.3**	37.1	0.0	**5.8**
2.2	2.32	13.8	0.97	**4.2**	2.3	0.60	6.80	5.07	68.0	**1.7**	14.7	21.9	**4.9**
6.6	1.64	5.5	0.66	**6.9**	4.6	1.65	13.78	4.38	59.0	**2.4**	37.5	26.2	**7.6**
2.5	2.28	18.1	0.66	**4.6**	3.0	0.95	10.35	4.57	62.8	**0.6**	4.3	39.1	**5.1**
6.3	0.19	1.0	0.24	**5.6**	6.0	0.90	5.43	3.83	59.0	**2.8**	18.7	15.6	**7.9**
7.0	0.40	2.6	0.40	**6.9**	8.3	1.29	11.36	4.25	49.5	**1.6**	7.1	21.2	**7.5**
7.7	0.09	0.3	0.05	**3.1**	0.3	0.37	3.20	3.72	88.0	**4.9**	40.2	10.6	**6.3**
1.2	2.46	18.4	0.58	**4.7**	1.9	1.07	8.80	4.33	65.5	**2.0**	18.3	19.4	**6.8**
1.7	2.27	15.4	0.83	**2.8**	0.8	0.33	2.88	4.00	83.8	**3.8**	25.2	11.0	**6.0**
3.0	1.90	11.9	0.67	**4.6**	2.3	0.85	8.02	3.95	61.6	**3.5**	27.7	13.5	**6.3**
6.0	0.38	1.7	0.58	**3.9**	0.4	0.60	4.78	3.94	90.4	**2.5**	36.1	23.4	**5.7**
8.2	0.06	0.4	0.04	**4.8**	2.6	1.00	9.06	4.35	72.1	**3.9**	32.0	12.8	**6.4**
2.9	2.71	17.9	0.56	**2.9**	0.8	0.34	3.62	3.69	78.2	**3.7**	29.1	13.0	**5.4**
1.4	5.50	37.6	2.20	**0.0**	-3.1	-1.14	-19.20	3.66	83.8	**3.3**	28.2	14.7	**1.9**
1.5	5.51	32.6	2.49	**0.3**	-0.7	-0.78	-7.77	4.44	91.0	**3.0**	24.1	15.0	**5.4**
4.2	0.85	7.4	0.12	**8.0**	3.3	1.71	21.20	5.75	69.4	**1.2**	6.8	26.3	**6.6**
3.5	2.69	16.3	0.51	**4.3**	0.6	0.72	7.66	4.26	63.2	**2.2**	27.6	19.7	**4.8**
3.7	1.92	11.3	0.78	**1.5**	-0.3	-0.19	-2.11	4.02	73.7	**5.0**	28.3	4.9	**5.2**
3.2	8.57	23.1	1.51	**4.8**	1.5	0.54	3.02	3.60	62.3	**2.9**	41.4	22.5	**9.7**
3.9	1.77	15.2	0.10	**4.3**	1.1	0.73	9.39	3.67	70.4	**1.7**	21.3	24.1	**4.7**
6.4	1.22	4.6	0.20	**6.7**	0.9	1.48	10.15	4.71	63.6	**2.6**	29.8	18.7	**8.9**
2.7	1.61	14.1	0.10	**5.0**	5.3	1.24	13.44	4.12	61.6	**3.1**	15.4	13.4	**4.0**
4.7	0.94	7.0	0.01	**4.9**	1.2	1.07	13.10	3.72	71.6	**3.9**	28.5	11.8	**6.2**
3.3	2.51	15.7	1.30	**2.8**	1.4	0.37	3.89	3.66	79.2	**5.0**	29.1	5.2	**5.6**
5.0	0.83	5.9	0.73	**5.8**	0.7	0.76	9.42	5.26	70.1	**2.6**	25.5	16.9	**5.5**
6.6	0.19	0.8	0.08	**5.3**	0.7	0.87	6.88	3.04	61.2	**2.9**	43.2	22.9	**7.6**
8.6	0.06	0.2	0.15	**5.3**	5.1	1.28	10.98	3.91	68.1	**4.4**	36.8	12.1	**6.8**
4.7	1.34	4.1	5.42	**10.0**	15.8	2.41	12.31	7.88	38.5	**3.0**	24.5	14.9	**9.2**
4.2	2.06	11.0	1.33	**1.4**	1.5	0.37	3.90	3.56	73.1	**2.3**	24.0	18.4	**3.4**
0.0	4.08	26.3	0.46	**3.2**	14.5	0.38	4.32	3.77	73.2	**0.7**	12.4	44.3	**6.5**
4.2	0.72	5.4	0.24	**9.7**	7.1	2.33	29.94	4.36	48.0	**0.8**	15.5	36.2	**6.8**
4.3	0.88	5.0	0.14	**7.9**	3.2	1.79	16.52	5.09	57.2	**1.7**	25.3	24.4	**7.7**
4.7	0.49	3.1	0.35	**3.6**	0.2	0.45	4.82	4.60	80.9	**1.7**	29.9	29.0	**4.9**
6.6	0.94	5.0	0.21	**6.8**	1.0	1.66	16.74	4.64	62.5	**2.0**	14.9	19.1	**6.3**
5.7	0.71	4.4	-0.07	**5.8**	2.0	1.48	15.87	4.30	63.8	**1.3**	29.2	37.8	**4.8**
4.6	0.57	4.6	0.52	**5.6**	3.7	1.35	14.45	4.84	72.8	**1.6**	17.8	24.4	**6.1**
1.9	1.48	13.1	0.61	**8.0**	13.2	1.83	18.31	4.78	46.7	**0.6**	7.2	37.7	**7.7**
1.2	5.54	30.5	0.66	**3.8**	1.6	0.60	6.40	3.57	70.8	**2.3**	29.6	20.0	**5.1**
2.2	2.28	12.4	0.82	**3.1**	0.7	0.48	4.57	4.20	76.4	**1.8**	26.0	24.0	**5.4**
8.5	0.44	1.4	0.15	**5.5**	1.8	1.16	7.22	4.59	75.3	**3.9**	39.1	15.0	**8.6**
2.1	4.35	21.9	0.95	**1.5**	0.6	0.25	2.40	3.70	86.5	**1.9**	22.7	20.1	**4.4**
1.9	3.62	22.0	1.38	**0.3**	-0.1	-0.16	-1.79	3.76	100.4	**1.7**	25.4	25.5	**3.0**

Name	City	State	Rating	2008 Rating	2007 Rating	Total Assets ($Mil)	One Year Asset Growth	Asset Mix (As a % of Total Assets) Comm-ercial Loans	Cons-umer Loans	Home Mort-gages	Secur-ities	Capital-ization Index	Leverage Ratio	Risk-based Capital Ratio
FIRST NATIONAL BK & TRUST	MOUNTAIN HOME	AR	**A**	A	A	389	-1.40	4.3	2.5	26.7	21.1	**10.0**	11.4	17.0
FIRST NATIONAL BK & TRUST	CLINTON	IL	**B-**	B-	B	97	-4.07	3.3	2.4	18.3	38.0	**10.0**	11.3	23.0
▼ FIRST NATIONAL BK & TRUST	ROCHELLE	IL	**D+**	C+	B-	217	-1.81	1.7	2.1	12.1	52.8	**6.4**	8.4	17.3
▲ FIRST NATIONAL BK & TRUST	JUNCTION CITY	KS	**B-**	C	C+	103	2.08	3.9	1.3	8.4	48.7	**7.3**	9.2	13.5
FIRST NATIONAL BK & TRUST	LEAVENWORTH	KS	**B+**	B+	B+	101	-4.80	4.0	29.7	21.4	16.7	**8.3**	9.9	14.4
▼ FIRST NATIONAL BK & TRUST	IRON MOUNTAIN	MI	**C+**	B	B+	283	1.25	9.8	2.8	16.6	25.5	**6.1**	8.1	13.4
FIRST NATIONAL BK & TRUST	BOTTINEAU	ND	**B**	B+	B+	117	9.32	2.6	3.4	5.1	41.5	**10.0**	11.0	20.6
FIRST NATIONAL BK & TRUST	WILLISTON	ND	**B-**	B-	C+	285	19.80	14.2	3.0	5.0	24.3	**5.5**	7.5	13.5
▲ FIRST NATIONAL BK & TRUST	COLUMBUS	NE	**C**	C-	C+	403	3.16	6.8	2.6	7.5	21.3	**5.6**	7.6	13.6
FIRST NATIONAL BK & TRUST	FALLS CITY	NE	**C**	C	C+	92	14.97	1.2	2.8	9.3	45.8	**6.6**	8.6	21.2
FIRST NATIONAL BK & TRUST	ARDMORE	OK	**B-**	B-	B	414	18.68	7.5	5.1	8.3	49.9	**5.6**	7.6	15.6
FIRST NATIONAL BK & TRUST	BROKEN ARROW	OK	**D**	C-	C	182	-6.11	7.1	2.1	23.1	24.6	**6.5**	8.5	15.7
▼ FIRST NATIONAL BK & TRUST	CHICKASHA	OK	**B+**	A-	A	366	2.23	21.2	7.2	10.8	19.4	**10.0**	12.0	16.8
FIRST NATIONAL BK & TRUST	MCALESTER	OK	**B+**	B+	A-	448	5.28	5.2	2.9	9.3	48.8	**10.0**	11.1	23.9
FIRST NATIONAL BK & TRUST	MIAMI	OK	**B-**	B-	B-	151	16.80	7.7	8.2	15.2	18.2	**5.3**	7.3	12.8
▼ FIRST NATIONAL BK & TRUST	OKMULGEE	OK	**C**	B	A-	217	8.18	10.4	4.8	17.8	35.0	**8.9**	10.2	17.2
FIRST NATIONAL BK & TRUST	SHAWNEE	OK	**C**	C	C	201	1.79	7.9	2.0	11.4	46.1	**8.6**	10.1	18.4
FIRST NATIONAL BK & TRUST	VINITA	OK	**C+**	B-	B-	223	-0.15	7.3	13.3	18.2	31.7	**6.7**	8.9	12.2
FIRST NATIONAL BK & TRUST	WEATHERFORD	OK	**A-**	A	A	117	11.95	18.9	6.5	9.2	3.3	**10.0**	14.3	21.3
FIRST NATIONAL BK & TRUST	NEWTOWN	PA	**B+**	A-	A	730	6.17	1.2	3.3	15.3	36.7	**9.9**	10.9	21.6
FIRST NATIONAL BK & TRUST	WEATHERFORD	TX	**C**	C-	C	193	4.97	11.8	3.7	9.6	5.6	**8.6**	10.0	14.2
FIRST NATIONAL BK & TRUST	BELOIT	WI	**C+**	C+	B-	861	4.25	4.3	1.5	11.8	37.7	**6.3**	8.3	13.3
FIRST NATIONAL BK & TRUST	POWELL	WY	**C**	C-	D	352	18.97	6.9	2.6	4.0	43.8	**10.0**	11.8	20.0
FIRST NATIONAL BK - FOX V	NEENAH	WI	**C**	C-	C-	307	20.31	17.0	1.7	17.2	12.2	**7.1**	9.0	13.6
▼ FIRST NATIONAL BK ALAMOGO	ALAMOGORDO	NM	**A-**	A	A	273	6.17	3.0	2.3	5.2	44.6	**7.7**	9.5	21.9
FIRST NATIONAL BK ALASKA	ANCHORAGE	AK	**A-**	B+	B+	2,726	2.80	9.5	0.7	3.6	48.5	**10.0**	14.8	23.7
FIRST NATIONAL BK AMES IO	AMES	IA	**B+**	B+	B+	520	10.31	5.3	0.3	5.8	56.8	**8.6**	10.0	14.0
FIRST NATIONAL BK ARENZVI	ARENZVILLE	IL	**D+**	C-	C-	62	10.84	12.1	8.5	18.1	23.2	**5.3**	7.3	11.5
FIRST NATIONAL BK ASSUMPT	ASSUMPTION	IL	**C**	C	C-	17	-6.16	3.1	8.6	18.2	42.7	**10.0**	11.8	17.5
FIRST NATIONAL BK AT PARI	PARIS	AR	**B-**	B-	B-	124	10.40	3.8	7.0	28.8	7.8	**8.9**	10.2	16.6
FIRST NATIONAL BK AUDRAIN	MEXICO	MO	**C+**	B-	B	148	-2.92	4.0	4.5	19.8	23.0	**5.4**	7.4	12.0
FIRST NATIONAL BK BALDWIN	FOLEY	AL	**E-**	D-	D+	249	-5.63	7.0	0.5	23.8	10.5	**0.5**	4.0	7.1
FIRST NATIONAL BK BATTLE	BATTLE LAKE	MN	**B+**	B	B	61	6.63	1.7	3.1	14.1	41.7	**9.3**	10.5	17.8
FIRST NATIONAL BK BEARDST	BEARDSTOWN	IL	**A-**	A	A-	93	7.58	8.9	13.0	19.1	11.7	**8.8**	10.2	15.7
FIRST NATIONAL BK BELLS/S	BELLS	TX	**C-**	C	B-	45	5.91	6.3	2.5	14.2	44.6	**10.0**	14.2	32.2
FIRST NATIONAL BK BERRYVI	BERRYVILLE	AR	**B**	C+	B-	134	2.30	7.8	7.6	38.0	3.4	**10.0**	13.8	19.4
▲ FIRST NATIONAL BK BLANCHE	BLANCHESTER	OH	**B+**	B	B	51	3.34	0.4	7.3	48.5	17.7	**10.0**	11.8	19.1
▼ FIRST NATIONAL BK BOSQUE	VALLEY MILLS	TX	**C+**	B-	B-	98	-3.70	11.0	10.3	21.1	1.4	**8.0**	9.6	18.5
FIRST NATIONAL BK BROOKFI	BROOKFIELD	IL	**E-**	E	D-	180	-22.21	2.7	0.4	30.5	3.6	**3.1**	6.3	10.1
▼ FIRST NATIONAL BK BROOKSV	BROOKSVILLE	KY	**B**	B+	A-	67	3.04	1.8	5.2	41.0	29.2	**8.4**	9.9	20.0
FIRST NATIONAL BK	BROWNSTOWN	IL	**C+**	C+	C	31	7.05	6.8	7.5	15.1	30.0	**8.3**	9.8	19.6
▲ FIRST NATIONAL BK CARROLL	CARROLLTON	KY	**B+**	A-	A-	93	10.21	2.6	3.6	44.4	20.1	**10.0**	11.1	18.1
▼ FIRST NATIONAL BK CARROLL	CARROLLTON	MO	**B**	B+	B-	50	5.16	1.2	1.5	5.8	44.7	**7.6**	9.4	20.6
FIRST NATIONAL BK CENTRAL	TUSCALOOSA	AL	**D+**	C	C+	241	-1.71	9.6	1.2	17.9	18.3	**7.6**	9.4	15.0
FIRST NATIONAL BK CENTRAL	WINTER PARK	FL	**E-**	D-	D-	352	-20.85	6.2	0.2	10.0	10.7	**0.0**	1.4	3.3
FIRST NATIONAL BK CENTRAL	WACO	TX	**B**	C+	B	563	16.30	11.1	3.7	15.6	5.1	**5.4**	8.0	11.3
FIRST NATIONAL BK	CHATSWORTH	GA	**E-**	D-	C	126	-9.98	7.8	3.1	19.9	13.3	**0.0**	3.0	5.5
▲ FIRST NATIONAL BK CHILLIC	CHILLICOTHE	IL	**D+**	E-	C	67	-0.84	3.9	20.9	31.2	23.1	**8.2**	9.8	15.2
▼ FIRST NATIONAL BK CHILLIC	CHILLICOTHE	TX	**B-**	B	B	44	7.82	3.7	9.6	9.9	27.8	**10.0**	11.3	19.5
FIRST NATIONAL BK CLARKSD	CLARKSDALE	MS	**B+**	B	B	311	-0.53	14.7	4.3	8.3	27.4	**7.4**	9.3	13.5
▲ FIRST NATIONAL BK COFFEE	DOUGLAS	GA	**D+**	D-	B	119	-11.54	7.3	2.0	15.1	15.1	**10.0**	13.0	20.8
FIRST NATIONAL BK COLD SP	COLD SPRING	MN	**D**	D-	B-	83	-1.64	9.0	4.4	13.3	9.0	**6.9**	8.9	13.9
FIRST NATIONAL BK CORTEZ	CORTEZ	CO	**B-**	B-	C+	82	7.31	0.8	2.2	12.5	52.5	**7.0**	9.0	20.4
FIRST NATIONAL BK CUNNING	CUNNINGHAM	KS	**B-**	B-	C+	27	6.59	6.2	3.3	7.3	48.9	**7.2**	9.1	19.1
FIRST NATIONAL BK DARLING	DARLINGTON	WI	**B**	B	B	90	4.79	4.9	6.1	8.6	27.9	**10.0**	11.8	17.4
FIRST NATIONAL BK DECATUR	BAINBRIDGE	GA	**D+**	C-	B-	115	7.66	6.6	4.6	13.0	15.2	**10.0**	12.1	18.6
FIRST NATIONAL BK EAGLE L	EAGLE LAKE	TX	**D+**	C-	C	94	-5.13	14.5	2.3	5.5	22.7	**7.5**	9.3	16.2
FIRST NATIONAL BK EAGLE R	EAGLE RIVER	WI	**D+**	C-	C	147	-7.89	1.4	1.5	44.8	20.2	**6.6**	8.7	15.0
FIRST NATIONAL BK EASTERN	FORREST CITY	AR	**B-**	B	A-	326	4.99	0.2	4.9	6.1	38.8	**9.2**	10.4	26.0
▲ FIRST NATIONAL BK ESTES P	ESTES PARK	CO	**A**	A	A	99	2.60	3.6	1.1	12.0	14.9	**10.0**	11.4	18.8

Asset Quality Index	Non-Performing Loans as a % of Total Loans	Non-Performing Loans as a % of Capital	Net Charge-offs Avg Loans	Profitability Index	Net Income ($Mil)	Return on Assets (R.O.A.)	Return on Equity (R.O.E.)	Net Interest Spread	Overhead Efficiency Ratio	Liquidity Index	Liquidity Ratio	Hot Money Ratio	Stability Index
7.1	0.21	1.1	0.20	**7.5**	5.7	1.45	9.87	4.59	60.9	**3.5**	9.5	11.0	**8.7**
9.2	0.30	1.1	0.07	**2.9**	0.4	0.41	3.56	2.75	83.9	**3.9**	28.5	11.8	**7.0**
1.3	7.95	32.1	0.50	**3.6**	1.5	0.66	7.42	3.57	78.8	**4.4**	32.9	10.8	**5.5**
4.5	0.02	0.1	0.19	**7.0**	1.3	1.26	9.93	4.04	58.9	**1.8**	20.6	21.2	**6.4**
6.1	0.38	2.5	-0.02	**5.3**	1.0	0.95	9.45	4.35	70.1	**4.0**	19.0	9.6	**6.5**
3.7	2.35	15.9	0.41	**4.2**	2.1	0.74	8.38	3.62	66.5	**2.2**	32.4	25.1	**5.4**
6.1	2.36	9.4	0.25	**4.0**	0.8	0.70	6.02	3.29	69.9	**5.4**	43.8	8.7	**8.1**
6.1	0.48	2.9	0.08	**6.9**	4.1	1.60	17.58	3.83	52.1	**4.5**	40.5	12.5	**5.0**
5.6	0.08	0.7	0.07	**5.3**	5.2	1.28	14.50	4.13	58.3	**4.3**	11.3	6.2	**4.2**
8.7	0.00	0.0	0.00	**2.9**	0.8	0.88	8.36	3.47	68.6	**6.0**	60.9	7.9	**4.1**
4.7	0.70	3.4	0.32	**5.1**	4.6	1.25	13.25	4.17	72.3	**2.8**	32.1	18.2	**5.7**
2.9	3.96	23.5	1.27	**0.4**	-0.2	-0.10	-1.24	3.30	96.5	**4.7**	30.3	7.5	**2.9**
3.6	1.63	9.0	0.35	**9.3**	5.4	1.48	10.03	5.24	53.8	**3.5**	21.5	12.0	**9.3**
5.0	3.27	12.3	0.12	**9.8**	10.4	2.35	18.31	4.20	41.5	**3.1**	42.2	20.3	**9.1**
6.2	0.17	1.2	0.66	**4.5**	0.9	0.64	8.55	3.61	72.4	**4.1**	25.3	9.2	**4.1**
2.1	3.85	19.7	0.85	**7.3**	3.5	1.63	13.69	4.35	57.2	**2.1**	14.7	18.3	**8.5**
3.5	3.94	15.3	0.31	**2.5**	0.7	0.35	3.06	4.50	86.7	**4.5**	43.9	13.3	**4.9**
2.7	2.59	16.0	0.60	**6.4**	3.7	1.58	17.90	4.48	65.6	**0.8**	11.6	33.3	**6.6**
7.8	0.58	2.6	0.12	**6.1**	1.6	1.36	8.71	4.68	71.1	**3.3**	29.6	15.1	**9.1**
4.9	1.80	8.0	0.01	**5.5**	7.3	1.03	9.55	3.85	66.8	**5.4**	39.0	6.8	**8.3**
2.3	1.43	10.5	0.40	**4.8**	1.4	0.75	7.51	4.77	71.0	**1.4**	15.3	25.7	**5.1**
5.1	0.69	4.1	0.62	**3.9**	5.2	0.64	6.64	3.27	68.3	**2.9**	24.5	15.3	**5.8**
2.8	6.42	22.4	0.40	**3.4**	2.1	0.69	5.42	3.93	69.8	**3.5**	33.1	15.1	**6.7**
2.6	1.87	14.4	0.54	**4.1**	2.1	0.75	8.09	3.91	66.3	**0.9**	25.1	52.0	**3.9**
7.5	0.78	2.4	0.20	**7.3**	4.7	1.79	16.49	4.10	65.5	**4.1**	42.6	15.3	**7.7**
5.4	2.86	8.3	0.21	**9.2**	40.4	1.50	9.13	4.40	58.9	**5.7**	29.5	5.3	**10.0**
5.1	2.41	8.5	0.05	**7.0**	6.9	1.43	13.64	3.46	48.6	**5.4**	48.7	10.4	**7.0**
4.1	0.74	6.4	0.19	**3.3**	0.3	0.46	6.49	3.72	78.9	**2.8**	21.4	15.4	**3.9**
6.2	0.58	1.8	-0.05	**3.4**	0.2	0.83	7.02	4.29	78.6	**4.6**	38.6	9.2	**5.3**
5.3	0.15	1.0	0.12	**6.7**	1.9	1.58	10.74	4.81	65.6	**1.1**	18.2	30.8	**7.5**
4.1	1.54	10.8	0.15	**8.3**	2.0	1.35	16.71	4.00	52.4	**2.8**	18.6	15.2	**6.0**
1.7	1.98	22.0	2.78	**0.0**	-4.7	-1.88	-27.21	3.01	108.2	**1.1**	16.6	31.4	**2.0**
5.8	1.80	7.8	0.18	**6.0**	0.8	1.45	12.84	3.88	64.1	**4.6**	42.9	12.4	**7.1**
5.4	0.52	3.3	0.42	**5.7**	1.0	1.13	9.41	4.50	76.4	**2.8**	20.3	15.4	**8.5**
9.1	0.06	0.2	0.22	**1.1**	0.0	0.07	0.49	3.62	110.0	**2.7**	57.2	33.3	**6.6**
4.9	1.45	8.6	0.49	**4.9**	1.2	0.91	6.47	5.37	75.2	**2.7**	6.2	14.9	**9.5**
8.4	0.12	0.7	0.13	**5.4**	0.5	0.95	7.18	4.56	70.8	**2.5**	15.3	16.6	**7.3**
4.5	1.28	7.0	0.11	**3.3**	0.5	0.54	5.58	3.50	83.5	**4.1**	39.8	14.4	**5.4**
0.3	13.17	104.9	3.43	**0.0**	-6.0	-2.81	-39.87	3.56	110.8	**2.7**	12.3	15.4	**1.8**
7.5	0.63	3.8	0.18	**4.5**	0.6	0.87	8.31	4.15	75.7	**3.7**	12.5	10.1	**6.6**
4.1	2.88	12.9	0.15	**3.8**	0.2	0.67	6.34	3.64	77.2	**4.4**	40.0	13.0	**6.0**
5.4	2.67	16.0	0.07	**6.2**	1.0	1.05	9.40	3.90	63.7	**1.2**	22.2	30.9	**7.3**
5.8	1.83	6.5	0.06	**7.8**	0.7	1.57	14.61	3.70	56.3	**5.5**	47.7	8.4	**8.0**
3.9	2.48	15.2	1.75	**1.1**	-0.3	-0.12	-1.24	3.70	78.2	**1.8**	18.8	20.6	**5.6**
0.0	26.60	402.0	5.90	**0.0**	-31.0	-7.65	-114.42	2.38	232.0	**0.7**	12.5	42.0	**0.8**
7.6	0.15	1.4	0.01	**7.7**	9.2	1.80	21.66	4.11	55.0	**2.2**	14.9	18.1	**7.0**
0.3	9.19	114.1	6.60	**0.0**	-6.0	-4.51	-65.93	4.65	113.5	**1.6**	16.3	22.8	**1.3**
3.0	1.43	9.2	0.09	**4.2**	0.4	0.63	7.12	3.49	65.3	**2.2**	29.0	20.7	**3.5**
5.7	2.04	9.0	0.11	**3.7**	0.4	0.79	6.78	3.69	82.1	**2.1**	39.2	32.8	**6.8**
8.3	0.02	0.1	0.12	**5.9**	3.5	1.09	11.57	4.37	61.1	**1.6**	21.5	25.5	**6.1**
0.3	7.47	34.8	-0.03	**5.1**	2.1	1.65	13.90	3.47	78.6	**1.4**	17.3	25.9	**4.9**
1.5	1.27	9.0	1.61	**2.3**	0.0	0.03	0.29	4.31	78.3	**1.5**	24.9	27.5	**4.9**
4.7	1.67	5.5	-0.01	**4.2**	0.6	0.81	8.24	4.16	77.9	**1.6**	19.8	24.6	**5.4**
8.7	0.11	0.5	0.13	**4.8**	0.3	1.06	10.38	4.34	74.2	**5.2**	53.7	11.2	**6.4**
4.7	2.55	11.4	0.29	**4.4**	0.7	0.84	6.80	3.77	65.2	**4.9**	46.5	11.8	**6.9**
1.1	6.15	30.8	2.09	**2.3**	0.3	0.31	3.06	3.46	58.7	**2.3**	35.8	26.0	**4.7**
3.6	0.87	4.7	0.57	**1.7**	0.2	0.25	2.57	4.71	100.1	**4.6**	29.3	7.8	**4.4**
1.8	3.84	27.6	1.59	**1.1**	-1.0	-0.66	-8.08	3.39	81.2	**2.8**	10.7	14.7	**4.3**
8.1	0.64	2.0	0.12	**3.8**	2.6	0.83	7.45	3.15	73.9	**3.3**	50.8	23.4	**6.8**
7.7	0.00	0.0	0.00	**6.9**	1.5	1.49	12.83	4.45	67.3	**5.2**	34.4	6.1	**9.3**

Name	City	State	Rating	2008 Rating	2007 Rating	Total Assets ($Mil)	One Year Asset Growth	Asset Mix (As a % of Total Assets)				Capital-ization Index	Leverage Ratio	Risk-based Capital Ratio
								Comm-ercial Loans	Cons-umer Loans	Home Mort-gages	Secur-ities			
FIRST NATIONAL BK FALFURR	FALFURRIAS	TX	**B+**	B+	B+	72	-2.04	9.0	10.0	1.7	58.0	**10.0**	11.1	34.3
FIRST NATIONAL BK FORT SM	FORT SMITH	AR	**B-**	B	B	1,087	2.93	16.9	2.6	9.1	13.3	**10.0**	11.7	16.4
FIRST NATIONAL BK GEORGET	GEORGETOWN	IL	**C-**	B-	C+	40	6.38	6.2	0.6	5.0	16.5	**3.6**	7.9	10.3
▼ FIRST NATIONAL BK GERMANT	GERMANTOWN	OH	**E**	D	D-	61	10.06	9.4	4.2	23.5	13.1	**4.0**	6.1	11.0
▼ FIRST NATIONAL BK GRANT P	GRANT PARK	IL	**D-**	D-	D	122	-4.16	9.5	0.3	16.5	34.9	**5.6**	7.6	13.5
FIRST NATIONAL BK GREEN F	GREEN FOREST	AR	**B**	B-	C-	349	3.12	5.4	3.0	12.2	25.6	**8.9**	10.3	15.5
▼ FIRST NATIONAL BK GULF CO	NAPLES	FL	**D-**	C	C	299	145.18	4.3	3.4	4.9	46.9	**6.3**	8.3	16.2
FIRST NATIONAL BK HARTFOR	HARTFORD	WI	**C+**	C+	C+	162	0.04	7.9	0.6	11.2	26.3	**10.0**	12.2	20.2
FIRST NATIONAL BK HARVEYV	HARVEYVILLE	KS	**C**	C+	C+	14	17.57	6.5	4.3	32.0	35.8	**8.1**	9.8	20.1
FIRST NATIONAL BK HEBBRON	HEBBRONVILLE	TX	**A-**	A-	A-	120	6.21	3.9	7.0	2.1	75.2	**10.0**	11.9	34.7
FIRST NATIONAL BK HUNTSVI	HUNTSVILLE	TX	**B**	B+	B+	390	14.98	5.3	6.1	12.3	50.1	**6.6**	8.6	18.6
FIRST NATIONAL BK HUTCHIN	HUTCHINSON	KS	**C**	C+	B-	550	-4.88	8.1	0.9	7.3	34.7	**8.2**	9.8	18.4
FIRST NATIONAL BK IN ALTU	ALTUS	OK	**B-**	B-	B-	286	1.86	7.0	0.5	3.5	64.1	**6.4**	8.4	21.8
FIRST NATIONAL BK IN AMBO	AMBOY	IL	**B-**	B-	B	168	8.93	5.7	1.5	8.7	41.1	**7.4**	9.3	16.7
FIRST NATIONAL BK IN CARL	CARLYLE	IL	**B+**	B+	B	151	3.95	0.8	2.0	11.3	46.0	**10.0**	11.8	22.4
▼ FIRST NATIONAL BK IN CIMA	CIMARRON	KS	**C+**	B-	C	85	18.85	5.5	4.0	7.6	34.7	**4.3**	6.4	12.1
FIRST NATIONAL BK IN COOP	COOPER	TX	**B-**	B	B	41	3.29	5.0	10.0	17.0	35.5	**7.4**	12.5	12.9
▲ FIRST NATIONAL BK IN CRES	CRESTON	IA	**C+**	C	C	201	4.46	11.4	4.6	14.7	21.3	**6.4**	8.4	12.6
FIRST NATIONAL BK IN DALH	DALHART	TX	**C-**	C+	C-	66	32.61	9.4	1.5	1.1	11.9	**4.6**	6.6	11.4
FIRST NATIONAL BK IN DE R	DE RIDDER	LA	**A-**	A	A	181	-5.13	3.0	5.6	26.4	38.1	**10.0**	13.5	26.9
▼ FIRST NATIONAL BK IN EXET	EXETER	NE	**C**	C+	C+	28	11.35	9.8	1.6	11.5	14.3	**7.7**	9.5	13.8
FIRST NATIONAL BK IN FAIR	FAIRFIELD	IA	**C+**	C+	B-	124	9.22	26.7	2.1	17.2	7.9	**6.0**	8.0	11.7
FIRST NATIONAL BK IN FRAN	FRANKFORT	KS	**C**	C-	C-	33	1.69	9.1	4.0	10.1	47.5	**7.8**	9.6	19.8
FIRST NATIONAL BK IN FRED	FREDONIA	KS	**A-**	A-	A-	97	12.48	5.4	9.5	11.0	57.3	**10.0**	12.9	26.0
FIRST NATIONAL BK IN GRAH	GRAHAM	TX	**C-**	C+	B-	225	3.06	5.3	9.9	9.8	22.4	**9.2**	10.5	16.9
FIRST NATIONAL BK IN HOMI	HOMINY	OK	**C**	C	C-	41	3.13	7.0	10.3	7.9	54.0	**6.1**	8.1	20.7
FIRST NATIONAL BK IN HOWE	HOWELL	MI	**E-**	E-	D-	307	-7.67	5.3	1.5	10.1	8.9	**0.1**	4.0	6.2
FIRST NATIONAL BK IN MAHN	MAHNOMEN	MN	**D+**	D+	C-	68	1.96	14.2	8.1	13.0	20.3	**6.6**	8.6	15.5
FIRST NATIONAL BK IN MARL	MARLOW	OK	**B+**	B+	B+	64	-0.61	5.7	8.2	13.9	40.2	**8.9**	10.3	17.9
▲ FIRST NATIONAL BK IN MUND	MUNDAY	TX	**C+**	C-	C+	82	7.54	8.2	5.8	6.5	10.6	**8.3**	9.9	14.2
FIRST NATIONAL BK IN OKEE	OKEENE	OK	**B-**	C+	C+	58	-8.37	4.8	0.4	0.5	49.9	**10.0**	31.0	55.9
FIRST NATIONAL BK IN OLNE	OLNEY	IL	**B-**	B-	B-	285	4.14	7.0	3.4	15.7	40.0	**5.1**	7.1	13.7
FIRST NATIONAL BK IN ORD	ORD	NE	**C+**	C+	B+	88	-1.23	5.4	3.2	13.1	24.4	**9.0**	10.4	17.7
FIRST NATIONAL BK IN PAWH	PAWHUSKA	OK	**D-**	D-	D	30	-1.34	6.0	13.0	16.0	10.7	**7.9**	9.6	16.6
FIRST NATIONAL BK IN PAXT	PAXTON	IL	**B-**	B	A	74	0.76	2.2	2.4	10.9	22.4	**9.5**	10.7	24.4
FIRST NATIONAL BK IN PHIL	PHILIP	SD	**A-**	A	A	161	6.24	3.7	1.6	0.3	26.6	**10.0**	12.0	17.0
FIRST NATIONAL BK IN PRAT	PRATT	KS	**C**	C-	B-	102	12.06	7.2	1.9	6.2	43.9	**6.8**	8.8	16.8
FIRST NATIONAL BK IN QUAN	QUANAH	TX	**D**	C-	C-	53	1.05	11.0	13.4	16.9	5.7	**5.2**	8.2	11.1
FIRST NATIONAL BK IN STAU	STAUNTON	IL	**B**	B-	B-	446	-2.97	4.2	3.3	22.1	27.0	**7.8**	9.5	16.0
FIRST NATIONAL BK IN TIGE	TIGERTON	WI	**B-**	B	B	21	0.89	2.0	3.1	39.1	23.2	**10.0**	15.2	38.7
FIRST NATIONAL BK IN TREM	TREMONT	IL	**D+**	C-	C-	116	-0.07	7.1	3.7	20.4	30.1	**6.5**	8.5	16.0
FIRST NATIONAL BK IN TRIN	TRINIDAD	CO	**B-**	B+	A-	180	0.27	1.7	3.0	46.4	4.0	**10.0**	11.9	27.5
FIRST NATIONAL BK IN WADE	WADENA	MN	**D**	D	D	58	5.47	4.8	3.1	26.0	11.5	**6.0**	8.0	16.1
FIRST NATIONAL BK IN WEWO	WEWOKA	OK	**B**	B	B	45	-1.90	2.9	6.6	13.9	57.5	**10.0**	13.8	32.8
▼ FIRST NATIONAL BK IN WHIT	WHITNEY	TX	**B-**	B	B+	59	7.20	3.2	4.8	1.1	64.4	**7.8**	9.5	30.2
▲ FIRST NATIONAL BK INDEPEN	INDEPENDENCE	KS	**B**	B-	B-	83	5.76	15.5	3.0	20.9	3.3	**7.3**	9.4	12.7
FIRST NATIONAL BK IZARD C	CALICO ROCK	AR	**A**	A+	A+	145	4.05	2.8	4.7	15.7	24.7	**10.0**	29.4	47.9
FIRST NATIONAL BK JEANERE	JEANERETTE	LA	**B-**	B	B+	184	11.56	5.3	5.7	27.7	11.9	**5.7**	7.8	11.6
▲ FIRST NATIONAL BK LAKE JA	LAKE JACKSON	TX	**B**	B-	C	244	4.15	1.7	1.1	0.9	73.3	**7.9**	9.6	37.6
FIRST NATIONAL BK LAS ANI	LAS ANIMAS	CO	**B**	B-	B-	232	-1.35	3.1	2.0	10.6	16.3	**8.6**	10.0	14.6
FIRST NATIONAL BK	WALNUT RIDGE	AR	**A-**	A-	A-	167	4.07	9.0	5.3	14.2	19.6	**9.2**	10.5	16.2
▼ FIRST NATIONAL BK LITCHFI	LITCHFIELD	IL	**C+**	B-	B-	87	10.51	7.8	4.5	11.0	14.1	**5.0**	9.0	11.0
FIRST NATIONAL BK LIVINGS	LIVINGSTON	TX	**A+**	A+	A+	272	7.05	2.8	4.9	9.4	44.8	**10.0**	14.3	35.8
FIRST NATIONAL BK LONG IS	GLEN HEAD	NY	**B+**	B+	A-	1,710	2.09	2.3	0.3	20.3	43.5	**7.6**	9.4	21.8
FIRST NATIONAL BK MANCHES	MANCHESTER	KY	**C+**	C-	C	148	0.94	3.2	3.0	17.6	44.2	**10.0**	13.3	26.6
FIRST NATIONAL BK MANCHES	MANCHESTER	TN	**B+**	B+	B+	198	9.25	11.8	7.0	19.3	24.3	**10.0**	12.2	19.6
▼ FIRST NATIONAL BK MCMINNV	MCMINNVILLE	TN	**B**	A-	A	405	11.03	7.9	0.8	22.0	28.9	**10.0**	13.1	22.6
FIRST NATIONAL BK	MENAHGA	MN	**B**	B	B	78	1.68	11.7	5.1	24.2	17.9	**10.0**	11.4	20.5
FIRST NATIONAL BK MERCERS	MERCERSBURG	PA	**C-**	C-	B-	186	-1.57	3.7	2.6	32.6	8.4	**6.3**	8.4	12.6
FIRST NATIONAL BK MIDWEST	OSKALOOSA	IA	**D-**	E+	D-	98	-10.54	3.1	14.3	13.2	0.1	**7.3**	9.4	12.8

Asset Quality Index	Non-Performing Loans as a % of Total Loans	Non-Performing Loans as a % of Capital	Net Charge-offs / Avg Loans	Profitability Index	Net Income ($Mil)	Return on Assets (R.O.A.)	Return on Equity (R.O.E.)	Net Interest Spread	Overhead Efficiency Ratio	Liquidity Index	Liquidity Ratio	Hot Money Ratio	Stability Index
8.5	1.03	2.4	0.16	**5.2**	0.8	1.13	9.57	3.04	69.3	**5.5**	41.5	7.3	**6.1**
4.1	1.60	9.2	0.37	**6.1**	11.9	1.12	8.25	4.35	58.3	**1.7**	16.7	22.9	**8.2**
5.5	0.37	3.0	0.00	**6.0**	0.4	1.05	9.62	4.17	56.9	**1.8**	13.7	19.8	**5.2**
0.3	6.19	55.3	1.87	**0.0**	-0.5	-0.93	-12.53	4.15	106.6	**5.1**	34.8	7.3	**2.1**
0.3	9.57	54.6	2.83	**0.0**	-1.6	-1.24	-13.23	3.88	99.4	**4.4**	38.8	12.8	**3.4**
4.5	0.84	4.7	0.19	**6.0**	5.3	1.54	14.78	4.35	63.1	**1.5**	21.8	26.4	**7.5**
7.1	0.77	3.1	1.29	**0.0**	-5.4	-2.22	-16.50	2.57	187.4	**4.9**	35.6	8.5	**0.8**
3.2	2.72	11.1	0.34	**3.5**	1.0	0.61	4.55	3.73	77.7	**5.4**	43.4	8.7	**6.8**
8.8	0.00	0.0	0.08	**3.0**	0.1	0.36	3.43	3.73	87.9	**2.4**	19.5	17.1	**5.4**
4.5	11.01	15.5	0.06	**6.0**	1.6	1.35	9.86	3.06	56.6	**3.2**	73.4	46.4	**8.1**
8.2	0.13	0.6	0.03	**5.0**	3.3	0.94	8.77	3.33	65.7	**2.6**	35.4	20.8	**6.4**
4.7	0.79	3.4	0.01	**2.7**	3.0	0.55	5.38	2.92	86.5	**3.8**	28.5	12.0	**6.0**
5.8	0.00	0.0	0.89	**4.9**	3.6	1.29	12.15	3.57	57.2	**2.3**	45.8	35.3	**5.8**
4.1	2.14	10.7	0.86	**4.1**	1.3	0.80	7.77	3.59	70.1	**4.0**	33.9	13.1	**5.6**
8.4	0.66	2.5	0.00	**4.9**	1.5	1.00	8.30	3.36	61.2	**4.4**	28.6	8.8	**7.0**
8.3	0.11	0.8	0.03	**5.5**	1.0	1.32	15.96	4.68	71.0	**3.7**	33.8	14.7	**4.2**
6.3	1.78	5.9	0.29	**6.1**	0.5	1.14	8.66	3.70	60.1	**3.2**	57.1	25.1	**5.7**
4.3	1.02	7.7	0.14	**7.5**	3.3	1.71	18.71	4.57	67.9	**4.1**	24.1	9.4	**6.6**
8.3	0.00	0.0	0.00	**4.2**	0.6	0.96	12.02	4.32	74.4	**3.6**	26.6	12.7	**4.4**
5.3	3.41	13.0	0.08	**7.8**	2.6	1.41	10.75	4.70	55.3	**3.1**	20.1	14.1	**8.4**
2.1	1.44	9.8	-0.01	**4.3**	0.3	1.04	7.99	4.37	74.2	**3.9**	23.5	10.3	**6.1**
5.4	0.47	3.8	-0.02	**4.3**	0.8	0.72	8.57	4.18	69.6	**3.8**	20.4	10.3	**4.6**
7.0	0.15	0.6	1.95	**3.2**	0.3	0.88	8.39	3.64	71.7	**3.8**	50.9	17.9	**4.4**
5.8	3.14	8.6	0.87	**7.3**	1.4	1.52	9.89	4.24	55.0	**3.6**	54.8	19.3	**8.8**
2.9	3.27	17.1	0.09	**7.0**	3.4	1.57	14.81	4.38	62.5	**1.7**	24.4	24.7	**6.4**
6.0	0.82	3.1	0.33	**4.3**	0.4	1.01	10.37	3.74	74.7	**4.8**	48.0	12.3	**5.5**
0.0	11.79	114.0	4.22	**0.0**	-2.3	-0.73	-17.28	4.40	87.2	**3.2**	17.3	13.1	**1.8**
2.1	2.56	16.1	0.38	**4.8**	0.7	1.05	11.91	4.58	67.1	**2.2**	18.8	18.6	**3.9**
8.5	0.17	0.8	0.52	**6.7**	1.0	1.52	13.40	5.08	66.0	**3.4**	39.1	17.8	**7.8**
7.1	0.22	1.5	0.05	**4.7**	0.6	0.82	8.68	3.93	74.1	**3.4**	19.2	12.6	**5.3**
9.0	0.00	0.0	-0.81	**7.8**	1.1	1.90	6.07	3.90	51.5	**2.0**	31.8	27.2	**5.7**
6.8	0.35	2.5	0.03	**5.3**	2.7	0.99	10.70	3.58	60.1	**3.4**	31.3	15.0	**5.4**
8.2	0.00	0.0	0.18	**3.5**	0.6	0.74	7.01	3.26	74.3	**2.1**	26.7	19.9	**6.6**
0.3	8.46	39.2	0.83	**1.4**	0.0	0.06	0.66	5.15	88.7	**5.2**	47.3	10.2	**4.3**
5.0	2.72	10.1	0.05	**4.4**	0.7	0.96	8.69	3.00	70.7	**4.3**	48.7	14.8	**6.4**
6.8	0.60	3.1	-0.03	**6.3**	1.8	1.17	9.61	3.70	53.5	**1.8**	25.7	23.7	**8.6**
8.3	0.00	0.0	0.02	**3.1**	0.7	0.67	6.38	3.19	78.5	**5.4**	44.1	9.0	**4.8**
2.5	1.23	10.8	1.53	**1.1**	-0.2	-0.36	-4.41	4.85	85.3	**1.3**	6.5	25.1	**4.7**
5.2	0.89	5.2	0.18	**4.9**	5.2	1.13	10.97	3.60	66.0	**3.9**	19.4	9.8	**6.9**
9.4	0.32	1.2	-0.02	**4.1**	0.2	0.87	5.88	3.63	76.2	**4.4**	31.3	7.6	**8.4**
2.5	3.54	19.9	0.78	**2.6**	0.5	0.38	4.06	4.11	72.8	**3.2**	34.6	17.3	**3.9**
5.0	1.45	7.1	0.27	**3.0**	0.7	0.38	3.19	3.82	87.0	**2.4**	32.9	21.7	**7.3**
3.2	2.60	18.4	0.67	**3.5**	0.4	0.65	8.28	4.34	78.1	**3.9**	32.0	13.1	**2.3**
8.6	0.49	1.1	0.19	**3.9**	0.4	0.84	5.37	4.07	76.9	**3.3**	68.9	30.5	**7.9**
8.8	0.01	0.0	0.52	**3.7**	0.5	0.84	8.45	2.59	78.8	**6.5**	77.0	7.9	**5.5**
6.6	0.33	2.4	0.03	**5.7**	1.1	1.29	13.08	5.30	73.1	**1.1**	15.9	31.6	**6.6**
6.8	2.88	5.2	0.08	**9.7**	2.3	1.61	5.51	5.05	52.0	**3.1**	44.9	22.0	**9.7**
4.9	1.31	9.5	0.68	**6.4**	2.4	1.44	18.48	4.46	60.7	**1.9**	29.3	26.5	**6.1**
10.0	0.00	0.0	0.06	**5.8**	3.3	1.40	12.43	2.61	46.9	**2.3**	33.9	24.2	**6.0**
5.1	0.65	4.0	0.88	**7.2**	3.9	1.69	16.27	4.78	52.1	**1.6**	18.7	24.8	**7.9**
7.4	0.43	2.5	0.20	**6.3**	1.8	1.14	9.87	4.18	59.9	**1.0**	16.1	31.7	**6.8**
3.6	0.66	5.8	0.08	**4.8**	0.9	1.12	11.54	4.11	67.7	**1.6**	4.5	20.3	**5.8**
8.7	0.04	0.1	0.20	**8.6**	5.2	2.01	11.83	4.21	64.7	**6.7**	74.7	8.1	**9.2**
8.9	0.44	2.3	0.04	**5.7**	18.9	1.16	13.77	3.90	56.5	**4.3**	32.2	13.8	**7.9**
3.5	7.17	20.7	0.33	**2.9**	0.9	0.58	4.11	4.14	84.6	**2.7**	50.0	31.3	**6.3**
4.9	2.12	9.4	0.07	**6.2**	2.0	1.06	8.60	4.04	59.6	**2.0**	30.5	25.7	**7.0**
8.3	0.36	1.6	2.52	**2.3**	0.2	0.04	0.27	3.60	61.1	**0.9**	19.9	37.3	**8.1**
3.7	2.44	12.7	0.25	**8.1**	1.5	1.87	14.19	4.67	59.7	**3.5**	28.5	13.6	**8.8**
1.7	2.82	22.4	0.61	**2.5**	0.7	0.36	4.92	3.87	77.3	**1.5**	13.4	23.6	**4.8**
0.3	8.86	56.9	0.47	**0.7**	0.0	0.03	0.29	3.95	93.5	**4.0**	14.7	8.6	**3.7**

	Name	City	State	Rating	2008 Rating	2007 Rating	Total Assets ($Mil)	One Year Asset Growth	Asset Mix (As a % of Total Assets) Comm-ercial Loans	Cons-umer Loans	Home Mort-gages	Secur-ities	Capital-ization Index	Leverage Ratio	Risk-based Capital Ratio
	FIRST NATIONAL BK MIFFLIN	MIFFLINTOWN	PA	**B-**	B-	B-	373	5.15	5.2	1.4	38.2	28.3	**6.4**	8.4	16.7
	FIRST NATIONAL BK MINERSV	MINERSVILLE	PA	**B**	B	B-	86	-3.57	3.4	4.5	32.2	32.4	**10.0**	12.8	25.7
	FIRST NATIONAL BK MINNESO	SAINT PETER	MN	**D**	C-	C-	186	-11.09	11.8	5.3	10.6	22.5	**8.4**	9.9	16.1
	FIRST NATIONAL BK MOOSE L	MOOSE LAKE	MN	**B-**	C	C-	68	4.95	4.8	2.4	18.0	11.3	**10.0**	11.1	16.3
	FIRST NATIONAL BK MOUNT D	MOUNT DORA	FL	**D**	D	A	200	-3.31	2.3	2.1	28.7	16.4	**10.0**	11.8	17.6
	FIRST NATIONAL BK MOUNT V	MOUNT VERNON	TX	**A-**	B+	B+	137	-0.08	2.5	4.7	28.3	48.0	**8.7**	10.1	24.8
	FIRST NATIONAL BK NEVADA	NEVADA	MO	**B-**	B-	B-	80	7.94	4.1	2.0	16.1	46.7	**10.0**	12.5	25.7
	FIRST NATIONAL BK NEW BRE	NEW BREMEN	OH	**B+**	B+	B+	223	6.08	4.5	3.2	15.9	31.1	**6.6**	8.6	18.7
	FIRST NATIONAL BK NEW MEX	CLAYTON	NM	**C+**	C+	C+	173	-5.33	7.5	3.6	7.3	21.2	**5.8**	7.8	12.7
	FIRST NATIONAL BK NORTHEA	LYONS	NE	**B**	B-	B-	228	6.49	4.8	8.1	4.4	21.3	**6.1**	9.2	11.8
	FIRST NATIONAL BK NORTHER	SOUTH SAN FRANCISCO	CA	**D**	D+	C-	716	1.03	8.5	0.3	4.4	17.6	**9.2**	10.5	14.9
	FIRST NATIONAL BK NORTHFI	NORTHFIELD	MN	**D**	C-	B-	125	-3.47	13.3	2.4	18.5	18.2	**6.3**	8.3	13.6
	FIRST NATIONAL BK	PANAMA CITY	FL	**D**	C-	B	119	-0.42	1.9	0.4	15.7	18.1	**10.0**	14.0	25.2
	FIRST NATIONAL BK OF ABSE	ABSECON	NJ	**C-**	C	B-	155	3.87	0.7	0.2	24.2	45.9	**6.2**	8.3	20.9
	FIRST NATIONAL BK OF ALBA	ALBANY	TX	**A-**	A-	A-	360	1.72	10.3	7.9	11.7	39.6	**8.2**	9.8	18.7
	FIRST NATIONAL BK OF ALLE	ALLENDALE	IL	**A-**	A-	A-	150	12.89	10.2	8.9	23.0	27.3	**9.2**	10.5	16.7
	FIRST NATIONAL BK OF ALTA	ALTAVISTA	VA	**D+**	C-	C+	337	1.45	6.8	14.0	18.0	7.9	**5.5**	8.4	11.4
	FIRST NATIONAL BK OF ALVI	ALVIN	TX	**A+**	A+	A+	108	-0.41	4.8	1.5	1.9	63.2	**10.0**	14.9	34.7
	FIRST NATIONAL BK OF AMER	EAST LANSING	MI	**C**	C-	C	468	-1.65	0.0	0.1	55.6	7.8	**10.0**	14.8	25.8
	FIRST NATIONAL BK OF AMHE	AMHERST	TX	**C-**	C	C-	20	3.65	4.7	2.2	0.1	42.3	**10.0**	16.1	64.1
	FIRST NATIONAL BK OF ANDE	ANDERSON	TX	**B-**	B	B+	142	6.65	9.2	8.8	12.4	15.6	**7.1**	9.1	14.7
	FIRST NATIONAL BK OF ANSO	ANSON	TX	**C+**	B-	C+	55	-1.76	8.1	8.2	11.6	28.6	**8.6**	10.0	20.4
	FIRST NATIONAL BK OF ARCO	ARCOLA	IL	**B**	B	C+	111	7.38	1.6	0.4	4.9	79.1	**10.0**	12.1	32.2
	FIRST NATIONAL BK OF ASPE	ASPERMONT	TX	**A-**	A-	A-	42	7.26	7.2	2.3	0.8	71.1	**10.0**	24.0	64.5
	FIRST NATIONAL BK OF AVA	AVA	IL	**A-**	A-	B+	59	6.34	5.3	5.4	20.1	39.2	**10.0**	11.3	18.9
▼	FIRST NATIONAL BK OF BAGL	BAGLEY	MN	**D+**	C-	C-	75	9.55	10.1	7.8	13.3	30.1	**5.6**	7.6	11.5
	FIRST NATIONAL BK OF BAIR	BAIRD	TX	**C+**	C	B-	199	-2.21	23.4	5.8	17.1	5.0	**9.4**	10.6	15.3
	FIRST NATIONAL BK OF BALL	BALLINGER	TX	**B**	B	B-	122	1.46	7.9	4.8	14.2	21.7	**6.5**	8.5	15.6
	FIRST NATIONAL BK OF BANC	BANCROFT	NE	**B-**	B-	B-	21	3.29	5.8	4.3	7.7	18.9	**10.0**	15.8	21.6
▼	FIRST NATIONAL BK OF BANG	BANGOR	WI	**B**	B+	B+	199	3.01	4.5	2.4	20.8	13.7	**10.0**	19.3	27.9
▲	FIRST NATIONAL BK OF BARR	BARRY	IL	**B-**	C+	C-	125	5.57	8.8	5.4	10.3	13.6	**10.0**	12.4	18.6
	FIRST NATIONAL BK OF BAST	BASTROP	TX	**B**	A-	A-	339	9.46	4.0	3.4	19.8	27.4	**10.0**	11.0	18.8
	FIRST NATIONAL BK OF BEEV	BEEVILLE	TX	**C+**	C+	B	241	25.12	14.1	1.7	2.9	8.1	**6.2**	8.2	15.7
	FIRST NATIONAL BK OF BELL	BELLEVUE	OH	**C-**	C-	D+	122	3.58	10.1	1.6	7.6	24.6	**6.6**	8.6	12.6
	FIRST NATIONAL BK OF BELL	BELLVILLE	TX	**B+**	B+	B+	346	22.91	3.5	3.1	14.3	53.2	**6.2**	8.2	19.0
	FIRST NATIONAL BK OF BELO	BELOIT	KS	**B+**	B+	B+	67	5.31	9.9	3.6	8.4	25.1	**10.0**	11.8	18.1
	FIRST NATIONAL BK OF BEMI	BEMIDJI	MN	**A-**	A-	A	529	2.07	9.7	6.5	20.0	37.7	**10.0**	12.2	21.4
	FIRST NATIONAL BK OF BENT	BENTON	LA	**B**	B+	B+	55	3.64	2.4	1.6	20.5	29.3	**10.0**	14.3	55.4
	FIRST NATIONAL BK OF BERL	BERLIN	WI	**D+**	D-	D	250	-5.25	9.4	2.7	13.4	18.8	**8.0**	9.7	14.7
▲	FIRST NATIONAL BK OF BORG	BORGER	TX	**C+**	C+	C+	8	-78.87	0.4	2.7	2.6	0.0	**10.0**	518.3	30.6
	FIRST NATIONAL BK OF BRUN	BRUNDIDGE	AL	**C+**	C-	B-	102	-6.39	6.1	4.9	16.7	37.0	**10.0**	11.1	21.1
▲	FIRST NATIONAL BK OF BUFF	BUFFALO	WY	**C-**	D+	C+	211	12.87	9.7	4.0	10.7	26.9	**6.3**	8.4	14.5
▼	FIRST NATIONAL BK OF BUHL	BUHL	MN	**E+**	D-	D	26	-1.43	15.0	7.8	21.6	3.7	**6.1**	8.1	12.6
	FIRST NATIONAL BK OF BURL	BURLESON	TX	**B-**	B	B	187	11.02	37.6	1.5	1.2	31.3	**6.3**	8.3	21.3
	FIRST NATIONAL BK OF BYER	BYERS	TX	**C-**	B-	B	94	8.95	7.2	10.6	8.6	19.3	**9.5**	10.7	17.6
▼	FIRST NATIONAL BK OF CAMB	CAMBRIDGE	NE	**B-**	B	B	50	11.50	2.3	4.6	4.3	25.8	**8.6**	10.1	17.6
	FIRST NATIONAL BK OF CANT	CANTON	TX	**B**	B	B	109	-1.35	4.1	7.1	22.4	13.5	**7.3**	9.2	17.7
	FIRST NATIONAL BK OF CARM	CARMI	IL	**C+**	C-	C+	287	7.79	14.0	4.2	8.2	18.9	**6.0**	8.0	11.9
	FIRST NATIONAL BK OF CATL	CATLIN	IL	**D**	D-	D-	43	-1.29	4.1	1.3	25.4	38.3	**6.1**	8.1	16.0
	FIRST NATIONAL BK OF CENT	CENTRALIA	KS	**A-**	B+	B-	106	1.42	10.8	1.7	6.2	51.8	**9.8**	10.9	21.3
	FIRST NATIONAL BK OF CHAD	CHADRON	NE	**A**	A	A	107	2.35	6.7	2.5	1.5	13.0	**9.5**	10.7	16.2
▲	FIRST NATIONAL BK OF CHIS	CHISHOLM	MN	**D+**	C	C-	80	2.55	5.6	4.1	7.8	67.0	**5.5**	7.5	15.9
	FIRST NATIONAL BK OF CHRI	CHRISMAN	IL	**B-**	B-	B-	38	1.47	5.4	4.7	5.7	24.7	**10.0**	12.5	19.0
	FIRST NATIONAL BK OF CLIN	CLINTON	MO	**B**	B-	C	70	-15.82	13.3	4.4	12.9	19.2	**10.0**	12.5	21.2
	FIRST NATIONAL BK OF COKA	COKATO	MN	**C-**	C	C-	33	5.84	7.5	3.4	8.7	16.9	**8.8**	10.2	19.3
	FIRST NATIONAL BK OF COLE	COLERAINE	MN	**C-**	C-	C-	73	3.47	2.3	2.8	20.9	53.7	**5.2**	7.2	17.7
	FIRST NATIONAL BK OF COLO	COLORADO CITY	TX	**C**	C	C-	39	5.08	17.7	3.8	3.2	45.3	**6.9**	8.9	29.4
	FIRST NATIONAL BK OF COWE	COWETA	OK	**D+**	C-	D+	65	-3.28	13.1	8.8	19.5	35.3	**5.9**	7.9	16.0
▼	FIRST NATIONAL BK OF CRES	CRESTVIEW	FL	**E-**	D-	B	130	-14.66	1.4	0.4	7.6	32.5	**3.6**	5.8	10.3
▼	FIRST NATIONAL BK OF CROS	CROSSETT	AR	**D**	C-	C-	150	-5.70	12.3	7.8	8.3	18.9	**7.3**	9.2	15.5

Asset Quality Index	Non-Performing Loans as a % of Total Loans	Non-Performing Loans as a % of Capital	Net Charge-offs Avg Loans	Profitability Index	Net Income ($Mil)	Return on Assets (R.O.A.)	Return on Equity (R.O.E.)	Net Interest Spread	Overhead Efficiency Ratio	Liquidity Index	Liquidity Ratio	Hot Money Ratio	Stability Index
5.2	0.43	3.1	0.45	**5.1**	3.8	1.06	12.47	3.65	64.1	**2.5**	20.7	16.8	**5.3**
5.5	2.82	10.3	0.01	**3.8**	0.6	0.67	5.31	4.14	78.5	**3.6**	38.0	16.2	**7.2**
0.7	5.56	29.7	0.96	**0.5**	-0.3	-0.17	-1.59	3.90	94.0	**3.7**	19.9	11.1	**4.4**
3.6	2.52	15.6	0.19	**5.8**	0.9	1.36	12.20	4.86	70.5	**3.1**	20.9	14.2	**8.0**
0.3	5.59	29.2	1.00	**4.5**	1.2	0.58	5.13	4.55	63.5	**1.9**	18.2	20.1	**6.5**
7.4	0.28	1.3	0.09	**6.9**	2.5	1.86	16.55	4.16	61.0	**3.2**	45.4	21.7	**7.3**
6.3	2.79	9.4	0.10	**3.8**	0.6	0.70	5.38	3.87	74.7	**4.2**	57.3	16.8	**7.3**
5.0	2.30	10.7	0.11	**5.0**	2.7	1.22	12.30	3.65	61.1	**4.8**	46.0	12.6	**6.8**
5.1	0.73	5.2	0.24	**4.4**	1.8	1.03	12.87	4.94	80.5	**1.5**	17.6	26.0	**4.8**
7.7	0.00	0.0	0.05	**6.2**	2.5	1.13	11.58	3.94	51.5	**3.0**	9.2	13.5	**5.8**
0.5	3.01	17.2	0.44	**3.1**	3.7	0.51	4.57	4.48	80.9	**3.2**	15.6	13.1	**6.8**
2.6	4.18	29.8	0.77	**0.9**	-0.2	-0.15	-1.76	4.19	87.1	**3.8**	25.9	11.1	**3.5**
0.3	12.83	51.2	0.51	**0.6**	-0.5	-0.43	-2.92	3.84	91.0	**1.7**	32.8	32.2	**7.6**
7.0	2.07	7.9	0.14	**2.1**	0.3	0.18	2.23	3.46	93.4	**6.9**	68.1	5.2	**3.9**
7.4	0.40	1.7	0.05	**9.1**	8.0	2.22	21.51	4.17	45.0	**3.1**	49.4	25.2	**8.3**
5.7	0.44	2.6	0.44	**5.5**	1.4	1.03	9.18	4.04	56.4	**1.8**	16.4	20.4	**6.6**
1.3	2.91	24.3	0.59	**2.1**	0.9	0.26	3.09	3.37	77.5	**2.7**	18.0	16.0	**4.2**
9.7	0.00	0.0	0.38	**9.6**	2.4	2.21	13.66	4.35	51.8	**4.7**	76.1	18.7	**9.5**
2.1	6.82	30.2	1.97	**6.3**	6.3	1.35	8.98	7.23	54.8	**0.7**	17.8	48.8	**7.8**
9.6	0.00	0.0	-0.07	**0.0**	-0.2	-0.75	-4.04	3.15	155.1	**3.8**	87.1	26.4	**6.9**
5.3	0.84	5.1	0.19	**3.9**	0.9	0.66	7.30	3.48	68.5	**1.2**	28.3	36.1	**4.8**
4.6	1.63	6.7	1.13	**3.2**	0.2	0.44	4.50	4.54	86.5	**4.2**	41.5	14.3	**4.9**
10.0	0.00	0.0	-0.01	**4.5**	1.2	1.08	8.40	3.65	65.1	**4.4**	74.4	19.8	**7.6**
9.7	0.02	0.0	0.81	**5.4**	0.5	1.09	4.28	3.91	64.5	**3.6**	85.7	32.5	**9.2**
6.8	0.91	4.1	0.06	**7.0**	0.8	1.32	11.17	4.57	58.7	**3.8**	41.9	16.2	**8.0**
4.1	0.84	5.1	0.59	**2.5**	0.2	0.31	3.25	4.27	86.7	**4.7**	16.5	4.5	**3.8**
3.9	0.82	6.2	0.86	**5.1**	1.6	0.78	7.52	4.83	67.5	**1.0**	5.8	29.5	**5.7**
6.7	0.42	2.4	0.01	**6.0**	1.7	1.39	14.90	4.33	67.2	**1.5**	27.7	30.7	**5.7**
7.8	0.32	1.3	0.44	**5.2**	0.2	1.04	6.45	4.27	64.5	**4.3**	36.6	10.3	**8.0**
3.0	5.85	22.4	0.14	**9.8**	3.1	1.60	8.31	4.65	24.5	**4.6**	19.3	5.5	**8.4**
3.4	3.25	16.6	0.51	**3.4**	0.8	0.71	4.81	3.97	72.5	**2.2**	26.5	19.7	**6.4**
3.4	4.12	21.5	0.12	**6.7**	4.8	1.50	12.33	4.50	66.3	**2.6**	23.0	16.8	**8.3**
5.8	0.02	0.1	0.04	**4.2**	1.6	0.74	9.50	3.42	65.0	**4.5**	48.4	14.5	**3.1**
1.6	4.66	31.7	0.54	**3.0**	0.1	0.04	0.41	4.42	79.6	**3.5**	12.5	11.4	**4.7**
7.2	0.00	0.0	0.04	**7.1**	5.3	1.68	11.58	4.30	51.5	**1.8**	39.1	46.7	**8.5**
7.4	1.13	5.5	0.26	**4.9**	0.6	0.93	7.93	4.18	66.7	**3.2**	16.4	13.1	**6.8**
5.9	1.18	5.0	0.38	**7.5**	9.3	1.75	13.75	3.85	49.5	**1.8**	25.2	23.0	**9.7**
8.5	1.03	2.4	-0.15	**3.6**	0.3	0.51	3.51	2.70	75.2	**4.0**	42.7	15.3	**8.3**
1.9	2.69	16.5	0.81	**2.9**	1.6	0.62	7.05	4.00	71.1	**4.0**	22.2	9.6	**3.4**
5.6	0.00	0.0	0.00	**4.5**	0.3	0.97	7.46	1.03	0.7	**2.3**	1.3	16.3	**7.8**
5.8	1.54	6.3	2.08	**2.5**	0.4	0.43	3.91	4.46	74.9	**2.1**	41.8	36.7	**3.7**
2.0	2.94	17.7	0.38	**4.7**	2.0	1.01	11.27	4.68	74.0	**1.9**	23.5	20.4	**5.4**
0.7	3.01	24.7	0.75	**0.3**	-0.2	-0.78	-8.13	4.02	108.1	**1.4**	20.8	27.0	**3.0**
4.2	1.38	9.4	0.01	**8.8**	3.2	1.84	20.78	4.18	59.1	**4.5**	29.7	8.9	**6.3**
4.7	1.29	6.6	1.15	**1.3**	-0.2	-0.18	-1.57	4.33	92.6	**3.1**	36.7	18.1	**6.0**
7.7	0.37	1.8	0.00	**4.2**	0.4	0.86	8.00	3.51	78.9	**4.5**	39.9	12.3	**5.7**
7.5	0.29	1.5	0.20	**5.3**	1.4	1.26	13.60	3.81	67.5	**3.2**	46.2	21.8	**6.3**
3.9	0.55	4.4	0.47	**4.5**	2.2	0.79	8.93	4.04	70.6	**3.0**	24.4	15.0	**5.0**
2.2	3.93	23.1	0.75	**1.4**	0.0	0.09	1.01	4.59	96.3	**2.4**	33.0	22.4	**3.7**
5.7	1.17	4.3	0.15	**5.9**	1.7	1.63	13.31	3.99	63.5	**1.3**	23.8	29.6	**7.5**
6.6	0.00	0.0	-0.01	**8.4**	2.0	1.82	12.55	4.71	60.6	**2.9**	23.5	15.4	**8.9**
5.8	1.53	5.1	0.80	**2.1**	0.6	0.75	8.74	3.10	90.7	**5.6**	45.6	7.1	**3.8**
8.3	0.03	0.1	0.00	**3.9**	0.4	0.94	7.55	3.43	72.9	**4.7**	38.1	11.1	**7.0**
5.4	1.42	6.3	1.29	**3.7**	0.6	0.86	7.01	4.39	71.7	**3.5**	36.6	16.5	**7.0**
8.4	0.36	1.5	0.11	**2.3**	0.1	0.27	2.56	3.61	89.5	**5.1**	49.6	10.9	**5.2**
7.1	0.87	4.1	0.03	**3.2**	0.4	0.57	7.41	3.32	81.7	**2.9**	41.2	22.2	**3.5**
9.1	0.00	0.0	0.00	**3.2**	0.2	0.45	5.10	3.15	81.6	**4.7**	23.3	5.3	**4.5**
4.4	2.11	11.3	0.31	**2.6**	0.2	0.30	3.73	3.99	87.1	**3.9**	38.0	14.7	**3.7**
0.1	25.57	142.3	7.63	**0.0**	-7.3	-5.16	-66.71	2.73	117.9	**2.7**	9.5	14.9	**3.6**
0.3	7.76	40.9	3.32	**2.7**	-0.8	-0.46	-4.47	4.66	65.9	**1.4**	23.9	28.0	**5.2**

Name	City	State	Rating	2008 Rating	2007 Rating	Total Assets ($Mil)	One Year Asset Growth	Asset Mix (As a % of Total Assets) Comm-ercial Loans	Cons-umer Loans	Home Mort-gages	Secur-ities	Capital-ization Index	Leverage Ratio	Risk-based Capital Ratio
▼ FIRST NATIONAL BK OF DAVI	DAVIS	OK	**F**	C-	D+	90	20.61	17.2	17.1	9.2	30.2	**6.1**	8.1	13.9
FIRST NATIONAL BK OF DEER	DEERWOOD	MN	**C**	D+	C-	235	1.59	14.9	2.3	14.9	7.9	**7.8**	9.6	13.6
FIRST NATIONAL BK OF DENN	DENNISON	OH	**B-**	B	B+	177	6.78	3.8	17.6	14.8	32.5	**8.6**	10.1	17.2
FIRST NATIONAL BK OF DIET	DIETERICH	IL	**B-**	B-	B-	318	13.58	9.0	3.3	8.9	35.8	**6.6**	8.6	14.3
FIRST NATIONAL BK OF DIGH	DIGHTON	KS	**B-**	C+	B+	50	5.15	9.4	3.8	2.3	39.7	**10.0**	22.0	44.9
FIRST NATIONAL BK OF DOZI	DOZIER	AL	**B-**	B-	B	36	-2.37	5.6	3.1	6.6	59.0	**10.0**	12.6	32.0
▼ FIRST NATIONAL BK OF DRYD	DRYDEN	NY	**A-**	A	A-	102	1.86	4.0	10.6	16.0	48.1	**10.0**	11.7	32.0
FIRST NATIONAL BK OF DUBL	DUBLIN	TX	**B-**	B-	B-	70	6.27	12.5	9.7	7.4	5.6	**8.1**	9.8	15.6
FIRST NATIONAL BK OF DURA	DURANGO	CO	**C-**	C-	B-	396	4.94	3.5	1.0	8.6	40.1	**8.2**	9.8	15.9
FIRST NATIONAL BK OF DWIG	DWIGHT	IL	**A**	A+	A+	123	-0.92	2.6	1.1	8.8	32.8	**10.0**	11.5	17.6
FIRST NATIONAL BK OF EDGE	EDGEWOOD	TX	**C**	C+	C+	18	1.68	1.7	4.9	19.2	41.9	**8.4**	9.9	21.4
FIRST NATIONAL BK OF ELDO	ELDORADO	TX	**B+**	B	B	51	8.00	6.1	3.1	8.6	37.2	**10.0**	13.2	25.7
FIRST NATIONAL BK OF ELK	ELK RIVER	MN	**D-**	D-	D	322	-19.87	11.3	1.3	8.8	24.6	**6.8**	8.8	14.5
FIRST NATIONAL BK OF ELKH	ELKHART	KS	**C**	C	B+	76	4.16	3.4	5.3	5.2	19.2	**9.8**	10.9	17.2
▲ FIRST NATIONAL BK OF ELME	ELMER	NJ	**B-**	B-	B-	219	-0.87	4.8	1.1	30.8	4.2	**7.3**	9.2	13.5
▼ FIRST NATIONAL BK OF ELY	ELY	NV	**C+**	A-	A	79	6.75	5.6	1.2	7.3	68.0	**6.5**	8.5	22.0
▲ FIRST NATIONAL BK OF EMOR	EMORY	TX	**B+**	B	B+	100	-6.48	5.1	3.4	14.4	42.1	**9.0**	10.3	26.7
FIRST NATIONAL BK OF EVAN	EVANT	TX	**C**	C	C	64	12.07	6.9	8.6	20.5	4.5	**5.8**	7.8	16.2
FIRST NATIONAL BK OF FAIR	FAIRBURY	NE	**A-**	B+	B	138	8.84	4.0	3.0	3.3	54.3	**10.0**	17.3	29.8
FIRST NATIONAL BK OF FAIR	FAIRFAX	MN	**A-**	A-	B+	27	-3.22	5.2	1.7	4.0	1.8	**10.0**	39.5	40.4
▲ FIRST NATIONAL BK OF FARR	SHENANDOAH	IA	**D**	D-	D	35	0.62	6.7	3.8	10.6	41.6	**6.6**	8.6	15.5
FIRST NATIONAL BK OF FLEM	FLEMING	CO	**E+**	C-	C-	19	11.23	8.1	7.4	13.6	8.5	**6.0**	8.0	15.3
▲ FIRST NATIONAL BK OF FLET	FLETCHER	OK	**C**	C	C+	17	-4.86	7.0	7.2	7.7	54.4	**10.0**	12.2	22.1
FIRST NATIONAL BK OF FLOR	MILTON	FL	**E-**	D-	D-	313	-15.92	1.8	0.2	11.9	11.7	**0.3**	4.1	6.6
FIRST NATIONAL BK OF FLOY	FLOYDADA	TX	**A-**	A	A	103	8.97	2.8	1.1	3.7	18.7	**10.0**	11.5	18.2
▼ FIRST NATIONAL BK OF FRED	FREDERICK	SD	**C-**	C	C	18	19.51	2.8	0.7	0.6	42.2	**10.0**	14.0	26.9
▲ FIRST NATIONAL BK OF FRIE	FRIEND	NE	**C+**	C	C+	38	-5.79	13.6	1.7	9.1	7.9	**8.5**	10.0	15.9
FIRST NATIONAL BK OF GIDD	GIDDINGS	TX	**C+**	C+	C+	149	4.20	6.4	3.0	10.5	47.6	**7.0**	9.0	19.2
FIRST NATIONAL BK OF GILB	GILBERT	MN	**C**	C	B-	25	-0.73	8.0	7.7	25.1	17.1	**10.0**	13.6	28.6
FIRST NATIONAL BK OF GILL	GILLETTE	WY	**B**	C+	C+	390	-5.60	6.5	3.7	6.6	55.6	**8.6**	10.1	26.0
FIRST NATIONAL BK OF GILM	GILMER	TX	**B-**	B-	B-	196	5.13	9.5	7.5	17.9	24.8	**8.2**	9.8	16.4
FIRST NATIONAL BK OF GIRA	GIRARD	KS	**B-**	B-	B-	75	-5.16	9.1	4.1	16.3	33.7	**9.4**	10.6	18.3
FIRST NATIONAL BK OF GORD	GORDON	NE	**A-**	A	A	150	-0.86	7.2	3.6	0.5	45.0	**10.0**	11.4	24.0
FIRST NATIONAL BK OF GRAN	GRANBURY	TX	**B+**	B+	B+	390	1.33	2.6	4.0	17.3	40.0	**8.6**	10.0	20.8
FIRST NATIONAL BK OF GRAY	GRAYSON	KY	**B**	B	B-	208	5.81	2.5	14.8	23.9	32.4	**6.5**	8.5	17.0
FIRST NATIONAL BK OF GRIF	GRIFFIN	GA	**D-**	D-	D-	261	-6.62	4.8	2.9	8.8	19.1	**6.0**	8.0	14.1
FIRST NATIONAL BK OF GROT	GROTON	NY	**A**	A	A	128	7.65	5.7	11.6	20.8	40.6	**10.0**	13.1	26.7
FIRST NATIONAL BK OF HAMP	HAMPTON	IA	**A-**	A-	A-	114	0.67	9.2	3.7	12.6	32.5	**10.0**	11.7	17.1
▼ FIRST NATIONAL BK OF HART	HARTFORD	AL	**B-**	B	B+	137	10.40	3.8	13.3	8.7	56.4	**9.8**	10.9	23.8
FIRST NATIONAL BK OF HENN	OTTERTAIL	MN	**B**	B	B	89	0.64	12.8	4.8	19.1	21.3	**9.2**	10.5	14.4
▲ FIRST NATIONAL BK OF HERE	HEREFORD	TX	**B**	B-	B-	129	21.37	17.2	2.3	11.2	7.2	**7.3**	9.2	14.3
FIRST NATIONAL BK OF HERM	HERMAN	MN	**B-**	B-	B-	24	3.07	9.4	2.7	1.7	41.6	**9.4**	10.6	20.8
▲ FIRST NATIONAL BK OF HICO	HICO	TX	**B+**	B	B	36	-1.20	3.5	8.1	11.6	50.0	**9.6**	10.7	21.6
FIRST NATIONAL BK OF HOLC	HOLCOMB	KS	**B+**	B+	B+	49	3.45	10.0	15.1	8.2	42.7	**10.0**	13.3	23.7
▼ FIRST NATIONAL BK OF HOLD	HOLDREGE	NE	**C-**	C+	B+	95	12.84	11.0	1.1	1.9	44.1	**6.5**	8.5	16.3
FIRST NATIONAL BK OF HOOK	HOOKER	OK	**A-**	A-	B+	56	1.31	5.0	2.4	7.5	51.7	**10.0**	12.5	23.2
▼ FIRST NATIONAL BK OF HOPE	HOPE	KS	**C+**	C+	C+	45	6.50	9.5	2.1	1.9	19.8	**9.5**	12.4	14.6
FIRST NATIONAL BK OF HOWA	HOWARD	KS	**B**	B+	B+	10	13.11	4.8	0.4	1.3	11.3	**10.0**	17.1	26.6
▲ FIRST NATIONAL BK OF HUGO	HUGO	CO	**B**	A-	B-	99	2.16	4.1	2.4	9.3	27.8	**9.2**	10.5	19.4
FIRST NATIONAL BK OF ILLI	LANSING	IL	**D-**	D-	C+	388	-4.92	9.4	1.9	9.0	32.4	**5.7**	7.7	12.5
▲ FIRST NATIONAL BK OF IPSW	IPSWICH	MA	**D+**	D+	D	268	4.51	12.6	0.3	21.5	6.8	**7.1**	9.1	13.4
FIRST NATIONAL BK OF IVES	IVESDALE	IL	**B-**	B-	B	12	-3.06	1.2	9.1	4.5	24.6	**10.0**	15.4	31.5
FIRST NATIONAL BK OF JACK	JACKSBORO	TX	**D**	D	D-	476	4.51	14.6	2.8	14.3	19.9	**10.0**	13.0	20.1
FIRST NATIONAL BK OF JACK	JACKSON	KY	**C+**	C+	C+	114	4.66	6.3	6.3	20.0	35.5	**10.0**	13.2	26.7
FIRST NATIONAL BK OF JASP	JASPER	TX	**B+**	B+	B+	218	3.50	2.3	6.6	12.6	51.3	**10.0**	11.1	26.3
FIRST NATIONAL BK OF JEFF	JEFFERSONVILLE	NY	**C-**	C+	B+	430	1.97	6.0	1.7	25.8	25.7	**9.1**	10.4	17.0
FIRST NATIONAL BK OF JOHN	JOHNSON	NE	**B-**	B-	B+	73	8.71	2.7	2.9	2.8	55.3	**10.0**	18.3	43.5
FIRST NATIONAL BK OF KANS	BURLINGTON	KS	**C-**	C+	C	68	-4.99	5.9	3.3	6.7	58.1	**6.8**	8.8	17.7
▼ FIRST NATIONAL BK OF KEMP	KEMP	TX	**C-**	B	B+	56	-8.63	4.0	4.3	14.0	18.4	**7.9**	9.6	18.0
FIRST NATIONAL BK OF KINM	KINMUNDY	IL	**B-**	C+	C	34	0.52	4.0	16.2	26.7	14.0	**6.1**	8.1	13.9

Asset Quality Index	Non-Performing Loans as a % of Total Loans	Non-Performing Loans as a % of Capital	Net Charge-offs Avg Loans	Profitability Index	Net Income ($Mil)	Return on Assets (R.O.A.)	Return on Equity (R.O.E.)	Net Interest Spread	Overhead Efficiency Ratio	Liquidity Index	Liquidity Ratio	Hot Money Ratio	Stability Index
2.4	1.68	12.0	1.13	**5.3**	1.2	1.42	15.95	4.31	61.3	**0.4**	5.8	66.7	**3.7**
3.3	1.48	10.4	0.53	**4.4**	2.3	0.98	9.14	4.63	73.3	**4.3**	10.2	6.2	**6.0**
6.6	0.49	2.6	0.18	**3.9**	1.1	0.65	6.26	4.13	78.7	**4.5**	30.1	8.9	**6.2**
7.4	0.29	1.7	0.19	**4.3**	2.8	0.95	10.24	3.24	61.4	**4.0**	38.1	14.3	**5.1**
7.4	2.98	5.1	-0.01	**3.7**	0.3	0.69	2.97	3.54	76.6	**6.4**	64.6	6.1	**6.5**
9.4	0.01	0.0	0.07	**2.9**	0.2	0.53	4.11	3.43	81.6	**3.3**	61.8	26.5	**6.6**
8.2	0.59	1.7	0.26	**5.6**	1.2	1.10	8.85	4.42	64.6	**4.9**	36.5	8.9	**7.3**
5.6	0.66	4.3	0.16	**5.1**	0.7	1.09	11.03	4.78	76.9	**3.6**	32.5	14.7	**6.0**
1.6	5.13	23.5	0.62	**4.2**	3.6	0.95	8.79	4.48	69.2	**5.3**	42.6	9.1	**4.8**
9.1	0.00	0.0	0.12	**6.1**	1.8	1.48	12.37	3.17	57.3	**3.6**	37.0	15.8	**9.0**
7.9	0.42	1.5	-0.45	**3.1**	0.1	0.39	3.76	4.18	90.9	**5.6**	56.2	7.2	**5.0**
9.2	0.54	1.2	0.00	**5.8**	0.7	1.54	11.03	5.13	71.3	**4.9**	42.1	11.0	**7.0**
1.5	6.84	38.2	1.04	**0.0**	-2.8	-0.77	-8.93	2.35	113.2	**2.1**	20.9	19.2	**3.0**
3.3	1.98	11.3	1.20	**6.3**	0.7	1.03	9.65	4.02	59.7	**1.4**	28.6	32.2	**5.6**
4.5	1.59	12.7	0.15	**4.8**	1.6	0.72	7.87	4.69	72.2	**3.1**	15.3	13.8	**5.8**
3.1	9.34	23.5	0.03	**4.8**	1.1	1.41	15.30	3.71	62.4	**7.2**	60.3	0.0	**6.9**
6.0	3.46	12.1	0.08	**5.5**	1.3	1.32	11.09	3.85	62.9	**1.9**	30.6	26.5	**6.9**
2.9	2.97	19.9	0.04	**5.5**	0.8	1.39	17.24	4.29	65.9	**2.8**	37.9	20.6	**4.9**
9.0	0.03	0.1	0.13	**6.4**	2.2	1.61	9.03	4.03	60.0	**3.0**	38.5	19.7	**7.1**
6.5	1.49	3.0	1.07	**6.6**	0.4	1.42	3.55	4.79	70.1	**4.9**	27.4	5.1	**8.3**
2.2	3.45	17.9	1.32	**2.6**	0.2	0.66	7.78	4.16	80.1	**4.7**	40.5	11.4	**3.5**
3.0	1.66	12.6	0.15	**3.6**	0.1	0.54	7.88	4.28	67.9	**0.8**	18.8	40.0	**1.7**
6.6	3.13	7.3	0.29	**4.3**	0.1	0.66	4.82	5.14	82.8	**4.9**	59.3	11.8	**6.2**
0.0	30.31	276.1	4.07	**0.0**	-10.8	-3.21	-40.92	2.17	217.8	**1.0**	19.5	33.4	**2.5**
9.1	0.00	0.0	0.01	**6.2**	1.4	1.51	11.23	3.24	51.0	**4.0**	61.5	20.4	**9.2**
6.4	3.64	8.5	0.64	**1.9**	0.0	0.03	0.18	3.66	83.7	**4.3**	69.7	16.9	**7.0**
8.0	0.18	1.1	-0.09	**5.1**	0.5	1.20	12.54	3.66	62.2	**3.4**	24.0	13.0	**5.6**
5.2	1.43	6.4	0.56	**3.8**	1.2	0.83	8.92	3.50	72.2	**3.7**	34.2	14.8	**5.8**
3.7	5.87	20.0	0.41	**2.0**	0.0	0.05	0.38	4.10	91.2	**4.1**	45.2	13.4	**6.7**
5.0	3.71	9.7	0.52	**6.7**	7.4	1.74	16.16	3.21	57.2	**3.7**	62.8	26.3	**6.5**
3.3	1.26	6.9	0.04	**6.8**	2.7	1.42	12.82	4.98	69.2	**2.4**	27.9	19.2	**5.3**
6.5	0.56	2.9	0.11	**4.9**	0.8	1.12	10.53	3.74	63.6	**2.7**	14.1	15.4	**4.8**
5.6	2.70	10.5	0.58	**9.1**	3.2	2.10	17.58	4.56	45.1	**1.8**	25.3	24.1	**8.2**
5.9	1.60	6.7	0.23	**4.8**	3.4	0.89	8.66	3.62	65.6	**5.2**	53.9	12.6	**5.5**
6.1	0.62	3.7	0.27	**7.8**	2.5	1.22	14.41	4.00	61.5	**2.0**	27.9	22.2	**5.6**
1.4	7.74	43.1	2.60	**0.0**	-0.8	-0.28	-3.08	4.04	89.3	**2.6**	23.0	16.7	**2.6**
6.3	1.47	5.5	0.91	**7.3**	1.5	1.22	8.91	5.00	59.2	**3.6**	30.1	13.4	**8.2**
7.0	0.73	3.3	0.16	**6.4**	1.7	1.44	11.64	4.27	53.6	**5.1**	42.0	9.8	**7.7**
3.2	2.28	7.1	0.81	**3.9**	1.1	0.82	7.12	3.98	66.9	**3.0**	59.8	38.0	**6.2**
4.6	1.16	7.3	0.42	**5.9**	1.3	1.44	13.09	4.30	63.8	**3.5**	19.0	11.7	**6.5**
4.7	1.31	8.5	0.10	**5.0**	0.8	0.71	7.56	4.31	66.4	**2.1**	34.1	28.2	**5.9**
8.9	0.00	0.0	0.11	**4.0**	0.2	0.72	6.08	3.78	78.6	**4.2**	61.7	16.1	**6.8**
9.1	0.00	0.0	-0.01	**6.1**	0.5	1.36	12.82	4.52	70.5	**3.9**	60.1	19.0	**7.3**
7.7	0.37	1.4	0.11	**6.3**	0.5	1.10	8.32	4.92	63.4	**1.6**	23.1	26.0	**7.8**
5.5	1.01	4.7	1.04	**1.6**	0.0	-0.03	-0.36	3.42	89.6	**4.6**	22.3	5.7	**5.4**
8.2	0.09	0.3	0.04	**6.7**	0.8	1.43	10.11	5.46	69.0	**4.5**	50.3	14.3	**8.4**
3.1	1.59	8.3	0.13	**5.1**	0.6	1.33	10.27	4.04	62.9	**2.4**	20.8	17.4	**7.3**
8.8	0.48	1.4	-0.07	**4.2**	0.1	0.84	4.70	3.21	75.8	**2.7**	47.2	22.9	**8.0**
4.8	2.17	9.6	0.76	**5.0**	1.1	1.07	8.83	4.35	67.4	**3.8**	34.2	14.1	**8.4**
0.3	10.12	61.1	3.22	**0.2**	-1.7	-0.41	-4.52	3.35	88.9	**3.7**	19.7	11.1	**4.6**
2.8	1.66	13.0	1.45	**1.4**	0.4	0.16	1.54	4.43	85.4	**3.8**	13.0	9.7	**4.8**
8.6	0.00	0.0	0.00	**2.7**	0.0	0.34	2.24	3.51	91.3	**3.3**	64.1	21.8	**6.8**
4.9	0.87	3.7	0.93	**0.0**	-8.3	-1.87	-13.63	3.13	172.2	**1.5**	27.8	30.7	**1.5**
7.8	0.17	0.6	0.15	**2.6**	0.5	0.42	3.03	3.37	84.5	**1.3**	30.4	45.0	**6.5**
8.0	1.28	4.3	0.15	**4.2**	-1.4	-0.66	-6.25	4.51	69.5	**2.3**	30.8	20.8	**5.8**
2.2	4.43	25.4	0.70	**4.7**	3.3	0.75	7.49	4.66	72.0	**2.2**	19.5	18.4	**6.7**
9.0	0.94	1.0	-0.31	**3.0**	0.4	0.56	2.84	2.43	77.0	**6.8**	85.6	7.6	**7.5**
7.8	0.71	2.5	0.09	**3.8**	0.7	0.93	9.70	3.48	78.2	**2.3**	24.2	18.4	**4.3**
4.5	2.74	11.6	1.37	**1.7**	-0.2	-0.29	-2.62	4.23	92.9	**2.6**	34.8	20.6	**6.4**
5.9	0.09	0.8	0.00	**10.0**	0.8	2.31	18.79	6.21	48.3	**4.3**	17.7	7.2	**5.7**

Name	City	State	Rating	2008 Rating	2007 Rating	Total Assets ($Mil)	One Year Asset Growth	Comm-ercial Loans	Cons-umer Loans	Home Mort-gages	Secur-ities	Capital-ization Index	Leverage Ratio	Risk-based Capital Ratio
								Asset Mix (As a % of Total Assets)						
▼ FIRST NATIONAL BK OF LA G	LA GRANGE	IL	**C**	B	A-	320	11.33	5.6	0.7	17.6	38.7	**5.5**	7.5	16.2
FIRST NATIONAL BK OF LACO	LACON	IL	**C-**	C-	D+	57	10.22	9.2	4.7	12.6	14.4	**6.1**	8.1	11.9
FIRST NATIONAL BK OF LAYT	LAYTON	UT	**C-**	D+	D-	256	-6.86	7.1	1.6	16.5	23.9	**10.0**	12.0	16.6
FIRST NATIONAL BK OF LE C	LE CENTER	MN	**B-**	C	B	80	1.64	3.8	3.1	14.0	16.9	**10.0**	11.8	18.8
FIRST NATIONAL BK OF LIBE	LIBERAL	KS	**C+**	C	B+	235	5.49	8.9	5.1	2.6	39.9	**6.6**	8.6	15.5
FIRST NATIONAL BK OF LILL	LILLY	PA	**C+**	C+	C+	23	0.77	1.3	9.0	13.3	60.3	**10.0**	14.7	32.7
▼ FIRST NATIONAL BK OF LIND	LINDSAY	OK	**D-**	D+	E-	38	42.23	8.2	2.8	7.4	23.1	**5.2**	7.2	14.7
▼ FIRST NATIONAL BK OF LIPA	LIPAN	TX	**D+**	C-	D+	17	14.77	9.0	18.9	12.8	11.5	**7.0**	9.0	18.4
▼ FIRST NATIONAL BK OF LIVE	LIVERPOOL	PA	**B+**	A-	A-	44	-2.74	1.6	3.3	61.7	9.2	**10.0**	14.7	27.8
▲ FIRST NATIONAL BK OF LOGA	LOGAN	IA	**C+**	C+	B	23	-4.61	3.1	2.4	6.2	7.8	**10.0**	14.6	21.0
FIRST NATIONAL BK OF LOUI	LOUISBURG	KS	**A**	A	A	77	-2.14	5.1	3.4	18.7	44.9	**10.0**	19.6	37.0
FIRST NATIONAL BK OF LOUI	CROWLEY	LA	**B+**	B+	A-	249	14.47	11.7	2.3	15.1	13.6	**6.4**	8.4	14.4
FIRST NATIONAL BK OF MANN	MANNING	IA	**A-**	A-	A-	79	6.94	4.2	1.0	6.8	22.1	**10.0**	15.1	27.1
▼ FIRST NATIONAL BK OF MCGE	MCGEHEE	AR	**C-**	B	B	50	3.00	8.9	5.3	5.8	41.8	**10.0**	12.2	24.1
FIRST NATIONAL BK OF MCGR	MCGREGOR	TX	**B-**	C+	C-	111	-0.59	10.9	9.4	41.0	0.0	**6.2**	8.2	12.5
FIRST NATIONAL BK OF MCHE	MCHENRY	IL	**C**	D+	C	145	2.11	3.6	1.7	23.2	42.1	**7.5**	9.3	18.2
FIRST NATIONAL BK OF MCIN	MCINTOSH	MN	**B**	B	B+	26	0.60	2.5	4.5	8.8	17.7	**10.0**	26.2	66.4
▼ FIRST NATIONAL BK OF MERT	MERTZON	TX	**B-**	B	B+	193	11.68	5.2	3.0	4.2	56.9	**7.4**	9.3	27.8
FIRST NATIONAL BK OF MICH	KALAMAZOO	MI	**B**	C	C	177	9.70	20.8	1.4	5.1	13.6	**8.8**	10.9	14.0
▼ FIRST NATIONAL BK OF MILA	MILACA	MN	**C-**	B-	A-	168	0.49	15.8	7.1	20.0	21.3	**8.9**	10.3	17.9
▼ FIRST NATIONAL BK OF MINE	MINEOLA	TX	**C-**	D+	D+	28	-11.10	1.7	6.9	12.9	63.1	**7.1**	9.1	29.0
FIRST NATIONAL BK OF MONT	MONTEREY	IN	**B-**	B-	B-	286	11.83	3.0	1.8	12.3	35.6	**8.6**	10.1	15.9
FIRST NATIONAL BK OF MOOD	MOODY	TX	**B+**	B+	A-	53	16.89	5.8	3.6	12.9	42.1	**10.0**	15.1	33.1
FIRST NATIONAL BK OF MUSC	MUSCATINE	IA	**C+**	C+	B-	292	-0.73	11.1	3.2	27.3	6.6	**8.3**	9.8	15.8
FIRST NATIONAL BK OF MUSK	MUSKOGEE	OK	**C+**	B-	C+	169	16.81	13.8	3.4	15.6	8.6	**5.8**	8.0	11.6
FIRST NATIONAL BK OF NASH	NASH	OK	**D**	D	C-	12	-3.47	3.7	9.8	4.9	0.0	**5.5**	7.5	15.8
FIRST NATIONAL BK OF NIAG	NIAGARA	WI	**C**	C	B-	65	2.07	6.7	7.8	27.7	19.4	**9.0**	10.3	20.2
▲ FIRST NATIONAL BK OF NOKO	NOKOMIS	IL	**A-**	B+	A-	135	7.08	3.6	4.7	18.1	24.7	**9.5**	10.7	17.8
FIRST NATIONAL BK OF NORW	NORWAY	MI	**B+**	B+	A-	87	1.64	11.9	2.5	33.7	16.7	**10.0**	11.5	18.0
▼ FIRST NATIONAL BK OF ODON	ODON	IN	**C-**	C+	C+	68	16.68	3.0	4.5	15.9	47.5	**5.7**	7.7	14.3
FIRST NATIONAL BK OF OGDE	OGDEN	IL	**C-**	B-	C+	86	2.34	10.1	1.0	6.8	24.9	**5.2**	7.2	12.4
FIRST NATIONAL BK OF OKAW	OKAWVILLE	IL	**C**	C-	B-	51	5.97	6.3	3.1	10.2	41.5	**10.0**	12.0	19.8
FIRST NATIONAL BK OF OKLA	PONCA CITY	OK	**B-**	B-	B-	242	12.31	7.9	3.7	12.8	8.0	**5.4**	7.8	11.3
FIRST NATIONAL BK OF OLAT	OLATHE	KS	**E-**	E-	D+	579	-36.13	8.6	0.7	5.1	10.7	**0.0**	2.8	5.2
▲ FIRST NATIONAL BK OF OMAH	OMAHA	NE	**C+**	C-	C	13,128	49.07	11.3	27.6	5.1	14.8	**6.9**	8.9	13.5
FIRST NATIONAL BK OF ONEI	ONEIDA	TN	**C-**	B+	B+	202	-1.14	2.3	4.4	30.1	15.6	**7.9**	9.6	14.9
FIRST NATIONAL BK OF ORDW	ORDWAY	CO	**C-**	C-	C+	45	-6.37	7.1	1.2	10.4	9.9	**8.4**	9.9	16.2
FIRST NATIONAL BK OF ORWE	ORWELL	VT	**D+**	C-	C	40	-2.09	5.4	3.7	57.3	0.0	**6.1**	8.1	15.2
▼ FIRST NATIONAL BK OF OSAK	OSAKIS	MN	**C+**	B+	A-	61	2.57	9.3	3.5	20.5	31.7	**10.0**	11.6	20.6
▼ FIRST NATIONAL BK OF OTTA	OTTAWA	IL	**D+**	D+	B-	286	1.01	7.4	0.9	8.6	17.7	**4.9**	6.9	13.2
FIRST NATIONAL BK OF OXFO	OXFORD	MS	**B**	B	A-	254	-1.46	5.2	2.6	18.8	32.2	**10.0**	11.3	21.9
▼ FIRST NATIONAL BK OF PADU	PADUCAH	TX	**D**	C+	B	60	0.33	6.9	10.7	1.3	34.2	**6.8**	8.8	17.1
FIRST NATIONAL BK OF PALM	PALMERTON	PA	**B**	A	A-	673	8.57	3.8	1.1	24.1	37.9	**10.0**	12.9	25.3
▲ FIRST NATIONAL BK OF PANA	PANA	IL	**B+**	B+	A-	126	-2.07	6.2	3.9	25.5	15.8	**10.0**	11.2	17.1
▲ FIRST NATIONAL BK OF PAND	PANDORA	OH	**C+**	C+	B-	129	4.71	7.1	1.9	13.0	28.6	**6.3**	8.3	13.6
FIRST NATIONAL BK OF PASC	DADE CITY	FL	**D+**	B-	B+	176	-0.83	0.3	17.1	30.3	23.5	**7.1**	9.1	15.6
FIRST NATIONAL BK OF PAWN	PAWNEE	OK	**B+**	B+	B+	62	2.50	6.3	7.8	9.3	28.4	**10.0**	11.7	17.5
▲ FIRST NATIONAL BK OF PICA	PICAYUNE	MS	**C+**	B-	B	208	-0.54	2.8	5.8	33.5	6.9	**9.6**	10.7	16.3
▲ FIRST NATIONAL BK OF PIKE	PIKEVILLE	TN	**C**	B-	B	97	6.26	5.5	5.3	19.2	13.0	**7.8**	10.4	13.2
FIRST NATIONAL BK OF PLAI	PLAINVIEW	MN	**D**	C-	C+	136	1.01	5.0	3.0	35.9	8.5	**6.0**	8.3	11.8
FIRST NATIONAL BK OF PONT	PONTOTOC	MS	**B-**	B-	B-	232	5.39	3.2	5.3	17.7	42.3	**10.0**	13.6	30.0
▼ FIRST NATIONAL BK OF PRIM	PRIMGHAR	IA	**B-**	B-	C+	29	9.48	3.0	1.6	7.4	32.1	**10.0**	21.0	31.1
FIRST NATIONAL BK OF PROC	PROCTOR	MN	**C-**	C-	D+	25	1.98	1.6	4.7	33.2	13.5	**6.9**	8.9	19.9
▼ FIRST NATIONAL BK OF PULA	PULASKI	TN	**C-**	C+	B+	601	-1.36	5.8	3.8	11.0	31.8	**6.6**	8.6	13.8
FIRST NATIONAL BK OF QUIT	QUITAQUE	TX	**B-**	B-	B	44	-2.19	5.6	5.3	0.0	19.9	**10.0**	15.4	29.1
FIRST NATIONAL BK OF RAYM	RAYMOND	IL	**B-**	B-	B-	127	6.74	2.9	5.9	7.9	29.8	**5.8**	9.0	11.6
FIRST NATIONAL BK OF REMB	REMBRANDT	IA	**B+**	B+	B+	46	7.15	6.6	5.6	11.4	15.5	**10.0**	16.8	26.4
▼ FIRST NATIONAL BK OF RUID	RUIDOSO	NM	**A-**	A	A	58	6.03	2.1	2.8	11.2	28.1	**10.0**	11.0	19.5
FIRST NATIONAL BK OF SAND	SANDOVAL	IL	**C**	C+	B	46	18.63	1.9	11.6	24.7	35.8	**6.0**	8.0	17.2
FIRST NATIONAL BK OF SANT	SANTA FE	NM	**B**	B	B+	707	-1.65	2.3	0.9	12.4	14.7	**9.0**	10.3	16.1

Asset Quality Index	Non-Performing Loans as a % of Total Loans	Non-Performing Loans as a % of Capital	Net Charge-offs / Avg Loans	Profitability Index	Net Income ($Mil)	Return on Assets (R.O.A.)	Return on Equity (R.O.E.)	Net Interest Spread	Overhead Efficiency Ratio	Liquidity Index	Liquidity Ratio	Hot Money Ratio	Stability Index
3.4	2.38	14.1	0.17	**6.1**	4.3	1.40	17.30	3.20	65.8	**5.1**	49.6	11.9	**5.6**
5.4	0.57	4.7	0.57	**3.2**	0.5	0.90	10.66	4.04	68.2	**2.0**	17.3	19.3	**3.3**
3.3	4.02	16.9	0.95	**1.6**	1.0	0.37	3.16	3.68	92.2	**2.8**	34.2	18.9	**6.1**
3.9	0.70	3.3	0.29	**4.4**	0.8	0.97	7.99	3.50	70.6	**4.1**	31.2	11.4	**7.0**
5.4	0.52	2.8	0.93	**4.2**	2.1	0.93	10.73	4.25	68.1	**1.6**	24.6	26.1	**4.1**
7.1	2.96	5.9	-0.01	**2.7**	0.1	0.45	2.82	3.53	90.6	**4.4**	72.1	16.7	**7.8**
2.9	3.83	18.3	0.16	**4.3**	0.3	1.05	12.02	3.51	70.7	**5.1**	53.6	11.9	**1.7**
7.5	0.04	0.2	0.00	**2.3**	0.0	0.19	2.07	4.38	90.7	**3.0**	54.8	22.9	**4.4**
8.5	0.66	3.2	0.09	**8.6**	0.6	1.46	10.26	4.59	52.6	**2.0**	23.4	19.7	**5.7**
5.9	0.54	2.8	0.21	**4.6**	0.2	0.96	6.60	4.54	78.6	**4.7**	5.7	2.4	**7.6**
8.5	1.46	3.4	0.03	**6.6**	1.1	1.44	7.03	4.21	67.9	**5.2**	45.0	9.8	**9.9**
4.5	1.44	10.1	0.06	**7.5**	3.5	1.49	17.12	4.66	62.6	**2.9**	29.8	17.3	**6.1**
9.1	0.23	0.7	-0.01	**5.3**	0.7	1.01	6.63	3.67	62.9	**6.1**	64.4	8.4	**8.4**
1.7	11.13	36.2	1.58	**2.5**	0.1	0.14	1.08	4.18	74.7	**5.1**	52.3	11.4	**7.6**
8.0	0.10	1.0	0.25	**4.3**	0.8	0.73	9.00	5.01	75.0	**0.6**	5.7	41.3	**4.3**
3.5	1.98	9.3	0.67	**2.7**	1.0	0.69	7.15	3.92	78.7	**3.5**	28.9	14.0	**3.4**
9.0	0.41	0.5	0.05	**3.7**	0.2	0.74	2.80	2.34	71.6	**4.3**	69.1	18.4	**9.0**
9.8	0.04	0.1	-0.05	**4.0**	1.3	0.76	7.74	3.26	68.6	**4.1**	65.6	21.1	**5.1**
7.3	0.00	0.0	0.01	**4.7**	1.5	0.95	8.10	4.04	57.9	**0.8**	14.2	35.3	**6.0**
2.1	3.82	22.0	1.40	**3.6**	0.7	0.39	3.64	4.26	58.7	**4.0**	23.6	9.7	**7.9**
7.9	1.71	4.1	0.05	**1.8**	0.3	1.09	12.62	2.63	97.6	**5.6**	75.7	12.5	**3.5**
6.3	1.04	5.2	0.21	**3.7**	1.7	0.65	6.22	3.03	69.6	**5.7**	45.8	7.4	**5.9**
5.0	5.84	13.9	0.28	**5.0**	0.6	1.15	7.17	3.62	73.5	**2.5**	57.7	41.6	**8.0**
3.6	1.84	12.1	0.19	**5.3**	2.9	0.99	10.07	3.45	57.9	**3.5**	19.4	12.0	**5.8**
2.7	1.15	9.3	0.15	**7.5**	2.7	1.81	21.48	4.42	61.5	**2.0**	23.3	20.1	**5.3**
8.3	0.00	0.0	0.00	**2.0**	0.0	0.14	1.95	3.31	95.3	**3.5**	59.5	19.0	**4.5**
3.3	3.60	17.5	0.04	**3.3**	0.3	0.51	4.98	4.18	80.1	**4.1**	42.8	14.8	**6.1**
6.8	0.10	0.6	0.00	**6.4**	2.1	1.58	12.72	3.85	58.8	**2.6**	32.8	19.5	**8.3**
5.9	1.32	7.9	0.30	**4.7**	0.8	0.91	7.94	4.22	70.6	**2.8**	23.6	15.9	**7.1**
5.3	1.54	7.4	0.33	**3.4**	0.3	0.48	5.66	4.63	85.1	**7.0**	64.0	2.2	**2.8**
3.7	3.08	23.9	0.00	**6.2**	0.9	1.03	14.41	3.68	58.9	**2.0**	19.1	19.5	**4.4**
9.0	0.18	0.7	-0.04	**2.1**	0.3	0.53	4.33	3.74	88.9	**5.6**	50.2	8.4	**5.6**
5.0	0.43	3.5	0.06	**5.9**	3.7	1.57	19.47	4.22	61.7	**1.1**	23.6	32.8	**5.3**
0.0	24.49	214.6	5.01	**0.0**	-24.1	-2.97	-77.80	1.89	157.6	**1.2**	18.5	29.9	**1.5**
3.2	2.79	16.4	5.74	**7.8**	192.0	1.57	19.92	6.35	50.5	**4.3**	16.0	7.4	**6.3**
2.6	3.29	22.4	0.88	**6.2**	2.5	1.23	12.15	4.42	59.7	**1.3**	12.4	26.2	**7.5**
3.6	2.34	12.6	0.41	**3.3**	0.3	0.60	6.33	4.15	78.0	**0.9**	25.2	46.9	**4.3**
1.1	5.04	44.8	-0.01	**4.3**	0.3	0.63	7.91	4.75	77.6	**1.9**	14.6	19.7	**5.2**
2.7	5.50	25.7	0.19	**5.8**	0.7	1.23	10.00	4.29	54.8	**4.3**	28.5	9.5	**9.0**
1.6	5.55	32.6	2.62	**1.1**	-1.2	-0.41	-4.64	3.92	82.9	**3.9**	30.5	12.2	**5.2**
6.5	0.40	1.6	0.71	**4.4**	1.9	0.73	6.43	4.34	67.2	**2.1**	23.8	19.4	**6.2**
1.7	6.95	24.8	1.44	**1.5**	0.1	0.19	2.20	2.20	74.4	**2.9**	45.3	24.7	**2.7**
3.7	5.76	23.3	0.25	**5.3**	6.8	1.04	7.59	3.92	62.9	**3.7**	43.1	17.2	**9.0**
5.3	2.01	11.5	-0.05	**5.6**	1.2	0.93	8.45	3.82	64.3	**3.5**	22.8	12.1	**7.3**
4.3	1.16	7.4	0.65	**4.1**	0.8	0.67	7.56	4.12	72.1	**2.0**	21.9	19.9	**5.3**
1.3	3.98	26.8	1.44	**2.6**	0.2	0.12	1.33	4.20	66.8	**2.1**	27.1	20.7	**5.0**
6.4	0.84	4.1	0.70	**4.7**	0.6	0.90	7.47	4.57	76.8	**3.2**	16.5	13.1	**6.9**
2.6	2.24	15.2	0.25	**9.1**	3.7	1.78	16.60	4.91	64.1	**1.5**	17.7	25.5	**8.2**
2.8	3.15	17.6	0.83	**3.3**	0.4	0.38	3.63	4.32	73.1	**1.0**	25.3	35.9	**5.5**
0.9	3.60	32.4	0.44	**4.1**	1.1	0.82	9.69	3.62	71.6	**1.6**	10.9	21.1	**5.0**
6.4	2.06	6.1	0.40	**3.7**	1.7	0.74	5.35	3.74	75.4	**2.3**	36.4	26.3	**6.5**
6.6	2.42	6.2	0.00	**3.3**	0.1	0.46	2.11	4.10	82.4	**5.8**	55.8	8.3	**7.9**
5.0	0.00	0.0	0.02	**3.0**	0.1	0.40	4.28	4.02	86.7	**4.8**	46.4	10.3	**5.2**
2.4	3.85	21.9	1.07	**3.8**	4.2	0.68	7.93	4.14	64.8	**1.6**	22.1	25.8	**5.1**
7.8	0.24	0.7	0.19	**4.1**	0.4	0.82	5.54	3.35	72.4	**3.0**	47.2	23.8	**7.6**
4.6	1.11	7.1	0.27	**4.8**	1.5	1.24	12.44	3.87	71.4	**2.6**	32.8	19.7	**5.7**
5.0	2.01	7.4	0.03	**5.6**	0.5	1.03	5.93	3.40	52.0	**5.0**	39.2	9.4	**8.4**
6.2	2.53	10.5	0.34	**4.8**	0.5	0.96	8.08	4.79	75.1	**2.7**	32.8	19.1	**7.8**
6.1	0.64	3.5	0.15	**4.1**	0.3	0.71	8.59	3.65	77.8	**3.8**	40.6	16.1	**4.9**
6.8	0.17	0.9	0.11	**5.0**	7.7	1.08	10.67	3.80	73.8	**3.1**	25.5	14.5	**8.6**

Name	City	State	Rating	2008 Rating	2007 Rating	Total Assets ($Mil)	One Year Asset Growth	Asset Mix (As a % of Total Assets) Comm-ercial Loans	Cons-umer Loans	Home Mort-gages	Secur-ities	Capital-ization Index	Leverage Ratio	Risk-based Capital Ratio
FIRST NATIONAL BK OF SCOT	SCOTIA	NY	**C+**	C+	C	350	4.02	8.5	37.2	14.2	10.5	**5.2**	7.5	11.1
▼ FIRST NATIONAL BK OF SEDA	SEDAN	KS	**B-**	B	B+	54	5.13	6.5	2.7	6.1	57.8	**7.2**	9.2	17.5
FIRST NATIONAL BK OF SEIL	SEILING	OK	**B+**	B+	B-	67	3.18	5.4	3.2	7.5	36.1	**10.0**	12.8	20.2
FIRST NATIONAL BK OF SEYM	SEYMOUR	TX	**B-**	B	B+	46	6.42	4.5	1.6	0.1	61.8	**8.8**	10.2	27.9
▼ FIRST NATIONAL BK OF SHEL	SHELBY	NC	**D**	B-	B+	995	-4.30	5.2	1.9	10.9	34.1	**7.3**	9.2	14.4
FIRST NATIONAL BK OF SHIN	SHINER	TX	**B-**	B	A	134	16.39	2.8	1.6	2.0	62.1	**7.8**	9.6	22.7
▼ FIRST NATIONAL BK OF SONO	SONORA	TX	**C**	B-	A-	234	7.63	9.1	6.3	17.1	16.5	**8.1**	9.7	15.5
FIRST NATIONAL BK OF SPAR	SPARTA	IL	**B-**	B-	B	78	10.55	4.3	8.7	22.5	42.1	**9.2**	10.5	21.3
FIRST NATIONAL BK OF ST I	SAINT IGNACE	MI	**C+**	C-	D+	218	9.13	3.5	2.0	12.2	48.7	**7.7**	9.5	18.2
FIRST NATIONAL BK OF ST L	CLAYTON	MO	**C-**	C+	B-	1,362	-8.40	6.0	1.0	12.5	9.4	**7.8**	9.5	13.5
FIRST NATIONAL BK OF STAN	STANTON	TX	**B**	B+	A-	85	15.91	4.4	3.9	1.5	67.6	**10.0**	11.5	29.0
FIRST NATIONAL BK OF STAR	STARBUCK	MN	**D-**	D-	C	21	10.10	6.2	0.7	6.6	0.0	**7.8**	9.6	14.5
FIRST NATIONAL BK OF STIG	STIGLER	OK	**B**	B	B-	100	1.88	5.4	3.5	6.4	52.6	**5.4**	7.4	16.7
FIRST NATIONAL BK OF SUFF	SUFFIELD	CT	**B+**	B+	B+	209	3.95	8.9	0.5	44.1	9.1	**9.4**	10.6	21.6
FIRST NATIONAL BK OF SULL	SULLIVAN	IL	**C-**	C	C	75	3.56	9.6	6.8	26.7	21.9	**5.9**	7.9	13.5
FIRST NATIONAL BK OF SYCA	SYCAMORE	OH	**C**	C-	B	98	4.70	4.0	3.5	20.5	41.6	**10.0**	11.6	22.8
FIRST NATIONAL BK OF SYRA	SYRACUSE	KS	**C-**	C-	B	172	-11.78	7.0	0.8	11.6	25.7	**7.7**	9.5	15.1
FIRST NATIONAL BK OF TAHO	TAHOKA	TX	**B**	B	B	65	-2.33	4.6	3.0	3.9	28.1	**7.5**	9.4	22.3
FIRST NATIONAL BK OF TALL	TALLADEGA	AL	**A-**	A	A	413	6.80	2.7	2.2	9.4	43.4	**9.2**	10.8	14.3
FIRST NATIONAL BK OF TENN	LIVINGSTON	TN	**B+**	B+	A	597	2.97	12.1	5.3	19.1	6.4	**10.0**	11.0	16.7
FIRST NATIONAL BK OF TEXH	TEXHOMA	OK	**B+**	A-	B	145	16.41	6.2	9.0	5.6	36.2	**8.4**	9.9	15.4
▼ FIRST NATIONAL BK OF THE	NAVARRE	MN	**D-**	C-	C+	57	-11.69	12.3	6.2	1.3	6.2	**8.2**	9.8	18.1
FIRST NATIONAL BK OF THE	SANDSTONE	MN	**D+**	C	B-	71	11.97	5.9	6.5	23.3	24.7	**6.7**	8.7	13.1
FIRST NATIONAL BK OF THOM	THOMAS	OK	**B+**	B+	B+	38	9.86	5.9	2.5	5.4	46.2	**10.0**	15.8	30.4
FIRST NATIONAL BK OF TOM	TOM BEAN	TX	**D+**	C-	C-	45	9.50	13.4	8.9	13.3	25.6	**7.5**	9.3	19.6
FIRST NATIONAL BK OF TREN	TRENTON	TX	**D**	C-	D-	142	-3.27	2.1	1.5	27.7	36.1	**7.9**	9.6	19.9
FIRST NATIONAL BK OF TRIN	TRINITY	TX	**C+**	C+	C+	49	3.46	2.8	10.1	5.7	52.0	**6.7**	8.7	22.1
FIRST NATIONAL BK OF VOLG	VOLGA	SD	**C-**	B	B	43	10.45	5.7	10.1	14.5	15.8	**7.7**	9.5	16.2
▼ FIRST NATIONAL BK OF WAHO	WAHOO	NE	**C+**	B+	B+	179	56.38	5.0	2.1	10.8	33.8	**6.6**	8.6	14.0
▲ FIRST NATIONAL BK OF WAKE	WAKEFIELD	MI	**D+**	C-	B-	49	1.29	3.4	8.4	24.4	34.5	**7.7**	9.4	19.4
FIRST NATIONAL BK OF WALK	WALKER	MN	**B**	B-	B	285	4.47	6.1	3.5	26.1	24.4	**10.0**	11.2	18.7
FIRST NATIONAL BK OF WAME	WAMEGO	KS	**D+**	C-	C	156	1.94	7.8	1.6	15.0	21.5	**5.9**	7.9	12.3
FIRST NATIONAL BK OF WASE	WASECA	MN	**B-**	B-	B-	110	-2.03	5.7	3.5	24.8	3.3	**4.6**	9.3	10.8
FIRST NATIONAL BK OF WATE	WATERLOO	IL	**C**	C	C+	324	4.94	2.2	1.0	16.3	42.7	**6.6**	8.6	17.7
▼ FIRST NATIONAL BK OF WAUC	WAUCHULA	FL	**C+**	B	B	79	-4.47	8.5	3.2	31.8	17.6	**10.0**	11.9	19.9
FIRST NATIONAL BK OF WAVE	WAVERLY	OH	**C**	B-	B-	145	-2.12	6.0	1.6	21.5	20.1	**7.6**	9.4	14.1
▼ FIRST NATIONAL BK OF WAYN	WAYNE	NE	**E**	D	D+	33	-8.97	11.0	4.6	2.2	22.0	**4.0**	6.0	10.8
FIRST NATIONAL BK OF WELL	WELLSTON	OH	**B**	B-	B+	94	-1.29	1.4	14.9	45.0	20.0	**10.0**	12.1	22.3
FIRST NATIONAL BK OF WINN	WINNSBORO	TX	**C+**	A-	A+	148	1.45	3.1	2.2	12.3	10.2	**10.0**	15.3	22.3
▼ FIRST NATIONAL BK OF WOOD	WOODSBORO	TX	**C**	B	B	39	16.38	5.7	6.3	11.3	43.8	**10.0**	11.1	29.1
▼ FIRST NATIONAL BK OF WYNN	WYNNE	AR	**D+**	D+	C-	262	-3.28	7.2	2.8	6.9	20.8	**8.7**	10.1	14.5
FIRST NATIONAL BK OF WYOM	WYOMING	DE	**D**	B-	B+	289	-1.20	2.0	1.5	20.3	16.3	**10.0**	14.3	20.8
FIRST NATIONAL BK OF WYOM	LARAMIE	WY	**D**	D	C-	179	-12.24	6.5	0.9	6.8	20.2	**9.3**	10.5	19.0
FIRST NATIONAL BK PARK FA	PARK FALLS	WI	**B+**	B+	A-	100	8.60	15.4	2.0	23.1	29.2	**8.9**	10.3	16.8
▲ FIRST NATIONAL BK PENNSYL	GREENVILLE	PA	**C**	C-	C	8,759	3.01	11.7	7.1	16.3	19.4	**6.3**	8.3	12.3
FIRST NATIONAL BK PETERST	PETERSTOWN	WV	**B**	B-	B-	55	9.59	1.0	6.2	39.1	28.8	**8.7**	10.1	20.2
FIRST NATIONAL BK PLATTEV	PLATTEVILLE	WI	**D**	D-	D+	127	-6.07	9.2	1.8	12.7	13.8	**7.6**	9.4	13.5
▼ FIRST NATIONAL BK POLK CO	CEDARTOWN	GA	**D-**	C-	B	163	-5.44	1.4	3.9	33.1	13.7	**6.6**	8.6	15.9
▼ FIRST NATIONAL BK PORT LA	PORT LAVACA	TX	**B-**	B	B	207	8.07	2.2	5.1	12.2	52.4	**10.0**	11.2	26.9
FIRST NATIONAL BK RIVER F	RIVER FALLS	WI	**D-**	D-	C-	283	-0.02	4.9	5.3	13.3	26.5	**7.0**	9.0	16.2
▼ FIRST NATIONAL BK S CAROL	HOLLY HILL	SC	**C+**	B-	A	152	0.35	4.1	3.9	12.2	20.9	**10.0**	15.4	24.5
FIRST NATIONAL BK SAINT J	SAINT JAMES	MN	**D+**	D	D	26	-8.64	5.4	4.2	23.9	13.9	**7.2**	9.1	15.0
FIRST NATIONAL BK SALLISA	SALLISAW	OK	**B+**	B	B-	207	-1.21	6.0	2.9	19.4	12.6	**6.1**	8.1	12.1
FIRST NATIONAL BK SCOTT C	SCOTT CITY	KS	**C+**	C+	B	91	24.32	8.7	6.2	3.8	13.1	**6.2**	10.6	11.9
▲ FIRST NATIONAL BK SCOTTSD	SCOTTSDALE	AZ	**D+**	C	C	65	16.64	0.0	0.1	0.5	3.5	**10.0**	33.3	180.4
▲ FIRST NATIONAL BK SIOUX F	SIOUX FALLS	SD	**C**	C-	B-	1,093	-2.54	13.5	0.6	11.4	31.9	**9.6**	10.7	19.5
FIRST NATIONAL BK SMITH C	SMITH CENTER	KS	**C-**	C-	D+	43	-10.02	5.3	1.3	2.5	36.1	**9.2**	10.5	19.1
FIRST NATIONAL BK SOUTH	ALMA	GA	**C+**	B	B	324	0.50	10.5	6.0	18.0	2.1	**9.6**	10.7	14.9
FIRST NATIONAL BK SOUTH D	YANKTON	SD	**D+**	D+	C	403	-6.48	7.8	4.5	2.7	15.2	**6.8**	8.8	14.3
FIRST NATIONAL BK SOUTH M	SOUTH MIAMI	FL	**D+**	D-	C+	372	10.21	5.8	0.2	1.6	47.9	**9.2**	10.5	18.8

Asset Quality Index	Non-Performing Loans as a % of Total Loans	Non-Performing Loans as a % of Capital	Net Charge-offs Avg Loans	Profitability Index	Net Income ($Mil)	Return on Assets (R.O.A.)	Return on Equity (R.O.E.)	Net Interest Spread	Overhead Efficiency Ratio	Liquidity Index	Liquidity Ratio	Hot Money Ratio	Stability Index
5.9	0.25	2.3	0.08	3.9	2.1	0.61	8.51	4.18	77.3	4.2	15.0	7.3	4.3
4.6	3.08	12.4	0.12	5.3	0.8	1.52	13.62	3.46	65.5	2.3	26.1	19.0	6.9
8.2	0.78	3.2	0.14	3.6	0.4	0.64	4.45	4.10	78.6	0.7	14.1	40.6	8.0
9.6	0.00	0.0	0.40	3.6	0.3	0.64	5.94	3.02	80.5	6.5	83.4	9.0	5.7
1.7	8.48	42.9	1.86	1.0	-8.0	-0.76	-7.44	3.22	80.4	0.8	18.9	39.9	6.9
7.6	0.37	1.1	-0.01	3.2	0.3	0.95	7.19	3.92	71.4	3.5	66.0	29.7	5.7
4.2	2.18	12.5	0.18	2.5	0.4	0.18	1.83	4.49	75.1	1.2	26.3	33.6	6.2
5.1	1.95	8.8	0.06	4.0	0.7	0.89	7.91	3.82	78.2	3.8	30.4	12.7	5.9
4.7	2.15	7.8	0.04	3.6	1.6	0.74	7.20	3.63	76.7	4.8	58.8	15.7	4.8
0.2	3.28	22.9	0.78	7.3	17.7	1.21	11.05	4.28	47.5	3.0	6.6	13.1	7.5
9.2	0.92	1.7	0.06	3.9	0.6	0.76	6.13	3.27	72.2	3.9	66.0	20.1	6.8
2.1	2.62	12.9	0.00	3.1	0.1	2.15	17.57	4.76	70.4	5.8	46.0	3.2	3.7
7.8	0.71	3.4	-0.01	8.9	2.3	2.31	26.48	4.05	54.0	5.0	47.3	11.9	6.5
5.8	1.65	9.9	0.09	5.2	1.7	0.80	7.72	3.56	66.5	2.5	25.2	17.5	6.8
4.5	1.16	8.5	0.19	3.0	0.4	0.50	6.20	3.44	82.9	3.7	14.7	10.3	4.3
2.4	5.44	22.1	0.33	4.2	0.9	0.94	6.98	4.12	72.0	3.1	32.6	17.0	8.0
4.9	0.28	1.7	1.97	1.2	-3.9	-2.12	-19.43	3.99	82.8	1.2	27.7	37.1	4.5
9.2	0.00	0.0	-0.05	4.8	0.7	1.09	10.93	2.88	65.5	2.8	64.3	35.0	6.6
6.3	1.25	4.6	0.68	7.7	5.8	1.46	13.07	4.19	41.0	1.7	35.0	35.8	7.1
4.8	1.72	10.8	0.33	3.8	3.1	0.52	4.63	3.66	67.3	1.8	19.1	20.9	8.2
8.0	0.15	0.9	0.49	4.9	1.5	1.19	11.07	4.08	68.4	1.6	35.5	43.7	6.5
5.5	1.83	7.2	0.67	0.5	-0.4	-0.58	-6.07	3.61	102.7	6.5	54.8	3.4	3.6
2.0	2.76	20.3	0.90	4.1	0.5	0.68	7.87	5.04	67.4	4.6	18.3	5.2	4.6
7.2	0.28	0.7	1.53	4.3	0.3	0.91	5.33	4.03	77.7	3.6	60.4	20.8	8.3
4.4	2.01	10.0	0.14	1.4	0.1	0.13	1.33	4.29	97.1	3.1	45.2	21.2	3.8
5.6	0.58	2.8	0.48	0.7	0.2	0.10	1.01	3.38	101.9	3.4	29.7	14.3	5.3
5.8	2.00	6.7	0.26	6.1	0.7	1.44	16.77	4.15	73.4	6.1	62.7	7.7	5.0
3.7	1.07	6.4	0.03	4.2	0.3	0.75	7.57	4.24	78.5	1.9	23.7	21.4	6.0
2.9	2.57	15.8	0.00	6.1	1.6	1.05	11.64	3.88	56.3	4.8	26.2	5.4	6.0
1.9	4.21	21.7	0.22	4.6	0.5	0.93	9.63	4.77	74.6	3.3	44.5	19.4	6.0
4.6	2.46	13.3	0.53	7.8	5.0	1.82	15.67	3.90	54.7	2.1	27.4	20.3	7.6
2.7	2.05	15.5	2.25	1.7	-0.2	-0.12	-1.49	3.77	66.5	1.7	18.6	22.7	4.2
3.8	1.29	9.4	0.28	7.8	2.1	1.84	17.67	5.35	60.8	4.1	10.5	7.6	7.8
4.3	1.82	8.7	0.24	3.0	1.8	0.56	6.13	2.98	77.7	3.3	32.9	16.1	5.0
5.0	1.87	10.0	0.85	2.1	0.0	0.00	0.02	4.70	88.9	0.8	19.6	45.8	6.6
3.4	2.53	16.6	0.08	4.0	1.1	0.74	7.69	3.75	74.6	3.1	7.2	12.6	6.1
0.3	8.10	45.0	5.69	0.0	-1.8	-4.88	-52.65	4.14	130.0	5.4	30.2	3.1	3.1
4.3	2.27	12.7	0.32	4.8	0.8	0.81	6.50	4.59	72.5	3.6	23.8	12.1	6.2
0.3	6.47	24.0	1.17	3.0	-0.2	-0.15	-0.98	4.78	77.7	1.0	19.6	32.6	8.5
8.9	0.58	1.6	-0.01	1.5	0.0	-0.10	-0.82	3.93	102.1	5.8	58.2	8.8	5.5
1.4	4.28	21.0	2.33	2.3	0.2	0.07	0.56	4.09	72.7	2.0	27.2	21.6	5.9
0.3	14.18	54.9	4.22	2.1	-8.0	-2.68	-15.46	3.76	57.2	2.2	24.0	19.1	8.4
2.6	3.81	17.4	0.39	0.7	-0.4	-0.19	-1.78	3.93	96.0	2.9	35.9	19.0	4.2
8.7	0.12	0.7	0.06	5.6	1.3	1.32	11.68	4.40	67.8	2.4	31.2	20.2	6.8
2.7	1.94	14.6	0.68	4.6	70.0	0.87	6.73	3.61	60.8	3.8	6.4	9.1	8.2
6.8	0.67	3.7	0.00	4.6	0.4	0.77	7.16	4.27	69.8	2.9	41.6	21.8	6.5
2.6	2.17	15.2	0.02	1.0	0.1	0.07	0.63	3.72	94.9	2.2	14.7	18.2	3.4
0.3	8.82	54.1	3.96	0.0	-4.1	-2.39	-23.26	4.13	88.2	3.5	21.6	11.9	4.2
8.3	1.09	3.4	0.68	2.9	0.8	0.38	3.02	3.03	76.2	2.8	52.1	32.1	7.1
0.3	4.45	26.6	0.67	4.2	2.3	0.78	8.35	3.94	68.2	4.0	21.4	9.8	5.5
3.2	6.33	21.9	0.30	4.7	1.3	0.82	5.49	4.19	70.6	3.7	32.9	14.0	7.0
1.5	4.56	30.7	0.20	2.6	0.1	0.19	2.08	4.66	94.1	3.4	18.5	12.4	4.3
4.6	0.67	5.6	0.17	8.8	4.7	2.26	14.56	4.88	54.3	1.3	4.3	23.6	8.3
3.6	1.33	8.5	0.73	4.4	0.6	0.71	6.27	4.37	60.9	3.0	18.8	14.5	6.0
9.4	0.00	0.0	0.00	0.0	-0.6	-6.58	-51.44	0.93	713.8	4.2	120.5	38.5	1.7
3.2	4.38	18.7	0.20	3.1	5.3	0.48	4.16	3.03	78.1	2.5	27.8	24.6	6.8
5.9	0.00	0.0	1.77	1.9	0.1	0.31	2.95	3.74	77.7	6.3	58.2	5.4	3.7
2.9	3.03	20.0	3.07	4.1	1.7	0.53	4.98	4.68	48.1	1.0	8.1	29.5	5.7
2.0	1.64	11.6	2.15	2.3	0.7	0.18	1.39	4.63	66.1	3.1	26.4	14.9	5.3
4.4	1.88	6.7	-1.08	1.1	0.5	0.12	1.29	2.73	104.4	2.6	35.9	22.6	2.7

Name	City	State	Rating	2008 Rating	2007 Rating	Total Assets ($Mil)	One Year Asset Growth	Comm-ercial Loans	Cons-umer Loans	Home Mort-gages	Secur-ities	Capital-ization Index	Leverage Ratio	Risk-based Capital Ratio
								Asset Mix (As a % of Total Assets)						
FIRST NATIONAL BK SOUTHER	RIVERSIDE	CA	**D-**	D-	C+	173	-20.65	8.9	0.3	3.2	11.2	**9.7**	10.8	15.3
▼ FIRST NATIONAL BK SOUTHER	MOUNT HOPE	KS	**D+**	C-	D+	67	10.85	17.7	3.0	4.6	13.0	**5.8**	7.8	13.1
FIRST NATIONAL BK SPEARVI	SPEARVILLE	KS	**B**	B+	B	31	3.31	5.0	3.9	0.0	17.6	**10.0**	12.1	20.1
FIRST NATIONAL BK STEELEV	STEELEVILLE	IL	**B**	B	B+	203	3.18	6.3	4.5	15.8	51.3	**8.5**	10.0	20.3
FIRST NATIONAL BK TAYLORV	TAYLORVILLE	IL	**A-**	B+	A-	167	2.38	5.4	4.8	13.0	49.2	**10.0**	11.5	15.9
FIRST NATIONAL BK TEXAS	KILLEEN	TX	**B**	B	B-	942	8.26	1.4	3.7	5.2	50.4	**5.0**	7.0	21.0
FIRST NATIONAL BK THE ROC	GRAND JUNCTION	CO	**D-**	D+	B-	335	-10.65	6.6	0.9	4.7	43.0	**7.2**	9.2	16.2
▼ FIRST NATIONAL BK	THROCKMORTON	TX	**C+**	B-	B	29	17.14	4.8	3.9	1.2	0.0	**7.8**	9.5	15.9
FIRST NATIONAL BK USA	BOUTTE	LA	**D-**	D-	D-	161	-12.99	3.6	1.1	29.7	3.4	**7.6**	9.4	15.9
FIRST NATIONAL BK WASHING	WASHINGTON	KS	**A-**	A-	A-	71	2.92	2.5	2.7	11.1	44.5	**10.0**	20.1	39.5
FIRST NATIONAL BK	WAYNESBORO	GA	**A-**	A-	A-	107	4.78	6.8	10.0	20.9	20.9	**10.0**	13.7	27.1
FIRST NATIONAL BK WELLING	WELLINGTON	KS	**C-**	C-	B-	84	-3.04	14.0	4.7	12.0	18.3	**6.8**	8.8	13.0
FIRST NATIONAL BK WEST UN	WEST UNION	IA	**C+**	B-	B-	104	4.29	4.4	2.9	15.8	24.3	**6.1**	8.1	13.4
FIRST NATIONAL BK WILLIAM	WILLIAMSON	WV	**B+**	B+	B+	98	-1.39	11.5	10.9	24.5	32.9	**10.0**	12.5	24.2
▼ FIRST NATIONAL COMMUNITY	DUNMORE	PA	**E+**	C-	B	1,173	-15.95	17.0	6.2	7.8	21.5	**2.6**	5.9	9.6
FIRST NATIONAL COMMUNITY	NEW RICHMOND	WI	**D+**	D	D	153	0.12	4.6	3.1	13.7	18.8	**6.9**	8.9	13.3
FIRST NATIONAL TRUST CO	PITTSBURGH	PA	**U**	U	U	22	1.71	0.0	0.0	0.0	0.0	**10.0**	73.8	131.4
FIRST NATIONS BANK	CHICAGO	IL	**B-**	B-	B-	289	1.95	6.4	0.8	7.5	12.0	**7.3**	9.2	13.2
▼ FIRST NAVY BANK	PENSACOLA	FL	**C**	C+	C+	63	16.43	0.0	6.8	0.0	74.8	**10.0**	21.4	140.1
FIRST NB IN PINCKNEYVILLE	PINCKNEYVILLE	IL	**A-**	A-	B	76	-0.74	0.8	9.9	27.4	40.1	**10.0**	13.3	29.4
FIRST NB MCCONNELSVILLE	MCCONNELSVILLE	OH	**C-**	D+	C-	134	-0.93	1.0	5.8	46.2	14.8	**4.9**	6.9	14.7
FIRST NB MUHLENBERG	CENTRAL CITY	KY	**B-**	B-	B-	144	4.95	6.6	3.3	35.0	25.8	**8.6**	10.0	17.7
FIRST NB OF CRYSTAL FALLS	CRYSTAL FALLS	MI	**C+**	B-	B	67	2.30	6.6	3.4	20.0	8.9	**10.0**	13.2	26.7
FIRST NB OF FORT STOCKTON	FORT STOCKTON	TX	**C+**	C+	B	63	6.45	5.5	3.6	4.9	67.5	**8.8**	10.2	26.2
FIRST NB OF FREDERICKSBUR	FREDERICKSBURG	PA	**D+**	D+	C	189	2.08	2.3	18.0	24.6	6.7	**5.9**	8.1	11.7
FIRST NB OF HUGHES SPRING	HUGHES SPRINGS	TX	**A-**	A-	A-	167	1.87	11.6	7.1	12.5	28.3	**8.5**	10.0	20.2
▼ FIRST NB OF PORT ALLEGANY	PORT ALLEGANY	PA	**C-**	C	C	102	-6.02	1.2	3.0	32.6	39.5	**7.3**	9.2	19.2
FIRST NB OF POWHATAN POIN	POWHATAN POINT	OH	**B-**	B-	B-	25	4.53	8.7	7.8	12.2	51.6	**9.4**	10.6	25.3
FIRST NB OF RUSSELL SPRIN	RUSSELL SPRINGS	KY	**A-**	A-	A	176	1.72	11.3	3.2	11.6	31.1	**10.0**	12.8	19.2
FIRST NB OF S PADRE ISLAN	SOUTH PADRE ISLAND	TX	**B-**	B-	B-	57	1.26	3.5	1.0	29.1	31.5	**6.4**	8.4	18.6
FIRST NB OF STERLING CITY	STERLING CITY	TX	**B**	B+	B+	83	3.15	5.1	6.2	6.0	55.1	**7.9**	9.6	21.6
▲ FIRST NB OF THE MID-CITIE	BEDFORD	TX	**C+**	C-	C+	35	6.91	14.0	5.1	12.8	0.0	**7.1**	9.0	15.1
FIRST NBC BANK	NEW ORLEANS	LA	**C**	C-	C-	1,461	46.92	26.0	0.5	9.1	15.1	**5.3**	9.1	11.2
FIRST NEBRASKA BANK	VALLEY	NE	**B**	B	B	172	0.56	12.7	2.8	8.3	25.6	**5.9**	8.7	11.6
FIRST NEIGHBOR BANK NA	TOLEDO	IL	**B**	B	B	238	5.52	11.6	5.9	18.0	17.6	**10.0**	12.1	16.6
FIRST NEIGHBORHOOD BANK	SPENCER	WV	**C**	C	C-	141	10.51	9.0	3.0	33.1	21.1	**6.5**	8.6	15.0
FIRST NEODESHA BANK	NEODESHA	KS	**B**	B	B	65	0.35	9.7	6.7	17.7	16.9	**5.9**	7.9	13.1
FIRST NEW MEXICO BANK	DEMING	NM	**A**	A	A	184	11.62	2.2	3.2	10.1	42.0	**9.8**	10.9	21.9
FIRST NEW MEXICO BK LAS C	LAS CRUCES	NM	**A**	A	A-	94	11.08	3.1	7.2	17.1	20.8	**10.0**	13.2	24.0
FIRST NEWTON NATIONAL BK	NEWTON	IA	**C**	C	C-	74	-15.81	7.8	1.2	15.1	32.5	**6.7**	8.7	15.8
FIRST NIAGARA BANK NA	BUFFALO	NY	**D+**	NR	NR	21,030	N/A	11.2	1.3	12.2	39.6	**4.6**	6.6	11.9
FIRST NM BANK OF SILVER C	SILVER CITY	NM	**A**	A	A	79	7.72	1.1	3.0	11.1	41.7	**10.0**	11.0	21.8
▲ FIRST NORTHERN BANK OF DI	DIXON	CA	**D+**	D+	C-	737	-1.39	11.1	0.4	8.2	14.6	**8.0**	9.7	16.5
▼ FIRST OKLAHOMA BANK	TULSA	OK	**D-**	C	C-	105	151.96	15.9	2.2	13.1	8.2	**6.6**	12.1	12.2
FIRST OPTION BANK	OSAWATOMIE	KS	**B-**	B-	B-	202	5.40	2.2	1.7	30.3	35.2	**5.7**	7.7	16.1
FIRST PALMETTO SAVINGS BA	CAMDEN	SC	**D**	D	C	673	-15.57	1.4	1.8	27.8	2.5	**8.8**	10.9	14.0
FIRST PEOPLES BANK	PORT SAINT LUCIE	FL	**E-**	E-	D-	232	-6.36	5.7	2.3	4.3	16.2	**0.0**	3.0	5.6
FIRST PEOPLES BANK	PINE MOUNTAIN	GA	**C**	C+	B	79	-14.69	2.9	7.6	29.5	10.3	**10.0**	13.7	22.3
FIRST PEOPLES BANK	MULLENS	WV	**C+**	C+	A	122	2.84	0.2	4.4	12.4	29.5	**10.0**	15.5	20.8
▲ FIRST PEOPLES BANK OF TEN	JEFFERSON CITY	TN	**D**	D	B-	131	2.44	11.4	3.6	21.2	20.2	**6.7**	8.8	12.3
FIRST PERSONAL BANK	ORLAND PARK	IL	**E-**	E	E+	181	1.75	17.2	0.1	26.3	6.1	**2.5**	5.2	9.5
FIRST PIEDMONT FS&LA OF G	GAFFNEY	SC	**A**	A	A+	279	1.97	1.2	2.5	30.3	0.0	**10.0**	24.6	32.3
▼ FIRST PIONEER NATIONAL BK	WRAY	CO	**B-**	B	A-	147	4.89	4.0	3.5	1.6	38.8	**10.0**	12.3	22.1
FIRST PLACE BANK	WARREN	OH	**D-**	D	D-	3,155	-2.55	3.7	0.5	38.7	6.6	**6.3**	8.3	12.6
FIRST PORT CITY BANK	BAINBRIDGE	GA	**C+**	C+	B+	129	3.15	6.4	1.6	14.2	21.3	**10.0**	11.8	17.7
FIRST PREMIER BANK	SIOUX FALLS	SD	**A**	A	A	1,115	8.17	8.5	16.3	6.2	26.4	**10.0**	14.6	23.2
FIRST PRIORITY BANK	MALVERN	PA	**D-**	D	C-	268	14.18	15.0	4.6	30.1	9.3	**7.6**	10.0	13.0
FIRST PRIVATE BANK & TRUS	ENCINO	CA	**C-**	C-	C-	505	-3.50	7.6	0.4	30.3	2.8	**7.5**	9.4	14.8
FIRST PRIVATE BANK OF TEX	DALLAS	TX	**C-**	C	C-	208	50.55	12.0	3.1	27.8	35.4	**10.0**	14.0	24.5
▼ FIRST PROGRESSIVE BANK	BREWTON	AL	**C**	C+	B	28	-6.61	5.0	6.3	10.5	53.5	**10.0**	27.3	71.1

Asset Quality Index	Non-Performing Loans as a % of Total Loans	Non-Performing Loans as a % of Capital	Net Charge-offs / Avg Loans	Profitability Index	Net Income ($Mil)	Return on Assets (R.O.A.)	Return on Equity (R.O.E.)	Net Interest Spread	Overhead Efficiency Ratio	Liquidity Index	Liquidity Ratio	Hot Money Ratio	Stability Index
0.0	14.03	76.9	2.44	**0.0**	-4.4	-2.26	-20.98	4.51	91.6	**2.5**	17.4	16.8	**3.5**
3.9	2.46	14.8	-0.07	**1.0**	0.0	-0.06	-0.76	4.37	93.8	**4.1**	32.7	12.0	**3.6**
5.0	0.68	3.1	0.63	**5.3**	0.2	0.62	3.90	3.48	57.3	**2.2**	30.9	22.4	**8.9**
4.6	1.90	7.5	0.57	**4.4**	2.1	1.06	9.52	3.18	63.5	**2.3**	26.2	19.0	**7.2**
6.8	1.08	4.2	0.37	**6.3**	2.2	1.33	10.66	4.00	48.7	**4.2**	45.9	15.4	**6.0**
5.5	1.70	5.8	1.62	**9.8**	22.7	2.50	30.03	3.98	87.7	**6.4**	76.4	10.1	**6.4**
0.3	12.92	48.6	4.69	**0.2**	-9.9	-2.78	-29.71	4.76	99.5	**1.7**	15.4	21.2	**3.2**
6.9	0.32	1.9	0.02	**4.8**	0.3	1.23	12.08	3.28	64.8	**4.5**	47.4	13.7	**4.3**
0.3	8.52	52.0	2.24	**0.0**	-7.7	-4.44	-47.86	3.64	227.7	**1.2**	17.4	29.3	**4.1**
9.3	0.05	0.1	-0.03	**6.6**	0.8	1.20	5.62	3.37	52.7	**3.0**	44.0	21.3	**8.8**
7.6	0.67	2.5	0.32	**5.8**	1.2	1.08	8.15	5.37	66.5	**2.3**	32.6	23.4	**7.7**
3.3	2.03	15.1	1.54	**1.9**	0.1	0.08	1.04	4.31	71.3	**1.6**	17.9	24.2	**4.3**
3.9	2.23	16.3	-0.03	**5.0**	1.3	1.22	13.73	4.26	65.8	**3.6**	28.7	13.5	**5.9**
4.5	2.25	9.8	0.46	**7.5**	1.7	1.73	12.65	5.07	60.9	**1.6**	30.7	31.5	**8.6**
1.7	2.96	23.4	3.86	**0.0**	-55.8	-4.14	-51.06	3.24	85.8	**1.6**	9.7	22.3	**4.3**
1.6	1.84	12.2	0.64	**3.2**	1.1	0.69	7.33	4.00	80.7	**3.4**	18.4	12.3	**4.6**
6.5	0.00	0.0	0.00	**10.0**	2.9	14.69	17.05	0.20	78.1	**3.8**	133.9	101.0	**4.3**
5.8	0.00	0.0	0.83	**4.6**	2.1	0.72	7.80	4.09	41.2	**0.8**	15.9	40.6	**5.9**
9.6	0.00	0.0	0.58	**0.6**	-0.1	-0.15	-0.65	2.45	107.5	**7.6**	111.9	6.2	**5.5**
8.2	0.78	2.6	0.13	**7.0**	1.0	1.32	9.21	4.51	60.7	**4.9**	30.1	6.5	**8.1**
2.2	1.26	11.7	0.32	**3.5**	0.7	0.52	4.64	4.33	80.4	**3.5**	16.2	11.9	**6.3**
4.5	1.96	12.3	0.37	**5.3**	1.4	0.99	9.31	4.15	61.3	**1.0**	19.1	33.6	**6.4**
8.9	0.11	0.4	0.25	**2.3**	0.2	0.26	1.97	3.37	91.2	**4.3**	46.1	14.6	**7.2**
6.2	1.76	4.1	-0.15	**3.3**	0.5	0.74	6.76	3.08	85.0	**3.5**	38.0	16.6	**6.8**
2.1	2.11	17.3	0.22	**3.4**	0.8	0.44	5.77	5.40	81.3	**4.2**	18.0	7.7	**3.8**
5.9	1.36	5.8	0.28	**5.4**	1.4	0.72	6.54	5.68	82.7	**2.4**	9.9	16.7	**8.6**
1.7	2.71	14.0	0.18	**4.0**	0.9	0.83	9.34	3.66	73.0	**2.1**	29.8	23.3	**4.6**
8.8	0.00	0.0	0.03	**3.7**	0.2	0.66	5.62	3.79	80.3	**5.7**	64.2	10.4	**7.4**
7.8	0.68	3.1	0.09	**5.3**	2.0	1.12	8.39	4.27	61.3	**2.2**	21.5	18.7	**8.1**
3.5	5.10	29.0	0.21	**6.3**	0.8	1.41	14.72	4.28	58.9	**4.2**	45.3	14.8	**7.1**
6.1	1.32	4.5	0.57	**5.3**	0.9	1.12	9.39	4.41	69.6	**3.4**	30.5	14.8	**6.7**
5.1	0.82	5.1	0.52	**2.5**	0.2	0.47	5.38	4.99	86.3	**2.6**	29.9	18.8	**3.8**
6.9	0.34	2.7	0.10	**3.5**	10.4	0.87	10.34	3.39	66.4	**1.0**	16.3	33.5	**5.6**
4.8	2.10	14.2	0.22	**6.3**	2.9	1.64	18.23	3.92	65.5	**3.9**	16.4	9.5	**5.9**
5.0	1.30	7.3	0.06	**6.1**	2.5	1.08	8.53	4.42	61.7	**2.2**	11.2	17.5	**6.5**
4.9	0.28	2.0	0.29	**3.2**	0.8	0.62	7.07	3.93	79.4	**3.1**	27.4	15.1	**3.2**
8.1	0.00	0.0	0.02	**6.3**	0.9	1.37	17.19	3.71	65.3	**1.7**	12.2	20.6	**5.7**
6.9	2.03	7.1	0.33	**8.6**	2.3	1.34	12.22	4.84	53.4	**6.0**	48.5	6.2	**7.5**
5.7	2.81	10.0	0.42	**9.5**	1.3	1.42	10.59	5.41	59.5	**4.5**	50.1	14.5	**7.0**
8.8	0.24	1.4	0.04	**2.6**	0.4	0.53	5.88	3.73	87.9	**4.7**	42.8	11.8	**3.8**
3.1	1.38	10.3	0.00	**1.5**	158.4	0.76	6.24	N/,	63.9	**3.9**	8.3	8.5	**4.9**
9.8	0.00	0.0	0.01	**8.1**	1.0	1.35	12.30	5.28	62.9	**6.0**	55.6	6.7	**8.0**
2.3	2.68	14.7	1.24	**1.5**	2.7	0.37	3.51	3.84	79.8	**4.3**	32.2	10.9	**5.2**
6.8	0.52	3.3	0.00	**0.0**	-2.1	-2.99	-16.59	3.51	219.8	**1.0**	24.2	38.0	**4.7**
5.1	0.19	1.3	1.03	**4.8**	2.0	1.10	13.04	4.02	67.7	**4.2**	20.0	8.0	**5.3**
1.2	5.08	35.5	0.31	**2.3**	0.7	0.10	0.97	3.87	54.6	**0.6**	6.2	35.0	**5.8**
0.0	6.38	88.3	3.10	**0.0**	-7.7	-3.06	-69.27	3.34	132.4	**1.0**	9.6	30.8	**0.1**
1.9	6.45	29.2	1.06	**3.8**	0.3	0.39	2.83	5.08	74.0	**1.7**	20.6	23.7	**6.6**
9.6	0.45	0.7	0.00	**2.5**	0.5	0.41	2.50	1.85	83.6	**5.8**	76.2	13.0	**6.1**
3.5	1.18	9.0	0.00	**1.6**	0.1	0.15	2.05	4.39	85.5	**2.7**	20.9	16.3	**3.5**
0.3	7.35	70.7	1.73	**0.1**	-1.0	-0.55	-8.02	3.65	89.2	**1.9**	24.5	21.6	**0.0**
7.8	0.94	2.9	0.00	**6.7**	4.5	1.61	6.26	5.17	55.3	**2.5**	24.1	17.6	**9.0**
4.5	3.44	12.8	1.39	**2.5**	0.3	0.24	1.81	3.40	72.1	**3.3**	40.0	18.7	**6.3**
0.7	3.97	32.8	3.34	**0.0**	-27.1	-0.86	-9.63	3.88	67.5	**3.1**	9.4	13.3	**4.6**
8.8	0.32	1.5	0.04	**3.2**	0.9	0.76	6.52	3.13	65.3	**2.9**	31.8	17.6	**4.9**
7.1	0.58	2.0	1.00	**6.7**	16.1	1.47	9.66	3.37	58.4	**1.5**	15.2	26.3	**9.6**
4.3	0.58	4.8	0.67	**0.2**	0.1	0.06	0.52	3.38	97.1	**0.6**	6.8	39.4	**1.0**
2.0	2.61	18.0	-0.44	**1.2**	0.9	0.18	1.59	4.18	97.8	**1.1**	16.5	31.6	**5.3**
8.7	0.00	0.0	0.00	**0.2**	-0.4	-0.20	-1.28	2.73	102.8	**2.1**	44.0	46.4	**1.7**
9.4	1.30	1.4	0.00	**2.0**	0.0	0.14	0.52	3.27	96.5	**4.6**	96.2	20.4	**6.9**

Name	City	State	Rating	2008 Rating	2007 Rating	Total Assets ($Mil)	One Year Asset Growth	Asset Mix (As a % of Total Assets) Comm-ercial Loans	Cons-umer Loans	Home Mort-gages	Secur-ities	Capital-ization Index	Leverage Ratio	Risk-based Capital Ratio
FIRST PRYORITY BANK	PRYOR	OK	**D**	D+	D	107	-3.39	15.8	13.6	5.5	12.1	**8.4**	9.9	15.0
FIRST RELIANCE BANK	FLORENCE	SC	**D**	D	D+	529	-18.02	7.3	1.2	10.6	16.0	**6.9**	8.9	13.1
FIRST REPUBLIC BANK	SAN FRANCISCO	CA	**D+**	NR	NR	22,378	N/A	4.7	1.3	49.6	4.6	**7.4**	9.2	14.6
▲ FIRST RESOURCE BANK	SAVAGE	MN	**D**	E-	D+	25	35.04	13.6	0.2	2.8	1.2	**10.0**	39.9	71.9
▲ FIRST RESOURCE BANK	EXTON	PA	**C**	D	D	126	-4.30	8.1	0.7	27.8	5.6	**10.0**	11.3	15.4
FIRST ROBINSON SB NA	ROBINSON	IL	**C+**	C+	B	209	15.03	7.5	7.3	21.1	22.2	**4.7**	6.7	11.9
FIRST SAFETY BANK	SAINT BERNARD	OH	**B-**	B	B-	56	-0.21	1.7	1.0	34.4	15.9	**10.0**	16.8	31.7
FIRST SAVANNA SB	SAVANNA	IL	**D**	D	D	14	10.11	0.0	5.4	44.9	34.6	**10.0**	11.5	27.6
FIRST SAVINGS & LOAN ASSN	MEBANE	NC	**C+**	C+	C+	59	1.13	0.0	0.0	45.3	36.9	**10.0**	17.5	45.8
FIRST SAVINGS BANK	BERESFORD	SD	**C+**	C+	C+	439	-2.62	6.3	6.0	5.4	17.0	**10.0**	13.4	20.2
FIRST SAVINGS BANK FSB	CLARKSVILLE	IN	**C+**	B-	C-	507	4.90	5.3	3.7	33.0	24.1	**6.0**	8.0	12.8
FIRST SB	DANVILLE	IL	**B**	B-	B-	38	2.19	0.0	0.4	38.0	39.8	**10.0**	20.3	62.1
FIRST SB NORTHWEST	RENTON	WA	**D-**	D	B-	1,183	-9.16	0.0	0.1	32.9	13.9	**10.0**	11.7	19.7
FIRST SB OF HEGEWISCH	CHICAGO	IL	**B-**	C+	C+	532	-0.08	0.0	0.1	53.1	27.6	**9.4**	10.6	30.3
FIRST SB OF PERKASIE	PERKASIE	PA	**C-**	B-	B	1,034	-3.82	3.1	0.2	33.6	17.9	**10.0**	12.4	20.2
▲ FIRST SECURITY BANK	SEARCY	AR	**B**	B	B-	3,510	14.78	6.2	2.3	10.7	46.6	**5.8**	7.8	13.0
▲ FIRST SECURITY BANK	MACKINAW	IL	**D**	C	D+	74	-16.94	15.1	1.6	19.3	9.5	**6.1**	8.2	12.5
FIRST SECURITY BANK	OVERBROOK	KS	**C+**	C	C-	34	30.87	5.8	2.6	9.2	0.0	**9.2**	10.4	17.3
▲ FIRST SECURITY BANK	BYRON	MN	**D+**	D	D	49	-0.95	8.4	2.0	10.5	11.2	**6.5**	8.6	12.1
▼ FIRST SECURITY BANK	UNION STAR	MO	**D-**	D	E+	20	1.67	6.3	5.7	33.3	17.9	**6.1**	8.1	15.0
FIRST SECURITY BANK	BATESVILLE	MS	**C-**	C-	C	499	4.70	3.9	4.3	13.6	31.5	**9.0**	10.3	18.5
▼ FIRST SECURITY BANK	BOZEMAN	MT	**D-**	C-	B	604	6.96	7.0	2.0	13.4	25.8	**5.9**	7.9	13.0
FIRST SECURITY BANK	BEAVER	OK	**B-**	B-	B-	100	6.63	11.6	2.6	8.6	16.0	**5.5**	8.6	11.4
FIRST SECURITY BANK & TRU	CHARLES CITY	IA	**B**	B+	B+	427	5.26	11.5	2.6	11.0	26.8	**6.7**	8.7	12.8
FIRST SECURITY BANK & TRU	NORTON	KS	**D**	D-	C+	57	-26.26	7.6	4.7	2.0	31.9	**10.0**	12.8	19.7
FIRST SECURITY BANK & TRU	OKLAHOMA CITY	OK	**D**	C-	D-	42	-9.13	21.0	2.3	28.2	11.5	**6.5**	8.5	13.1
FIRST SECURITY BANK - WES	BEULAH	ND	**B**	B-	B	81	1.06	5.4	2.7	2.7	29.5	**9.5**	10.7	20.9
▲ FIRST SECURITY BANK CANBY	CANBY	MN	**B-**	C	C	31	3.82	6.2	2.8	1.1	20.5	**9.5**	10.7	17.3
FIRST SECURITY BANK DEER	DEER LODGE	MT	**C**	C+	B	28	-3.00	9.2	5.3	20.9	4.9	**6.9**	8.9	16.1
FIRST SECURITY BANK KENTU	CALHOUN	KY	**D**	D	D-	61	31.26	6.9	7.1	25.1	4.2	**4.7**	8.0	10.9
FIRST SECURITY BANK MISSO	MISSOULA	MT	**C-**	C	B+	1,006	12.75	7.5	2.5	9.2	36.9	**9.7**	10.8	16.6
FIRST SECURITY BANK NA	FLOWER MOUND	TX	**D+**	C-	C	154	1.57	6.5	4.0	12.8	10.0	**10.0**	11.2	15.7
▲ FIRST SECURITY BANK OF HE	HELENA	MT	**C**	D-	D-	43	-4.46	14.0	8.8	48.2	2.8	**8.8**	10.2	16.0
FIRST SECURITY BANK OF MA	MALTA	MT	**C**	C-	C-	33	2.27	5.6	18.7	2.3	19.5	**6.8**	8.8	15.5
FIRST SECURITY BANK OF NE	LAS VEGAS	NV	**D**	D	D+	106	-12.06	18.0	0.2	2.9	2.0	**10.0**	12.1	16.8
▼ FIRST SECURITY BANK OF RO	ROUNDUP	MT	**B+**	A-	A-	46	5.08	9.8	4.1	4.6	25.3	**8.2**	9.8	15.9
FIRST SECURITY BANK	OWENSBORO	KY	**C**	C+	C+	337	54.72	9.8	11.9	19.0	7.7	**6.3**	8.8	12.0
FIRST SECURITY	HENDRICKS	MN	**C-**	C-	D	20	0.69	6.5	4.5	8.6	14.3	**7.8**	9.6	19.4
▲ FIRST SECURITY BANK-SLEEP	SLEEPY EYE	MN	**B-**	C	C	156	-7.74	6.4	3.2	8.1	22.7	**9.5**	10.9	14.6
▲ FIRST SECURITY BK-LAKE BE	LAKE BENTON	MN	**B-**	C	C	24	1.81	6.7	3.3	5.3	30.1	**9.0**	10.3	17.9
▼ FIRST SECURITY BUSINESS B	ORANGE	CA	**B-**	A	A+	551	70.55	0.0	0.0	0.0	17.5	**6.0**	8.0	16.5
FIRST SECURITY STATE BK	EVANSDALE	IA	**D**	D	D+	83	-6.05	16.6	33.4	6.0	9.3	**7.9**	9.6	13.4
FIRST SECURITY STATE BK	CRANFILLS GAP	TX	**C+**	C+	C+	91	5.83	2.8	6.7	13.2	35.3	**4.5**	6.5	15.5
▲ FIRST SECURITY TRUST & SB	ELMWOOD PARK	IL	**D**	D-	C-	210	2.08	4.2	0.2	21.0	39.3	**10.0**	13.4	22.1
FIRST SECURITY TRUST BANK	FLORENCE	KY	**C-**	C	C	134	6.57	4.1	0.5	13.0	24.2	**7.0**	9.0	13.6
▲ FIRST SENTINEL BANK	RICHLANDS	VA	**C-**	C	C+	171	2.48	6.8	17.3	29.9	5.2	**6.4**	8.5	13.3
FIRST SENTRY BANK INC	HUNTINGTON	WV	**C**	C-	C+	491	0.51	17.7	3.5	13.5	17.2	**5.2**	7.2	11.6
FIRST SERVICE BANK	GREENBRIER	AR	**D+**	C	C+	216	-0.35	5.5	4.8	22.7	10.6	**6.5**	8.5	13.5
▼ FIRST SHORE FS&LA	SALISBURY	MD	**C**	C+	C+	335	1.16	1.7	5.1	50.2	7.9	**8.5**	10.0	16.6
FIRST SOUND BANK	SEATTLE	WA	**E-**	E-	D+	147	-25.64	23.4	0.3	0.4	0.7	**0.0**	4.0	6.1
▼ FIRST SOUTH BANK	WASHINGTON	NC	**D-**	C-	C-	791	-4.32	2.7	0.8	19.5	12.5	**7.1**	9.1	13.4
▼ FIRST SOUTH BANK	SPARTANBURG	SC	**E-**	D-	B-	464	-0.92	7.7	0.0	9.2	22.8	**2.1**	5.8	9.1
▲ FIRST SOUTH BANK	BOLIVAR	TN	**C+**	B-	B-	443	2.42	6.9	2.0	13.5	28.5	**6.4**	8.5	14.9
FIRST SOUTHEAST BANK	HARMONY	MN	**D+**	C	C-	59	9.50	12.2	4.0	9.1	6.7	**5.9**	8.6	11.7
▲ FIRST SOUTHERN BANK	FLORENCE	AL	**C+**	C-	C	154	18.65	13.4	2.8	22.9	13.2	**6.5**	8.6	14.3
FIRST SOUTHERN BANK	BOCA RATON	FL	**D**	D-	D	547	39.43	3.5	0.0	3.0	23.1	**10.0**	14.5	21.3
FIRST SOUTHERN BANK	CARBONDALE	IL	**C+**	C+	C	237	5.85	10.3	3.8	29.9	13.6	**6.2**	8.2	12.0
FIRST SOUTHERN BANK	COLUMBIA	MS	**C**	C	C-	186	-1.53	9.2	7.7	17.8	7.1	**5.5**	8.2	11.4
▼ FIRST SOUTHERN NATIONAL B	STATESBORO	GA	**E-**	D-	D+	174	-26.49	9.8	5.9	18.2	11.7	**0.0**	3.3	6.0
FIRST SOUTHERN NATIONAL B	LANCASTER	KY	**B-**	C+	C+	655	0.76	4.4	2.4	19.4	26.9	**7.4**	9.3	16.9

Asset Quality Index	Non-Performing Loans as a % of Total Loans	Non-Performing Loans as a % of Capital	Net Charge-offs Avg Loans	Profitability Index	Net Income ($Mil)	Return on Assets (R.O.A.)	Return on Equity (R.O.E.)	Net Interest Spread	Overhead Efficiency Ratio	Liquidity Index	Liquidity Ratio	Hot Money Ratio	Stability Index
0.4	7.69	36.0	1.48	**0.0**	-1.3	-1.15	-11.69	3.39	131.6	**2.2**	19.0	18.6	**3.5**
1.5	6.06	38.9	1.73	**0.6**	0.6	0.10	1.07	3.41	90.4	**1.0**	20.8	34.3	**3.7**
8.7	0.10	0.9	0.00	**1.4**	142.4	0.65	7.11	N/,	51.8	**1.7**	12.7	21.2	**4.7**
4.9	8.48	8.0	0.09	**0.0**	-0.2	-5.53	-58.18	3.29	174.6	**3.1**	89.7	60.1	**1.5**
4.2	2.23	16.0	0.49	**2.2**	0.5	0.38	3.39	3.40	69.3	**1.3**	3.1	23.4	**3.9**
8.0	0.23	2.0	0.04	**4.8**	1.8	0.95	12.82	3.38	64.3	**3.6**	21.8	11.8	**3.0**
6.1	1.67	5.9	0.31	**3.5**	0.4	0.77	4.51	3.07	72.8	**4.0**	42.6	15.3	**7.6**
2.8	6.45	28.4	0.12	**0.1**	0.0	-0.22	-1.84	2.81	112.6	**3.3**	42.7	16.6	**6.2**
7.2	2.86	8.0	0.07	**2.9**	0.3	0.42	2.44	3.33	75.2	**2.6**	59.7	37.9	**6.9**
2.8	4.63	18.4	3.51	**3.7**	2.3	0.53	3.97	5.23	62.3	**3.5**	34.5	15.7	**6.7**
3.2	1.51	11.8	-0.04	**3.4**	3.4	0.68	7.00	4.37	73.9	**2.2**	29.3	20.7	**5.2**
8.0	3.87	7.2	0.00	**3.9**	0.3	0.82	4.00	3.25	65.0	**3.7**	73.6	26.0	**8.0**
0.3	7.24	38.3	6.38	**0.0**	-51.1	-3.98	-35.62	2.59	92.1	**0.8**	18.7	54.3	**6.1**
9.2	0.27	1.4	0.14	**4.3**	4.0	0.73	7.21	2.92	56.3	**3.2**	45.9	21.3	**6.6**
1.7	4.40	22.4	2.85	**1.2**	-1.0	-0.09	-0.66	2.89	59.6	**3.0**	17.6	14.9	**9.1**
5.4	1.35	7.0	0.47	**8.4**	66.9	2.05	20.88	5.14	47.1	**2.2**	24.0	23.2	**8.3**
2.2	2.66	21.7	2.91	**1.2**	-1.0	-1.18	-14.84	3.67	72.4	**1.6**	12.0	21.6	**5.3**
7.8	0.00	0.0	0.01	**3.0**	0.1	0.26	2.11	4.72	88.4	**3.2**	34.1	17.1	**3.8**
4.6	0.75	5.6	0.19	**2.6**	0.3	0.50	5.98	4.21	78.1	**2.2**	20.8	18.6	**3.2**
0.9	5.37	37.3	0.06	**3.0**	0.1	0.50	6.14	4.34	87.4	**3.2**	25.7	13.8	**5.1**
2.7	3.45	15.2	0.88	**2.6**	2.0	0.41	3.55	3.82	80.4	**2.0**	24.6	19.9	**6.1**
0.3	7.34	48.7	2.57	**1.6**	-5.7	-0.99	-9.79	4.09	70.5	**4.0**	25.4	9.9	**7.9**
5.7	0.66	5.5	0.11	**4.9**	1.1	1.19	14.10	2.87	59.6	**0.7**	10.5	37.8	**6.0**
5.0	0.49	3.4	0.69	**7.3**	6.7	1.58	15.50	4.31	55.6	**4.6**	31.1	8.9	**7.3**
1.6	4.90	20.2	5.38	**0.0**	-0.8	-1.18	-8.76	4.26	87.3	**1.5**	16.2	24.7	**5.3**
1.5	4.64	37.8	0.51	**3.6**	0.3	0.67	7.93	5.26	85.9	**1.4**	8.0	23.6	**3.6**
8.1	0.00	0.0	0.63	**4.6**	0.9	1.10	10.97	4.01	67.6	**5.5**	54.9	9.8	**5.2**
7.2	0.00	0.0	0.70	**5.8**	0.5	1.52	11.43	4.33	65.0	**5.9**	42.5	4.6	**5.7**
4.8	1.15	7.0	0.96	**3.4**	0.1	0.31	3.47	4.15	78.4	**4.6**	41.1	12.1	**4.5**
4.3	1.08	9.2	0.25	**2.4**	0.2	0.32	4.03	4.60	86.1	**0.9**	19.6	36.9	**2.3**
1.4	6.16	28.6	1.29	**6.4**	10.3	1.10	8.31	4.55	47.7	**2.7**	29.4	23.6	**7.5**
0.0	4.61	27.7	0.48	**7.7**	2.6	1.67	13.11	4.61	50.4	**1.1**	16.4	31.6	**6.8**
4.0	1.62	12.0	1.37	**3.3**	0.3	0.56	5.80	5.29	69.3	**1.0**	8.1	30.1	**4.0**
4.0	1.00	5.6	0.44	**5.1**	0.2	0.75	7.84	5.31	78.1	**4.0**	45.7	15.7	**4.3**
0.0	21.36	97.2	1.78	**0.0**	-5.4	-4.89	-36.24	3.17	276.9	**1.6**	21.4	24.7	**1.7**
5.0	2.93	15.1	0.02	**6.2**	0.4	0.93	8.45	5.09	81.8	**4.7**	28.9	7.0	**7.8**
3.3	0.89	7.8	0.39	**3.7**	2.0	0.73	8.46	4.08	77.4	**2.3**	8.5	16.7	**5.1**
5.8	1.33	4.9	0.14	**5.0**	0.2	1.09	11.86	4.39	69.7	**5.9**	60.0	6.5	**3.7**
7.0	0.12	0.6	0.00	**7.4**	3.1	1.99	18.85	4.98	62.5	**4.4**	23.5	7.1	**4.7**
7.5	0.05	0.2	0.32	**6.5**	0.4	1.59	16.26	5.55	67.7	**5.8**	45.4	2.8	**5.3**
3.7	1.32	5.4	0.00	**7.7**	4.2	1.07	12.04	2.86	25.9	**7.2**	74.5	4.6	**7.4**
0.8	2.09	14.2	1.18	**4.2**	1.1	1.26	14.24	4.20	67.9	**1.5**	19.1	25.0	**3.7**
6.6	0.53	3.0	0.28	**5.6**	1.1	1.23	15.94	3.84	69.7	**5.0**	57.1	12.6	**6.1**
0.3	31.60	74.4	1.36	**0.0**	-3.9	-1.77	-12.45	2.58	200.4	**3.7**	61.3	25.7	**5.0**
2.6	2.03	14.4	0.62	**1.3**	0.4	0.28	3.04	3.45	86.7	**2.0**	27.8	23.0	**4.4**
2.9	2.01	15.9	0.90	**4.4**	1.1	0.62	7.38	5.20	62.7	**1.8**	17.7	20.3	**4.3**
4.4	1.25	11.0	1.35	**3.6**	2.8	0.57	7.31	3.75	54.0	**0.8**	15.7	36.1	**3.1**
1.7	3.25	22.5	0.72	**4.4**	1.8	0.82	9.46	4.96	74.1	**1.4**	15.7	25.6	**5.4**
5.3	0.65	4.8	0.09	**2.5**	0.7	0.21	2.19	3.08	70.2	**1.5**	17.2	25.8	**5.9**
0.3	12.59	133.4	8.69	**0.0**	-6.4	-3.80	-118.32	4.37	141.6	**0.6**	16.7	62.9	**3.3**
0.0	7.04	47.9	2.56	**2.7**	-2.0	-0.25	-2.42	4.57	60.8	**1.1**	19.4	32.2	**7.7**
0.0	15.78	124.2	2.25	**0.1**	-4.1	-0.87	-11.88	2.58	100.7	**0.8**	21.8	49.6	**2.2**
3.8	1.55	9.7	1.19	**3.7**	2.9	0.67	6.22	3.99	64.4	**2.0**	25.4	20.5	**6.7**
2.5	1.00	8.7	0.20	**6.5**	0.8	1.37	15.77	4.61	62.3	**1.0**	12.3	31.7	**5.7**
3.5	1.51	11.2	-0.21	**3.4**	0.7	0.48	5.71	3.72	86.5	**4.2**	25.0	8.5	**5.2**
0.1	9.56	36.0	6.28	**0.0**	-37.0	-7.85	-43.71	3.57	154.8	**1.6**	22.9	24.6	**5.3**
4.2	1.75	13.4	0.62	**4.7**	2.0	0.84	10.19	4.42	51.2	**1.6**	14.4	23.4	**4.7**
4.3	0.95	8.0	0.69	**2.9**	1.0	0.50	6.27	4.40	77.9	**1.4**	9.4	24.2	**4.1**
0.0	14.73	159.8	7.60	**0.0**	-14.4	-6.79	-83.89	3.05	151.9	**0.7**	17.6	55.1	**0.8**
4.4	0.79	4.5	0.07	**5.9**	7.6	1.16	9.32	4.21	65.7	**2.5**	23.6	17.2	**7.9**

Name	City	State	Rating	2008 Rating	2007 Rating	Total Assets ($Mil)	One Year Asset Growth	Asset Mix (As a % of Total Assets) Comm-ercial Loans	Cons-umer Loans	Home Mort-gages	Secur-ities	Capital-ization Index	Leverage Ratio	Risk-based Capital Ratio
▲ FIRST SOUTHERN STATE BK	STEVENSON	AL	**C**	C-	B-	340	4.25	3.2	7.8	17.4	27.0	**7.2**	9.1	14.5
▼ FIRST SOUTHWEST BANK	ALAMOSA	CO	**D-**	D	C-	239	-12.11	5.6	1.0	12.4	6.1	**6.3**	8.3	12.4
FIRST STAR BANK	BETHLEHEM	PA	**D+**	D+	C-	484	-20.64	1.1	0.8	23.4	31.2	**5.2**	7.2	13.3
FIRST STAR BANK SSB	BREMOND	TX	**B-**	C+	C+	193	2.40	3.3	6.2	40.1	23.4	**6.5**	8.5	16.8
FIRST STATE B&TC OF LARNE	LARNED	KS	**B+**	B+	A-	105	0.53	7.9	2.5	9.7	21.9	**10.0**	11.4	18.5
▲ FIRST STATE BK	CROSSETT	AR	**D+**	D+	C-	35	-11.91	9.1	11.0	20.1	27.9	**6.9**	8.9	16.8
▼ FIRST STATE BK	LONOKE	AR	**D-**	D+	B-	283	-12.24	3.9	0.8	15.1	11.2	**5.6**	7.6	12.3
FIRST STATE BK	RUSSELLVILLE	AR	**D+**	D	C+	192	-4.15	8.8	2.1	21.8	13.9	**8.1**	9.7	14.6
FIRST STATE BK	STOCKBRIDGE	GA	**E-**	E-	E	564	-8.25	1.9	0.9	7.7	12.0	**0.0**	2.7	4.4
FIRST STATE BK	WRENS	GA	**D-**	D-	D+	93	-13.12	6.1	6.8	25.4	10.6	**5.2**	7.2	12.0
FIRST STATE BK	BELMOND	IA	**B-**	C+	B	81	5.22	9.3	2.3	10.5	43.5	**10.0**	11.6	19.4
FIRST STATE BK	BRITT	IA	**A**	A-	B+	80	6.53	3.2	1.7	13.5	42.6	**10.0**	11.5	21.1
FIRST STATE BK	HAWARDEN	IA	**C**	C-	C	45	5.94	12.8	2.5	9.9	0.7	**5.7**	7.7	12.1
FIRST STATE BK	IDA GROVE	IA	**B-**	C+	C	119	0.98	6.3	4.1	7.2	33.8	**5.6**	8.5	11.4
FIRST STATE BK	LYNNVILLE	IA	**B-**	C+	C+	94	7.99	5.2	1.9	6.3	16.3	**7.9**	9.6	13.3
▼ FIRST STATE BK	MANCHESTER	IA	**B**	B	A-	144	5.96	10.5	3.1	9.8	33.7	**8.9**	10.3	15.8
FIRST STATE BK	NASHUA	IA	**B-**	B	B-	43	6.13	10.8	2.4	12.8	23.0	**7.6**	9.4	15.6
FIRST STATE BK	SIOUX RAPIDS	IA	**B+**	B+	B+	30	9.46	1.8	1.2	2.8	67.9	**10.0**	14.8	34.4
FIRST STATE BK	STUART	IA	**B-**	C+	C+	93	4.22	9.6	2.7	12.3	30.2	**6.0**	8.0	14.8
FIRST STATE BK	SUMNER	IA	**C+**	C+	B-	96	2.61	5.9	2.6	12.5	44.9	**7.6**	9.4	17.9
FIRST STATE BK	WEBSTER CITY	IA	**C**	C-	C-	251	-0.27	7.5	1.2	5.6	18.9	**5.5**	9.3	11.4
FIRST STATE BK	MENDOTA	IL	**B**	B-	C	611	16.98	5.7	1.5	44.3	11.1	**5.3**	7.3	12.0
FIRST STATE BK	MONTICELLO	IL	**B-**	C	B	223	1.00	5.3	3.4	22.5	25.5	**6.8**	8.8	14.4
FIRST STATE BK	NESS CITY	KS	**A-**	A-	A-	59	11.06	6.2	2.1	2.8	48.8	**10.0**	13.7	22.9
FIRST STATE BK	NORTON	KS	**B-**	C+	B-	274	2.92	11.3	3.0	3.4	43.3	**5.8**	7.8	13.1
FIRST STATE BK	IRVINGTON	KY	**A-**	A-	A-	142	1.06	4.1	4.5	34.1	26.6	**10.0**	11.7	24.6
FIRST STATE BK	HOLLY SPRINGS	MS	**C**	C	B+	101	-2.70	5.2	3.4	19.4	19.8	**10.0**	13.4	17.0
FIRST STATE BK	WAYNESBORO	MS	**B**	A-	A-	447	5.71	10.2	3.5	17.4	31.5	**9.0**	10.4	16.3
▲ FIRST STATE BK	BUXTON	ND	**D+**	C-	B-	139	6.35	8.0	1.7	16.7	5.7	**6.7**	9.6	12.3
FIRST STATE BK	BEAVER CITY	NE	**B**	B-	C-	48	3.57	6.9	6.7	1.4	31.6	**10.0**	15.1	21.1
FIRST STATE BK	FARNAM	NE	**C-**	D+	C	45	-7.47	13.3	3.8	7.7	24.6	**10.0**	14.4	21.7
FIRST STATE BK	GOTHENBURG	NE	**C-**	D+	D+	301	-9.00	9.2	1.2	6.2	26.2	**10.0**	11.9	16.3
FIRST STATE BK	HORDVILLE	NE	**B-**	B-	B-	29	7.73	8.2	1.5	7.4	15.7	**10.0**	12.3	16.3
▲ FIRST STATE BK	LINCOLN	NE	**C**	C	C	343	21.41	13.1	3.7	15.8	11.4	**4.6**	7.2	10.8
FIRST STATE BK	LOOMIS	NE	**B-**	C+	C	86	-3.41	9.0	6.4	8.4	12.7	**5.5**	8.0	11.4
FIRST STATE BK	RANDOLPH	NE	**A-**	A-	A-	44	14.35	2.4	2.6	6.4	7.1	**10.0**	14.7	17.7
FIRST STATE BK	SCOTTSBLUFF	NE	**B-**	C+	C+	220	8.71	8.2	2.2	10.0	12.4	**6.3**	8.3	12.8
▼ FIRST STATE BK	SHELTON	NE	**D-**	D-	D	30	-10.33	5.4	5.3	10.6	18.3	**7.9**	9.6	15.2
▼ FIRST STATE BK	CRANFORD	NJ	**E-**	E+	E	229	-12.83	4.5	14.7	8.7	5.1	**0.4**	4.2	6.7
FIRST STATE BK	SOCORRO	NM	**B**	B-	C+	119	-6.74	0.5	0.9	9.0	81.9	**7.3**	9.2	35.5
FIRST STATE BK	WINCHESTER	OH	**B**	B-	B-	216	8.41	3.0	7.8	23.7	22.8	**6.7**	8.8	15.5
FIRST STATE BK	ANADARKO	OK	**A**	A	A	85	9.03	3.5	4.4	4.8	53.1	**10.0**	16.3	36.6
FIRST STATE BK	BOISE CITY	OK	**D+**	C	C	54	12.85	1.7	9.9	4.7	13.4	**7.1**	9.1	12.8
FIRST STATE BK	CANUTE	OK	**D**	C-	C+	91	27.35	36.8	1.4	11.1	7.2	**6.4**	9.1	12.1
▼ FIRST STATE BK	COMMERCE	OK	**D+**	C-	E+	13	-5.71	11.6	13.7	21.5	21.0	**6.6**	8.6	14.0
▼ FIRST STATE BK	ELMORE CITY	OK	**D+**	C	C	8	-6.05	6.2	6.0	10.5	25.7	**6.1**	8.1	19.3
▼ FIRST STATE BK	FAIRFAX	OK	**D+**	C-	C-	38	-3.44	13.2	6.2	3.8	41.5	**10.0**	14.2	26.4
▼ FIRST STATE BK	GRANDFIELD	OK	**D+**	C	D+	31	6.28	1.4	4.5	12.8	40.8	**5.1**	7.1	14.1
FIRST STATE BK	NOBLE	OK	**D+**	D	D+	54	5.28	3.9	11.4	14.6	27.4	**5.5**	7.5	12.3
FIRST STATE BK	RYAN	OK	**D**	D+	C-	47	4.78	6.8	18.4	22.5	0.1	**8.0**	9.6	15.0
FIRST STATE BK	TAHLEQUAH	OK	**D-**	D+	D+	89	-3.81	3.6	1.0	12.3	8.6	**7.0**	9.3	12.5
▼ FIRST STATE BK	VALLIANT	OK	**D**	C-	C	54	-7.49	9.9	42.5	17.0	4.9	**6.7**	8.7	13.2
FIRST STATE BK	WATONGA	OK	**C-**	B-	B+	42	5.72	7.9	9.6	5.9	31.4	**8.6**	10.1	17.0
FIRST STATE BK	WAYNOKA	OK	**C+**	C+	C	20	-0.78	4.3	4.7	8.3	58.1	**10.0**	13.7	33.2
FIRST STATE BK	YUKON	OK	**C-**	C	C-	15	-0.30	18.2	13.5	26.2	0.0	**7.2**	9.1	12.9
FIRST STATE BK	ARMOUR	SD	**B**	B+	B+	91	7.46	6.8	4.6	2.1	21.4	**5.0**	7.6	11.0
▼ FIRST STATE BK	WILMOT	SD	**D+**	D+	D+	37	-6.75	8.8	4.3	0.5	35.1	**6.9**	8.9	13.1
▲ FIRST STATE BK	UNION CITY	TN	**C-**	D	D+	1,477	5.34	7.4	8.0	15.7	25.4	**7.1**	9.0	14.2
FIRST STATE BK	ABERNATHY	TX	**C+**	C+	C-	22	-5.61	2.7	9.6	2.7	9.1	**7.4**	9.3	17.2
FIRST STATE BK	ABILENE	TX	**C-**	C	C-	33	-1.14	11.2	5.8	10.0	4.7	**5.0**	7.0	14.0

Asset Quality Index	Non-Performing Loans as a % of Total Loans	Non-Performing Loans as a % of Capital	Net Charge-offs Avg Loans	Profitability Index	Net Income ($Mil)	Return on Assets (R.O.A.)	Return on Equity (R.O.E.)	Net Interest Spread	Overhead Efficiency Ratio	Liquidity Index	Liquidity Ratio	Hot Money Ratio	Stability Index
3.2	1.54	9.4	1.56	2.9	2.0	0.59	6.18	4.03	62.4	1.8	21.8	22.1	3.5
0.0	6.54	46.0	1.09	0.8	-0.8	-0.31	-3.10	3.79	89.5	1.3	7.4	25.1	5.2
3.1	4.25	23.5	0.01	1.6	-1.1	-0.21	-3.28	1.45	94.6	3.6	34.7	15.1	3.0
6.3	0.97	6.7	0.07	7.3	3.1	1.60	19.79	4.38	59.4	1.5	11.2	23.3	5.3
7.8	0.08	0.4	0.26	4.5	1.0	1.01	8.53	4.21	66.3	3.1	25.3	14.9	6.9
3.5	1.46	7.2	0.64	1.7	-0.2	-0.47	-5.75	4.24	84.8	2.2	37.8	30.4	4.3
0.0	1.73	13.1	4.62	0.0	-4.9	-1.63	-18.10	3.84	82.8	1.6	17.0	24.0	3.2
1.8	3.81	24.5	0.19	4.0	1.2	0.61	6.20	3.99	68.2	1.7	13.8	21.8	4.1
0.0	23.27	342.4	0.89	0.0	-6.2	-1.05	-29.21	1.91	165.0	1.1	13.9	29.5	1.4
0.0	14.86	108.2	2.05	0.0	-2.0	-2.05	-23.99	3.92	123.0	1.7	22.6	23.2	1.8
4.0	4.68	18.8	0.93	5.2	0.9	1.22	9.58	4.12	50.7	5.8	48.1	6.5	5.9
7.9	0.20	0.8	-0.04	8.7	1.3	1.65	13.85	4.17	39.6	3.4	49.0	19.8	7.8
6.4	0.22	2.1	-0.03	4.7	0.5	1.05	12.70	3.56	67.6	3.7	22.3	11.5	4.3
4.1	0.09	0.6	0.73	5.9	1.9	1.62	18.57	4.73	59.2	2.9	38.2	20.0	5.3
4.3	0.54	3.6	0.39	4.8	0.9	0.99	9.77	4.57	56.8	1.6	22.2	24.4	4.1
4.3	2.60	12.6	0.28	5.6	1.8	1.27	11.93	3.64	58.0	3.8	48.7	18.1	6.7
5.0	1.53	8.5	0.49	5.1	0.4	0.88	8.59	2.98	53.3	2.2	36.8	28.2	6.0
9.9	0.15	0.3	-0.28	4.9	0.3	0.99	6.49	3.59	70.1	6.6	84.6	8.6	8.1
8.7	0.00	0.0	0.42	3.7	0.6	0.69	8.44	3.77	74.3	4.3	42.9	13.8	5.2
6.5	0.04	0.2	0.79	4.8	0.9	0.93	8.30	3.85	60.7	3.3	47.8	19.6	5.3
5.6	0.12	0.9	0.14	7.6	3.4	1.32	12.72	3.93	60.5	3.1	14.5	13.6	5.0
6.4	0.38	3.7	1.14	7.7	6.0	1.31	16.23	3.91	69.8	0.5	3.5	39.4	5.1
4.3	1.14	7.6	0.23	4.7	2.4	1.07	10.68	4.20	66.6	1.7	16.1	21.6	5.2
8.9	0.18	0.5	0.05	7.0	0.9	1.65	10.97	4.70	55.7	4.6	44.2	12.5	9.1
4.3	1.13	6.7	0.14	6.8	4.7	1.74	17.34	4.17	53.4	1.7	18.7	22.1	5.0
8.2	0.18	0.9	0.11	9.4	2.1	1.53	12.75	4.61	58.7	4.7	29.0	7.4	8.3
1.8	4.97	22.3	0.90	1.9	-0.4	-0.39	-3.22	3.61	94.8	1.2	16.6	29.1	5.8
4.8	1.75	9.1	0.88	4.5	3.6	0.86	7.94	4.26	64.8	1.6	21.1	24.4	7.1
1.4	2.96	23.7	0.00	5.6	1.7	1.27	13.16	4.47	64.9	0.7	7.1	34.0	6.8
6.9	0.92	3.0	0.51	5.6	0.7	1.41	8.33	3.22	53.8	3.3	45.7	19.4	7.7
3.5	2.59	9.6	0.70	4.6	0.3	0.72	4.14	4.29	69.6	2.7	30.4	18.3	5.0
0.9	7.37	33.4	1.92	4.5	2.6	0.85	6.88	4.17	48.6	1.3	19.6	29.5	5.2
7.3	0.21	1.1	-0.39	3.3	0.1	0.42	3.37	3.32	82.2	4.0	25.9	10.1	7.6
3.4	1.15	10.7	0.30	4.6	3.2	1.00	9.47	4.00	65.5	2.9	12.2	14.2	7.2
5.8	0.03	0.3	0.07	7.7	1.2	1.33	13.05	4.31	53.7	2.2	12.1	17.7	5.7
8.3	0.02	0.1	0.13	6.8	0.6	1.60	10.56	3.62	55.3	5.9	47.5	5.7	9.4
4.5	0.80	5.5	0.87	7.7	3.6	1.64	19.43	4.37	49.7	2.3	28.7	19.9	6.8
0.1	9.47	52.1	2.27	1.1	0.0	0.01	0.10	3.53	97.8	2.4	22.6	17.6	3.6
0.0	4.40	57.9	2.95	0.0	-4.4	-1.72	-33.65	3.50	92.2	1.3	20.8	28.9	0.0
10.0	0.52	0.7	1.35	5.3	1.2	0.98	11.90	4.58	68.7	5.0	38.5	9.6	4.8
7.8	0.20	1.2	0.16	6.9	2.4	1.16	11.82	4.44	57.4	3.6	20.8	11.4	6.0
8.8	1.33	2.4	0.35	6.3	1.2	1.51	8.55	3.92	63.3	4.9	50.2	12.3	9.7
1.7	2.40	17.4	0.25	6.1	0.6	1.26	13.76	4.56	63.9	1.4	20.1	27.9	4.2
5.7	0.05	0.4	0.12	0.4	-0.2	-0.23	-2.31	3.89	99.7	2.0	9.3	18.3	5.9
6.5	0.50	3.0	1.07	4.0	0.1	0.88	10.08	6.06	72.2	3.7	33.8	12.2	3.0
9.0	0.00	0.0	0.00	1.0	0.0	-0.46	-5.32	4.36	108.9	7.0	65.1	0.0	4.4
4.5	4.05	13.5	0.86	0.0	-0.2	-0.56	-3.72	3.53	109.0	2.7	38.6	23.4	6.0
2.6	3.07	20.5	-0.02	5.4	0.4	1.25	14.59	4.13	69.1	2.6	38.6	24.0	4.7
2.5	3.56	18.7	0.75	4.0	0.4	0.79	9.80	5.01	82.4	3.0	39.1	19.6	3.7
0.8	3.16	23.4	1.62	4.4	0.3	0.61	6.32	4.63	51.5	1.0	23.9	35.7	4.6
0.0	4.36	31.9	0.03	3.7	0.4	0.46	5.22	3.50	73.3	0.8	15.5	38.1	5.7
1.0	3.90	26.1	3.05	3.2	-0.4	-0.60	-6.38	6.94	53.0	0.8	18.6	38.8	7.0
1.4	3.56	19.2	0.10	8.8	0.7	1.75	15.70	5.16	61.6	2.7	30.1	18.4	8.8
5.8	2.79	5.9	0.57	3.5	0.1	0.54	3.74	4.48	83.9	5.4	71.5	11.7	6.7
7.5	0.18	1.5	0.00	4.0	0.1	0.75	8.12	5.54	88.2	1.2	16.3	28.0	3.7
6.8	0.02	0.2	0.04	8.3	1.6	1.89	23.10	4.36	61.5	3.6	12.1	10.5	6.6
2.2	3.72	17.8	2.31	0.5	-0.3	-0.70	-8.08	4.78	78.1	2.3	33.7	24.8	2.9
3.8	1.22	7.9	1.28	2.5	8.0	0.55	5.85	3.90	70.8	1.3	22.8	37.4	5.0
3.4	1.17	5.4	0.02	7.5	0.4	1.72	17.43	5.03	69.9	2.8	38.4	18.3	8.1
8.0	0.00	0.0	0.10	3.7	0.2	0.62	7.04	3.70	79.1	3.2	42.3	19.6	5.4

Name	City	State	Rating	2008 Rating	2007 Rating	Total Assets ($Mil)	One Year Asset Growth	Asset Mix (As a % of Total Assets) Commercial Loans	Consumer Loans	Home Mortgages	Securities	Capitalization Index	Leverage Ratio	Risk-based Capital Ratio
▼ FIRST STATE BK	ATHENS	TX	B+	A-	B+	330	-2.27	5.6	5.4	19.2	21.2	9.0	10.4	18.5
FIRST STATE BK	AVINGER	TX	B	B	B-	22	-4.75	3.8	2.1	18.0	0.0	5.0	7.0	16.1
FIRST STATE BK	BEDIAS	TX	B-	B-	B+	130	13.53	10.5	7.4	11.2	27.3	8.4	10.1	13.6
▼ FIRST STATE BK	CHICO	TX	B-	B-	B-	215	4.98	15.0	11.4	14.5	18.2	5.3	7.3	11.4
FIRST STATE BK	CLUTE	TX	B-	B-	B	118	1.42	14.7	13.5	8.9	22.8	8.8	10.2	17.2
FIRST STATE BK	COLUMBUS	TX	A	A	A	100	1.51	2.5	3.4	3.9	29.9	10.0	15.6	44.5
FIRST STATE BK	GAINESVILLE	TX	C+	B-	B-	488	6.87	6.4	3.1	10.6	34.7	5.2	7.2	13.6
FIRST STATE BK	GRAHAM	TX	B	B+	B+	124	2.10	9.2	8.0	19.4	0.0	6.5	8.5	15.0
▼ FIRST STATE BK	HALLSVILLE	TX	C-	C	C	38	1.35	1.3	5.8	19.7	53.5	6.9	8.9	23.2
▼ FIRST STATE BK	HEMPHILL	TX	C	B-	B-	51	1.88	2.8	1.9	2.1	59.3	10.0	14.8	33.7
FIRST STATE BK	JUNCTION	TX	B-	C+	C+	35	-11.07	4.0	4.9	18.3	41.5	8.3	9.9	18.0
FIRST STATE BK	LOUISE	TX	B	B	B	264	15.42	6.8	7.8	16.2	34.9	5.2	7.2	13.1
▼ FIRST STATE BK	MESQUITE	TX	D+	C	B	227	2.86	12.3	4.1	17.0	8.1	10.0	11.0	18.8
FIRST STATE BK	NEW BRAUNFELS	TX	B	B+	B	281	14.07	10.4	2.2	11.4	5.5	7.5	9.3	13.2
FIRST STATE BK	OVERTON	TX	B+	B+	B-	46	1.97	12.9	2.3	8.2	36.0	10.0	17.1	42.5
FIRST STATE BK	RICE	TX	D	D+	D+	115	47.70	12.0	6.2	8.4	38.8	9.1	10.4	17.7
FIRST STATE BK	SHALLOWATER	TX	B+	B+	B+	48	-12.20	8.2	3.5	6.7	10.2	10.0	14.6	27.7
FIRST STATE BK	SPEARMAN	TX	B-	B+	B+	108	7.11	7.6	1.8	1.2	39.1	6.9	8.9	15.4
▲ FIRST STATE BK	STRATFORD	TX	A-	B	B+	179	4.98	10.2	2.6	8.1	22.9	8.3	9.8	15.8
FIRST STATE BK	THREE RIVERS	TX	A-	A-	B+	108	2.20	9.4	5.3	6.8	27.1	10.0	11.2	28.1
FIRST STATE BK	VAN	TX	B+	B+	B+	43	0.21	5.4	17.2	35.1	9.0	10.0	15.4	26.1
FIRST STATE BK	YOAKUM	TX	A	A	A	122	4.61	6.0	9.7	19.2	29.2	10.0	11.4	23.5
FIRST STATE BK	DANVILLE	VA	E-	E-	D-	35	25.69	5.8	6.1	17.1	14.6	0.1	3.3	6.3
FIRST STATE BK	NEW LONDON	WI	D-	D-	C-	305	-9.58	4.7	1.1	9.7	20.9	8.7	10.1	16.0
FIRST STATE BK	BARBOURSVILLE	WV	D+	D	D+	248	12.85	11.5	2.9	29.9	5.3	6.3	8.3	13.3
FIRST STATE BK	WHEATLAND	WY	B-	B-	B-	271	6.48	9.8	5.3	6.4	24.0	5.9	7.9	13.0
FIRST STATE BK & TRUST	TONGANOXIE	KS	D-	D-	D+	290	-9.81	4.3	3.6	23.3	6.3	4.0	6.0	11.2
FIRST STATE BK & TRUST	BAYPORT	MN	C+	C+	C+	206	-0.16	8.4	5.2	25.9	29.9	5.7	7.7	14.4
▼ FIRST STATE BK & TRUST CO	FREMONT	NE	D+	C+	B-	203	-9.97	18.8	3.2	11.6	13.2	6.2	8.2	12.3
FIRST STATE BK & TRUST CO	CARTHAGE	TX	A	A	A	445	9.00	1.9	7.3	12.2	57.8	10.0	12.5	30.9
FIRST STATE BK & TRUST CO	CARUTHERSVILLE	MO	B	B	B	338	1.92	4.3	4.9	20.4	12.4	8.9	10.2	17.5
▼ FIRST STATE BK BOURBON IN	BOURBON	IN	B	B+	B+	80	-2.78	4.9	1.4	21.4	32.7	10.0	18.8	43.9
FIRST STATE BK CAMPBELL H	CAMPBELL HILL	IL	C+	C	C	95	4.80	6.1	4.6	28.6	24.1	6.1	8.1	13.4
▲ FIRST STATE BK CENTRAL TE	AUSTIN	TX	C	C-	B	1,068	8.12	11.0	2.1	3.9	33.5	9.1	10.4	15.7
FIRST STATE BK FLORIDA KE	KEY WEST	FL	D-	D	D+	777	-8.49	2.1	1.0	26.0	33.6	5.4	7.4	14.3
FIRST STATE BK IN TEMPLE	TEMPLE	OK	B	B	B	22	-9.92	5.6	6.0	10.0	40.6	10.0	18.7	38.3
FIRST STATE BK IN TUSCOLA	TUSCOLA	TX	C-	C	D+	19	-1.47	4.1	7.4	7.3	24.6	7.4	9.3	20.2
FIRST STATE BK KIOWA KANS	KIOWA	KS	B	B+	B+	55	20.28	2.8	1.9	4.5	27.6	7.5	9.3	14.9
FIRST STATE BK MINERAL WE	MINERAL WELLS	TX	A-	A-	B+	84	10.26	7.0	3.8	17.2	9.4	10.0	11.9	22.5
FIRST STATE BK MINNESOTA	LE ROY	MN	C+	B-	C+	58	-1.15	10.2	2.9	5.3	30.9	6.5	8.5	14.6
FIRST STATE BK OF ALEXAND	ALEXANDRIA	MN	D-	C-	C	116	3.36	12.0	3.7	13.8	11.7	6.0	8.5	11.7
FIRST STATE BK OF ARCADIA	ARCADIA	FL	C-	C	B-	129	-6.12	2.7	3.1	25.9	19.9	6.7	8.7	13.6
FIRST STATE BK OF ASHBY	ASHBY	MN	D+	C	C-	30	-4.45	8.1	4.7	20.2	12.8	5.4	7.4	14.1
▲ FIRST STATE BK OF BEECHER	BEECHER CITY	IL	B-	B	B	57	12.10	9.7	14.6	21.7	13.8	10.0	12.5	17.8
FIRST STATE BK OF BEN WHE	BEN WHEELER	TX	B	B	B	103	8.53	5.9	6.3	12.1	54.1	9.3	10.6	23.2
▲ FIRST STATE BK OF BIGFORK	BIGFORK	MN	C	C	D+	43	0.04	5.2	4.2	39.5	10.3	9.6	10.8	20.5
FIRST STATE BK OF BLAKELY	BLAKELY	GA	B+	B-	A-	321	9.83	8.2	3.4	16.9	7.3	10.0	11.0	17.0
FIRST STATE BK OF BLOOMIN	BLOOMINGTON	IL	C+	C	B	93	-3.02	8.4	1.4	16.0	26.3	6.4	8.4	13.5
FIRST STATE BK OF	BROWNSBORO	TX	C	C+	C	89	-2.61	6.5	10.9	14.3	32.7	6.6	8.6	15.0
FIRST STATE BK OF BURLING	BURLINGAME	KS	E-	E-	E-	29	-17.73	16.1	4.2	22.5	15.6	0.1	3.2	6.3
FIRST STATE BK OF BURNET	BURNET	TX	A+	A+	A+	186	5.11	6.2	4.3	11.1	54.2	10.0	12.1	26.7
FIRST STATE BK OF CANDO	CANDO	ND	D-	D	C+	48	-0.66	6.1	6.2	3.1	23.5	6.1	8.1	12.3
FIRST STATE BK OF CLAREMO	GROTON	SD	B+	B+	A-	49	2.08	13.3	4.2	0.5	16.9	9.7	11.1	14.8
FIRST STATE BK OF CLEARBR	CLEARBROOK	MN	B	B	B-	35	6.99	6.2	7.0	7.6	30.2	8.2	9.8	17.1
FIRST STATE BK OF COLFAX	COLFAX	IA	A	A	A	66	-2.36	2.0	1.4	23.4	35.7	10.0	12.0	19.0
FIRST STATE BK OF COLORAD	HOTCHKISS	CO	C+	C	C-	193	246.29	3.7	2.2	16.9	16.1	10.0	11.1	16.4
FIRST STATE BK OF DE QUEE	DE QUEEN	AR	C+	C+	C	169	12.51	10.3	7.9	18.4	23.7	6.1	8.1	13.4
FIRST STATE BK OF DECATUR	DECATUR	MI	B	B-	B	58	6.29	6.1	2.9	42.3	27.0	10.0	16.9	35.9
FIRST STATE BK OF DEKALB	FORT PAYNE	AL	C+	B-	B+	95	2.87	8.2	6.3	21.3	21.8	10.0	14.3	20.1
▲ FIRST STATE BK OF DIX	DIX	IL	D+	D+	D+	44	0.97	5.0	7.5	23.8	14.0	5.1	7.1	13.4

Asset Quality Index	Non-Performing Loans as a % of Total Loans	Non-Performing Loans as a % of Capital	Net Charge-offs Avg Loans	Profitability Index	Net Income ($Mil)	Return on Assets (R.O.A.)	Return on Equity (R.O.E.)	Net Interest Spread	Overhead Efficiency Ratio	Liquidity Index	Liquidity Ratio	Hot Money Ratio	Stability Index
4.6	0.89	4.7	0.12	**9.1**	4.9	1.47	13.00	4.90	58.0	**3.3**	21.5	13.0	**7.4**
9.0	0.00	0.0	0.00	**5.9**	0.3	1.33	19.57	3.01	57.2	**2.4**	52.1	30.1	**6.7**
4.5	0.87	5.3	0.87	**8.3**	2.3	1.95	18.08	4.91	42.3	**1.5**	33.5	45.9	**6.5**
5.0	1.00	8.6	1.71	**4.4**	1.9	0.86	11.28	4.81	57.4	**1.1**	11.2	29.9	**5.6**
4.5	1.58	7.7	0.99	**3.6**	0.5	0.45	4.14	4.27	74.7	**3.2**	38.9	18.7	**6.1**
9.7	0.07	0.1	-0.01	**8.9**	2.2	2.22	14.07	3.60	47.4	**3.5**	65.1	29.4	**9.2**
5.1	1.02	6.4	0.62	**4.9**	5.0	1.06	12.53	4.53	71.2	**3.6**	35.4	15.5	**5.3**
7.3	0.10	0.6	0.06	**5.2**	1.5	1.23	14.25	3.42	65.9	**2.2**	42.7	34.2	**6.0**
8.8	0.03	0.1	0.00	**2.1**	0.1	0.36	3.95	3.49	95.9	**3.7**	63.8	21.6	**4.9**
8.0	0.47	0.4	-0.01	**1.8**	0.1	0.22	1.40	1.84	96.9	**4.2**	82.4	22.1	**6.9**
6.2	1.10	4.9	-0.01	**6.4**	0.3	0.94	9.14	5.84	69.1	**3.9**	16.6	9.7	**5.7**
5.2	0.93	6.9	0.12	**7.9**	4.7	1.90	22.86	5.07	64.8	**3.3**	33.3	16.4	**6.0**
2.6	5.92	23.7	3.71	**0.3**	-3.7	-1.63	-13.35	4.77	71.3	**5.1**	38.2	8.6	**5.3**
5.2	0.98	7.1	0.25	**6.5**	4.0	1.52	15.61	4.74	64.1	**2.2**	26.6	19.5	**6.4**
9.3	0.04	0.1	0.09	**2.7**	0.2	0.36	1.90	3.32	89.1	**4.8**	69.8	15.8	**8.0**
4.2	1.88	8.7	0.02	**1.0**	0.3	0.34	2.64	3.16	88.2	**2.5**	33.3	20.8	**6.0**
7.2	0.14	0.5	0.43	**6.2**	0.6	1.30	7.38	4.49	69.8	**1.9**	31.2	27.2	**7.7**
4.1	2.49	12.7	0.00	**5.6**	1.3	1.29	13.83	3.60	64.9	**1.7**	33.3	33.6	**6.5**
8.3	0.00	0.0	0.02	**6.0**	2.5	1.41	13.43	4.00	66.5	**2.8**	31.4	18.1	**7.8**
6.2	2.91	9.8	-0.04	**5.6**	1.4	1.34	10.51	3.56	65.0	**2.4**	40.3	29.4	**7.6**
7.7	0.00	0.0	0.14	**6.7**	0.5	1.09	7.25	4.54	65.6	**1.6**	22.4	25.7	**8.6**
7.8	0.70	2.6	0.13	**6.2**	1.7	1.38	11.14	3.97	63.2	**4.7**	50.4	14.3	**8.9**
0.0	4.93	73.4	0.81	**1.5**	-0.4	-1.21	-25.75	4.75	127.1	**0.7**	10.1	40.2	**0.8**
1.5	6.58	33.2	2.11	**0.2**	-1.8	-0.57	-5.22	3.84	89.0	**2.4**	34.4	23.0	**4.5**
1.6	2.41	20.1	0.82	**7.2**	3.9	1.66	20.35	4.47	63.0	**0.7**	17.9	52.7	**6.2**
6.6	0.17	1.2	0.09	**5.5**	2.6	0.99	12.47	3.72	57.8	**1.2**	19.6	30.4	**5.0**
0.3	4.10	37.8	2.57	**0.0**	-4.5	-1.44	-18.24	4.07	105.6	**2.6**	10.3	15.5	**3.0**
4.7	0.98	6.7	0.77	**3.5**	1.4	0.67	8.16	4.14	77.1	**2.5**	32.3	19.9	**4.0**
2.4	2.75	19.9	2.58	**3.4**	0.3	0.13	1.54	4.08	58.4	**2.2**	14.5	17.8	**5.4**
8.8	0.19	0.5	0.17	**8.3**	6.2	1.50	10.72	4.05	46.6	**1.2**	29.1	45.6	**7.3**
5.2	1.08	6.2	0.32	**5.0**	3.0	0.92	8.91	4.35	65.3	**1.9**	23.2	20.4	**6.2**
9.6	0.28	0.7	0.04	**4.1**	0.6	0.73	2.54	4.11	73.4	**5.4**	61.9	11.5	**7.3**
4.6	1.35	9.9	0.08	**4.5**	0.7	0.75	8.42	4.32	65.1	**2.9**	26.3	15.9	**4.7**
3.2	2.50	12.2	0.36	**4.0**	8.1	0.80	6.95	4.37	67.4	**2.2**	28.0	29.2	**8.7**
0.3	6.52	43.3	2.82	**0.3**	-11.1	-1.30	-19.41	2.98	79.3	**2.3**	13.8	17.6	**3.2**
6.3	2.10	5.8	0.49	**4.9**	0.2	0.85	4.27	5.77	79.1	**0.9**	25.5	34.8	**7.4**
7.2	0.02	0.1	0.58	**3.9**	0.2	0.79	8.27	4.46	83.7	**5.2**	50.2	8.7	**5.8**
7.5	0.12	0.7	0.00	**5.3**	0.4	0.82	8.11	3.94	60.8	**1.8**	27.3	25.8	**6.3**
6.0	1.84	8.1	0.14	**5.3**	1.0	1.24	10.26	4.24	71.4	**3.4**	41.4	18.0	**7.3**
6.0	0.72	4.4	0.30	**5.2**	0.7	1.15	13.12	4.35	67.7	**6.2**	38.5	1.0	**5.0**
0.3	4.00	33.5	0.29	**5.3**	0.9	0.82	5.29	4.37	63.1	**2.9**	17.9	14.8	**5.8**
3.6	2.25	15.4	1.10	**5.3**	1.4	1.04	12.17	5.28	62.0	**1.7**	23.9	24.4	**4.9**
5.3	1.24	8.5	0.32	**3.2**	0.2	0.64	8.76	3.40	78.4	**4.0**	34.5	13.1	**5.0**
3.6	2.67	15.0	1.17	**8.5**	0.9	1.70	12.84	5.23	49.6	**1.7**	10.1	20.0	**9.1**
5.3	1.84	6.6	0.41	**7.5**	2.1	2.08	19.91	4.24	54.9	**2.3**	45.1	35.2	**6.2**
2.9	3.25	19.0	0.35	**4.1**	0.2	0.56	5.12	4.92	78.8	**5.0**	30.0	5.8	**6.2**
7.9	0.38	2.2	0.47	**5.0**	2.6	0.83	7.21	3.92	62.3	**0.9**	24.5	52.7	**6.0**
6.5	0.61	4.2	0.02	**3.8**	1.0	1.04	10.68	3.91	72.4	**0.9**	22.1	39.8	**4.3**
3.2	2.76	16.4	0.11	**5.4**	1.3	1.43	17.39	4.59	73.0	**1.8**	25.4	22.8	**4.4**
0.3	1.70	23.7	2.45	**0.0**	-0.3	-0.80	-23.36	3.66	98.7	**1.3**	15.3	27.4	**0.0**
8.0	1.14	3.6	0.59	**8.6**	3.4	1.88	13.50	4.44	55.6	**3.4**	56.8	26.2	**9.5**
1.3	1.95	14.5	1.92	**0.9**	-0.3	-0.63	-7.20	4.01	87.7	**3.4**	19.3	12.5	**3.8**
6.7	0.01	0.1	0.17	**6.2**	0.7	1.33	10.65	5.12	70.5	**3.8**	25.9	11.5	**9.4**
6.3	1.14	5.8	-0.01	**6.1**	0.5	1.40	13.52	4.14	67.9	**4.7**	37.5	10.7	**7.9**
4.9	4.01	17.5	0.01	**10.0**	1.8	2.63	18.65	4.96	32.7	**4.6**	45.8	12.9	**8.8**
3.4	3.52	19.1	1.06	**4.4**	1.0	0.64	5.44	5.66	71.1	**2.6**	19.5	16.2	**6.8**
5.2	0.66	5.0	0.34	**4.2**	1.6	0.99	12.05	4.07	61.8	**0.7**	13.0	46.0	**3.7**
4.6	4.12	13.8	0.55	**4.5**	0.5	0.90	5.23	3.99	67.6	**3.0**	45.0	22.0	**7.4**
2.0	6.54	26.4	0.34	**3.4**	0.3	0.33	2.19	3.86	85.0	**1.2**	18.1	29.8	**7.1**
5.5	0.53	3.7	0.90	**3.4**	0.3	0.66	8.87	3.79	74.1	**2.8**	41.4	23.5	**3.0**

Name	City	State	Rating	2008 Rating	2007 Rating	Total Assets ($Mil)	One Year Asset Growth	Asset Mix (As a % of Total Assets) Comm-ercial Loans	Cons-umer Loans	Home Mort-gages	Secur-ities	Capital-ization Index	Leverage Ratio	Risk-based Capital Ratio
▼ FIRST STATE BK OF DONGOLA	DONGOLA	IL	**C-**	C	C	20	7.63	2.3	16.8	50.6	4.4	**9.1**	10.4	16.9
▲ FIRST STATE BK OF EAST DE	SAINT CLAIR SHORES	MI	**D**	D-	D-	585	-3.77	6.1	0.5	20.5	24.6	**7.1**	9.1	18.6
FIRST STATE BK OF FERTILE	FERTILE	MN	**B-**	B-	B	33	1.22	8.3	7.0	4.4	34.0	**10.0**	15.4	27.7
FIRST STATE BK OF FORREST	FORREST	IL	**B**	C+	C+	61	-3.38	6.4	4.7	43.6	6.1	**7.4**	9.3	14.5
FIRST STATE BK OF FORSYTH	FORSYTH	MT	**B**	B+	B	104	15.80	2.8	5.2	9.2	49.0	**7.2**	9.1	18.6
FIRST STATE BK OF FOUNTAI	FOUNTAIN	MN	**C+**	B-	C+	32	-3.24	4.7	2.6	18.7	15.9	**10.0**	11.6	19.7
FIRST STATE BK OF GOLVA	GOLVA	ND	**B**	B	B-	56	6.34	7.8	2.3	3.1	31.4	**6.7**	8.7	15.0
FIRST STATE BK OF GROVE C	GROVE CITY	MN	**B-**	B	B+	23	9.01	9.6	5.1	9.9	5.2	**10.0**	17.4	29.8
FIRST STATE BK OF HARVEY	HARVEY	ND	**C+**	C+	B-	67	1.87	7.8	2.7	3.8	47.8	**7.7**	9.5	19.9
FIRST STATE BK OF HEALY	HEALY	KS	**B**	C+	B	65	4.17	14.6	1.0	1.8	35.0	**10.0**	18.3	23.1
FIRST STATE BK OF ILLINOI	LA HARPE	IL	**C-**	D+	C-	252	12.17	12.2	2.1	10.7	15.2	**5.9**	8.5	11.7
FIRST STATE BK OF JOPLIN	JOPLIN	MO	**A-**	A-	B+	172	-3.71	10.7	1.8	17.9	27.7	**8.9**	10.3	17.4
▲ FIRST STATE BK OF KANSAS	KANSAS CITY	KS	**D**	D+	C	77	7.28	23.2	3.5	8.4	19.9	**9.3**	10.5	14.9
FIRST STATE BK OF KENSING	KENSINGTON	MN	**C-**	D	E+	53	-6.89	4.9	2.0	8.8	16.5	**7.7**	9.4	14.8
FIRST STATE BK OF KIESTER	KIESTER	MN	**E-**	E-	D-	17	-14.00	14.5	1.8	5.5	8.2	**4.0**	6.0	10.8
FIRST STATE BK OF LE CENT	LE CENTER	MN	**B-**	B-	B-	65	2.50	17.8	7.9	21.8	16.3	**8.9**	10.2	15.3
FIRST STATE BK OF LIVINGS	LIVINGSTON	TX	**A-**	A	A-	280	3.49	3.3	6.3	5.8	41.5	**10.0**	12.9	27.2
FIRST STATE BK OF MALTA	MALTA	MT	**A-**	A	A	119	4.32	6.1	3.0	1.1	41.1	**10.0**	14.0	27.1
FIRST STATE BK OF MAPLETO	MAPLETON	IA	**B**	B	B+	44	-5.13	11.0	5.6	13.8	8.5	**5.7**	7.7	12.6
FIRST STATE BK OF MIAMI T	MIAMI	TX	**D+**	C-	C-	40	12.01	15.2	15.3	7.7	11.3	**4.2**	7.0	10.6
FIRST STATE BK OF MIDDLEB	MIDDLEBURY	IN	**D+**	D+	D+	390	2.98	11.7	2.4	24.2	16.0	**6.8**	8.8	13.6
▼ FIRST STATE BK OF MOBEETI	MOBEETIE	TX	**C-**	C	C	96	17.18	4.5	3.1	1.8	51.0	**5.1**	7.1	20.5
▲ FIRST STATE BK OF MUNICH	MUNICH	ND	**B**	B	B-	104	4.90	5.0	2.6	3.9	13.5	**8.5**	10.1	13.8
▲ FIRST STATE BK OF	MURDOCK	MN	**C-**	D	C	9	-3.03	4.5	5.1	16.1	4.5	**10.0**	11.6	16.0
FIRST STATE BK OF NEWCAST	NEWCASTLE	WY	**A+**	A+	A+	137	4.82	6.6	8.6	8.7	61.2	**10.0**	11.6	25.2
▲ FIRST STATE BK OF NORTH D	ARTHUR	ND	**D+**	C-	B-	278	34.79	8.8	2.9	4.4	6.9	**3.6**	10.3	10.3
▼ FIRST STATE BK OF	HUNTSVILLE	AR	**C**	B-	B-	80	8.71	8.7	1.3	12.7	10.1	**10.0**	13.4	18.7
FIRST STATE BK OF ODEM	ODEM	TX	**D**	C+	C+	101	10.52	11.4	3.9	3.5	50.9	**5.0**	7.0	17.2
FIRST STATE BK OF OLMSTED	OLMSTED	IL	**B-**	B-	B-	34	11.59	10.4	6.5	31.0	14.7	**10.0**	11.4	21.0
FIRST STATE BK OF PAINT R	PAINT ROCK	TX	**B-**	B	B	68	6.82	5.1	4.7	6.7	28.7	**10.0**	11.3	19.8
FIRST STATE BK OF PORTER	PORTER	IN	**D+**	C-	C-	149	10.52	1.8	0.6	22.9	42.0	**8.6**	10.1	19.8
FIRST STATE BK OF PORTER	PORTER	OK	**A-**	B+	B	35	3.72	12.2	10.7	17.2	0.1	**10.0**	14.3	18.9
FIRST STATE BK OF PURDY	MONETT	MO	**C-**	C	B-	143	17.21	8.6	1.4	7.1	15.5	**5.9**	7.9	14.7
FIRST STATE BK OF RANDOLP	CUTHBERT	GA	**C-**	B-	B+	56	2.49	10.7	5.6	5.5	15.9	**9.1**	10.4	15.2
FIRST STATE BK OF RANSOM	RANSOM	KS	**A-**	A-	A-	41	8.43	8.6	0.8	0.5	51.8	**10.0**	19.7	40.8
FIRST STATE BK OF RED BUD	RED BUD	IL	**D-**	E	D-	96	5.13	3.6	1.2	19.6	45.2	**6.5**	8.5	17.2
FIRST STATE BK OF RED WIN	RED WING	MN	**B-**	B-	B	47	-2.95	8.3	5.9	8.5	58.0	**10.0**	13.6	27.0
FIRST STATE BK OF ROSCOE	ROSCOE	SD	**C+**	C+	C+	87	6.92	19.8	1.0	0.0	16.2	**6.4**	8.4	13.4
▼ FIRST STATE BK OF	ROSEMOUNT	MN	**D**	C-	C+	59	-7.57	6.9	3.9	12.1	47.5	**6.9**	9.0	17.7
FIRST STATE BK OF SAN DIE	SAN DIEGO	TX	**B-**	B-	B-	63	6.64	10.0	10.1	7.3	38.7	**5.8**	7.8	17.2
FIRST STATE BK OF SAUK CE	SAUK CENTRE	MN	**B+**	A-	A-	98	4.21	7.3	3.8	8.8	43.7	**10.0**	12.0	25.4
FIRST STATE BK OF SHARON	ANETA	ND	**C**	C	D	40	-1.45	5.3	2.3	2.4	5.0	**6.6**	8.6	15.4
FIRST STATE BK OF SHELBY	SHELBY	MT	**A**	A	A	109	13.09	7.7	1.4	0.0	61.2	**10.0**	17.5	44.1
FIRST STATE BK OF ST CHAR	SAINT CHARLES	MO	**B**	B+	B+	206	10.23	8.3	0.3	31.1	17.2	**10.0**	14.8	19.7
FIRST STATE BK OF ST PETE	SAINT PETER	IL	**A-**	A-	B	28	7.49	4.4	5.2	7.2	62.0	**10.0**	13.9	30.5
▼ FIRST STATE BK OF ST ROBE	SAINT ROBERT	MO	**B-**	B	B-	89	-0.58	3.0	6.7	27.9	22.5	**7.2**	9.1	17.5
▲ FIRST STATE BK OF SWANVIL	SWANVILLE	MN	**C-**	C-	C+	27	3.12	22.4	5.1	9.3	10.2	**10.0**	11.6	15.0
FIRST STATE BK OF THE SOU	SULLIGENT	AL	**B**	B	B-	92	-2.68	3.5	9.8	15.8	45.5	**10.0**	13.9	23.6
FIRST STATE BK OF UVALDE	UVALDE	TX	**B**	B	B	662	18.12	3.5	2.3	5.6	59.7	**5.6**	7.6	20.5
FIRST STATE BK OF VAN ORI	VAN ORIN	IL	**C+**	C+	C+	35	0.54	3.5	2.3	6.8	36.0	**6.5**	8.6	17.2
FIRST STATE BK OF WABASHA	WABASHA	MN	**D+**	C-	C-	114	5.40	3.4	2.5	10.8	45.8	**6.2**	8.2	17.3
▲ FIRST STATE BK OF WARNER	WARNER	SD	**D-**	D-	D	49	-4.70	12.1	4.7	2.1	9.7	**3.8**	6.4	10.4
FIRST STATE BK OF WARREN	WARREN	AR	**B+**	B	B+	102	-1.32	14.9	5.3	10.0	45.6	**8.6**	10.1	17.4
FIRST STATE BK OF WEST SA	WEST SALEM	IL	**B**	B	B	16	-0.77	2.6	4.4	13.3	49.8	**10.0**	20.3	43.4
FIRST STATE BK OF WILTON	WILTON	ND	**B+**	B+	B	33	8.02	6.1	1.5	0.9	44.7	**10.0**	11.1	18.3
▲ FIRST STATE BK OF WYOMING	WYOMING	MN	**C**	C+	B+	143	-0.03	5.3	2.4	12.2	43.4	**10.0**	15.0	25.4
FIRST STATE BK OKABENA (I	OKABENA	MN	**C-**	C-	C	18	-6.56	7.2	2.1	6.1	28.8	**10.0**	19.0	33.4
FIRST STATE BK POND CREEK	POND CREEK	OK	**C-**	C	C	39	4.41	20.4	7.6	14.5	17.6	**6.8**	8.8	13.6
FIRST STATE BK	SHANNON	IL	**C+**	D+	B-	145	1.86	4.7	3.1	12.0	30.6	**6.2**	8.2	12.3
FIRST STATE BK SOUTHWEST	PIPESTONE	MN	**B+**	B+	B	186	2.50	11.4	7.2	4.3	27.6	**7.5**	9.3	15.0

Asset Quality Index	Non-Performing Loans as a % of Total Loans	Non-Performing Loans as a % of Capital	Net Charge-offs Avg Loans	Profitability Index	Net Income ($Mil)	Return on Assets (R.O.A.)	Return on Equity (R.O.E.)	Net Interest Spread	Overhead Efficiency Ratio	Liquidity Index	Liquidity Ratio	Hot Money Ratio	Stability Index
1.8	3.51	24.1	0.18	2.6	0.1	0.32	3.00	4.08	87.9	2.9	15.6	14.4	6.5
1.7	4.89	22.3	1.87	2.0	0.7	0.11	1.13	4.14	68.6	5.0	47.8	12.0	4.3
7.7	0.42	1.1	0.32	3.2	0.2	0.56	3.52	4.19	85.4	5.9	53.0	7.2	6.9
4.9	0.84	6.6	0.00	7.7	1.2	1.86	20.65	4.33	54.8	2.9	9.5	13.8	7.9
7.0	0.57	2.2	-0.02	4.8	1.0	0.96	9.57	3.22	58.8	3.5	57.2	24.7	5.3
8.1	0.15	0.8	0.04	2.4	0.1	0.14	1.19	4.40	93.5	5.2	37.0	7.5	6.4
7.6	0.48	2.9	0.00	7.3	0.9	1.58	17.32	4.96	59.1	2.9	15.6	14.7	6.3
4.7	3.41	11.1	2.85	4.0	0.0	0.18	0.97	4.53	54.9	2.4	43.8	23.7	9.2
5.3	2.20	7.9	0.62	3.6	0.5	0.80	7.67	3.37	70.3	5.9	60.2	8.7	5.3
6.7	0.26	0.7	2.55	4.1	0.6	0.87	4.60	4.26	53.8	2.5	39.5	26.4	7.6
5.5	0.53	4.4	0.11	2.5	1.0	0.41	3.09	3.92	79.8	1.4	12.2	25.6	4.7
6.4	0.17	0.8	0.01	5.9	3.0	1.71	16.10	4.42	66.4	3.9	30.9	12.3	8.2
0.9	5.23	29.3	0.67	1.5	0.1	0.06	0.58	4.36	89.4	1.1	13.3	29.7	4.3
3.6	1.26	7.7	0.43	3.0	0.3	0.51	5.36	3.68	90.8	4.3	29.2	10.1	3.2
1.5	3.58	34.6	1.01	0.0	-0.4	-2.01	-32.46	4.18	173.3	4.2	26.3	8.2	0.9
3.9	2.07	12.2	0.48	7.5	1.1	1.72	15.77	5.16	62.1	3.7	21.4	11.4	7.7
7.2	0.74	2.8	0.23	6.3	3.1	1.11	8.36	3.95	67.5	3.0	38.5	19.4	7.9
5.1	3.40	9.6	0.74	7.7	1.3	1.12	7.48	3.99	43.9	2.9	35.7	18.9	8.9
7.6	0.30	2.2	2.08	3.0	0.1	0.30	3.78	3.22	61.6	2.6	22.8	16.6	6.5
6.0	0.27	2.3	0.10	3.4	0.2	0.42	5.11	4.70	83.9	1.5	16.4	24.8	3.0
1.9	2.42	16.6	0.63	3.1	2.1	0.53	6.00	3.99	70.7	1.8	21.6	21.5	4.2
6.9	0.95	2.4	0.03	3.5	0.6	0.73	8.90	2.70	71.6	3.4	54.3	21.1	3.2
5.9	0.06	0.4	0.06	7.7	1.3	1.32	13.00	4.40	54.1	1.4	13.5	24.8	6.8
5.2	0.24	1.4	1.11	1.2	0.0	-0.49	-4.77	4.86	98.6	5.1	30.1	2.6	6.0
8.4	0.73	2.1	0.17	8.0	2.4	1.79	13.07	4.08	51.5	2.9	46.3	26.1	9.0
2.0	0.58	5.6	0.79	6.0	2.4	1.12	9.36	5.25	56.4	2.2	6.0	17.1	7.1
1.8	6.59	26.4	2.75	7.9	1.4	1.84	13.27	3.82	53.2	1.4	16.7	26.4	7.7
6.6	1.63	6.2	2.26	1.0	0.1	0.10	1.33	3.66	85.0	4.2	48.3	15.9	2.9
6.2	1.04	5.4	-0.01	4.1	0.2	0.72	6.09	4.02	77.4	2.9	28.4	16.9	6.4
4.4	2.25	9.4	0.39	4.7	0.8	1.25	11.15	4.15	65.3	2.5	36.3	23.2	5.6
3.9	2.29	10.5	0.63	1.6	0.6	0.45	4.35	2.94	81.4	2.5	49.9	36.3	4.7
7.5	0.11	0.6	0.18	9.3	0.8	2.22	16.06	7.02	65.7	0.9	15.2	34.2	9.5
4.2	2.44	14.2	1.47	2.8	0.5	0.36	4.48	3.67	72.6	2.3	44.2	33.6	3.1
3.2	2.42	12.8	1.49	2.9	0.1	0.21	1.94	4.43	62.3	4.2	34.0	12.1	6.6
7.3	3.12	5.0	-0.01	5.9	0.4	0.99	4.72	3.70	63.6	6.7	67.9	4.9	8.4
2.0	4.39	17.9	4.64	0.0	-2.1	-2.31	-25.26	2.70	155.7	4.8	35.5	9.3	4.5
5.5	3.64	9.1	1.69	3.0	0.2	0.35	2.62	3.59	70.4	4.4	67.4	17.4	5.6
3.7	1.98	13.6	0.34	3.8	0.7	0.83	9.48	3.05	67.1	2.2	29.2	21.0	5.5
2.5	5.81	25.3	2.25	0.5	-0.4	-0.69	-6.95	3.67	91.0	4.4	48.4	14.3	4.7
6.6	0.31	1.5	0.12	6.6	0.9	1.54	16.94	4.08	66.4	1.8	21.7	22.1	5.7
6.2	2.42	8.3	0.67	4.7	1.0	1.02	7.67	3.58	60.2	4.4	51.3	14.7	7.9
3.7	1.29	8.0	-0.02	3.4	0.3	0.63	6.24	N/,	26.1	4.6	42.7	12.2	3.6
6.9	4.69	6.4	0.19	8.4	1.4	1.38	7.30	4.38	49.6	6.1	90.6	13.5	9.1
6.5	0.64	2.7	1.06	4.1	1.7	0.87	5.51	4.34	71.7	2.4	18.9	17.4	6.8
9.2	0.02	0.1	0.05	7.6	0.4	1.35	9.20	4.36	54.2	6.2	61.6	7.1	8.9
8.6	0.00	0.0	0.45	4.2	0.7	0.73	8.15	4.30	73.8	2.7	21.6	16.4	5.6
1.3	4.76	27.5	0.18	1.8	0.0	0.04	0.34	4.74	93.1	0.7	13.4	42.4	6.4
8.3	0.91	2.5	0.12	4.7	1.0	1.03	7.56	4.49	69.8	3.2	46.7	20.6	7.0
5.6	2.62	9.1	0.30	5.6	7.0	1.16	12.77	3.48	49.9	2.9	50.0	29.2	6.7
5.0	1.75	7.5	0.07	3.2	0.2	0.66	6.24	3.82	83.4	4.6	42.0	12.6	6.3
1.6	5.66	23.6	0.85	2.0	0.7	0.59	6.68	3.38	75.7	2.7	37.0	21.7	3.9
4.0	0.53	4.2	2.89	0.5	-1.3	-2.54	-40.35	3.76	91.9	3.7	23.0	11.4	3.5
6.5	1.46	6.4	0.56	5.7	1.1	1.04	10.15	3.84	66.7	2.8	43.8	26.3	5.8
9.1	0.08	0.2	0.03	3.5	0.1	0.43	2.03	3.62	84.7	6.8	71.4	2.5	7.5
8.5	0.00	0.0	0.05	7.0	0.5	1.53	13.20	3.88	57.4	5.7	37.4	4.4	7.0
3.4	6.28	18.7	2.24	2.4	0.3	0.18	1.17	3.88	62.4	3.8	48.8	18.4	7.2
7.1	0.58	1.3	1.65	1.2	0.0	0.18	0.97	3.66	88.5	3.1	59.4	23.0	5.0
3.8	1.77	11.8	0.46	4.4	0.4	0.93	10.78	3.87	76.4	2.4	31.5	21.2	5.0
5.2	0.45	2.8	0.37	3.5	1.4	0.92	9.83	3.31	68.9	3.1	14.3	13.2	4.5
6.5	0.22	1.3	0.09	6.6	2.3	1.33	13.48	4.35	62.3	3.8	22.6	10.9	6.5

Name	City	State	Rating	2008 Rating	2007 Rating	Total Assets ($Mil)	One Year Asset Growth	Asset Mix (As a % of Total Assets) Commercial Loans	Consumer Loans	Home Mortgages	Securities	Capitalization Index	Leverage Ratio	Risk-based Capital Ratio
▼ FIRST STATE COMMUNITY	FARMINGTON	MO	**B-**	B	B+	1,225	20.21	3.7	2.2	30.5	15.7	**6.4**	8.4	12.3
FIRST STATE FINANCIAL INC	PINEVILLE	KY	**D-**	D-	C-	413	2.02	7.3	5.3	19.2	9.8	**6.7**	8.7	12.9
▲ FIRST TENNESSEE BANK NA	MEMPHIS	TN	**C-**	D	D	24,482	-5.26	15.6	1.2	15.9	11.5	**10.0**	12.3	20.3
FIRST TEXAS BANK	GEORGETOWN	TX	**B+**	B+	A-	307	-1.06	4.4	1.5	4.4	56.0	**8.0**	9.7	20.8
FIRST TEXAS BANK	KILLEEN	TX	**A-**	A-	A-	227	-2.58	1.8	1.3	9.5	47.5	**10.0**	12.1	20.3
FIRST TEXAS BANK	LAMPASAS	TX	**A-**	A-	A-	107	4.84	1.7	3.3	7.7	52.9	**10.0**	13.0	30.4
▼ FIRST TEXAS BANK	ROUND ROCK	TX	**B+**	A-	A-	170	2.97	9.7	2.1	3.7	40.1	**6.8**	8.8	15.2
FIRST TEXOMA NATIONAL BK	DURANT	OK	**D**	D-	D+	195	-18.16	8.8	4.2	16.6	11.4	**7.4**	9.3	14.2
FIRST TRADE UNION BANK	BOSTON	MA	**D-**	C-	B-	615	-8.31	9.3	2.3	21.2	16.1	**6.7**	8.8	14.4
▼ FIRST TRI-COUNTY BANK	SWANTON	NE	**D+**	D+	D	50	11.59	13.0	7.2	16.1	2.5	**4.1**	7.4	10.6
FIRST TRUST & SB	CORALVILLE	IA	**D-**	D+	D-	48	0.15	7.5	1.1	4.6	47.9	**7.3**	9.2	15.1
FIRST TRUST & SB	MARCUS	IA	**C+**	B-	B	44	9.79	9.5	6.4	5.5	32.5	**9.3**	10.6	16.5
FIRST TRUST & SB	MOVILLE	IA	**B**	B	B	104	8.44	0.8	1.0	3.4	43.0	**10.0**	17.9	36.2
▲ FIRST TRUST & SB	WHEATLAND	IA	**B-**	C+	C	117	5.65	15.9	4.8	8.8	6.9	**5.7**	8.8	11.5
FIRST TRUST & SB OF ALBAN	ALBANY	IL	**A-**	A-	A-	126	6.78	5.5	4.6	20.7	24.0	**10.0**	11.2	16.6
▲ FIRST TRUST & SB OF WATSE	WATSEKA	IL	**A**	A	A	188	4.20	8.4	3.3	11.9	24.7	**10.0**	12.4	22.9
FIRST TRUST & SB ONEIDA T	ONEIDA	TN	**D+**	C-	B-	146	7.45	3.5	12.0	36.7	9.6	**8.2**	9.8	14.8
FIRST TRUST BANK	CHARLOTTE	NC	**D-**	B-	B	445	-2.34	5.3	0.2	4.9	26.3	**7.4**	9.3	13.8
FIRST TRUST BANK OF ILLIN	KANKAKEE	IL	**B**	B-	C+	215	11.92	15.1	2.1	6.0	39.5	**6.5**	8.5	14.5
FIRST TUSKEGEE BANK	TUSKEGEE	AL	**D-**	D-	D-	72	-0.80	5.1	3.2	16.2	20.7	**5.9**	7.9	12.8
FIRST UNITED BANK	CRETE	IL	**E-**	D-	D-	400	-12.17	8.1	1.5	10.1	23.9	**1.2**	4.4	8.2
FIRST UNITED BANK	PARK RIVER	ND	**C**	C-	D+	127	0.70	8.9	5.4	8.3	10.7	**5.3**	8.6	11.2
▲ FIRST UNITED BANK	DIMMITT	TX	**B**	B-	C+	1,009	12.54	9.5	1.8	5.2	40.7	**5.4**	7.4	12.9
FIRST UNITED BANK & TRUST	OAKLAND	MD	**D+**	D+	C+	1,688	-2.80	3.8	4.6	16.4	13.6	**5.7**	7.7	11.5
FIRST UNITED BANK & TRUST	MADISONVILLE	KY	**B-**	B-	B-	209	-1.15	8.5	4.0	31.6	33.7	**6.8**	8.8	16.8
FIRST UNITED BANK & TRUST	DURANT	OK	**D**	D+	D+	2,061	-5.90	11.6	4.5	11.9	15.6	**6.1**	8.1	12.2
FIRST UNITED NATIONAL BK	FRYBURG	PA	**B-**	B	B	249	8.17	4.4	9.0	37.9	20.1	**5.4**	7.4	16.1
▼ FIRST UNITED SECURITY BAN	THOMASVILLE	AL	**C-**	D+	D+	626	-9.38	6.2	10.1	13.1	21.9	**10.0**	11.4	17.2
FIRST UTAH BANK	SALT LAKE CITY	UT	**E+**	D-	D-	306	-8.80	8.0	0.7	8.8	14.0	**4.2**	6.2	10.8
▲ FIRST VALLEY BANK	SEELEY LAKE	MT	**C+**	C-	C-	53	0.36	8.2	2.8	24.6	0.4	**6.4**	8.4	12.4
FIRST VICTORIA NATIONAL B	VICTORIA	TX	**B-**	B-	B-	1,731	9.90	15.9	4.1	14.8	13.9	**6.5**	8.5	12.2
FIRST VIRGINIA COMMUNITY	FAIRFAX	VA	**D**	C	C	207	46.09	10.6	0.7	17.3	10.5	**9.3**	12.6	14.4
FIRST VISION BANK OF TENN	TULLAHOMA	TN	**C**	C-	C-	121	5.01	9.4	3.1	21.0	8.2	**10.0**	13.3	17.9
FIRST VOLUNTEER BANK OF T	CHATTANOOGA	TN	**C-**	C-	C+	668	4.33	7.0	2.5	17.6	9.9	**6.8**	8.9	13.1
FIRST WESTERN BANK	BOONEVILLE	AR	**D**	D-	D	273	-2.94	5.2	3.2	28.2	13.5	**6.2**	8.3	12.2
FIRST WESTERN BANK &	EDEN PRAIRIE	MN	**B-**	B-	B	46	13.29	16.4	0.1	0.7	1.6	**10.0**	20.6	27.0
FIRST WESTERN BANK &	MINOT	ND	**B-**	B-	B	605	5.46	12.5	3.9	3.6	38.6	**6.4**	8.4	13.5
FIRST WESTERN FSB	RAPID CITY	SD	**B+**	B+	B	37	20.64	0.9	2.2	55.0	0.0	**10.0**	15.0	22.7
FIRST WESTERN TRUST BANK	SCOTTSDALE	AZ	**D**	C	C	66	4.75	33.4	7.6	12.2	4.9	**10.0**	15.0	20.0
FIRST WESTERN TRUST BANK	DENVER	CO	**D**	D	D+	494	6.98	20.9	5.2	16.0	7.4	**5.3**	8.7	11.3
FIRST WESTROADS BANK INC	OMAHA	NE	**C+**	B-	B	188	-8.06	7.8	1.2	7.2	10.9	**10.0**	11.0	15.2
FIRST WHITNEY BANK & TRUS	ATLANTIC	IA	**A**	A-	A	154	7.68	13.6	1.5	4.2	28.7	**8.4**	11.2	13.7
FIRST-CITIZENS BANK & TRU	RALEIGH	NC	**B**	B	B	17,903	13.32	8.5	3.7	5.2	24.0	**6.4**	8.4	16.7
FIRST-LOCKHART NATIONAL B	LOCKHART	TX	**B+**	B	B	154	4.10	8.9	4.0	12.4	19.2	**6.6**	8.6	14.3
▲ FIRSTATLANTIC BANK	JACKSONVILLE	FL	**C**	C-	C-	208	8.96	1.2	0.4	19.0	35.0	**10.0**	18.3	35.2
FIRSTBANK	LAKEWOOD	CO	**B**	B	B	10,385	952.55	0.7	1.0	22.6	50.5	**5.6**	7.6	16.5
FIRSTBANK	MOUNT PLEASANT	MI	**D**	C-	C-	394	5.01	10.1	4.5	19.1	16.6	**6.7**	8.7	13.1
FIRSTBANK	ANTLERS	OK	**B+**	B+	B	208	6.96	8.9	15.1	32.7	1.5	**5.7**	7.7	11.6
▲ FIRSTBANK - WEST MICHIGAN	IONIA	MI	**D**	D	C-	199	-4.75	8.9	2.4	25.2	17.5	**6.8**	8.8	15.4
FIRSTBANK OF ARIZONA INC	PHOENIX	AZ	**B-**	B-	B-	134	0.75	0.2	0.1	15.9	4.5	**10.0**	24.0	29.8
FIRSTBANK PUERTO RICO	SAN JUAN	PR	**D-**	D-	D	15,677	-20.08	11.0	8.9	21.1	20.6	**5.6**	7.6	11.9
FIRSTBANK SOUTHWEST	AMARILLO	TX	**A**	A-	A-	751	7.01	10.9	3.9	6.1	38.7	**8.4**	9.9	17.7
FIRSTBANK-ALMA	ALMA	MI	**D+**	C-	C-	257	-7.06	6.9	3.4	16.1	33.5	**5.5**	7.5	15.2
FIRSTBANK-ST JOHNS	SAINT JOHNS	MI	**D**	C-	C-	95	-6.51	12.9	10.9	10.9	15.8	**6.2**	8.3	12.7
FIRSTBANK-WEST BRANCH	WEST BRANCH	MI	**D+**	C	C	244	-3.48	6.6	5.9	27.0	10.3	**6.6**	8.6	13.6
FIRSTCAPITAL BANK OF TEXA	MIDLAND	TX	**C+**	C+	C+	481	27.73	19.1	2.5	14.8	10.9	**6.5**	8.5	12.9
▼ FIRSTCITY BANK OF	NORTH PALM BEACH	FL	**D-**	C	D+	66	42.45	22.1	0.0	3.6	29.5	**7.4**	9.3	13.5
FIRSTIER BANK	KIMBALL	NE	**D-**	D-	B+	257	-26.14	4.8	3.1	4.0	1.6	**7.5**	9.3	13.0
FIRSTMERIT BANK NA	AKRON	OH	**D+**	C+	B-	14,124	34.23	14.3	8.8	7.1	21.6	**4.8**	6.8	11.7
FIRSTRUST SB	CONSHOHOCKEN	PA	**C+**	C	B-	2,390	1.66	20.6	5.2	9.5	10.2	**8.9**	10.3	14.0

Asset Quality Index	Non-Performing Loans as a % of Total Loans	Non-Performing Loans as a % of Capital	Net Charge-offs / Avg Loans	Profitability Index	Net Income ($Mil)	Return on Assets (R.O.A.)	Return on Equity (R.O.E.)	Net Interest Spread	Overhead Efficiency Ratio	Liquidity Index	Liquidity Ratio	Hot Money Ratio	Stability Index
3.7	0.51	4.2	0.11	**6.8**	13.9	1.22	11.38	4.12	56.2	**1.7**	5.0	19.6	**8.7**
0.0	6.28	50.2	0.94	**3.6**	2.4	0.58	6.68	3.67	67.2	**0.7**	12.4	36.2	**4.3**
1.8	4.75	21.4	2.99	**1.0**	90.6	0.36	2.64	3.28	77.2	**3.7**	10.5	10.4	**6.9**
3.7	6.09	20.7	1.28	**5.8**	2.4	0.76	8.99	3.65	53.7	**5.8**	57.7	10.6	**6.8**
7.7	2.95	8.8	-0.05	**5.9**	2.1	0.93	7.52	4.13	69.7	**6.1**	61.9	9.8	**7.7**
9.6	0.02	0.0	0.12	**5.6**	0.9	0.90	6.65	4.03	65.6	**6.8**	76.5	7.4	**6.7**
9.5	0.07	0.4	0.01	**6.4**	1.7	1.03	11.26	4.52	68.6	**3.4**	42.5	18.6	**6.7**
1.2	4.14	27.7	2.06	**0.5**	-3.0	-1.35	-15.37	4.28	96.0	**2.6**	14.5	15.8	**4.9**
0.1	3.98	26.6	2.53	**1.1**	-2.6	-0.40	-4.46	3.71	70.2	**3.2**	27.4	14.6	**3.8**
1.8	0.82	8.2	0.06	**4.8**	0.4	0.83	10.01	4.33	65.6	**3.7**	11.5	10.2	**4.6**
6.1	2.52	10.8	0.59	**0.9**	0.1	0.29	2.95	3.94	107.0	**2.3**	34.1	24.5	**3.3**
8.3	0.10	0.5	-0.08	**3.3**	0.2	0.49	4.63	3.73	83.4	**4.1**	40.6	14.5	**4.9**
9.6	0.98	1.2	-0.57	**4.2**	0.9	0.85	4.49	2.93	59.2	**6.9**	94.5	9.6	**7.8**
4.1	0.48	4.1	0.08	**4.7**	1.2	1.08	11.51	3.84	66.6	**2.7**	15.1	15.3	**6.3**
6.2	0.71	4.2	0.05	**8.6**	2.4	2.03	15.00	4.59	48.5	**3.1**	23.7	14.3	**8.4**
7.6	0.78	3.0	0.26	**7.8**	2.4	1.33	10.30	3.97	48.4	**3.5**	38.8	17.0	**8.2**
0.2	7.45	53.7	0.54	**4.6**	1.3	0.90	8.99	4.53	60.5	**0.9**	12.4	32.7	**5.4**
0.0	11.42	61.0	4.25	**1.4**	-3.9	-0.85	-8.44	3.88	48.6	**0.8**	24.4	53.2	**5.9**
4.8	1.15	6.2	0.11	**5.6**	2.2	1.08	11.88	3.59	56.0	**2.4**	33.0	22.3	**4.9**
0.3	8.18	52.0	1.65	**1.5**	0.1	0.13	1.64	4.72	89.1	**1.5**	18.0	25.4	**2.7**
0.3	13.28	94.7	1.33	**0.0**	-12.6	-2.97	-49.29	3.58	99.0	**2.1**	19.7	19.2	**1.5**
3.1	1.08	9.3	0.27	**6.9**	1.9	1.55	18.29	4.71	59.3	**3.7**	5.9	9.6	**5.5**
5.3	0.62	4.0	0.30	**6.2**	14.1	1.52	17.14	3.92	60.5	**1.0**	20.1	37.9	**7.6**
1.9	3.70	24.0	1.26	**1.1**	-7.8	-0.44	-5.81	2.81	79.9	**1.6**	26.2	37.9	**5.2**
5.9	0.92	5.3	0.25	**5.2**	2.1	0.97	10.66	3.83	64.9	**2.7**	14.5	15.4	**4.6**
1.2	3.12	24.6	1.11	**4.7**	20.3	0.96	10.67	4.38	65.4	**1.0**	5.0	28.8	**8.5**
6.4	0.58	4.4	0.11	**5.4**	2.5	1.05	13.86	3.60	57.1	**2.5**	32.8	20.1	**4.8**
1.6	4.61	22.2	1.97	**3.1**	2.4	0.34	2.75	6.02	67.3	**1.4**	14.0	25.7	**6.7**
0.3	8.05	50.7	5.12	**0.0**	-16.1	-4.98	-77.88	3.12	172.7	**0.8**	18.9	42.2	**1.9**
5.1	0.55	4.5	0.07	**6.3**	0.7	1.36	17.34	3.46	59.3	**2.4**	20.8	17.6	**5.0**
4.2	1.42	11.1	0.66	**4.8**	13.1	0.80	8.22	4.40	66.1	**1.7**	10.2	21.3	**7.6**
4.3	2.37	14.4	0.54	**1.2**	0.8	0.48	3.92	4.23	83.2	**0.7**	19.9	55.0	**2.1**
7.5	0.56	3.2	0.66	**2.6**	0.6	0.53	4.09	4.00	76.8	**0.7**	13.5	39.3	**4.1**
2.5	1.34	9.9	1.42	**4.6**	4.0	0.60	6.05	4.72	63.1	**1.9**	18.9	20.0	**6.6**
2.1	1.01	8.0	0.71	**1.1**	1.0	0.37	4.44	4.35	92.2	**0.7**	8.6	36.1	**2.8**
0.0	5.78	18.6	6.34	**0.0**	-0.5	-1.13	-5.06	3.56	86.5	**1.4**	31.0	40.4	**5.3**
4.1	0.48	2.6	1.46	**4.0**	2.3	0.40	4.17	3.48	59.9	**2.9**	29.7	17.2	**4.8**
4.8	2.08	12.3	0.00	**10.0**	1.2	3.44	22.45	6.84	42.8	**0.5**	3.7	43.6	**8.8**
7.8	0.00	0.0	0.00	**0.9**	0.1	0.19	1.33	4.34	93.7	**1.1**	6.8	28.1	**2.9**
0.9	3.42	30.4	0.15	**4.5**	4.1	0.90	9.64	4.22	64.5	**0.7**	10.6	35.2	**4.9**
3.7	1.27	8.1	0.40	**7.6**	3.3	1.70	15.65	4.75	56.8	**3.2**	18.9	13.5	**7.7**
7.7	0.28	1.6	0.00	**9.8**	3.3	2.34	20.82	4.49	41.3	**4.3**	37.9	12.6	**8.5**
5.3	1.48	9.8	0.60	**6.7**	207.7	1.15	13.87	4.38	58.6	**2.7**	18.2	16.1	**8.3**
8.4	0.00	0.0	0.09	**5.7**	2.0	1.39	14.86	4.41	69.3	**2.7**	26.4	17.1	**6.2**
6.5	1.83	5.4	0.00	**2.0**	0.5	0.23	1.49	3.12	83.1	**2.9**	49.3	28.7	**2.0**
6.1	1.27	6.7	1.43	**10.0**	163.6	5.00	94.60	14.44	47.3	**5.9**	45.7	9.1	**6.4**
1.6	2.92	21.9	0.52	**4.8**	3.3	0.86	8.65	4.00	60.8	**1.6**	23.2	25.8	**5.0**
5.9	0.21	2.1	0.33	**9.7**	4.6	2.31	27.87	6.67	63.0	**0.7**	12.4	36.1	**6.0**
1.5	1.68	10.3	1.42	**0.4**	-0.1	-0.04	-0.28	4.17	99.3	**4.0**	23.2	9.7	**4.8**
6.7	0.88	2.3	0.78	**0.0**	-3.3	-2.51	-9.69	4.63	187.7	**1.5**	9.1	22.3	**7.0**
0.0	10.73	72.9	4.69	**0.0**	-421.7	-2.37	-26.89	2.74	72.5	**0.5**	8.7	63.3	**5.1**
8.4	0.20	0.9	0.02	**7.3**	11.0	1.55	14.13	3.61	62.1	**3.1**	36.1	18.3	**8.4**
1.8	1.03	6.8	1.20	**3.9**	1.7	0.61	7.86	3.08	63.1	**3.8**	29.9	12.8	**4.5**
0.4	6.06	42.5	1.39	**1.1**	-0.1	-0.11	-1.40	3.85	68.6	**1.6**	25.5	26.7	**4.2**
1.8	1.63	13.2	0.47	**6.6**	2.7	1.07	12.64	4.88	57.1	**2.9**	13.7	14.6	**5.2**
6.9	0.00	0.0	0.65	**4.2**	3.2	0.75	8.92	4.13	68.2	**2.1**	35.1	28.3	**3.8**
7.6	0.26	1.5	0.82	**0.0**	-1.1	-1.92	-15.87	4.12	132.5	**2.6**	38.6	25.2	**0.8**
0.0	13.22	84.2	2.25	**0.1**	-8.1	-2.69	-28.19	2.91	116.7	**1.2**	15.7	29.5	**6.0**
2.1	1.49	12.3	1.00	**4.6**	106.3	0.79	9.33	3.92	65.1	**3.5**	10.9	11.2	**5.4**
3.7	2.20	12.6	0.63	**3.1**	12.3	0.53	4.71	4.46	74.5	**3.9**	22.9	12.0	**7.0**

Name	City	State	Rating	2008 Rating	2007 Rating	Total Assets ($Mil)	One Year Asset Growth	Asset Mix (As a % of Total Assets) Commercial Loans	Consumer Loans	Home Mortgages	Securities	Capitalization Index	Leverage Ratio	Risk-based Capital Ratio
FIRSTSECURE BANK & TRUST	PALOS HILLS	IL	**E-**	E-	E-	68	-7.71	2.5	0.7	22.3	4.8	**0.9**	4.9	7.9
▼ FIRSTSTATE BK	LINEVILLE	AL	**D+**	C	C+	186	5.77	3.4	5.8	14.9	40.3	**5.8**	7.8	12.9
▲ FISHER NATIONAL BK	FISHER	IL	**C-**	D-	D+	74	6.12	4.6	4.6	31.3	24.1	**6.5**	8.5	14.7
FIVE POINTS BANK	GRAND ISLAND	NE	**A-**	B+	B	618	10.52	18.4	2.4	5.5	25.6	**8.9**	10.3	14.9
FIVE POINTS BANK OF HASTI	HASTINGS	NE	**B+**	B	B	190	9.94	10.3	1.5	4.9	28.9	**6.8**	8.8	13.4
FIVE STAR BANK	ROCKLIN	CA	**C-**	C-	B-	399	4.74	7.1	0.0	5.7	3.7	**7.8**	10.9	13.1
FIVE STAR BANK	WARSAW	NY	**B-**	B-	B-	2,207	7.45	7.0	20.1	10.8	31.5	**5.2**	7.2	12.0
FLAGLER BANK	WEST PALM BEACH	FL	**D-**	D-	D	125	0.24	7.0	0.1	4.5	19.5	**4.4**	6.6	10.7
▼ FLAGSHIP BANK MINNESOTA	WAYZATA	MN	**E-**	D	D+	126	4.55	16.7	2.7	7.8	5.1	**1.1**	5.2	8.1
▼ FLAGSHIP BANK WINSTED	WINSTED	MN	**E+**	D+	C-	46	-1.91	6.3	3.1	10.8	7.6	**5.7**	7.7	13.1
FLAGSHIP COMMUNITY BANK	CLEARWATER	FL	**D-**	D	C	89	4.84	14.4	0.5	8.7	0.0	**8.6**	11.7	13.9
FLAGSTAR BANK FSB	TROY	MI	**D-**	D-	E	13,620	-5.88	5.3	0.6	57.1	4.7	**7.9**	9.6	18.6
▼ FLANAGAN STATE BK	FLANAGAN	IL	**C-**	C	C	131	4.33	7.7	1.9	13.1	31.4	**6.9**	9.0	14.8
FLATBUSH FS&LA	BROOKLYN	NY	**D+**	C-	C-	147	-5.68	0.0	0.1	48.8	14.9	**10.0**	11.5	20.3
▼ FLATHEAD BANK OF BIGFORK	KALISPELL	MT	**D+**	C-	B+	218	-6.58	12.1	3.3	16.7	12.5	**10.0**	11.1	15.9
▼ FLATIRONS BANK	BOULDER	CO	**D-**	C-	B-	86	-12.63	15.1	0.2	2.8	46.4	**4.6**	6.6	12.8
FLEETWOOD BANK	FLEETWOOD	PA	**C+**	C+	C+	225	3.46	1.0	0.5	34.5	31.1	**6.2**	8.2	16.2
FLINT COMMUNITY BANK	ALBANY	GA	**C**	C-	C-	111	6.49	12.0	2.0	30.3	2.3	**7.1**	9.1	13.0
FLINT CREEK VALLEY BANK	PHILIPSBURG	MT	**C+**	B-	C	57	7.03	14.8	3.5	12.0	6.0	**7.0**	9.0	12.9
FLINT HILLS BANK OF ESKRI	ESKRIDGE	KS	**A-**	B+	B	90	5.99	6.9	3.8	11.3	42.6	**9.0**	10.3	18.8
FLINT RIVER NATIONAL BK	CAMILLA	GA	**D-**	D-	D	31	3.80	6.2	2.5	10.9	4.0	**9.7**	10.8	14.9
FLORA BANK & TRUST	FLORA	IL	**C+**	C+	C+	68	14.17	5.1	6.4	17.5	15.4	**7.2**	9.1	17.6
FLORA SB	FLORA	IL	**D+**	C-	C-	29	1.36	9.9	8.7	47.1	9.9	**9.2**	10.5	17.6
FLORENCE SB	FLORENCE	MA	**C+**	C+	C+	1,071	-1.00	2.0	0.2	41.6	30.9	**6.3**	8.3	14.4
▼ FLORIDA BANK	TAMPA	FL	**E+**	D-	D-	840	3.18	5.7	0.7	11.7	21.1	**4.5**	6.5	11.0
▼ FLORIDA BANK OF	ORLANDO	FL	**D-**	D-	D-	230	35.78	8.9	0.7	5.9	10.5	**6.4**	8.9	12.0
FLORIDA BUSINESS BANK	MELBOURNE	FL	**D**	D	D-	113	4.12	4.4	0.1	4.0	33.6	**10.0**	12.2	20.4
FLORIDA CAPITAL BANK NA	JACKSONVILLE	FL	**E-**	E+	E+	979	1.72	2.5	0.2	30.4	13.7	**1.9**	4.6	9.8
▲ FLORIDA CITIZENS BANK	GAINESVILLE	FL	**E+**	C-	B-	285	-1.55	16.0	1.4	4.6	13.7	**3.6**	7.0	10.3
FLORIDA GULF BANK	FORT MYERS	FL	**D+**	D+	C-	348	-5.03	12.1	3.9	12.1	8.6	**6.2**	8.2	13.1
FLORIDA PARISHES BANK	HAMMOND	LA	**B-**	B-	B-	173	5.55	2.5	4.9	28.9	18.9	**8.2**	9.8	16.7
▼ FLORIDA SHORES	POMPANO BEACH	FL	**D-**	C-	C-	139	53.04	13.0	0.5	6.9	13.3	**6.9**	10.2	12.4
▲ FLORIDA SHORES	VENICE	FL	**D+**	C-	C	257	43.12	8.9	1.5	5.6	45.5	**8.7**	10.2	17.6
FLORIDA TRADITIONS BANK	DADE CITY	FL	**D+**	C	C	194	19.31	20.0	1.6	5.9	11.0	**7.9**	10.7	13.3
FLORIDIAN BANK	DAYTONA BEACH	FL	**D-**	C-	C	154	-3.24	10.4	0.5	11.1	4.2	**6.0**	8.0	11.7
FLORIDIAN COMMUNITY BANK	DAVIE	FL	**D+**	D-	C-	221	14.35	13.2	0.3	12.4	15.2	**6.2**	8.2	13.2
FLOWERS NATIONAL BK	CAINSVILLE	MO	**D+**	C-	C-	26	16.06	7.6	2.1	9.9	24.0	**10.0**	14.2	21.1
FLUSHING COMMERCIAL BANK	NEW HYDE PARK	NY	**B-**	C+	B-	629	56.11	0.0	0.0	0.0	4.0	**6.9**	8.9	62.7
FLUSHING SAVINGS BANK FSB	NEW HYDE PARK	NY	**D**	C-	C+	4,308	4.34	6.6	0.0	21.0	18.6	**7.3**	9.2	14.3
FMB BANK	WRIGHT CITY	MO	**D-**	D+	D+	36	8.43	6.4	10.1	20.3	18.8	**6.9**	8.9	14.9
▲ FNB BANK	SCOTTSBORO	AL	**C**	C	B+	331	9.19	6.7	4.1	13.5	23.9	**10.0**	11.2	17.7
FNB BANK INC	MAYFIELD	KY	**B-**	B-	B-	339	76.92	11.8	3.0	13.0	27.3	**6.7**	8.7	13.0
FNB BANK INC	ROMNEY	WV	**B**	B	B+	152	10.90	4.6	4.1	22.2	39.0	**9.4**	10.6	18.0
FNB BANK NA	DANVILLE	PA	**C**	C+	B-	389	-3.27	3.7	9.4	24.5	19.7	**5.2**	7.2	14.4
FNBT.COM BANK	FORT WALTON BEACH	FL	**C**	C	A-	360	2.60	2.2	1.8	12.7	5.8	**10.0**	12.0	19.5
FOCUS BANK	CHARLESTON	MO	**C+**	C+	C	603	-0.75	8.0	3.8	23.7	8.1	**7.7**	9.5	13.3
FOCUS BUSINESS BANK	SAN JOSE	CA	**D**	D	C-	132	22.23	21.8	1.0	1.0	22.7	**10.0**	16.5	28.5
▼ FOLSOM LAKE BANK	FOLSOM	CA	**D-**	C-	C-	112	9.15	4.4	0.2	7.1	26.2	**8.7**	10.2	15.4
FOOTHILLS BANK	YUMA	AZ	**C**	B-	B+	205	0.12	6.0	1.1	8.0	0.1	**8.3**	11.2	13.6
▼ FOOTHILLS BANK & TRUST	MARYVILLE	TN	**D+**	C-	C-	131	25.44	7.5	1.6	13.7	21.4	**10.0**	12.8	18.1
FORCHT BANK NA	LEXINGTON	KY	**C-**	B-	B+	1,051	-4.81	3.3	3.8	26.7	25.8	**6.6**	8.6	14.6
FORD COUNTY STATE BK	SPEARVILLE	KS	**B**	B	B	31	9.00	15.5	2.7	3.3	18.7	**10.0**	13.1	18.9
▼ FORDYCE BANK & TRUST CO	FORDYCE	AR	**B**	B+	B+	122	8.06	10.9	9.0	21.2	40.3	**8.5**	10.0	18.4
FOREST COMMERCIAL BANK	ASHEVILLE	NC	**C-**	C	C	102	33.19	7.5	0.2	3.0	22.4	**10.0**	17.3	22.1
FOREST PARK NATIONAL BK &	FOREST PARK	IL	**C-**	C-	D+	187	7.56	7.0	0.8	13.0	17.3	**6.3**	8.3	12.6
FORETHOUGHT FSB	BATESVILLE	IN	**C-**	C-	C	134	5.00	0.0	0.0	0.0	95.7	**4.9**	6.9	16.4
▼ FORREST CITY BANK NA	FORREST CITY	AR	**D+**	C-	C	54	3.21	5.0	4.1	24.0	26.8	**9.9**	10.9	16.0
FORRESTON STATE BK	FORRESTON	IL	**D**	D-	D+	103	-9.00	6.0	0.4	9.4	18.9	**8.4**	10.9	13.7
▲ FORT DAVIS STATE BK	FORT DAVIS	TX	**D+**	C-	B	78	8.15	11.7	10.4	13.9	17.9	**6.6**	8.6	14.6
FORT GIBSON STATE BK	FORT GIBSON	OK	**D+**	C-	D+	57	-5.41	6.3	15.6	12.0	32.6	**4.9**	6.9	13.1

Asset Quality Index	Non-Performing Loans as a % of Total Loans	Non-Performing Loans as a % of Capital	Net Charge-offs Avg Loans	Profitability Index	Net Income ($Mil)	Return on Assets (R.O.A.)	Return on Equity (R.O.E.)	Net Interest Spread	Overhead Efficiency Ratio	Liquidity Index	Liquidity Ratio	Hot Money Ratio	Stability Index
0.0	15.44	149.2	0.93	**0.0**	-1.4	-2.00	-31.69	3.57	97.2	**0.9**	18.2	35.3	**1.4**
1.6	3.72	21.4	0.75	**3.9**	1.5	0.80	10.52	4.40	64.2	**0.9**	19.2	36.2	**3.5**
2.1	2.36	15.9	0.71	**3.8**	0.6	0.85	9.49	4.33	73.1	**3.0**	27.6	15.8	**4.8**
7.4	0.44	2.5	0.04	**8.0**	11.6	2.04	19.46	4.15	51.2	**4.2**	30.7	10.8	**7.2**
7.0	0.84	5.1	0.27	**5.9**	2.1	1.21	14.77	3.73	52.3	**4.9**	39.6	10.2	**6.0**
0.4	1.91	12.1	0.81	**4.7**	4.1	1.04	9.91	4.30	51.2	**0.8**	19.1	46.1	**6.9**
5.5	0.50	3.8	0.54	**5.8**	22.9	1.06	11.07	4.16	59.2	**3.7**	5.3	9.7	**6.8**
0.0	14.95	93.7	3.11	**0.2**	-1.3	-0.99	-14.05	3.58	84.9	**1.3**	20.1	28.7	**3.9**
0.3	6.51	61.9	2.61	**0.0**	-1.9	-1.51	-17.18	3.39	139.6	**0.7**	16.9	52.1	**2.7**
1.4	5.61	36.4	0.74	**2.4**	0.0	0.06	0.66	3.93	82.4	**3.2**	33.3	16.7	**1.0**
0.0	5.31	35.9	2.01	**0.4**	-0.2	-0.26	-1.93	4.62	76.8	**0.5**	1.5	36.5	**1.3**
0.2	3.12	20.4	2.13	**0.0**	-354.9	-2.54	-28.22	1.68	89.8	**0.8**	13.0	37.4	**3.4**
1.8	4.22	25.5	0.56	**5.0**	1.6	1.25	12.86	4.05	66.9	**2.9**	31.1	17.7	**6.0**
0.8	7.04	43.3	0.00	**2.5**	0.5	0.31	3.23	4.19	76.2	**1.4**	22.7	28.9	**4.5**
0.3	3.59	20.4	2.36	**3.3**	0.4	0.17	1.35	4.58	61.4	**3.2**	11.5	12.7	**7.4**
4.0	0.00	0.0	2.33	**0.0**	-10.3	-10.11	-71.46	4.29	319.2	**1.5**	22.7	26.6	**5.2**
6.6	0.98	6.1	0.01	**3.1**	1.0	0.45	5.40	3.44	82.2	**2.9**	37.0	19.7	**4.8**
4.8	1.09	9.3	0.27	**3.3**	0.6	0.57	6.32	4.05	70.3	**0.7**	9.4	34.4	**4.6**
3.2	2.25	17.2	0.28	**5.2**	0.3	0.64	6.83	5.74	74.2	**3.3**	18.0	12.8	**5.6**
8.4	0.01	0.1	-0.18	**6.3**	1.3	1.51	13.11	3.66	56.7	**1.8**	26.5	25.1	**7.8**
1.5	4.51	26.9	0.20	**0.0**	-0.3	-0.90	-8.13	3.64	116.2	**1.1**	29.0	60.2	**4.2**
5.5	1.98	11.1	0.03	**3.3**	0.3	0.46	4.79	3.50	84.2	**3.9**	32.0	12.9	**4.8**
2.8	2.70	18.1	0.43	**1.0**	0.0	-0.09	-0.87	2.86	89.4	**1.0**	21.5	33.7	**6.0**
3.7	1.29	9.1	0.25	**3.3**	4.1	0.38	4.81	3.14	71.8	**3.6**	28.1	16.0	**5.9**
0.3	9.62	72.7	3.99	**0.0**	-42.3	-5.01	-50.51	2.82	105.5	**1.6**	26.2	26.8	**2.9**
2.7	2.39	16.5	1.85	**0.0**	-1.7	-0.78	-8.00	4.02	93.8	**1.2**	15.6	28.5	**0.8**
0.1	7.58	32.5	1.34	**0.2**	0.1	0.10	0.75	3.12	118.5	**1.4**	19.2	27.2	**4.9**
0.3	10.12	109.9	4.24	**0.0**	-27.2	-2.70	-55.05	2.08	99.4	**0.9**	20.5	40.6	**2.9**
0.3	2.95	26.1	2.98	**0.3**	-6.9	-2.30	-31.90	2.80	86.0	**0.7**	10.3	37.4	**4.2**
1.7	0.93	7.1	1.22	**1.7**	0.4	0.10	1.24	3.74	64.2	**3.2**	12.1	12.8	**3.5**
5.0	1.03	6.3	0.35	**5.6**	2.3	1.37	14.07	5.11	60.1	**3.4**	26.9	13.6	**5.9**
5.1	0.51	3.8	0.86	**0.0**	-0.9	-0.88	-7.10	4.03	101.8	**0.9**	23.4	37.9	**1.2**
7.2	0.28	1.3	0.09	**1.0**	1.0	0.49	5.56	3.00	92.4	**3.1**	38.9	19.0	**1.5**
3.7	0.78	5.2	0.73	**1.3**	0.4	0.24	1.90	3.67	70.5	**0.7**	8.3	33.8	**2.3**
0.0	4.93	37.1	3.56	**0.0**	-3.5	-2.26	-27.49	3.61	86.3	**1.8**	25.6	23.7	**1.3**
3.5	1.58	11.0	-0.03	**2.1**	0.9	0.42	5.29	3.95	76.4	**2.5**	26.6	17.8	**3.5**
4.3	3.92	14.4	-0.01	**0.4**	-0.1	-0.40	-2.00	5.57	105.2	**3.2**	40.1	19.0	**5.1**
10.0	0.00	0.0	0.00	**4.5**	4.2	0.76	8.23	1.70	19.5	**8.6**	105.6	0.0	**6.0**
0.8	3.43	26.5	0.42	**4.3**	39.9	0.94	10.09	3.61	47.2	**1.4**	21.6	31.2	**6.5**
1.5	3.95	22.1	0.32	**0.7**	0.0	-0.09	-1.07	4.07	96.2	**3.2**	20.4	13.6	**3.3**
2.1	3.74	18.2	1.62	**2.8**	1.7	0.52	4.44	3.55	74.1	**1.9**	24.1	20.6	**5.5**
7.3	0.09	0.7	0.17	**4.4**	1.9	0.79	6.25	4.19	68.4	**3.7**	20.6	10.9	**6.9**
3.7	3.48	15.4	0.53	**4.4**	1.1	0.80	6.99	4.62	74.8	**2.2**	31.1	23.5	**5.4**
5.1	0.72	5.6	0.20	**6.6**	4.9	1.23	15.68	3.45	56.6	**2.3**	26.0	18.7	**4.3**
2.9	2.95	9.4	1.48	**3.4**	2.1	0.56	4.45	2.92	79.0	**5.1**	46.7	11.1	**7.5**
4.4	1.38	10.5	0.20	**3.8**	4.1	0.68	7.32	3.44	63.7	**0.9**	8.4	31.7	**5.9**
5.6	0.13	0.4	-0.47	**0.1**	-0.2	-0.17	-0.96	3.30	109.7	**4.8**	56.4	15.3	**1.6**
0.0	4.22	23.4	0.91	**1.1**	0.4	0.32	3.00	3.74	86.2	**1.1**	26.1	35.7	**1.3**
2.4	1.85	12.6	0.75	**6.7**	2.3	1.10	8.90	5.88	55.4	**2.4**	13.4	16.8	**6.6**
6.3	0.91	4.7	0.19	**0.7**	0.2	0.18	1.27	3.26	87.9	**2.6**	22.5	16.6	**2.2**
1.8	1.62	11.1	1.30	**4.5**	10.8	1.02	9.56	4.77	69.7	**3.4**	13.9	12.0	**7.8**
4.7	1.71	7.4	-0.02	**5.1**	0.3	0.94	7.01	4.74	66.8	**3.0**	30.8	17.1	**7.9**
6.3	0.89	3.8	0.55	**4.5**	1.1	0.91	8.65	4.33	72.6	**2.7**	44.5	28.6	**6.2**
7.5	0.00	0.0	0.00	**0.8**	0.0	0.04	0.21	3.62	91.3	**1.4**	26.9	30.2	**2.3**
2.2	2.36	17.4	0.60	**2.6**	0.4	0.21	2.49	4.48	89.3	**3.3**	20.5	13.1	**4.6**
9.9	0.00	0.0	0.00	**2.2**	0.4	0.26	3.26	1.28	86.3	**8.5**	106.6	0.6	**1.6**
3.5	4.03	18.7	0.09	**0.9**	-0.2	-0.47	-5.39	3.40	98.8	**1.8**	18.3	21.1	**3.1**
1.8	4.05	24.8	1.57	**0.9**	0.1	0.06	0.70	3.87	82.0	**1.2**	17.1	29.6	**2.8**
1.8	3.03	19.6	1.35	**2.7**	0.1	0.08	0.85	4.71	89.7	**1.7**	27.0	26.1	**6.0**
7.5	0.00	0.0	0.38	**4.5**	0.5	0.82	12.11	4.85	76.8	**1.3**	24.2	29.7	**3.0**

Name	City	State	Rating	2008 Rating	2007 Rating	Total Assets ($Mil)	One Year Asset Growth	Asset Mix (As a % of Total Assets) Comm-ercial Loans	Cons-umer Loans	Home Mort-gages	Secur-ities	Capital-ization Index	Leverage Ratio	Risk-based Capital Ratio
FORT HOOD NATIONAL BK	FORT HOOD	TX	**B**	B-	B-	214	-3.07	0.0	1.9	1.2	65.1	**5.0**	7.0	33.8
FORT JENNINGS STATE BK	FORT JENNINGS	OH	**C+**	C+	C+	142	5.71	8.1	4.5	24.4	8.8	**5.6**	7.6	12.1
▼FORT LEE FEDERAL SAVINGS	FORT LEE	NJ	**E-**	D-	D+	56	-17.01	12.9	21.0	24.8	0.9	**1.7**	4.7	8.7
FORT MADISON BANK &	FORT MADISON	IA	**C**	D	D	140	13.98	31.7	2.4	28.7	13.2	**7.3**	9.2	14.0
FORT MORGAN STATE BK	FORT MORGAN	CO	**C-**	C+	C	82	24.27	23.0	3.8	12.0	11.8	**7.0**	9.1	12.5
FORT SILL NATIONAL BK	FORT SILL	OK	**A**	A	A	334	-1.08	0.1	7.8	6.4	59.5	**6.7**	8.8	21.6
▼FORT WASHINGTON SAVINGS	CINCINNATI	OH	**D**	C	B	107	13.17	0.0	0.0	24.3	61.5	**6.8**	8.8	29.4
FORTUNE BANK	SEATTLE	WA	**D-**	C-	C-	132	11.53	22.4	1.0	6.2	8.4	**9.5**	10.6	15.0
FORTUNEBANK	ARNOLD	MO	**D+**	C	D+	146	5.75	14.3	1.3	14.3	19.7	**7.2**	9.1	14.1
FORWARD FINANCIAL BANK	MARSHFIELD	WI	**D+**	D+	C+	267	0.02	8.1	2.1	24.2	9.6	**6.4**	8.7	12.1
FOSTER BANK	CHICAGO	IL	**D-**	D-	C-	533	-4.26	17.9	0.2	14.3	2.1	**6.5**	8.8	12.1
▲FOUNDATION BANK	CINCINNATI	OH	**B**	B-	C+	175	32.79	1.8	0.6	22.9	0.4	**10.0**	11.5	18.3
FOUNDATION BANK	BELLEVUE	WA	**D-**	D+	C+	368	-19.78	27.4	0.3	7.4	11.1	**5.7**	7.7	11.7
▼FOUNDATION FIRST BANK	WATERLOO	NE	**D+**	C-	C-	39	60.27	16.4	4.8	15.4	12.1	**10.0**	17.4	20.3
▲FOUNDATIONS BANK	PEWAUKEE	WI	**E+**	E	D	203	-12.87	11.5	1.3	8.2	8.6	**5.6**	7.8	11.4
FOUNDERS BANK & TRUST	GRAND RAPIDS	MI	**C+**	C+	C+	408	4.98	16.0	0.8	27.4	11.9	**6.6**	8.6	12.2
FOUNDERS BANK SSB	SUGAR LAND	TX	**D**	C	C	140	7.11	11.6	1.1	14.1	7.3	**10.0**	11.6	19.9
FOUNDERS COMMUNITY BANK	SAN LUIS OBISPO	CA	**C-**	D+	C	110	1.66	18.9	0.7	7.7	4.5	**7.5**	9.4	13.8
FOUNTAIN TRUST CO	COVINGTON	IN	**B**	B	A-	251	8.55	4.4	3.3	21.2	35.8	**10.0**	11.7	24.0
FOUR CORNERS COMMUNITY	FARMINGTON	NM	**C**	B-	B-	210	7.58	10.0	1.2	9.8	27.8	**7.2**	9.1	16.0
FOUR COUNTY BANK	ALLENTOWN	GA	**E-**	E-	D+	67	-10.75	8.5	6.4	20.8	7.6	**1.3**	5.2	8.3
▼FOUR OAKS BANK & TRUST	FOUR OAKS	NC	**E**	D	C-	947	-2.75	4.3	1.4	13.1	13.8	**3.2**	6.2	10.1
FOWLER STATE BK	FOWLER	CO	**B**	B-	C-	63	0.73	4.4	3.0	12.9	30.7	**10.0**	12.1	23.1
FOWLER STATE BK	FOWLER	IN	**C+**	B	B	136	5.15	5.9	4.2	13.0	41.4	**9.8**	10.9	18.5
▼FOWLER STATE BK	FOWLER	KS	**C+**	B+	B+	63	20.22	8.8	6.4	5.7	41.9	**10.0**	11.2	20.6
FOX CHASE BANK	HATBORO	PA	**C**	C-	C	1,099	-6.63	8.9	0.5	27.0	33.2	**10.0**	13.6	23.8
FOX RIVER STATE BK	BURLINGTON	WI	**D-**	D-	D+	100	-5.96	13.0	1.8	13.6	12.8	**5.4**	8.3	11.3
FOX VALLEY SAVINGS BANK	FOND DU LAC	WI	**D**	D	D+	330	-7.42	0.0	0.9	28.1	37.5	**9.3**	10.5	18.5
FOXBORO FEDERAL SAVINGS	FOXBORO	MA	**B-**	B-	B	137	6.87	0.0	0.3	52.6	21.0	**10.0**	14.8	29.9
▲FPC FINANCIAL FSB	MADISON	WI	**A-**	B	B+	1,895	1.73	0.2	100.4	0.0	0.2	**10.0**	16.4	17.5
FRAMINGHAM CO-OP BANK	FRAMINGHAM	MA	**A-**	B-	B	382	3.56	11.4	0.4	18.0	13.5	**10.0**	21.1	27.2
▲FRANDSEN BANK & TRUST	LONSDALE	MN	**D+**	C-	C-	997	34.80	10.2	2.5	12.4	25.4	**6.6**	8.6	13.0
▼FRANKLIN BANK	FRANKLIN	IL	**B+**	A-	B+	33	7.86	1.9	5.4	20.3	34.1	**8.4**	9.9	19.0
FRANKLIN BANK	PILESGROVE	NJ	**C-**	D	D	253	-0.14	2.0	5.9	50.4	21.2	**5.9**	7.9	15.9
FRANKLIN BANK & TRUST CO	FRANKLIN	KY	**B-**	C+	B-	347	7.77	14.9	3.3	23.8	13.1	**7.5**	9.4	13.9
FRANKLIN COMMUNITY BANK	ROCKY MOUNT	VA	**D+**	D+	C	214	-4.78	5.5	1.1	22.9	12.6	**7.9**	9.6	14.8
▼FRANKLIN COUNTY UNITED BA	DECHERD	TN	**D**	C+	B-	100	2.05	10.3	2.7	12.1	11.1	**9.5**	10.7	14.6
▲FRANKLIN FSB	GLEN ALLEN	VA	**C-**	D+	D+	960	-1.87	1.0	0.0	10.5	32.6	**10.0**	11.1	15.7
FRANKLIN GROVE BANK	FRANKLIN GROVE	IL	**B+**	B+	B+	31	9.33	29.2	3.7	8.8	30.7	**10.0**	17.0	28.5
FRANKLIN NB OF MINNEAPOLI	MINNEAPOLIS	MN	**C-**	C	B-	130	0.69	13.2	0.6	5.4	9.3	**10.0**	14.2	18.4
FRANKLIN SAVINGS & LOAN C	CINCINNATI	OH	**D-**	D	D+	271	-10.13	1.7	2.0	46.5	7.3	**5.4**	7.4	11.5
FRANKLIN SB	FARMINGTON	ME	**A-**	A-	A	320	2.69	5.1	4.6	37.2	4.1	**10.0**	25.2	38.2
▲FRANKLIN SB	FRANKLIN	NH	**C**	C-	C+	358	3.70	1.7	1.4	38.4	22.5	**9.2**	10.5	17.6
FRANKLIN SECURITY BANK	PLAINS	PA	**C+**	C	C-	204	-2.58	6.8	32.9	13.3	24.2	**6.9**	8.9	14.7
FRANKLIN STATE BK	FRANKLIN	MN	**C+**	C+	C+	24	-0.69	2.2	3.6	11.9	6.3	**10.0**	12.0	19.2
FRANKLIN STATE BK	FRANKLIN	NE	**B**	B	B+	46	8.50	3.3	3.4	1.8	54.2	**10.0**	17.7	34.8
FRANKLIN STATE BK & TRUST	WINNSBORO	LA	**B+**	B+	A-	122	-2.93	8.0	8.9	18.0	29.7	**7.2**	9.2	17.1
FRANKLIN SYNERGY BANK	FRANKLIN	TN	**D+**	D	C-	350	28.31	2.9	0.6	20.9	36.2	**8.6**	10.1	16.6
FRANKLIN TEMPLETON BANK	SALT LAKE CITY	UT	**C**	C-	C-	315	-8.41	2.0	43.0	16.4	28.3	**9.9**	10.9	15.7
FRATERNITY FS&LA	BALTIMORE	MD	**D**	C-	C-	170	1.64	0.0	0.6	50.8	12.6	**7.8**	9.5	19.0
FREDERICK COUNTY BANK	FREDERICK	MD	**C-**	C+	C+	288	11.86	8.9	0.6	8.9	10.4	**8.2**	9.8	13.8
FREDONIA VALLEY BANK	FREDONIA	KY	**B+**	B	B-	69	0.06	3.8	5.6	49.3	19.8	**10.0**	11.5	19.7
FREEDOM BANK	STERLING	IL	**D+**	D+	D+	75	-5.09	10.7	0.4	5.5	24.5	**7.2**	9.2	14.3
FREEDOM BANK	HUNTINGBURG	IN	**B**	B	B	275	9.85	5.6	6.8	36.1	0.1	**7.1**	9.1	13.1
FREEDOM BANK	OVERLAND PARK	KS	**C**	C-	C	113	21.82	21.2	0.5	8.3	18.7	**5.6**	7.6	11.5
▲FREEDOM BANK	COLUMBIA FALLS	MT	**E+**	E	D-	51	-25.11	11.2	3.1	14.2	1.0	**5.4**	8.2	11.3
FREEDOM BANK	ORADELL	NJ	**C**	C-	C	118	4.59	13.5	0.3	9.5	8.0	**7.5**	9.4	13.1
FREEDOM BANK INC	BELINGTON	WV	**D+**	C	B-	166	4.32	18.1	4.9	26.8	1.3	**6.5**	8.5	12.5
▼FREEDOM BANK OF AMERICA	SAINT PETERSBURG	FL	**E-**	E	D	87	-13.05	6.6	3.1	2.5	4.6	**1.5**	6.1	8.5
FREEDOM BANK OF	TULSA	OK	**C-**	C-	B-	42	-3.63	5.1	6.5	36.3	13.2	**10.0**	11.5	20.5

Asset Quality Index	Non-Performing Loans as a % of Total Loans	Non-Performing Loans as a % of Capital	Net Charge-offs Avg Loans	Profitability Index	Net Income ($Mil)	Return on Assets (R.O.A.)	Return on Equity (R.O.E.)	Net Interest Spread	Overhead Efficiency Ratio	Liquidity Index	Liquidity Ratio	Hot Money Ratio	Stability Index
9.9	0.05	0.1	2.06	**4.9**	2.1	1.04	10.97	3.63	92.9	**7.0**	73.1	5.8	**5.8**
7.0	0.49	4.1	0.39	**4.5**	1.1	0.78	9.88	4.16	64.5	**2.0**	25.6	20.7	**4.1**
0.0	10.77	109.3	5.79	**0.5**	-1.7	-2.48	-31.74	4.85	72.9	**1.0**	21.9	34.0	**1.8**
4.3	0.54	4.1	1.03	**3.0**	1.1	0.88	8.12	3.97	75.2	**3.5**	22.0	12.2	**3.2**
2.5	1.70	12.2	0.06	**6.8**	1.2	1.59	17.59	4.54	64.1	**1.2**	13.5	29.3	**6.8**
8.5	0.84	1.7	9.08	**9.7**	6.8	1.93	13.92	4.20	73.9	**6.9**	63.9	4.8	**7.8**
6.4	2.55	7.4	0.00	**0.7**	-1.3	-1.20	-11.35	1.98	187.8	**7.0**	81.3	6.8	**5.5**
1.1	2.46	15.1	0.47	**0.4**	-0.2	-0.14	-1.26	4.18	96.5	**0.8**	15.7	37.8	**1.4**
1.7	3.48	23.1	0.34	**2.4**	0.4	0.29	3.29	3.20	80.5	**1.7**	29.2	28.2	**2.5**
2.1	2.13	17.4	0.93	**1.7**	0.4	0.14	1.25	3.85	78.7	**2.5**	16.2	16.5	**5.3**
0.0	5.01	40.4	1.32	**1.1**	-2.2	-0.39	-4.11	4.15	72.7	**0.6**	6.4	39.5	**7.0**
4.8	0.77	4.9	0.17	**7.7**	5.5	3.42	25.46	3.39	37.7	**1.5**	20.6	26.5	**6.7**
0.3	8.03	48.1	2.93	**0.0**	-13.3	-2.95	-35.80	3.37	82.3	**1.7**	16.5	21.5	**4.1**
7.5	0.49	2.4	0.01	**0.0**	-0.4	-1.21	-6.08	4.14	110.7	**1.4**	23.6	28.1	**5.6**
0.0	6.19	46.0	3.63	**0.0**	-4.1	-1.88	-24.24	2.76	94.4	**0.8**	15.9	41.8	**0.5**
4.3	1.15	9.4	0.70	**4.4**	3.4	0.84	9.68	3.76	63.4	**1.2**	8.7	26.6	**4.6**
6.9	0.00	0.0	1.99	**0.0**	-2.2	-1.69	-13.12	3.24	112.9	**5.3**	41.0	8.6	**2.0**
7.8	0.04	0.3	0.97	**2.0**	0.3	0.30	3.10	4.96	83.3	**2.8**	28.7	17.0	**3.0**
6.1	1.55	6.2	0.35	**4.2**	1.6	0.67	5.23	3.74	66.4	**5.2**	52.5	12.0	**6.8**
3.4	3.00	17.5	0.36	**7.1**	3.4	1.68	18.12	4.30	50.6	**0.9**	18.9	36.9	**6.2**
1.2	3.81	42.3	4.70	**0.9**	-0.2	-0.34	-6.56	3.79	74.4	**0.8**	17.2	44.9	**0.0**
0.0	6.61	57.6	3.82	**0.0**	-25.1	-2.63	-33.94	3.62	77.8	**0.7**	15.9	48.2	**3.1**
4.0	4.67	18.5	1.00	**3.7**	0.5	0.75	6.28	3.13	57.7	**2.9**	47.2	24.9	**7.0**
4.8	2.38	9.5	1.40	**3.1**	0.6	0.45	3.99	3.95	64.3	**3.5**	37.5	16.7	**6.0**
7.0	1.77	6.8	0.18	**2.0**	0.1	0.11	0.86	3.40	84.2	**4.7**	51.5	13.3	**7.5**
3.2	3.44	14.2	0.29	**2.2**	2.9	0.25	2.08	2.43	66.9	**5.0**	42.9	13.4	**7.4**
0.3	6.32	40.7	1.88	**1.9**	0.3	0.29	2.78	3.60	67.5	**0.5**	6.8	49.9	**4.1**
1.9	5.11	21.5	0.14	**0.9**	-0.3	-0.09	-0.80	2.23	79.3	**3.1**	48.3	25.1	**3.9**
8.6	0.00	0.0	0.00	**3.9**	1.1	0.84	5.59	3.20	64.3	**3.7**	46.2	18.3	**8.0**
5.1	0.33	1.8	2.07	**9.4**	73.2	3.51	27.06	11.06	33.9	**0.0**	0.3	99.2	**9.8**
7.0	1.31	4.5	0.23	**7.3**	5.8	1.54	7.58	4.50	53.0	**1.0**	25.7	35.9	**6.5**
0.7	2.63	17.3	0.66	**4.9**	8.3	0.91	6.93	4.53	68.4	**4.3**	17.7	6.8	**7.3**
8.7	0.02	0.1	-0.01	**7.1**	0.5	1.65	15.24	4.28	58.3	**4.6**	42.1	12.4	**6.3**
4.8	1.15	9.2	0.00	**2.0**	0.9	0.37	4.69	3.12	84.5	**2.4**	30.7	20.3	**3.5**
4.6	0.80	6.2	1.00	**4.1**	2.0	0.61	6.67	4.29	58.4	**2.9**	16.5	14.6	**5.5**
1.5	5.43	35.2	0.60	**1.9**	0.8	0.35	3.63	3.35	77.8	**1.2**	15.6	28.7	**5.0**
1.0	3.93	21.8	2.43	**0.4**	-1.2	-1.18	-10.04	4.42	77.4	**1.0**	18.1	33.6	**5.4**
2.7	5.37	22.5	0.56	**2.2**	3.5	0.36	3.27	2.85	50.3	**4.2**	46.4	15.8	**6.0**
8.7	0.00	0.0	0.00	**6.8**	0.4	1.21	6.95	4.36	54.3	**3.1**	48.0	22.9	**8.6**
2.0	2.29	11.7	0.87	**2.9**	0.5	0.37	2.51	5.69	80.3	**2.1**	11.6	18.3	**6.6**
0.5	3.75	35.6	0.57	**0.8**	-0.7	-0.26	-3.40	2.80	96.0	**1.5**	11.5	22.8	**1.9**
6.7	1.72	5.3	0.26	**6.2**	3.3	1.02	4.37	5.01	67.9	**3.2**	11.7	12.8	**7.7**
3.8	1.23	7.4	0.70	**2.6**	1.2	0.34	3.12	3.69	83.4	**3.5**	23.3	12.3	**5.6**
3.3	1.28	8.3	0.52	**3.6**	1.6	0.77	8.36	3.48	62.1	**1.9**	37.8	35.2	**3.2**
6.2	0.39	2.1	0.09	**5.0**	0.2	0.90	7.72	3.82	62.8	**3.2**	29.3	13.8	**6.9**
5.5	4.09	8.8	0.10	**4.1**	0.3	0.77	4.17	3.68	71.8	**5.7**	54.8	8.8	**7.1**
6.8	0.65	3.7	0.12	**5.9**	1.6	1.34	13.99	4.45	70.3	**2.1**	25.9	19.6	**6.7**
4.1	1.40	8.0	0.16	**1.3**	1.3	0.43	3.97	3.19	88.8	**1.1**	17.3	31.0	**2.2**
5.2	0.65	3.7	1.62	**3.1**	1.9	0.60	5.59	2.69	62.2	**1.5**	32.6	40.8	**5.7**
5.3	0.59	3.8	0.40	**0.8**	-0.9	-0.51	-5.14	2.30	101.3	**1.9**	30.8	27.4	**5.0**
2.3	1.05	6.9	0.50	**3.5**	1.4	0.51	5.17	4.10	68.7	**2.2**	25.5	19.1	**5.3**
4.6	2.60	14.6	0.13	**6.2**	0.9	1.29	11.37	4.95	61.4	**4.2**	23.9	8.4	**6.8**
4.1	2.32	14.5	1.75	**1.0**	0.3	0.40	4.62	3.11	69.3	**1.4**	8.3	23.4	**3.4**
4.5	0.92	7.7	0.15	**8.2**	3.6	1.35	15.05	3.98	40.9	**2.6**	9.5	15.2	**6.3**
4.4	0.91	7.9	0.35	**3.5**	0.7	0.71	8.95	3.85	71.1	**1.9**	10.2	18.9	**4.2**
0.0	14.42	111.2	2.22	**0.0**	-1.3	-2.10	-30.80	3.10	124.3	**0.7**	12.8	43.3	**0.1**
2.3	1.94	14.6	0.75	**2.7**	1.0	0.87	9.56	4.19	61.2	**1.4**	21.3	28.6	**3.7**
1.5	5.58	46.5	0.30	**2.9**	0.3	0.16	1.78	4.44	73.9	**1.6**	13.2	22.9	**5.1**
0.0	2.12	19.9	3.01	**0.0**	-1.9	-1.86	-21.11	3.43	115.4	**0.6**	7.4	46.4	**0.0**
3.3	4.22	21.8	0.14	**1.7**	0.1	0.16	1.38	4.20	93.4	**1.0**	20.1	34.2	**5.1**

Name	City	State	Rating	2008 Rating	2007 Rating	Total Assets ($Mil)	One Year Asset Growth	Asset Mix (As a % of Total Assets) Comm-ercial Loans	Cons-umer Loans	Home Mort-gages	Secur-ities	Capital-ization Index	Leverage Ratio	Risk-based Capital Ratio
FREEDOM BANK OF	CASSVILLE	MO	**C+**	C	C	117	15.89	12.0	4.6	22.4	5.9	**6.5**	8.5	12.9
▲ FREEDOM BANK OF VIRGINIA	FAIRFAX	VA	**C**	D	D+	171	8.92	18.7	1.3	8.5	4.6	**10.0**	12.4	16.1
FREEDOM FINANCIAL BANK	WEST DES MOINES	IA	**C-**	C+	D+	164	-3.65	10.1	2.4	4.6	3.2	**7.2**	10.4	12.7
▼ FREEDOM NATIONAL BK	GREENVILLE	RI	**C-**	C	C+	86	-0.02	8.7	0.3	8.1	14.5	**7.0**	9.0	13.3
FREEDOM SECURITY BANK	CORALVILLE	IA	**C-**	C	B	87	1.64	8.8	1.7	20.5	29.5	**8.1**	9.7	16.6
FREEDOM STATE BK	FREEDOM	OK	**C-**	C-	D+	18	5.51	3.9	11.5	7.0	25.8	**8.0**	9.6	17.6
FREEDOMBANK	ELKADER	IA	**C-**	D	C-	225	-2.51	8.9	3.3	17.8	16.4	**7.6**	9.4	13.8
FREEHOLD SAVINGS BANK	FREEHOLD	NJ	**B-**	B-	B	251	2.75	0.0	0.1	26.0	60.6	**10.0**	12.2	38.5
FREELAND STATE BK	FREELAND	MI	**C-**	C-	C+	54	-1.68	0.8	2.0	28.7	44.5	**10.0**	16.8	45.8
FREEPORT STATE BK	HARPER	KS	**E-**	D	D-	23	10.76	4.8	1.7	10.9	36.7	**5.0**	7.0	12.4
FREEPORT STATE BK	FREEPORT	MN	**C+**	C	C-	85	7.56	12.7	4.0	10.0	10.8	**5.6**	8.6	11.4
▲ FREESTAR BANK NA	PONTIAC	IL	**B-**	C	C	403	-4.52	11.7	1.9	12.1	22.3	**5.9**	7.9	12.2
FREMONT BANK	FREMONT	CA	**C-**	C+	B	2,420	2.56	5.5	0.2	31.0	8.6	**6.0**	8.0	12.7
▲ FREMONT NATIONAL BK &	FREMONT	NE	**C**	D	C-	294	-6.16	6.1	1.0	20.7	25.9	**6.2**	8.2	19.0
FRESNO FIRST BANK	FRESNO	CA	**C+**	C-	C-	143	16.91	16.5	0.6	7.4	28.6	**10.0**	11.1	19.6
FRIENDLY HILLS BANK	WHITTIER	CA	**D**	C-	C	95	16.95	9.6	0.2	19.1	29.9	**10.0**	12.1	19.7
▼ FRIENDS BANK	NEW SMYRNA BEACH	FL	**E+**	D+	B-	147	-6.80	0.4	0.4	9.4	9.5	**2.3**	6.0	9.3
FRIENDSHIP STATE BK	FRIENDSHIP	IN	**B-**	C+	B-	279	3.89	2.4	3.9	46.3	14.0	**6.1**	8.1	14.3
FRONT RANGE BANK	LAKEWOOD	CO	**D-**	D-	D-	135	2.92	4.6	0.3	18.5	41.1	**6.5**	8.6	15.7
▼ FRONTENAC BANK	EARTH CITY	MO	**E-**	D-	D+	386	-7.89	3.3	0.2	10.3	8.4	**3.9**	7.0	10.4
▲ FRONTIER BANK	LAMAR	CO	**A-**	B-	B-	187	5.64	5.4	1.2	9.6	45.4	**10.0**	11.8	21.6
FRONTIER BANK	LAGRANGE	GA	**D-**	C-	C	312	-2.58	4.8	1.8	16.1	15.3	**5.4**	7.6	11.3
FRONTIER BANK	ROCK RAPIDS	IA	**D+**	E-	E-	154	-4.70	16.4	1.9	6.4	33.4	**5.5**	7.6	11.4
FRONTIER BANK	DAVENPORT	NE	**C+**	C+	C	23	0.89	13.0	2.2	2.3	5.5	**10.0**	17.2	20.3
FRONTIER BANK	MADISON	NE	**C+**	C+	C+	114	22.73	19.4	2.7	21.3	6.8	**5.2**	9.6	11.1
▼ FRONTIER BANK FSB	PALM DESERT	CA	**E-**	C-	B-	313	-15.11	4.9	1.8	35.9	1.5	**2.3**	5.4	9.3
FRONTIER BANK OF TEXAS	ELGIN	TX	**C-**	C	C	93	29.94	6.1	4.7	19.1	17.0	**10.0**	26.9	52.1
FRONTIER COMMUNITY BANK	WAYNESBORO	VA	**D-**	C	C	70	29.84	9.3	0.6	14.1	0.0	**8.1**	10.4	13.4
FRONTIER SB	COUNCIL BLUFFS	IA	**C**	B-	B	31	2.31	5.9	0.4	5.4	4.9	**10.0**	12.1	20.8
▲ FRONTIER STATE BK	OKLAHOMA CITY	OK	**C**	C	B-	510	-6.77	16.4	2.3	11.3	32.4	**7.8**	9.5	13.7
FROST NATIONAL BK	SAN ANTONIO	TX	**B-**	B-	A-	17,647	7.97	19.3	1.8	3.4	30.7	**6.3**	8.3	14.4
FROST STATE BK	FROST	MN	**D+**	C-	D	31	17.67	10.2	5.5	8.0	3.9	**6.3**	9.4	11.9
FSGBANK NA	CHATTANOOGA	TN	**D-**	D	B-	1,167	-13.64	7.1	2.9	14.6	13.2	**5.1**	7.1	12.2
FULLERTON COMMUNITY	FULLERTON	CA	**D-**	D	D	688	-6.34	6.7	0.2	6.1	2.6	**6.7**	8.7	13.0
FULLERTON FEDERAL	BALTIMORE	MD	**E+**	D	C	9	-0.69	0.0	0.0	32.1	13.8	**5.6**	7.6	19.5
FULLERTON NATIONAL BK	FULLERTON	NE	**B-**	B-	B-	31	3.95	6.2	5.5	10.8	9.0	**8.5**	10.4	13.7
FULTON BANK NA	LANCASTER	PA	**C-**	C	B-	8,801	4.41	11.8	1.8	11.8	13.5	**7.2**	9.2	12.7
FULTON SB	FULTON	NY	**A-**	A-	B+	401	-0.05	0.8	1.4	49.4	21.7	**10.0**	16.9	27.7
FULTON STATE BK	FULTON	SD	**B-**	B	B+	51	7.24	18.2	3.3	0.2	33.2	**9.3**	10.6	17.5
G W JONES EXCHANGE BANK	MARCELLUS	MI	**C**	C	C+	59	-3.61	4.0	1.7	38.5	13.0	**7.8**	9.5	22.7
GALENA STATE BK & TRUST C	GALENA	IL	**C**	C-	C	278	-4.48	10.0	0.8	14.1	35.8	**6.3**	8.3	14.5
GALION BUILDING & LOAN BA	GALION	OH	**C**	C	C+	64	7.86	1.6	3.7	62.8	8.3	**8.2**	9.8	20.5
GARDEN CITY STATE BK	GARDEN CITY	KS	**B**	B-	B	61	4.98	27.7	1.6	11.8	4.5	**10.0**	13.1	15.7
GARDEN PLAIN STATE BK	WICHITA	KS	**B**	B	B+	73	7.04	12.9	3.5	21.6	23.0	**8.3**	9.9	13.7
▲ GARDNER BANK	GARDNER	KS	**C-**	C	C	90	-0.07	11.1	1.8	20.2	4.8	**6.0**	8.7	11.8
▲ GARFIELD COUNTY BANK	JORDAN	MT	**B-**	C+	B-	43	5.47	4.6	4.1	4.0	9.8	**10.0**	11.8	15.2
GARNAVILLO SB	GARNAVILLO	IA	**D**	C-	D+	40	5.86	13.9	4.6	6.7	9.6	**6.1**	8.1	12.3
GARNETT STATE SB	GARNETT	KS	**C+**	C+	B	108	0.33	4.8	3.1	9.6	48.6	**9.1**	10.4	19.6
GARRETT STATE BK	GARRETT	IN	**B**	B-	B-	170	2.68	2.9	2.4	50.0	21.7	**6.4**	8.4	16.8
GARRISON STATE BK & TRUST	GARRISON	ND	**B-**	B	B	75	8.32	9.6	5.5	3.2	20.5	**7.9**	9.6	14.2
GARY STATE BK	GARY	MN	**C+**	C	C-	11	-0.26	9.1	6.4	5.5	1.9	**10.0**	12.9	19.3
GATE CITY BANK	FARGO	ND	**B+**	B+	A-	1,216	6.11	0.2	27.3	48.2	5.1	**10.0**	12.0	19.5
▼ GATES BANKING & TRUST CO	GATES	TN	**B**	B+	A-	42	8.12	3.0	1.6	4.9	58.8	**6.9**	8.9	19.0
▲ GATEWAY BANK	MENDOTA HEIGHTS	MN	**B-**	C+	C	94	11.06	35.8	4.3	9.1	4.6	**6.8**	9.3	12.4
▼ GATEWAY BANK & TRUST	RINGGOLD	GA	**D+**	C-	C+	267	0.45	8.9	1.5	15.5	14.4	**7.4**	9.2	14.2
GATEWAY BANK FSB	SAN FRANCISCO	CA	**D-**	D-	D	306	-28.00	0.4	0.0	51.9	7.0	**6.2**	8.2	17.6
GATEWAY BANK OF CENTRAL	OCALA	FL	**D**	C	C-	202	15.39	6.3	1.0	10.7	12.6	**6.2**	8.6	11.9
GATEWAY BANK OF FLORIDA	DAYTONA BEACH	FL	**D-**	D	C	191	3.64	5.8	0.5	5.0	38.8	**5.9**	7.9	14.3
▲ GATEWAY BANK OF	MCMURRAY	PA	**C**	C-	C-	123	4.15	22.3	0.6	14.7	8.9	**10.0**	11.4	15.0
▼ GATEWAY BANK OF	SARASOTA	FL	**D-**	C	C	160	47.37	6.3	1.0	9.6	37.6	**7.4**	9.3	15.2

Asset Quality Index	Non-Performing Loans as a % of Total Loans	Non-Performing Loans as a % of Capital	Net Charge-offs / Avg Loans	Profitability Index	Net Income ($Mil)	Return on Assets (R.O.A.)	Return on Equity (R.O.E.)	Net Interest Spread	Overhead Efficiency Ratio	Liquidity Index	Liquidity Ratio	Hot Money Ratio	Stability Index
3.6	1.44	13.1	0.31	5.1	1.3	1.18	14.48	4.45	62.5	0.6	7.3	37.6	5.3
2.8	1.63	9.9	0.27	3.4	2.4	1.42	12.14	4.20	73.1	0.8	16.0	43.6	4.5
6.7	0.24	1.8	0.85	2.0	0.4	0.22	2.17	2.45	72.2	0.6	14.7	60.2	6.5
1.0	3.24	22.6	0.06	2.1	0.2	0.23	2.48	3.36	75.9	1.8	21.7	22.2	4.5
3.2	1.62	8.8	1.13	0.9	-0.1	-0.06	-0.58	3.93	87.4	4.1	35.8	13.0	5.2
2.9	3.90	18.9	0.04	3.4	0.1	0.58	5.90	3.92	83.4	3.6	50.4	16.9	5.5
2.6	1.49	10.5	0.49	5.9	3.3	1.45	12.60	4.48	61.1	3.5	16.1	11.4	6.2
8.4	0.12	0.3	0.00	3.4	1.3	0.54	4.48	2.10	62.2	4.0	77.6	27.0	7.0
4.9	7.96	16.9	1.82	0.4	-0.1	-0.23	-1.35	2.62	102.0	6.3	73.7	8.6	6.7
4.9	1.46	9.9	0.68	0.3	-0.1	-0.63	-8.11	3.57	109.6	4.0	16.9	8.3	0.0
5.2	1.53	12.9	0.00	6.1	0.9	1.06	12.52	5.27	68.6	2.7	13.3	15.6	4.7
4.3	0.66	5.1	0.13	5.6	4.9	1.17	12.08	4.63	67.5	2.4	6.7	16.2	5.7
2.7	2.57	20.6	1.47	4.0	30.5	1.24	14.44	3.76	58.5	4.0	5.1	7.7	6.5
4.8	0.30	2.2	0.18	5.9	4.7	1.53	17.34	4.11	57.1	3.1	12.6	13.2	4.2
3.7	0.22	1.1	0.41	3.8	1.5	1.12	9.76	4.53	66.4	2.0	37.4	32.6	5.2
2.5	4.94	22.8	1.60	0.0	-0.7	-0.70	-5.13	4.28	102.7	4.2	23.4	8.5	1.7
0.0	30.54	225.1	3.06	0.0	-4.1	-2.56	-28.34	2.77	83.9	1.4	21.1	28.4	5.4
5.4	0.64	5.4	0.29	5.6	2.6	0.95	11.16	4.52	66.8	2.5	19.9	16.9	4.9
0.3	7.83	43.7	0.00	0.4	0.0	0.00	0.00	N/,	0.0	1.0	21.9	34.6	2.8
0.0	4.45	35.2	1.98	0.0	-3.2	-0.78	-9.42	2.56	98.5	0.8	18.9	38.2	2.8
6.3	0.99	3.8	0.58	8.1	4.2	2.25	17.53	4.33	52.4	3.1	32.6	17.1	7.6
0.3	8.46	63.5	1.59	1.8	0.8	0.26	3.27	3.66	81.1	2.5	9.8	15.9	3.2
5.5	0.30	2.0	0.12	2.7	0.8	0.48	6.98	3.04	77.1	2.5	40.9	27.9	1.9
7.2	0.81	3.5	0.00	9.2	0.3	1.18	7.55	5.32	43.0	3.4	18.3	12.2	5.0
4.9	0.12	1.1	-0.05	2.7	0.1	0.13	1.10	3.42	87.6	2.7	5.6	14.6	6.0
0.3	11.39	122.9	0.03	0.1	-13.3	-3.89	-52.47	4.45	106.3	1.2	19.0	30.1	0.3
8.7	0.00	0.0	0.05	1.6	0.1	0.11	0.36	4.08	96.0	3.4	60.2	24.5	3.1
4.6	0.00	0.0	0.00	0.0	-0.4	-0.66	-5.68	3.22	106.8	0.9	6.7	31.1	0.8
7.1	0.00	0.0	0.00	2.5	0.1	0.18	1.48	4.11	93.8	5.5	50.6	9.3	5.9
2.8	4.08	20.8	0.69	7.0	6.5	1.25	12.28	4.06	52.2	1.1	28.9	55.8	5.3
4.3	1.96	10.2	0.52	7.0	218.0	1.28	10.33	4.12	61.5	6.1	38.9	5.9	10.0
1.7	1.96	16.0	0.22	8.0	0.4	1.41	15.07	4.40	37.7	0.7	15.6	48.4	5.3
0.3	8.10	53.9	4.26	0.0	-43.9	-3.36	-36.36	2.98	101.0	1.7	28.2	44.5	4.6
0.0	3.66	28.1	0.14	1.3	-0.9	-0.13	-1.50	3.62	86.1	1.4	18.6	27.6	4.2
3.5	5.35	21.8	0.00	0.0	-0.2	-1.75	-12.82	1.73	184.9	4.7	65.4	14.0	5.3
3.5	2.50	16.1	0.00	6.2	0.4	1.49	14.31	4.23	63.6	2.9	19.2	15.0	7.7
2.1	2.43	17.6	1.06	5.9	91.6	1.08	10.32	3.83	51.3	3.2	5.8	12.3	6.1
8.2	1.21	4.5	0.25	6.2	5.2	1.28	8.27	4.51	64.7	3.4	25.7	13.4	8.1
6.1	0.37	1.5	-0.05	4.3	0.4	0.75	6.85	4.19	71.7	3.5	47.8	18.6	6.1
4.1	2.39	13.4	0.27	2.3	0.1	0.18	1.88	3.89	90.6	5.1	39.7	8.9	4.9
2.2	3.95	25.0	0.76	7.1	3.9	1.36	16.33	3.65	49.6	3.9	22.9	10.1	5.0
5.1	1.04	7.6	0.19	2.9	0.3	0.41	4.15	3.66	82.6	4.1	23.1	9.1	4.5
5.1	1.43	8.3	0.15	7.5	1.3	2.11	16.97	5.26	56.0	1.5	9.2	23.1	7.9
6.1	0.54	3.2	0.17	5.7	0.7	0.95	9.12	4.52	61.9	2.1	29.1	22.2	6.8
3.3	0.18	1.5	0.79	2.2	0.1	0.14	1.62	4.19	76.4	3.4	7.9	11.2	5.1
2.3	3.01	17.3	0.02	8.7	0.5	1.24	10.27	4.60	52.7	0.8	18.3	37.0	9.4
0.5	2.70	22.8	1.13	3.5	0.2	0.49	6.10	4.51	61.5	2.1	19.1	18.9	5.4
5.1	1.55	6.2	0.18	3.0	0.5	0.41	3.93	3.20	82.5	4.3	35.0	12.0	5.4
5.7	0.58	4.5	0.17	5.6	2.3	1.35	15.38	3.69	60.8	1.8	27.6	25.7	5.9
6.0	0.39	2.5	-0.04	4.7	0.6	0.80	7.86	4.33	72.4	3.9	17.6	9.5	6.1
7.0	0.00	0.0	-0.22	5.9	0.2	1.40	11.09	4.91	74.4	3.2	28.7	13.8	5.7
6.9	0.26	1.6	0.11	4.5	10.5	0.89	7.44	3.60	67.9	3.5	17.8	12.1	9.5
5.5	2.81	8.1	0.01	6.0	0.5	1.20	11.21	3.92	56.8	2.1	46.9	47.8	6.6
7.4	0.00	0.0	0.17	5.9	1.4	1.55	16.97	4.46	57.3	2.0	20.5	19.8	5.6
1.3	3.70	24.0	1.46	2.6	1.0	0.37	4.01	4.01	67.5	3.5	22.2	12.3	4.2
0.5	6.62	34.5	0.00	0.0	-5.3	-1.51	-21.18	3.70	91.6	2.3	37.7	27.7	1.9
1.7	3.74	28.5	1.04	0.9	0.1	0.06	0.64	4.02	70.1	1.3	17.8	27.9	2.3
0.3	2.82	13.7	4.62	0.0	-2.4	-1.25	-14.26	3.51	65.4	1.6	34.2	34.6	2.3
8.6	0.00	0.0	0.01	1.8	0.5	0.36	3.20	3.24	83.5	0.6	11.6	52.5	7.0
3.7	1.38	7.5	0.30	0.0	-0.4	-0.28	-2.37	3.47	110.2	5.3	41.4	8.7	1.8

Name	City	State	Rating	2008 Rating	2007 Rating	Total Assets ($Mil)	One Year Asset Growth	Asset Mix (As a % of Total Assets): Comm-ercial Loans	Cons-umer Loans	Home Mort-gages	Secur-ities	Capital-ization Index	Leverage Ratio	Risk-based Capital Ratio
▲ GATEWAY BUSINESS BANK	CERRITOS	CA	**D+**	D	C	198	-8.38	7.5	0.1	29.1	0.1	**10.0**	13.5	31.2
▼ GATEWAY COMMERCIAL BANK	MESA	AZ	**D+**	C	C	71	30.69	8.7	0.4	2.2	32.8	**10.0**	15.0	25.7
GATEWAY COMMUNITY BANK	ROSCOE	IL	**C-**	D+	D+	85	2.05	11.4	2.1	15.0	24.5	**7.7**	9.4	13.7
▼ GATEWAY STATE BK	CLINTON	IA	**C+**	B	B+	115	5.58	10.5	2.6	12.7	19.8	**5.4**	7.4	12.0
GBC INTERNATIONAL BK	LOS ANGELES	CA	**D+**	C-	C-	386	27.61	16.0	0.2	2.2	5.1	**6.0**	8.0	13.1
▲ GCF BANK	SEWELL	NJ	**D+**	D	C-	348	0.06	1.9	10.3	34.2	32.5	**5.4**	7.4	12.5
GE CAPITAL FINANCIAL INC	SALT LAKE CITY	UT	**A**	A-	A-	7,545	-20.70	60.7	0.0	0.0	6.1	**10.0**	21.2	20.8
▲ GE MONEY BANK	DRAPER	UT	**B-**	C+	C+	22,237	18.24	4.8	92.2	0.2	0.5	**10.0**	23.5	20.4
GEAUGA SB	NEWBURY	OH	**D-**	D-	D+	424	-4.33	0.0	0.0	38.5	32.6	**8.4**	9.9	19.0
GEDDES FS&LA	SYRACUSE	NY	**B-**	B-	B-	461	13.36	0.0	0.2	86.1	0.1	**10.0**	12.4	24.5
▼ GENERATIONS BANK	CENTRE	AL	**D**	C	C	62	19.91	8.2	3.2	10.0	15.4	**10.0**	11.4	15.3
GENERATIONS BANK	OVERLAND PARK	KS	**D-**	D	C-	44	-44.44	12.2	0.3	29.2	43.4	**5.3**	7.3	15.2
GENESEE REGIONAL BANK	ROCHESTER	NY	**C**	C-	C+	270	31.71	16.5	1.6	2.8	25.2	**5.4**	7.4	11.6
GENEVA STATE BK	GENEVA	NE	**C+**	C	C-	217	3.43	2.9	1.8	3.8	21.8	**4.8**	8.5	10.9
GENOA BANKING CO	GENOA	OH	**C+**	C+	C+	249	0.94	6.1	6.4	27.5	19.0	**5.9**	7.9	13.2
GENOA NATIONAL BK	GENOA	NE	**D**	D+	D	55	0.75	4.4	3.4	5.2	28.1	**8.0**	9.6	14.0
GEO D WARTHEN BANK	SANDERSVILLE	GA	**D+**	C	B-	171	6.61	8.2	7.7	18.3	30.0	**7.1**	9.1	14.4
▲ GEORGETOWN SAVINGS	GEORGETOWN	MA	**C+**	C-	D+	205	2.85	4.8	0.4	42.4	5.1	**6.8**	8.8	12.3
GEORGIA BANKING CO	ATLANTA	GA	**D**	D	D	243	19.38	3.0	0.5	63.9	13.2	**6.8**	8.8	19.5
GEORGIA BK & TRUST CO AUG	AUGUSTA	GA	**C-**	D+	D	1,431	7.74	5.2	1.1	10.3	38.4	**5.2**	7.2	13.4
GEORGIA COMMERCE BANK	ATLANTA	GA	**B**	B	B-	395	13.79	23.3	1.3	14.5	4.4	**10.0**	12.0	15.7
GEORGIA HERITAGE BANK	DALLAS	GA	**E-**	D-	E-	81	-8.08	4.6	2.0	6.7	17.3	**1.7**	5.1	8.7
▼ GEORGIA PRIMARY BANK	ATLANTA	GA	**D**	C+	C	295	16.95	39.0	0.0	6.5	1.5	**6.8**	9.8	12.3
GEORGIA TRUST BANK	BUFORD	GA	**E-**	E	D-	144	-9.60	9.1	1.1	7.0	15.1	**0.0**	2.9	5.4
GERBER STATE BK	ARGENTA	IL	**B-**	B-	B+	64	5.54	1.0	1.6	16.3	46.5	**6.7**	10.7	12.3
GERMAN AMERICAN	JASPER	IN	**B+**	B+	B	1,366	10.49	13.7	2.3	7.6	25.2	**6.7**	8.7	13.2
GERMAN-AMERICAN STATE	GERMAN VALLEY	IL	**C+**	C	C	185	5.66	16.1	3.7	14.9	22.9	**6.8**	8.8	12.5
GERMANTOWN TRUST & SB	BREESE	IL	**A+**	A+	A	314	2.44	2.3	1.1	13.0	56.3	**10.0**	13.0	26.5
▲ GIBRALTAR BANK	OAK RIDGE	NJ	**C+**	C-	D	96	-2.64	0.4	0.0	62.7	12.8	**10.0**	11.8	24.1
GIBRALTAR PRIVATE BANK &	CORAL GABLES	FL	**D**	D-	C-	1,643	11.33	2.0	1.9	41.3	4.8	**7.0**	9.0	14.4
GIBSLAND BANK & TRUST CO	GIBSLAND	LA	**B-**	B-	C+	232	21.26	7.6	6.6	16.6	15.8	**5.8**	8.7	11.6
GIFFORD STATE BK	GIFFORD	IL	**C+**	C+	B-	104	11.38	5.2	4.7	20.4	7.7	**4.2**	8.3	10.6
GILMER NATIONAL BK	GILMER	TX	**B**	B-	B-	187	1.29	4.4	15.4	18.2	31.6	**10.0**	12.9	23.4
▲ GILMORE BANK	LOS ANGELES	CA	**D+**	D-	D	179	-3.45	20.7	3.6	7.7	16.1	**8.3**	9.9	15.5
GIRARD NATIONAL BK	GIRARD	KS	**D**	C-	C+	498	0.05	14.3	4.0	11.5	19.2	**7.3**	9.6	12.7
GLACIER BANK	KALISPELL	MT	**C-**	C-	B+	1,374	3.25	4.5	1.0	13.7	32.8	**10.0**	12.0	17.9
GLADEWATER NATIONAL BK	GLADEWATER	TX	**D**	C	B	31	10.43	25.4	7.5	17.6	6.3	**10.0**	11.3	18.8
GLASFORD STATE BK	GLASFORD	IL	**B**	B	B+	31	4.56	1.2	6.9	27.8	29.9	**6.5**	8.6	23.4
▼ GLASGOW SB	GLASGOW	MO	**E**	C-	C	32	-11.70	5.0	3.8	12.9	17.8	**3.4**	5.4	10.3
GLEN BURNIE MUTUAL SB	GLEN BURNIE	MD	**C-**	C-	C-	71	4.30	0.0	0.0	69.7	2.3	**6.8**	8.8	18.8
▲ GLEN ROCK SB	GLEN ROCK	NJ	**C**	C-	C-	147	-1.37	0.0	0.2	69.1	21.9	**4.8**	6.8	13.8
GLENMEDE TRUST CO NA	PHILADELPHIA	PA	**U**	U	U	51	-1.36	0.0	0.0	0.0	12.9	**10.0**	47.1	82.1
▲ GLENNVILLE BANK	GLENNVILLE	GA	**C+**	C+	B	138	4.85	4.7	4.3	20.0	20.3	**8.2**	9.8	16.7
GLENS FALLS NATIONAL BK &	GLENS FALLS	NY	**A-**	A-	B+	1,641	4.41	4.3	16.9	19.1	37.7	**6.3**	8.3	15.5
GLENVIEW STATE BK	GLENVIEW	IL	**B**	B	B	1,134	9.97	5.4	10.7	7.5	55.8	**7.8**	9.5	16.2
GLENWOOD STATE BK	GLENWOOD	IA	**C**	B-	B+	140	4.46	1.1	3.3	5.9	42.0	**8.1**	9.7	25.5
GLENWOOD STATE BK	GLENWOOD	MN	**C**	C-	C+	181	3.25	25.9	1.9	13.0	2.0	**6.0**	9.3	11.8
GLOBAL BANK	NEW YORK	NY	**D-**	D	C-	123	-4.91	1.3	0.1	35.5	27.5	**9.1**	10.4	22.5
▼ GLOBAL COMMERCE BANK	DORAVILLE	GA	**E**	D-	B+	157	-11.36	3.7	0.3	0.5	22.0	**2.2**	5.5	9.2
▼ GLOBAL TRUST BANK	MOUNTAIN VIEW	CA	**D**	C	C	66	27.04	24.4	1.1	1.2	0.0	**10.0**	25.2	39.2
GOGEBIC RANGE BANK	IRONWOOD	MI	**C+**	B	B	62	0.08	29.2	8.0	11.7	6.6	**8.3**	10.4	13.6
▼ GOLD CANYON BANK	GOLD CANYON	AZ	**E+**	C-	D+	59	-9.60	8.0	4.7	2.7	38.6	**3.4**	5.4	10.3
▲ GOLD COAST BANK	CHICAGO	IL	**B-**	C+	C-	182	18.53	7.6	0.3	26.0	0.0	**7.7**	9.4	14.1
▼ GOLD COAST BANK	ISLANDIA	NY	**D**	C	C	119	28.98	7.3	1.3	0.0	28.4	**10.0**	13.4	21.9
▼ GOLD COUNTRY BANK NA	MARYSVILLE	CA	**D-**	D	D-	123	24.75	10.6	1.3	10.2	5.1	**8.7**	10.2	17.8
GOLDEN BANK NA	HOUSTON	TX	**C**	B-	B+	506	-0.36	4.8	0.3	2.4	19.0	**10.0**	12.1	18.8
GOLDEN BELT BANK FSA	ELLIS	KS	**C**	C	B+	135	2.25	10.8	3.2	25.0	22.8	**8.9**	10.3	15.0
GOLDEN COAST BANK	LONG BEACH	CA	**D**	E	D	35	-3.57	0.6	0.0	4.7	7.2	**10.0**	33.3	38.5
GOLDEN EAGLE COMMUNITY	WOODSTOCK	IL	**D-**	D+	C	153	14.26	5.5	0.6	14.0	14.6	**8.6**	10.1	14.4
▼ GOLDEN SECURITY BANK	ROSEMEAD	CA	**E-**	D-	D-	148	-10.26	0.0	0.0	0.0	0.0	**2.6**	6.4	9.6

Asset Quality Index	Non-Performing Loans as a % of Total Loans	Non-Performing Loans as a % of Capital	Net Charge-offs Avg Loans	Profitability Index	Net Income ($Mil)	Return on Assets (R.O.A.)	Return on Equity (R.O.E.)	Net Interest Spread	Overhead Efficiency Ratio	Liquidity Index	Liquidity Ratio	Hot Money Ratio	Stability Index
2.2	3.75	15.6	1.91	**1.8**	0.4	0.20	1.38	3.26	90.2	**2.2**	37.7	29.7	**4.9**
6.3	0.00	0.0	0.50	**0.7**	0.1	0.16	0.93	3.37	87.4	**4.2**	57.2	16.8	**2.2**
2.3	3.25	21.7	0.45	**3.5**	0.8	0.88	9.97	4.24	73.4	**1.5**	23.3	27.3	**4.6**
4.3	0.60	4.9	0.11	**3.8**	0.7	0.61	6.86	3.59	75.7	**2.0**	22.2	19.9	**5.8**
1.1	2.49	20.0	0.50	**7.9**	6.3	1.88	21.02	4.45	49.0	**0.8**	19.4	40.6	**4.8**
3.0	1.73	12.2	0.20	**1.3**	-0.7	-0.20	-2.58	3.24	109.5	**2.6**	40.3	25.7	**3.2**
6.6	0.58	2.3	0.00	**10.0**	201.3	2.44	9.91	3.78	40.4	**0.3**	12.6	99.2	**9.0**
2.8	2.12	7.0	6.81	**5.4**	849.0	4.30	16.37	15.28	35.2	**0.1**	2.2	98.4	**9.5**
0.3	8.74	44.7	1.73	**0.2**	-1.1	-0.24	-2.46	3.08	74.5	**0.7**	19.7	54.5	**3.8**
8.8	0.51	3.7	0.01	**3.9**	3.6	0.80	6.44	2.77	52.4	**0.8**	9.9	32.9	**7.2**
8.5	0.00	0.0	0.25	**0.3**	-0.1	-0.15	-1.25	3.72	94.2	**1.0**	18.0	33.7	**2.2**
6.5	0.00	0.0	-0.44	**0.0**	-1.6	-2.62	-32.19	2.92	99.9	**2.2**	52.1	55.5	**3.8**
4.9	0.44	3.5	0.11	**4.9**	2.0	0.90	12.59	3.83	61.3	**1.7**	35.2	37.9	**2.7**
6.8	0.15	1.2	0.39	**5.5**	2.2	1.11	12.72	4.40	65.4	**2.2**	10.8	17.4	**4.5**
4.2	1.65	13.6	0.52	**3.4**	1.4	0.56	6.94	4.04	76.4	**2.2**	13.4	17.9	**4.4**
0.7	4.65	27.8	0.28	**3.8**	0.5	0.81	8.71	3.52	65.1	**1.2**	16.8	29.1	**5.5**
1.7	3.91	25.1	0.52	**3.1**	0.7	0.41	4.52	4.19	80.4	**2.6**	24.0	17.0	**4.8**
7.7	0.01	0.1	0.05	**3.6**	1.5	0.72	8.69	4.01	72.2	**2.7**	7.4	14.9	**3.0**
1.7	4.45	34.2	1.70	**1.4**	0.5	0.22	2.16	3.59	77.9	**0.5**	11.4	65.7	**2.9**
3.5	2.81	16.5	1.30	**2.6**	6.8	0.49	6.50	3.27	62.1	**2.2**	26.1	26.7	**4.6**
4.0	0.00	0.0	0.54	**4.3**	2.1	0.61	5.34	4.06	56.7	**1.2**	25.9	32.8	**6.1**
0.3	4.59	38.6	1.49	**0.0**	-3.1	-3.61	-50.65	2.62	723.0	**1.5**	27.1	29.7	**0.0**
0.3	8.96	64.3	0.96	**3.3**	1.0	0.36	3.53	3.96	37.6	**2.8**	13.0	14.8	**1.3**
0.3	14.42	180.9	2.36	**0.0**	-6.6	-4.19	-86.79	1.64	-1,533.3	**1.0**	24.9	36.5	**0.0**
4.6	1.94	7.7	0.47	**3.4**	0.5	0.78	6.69	3.25	65.9	**4.7**	39.6	11.4	**7.0**
5.6	1.11	7.8	0.32	**6.3**	14.9	1.13	10.67	4.22	60.0	**4.4**	21.5	8.1	**8.2**
3.9	1.25	9.5	0.70	**6.4**	2.6	1.48	16.32	3.93	48.4	**1.5**	17.1	24.5	**4.9**
9.4	0.00	0.0	0.02	**8.5**	6.1	1.94	13.84	2.99	36.7	**5.1**	54.9	13.2	**9.5**
4.6	2.05	12.9	0.13	**2.8**	0.6	0.57	5.12	3.51	79.5	**1.7**	19.8	22.6	**6.4**
1.3	3.68	29.0	0.11	**0.3**	-9.5	-0.60	-6.38	3.79	87.4	**1.2**	12.6	28.9	**5.5**
4.4	1.23	9.5	0.36	**8.4**	2.8	1.38	16.89	5.51	63.2	**0.9**	24.3	41.5	**4.5**
6.3	0.62	5.1	0.24	**4.5**	1.0	0.98	11.88	3.82	70.3	**1.3**	15.1	27.7	**5.2**
4.6	2.69	10.8	0.71	**4.1**	1.7	0.89	6.75	4.16	64.6	**2.3**	44.8	34.6	**6.2**
2.4	2.37	15.7	-0.26	**2.1**	1.1	0.62	6.46	4.42	91.1	**3.4**	24.2	13.2	**3.7**
0.8	3.58	23.9	1.08	**3.8**	2.7	0.54	4.78	4.02	67.6	**2.1**	9.7	17.9	**6.8**
1.3	6.66	29.3	2.75	**5.6**	13.2	0.99	8.10	4.36	43.1	**4.4**	20.6	7.9	**7.3**
0.2	7.74	39.0	0.14	**2.1**	0.1	0.29	2.40	4.11	88.1	**2.3**	35.7	25.8	**3.7**
4.3	1.73	9.4	0.49	**2.1**	0.1	0.20	2.05	3.40	88.3	**5.6**	32.3	2.9	**5.8**
1.7	7.14	45.3	1.96	**0.0**	-3.0	-8.43	-70.04	2.75	377.8	**2.2**	27.9	20.1	**4.2**
6.1	0.91	7.4	0.00	**1.6**	0.1	0.15	1.71	1.07	85.5	**5.5**	25.2	0.0	**4.9**
5.2	1.52	14.6	0.00	**3.9**	1.0	0.67	11.05	3.37	65.9	**2.2**	9.2	17.3	**3.1**
10.0	0.00	0.0	0.00	**9.5**	5.4	9.66	24.13	0.72	91.1	**2.8**	80.8	101.0	**7.0**
3.6	1.66	9.5	0.94	**5.5**	1.3	0.98	9.97	3.79	57.9	**1.1**	27.1	35.8	**5.5**
6.9	0.47	2.9	0.06	**6.5**	18.7	1.16	13.00	3.59	62.0	**4.3**	16.2	7.4	**8.3**
8.4	0.16	0.5	0.05	**4.6**	12.8	1.18	11.11	2.83	66.6	**5.8**	56.6	11.7	**9.3**
6.7	0.59	1.7	0.13	**2.7**	0.6	0.42	4.25	3.07	85.8	**6.5**	65.7	7.4	**5.4**
2.5	1.82	14.7	0.49	**4.4**	1.8	0.99	10.70	4.15	63.6	**1.6**	8.4	21.5	**6.3**
6.5	0.00	0.0	0.56	**0.2**	0.1	0.11	1.12	3.21	99.7	**1.2**	9.7	27.4	**1.5**
0.0	10.59	78.0	4.44	**0.0**	-6.4	-3.70	-49.55	2.28	134.8	**1.0**	20.3	33.5	**3.5**
8.6	0.00	0.0	0.00	**0.0**	-1.6	-2.56	-9.34	3.03	159.6	**2.5**	56.6	36.0	**1.5**
3.9	1.50	10.6	0.72	**7.0**	0.8	1.18	11.82	5.02	53.4	**1.7**	15.2	20.9	**7.2**
3.7	3.26	24.0	3.38	**0.0**	-1.7	-2.50	-38.05	3.07	137.5	**2.9**	45.1	24.0	**0.5**
5.5	0.55	3.7	0.58	**4.4**	1.3	0.75	8.19	4.77	42.2	**0.7**	13.2	44.3	**5.4**
7.9	0.19	0.8	0.00	**0.1**	-0.6	-0.53	-3.49	3.91	99.6	**4.7**	31.7	8.4	**1.6**
3.4	0.97	5.1	0.44	**0.0**	-2.3	-3.07	-28.23	5.17	129.2	**4.1**	43.1	15.5	**2.9**
1.8	6.45	29.0	0.37	**2.4**	1.0	0.19	1.51	3.65	77.4	**3.6**	35.0	15.5	**7.7**
2.6	2.68	15.7	0.00	**5.6**	1.6	1.23	10.95	4.06	56.3	**4.9**	36.1	8.7	**7.2**
6.0	0.00	0.0	0.15	**0.0**	-0.6	-1.62	-10.62	1.98	163.2	**1.5**	34.3	54.4	**2.0**
0.0	4.80	30.0	0.25	**3.0**	0.9	0.61	5.93	3.77	69.1	**1.2**	23.3	31.2	**1.0**
0.0	7.09	61.5	1.66	**0.2**	-2.3	-1.41	-22.25	4.16	107.2	**4.6**	17.1	4.9	**4.3**

Name	City	State	Rating	2008 Rating	2007 Rating	Total Assets ($Mil)	One Year Asset Growth	Asset Mix (As a % of Total Assets) Comm-ercial Loans	Cons-umer Loans	Home Mort-gages	Secur-ities	Capital-ization Index	Leverage Ratio	Risk-based Capital Ratio
▼ GOLDEN STATE BK	UPLAND	CA	E-	E+	D+	123	-22.91	18.3	1.4	6.1	0.0	1.7	6.0	8.7
▲ GOLDEN VALLEY BANK	CHICO	CA	B-	C	C	102	10.04	7.6	0.2	8.6	13.9	10.0	15.7	23.0
GOLDMAN SACHS BANK USA	NEW YORK	NY	A-	B+	NR	89,447	-1.72	0.9	0.3	1.1	0.0	10.0	19.5	23.9
GOLDMAN SACHS TRUST CO	NEW YORK	NY	U	U	U	36	6.15	0.0	0.0	0.0	75.4	10.0	88.2	498.3
GOLDWATER BANK NA	SCOTTSDALE	AZ	E-	E	D+	192	-2.44	3.0	2.8	24.5	20.4	2.0	4.6	13.3
▲ GOODFIELD STATE BK	GOODFIELD	IL	B+	B-	B-	71	8.48	10.8	4.8	19.1	22.7	7.7	10.9	13.1
▼ GOOSE RIVER BANK	MAYVILLE	ND	D	D+	D+	105	6.34	10.7	4.8	2.4	22.6	5.2	7.2	12.3
GOPPERT FINANCIAL BANK	LATHROP	MO	C+	C+	B-	69	6.08	12.3	1.6	12.3	29.4	8.4	9.9	14.9
GORHAM SB	GORHAM	ME	C	C	C	897	2.55	7.2	0.9	26.0	21.0	6.1	8.1	13.5
GORHAM STATE BK	GORHAM	KS	C-	C	D+	22	-1.08	10.5	4.2	8.7	3.0	6.0	8.0	16.3
▼ GOTHAM BANK OF NEW YORK	NEW YORK	NY	C-	C-	B-	385	4.09	19.0	0.0	4.4	52.4	5.3	7.3	19.1
GOTHENBURG STATE BK	GOTHENBURG	NE	A-	B+	B	111	7.22	14.5	4.1	3.2	12.1	10.0	11.8	15.2
GOUVERNEUR SAVINGS &	GOUVERNEUR	NY	B+	B+	A-	147	1.64	1.5	4.1	59.5	12.6	10.0	15.8	29.1
GRABILL BANK	GRABILL	IN	B-	C	C	604	3.66	11.6	0.7	9.0	18.4	7.8	9.5	14.2
GRAHAM SAVINGS & LOAN	GRAHAM	TX	B+	B+	B	132	6.16	0.7	2.7	61.0	5.9	7.2	9.2	16.3
▲ GRAND BANK	TULSA	OK	C+	C	C+	218	-9.73	17.2	0.9	10.5	16.6	10.0	11.5	15.2
GRAND BANK	DALLAS	TX	C+	B-	B-	411	-0.85	5.4	1.3	5.6	18.1	5.9	7.9	26.0
▼ GRAND BANK & TRUST OF FLO	WEST PALM BEACH	FL	E-	D-	C-	453	-5.87	8.0	0.8	4.6	16.0	3.0	5.8	10.0
▼ GRAND BANK FOR SAVINGS	HATTIESBURG	MS	D+	C+	B	138	-1.16	2.3	0.8	50.6	0.0	7.3	9.2	17.3
GRAND BANK NA	HAMILTON	NJ	D+	D+	C	425	22.69	3.6	0.3	54.2	2.1	6.6	8.6	17.7
▼ GRAND BANK OF TEXAS	GRAND PRAIRIE	TX	D	D+	C	119	2.85	10.0	3.3	30.5	4.5	5.4	7.4	11.6
▲ GRAND MARAIS STATE BK	GRAND MARAIS	MN	B-	B+	B	69	5.68	6.6	1.8	31.4	26.0	7.0	9.0	15.1
GRAND MARSH STATE BK	GRAND MARSH	WI	A	A	A	119	1.79	4.5	2.3	25.0	37.7	10.0	16.1	29.4
GRAND MOUNTAIN BANK FSB	GRANBY	CO	D-	D+	C	125	-14.26	5.9	1.0	27.9	4.3	6.4	8.4	13.7
GRAND RAPIDS STATE BK	GRAND RAPIDS	MN	B	B	A-	229	-2.83	10.0	3.5	14.9	26.5	9.7	10.8	15.4
▼ GRAND RIDGE NATIONAL BK	WHEATON	IL	C-	B-	B-	42	20.22	8.7	1.1	6.5	37.7	10.0	22.6	43.1
GRAND RIVER BANK	GRANDVILLE	MI	D	C	NR	52	73.75	8.7	0.0	3.9	7.3	10.0	21.7	26.0
▼ GRAND RIVERS COMMUNITY	GRAND CHAIN	IL	E	C-	D	16	9.06	19.8	7.4	23.7	8.9	6.3	8.4	12.3
GRAND SB	GROVE	OK	C	C	B-	231	6.14	6.3	16.0	29.5	0.5	6.7	9.3	12.3
▼ GRAND TIMBER BANK	MCGREGOR	MN	C-	D	D	43	-5.16	9.6	7.1	21.7	9.7	10.0	11.3	15.6
GRAND VALLEY BANK	HEBER CITY	UT	D	D+	C+	255	1.86	2.9	0.5	5.6	54.0	7.1	9.1	19.5
GRANDPOINT BANK	LOS ANGELES	CA	D	C	C	491	1761.50	15.3	0.5	3.7	19.8	10.0	39.3	15.2
GRANDSOUTH BANK	GREENVILLE	SC	D	D-	C-	363	-5.15	15.4	1.1	13.7	11.0	10.0	11.6	15.5
GRANDVIEW BANK	GRANDVIEW	TX	B	B	B	101	13.93	13.4	9.8	17.2	14.7	6.8	9.1	12.4
GRANGER NATIONAL BK	GRANGER	TX	B	B-	B-	28	3.86	1.1	2.5	4.6	55.8	10.0	13.8	34.3
GRANITE FALLS BANK	GRANITE FALLS	MN	B	B	C+	187	2.09	4.2	1.2	1.3	60.5	6.2	8.2	16.5
GRANITE SB	ROCKPORT	MA	C	C	C+	72	6.40	0.0	0.4	39.0	23.1	10.0	13.8	24.4
▲ GRANT COUNTY BANK	ULYSSES	KS	C	B	B+	180	2.10	7.2	4.8	18.9	24.7	8.8	10.2	15.9
▼ GRANT COUNTY BANK	MEDFORD	OK	B-	B+	B	75	8.47	7.4	7.3	7.7	42.6	10.0	12.3	23.9
GRANT COUNTY BANK	PETERSBURG	WV	C-	C	B-	244	-1.40	4.7	5.2	33.6	6.1	8.9	10.3	14.6
▲ GRANT COUNTY DEPOSIT	WILLIAMSTOWN	KY	C-	C+	C+	91	0.13	0.8	3.7	29.7	20.9	9.1	10.4	18.5
GRANT COUNTY STATE BK	SWAYZEE	IN	B-	B-	B	81	13.98	3.7	8.3	34.4	13.3	6.9	8.9	15.6
GRANT COUNTY STATE BK	CARSON	ND	B	B	B	29	0.92	1.5	0.9	0.0	0.0	8.4	9.9	17.6
GRANTS STATE BK	GRANTS	NM	C-	C-	B-	110	5.94	2.3	2.0	3.7	59.7	6.8	8.8	19.3
GRANVILLE NATIONAL BK	GRANVILLE	IL	C	D+	D	46	5.26	2.6	5.2	26.9	29.7	7.3	9.2	20.3
GRAPELAND STATE BK	GRAPELAND	TX	D	C	C-	26	-1.10	4.6	26.7	16.2	28.6	5.3	7.3	12.5
GRATIOT STATE BK	GRATIOT	WI	C+	C-	B-	39	8.24	2.6	1.5	8.0	62.8	10.0	11.2	24.9
GRATZ NATIONAL BK	GRATZ	PA	A	A	A	144	5.63	9.3	1.1	39.7	13.6	10.0	12.0	21.1
GRAYSON NATIONAL BK	INDEPENDENCE	VA	D+	D	C-	368	-0.38	3.5	3.3	32.3	13.0	6.3	8.3	13.6
▼ GRAYSTONE TOWER BANK	LANCASTER	PA	C	C	C-	2,745	87.06	9.1	0.6	21.1	3.7	6.1	12.6	11.8
GREAT AMERICAN BANK	DE SOTO	KS	C+	C+	C+	52	1.93	3.2	0.6	15.0	4.8	10.0	11.6	19.1
GREAT EASTERN BANK OF	MIAMI	FL	D-	D-	D	62	-4.83	8.8	0.6	8.9	17.0	10.0	11.7	16.4
▼ GREAT FLORIDA BANK	MIAMI LAKES	FL	E-	D-	D-	1,556	-12.19	5.7	0.4	21.7	25.0	0.9	4.1	8.4
GREAT LAKES BANK NA	BLUE ISLAND	IL	C-	C-	B-	642	-3.91	7.9	0.3	10.8	40.6	7.2	9.1	14.4
GREAT LAKES BANKERS BANK	WORTHINGTON	OH	C	C-	C	106	14.73	1.9	0.0	0.7	33.1	6.7	8.7	19.7
GREAT MIDWEST BANK SSB	BROOKFIELD	WI	B-	B-	C+	544	-2.15	0.1	0.3	61.3	16.9	10.0	17.0	28.3
GREAT NATIONS BANK	NORMAN	OK	D	C	NR	28	57.67	9.8	0.6	7.3	6.5	10.0	36.5	54.0
GREAT NORTHERN BANK	SAINT MICHAEL	MN	E-	E-	E-	70	-14.43	9.2	1.7	19.3	10.7	1.1	5.0	8.1
▲ GREAT PLAINS BANK	EUREKA	SD	C-	C+	C+	90	9.27	12.1	1.8	2.0	10.3	4.8	8.9	10.9
GREAT PLAINS NATIONAL BK	BELFIELD	ND	B	B	B-	137	26.17	7.4	3.4	3.9	20.7	6.5	8.5	12.1

Asset Quality Index	Non-Performing Loans as a % of Total Loans	Non-Performing Loans as a % of Capital	Net Charge-offs Avg Loans	Profitability Index	Net Income ($Mil)	Return on Assets (R.O.A.)	Return on Equity (R.O.E.)	Net Interest Spread	Overhead Efficiency Ratio	Liquidity Index	Liquidity Ratio	Hot Money Ratio	Stability Index
0.0	16.24	143.2	2.07	**0.0**	-2.9	-2.01	-30.76	4.18	104.2	**0.7**	13.9	42.3	**3.0**
4.5	3.42	13.6	0.57	**3.5**	0.8	0.86	5.36	4.76	70.2	**3.5**	29.7	14.3	**5.2**
10.0	0.00	0.0	0.00	**7.9**	1,199.0	1.28	6.64	-0.33	42.2	**4.2**	106.2	38.0	**7.0**
10.0	0.00	0.0	0.00	**7.0**	1.6	4.84	5.47	0.15	88.6	**5.0**	562.8	101.0	**7.0**
0.3	9.64	68.5	3.23	**0.0**	-1.6	-0.82	-15.37	4.21	101.5	**2.2**	45.6	48.6	**0.0**
8.5	0.09	0.5	-0.11	**8.9**	2.2	3.38	32.03	4.91	41.5	**2.9**	31.5	17.7	**5.6**
2.8	0.32	2.4	1.18	**2.0**	0.1	0.13	1.69	3.83	71.7	**2.8**	27.9	17.2	**2.9**
6.7	0.38	2.2	0.18	**3.1**	0.3	0.47	4.56	3.94	82.9	**2.8**	26.5	16.6	**5.1**
2.4	3.06	23.7	0.10	**2.7**	5.7	0.63	7.84	2.89	82.5	**0.9**	2.9	30.5	**5.5**
8.7	0.17	0.9	0.00	**3.7**	0.1	0.60	7.47	3.72	75.8	**5.2**	50.0	9.0	**3.7**
7.0	0.50	2.3	0.98	**1.9**	1.8	0.47	6.18	2.43	76.9	**2.6**	51.5	37.5	**3.3**
7.9	0.12	0.7	0.12	**8.4**	1.9	1.78	15.19	4.70	60.4	**1.4**	15.9	26.2	**7.3**
5.6	1.59	7.6	0.13	**5.4**	1.8	1.24	8.13	4.66	58.7	**3.5**	16.6	11.9	**8.2**
4.6	1.16	7.4	0.21	**6.5**	7.2	1.22	12.47	3.64	51.7	**1.6**	21.9	25.8	**6.6**
5.2	1.24	10.4	0.03	**7.0**	2.1	1.65	18.61	3.65	56.5	**0.8**	15.5	39.9	**6.7**
3.9	2.63	15.6	2.37	**3.5**	1.0	0.44	3.78	4.58	61.8	**0.8**	2.0	31.5	**5.9**
9.5	0.00	0.0	0.16	**3.0**	2.2	0.56	6.74	1.92	78.2	**6.8**	60.3	4.8	**4.3**
0.3	7.83	64.6	5.32	**0.0**	-18.1	-3.78	-46.06	2.82	96.3	**1.8**	28.5	26.8	**1.7**
2.3	3.75	28.8	0.00	**1.4**	0.0	-0.02	-0.25	5.88	78.9	**1.0**	23.2	34.8	**4.4**
1.5	2.90	26.8	1.64	**5.4**	5.0	1.37	15.53	3.62	84.6	**0.5**	6.6	49.0	**3.6**
0.7	4.83	42.3	1.05	**1.1**	-0.5	-0.38	-5.16	4.66	89.5	**3.6**	17.3	11.3	**3.7**
9.0	0.11	0.8	0.00	**8.8**	1.3	1.97	22.83	4.68	61.5	**3.5**	25.8	12.9	**5.0**
6.2	1.76	5.9	0.21	**7.3**	1.5	1.31	8.48	3.62	44.7	**4.0**	49.7	17.5	**8.3**
0.3	12.50	81.4	1.33	**0.2**	-2.1	-1.54	-17.91	3.69	95.4	**1.5**	27.9	29.8	**3.0**
5.8	0.63	3.1	0.34	**5.5**	2.8	1.23	10.74	4.73	66.5	**3.1**	27.7	15.6	**6.3**
7.9	1.22	2.2	0.00	**0.6**	-0.2	-1.13	-8.27	3.29	164.4	**3.1**	56.5	27.3	**6.5**
7.7	0.00	0.0	0.00	**0.0**	-1.2	-2.93	-10.65	3.11	166.3	**2.1**	19.8	18.9	**1.5**
2.0	4.08	34.9	1.35	**1.6**	0.0	0.03	0.38	4.83	99.5	**0.9**	17.1	34.0	**0.7**
3.6	0.77	6.6	0.50	**7.4**	3.7	1.66	17.50	4.78	58.7	**1.3**	8.1	25.0	**6.1**
0.3	5.23	30.6	1.05	**2.4**	-0.1	-0.28	-2.38	5.04	78.3	**3.8**	8.9	9.0	**7.1**
1.3	8.34	32.8	1.25	**4.0**	1.6	0.64	6.50	4.13	73.3	**5.7**	57.0	10.7	**5.7**
2.3	1.43	8.2	0.00	**0.0**	-3.3	-6.49	-12.52	3.42	131.8	**3.7**	19.6	10.8	**1.7**
0.7	3.65	21.5	2.47	**1.3**	-0.5	-0.14	-1.19	4.60	60.9	**1.0**	14.2	31.5	**4.6**
7.3	0.27	1.9	0.32	**6.3**	1.1	1.22	12.04	5.16	67.6	**2.4**	26.2	18.6	**6.0**
9.4	0.00	0.0	0.26	**4.3**	0.3	1.14	7.77	4.26	79.1	**4.8**	82.1	17.6	**7.6**
7.9	0.02	0.1	0.45	**7.0**	2.5	1.43	15.43	3.79	46.2	**5.4**	42.2	7.8	**5.6**
9.7	0.50	2.0	0.05	**1.7**	0.1	0.18	1.27	3.00	89.5	**2.5**	40.9	27.4	**7.0**
3.1	0.73	4.1	0.41	**5.1**	2.0	1.12	10.56	4.49	55.8	**0.7**	9.7	34.2	**6.7**
5.3	3.30	9.2	1.61	**2.7**	0.5	0.66	4.84	2.99	68.2	**1.6**	34.5	35.2	**8.3**
1.7	2.40	17.7	0.53	**5.2**	1.5	0.61	5.82	4.61	63.0	**1.7**	9.2	19.8	**5.6**
2.4	3.87	22.4	1.16	**2.5**	0.1	0.11	1.05	4.65	81.7	**1.9**	19.0	20.3	**6.0**
5.1	0.86	6.1	0.04	**5.3**	1.0	1.32	14.23	4.03	57.4	**2.0**	28.3	24.0	**5.2**
7.4	0.00	0.0	0.03	**4.3**	0.3	0.96	9.57	3.49	71.9	**3.9**	42.2	15.9	**7.8**
2.9	5.35	13.3	0.07	**5.0**	1.3	1.25	10.13	4.34	69.4	**4.9**	57.9	15.2	**5.7**
4.5	2.78	13.7	0.16	**2.9**	0.2	0.48	4.91	3.75	80.3	**5.5**	45.2	7.8	**4.9**
3.6	1.93	15.0	0.28	**3.1**	0.1	0.53	7.58	4.18	85.4	**1.6**	26.7	27.9	**3.0**
5.8	2.22	6.0	2.43	**2.6**	0.3	0.66	5.49	3.05	65.0	**5.4**	71.2	13.3	**4.1**
8.9	0.53	2.8	0.12	**6.8**	1.8	1.28	10.47	4.21	49.6	**2.5**	28.1	18.6	**7.7**
1.6	6.58	47.3	0.58	**2.7**	1.3	0.36	4.39	3.65	74.7	**1.7**	20.7	23.3	**3.9**
6.1	0.86	7.8	0.36	**2.4**	3.5	0.22	1.89	3.85	79.8	**1.7**	10.6	20.9	**4.6**
3.3	0.82	4.4	0.31	**5.6**	0.8	1.47	7.95	7.29	68.4	**1.4**	24.2	28.3	**6.7**
0.0	6.25	34.4	2.76	**0.0**	-2.0	-3.07	-28.70	3.89	180.2	**1.7**	24.7	24.2	**4.2**
0.1	14.61	160.5	3.01	**0.0**	-41.1	-2.40	-42.98	1.79	165.4	**1.2**	22.1	40.3	**2.6**
2.5	4.52	22.6	1.79	**2.1**	1.4	0.22	2.40	3.75	70.1	**5.1**	35.2	7.1	**4.4**
3.1	3.02	12.0	0.84	**3.1**	0.2	0.17	1.85	3.67	87.2	**7.6**	65.0	0.3	**4.2**
4.9	2.40	10.3	0.40	**3.2**	2.5	0.45	2.70	3.06	68.1	**1.8**	23.6	22.8	**8.2**
9.5	0.00	0.0	0.00	**0.0**	-1.2	-5.21	-11.71	1.39	702.0	**3.2**	63.7	28.7	**1.5**
0.3	1.96	17.3	3.46	**0.0**	-1.8	-2.48	-43.15	4.99	109.2	**3.3**	14.8	12.3	**0.9**
2.3	1.77	14.3	-0.02	**7.1**	1.4	1.59	18.17	4.05	56.2	**1.3**	8.4	24.9	**7.4**
8.1	0.01	0.1	0.00	**6.4**	1.8	1.44	16.86	4.32	57.1	**3.9**	22.5	10.3	**6.3**

Name	City	State	Rating	2008 Rating	2007 Rating	Total Assets ($Mil)	One Year Asset Growth	Asset Mix (As a % of Total Assets) Comm-ercial Loans	Cons-umer Loans	Home Mort-gages	Secur-ities	Capital-ization Index	Leverage Ratio	Risk-based Capital Ratio
GREAT PLAINS NATIONAL BK	ELK CITY	OK	**C+**	C+	C+	351	7.28	14.0	8.4	21.8	6.4	**6.5**	8.8	12.2
▲GREAT SOUTHERN BANK	SPRINGFIELD	MO	**B**	B-	C+	3,410	-6.32	4.1	4.5	9.7	22.5	**6.3**	8.3	15.8
GREAT SOUTHERN NATIONAL	MERIDIAN	MS	**A-**	B+	B+	257	1.22	7.3	12.6	15.9	40.0	**7.8**	9.5	19.2
▼GREAT STATE BK	WILKESBORO	NC	**D+**	C	C	56	35.31	12.0	0.4	14.0	20.2	**10.0**	14.9	20.9
▲GREAT WESTERN BANK	SIOUX FALLS	SD	**D+**	B-	B	8,258	54.86	10.8	1.6	7.1	18.5	**5.1**	7.1	12.7
▲GREATER HUDSON BANK NA	MIDDLETOWN	NY	**B-**	D+	D	258	49.28	8.7	0.0	0.5	44.3	**10.0**	12.6	18.7
▼GREATER ROME BANK	ROME	GA	**D**	C	C+	167	-8.14	8.4	3.6	16.5	25.3	**5.0**	7.0	12.8
GREATER SOUTH TEXAS	FALFURRIAS	TX	**D-**	C-	D+	51	9.93	6.6	6.5	19.4	14.2	**9.3**	10.6	16.9
GREEN BANK NA	HOUSTON	TX	**D+**	D	C-	865	58.90	27.7	0.8	6.4	14.5	**10.0**	15.4	20.9
▼GREEN BELT BANK & TRUST	IOWA FALLS	IA	**B-**	B	B	288	32.06	8.9	3.6	9.6	6.7	**4.9**	8.5	10.9
▼GREENBANK	GREENEVILLE	TN	**D-**	D	C-	2,403	-8.11	6.7	2.7	13.5	8.4	**6.9**	8.9	13.2
▲GREENCHOICE BANK FSB	CICERO	IL	**D-**	E-	D-	61	0.84	0.0	0.1	31.7	2.3	**10.0**	11.1	15.5
GREENE COUNTY	CATSKILL	NY	**B+**	B+	B+	152	43.07	0.0	0.0	0.0	93.1	**6.7**	8.7	42.1
▼GREENEVILLE FEDERAL BANK	GREENEVILLE	TN	**D**	C	B-	202	9.81	6.7	3.4	26.8	4.0	**6.0**	8.3	11.7
GREENFIELD BANKING CO	GREENFIELD	IN	**B-**	C	B-	380	-2.18	4.0	3.6	10.9	28.9	**9.2**	10.5	19.6
GREENFIELD BANKING CO	GREENFIELD	TN	**C+**	B-	B-	51	-0.73	9.6	12.6	22.4	15.8	**9.3**	11.4	14.4
GREENFIELD CO-OP BANK	GREENFIELD	MA	**B-**	B-	B-	288	1.74	4.9	0.2	39.5	26.3	**10.0**	11.7	21.3
GREENFIELD SB	GREENFIELD	MA	**C**	C	C	625	1.36	2.5	0.1	41.8	26.4	**8.0**	9.7	18.1
GREENLEAF WAYSIDE BANK	GREENLEAF	WI	**C+**	C+	C	66	5.68	6.5	1.8	23.8	11.9	**6.8**	8.8	14.9
GREENSBURG STATE BK	GREENSBURG	KS	**A**	A	A-	55	-6.23	2.1	5.1	4.1	69.1	**10.0**	18.2	49.4
GREENVILLE BANKING CO	GREENVILLE	GA	**B-**	B	B	30	1.92	5.1	2.1	13.3	21.0	**10.0**	14.0	20.3
GREENVILLE FEDERAL	GREENVILLE	OH	**D+**	C-	D+	125	1.24	1.2	1.6	68.0	9.6	**6.9**	8.9	14.8
GREENVILLE NATIONAL BK	GREENVILLE	OH	**B**	B	B+	348	2.95	2.5	7.9	29.7	21.3	**6.4**	8.4	15.0
GREENVILLE SB	GREENVILLE	PA	**B-**	C+	C+	200	9.34	1.9	1.3	52.0	17.0	**8.8**	10.2	19.5
GREENWOODS STATE BK	LAKE MILLS	WI	**D**	D-	B-	61	-3.94	11.2	2.1	28.0	10.9	**8.2**	9.9	13.5
GREER STATE BK	GREER	SC	**E+**	C-	D-	456	-3.97	8.1	1.3	11.8	29.1	**4.5**	6.5	10.9
GREYSTONE BANK	RALEIGH	NC	**D-**	D-	D-	318	-53.90	2.7	0.1	17.6	4.7	**8.6**	10.1	15.2
GRIFFITH SB	GRIFFITH	IN	**D-**	D-	D+	90	-16.77	0.0	3.1	64.0	6.1	**5.2**	7.2	14.4
▲GRINNELL STATE BK	GRINNELL	IA	**A**	A-	B	167	5.81	6.1	0.9	7.4	22.6	**10.0**	12.5	15.2
GRUNDY BANK	MORRIS	IL	**D**	D	C-	245	6.40	6.8	1.0	15.1	15.1	**5.6**	7.6	13.2
GRUNDY NATIONAL BK	GRUNDY	VA	**A-**	A-	A	362	13.40	10.6	7.0	8.0	42.7	**10.0**	16.8	29.2
GRUNDY NB OF GRUNDY	GRUNDY CENTER	IA	**B-**	B-	B-	180	5.77	10.2	0.9	5.1	31.8	**7.6**	9.4	13.3
GRUVER STATE BK	GRUVER	TX	**A-**	A-	A-	54	4.00	19.0	6.2	2.5	37.2	**10.0**	13.1	22.5
GSL SB	GUTTENBERG	NJ	**C**	C-	C-	92	0.84	0.0	0.0	30.2	56.4	**10.0**	15.5	45.3
▲GUADALUPE NATIONAL BK	KERRVILLE	TX	**C-**	C	C	79	34.21	14.4	3.8	20.0	4.8	**8.2**	9.8	14.1
GUARANTY BANK	MAMOU	LA	**C+**	B	B	126	10.17	6.1	6.6	19.4	22.3	**8.4**	9.9	20.7
GUARANTY BANK	SPRINGFIELD	MO	**D+**	D	D	682	-7.45	12.5	0.5	15.8	14.2	**7.2**	9.2	13.1
GUARANTY BANK	MILWAUKEE	WI	**E+**	E+	D-	1,267	-3.75	0.3	3.1	43.5	1.5	**2.8**	6.1	9.8
GUARANTY BANK & TRUST CO	DENVER	CO	**D-**	D-	D+	1,868	-12.06	9.6	0.3	3.4	21.4	**7.5**	9.3	14.1
GUARANTY BANK & TRUST CO	CEDAR RAPIDS	IA	**D+**	D+	C-	241	-3.24	6.6	0.6	13.5	40.2	**6.1**	8.1	13.2
GUARANTY BANK & TRUST CO	NEW ROADS	LA	**C-**	C	B-	123	6.17	5.3	5.0	34.5	10.9	**7.9**	9.6	15.1
GUARANTY BANK & TRUST CO	BELZONI	MS	**C**	C-	B-	491	-0.72	12.0	3.4	14.0	19.3	**9.7**	10.9	14.8
GUARANTY BANK & TRUST CO	DELHI	LA	**A-**	A-	A	121	-0.80	6.5	7.6	17.6	13.7	**7.5**	9.3	13.7
GUARANTY BOND BANK	MOUNT PLEASANT	TX	**B**	B-	B-	971	9.56	9.0	4.5	18.0	36.1	**6.6**	8.7	15.5
GUARANTY SAVINGS BANK	METAIRIE	LA	**C-**	C	C+	262	-3.40	2.9	0.6	30.3	18.5	**9.0**	10.3	17.5
GUARANTY STATE BK &	BELOIT	KS	**B**	C+	B-	159	9.13	5.0	0.9	8.9	18.2	**6.9**	9.7	12.4
GUARDIAN BANK	VALDOSTA	GA	**B-**	B	B	206	11.00	8.5	1.8	26.7	10.7	**8.7**	10.1	14.4
GUARDIAN SAVINGS BANK	GRANITE CITY	IL	**B-**	B-	B-	40	-1.28	0.0	0.3	29.2	46.2	**10.0**	18.6	58.5
GUARDIAN SAVINGS BANK A F	CINCINNATI	OH	**C+**	C+	C+	736	7.37	0.0	0.0	74.5	0.4	**5.3**	7.3	14.2
GUARDIAN TRUST CO FSB	NEW YORK	NY	**C-**	C	C	4	-43.48	0.0	0.0	0.0	82.7	**10.0**	97.0	478.7
GUERNSEY BANK	WORTHINGTON	OH	**D+**	D+	D+	135	6.72	3.5	0.5	22.5	12.2	**6.1**	8.1	12.3
GUIDE ROCK STATE BK	GUIDE ROCK	NE	**C**	C-	D+	26	-11.31	11.0	8.3	3.9	11.1	**10.0**	12.1	16.7
GUILFORD SB	GUILFORD	CT	**B**	C+	B-	509	0.57	0.6	0.3	50.5	22.3	**10.0**	12.5	23.2
GULF COAST BANK	ABBEVILLE	LA	**A-**	A-	A	295	16.49	6.2	10.0	19.3	2.4	**10.0**	13.3	21.3
▲GULF COAST BANK & TRUST C	NEW ORLEANS	LA	**D**	D-	C-	890	-9.55	10.9	1.4	26.0	10.0	**6.1**	8.1	12.9
▼GULF COAST COMMUNITY	PENSACOLA	FL	**E-**	D-	C-	244	-7.23	6.0	0.5	12.6	10.3	**1.9**	6.4	8.9
▼GULFSHORE BANK	TAMPA	FL	**D-**	C-	C-	149	92.06	6.5	0.7	8.0	22.6	**7.1**	9.1	17.4
▼GULFSOUTH PRIVATE BANK	DESTIN	FL	**E+**	D-	B	197	-5.88	4.2	3.8	23.2	4.3	**4.3**	7.0	10.7
GULFSTREAM BUSINESS	STUART	FL	**C-**	C-	B-	551	-2.38	21.7	0.3	4.3	13.5	**9.3**	10.5	15.0
GUNNISON BANK & TRUST CO	GUNNISON	CO	**C-**	D	C+	68	-0.06	5.5	1.2	11.9	2.5	**7.7**	9.4	13.7

Asset Quality Index	Non-Performing Loans as a % of Total Loans	Non-Performing Loans as a % of Capital	Net Charge-offs Avg Loans	Profitability Index	Net Income ($Mil)	Return on Assets (R.O.A.)	Return on Equity (R.O.E.)	Net Interest Spread	Overhead Efficiency Ratio	Liquidity Index	Liquidity Ratio	Hot Money Ratio	Stability Index
3.9	0.66	6.0	0.41	8.6	7.0	2.10	23.26	5.91	62.4	1.0	5.3	28.8	6.2
5.1	1.52	9.1	1.70	5.2	25.0	0.71	8.66	4.32	58.8	1.3	15.0	28.8	7.3
6.6	0.95	4.8	0.33	8.0	3.6	1.38	13.94	5.84	67.5	4.2	41.5	14.5	6.3
6.7	1.37	6.3	0.02	0.0	-0.1	-0.23	-1.38	3.18	98.2	2.1	29.7	23.2	1.5
1.3	2.26	20.2	0.63	5.0	65.0	0.91	5.46	4.36	54.7	1.6	12.7	22.5	9.3
7.8	0.42	1.6	0.28	4.0	4.1	1.74	13.30	3.76	67.0	2.5	36.5	23.9	5.0
1.5	3.77	25.3	1.33	0.8	-0.6	-0.35	-4.56	3.37	90.2	3.1	31.0	16.5	3.6
2.6	2.28	12.6	0.52	0.3	-0.5	-1.05	-9.59	4.72	116.2	0.7	16.2	46.4	4.1
5.4	2.60	11.3	0.15	1.3	1.7	0.27	1.69	3.61	78.2	2.0	37.2	31.6	6.0
7.2	0.28	2.4	0.02	6.4	3.6	1.51	15.73	3.62	59.1	1.9	19.1	20.0	5.1
0.3	8.35	51.5	2.83	0.0	-77.6	-3.09	-26.30	3.82	92.0	2.8	16.6	15.6	6.0
0.3	18.52	113.3	0.00	0.0	-2.8	-4.72	-57.00	2.56	339.5	0.8	18.5	37.6	3.6
10.0	0.00	0.0	0.00	9.4	1.9	1.62	14.67	2.95	11.7	5.1	8.0	0.4	6.5
1.1	5.27	38.9	0.62	0.7	-6.1	-3.21	-32.05	4.21	69.4	0.8	13.8	35.4	4.5
5.2	1.69	7.3	0.54	3.9	3.1	0.86	8.27	4.31	74.8	6.1	47.1	5.0	5.4
3.8	1.87	10.6	0.11	3.7	0.3	0.51	4.34	3.88	74.9	1.8	31.2	29.4	6.6
6.7	0.90	4.4	0.01	3.6	1.7	0.61	5.13	3.20	70.5	4.3	37.0	12.3	6.8
6.4	0.54	3.5	0.14	3.5	4.2	0.68	6.71	3.14	79.9	2.2	26.6	19.3	6.4
5.7	0.74	4.7	0.17	4.9	0.7	1.19	12.85	3.94	71.1	5.0	34.7	7.9	5.1
8.6	3.01	3.2	0.46	7.8	0.8	1.43	7.96	4.31	49.1	6.1	55.4	6.1	9.3
8.5	0.30	1.0	0.59	3.6	0.2	0.60	4.27	4.78	85.5	5.4	40.6	7.5	7.2
4.2	0.73	6.3	0.00	2.1	0.5	0.40	4.34	3.79	74.4	2.5	14.5	16.6	3.9
5.1	0.96	7.1	0.19	6.5	3.9	1.14	13.53	3.98	58.7	3.6	18.6	11.5	6.0
7.3	0.65	4.1	0.11	4.2	1.6	0.79	7.94	3.01	59.2	3.5	32.7	15.2	6.0
1.4	2.93	19.1	2.95	0.6	-0.4	-0.52	-4.34	3.68	78.7	2.1	19.6	18.8	5.0
0.3	6.90	50.6	1.89	0.0	-6.6	-1.44	-19.05	2.92	86.6	1.5	16.1	24.4	2.2
0.0	9.34	59.1	0.32	0.0	-17.1	-3.29	-36.39	2.47	-258.0	0.4	17.4	96.2	0.5
0.3	9.35	77.4	1.87	0.0	-1.7	-1.62	-20.17	2.82	73.2	1.2	17.5	29.0	2.7
8.4	0.27	1.4	0.23	6.2	1.9	1.14	9.00	4.51	62.1	3.9	30.0	11.9	7.8
1.4	4.16	30.2	0.90	4.5	2.4	0.94	10.86	3.38	58.9	1.6	17.9	24.2	6.7
6.7	1.40	4.0	0.02	6.6	4.0	1.20	6.77	4.45	53.2	2.9	48.6	28.5	7.3
4.5	0.97	5.5	0.54	4.8	1.9	1.07	9.78	3.68	68.3	1.2	21.7	31.6	6.1
5.7	0.00	0.0	-0.23	5.6	0.8	1.41	10.95	3.50	62.9	1.9	28.8	25.1	9.6
9.6	0.14	0.3	0.00	2.5	0.2	0.25	1.62	3.32	86.9	3.9	74.1	22.4	7.3
8.3	0.00	0.0	0.01	1.2	0.2	0.26	2.56	3.94	91.5	1.5	11.9	23.1	2.0
4.3	1.54	7.7	0.00	4.1	0.9	0.72	6.92	4.31	77.5	3.3	45.9	20.7	6.6
1.4	4.44	30.3	1.20	2.0	2.6	0.36	3.97	2.77	65.3	2.4	9.9	16.6	5.0
0.5	3.59	24.1	0.95	0.0	-20.2	-1.54	-25.08	3.69	107.6	5.1	14.5	1.9	4.4
0.6	7.46	40.1	2.85	0.0	-28.5	-1.44	-13.61	3.72	95.3	1.5	9.6	23.1	6.0
6.3	0.96	5.6	0.99	2.3	0.0	0.00	-0.07	3.72	82.8	3.9	28.8	11.6	1.7
2.3	1.62	12.6	0.16	6.8	1.4	1.13	12.41	4.76	62.9	2.3	15.2	17.5	6.1
2.9	2.14	12.2	1.32	5.0	3.8	0.75	7.38	4.61	62.8	1.6	22.2	25.6	6.4
8.5	0.08	0.5	0.11	8.3	2.3	1.92	19.78	4.41	60.3	3.2	37.5	18.1	7.5
5.1	1.04	6.2	0.17	6.5	16.2	1.77	20.94	3.60	63.3	1.8	26.0	24.4	6.5
2.3	3.24	21.4	-0.06	1.6	0.5	0.18	1.80	3.66	69.7	1.9	25.0	21.4	6.5
7.3	0.01	0.1	-0.20	7.2	2.2	1.52	15.67	3.76	58.4	2.3	8.1	16.6	5.2
5.6	0.85	5.7	0.43	4.4	2.0	0.97	10.05	3.61	60.2	1.3	17.1	28.3	5.7
10.0	0.39	0.6	0.00	3.2	0.2	0.40	2.20	2.58	77.0	5.5	84.6	14.2	7.0
4.1	1.02	10.9	0.04	6.4	10.9	1.55	21.34	2.74	44.3	1.7	9.2	20.0	4.6
8.6	0.00	0.0	0.00	4.2	0.1	0.91	1.28	3.70	85.9	5.0	2,193.2	101.0	0.0
3.0	0.98	8.2	-0.17	1.5	0.7	0.54	6.55	3.25	93.1	2.7	23.4	16.2	2.8
2.4	2.97	14.8	0.70	2.9	0.1	0.42	3.57	4.04	80.0	2.8	24.9	15.8	5.6
8.0	1.34	7.0	0.02	4.2	3.6	0.71	5.85	3.61	71.8	3.4	25.5	13.2	7.7
6.6	0.65	3.4	0.24	7.0	2.6	0.96	6.78	5.24	72.6	3.5	26.1	12.7	8.6
1.5	5.21	41.7	1.26	4.8	8.1	1.15	15.85	6.16	74.6	1.2	16.5	29.7	3.9
0.0	26.92	259.3	5.04	0.0	-9.5	-3.72	-43.68	2.45	122.0	1.5	16.7	25.7	2.8
6.2	1.79	10.2	0.05	0.0	-0.5	-0.42	-3.79	2.66	109.2	4.3	49.3	16.0	0.8
0.0	14.04	116.6	3.11	0.0	-3.7	-1.80	-19.22	2.30	104.9	0.8	15.8	37.3	0.2
2.0	1.25	6.2	0.66	3.0	1.7	0.30	2.87	3.89	50.3	2.3	24.8	18.4	6.3
0.7	2.11	14.0	1.16	4.8	0.4	0.57	5.98	5.48	69.2	1.1	22.7	33.1	4.9

Name	City	State	Rating	2008 Rating	2007 Rating	Total Assets ($Mil)	One Year Asset Growth	Asset Mix (As a % of Total Assets) Comm-ercial Loans	Cons-umer Loans	Home Mort-gages	Secur-ities	Capital-ization Index	Leverage Ratio	Risk-based Capital Ratio
GUNNISON SAVINGS & LOAN A	GUNNISON	CO	**C-**	C	C	106	8.23	0.4	1.5	57.8	0.2	**7.4**	9.3	20.2
▲ GUNNISON VALLEY BANK	GUNNISON	UT	**D-**	E-	D-	68	-3.92	15.8	22.4	2.9	0.0	**7.1**	9.7	12.6
GUTHRIE COUNTY STATE BK	PANORA	IA	**D+**	C-	D+	103	4.59	8.9	4.2	23.3	26.8	**4.9**	6.9	12.5
GWINNETT COMMUNITY BANK	DULUTH	GA	**E-**	E-	D-	507	3.66	8.4	0.5	11.7	17.1	**0.6**	4.5	7.2
▼ H F GEHANT BANKING CO	WEST BROOKLYN	IL	**B-**	B-	B-	53	5.51	3.8	4.1	25.3	15.5	**10.0**	11.1	17.7
H&R BLOCK BANK	KANSAS CITY	MO	**D+**	D	D	1,794	-18.64	0.0	39.5	30.5	1.1	**10.0**	23.0	36.4
HABIB AMERICAN BANK	NEW YORK	NY	**B-**	B	B	680	-0.23	10.3	2.2	3.7	4.7	**6.0**	8.1	14.8
HADDON SB	HADDON HEIGHTS	NJ	**C-**	C-	D	321	4.68	0.0	0.0	29.1	65.1	**7.3**	9.2	25.9
HALSTEAD BANK	HALSTEAD	KS	**C-**	C	C-	73	5.35	11.7	6.6	12.0	16.3	**5.6**	8.2	11.5
▼ HAMILTON BANK	HAMILTON	MO	**B-**	B	B-	48	-1.58	5.0	4.3	15.0	22.5	**9.9**	10.9	17.7
HAMILTON FEDERAL BANK	BALTIMORE	MD	**C**	C	C-	330	9.66	5.4	0.4	38.7	25.6	**7.7**	9.4	17.8
HAMILTON STATE BK	HOSCHTON	GA	**D-**	D	D+	245	-9.55	9.9	1.3	10.6	4.0	**8.7**	10.2	14.3
HAMLER STATE BK	HAMLER	OH	**B+**	B	B+	60	4.62	2.0	1.5	17.6	36.9	**10.0**	16.0	31.6
HAMLIN BANK & TRUST CO	SMETHPORT	PA	**A**	A	A	380	9.06	2.3	5.3	31.5	45.8	**10.0**	15.2	28.4
▼ HAMLIN NATIONAL BK	HAMLIN	TX	**C-**	B+	B+	87	7.64	11.8	4.7	6.7	21.9	**10.0**	16.6	25.7
HAMPDEN BANK	SPRINGFIELD	MA	**C**	C	C	552	-0.91	6.4	4.8	27.3	19.6	**10.0**	12.9	19.6
HAMPSHIRE FIRST BANK	MANCHESTER	NH	**C-**	C	C-	236	28.91	8.2	0.1	11.8	8.0	**9.1**	12.0	14.2
HAMPTON STATE BK	HAMPTON	IA	**A-**	A-	A-	66	2.47	4.5	3.3	18.1	27.5	**9.9**	10.9	16.5
HAMPTONS STATE BK	SOUTHAMPTON	NY	**D**	D-	D-	68	7.51	13.7	0.9	0.0	34.9	**5.4**	7.4	12.0
HANCOCK BANK	GULFPORT	MS	**B-**	B-	B-	5,082	-4.14	4.1	5.2	15.5	17.9	**6.0**	8.0	16.5
HANCOCK BANK & TRUST CO	HAWESVILLE	KY	**C+**	C	C+	336	10.58	10.3	2.2	31.1	13.0	**6.0**	8.0	12.4
▼ HANCOCK BANK OF ALABAMA	MOBILE	AL	**C**	B-	B-	200	9.15	19.5	11.1	10.4	4.0	**10.0**	16.4	17.4
HANCOCK BANK OF	BATON ROUGE	LA	**B-**	B-	B-	2,919	0.77	7.0	6.9	9.9	28.2	**10.0**	11.3	15.7
HANCOCK COUNTY SAVINGS	CHESTER	WV	**B**	B	B	297	5.59	0.2	2.0	80.6	6.9	**10.0**	16.1	33.3
HANMI BANK	LOS ANGELES	CA	**E+**	D-	D	2,900	-8.10	12.1	0.4	2.2	14.3	**6.5**	8.6	12.2
▼ HANOVER COMMUNITY BANK	GARDEN CITY PARK	NY	**D-**	C	NR	58	-20.50	5.1	0.1	27.2	16.0	**9.7**	10.8	17.9
HANTZ BANK	DAVISON	MI	**D**	E-	D-	43	12.32	10.0	0.6	5.0	16.5	**10.0**	12.7	17.2
HAPPY STATE BK	HAPPY	TX	**B-**	B-	B	1,577	19.38	15.2	3.5	8.7	23.4	**3.5**	7.6	10.3
▼ HARBOR BANK OF MARYLAND	BALTIMORE	MD	**E+**	D-	D-	250	-18.06	20.4	0.9	8.7	9.0	**4.4**	7.3	10.7
HARBOR NATIONAL BK	CHARLESTON	SC	**D**	C-	C-	234	2.70	5.0	0.3	15.2	9.5	**8.7**	11.2	13.9
HARDIN COUNTY BANK	SAVANNAH	TN	**C+**	C	B-	345	8.50	9.9	5.6	28.9	11.1	**5.5**	8.1	11.4
▲ HARDIN COUNTY SB	ELDORA	IA	**C-**	D	D	142	2.66	4.7	1.4	3.9	38.9	**6.7**	8.7	12.7
HARDWARE STATE BK	LOVINGTON	IL	**C-**	C-	C-	23	-1.05	5.3	2.1	7.2	13.3	**6.3**	8.3	15.7
▲ HARFORD BANK	ABERDEEN	MD	**C-**	C+	B+	277	8.19	4.9	7.5	18.1	9.6	**7.5**	9.3	13.1
HARLEYSVILLE SB	HARLEYSVILLE	PA	**C**	C	C	857	2.00	0.8	0.1	42.0	33.0	**4.3**	6.3	12.2
HARMONY BANK	JACKSON	NJ	**D**	C	C	91	61.39	1.0	0.4	7.7	4.6	**10.0**	13.8	16.6
HARRINGTON BANK FSB	CHAPEL HILL	NC	**D-**	D	D+	303	2.28	6.2	1.2	21.9	9.8	**6.7**	8.7	12.8
▼ HARRIS BANK NA	SCOTTSDALE	AZ	**D**	D	C-	618	-9.70	4.0	3.5	45.5	2.3	**8.0**	9.7	14.7
▲ HARRIS CENTRAL NA	CHICAGO	IL	**C**	C	C-	5	0.98	0.0	0.0	0.0	87.8	**10.0**	89.1	4,501.1
▼ HARRIS NA	CHICAGO	IL	**D+**	C-	C-	50,026	13.77	5.4	10.0	11.4	11.3	**8.0**	9.6	17.9
▼ HARRISON BUILDING & LOAN	HARRISON	OH	**C-**	C-	D+	221	4.27	2.4	0.5	35.3	34.7	**10.0**	12.7	27.7
HARRISON COUNTY BANK	LOST CREEK	WV	**B-**	B-	B-	96	9.45	2.1	5.7	19.4	54.8	**6.7**	8.7	20.8
HARRISON DEPOSIT BANK & T	CYNTHIANA	KY	**B+**	B+	B+	54	-1.21	1.0	3.2	25.1	28.7	**9.0**	10.3	21.2
HART COUNTY BANK & TRUST	MUNFORDVILLE	KY	**C-**	C-	B	28	1.66	5.5	1.5	2.3	29.3	**10.0**	14.7	26.7
HARTFORD SB	HARTFORD	WI	**D-**	D+	C-	219	-1.38	0.0	0.4	38.4	21.4	**6.4**	8.4	13.6
▲ HARTSBURG STATE BK	HARTSBURG	IL	**C**	C	C	17	9.79	5.5	3.7	8.3	10.8	**9.2**	11.5	14.3
▼ HARTWICK STATE BK	HARTWICK	IA	**C-**	D+	C-	25	-2.38	3.8	1.9	19.5	33.4	**6.7**	8.7	17.9
HARVARD SB	HARVARD	IL	**D**	D	D	168	6.42	2.8	3.7	28.0	4.6	**8.8**	10.2	15.8
HARVARD STATE BK	HARVARD	IL	**D-**	D	C	241	-3.88	4.8	5.7	14.0	26.8	**6.0**	8.0	13.1
HARVEST BANK OF	GAITHERSBURG	MD	**E-**	E+	D-	162	-28.89	5.9	0.2	16.0	16.3	**0.0**	3.1	5.7
HARVEST COMMUNITY BANK	PENNSVILLE	NJ	**D**	D+	C-	200	4.05	19.3	0.2	16.0	19.3	**5.9**	7.9	12.2
▼ HARWOOD STATE BK	HARWOOD	ND	**D**	C-	C	31	11.26	14.1	4.4	7.5	6.5	**6.9**	9.0	13.7
HASKELL NATIONAL BK	HASKELL	TX	**B**	B	B-	64	-5.58	3.6	8.6	13.2	29.5	**10.0**	11.5	21.5
HASTINGS CITY BANK	HASTINGS	MI	**C**	C	C	241	1.13	3.3	2.2	33.0	20.2	**7.1**	9.1	18.5
HASTINGS STATE BK	HASTINGS	NE	**E+**	D-	E+	147	-1.26	9.6	1.7	8.5	39.3	**5.3**	7.3	13.3
HATBORO FEDERAL SAVINGS	HATBORO	PA	**B-**	B-	B	538	-4.61	0.0	0.0	71.6	10.0	**10.0**	16.2	33.4
HAVANA NATIONAL BK	HAVANA	IL	**C+**	C	C+	172	5.30	4.7	2.7	13.0	26.6	**5.7**	7.7	12.5
HAVEN SB	HOBOKEN	NJ	**B**	C	C-	690	-4.81	0.2	0.0	56.2	27.2	**10.0**	11.8	27.3
HAVERFORD TRUST CO	RADNOR	PA	**B+**	B-	B-	106	-3.58	10.2	57.5	1.6	13.0	**10.0**	15.7	16.1
HAVERHILL BANK	HAVERHILL	MA	**C-**	D	D+	249	3.02	0.6	1.4	51.8	17.6	**10.0**	11.4	20.0

Asset Quality Index	Non-Performing Loans as a % of Total Loans	Non-Performing Loans as a % of Capital	Net Charge-offs Avg Loans	Profitability Index	Net Income ($Mil)	Return on Assets (R.O.A.)	Return on Equity (R.O.E.)	Net Interest Spread	Overhead Efficiency Ratio	Liquidity Index	Liquidity Ratio	Hot Money Ratio	Stability Index
4.7	1.71	11.7	0.06	**2.2**	0.1	0.08	0.88	2.39	93.3	**2.2**	33.0	24.8	**5.3**
0.2	12.09	84.5	1.80	**3.3**	0.3	0.42	6.09	5.36	75.2	**2.3**	11.3	17.2	**4.7**
2.4	2.37	18.0	0.89	**3.6**	0.7	0.65	8.44	3.92	72.8	**2.7**	19.1	15.8	**3.9**
0.3	12.56	132.3	2.55	**0.5**	0.7	0.14	3.99	1.66	74.1	**0.8**	18.0	48.4	**0.0**
3.3	2.03	12.5	0.09	**4.6**	0.6	1.10	10.05	3.62	61.6	**1.6**	26.5	26.9	**6.9**
1.1	8.51	23.6	0.97	**6.7**	44.9	2.91	11.54	6.61	40.8	**2.0**	35.6	65.9	**2.1**
3.2	2.33	14.7	0.33	**5.5**	6.6	0.90	11.08	2.22	57.7	**1.9**	40.9	54.5	**6.2**
8.5	0.76	2.5	0.00	**2.1**	0.7	0.21	2.36	1.85	82.1	**5.8**	62.2	11.4	**4.5**
6.0	0.47	3.6	0.18	**3.8**	0.5	0.76	8.97	4.61	79.0	**2.4**	12.9	16.8	**4.9**
3.5	3.10	16.2	-0.02	**3.3**	0.2	0.47	3.88	4.29	90.6	**3.5**	32.0	14.9	**7.6**
6.7	0.88	5.0	0.00	**2.8**	1.2	0.37	3.57	2.45	75.4	**2.8**	45.9	27.6	**5.6**
0.0	3.31	22.6	1.57	**0.0**	-1.6	-0.62	-4.35	3.93	95.3	**2.3**	15.1	17.5	**5.0**
7.2	1.49	4.7	0.27	**5.5**	0.8	1.32	8.21	3.84	52.1	**3.9**	46.1	16.6	**7.5**
6.5	2.78	7.9	0.38	**8.1**	5.2	1.45	8.09	4.59	50.2	**5.0**	52.8	13.2	**7.6**
1.6	13.09	39.4	0.67	**5.3**	1.0	1.28	7.31	5.25	68.0	**3.4**	30.7	14.8	**7.0**
3.7	2.13	11.0	0.60	**2.8**	2.4	0.44	3.39	3.38	73.4	**1.3**	23.2	30.7	**6.9**
1.8	1.09	7.6	0.10	**3.2**	1.1	0.54	4.08	3.72	62.4	**0.7**	10.8	39.1	**4.4**
8.4	0.13	0.7	0.02	**6.1**	1.0	1.42	11.81	3.86	61.2	**2.0**	23.5	19.6	**8.2**
4.0	2.10	14.8	0.39	**1.8**	0.2	0.22	3.05	3.96	92.7	**1.1**	24.1	33.4	**3.3**
5.5	1.31	8.3	1.13	**3.4**	18.8	0.35	4.18	3.53	78.1	**1.9**	15.6	20.5	**6.5**
4.6	0.90	8.1	0.23	**3.8**	2.9	0.90	10.74	3.39	66.9	**1.1**	8.3	27.8	**4.5**
3.6	1.88	9.0	1.17	**0.3**	-0.3	-0.14	-1.19	4.09	73.4	**1.2**	6.7	26.8	**6.3**
4.9	1.87	10.3	0.81	**6.6**	34.7	1.22	9.75	4.37	54.5	**2.7**	10.4	15.2	**7.5**
8.2	0.74	3.8	0.19	**4.3**	2.7	0.91	5.68	4.22	59.6	**3.5**	13.7	11.6	**8.0**
0.0	6.85	39.1	4.77	**0.0**	-82.6	-2.76	-40.49	3.72	66.2	**1.0**	20.6	45.2	**5.8**
9.1	0.00	0.0	0.13	**0.0**	-2.1	-3.47	-29.55	3.80	175.7	**1.1**	28.5	46.8	**1.0**
1.7	4.79	17.4	0.33	**0.0**	-0.3	-1.03	-8.03	3.62	123.8	**3.6**	42.9	17.5	**3.6**
7.6	0.16	1.4	0.22	**4.9**	15.2	1.11	11.72	4.24	71.1	**2.3**	7.7	17.1	**7.3**
0.0	4.29	34.1	1.71	**0.0**	-4.1	-1.41	-15.41	4.06	112.6	**2.0**	10.7	18.5	**3.4**
0.6	4.55	30.4	1.55	**1.5**	0.1	0.05	0.41	3.65	62.7	**1.3**	10.0	26.5	**1.9**
5.4	0.92	8.5	0.25	**6.0**	3.8	1.15	15.05	4.51	64.2	**0.7**	10.8	35.4	**4.5**
2.5	3.21	17.6	0.66	**3.2**	1.4	0.99	11.01	3.79	76.0	**4.2**	38.1	13.5	**2.7**
8.8	0.00	0.0	0.00	**2.8**	0.1	0.37	4.48	3.29	84.8	**3.3**	42.2	16.5	**4.8**
2.7	0.46	3.5	0.62	**4.4**	2.0	0.74	7.79	4.49	64.9	**1.9**	11.4	19.2	**5.7**
7.2	0.61	5.5	0.03	**3.6**	5.5	0.65	10.51	2.38	60.4	**3.5**	23.8	12.2	**3.8**
7.7	0.00	0.0	0.00	**0.0**	-1.0	-1.29	-7.73	3.24	121.0	**2.2**	21.9	18.7	**1.5**
0.8	5.05	41.1	0.22	**1.8**	0.1	0.03	0.38	3.71	76.4	**1.3**	18.3	28.0	**4.0**
1.0	4.48	32.4	1.53	**3.2**	5.3	0.82	7.67	3.35	66.6	**4.4**	14.8	6.3	**4.6**
10.0	0.00	0.0	0.00	**5.8**	0.0	0.90	1.02	0.26	-580.0	**10.0**	880.6	0.0	**2.3**
3.8	3.46	15.1	1.31	**0.6**	0.1	0.04	0.40	2.24	80.9	**5.2**	41.4	12.0	**5.3**
5.3	2.80	10.5	0.32	**1.5**	0.0	-0.01	-0.04	2.93	85.7	**4.3**	53.7	16.9	**6.8**
8.4	0.29	1.1	0.30	**4.3**	0.6	0.63	6.80	3.62	72.5	**2.1**	30.4	24.2	**4.7**
9.2	0.00	0.0	0.05	**4.8**	0.6	1.18	10.62	3.27	64.5	**3.1**	38.7	19.0	**6.6**
10.0	0.29	0.6	-0.44	**1.9**	0.1	0.20	1.28	3.53	85.2	**6.2**	75.8	9.5	**7.5**
0.3	7.05	54.6	0.51	**1.6**	0.5	0.22	2.45	3.21	80.6	**1.7**	15.2	22.2	**4.6**
7.1	0.00	0.0	0.02	**3.4**	0.1	0.43	3.67	3.53	71.5	**1.3**	28.9	30.0	**6.1**
7.1	0.66	3.3	-0.02	**2.7**	0.1	0.30	3.17	3.51	89.0	**4.8**	56.3	12.2	**5.2**
3.1	2.77	17.0	0.38	**1.4**	0.2	0.14	1.50	3.51	77.8	**1.9**	22.5	20.5	**4.8**
0.5	5.03	35.6	0.80	**4.3**	1.9	0.78	8.25	4.40	74.3	**1.1**	10.9	29.3	**5.9**
0.3	14.76	210.4	2.47	**0.0**	-12.4	-6.27	-94.63	2.37	194.6	**1.9**	19.2	20.2	**0.6**
0.3	6.86	54.0	1.20	**2.7**	0.6	0.32	3.93	3.89	70.4	**3.0**	27.9	16.0	**4.2**
4.5	1.54	9.1	0.14	**1.4**	0.1	0.27	2.86	3.31	92.3	**4.7**	47.0	12.7	**2.9**
8.4	0.36	1.5	0.07	**4.0**	0.4	0.62	5.41	4.32	79.1	**4.2**	42.0	14.3	**6.2**
4.2	1.12	6.6	0.84	**2.7**	1.2	0.52	5.33	3.88	80.5	**4.8**	31.6	7.6	**5.2**
4.0	0.45	2.7	1.21	**0.0**	-2.4	-1.67	-25.86	3.79	104.6	**2.1**	27.5	20.5	**0.3**
6.1	1.21	5.6	0.06	**3.5**	3.6	0.61	4.16	2.16	57.7	**1.7**	22.8	23.8	**8.3**
5.3	0.71	5.2	0.26	**3.7**	1.2	0.71	8.18	3.59	70.4	**1.7**	18.1	21.7	**4.4**
9.4	0.47	2.4	0.09	**4.1**	5.2	0.73	6.57	3.06	60.2	**1.5**	23.5	26.9	**7.1**
5.6	0.00	0.0	0.49	**7.4**	2.5	2.26	14.40	2.33	87.2	**1.0**	29.4	78.9	**8.7**
4.1	0.91	5.4	0.57	**1.9**	0.7	0.28	2.37	3.78	83.3	**1.4**	22.2	28.4	**4.9**

Name	City	State	Rating	2008 Rating	2007 Rating	Total Assets ($Mil)	One Year Asset Growth	Asset Mix (As a % of Total Assets) Comm-ercial Loans	Cons-umer Loans	Home Mort-gages	Secur-ities	Capital-ization Index	Leverage Ratio	Risk-based Capital Ratio
HAVILAND STATE BK	HAVILAND	KS	**B+**	B+	B+	33	12.77	3.9	1.7	4.0	25.4	**10.0**	11.4	18.4
HAWAII NATIONAL BK	HONOLULU	HI	**C-**	C+	B	582	1.24	15.5	1.3	6.9	32.3	**6.8**	8.8	15.7
HAWTHORN BANK	JEFFERSON CITY	MO	**C-**	C-	C+	1,186	-2.63	9.4	2.6	16.3	15.1	**9.0**	10.3	14.6
▼HBANK TEXAS	GRAPEVINE	TX	**B-**	B	B	107	6.93	11.7	4.0	14.0	8.4	**8.2**	9.8	19.6
HCSB A STATE BANKING ASSN	PLAINVIEW	TX	**C+**	C+	B-	361	-0.56	7.5	3.4	9.9	28.0	**6.3**	8.3	13.4
HEADLAND NATIONAL BK	HEADLAND	AL	**D+**	C+	B	111	-2.69	9.1	3.9	15.9	23.5	**9.7**	10.8	17.2
▲HEADWATERS STATE BK	LAND O'LAKES	WI	**B+**	A-	A-	65	2.63	1.8	4.1	35.0	24.9	**10.0**	13.1	22.1
HEARTLAND BANK	SOMERS	IA	**A**	A	A-	98	8.99	5.9	3.4	8.9	31.0	**10.0**	13.2	17.1
▼HEARTLAND BANK	LEAWOOD	KS	**E-**	D-	D+	136	-23.38	17.3	0.2	6.1	0.1	**1.2**	4.5	8.2
▼HEARTLAND BANK	SAINT LOUIS	MO	**E+**	D-	D	889	-5.50	21.8	1.3	14.5	9.5	**4.2**	7.2	10.6
HEARTLAND BANK	GAHANNA	OH	**D+**	C-	C	536	2.56	5.4	1.7	15.6	22.6	**6.2**	8.2	12.9
HEARTLAND BANK & TRUST	BLOOMINGTON	IL	**B-**	B	B+	1,641	13.27	11.7	0.7	16.9	16.0	**6.4**	8.4	13.1
HEARTLAND COMMUNITY	BRYANT	AR	**C+**	B-	C+	162	21.28	36.6	1.6	14.4	8.2	**9.1**	11.5	14.2
HEARTLAND COMMUNITY	FRANKLIN	IN	**D**	D	C-	233	-4.08	10.1	3.7	18.2	24.7	**7.6**	9.4	14.9
HEARTLAND COMMUNITY	BENNET	NE	**D+**	C-	D+	53	11.89	26.1	7.7	12.6	17.5	**5.1**	7.1	11.7
HEARTLAND NATIONAL BK	SEBRING	FL	**D**	D+	B-	289	-1.41	7.6	4.4	11.7	10.8	**6.5**	8.5	13.7
HEARTLAND STATE BK	EDGELEY	ND	**C+**	B	B	59	5.82	4.5	2.8	1.5	27.7	**7.4**	9.3	14.8
▲HEARTLAND STATE BK	REDFIELD	SD	**C+**	C	D	64	8.42	10.1	8.6	1.9	9.4	**5.8**	8.7	11.6
HEBER SPRINGS STATE BK	HEBER SPRINGS	AR	**B+**	B-	C-	189	7.04	5.8	3.0	9.0	51.4	**8.9**	10.2	20.8
HEBRON SB	HEBRON	MD	**D-**	D+	B-	469	5.11	7.3	1.0	30.9	7.1	**5.5**	7.5	11.4
HEDRICK SB	OTTUMWA	IA	**C-**	D	D+	62	-4.01	12.1	2.5	15.8	29.1	**6.9**	8.9	14.5
HELENA NATIONAL BK	HELENA	AR	**B**	B	B+	171	1.09	8.5	3.9	3.9	35.3	**10.0**	13.4	24.4
HELM BANK USA	MIAMI	FL	**D-**	D-	D+	754	7.03	5.1	1.4	27.6	55.6	**5.1**	7.1	20.3
▲HENDERSON FSB	HENDERSON	TX	**A-**	B+	B+	104	7.48	2.8	3.7	60.6	15.1	**10.0**	14.6	29.2
HENDERSON STATE BK	HENDERSON	NE	**C+**	C+	C	153	10.25	13.6	0.7	0.8	7.4	**4.3**	8.8	10.6
HENDRICKS COUNTY BANK &	BROWNSBURG	IN	**B-**	B-	B	151	-0.50	3.4	0.8	16.1	15.7	**10.0**	12.1	21.9
HENRY COUNTY BANK	NAPOLEON	OH	**B-**	C	C+	229	0.21	5.8	7.1	15.5	35.4	**7.8**	9.5	16.9
▲HENRY STATE BK	HENRY	IL	**A-**	A-	A-	103	1.07	8.4	7.7	9.7	25.7	**10.0**	11.8	17.5
HERALD NATIONAL BK	NEW YORK	NY	**D+**	C	C	505	13.88	24.4	1.0	3.5	28.9	**10.0**	11.0	16.4
HERGET BANK NA	PEKIN	IL	**C-**	C-	B-	265	0.10	4.0	1.3	13.4	34.7	**6.8**	8.9	17.5
▼HERITAGE BANK	HINESVILLE	GA	**E-**	C+	B-	960	-2.25	7.1	2.2	15.3	12.0	**0.8**	4.3	7.7
HERITAGE BANK	JONESBORO	GA	**E-**	E-	D-	395	-3.80	2.9	0.6	6.7	15.4	**0.8**	4.6	7.5
HERITAGE BANK	MARION	IA	**C-**	C-	C-	34	5.31	11.0	1.6	21.0	39.6	**8.6**	10.0	18.5
HERITAGE BANK	TOPEKA	KS	**E-**	E-	E-	54	10.61	21.1	0.6	29.5	0.2	**3.0**	6.8	10.0
HERITAGE BANK	HOPKINSVILLE	KY	**C+**	C	C+	1,060	3.52	5.1	1.7	17.8	33.8	**7.6**	9.4	16.2
▼HERITAGE BANK	LUCAMA	NC	**D+**	C-	B	263	3.82	5.4	1.6	15.2	36.0	**9.2**	10.5	21.8
▲HERITAGE BANK	WOOD RIVER	NE	**A-**	B+	B	513	3.66	10.3	2.1	4.7	37.5	**9.4**	10.6	18.4
HERITAGE BANK	PEARLAND	TX	**C-**	C	B-	49	40.93	8.0	3.0	8.8	0.7	**10.0**	15.9	21.7
▼HERITAGE BANK	SAINT GEORGE	UT	**B+**	A	A+	95	13.75	0.0	0.0	2.2	70.0	**9.8**	10.8	49.8
HERITAGE BANK	NORFOLK	VA	**B-**	C+	C	264	-2.94	11.3	0.7	12.9	6.6	**10.0**	12.2	15.8
▲HERITAGE BANK	OLYMPIA	WA	**C+**	C	C+	1,204	39.94	16.9	1.8	9.6	10.9	**10.0**	12.4	19.1
▼HERITAGE BANK	SPENCER	WI	**C-**	B-	B	91	5.13	14.1	2.7	29.5	12.0	**8.0**	9.7	14.2
HERITAGE BANK & TRUST	COLUMBIA	TN	**D-**	D	D	139	0.65	11.0	3.1	18.4	9.2	**4.5**	8.0	10.8
HERITAGE BANK INC	ERLANGER	KY	**C-**	C	C	393	1.66	6.6	1.4	22.9	11.5	**6.9**	8.9	13.1
▼HERITAGE BANK NA	JONESBORO	AR	**B-**	B-	B-	265	-4.50	8.1	3.5	20.8	10.7	**8.6**	10.1	16.2
HERITAGE BANK NA	PHOENIX	AZ	**D-**	D	C-	121	-18.56	13.9	3.4	10.1	16.4	**8.5**	10.0	18.1
HERITAGE BANK NA	HOLSTEIN	IA	**D+**	D+	D+	140	0.36	11.6	4.0	8.6	16.4	**7.9**	9.6	13.6
HERITAGE BANK NA	SPICER	MN	**C-**	D+	D+	184	-4.93	12.2	4.5	13.1	20.5	**7.4**	9.3	12.9
HERITAGE BANK OF CENTRAL	TRIVOLI	IL	**D-**	D	D	325	-12.99	24.3	1.2	11.5	19.9	**8.0**	9.6	14.5
HERITAGE BANK OF	SAN JOSE	CA	**D**	D-	C	1,243	-8.68	24.6	0.5	1.9	18.7	**10.0**	12.1	18.1
HERITAGE BANK OF FLORIDA	LUTZ	FL	**E+**	C	B+	254	-5.88	16.0	1.7	24.0	0.0	**2.1**	5.9	9.1
▼HERITAGE BANK OF NEVADA	RENO	NV	**C**	B	A-	452	12.44	16.8	0.3	3.1	15.1	**7.7**	9.5	15.4
HERITAGE BANK OF NORTH FL	ORANGE PARK	FL	**E-**	D-	D-	143	-9.63	6.7	3.0	7.3	4.4	**0.5**	4.9	7.0
HERITAGE BANK OF	SCHAUMBURG	IL	**D-**	D+	B-	121	3.66	1.4	0.2	19.1	1.8	**6.2**	8.2	12.2
HERITAGE BANK OF THE	LEBANON	MO	**C-**	C-	C	43	-3.07	3.6	3.6	27.5	5.4	**9.8**	10.8	15.8
▲HERITAGE BANK OF THE	ALBANY	GA	**C-**	C	C+	728	27.91	7.0	4.2	19.2	29.3	**10.0**	12.2	19.9
HERITAGE BANKING GROUP	CARTHAGE	MS	**E-**	E-	E+	226	-11.95	4.5	5.0	15.6	3.2	**0.0**	2.2	4.0
HERITAGE COMMUNITY BANK	CHAMOIS	MO	**C-**	C-	C-	57	8.52	5.6	2.1	10.6	12.9	**10.0**	13.1	16.9
HERITAGE COMMUNITY BANK	RANDOLPH	NJ	**E-**	D-	D-	140	6.45	35.8	0.5	5.0	4.3	**2.7**	7.9	9.7
▲HERITAGE COMMUNITY BANK	HARTSVILLE	SC	**C-**	D+	C-	105	-0.95	5.3	2.8	16.2	4.8	**7.8**	9.8	13.2

Asset Quality Index	Non-Performing Loans as a % of Total Loans	Non-Performing Loans as a % of Capital	Net Charge-offs Avg Loans	Profitability Index	Net Income ($Mil)	Return on Assets (R.O.A.)	Return on Equity (R.O.E.)	Net Interest Spread	Overhead Efficiency Ratio	Liquidity Index	Liquidity Ratio	Hot Money Ratio	Stability Index
3.9	3.63	18.0	0.05	**5.9**	0.4	1.15	8.59	4.73	66.0	**3.0**	23.6	14.8	**8.3**
3.6	2.88	16.5	0.15	**2.1**	1.7	0.30	3.43	4.15	99.5	**2.2**	29.3	21.8	**5.6**
2.0	4.16	26.9	1.64	**2.2**	4.0	0.33	3.14	4.00	62.0	**2.5**	7.7	15.8	**7.6**
7.0	0.00	0.0	0.19	**3.8**	0.6	0.60	6.08	3.44	65.1	**2.8**	51.1	31.7	**5.4**
3.4	1.76	11.8	0.01	**4.6**	4.0	1.14	14.43	4.48	77.2	**4.7**	29.0	7.3	**4.0**
1.6	4.48	21.8	1.41	**2.6**	0.4	0.32	2.88	3.86	70.8	**2.0**	25.9	20.7	**6.1**
5.1	2.26	11.5	0.36	**8.2**	1.1	1.84	14.25	5.49	58.8	**2.5**	35.0	21.8	**8.3**
8.1	0.22	1.0	0.03	**8.8**	2.0	2.11	15.23	4.81	55.6	**2.2**	14.9	18.1	**9.1**
0.0	9.27	87.4	7.04	**0.0**	-12.5	-7.91	-94.05	2.52	122.7	**1.3**	20.9	29.2	**2.0**
0.0	6.84	51.3	2.16	**0.7**	-4.5	-0.49	-6.24	4.46	76.3	**1.7**	18.9	22.8	**3.5**
1.5	1.46	11.7	0.32	**4.8**	4.9	0.90	10.34	4.10	63.7	**1.9**	16.9	20.0	**5.5**
4.4	1.51	11.3	0.43	**7.4**	30.1	1.86	17.52	4.52	47.6	**3.6**	14.1	11.5	**9.6**
3.7	1.08	7.1	0.20	**8.1**	2.9	1.98	16.76	4.97	52.8	**1.7**	13.8	20.6	**4.5**
2.4	3.20	18.7	2.04	**1.0**	0.3	0.11	1.22	4.53	79.5	**4.4**	30.1	9.9	**3.4**
3.2	1.59	13.1	0.24	**4.5**	0.5	0.99	14.13	4.29	77.7	**4.8**	31.0	7.5	**2.7**
0.8	4.94	30.7	2.28	**0.6**	-2.0	-0.70	-8.40	3.77	68.2	**2.0**	29.1	23.8	**4.4**
7.9	0.00	0.0	1.84	**3.0**	0.1	0.11	1.03	3.88	67.2	**1.7**	26.6	26.4	**7.3**
6.0	0.00	0.0	0.01	**7.4**	1.1	1.77	21.00	5.65	62.9	**2.0**	10.3	18.7	**5.0**
8.3	0.19	0.7	0.43	**5.7**	2.0	1.07	9.81	4.08	60.9	**4.2**	49.0	16.2	**6.1**
0.3	1.78	17.8	0.84	**3.2**	1.8	0.39	5.03	3.62	62.3	**1.0**	4.8	28.5	**3.8**
4.7	1.15	6.7	0.54	**3.1**	0.6	0.88	9.55	4.08	77.1	**4.3**	21.9	7.8	**3.4**
6.8	2.42	7.6	0.36	**4.1**	1.7	1.01	7.58	4.22	70.2	**1.5**	27.2	30.2	**6.7**
0.3	5.84	26.4	2.73	**2.2**	9.4	1.24	18.25	3.28	70.4	**6.2**	64.2	9.7	**3.2**
8.4	0.34	1.7	0.03	**5.5**	1.3	1.29	8.71	4.39	52.9	**1.1**	23.7	33.9	**8.3**
3.8	1.43	13.3	0.01	**5.9**	1.7	1.20	13.76	4.08	56.6	**0.5**	2.3	38.4	**4.8**
5.4	2.62	11.7	0.18	**2.8**	0.5	0.30	2.47	3.53	86.2	**4.3**	40.3	13.5	**6.7**
3.6	2.38	12.7	0.32	**4.3**	2.2	0.94	9.31	4.15	66.1	**0.7**	12.3	44.1	**5.6**
7.4	0.36	1.9	1.15	**5.4**	1.3	1.28	10.56	3.78	49.8	**1.9**	24.7	21.0	**7.4**
7.4	0.13	0.7	0.61	**0.0**	-5.4	-1.14	-10.59	4.09	106.5	**4.2**	23.5	8.7	**1.0**
3.6	3.08	16.0	1.55	**2.9**	1.2	0.45	4.94	3.34	70.5	**3.2**	41.1	19.0	**3.9**
0.3	9.27	83.5	4.19	**1.1**	-42.0	-4.31	-55.02	3.51	100.0	**0.8**	17.5	42.6	**3.9**
0.0	7.48	75.7	1.03	**0.0**	-6.4	-1.56	-29.08	3.00	110.5	**1.0**	17.4	32.2	**1.1**
9.0	0.00	0.0	-0.01	**1.7**	0.1	0.14	1.38	4.28	96.4	**6.1**	49.8	5.2	**4.7**
0.8	4.34	41.5	2.67	**0.0**	-1.1	-2.10	-30.15	4.80	105.0	**0.9**	2.8	29.4	**2.5**
5.6	0.83	4.8	0.75	**4.0**	7.4	0.69	7.43	3.15	62.3	**2.6**	41.9	35.1	**6.2**
3.5	2.89	13.8	0.82	**1.4**	0.2	0.08	0.68	3.76	94.1	**4.4**	34.1	11.1	**4.9**
5.9	0.54	2.4	0.01	**8.7**	10.7	2.14	18.14	3.95	47.0	**2.7**	22.4	16.0	**9.6**
7.0	0.43	1.7	0.27	**0.0**	-1.0	-2.38	-10.66	3.80	194.1	**1.9**	28.3	24.7	**4.8**
8.3	5.99	1.9	4.56	**5.0**	0.2	0.20	1.48	1.81	93.3	**2.7**	78.5	189.1	**6.7**
7.6	0.00	0.0	0.03	**3.7**	2.2	0.80	6.50	3.99	74.8	**5.1**	11.5	0.8	**6.8**
1.5	4.74	25.5	2.15	**5.7**	12.5	1.26	10.25	4.67	53.7	**1.8**	12.6	20.1	**6.8**
6.1	0.43	3.0	1.69	**2.2**	0.2	0.17	1.71	4.08	66.8	**1.4**	12.2	24.5	**5.8**
0.0	10.72	84.8	0.79	**0.4**	-0.6	-0.42	-4.85	3.99	80.5	**0.6**	4.1	36.2	**1.3**
2.1	2.90	21.9	0.33	**5.1**	3.3	0.85	9.69	3.99	57.8	**1.1**	14.3	30.6	**5.5**
5.4	0.87	5.1	0.15	**3.7**	1.4	0.52	3.43	4.25	59.6	**1.8**	17.6	21.2	**6.8**
0.0	11.05	65.0	4.09	**0.0**	-4.2	-2.94	-24.51	3.17	126.4	**0.8**	6.8	32.7	**1.7**
1.9	2.66	18.7	1.66	**2.4**	0.4	0.32	3.29	4.44	69.7	**3.1**	20.8	14.2	**4.4**
2.8	1.72	11.2	1.68	**4.1**	1.5	0.84	9.01	4.70	62.8	**2.8**	25.3	16.0	**5.4**
0.6	6.71	44.0	1.60	**1.3**	0.4	0.11	1.17	3.36	70.1	**2.0**	11.2	18.7	**3.2**
2.1	3.58	16.7	3.12	**0.0**	-52.2	-3.92	-29.03	3.91	163.7	**2.1**	24.5	24.7	**7.2**
0.3	7.38	65.5	4.08	**0.9**	-7.5	-2.77	-36.99	3.02	67.3	**1.4**	12.2	24.5	**4.7**
2.4	2.70	17.3	1.25	**7.3**	5.3	1.20	12.74	4.79	44.3	**2.7**	27.3	17.1	**6.9**
0.0	12.55	141.9	0.80	**0.0**	-4.3	-2.84	-33.44	3.60	184.4	**0.6**	9.5	40.4	**2.6**
0.3	2.36	19.1	0.85	**4.2**	1.1	0.90	6.22	4.03	66.2	**3.9**	27.9	11.7	**8.4**
2.1	3.00	19.4	0.60	**4.7**	0.4	0.97	9.63	5.09	78.7	**1.4**	17.3	27.3	**6.1**
4.2	2.37	10.9	0.97	**1.8**	2.1	0.33	3.56	3.83	78.2	**3.0**	29.4	16.2	**4.9**
0.1	10.92	153.2	2.79	**0.0**	-10.4	-4.33	-91.83	3.46	133.1	**0.8**	17.3	38.2	**0.7**
7.3	0.65	3.6	0.16	**1.0**	0.0	0.01	0.10	3.59	82.6	**1.9**	16.2	19.7	**5.7**
1.7	2.83	25.5	0.71	**0.6**	0.0	0.03	0.40	3.89	78.0	**1.4**	14.1	26.0	**0.5**
2.5	0.95	6.6	0.15	**2.6**	0.3	0.31	3.22	4.43	85.3	**1.2**	11.0	27.9	**4.7**

	Name	City	State	Rating	2008 Rating	2007 Rating	Total Assets ($Mil)	One Year Asset Growth	Comm-ercial Loans	Cons-umer Loans	Home Mort-gages	Secur-ities	Capital-ization Index	Leverage Ratio	Risk-based Capital Ratio
									Asset Mix (As a % of Total Assets)						
	HERITAGE COMMUNITY BANK	GREENEVILLE	TN	**D-**	D-	C-	121	-1.21	2.7	4.6	28.4	3.1	**6.1**	8.1	12.6
	HERITAGE FIRST BANK	GULF SHORES	AL	**E-**	D-	E+	57	1.68	2.9	5.4	24.4	6.5	**1.8**	4.8	8.8
▲	HERITAGE FIRST BANK	ROME	GA	**E**	D-	E	102	7.97	6.1	8.3	26.0	3.0	**5.4**	7.4	11.9
	HERITAGE OAKS BANK	PASO ROBLES	CA	**D-**	D-	C-	979	4.09	14.9	0.8	3.4	22.9	**9.3**	10.5	14.8
	HERITAGE STATE BK	LAWRENCEVILLE	IL	**B**	B+	B+	75	-14.15	6.3	0.5	8.3	11.0	**4.9**	8.1	10.9
	HERITAGE STATE BK	NEVADA	MO	**B**	B-	B-	109	-6.51	8.1	3.2	26.3	13.3	**7.7**	9.5	13.7
	HERNDON NATIONAL BK	HERNDON	PA	**B-**	B-	B	31	1.40	3.9	1.5	17.8	49.7	**10.0**	27.2	71.2
▲	HERRIN SECURITY BANK	HERRIN	IL	**C-**	D-	D-	108	-5.58	6.5	2.6	14.1	41.9	**7.4**	9.2	20.3
	HERRING BANK	AMARILLO	TX	**C**	C-	B-	530	6.80	13.1	5.5	8.2	17.7	**7.7**	9.4	15.4
	HERSHEY STATE BK	HERSHEY	NE	**A-**	A-	A-	48	8.14	16.1	10.4	14.7	4.8	**10.0**	14.0	20.5
	HERTFORD SB SSB	HERTFORD	NC	**C+**	C	D+	15	-1.83	0.0	1.2	51.9	0.0	**10.0**	11.9	23.6
	HIAWATHA BANK & TRUST CO	HIAWATHA	IA	**B**	B	B	39	14.09	9.5	3.0	32.2	0.0	**9.2**	10.4	14.4
	HIAWATHA NATIONAL BK	HAGER CITY	WI	**C-**	C	D	80	62.91	4.5	1.8	16.8	21.6	**10.0**	12.7	23.0
	HIBERNIA HOMESTEAD BANK	NEW ORLEANS	LA	**C-**	C	C	77	16.11	3.1	0.0	54.0	5.5	**10.0**	25.6	36.7
	HICKORY POINT BANK & TRUS	DECATUR	IL	**C+**	C+	C+	867	0.16	6.4	7.6	5.6	53.4	**6.0**	8.0	23.2
	HICKSVILLE BANK	HICKSVILLE	OH	**D**	D-	E+	119	-11.45	4.7	5.0	25.4	25.5	**6.1**	8.1	13.6
	HIGH COUNTRY BANK	SALIDA	CO	**B**	C	NR	181	-6.56	7.2	3.0	35.3	6.3	**10.0**	11.4	18.3
	HIGH DESERT BANK	BEND	OR	**E+**	D-	C	38	-9.28	10.2	0.0	16.9	0.0	**5.5**	7.6	11.4
▼	HIGH PLAINS BANK	FLAGLER	CO	**C-**	C+	B+	95	1.02	7.6	2.5	16.8	11.1	**8.5**	10.0	15.3
▲	HIGH PLAINS BANK	KEYES	OK	**D+**	D-	E-	53	15.46	9.9	1.5	1.2	1.4	**6.6**	10.4	12.2
▼	HIGH POINT BANK & TRUST C	HIGH POINT	NC	**C-**	C	B+	775	-0.81	10.0	0.7	11.4	16.1	**10.0**	11.9	16.8
	HIGH TRUST BANK	STOCKBRIDGE	GA	**E-**	E+	D	197	-5.57	1.0	0.7	7.4	8.3	**0.0**	3.5	5.3
	HIGHLAND BANK	SAINT MICHAEL	MN	**E+**	E	D	476	-14.94	12.7	1.0	9.2	31.7	**4.3**	6.3	11.0
	HIGHLAND COMMERCIAL	MARIETTA	GA	**D-**	D-	D+	130	-9.38	11.5	0.9	9.8	11.8	**6.7**	8.7	12.2
	HIGHLAND COMMUNITY BANK	CHICAGO	IL	**E-**	D-	D-	102	-13.44	6.5	0.9	9.7	28.1	**4.4**	6.4	11.2
▼	HIGHLAND FALLS FS&LA	HIGHLAND FALLS	NY	**D**	C-	C	40	-1.55	0.0	1.1	43.3	19.6	**10.0**	15.6	33.0
	HIGHLAND FS&LA	CROSSVILLE	TN	**B-**	B-	B-	67	-1.92	0.0	0.4	44.1	0.0	**10.0**	19.4	28.3
	HIGHLAND STATE BK	HIGHLAND	WI	**C+**	C+	C	28	1.25	16.6	6.7	35.9	3.2	**7.1**	9.1	15.0
	HIGHLANDS BANK	JACKSON	LA	**B+**	A-	A-	134	0.23	11.7	1.6	14.5	11.5	**9.6**	10.7	15.7
	HIGHLANDS COMMUNITY	COVINGTON	VA	**B-**	B-	A	104	14.36	4.1	9.2	19.7	37.0	**7.6**	9.4	16.2
	HIGHLANDS INDEPENDENT	SEBRING	FL	**D-**	D-	B-	292	-9.23	6.9	2.8	17.8	16.6	**4.8**	6.8	11.5
	HIGHLANDS STATE BK	VERNON	NJ	**D**	D-	D+	164	-1.04	10.3	0.1	12.2	10.6	**6.6**	9.1	12.2
	HIGHLANDS UNION BANK	ABINGDON	VA	**E+**	D	C-	657	1.83	6.2	4.1	28.9	8.5	**3.6**	6.2	10.3
	HILL BANK & TRUST CO	WEIMAR	TX	**B**	B	B+	101	10.26	1.0	1.1	2.7	67.8	**10.0**	18.9	34.4
▲	HILL-DODGE BANKING CO	WARSAW	IL	**B-**	C+	C+	38	2.01	11.6	5.5	12.5	13.9	**8.3**	9.9	14.5
	HILLCREST BANK NA	OVERLAND PARK	KS	**C-**	NR	NR	1,360	N/A	7.9	0.2	1.0	22.5	**10.0**	14.3	80.5
	HILLS BANK & TRUST CO	HILLS	IA	**B**	B	B+	1,930	5.49	7.3	1.2	30.6	10.7	**8.0**	9.7	13.5
	HILLSBORO BANK	PLANT CITY	FL	**C+**	B	A-	97	0.98	9.3	1.1	6.7	36.7	**10.0**	13.0	22.0
	HILLSBORO STATE BK	HILLSBORO	KS	**C-**	C-	C	14	2.64	4.8	5.4	21.0	15.6	**7.6**	9.4	18.2
	HILLSDALE COUNTY	HILLSDALE	MI	**C-**	C-	B	347	5.02	11.9	6.6	22.2	6.4	**6.3**	8.5	12.0
	HILLTOP COMMUNITY BANK	SUMMIT	NJ	**C+**	C	C	157	-5.33	8.0	0.3	8.4	20.2	**10.0**	11.0	16.0
	HILLTOP NATIONAL BK	CASPER	WY	**A-**	B+	B+	482	4.74	5.6	5.7	19.3	45.4	**7.5**	9.3	20.6
▲	HINGHAM INSTITUTION FOR S	HINGHAM	MA	**B-**	C+	B-	1,018	9.97	0.0	0.1	40.8	9.4	**5.2**	7.2	12.7
	HINSDALE BANK & TRUST CO	HINSDALE	IL	**C-**	D+	C-	1,463	1.64	18.6	12.9	3.3	10.0	**7.2**	9.2	12.7
	HNB NATIONAL BK	HANNIBAL	MO	**B-**	C-	C-	326	1.32	7.6	4.7	24.5	5.6	**5.9**	9.8	11.6
	HOCKING VALLEY BANK	ATHENS	OH	**B**	B	B	233	6.63	6.4	3.7	26.9	20.6	**6.9**	8.9	16.7
	HODGE BANK & TRUST CO	HODGE	LA	**B+**	B+	B	63	6.25	7.5	10.3	19.7	32.1	**10.0**	11.8	24.4
	HOLBROOK CO-OP BANK	HOLBROOK	MA	**D**	D	C	108	-6.20	7.5	0.5	16.5	10.1	**5.0**	7.0	11.9
▲	HOLCOMB STATE BK	HOLCOMB	IL	**C**	B-	B-	156	5.96	9.2	3.3	10.3	13.7	**6.0**	8.0	11.9
	HOLLADAY BANK & TRUST	SALT LAKE CITY	UT	**D**	D	D	57	-2.26	3.2	0.9	12.4	0.6	**10.0**	11.4	18.4
▲	HOLMES COUNTY BANK &	LEXINGTON	MS	**C**	C	B-	119	-1.06	4.2	16.6	16.5	13.7	**8.9**	10.3	15.6
▼	HOME BANK	LAFAYETTE	LA	**B-**	B+	B+	683	36.81	7.1	3.7	20.1	16.3	**10.0**	15.5	23.7
▲	HOME BANK & TRUST CO	EUREKA	KS	**C-**	D-	C-	78	-4.07	13.2	4.7	18.4	6.5	**4.8**	7.2	10.9
	HOME BANK OF ARKANSAS	GREENBRIER	AR	**D**	D+	D-	80	0.75	15.8	5.0	22.6	6.4	**6.5**	8.6	12.6
▲	HOME BANK OF CALIFORNIA	SAN DIEGO	CA	**D+**	D	C	147	-10.08	0.0	0.0	11.0	0.0	**10.0**	11.3	16.0
	HOME BANK SB	MARTINSVILLE	IN	**C-**	C	B-	230	-1.36	0.9	0.7	52.6	10.9	**10.0**	12.6	18.9
	HOME BANKING CO	SELMER	TN	**B-**	B-	C+	65	10.20	1.4	9.4	20.3	31.0	**9.2**	10.5	15.9
	HOME BUILDERS ASSN	LYNCHBURG	OH	**C+**	C	C	26	7.41	2.7	4.8	63.6	0.3	**10.0**	17.2	28.5
	HOME BUILDING & LOAN CO	GREENFIELD	OH	**C-**	C-	C	45	3.42	0.0	0.1	40.1	15.0	**10.0**	15.2	41.9
	HOME CITY FSB OF SPRINGFI	SPRINGFIELD	OH	**D+**	D+	D+	146	0.28	7.9	0.6	44.7	0.1	**6.4**	8.4	14.4

Asset Quality Index	Non-Performing Loans as a % of Total Loans	Non-Performing Loans as a % of Capital	Net Charge-offs Avg Loans	Profitability Index	Net Income ($Mil)	Return on Assets (R.O.A.)	Return on Equity (R.O.E.)	Net Interest Spread	Overhead Efficiency Ratio	Liquidity Index	Liquidity Ratio	Hot Money Ratio	Stability Index
0.3	6.08	45.9	2.02	0.2	-0.6	-0.48	-6.16	3.38	79.4	1.5	20.1	26.2	3.6
0.3	4.10	38.9	2.02	0.0	-1.3	-2.24	-36.93	4.54	112.6	1.2	18.8	30.8	1.4
2.0	2.42	21.1	0.53	0.6	-0.4	-0.36	-5.24	3.42	89.2	1.8	18.5	21.8	1.7
0.0	4.68	25.4	2.95	0.0	-18.4	-1.86	-14.44	4.71	77.2	3.2	27.5	14.8	5.7
5.5	0.53	4.3	0.03	9.7	2.2	2.53	30.97	5.03	51.9	4.1	13.0	7.7	7.6
5.3	1.10	7.9	0.06	5.3	1.2	1.14	12.44	4.55	74.0	2.9	8.8	13.7	5.5
8.4	3.72	3.8	0.01	3.0	0.2	0.50	1.86	4.41	79.6	8.2	97.5	0.0	7.6
2.1	3.92	17.3	0.84	2.9	0.8	0.69	6.97	4.26	78.3	4.0	41.4	15.2	3.1
3.3	1.56	9.8	0.51	5.9	7.9	1.51	15.89	4.40	67.1	1.5	18.6	25.5	6.0
5.6	1.11	5.7	0.17	9.9	0.8	1.66	11.14	5.36	53.5	1.2	12.0	27.9	8.8
7.4	1.48	8.5	0.00	2.9	0.1	0.71	6.22	3.14	73.5	3.7	32.5	12.2	6.3
4.7	0.65	5.1	0.51	6.1	0.4	1.01	9.31	4.78	61.6	1.8	3.5	19.1	6.3
4.3	3.10	12.4	0.92	1.2	-0.7	-1.13	-7.79	4.41	101.8	4.9	45.9	11.5	6.3
8.1	1.82	6.0	0.00	0.8	0.0	-0.01	-0.05	4.12	96.8	1.2	15.3	28.5	2.5
7.1	0.60	2.4	0.06	3.7	5.5	0.62	7.46	2.09	76.2	6.0	72.6	11.5	5.0
1.7	2.26	15.3	0.92	2.7	0.6	0.48	5.63	4.31	80.7	1.7	18.7	23.0	2.7
4.8	2.11	13.0	0.42	5.9	1.8	0.95	8.66	4.85	65.3	2.4	12.2	16.8	6.0
0.9	3.56	24.9	0.53	0.0	-0.9	-2.23	-26.26	4.78	108.1	1.4	21.4	27.4	0.0
1.7	6.98	41.7	2.31	3.8	0.6	0.59	5.56	4.69	65.8	2.2	13.9	18.0	7.0
5.0	0.15	1.1	0.07	3.6	0.5	1.00	8.89	4.61	71.3	1.2	11.0	28.4	3.4
1.8	4.51	23.3	1.25	2.0	1.5	0.19	1.54	4.00	74.4	1.2	20.5	30.0	6.4
0.0	23.29	292.9	1.33	0.0	-3.7	-1.80	-38.21	1.80	159.9	0.5	10.8	67.6	2.0
1.2	6.90	48.5	1.29	1.4	0.9	0.18	2.94	3.84	83.8	1.9	24.9	21.2	2.3
0.0	5.61	40.6	1.04	0.0	-0.7	-0.53	-6.12	3.42	96.4	1.5	13.5	23.9	3.7
0.3	11.36	78.7	4.39	0.0	-1.4	-1.18	-17.49	3.36	94.2	1.1	9.8	28.5	2.3
4.6	3.70	11.5	0.00	0.1	-0.8	-1.89	-12.17	2.65	-813.6	3.7	53.6	18.7	6.3
7.9	0.62	1.8	0.15	2.9	0.3	0.37	1.93	3.30	83.6	2.6	43.8	27.8	7.1
6.4	0.06	0.4	0.22	4.7	0.3	0.96	10.67	4.23	69.7	4.5	20.2	6.1	5.7
5.0	0.68	4.3	0.49	5.9	1.9	1.43	13.56	4.19	60.1	0.9	19.4	38.2	7.9
4.4	2.08	11.3	0.66	3.4	0.8	0.80	7.79	3.49	68.0	2.6	47.0	31.9	5.2
1.5	6.97	45.4	2.95	0.0	-3.6	-1.17	-13.06	3.32	87.7	2.0	25.9	20.4	3.6
2.2	2.86	21.0	0.35	1.2	0.5	0.28	2.93	3.60	84.0	4.1	15.6	7.9	2.0
0.3	4.19	37.7	1.28	0.4	-0.6	-0.09	-1.49	3.42	86.2	2.1	14.6	18.5	3.0
10.0	0.00	0.0	-0.07	5.0	0.9	0.97	5.03	2.86	52.6	5.3	93.4	17.6	7.3
4.1	1.21	7.9	0.07	7.8	0.6	1.81	17.99	4.32	52.8	3.2	20.2	13.7	7.4
1.5	7.34	27.0	0.00	3.7	38.9	2.86	18.80	N/,	8.1	2.0	30.5	38.3	3.9
4.6	0.84	6.3	0.57	6.4	23.6	1.27	12.98	3.86	52.0	3.3	10.9	12.5	8.6
6.6	1.01	3.4	3.18	2.7	0.4	0.35	2.76	4.13	66.4	2.8	50.5	28.0	6.8
8.7	0.00	0.0	0.04	3.1	0.1	0.65	6.98	3.83	82.0	4.1	40.1	12.2	3.6
1.7	1.84	15.9	0.20	5.0	3.0	0.88	9.43	4.82	68.5	3.7	14.1	10.6	6.2
1.9	3.69	19.6	0.29	3.2	0.6	0.37	3.28	4.00	77.6	2.8	31.6	18.0	6.1
7.2	0.36	1.6	0.03	7.3	8.5	1.75	17.54	4.19	63.5	4.6	48.3	13.9	7.5
5.9	0.72	7.2	0.02	6.1	10.2	1.05	14.81	3.42	45.2	1.5	9.0	23.7	6.1
3.1	1.99	14.3	0.82	3.2	9.4	0.66	5.42	3.77	56.3	1.3	15.1	28.8	5.8
5.0	0.82	6.2	0.34	6.8	6.4	1.97	21.49	4.49	58.2	2.5	8.1	16.0	5.5
7.2	0.15	0.9	0.11	4.8	1.8	0.80	8.42	4.26	68.2	1.9	14.9	19.3	5.8
6.0	0.94	3.7	0.51	6.0	0.9	1.41	11.76	4.31	57.4	3.4	47.2	19.3	7.5
2.4	2.13	16.2	1.04	0.9	-0.3	-0.29	-4.02	4.27	86.4	2.0	24.9	20.4	3.4
3.4	1.06	7.9	1.15	3.5	0.8	0.56	6.58	3.95	69.0	1.3	19.5	29.1	5.1
0.1	15.88	70.8	1.72	0.3	-0.4	-0.63	-5.10	4.07	100.9	2.1	33.4	26.6	5.7
3.1	1.40	7.5	1.26	5.3	1.5	1.21	12.55	4.37	64.5	1.4	24.1	28.0	6.9
4.0	3.79	15.4	0.07	3.9	4.4	0.67	4.22	4.78	76.5	3.2	27.1	14.7	8.2
7.1	0.42	3.9	0.03	3.3	0.5	0.66	9.57	4.08	78.7	1.6	16.2	22.7	3.7
0.7	4.68	36.3	0.26	2.0	0.0	0.01	0.14	4.53	80.4	0.5	6.4	45.6	5.4
1.0	4.10	27.0	0.46	8.9	3.2	2.02	19.82	4.24	46.9	0.7	10.8	40.4	8.7
2.5	5.40	32.1	0.02	1.4	-0.3	-0.14	-1.14	3.32	79.9	1.8	16.2	20.0	5.6
6.4	0.53	2.6	0.11	4.5	0.5	0.81	7.75	4.88	76.5	2.4	35.2	24.9	5.4
4.8	3.25	16.4	0.00	3.2	0.1	0.46	2.69	4.07	75.7	1.5	9.8	22.2	6.8
2.3	12.37	32.1	0.97	1.6	0.0	-0.02	-0.12	2.48	78.3	7.3	64.9	0.0	6.3
1.7	2.36	19.0	0.84	2.5	0.6	0.40	4.92	3.05	70.4	1.0	17.6	33.3	3.6

Name	City	State	Rating	2008 Rating	2007 Rating	Total Assets ($Mil)	One Year Asset Growth	Asset Mix (As a % of Total Assets) Comm-ercial Loans	Cons-umer Loans	Home Mort-gages	Secur-ities	Capital-ization Index	Leverage Ratio	Risk-based Capital Ratio
HOME EXCHANGE BANK	JAMESPORT	MO	**B-**	C	A-	100	6.33	2.0	1.2	3.7	55.0	**7.0**	9.0	18.2
▲ HOME FEDERAL BANK	NAMPA	ID	**C-**	C	B	1,351	71.12	7.2	0.6	12.0	30.0	**9.4**	10.6	26.6
HOME FEDERAL BANK	SHREVEPORT	LA	**B-**	B-	B	211	21.94	4.5	0.2	23.6	24.4	**10.0**	19.0	38.5
HOME FEDERAL BANK	SIOUX FALLS	SD	**C-**	B-	B-	1,220	4.38	19.9	2.5	10.6	21.4	**6.6**	9.1	12.2
HOME FEDERAL BANK CORP	MIDDLESBORO	KY	**B-**	B-	B-	348	1.61	2.8	1.9	35.5	17.9	**7.3**	9.2	15.2
▲ HOME FEDERAL BANK OF	HALLANDALE BEACH	FL	**E+**	D-	D-	84	-0.08	1.3	0.0	28.4	0.0	**6.4**	8.4	14.9
HOME FEDERAL BANK OF	KNOXVILLE	TN	**B**	B	B+	1,975	2.98	2.8	0.9	18.0	49.2	**10.0**	15.6	28.5
HOME FS&LA	ASHLAND	KY	**B-**	C	C-	288	5.64	3.4	3.3	51.9	25.4	**7.8**	9.5	20.4
HOME FS&LA	BAMBERG	SC	**C-**	C	C+	36	8.19	0.2	7.1	71.6	0.6	**8.5**	10.0	16.7
▼ HOME FS&LA OF COLLINSVILL	COLLINSVILLE	IL	**D-**	D+	D-	113	-13.08	0.0	0.1	63.6	19.9	**8.9**	10.3	18.8
HOME FS&LA OF GRAND	GRAND ISLAND	NE	**C+**	C+	C+	196	4.95	11.7	3.7	16.1	30.4	**7.7**	9.5	16.4
HOME FS&LA OF NEBRASKA	LEXINGTON	NE	**D-**	D+	D+	56	-9.30	25.9	4.3	11.8	7.4	**8.5**	10.0	15.8
▲ HOME FS&LA OF NILES	NILES	OH	**C+**	C+	B	106	2.43	0.1	0.4	22.5	61.8	**10.0**	12.6	35.4
HOME FSB	ROCHESTER	MN	**D-**	D	D+	881	-14.92	19.7	0.6	13.2	17.2	**4.9**	7.6	11.0
▲ HOME LOAN INVESTMENT	WARWICK	RI	**D**	D-	D	214	1.52	0.0	0.0	39.8	2.8	**10.0**	11.7	22.0
▲ HOME LOAN SB	COSHOCTON	OH	**C**	B-	B	164	1.69	11.4	6.1	44.6	5.6	**10.0**	11.1	16.3
▲ HOME LOAN STATE BK	GRAND JUNCTION	CO	**D**	D-	D+	43	-1.58	15.3	18.0	5.6	27.1	**6.9**	8.9	22.0
HOME NATIONAL BK	RACINE	OH	**B-**	B	B-	61	7.15	5.1	12.2	35.6	25.0	**10.0**	13.4	19.9
HOME NATIONAL BK OF	THORNTOWN	IN	**C-**	C	C+	85	5.40	14.0	3.3	21.0	32.8	**5.4**	7.4	13.5
HOME S&LA OF NORBORNE	NORBORNE	MO	**C+**	C+	B+	83	6.90	3.1	4.4	54.7	12.5	**10.0**	16.4	32.1
HOME SAVINGS & LOAN CO	YOUNGSTOWN	OH	**D-**	D-	D	2,210	-5.52	2.1	2.7	39.7	16.4	**6.2**	8.2	13.0
▼ HOME SAVINGS & LOAN CO OF	KENTON	OH	**B+**	A	A	109	3.70	7.3	3.7	51.3	18.4	**10.0**	27.4	50.3
▲ HOME SAVINGS BANK	CHANUTE	KS	**C-**	C	C-	61	5.65	0.4	2.4	27.8	42.6	**10.0**	22.5	50.2
HOME SAVINGS BANK	JEFFERSON CITY	MO	**D**	D	D+	31	-0.37	0.0	3.6	61.2	0.0	**7.6**	9.4	17.6
HOME SAVINGS BANK FSB	LUDLOW	KY	**C-**	D+	C-	35	-3.67	0.0	0.2	45.4	21.5	**10.0**	12.8	25.5
HOME SAVINGS BANK OF	WAPAKONETA	OH	**C-**	C-	B-	35	0.34	0.0	0.7	60.0	0.9	**9.1**	10.4	22.1
▼ HOME SAVINGS OF AMERICA	LITTLE FALLS	MN	**E-**	E+	D-	454	-4.19	0.4	0.1	64.7	0.0	**2.7**	4.9	11.0
▼ HOME SB	KENT	OH	**C-**	C	C-	143	13.44	5.8	3.4	26.7	10.4	**5.4**	7.4	11.4
▲ HOME SB	SALT LAKE CITY	UT	**D**	D-	D-	120	-11.97	0.0	0.7	24.2	0.0	**10.0**	11.2	15.7
▼ HOME SB	MADISON	WI	**D-**	D	D	150	0.65	2.1	2.1	37.5	3.1	**4.7**	6.7	11.3
▲ HOME SB OF ALBEMARLE SSB	ALBEMARLE	NC	**C**	C-	C-	306	1.15	5.5	1.0	38.3	5.5	**5.9**	7.9	11.8
HOME STATE B&TC OF	MCPHERSON	KS	**C+**	C+	C+	130	4.10	16.2	6.4	15.8	37.2	**6.1**	8.1	11.8
▲ HOME STATE BK	LOVELAND	CO	**D**	D-	C	566	1.06	5.7	0.8	7.0	33.1	**7.0**	9.0	14.6
▲ HOME STATE BK	JEFFERSON	IA	**A-**	A-	A-	140	7.47	15.3	1.7	10.8	12.0	**7.4**	9.6	12.9
HOME STATE BK	ROYAL	IA	**A-**	A-	A-	38	-1.58	1.7	1.2	2.9	43.9	**10.0**	29.5	47.6
▲ HOME STATE BK	LITCHFIELD	MN	**C+**	C	C+	121	-2.52	14.0	4.1	14.1	16.6	**10.0**	11.2	15.1
▲ HOME STATE BK	LOUISVILLE	NE	**A-**	B+	A-	81	-3.94	5.8	4.2	19.7	10.4	**7.8**	11.8	13.2
▲ HOME STATE BK NA	CRYSTAL LAKE	IL	**D+**	D-	C+	666	-9.82	8.1	1.6	14.4	14.6	**7.5**	9.4	14.9
HOME TRUST & SB	OSAGE	IA	**B**	B-	B-	185	10.92	10.3	2.0	11.7	33.8	**6.1**	8.1	14.5
▼ HOMEBANC NA	LAKE MARY	FL	**D+**	D	C	318	17.45	0.5	0.0	68.9	5.8	**5.3**	7.3	19.8
HOMEBANK @	SEAGOVILLE	TX	**C-**	C-	C+	101	2.59	13.2	3.1	21.6	16.8	**8.1**	9.8	16.7
HOMELAND COMMUNITY BANK	MCMINNVILLE	TN	**C+**	C	B-	118	11.53	5.7	3.2	23.6	12.2	**7.1**	9.1	13.6
HOMELAND FSB	COLUMBIA	LA	**C**	C	C-	143	5.58	9.4	15.4	31.4	9.1	**8.1**	9.7	15.7
HOMESTAR BANK &	MANTENO	IL	**E-**	D	D+	395	-10.20	3.7	5.7	24.4	3.0	**1.1**	4.6	8.1
HOMESTEAD BANK	COZAD	NE	**A-**	B+	A-	114	4.65	9.4	2.8	3.8	14.3	**10.0**	14.8	21.3
HOMESTEAD SAVINGS BANK	ALBION	MI	**D-**	D	C-	79	-4.76	1.1	0.7	50.4	8.1	**5.4**	7.4	14.3
HOMESTREET BANK	SEATTLE	WA	**E-**	E-	D	2,480	-22.23	3.3	0.0	28.9	12.3	**2.1**	5.2	9.2
HOMETOWN BANK	REDWOOD FALLS	MN	**B-**	B-	B-	174	-0.76	16.3	4.2	17.3	15.6	**7.0**	9.0	12.9
HOMETOWN BANK	ROANOKE	VA	**D-**	D	D+	353	4.53	9.9	0.9	13.6	14.6	**5.8**	7.8	11.7
▲ HOMETOWN BANK	FOND DU LAC	WI	**B**	C-	B-	189	-10.06	26.7	1.8	6.0	0.0	**10.0**	13.1	16.8
▼ HOMETOWN BANK A	WEBSTER	MA	**C+**	B	B+	222	4.59	2.7	0.6	43.5	6.7	**9.6**	10.8	17.3
▼ HOMETOWN BANK NA	CARTHAGE	MO	**D-**	D	D-	198	-16.07	13.2	3.2	15.6	5.2	**8.1**	9.7	13.5
HOMETOWN BANK NA	GALVESTON	TX	**C+**	C+	B-	365	6.54	4.9	4.0	18.7	29.0	**6.6**	8.6	15.2
HOMETOWN BANK OF	ONEONTA	AL	**C+**	C	B	256	21.61	4.9	8.9	20.7	35.7	**8.6**	10.1	16.6
▲ HOMETOWN BANK OF CORBIN	CORBIN	KY	**C-**	D+	C-	131	2.87	6.0	5.4	23.7	12.3	**6.8**	8.8	13.5
HOMETOWN BANK OF	BEDFORD	PA	**C-**	C-	C-	90	30.42	8.7	1.9	32.9	1.0	**7.2**	9.2	13.2
HOMETOWN COMMUNITY	BRASELTON	GA	**E-**	E-	D	136	-2.71	2.4	1.0	8.3	29.6	**0.0**	2.4	5.1
▼ HOMETOWN COMMUNITY	CYRUS	MN	**D-**	D	D-	26	-0.67	6.2	4.4	17.8	17.8	**4.2**	6.2	11.5
HOMETOWN NATIONAL BK	LASALLE	IL	**C-**	D+	C+	166	-1.90	10.8	1.1	9.2	11.0	**7.3**	9.2	15.3
HOMETOWN NATIONAL BK	LONGVIEW	WA	**E-**	E-	D+	20	-26.84	4.7	1.3	7.1	4.9	**2.6**	4.9	9.7

Asset Quality Index	Non-Performing Loans as a % of Total Loans	Non-Performing Loans as a % of Capital	Net Charge-offs Avg Loans	Profitability Index	Net Income ($Mil)	Return on Assets (R.O.A.)	Return on Equity (R.O.E.)	Net Interest Spread	Overhead Efficiency Ratio	Liquidity Index	Liquidity Ratio	Hot Money Ratio	Stability Index
5.1	4.79	18.4	0.47	**4.6**	1.3	1.42	13.95	3.30	53.4	**0.8**	5.1	32.3	**5.4**
2.4	3.92	14.6	2.86	**0.7**	-5.4	-0.52	-3.55	3.11	93.1	**4.7**	51.1	16.6	**7.6**
8.7	0.10	0.3	0.00	**4.1**	1.5	0.78	4.40	3.75	67.9	**3.3**	51.7	24.9	**7.4**
1.6	3.58	26.0	0.24	**3.7**	7.2	0.58	6.58	3.51	67.0	**2.1**	25.1	26.4	**7.0**
4.6	1.61	11.5	0.38	**3.7**	2.0	0.57	6.12	4.00	70.4	**1.8**	15.2	19.9	**5.5**
0.3	13.52	85.1	0.00	**0.3**	-3.1	-3.65	-58.59	2.46	154.1	**0.8**	24.4	52.9	**4.1**
6.1	3.02	8.3	0.47	**3.7**	12.1	0.62	4.00	3.08	66.7	**4.0**	63.2	25.5	**9.0**
5.6	0.86	5.5	0.04	**3.5**	1.7	0.59	6.15	3.07	68.1	**1.7**	33.4	32.4	**5.3**
3.6	1.79	16.5	0.01	**2.8**	0.1	0.33	3.21	3.82	78.6	**0.5**	3.7	44.2	**4.8**
1.7	4.30	28.2	-0.01	**0.0**	-1.3	-1.03	-10.73	2.96	89.3	**1.6**	25.0	26.3	**3.5**
4.9	1.21	6.1	-0.01	**3.4**	1.0	0.54	5.51	3.44	75.1	**4.5**	43.0	13.4	**5.9**
3.2	0.94	5.6	2.09	**0.0**	-1.4	-2.45	-22.77	3.91	110.7	**4.4**	31.2	9.9	**3.9**
5.0	5.17	11.9	-2.69	**4.0**	1.0	0.95	8.07	2.24	77.9	**3.3**	74.9	38.5	**6.1**
0.3	6.53	51.6	0.72	**0.0**	-27.8	-2.88	-32.50	3.39	68.2	**1.5**	21.3	26.4	**3.4**
0.0	15.54	67.6	1.68	**0.0**	-12.0	-5.54	-62.86	3.28	165.0	**2.3**	28.3	19.6	**5.0**
3.7	2.30	15.6	0.20	**5.4**	1.7	1.06	9.66	4.40	54.4	**1.6**	8.7	21.5	**6.0**
6.2	0.38	2.2	1.73	**0.0**	-0.2	-0.46	-3.39	4.01	97.4	**0.8**	2.4	31.0	**4.6**
3.4	3.21	16.7	0.22	**6.4**	0.6	1.05	8.02	5.40	66.6	**0.8**	13.4	34.8	**7.3**
2.9	3.20	23.2	0.07	**3.6**	0.4	0.51	6.87	3.55	77.9	**2.7**	24.7	16.7	**4.2**
4.5	3.61	15.2	0.30	**2.5**	0.2	0.27	1.63	2.56	74.3	**2.4**	31.5	20.3	**6.5**
0.3	8.26	61.1	2.90	**0.0**	-28.3	-1.23	-14.26	3.30	77.0	**3.4**	13.0	12.3	**4.4**
8.6	0.83	2.2	0.23	**5.0**	1.1	1.05	3.79	3.67	54.3	**3.3**	34.2	16.7	**8.5**
5.9	0.29	0.5	0.00	**2.5**	0.3	0.50	2.13	2.73	97.9	**6.0**	69.2	9.7	**5.1**
3.3	2.25	17.2	0.18	**1.2**	0.0	-0.09	-1.01	3.14	102.1	**1.4**	17.6	26.7	**2.4**
9.3	0.77	3.3	0.06	**1.8**	0.1	0.16	1.31	3.13	90.6	**2.4**	44.6	31.2	**4.3**
9.7	0.00	0.0	0.00	**2.3**	0.1	0.19	1.83	2.74	89.3	**3.5**	29.6	14.1	**4.9**
0.3	5.91	71.9	1.01	**1.0**	-2.1	-0.46	-8.02	1.70	99.9	**0.9**	21.3	41.8	**0.3**
2.6	2.05	20.0	0.13	**3.5**	0.7	0.52	6.96	4.11	74.5	**1.6**	14.8	23.2	**3.2**
1.9	1.65	10.1	2.02	**1.2**	-0.5	-0.36	-3.45	4.54	72.2	**0.7**	9.7	37.2	**4.6**
1.2	2.94	30.8	1.19	**0.4**	-0.7	-0.49	-7.03	3.48	87.4	**1.2**	10.2	27.5	**2.9**
4.0	1.00	9.0	0.02	**2.8**	1.1	0.37	4.94	3.15	73.2	**0.8**	11.3	34.2	**3.8**
5.2	1.35	8.1	0.08	**4.0**	1.2	0.90	10.91	4.06	78.1	**2.5**	22.8	17.5	**4.4**
1.4	7.72	44.6	1.79	**2.3**	1.8	0.33	3.51	4.11	73.9	**3.4**	27.9	14.0	**5.2**
8.1	0.14	1.1	0.08	**6.9**	2.3	1.61	16.71	3.80	55.2	**3.7**	13.6	10.5	**7.8**
8.1	0.76	1.2	0.50	**9.4**	0.8	2.14	7.03	4.22	42.7	**6.7**	62.4	3.5	**10.0**
6.9	0.01	0.0	1.16	**3.5**	0.8	0.65	5.85	4.99	72.9	**1.6**	16.7	23.9	**6.3**
6.9	0.00	0.0	0.31	**9.9**	2.4	2.77	25.42	4.77	48.5	**1.7**	16.4	21.2	**9.1**
1.3	6.09	34.7	2.39	**1.3**	1.5	0.21	2.24	3.33	80.4	**1.9**	20.4	20.6	**4.7**
7.2	0.36	2.3	0.00	**5.7**	2.4	1.43	13.96	2.94	45.0	**3.9**	50.2	18.2	**5.9**
2.7	2.16	18.6	0.69	**2.4**	2.0	0.66	6.56	2.11	83.7	**0.6**	11.4	54.0	**3.0**
7.2	0.08	0.5	0.42	**2.7**	0.3	0.32	3.13	4.69	87.2	**4.1**	35.0	12.9	**5.1**
5.9	0.90	6.9	0.74	**3.3**	0.5	0.48	4.87	3.56	65.5	**0.7**	11.6	37.7	**5.4**
2.6	2.09	13.9	0.45	**6.4**	2.1	1.47	15.34	5.60	56.5	**0.9**	22.0	40.2	**6.1**
0.3	8.45	87.8	6.12	**0.0**	-16.2	-3.78	-58.34	3.51	83.3	**3.5**	18.9	11.8	**1.5**
6.4	0.86	3.5	0.05	**6.8**	1.7	1.49	10.18	4.20	68.7	**4.8**	32.7	8.0	**9.5**
2.7	2.19	18.8	0.28	**0.6**	-0.2	-0.21	-2.81	3.46	91.5	**3.8**	24.0	10.9	**0.0**
0.3	7.01	63.7	3.88	**0.3**	-11.6	-0.40	-8.15	1.63	85.2	**1.6**	13.0	23.8	**0.0**
3.9	1.12	8.4	0.48	**4.4**	1.7	0.94	8.65	4.54	62.0	**4.9**	21.5	3.6	**6.0**
4.2	1.39	11.2	1.55	**0.0**	-3.8	-1.09	-12.67	3.25	77.0	**1.5**	18.9	25.4	**0.8**
4.4	1.52	8.9	0.60	**4.3**	1.4	0.74	5.99	3.57	62.9	**1.5**	12.2	23.8	**5.3**
3.1	3.29	22.6	0.21	**6.7**	2.3	1.07	10.13	4.19	49.9	**1.3**	14.7	27.5	**6.6**
0.8	7.02	42.4	0.68	**0.0**	-2.9	-1.32	-13.30	3.79	96.8	**1.2**	6.1	25.7	**4.4**
5.5	0.79	5.3	0.15	**6.5**	4.6	1.29	14.39	4.87	58.6	**1.3**	24.8	30.1	**6.2**
3.9	1.58	8.9	0.75	**6.6**	2.6	1.18	11.45	4.41	55.8	**1.1**	22.4	32.2	**4.5**
2.1	1.33	9.6	0.92	**2.3**	0.5	0.40	4.59	4.10	82.3	**1.9**	19.7	19.8	**4.1**
8.8	0.00	0.0	0.01	**2.7**	0.6	0.70	7.16	4.01	77.7	**1.4**	20.9	27.4	**3.5**
0.3	13.67	172.8	1.88	**0.0**	-4.7	-3.30	-74.49	1.30	242.3	**0.5**	12.3	65.0	**0.0**
4.3	0.75	6.1	1.29	**1.0**	-0.3	-0.95	-12.95	3.98	91.4	**2.4**	23.6	18.1	**3.0**
3.1	1.65	9.9	0.55	**2.3**	0.7	0.45	4.67	4.17	74.5	**4.2**	26.3	9.3	**3.9**
0.0	6.88	50.3	-0.96	**0.0**	-0.6	-2.48	-43.52	4.50	140.0	**1.7**	19.8	22.1	**3.0**

Name	City	State	Rating	2008 Rating	2007 Rating	Total Assets ($Mil)	One Year Asset Growth	Asset Mix (As a % of Total Assets) Comm-ercial Loans	Cons-umer Loans	Home Mort-gages	Secur-ities	Capital-ization Index	Leverage Ratio	Risk-based Capital Ratio
▼ HOMETRUST BANK	CLYDE	NC	D	C-	B	1,669	14.84	8.5	0.2	34.9	5.2	8.5	10.0	14.2
HOMEWOOD FSB	BALTIMORE	MD	B-	B-	B	76	-1.11	0.0	9.3	45.2	8.8	10.0	16.9	34.2
HONDO NATIONAL BK	HONDO	TX	B-	B-	C+	139	12.85	7.4	4.5	14.7	32.5	6.2	8.2	13.9
▲ HONESDALE NATIONAL BK	HONESDALE	PA	A-	B	B	521	1.19	9.6	9.0	25.8	19.1	10.0	11.6	16.3
HONOR BANK	HONOR	MI	D-	C-	D+	197	-2.95	9.5	3.4	15.5	15.0	5.9	7.9	12.1
▲ HOOSAC BANK	NORTH ADAMS	MA	C	C-	C-	340	-6.75	5.4	0.5	18.1	32.8	10.0	11.1	16.2
▼ HOOSIER HEARTLAND STATE	CRAWFORDSVILLE	IN	D+	C	C-	133	5.27	4.2	6.8	12.9	27.8	5.9	7.9	13.2
HOPETON STATE BK	HOPETON	OK	C+	C+	C+	23	-2.90	0.4	6.0	0.0	66.6	10.0	19.5	53.2
HOPEWELL VALLEY	PENNINGTON	NJ	C	C-	C-	352	11.98	2.7	0.2	10.8	20.1	5.8	7.8	12.4
HOPKINS FSB	BALTIMORE	MD	C+	C+	B	355	17.93	1.0	0.5	12.8	56.9	6.1	8.1	19.8
HORATIO STATE BK	HORATIO	AR	B	B+	B+	117	9.26	3.6	19.9	31.6	13.6	8.7	10.1	17.4
HORICON BANK	HORICON	WI	D+	D+	C-	512	-6.33	12.0	1.6	25.9	3.0	7.1	10.3	12.6
HORIZON BANK	FYFFE	AL	C-	B-	B+	97	-1.20	3.1	7.4	25.7	6.2	10.0	14.6	20.5
HORIZON BANK	WAVERLY	NE	A-	B+	B+	169	8.16	32.1	6.7	7.4	11.5	5.9	9.6	11.7
HORIZON BANK NA	MICHIGAN CITY	IN	B-	B-	B-	1,398	1.02	3.8	10.5	17.5	28.0	6.6	8.6	14.0
HORIZON BANK SSB	AUSTIN	TX	B+	B	B-	210	16.21	12.9	4.6	16.6	10.6	6.2	8.2	12.2
HORIZON COMMUNITY BANK	LAKE HAVASU CITY	AZ	D-	D-	D-	156	-5.50	7.4	1.6	10.2	5.9	6.8	8.8	13.6
HORIZON STATE BK	CAMERON	MO	C-	C	C-	19	-3.74	6.4	4.4	18.3	6.0	6.4	8.4	13.6
▼ HORRY COUNTY STATE BK	LORIS	SC	E-	D	C-	791	4.13	6.9	1.6	12.8	33.5	2.2	5.1	9.2
HOT SPRINGS BANK & TRUST	HOT SPRINGS	AR	C+	C+	C	105	10.11	8.6	2.6	18.5	20.6	6.4	8.4	14.2
HOUGHTON STATE BK	RED OAK	IA	C	C	C+	144	5.32	25.6	1.8	6.7	10.9	5.0	7.9	11.0
HOUSTON BUSINESS BANK	HOUSTON	TX	B-	B-	NR	25	42.06	16.4	0.0	0.0	12.2	10.0	39.8	51.7
HOUSTON COMMUNITY BANK	HOUSTON	TX	B+	B	B-	245	4.47	8.3	9.7	6.4	1.1	7.1	9.1	13.9
▲ HOWARD BANK	ELLICOTT CITY	MD	D+	D+	D+	300	4.88	28.2	0.4	8.6	5.0	6.1	9.1	11.8
HOWARD STATE BK HOWARD	HOWARD	KS	B-	B-	B-	44	2.12	8.0	5.4	8.8	17.0	8.4	9.9	18.1
HOYNE SB	CHICAGO	IL	C-	C-	C	302	-1.74	0.0	0.0	63.9	18.8	10.0	18.2	44.9
▲ HSBC BANK NEVADA NA	LAS VEGAS	NV	B	C	C-	1,985	4.18	0.0	0.0	0.0	59.5	10.0	63.3	92.7
HSBC BANK USA NA	MCLEAN	VA	C-	D	D+	181,119	8.35	7.8	14.0	8.4	26.8	6.3	8.3	18.4
HSBC TRUST CO (DELAWARE)	WILMINGTON	DE	B-	C	C	58	-18.54	0.0	0.0	0.0	17.7	4.8	6.8	16,089.5
HUDSON CITY SAVINGS BANK	PARAMUS	NJ	B-	B-	B	60,471	0.76	0.0	0.0	50.8	45.6	6.0	8.0	22.7
▲ HUDSON VALLEY BANK NA	YONKERS	NY	C	C+	B+	2,667	5.41	9.2	1.1	7.0	17.2	6.8	8.8	14.0
HULL FSB	BALTIMORE	MD	D-	D-	C-	27	4.20	0.0	0.3	85.8	0.4	7.3	9.2	18.5
HULL STATE BK	HULL	TX	C	C	B	47	3.48	9.3	15.8	3.2	26.2	7.9	9.6	15.3
HUNTINGDON SB	HUNTINGDON	PA	C+	C+	C+	16	7.85	0.0	0.1	71.7	0.0	10.0	21.0	39.4
HUNTINGDON VALLEY BANK	WARMINSTER	PA	D+	D-	D	137	-4.58	0.5	0.1	52.9	14.6	5.9	7.9	12.4
HUNTINGTON FSB	HUNTINGTON	WV	B-	B-	B	485	4.65	0.0	0.2	33.5	42.6	10.0	13.4	35.1
HUNTINGTON NATIONAL BK	COLUMBUS	OH	D	D-	D	53,407	4.49	15.4	11.7	15.0	17.9	5.0	7.0	12.8
HUNTINGTON STATE BK	HUNTINGTON	TX	D-	C	C+	269	4.33	5.8	15.9	13.8	8.2	6.1	8.1	11.9
HURON COMMUNITY BANK	EAST TAWAS	MI	C-	C-	C	190	-2.56	41.4	0.8	22.2	10.8	9.8	10.9	16.9
HURON NATIONAL BK	ROGERS CITY	MI	B	B+	B+	54	5.99	4.1	4.5	37.7	12.9	10.0	13.0	22.2
▲ HURON VALLEY STATE BK	MILFORD	MI	D+	C-	C	58	19.71	12.2	1.3	5.1	4.2	6.3	9.6	12.0
HUSTISFORD STATE BK	HUSTISFORD	WI	B+	B	B+	53	4.81	3.6	4.0	52.6	7.3	10.0	13.2	20.9
▼ HYDE PARK BANK & TRUST	CHICAGO	IL	D+	C-	C-	369	2.97	1.1	0.1	4.4	53.5	7.0	9.0	17.9
HYDE PARK SB	BOSTON	MA	B	B	C	910	0.49	0.1	0.1	21.4	59.8	10.0	15.2	35.6
▲ HYDEN CITIZENS BANK	HYDEN	KY	C	C+	B	120	-5.14	22.6	5.8	24.6	29.1	6.3	8.3	14.1
▲ HYPERION BANK	PHILADELPHIA	PA	D+	D-	C	90	1.79	11.9	0.2	24.9	9.9	6.3	8.7	12.0
I BANK TEXAS SSB	AUSTIN	TX	B	B-	B	157	-4.33	5.5	0.7	34.6	0.0	10.0	11.6	19.4
▲ IBERIABANK	LAFAYETTE	LA	B	C	C+	8,316	2.47	9.7	4.1	13.7	21.7	6.1	8.1	15.7
IBERVILLE BANK	PLAQUEMINE	LA	D	D+	C	227	-1.47	1.6	2.7	15.0	8.2	7.6	9.4	15.4
ICE TRUST US LLC	NEW YORK	NY	U	U	NR	8,317	32.37	0.0	0.0	0.0	0.0	0.0	0.7	1,168.1
ICON BANK OF TEXAS NA	HOUSTON	TX	B-	C	C-	298	21.42	21.8	2.0	18.3	5.6	8.6	10.1	15.2
IDABEL NATIONAL BK	IDABEL	OK	B+	B	B-	107	5.13	4.8	5.9	14.7	44.6	6.5	8.5	15.7
IDAHO BANKING CO	BOISE	ID	E-	E+	D+	186	-18.71	15.2	1.1	8.7	14.5	0.5	4.7	7.1
IDAHO FIRST BANK	MCCALL	ID	E-	E-	D-	77	4.49	14.2	2.2	12.6	3.9	3.5	5.9	10.3
IDAHO INDEPENDENT BANK	COEUR D'ALENE	ID	D	D+	B-	442	-10.46	9.7	2.0	6.1	6.6	10.0	11.8	16.9
IDAHO TRUST BANK	BOISE	ID	D	C-	D	89	0.74	22.7	0.3	5.3	1.6	10.0	15.4	26.5
▲ ILLINI BANK	SPRINGFIELD	IL	B	B	B	247	-1.51	12.5	1.3	6.0	24.9	6.6	8.6	13.6
ILLINI STATE BK	OGLESBY	IL	A-	B+	B+	84	12.57	1.7	2.5	13.0	49.0	10.0	11.0	24.1
▼ ILLINOIS NATIONAL BK	SPRINGFIELD	IL	D	C-	D+	565	-7.66	8.5	2.9	6.8	13.6	6.0	8.0	15.0
▲ ILLINOIS-SERVICE FS&LA	CHICAGO	IL	D+	D+	C-	149	1.20	0.4	0.6	24.5	47.0	7.8	9.5	23.1

Asset Quality Index	Non-Performing Loans as a % of Total Loans	Non-Performing Loans as a % of Capital	Net Charge-offs Avg Loans	Profitability Index	Net Income ($Mil)	Return on Assets (R.O.A.)	Return on Equity (R.O.E.)	Net Interest Spread	Overhead Efficiency Ratio	Liquidity Index	Liquidity Ratio	Hot Money Ratio	Stability Index
1.1	3.67	25.3	1.77	**2.8**	5.7	0.35	3.29	3.31	63.3	**1.0**	15.2	33.2	**6.7**
4.9	2.75	10.4	-0.77	**3.7**	0.5	0.67	3.99	3.00	53.2	**3.1**	38.0	19.0	**7.8**
7.0	0.51	3.4	0.12	**5.4**	1.4	1.31	15.85	4.31	69.2	**1.8**	35.7	34.1	**4.9**
5.7	0.70	3.9	0.31	**7.4**	6.9	1.31	11.62	4.04	55.3	**2.5**	18.8	16.7	**9.1**
1.7	2.91	22.2	2.10	**0.2**	-0.9	-0.46	-5.36	4.36	83.4	**3.5**	23.2	12.5	**3.7**
6.0	2.72	12.2	0.28	**2.5**	0.9	0.26	2.18	2.62	87.6	**3.3**	20.5	13.2	**5.5**
1.9	2.68	17.1	0.47	**3.7**	0.9	0.71	7.94	4.54	75.9	**2.7**	34.8	19.9	**2.7**
7.3	3.17	4.0	-0.35	**2.8**	0.1	0.57	3.01	4.16	89.7	**3.7**	87.5	27.5	**6.4**
6.8	0.53	4.0	0.05	**3.2**	1.6	0.46	5.88	3.54	75.7	**1.9**	25.4	21.7	**4.1**
2.8	7.06	23.9	0.00	**4.3**	2.9	0.87	9.59	2.22	45.2	**3.5**	76.1	34.0	**4.7**
5.0	0.55	3.5	0.41	**6.3**	1.2	1.04	10.28	4.07	52.0	**1.1**	26.1	37.2	**6.7**
1.5	3.01	22.5	0.69	**5.6**	7.3	1.38	13.93	4.70	53.1	**2.4**	3.3	15.7	**6.1**
1.7	6.09	27.8	0.53	**6.4**	1.1	1.16	7.90	4.44	51.6	**1.7**	16.3	22.5	**8.7**
7.7	0.00	0.0	0.00	**10.0**	2.8	1.76	16.80	4.74	44.0	**2.1**	10.4	18.0	**7.7**
3.8	2.04	13.0	0.94	**4.4**	11.8	0.85	8.84	3.99	61.2	**1.7**	10.8	20.8	**6.8**
7.3	0.24	2.1	0.24	**7.0**	3.7	1.86	20.90	5.42	64.3	**1.7**	13.2	20.7	**6.3**
0.9	6.04	36.0	2.55	**0.0**	-1.9	-1.17	-14.28	3.25	101.2	**2.0**	30.4	25.3	**2.7**
8.5	0.03	0.2	0.09	**2.2**	0.0	0.16	1.83	5.63	96.7	**3.5**	25.9	11.9	**5.2**
0.3	5.65	45.6	3.33	**0.0**	-13.0	-1.64	-25.65	2.59	86.2	**0.9**	19.4	37.2	**2.6**
1.8	2.16	14.2	0.89	**0.2**	-0.8	-0.74	-7.92	3.75	99.1	**2.1**	21.7	19.3	**6.0**
5.1	0.43	3.8	0.09	**8.6**	2.0	1.44	12.70	4.48	46.4	**4.1**	22.3	8.8	**7.0**
8.5	0.00	0.0	0.00	**0.0**	-0.5	-2.17	-5.03	4.41	146.3	**2.5**	56.8	37.5	**5.3**
6.6	0.37	2.7	0.06	**8.5**	4.6	1.94	21.26	5.44	61.1	**1.1**	27.8	49.5	**7.3**
2.8	1.81	15.0	0.63	**2.6**	1.2	0.41	4.55	3.94	69.6	**1.0**	6.5	29.0	**3.2**
6.5	0.25	1.3	0.18	**5.9**	0.5	1.31	12.03	4.50	66.5	**4.8**	32.2	8.0	**5.7**
6.0	3.99	14.4	0.26	**1.2**	-0.3	-0.05	-0.26	3.03	90.8	**3.2**	34.4	17.1	**7.2**
6.5	0.00	0.0	0.00	**7.0**	49.7	2.57	3.77	1.88	90.6	**4.9**	190.8	99.4	**7.0**
2.6	3.75	16.3	3.63	**3.3**	1,623.2	0.89	9.50	2.70	53.1	**5.3**	47.4	13.1	**6.0**
10.0	0.00	0.0	0.00	**4.5**	4.7	0.59	8.81	0.16	67.1	**10.0**	1,095.3	0.0	**6.4**
5.6	2.62	16.1	0.31	**4.3**	530.0	0.87	10.53	1.99	19.8	**3.9**	51.0	22.3	**7.6**
3.3	3.06	19.0	2.60	**3.7**	4.8	0.17	1.88	4.26	58.5	**4.6**	21.0	6.4	**8.5**
0.3	7.27	63.4	0.00	**1.3**	-0.1	-0.38	-4.34	3.78	36.0	**5.2**	10.6	0.0	**3.9**
3.7	1.10	5.0	0.14	**3.5**	0.2	0.39	3.89	4.98	87.3	**3.8**	42.8	16.7	**4.5**
7.6	2.01	8.6	0.00	**3.1**	0.1	0.47	2.83	2.46	75.1	**1.8**	30.2	23.3	**7.8**
3.7	1.97	16.1	0.42	**1.4**	0.3	0.22	2.83	3.71	96.0	**3.7**	12.8	10.1	**2.9**
4.4	5.26	17.9	0.35	**3.1**	2.2	0.45	3.41	2.97	61.8	**3.9**	58.0	20.1	**7.3**
0.9	2.17	17.1	2.24	**2.5**	345.0	0.69	10.96	3.36	60.3	**4.1**	12.6	8.1	**4.7**
0.3	4.72	36.2	0.55	**2.8**	0.8	0.29	3.84	4.94	69.7	**1.5**	11.9	23.8	**3.8**
2.1	2.29	14.0	0.27	**4.5**	1.8	0.91	8.50	4.39	69.3	**3.9**	15.9	9.2	**6.5**
3.5	4.33	22.0	0.23	**5.8**	0.6	1.08	8.13	4.06	57.4	**3.2**	35.4	17.6	**7.2**
4.1	0.46	3.5	0.03	**1.4**	0.2	0.39	3.83	4.42	80.4	**1.4**	13.2	25.8	**2.3**
5.3	2.00	11.5	0.14	**5.6**	0.5	0.90	6.54	4.63	59.0	**1.4**	12.2	25.0	**8.2**
3.0	5.41	20.2	1.79	**1.4**	2.0	0.49	6.23	3.04	85.7	**2.6**	20.7	16.8	**3.0**
9.7	0.78	1.2	0.39	**4.6**	29.2	3.33	21.46	2.74	69.6	**4.1**	85.6	28.0	**8.4**
4.1	0.97	6.3	0.59	**5.3**	1.6	1.28	15.05	4.36	69.5	**1.6**	9.8	20.7	**5.6**
1.5	4.33	37.6	0.77	**2.2**	1.7	1.91	21.19	4.16	97.6	**0.5**	4.8	50.4	**2.8**
5.0	0.00	0.0	0.45	**5.5**	1.4	0.87	7.95	3.77	50.3	**3.5**	18.8	11.9	**6.5**
5.1	0.45	2.8	0.29	**5.8**	65.3	0.76	8.71	3.48	58.3	**2.1**	14.0	19.0	**9.4**
1.5	5.91	33.9	0.98	**1.2**	-1.7	-0.75	-7.51	3.53	94.6	**4.8**	36.5	10.0	**5.0**
10.0	0.00	0.0	0.00	**1.3**	3.7	0.05	7.24	N/,	91.1	**3.7**	100.7	101.0	**0.8**
8.1	0.20	1.4	0.22	**3.9**	2.9	1.07	11.62	5.41	73.3	**1.6**	22.3	25.7	**4.8**
6.9	0.45	2.6	0.42	**7.5**	2.0	1.94	19.46	4.43	54.8	**1.8**	33.8	31.7	**6.2**
0.0	14.32	102.1	4.54	**0.0**	-8.8	-4.16	-66.61	3.33	122.7	**1.0**	13.3	31.3	**2.4**
0.3	3.52	32.1	3.24	**0.0**	-2.0	-2.40	-58.49	2.65	127.0	**1.0**	28.4	61.4	**0.0**
0.2	10.60	47.3	4.71	**0.2**	-5.7	-1.17	-9.37	4.08	82.0	**4.3**	27.2	9.3	**5.4**
2.9	6.38	21.3	8.16	**0.0**	-4.2	-4.58	-21.71	2.91	122.7	**2.9**	39.4	20.6	**5.0**
4.8	1.03	6.3	0.55	**6.2**	3.0	1.19	13.35	3.94	62.7	**4.7**	31.3	8.4	**5.6**
7.1	0.32	1.2	0.72	**5.5**	1.1	1.30	10.00	4.19	62.9	**5.2**	42.8	9.4	**7.3**
1.6	5.25	28.9	1.36	**0.8**	-1.1	-0.17	-2.12	2.72	92.3	**4.5**	37.0	11.7	**4.8**
2.5	6.35	24.9	0.59	**1.6**	0.1	0.05	0.51	3.41	82.8	**4.8**	62.6	16.4	**4.5**

Name	City	State	Rating	2008 Rating	2007 Rating	Total Assets ($Mil)	One Year Asset Growth	Asset Mix (As a % of Total Assets) Comm-ercial Loans	Cons-umer Loans	Home Mort-gages	Secur-ities	Capital-ization Index	Leverage Ratio	Risk-based Capital Ratio
INCOMMONS BANK NA	MEXIA	TX	**C+**	C	B	100	7.69	8.6	7.9	27.7	18.8	**7.3**	9.2	15.5
INDEPENDENCE BANK	NEWPORT BEACH	CA	**D**	D-	D	323	-9.41	3.3	0.6	0.0	15.7	**8.9**	10.7	14.1
▼ INDEPENDENCE BANK	HAVRE	MT	**B+**	B+	B-	400	5.19	9.7	3.2	4.4	11.2	**9.5**	11.2	14.6
▼ INDEPENDENCE BANK	INDEPENDENCE	OH	**C**	C	C	162	8.63	30.6	0.6	4.6	19.6	**9.5**	10.6	14.7
INDEPENDENCE BANK	EAST GREENWICH	RI	**C-**	C-	D+	71	-4.65	26.5	0.0	16.5	12.1	**7.1**	9.0	23.2
INDEPENDENCE BANK NA	HOUSTON	TX	**D+**	C-	C+	167	11.60	13.6	1.4	18.5	14.0	**10.0**	11.8	17.1
▼ INDEPENDENCE BANK OF	BRASELTON	GA	**D**	C	C	95	69.23	9.0	1.1	11.2	13.3	**10.0**	17.4	23.0
INDEPENDENCE BANK OF	OWENSBORO	KY	**C+**	C	C-	990	12.20	7.1	1.8	21.0	26.1	**4.3**	6.7	10.6
INDEPENDENCE FEDERAL	INDEPENDENCE	IA	**D-**	D	D+	23	-3.72	0.0	2.6	53.3	39.8	**7.8**	9.5	22.9
INDEPENDENCE FSB	WASHINGTON	DC	**E-**	E-	D-	111	-29.26	0.6	6.4	54.5	4.1	**2.0**	4.6	9.5
▼ INDEPENDENCE NATIONAL BK	GREENVILLE	SC	**E+**	D-	C-	122	-9.98	10.1	1.4	15.7	8.8	**5.7**	8.4	11.5
▲ INDEPENDENCE STATE BK	INDEPENDENCE	WI	**D-**	E	E	59	-3.85	8.6	2.5	9.5	28.1	**6.1**	8.1	11.9
INDEPENDENCE TRUST CO	FRANKLIN	TN	**C**	C	C+	4	5.76	0.0	0.0	0.0	51.2	**10.0**	81.3	249.6
INDEPENDENT BANK	IONIA	MI	**D-**	D-	D-	2,536	-14.42	5.7	13.0	28.7	2.7	**4.6**	6.6	11.1
▼ INDEPENDENT BANK	MEMPHIS	TN	**C-**	C	C-	793	-0.26	7.4	66.7	1.3	3.5	**5.9**	8.9	11.7
▲ INDEPENDENT BANK	MCKINNEY	TX	**C+**	B-	C	1,098	21.35	10.2	2.9	19.2	4.8	**6.3**	8.6	12.0
▼ INDEPENDENT BANK OF	IRVING	TX	**D-**	D-	D-	98	10.53	17.8	2.9	11.8	7.5	**6.4**	8.4	13.9
▲ INDEPENDENT BANKERS	LAKE MARY	FL	**D**	E+	D	298	-37.20	0.0	0.0	2.9	15.9	**5.2**	7.2	12.6
INDEPENDENT FARMERS	MAYSVILLE	MO	**C-**	C	C+	92	7.31	5.3	4.5	10.2	42.3	**6.4**	8.4	14.6
INDIANA BANK & TRUST CO	COLUMBUS	IN	**C-**	D+	C-	1,042	3.26	11.8	1.1	13.2	21.7	**7.4**	9.3	12.9
INDIANA BUSINESS BANK	INDIANAPOLIS	IN	**D-**	D	D-	81	-8.86	13.0	1.1	7.1	8.8	**7.6**	9.4	13.8
INDIANA COMMUNITY BANK	GOSHEN	IN	**E**	D	C-	129	58.45	15.7	0.6	19.7	0.0	**2.5**	6.3	9.5
INDIANA FIRST SB	INDIANA	PA	**C+**	C+	C-	256	5.43	3.8	0.8	59.1	12.0	**7.8**	9.6	16.5
▼ INDUS AMERICAN BANK	ISELIN	NJ	**E**	D+	C-	212	11.93	6.0	0.3	7.6	14.9	**4.1**	8.1	10.6
INDUSTRIAL BANK	WASHINGTON	DC	**D+**	C-	C-	382	5.93	6.0	0.6	25.2	31.6	**6.5**	8.5	14.6
INDUSTRIAL STATE BK	KANSAS CITY	KS	**C-**	B-	B	151	-2.51	11.6	1.9	1.8	20.9	**10.0**	19.9	25.9
INDUSTRY STATE BK	INDUSTRY	TX	**B+**	B	B	376	18.19	5.2	2.8	5.1	59.9	**5.8**	7.8	18.2
INEZ DEPOSIT BANK	INEZ	KY	**C+**	C+	B-	115	3.58	0.6	5.9	32.4	39.0	**8.7**	10.2	22.8
INEZ DEPOSIT BANK FSB	LOUISA	KY	**C**	C	B	50	3.58	1.2	4.9	28.1	32.7	**9.9**	11.0	20.0
▲ ING BANK FSB	WILMINGTON	DE	**C-**	D	C-	87,611	-2.76	0.5	0.1	44.9	49.9	**8.6**	10.1	28.1
ING NATIONAL TRUST	MINNEAPOLIS	MN	**U**	U	U	7	5.04	0.0	0.0	0.0	30.8	**10.0**	85.8	474.9
▼ INLAND BANK & TRUST	OAK BROOK	IL	**D-**	D+	D-	1,204	5.96	4.9	0.2	6.9	18.6	**7.6**	9.4	14.2
▼ INLAND COMMUNITY BANK NA	ONTARIO	CA	**D**	D-	D+	264	-6.41	5.4	0.2	2.1	16.0	**8.6**	10.1	16.1
INLAND NORTHWEST BANK	SPOKANE	WA	**D-**	D-	D+	393	0.19	11.9	2.0	6.7	17.7	**8.3**	10.1	13.6
INSBANK	NASHVILLE	TN	**D-**	D	C-	134	-1.11	6.7	3.1	8.3	16.0	**7.5**	9.6	12.9
INSIGHT BANK	COLUMBUS	OH	**C**	C-	C	133	34.67	6.3	0.6	22.9	0.0	**10.0**	12.0	17.5
INSIGNIA BANK	SARASOTA	FL	**D-**	D-	D	149	11.10	0.3	1.6	14.7	11.1	**7.6**	9.6	13.0
INSOUTH BANK	BROWNSVILLE	TN	**E+**	D-	D-	353	-7.08	6.5	1.8	19.0	16.4	**4.4**	6.4	11.6
INST FOR SVGS IN	NEWBURYPORT	MA	**B**	B-	B-	1,193	12.37	0.5	0.3	50.1	24.3	**10.0**	12.4	24.8
INSURBANC	FARMINGTON	CT	**B-**	B-	B-	155	-0.99	19.3	0.2	8.6	35.5	**10.0**	12.7	23.1
INTEGRA BANK NA	EVANSVILLE	IN	**E-**	E	D	2,419	-17.13	7.4	2.6	8.7	21.8	**0.4**	3.5	7.7
▼ INTEGRITY BANK	CAMP HILL	PA	**C-**	C-	C+	541	14.79	13.6	2.6	13.6	0.8	**5.6**	7.8	11.4
INTEGRITY BANK & TRUST	MONUMENT	CO	**D-**	D	C	107	0.58	6.0	1.1	17.8	10.7	**7.9**	9.6	14.3
INTEGRITY BANK PLUS	WABASSO	MN	**C**	C-	D+	50	5.67	5.6	1.3	9.1	15.6	**6.7**	8.7	12.6
▲ INTEGRITY BANK SSB	HOUSTON	TX	**C**	C	C	212	25.14	17.4	1.3	7.6	12.2	**10.0**	13.3	20.4
▼ INTEGRITY FIRST BANK	WAUSAU	WI	**E-**	D-	D+	109	-21.18	17.1	0.6	16.0	13.2	**3.0**	6.3	10.0
INTER NATIONAL BK	MCALLEN	TX	**D-**	D-	B-	2,262	6.10	8.4	0.8	10.4	28.1	**7.0**	9.0	18.6
INTER SAVINGS BANK FSB	MAPLE GROVE	MN	**E-**	E-	E-	603	-13.97	0.5	0.1	44.0	13.4	**0.0**	2.2	4.3
INTER-STATE FS&LA OF KANS	KANSAS CITY	KS	**C+**	C+	B-	214	0.71	0.0	0.0	24.6	69.5	**10.0**	24.0	174.4
INTERAMERICAN BANK A FSB	MIAMI	FL	**D**	C	B	248	-5.73	5.6	1.2	24.5	0.1	**9.7**	10.8	16.0
INTERAUDI BANK	NEW YORK	NY	**C+**	C+	C+	1,279	-2.53	7.0	0.4	6.7	41.5	**6.2**	8.2	18.4
▲ INTERBANK	OKLAHOMA CITY	OK	**B-**	C+	C+	1,656	129.51	8.6	3.6	8.3	0.0	**7.7**	10.1	13.0
INTERCITY STATE BK	SCHOFIELD	WI	**B-**	B-	B	166	8.87	2.4	4.2	24.9	4.6	**10.0**	16.2	20.0
INTERCONTINENTAL BANK	WEST MIAMI	FL	**B-**	B	B+	143	-3.09	3.7	0.6	1.6	77.0	**10.0**	11.4	34.8
INTERCREDIT BANK NA	MIAMI	FL	**D-**	D-	D-	253	-12.81	11.9	1.3	26.7	16.9	**7.0**	9.0	15.9
INTERNATIONAL BK	RATON	NM	**B-**	C+	C+	324	2.75	15.8	1.2	11.2	15.0	**7.7**	9.5	13.4
INTERNATIONAL BK OF	AMHERST	WI	**B+**	B+	B	46	2.89	10.4	2.3	29.4	18.2	**10.0**	14.7	25.4
INTERNATIONAL BK OF CHICA	CHICAGO	IL	**D-**	C-	C-	240	9.43	2.8	0.5	21.5	22.3	**8.4**	9.9	15.4
INTERNATIONAL BK OF	BROWNSVILLE	TX	**A-**	B+	B+	888	7.15	7.6	0.8	5.4	47.3	**10.0**	12.8	25.6
INTERNATIONAL BK OF	LAREDO	TX	**A-**	B	B	9,833	-0.78	7.9	1.2	8.3	40.4	**7.5**	9.4	16.5

Asset Quality Index	Non-Performing Loans as a % of Total Loans	Non-Performing Loans as a % of Capital	Net Charge-offs Avg Loans	Profitability Index	Net Income ($Mil)	Return on Assets (R.O.A.)	Return on Equity (R.O.E.)	Net Interest Spread	Overhead Efficiency Ratio	Liquidity Index	Liquidity Ratio	Hot Money Ratio	Stability Index
6.7	0.32	2.1	0.29	**3.4**	0.5	0.46	4.82	4.82	88.9	**3.9**	20.4	9.8	**5.3**
0.6	3.92	24.8	0.53	**2.4**	1.2	0.36	3.64	3.90	81.4	**1.1**	18.2	30.9	**3.3**
4.5	1.34	8.4	0.02	**10.0**	7.5	1.88	16.14	5.19	38.9	**0.8**	6.5	32.8	**9.0**
2.0	4.48	21.4	0.72	**3.7**	1.1	0.67	6.05	4.52	63.0	**0.8**	22.4	47.9	**6.6**
5.9	1.52	7.5	0.00	**2.7**	0.3	0.43	4.83	3.05	84.5	**2.3**	36.0	26.2	**3.8**
6.7	1.26	6.5	0.51	**1.6**	0.6	0.32	3.30	3.68	85.4	**1.3**	32.1	54.3	**4.8**
7.5	0.00	0.0	0.00	**0.1**	-0.4	-0.51	-2.46	3.84	98.2	**1.9**	27.5	23.5	**1.6**
6.2	0.48	4.5	0.11	**8.2**	13.9	1.47	22.00	4.58	53.0	**2.0**	4.7	17.9	**4.3**
2.7	3.53	19.5	0.05	**0.8**	-0.1	-0.51	-5.01	1.73	119.8	**3.7**	46.2	15.5	**3.7**
0.3	9.74	118.1	0.61	**1.2**	0.2	0.11	2.91	3.37	88.3	**1.2**	16.2	29.1	**0.3**
0.0	12.73	89.5	1.86	**0.0**	-6.4	-4.86	-49.14	2.29	164.4	**0.8**	16.7	44.7	**0.5**
1.9	3.68	23.8	1.70	**0.0**	-1.3	-2.12	-25.03	4.06	115.5	**3.5**	34.0	15.7	**2.5**
7.0	0.00	0.0	0.00	**10.0**	0.2	4.24	5.30	4.16	87.8	**5.0**	363.2	100.0	**1.4**
0.0	3.62	28.2	2.91	**0.0**	-28.5	-1.02	-15.79	4.64	90.2	**2.2**	18.3	18.6	**3.6**
2.3	0.93	8.3	0.61	**5.4**	7.5	0.96	11.03	4.30	57.2	**0.9**	7.3	30.9	**5.2**
3.8	0.93	7.9	0.31	**7.0**	16.4	1.69	16.54	4.64	59.8	**2.1**	9.7	18.3	**8.6**
2.4	3.04	22.0	0.85	**0.4**	-0.2	-0.19	-2.14	3.74	93.0	**2.4**	23.5	17.7	**2.8**
0.0	18.88	98.5	4.43	**0.0**	-7.6	-2.07	-29.87	2.35	96.1	**0.8**	15.0	37.7	**3.3**
2.7	3.43	20.1	0.56	**5.0**	0.9	1.06	11.63	4.50	64.4	**2.0**	24.7	20.0	**5.2**
2.2	2.70	17.8	0.76	**2.8**	6.1	0.58	6.27	3.40	65.0	**4.1**	25.2	12.0	**6.1**
0.0	6.42	43.8	3.04	**0.0**	-1.7	-1.96	-19.59	3.54	77.8	**1.1**	11.0	29.6	**5.0**
0.3	6.44	59.0	2.30	**0.0**	-5.1	-3.14	-45.89	3.28	138.9	**0.6**	11.1	48.0	**3.1**
6.4	0.50	3.8	0.11	**3.5**	1.6	0.63	6.66	3.36	72.7	**1.7**	13.3	21.6	**5.7**
0.0	5.37	44.7	0.92	**0.4**	-0.3	-0.13	-1.48	4.26	73.5	**0.7**	5.4	34.4	**0.8**
1.5	5.52	36.3	0.40	**2.2**	0.3	0.08	0.99	4.64	88.2	**1.5**	15.9	24.3	**3.4**
2.7	0.12	0.4	0.31	**6.5**	1.7	1.06	5.56	4.32	60.9	**3.8**	37.2	15.0	**7.3**
5.8	2.47	9.3	0.20	**7.0**	5.7	1.68	19.16	3.82	60.9	**2.7**	54.7	37.2	**6.2**
4.4	3.18	12.6	0.28	**3.3**	0.6	0.47	4.38	3.62	84.0	**3.0**	45.8	24.8	**6.4**
4.9	2.87	10.1	0.03	**2.4**	0.1	0.23	1.93	3.68	92.2	**3.5**	61.9	23.6	**5.5**
4.3	3.93	17.0	0.93	**1.7**	264.0	0.29	3.11	1.80	43.8	**7.3**	56.3	2.2	**4.8**
10.0	0.00	0.0	0.00	**9.1**	0.1	1.85	2.06	1.34	95.6	**5.0**	459.5	101.0	**6.1**
0.0	13.42	78.7	1.09	**2.1**	4.9	0.41	3.42	3.25	63.3	**2.1**	23.6	24.4	**6.6**
0.4	5.29	27.5	0.20	**3.1**	1.6	0.56	5.63	4.51	75.8	**1.4**	16.0	25.6	**3.6**
0.4	4.44	26.9	1.01	**1.7**	1.4	0.36	3.64	4.29	75.0	**1.9**	22.4	21.2	**4.4**
2.7	0.25	1.7	0.10	**0.7**	0.1	0.05	0.53	3.14	75.2	**0.5**	3.3	41.3	**4.7**
7.0	0.55	3.7	0.00	**2.7**	0.7	0.65	6.04	4.25	80.5	**0.7**	15.2	43.5	**4.2**
0.9	1.84	12.3	0.86	**0.1**	-0.5	-0.35	-2.69	3.78	100.3	**1.8**	21.4	21.6	**1.1**
0.3	9.17	67.3	1.85	**0.0**	-3.4	-0.94	-14.11	3.72	105.7	**1.3**	20.7	28.6	**1.3**
9.3	0.76	3.7	0.03	**4.4**	11.2	1.02	7.51	2.87	59.0	**2.8**	37.3	28.6	**9.2**
3.7	5.78	22.3	0.07	**3.2**	0.7	0.41	3.27	3.15	75.1	**3.4**	54.5	25.4	**7.5**
0.1	14.06	102.5	6.17	**0.0**	-110.9	-3.89	-78.25	2.34	88.6	**2.0**	28.7	33.5	**3.9**
2.1	1.09	10.6	0.56	**3.7**	2.7	0.51	10.67	3.60	61.2	**1.3**	7.0	24.6	**3.1**
0.3	5.26	35.1	0.74	**0.2**	-0.6	-0.55	-5.69	3.62	96.8	**1.6**	19.7	24.5	**4.3**
3.6	0.66	5.2	0.16	**4.7**	0.5	1.07	10.89	5.38	73.4	**4.0**	11.2	8.2	**5.5**
4.6	0.36	1.8	0.30	**2.2**	0.8	0.38	2.72	3.68	76.7	**3.1**	28.7	15.6	**3.7**
1.0	3.71	29.6	4.89	**0.0**	-4.6	-3.83	-49.42	3.14	88.6	**0.8**	15.8	40.2	**0.0**
0.2	12.22	59.1	1.48	**1.9**	-2.1	-0.10	-0.53	3.21	83.8	**2.3**	37.7	51.7	**9.2**
0.3	5.83	108.3	2.99	**0.0**	-13.6	-2.09	-67.84	2.25	95.0	**1.2**	22.3	31.1	**0.0**
10.0	0.20	0.2	0.00	**2.2**	0.2	0.10	0.42	1.84	91.2	**7.1**	96.4	9.1	**7.5**
1.0	4.72	31.2	0.26	**0.6**	-5.6	-2.20	-18.35	3.65	92.4	**1.0**	10.3	29.9	**5.9**
7.9	1.42	5.5	0.00	**3.2**	6.6	0.53	6.32	1.69	68.6	**3.1**	61.9	60.1	**5.6**
4.3	1.31	10.1	0.05	**7.8**	30.7	3.11	22.31	7.40	55.9	**1.7**	11.1	20.7	**10.0**
2.5	2.88	14.2	0.10	**9.7**	2.4	1.54	9.56	4.02	42.2	**2.6**	16.5	16.3	**7.4**
9.5	2.11	2.4	0.75	**3.8**	1.0	0.65	6.00	2.19	69.7	**3.7**	91.7	40.3	**5.3**
0.3	6.53	43.9	2.89	**0.0**	-8.3	-3.09	-34.08	3.15	155.1	**0.9**	22.7	44.3	**3.4**
4.5	1.70	11.5	0.28	**8.8**	4.1	1.26	13.38	5.40	56.3	**1.5**	8.5	22.1	**6.5**
4.3	3.64	16.7	0.05	**6.7**	0.6	1.41	9.76	4.79	67.0	**4.7**	29.8	7.6	**9.2**
0.0	0.99	6.3	0.48	**3.6**	1.8	0.77	7.85	3.72	57.6	**0.8**	23.3	58.0	**5.2**
7.7	1.54	5.4	0.06	**9.8**	15.9	1.98	14.09	4.08	44.1	**1.6**	34.7	39.3	**8.9**
5.8	1.62	7.9	0.44	**6.4**	113.8	1.21	9.64	3.64	64.2	**1.9**	24.1	26.9	**9.1**

Name	City	State	Rating	2008 Rating	2007 Rating	Total Assets ($Mil)	One Year Asset Growth	Asset Mix (As a % of Total Assets) Commercial Loans	Consumer Loans	Home Mortgages	Securities	Capitalization Index	Leverage Ratio	Risk-based Capital Ratio
INTERNATIONAL BK OF	ZAPATA	TX	A-	B+	B+	519	14.25	4.3	3.7	11.0	61.9	9.9	10.9	31.0
▲ INTERNATIONAL CITY BANK N	LONG BEACH	CA	C-	D	D	180	-16.32	19.7	0.1	0.7	30.9	10.0	11.5	20.2
INTERNATIONAL FINANCE BAN	MIAMI	FL	D-	D-	C-	505	2.27	9.5	1.8	23.0	26.7	5.7	7.7	12.8
INTERSTATE BK SSB	PERRYTON	TX	C-	B-	C+	122	5.68	13.8	10.4	13.4	27.5	6.3	8.3	13.8
INTERSTATE FS&LA OF	MCGREGOR	IA	C-	C	C	9	-0.01	0.0	1.6	71.0	0.1	10.0	18.4	35.5
▲ INTERVEST NATIONAL BK	NEW YORK	NY	D+	D-	D-	2,055	-13.50	0.1	0.0	0.0	29.5	7.9	9.6	14.2
INTRACOASTAL BANK	PALM COAST	FL	C+	C	C	113	32.26	2.6	0.6	3.6	33.5	10.0	12.7	19.2
INTRUST BANK NA	WICHITA	KS	B-	B	A-	3,705	0.30	29.5	5.3	5.3	28.5	7.1	9.1	12.9
INVESCO NATIONAL TRUST	ATLANTA	GA	B+	B+	B+	154	11.17	0.0	0.0	0.0	13.0	10.0	46.6	78.8
INVESTAR BANK	BATON ROUGE	LA	C-	C-	C	210	20.44	4.0	28.7	16.4	10.9	5.5	8.1	11.4
INVESTMENT SB	ALTOONA	PA	B-	C+	C+	123	-3.06	2.1	1.6	53.2	25.9	10.0	14.1	27.4
INVESTORS COMMUNITY	MANITOWOC	WI	D+	C	C+	669	2.32	7.2	0.1	4.8	7.1	6.5	9.8	12.1
INVESTORS NATIONAL BK	CHILLICOTHE	MO	B	B	B-	65	8.88	0.9	3.0	26.6	48.8	10.0	11.5	26.1
INVESTORS SB	SHORT HILLS	NJ	C+	C	C-	9,577	14.59	0.6	0.1	53.7	11.6	6.6	8.6	13.8
INVESTORSBANK	WAUKESHA	WI	D	D	D-	252	-3.64	13.4	0.1	15.0	4.5	10.0	12.7	16.2
INVESTRUST NA	OKLAHOMA CITY	OK	U	U	U	3	2.93	0.0	0.0	0.0	82.1	10.0	98.3	123.4
INWOOD NATIONAL BK	DALLAS	TX	A	A	A-	1,293	-0.38	6.3	0.8	13.1	15.1	9.3	10.6	19.1
IOWA FALLS STATE BK	IOWA FALLS	IA	B+	B-	B-	102	1.16	9.8	2.8	7.4	27.4	7.9	10.5	13.3
IOWA PRAIRIE BANK	BRUNSVILLE	IA	C-	C-	C+	62	-12.86	7.0	3.5	6.5	32.5	5.7	7.7	14.9
IOWA SB	CARROLL	IA	C+	C	D	156	-0.09	11.2	1.7	4.4	32.4	6.3	8.3	14.5
IOWA STATE BK	ALGONA	IA	C	D+	C+	242	0.59	10.2	2.7	7.9	26.5	7.4	9.3	13.2
IOWA STATE BK	CLARKSVILLE	IA	C-	C-	D+	217	25.20	9.4	1.2	2.2	28.1	3.5	6.7	10.2
IOWA STATE BK	DES MOINES	IA	A	A-	A-	294	0.80	5.2	0.6	10.3	36.5	10.0	12.8	23.8
▼ IOWA STATE BK	HULL	IA	C-	C+	B-	339	5.18	10.8	2.7	8.4	18.0	6.1	8.9	11.9
IOWA STATE BK	SAC CITY	IA	C-	C-	C-	106	-0.49	8.7	5.0	17.6	24.6	5.9	7.9	12.5
▼ IOWA STATE BK	WAPELLO	IA	C-	D+	C	81	10.61	8.7	5.1	13.5	3.1	10.0	11.4	16.4
▲ IOWA STATE BK & TRUST CO	FAIRFIELD	IA	C	D+	C+	87	-16.74	20.3	2.7	17.7	7.5	7.9	9.6	15.8
IOWA STATE SB	CRESTON	IA	C+	C	C	176	0.67	4.7	3.6	11.1	26.1	5.2	7.2	11.4
IOWA STATE SB	KNOXVILLE	IA	C+	C+	B-	99	2.69	19.7	8.6	9.3	20.1	6.1	8.1	12.2
▲ IOWA TRUST & SB	CENTERVILLE	IA	A	A-	A	158	7.54	4.6	3.2	12.3	43.9	10.0	11.2	16.7
IOWA TRUST & SB	EMMETSBURG	IA	C-	B	B+	144	-2.57	5.9	3.1	7.8	25.3	6.7	8.7	12.8
IOWA-NEBRASKA STATE BK	SOUTH SIOUX CITY	NE	D-	D+	D+	191	-5.23	12.1	4.0	12.6	21.3	5.8	7.8	11.9
IPAVA STATE BK	IPAVA	IL	B-	B-	B-	86	7.51	10.6	5.5	14.4	17.1	5.3	8.7	11.2
IPSWICH STATE BK	IPSWICH	SD	B+	B+	B+	51	21.30	5.7	2.4	0.3	22.7	10.0	15.9	24.7
▲ IRELAND BANK	MALAD CITY	ID	C	C-	C	207	1.80	16.4	3.5	4.5	23.6	6.8	8.8	13.1
IRON WORKERS SB	ASTON	PA	C	C-	C-	163	-0.51	0.5	0.0	49.3	3.3	5.8	7.8	12.9
IROQUOIS FARMERS STATE	IROQUOIS	IL	B	B-	B-	79	94.67	3.9	5.5	13.0	32.7	9.2	10.4	16.3
IROQUOIS FS&LA	WATSEKA	IL	C+	C+	C+	405	4.46	3.8	4.2	36.6	34.1	6.9	8.9	17.3
ISABELLA BANK	MOUNT PLEASANT	MI	B-	B-	B-	1,169	7.46	7.0	2.7	22.5	28.1	5.6	7.6	12.8
ISB COMMUNITY BANK	IXONIA	WI	D-	D	C-	412	-2.88	6.7	0.5	9.3	11.5	6.3	8.5	12.0
ISLANDERS BANK	FRIDAY HARBOR	WA	D	C-	C-	240	9.56	3.0	2.1	18.3	0.0	9.4	11.3	14.5
ISRAEL DISCOUNT BK OF NEW	NEW YORK	NY	C+	C	C	9,315	-2.09	25.3	0.8	0.1	48.9	6.2	8.2	14.6
ITASCA BANK & TRUST CO	ITASCA	IL	D+	C-	C	428	1.27	23.1	0.4	12.3	20.8	6.4	8.4	12.9
ITS BANK	JOHNSTON	IA	B	B	B	5	2.51	0.0	0.0	0.0	77.7	10.0	90.0	428.5
IUKA STATE BK	IUKA	IL	B-	B-	B-	20	-1.97	8.9	8.5	35.1	15.7	10.0	13.3	21.0
JACKSBORO NATIONAL BK	JACKSBORO	TX	B+	B	B	173	2.81	9.2	3.7	11.0	41.9	7.2	9.1	16.9
JACKSON COUNTY BANK	SEYMOUR	IN	D+	C	B-	372	-6.96	14.0	2.2	21.9	12.8	9.0	10.3	15.0
JACKSON COUNTY BANK	MCKEE	KY	A	A	A	138	-1.47	2.2	9.9	19.7	46.3	10.0	20.6	40.1
JACKSON COUNTY BANK	BLACK RIVER FALLS	WI	B	B-	B-	213	0.44	1.7	4.2	20.8	13.6	7.3	9.2	15.7
JACKSON FS&LA	JACKSON	MN	B-	C+	B-	33	6.91	4.4	3.0	30.4	38.0	10.0	19.6	41.1
JACKSON PARISH BANK	JONESBORO	LA	C+	B-	B-	70	6.38	4.1	5.9	8.4	27.1	10.0	11.7	27.7
JACKSON SB SSB	SYLVA	NC	B	B	B	37	6.40	0.0	0.8	67.6	0.0	10.0	16.6	30.6
JACKSONVILLE BANK	JACKSONVILLE	FL	D-	D+	C-	646	47.44	5.6	0.8	12.1	9.7	3.2	8.8	10.1
▲ JACKSONVILLE SB	JACKSONVILLE	IL	C+	C	C	301	4.47	8.3	5.7	18.8	31.5	7.4	9.3	14.8
JAMES POLK STONE	PORTALES	NM	B	B	B	171	12.03	5.2	8.3	21.5	18.6	7.4	9.3	15.4
JAMESTOWN STATE BK	JAMESTOWN	KS	B-	B-	C	19	1.98	2.8	3.2	3.4	46.0	10.0	16.0	34.6
JANESVILLE STATE BK	JANESVILLE	MN	A-	B+	B-	54	5.13	3.1	2.0	17.9	13.4	10.0	12.0	16.3
▲ JARRETTSVILLE FS&LA	JARRETTSVILLE	MD	A-	B+	A-	96	7.34	0.0	0.1	71.1	8.6	10.0	14.1	28.2
▼ JASPER BANKING CO	JASPER	GA	E+	D-	C-	238	-9.16	4.3	1.9	11.0	26.3	4.4	6.8	10.7
JEFF DAVIS BANK & TRUST C	JENNINGS	LA	A-	A-	A-	536	6.47	6.9	7.9	17.0	31.0	9.3	10.6	18.5

Asset Quality Index	Non-Performing Loans as a % of Total Loans	Non-Performing Loans as a % of Capital	Net Charge-offs Avg Loans	Profitability Index	Net Income ($Mil)	Return on Assets (R.O.A.)	Return on Equity (R.O.E.)	Net Interest Spread	Overhead Efficiency Ratio	Liquidity Index	Liquidity Ratio	Hot Money Ratio	Stability Index
8.1	0.54	1.3	0.28	**9.7**	7.9	1.73	12.56	3.81	48.3	**1.5**	34.0	43.6	**8.0**
4.1	3.24	10.0	2.35	**2.1**	0.8	0.39	3.68	3.69	84.7	**0.6**	7.8	47.9	**4.2**
0.3	3.34	23.4	1.53	**1.8**	1.3	0.24	3.20	3.87	74.0	**1.4**	31.5	40.8	**4.4**
2.1	2.56	16.9	0.24	**4.0**	1.0	0.82	8.58	4.12	80.2	**2.1**	35.9	30.1	**5.9**
9.1	0.00	0.0	0.04	**2.6**	0.0	0.33	1.86	3.48	86.6	**4.5**	23.5	6.2	**6.3**
0.6	4.40	25.2	6.51	**0.6**	-50.2	-2.30	-22.69	2.27	75.7	**2.1**	31.9	35.6	**7.9**
8.9	0.00	0.0	0.02	**3.0**	1.2	1.18	8.78	3.50	75.6	**2.1**	38.3	32.3	**4.5**
4.1	0.85	5.5	2.38	**4.9**	34.0	0.93	9.99	3.31	62.3	**3.7**	20.5	11.6	**8.3**
6.5	0.00	0.0	0.00	**10.0**	10.4	7.54	9.29	1.00	84.2	**3.3**	92.6	100.0	**6.7**
1.9	2.24	20.3	0.64	**2.4**	0.7	0.35	4.55	3.24	76.2	**2.9**	14.9	14.6	**2.8**
9.5	0.39	1.7	0.07	**3.3**	0.7	0.57	3.91	3.29	73.4	**2.3**	36.1	26.0	**7.4**
1.4	2.00	15.4	0.76	**4.8**	6.4	0.98	10.55	3.18	42.2	**0.4**	4.6	58.0	**5.8**
5.7	2.96	10.6	0.26	**5.2**	0.7	1.16	10.14	4.04	67.4	**3.4**	53.6	20.2	**6.5**
4.8	2.02	18.2	0.43	**4.0**	61.9	0.70	7.79	3.19	44.0	**1.9**	4.4	18.4	**6.5**
0.0	8.50	50.9	0.88	**4.2**	1.5	0.60	4.74	3.12	54.6	**0.6**	8.4	46.7	**8.0**
10.0	0.00	0.0	0.00	**7.9**	0.1	2.57	2.49	1.45	96.1	**5.0**	2,147.9	101.0	**5.9**
8.1	0.21	1.1	0.10	**7.9**	23.0	1.76	14.06	3.85	52.2	**3.5**	31.1	17.9	**10.0**
5.4	1.82	10.6	0.01	**6.5**	1.5	1.52	13.58	4.77	58.5	**3.8**	34.1	14.1	**7.1**
8.1	0.06	0.4	0.05	**4.0**	0.6	0.93	12.57	3.43	68.9	**2.6**	14.7	15.9	**3.1**
4.9	1.39	8.0	-0.01	**4.2**	1.6	1.06	11.77	3.77	73.6	**5.5**	42.4	7.4	**4.4**
3.4	0.86	5.8	0.43	**5.5**	2.5	1.06	10.06	4.09	60.2	**3.1**	20.6	14.1	**5.3**
4.6	0.43	3.7	0.27	**4.0**	2.1	1.02	15.21	3.09	57.3	**5.7**	35.0	2.8	**3.1**
6.3	1.33	4.8	0.47	**7.9**	6.0	2.03	16.01	4.13	55.5	**5.0**	41.5	10.2	**8.0**
2.5	1.67	12.1	0.09	**7.4**	4.3	1.34	13.51	4.13	52.4	**4.0**	21.2	9.3	**4.9**
1.6	2.97	22.7	0.42	**4.4**	1.1	1.04	10.71	3.32	57.2	**3.9**	25.9	10.7	**5.8**
1.1	6.05	32.8	0.19	**1.8**	0.3	0.34	3.17	3.33	76.8	**1.4**	21.0	28.0	**4.5**
2.9	2.36	14.5	1.33	**3.2**	0.6	0.61	6.82	3.57	78.0	**4.4**	29.8	9.8	**3.7**
6.1	0.20	1.6	0.01	**4.3**	1.4	0.78	9.06	4.53	76.6	**4.1**	16.4	8.2	**5.0**
3.7	0.83	6.0	0.85	**6.2**	1.3	1.35	15.57	5.29	67.2	**5.0**	19.7	2.9	**5.4**
7.4	0.17	0.8	0.36	**8.1**	3.3	2.18	18.87	4.15	51.2	**3.0**	27.1	15.6	**8.0**
2.6	3.19	21.5	0.86	**4.5**	0.9	0.63	6.47	4.49	59.2	**2.5**	18.0	16.8	**6.5**
0.3	5.30	36.6	1.70	**0.1**	-2.0	-0.99	-11.90	3.33	87.7	**3.9**	9.6	8.8	**3.5**
7.1	0.19	1.4	0.11	**5.8**	1.2	1.48	16.02	4.37	67.4	**1.7**	18.4	22.5	**5.9**
7.8	0.51	1.6	0.29	**5.7**	0.5	1.09	6.31	4.38	59.3	**2.5**	37.3	24.9	**8.3**
3.8	1.83	12.8	0.08	**2.8**	1.2	0.56	6.17	4.77	88.6	**2.5**	10.5	15.9	**3.7**
7.1	0.21	1.9	0.00	**3.4**	0.8	0.49	6.58	3.70	76.8	**2.6**	23.3	16.8	**4.1**
4.9	1.26	6.5	0.15	**4.6**	0.7	1.03	9.55	4.31	74.4	**3.7**	36.5	15.3	**6.4**
4.3	1.47	9.4	0.03	**3.8**	3.0	0.76	8.12	3.14	60.8	**2.6**	39.6	26.0	**4.6**
5.2	0.82	6.0	0.75	**4.4**	10.8	0.96	11.68	4.03	64.7	**1.7**	17.3	23.2	**6.5**
0.0	4.56	33.7	2.12	**0.8**	0.4	0.11	1.23	3.20	69.8	**1.0**	17.2	33.0	**4.2**
1.0	3.28	21.6	0.21	**7.4**	3.2	1.41	11.55	5.24	53.2	**1.3**	15.2	27.7	**5.4**
5.8	1.58	7.5	1.27	**3.2**	50.6	0.54	6.87	2.34	63.2	**1.7**	28.2	51.0	**5.1**
1.3	4.11	29.2	0.91	**3.0**	2.2	0.50	5.90	3.92	69.8	**1.1**	15.3	31.2	**4.3**
10.0	0.00	0.0	0.00	**10.0**	0.2	3.19	3.55	2.69	28.5	**5.0**	1,009.2	100.0	**6.0**
7.1	0.84	4.2	0.65	**3.4**	0.1	0.31	2.21	4.56	78.0	**2.2**	17.4	17.9	**7.7**
5.7	0.69	3.7	0.45	**6.3**	2.4	1.47	13.83	4.86	69.8	**3.0**	34.3	18.3	**7.0**
2.2	2.95	19.8	0.41	**3.7**	2.5	0.65	6.59	3.82	71.2	**2.4**	15.0	17.2	**5.2**
7.4	1.45	3.2	0.72	**7.0**	1.8	1.26	6.25	4.00	53.3	**2.9**	48.8	28.8	**8.4**
4.8	1.22	8.1	0.33	**8.4**	4.2	1.91	19.95	3.68	48.1	**2.2**	15.8	18.2	**7.8**
6.4	2.18	5.0	0.01	**4.0**	0.3	0.85	4.31	3.85	68.3	**6.1**	55.7	5.9	**6.7**
3.7	9.12	21.4	0.63	**2.2**	0.1	0.23	1.93	3.36	87.7	**6.2**	61.5	6.8	**4.5**
4.5	2.86	14.0	0.00	**3.7**	0.2	0.59	3.48	3.34	71.3	**1.7**	16.7	22.6	**8.0**
0.0	8.90	78.5	0.84	**0.5**	-10.3	-2.17	-24.82	3.85	231.2	**1.1**	12.8	29.2	**4.3**
4.2	1.74	10.1	0.59	**3.7**	2.2	0.74	7.92	3.75	70.2	**1.9**	26.5	22.9	**4.5**
5.1	0.82	4.9	0.16	**6.2**	2.2	1.42	15.42	6.00	74.1	**4.9**	27.5	4.8	**5.3**
8.9	0.26	0.6	0.00	**3.2**	0.1	0.51	3.00	4.27	88.1	**6.0**	64.9	6.5	**6.8**
8.8	0.07	0.4	0.05	**6.4**	0.8	1.53	12.53	4.17	61.0	**4.1**	26.1	10.0	**8.3**
7.8	0.73	4.1	0.06	**5.4**	1.2	1.25	9.04	3.64	34.7	**3.4**	19.2	12.2	**8.1**
0.3	16.46	99.3	1.46	**0.0**	-2.0	-0.81	-11.19	2.39	109.4	**1.4**	15.3	26.6	**2.2**
5.9	0.95	4.7	0.20	**6.7**	6.4	1.26	10.97	4.77	66.4	**2.3**	29.8	20.8	**7.6**

Name	City	State	Rating	2008 Rating	2007 Rating	Total Assets ($Mil)	One Year Asset Growth	Asset Mix (As a % of Total Assets) Commercial Loans	Consumer Loans	Home Mortgages	Securities	Capitalization Index	Leverage Ratio	Risk-based Capital Ratio
▲JEFFERSON BANK	FAYETTE	MS	**B**	B-	B	95	76.53	7.6	4.2	3.2	34.1	**10.0**	12.0	25.5
JEFFERSON BANK	DALLAS	TX	**E-**	E-	E	205	-35.28	12.2	0.4	5.8	23.8	**3.5**	5.5	11.2
JEFFERSON BANK	SAN ANTONIO	TX	**B-**	B-	B	769	12.68	10.3	2.4	18.8	24.6	**8.1**	9.7	14.0
JEFFERSON BANK & TRUST	EUREKA	MO	**D-**	D-	C	713	-13.26	12.5	0.6	3.6	11.1	**6.1**	8.1	11.9
▼JEFFERSON BANK OF	OLDSMAR	FL	**D**	C	C	114	29.39	7.7	0.5	3.6	44.8	**10.0**	13.3	22.5
JEFFERSON BANK OF	JEFFERSON CITY	MO	**C+**	C+	C+	474	-3.27	8.3	19.9	13.6	18.8	**7.2**	9.2	13.4
JEFFERSON COUNTY BANK	DAYKIN	NE	**B**	B	B	40	-0.30	4.9	1.2	3.6	30.8	**10.0**	11.4	20.2
JEFFERSON FEDERAL BANK	MORRISTOWN	TN	**D**	D+	D+	614	-8.48	9.7	1.0	20.2	7.5	**5.7**	7.7	12.5
JEFFERSON SECURITY BANK	SHEPHERDSTOWN	WV	**C-**	C	C+	265	7.12	1.5	1.2	23.1	37.8	**5.7**	7.7	14.2
▼JERSEY SHORE STATE BK	WILLIAMSPORT	PA	**B**	B+	B+	682	2.14	4.7	1.4	24.3	29.4	**6.2**	8.2	13.8
JERSEY STATE BK	JERSEYVILLE	IL	**B-**	B-	B-	138	6.80	6.8	1.8	9.4	45.3	**7.8**	9.6	19.7
JEWETT CITY SB	JEWETT CITY	CT	**B-**	B-	B	242	5.49	3.4	0.8	42.6	23.4	**10.0**	14.9	28.3
JGB BANK NA	MIAMI	FL	**D**	D-	C-	366	24.98	28.9	0.7	9.1	10.6	**10.0**	11.5	18.3
▲JIM THORPE NATIONAL BK	JIM THORPE	PA	**C**	C+	C+	157	-6.97	0.8	1.0	37.3	30.2	**6.0**	8.0	17.7
JOHN MARSHALL BANK	ALEXANDRIA	VA	**C+**	C	C	310	32.06	18.6	0.3	3.9	8.2	**6.5**	10.6	12.1
JOHN O MELBY & CO BANK	WHITEHALL	WI	**B-**	B-	B-	42	3.42	7.3	3.7	21.5	23.2	**10.0**	11.3	19.6
JOHNSON BANK	RACINE	WI	**D-**	D+	C+	4,936	-11.43	12.6	0.9	16.9	12.1	**3.2**	5.8	10.1
JOHNSON CITY BANK	JOHNSON CITY	TX	**A-**	A-	A-	89	9.65	4.2	13.8	26.3	1.6	**10.0**	12.8	18.9
▼JOHNSON COUNTY BANK	MOUNTAIN CITY	TN	**C**	B+	B+	117	-2.95	0.9	4.6	48.9	8.5	**10.0**	12.3	22.6
JOHNSON STATE BK	JOHNSON	KS	**B-**	B-	B+	68	-0.07	4.4	2.4	3.3	41.0	**10.0**	12.8	20.7
JONAH BANK OF WYOMING	CASPER	WY	**B-**	B	C	182	35.59	21.9	1.0	9.5	6.8	**6.8**	8.8	16.1
▼JONES NATIONAL BK & TRUST	SEWARD	NE	**B-**	B	B+	217	7.58	11.8	3.0	8.6	34.1	**6.8**	8.8	13.5
JONESBORO STATE BK	JONESBORO	LA	**B+**	A	A	116	-3.80	5.8	4.6	8.1	61.5	**10.0**	14.2	40.6
JONESBURG STATE BK	JONESBURG	MO	**C+**	C+	C+	72	13.59	2.7	2.1	28.9	2.1	**5.6**	7.6	12.7
JONESTOWN BANK & TRUST	JONESTOWN	PA	**D**	C	B-	349	4.49	2.1	22.3	29.2	8.4	**5.1**	8.6	11.1
▼JOURDANTON STATE BK	JOURDANTON	TX	**B+**	A-	A-	97	8.45	8.5	6.3	3.1	45.3	**10.0**	15.3	30.3
JOY STATE BK	JOY	IL	**D+**	D+	D	41	5.56	3.9	7.4	23.1	26.4	**5.9**	7.9	13.1
▼JPMORGAN BANK & TRUST CO	SAN FRANCISCO	CA	**D**	C+	C+	22,400	122.92	0.0	0.4	38.5	0.0	**5.5**	7.5	11.6
▼JPMORGAN CHASE BANK	DEARBORN	MI	**D+**	C	C+	65	4.66	0.0	0.0	0.0	0.0	**10.0**	65.8	385.3
JPMORGAN CHASE BANK NA	COLUMBUS	OH	**D**	C	C+	1,631,621	0.24	5.6	4.8	8.7	18.8	**3.7**	5.7	13.5
JUNCTION NATIONAL BK	JUNCTION	TX	**A-**	A-	A-	45	4.56	8.7	6.7	5.8	39.4	**10.0**	12.7	24.1
JUNIATA VALLEY BANK	MIFFLINTOWN	PA	**B**	A-	A-	430	-1.48	7.6	1.7	40.6	18.1	**8.8**	10.2	17.5
▲JUSTIN STATE BK	JUSTIN	TX	**B**	C	B	66	-4.17	5.9	1.7	38.7	1.5	**10.0**	11.0	17.1
▼KAHOKA STATE BK	KAHOKA	MO	**D+**	C	C+	52	8.81	7.3	5.6	20.4	29.9	**6.0**	8.0	16.1
▲KAISER FEDERAL BANK	COVINA	CA	**D+**	C	B-	877	0.74	0.0	4.1	34.1	0.7	**10.0**	12.7	20.7
KALAMAZOO COUNTY STATE	SCHOOLCRAFT	MI	**C**	C	C-	85	7.99	2.6	6.2	20.5	36.1	**10.0**	12.4	24.1
▼KANABEC STATE BK	MORA	MN	**B+**	B	A-	133	1.98	4.7	3.5	9.7	44.7	**10.0**	11.8	23.8
KANSAS STATE BK	OTTAWA	KS	**B-**	B-	B-	105	-12.46	3.0	0.9	9.9	49.4	**8.4**	9.9	28.0
KANSAS STATE BK OF	MANHATTAN	KS	**B**	B	B-	733	7.95	13.5	1.2	17.2	6.1	**6.9**	8.9	14.7
KANSAS STATE BK	OVERBROOK	KS	**B-**	B-	B-	47	-0.73	7.6	6.1	10.9	41.9	**9.6**	10.8	19.1
▼KANSASLAND BANK	QUINTER	KS	**D+**	C-	C-	42	13.20	6.1	3.4	13.8	23.9	**5.5**	7.5	11.8
KANZA BANK	KINGMAN	KS	**C+**	C	B-	185	-9.78	8.3	1.5	17.7	17.3	**7.0**	9.0	13.2
KAPLAN STATE BK	KAPLAN	LA	**A-**	A-	A-	92	0.62	1.6	4.7	11.1	62.5	**9.1**	10.4	25.7
▼KARNES COUNTY NATIONAL	KARNES CITY	TX	**D+**	C-	C+	114	28.00	2.4	4.0	7.3	60.0	**6.1**	8.1	18.2
KASSON STATE BK	KASSON	MN	**C**	C	C	61	1.54	14.7	14.8	10.9	17.2	**6.6**	8.7	12.2
KATAHDIN TRUST CO	PATTEN	ME	**C**	C	B-	509	2.88	20.7	3.9	17.3	12.2	**9.2**	10.6	14.3
KAW VALLEY BANK	TOPEKA	KS	**C**	C	C+	493	9.05	29.8	2.2	7.9	21.5	**6.9**	8.9	13.6
KAW VALLEY STATE BK	EUDORA	KS	**D**	D-	D-	38	6.69	10.1	9.2	18.4	36.7	**6.4**	8.4	15.8
KAW VALLEY STATE BK & TRU	WAMEGO	KS	**B+**	B-	B-	129	-1.19	12.0	3.6	12.8	32.6	**9.5**	10.7	18.3
▲KCB BANK	KEARNEY	MO	**C+**	C	D-	154	7.68	8.9	0.9	15.7	25.9	**9.1**	10.4	16.8
▲KEARNEY TRUST CO	KEARNEY	MO	**C+**	C+	B-	132	-3.85	6.5	4.8	17.8	22.9	**8.4**	9.9	16.3
KEARNY COUNTY BANK	LAKIN	KS	**A-**	B+	B+	119	-1.13	6.1	3.1	8.3	43.8	**10.0**	20.8	37.8
KEARNY FSB	FAIRFIELD	NJ	**C+**	C+	C+	2,749	30.37	3.7	0.1	26.4	43.0	**10.0**	12.0	24.9
KENDALL STATE BK	VALLEY FALLS	KS	**E+**	D	D-	35	2.27	24.3	2.0	10.9	9.2	**5.6**	7.6	12.5
KENNEBEC FS&LA OF	WATERVILLE	ME	**D+**	D+	D-	79	2.07	0.2	0.3	62.6	3.3	**5.4**	7.9	11.3
KENNEBEC SB	AUGUSTA	ME	**C+**	C+	B-	777	7.78	3.9	0.5	63.3	9.3	**8.7**	10.1	17.1
▲KENNEBUNK SB	KENNEBUNK	ME	**C**	C+	C+	795	0.01	1.8	0.5	30.1	10.6	**8.3**	9.8	13.9
KENNETT NATIONAL BK	KENNETT	MO	**B+**	B+	B	98	-12.11	8.5	4.7	25.9	9.1	**8.6**	10.1	15.1
▼KENNEY BANK & TRUST	KENNEY	IL	**D+**	B-	B-	73	79.88	9.6	0.4	10.9	0.4	**9.0**	10.4	40.0
KENT BANK	KENT	IL	**D**	D-	D	89	0.30	5.2	1.5	17.0	19.9	**7.7**	9.5	15.0

Asset Quality Index	Non-Performing Loans as a % of Total Loans	Non-Performing Loans as a % of Capital	Net Charge-offs Avg Loans	Profitability Index	Net Income ($Mil)	Return on Assets (R.O.A.)	Return on Equity (R.O.E.)	Net Interest Spread	Overhead Efficiency Ratio	Liquidity Index	Liquidity Ratio	Hot Money Ratio	Stability Index
5.3	4.73	14.3	0.08	**8.1**	6.6	7.97	75.11	4.81	42.5	**2.3**	47.6	33.8	**6.5**
0.3	4.19	27.9	3.28	**0.0**	-2.5	-0.91	-16.99	2.41	174.2	**1.4**	32.3	45.0	**0.7**
3.7	1.44	9.2	0.02	**6.5**	11.3	1.56	17.06	4.68	67.2	**4.4**	30.2	9.9	**5.9**
0.0	4.68	33.2	2.38	**0.2**	-4.7	-0.60	-7.30	2.59	72.2	**1.8**	17.5	20.4	**3.8**
8.9	0.00	0.0	3.79	**0.0**	-1.4	-1.40	-8.12	3.77	88.1	**1.3**	9.7	26.1	**1.5**
3.5	0.90	5.8	0.55	**9.6**	8.1	1.67	15.96	4.49	46.6	**2.8**	23.1	15.9	**6.2**
7.0	1.21	4.5	0.00	**6.3**	0.6	1.59	14.22	4.06	52.9	**4.3**	41.4	13.5	**6.9**
1.3	3.18	23.7	1.18	**0.3**	-23.3	-3.60	-33.92	3.30	192.4	**1.7**	21.6	22.7	**2.0**
2.4	3.88	23.8	0.49	**2.2**	0.9	0.33	4.43	3.50	85.7	**2.7**	13.2	15.2	**3.2**
3.9	1.47	10.0	0.19	**7.5**	11.0	1.59	19.02	4.60	56.7	**3.4**	19.4	12.2	**6.9**
4.6	2.31	9.1	0.30	**4.1**	1.0	0.79	7.49	3.47	66.2	**4.9**	48.6	12.5	**5.3**
5.5	2.39	10.1	0.22	**3.2**	0.8	0.34	2.11	3.77	81.1	**4.6**	37.6	11.0	**7.2**
0.6	5.91	30.2	1.57	**0.5**	-0.8	-0.25	-2.61	3.78	96.1	**0.9**	20.0	35.9	**3.1**
4.6	2.02	12.2	0.27	**3.1**	0.8	0.54	6.43	3.50	78.9	**4.0**	27.4	10.6	**4.7**
3.7	0.72	5.4	0.09	**3.6**	4.3	1.54	13.69	4.45	70.3	**0.5**	3.4	44.3	**4.4**
3.7	1.62	8.5	0.06	**3.7**	0.3	0.73	4.08	3.99	79.0	**4.0**	40.0	15.2	**6.9**
0.3	5.98	51.8	4.19	**0.0**	-135.4	-2.58	-32.48	3.39	65.8	**1.4**	11.0	25.3	**5.0**
6.9	0.78	4.3	0.59	**5.7**	1.1	1.27	10.33	4.61	60.9	**1.1**	27.0	43.2	**7.7**
1.7	4.46	22.8	0.67	**4.9**	0.9	0.75	6.15	4.10	62.3	**1.0**	18.5	33.3	**7.6**
7.8	0.82	2.4	-0.04	**3.7**	0.5	0.70	4.93	3.86	77.9	**2.9**	40.5	21.7	**6.5**
7.0	0.65	4.4	0.01	**4.3**	1.4	0.96	9.91	4.24	79.1	**2.6**	36.5	21.9	**5.1**
7.5	0.16	1.0	0.26	**4.5**	1.9	0.92	9.74	3.60	68.2	**1.6**	11.3	21.2	**6.4**
7.7	1.79	2.8	0.20	**4.5**	1.1	0.87	6.15	2.64	59.2	**4.0**	34.5	13.2	**8.3**
7.8	0.02	0.2	0.11	**5.9**	1.0	1.41	18.53	4.30	65.4	**2.4**	25.8	18.1	**5.0**
0.6	2.23	19.3	0.65	**5.7**	3.6	1.06	12.47	3.97	59.4	**1.9**	8.7	19.1	**5.9**
5.3	0.00	0.0	0.84	**6.6**	1.2	1.28	7.35	5.05	77.3	**6.8**	70.1	4.9	**7.8**
2.0	3.10	21.5	0.44	**4.4**	0.4	0.89	9.91	4.41	64.0	**2.9**	29.0	16.9	**4.8**
1.7	2.95	32.5	1.38	**7.0**	119.3	0.96	8.86	3.76	3.7	**0.4**	14.4	100.0	**3.7**
10.0	0.00	0.0	0.00	**3.5**	0.3	0.39	0.50	0.41	24.2	**5.0**	455.0	98.6	**2.3**
0.8	5.74	27.9	1.98	**3.4**	11,826.0	0.73	9.18	2.44	68.8	**6.7**	55.5	6.5	**5.3**
8.5	0.55	1.6	0.45	**7.7**	0.8	1.80	12.43	4.82	64.4	**3.9**	55.5	18.3	**8.9**
3.9	2.33	15.1	0.21	**6.3**	4.8	1.11	10.73	4.26	63.9	**4.0**	18.8	9.1	**6.6**
4.9	2.74	17.2	0.06	**6.5**	0.9	1.35	12.26	5.49	71.8	**3.8**	9.6	9.0	**7.5**
4.4	2.00	12.3	1.23	**1.6**	0.0	-0.05	-0.55	2.92	77.2	**2.4**	35.7	25.2	**4.5**
1.6	3.04	18.9	0.05	**4.2**	7.2	0.83	8.25	3.41	53.1	**1.5**	13.8	23.5	**6.2**
2.8	1.34	5.3	1.04	**1.9**	0.3	0.36	2.72	4.01	84.8	**5.0**	50.0	11.7	**6.0**
4.3	3.34	11.2	0.78	**2.0**	0.4	0.31	2.54	3.27	73.6	**3.2**	15.9	13.0	**7.9**
6.8	1.75	4.4	0.35	**2.9**	0.5	0.46	4.79	3.25	88.0	**3.9**	29.1	11.7	**4.9**
4.9	0.92	7.3	0.32	**6.8**	10.9	1.59	17.65	4.10	49.4	**1.5**	12.2	23.3	**7.4**
5.1	1.48	5.7	0.38	**3.8**	0.4	0.80	6.87	4.01	66.3	**4.4**	45.9	14.1	**6.2**
5.2	1.01	8.1	0.48	**2.2**	0.1	0.18	1.92	4.21	85.9	**0.9**	11.3	32.5	**4.6**
5.0	0.64	4.6	1.17	**4.0**	1.3	0.67	6.93	4.56	74.4	**1.9**	10.4	19.1	**4.8**
6.1	1.88	5.0	0.10	**9.6**	2.0	2.16	17.40	4.62	55.1	**4.3**	49.9	15.0	**8.6**
5.8	3.05	11.8	-0.17	**3.0**	0.8	0.78	8.65	4.35	79.0	**3.5**	57.2	24.8	**3.2**
4.4	0.90	6.5	0.50	**3.3**	0.2	0.40	4.42	4.08	71.5	**3.1**	31.8	16.7	**4.3**
2.6	1.65	11.5	0.32	**5.6**	4.9	0.98	8.54	4.53	66.0	**4.0**	7.8	7.8	**6.8**
2.3	0.65	4.4	0.36	**3.9**	3.8	0.76	8.38	3.02	56.6	**0.7**	17.0	47.8	**5.1**
2.5	2.96	15.3	1.19	**2.8**	0.3	0.80	9.10	4.20	75.9	**4.7**	29.8	7.5	**2.3**
4.9	1.62	8.0	0.41	**6.8**	2.5	1.86	16.86	3.67	63.8	**3.3**	32.7	16.2	**6.7**
3.7	3.13	16.5	0.50	**3.8**	1.5	1.01	9.78	4.35	75.5	**3.2**	16.9	13.2	**4.9**
3.9	1.38	7.8	1.00	**4.3**	1.2	0.88	8.78	4.18	66.7	**3.4**	26.1	13.6	**5.5**
5.7	3.90	8.4	0.07	**8.5**	2.4	1.97	9.47	3.81	47.4	**4.5**	30.6	9.0	**9.1**
5.3	2.33	9.2	0.00	**2.6**	5.2	0.22	1.12	2.72	79.8	**3.9**	56.0	23.2	**8.3**
0.3	4.96	35.4	2.96	**0.0**	-0.9	-2.58	-29.12	4.33	82.1	**1.6**	19.5	24.3	**3.0**
6.6	0.36	3.7	0.00	**2.5**	0.3	0.38	5.08	3.18	82.4	**1.4**	10.3	25.0	**3.7**
6.9	0.65	5.0	0.02	**3.6**	4.6	0.61	6.23	2.86	67.8	**1.7**	12.0	21.1	**6.7**
3.4	2.50	17.5	0.61	**4.0**	5.1	0.63	6.67	4.52	75.0	**4.5**	8.4	4.6	**6.2**
6.1	0.37	2.2	0.97	**5.0**	0.8	0.76	7.04	5.26	71.7	**2.4**	23.7	17.6	**5.8**
3.7	8.27	15.6	6.15	**0.3**	-0.7	-0.89	-8.03	1.93	93.1	**7.6**	85.4	1.6	**6.1**
0.5	6.69	43.8	1.55	**2.7**	0.5	0.50	5.22	3.98	65.9	**2.3**	27.6	19.2	**3.3**

Name	City	State	Rating	2008 Rating	2007 Rating	Total Assets ($Mil)	One Year Asset Growth	Asset Mix (As a % of Total Assets) Comm-ercial Loans	Cons-umer Loans	Home Mort-gages	Secur-ities	Capital-ization Index	Leverage Ratio	Risk-based Capital Ratio
KENT STATE BK	KENT	MN	**C-**	C	C-	7	3.41	3.5	6.5	0.0	0.1	**9.3**	10.6	19.7
KENTLAND BANK	KENTLAND	IN	**B+**	B+	A	238	-2.24	8.3	2.5	11.2	27.7	**10.0**	12.5	18.7
▲ KENTLAND FS&LA	KENTLAND	IN	**C+**	C	C-	4	6.59	0.0	1.0	76.1	12.5	**10.0**	16.6	40.1
KENTUCKY BANK	PARIS	KY	**C-**	C-	C	659	-2.56	2.2	3.0	17.7	26.9	**6.7**	8.7	13.5
KENTUCKY FARMERS BANK	ASHLAND	KY	**A+**	A+	A+	164	6.02	7.8	6.7	17.7	48.0	**10.0**	21.5	35.6
▼ KENTUCKY FS&LA	COVINGTON	KY	**D-**	D	D+	41	9.31	0.0	0.7	65.3	12.3	**5.8**	7.8	18.1
KENTUCKY HOME BANK	BARDSTOWN	KY	**B-**	B-	C	98	-0.14	2.9	4.5	31.2	5.7	**10.0**	12.5	18.2
KENTUCKY NEIGHBORHOOD	ELIZABETHTOWN	KY	**C-**	C+	C	115	-3.02	4.5	2.1	37.1	11.2	**7.8**	10.6	13.1
KEOKUK COUNTY STATE BK	SIGOURNEY	IA	**C**	C	C-	100	42.93	12.7	3.6	10.4	6.3	**5.5**	8.8	11.4
KERNDT BROTHERS SB	LANSING	IA	**B-**	C-	D+	220	-1.20	8.9	1.2	7.1	20.5	**10.0**	11.0	15.9
KEVIL BANK	KEVIL	KY	**B**	B	B	29	0.90	0.9	2.5	8.4	72.6	**10.0**	12.7	34.5
▼ KEY COMMUNITY BANK	INVER GROVE HEIGHTS	MN	**D**	C-	D+	63	-8.06	15.1	2.0	9.2	18.5	**8.0**	9.7	13.6
▲ KEYBANK NA	CLEVELAND	OH	**C-**	D-	C-	88,592	-1.76	14.8	11.3	4.6	24.8	**9.0**	10.4	16.5
KEYSAVINGS BANK	WISCONSIN RAPIDS	WI	**C-**	C-	C-	81	-0.84	0.0	0.4	46.0	29.5	**10.0**	13.7	32.8
KEYSOURCE COMMERCIAL	DURHAM	NC	**C-**	C-	C-	218	13.15	14.6	0.3	5.5	8.2	**6.8**	8.8	15.5
▲ KEYSTONE BANK	AUBURN	AL	**C**	C	C-	188	13.62	8.2	3.4	22.1	13.1	**8.1**	9.7	14.3
▲ KEYSTONE COMMUNITY BANK	KALAMAZOO	MI	**D**	C-	C-	266	2.28	20.5	1.3	7.6	10.4	**6.8**	9.2	12.4
KEYSTONE SB	KEYSTONE	IA	**C-**	C-	C+	72	9.63	4.8	3.7	22.5	25.5	**5.9**	7.9	11.8
KEYTRUST CO NA	ANCHORAGE	AK	**U**	U	U	16	2.78	0.0	0.0	0.0	0.0	**10.0**	100.9	456.3
KEYWORTH BANK	DULUTH	GA	**D**	C-	C	289	37.30	4.1	0.2	1.5	44.3	**9.9**	10.9	19.4
KILGORE NATIONAL BK	KILGORE	TX	**C+**	B-	B	79	10.47	8.4	4.5	25.4	1.5	**7.8**	9.5	17.2
KILLBUCK SB CO	KILLBUCK	OH	**B+**	A-	A	404	8.88	9.8	1.7	19.1	28.7	**9.0**	10.4	19.2
KINDERHOOK STATE BK	KINDERHOOK	IL	**D-**	D-	D	16	-8.44	6.4	6.1	12.8	14.4	**7.8**	9.5	14.1
KINDRED STATE BK	KINDRED	ND	**D**	C-	C-	22	1.66	8.3	9.3	5.7	26.5	**5.1**	7.1	15.0
▼ KING SOUTHERN BANK	CHAPLIN	KY	**C**	C	C	174	1.50	7.9	0.8	27.4	9.2	**6.1**	8.1	11.8
KINGSLEY STATE BK	KINGSLEY	IA	**A-**	A-	B+	128	-0.01	7.1	3.1	11.4	39.0	**10.0**	13.7	24.4
KINGSTON NATIONAL BK	KINGSTON	OH	**B+**	B+	B+	184	4.91	12.0	2.9	22.3	23.6	**9.4**	10.6	17.1
KINGSTREE FS&LA	KINGSTREE	SC	**C-**	C	C	29	14.99	0.5	0.8	54.2	12.4	**10.0**	15.5	36.1
KIRKPATRICK BANK	EDMOND	OK	**C-**	C-	C-	517	4.57	2.2	0.6	6.5	24.9	**8.1**	9.7	15.4
KIRKWOOD BANK & TRUST CO	BISMARCK	ND	**D+**	D+	C-	159	7.71	15.8	3.4	7.2	5.3	**6.1**	8.1	12.0
KIRKWOOD BANK OF NEVADA	LAS VEGAS	NV	**C-**	C	C	36	48.39	8.9	0.0	1.8	0.0	**10.0**	24.2	47.2
KISHACOQUILLAS VALLEY NB	BELLEVILLE	PA	**C+**	C+	C+	554	5.84	11.1	1.5	20.9	21.7	**6.1**	8.1	11.8
KIT CARSON STATE BK	KIT CARSON	CO	**B-**	C	C-	65	9.37	8.2	1.4	1.7	17.7	**9.1**	10.4	16.8
▲ KITSAP BANK	PORT ORCHARD	WA	**C-**	C-	C+	888	0.21	6.4	1.4	8.1	34.0	**5.8**	7.8	13.9
▼ KLEBERG FIRST NB OF KINGS	KINGSVILLE	TX	**C+**	B-	B-	369	1.01	6.3	17.5	13.2	26.0	**6.5**	8.5	14.5
KLEINBANK	CHASKA	MN	**C-**	C-	B	1,496	-0.93	6.3	1.3	9.5	30.4	**5.9**	7.9	12.9
KODABANK	DRAYTON	ND	**B+**	B+	B	84	69.15	8.8	11.3	5.4	19.8	**8.9**	10.3	16.9
KOPERNIK FEDERAL BANK	BALTIMORE	MD	**C**	C	C+	38	0.66	0.0	0.7	62.5	13.4	**10.0**	11.0	24.4
▼ KOSCIUSZKO FSB	BALTIMORE	MD	**C**	C+	C+	13	3.53	0.0	0.1	61.5	0.7	**10.0**	17.7	34.6
KRESS NATIONAL BK	KRESS	TX	**B+**	B+	B+	40	13.42	5.5	4.2	0.7	18.1	**10.0**	11.3	22.1
KS BANK INC	SMITHFIELD	NC	**D+**	D+	C+	335	-3.80	4.4	0.8	27.1	26.1	**7.4**	9.3	15.8
KSB BANK	KEOKUK	IA	**B-**	C-	D	101	-2.67	9.3	2.3	20.1	17.8	**6.7**	8.8	13.0
▲ LA FARGE STATE BK	LA FARGE	WI	**C+**	B	A	49	9.40	1.5	3.2	3.9	34.1	**10.0**	31.1	43.2
LA MONTE COMMUNITY BANK	LA MONTE	MO	**B-**	B	A-	24	-0.72	2.2	2.7	25.9	14.3	**10.0**	12.9	19.9
LA SALLE STATE BK	LA SALLE	IL	**C**	C+	C	112	5.10	6.4	4.6	15.5	27.0	**6.2**	8.2	15.4
LABETTE BANK	ALTAMONT	KS	**B**	B-	B-	277	3.71	2.1	3.8	24.5	32.8	**6.9**	9.0	16.9
LACONIA SB	LACONIA	NH	**C**	C+	C+	1,061	1.69	4.7	1.8	26.3	20.9	**6.5**	8.5	13.7
LADYSMITH FS&LA	LADYSMITH	WI	**D-**	C-	C	47	12.42	8.0	2.4	39.3	35.2	**6.9**	8.9	17.8
LAFAYETTE AMBASSADOR	EASTON	PA	**C**	C+	B	1,403	-2.63	6.1	2.9	12.6	23.0	**6.3**	8.3	12.7
LAFAYETTE COMMUNITY	LAFAYETTE	IN	**D-**	D	D-	131	7.89	4.1	0.2	23.1	26.1	**6.8**	8.8	13.5
LAFAYETTE SAVINGS BANK FS	LAFAYETTE	IN	**D-**	D	D+	372	0.21	4.4	0.3	31.6	3.1	**7.6**	9.4	13.8
LAFAYETTE STATE BK	MAYO	FL	**C-**	C-	C+	84	10.78	4.3	5.5	15.5	5.7	**7.4**	10.0	12.9
▲ LAGRANGE BANKING CO	LAGRANGE	GA	**D+**	D	C	95	15.61	5.4	2.3	13.5	9.6	**10.0**	12.1	17.1
LAKE AREA BANK	LINDSTROM	MN	**D-**	D-	D	284	-7.44	9.7	0.9	11.9	16.6	**6.2**	8.3	13.3
▼ LAKE BANK	TWO HARBORS	MN	**D-**	D	D+	104	3.95	5.8	0.8	31.0	12.0	**6.5**	8.5	13.7
LAKE CITY BANK	WARSAW	IN	**B-**	B	B-	2,679	4.22	24.8	1.9	4.1	16.6	**7.7**	9.8	13.1
▲ LAKE CITY FEDERAL BANK	LAKE CITY	MN	**D**	D	D	80	-3.97	6.3	4.1	49.1	6.8	**7.0**	9.0	14.9
LAKE COMMUNITY BANK	LONG LAKE	MN	**D**	D-	D	145	-0.82	9.8	1.6	7.7	23.4	**7.0**	9.0	13.8
LAKE COUNTRY COMMUNITY	MORRISTOWN	MN	**E-**	E-	E	33	-17.55	9.9	2.8	43.6	3.0	**0.2**	3.6	6.4
LAKE COUNTY BANK	SAINT IGNATIUS	MT	**D**	D+	B-	29	-4.83	9.4	11.1	6.1	1.6	**10.0**	14.4	22.9

Asset Quality Index	Non-Performing Loans as a % of Total Loans	Non-Performing Loans as a % of Capital	Net Charge-offs Avg Loans	Profitability Index	Net Income ($Mil)	Return on Assets (R.O.A.)	Return on Equity (R.O.E.)	Net Interest Spread	Overhead Efficiency Ratio	Liquidity Index	Liquidity Ratio	Hot Money Ratio	Stability Index
8.1	0.00	0.0	0.00	**1.8**	0.0	0.04	0.38	4.22	99.1	**6.3**	45.9	0.0	**5.8**
5.0	2.33	10.4	2.46	**4.5**	1.4	0.60	4.44	4.20	57.2	**1.8**	19.2	20.9	**7.8**
9.7	0.00	0.0	0.00	**3.0**	0.0	0.46	2.73	4.71	90.1	**1.9**	23.6	20.0	**5.9**
1.8	3.20	21.3	1.41	**3.4**	5.2	0.75	7.30	3.57	75.8	**1.6**	8.0	20.7	**7.0**
8.6	1.10	2.2	0.20	**10.0**	6.1	3.79	16.37	6.74	44.8	**4.5**	57.0	16.8	**9.4**
5.9	0.47	4.1	0.00	**1.8**	0.0	0.06	0.70	3.24	97.7	**1.7**	26.2	26.4	**1.7**
3.7	2.26	13.3	0.19	**6.0**	1.1	1.15	9.51	4.22	58.4	**1.7**	15.7	21.9	**6.7**
1.7	3.29	22.6	0.12	**4.6**	1.0	0.85	8.07	4.56	75.6	**1.6**	12.8	22.4	**5.7**
4.9	0.91	7.1	0.23	**5.2**	0.8	0.88	10.27	5.04	62.0	**3.4**	16.1	11.9	**5.1**
4.7	1.34	7.2	0.74	**4.1**	2.1	0.95	7.88	3.85	65.1	**3.1**	35.8	17.9	**5.5**
9.2	1.26	2.3	0.03	**4.3**	0.3	0.89	5.84	3.58	76.9	**5.9**	68.0	10.1	**8.2**
1.7	5.69	36.1	0.27	**0.0**	-1.1	-1.67	-15.43	4.32	131.8	**3.7**	14.8	10.4	**3.5**
2.9	2.60	13.7	2.77	**2.5**	636.8	0.73	7.34	3.15	63.9	**3.8**	14.7	10.3	**6.3**
6.5	2.84	10.5	0.29	**0.6**	0.0	-0.05	-0.32	2.46	99.4	**4.1**	45.1	15.3	**6.9**
2.3	2.28	17.8	0.59	**2.6**	0.9	0.45	5.05	3.53	66.5	**0.7**	17.3	52.7	**3.3**
6.0	0.45	3.0	0.48	**2.8**	1.3	0.70	7.43	3.34	64.5	**1.5**	25.4	27.6	**3.8**
0.5	3.63	25.7	1.75	**0.0**	-2.3	-0.89	-5.94	3.64	71.5	**2.4**	19.6	17.4	**5.5**
4.2	1.67	12.3	0.01	**3.4**	0.4	0.63	7.18	4.25	80.9	**3.2**	32.8	16.6	**3.1**
10.0	0.00	0.0	0.00	**9.5**	0.5	2.93	2.91	N/,	34.6	**5.0**	5,138.7	101.0	**4.3**
4.3	1.81	7.1	1.39	**0.4**	0.1	0.05	0.36	3.06	79.7	**2.8**	44.3	26.1	**1.2**
4.9	0.83	4.7	0.07	**3.6**	0.2	0.28	2.89	4.51	86.2	**3.1**	38.6	19.0	**5.2**
9.1	0.05	0.2	0.00	**4.6**	3.3	0.86	7.71	3.17	67.1	**2.6**	34.8	21.5	**7.3**
4.6	0.66	4.0	0.84	**0.0**	-0.4	-2.50	-24.81	3.72	183.3	**1.6**	33.1	27.6	**3.5**
4.3	1.19	6.1	-0.01	**3.5**	0.1	0.54	7.31	4.17	85.6	**4.2**	44.2	12.6	**2.3**
4.8	2.14	19.5	0.43	**5.0**	2.4	1.41	18.06	4.44	61.4	**0.6**	7.8	35.9	**4.2**
7.5	0.97	3.1	-0.05	**5.9**	1.9	1.47	10.77	3.37	50.7	**4.1**	58.3	18.9	**8.4**
5.6	0.75	4.5	0.20	**5.8**	2.1	1.14	10.48	4.45	61.1	**1.7**	19.1	23.2	**7.2**
6.7	1.00	4.0	0.00	**0.6**	-0.5	-1.71	-10.57	2.66	313.3	**1.7**	37.4	45.7	**6.2**
3.3	2.74	14.7	0.22	**2.6**	2.4	0.47	4.83	3.44	70.4	**2.8**	25.6	16.4	**5.6**
3.2	1.04	6.8	-0.47	**3.2**	1.3	0.88	10.77	3.93	77.0	**4.8**	32.8	8.1	**2.7**
8.8	1.07	2.1	0.00	**0.0**	-0.3	-0.96	-3.18	3.20	125.5	**3.0**	69.0	34.7	**3.0**
4.0	1.21	8.8	0.27	**4.0**	4.4	0.80	9.70	3.73	74.7	**2.8**	10.3	14.7	**6.2**
6.8	0.25	1.4	0.15	**4.8**	0.6	0.95	8.72	5.10	70.4	**0.9**	19.6	37.7	**5.5**
3.4	1.08	6.7	1.49	**2.0**	2.4	0.29	3.11	3.65	82.8	**4.6**	38.4	11.6	**6.0**
3.2	1.33	8.9	0.34	**4.5**	3.3	0.92	6.39	4.88	82.4	**3.3**	24.5	13.4	**7.7**
2.2	3.53	22.7	2.17	**1.7**	6.2	0.40	4.11	4.38	77.8	**4.0**	23.4	11.9	**6.5**
5.6	0.40	2.4	0.33	**9.4**	1.4	1.88	15.96	4.62	49.4	**1.8**	23.5	21.8	**7.4**
5.3	2.25	14.0	0.00	**2.8**	0.1	0.38	3.50	3.01	75.3	**1.9**	32.1	28.7	**5.8**
6.3	1.69	7.3	0.00	**3.0**	0.1	0.39	2.23	3.93	76.1	**1.8**	25.6	22.2	**6.4**
8.7	0.00	0.0	0.00	**7.9**	0.6	1.75	14.35	4.78	64.2	**3.5**	58.5	21.7	**8.0**
1.7	3.54	22.0	0.66	**1.7**	1.4	0.40	4.40	3.71	86.5	**1.0**	20.2	34.1	**4.0**
4.7	1.01	6.8	0.01	**5.1**	1.0	1.02	9.41	4.31	78.9	**4.3**	25.1	8.1	**5.6**
3.5	9.04	16.8	0.00	**10.0**	1.0	2.18	7.01	4.93	31.8	**6.1**	60.3	7.5	**7.9**
8.4	0.42	2.3	0.02	**4.9**	0.2	0.85	6.88	4.26	70.1	**4.0**	14.1	8.5	**6.6**
5.5	1.04	6.3	0.08	**3.0**	0.6	0.56	5.89	3.52	85.6	**3.4**	26.3	13.5	**4.3**
5.8	0.66	4.0	0.35	**4.4**	1.7	0.62	6.27	4.10	73.8	**1.5**	16.5	25.4	**6.1**
3.7	1.73	12.2	0.29	**3.2**	4.9	0.47	4.61	4.00	81.7	**2.8**	16.6	15.5	**8.2**
1.1	6.36	36.7	0.01	**1.8**	0.2	0.35	3.79	2.48	72.5	**2.5**	46.6	30.6	**3.4**
3.7	1.84	14.6	0.42	**8.2**	20.8	1.45	16.12	4.07	50.0	**3.1**	3.9	12.5	**6.7**
4.0	2.62	15.4	3.24	**0.1**	-0.6	-0.46	-4.49	3.96	90.6	**4.4**	30.9	10.2	**4.1**
0.0	5.29	43.5	0.22	**3.7**	2.3	0.60	6.53	3.63	60.8	**1.4**	7.5	23.8	**4.3**
2.6	2.22	16.3	0.23	**4.3**	0.5	0.65	6.39	4.69	79.3	**0.8**	7.3	32.7	**5.1**
3.9	2.80	16.2	0.84	**0.3**	-0.2	-0.21	-1.74	4.36	86.8	**3.1**	13.6	13.3	**2.0**
0.1	8.61	58.4	2.28	**0.2**	-2.0	-0.68	-7.47	3.95	85.0	**1.8**	23.9	22.5	**3.9**
0.3	2.41	18.2	0.11	**3.0**	0.5	0.46	5.25	4.13	78.3	**2.2**	9.7	17.7	**3.2**
4.2	1.76	11.9	0.54	**5.7**	25.8	0.98	9.85	3.79	44.8	**1.2**	9.3	28.2	**8.3**
2.1	2.10	16.7	0.04	**0.9**	-0.2	-0.23	-2.72	3.50	76.7	**2.9**	12.7	14.1	**4.1**
0.3	10.44	61.6	2.25	**0.1**	-0.4	-0.30	-3.18	3.82	90.9	**1.7**	18.2	23.1	**2.8**
2.0	2.65	27.5	1.86	**0.0**	-0.3	-0.89	-14.36	3.78	105.1	**4.2**	20.6	7.8	**1.8**
0.6	10.39	30.8	1.11	**2.1**	0.0	0.07	0.47	4.33	97.0	**5.1**	45.1	10.3	**5.1**

	Name	City	State	Rating	2008 Rating	2007 Rating	Total Assets ($Mil)	One Year Asset Growth	Comm-ercial Loans	Cons-umer Loans	Home Mort-gages	Secur-ities	Capital-ization Index	Leverage Ratio	Risk-based Capital Ratio
	LAKE ELMO BANK	LAKE ELMO	MN	**D-**	D+	C+	272	-1.10	4.0	1.0	20.5	24.6	**6.3**	8.3	13.2
	LAKE FEDERAL BANK FSB	HAMMOND	IN	**B-**	B-	B-	77	3.18	1.2	0.8	63.2	7.0	**10.0**	17.4	34.7
▼	LAKE FOREST BANK & TRUST	LAKE FOREST	IL	**C-**	C	C+	2,408	32.56	46.7	7.0	4.4	9.5	**4.6**	6.6	11.3
	LAKE NATIONAL BK	MENTOR	OH	**B-**	C	C-	110	15.40	7.2	0.9	26.8	2.5	**8.1**	9.8	15.8
▼	LAKE REGION BANK	NEW LONDON	MN	**E+**	D-	D+	97	-4.20	16.4	4.3	10.2	21.6	**4.5**	6.5	11.4
	LAKE SHORE SAVINGS BANK	DUNKIRK	NY	**C+**	C+	C+	475	12.88	2.2	0.4	40.3	32.1	**8.9**	10.3	20.4
	LAKE SUNAPEE BANK FSB	NEWPORT	NH	**B-**	B-	B-	964	3.51	7.7	0.9	36.3	20.2	**6.3**	8.3	12.7
	LAKE-OSCEOLA STATE BK	BALDWIN	MI	**C-**	C-	C-	167	3.26	1.2	2.2	42.4	10.7	**8.4**	9.9	16.5
▼	LAKELAND BANK	OAK RIDGE	NJ	**C**	C-	B-	2,787	2.72	6.8	2.0	19.4	19.5	**6.7**	8.7	13.0
	LAKES STATE BK	PEQUOT LAKES	MN	**B**	B-	B	104	2.40	4.2	5.4	28.5	17.4	**7.9**	9.6	15.8
▲	LAKESIDE BANK	CHICAGO	IL	**D**	D	D+	1,052	-3.29	4.9	0.1	8.7	3.4	**10.0**	12.5	15.2
▼	LAKESIDE BANK	LAKE CHARLES	LA	**D**	NR	NR	19	N/A	6.8	0.2	1.3	30.1	**10.0**	74.3	153.8
	LAKESIDE BANK OF SALINA	SALINA	OK	**C-**	C	C-	31	2.72	4.8	24.3	43.9	1.9	**7.8**	9.6	14.3
▲	LAKESIDE NATIONAL BK	ROCKWALL	TX	**C**	C+	B-	55	11.13	4.6	7.6	5.0	32.9	**6.5**	8.5	21.6
	LAKESIDE STATE BK	NEW TOWN	ND	**B**	B+	A-	183	13.79	5.9	3.8	2.2	38.2	**6.3**	8.3	16.1
	LAKESIDE STATE BK	OOLOGAH	OK	**B-**	B-	B-	52	-3.52	4.1	11.4	13.7	51.4	**7.4**	9.3	21.0
	LAKEVIEW BANK	LAKEVILLE	MN	**E-**	E+	D-	59	-9.60	14.1	1.1	17.4	4.3	**3.0**	6.7	10.0
▼	LAKEWOOD BANK NA	BAXTER	MN	**D-**	D	D+	142	0.66	8.9	3.2	23.9	7.3	**6.6**	8.6	12.6
	LAMAR BANK & TRUST CO	LAMAR	MO	**A-**	A-	A-	121	1.60	4.5	3.2	29.7	8.4	**7.6**	9.4	15.5
	LAMAR NATIONAL BK	PARIS	TX	**A**	A-	A-	128	3.32	10.7	7.0	23.6	29.7	**8.4**	9.9	21.3
▲	LAMESA NATIONAL BK	LAMESA	TX	**B**	B	B	273	18.11	5.4	0.3	0.1	28.2	**8.6**	10.1	17.5
	LAMONT BANK OF ST JOHN	SAINT JOHN	WA	**C+**	B-	B	46	21.24	2.6	2.6	0.0	76.4	**6.5**	8.5	26.2
▲	LANDMANDS BANK	AUDUBON	IA	**C+**	D+	C	57	-9.45	8.3	3.7	5.9	13.6	**7.3**	9.4	12.7
	LANDMARK BANK	CLINTON	LA	**B-**	B	B+	96	2.60	4.0	3.4	21.6	22.8	**8.0**	9.7	16.3
	LANDMARK BANK NA	FORT LAUDERDALE	FL	**D-**	D-	C	330	-1.81	1.6	0.0	2.1	0.8	**7.7**	9.5	14.5
	LANDMARK BANK NA	COLUMBIA	MO	**B-**	B	C+	1,488	1.60	9.2	4.4	22.4	14.4	**6.4**	8.4	12.2
	LANDMARK BANK OF FLORIDA	SARASOTA	FL	**E-**	E-	D-	288	-12.65	4.0	0.9	11.1	7.4	**0.0**	3.0	5.9
	LANDMARK COMMUNITY BANK	PITTSTON	PA	**C+**	C+	C-	203	8.70	29.4	0.5	10.7	16.7	**6.6**	8.8	12.2
	LANDMARK COMMUNITY BANK	COLLIERVILLE	TN	**D**	D	D	253	34.31	10.3	2.1	37.9	21.1	**6.6**	8.6	15.4
▲	LANDMARK COMMUNITY BANK	ISANTI	MN	**D+**	D-	D+	104	1.08	11.8	1.1	12.1	15.3	**4.7**	6.9	10.9
	LANDMARK NATIONAL BK	MANHATTAN	KS	**C**	C-	C+	560	-3.89	11.3	1.0	16.4	27.3	**9.3**	10.5	17.0
	LAONA STATE BK	LAONA	WI	**D**	D	D+	147	0.78	11.6	4.7	30.9	21.3	**7.4**	9.2	14.7
▲	LAPEER COUNTY BANK &	LAPEER	MI	**D**	D+	D+	289	-1.65	6.2	1.5	17.1	25.0	**7.1**	9.1	14.8
	LAPORTE SB	LA PORTE	IN	**C**	C	C-	443	9.46	3.7	2.1	16.2	26.9	**8.4**	9.9	15.2
	LATIMER STATE BK	WILBURTON	OK	**A-**	A-	A	77	0.51	7.9	6.1	11.8	22.7	**10.0**	17.1	40.3
	LAUDERDALE COUNTY BANK	HALLS	TN	**C-**	C-	C-	44	3.45	16.3	5.8	15.6	22.7	**6.8**	8.8	16.1
	LAURA STATE BK	WILLIAMSFIELD	IL	**C-**	C	C	14	6.70	3.5	8.9	9.8	6.2	**10.0**	13.8	30.7
	LAURENS STATE BK	LAURENS	IA	**A-**	B+	B	58	2.76	5.4	3.4	9.3	39.6	**10.0**	11.2	22.8
	LAWRENCE BANK	LAWRENCE	KS	**C**	C	B-	70	0.68	7.7	1.5	22.5	0.0	**7.2**	9.3	12.6
	LAWRENCEBURG FEDERAL	LAWRENCEBURG	TN	**B-**	B-	B-	46	-0.41	0.0	1.9	80.0	0.0	**10.0**	23.4	45.9
▼	LAWSON BANK	LAWSON	MO	**C**	C	C	119	6.79	8.5	1.0	14.1	32.8	**6.6**	8.6	15.4
	LAYTON STATE BK	MILWAUKEE	WI	**D-**	D	D	144	9.22	14.0	0.2	7.8	11.9	**8.4**	9.9	15.4
	LCA BANK CORP	PARK CITY	UT	**B+**	B+	B+	59	40.69	1.3	0.0	0.0	0.6	**8.7**	12.4	14.0
	LCNB NATIONAL BK	LEBANON	OH	**C+**	B-	B	758	3.43	4.8	2.6	20.3	32.6	**5.9**	7.9	13.5
	LEA COUNTY STATE BK	HOBBS	NM	**B-**	B-	B-	212	-2.83	5.0	1.1	1.4	76.9	**6.3**	8.3	20.7
▼	LEAD BANK	GARDEN CITY	MO	**E-**	D-	D	85	-10.08	8.2	1.7	34.0	11.6	**3.3**	5.9	10.2
▲	LEADER BANK NA	ARLINGTON	MA	**A-**	B-	C+	366	17.11	1.5	0.1	43.5	3.1	**10.0**	11.4	19.4
	LEADERS BANK	OAK BROOK	IL	**E-**	D-	D+	630	-6.82	20.7	0.2	2.9	6.3	**1.5**	4.6	8.5
	LEDYARD NATIONAL BK	HANOVER	NH	**C+**	C+	B	395	0.28	6.3	2.1	22.5	36.3	**6.3**	8.3	15.8
▼	LEE BANK	LEE	MA	**C-**	C	C+	271	-3.86	5.4	0.6	34.1	9.3	**8.3**	9.9	14.0
	LEE BANK & TRUST CO	PENNINGTON GAP	VA	**D**	D+	B	177	5.73	7.6	8.9	25.8	12.0	**10.0**	11.6	17.3
	LEE COUNTY BANK & TRUST N	FORT MADISON	IA	**C**	C+	B	168	5.36	14.8	1.7	32.9	0.3	**6.4**	8.4	14.0
	LEESBURG FSB	LEESBURG	OH	**C+**	C+	C+	62	0.74	6.1	13.8	54.8	0.0	**10.0**	11.9	19.0
	LEGACY BANK	WILEY	CO	**C-**	C-	B-	242	-3.74	13.7	1.5	11.3	14.7	**9.6**	10.7	15.9
	LEGACY BANK	ALTOONA	IA	**D-**	D	D-	83	-5.24	17.9	4.3	27.6	13.3	**6.1**	8.1	13.3
	LEGACY BANK	WICHITA	KS	**C-**	C-	B-	247	6.09	13.5	1.3	18.0	6.2	**5.3**	8.7	11.2
	LEGACY BANK	HINTON	OK	**D**	D	C-	431	-8.14	17.9	1.7	8.5	8.4	**6.6**	8.8	12.2
▼	LEGACY BANK	MILWAUKEE	WI	**F**	D-	D	190	-15.06	4.4	0.3	24.0	10.3	**0.0**	0.7	1.8
	LEGACY BANK & TRUST CO	ROGERSVILLE	MO	**C-**	C+	B-	127	-4.83	6.5	2.4	23.3	8.6	**5.8**	7.8	12.5
	LEGACY BANK OF FLORIDA	BOCA RATON	FL	**E-**	D-	D	326	3.04	4.4	0.3	3.1	22.0	**1.2**	5.4	8.2

Asset Mix columns (Comm-ercial Loans, Cons-umer Loans, Home Mort-gages, Secur-ities) are As a % of Total Assets.

Asset Quality Index	Non-Performing Loans as a % of Total Loans	Non-Performing Loans as a % of Capital	Net Charge-offs Avg Loans	Profitability Index	Net Income ($Mil)	Return on Assets (R.O.A.)	Return on Equity (R.O.E.)	Net Interest Spread	Overhead Efficiency Ratio	Liquidity Index	Liquidity Ratio	Hot Money Ratio	Stability Index
1.7	4.41	28.0	2.55	**0.3**	-2.6	-0.96	-10.61	3.94	73.3	**4.0**	26.1	10.5	**4.1**
9.5	0.20	0.8	0.03	**3.3**	0.4	0.59	3.36	3.67	69.0	**1.3**	25.5	31.6	**7.6**
3.4	1.03	10.5	1.39	**6.9**	25.5	1.00	15.14	3.62	42.3	**1.5**	9.4	24.2	**5.7**
3.5	3.04	20.1	0.01	**4.1**	0.9	0.93	8.97	4.10	59.1	**1.6**	23.1	25.6	**6.0**
1.1	3.62	28.7	3.19	**0.4**	-1.3	-1.32	-16.71	4.57	95.2	**5.2**	34.3	5.9	**2.7**
5.9	0.89	4.7	0.02	**3.6**	3.1	0.69	6.42	3.20	65.8	**3.1**	43.3	20.5	**5.0**
3.8	1.46	11.2	0.24	**4.3**	8.8	0.90	8.14	3.51	64.1	**2.0**	26.4	20.7	**7.2**
2.3	2.11	14.7	0.82	**4.2**	1.1	0.65	6.40	4.58	69.0	**2.7**	17.6	16.0	**5.7**
2.6	2.19	16.8	0.88	**3.9**	23.1	0.84	7.01	4.16	56.6	**4.1**	10.1	7.9	**6.7**
5.0	0.27	1.7	0.89	**5.0**	1.0	0.97	8.74	4.11	70.5	**1.4**	23.6	29.1	**7.0**
0.2	4.33	26.4	1.20	**4.7**	11.3	1.04	8.74	4.03	42.5	**0.7**	8.7	39.0	**9.6**
9.9	0.00	0.0	0.00	**0.0**	-0.6	-3.65	-5.39	N/,	1,025.5	**5.3**	188.0	35.1	**2.0**
1.4	3.31	24.2	1.09	**9.5**	0.5	1.46	14.74	6.45	54.3	**1.7**	15.5	21.4	**5.2**
5.8	3.93	12.4	0.18	**3.0**	0.2	0.38	4.41	3.53	85.5	**4.9**	74.9	16.2	**5.2**
6.0	0.73	3.3	0.78	**6.0**	2.2	1.29	13.68	3.79	51.2	**4.4**	36.0	11.5	**6.6**
4.6	2.65	10.9	0.15	**4.8**	0.6	1.04	8.99	4.97	80.3	**2.7**	37.9	22.5	**6.3**
0.3	10.68	88.4	2.21	**0.1**	-0.7	-1.19	-12.81	3.74	83.5	**2.3**	11.9	17.3	**0.0**
0.3	4.27	34.1	0.52	**4.4**	0.9	0.62	4.48	4.22	68.0	**2.5**	18.4	17.0	**5.4**
8.6	0.06	0.4	0.05	**9.9**	2.8	2.36	24.94	4.57	50.4	**2.0**	18.9	19.3	**7.8**
8.7	0.07	0.3	0.02	**7.8**	2.2	1.74	16.43	4.97	61.6	**2.5**	36.8	23.9	**7.4**
5.2	1.82	5.7	0.74	**4.9**	2.7	1.13	10.23	2.73	48.6	**3.5**	60.5	28.4	**6.4**
9.7	0.26	0.4	1.77	**3.2**	0.2	0.37	3.67	2.60	59.9	**8.0**	91.1	0.0	**4.1**
4.0	0.06	0.4	0.31	**8.8**	1.2	2.08	19.11	4.62	62.5	**2.3**	20.2	17.9	**5.7**
4.1	2.21	13.4	0.24	**5.3**	1.2	1.25	12.29	4.35	69.6	**2.3**	29.2	19.9	**6.6**
0.0	9.49	59.2	5.87	**0.5**	-7.4	-2.16	-20.30	4.02	56.8	**0.9**	19.8	39.7	**5.9**
5.3	1.02	7.8	0.93	**4.4**	10.6	0.71	8.43	4.49	70.4	**1.7**	9.5	21.2	**6.6**
0.0	15.70	207.5	1.18	**0.0**	-6.7	-2.11	-57.21	3.08	99.4	**0.6**	7.8	41.4	**0.2**
2.8	2.04	15.5	0.13	**4.2**	1.5	0.77	8.60	4.10	69.1	**2.7**	11.8	15.4	**5.5**
4.4	1.63	12.7	0.35	**1.3**	1.3	0.55	6.11	3.58	79.4	**0.7**	12.5	37.1	**3.5**
4.2	1.09	8.3	1.80	**0.0**	-1.9	-1.77	-23.46	4.09	106.2	**2.2**	21.2	18.5	**2.4**
3.3	1.49	7.7	1.86	**2.9**	2.7	0.46	3.60	4.02	71.1	**3.6**	16.8	11.4	**7.6**
0.3	5.46	38.1	0.29	**3.9**	1.0	0.72	7.01	3.39	68.2	**2.0**	26.2	21.5	**5.6**
1.6	1.55	10.3	2.31	**1.3**	0.8	0.27	2.87	3.98	65.0	**3.8**	28.4	12.1	**4.2**
3.0	2.23	13.5	0.85	**3.3**	2.9	0.69	5.59	3.64	64.2	**2.8**	22.7	15.6	**6.7**
5.7	4.94	8.9	0.93	**5.8**	0.9	1.22	7.30	2.92	56.2	**2.7**	61.1	35.2	**9.1**
3.9	0.67	3.7	0.45	**2.9**	0.2	0.44	4.67	4.23	83.2	**2.1**	38.8	31.7	**3.0**
4.5	4.28	12.5	0.27	**1.1**	0.0	-0.10	-0.76	3.07	97.6	**6.5**	64.3	3.5	**6.9**
8.5	0.00	0.0	-0.19	**6.5**	0.9	1.53	13.84	3.82	59.8	**5.2**	56.6	12.0	**7.1**
3.6	0.57	4.3	0.84	**2.3**	0.2	0.24	1.52	4.20	72.1	**1.1**	13.8	29.8	**5.9**
6.1	2.31	8.3	0.05	**4.5**	0.5	1.00	4.32	4.96	65.5	**2.8**	12.7	14.8	**7.3**
7.0	0.38	2.1	0.46	**3.1**	0.9	0.72	8.21	4.19	76.7	**2.3**	30.4	21.3	**4.2**
0.3	5.64	33.3	0.73	**1.6**	0.3	0.18	1.74	4.36	79.7	**3.1**	28.6	15.6	**4.8**
8.1	0.22	1.4	1.10	**10.0**	1.4	2.71	21.84	11.36	48.9	**0.2**	7.4	99.1	**6.5**
3.1	0.76	5.5	0.44	**5.7**	9.2	1.21	13.70	3.95	63.0	**3.2**	16.6	13.1	**6.3**
9.4	0.39	0.7	-0.03	**4.7**	3.4	1.62	19.12	3.76	82.1	**5.2**	61.4	13.9	**4.5**
0.3	9.18	69.8	5.32	**0.0**	-5.5	-5.72	-71.25	2.02	206.3	**0.8**	17.9	36.7	**2.8**
8.4	0.23	1.6	0.12	**9.4**	8.7	2.58	25.55	3.51	38.4	**0.7**	8.7	35.5	**5.9**
0.0	8.80	86.3	2.40	**0.0**	-24.0	-3.58	-52.33	2.94	84.5	**0.6**	16.5	64.6	**2.7**
4.5	2.29	12.4	0.24	**3.8**	2.6	0.65	7.61	3.48	80.3	**4.2**	29.7	10.6	**4.8**
3.0	1.19	8.9	0.27	**3.8**	1.5	0.53	5.93	3.62	70.0	**1.9**	11.0	19.1	**5.1**
0.2	6.37	36.3	1.75	**0.8**	-0.8	-0.45	-3.83	3.85	81.3	**1.0**	15.6	32.8	**5.9**
2.5	2.63	22.0	1.79	**2.7**	0.3	0.19	2.18	3.55	61.4	**4.9**	22.3	3.6	**5.0**
4.0	1.67	11.0	0.49	**3.3**	0.3	0.48	4.27	4.89	71.3	**1.5**	9.3	23.2	**5.4**
1.1	3.01	17.5	1.23	**3.1**	0.6	0.25	1.90	4.41	66.8	**1.4**	14.6	26.4	**6.8**
0.3	10.05	74.3	1.25	**1.1**	-0.2	-0.26	-3.07	4.30	83.1	**4.0**	6.3	7.3	**4.0**
2.2	2.29	19.2	0.58	**3.7**	1.2	0.49	5.64	4.29	68.4	**0.8**	9.6	32.8	**5.4**
1.2	4.85	35.7	1.32	**0.9**	0.1	0.03	0.31	4.41	77.8	**4.1**	14.1	8.0	**3.2**
0.0	24.79	180.0	0.95	**0.0**	-9.3	-4.34	-122.07	3.37	118.0	**0.6**	13.5	59.7	**3.1**
1.5	2.09	15.9	1.50	**1.7**	0.3	0.25	2.46	4.21	75.6	**3.0**	16.0	14.0	**4.6**
0.0	6.06	62.9	3.98	**0.0**	-11.6	-3.54	-45.07	3.22	84.7	**4.1**	22.9	9.4	**0.0**

Name	City	State	Rating	2008 Rating	2007 Rating	Total Assets ($Mil)	One Year Asset Growth	Asset Mix (As a % of Total Assets) Comm-ercial Loans	Cons-umer Loans	Home Mort-gages	Secur-ities	Capital-ization Index	Leverage Ratio	Risk-based Capital Ratio
LEGACY BANKS	PITTSFIELD	MA	**D-**	D	C	905	-2.28	2.8	0.3	31.0	19.2	**5.2**	7.2	12.0
LEGACY NATIONAL BK	SPRINGDALE	AR	**D-**	D-	D-	248	4.22	9.4	1.3	16.2	6.2	**8.6**	10.1	13.8
LEGACY STATE BK	LOGANVILLE	GA	**D-**	D-	D-	92	-22.67	3.8	0.3	4.0	30.4	**5.8**	7.8	13.7
LEGACY TRUST CO NA	HOUSTON	TX	**U**	U	U	14	8.19	0.0	0.0	0.0	81.1	**10.0**	91.5	120.5
LEGACYTEXAS BANK	PLANO	TX	**D-**	D	C	1,535	-8.76	11.8	0.7	6.6	15.6	**6.6**	8.6	13.1
LEGENCE BANK	ELDORADO	IL	**C+**	C+	C+	179	2.89	4.9	3.4	12.4	26.9	**6.5**	8.5	13.9
LEGEND BANK NA	BOWIE	TX	**C-**	C-	B	548	-3.91	9.3	2.4	7.2	34.1	**6.7**	8.7	13.9
LEGENDS BANK	LINN	MO	**A**	A	A	255	5.16	3.4	5.2	25.3	18.4	**10.0**	14.7	23.2
LEGENDS BANK	CLARKSVILLE	TN	**C+**	C	C	342	9.90	10.9	1.2	9.9	25.1	**6.5**	8.8	12.1
▲ LEGG MASON INVESTMENT	BALTIMORE	MD	**D+**	C	C	70	-17.94	0.0	0.0	0.0	12.0	**10.0**	60.2	111.4
LEIGHTON STATE BK	PELLA	IA	**B-**	B-	C+	102	6.13	7.0	3.1	17.3	19.0	**9.3**	10.5	14.4
LEITCHFIELD DEPOSIT BANK	LEITCHFIELD	KY	**A**	A-	B+	103	6.15	8.1	3.7	15.1	9.9	**10.0**	16.4	22.3
▼ LEMONT NATIONAL BK	LEMONT	IL	**D+**	C-	C-	60	-5.07	0.0	0.2	10.3	14.3	**5.8**	7.8	29.5
LENA STATE BK	LENA	IL	**C**	C	C+	83	-0.68	19.8	0.8	6.5	37.1	**8.5**	10.0	16.6
LENOX NATIONAL BK	LENOX	MA	**B**	C+	B-	55	-2.20	2.5	2.1	29.4	44.7	**10.0**	13.3	31.0
LEONARDVILLE STATE BK	LEONARDVILLE	KS	**C+**	C	C-	13	34.92	8.9	1.4	2.2	15.9	**6.0**	8.0	14.2
▲ LEVEL ONE BANK	FARMINGTON HILLS	MI	**B-**	C	C	425	149.33	15.6	0.3	12.3	12.0	**10.0**	15.7	19.6
▲ LEWIS & CLARK BANK	OREGON CITY	OR	**D+**	C-	D	120	6.17	5.2	0.0	10.2	13.1	**9.6**	10.7	16.2
LEWISBURG BANKING CO	LEWISBURG	KY	**A-**	A-	A-	76	11.38	20.3	7.8	27.2	15.3	**10.0**	13.6	19.5
▲ LEWISTON STATE BK	LEWISTON	UT	**C-**	D+	B-	233	2.06	12.5	3.0	8.5	18.9	**8.9**	10.5	14.1
▲ LIBERTAD BANK SSB	AUSTIN	TX	**C-**	D	C-	39	-6.90	5.5	0.3	25.0	7.1	**10.0**	17.3	29.3
LIBERTY BANK	GERALDINE	AL	**A-**	A-	A-	102	2.92	1.2	12.3	15.7	43.4	**10.0**	12.6	22.7
LIBERTY BANK	SOUTH SAN FRANCISCO	CA	**D-**	C-	C+	237	2.81	15.4	0.7	1.8	15.9	**8.6**	11.0	13.8
LIBERTY BANK	MIDDLETOWN	CT	**B-**	B+	A-	3,390	9.26	14.0	2.1	17.1	19.1	**10.0**	14.0	18.8
LIBERTY BANK	ALTON	IL	**B-**	B-	C+	292	5.55	11.9	1.6	9.5	41.6	**7.1**	9.1	15.4
LIBERTY BANK	SPRINGFIELD	MO	**B+**	B	C+	973	2.45	12.2	1.4	21.9	0.1	**9.0**	10.4	14.8
▼ LIBERTY BANK	NORTH RICHLAND HILLS	TX	**D**	C-	D	271	25.03	14.1	3.0	13.0	14.6	**7.5**	9.4	14.0
LIBERTY BANK	SALT LAKE CITY	UT	**E-**	D	C-	13	-18.37	0.4	0.2	56.3	0.0	**4.6**	6.6	13.0
LIBERTY BANK & TRUST CO	NEW ORLEANS	LA	**C+**	C	C	464	9.59	2.2	5.6	22.6	34.6	**5.4**	7.4	15.5
LIBERTY BANK FOR SAVINGS	CHICAGO	IL	**B-**	B	B-	846	2.92	0.0	0.1	27.4	61.5	**10.0**	19.2	55.7
LIBERTY BANK FSB	WEST DES MOINES	IA	**D-**	C-	C+	1,140	5.53	16.9	1.5	12.9	0.7	**5.3**	8.0	11.2
LIBERTY BANK NA	BEACHWOOD	OH	**D-**	D-	C	249	13.54	17.0	12.7	5.5	4.0	**5.5**	7.7	11.4
▲ LIBERTY BANK OF ARKANSAS	JONESBORO	AR	**B-**	C+	C+	2,543	-0.14	9.7	1.7	12.0	24.5	**9.3**	10.5	16.1
▼ LIBERTY BAY BANK	POULSBO	WA	**D**	C	NR	42	102.15	15.7	1.5	2.3	8.8	**10.0**	18.8	30.3
LIBERTY BELL BANK	MARLTON	NJ	**D-**	D-	D	174	2.25	16.8	0.1	12.2	10.1	**4.7**	7.5	10.8
LIBERTY CAPITAL BANK	ADDISON	TX	**C-**	C	C	76	64.16	11.6	2.1	8.7	0.0	**10.0**	12.0	22.7
LIBERTY FIRST BANK	MONROE	GA	**D**	C-	D	96	1.69	6.0	1.5	22.7	20.1	**10.0**	11.4	16.9
▲ LIBERTY FS&LA	BALTIMORE	MD	**D+**	D	C-	49	3.33	0.0	1.1	53.7	23.7	**10.0**	12.6	27.7
LIBERTY FSB	IRONTON	OH	**B-**	B-	B	53	4.39	0.0	4.5	45.4	12.2	**10.0**	12.0	23.0
LIBERTY FSB	ENID	OK	**E-**	D	D	134	-20.74	1.0	0.8	38.6	1.3	**0.5**	4.1	7.0
LIBERTY NATIONAL BK	SIOUX CITY	IA	**C**	C-	C	218	20.76	14.3	1.2	6.1	20.1	**5.7**	7.7	12.0
LIBERTY NATIONAL BK	ADA	OH	**C-**	C-	C-	203	5.61	6.6	1.5	16.4	17.5	**6.9**	8.9	14.3
LIBERTY NATIONAL BK	LAWTON	OK	**C**	D	D-	206	13.65	7.1	4.2	17.1	36.5	**6.3**	8.3	15.3
▼ LIBERTY NATIONAL BK IN PA	PARIS	TX	**A-**	A	A-	246	0.11	4.2	5.1	18.3	52.1	**10.0**	16.3	37.4
▼ LIBERTY SAVINGS ASSN FSA	FORT SCOTT	KS	**C-**	C+	C+	38	-4.61	0.8	2.0	25.4	53.0	**10.0**	16.3	50.4
LIBERTY SAVINGS BANK FSB	WHITING	IN	**D-**	D	C-	71	-14.07	0.0	0.1	69.1	9.0	**6.2**	8.2	17.6
LIBERTY SAVINGS BANK FSB	SAINT CLOUD	MN	**A**	A	A	161	8.91	0.1	2.2	39.4	3.2	**9.6**	10.8	18.3
LIBERTY SAVINGS BANK FSB	WILMINGTON	OH	**D-**	D-	D-	999	-21.48	1.5	0.2	29.4	15.3	**5.1**	7.1	12.6
LIBERTY SAVINGS BANK FSB	POTTSVILLE	PA	**E-**	D	D-	33	0.80	0.9	4.5	55.3	5.7	**4.3**	6.3	14.9
LIBERTY STATE BK	POWERS LAKE	ND	**B**	B	B+	48	19.93	5.1	4.9	6.7	37.6	**6.4**	8.4	14.1
LIBERTY STATE BK	LIBERTY	TN	**C+**	B-	B	134	2.96	5.7	8.8	31.4	27.0	**8.3**	9.9	17.3
LIBERTY TRUST & SB	DURANT	IA	**A**	A	A	121	0.78	4.8	3.2	9.0	39.6	**10.0**	16.6	28.7
LIBERTYVILLE BANK & TRUST	LIBERTYVILLE	IL	**D+**	D+	C	1,131	7.26	17.0	8.6	5.9	10.1	**5.5**	7.5	13.2
▼ LIBERTYVILLE SB	FAIRFIELD	IA	**D+**	D+	C-	174	0.23	12.1	3.0	15.6	19.6	**8.8**	10.2	14.2
LIFESTORE BANK	WEST JEFFERSON	NC	**D-**	C-	B-	292	-3.28	6.7	2.4	28.7	11.2	**6.1**	8.1	12.8
LIGHTHOUSE BANK	SANTA CRUZ	CA	**C**	C-	D	117	28.17	7.4	0.0	3.3	2.3	**10.0**	15.2	22.0
▼ LINCOLN COMMUNITY BANK	MERRILL	WI	**D+**	C-	C-	67	-5.01	5.1	1.5	18.0	13.5	**8.1**	9.8	15.9
▲ LINCOLN FSB OF NEBRASKA	LINCOLN	NE	**C+**	C-	C	339	-4.75	6.1	0.1	35.9	1.8	**7.8**	9.6	15.1
LINCOLN NB OF HODGENVILLE	HODGENVILLE	KY	**A-**	B+	A-	147	5.59	1.6	5.5	38.2	17.9	**10.0**	17.6	28.1
LINCOLN PARK SB	LINCOLN PARK	NJ	**C**	C	C-	160	8.31	0.6	0.2	35.5	49.1	**6.3**	8.4	20.0

Asset Quality Index	Non-Performing Loans as a % of Total Loans	Non-Performing Loans as a % of Capital	Net Charge-offs Avg Loans	Profitability Index	Net Income ($Mil)	Return on Assets (R.O.A.)	Return on Equity (R.O.E.)	Net Interest Spread	Overhead Efficiency Ratio	Liquidity Index	Liquidity Ratio	Hot Money Ratio	Stability Index
2.4	2.04	17.1	1.93	**0.0**	-7.8	-0.84	-8.54	3.14	110.0	**1.7**	15.0	21.5	**5.9**
1.1	6.89	40.8	1.08	**0.0**	-1.8	-0.72	-5.84	2.98	108.0	**0.7**	10.7	35.7	**4.6**
0.3	14.82	75.6	3.00	**0.0**	-3.1	-3.23	-37.17	1.99	266.9	**1.5**	30.1	32.5	**2.8**
10.0	0.00	0.0	0.00	**10.0**	1.2	8.80	9.65	3.55	80.6	**5.0**	894.7	101.0	**7.0**
0.0	5.64	37.2	0.85	**1.3**	-0.7	-0.04	-0.50	3.76	81.2	**1.7**	20.2	25.3	**6.5**
3.8	1.13	7.7	0.45	**5.6**	2.3	1.36	12.56	5.93	73.4	**2.3**	22.6	18.2	**6.0**
2.8	2.81	16.3	1.03	**5.1**	5.6	0.97	9.03	4.24	64.6	**2.3**	20.8	18.1	**7.2**
6.1	1.32	6.1	0.08	**6.9**	2.8	1.12	7.71	3.92	58.4	**2.2**	12.9	18.0	**8.7**
6.7	0.37	2.6	0.19	**3.7**	2.4	0.74	8.05	3.86	74.3	**0.6**	9.4	40.9	**4.1**
6.5	0.00	0.0	0.00	**0.0**	-16.9	-19.83	-21.95	4.48	148.7	**8.6**	115.5	0.0	**1.3**
3.8	1.82	11.8	0.11	**7.0**	1.7	1.71	15.61	4.53	56.2	**1.6**	20.4	25.0	**6.3**
7.2	0.60	2.5	-0.03	**8.1**	1.4	1.34	7.77	5.07	59.7	**1.8**	17.5	20.4	**9.4**
10.0	0.00	0.0	0.00	**0.0**	-0.6	-0.95	-9.99	1.89	176.5	**6.5**	78.8	8.1	**4.1**
6.0	1.01	5.2	0.15	**4.9**	0.8	1.00	9.48	3.69	57.0	**2.5**	34.3	21.0	**6.1**
7.6	1.56	5.1	0.00	**3.9**	0.3	0.56	4.27	3.50	74.0	**3.1**	57.1	26.6	**7.2**
8.3	0.00	0.0	-0.06	**0.0**	-0.3	-2.62	-23.76	2.77	200.9	**6.0**	51.6	3.9	**4.4**
6.3	0.03	0.2	0.18	**5.8**	6.5	3.12	27.92	4.17	44.8	**1.0**	12.5	30.7	**6.5**
1.4	5.34	30.8	0.14	**2.1**	0.3	0.28	2.59	3.91	82.6	**1.9**	28.9	25.5	**2.7**
6.4	1.30	7.0	0.01	**8.2**	1.3	1.84	13.33	4.80	61.4	**2.6**	15.0	16.2	**9.5**
0.8	4.00	24.1	1.22	**4.7**	1.6	0.68	6.30	4.84	59.1	**1.6**	22.2	24.6	**6.3**
8.0	0.88	3.4	-0.29	**1.3**	0.1	0.16	0.94	5.06	98.8	**1.8**	30.3	27.6	**3.0**
5.6	2.36	7.3	0.10	**5.8**	1.1	1.04	8.06	4.87	65.8	**4.0**	54.9	18.9	**6.8**
0.0	6.89	37.0	2.97	**0.4**	-3.3	-1.37	-13.86	4.32	79.1	**1.0**	25.6	42.8	**5.8**
3.7	4.12	19.1	0.13	**3.5**	16.7	0.52	3.69	3.31	68.3	**4.2**	31.2	14.3	**10.0**
3.7	2.42	12.7	0.61	**4.2**	2.3	0.80	7.09	3.99	65.2	**3.0**	25.0	15.0	**5.5**
5.5	0.39	3.0	0.61	**7.0**	13.0	1.36	13.37	4.39	49.8	**3.3**	7.9	11.8	**6.4**
2.9	1.01	7.3	0.38	**0.6**	-0.3	-0.12	-0.68	4.60	100.7	**1.0**	25.6	37.3	**6.4**
1.7	5.77	45.2	1.42	**0.0**	-0.9	-6.71	-74.03	3.80	282.4	**0.9**	22.3	35.1	**3.7**
3.7	3.05	16.2	0.53	**3.3**	2.2	0.52	6.44	4.87	88.7	**2.2**	23.6	18.9	**3.3**
7.1	3.58	6.3	0.33	**3.3**	4.8	0.57	2.81	3.08	65.2	**5.1**	78.7	17.0	**8.6**
0.3	6.86	56.2	2.23	**0.2**	-45.6	-3.82	-36.37	3.98	124.6	**1.3**	14.4	28.8	**5.6**
1.0	4.76	36.5	0.98	**0.1**	-0.6	-0.23	-2.86	3.32	78.5	**2.9**	27.6	16.3	**2.4**
4.3	1.16	6.5	1.57	**4.0**	15.6	0.61	4.43	3.87	58.2	**1.0**	8.1	30.5	**7.6**
9.0	0.00	0.0	0.00	**0.0**	-1.9	-5.88	-23.53	2.66	295.7	**3.0**	48.1	24.0	**1.5**
0.3	6.85	62.7	0.16	**1.2**	0.2	0.12	1.54	3.50	89.9	**1.9**	14.1	19.5	**2.9**
8.8	0.00	0.0	0.00	**1.2**	0.1	0.24	1.65	3.73	85.8	**5.4**	61.1	11.4	**2.7**
0.3	5.39	31.2	0.29	**2.4**	0.6	0.63	5.57	3.41	76.4	**1.0**	24.4	36.8	**2.3**
3.4	3.12	15.2	0.00	**0.2**	-1.5	-3.02	-22.47	3.19	127.3	**3.1**	35.8	18.0	**4.7**
5.3	1.23	6.7	0.02	**3.6**	0.3	0.53	3.22	4.03	83.1	**3.9**	28.9	12.1	**7.2**
0.3	5.79	71.4	0.73	**0.0**	-11.5	-7.20	-124.89	2.25	159.0	**1.3**	10.1	25.8	**0.3**
3.0	1.14	8.1	0.20	**2.5**	0.8	0.40	2.87	3.98	79.7	**2.4**	35.8	25.1	**6.0**
2.6	1.95	13.8	0.44	**4.6**	1.9	0.95	9.34	4.22	66.8	**1.7**	13.7	21.8	**6.5**
4.4	1.43	9.0	0.64	**4.3**	2.2	1.10	12.08	4.66	74.4	**1.5**	17.5	25.8	**3.1**
8.8	1.35	2.6	0.19	**6.5**	3.0	1.21	6.92	3.82	51.9	**4.7**	54.1	15.0	**8.3**
7.0	3.00	6.7	0.31	**0.9**	-0.2	-0.44	-2.72	2.57	91.1	**4.6**	72.4	17.5	**6.1**
1.8	3.71	30.9	1.11	**0.2**	-0.8	-0.96	-12.35	2.68	94.9	**1.5**	23.2	26.9	**1.3**
7.2	0.00	0.0	0.28	**8.3**	3.0	1.96	16.98	3.63	66.1	**4.9**	33.6	7.6	**9.1**
0.4	6.45	45.0	-0.05	**0.0**	-19.6	-1.84	-23.92	2.87	106.4	**3.8**	29.9	12.9	**2.5**
3.5	0.69	6.8	-0.02	**1.1**	-0.1	-0.20	-2.73	4.09	105.3	**3.2**	27.8	15.0	**0.3**
8.3	0.00	0.0	0.01	**9.4**	0.9	2.05	23.03	4.32	45.8	**4.1**	21.1	9.0	**6.3**
1.5	4.17	24.2	0.67	**4.7**	1.2	0.87	8.74	3.87	59.6	**1.6**	10.0	21.8	**6.2**
7.7	0.70	2.1	1.17	**6.2**	1.7	1.41	8.46	4.27	55.2	**5.0**	53.3	13.2	**8.7**
1.6	2.83	24.1	1.67	**1.3**	-0.5	-0.05	-0.64	3.55	57.5	**1.1**	15.8	32.3	**4.5**
1.0	4.90	31.9	1.47	**4.7**	1.9	1.16	11.79	4.75	51.6	**3.1**	26.7	15.2	**5.0**
0.5	5.10	39.0	0.93	**0.7**	-2.5	-0.82	-10.22	3.43	85.8	**1.8**	22.7	21.7	**3.7**
4.6	2.71	9.8	0.00	**2.8**	0.7	0.63	3.85	4.63	76.5	**4.0**	42.9	15.7	**4.3**
1.4	4.97	28.4	0.95	**1.8**	0.1	0.14	1.35	4.46	74.6	**3.5**	37.7	16.6	**4.3**
4.0	1.31	10.3	0.01	**3.7**	2.3	0.66	6.42	3.61	62.3	**1.6**	9.0	21.7	**5.6**
8.8	0.35	1.3	0.06	**6.1**	1.6	1.13	6.33	4.28	60.4	**2.0**	24.6	20.3	**8.1**
3.6	3.68	18.9	0.28	**3.1**	0.7	0.44	5.36	2.92	68.8	**3.0**	27.2	15.9	**4.0**

Name	City	State	Rating	2008 Rating	2007 Rating	Total Assets ($Mil)	One Year Asset Growth	Asset Mix (As a % of Total Assets) Comm-ercial Loans	Cons-umer Loans	Home Mort-gages	Secur-ities	Capital-ization Index	Leverage Ratio	Risk-based Capital Ratio
▼LINCOLN SB	REINBECK	IA	**C+**	B-	C+	553	1.43	11.5	1.4	8.5	23.5	**5.8**	7.8	11.9
LINCOLN STATE BK	HANKINSON	ND	**C-**	C	D+	50	9.71	8.1	5.8	4.7	40.3	**5.7**	7.7	15.8
LINCOLN STATE BK SB	ROCHELLE	IL	**D+**	D	D-	47	8.56	8.2	4.2	26.2	9.8	**6.2**	8.2	13.0
LINCOLNWAY COMMUNITY	NEW LENOX	IL	**D-**	D-	C	131	-6.01	17.0	0.1	17.8	5.8	**6.5**	8.5	13.6
LINDALE STATE BK	LINDALE	TX	**B**	B	B-	105	-6.37	9.1	5.2	22.0	16.6	**8.3**	9.9	15.9
▼LINDELL BANK & TRUST CO	SAINT LOUIS	MO	**B-**	B+	A	506	-6.36	7.1	0.3	13.0	48.1	**7.8**	9.6	23.1
LINN COUNTY STATE BK	COGGON	IA	**C**	C-	C+	25	5.28	16.9	6.3	16.0	5.4	**10.0**	12.0	18.8
LISCO STATE BK	LISCO	NE	**B**	B	B	16	11.05	4.2	0.4	4.0	20.0	**10.0**	13.8	19.6
LISLE SB	LISLE	IL	**D**	D	C-	517	3.22	0.0	0.0	50.3	21.9	**10.0**	16.7	36.7
▼LITCHFIELD BANCORP	LITCHFIELD	CT	**C-**	C	C	222	3.99	0.9	1.4	31.3	34.5	**5.4**	7.4	15.4
▼LITCHFIELD NATIONAL BK	LITCHFIELD	IL	**C**	C+	C+	89	3.54	2.9	3.8	16.4	24.2	**5.2**	7.2	13.0
▲LITTLE BANK INC	KINSTON	NC	**B-**	C+	C+	299	-1.38	6.1	0.9	11.8	25.9	**10.0**	11.1	16.6
LITTLE HORN STATE BK	HARDIN	MT	**D**	D	D-	65	-4.63	5.2	3.5	11.2	29.7	**7.5**	9.4	16.6
LITTLE RIVER BANK	LEPANTO	AR	**C-**	B-	B-	44	-8.97	7.8	9.4	21.3	22.2	**8.9**	10.3	22.7
▼LIVE OAK BANKING CO	WILMINGTON	NC	**D+**	B-	D	245	89.79	31.4	0.0	0.0	2.5	**6.8**	8.8	16.0
LIVE OAK STATE BK	DALLAS	TX	**B**	B	B+	108	-1.12	3.6	1.1	18.3	21.3	**10.0**	11.1	20.5
LIVINGSTON STATE BK	LIVINGSTON	WI	**D**	D	C-	152	-5.60	5.4	4.1	19.8	10.1	**6.7**	8.7	13.2
LLANO NATIONAL BK	LLANO	TX	**C-**	C	B	118	6.64	4.1	7.7	14.4	25.0	**8.5**	10.0	15.8
LLEWELLYN-EDISON SAVINGS	WEST ORANGE	NJ	**C**	C+	B-	139	-2.91	1.3	0.0	18.3	51.3	**10.0**	15.8	41.2
▼LOGAN BANK & TRUST CO	LOGAN	WV	**B+**	A-	A-	233	3.12	7.1	5.6	26.8	14.0	**7.4**	9.3	21.7
LOGAN COUNTY BANK	SCRANTON	AR	**A-**	B+	A-	68	6.95	3.1	5.8	16.7	61.4	**10.0**	17.3	46.0
LOGAN COUNTY BANK	LINCOLN	IL	**B-**	C+	B-	95	-0.96	4.1	1.5	10.6	45.6	**6.8**	8.8	14.7
LOGANSPORT SAVINGS BANK	LOGANSPORT	IN	**B**	B	B+	151	-6.70	20.2	2.0	27.7	17.1	**10.0**	12.7	19.0
LONE STAR BANK	HOUSTON	TX	**D-**	D-	D	128	-5.82	14.2	1.1	11.2	10.1	**8.3**	9.9	13.8
LONE STAR BANK SSB	MOULTON	TX	**B-**	C+	C+	183	6.55	3.9	2.0	44.2	7.2	**6.0**	8.1	15.2
LONE STAR CAPITAL BANK NA	SAN ANTONIO	TX	**D+**	C-	C-	132	1.14	10.0	2.2	6.5	39.0	**5.5**	7.5	16.2
LONE STAR NATIONAL BK	MCALLEN	TX	**C**	C-	B-	2,091	12.65	10.0	1.9	9.9	31.3	**7.5**	9.3	16.2
LONE STAR STATE BK	LONE STAR	TX	**B**	B	B	37	-11.34	7.1	6.0	17.3	0.0	**5.8**	7.8	14.6
▲LONE STAR STATE BK OF	LUBBOCK	TX	**C**	C	C-	384	13.50	25.5	2.5	5.6	8.5	**5.9**	9.1	11.7
▼LONE SUMMIT BANK	LAKE LOTAWANA	MO	**E-**	D	D	33	23.65	7.1	1.4	7.4	0.0	**3.4**	6.4	10.2
LONGVIEW STATE BK	SIDNEY	IL	**C-**	B-	C+	58	-5.33	5.5	2.7	21.5	6.0	**6.6**	8.6	13.9
LOOMIS FS&LA	CHICAGO	IL	**B-**	B-	C+	98	7.50	12.0	0.1	43.3	32.4	**10.0**	15.8	43.7
LORAIN NATIONAL BK	LORAIN	OH	**D-**	D	D+	1,152	0.29	5.3	14.3	8.9	19.3	**6.6**	8.6	12.9
▼LORRAINE STATE BK	LORRAINE	KS	**C+**	B-	C+	22	12.97	4.1	10.1	6.7	26.3	**8.9**	10.3	14.1
LOS ALAMOS NATIONAL BK	LOS ALAMOS	NM	**D+**	D	D+	1,557	-6.67	9.6	2.7	24.1	11.2	**8.0**	9.6	14.3
▼LOS ANGELES NATIONAL BK	BUENA PARK	CA	**D+**	B-	B+	202	-4.80	6.6	0.0	1.4	11.5	**10.0**	12.9	18.0
LOTUS BANK	NOVI	MI	**D+**	C	C	68	19.53	24.3	0.5	6.1	8.7	**9.2**	11.2	14.3
LOUISA COMMUNITY BANK	LOUISA	KY	**D**	D+	C-	26	5.07	15.6	4.7	24.8	11.8	**10.0**	15.0	21.1
LOVELADY STATE BK	LOVELADY	TX	**B-**	B-	C	34	4.80	9.8	18.7	15.7	10.9	**8.7**	10.2	16.7
▲LOWELL CO-OP BANK	LOWELL	MA	**D-**	E	E-	117	30.86	3.1	0.6	58.1	2.7	**6.9**	9.5	12.4
LOWELL FIVE CENT SB	LOWELL	MA	**C**	C-	D+	701	2.51	2.7	0.6	32.1	30.4	**10.0**	14.3	23.1
▲LOWRY STATE BK	LOWRY	MN	**C-**	C-	D	37	3.09	16.4	7.5	19.2	0.5	**6.4**	8.7	12.0
LUANA SB	LUANA	IA	**B**	B-	B-	389	15.61	5.4	2.4	21.9	15.7	**6.2**	8.5	11.9
LUBBOCK NATIONAL BK	LUBBOCK	TX	**C-**	C-	B	710	-0.77	11.5	1.2	6.7	35.3	**6.1**	8.1	14.1
LUMBEE GUARANTY BANK	PEMBROKE	NC	**C+**	B-	A-	283	6.35	2.9	4.6	18.4	22.2	**8.6**	10.1	16.6
LUSITANIA SAVINGS BANK FS	NEWARK	NJ	**B+**	B	A-	251	2.36	0.5	1.7	39.6	9.7	**10.0**	11.7	24.7
LUSK STATE BK	LUSK	WY	**B-**	C+	C-	44	4.02	3.8	5.2	6.8	7.0	**7.3**	9.2	15.0
▲LUTHER BURBANK SAVINGS	SANTA ROSA	CA	**C+**	C	B+	3,451	-2.40	0.0	0.0	19.8	0.3	**9.6**	10.7	15.4
LUZERNE BANK	LUZERNE	PA	**B**	B-	B	280	4.66	19.7	1.8	17.2	8.8	**7.3**	9.4	12.7
LYDIAN PRIVATE BANK	PALM BEACH	FL	**E**	D-	D	1,758	-16.65	6.7	3.8	46.7	11.6	**4.6**	6.7	12.2
LYNDON STATE BK	LYNDON	KS	**C-**	C	C-	85	-4.65	8.0	4.4	30.8	26.6	**6.2**	8.2	14.4
▼LYNNVILLE NATIONAL BK	LYNNVILLE	IN	**C+**	B-	B-	97	-0.38	1.0	4.9	47.2	9.9	**8.3**	9.9	17.0
LYON COUNTY STATE BK	EMPORIA	KS	**B-**	B-	B-	79	-5.74	2.9	3.4	12.5	47.8	**7.0**	9.0	20.7
LYONS FEDERAL BANK	LYONS	KS	**C+**	B-	B-	77	8.10	16.4	3.3	18.0	0.3	**8.4**	9.9	15.4
LYONS NATIONAL BK	LYONS	NY	**B-**	C+	C+	513	12.11	7.6	5.3	18.2	31.1	**6.2**	8.2	14.2
▼LYONS STATE BK	LYONS	KS	**D+**	C-	D+	110	10.08	9.8	3.4	7.1	29.7	**5.4**	7.4	11.7
LYTLE STATE BK OF LYTLE T	LYTLE	TX	**B+**	B+	B+	71	-1.86	4.4	16.1	9.5	50.9	**10.0**	16.7	26.9
M C BANK & TRUST CO	MORGAN CITY	LA	**A-**	A-	A-	304	8.40	7.4	3.9	8.3	53.0	**10.0**	13.6	28.3
M&I BANK FSB	LAS VEGAS	NV	**D-**	D	C-	1,306	-28.48	4.1	23.8	20.8	6.1	**6.3**	10.2	12.0
▼M&I BANK OF MAYVILLE	MAYVILLE	WI	**C-**	C	C-	3	2.47	0.0	0.0	0.0	0.0	**10.0**	76.9	392.6

Asset Quality Index	Non-Performing Loans as a % of Total Loans	Non-Performing Loans as a % of Capital	Net Charge-offs Avg Loans	Profitability Index	Net Income ($Mil)	Return on Assets (R.O.A.)	Return on Equity (R.O.E.)	Net Interest Spread	Overhead Efficiency Ratio	Liquidity Index	Liquidity Ratio	Hot Money Ratio	Stability Index
2.9	1.95	15.3	0.23	**4.6**	5.4	0.98	8.89	4.17	67.2	**4.3**	20.2	7.4	**7.0**
5.4	1.14	7.2	0.42	**4.5**	0.5	1.04	12.55	3.88	73.7	**4.2**	29.9	10.5	**3.7**
4.6	0.99	7.8	0.14	**4.1**	0.6	1.25	15.48	4.07	76.7	**1.6**	20.6	24.3	**3.6**
0.3	8.44	57.0	1.68	**0.5**	-0.8	-0.54	-6.24	3.57	70.0	**0.9**	22.7	35.3	**0.8**
8.3	0.27	1.5	0.49	**1.3**	0.2	0.14	1.36	3.35	81.3	**1.9**	25.2	21.1	**5.9**
5.0	3.36	12.9	2.94	**3.2**	2.6	0.50	3.93	4.44	44.9	**4.2**	33.0	11.4	**7.5**
5.7	0.06	0.3	-0.40	**4.0**	0.1	0.57	3.13	4.90	78.9	**5.1**	25.0	2.6	**6.4**
5.3	2.49	11.0	0.27	**7.3**	0.3	1.71	11.12	4.28	54.9	**4.3**	21.7	7.2	**9.3**
2.3	6.22	22.0	2.31	**0.3**	-0.9	-0.17	-0.98	2.99	67.4	**2.3**	31.0	21.6	**6.5**
5.7	0.69	4.7	0.02	**1.8**	0.3	0.15	1.91	3.23	95.3	**3.7**	40.1	16.5	**4.2**
3.7	3.36	25.4	0.34	**3.3**	0.2	0.27	3.60	3.60	76.5	**4.5**	30.4	9.4	**4.2**
5.0	1.86	10.3	0.80	**4.0**	1.7	0.57	5.27	3.53	61.1	**1.6**	30.2	31.1	**5.9**
2.1	3.79	18.5	1.22	**0.5**	-0.3	-0.50	-4.79	4.96	93.2	**4.6**	39.2	11.5	**4.6**
2.7	4.27	18.2	3.44	**3.1**	-0.1	-0.21	-1.93	4.95	64.2	**2.3**	41.3	31.6	**6.3**
1.2	1.08	9.0	0.67	**8.9**	9.0	4.51	51.48	1.98	52.8	**0.4**	13.7	80.9	**2.1**
8.1	0.00	0.0	0.96	**3.4**	0.6	0.56	5.11	3.67	73.8	**1.8**	28.1	26.4	**7.5**
1.1	2.33	17.0	2.02	**1.6**	-0.1	-0.06	-0.61	4.43	62.1	**1.6**	17.1	23.1	**4.8**
1.8	3.85	20.8	0.39	**5.2**	0.9	0.76	7.32	4.63	66.3	**2.4**	39.2	27.4	**6.8**
6.3	2.77	7.6	0.01	**2.6**	0.4	0.27	1.84	2.87	84.3	**4.6**	63.5	17.3	**7.3**
7.3	1.10	5.3	0.03	**5.0**	1.8	0.76	8.05	3.54	70.2	**4.5**	48.7	14.7	**6.5**
7.6	2.85	5.1	0.21	**6.2**	0.9	1.32	7.36	3.84	51.4	**3.8**	63.4	19.7	**8.1**
7.3	1.23	5.8	0.10	**5.0**	0.8	0.86	9.71	3.32	62.3	**4.3**	47.6	14.9	**5.4**
5.2	1.45	8.0	0.51	**4.1**	1.2	0.78	6.00	3.29	58.3	**1.7**	23.1	23.8	**6.4**
0.4	3.99	26.6	2.41	**0.0**	-1.6	-1.12	-11.56	3.10	106.8	**1.1**	9.7	29.3	**1.0**
5.1	0.68	5.9	0.17	**7.1**	2.4	1.31	16.61	5.16	64.2	**1.1**	13.3	29.3	**5.2**
5.4	0.02	0.1	1.10	**1.5**	0.2	0.14	1.00	3.23	87.1	**2.1**	44.6	53.9	**6.6**
2.6	3.89	22.0	1.95	**2.6**	4.5	0.23	2.35	3.75	62.3	**0.9**	20.1	46.7	**6.5**
8.3	0.00	0.0	0.00	**8.6**	0.9	1.99	27.75	3.45	45.3	**2.2**	36.4	28.7	**6.9**
3.4	0.88	7.1	0.40	**3.4**	2.9	0.80	6.74	3.91	70.8	**0.8**	14.7	35.5	**4.3**
0.7	3.46	27.6	0.45	**0.0**	-0.4	-1.18	-15.67	3.41	80.8	**1.1**	27.0	40.3	**4.0**
0.3	4.97	39.3	0.64	**5.7**	0.7	1.07	14.23	3.74	68.7	**3.2**	17.3	13.3	**4.0**
8.6	0.89	3.2	0.00	**3.5**	0.6	0.60	3.71	3.51	60.9	**4.7**	45.2	12.4	**7.6**
0.3	5.11	37.2	1.61	**2.6**	4.3	0.38	3.58	3.73	69.9	**1.5**	11.5	24.5	**6.0**
7.3	0.38	2.4	0.06	**5.3**	0.2	1.04	9.53	3.96	64.8	**2.6**	31.2	17.1	**5.0**
1.4	4.12	27.3	1.33	**2.7**	3.5	0.22	2.29	3.90	62.9	**1.7**	17.3	23.8	**6.1**
0.0	8.01	38.1	0.61	**3.5**	0.8	0.38	3.04	3.76	65.5	**0.9**	24.5	52.9	**7.6**
8.3	0.00	0.0	0.17	**1.2**	0.3	0.25	2.18	3.93	83.3	**1.8**	22.1	21.9	**2.2**
5.3	1.59	7.4	0.08	**0.0**	-0.2	-0.72	-4.43	4.40	97.1	**0.7**	15.6	44.6	**2.0**
3.7	1.05	6.1	0.31	**4.9**	0.4	1.14	10.61	5.11	72.6	**1.6**	25.2	26.4	**6.0**
2.5	2.29	21.2	0.20	**0.0**	-2.4	-2.47	-38.24	3.93	156.3	**0.8**	9.2	33.7	**1.4**
5.5	0.86	3.3	0.08	**2.4**	2.8	0.41	2.80	3.41	83.5	**3.9**	39.7	15.1	**7.3**
2.5	1.42	11.8	1.33	**6.4**	0.5	1.42	16.35	4.74	49.9	**3.4**	11.9	11.4	**5.7**
6.4	0.14	1.1	0.09	**7.9**	6.8	1.87	21.31	4.16	45.7	**0.9**	24.4	49.2	**5.9**
2.4	3.08	19.0	0.79	**2.8**	3.8	0.54	6.41	3.43	77.1	**2.4**	36.8	25.8	**4.6**
3.9	1.69	9.4	0.21	**3.6**	1.4	0.52	5.01	4.71	80.0	**1.5**	23.5	26.5	**5.9**
6.9	0.83	4.2	0.01	**4.6**	2.6	1.05	9.37	3.66	44.5	**3.3**	35.6	16.9	**7.1**
5.0	0.53	3.7	-0.02	**9.9**	1.0	2.39	25.95	5.72	53.0	**2.0**	24.3	20.3	**7.4**
2.1	2.01	16.3	0.03	**8.6**	80.1	2.31	22.57	4.10	23.9	**0.4**	2.1	50.3	**9.1**
7.8	0.25	1.9	0.17	**4.9**	2.6	0.96	10.52	4.22	64.7	**3.8**	19.1	10.2	**6.0**
0.6	3.55	32.4	-0.01	**0.3**	-12.8	-0.66	-12.31	3.13	73.9	**1.3**	18.7	29.5	**1.4**
1.9	3.26	23.7	0.95	**3.8**	0.4	0.51	6.26	4.65	70.8	**2.4**	18.0	17.4	**4.6**
2.5	3.36	21.7	0.11	**4.6**	1.0	0.99	10.20	4.55	76.7	**2.7**	14.2	15.2	**6.7**
9.4	0.17	0.7	0.18	**3.8**	0.6	0.69	7.40	3.70	86.4	**4.1**	35.0	12.6	**5.2**
5.3	0.46	2.7	0.00	**3.0**	0.3	0.41	4.10	3.03	80.1	**2.3**	31.9	22.4	**6.4**
4.2	1.69	10.9	0.30	**4.6**	4.5	0.92	11.06	4.11	65.5	**3.5**	20.8	12.3	**5.5**
2.9	2.63	19.1	-0.28	**2.8**	0.4	0.42	5.45	4.06	84.6	**1.9**	21.0	20.0	**3.4**
4.6	3.96	8.4	1.15	**6.7**	0.9	1.32	7.74	5.23	64.5	**3.1**	49.1	22.5	**7.6**
5.3	3.52	8.9	0.03	**6.3**	3.2	1.07	7.26	4.49	53.2	**4.3**	66.5	19.4	**8.3**
1.3	4.24	20.3	6.88	**0.4**	-30.9	-1.96	-15.48	3.85	64.3	**0.4**	9.9	78.5	**5.0**
10.0	0.00	0.0	0.00	**2.6**	0.0	0.13	0.17	0.27	99.5	**10.0**	427.9	0.0	**1.7**

Name	City	State	Rating	2008 Rating	2007 Rating	Total Assets ($Mil)	One Year Asset Growth	Asset Mix (As a % of Total Assets) Comm-ercial Loans	Cons-umer Loans	Home Mort-gages	Secur-ities	Capital-ization Index	Leverage Ratio	Risk-based Capital Ratio
M&I MARSHALL & ILSLEY BAN	MILWAUKEE	WI	**D**	D	C-	49,144	-2.21	20.1	1.2	13.5	12.9	**6.3**	8.3	13.5
▼ M&T BANK NA	OAKFIELD	NY	**C**	C	B-	798	-12.13	0.0	0.0	30.0	5.5	**10.0**	22.5	27.6
MACATAWA BANK	HOLLAND	MI	**E**	E	D-	1,576	-13.73	14.3	1.4	14.1	0.6	**2.7**	7.1	9.7
MACHIAS SB	MACHIAS	ME	**D+**	C-	C+	976	2.17	15.5	1.3	18.2	2.3	**8.4**	10.6	13.7
MACKINAC SAVINGS BANK	BOYNTON BEACH	FL	**D-**	D-	D-	127	-6.73	0.1	0.0	48.5	0.0	**4.6**	6.7	23.3
MACON BANK & TRUST CO	LAFAYETTE	TN	**B-**	B-	B-	314	4.78	3.5	6.4	12.7	43.4	**10.0**	11.1	22.5
MACON BANK INC	FRANKLIN	NC	**D-**	D	D+	1,030	-4.71	1.5	0.4	24.5	21.1	**6.4**	8.5	13.3
MACON-ATLANTA STATE BK	MACON	MO	**B+**	A-	B+	201	8.09	2.8	2.8	11.7	38.7	**8.5**	10.0	14.3
MADISON BANK	RICHMOND	KY	**D**	D+	C-	152	1.82	4.6	1.8	19.9	10.9	**6.6**	8.7	14.4
MADISON BANK OF	FOREST HILL	MD	**C-**	C-	C-	161	-5.13	0.0	0.5	53.5	11.6	**10.0**	12.0	22.7
MADISON COUNTY BANK	MADISON	NE	**A-**	B	B+	218	11.39	17.8	1.6	18.1	8.7	**10.0**	11.5	15.3
▲ MADISON COUNTY	MADISON	FL	**D**	C	B	93	14.34	7.8	3.8	9.2	22.0	**7.1**	9.0	16.3
MADISON NATIONAL BK	HAUPPAUGE	NY	**D-**	C-	C-	297	-8.82	12.5	0.1	0.0	6.9	**8.6**	10.5	13.8
MADISON SQUARE FSB	BALTIMORE	MD	**D**	D	D	154	4.40	3.1	0.9	37.2	28.3	**5.8**	7.8	16.6
MAGNA BANK	MEMPHIS	TN	**C-**	C+	D+	427	-2.47	6.1	1.3	28.9	9.4	**10.0**	12.2	15.9
▲ MAGNOLIA BANK INC	HODGENVILLE	KY	**B**	B-	B-	131	4.24	4.2	2.0	26.2	17.2	**7.0**	9.0	13.8
MAGNOLIA STATE BK	BAY SPRINGS	MS	**B-**	B	B	234	9.50	4.3	7.9	24.4	15.6	**6.1**	8.1	12.0
MAGYAR BANK	NEW BRUNSWICK	NJ	**D-**	D-	D-	527	-5.59	6.9	2.5	30.3	13.6	**5.9**	7.9	13.0
MAHOPAC NATIONAL BK	BREWSTER	NY	**C+**	B-	B-	855	1.57	7.3	0.3	16.0	27.0	**6.6**	8.7	13.9
MAIN BANK	ALBUQUERQUE	NM	**C**	C-	D+	79	19.36	8.9	0.4	11.8	14.2	**7.7**	9.5	18.7
▲ MAIN STREET BANK	BINGHAM FARMS	MI	**E**	D-	D+	86	58.60	22.1	0.4	11.9	2.4	**4.1**	7.3	10.6
MAIN STREET BANK	KINGWOOD	TX	**B-**	C+	C	350	-21.93	50.0	0.9	0.1	0.0	**9.5**	10.7	17.4
MAIN STREET BANK CORP	WHEELING	WV	**C-**	C-	C-	228	5.85	14.7	5.0	37.6	9.9	**6.5**	8.5	12.9
MAINLAND BANK	TEXAS CITY	TX	**B+**	B	B	97	-0.42	22.2	1.8	13.3	34.5	**6.0**	8.0	14.5
MAINLINE NATIONAL BK	EBENSBURG	PA	**C-**	C-	C	248	-2.84	10.6	8.0	21.7	36.4	**7.4**	9.3	13.6
MAINSOURCE BANK	GREENSBURG	IN	**D**	D-	D+	2,753	-4.57	5.1	2.6	20.5	29.3	**7.0**	9.0	15.7
MAINSTREET BANK	ASHLAND	MO	**C+**	C+	C	61	9.69	8.7	2.8	15.8	41.2	**6.6**	8.6	15.3
MAINSTREET BANK	HERNDON	VA	**D+**	C-	C	240	1.62	5.4	0.4	11.0	10.3	**6.8**	9.4	12.3
MAINSTREET COMMUNITY BK	DELAND	FL	**D**	D-	D+	186	8.41	7.6	2.0	13.3	13.5	**5.9**	9.3	11.7
MALAGA BANK FSB	PALOS VERDES	CA	**B+**	B	B	813	0.41	0.7	0.1	17.7	0.0	**10.0**	11.5	19.4
MALVERN FSB	PAOLI	PA	**D**	C-	C+	687	1.35	1.8	0.1	47.2	11.2	**6.5**	8.5	12.9
▲ MALVERN NATIONAL BK	MALVERN	AR	**C+**	C	B	471	6.08	6.0	1.8	9.2	42.1	**8.8**	10.2	16.6
MALVERN TRUST & SB	MALVERN	IA	**C+**	C+	B-	55	6.19	4.6	9.3	20.0	3.0	**6.5**	10.2	12.1
MANASQUAN SB	MANASQUAN	NJ	**C+**	C	C+	801	8.15	6.2	0.2	33.9	22.5	**7.5**	9.4	16.8
MANCOS VALLEY BANK	MANCOS	CO	**D**	C-	C	89	7.10	3.2	8.3	15.5	26.0	**5.9**	7.9	13.7
▲ MANHATTAN BANK	MANHATTAN	MT	**D**	D+	B-	112	-0.86	5.9	3.1	9.8	26.8	**8.0**	9.7	15.4
MANOR BANK	MANOR	PA	**C-**	C-	C+	22	14.15	1.5	1.2	33.3	30.8	**9.3**	10.5	24.0
MANSFIELD CO-OP BANK	MANSFIELD	MA	**C+**	C+	C+	330	4.24	2.3	0.2	30.5	19.9	**10.0**	11.1	17.5
▼ MANSFIELD STATE BK	MANSFIELD	SD	**C**	C-	C-	10	-4.36	2.0	0.8	0.3	18.4	**10.0**	16.3	46.4
▲ MANSON STATE BK	MANSON	IA	**C**	D+	C+	35	-4.77	6.2	1.5	9.4	58.1	**7.5**	9.3	20.0
▼ MANUFACTURERS &	BUFFALO	NY	**C+**	C-	C	67,055	-1.19	15.9	7.4	9.5	9.8	**6.5**	8.5	12.3
MANUFACTURERS BANK	LOS ANGELES	CA	**C-**	C	B	1,942	-1.26	26.7	0.0	1.3	44.6	**10.0**	14.1	20.0
▲ MANUFACTURERS BANK &	FOREST CITY	IA	**C**	D+	D+	251	8.72	8.9	2.8	11.2	30.2	**7.4**	9.2	13.8
MAPLE BANK	CHAMPLIN	MN	**D-**	D-	D	61	-1.70	17.7	1.5	6.3	5.6	**6.8**	8.8	14.6
▲ MAPLE CITY SAVINGS BANK F	HORNELL	NY	**B-**	C-	C-	48	1.04	1.9	2.1	68.1	0.8	**10.0**	13.3	21.8
MAQUOKETA STATE BK	MAQUOKETA	IA	**B+**	B+	A-	294	3.02	6.8	3.3	7.6	30.1	**10.0**	11.7	19.2
MARATHON NATIONAL BK OF	ASTORIA	NY	**D**	D	C	838	0.45	4.1	0.1	4.5	9.4	**9.2**	10.5	17.7
MARATHON SB	WAUSAU	WI	**C+**	B-	B-	169	2.23	0.6	1.1	32.1	40.9	**10.0**	11.7	20.9
MARATHON STATE BK	MARATHON	WI	**B**	B	B	106	-1.69	4.7	1.7	13.1	57.0	**10.0**	18.7	18.9
MARBLEHEAD BANK	MARBLEHEAD	MA	**C-**	C-	C-	169	-2.68	0.7	0.6	62.1	4.8	**7.9**	9.6	18.4
MARBLEHEAD BANK	MARBLEHEAD	OH	**C**	C+	B-	33	5.62	3.9	8.3	11.1	65.3	**9.8**	10.9	20.9
MARIES COUNTY BANK	VIENNA	MO	**B**	B	B-	306	8.12	2.7	6.0	16.7	30.2	**9.8**	10.8	16.1
MARINE BANK	SPRINGFIELD	IL	**C-**	D+	D+	584	-1.89	8.3	1.1	10.0	12.1	**5.4**	8.5	11.3
MARINE BANK & TRUST	CARTHAGE	IL	**B-**	C-	C	212	5.08	9.5	10.3	15.2	21.7	**5.5**	8.0	11.4
MARINE BANK & TRUST CO	VERO BEACH	FL	**E**	D-	D	145	-9.94	11.8	3.0	14.1	5.1	**1.3**	6.0	8.3
MARINERS BANK	EDGEWATER	NJ	**D-**	D-	D+	288	-13.46	14.2	0.7	14.5	6.0	**6.8**	8.8	12.5
MARION BANK & TRUST CO	MARION	AL	**B**	B-	B-	228	9.34	2.4	5.8	14.4	29.9	**7.7**	9.5	14.1
MARION CENTER BANK	MARION CENTER	PA	**D+**	D+	C-	242	7.53	10.8	2.1	20.8	37.4	**5.6**	7.6	13.4
▼ MARION COUNTY SB	SALEM	IL	**C+**	B-	B-	118	6.09	0.8	15.8	27.2	38.9	**7.4**	9.3	19.6
MARION COUNTY STATE BK	PELLA	IA	**B+**	B+	B+	219	0.33	11.8	1.3	12.3	30.4	**8.1**	9.8	14.9

Asset Quality Index	Non-Performing Loans as a % of Total Loans	Non-Performing Loans as a % of Capital	Net Charge-offs / Avg Loans	Profitability Index	Net Income ($Mil)	Return on Assets (R.O.A.)	Return on Equity (R.O.E.)	Net Interest Spread	Overhead Efficiency Ratio	Liquidity Index	Liquidity Ratio	Hot Money Ratio	Stability Index
1.1	4.24	29.0	4.57	**0.0**	-503.3	-1.00	-9.70	3.31	63.3	**1.9**	19.8	22.0	**6.6**
8.4	1.21	4.4	0.58	**4.4**	1.1	0.12	0.70	2.76	18.0	**0.4**	8.1	63.1	**3.7**
0.3	6.17	48.1	2.17	**0.0**	-15.6	-0.94	-14.19	3.45	90.7	**2.9**	16.6	15.1	**4.2**
1.3	3.64	24.8	0.98	**4.5**	6.8	0.72	6.83	4.33	55.6	**0.6**	11.0	47.5	**6.8**
1.7	4.77	36.5	0.28	**2.2**	0.2	0.15	2.42	3.00	82.4	**6.3**	48.0	4.3	**1.4**
7.5	0.78	3.0	0.38	**3.9**	2.5	0.80	6.98	3.54	75.8	**2.4**	48.2	35.3	**6.8**
0.3	7.45	50.8	2.61	**0.3**	-5.5	-0.52	-5.82	2.93	73.6	**1.0**	16.9	34.4	**5.8**
8.2	0.24	1.1	0.04	**5.7**	2.3	1.23	11.45	3.28	58.6	**2.7**	33.6	19.4	**5.8**
3.0	2.43	15.3	1.14	**1.2**	0.1	0.06	0.68	3.94	91.2	**1.1**	25.2	33.5	**3.9**
3.7	3.75	21.3	0.00	**1.1**	-0.2	-0.12	-0.96	3.01	86.4	**2.0**	23.7	19.8	**4.9**
6.3	0.19	1.2	0.02	**5.9**	2.8	1.37	11.36	4.19	53.6	**4.5**	11.5	4.9	**7.2**
1.6	4.43	26.8	0.25	**2.3**	0.3	0.32	3.27	3.38	81.8	**1.4**	32.3	43.1	**4.9**
0.0	6.00	41.2	1.13	**0.8**	-0.1	-0.02	-0.16	3.95	82.1	**1.1**	13.1	29.4	**1.0**
8.5	0.32	2.3	0.03	**1.0**	-0.1	-0.09	-1.40	2.58	97.4	**2.5**	42.9	30.2	**3.3**
1.6	4.56	27.0	0.08	**1.0**	-1.6	-0.36	-3.09	3.37	89.0	**1.7**	14.6	21.7	**6.2**
6.1	0.47	3.4	0.09	**5.4**	1.6	1.26	13.97	3.75	73.8	**2.7**	15.0	15.5	**5.4**
7.0	0.03	0.2	0.05	**5.6**	2.5	1.07	13.06	5.18	71.4	**2.8**	21.2	15.4	**5.3**
0.3	7.40	63.4	1.01	**1.4**	4.7	0.86	11.12	3.25	79.9	**1.6**	6.8	20.9	**3.0**
1.5	3.12	20.6	0.55	**4.0**	5.4	0.62	5.46	4.16	66.1	**3.3**	19.2	12.8	**6.6**
7.1	0.00	0.0	0.37	**4.9**	0.9	1.26	14.52	4.12	72.5	**4.8**	43.9	11.5	**3.4**
2.2	0.88	8.1	0.94	**0.0**	-0.4	-0.57	-6.81	4.43	91.0	**0.7**	20.5	57.7	**0.2**
4.1	1.78	9.2	0.95	**4.8**	4.8	1.09	10.83	5.58	70.0	**1.0**	21.5	34.3	**4.2**
2.0	2.23	19.2	0.28	**5.1**	2.0	0.90	10.84	3.98	58.3	**0.9**	9.5	31.2	**5.0**
5.9	0.06	0.4	-0.02	**9.5**	2.4	2.44	28.76	5.35	58.3	**4.2**	33.4	11.7	**6.8**
4.5	1.56	8.9	0.03	**1.9**	-0.7	-0.27	-3.38	3.22	86.6	**3.3**	29.2	14.9	**3.9**
1.3	4.11	23.7	2.22	**3.1**	19.3	0.68	5.91	4.23	60.9	**4.1**	23.1	11.2	**6.4**
5.8	0.92	4.2	1.60	**6.0**	0.4	0.67	7.14	4.83	51.7	**2.2**	46.4	43.0	**5.7**
3.9	0.43	3.2	0.50	**1.3**	0.4	0.17	1.83	3.78	81.6	**0.8**	14.3	36.6	**6.6**
1.8	2.47	16.2	1.79	**1.2**	0.4	0.24	2.47	4.02	71.4	**1.3**	19.4	28.1	**3.7**
7.3	0.00	0.0	0.00	**5.7**	11.3	1.38	12.68	3.65	34.5	**0.5**	3.1	42.6	**7.4**
1.3	3.21	26.6	1.54	**0.8**	-4.1	-0.59	-6.75	3.01	78.2	**1.5**	17.8	25.1	**4.6**
3.4	3.61	14.2	0.83	**4.2**	4.2	0.93	9.04	3.94	64.0	**2.2**	35.1	26.7	**6.2**
4.9	1.72	12.8	0.33	**3.8**	0.4	0.80	8.00	3.85	66.9	**1.5**	17.2	25.1	**6.0**
6.7	0.98	6.0	0.11	**3.4**	3.8	0.49	5.30	2.60	66.1	**2.2**	35.2	27.3	**6.2**
1.6	2.50	17.2	1.55	**3.0**	0.4	0.51	6.50	3.86	55.0	**2.3**	29.7	20.3	**3.2**
0.3	5.08	26.8	0.91	**3.8**	0.7	0.65	6.66	4.74	73.5	**4.5**	36.6	11.6	**5.3**
10.0	0.00	0.0	0.02	**0.3**	-0.1	-0.38	-3.28	3.77	123.8	**5.9**	57.8	5.9	**5.2**
5.2	2.50	15.1	0.32	**2.9**	1.0	0.30	2.64	3.76	84.3	**2.0**	24.7	19.9	**6.5**
9.5	0.00	0.0	0.00	**0.9**	0.0	-0.13	-0.73	3.08	105.0	**6.7**	91.3	7.1	**7.1**
3.5	1.68	6.1	1.80	**2.7**	0.3	0.83	7.33	2.94	77.1	**6.2**	68.1	8.1	**6.1**
1.7	2.40	19.5	0.68	**6.8**	815.8	1.21	9.38	3.98	52.8	**4.2**	6.5	6.3	**8.9**
5.0	3.37	11.1	1.10	**1.5**	1.3	0.07	0.48	2.24	86.1	**3.0**	32.9	22.0	**8.5**
2.9	1.81	10.8	0.47	**4.8**	2.7	1.09	10.79	4.08	67.7	**2.7**	32.8	19.3	**5.6**
0.3	12.96	67.2	-1.30	**2.0**	0.3	0.41	4.03	2.78	87.7	**1.1**	27.5	47.9	**4.9**
5.4	2.19	12.6	0.00	**1.4**	-0.1	-0.15	-1.13	4.54	97.4	**4.4**	19.8	6.4	**5.9**
5.7	1.23	5.5	0.04	**7.4**	4.7	1.65	13.84	3.72	50.2	**3.9**	31.8	12.5	**6.9**
1.5	1.72	9.4	0.28	**3.5**	5.2	0.62	4.94	3.89	74.7	**1.9**	27.2	24.1	**6.8**
2.3	8.23	33.3	0.98	**2.5**	0.6	0.35	2.97	3.28	71.2	**4.2**	48.0	16.0	**5.8**
9.8	0.04	0.1	0.18	**3.5**	0.6	0.59	3.13	2.59	61.5	**4.6**	83.2	20.1	**8.1**
4.6	2.15	16.5	0.22	**2.0**	0.2	0.14	1.33	3.71	92.4	**3.6**	17.2	11.3	**5.3**
5.4	3.12	7.5	0.12	**2.8**	0.2	0.74	6.37	3.84	92.9	**6.5**	63.1	4.9	**6.3**
4.7	1.04	5.2	0.44	**5.2**	3.3	1.08	9.94	4.49	63.0	**1.8**	23.4	21.8	**6.3**
2.2	1.54	12.8	0.72	**4.0**	6.5	1.09	13.09	3.64	65.3	**2.5**	8.5	15.7	**3.7**
5.0	0.58	5.0	0.00	**5.2**	2.2	1.26	13.80	3.78	60.7	**2.3**	16.3	17.4	**6.6**
0.0	6.88	64.9	2.49	**0.3**	-3.4	-2.24	-29.58	3.97	93.0	**1.7**	11.1	20.3	**4.5**
0.0	5.44	43.2	1.79	**0.9**	0.2	0.05	0.72	3.72	66.3	**0.8**	12.6	34.5	**3.9**
5.9	0.65	4.2	0.21	**5.5**	2.5	1.14	11.78	3.90	54.2	**1.4**	23.7	29.2	**5.5**
1.9	3.15	21.4	0.40	**2.3**	1.2	0.50	6.44	3.52	80.8	**2.8**	33.7	19.1	**3.6**
4.9	0.82	4.3	0.17	**3.8**	0.8	0.66	6.92	3.31	69.8	**3.5**	33.8	15.2	**5.2**
5.2	1.23	7.6	-0.02	**9.3**	4.6	2.08	21.76	4.08	44.0	**2.3**	28.9	19.8	**7.7**

Name	City	State	Rating	2008 Rating	2007 Rating	Total Assets ($Mil)	One Year Asset Growth	Asset Mix (As a % of Total Assets) Comm-ercial Loans	Cons-umer Loans	Home Mort-gages	Secur-ities	Capital-ization Index	Leverage Ratio	Risk-based Capital Ratio
▼MARION NATIONAL BK	MARION	KS	**D**	C-	C+	27	38.07	7.6	3.4	12.2	36.4	**5.3**	7.3	13.4
MARION STATE BK	MARION	LA	**C+**	C+	C+	129	-0.91	7.4	11.3	24.4	14.0	**7.0**	9.0	14.4
MARION STATE BK	MARION	TX	**A-**	A-	B+	62	7.77	5.8	7.0	3.6	62.6	**10.0**	13.8	28.9
MARKESAN STATE BK	MARKESAN	WI	**C+**	A-	A-	132	9.88	6.5	5.4	6.8	13.7	**8.8**	11.1	14.0
MARKLEBANK	MARKLE	IN	**C+**	C	C-	327	6.34	10.2	1.5	16.8	16.4	**6.2**	8.2	12.4
MARLBOROUGH SB	MARLBOROUGH	MA	**C+**	C+	C+	440	9.89	1.8	0.6	32.3	22.6	**8.2**	9.8	18.0
MARLIN BUSINESS BANK	SALT LAKE CITY	UT	**B+**	B+	B+	124	19.07	0.1	0.0	0.0	5.1	**10.0**	16.6	18.7
MAROA FORSYTH COMMUNITY	MAROA	IL	**B**	B-	B-	20	-4.96	5.6	6.2	17.6	43.6	**10.0**	12.0	17.9
MARQUETTE BANK	ORLAND PARK	IL	**D**	C-	C+	1,730	-3.82	0.8	0.1	18.3	27.9	**6.5**	8.5	14.2
MARQUETTE FARMERS STATE	MARQUETTE	KS	**C**	C	C-	30	2.73	7.2	6.5	16.8	25.1	**10.0**	13.3	24.4
MARQUETTE SB	ERIE	PA	**A-**	B	B	718	10.24	1.0	1.0	49.5	33.5	**10.0**	13.7	25.9
MARQUIS BANK	NORTH MIAMI BEACH	FL	**D**	D	C-	89	69.96	8.2	0.1	4.6	4.4	**10.0**	23.1	29.0
MARS NATIONAL BK	MARS	PA	**B-**	B-	B+	332	3.58	3.5	2.2	16.0	41.0	**8.4**	10.0	20.0
MARSEILLES BANK	MARSEILLES	IL	**B-**	B-	C+	40	10.87	0.2	7.3	37.0	39.1	**6.4**	8.4	18.4
MARSHALL & ILSLEY TRUST C	MILWAUKEE	WI	**U**	U	U	172	18.06	0.0	0.0	0.0	35.7	**10.0**	58.1	68.8
MARSHALL COUNTY STATE BK	VARNA	IL	**D**	D	D+	26	4.92	7.5	3.7	15.1	17.0	**10.0**	11.9	21.0
MARSHALL COUNTY STATE BK	NEWFOLDEN	MN	**B+**	B+	B+	27	-1.71	4.7	5.6	12.2	17.3	**10.0**	19.5	55.7
MARTHAS VINEYARD SB	EDGARTOWN	MA	**A-**	B+	B	498	2.87	8.9	0.5	48.4	10.3	**10.0**	11.7	20.4
MARTINSBURG BANK & TRUST	MEXICO	MO	**A-**	B+	A-	183	1.08	8.9	1.3	15.5	21.6	**10.0**	11.0	15.7
MARTINSVILLE FIRST SAVING	MARTINSVILLE	VA	**D**	D+	B-	47	3.21	0.0	0.3	55.4	22.9	**9.7**	10.8	24.5
MARYLAND BANK & TRUST CO	LEXINGTON PARK	MD	**D-**	D-	C-	348	-0.35	5.2	1.4	19.0	20.6	**6.8**	8.8	15.1
MARYLAND FINANCIAL BANK	TOWSON	MD	**D-**	D	D-	78	-6.55	5.6	4.3	5.4	6.6	**6.4**	8.4	12.2
MASCOMA SAVINGS BANK	LEBANON	NH	**B-**	B-	C+	998	9.78	6.7	2.0	36.0	20.3	**7.4**	9.2	15.2
MASON CITY NATIONAL BK	MASON CITY	IL	**B+**	B+	B	68	1.72	1.3	2.8	14.3	39.2	**10.0**	14.5	32.1
▲MASON NATIONAL BK	MASON	TX	**A-**	B+	A-	91	-2.35	5.2	8.3	11.1	49.2	**10.0**	13.7	29.2
MASON STATE BK	MASON	MI	**C-**	C+	B	123	-5.71	5.5	0.4	47.1	11.4	**8.3**	9.9	18.3
MASPETH FS&LA	MASPETH	NY	**B+**	A-	A	1,699	7.67	0.5	0.0	64.5	0.9	**10.0**	25.4	40.5
▼MASSENA SAVINGS & LOAN	MASSENA	NY	**C+**	B-	B-	139	0.30	1.1	9.9	64.4	0.0	**8.4**	9.9	17.4
▼MASSMUTUAL TRUST CO FSB	ENFIELD	CT	**C+**	B-	B-	17	-9.25	0.0	0.0	0.0	79.1	**10.0**	84.7	461.8
MAUCH CHUNK TRUST CO	JIM THORPE	PA	**B-**	C	C+	302	1.05	3.4	1.4	17.8	46.9	**7.4**	9.2	15.8
MAXWELL STATE BK	MAXWELL	IA	**A**	A	A	25	3.43	3.7	1.4	8.4	46.8	**9.2**	10.5	19.6
MAYFLOWER CO-OP BANK	MIDDLEBORO	MA	**C+**	C	C	242	-0.71	2.2	0.6	26.3	36.1	**6.2**	8.2	16.5
MAYNARD SB	MAYNARD	IA	**A**	A	A-	47	0.85	4.2	6.9	18.5	24.3	**10.0**	13.2	18.6
MAYVILLE SB	MAYVILLE	WI	**D+**	C-	D+	55	10.89	7.1	3.4	56.2	2.0	**7.2**	9.2	16.0
MAYVILLE STATE BK	MAYVILLE	MI	**B-**	B	B	89	3.20	0.7	1.9	47.0	26.3	**8.2**	9.8	20.1
MAZON STATE BK	MAZON	IL	**C-**	D+	E+	80	3.75	3.1	1.6	29.8	19.8	**6.5**	8.5	14.0
MB FINANCIAL BANK NA	CHICAGO	IL	**D**	D	C+	10,248	-5.45	21.1	2.2	5.0	15.5	**7.3**	9.2	15.6
MBANK	MANISTIQUE	MI	**D**	D	D	479	-7.10	13.0	1.1	12.7	7.1	**5.2**	8.1	11.2
MBANK	GRESHAM	OR	**E-**	E-	D-	209	-17.72	3.3	1.0	12.8	19.6	**0.6**	4.4	7.2
MBL BANK	MINDEN	LA	**B-**	C-	A-	247	17.27	4.9	7.5	21.5	25.3	**7.6**	9.4	20.3
MCCLAIN BANK	PURCELL	OK	**D+**	C+	C+	163	-8.57	5.8	5.3	20.9	29.0	**8.7**	10.1	18.6
▼MCCLAVE STATE BK	MCCLAVE	CO	**E+**	E	D-	21	4.67	8.7	2.2	5.7	21.2	**5.6**	7.6	12.4
MCCOOK NATIONAL BK	MCCOOK	NE	**B**	B	A	269	7.71	5.2	1.6	5.4	30.9	**10.0**	13.7	19.2
MCCURTAIN COUNTY	BROKEN BOW	OK	**B-**	B-	C+	156	9.46	3.9	13.4	21.2	11.0	**7.4**	9.3	13.4
MCFARLAND STATE BK	MCFARLAND	WI	**C-**	B-	B-	355	-2.35	6.8	0.4	12.3	1.1	**9.1**	10.4	15.3
▲MCGEHEE BANK	MCGEHEE	AR	**A**	A	A	111	-4.64	10.9	1.0	3.0	13.8	**10.0**	14.4	16.2
MCHENRY SB	MCHENRY	IL	**E-**	D-	D-	302	8.43	9.3	9.7	28.8	16.4	**1.9**	5.0	8.9
MCINTOSH COUNTY BANK	ASHLEY	ND	**D**	C	C	80	7.76	3.7	2.0	1.6	30.8	**6.9**	8.9	14.8
MCINTOSH STATE BK	JACKSON	GA	**E-**	E-	E+	342	-16.42	3.0	1.9	15.1	11.4	**0.0**	2.1	4.3
MCKENZIE BANKING CO	MCKENZIE	TN	**B**	B	B	115	2.91	3.7	6.9	23.0	5.9	**10.0**	12.5	26.9
▼MCKENZIE COUNTY BANK	WATFORD CITY	ND	**B-**	B	B+	83	28.81	9.2	8.4	16.1	28.7	**5.5**	7.5	13.1
MCNB BANK & TRUST CO	WELCH	WV	**C**	C	C	325	8.25	3.2	2.4	13.8	21.8	**6.0**	8.1	12.4
▲MCVILLE STATE BK	MCVILLE	ND	**D+**	D-	D	37	8.77	14.5	5.2	4.5	6.0	**5.8**	8.1	11.6
MEADE COUNTY BANK	BRANDENBURG	KY	**A-**	A-	A-	136	10.24	0.3	3.9	40.6	23.0	**8.5**	10.0	20.4
MEADOWS BANK	LAS VEGAS	NV	**C-**	C	C	207	50.97	21.7	0.1	1.0	14.6	**10.0**	18.2	22.8
MECHANICS & FARMERS	DURHAM	NC	**D-**	D+	D+	312	14.03	3.1	0.7	11.1	6.6	**9.1**	10.4	16.8
MECHANICS BANK	RICHMOND	CA	**C-**	C	B	2,892	-1.81	6.7	2.9	5.5	25.5	**8.4**	9.9	15.3
MECHANICS BANK	WATER VALLEY	MS	**C+**	C	C	194	-1.80	8.5	4.8	24.0	20.9	**6.5**	8.5	14.1
MECHANICS BANK	MANSFIELD	OH	**B-**	B-	B	361	2.74	1.5	1.3	64.0	8.6	**8.0**	9.7	20.8
MECHANICS CO-OP BANK	TAUNTON	MA	**C**	C	C+	369	-1.17	3.2	4.1	27.7	29.9	**5.7**	7.7	13.3

Asset Quality Index	Non-Performing Loans as a % of Total Loans	Non-Performing Loans as a % of Capital	Net Charge-offs / Avg Loans	Profitability Index	Net Income ($Mil)	Return on Assets (R.O.A.)	Return on Equity (R.O.E.)	Net Interest Spread	Overhead Efficiency Ratio	Liquidity Index	Liquidity Ratio	Hot Money Ratio	Stability Index
6.4	0.00	0.0	0.04	**1.1**	0.0	-0.10	-0.83	4.53	108.0	**4.2**	37.0	13.2	**5.8**
3.8	1.58	11.1	0.60	**3.8**	0.8	0.59	6.74	4.44	75.4	**1.1**	13.8	30.4	**4.8**
8.1	1.86	3.8	0.86	**7.2**	1.2	1.89	12.83	4.31	55.5	**2.9**	57.4	30.8	**8.1**
2.8	2.74	17.6	0.31	**6.2**	1.3	1.04	8.94	4.39	56.8	**2.3**	23.2	18.4	**7.9**
2.9	0.96	7.7	0.48	**4.9**	3.1	0.98	7.55	3.99	61.8	**1.5**	15.3	24.3	**6.5**
5.3	1.79	9.6	0.02	**3.9**	2.6	0.62	6.32	3.35	67.0	**3.1**	42.3	20.0	**5.8**
8.9	0.28	1.5	1.32	**10.0**	4.1	3.52	22.75	11.37	39.9	**0.3**	10.0	87.6	**6.7**
3.5	3.67	13.5	0.64	**3.1**	0.1	0.44	3.23	4.28	85.2	**3.4**	29.9	13.1	**6.8**
1.7	3.63	22.5	1.72	**0.8**	0.3	0.02	0.17	3.49	77.8	**4.4**	25.6	10.6	**7.0**
3.0	4.15	16.2	0.08	**2.5**	0.1	0.24	1.74	3.49	89.3	**2.7**	47.4	27.9	**7.0**
6.6	2.11	9.1	0.02	**5.5**	7.2	1.05	7.27	3.33	52.2	**3.5**	38.7	16.9	**8.3**
3.0	3.08	9.1	0.92	**0.0**	-1.9	-2.69	-10.36	3.29	114.8	**2.4**	32.8	21.1	**1.5**
5.5	1.89	7.9	0.06	**3.4**	1.6	0.47	4.35	3.58	85.8	**5.6**	43.1	7.2	**6.4**
7.1	0.44	2.6	0.54	**7.9**	0.7	1.72	18.93	4.77	60.2	**3.0**	45.4	22.9	**5.7**
6.5	0.00	0.0	0.00	**9.5**	18.2	11.82	17.01	1.40	87.0	**3.5**	101.7	101.0	**2.3**
3.2	3.67	14.9	-0.04	**0.0**	-0.2	-0.72	-5.08	2.87	123.5	**3.8**	47.0	17.4	**4.8**
9.1	0.06	0.1	-0.06	**4.8**	0.3	1.05	5.13	2.73	61.4	**6.6**	68.4	5.4	**9.6**
6.7	1.15	7.0	0.04	**5.8**	4.6	0.93	7.72	4.35	66.2	**3.2**	23.3	13.6	**7.8**
8.7	0.33	2.0	0.23	**5.8**	2.6	1.50	13.73	3.97	64.4	**3.0**	15.7	14.1	**7.0**
1.3	9.24	48.6	0.00	**0.9**	-0.2	-0.40	-3.55	3.04	98.5	**2.3**	41.8	30.9	**5.6**
1.1	6.50	38.4	1.41	**0.3**	-0.9	-0.25	-2.94	4.18	94.1	**3.0**	25.2	14.9	**4.0**
0.0	6.77	49.8	2.61	**0.4**	-0.3	-0.32	-4.02	2.83	75.1	**0.9**	27.7	75.6	**4.0**
5.1	0.49	3.5	0.10	**3.8**	6.6	0.70	7.27	3.51	74.0	**3.7**	26.0	11.6	**6.2**
9.1	0.64	1.9	0.05	**4.0**	0.6	0.88	5.86	2.92	71.1	**4.6**	57.7	15.1	**8.2**
6.5	0.13	0.4	0.34	**8.7**	1.8	1.96	12.42	4.10	53.0	**3.4**	53.2	20.5	**10.0**
3.4	2.79	19.0	0.17	**2.3**	0.3	0.24	2.34	2.73	86.6	**0.8**	18.3	37.9	**5.3**
3.1	6.08	21.2	-0.02	**7.0**	26.2	1.60	6.25	4.76	29.4	**2.3**	9.5	17.3	**10.0**
4.0	1.73	14.2	0.00	**3.4**	0.7	0.52	5.42	3.20	63.3	**1.9**	11.9	19.2	**5.4**
8.1	0.00	0.0	0.00	**4.4**	0.1	0.57	0.67	3.06	97.7	**10.0**	639.6	0.0	**0.9**
3.7	3.56	15.4	0.47	**4.4**	2.4	0.81	8.14	3.95	64.3	**3.7**	22.5	11.3	**5.2**
9.2	0.00	0.0	0.00	**8.6**	0.5	1.89	14.90	5.00	40.8	**4.2**	58.9	15.5	**8.4**
6.4	0.88	5.3	0.22	**3.5**	1.3	0.52	6.22	3.89	79.2	**3.9**	42.4	16.1	**4.6**
7.6	0.43	2.2	0.09	**9.1**	1.0	2.04	15.06	5.03	48.8	**4.5**	30.0	8.9	**8.5**
4.4	0.80	6.8	0.02	**1.8**	0.1	0.20	2.11	3.28	89.8	**1.4**	13.8	24.9	**4.6**
4.5	1.15	6.7	0.77	**3.6**	0.6	0.63	6.25	3.43	71.3	**5.0**	39.3	9.4	**6.1**
5.6	0.66	3.9	0.36	**2.3**	0.5	0.61	7.37	4.11	89.4	**3.7**	23.6	11.5	**4.1**
0.0	6.84	40.7	3.44	**1.2**	21.0	0.20	1.62	3.92	54.7	**1.8**	17.5	22.1	**6.5**
0.8	1.55	13.1	1.35	**1.0**	0.1	0.02	0.17	3.76	82.3	**1.4**	12.8	25.0	**5.0**
0.0	18.86	177.8	1.54	**0.0**	-3.1	-1.36	-26.93	2.92	141.2	**0.9**	20.6	40.2	**1.2**
6.5	0.39	2.1	0.07	**4.5**	2.3	1.08	10.17	3.54	51.5	**4.3**	49.8	16.0	**5.2**
1.7	6.44	31.6	0.47	**4.2**	1.2	0.72	7.19	4.64	75.4	**3.6**	20.6	11.3	**3.8**
4.5	0.44	3.1	1.50	**1.0**	0.1	0.23	2.53	4.64	88.6	**0.7**	17.1	40.5	**3.0**
4.8	1.99	8.4	0.25	**5.9**	2.8	1.10	7.54	3.67	56.2	**2.4**	24.0	17.8	**6.9**
4.3	1.01	7.3	0.02	**7.2**	1.8	1.27	14.03	4.54	57.2	**1.6**	16.9	24.0	**4.9**
2.3	0.41	3.1	0.04	**7.8**	7.0	1.92	19.26	3.62	46.2	**0.9**	6.9	31.5	**8.2**
8.6	0.08	0.3	0.02	**6.6**	1.8	1.54	10.74	3.97	63.3	**3.0**	43.7	23.0	**8.6**
0.3	6.57	71.5	1.74	**0.2**	-3.3	-1.16	-22.24	4.05	85.5	**1.0**	22.4	33.9	**0.0**
2.8	3.09	16.0	0.34	**6.3**	1.1	1.46	14.38	3.67	58.4	**3.1**	29.2	15.8	**5.4**
0.0	24.43	334.5	2.58	**0.0**	-12.1	-3.23	-107.88	2.45	141.7	**1.1**	13.4	29.4	**0.1**
4.0	4.88	17.0	0.18	**8.0**	1.6	1.36	10.81	5.25	68.3	**4.9**	56.2	14.7	**7.1**
4.1	0.94	6.6	1.53	**7.4**	1.1	1.58	18.80	4.86	48.8	**1.7**	25.2	24.3	**5.7**
3.1	0.99	7.2	0.10	**3.1**	1.6	0.51	6.28	3.36	77.2	**2.0**	24.8	20.5	**4.5**
3.3	0.22	2.0	0.10	**3.3**	0.2	0.70	7.51	4.27	78.6	**1.5**	13.4	24.7	**3.0**
8.3	0.05	0.3	0.15	**9.3**	2.0	1.50	14.81	4.36	50.1	**4.0**	28.5	11.0	**6.6**
7.0	0.80	2.9	0.49	**0.6**	0.3	0.19	0.93	4.50	78.3	**4.3**	34.2	11.4	**2.1**
0.0	8.09	46.7	0.11	**2.4**	0.9	0.32	2.78	4.16	86.0	**1.5**	34.1	43.5	**5.1**
1.7	2.52	14.0	1.38	**2.4**	11.0	0.38	3.75	4.39	72.9	**2.9**	22.6	16.6	**6.7**
4.9	0.71	4.9	0.32	**4.0**	1.8	0.88	10.20	4.08	74.5	**1.1**	20.8	32.2	**4.0**
4.2	1.35	9.8	0.18	**4.2**	2.2	0.61	6.40	3.83	72.7	**3.8**	20.2	10.3	**5.4**
5.1	1.54	11.4	0.07	**3.2**	2.1	0.57	7.31	3.13	74.5	**1.5**	23.6	26.9	**3.8**

Name	City	State	Rating	2008 Rating	2007 Rating	Total Assets ($Mil)	One Year Asset Growth	Asset Mix (As a % of Total Assets) Comm-ercial Loans	Cons-umer Loans	Home Mort-gages	Secur-ities	Capital-ization Index	Leverage Ratio	Risk-based Capital Ratio
MECHANICS SB	AUBURN	ME	**C-**	C-	C-	304	14.28	8.0	3.0	54.3	6.3	**9.9**	10.9	15.6
MEDALLION BANK	SALT LAKE CITY	UT	**A-**	B	B+	569	22.25	56.5	34.2	0.0	3.7	**10.0**	17.0	18.5
MEDIAPOLIS SB	MEDIAPOLIS	IA	**C+**	C+	C	126	-0.95	9.0	3.5	17.0	23.0	**6.1**	8.3	11.8
MEDINA BANKING CO	MEDINA	TN	**B**	B-	B	37	5.35	10.4	6.5	5.9	52.1	**10.0**	15.7	33.1
▲ MEDINA SAVINGS & LOAN ASS	MEDINA	NY	**C+**	C-	C-	37	1.76	2.6	5.6	38.1	30.3	**10.0**	11.9	27.5
MEETINGHOUSE BANK	DORCHESTER	MA	**C-**	D+	D	63	5.10	1.3	0.9	54.7	10.1	**5.8**	7.8	12.8
▲ MEGA BANK	SAN GABRIEL	CA	**C-**	C-	D	165	18.42	7.5	0.0	1.6	9.3	**10.0**	11.9	15.7
MELROSE CO-OP BANK	MELROSE	MA	**C+**	C+	B-	165	14.22	0.0	0.3	58.1	13.9	**9.5**	10.7	19.3
MELVIN SB	MELVIN	IA	**B+**	B+	B+	53	-1.84	8.7	3.9	5.8	47.5	**10.0**	20.0	29.9
▼ MEMBERS TRUST CO	TAMPA	FL	**C-**	C	C	25	-2.05	0.0	0.0	0.0	85.5	**10.0**	93.7	456.1
MEMORIAL CITY BANK	HOUSTON	TX	**C-**	C	C	165	19.16	21.5	0.7	13.7	8.6	**10.0**	12.1	15.0
MEMPHIS STATE BK	MEMPHIS	TX	**B-**	B	B+	33	4.46	3.6	2.9	1.2	61.5	**9.1**	10.4	26.7
▼ MENARD NATIONAL BK	MENARD	TX	**B-**	B+	B	35	9.20	3.8	3.5	12.7	38.6	**10.0**	11.6	21.4
▼ MENNO STATE BK	MENNO	SD	**B**	B+	B	33	4.59	4.6	1.2	4.4	32.6	**8.0**	9.6	17.7
MER ROUGE STATE BK	MER ROUGE	LA	**B**	B	B	40	9.30	8.1	1.8	7.0	18.8	**10.0**	11.7	21.6
MERAMEC VALLEY BANK	VALLEY PARK	MO	**D-**	E	D+	116	-11.11	9.1	1.2	19.4	5.4	**5.8**	7.8	12.0
MERCANTIL COMMERCEBANK	CORAL GABLES	FL	**D-**	D-	D+	6,479	8.11	17.6	0.7	2.6	34.9	**7.0**	9.0	18.1
MERCANTIL COMMERCEBANK	CORAL GABLES	FL	**U**	U	U	8	12.91	0.0	0.0	0.0	46.4	**10.0**	91.9	318.2
▼ MERCANTILE BANK	QUINCY	IL	**D-**	D+	C-	684	-13.75	15.4	8.7	18.2	14.3	**4.8**	7.1	10.9
▲ MERCANTILE BANK & TRUST C	BOSTON	MA	**B+**	B-	C-	167	1.26	53.0	0.2	6.7	3.4	**8.1**	10.4	13.4
MERCANTILE BANK OF MICHIG	GRAND RAPIDS	MI	**D-**	D-	D+	1,631	-14.35	15.5	0.4	4.2	13.5	**7.0**	9.1	12.5
MERCANTILE BK OF LOUISIAN	LOUISIANA	MO	**B+**	A-	A	105	2.92	5.9	1.5	28.8	15.7	**10.0**	21.2	28.5
MERCER COUNTY STATE BK	SANDY LAKE	PA	**B-**	C+	B-	287	3.19	4.6	4.0	21.4	36.0	**7.0**	9.0	15.5
MERCER SAVINGS BANK	CELINA	OH	**D+**	D+	C-	123	2.29	3.6	1.5	59.4	19.5	**6.3**	8.3	18.1
MERCHANTS & CITIZENS	MCRAE	GA	**C**	C+	C	97	-6.79	2.9	6.0	12.6	33.2	**10.0**	11.2	20.1
▼ MERCHANTS & FARMERS	EUTAW	AL	**C-**	C	B-	55	10.10	7.3	7.5	11.0	39.6	**7.5**	9.3	19.1
MERCHANTS & FARMERS	DUMAS	AR	**C**	C	C-	87	-0.99	10.5	3.1	6.0	28.3	**6.5**	8.5	16.3
MERCHANTS & FARMERS	MELVILLE	LA	**D**	D	D+	8	-6.83	1.8	5.9	20.3	9.7	**10.0**	11.3	39.6
MERCHANTS & FARMERS	SALISBURY	MO	**D+**	D+	C-	104	-0.12	4.9	1.5	18.0	28.5	**7.0**	9.0	15.3
▼ MERCHANTS & FARMERS	HOLLY SPRINGS	MS	**C-**	B-	C+	83	5.26	5.5	7.9	20.3	26.6	**9.0**	10.4	16.8
MERCHANTS & FARMERS	KOSCIUSKO	MS	**D**	D-	B-	1,599	-3.72	7.5	2.8	12.6	17.3	**5.3**	7.7	11.2
MERCHANTS & FARMERS	LEESVILLE	LA	**B+**	B+	A	254	5.75	4.9	2.4	13.2	45.8	**10.0**	14.0	26.6
MERCHANTS &	JOLIET	IL	**D+**	C	C-	160	1.68	27.0	16.8	4.9	9.7	**6.1**	8.6	11.8
MERCHANTS & MARINE BANK	PASCAGOULA	MS	**B**	B+	A-	503	11.75	5.4	5.9	8.7	45.8	**10.0**	11.1	19.7
▼ MERCHANTS & PLANTERS	CLARENDON	AR	**C+**	B-	C+	42	1.55	5.4	4.1	5.3	52.3	**7.6**	9.4	23.8
MERCHANTS & PLANTERS	NEWPORT	AR	**C+**	C+	C	202	3.18	5.9	6.5	7.9	43.3	**5.6**	7.6	14.0
MERCHANTS & PLANTERS	RAYMOND	MS	**D**	C-	B	85	-3.25	4.5	3.8	12.0	22.0	**6.7**	8.7	16.7
▼ MERCHANTS & PLANTERS	BOLIVAR	TN	**C-**	C	D+	91	1.05	6.3	5.3	22.0	14.8	**8.1**	9.8	15.7
▼ MERCHANTS & SOUTHERN	GAINESVILLE	FL	**D-**	C-	C+	389	-3.49	3.7	0.8	8.3	16.6	**5.8**	7.8	11.7
MERCHANTS BANK	JACKSON	AL	**D+**	C-	C+	210	7.45	8.9	4.7	18.2	17.5	**6.6**	8.6	13.9
MERCHANTS BANK	RUGBY	ND	**C+**	C+	B-	49	10.05	9.0	4.0	3.3	34.8	**6.0**	8.0	12.5
MERCHANTS BANK	SOUTH BURLINGTON	VT	**B**	B	B	1,491	3.62	6.1	0.4	25.5	31.3	**5.7**	7.7	15.7
MERCHANTS BANK & TRUST	WEST HARRISON	IN	**C**	C-	C-	216	-7.03	7.1	0.7	26.0	9.2	**7.6**	9.4	14.1
▲ MERCHANTS BANK NA	WINONA	MN	**C+**	C-	C	1,152	5.73	13.0	3.7	9.2	16.3	**8.5**	10.0	14.4
MERCHANTS BANK OF	CULLMAN	AL	**D-**	D-	D	248	1.30	9.8	4.4	22.1	13.0	**5.6**	7.6	11.7
MERCHANTS BANK OF	BANGOR	PA	**C**	C-	C	293	1.49	2.7	1.1	27.0	34.3	**7.0**	9.0	17.5
MERCHANTS BANK OF	LYNN	IN	**A-**	B+	A	432	10.20	7.4	1.4	0.9	33.0	**10.0**	11.9	17.6
▼ MERCHANTS BK OF	CARSON	CA	**C-**	C+	B+	87	14.00	18.1	0.3	2.3	5.6	**10.0**	14.5	24.6
MERCHANTS COMMERCIAL	SAINT THOMAS	VI	**D**	B-	C	84	-0.17	8.2	1.2	37.5	4.0	**10.0**	15.0	22.4
MERCHANTS NATIONAL BK	HILLSBORO	OH	**C-**	C	B-	569	4.28	5.2	4.0	28.7	10.6	**5.7**	7.7	11.8
MERCHANTS NB OF	SACRAMENTO	CA	**B**	B	B	173	5.98	1.2	0.3	13.0	60.7	**6.9**	8.9	25.1
MERCHANTS STATE BK	FREEMAN	SD	**C**	C	C-	126	2.87	6.7	1.8	3.3	26.7	**5.5**	8.0	11.4
MEREDITH VILLAGE SB	MEREDITH	NH	**B-**	C+	C+	622	3.32	3.8	4.5	33.2	11.2	**9.5**	10.7	15.9
MERIDIAN BANK	DEVON	PA	**D+**	D+	D+	369	26.38	12.9	0.7	22.0	3.3	**5.0**	8.4	11.0
MERIDIAN BANK NA	WICKENBURG	AZ	**D**	D-	D+	1,255	-22.03	34.9	0.1	0.9	26.5	**10.0**	12.2	17.4
MERIDIAN BANK TEXAS	FORT WORTH	TX	**D+**	C-	C-	240	5.31	18.5	1.3	2.6	23.5	**10.0**	12.1	16.8
▼ MERIT BANK	GOFF	KS	**D+**	C-	C-	54	16.93	18.3	3.9	40.0	4.9	**6.3**	8.3	14.1
MERRICK BANK	SOUTH JORDAN	UT	**C-**	C-	C-	1,117	-0.18	0.6	89.1	0.0	3.7	**10.0**	21.8	25.9
MERRILL FS&LA	MERRILL	WI	**C+**	C	C	41	6.94	10.1	5.2	43.9	0.0	**9.7**	10.8	19.9
MERRIMAC SB	MERRIMAC	MA	**D-**	D	E-	63	2.66	3.9	4.1	47.7	22.5	**4.0**	6.0	11.6

Asset Quality Index	Non-Performing Loans as a % of Total Loans	Non-Performing Loans as a % of Capital	Net Charge-offs Avg Loans	Profitability Index	Net Income ($Mil)	Return on Assets (R.O.A.)	Return on Equity (R.O.E.)	Net Interest Spread	Overhead Efficiency Ratio	Liquidity Index	Liquidity Ratio	Hot Money Ratio	Stability Index
1.4	4.59	30.8	0.36	**2.7**	1.0	0.35	2.98	4.48	75.3	**1.2**	7.6	26.3	**6.1**
5.6	0.61	3.0	2.53	**10.0**	11.2	2.20	12.27	7.83	26.5	**0.2**	8.0	100.0	**8.7**
3.8	1.32	10.2	0.51	**4.7**	1.3	1.04	12.16	3.89	53.0	**1.6**	20.7	23.9	**5.2**
5.8	5.10	10.1	0.49	**4.2**	0.3	0.82	4.84	4.32	75.6	**5.3**	76.9	14.5	**7.6**
6.3	1.56	6.4	-0.02	**4.5**	0.5	1.22	13.16	3.71	69.8	**6.0**	45.7	4.6	**3.9**
5.1	1.39	12.5	0.00	**4.2**	0.5	0.82	10.71	3.86	76.7	**1.0**	23.9	34.9	**4.3**
6.4	0.74	4.5	0.14	**1.9**	1.7	1.06	9.09	3.63	74.7	**0.7**	12.3	38.3	**3.6**
9.6	0.09	0.5	0.01	**3.5**	0.8	0.54	4.87	2.70	65.6	**2.7**	32.0	18.6	**5.2**
8.9	0.09	0.2	-0.71	**4.3**	0.4	0.83	4.02	3.45	67.4	**6.0**	75.2	10.8	**7.2**
8.8	0.00	0.0	0.00	**1.0**	0.0	0.05	0.06	3.05	99.8	**10.0**	1,530.5	0.0	**0.3**
8.6	0.00	0.0	0.11	**1.6**	0.7	0.50	3.88	4.04	85.2	**0.9**	22.2	38.4	**3.2**
8.4	0.00	0.0	0.03	**2.8**	0.2	0.79	6.33	3.04	91.5	**3.8**	49.4	17.5	**5.7**
7.4	0.00	0.0	0.02	**3.0**	0.1	0.26	2.12	3.99	90.0	**2.2**	46.1	38.1	**7.2**
8.2	0.70	2.6	0.22	**5.5**	0.3	0.96	8.69	3.59	59.6	**6.4**	57.8	4.6	**6.6**
6.3	0.68	2.5	0.43	**5.4**	0.4	1.06	8.25	4.70	69.3	**2.8**	45.7	26.0	**7.4**
1.8	2.88	21.1	0.94	**0.8**	0.1	0.08	1.09	3.94	109.5	**1.2**	14.2	29.3	**2.2**
0.3	8.27	47.5	2.56	**0.4**	1.2	0.02	0.18	2.37	72.9	**3.8**	25.5	13.8	**5.6**
10.0	0.00	0.0	0.00	**10.0**	0.8	10.64	11.19	2.57	51.9	**5.0**	4,048.3	101.0	**2.3**
1.0	4.20	32.8	2.18	**0.2**	-12.3	-1.69	-20.64	3.33	71.8	**0.9**	20.7	35.3	**3.1**
7.9	0.00	0.0	0.09	**6.1**	1.7	1.02	10.04	4.56	61.7	**1.3**	5.1	24.3	**5.8**
0.1	5.01	31.3	2.43	**0.0**	-11.0	-0.60	-6.56	3.43	67.0	**0.5**	6.0	55.7	**5.4**
3.7	0.78	2.5	0.59	**5.9**	1.2	1.19	5.27	4.29	48.5	**1.1**	20.7	32.0	**7.4**
4.6	1.83	10.1	0.21	**3.5**	1.8	0.62	6.15	3.80	76.2	**2.6**	32.9	19.6	**5.5**
2.7	2.75	22.0	0.09	**1.0**	-0.2	-0.17	-2.09	3.21	100.6	**4.0**	26.0	10.2	**3.2**
2.5	4.92	18.7	1.97	**2.5**	0.5	0.48	3.43	4.56	77.8	**2.2**	32.5	24.7	**6.0**
3.0	3.70	18.4	0.65	**2.2**	0.0	0.03	0.34	4.02	89.3	**3.9**	26.0	10.8	**3.8**
6.0	0.65	3.0	0.00	**3.6**	0.6	0.69	8.02	3.89	84.3	**2.8**	32.0	18.4	**4.2**
4.3	4.39	11.5	0.05	**0.0**	-0.1	-0.98	-8.70	3.64	122.3	**6.4**	67.6	4.3	**4.6**
1.7	1.06	6.5	0.36	**3.7**	1.0	0.97	11.07	3.87	66.2	**2.3**	29.9	20.6	**3.3**
2.3	4.01	20.6	0.25	**5.1**	1.0	1.15	10.59	4.66	71.9	**1.3**	25.1	30.4	**6.4**
0.9	3.20	25.2	1.63	**1.6**	5.4	0.34	4.04	3.54	78.9	**2.0**	13.6	19.1	**4.3**
8.9	0.67	2.2	0.37	**4.6**	2.3	0.92	6.70	4.27	75.2	**2.7**	40.6	24.9	**8.4**
4.1	0.65	5.6	1.21	**1.7**	0.2	0.10	1.21	4.18	76.8	**1.5**	4.9	21.9	**4.1**
5.4	1.83	6.9	0.40	**5.0**	5.0	1.01	9.59	3.82	69.8	**2.8**	27.1	16.5	**6.6**
5.5	2.56	7.7	0.14	**4.0**	0.4	0.85	7.97	3.42	70.4	**2.7**	44.4	26.4	**4.9**
5.2	1.70	9.1	0.33	**4.4**	1.5	0.77	10.04	3.94	74.9	**2.2**	34.2	26.3	**3.6**
4.7	2.63	10.3	5.49	**0.4**	-2.1	-2.30	-22.30	3.67	95.9	**2.5**	36.6	23.4	**5.2**
7.0	0.21	1.4	0.20	**2.3**	0.7	0.70	6.54	4.29	86.0	**1.8**	19.9	21.3	**4.4**
0.0	4.36	30.5	1.35	**1.3**	-1.4	-0.34	-4.02	3.87	73.1	**2.3**	17.6	17.7	**5.5**
2.4	2.90	19.6	0.87	**3.3**	1.1	0.55	6.15	4.07	72.6	**1.3**	25.2	30.9	**5.1**
8.6	0.00	0.0	0.16	**5.6**	0.5	1.00	10.80	4.51	63.0	**4.6**	32.7	9.4	**5.0**
6.9	0.41	3.0	-0.09	**5.4**	16.6	1.15	14.47	3.77	71.2	**3.6**	18.5	11.7	**7.5**
2.9	3.51	27.7	0.68	**3.2**	1.3	0.56	6.34	3.99	75.2	**3.7**	13.2	10.2	**3.4**
3.7	1.42	7.9	0.63	**5.3**	11.0	0.99	8.58	3.84	62.1	**2.9**	13.9	14.6	**9.4**
0.3	5.42	44.3	1.02	**2.3**	0.7	0.26	3.52	4.13	74.2	**2.2**	13.3	18.0	**2.9**
5.7	1.95	10.5	0.16	**3.2**	1.4	0.47	5.14	3.68	79.4	**4.1**	29.3	11.0	**4.6**
5.0	1.27	5.2	0.05	**10.0**	24.3	6.65	52.35	2.77	23.5	**3.2**	25.6	14.4	**9.4**
0.9	11.47	37.6	3.00	**2.6**	0.1	0.13	0.85	4.84	80.0	**1.9**	42.0	57.0	**5.6**
0.0	15.34	83.4	0.71	**3.2**	0.4	0.45	2.97	4.27	80.4	**2.4**	11.0	16.5	**2.0**
2.0	1.98	18.1	0.25	**6.2**	6.2	1.11	14.48	4.16	56.7	**2.5**	9.9	15.9	**5.6**
8.6	0.00	0.0	0.00	**4.8**	1.7	1.01	10.36	3.66	60.1	**3.5**	62.0	28.4	**5.9**
3.7	1.13	8.6	0.42	**4.2**	1.1	0.89	11.33	4.47	68.8	**3.9**	3.2	7.5	**3.0**
4.2	0.71	4.8	0.56	**3.6**	4.3	0.71	6.32	4.39	77.5	**2.4**	8.5	16.6	**6.8**
2.6	1.89	18.2	0.86	**2.6**	1.1	0.33	3.53	3.93	68.3	**0.4**	4.2	53.1	**4.1**
1.2	6.30	25.8	4.10	**0.0**	-27.9	-1.82	-15.02	4.74	105.5	**2.0**	33.6	60.9	**5.2**
1.2	5.11	27.5	0.34	**2.9**	1.7	0.70	5.66	3.81	76.0	**1.3**	30.7	48.5	**3.8**
5.4	1.10	9.3	0.42	**2.2**	0.1	0.28	2.79	4.08	68.3	**1.9**	17.6	20.0	**6.1**
1.8	4.11	10.4	18.07	**7.3**	47.2	4.28	20.93	18.59	29.5	**0.5**	10.5	74.4	**9.1**
6.0	0.24	1.9	0.20	**3.7**	0.3	0.68	6.32	4.34	65.5	**0.6**	4.0	35.3	**6.0**
4.4	0.60	6.2	0.68	**3.1**	0.3	0.53	9.01	4.36	83.0	**3.1**	29.1	16.0	**2.3**

	Name	City	State	Rating	2008 Rating	2007 Rating	Total Assets ($Mil)	One Year Asset Growth	Asset Mix (As a % of Total Assets) Comm-ercial Loans	Cons-umer Loans	Home Mort-gages	Secur-ities	Capital-ization Index	Leverage Ratio	Risk-based Capital Ratio
▲	MERRIMACK COUNTY SB	CONCORD	NH	**C+**	C	B-	614	3.74	4.7	4.0	24.6	20.2	**6.5**	8.5	14.8
	METABANK	STORM LAKE	IA	**C-**	D-	D	1,128	23.18	4.0	2.3	4.2	46.2	**4.8**	6.8	19.7
	METAIRIE BANK & TRUST CO	METAIRIE	LA	**B**	B	B+	331	2.06	3.3	2.9	32.0	21.4	**10.0**	11.1	20.6
	METAMORA STATE BK	METAMORA	OH	**D**	D+	C-	63	3.60	11.0	1.7	37.9	16.2	**5.5**	7.5	14.7
	METCALF BANK	LEE'S SUMMIT	MO	**C-**	C+	C+	1,188	17.40	10.8	3.3	8.6	13.1	**6.3**	8.3	12.0
	METHUEN CO-OP BANK	METHUEN	MA	**C-**	C-	C	81	5.49	0.4	2.6	52.8	8.9	**9.1**	10.4	20.8
	METLIFE BANK NA	BRIDGEWATER	NJ	**D**	C+	C	16,310	15.62	8.1	0.0	28.8	42.8	**5.1**	7.1	15.0
	METRO BANK	PELL CITY	AL	**B**	C	B-	597	10.90	6.0	5.1	19.2	17.5	**9.5**	10.7	15.8
	METRO BANK	DOUGLASVILLE	GA	**C-**	C	C	126	1.64	4.1	0.4	6.4	17.4	**10.0**	15.2	19.8
	METRO BANK	LOUISVILLE	KY	**C-**	D	D+	36	10.61	12.3	0.0	5.6	17.9	**10.0**	13.4	27.2
	METRO BANK	LEMOYNE	PA	**D+**	C-	C-	2,229	3.86	11.0	0.5	13.7	29.7	**7.6**	9.4	14.1
	METRO CITY BANK	DORAVILLE	GA	**C**	B-	B-	369	13.62	3.8	0.9	0.6	6.1	**10.0**	13.1	16.1
	METRO PHOENIX BANK	PHOENIX	AZ	**D**	D	C-	69	-0.28	23.6	0.1	6.9	0.7	**10.0**	12.8	16.2
	METRO UNITED BANK	SAN DIEGO	CA	**D-**	D-	C-	411	-13.81	3.5	0.2	2.4	0.0	**9.1**	10.8	14.3
	METROBANK NA	HOUSTON	TX	**D-**	D	C-	1,151	2.93	6.7	0.2	1.2	15.6	**9.5**	10.7	14.9
	METROPOLITAN BANK	OAKLAND	CA	**D-**	D-	D+	149	-3.60	4.2	0.2	19.9	8.5	**7.9**	9.6	14.8
	METROPOLITAN BANK	RIDGELAND	MS	**D+**	C-	C-	506	32.75	17.8	3.7	9.3	21.2	**9.4**	10.9	14.5
	METROPOLITAN BANK &	CHICAGO	IL	**D-**	D-	D	307	-8.37	1.6	0.1	17.7	11.5	**7.1**	9.1	13.9
	METROPOLITAN CAPITAL	CHICAGO	IL	**D+**	C-	C-	144	12.78	28.4	0.4	13.0	12.3	**6.5**	8.9	12.2
	METROPOLITAN NATIONAL BK	LITTLE ROCK	AR	**E-**	E-	D+	1,296	-12.44	6.2	1.8	12.9	18.0	**2.0**	5.5	9.0
	METROPOLITAN NATIONAL BK	SPRINGFIELD	MO	**D+**	C-	B-	542	-4.37	6.4	1.7	25.9	17.9	**9.2**	10.5	17.8
	METROPOLITAN NATIONAL BK	NEW YORK	NY	**D-**	D	C-	578	-1.67	7.0	0.0	7.7	7.8	**9.2**	10.5	15.4
	METUCHEN SB	METUCHEN	NJ	**D+**	C-	C	290	-10.63	1.2	0.0	39.1	34.2	**6.9**	8.9	22.9
	METZ BANKING CO	NEVADA	MO	**B-**	B-	B-	60	-0.55	9.5	1.8	9.2	22.1	**7.5**	9.3	14.1
	MIAMI SAVINGS BANK	MIAMITOWN	OH	**C+**	C	C	119	4.06	6.1	0.7	38.5	0.0	**10.0**	11.0	18.4
	MICHIGAN COMMERCE BANK	ANN ARBOR	MI	**E-**	E+	C-	934	-14.30	13.0	0.4	13.7	0.6	**0.0**	1.2	2.8
▲	MID AMERICA BANK	LINN	MO	**C+**	C	C	246	21.09	8.3	3.2	27.9	16.5	**5.0**	7.0	11.2
▲	MID AMERICA BANK	JANESVILLE	WI	**C-**	D-	D	115	37.70	20.8	0.5	28.6	18.6	**8.4**	9.9	15.1
▲	MID AMERICA BANK & TRUST	DIXON	MO	**C-**	D	D-	119	15.94	10.1	2.3	23.5	10.5	**6.2**	8.4	11.9
▼	MID CITY BANK INC	OMAHA	NE	**E-**	D	D+	178	-20.52	32.1	2.1	4.2	24.1	**0.0**	3.0	7.2
	MID PENN BANK	MILLERSBURG	PA	**D**	D+	C-	637	5.19	8.1	0.6	13.1	11.1	**5.4**	7.4	11.5
	MID-AMERICA BANK	BALDWIN CITY	KS	**C+**	C	C	58	-2.11	2.5	1.8	43.0	1.8	**6.9**	8.9	12.9
▲	MID-CENTRAL FSB	WADENA	MN	**C**	C-	C-	100	-4.54	5.0	12.6	51.1	1.7	**5.3**	7.3	13.0
	MID-MISSOURI BANK	SPRINGFIELD	MO	**D+**	D	D-	481	-9.07	7.0	2.0	24.4	3.3	**7.8**	9.6	13.9
	MID-SOUTHERN SAVINGS	SALEM	IN	**C-**	C	B-	193	1.73	3.0	3.4	46.4	4.3	**9.0**	10.3	17.0
	MID-WISCONSIN BANK	MEDFORD	WI	**D+**	D	C-	506	0.78	6.0	1.2	17.4	20.0	**6.9**	9.0	13.9
	MIDAMERICA NATIONAL BK	CANTON	IL	**B+**	B+	B+	339	4.26	3.9	3.4	11.1	46.2	**10.0**	11.2	23.1
	MIDCAROLINA BANK	BURLINGTON	NC	**C**	B-	B-	532	-1.64	11.5	0.5	14.2	17.0	**7.1**	9.0	13.0
	MIDCOAST COMMUNITY BANK	WILMINGTON	DE	**C-**	C-	C-	192	16.82	11.6	0.2	15.9	4.1	**8.3**	10.6	13.6
	MIDCOUNTRY BANK	MARION	IL	**D-**	D-	D-	711	-14.66	17.5	2.5	22.0	13.4	**9.3**	10.5	16.7
	MIDDLEBURG BANK	MIDDLEBURG	VA	**D+**	C+	C+	1,098	13.15	5.1	1.1	22.9	22.9	**6.6**	8.6	13.5
	MIDDLEFIELD BANKING CO	MIDDLEFIELD	OH	**D+**	C-	C+	550	14.12	8.8	0.8	25.0	35.1	**4.1**	6.1	11.5
	MIDDLESEX FEDERAL	SOMERVILLE	MA	**D-**	D	C-	373	-7.29	0.0	0.1	33.8	18.6	**8.9**	10.2	17.3
	MIDDLESEX SB	NATICK	MA	**C+**	C	C	4,032	2.02	5.1	0.3	25.2	40.6	**7.6**	9.4	16.8
	MIDDLETON COMMUNITY	MIDDLETON	WI	**C+**	B-	B	214	-1.40	14.9	1.6	9.6	21.5	**10.0**	11.1	15.6
	MIDDLETOWN STATE BK	MIDDLETOWN	IL	**C-**	C-	C-	24	-4.28	9.8	4.3	22.1	7.0	**5.2**	8.0	11.2
	MIDDLETOWN VALLEY BANK	MIDDLETOWN	MD	**A-**	A	A+	144	2.26	0.8	0.3	38.4	36.2	**10.0**	12.1	27.9
	MIDFIRST BANK	OKLAHOMA CITY	OK	**D+**	C-	B-	10,788	-15.83	5.4	0.3	40.0	9.9	**10.0**	11.0	16.7
▼	MIDLAND COMMUNITY BANK	KINCAID	IL	**C-**	C	B-	41	15.38	5.3	5.0	31.0	31.3	**7.1**	9.1	15.9
	MIDLAND FS&LA	BRIDGEVIEW	IL	**C-**	C-	C	120	1.99	0.0	0.4	59.2	19.1	**7.5**	9.3	21.7
	MIDLAND NATIONAL BK	NEWTON	KS	**C**	B+	B	134	-2.17	8.3	2.9	11.2	30.7	**7.2**	9.2	14.9
▼	MIDLAND STATES BANK	EFFINGHAM	IL	**D+**	B-	C+	1,654	45.08	8.9	2.7	7.6	25.6	**5.3**	7.3	11.8
	MIDSOUTH BANK	MURFREESBORO	TN	**D**	D-	D+	234	-6.46	11.4	1.1	12.9	22.7	**8.2**	9.8	14.6
	MIDSOUTH BANK NA	DOTHAN	AL	**C**	C	C	374	-2.99	10.9	2.2	15.6	12.3	**7.6**	9.4	14.9
▲	MIDSOUTH BANK NA	LAFAYETTE	LA	**C+**	C	B-	1,001	3.11	17.3	6.2	6.5	26.5	**9.7**	10.8	17.5
	MIDSTATE FS&LA	BALTIMORE	MD	**C-**	C	B	173	10.07	0.0	0.5	50.7	15.9	**10.0**	11.6	24.7
▲	MIDSTATES BANK NA	COUNCIL BLUFFS	IA	**B+**	C+	B-	314	0.00	2.5	1.0	10.7	38.8	**10.0**	11.0	17.3
	MIDTOWN BANK & TRUST CO	ATLANTA	GA	**D**	D-	D+	200	0.56	7.7	0.7	17.5	16.5	**8.4**	9.9	14.0
▲	MIDWEST BANK	DETROIT LAKES	MN	**C**	D+	C	263	3.99	17.0	3.2	14.8	2.7	**6.1**	9.5	11.8
	MIDWEST BANK NA	PIERCE	NE	**B**	C+	B	449	5.34	10.9	4.4	3.5	14.8	**8.3**	9.9	13.6

Asset Quality Index	Non-Performing Loans as a % of Total Loans	Non-Performing Loans as a % of Capital	Net Charge-offs Avg Loans	Profitability Index	Net Income ($Mil)	Return on Assets (R.O.A.)	Return on Equity (R.O.E.)	Net Interest Spread	Overhead Efficiency Ratio	Liquidity Index	Liquidity Ratio	Hot Money Ratio	Stability Index
3.7	1.22	8.6	0.23	**3.9**	3.9	0.65	6.25	3.52	74.0	**3.5**	17.5	11.8	**7.0**
3.6	3.03	12.8	4.80	**4.6**	12.8	1.28	17.52	3.76	74.0	**7.4**	68.5	3.5	**2.5**
9.0	0.30	1.6	0.06	**4.2**	2.4	0.73	6.28	4.21	79.6	**5.2**	34.2	5.9	**7.1**
1.7	3.49	29.3	0.54	**2.4**	0.2	0.24	3.12	4.33	77.3	**2.3**	21.8	18.2	**3.7**
1.3	1.16	8.6	0.53	**6.6**	11.3	1.08	6.44	4.84	57.8	**3.1**	7.2	12.9	**7.2**
3.7	3.35	19.7	0.13	**1.9**	0.2	0.27	2.56	3.41	86.9	**3.4**	35.1	16.1	**5.5**
0.1	0.88	5.4	0.77	**8.2**	218.3	1.48	20.05	2.00	67.5	**0.7**	10.8	49.0	**5.2**
4.8	0.96	5.8	0.78	**5.7**	5.6	0.98	9.23	4.51	57.0	**1.5**	21.5	26.1	**6.5**
5.2	1.57	7.1	0.59	**1.3**	0.4	0.32	2.09	3.85	84.4	**1.2**	19.7	30.3	**3.3**
1.7	8.54	24.0	0.19	**2.5**	0.3	0.91	6.45	1.96	81.5	**2.0**	50.0	83.4	**4.7**
2.9	3.77	22.8	0.96	**1.3**	-1.9	-0.09	-0.94	4.19	87.5	**4.2**	10.8	7.2	**5.3**
2.7	1.24	7.0	0.79	**6.4**	4.1	1.19	9.08	3.66	46.8	**0.6**	12.1	49.9	**4.3**
0.0	10.77	60.1	4.56	**0.0**	-3.3	-4.85	-29.78	4.33	111.4	**0.7**	13.2	41.2	**2.0**
0.0	4.87	30.8	0.41	**0.3**	-1.8	-0.41	-3.02	3.74	82.2	**0.9**	17.6	34.0	**4.2**
0.0	6.80	38.0	1.35	**2.4**	3.2	0.28	2.53	4.11	66.0	**1.2**	21.5	33.7	**5.5**
0.0	4.11	28.5	0.54	**6.9**	2.7	1.75	19.08	4.50	51.1	**2.4**	9.8	16.7	**6.9**
5.0	0.98	6.2	0.05	**1.0**	1.4	0.34	2.97	2.86	84.9	**0.9**	22.6	47.1	**5.4**
0.0	6.36	44.6	4.39	**0.6**	-4.5	-1.37	-15.81	4.98	58.5	**0.9**	7.2	30.8	**4.0**
8.5	0.08	0.6	0.00	**1.7**	0.6	0.43	4.77	4.16	82.7	**0.6**	14.4	54.8	**3.8**
0.3	14.97	115.1	2.72	**0.0**	-8.3	-0.60	-10.61	3.04	108.3	**1.2**	13.7	29.5	**2.9**
2.3	3.15	18.7	1.80	**1.3**	1.1	0.19	1.64	3.71	80.5	**3.1**	16.6	13.4	**6.7**
0.0	3.60	23.3	0.51	**3.1**	2.9	0.49	4.25	4.05	77.2	**1.6**	21.0	25.3	**6.7**
5.9	1.97	9.9	0.60	**1.8**	0.7	0.22	2.78	2.49	90.0	**5.1**	53.5	13.1	**3.6**
5.5	0.53	3.5	0.22	**6.5**	1.0	1.62	17.01	4.50	58.4	**2.3**	26.1	18.6	**7.3**
3.6	1.16	7.3	0.25	**3.1**	0.6	0.55	4.91	3.23	66.6	**0.9**	23.1	42.0	**6.4**
0.0	13.77	162.8	6.68	**0.0**	-73.6	-6.55	-233.67	3.10	116.3	**1.2**	12.2	28.7	**1.3**
5.4	0.57	5.2	1.14	**5.0**	2.8	1.12	17.58	3.88	52.7	**2.5**	17.3	16.7	**4.5**
4.8	0.43	2.8	0.47	**2.7**	0.7	0.74	5.76	3.77	81.0	**1.4**	17.2	26.7	**4.3**
2.8	2.12	17.4	0.22	**2.6**	0.6	0.49	4.78	4.30	79.3	**3.3**	15.6	12.6	**4.3**
0.2	25.36	110.6	7.56	**0.0**	-24.6	-11.66	-116.88	3.53	625.7	**3.2**	49.0	24.2	**4.7**
0.9	3.53	30.7	0.69	**2.9**	2.9	0.47	6.04	3.50	73.5	**2.9**	12.4	14.3	**3.9**
5.3	0.96	6.7	0.10	**6.4**	0.7	1.17	13.83	3.97	49.4	**1.2**	19.4	29.8	**6.1**
4.2	0.76	7.9	0.21	**3.9**	0.7	0.72	10.31	4.44	76.0	**4.2**	12.6	7.3	**3.3**
4.0	2.01	14.6	0.69	**1.5**	0.9	0.19	1.98	4.17	92.3	**2.3**	13.3	17.4	**3.6**
2.5	2.57	19.2	0.20	**3.3**	0.7	0.39	3.77	2.74	64.0	**1.4**	19.4	27.8	**6.1**
2.0	3.29	21.0	0.91	**1.7**	1.3	0.26	2.79	3.60	72.3	**2.7**	16.8	15.8	**3.4**
5.1	3.06	11.0	0.32	**4.3**	2.5	0.78	5.68	3.81	69.1	**4.7**	32.2	8.6	**7.4**
3.3	2.25	15.5	1.06	**2.5**	1.3	0.23	2.67	3.52	61.4	**0.9**	16.4	34.0	**5.6**
6.3	0.45	3.4	0.06	**2.3**	1.4	0.79	7.20	3.30	73.5	**0.8**	14.8	35.1	**3.3**
0.3	6.80	35.5	3.20	**1.3**	1.4	0.17	1.48	3.50	81.5	**3.9**	30.1	12.3	**5.1**
3.2	4.22	27.5	0.87	**1.3**	-1.6	-0.12	-1.32	3.63	84.5	**1.7**	23.3	29.6	**6.7**
1.4	4.65	38.8	0.33	**4.5**	4.6	0.87	12.53	3.52	60.1	**3.6**	31.3	14.3	**4.5**
0.8	6.61	37.7	1.60	**0.0**	-5.9	-1.52	-14.71	2.76	84.5	**1.4**	32.1	43.6	**4.0**
4.2	3.31	16.9	0.50	**3.9**	25.6	0.64	6.44	3.29	60.0	**3.6**	45.4	22.3	**7.6**
6.0	0.41	2.2	0.97	**2.7**	0.7	0.33	2.87	3.52	58.8	**1.1**	26.9	44.5	**6.4**
8.2	0.00	0.0	-0.01	**7.3**	0.5	1.82	23.07	3.73	48.5	**3.0**	11.2	13.3	**3.7**
3.7	2.71	10.1	0.16	**7.8**	1.7	1.21	10.20	4.36	57.3	**6.4**	51.4	4.4	**9.2**
0.3	3.23	20.0	0.21	**5.9**	175.3	1.49	20.73	3.38	54.7	**0.7**	13.6	48.8	**6.3**
3.6	2.40	14.8	0.00	**4.4**	0.3	0.84	8.47	3.47	67.0	**3.3**	37.6	17.6	**3.2**
3.3	2.76	19.2	0.05	**2.0**	0.2	0.13	1.31	3.56	95.3	**4.1**	31.8	11.8	**4.6**
3.0	1.76	9.4	2.57	**2.3**	-0.4	-0.30	-2.69	4.52	67.1	**3.9**	24.0	10.2	**6.5**
1.7	4.26	33.1	0.80	**5.8**	14.5	0.94	10.66	4.26	55.5	**1.7**	15.1	22.4	**7.8**
1.2	6.22	35.6	2.67	**1.0**	0.7	0.29	3.12	3.75	87.5	**1.7**	24.9	23.9	**3.4**
3.9	2.13	13.2	0.53	**2.6**	0.6	0.17	1.75	3.79	79.6	**1.5**	19.0	25.0	**5.0**
3.6	3.20	16.2	0.72	**3.9**	6.3	0.65	5.39	4.80	77.1	**4.8**	24.0	7.1	**6.9**
1.4	6.21	33.9	0.08	**2.1**	0.3	0.15	1.27	2.51	67.7	**1.4**	33.5	60.4	**6.0**
5.0	1.84	8.0	1.05	**5.8**	3.9	1.24	11.16	4.19	55.4	**5.1**	39.4	8.8	**7.2**
0.3	8.94	51.1	4.18	**0.5**	0.1	0.06	0.48	2.84	89.0	**1.7**	16.0	22.0	**4.5**
3.0	0.68	5.8	0.23	**6.9**	4.5	1.77	18.42	4.50	57.6	**3.7**	8.6	9.6	**5.8**
5.6	0.41	2.7	0.51	**6.0**	4.9	1.14	11.11	4.62	56.5	**1.8**	16.8	20.4	**6.8**

Name	City	State	Rating	2008 Rating	2007 Rating	Total Assets ($Mil)	One Year Asset Growth	Asset Mix (As a % of Total Assets) Commercial Loans	Consumer Loans	Home Mortgages	Securities	Capitalization Index	Leverage Ratio	Risk-based Capital Ratio
▼ MIDWEST BANK OF WESTERN	MONMOUTH	IL	**D+**	C-	C-	385	3.22	8.8	2.2	6.8	32.3	**6.2**	8.2	13.4
MIDWEST BANKCENTRE	LEMAY	MO	**B-**	B-	B-	1,092	-2.24	7.1	1.2	7.4	25.4	**9.1**	10.4	14.8
MIDWEST COMMUNITY BANK	FREEPORT	IL	**D**	C	C+	223	-1.00	2.3	0.3	19.0	0.8	**7.0**	9.0	15.0
MIDWEST COMMUNITY BANK	PLAINVILLE	KS	**E-**	E-	E+	82	-20.02	14.5	2.6	18.3	23.9	**0.0**	2.7	6.1
MIDWEST FS&LA OF ST JOSEP	SAINT JOSEPH	MO	**C-**	C-	C	33	48.27	1.8	0.4	40.7	10.6	**10.0**	19.8	50.6
MIDWEST HERITAGE BANK	WEST DES MOINES	IA	**B-**	C+	C+	144	2.49	3.8	31.7	19.6	19.5	**7.4**	9.3	14.0
MIDWEST INDEPENDENT	JEFFERSON CITY	MO	**D**	D	D-	266	-8.75	1.8	0.0	1.2	2.4	**6.6**	8.6	15.8
MIDWEST REGIONAL BANK	FESTUS	MO	**D**	D-	D+	99	34.90	13.9	2.3	8.5	5.8	**5.4**	8.7	11.3
▲ MIDWESTONE BANK	IOWA CITY	IA	**C**	D+	D+	1,562	2.23	12.4	1.4	12.8	29.7	**7.2**	9.1	13.2
MIFFLIN COUNTY SB	LEWISTOWN	PA	**B-**	C+	B-	122	1.73	5.2	3.9	48.9	11.4	**10.0**	11.1	17.3
MIFFLINBURG BANK & TRUST	MIFFLINBURG	PA	**A-**	A-	A-	311	4.09	8.4	5.6	17.8	25.4	**8.3**	9.8	15.4
MILE HIGH BANKS	LONGMONT	CO	**D-**	D	B-	1,163	-10.42	1.3	0.1	13.7	0.0	**1.8**	5.7	8.8
▲ MILESTONE BANK	DOYLESTOWN	PA	**C**	C	C	130	31.24	23.0	0.2	20.9	10.8	**8.6**	10.3	13.8
▼ MILFORD BANK	MILFORD	CT	**C-**	B-	C+	377	2.07	7.2	3.6	40.2	4.4	**8.9**	10.3	16.6
MILFORD BUILDING & LOAN A	MILFORD	IL	**E-**	D-	D-	24	8.82	0.0	0.2	59.8	0.2	**4.8**	6.8	15.7
MILFORD FS&LA	MILFORD	MA	**C**	C	C-	341	-1.63	0.0	0.5	68.0	7.5	**9.6**	10.8	21.9
MILFORD NATIONAL BK & TRU	MILFORD	MA	**C-**	C-	D+	276	-3.80	6.9	5.0	32.4	3.6	**6.4**	8.5	14.2
MILLBURY NATIONAL BK	MILLBURY	MA	**C-**	C-	B-	73	0.71	12.9	1.6	17.6	20.0	**8.7**	10.2	15.5
MILLBURY SB	MILLBURY	MA	**C**	C	C+	204	0.40	3.0	1.2	29.9	29.1	**8.6**	10.1	18.6
▲ MILLEDGEVILLE STATE BK	MILLEDGEVILLE	IL	**C+**	C	C-	77	5.18	15.2	1.8	8.1	30.4	**7.9**	9.6	14.1
▲ MILLENNIUM BANK	EDWARDS	CO	**E+**	D-	D+	273	-15.21	10.6	0.6	15.8	22.8	**3.9**	6.8	10.5
MILLENNIUM BANK	DES PLAINES	IL	**D-**	D	C-	46	10.10	18.8	0.3	2.5	10.8	**6.9**	8.9	12.9
▲ MILLENNIUM BANK	JUNCTION CITY	KS	**B-**	C-	C-	29	16.18	10.7	5.5	26.7	0.0	**10.0**	13.9	19.8
MILLENNIUM BANK NA	STERLING	VA	**E-**	E-	D-	196	-18.30	8.9	2.5	10.3	17.5	**1.0**	5.3	7.9
MILLINGTON SB	MILLINGTON	NJ	**D-**	D	C-	351	-3.61	2.6	0.3	51.5	14.0	**7.7**	9.5	15.7
MILLS COUNTY STATE BK	GOLDTHWAITE	TX	**B**	A-	A-	203	4.50	7.0	7.6	15.2	26.8	**9.0**	10.3	21.8
MILLS RESOLUTE BANK	SANBORN	MN	**D-**	C-	C-	20	20.43	4.9	7.8	10.5	1.3	**5.3**	7.3	11.8
MILLVILLE SAVINGS & LOAN	MILLVILLE	NJ	**C+**	B-	B-	135	5.05	0.5	0.1	25.6	54.8	**10.0**	11.2	35.2
MILTON BANKING CO	WELLSTON	OH	**C-**	D+	C	126	6.29	10.1	12.6	33.3	5.5	**4.8**	7.8	10.9
MILTON SAVINGS BANK	MILTON	PA	**B+**	B+	A-	65	4.86	0.0	0.6	68.4	5.5	**10.0**	16.5	37.0
▲ MILTON SB	MILTON	WI	**E**	E+	D-	16	-4.48	7.7	2.1	52.9	10.5	**5.1**	7.1	12.6
MINDEN EXCHANGE BANK &	MINDEN	NE	**A-**	B+	C	132	2.83	5.2	3.0	3.3	39.2	**10.0**	13.5	23.9
MINEOLA COMMUNITY BANK	MINEOLA	TX	**B**	B-	B-	153	-1.00	1.2	3.9	31.6	38.5	**10.0**	15.5	29.1
MINER COUNTY BANK	HOWARD	SD	**B-**	B	B+	39	2.13	4.2	2.9	3.6	30.3	**10.0**	11.1	18.7
MINERS & MERCHANTS BANK	THOMAS	WV	**B+**	B+	B+	52	8.70	0.3	3.8	28.3	46.5	**10.0**	14.2	40.4
▲ MINERS BANK	MINERSVILLE	PA	**C**	C-	C-	118	8.80	5.3	2.7	35.3	12.2	**6.5**	8.5	12.9
MINERS EXCHANGE BANK	COEBURN	VA	**C+**	C+	B-	130	25.79	0.7	9.6	27.4	21.1	**5.6**	7.6	14.6
▼ MINERS NATIONAL BK OF EVE	EVELETH	MN	**C-**	C	C	46	3.71	3.2	3.7	21.9	30.7	**8.8**	10.2	22.9
MINERS STATE BK	IRON RIVER	MI	**C**	C+	B-	134	-1.62	10.4	0.8	11.6	26.0	**5.7**	7.7	12.7
MINNESOTA BANK & TRUST	EDINA	MN	**C**	C	C+	58	18.36	38.2	0.1	0.6	32.4	**10.0**	23.6	31.5
MINNESOTA FIRST CREDIT &	ROCHESTER	MN	**B-**	B	B	29	-0.62	0.5	25.4	66.7	0.0	**10.0**	11.2	17.6
MINNESOTA NATIONAL BK	SAUK CENTRE	MN	**C**	C-	C-	190	-3.99	10.5	3.3	11.4	28.3	**6.9**	8.9	15.1
MINNSTAR BANK NA	LAKE CRYSTAL	MN	**D-**	D-	C	102	0.64	10.6	2.6	17.2	13.7	**6.2**	8.2	12.5
MINNWEST BANK CENTRAL	MONTEVIDEO	MN	**D+**	D	D	328	1.35	4.2	1.5	3.4	8.3	**5.7**	8.8	11.5
MINNWEST BANK LUVERNE	LUVERNE	MN	**D+**	D	D+	173	-2.89	9.2	1.2	4.2	10.1	**5.5**	7.8	11.4
MINNWEST BANK METRO	EAGAN	MN	**D**	D-	D	269	-21.33	10.1	0.2	3.8	13.2	**4.5**	6.5	10.9
MINNWEST BANK MV	REDWOOD FALLS	MN	**D+**	D	D+	527	-0.72	7.7	1.0	5.2	7.6	**7.0**	9.0	12.6
MINNWEST BANK SIOUX	SIOUX FALLS	SD	**D+**	D+	C-	117	-5.75	8.2	1.8	14.2	9.3	**5.6**	7.6	12.3
MINNWEST BANK SOUTH	TRACY	MN	**D**	D	D+	232	0.65	3.1	1.3	3.0	17.2	**4.9**	6.9	11.5
MINSTER BANK	MINSTER	OH	**B**	B	B	307	4.98	8.8	1.3	15.0	19.5	**5.5**	7.5	12.9
▼ MINT NATIONAL BK	KINGWOOD	TX	**D**	C	NR	32	70.42	6.5	1.0	20.7	0.0	**10.0**	21.8	41.5
MISSION BANK	KINGMAN	AZ	**D**	D+	C-	95	6.50	7.6	0.7	8.1	2.6	**7.7**	9.9	13.0
MISSION BANK	BAKERSFIELD	CA	**A-**	A	A-	233	8.71	14.2	0.0	4.3	16.0	**9.1**	10.4	16.9
MISSION BANK	MISSION	KS	**D+**	C	B-	574	-3.55	10.4	1.0	2.8	24.4	**10.0**	12.7	18.7
MISSION COMMUNITY BANK	SAN LUIS OBISPO	CA	**C-**	C-	D+	199	3.44	8.9	0.8	2.9	37.8	**8.8**	10.2	17.2
MISSION NATIONAL BK	SAN FRANCISCO	CA	**C**	C	B-	185	5.66	2.6	0.3	4.1	2.4	**7.5**	9.4	13.0
▲ MISSION OAKS NATIONAL BK	TEMECULA	CA	**E+**	D-	D	159	-19.59	12.0	0.8	2.9	16.5	**7.4**	9.3	13.7
▲ MISSION VALLEY BANK	SUN VALLEY	CA	**C-**	C-	B-	255	-3.37	29.5	0.3	0.9	8.8	**10.0**	12.7	17.8
MISSISSIPPI COUNTY S&LA	CHARLESTON	MO	**C-**	C-	D+	9	1.08	0.0	0.3	46.3	29.8	**10.0**	27.1	74.2
MISSISSIPPI NATL BANKERS	RIDGELAND	MS	**C+**	C	B-	133	-32.64	0.4	0.0	0.5	1.5	**10.0**	11.6	34.2

Asset Quality Index	Non-Performing Loans as a % of Total Loans	Non-Performing Loans as a % of Capital	Net Charge-offs Avg Loans	Profitability Index	Net Income ($Mil)	Return on Assets (R.O.A.)	Return on Equity (R.O.E.)	Net Interest Spread	Overhead Efficiency Ratio	Liquidity Index	Liquidity Ratio	Hot Money Ratio	Stability Index
1.6	3.26	20.5	0.99	**4.2**	3.1	0.82	7.05	3.67	57.2	**1.3**	16.5	28.3	**6.0**
6.5	1.25	6.6	0.22	**3.5**	7.2	0.66	6.31	3.06	72.3	**3.4**	14.2	12.2	**8.3**
1.4	1.72	12.4	0.88	**1.6**	0.2	0.08	0.85	2.97	80.8	**1.8**	17.2	20.9	**5.8**
0.3	5.64	57.9	2.30	**0.0**	-2.5	-2.48	-70.06	3.36	114.9	**1.0**	10.6	30.1	**0.2**
9.7	0.00	0.0	0.00	**0.0**	-0.3	-1.09	-4.19	2.52	139.5	**2.6**	61.9	48.4	**5.4**
6.2	0.17	1.2	0.08	**5.4**	1.9	1.28	14.15	4.46	73.2	**5.3**	33.4	4.8	**5.2**
0.8	6.28	28.7	1.77	**1.7**	0.8	0.25	2.47	3.48	76.8	**1.7**	27.1	26.5	**4.7**
4.5	0.27	2.3	0.13	**0.8**	0.1	0.15	1.19	3.17	95.0	**1.3**	20.3	28.6	**4.5**
2.7	3.04	19.0	0.70	**3.6**	11.3	0.73	7.23	3.84	63.5	**3.1**	28.2	18.4	**5.9**
5.5	1.02	6.5	0.20	**4.0**	0.9	0.69	6.40	3.34	64.1	**1.7**	22.0	24.1	**6.7**
6.9	0.72	4.1	0.11	**6.0**	3.6	1.19	11.48	3.91	60.0	**3.1**	19.9	13.7	**6.9**
0.0	2.86	27.5	4.00	**0.0**	-38.8	-3.04	-40.31	3.05	106.7	**0.7**	11.5	42.4	**6.4**
5.5	0.86	6.5	1.02	**3.3**	1.6	1.47	13.40	4.59	66.3	**1.7**	3.6	19.5	**4.1**
2.2	4.08	27.6	0.31	**2.7**	1.1	0.28	2.83	3.66	79.8	**3.1**	16.8	13.8	**6.4**
2.7	3.00	28.2	0.00	**3.2**	0.1	0.49	7.09	2.90	70.4	**2.6**	31.9	17.5	**0.3**
5.7	0.69	4.8	0.01	**3.2**	2.3	0.67	6.38	3.03	72.7	**3.3**	20.5	13.2	**5.9**
4.0	1.43	11.5	0.26	**2.8**	1.0	0.37	4.33	3.90	81.3	**3.0**	14.2	14.0	**4.1**
6.1	0.59	3.7	1.00	**1.2**	-0.1	-0.06	-0.60	3.61	94.7	**0.8**	10.3	32.9	**4.7**
7.1	1.08	5.9	0.25	**3.0**	0.8	0.38	3.75	3.17	76.2	**3.6**	41.4	17.2	**6.1**
5.3	0.91	5.4	1.55	**3.9**	0.8	1.09	10.58	4.15	50.1	**2.1**	31.6	25.8	**4.8**
0.3	7.16	54.0	3.81	**0.0**	-7.9	-2.66	-33.62	3.62	98.0	**0.8**	18.0	43.7	**2.6**
0.9	5.40	35.1	0.02	**0.0**	-0.8	-1.71	-17.32	2.88	155.8	**0.9**	22.1	46.1	**1.0**
8.3	0.00	0.0	0.04	**3.6**	0.3	0.92	6.28	4.80	75.6	**1.9**	14.9	19.3	**5.3**
0.3	1.65	12.2	2.10	**0.0**	-6.1	-2.70	-79.81	2.33	225.7	**0.9**	19.3	36.9	**0.0**
0.3	6.23	45.5	0.37	**2.1**	0.8	0.21	2.30	3.25	74.9	**2.2**	19.9	18.5	**5.0**
4.7	2.05	9.6	0.09	**5.7**	2.5	1.23	11.02	3.98	66.8	**2.9**	40.2	21.0	**7.5**
3.7	0.77	7.1	0.00	**2.6**	0.1	0.40	3.04	3.49	84.5	**3.4**	28.8	12.8	**1.7**
7.0	2.68	7.2	0.49	**3.2**	0.6	0.42	3.71	2.44	67.6	**5.6**	73.4	13.8	**6.8**
2.2	1.66	15.5	0.41	**5.1**	1.0	0.87	10.33	5.04	70.8	**1.7**	16.1	21.6	**4.6**
8.0	0.63	2.9	0.00	**4.2**	0.5	0.83	5.03	3.73	63.6	**3.5**	23.0	12.2	**7.8**
4.7	0.77	7.2	-0.15	**1.2**	0.1	0.28	3.84	4.40	98.0	**3.9**	22.6	10.1	**0.7**
8.6	0.02	0.1	0.28	**5.4**	1.3	0.94	6.77	3.32	64.7	**4.6**	32.3	9.4	**5.8**
9.1	0.38	1.2	0.66	**3.7**	0.7	0.49	3.19	3.70	70.3	**2.9**	51.1	30.1	**7.3**
7.1	0.00	0.0	0.18	**3.6**	0.2	0.59	5.06	4.15	83.7	**4.0**	31.8	12.0	**7.3**
8.8	0.79	2.0	0.05	**4.9**	0.4	0.79	5.41	3.79	71.6	**4.3**	69.9	18.3	**8.4**
4.7	1.19	10.3	0.13	**2.7**	0.5	0.48	5.23	4.19	81.8	**3.2**	14.1	12.9	**4.4**
3.8	0.46	3.2	0.12	**4.5**	0.9	0.79	10.04	5.05	74.2	**1.7**	28.3	28.6	**3.5**
8.7	0.11	0.4	0.07	**1.8**	0.0	0.10	0.89	4.22	98.6	**3.6**	48.7	18.5	**5.7**
5.7	0.45	3.3	0.49	**2.7**	0.7	0.52	6.34	3.30	82.9	**3.1**	31.7	16.5	**4.8**
8.6	0.02	0.1	0.09	**0.0**	-0.6	-1.06	-4.11	3.43	151.0	**5.8**	46.4	6.3	**4.9**
5.4	0.78	5.8	0.42	**4.1**	0.2	0.54	4.86	6.26	79.0	**4.1**	4.4	6.8	**6.4**
2.9	1.27	7.1	0.20	**3.7**	1.3	0.70	5.82	3.76	71.4	**2.6**	32.2	19.4	**5.7**
0.3	7.18	53.1	0.58	**1.0**	0.0	0.03	0.36	3.80	93.4	**3.0**	16.3	14.3	**2.9**
2.8	0.25	2.1	0.51	**4.3**	2.5	0.78	8.79	3.86	58.2	**1.0**	9.8	30.0	**4.3**
1.7	1.73	15.0	0.30	**2.9**	0.9	0.51	6.24	3.53	67.4	**3.1**	14.6	13.3	**3.7**
0.3	8.47	59.9	3.09	**0.0**	-9.8	-3.21	-42.05	2.82	224.2	**1.4**	25.7	30.0	**3.0**
1.6	1.34	10.2	1.12	**3.6**	2.4	0.46	5.02	3.81	57.8	**1.8**	13.9	19.7	**4.6**
0.3	2.63	21.5	1.54	**3.2**	0.4	0.29	3.87	3.84	56.3	**1.9**	24.2	21.2	**4.2**
1.0	2.36	17.6	1.71	**0.1**	-1.3	-0.57	-7.35	3.10	89.1	**3.2**	34.3	17.0	**3.4**
5.6	0.69	5.0	0.16	**7.3**	3.9	1.31	16.80	4.32	58.8	**4.1**	19.6	8.9	**5.8**
8.8	0.00	0.0	0.00	**0.0**	-0.4	-1.34	-5.68	3.28	124.9	**3.3**	43.0	18.8	**1.5**
4.4	0.04	0.3	0.84	**1.0**	-0.1	-0.15	-1.52	4.14	85.4	**1.5**	25.5	28.6	**4.7**
6.1	1.78	8.2	1.06	**6.3**	1.9	0.85	8.20	4.77	56.2	**3.7**	48.8	18.6	**7.7**
0.7	3.16	13.7	0.76	**2.3**	0.4	0.07	0.53	3.51	69.9	**2.0**	20.3	19.7	**6.9**
5.8	0.20	0.9	6.74	**0.0**	-5.6	-2.86	-27.15	3.78	103.1	**1.7**	34.8	35.0	**4.7**
2.7	1.91	12.8	0.24	**6.3**	1.7	0.94	10.36	5.02	62.1	**1.4**	21.9	28.1	**6.6**
0.0	10.62	58.5	2.80	**0.0**	-7.4	-4.04	-47.07	3.97	184.0	**1.1**	19.3	31.3	**3.7**
1.4	2.91	14.4	1.58	**3.3**	1.2	0.44	3.84	4.72	72.7	**0.9**	21.5	40.7	**6.0**
9.4	1.85	3.2	0.00	**0.0**	-0.1	-0.87	-3.23	3.89	132.7	**6.0**	68.5	7.2	**5.2**
4.7	5.87	14.6	2.51	**1.7**	0.1	0.03	0.23	1.61	67.7	**7.7**	66.4	0.0	**6.7**

Name	City	State	Rating	2008 Rating	2007 Rating	Total Assets ($Mil)	One Year Asset Growth	Asset Mix (As a % of Total Assets) Comm-ercial Loans	Cons-umer Loans	Home Mort-gages	Secur-ities	Capital-ization Index	Leverage Ratio	Risk-based Capital Ratio
MISSISSIPPI RIVER BANK	BELLE CHASSE	LA	**A-**	A-	A	201	18.25	10.6	1.5	8.2	48.8	**8.2**	9.8	24.9
MISSOURI B&TC OF KANSAS C	KANSAS CITY	MO	**B-**	B-	C+	435	-4.11	29.3	0.6	6.2	13.8	**4.7**	6.7	10.9
▼MISSOURI BANK	WARRENTON	MO	**B**	A-	B+	169	5.90	3.5	1.9	19.9	15.4	**8.0**	9.7	14.1
MITCHELL BANK	MILWAUKEE	WI	**D**	D	C+	65	-11.19	13.1	0.7	27.2	1.0	**10.0**	12.0	17.9
MITSUBISHI UFJ TRUST & BA	NEW YORK	NY	**B-**	B+	B	262	2.99	0.2	0.0	0.0	7.6	**10.0**	74.7	447.6
MIZUHO CORPORATE BANK	NEW YORK	NY	**C+**	B-	B-	3,253	-6.30	22.8	0.0	0.4	8.4	**10.0**	34.1	25.3
MIZUHO CORPORATE BANK	LOS ANGELES	CA	**B-**	B-	B-	117	-59.79	0.1	0.0	0.1	2.5	**10.0**	62.3	5,102.4
MIZUHO TRUST & BANKING CO	NEW YORK	NY	**C+**	B-	B	547	127.91	0.0	0.0	0.0	0.0	**4.3**	6.3	67.0
MODERN BANK NA	NEW YORK	NY	**D-**	D	D-	554	-8.99	8.2	2.6	18.6	39.2	**6.2**	8.2	16.2
MOHAVE STATE BK	LAKE HAVASU CITY	AZ	**D-**	D-	D	303	-18.91	5.2	0.3	7.6	10.9	**4.8**	7.8	10.9
▼MOJAVE DESERT BANK NA	MOJAVE	CA	**C+**	B-	B	98	7.76	9.2	1.0	9.1	10.3	**6.9**	8.9	16.4
MONADNOCK COMMUNITY	PETERBOROUGH	NH	**D-**	C-	C-	104	-9.70	8.6	3.9	24.2	18.4	**6.8**	8.8	17.7
MONARCH BANK	CHESAPEAKE	VA	**B-**	C+	C+	826	19.78	10.7	0.4	31.5	2.1	**6.9**	8.9	12.4
MONARCH COMMUNITY BANK	COLDWATER	MI	**E-**	D-	C	257	-8.63	2.5	1.3	37.1	4.4	**0.9**	4.5	7.9
MONITOR BANK	BIG PRAIRIE	OH	**C+**	B-	A-	36	13.12	20.7	5.4	16.4	3.7	**10.0**	13.3	23.3
MONONA STATE BK	MONONA	WI	**D-**	C-	B-	345	-0.68	10.2	0.9	15.6	10.2	**9.6**	11.0	14.7
▼MONROE BANK & TRUST	MONROE	MI	**E-**	E+	D+	1,259	-8.97	6.1	1.3	17.4	24.9	**3.3**	6.2	10.2
▼MONROE COUNTY BANK	FORSYTH	GA	**D-**	D+	C+	93	2.89	5.6	3.9	29.0	6.6	**6.7**	8.7	16.1
▼MONROE FS&LA	TIPP CITY	OH	**D**	C-	C-	93	-6.18	8.0	0.5	43.6	4.6	**9.5**	10.6	17.2
MONROE SAVINGS BANK SLA	WILLIAMSTOWN	NJ	**C+**	C+	B-	93	-5.68	0.2	8.1	43.3	20.9	**9.0**	10.4	21.6
▼MONROE STATE BK	MONROE	IA	**C**	C+	C	22	7.99	11.4	8.8	20.5	5.8	**10.0**	14.9	22.5
▲MONSON SB	MONSON	MA	**C+**	C+	C+	236	0.47	11.8	0.3	25.9	19.6	**6.7**	8.7	15.5
MONTANA STATE BK	PLENTYWOOD	MT	**B-**	B-	C+	63	10.44	3.6	2.6	0.4	15.6	**6.1**	8.1	17.9
MONTECITO BANK & TRUST	SANTA BARBARA	CA	**D**	C-	B-	941	-1.51	12.2	4.2	2.0	38.1	**7.0**	9.0	12.6
MONTEREY COUNTY BANK	MONTEREY	CA	**D**	D+	C-	263	-3.46	12.7	0.2	13.5	17.0	**7.4**	9.2	14.1
MONTEZUMA STATE BK	MONTEZUMA	IA	**B**	B	B	41	8.88	17.2	5.6	9.3	6.0	**10.0**	18.3	31.9
MONTEZUMA STATE BK	MONTEZUMA	KS	**B**	B	B	90	17.63	1.5	0.7	2.1	64.3	**5.6**	7.6	18.2
▲MONTGOMERY BANK & TRUST	AILEY	GA	**D-**	E-	D	230	-6.34	5.2	4.3	17.0	7.0	**5.8**	7.8	11.7
MONTGOMERY BANK NA	SIKESTON	MO	**D+**	C-	C-	910	-3.32	16.1	1.3	15.6	2.9	**5.0**	8.0	11.0
MONTICELLO BANKING CO	MONTICELLO	KY	**D**	C-	C-	606	6.60	10.6	9.3	16.9	21.1	**6.0**	8.1	12.5
MONTROSE SB	MONTROSE	MO	**B+**	B+	B+	38	8.87	7.9	4.6	17.8	20.8	**10.0**	12.6	19.1
▲MONTROSEBANK	MONTROSE	CO	**B**	B-	B+	209	3.51	4.3	3.5	15.7	22.7	**7.5**	9.3	15.2
MONUMENT BANK	BETHESDA	MD	**C+**	C+	C	313	26.87	7.3	0.6	11.5	18.9	**7.0**	9.0	13.2
MONUMENT BANK	DOYLESTOWN	PA	**D**	C	C	117	13.20	1.8	0.0	9.8	48.8	**7.4**	9.3	14.6
▲MOODY NATIONAL BK	GALVESTON	TX	**C+**	C	C+	919	-0.06	8.1	1.1	3.5	39.7	**6.6**	8.6	15.8
MORGAN FEDERAL BANK	FORT MORGAN	CO	**C-**	C+	C-	110	2.69	1.2	1.2	30.2	36.1	**6.0**	8.0	14.6
MORGAN STANLEY BANK NA	SALT LAKE CITY	UT	**C+**	C	C-	68,180	3.05	8.2	5.3	0.0	43.5	**10.0**	12.1	18.6
▼MORGAN STANLEY PRIVATE	NEW YORK	NY	**C**	NR	NR	7,503	N/A	0.0	0.0	26.7	0.0	**10.0**	12.4	37.3
MORGAN STANLEY TRUST NA	WILMINGTON	DE	**U**	U	U	30	54.36	0.0	0.0	0.0	86.5	**10.0**	105.1	979.2
MORGANTON FS&LA	MORGANTON	NC	**B-**	C+	B-	87	-1.02	0.0	0.5	26.4	0.8	**10.0**	27.3	37.0
MORGANTOWN BANK &	MORGANTOWN	KY	**D**	C	C	132	0.05	3.7	5.9	34.8	19.7	**7.6**	9.4	14.9
MORRILL & JANES BANK & TR	MERRIAM	KS	**B**	B	B-	599	11.36	10.0	0.8	5.4	45.2	**6.2**	8.2	15.3
MORRIS BANK	DUBLIN	GA	**B-**	C+	C	355	12.36	8.9	3.7	17.1	12.6	**6.6**	8.6	13.2
▲MORRIS COUNTY NATIONAL	NAPLES	TX	**C+**	C-	D	86	0.96	7.1	9.7	15.2	28.2	**6.5**	8.5	14.3
MORRIS PLAN CO OF TERRE H	TERRE HAUTE	IN	**B**	B	B+	66	9.96	1.8	68.8	17.6	0.8	**10.0**	15.8	19.3
MORRIS STATE BK	MORRIS	OK	**B-**	C+	B-	62	-1.65	4.8	16.5	37.2	2.7	**6.7**	8.7	13.8
MORTON COMMUNITY BANK	MORTON	IL	**B-**	B	B-	2,672	13.10	7.4	1.0	11.9	35.0	**6.1**	8.1	14.8
MOTHER LODE BANK	SONORA	CA	**D-**	E	D-	62	-2.81	5.4	0.5	16.2	9.8	**7.7**	9.5	14.9
MOUND CITY BANK	PLATTEVILLE	WI	**D+**	C-	C+	262	0.89	6.8	1.3	21.0	14.2	**6.7**	8.7	12.8
MOUNT GILEAD SAVINGS & LO	MOUNT GILEAD	NC	**C**	C	C-	12	14.20	0.0	0.5	80.4	0.0	**10.0**	14.7	30.9
MOUNT MCKINLEY BANK	FAIRBANKS	AK	**A**	A-	A	308	8.79	5.3	0.4	8.9	49.4	**10.0**	18.9	33.5
MOUNT VERNON BANK	MOUNT VERNON	GA	**B-**	C+	B	130	13.86	3.2	3.0	15.7	23.9	**6.8**	8.8	15.7
MOUNT VERNON BANK &	MOUNT VERNON	IA	**A-**	A-	A-	91	1.70	5.3	4.1	33.2	33.4	**10.0**	12.9	19.4
MOUNTAIN 1ST BANK & TRUST	HENDERSONVILLE	NC	**E-**	D-	C-	726	-8.47	9.1	0.6	13.9	18.4	**1.4**	4.5	8.4
MOUNTAIN COMMERCE BANK	ERWIN	TN	**D-**	D	D-	344	7.83	7.8	1.8	17.0	12.1	**6.9**	8.9	12.4
MOUNTAIN HERITAGE BANK	CLAYTON	GA	**E-**	E-	E	108	-8.84	2.5	2.3	14.8	16.9	**0.0**	2.5	5.0
MOUNTAIN NATIONAL BK	SEVIERVILLE	TN	**D-**	D-	B-	568	-11.04	4.4	0.9	16.8	15.4	**7.8**	9.6	14.6
▲MOUNTAIN PACIFIC BANK	EVERETT	WA	**D**	D-	D-	99	-10.01	9.1	0.7	7.7	15.2	**10.0**	13.1	19.0
MOUNTAIN VALLEY BANK	WALDEN	CO	**D**	C	B-	144	-4.08	11.5	2.6	13.4	11.9	**7.8**	9.6	13.9
MOUNTAIN VALLEY BANK	DUNLAP	TN	**D**	D+	C+	98	-1.57	1.4	10.8	38.7	14.1	**6.3**	8.3	14.5

Asset Quality Index	Non-Performing Loans as a % of Total Loans	Non-Performing Loans as a % of Capital	Net Charge-offs Avg Loans	Profitability Index	Net Income ($Mil)	Return on Assets (R.O.A.)	Return on Equity (R.O.E.)	Net Interest Spread	Overhead Efficiency Ratio	Liquidity Index	Liquidity Ratio	Hot Money Ratio	Stability Index
6.9	0.39	1.5	0.12	**9.6**	3.0	1.65	15.52	4.66	50.2	**5.2**	39.4	8.2	**7.4**
8.6	0.04	0.4	0.16	**3.7**	3.2	0.72	10.69	3.84	76.9	**2.0**	24.7	20.2	**4.8**
4.1	2.93	18.5	0.50	**6.5**	2.2	1.41	14.66	4.44	55.5	**3.5**	26.5	13.2	**6.5**
0.3	13.32	67.7	1.83	**0.0**	-0.7	-0.92	-7.41	4.46	82.4	**4.6**	14.7	4.4	**6.0**
8.6	76.27	0.2	0.00	**10.0**	11.0	4.47	5.30	0.63	59.7	**5.1**	431.4	91.7	**5.0**
8.6	0.00	0.0	0.00	**2.1**	6.7	0.22	0.64	1.35	78.0	**2.9**	52.0	50.2	**7.5**
10.0	12.85	0.1	0.10	**0.0**	-2.6	-1.20	-3.55	0.43	355.1	**5.5**	257.6	38.7	**6.3**
10.0	0.00	0.0	0.00	**2.5**	0.7	0.11	1.47	0.30	95.5	**8.5**	106.1	0.5	**7.1**
2.9	3.66	20.7	0.19	**0.0**	-4.1	-0.67	-7.81	2.48	124.3	**0.8**	23.4	56.3	**1.2**
0.0	10.69	71.0	4.42	**0.0**	-10.0	-2.84	-32.66	3.92	98.7	**2.1**	9.5	18.2	**4.9**
5.2	1.15	6.5	0.75	**3.0**	0.2	0.22	2.34	5.13	81.7	**3.9**	34.4	13.8	**4.7**
3.5	2.44	15.1	1.01	**0.3**	-1.2	-1.07	-11.47	2.17	123.6	**2.7**	37.6	21.6	**3.9**
4.5	1.23	10.6	1.30	**4.6**	6.4	0.87	9.44	4.35	77.6	**1.1**	5.2	26.9	**5.8**
0.1	9.41	87.7	3.96	**0.0**	-10.1	-3.74	-61.63	3.10	87.5	**1.1**	19.3	31.7	**0.0**
6.4	1.23	5.2	0.21	**2.1**	0.1	0.19	1.38	3.01	88.4	**3.6**	42.0	17.6	**7.4**
0.0	3.61	22.7	0.33	**3.6**	1.8	0.54	4.96	3.70	66.6	**1.5**	10.6	22.9	**6.5**
0.3	8.96	68.5	2.89	**0.0**	-11.6	-0.89	-14.12	3.21	82.1	**2.8**	21.5	16.7	**2.6**
3.7	4.38	28.6	1.16	**0.0**	-1.2	-1.24	-15.06	2.80	104.1	**1.6**	25.3	26.0	**3.3**
1.0	5.77	37.1	0.00	**2.1**	1.4	1.49	14.30	3.57	50.1	**3.5**	20.1	11.9	**5.5**
4.5	1.40	8.5	0.00	**3.1**	0.4	0.42	4.30	3.42	77.2	**3.1**	33.6	17.3	**5.2**
2.0	7.49	28.0	0.07	**4.2**	0.1	0.50	3.25	4.96	79.9	**5.6**	48.0	5.6	**7.5**
5.5	0.66	4.5	0.32	**4.0**	1.7	0.72	8.43	3.36	70.1	**2.3**	30.5	20.9	**5.2**
8.7	0.06	0.3	-0.03	**4.5**	0.6	0.99	10.62	3.57	71.8	**5.6**	48.9	7.8	**5.2**
0.7	5.95	32.2	2.91	**2.3**	3.1	0.33	3.21	4.17	65.3	**4.9**	35.8	8.6	**6.9**
1.3	7.04	38.1	0.23	**0.5**	-1.0	-0.34	-3.68	3.51	120.2	**0.8**	17.6	46.1	**5.2**
5.1	1.90	5.0	0.13	**3.5**	0.2	0.54	2.84	3.50	70.1	**6.1**	55.5	5.9	**7.0**
9.2	0.00	0.0	-0.02	**5.9**	1.2	1.55	17.10	4.23	66.5	**5.3**	38.1	7.2	**6.2**
0.3	25.82	171.5	2.49	**0.0**	-6.4	-2.79	-89.27	2.04	125.4	**1.0**	26.2	47.1	**1.2**
2.2	1.69	15.6	0.58	**2.0**	1.7	0.19	2.31	3.68	79.7	**4.1**	7.9	7.0	**4.6**
1.1	3.60	25.4	0.53	**3.7**	4.2	0.72	8.86	3.88	67.3	**0.9**	22.8	45.0	**5.3**
7.8	0.32	1.6	0.23	**8.1**	0.6	1.66	12.94	4.78	56.7	**3.1**	28.6	15.9	**8.0**
5.7	1.17	7.7	0.34	**9.7**	4.4	2.14	21.13	5.54	53.8	**4.6**	29.1	7.9	**7.9**
5.7	0.88	6.4	0.37	**3.7**	1.8	0.65	6.72	3.91	67.3	**1.7**	19.9	23.5	**4.5**
9.4	0.00	0.0	0.00	**1.0**	0.6	0.63	6.26	3.02	90.8	**1.2**	29.1	46.8	**2.0**
3.2	4.02	20.4	0.79	**2.7**	4.8	0.49	6.00	3.34	76.1	**2.7**	16.9	15.8	**5.4**
4.6	1.10	5.9	0.58	**2.2**	0.3	0.25	2.71	2.90	81.6	**3.8**	53.5	19.6	**5.2**
6.4	3.49	5.0	0.00	**3.4**	450.0	0.67	5.76	0.34	17.3	**4.0**	92.6	40.7	**7.2**
10.0	0.00	0.0	0.00	**1.5**	52.7	0.72	5.77	N/,	44.0	**4.5**	79.9	23.9	**6.4**
10.0	0.00	0.0	0.00	**5.5**	0.9	4.13	4.91	0.26	95.0	**5.0**	1,041.2	101.0	**6.7**
5.9	1.73	4.5	0.07	**3.9**	0.7	0.84	3.18	3.56	67.7	**1.4**	18.5	26.5	**7.6**
2.8	0.91	6.3	2.25	**0.6**	-0.6	-0.41	-4.27	3.86	90.3	**2.3**	13.3	17.4	**4.7**
4.9	0.61	3.3	0.75	**4.9**	5.4	0.95	8.92	3.33	52.9	**1.4**	7.0	23.9	**6.6**
4.5	0.44	3.3	0.58	**4.9**	4.0	1.20	14.76	3.60	49.1	**0.8**	20.3	43.2	**5.1**
3.9	2.35	13.6	0.77	**5.4**	1.3	1.57	17.64	4.71	68.8	**1.9**	22.0	20.1	**4.5**
3.3	1.47	6.4	1.79	**10.0**	2.3	3.69	24.76	11.25	27.3	**0.8**	5.8	32.7	**7.1**
4.1	0.69	5.5	0.26	**9.4**	1.4	2.24	25.55	4.91	54.7	**1.0**	18.9	32.6	**6.7**
3.7	1.72	11.0	0.14	**5.2**	37.3	1.46	17.42	3.01	50.3	**1.0**	13.5	33.0	**8.6**
2.0	1.19	7.0	3.19	**0.0**	-1.0	-1.56	-17.82	4.08	114.2	**4.4**	29.6	9.5	**3.9**
1.3	0.86	6.7	1.07	**2.1**	0.4	0.16	1.84	3.60	69.6	**1.9**	16.3	19.4	**4.5**
9.6	0.00	0.0	0.00	**2.9**	0.1	0.55	3.60	3.67	83.0	**1.5**	14.8	23.7	**6.1**
6.6	0.94	1.9	0.13	**6.7**	4.0	1.36	7.20	5.25	69.6	**5.2**	62.3	14.1	**9.0**
6.7	0.25	1.5	0.14	**4.5**	1.0	0.86	10.01	3.61	72.9	**2.6**	42.5	27.6	**3.8**
8.4	0.78	3.5	0.02	**6.6**	1.1	1.21	9.26	3.95	58.6	**5.0**	37.6	9.1	**8.1**
0.3	7.60	77.3	4.64	**0.0**	-4.1	-0.52	-9.68	2.86	90.4	**1.3**	26.3	32.2	**1.3**
0.0	5.67	43.8	0.82	**1.6**	0.7	0.22	2.34	3.79	84.8	**1.2**	9.9	27.5	**4.3**
0.2	15.13	202.1	1.98	**0.0**	-2.0	-1.68	-47.33	1.70	174.1	**0.6**	15.0	54.4	**0.0**
0.1	15.30	88.2	0.93	**0.8**	0.2	0.04	0.40	2.46	100.0	**1.2**	8.1	27.1	**5.3**
0.3	13.02	52.9	2.58	**0.0**	-2.8	-2.71	-23.51	2.31	164.0	**2.2**	10.3	17.3	**1.7**
1.1	6.51	45.1	1.01	**3.1**	0.6	0.41	4.32	4.35	80.0	**0.9**	20.6	35.4	**5.0**
0.6	5.45	40.0	1.05	**2.9**	0.2	0.20	2.36	4.56	78.7	**1.4**	12.7	24.7	**3.9**

Name	City	State	Rating	2008 Rating	2007 Rating	Total Assets ($Mil)	One Year Asset Growth	Asset Mix (As a % of Total Assets) Commercial Loans	Consumer Loans	Home Mortgages	Securities	Capitalization Index	Leverage Ratio	Risk-based Capital Ratio
MOUNTAIN VALLEY BANK NA	ELKINS	WV	**B**	B	A-	113	2.04	7.4	6.0	33.7	24.5	**10.0**	13.1	23.0
MOUNTAIN VALLEY	CLEVELAND	GA	**D-**	D+	D	140	-5.52	5.0	1.0	11.5	13.4	**8.1**	9.7	14.4
MOUNTAIN VIEW BANK OF	WESTMINSTER	CO	**D+**	C	C	60	19.13	9.2	0.1	3.8	0.0	**10.0**	12.0	19.3
MOUNTAIN WEST BANK	COEUR D'ALENE	ID	**C-**	C-	B	1,172	-0.45	6.6	0.7	24.1	20.9	**10.0**	13.3	20.1
MOUNTAIN WEST BANK NA	HELENA	MT	**D-**	D-	C	709	-11.81	9.6	2.3	10.9	12.5	**7.1**	9.1	13.0
MRV BANKS	SAINTE GENEVIEVE	MO	**D**	C-	C-	66	20.50	8.3	0.8	9.3	11.4	**8.2**	9.8	14.6
▼MT VICTORY STATE BK	MOUNT VICTORY	OH	**C+**	B-	B-	15	-4.17	2.9	7.2	5.9	59.5	**10.0**	12.0	31.8
MT WASHINGTON SAVINGS &	CINCINNATI	OH	**D+**	C-	C	72	4.50	0.0	0.5	80.8	6.6	**10.0**	20.4	37.1
MUENSTER STATE BK	MUENSTER	TX	**A+**	A+	A+	148	12.94	1.7	2.4	6.5	71.2	**10.0**	11.6	34.1
MULESHOE STATE BK	MULESHOE	TX	**C+**	C+	B-	99	7.54	9.2	6.6	6.1	23.7	**5.6**	7.6	13.2
MUNCY BANK & TRUST CO	MUNCY	PA	**B**	B	B+	289	11.64	9.0	4.6	45.3	14.2	**6.4**	8.4	12.1
▼MUNICIPAL TRUST & SB	BOURBONNAIS	IL	**B-**	B	A	261	-1.46	0.4	0.3	24.3	2.8	**10.0**	20.3	38.4
MURPHY BANK	FRESNO	CA	**C+**	C+	B	116	-4.10	10.3	54.9	10.9	0.7	**10.0**	14.8	20.5
MURPHY-WALL STATE BK &	PINCKNEYVILLE	IL	**B-**	B-	B-	93	13.16	6.5	2.6	19.7	30.0	**10.0**	11.6	20.1
MURRAY BANK	MURRAY	KY	**B-**	B-	B-	224	16.02	7.6	3.5	24.4	28.2	**5.6**	7.6	14.6
MURRAY STATE BK	MURRAY	NE	**B+**	B+	B+	44	0.63	10.9	4.8	20.9	15.2	**10.0**	16.1	26.0
MUTUAL BANK	WHITMAN	MA	**C+**	C	C	372	0.92	0.4	3.1	48.0	30.9	**6.4**	8.4	16.8
▼MUTUAL FEDERAL BANK	CHICAGO	IL	**D+**	C-	C	76	14.80	0.1	1.1	32.5	7.0	**10.0**	20.8	36.1
MUTUAL FSB A FSSB	SIDNEY	OH	**D-**	D-	C-	112	-2.96	8.9	12.9	31.3	8.9	**6.7**	8.8	14.4
MUTUAL OF OMAHA BANK	OMAHA	NE	**C-**	C-	C-	4,672	18.67	12.8	0.5	13.0	23.4	**5.2**	8.1	11.2
MUTUAL SAVINGS & LOAN ASS	METAIRIE	LA	**B**	B	B	37	-10.71	0.0	0.6	80.3	0.3	**10.0**	29.7	56.1
MUTUAL SAVINGS ASSN FSA	LEAVENWORTH	KS	**B-**	C+	B+	238	-16.19	1.9	1.5	32.2	34.8	**10.0**	23.0	24.8
MUTUAL SAVINGS BANK	HARTSVILLE	SC	**C-**	C	B	45	0.42	4.3	5.9	23.8	5.3	**10.0**	31.1	58.2
▼MUTUAL SB	FRANKLIN	IN	**D+**	C-	D+	118	-8.15	4.1	3.3	34.2	3.7	**9.7**	10.8	16.3
MUTUALBANK	MUNCIE	IN	**C-**	C-	C-	1,401	0.40	4.5	9.0	36.4	17.4	**7.3**	9.2	13.8
▲MVB BANK INC	FAIRMONT	WV	**C+**	B-	B-	414	17.41	3.3	3.2	14.9	16.7	**6.2**	8.2	13.3
MWABANK	ROCK ISLAND	IL	**D+**	D	D+	241	8.69	1.4	2.4	59.1	26.5	**6.7**	8.8	17.5
MY BANK	BELEN	NM	**D+**	C	C+	161	8.89	3.6	2.0	11.7	31.5	**7.1**	9.0	15.1
▼NAFH NATIONAL BK	MIAMI	FL	**D+**	NR	NR	1,199	N/A	3.5	0.5	14.1	5.1	**10.0**	12.0	16.9
NANTAHALA BANK & TRUST	FRANKLIN	NC	**E-**	D-	D-	190	-11.11	9.7	0.9	10.1	13.4	**2.6**	6.2	9.6
NAPOLEON BANK	NAPOLEON	MO	**B**	B	B	35	-8.70	4.3	2.8	10.2	59.6	**10.0**	20.2	48.3
NAPOLEON STATE BK	NAPOLEON	IN	**C+**	B-	B-	155	7.85	5.6	9.2	26.0	9.2	**7.2**	9.2	13.5
▼NARA BANK	LOS ANGELES	CA	**D+**	C-	B	2,959	-8.24	16.1	0.3	0.6	17.9	**10.0**	12.3	17.3
NASHUA BANK	NASHUA	NH	**D+**	C	C	111	8.40	6.2	0.4	12.3	33.5	**9.2**	10.5	20.9
NASHVILLE BANK & TRUST CO	NASHVILLE	TN	**C+**	C+	C+	207	12.59	13.1	4.5	18.4	8.6	**8.5**	10.0	15.7
NASHVILLE SB	NASHVILLE	IL	**B-**	B-	B-	45	15.14	3.5	2.0	28.8	20.7	**8.7**	10.1	19.1
NATBANK NA	HOLLYWOOD	FL	**D**	C-	C	107	14.27	1.0	1.6	59.3	1.2	**10.0**	13.6	25.0
NATICK FSB	NATICK	MA	**D+**	C-	C-	161	-1.40	0.0	0.5	39.2	21.0	**6.8**	8.8	18.3
NATIONAL ADVISORS TRUST C	OVERLAND PARK	KS	**B-**	A	C	5	-0.04	0.0	0.0	0.0	55.0	**10.0**	80.1	324.3
NATIONAL B&TC OF	SYCAMORE	IL	**D**	D+	B+	559	-1.65	7.4	5.6	5.5	22.7	**9.0**	10.3	18.0
NATIONAL BK	HILLSBORO	IL	**B-**	B	B	273	16.81	6.1	1.7	10.8	28.1	**6.7**	8.7	13.4
NATIONAL BK	GATESVILLE	TX	**B-**	B-	B	463	0.86	3.2	9.5	11.8	26.7	**8.1**	9.7	17.0
NATIONAL BK & TRUST	LA GRANGE	TX	**B**	B	B	187	7.57	0.7	5.8	11.1	70.0	**5.5**	7.5	22.2
NATIONAL BK & TRUST CO	WILMINGTON	OH	**B-**	B	B	690	6.19	8.4	1.4	16.9	19.4	**7.7**	9.5	16.3
NATIONAL BK OF ADAMS	WEST UNION	OH	**B**	B	A-	74	3.72	1.2	3.6	33.6	14.3	**10.0**	12.9	27.1
NATIONAL BK OF ANDREWS	ANDREWS	TX	**A-**	A-	B+	109	7.29	20.1	5.3	12.4	23.9	**7.1**	9.0	15.1
NATIONAL BK OF ARIZONA	PHOENIX	AZ	**D**	D	C-	4,407	-2.94	6.8	0.6	12.0	5.5	**10.0**	12.7	18.2
NATIONAL BK OF ARKANSAS	NORTH LITTLE ROCK	AR	**D+**	D-	D	196	-1.74	5.8	1.0	17.3	23.1	**6.4**	8.4	13.7
NATIONAL BK OF	BLACKSBURG	VA	**A-**	A-	A-	1,019	4.10	3.5	3.5	13.6	30.4	**10.0**	11.9	19.0
NATIONAL BK OF CALIFORNIA	LOS ANGELES	CA	**D**	D	C-	381	-2.76	17.9	2.6	2.3	7.5	**9.4**	10.6	14.9
▼NATIONAL BK OF CAMBRIDGE	CAMBRIDGE	MD	**D-**	C-	A-	219	-4.40	5.5	1.8	15.7	19.5	**7.5**	9.3	14.6
▲NATIONAL BK OF COMMERCE	BIRMINGHAM	AL	**D+**	D-	D	375	1.11	7.5	2.2	12.5	8.1	**10.0**	20.3	35.8
▲NATIONAL BK OF COMMERCE	SUPERIOR	WI	**D+**	C+	B	534	-6.27	12.1	1.1	10.7	18.0	**8.7**	10.1	14.9
NATIONAL BK OF COXSACKIE	COXSACKIE	NY	**A-**	A-	A	194	-0.53	3.7	5.2	29.4	29.8	**9.9**	10.9	19.3
NATIONAL BK OF DELAWARE	WALTON	NY	**B-**	B-	B-	253	0.46	4.6	3.0	21.9	42.9	**7.1**	9.1	18.2
NATIONAL BK OF EARLVILLE	EARLVILLE	IL	**C-**	C-	A-	61	6.77	1.9	4.3	28.8	17.6	**10.0**	15.8	23.9
NATIONAL BK OF GEORGIA	ATHENS	GA	**D-**	D	B-	305	3.83	4.9	0.8	22.9	1.2	**6.2**	8.2	12.1
NATIONAL BK OF HARVEY	HARVEY	ND	**D-**	D-	D	49	-14.21	18.2	1.5	2.1	37.1	**8.5**	10.0	19.0
NATIONAL BK OF INDIANAPOL	INDIANAPOLIS	IN	**C**	C	C+	1,438	16.81	14.9	2.1	12.2	13.4	**4.5**	6.5	11.2
NATIONAL BK OF KANSAS CIT	OVERLAND PARK	KS	**D-**	NR	NR	656	-7.33	4.6	0.2	22.7	38.7	**8.1**	9.8	16.3

Asset Quality Index	Non-Performing Loans as a % of Total Loans	Non-Performing Loans as a % of Capital	Net Charge-offs Avg Loans	Profitability Index	Net Income ($Mil)	Return on Assets (R.O.A.)	Return on Equity (R.O.E.)	Net Interest Spread	Overhead Efficiency Ratio	Liquidity Index	Liquidity Ratio	Hot Money Ratio	Stability Index
7.0	1.25	6.0	-0.04	**4.1**	0.8	0.67	5.17	4.43	76.2	**2.8**	22.5	15.8	**7.8**
0.3	9.32	58.0	0.65	**0.6**	0.1	0.07	0.73	3.43	79.1	**1.0**	16.3	32.0	**3.1**
5.2	1.54	8.2	0.00	**2.5**	0.2	0.34	2.52	3.66	76.8	**6.1**	34.9	0.6	**0.7**
0.7	7.88	34.1	5.21	**0.9**	-12.2	-1.02	-6.95	4.64	66.9	**2.9**	17.6	15.1	**6.1**
0.0	12.20	75.7	2.56	**0.6**	-4.4	-0.57	-6.24	3.57	79.6	**2.0**	21.1	19.7	**4.5**
7.2	0.36	2.3	0.00	**0.7**	0.1	0.10	0.84	3.01	88.9	**1.6**	21.8	24.3	**1.5**
9.0	0.15	0.3	0.09	**2.5**	0.0	0.23	1.91	3.13	91.8	**5.6**	67.5	9.6	**7.1**
0.8	8.45	33.5	0.03	**3.1**	0.3	0.43	2.08	3.37	77.7	**1.4**	11.3	24.9	**6.1**
7.5	0.00	0.0	-0.04	**9.8**	3.8	2.81	20.49	3.81	40.5	**4.0**	71.6	24.0	**9.1**
8.4	0.01	0.1	0.22	**3.3**	0.5	0.51	5.96	4.46	84.8	**3.4**	37.4	16.9	**4.2**
6.1	0.48	3.9	0.07	**5.7**	3.1	1.13	13.23	4.06	59.6	**1.4**	12.2	25.1	**5.4**
5.0	4.39	11.3	0.34	**5.4**	3.0	1.14	5.75	3.40	48.5	**4.5**	51.0	15.3	**9.3**
2.5	1.35	6.7	1.29	**9.1**	2.4	2.00	14.00	6.42	44.7	**0.8**	21.8	54.4	**9.1**
5.1	2.33	10.8	1.07	**4.0**	0.7	0.85	7.04	4.39	74.2	**4.3**	29.0	9.5	**6.1**
4.8	1.11	8.2	0.00	**4.5**	1.9	0.94	11.27	3.22	61.4	**2.9**	39.4	21.0	**4.7**
8.4	0.00	0.0	0.00	**4.8**	0.4	0.83	5.15	4.18	71.4	**2.8**	30.7	17.8	**8.4**
6.2	0.50	3.4	0.02	**3.7**	2.4	0.65	7.70	3.04	77.5	**4.6**	35.6	10.5	**4.2**
1.6	14.58	37.7	0.07	**0.0**	-2.9	-3.93	-15.83	2.93	213.8	**2.9**	45.3	23.5	**4.5**
0.0	4.58	35.5	1.08	**0.2**	-1.2	-0.95	-6.77	3.63	90.2	**2.1**	22.8	19.4	**4.6**
2.7	2.28	17.5	0.16	**2.7**	22.4	0.48	3.82	3.93	71.4	**4.0**	31.6	15.5	**7.4**
9.6	0.00	0.0	0.00	**4.2**	0.4	0.91	3.33	4.51	69.7	**0.7**	2.1	32.8	**7.3**
3.6	5.86	13.4	0.01	**4.1**	2.8	1.04	5.37	3.29	56.8	**2.4**	47.8	34.8	**6.3**
6.5	1.57	2.6	2.39	**1.0**	-0.2	-0.49	-1.55	3.65	78.1	**2.6**	57.0	34.5	**5.5**
5.1	0.34	2.0	1.80	**0.0**	-1.9	-1.52	-12.95	3.99	97.8	**3.8**	12.2	9.4	**5.5**
1.8	3.20	22.4	0.40	**3.3**	7.4	0.51	5.17	3.34	70.4	**2.1**	21.4	20.4	**7.2**
5.6	0.94	7.6	0.33	**3.5**	2.4	0.60	7.35	3.08	68.2	**1.5**	9.0	22.8	**4.5**
3.2	1.97	13.9	0.41	**1.4**	0.3	0.13	1.46	3.29	69.8	**5.3**	33.4	5.3	**3.0**
1.7	4.71	28.2	0.46	**4.2**	1.0	0.63	6.74	4.91	73.3	**2.9**	30.6	17.2	**5.4**
2.9	1.58	8.2	0.00	**3.7**	20.5	1.73	13.06	N/,	33.1	**1.2**	22.3	38.8	**4.0**
0.0	15.96	139.3	2.71	**0.0**	-7.7	-3.79	-66.88	2.91	140.0	**1.4**	15.7	26.6	**1.2**
9.2	1.38	2.2	0.04	**4.1**	0.3	0.74	3.76	3.84	73.8	**6.3**	80.6	9.8	**7.3**
5.1	0.55	4.2	0.52	**3.9**	0.9	0.61	6.51	3.76	64.9	**1.6**	22.8	25.5	**5.3**
2.4	2.13	10.9	3.72	**0.8**	-5.3	-0.18	-1.38	3.84	47.5	**2.7**	16.7	16.0	**7.3**
5.4	1.51	7.6	0.00	**1.1**	0.3	0.30	2.71	3.33	91.4	**3.5**	32.0	15.1	**2.4**
8.7	0.00	0.0	0.00	**3.7**	1.3	0.64	6.12	3.39	75.1	**2.5**	29.2	18.8	**6.7**
8.6	0.00	0.0	-0.02	**4.2**	0.3	0.75	7.30	3.07	63.1	**1.6**	21.7	24.5	**5.4**
3.4	4.30	19.9	1.16	**0.0**	-1.2	-1.20	-7.98	3.32	104.6	**1.8**	22.0	21.5	**5.1**
4.6	1.72	9.4	0.00	**1.3**	0.3	0.20	2.22	2.47	89.1	**3.7**	49.8	18.7	**3.7**
6.8	0.00	0.0	0.00	**10.0**	0.4	8.65	10.52	1.62	91.0	**5.0**	417.3	100.0	**1.3**
0.8	6.32	31.7	0.87	**2.9**	2.0	0.34	2.98	3.56	82.9	**2.0**	17.5	19.1	**6.0**
4.4	1.73	11.2	0.37	**4.5**	2.0	0.80	8.46	3.74	66.2	**4.0**	25.2	10.3	**4.7**
4.3	0.81	4.1	0.40	**6.3**	5.2	1.14	11.77	4.75	60.4	**4.2**	39.4	13.6	**5.5**
8.2	0.88	2.7	0.07	**6.2**	2.8	1.48	17.38	3.09	55.0	**3.3**	53.7	25.3	**5.7**
4.0	2.31	13.8	0.40	**6.7**	9.2	1.34	12.07	4.09	63.4	**4.4**	26.5	8.1	**6.5**
5.6	2.72	11.5	0.31	**4.5**	0.8	1.04	7.90	3.26	66.8	**2.8**	31.7	18.2	**8.0**
6.6	0.96	5.6	0.06	**8.9**	1.8	1.73	17.34	4.81	69.6	**4.0**	34.6	13.0	**8.1**
0.7	4.32	20.4	3.31	**0.3**	-7.9	-0.18	-1.25	4.32	77.6	**4.2**	17.6	8.1	**5.1**
1.5	4.52	30.8	0.78	**1.2**	0.3	0.17	1.94	3.54	95.3	**1.7**	18.9	22.1	**3.9**
5.8	1.62	7.5	0.45	**8.3**	15.9	1.62	12.73	4.45	48.2	**3.6**	27.8	15.8	**9.9**
3.4	2.71	15.1	3.33	**0.7**	-5.7	-1.46	-12.21	5.18	83.5	**3.2**	20.1	13.6	**5.9**
0.3	14.43	78.1	6.50	**0.0**	-8.3	-3.70	-29.29	2.90	105.6	**1.4**	20.3	26.9	**6.2**
3.6	4.89	12.8	5.00	**0.0**	-11.5	-3.24	-30.91	3.86	108.9	**3.4**	45.8	19.4	**5.0**
0.6	6.47	38.1	1.44	**3.7**	0.9	0.16	1.55	3.70	63.2	**1.4**	23.0	28.7	**6.7**
5.9	0.93	4.4	0.09	**5.4**	2.0	1.00	8.73	4.21	68.7	**3.3**	21.0	12.9	**7.3**
6.1	0.76	3.6	0.13	**3.6**	1.7	0.67	5.86	3.89	80.9	**1.8**	17.9	20.9	**7.0**
0.9	8.59	36.9	0.20	**4.4**	0.4	0.73	4.52	3.92	59.7	**2.9**	23.1	15.1	**6.7**
0.1	3.16	25.9	0.87	**2.6**	0.8	0.25	3.04	3.60	71.2	**2.7**	17.9	15.8	**4.1**
1.4	7.62	32.9	3.50	**0.2**	-0.4	-0.73	-7.35	3.66	68.8	**3.2**	21.4	13.5	**3.5**
5.0	1.24	10.7	0.33	**3.3**	6.2	0.47	7.10	3.35	76.2	**4.1**	21.8	10.5	**3.1**
0.3	11.20	49.1	3.25	**0.0**	-7.9	-1.17	-13.42	1.43	89.1	**1.6**	14.8	22.3	**4.7**

Name	City	State	Rating	2008 Rating	2007 Rating	Total Assets ($Mil)	One Year Asset Growth	Asset Mix (As a % of Total Assets) Comm-ercial Loans	Cons-umer Loans	Home Mort-gages	Secur-ities	Capital-ization Index	Leverage Ratio	Risk-based Capital Ratio
NATIONAL BK OF MALVERN	MALVERN	PA	**B-**	C+	B-	132	1.65	0.1	0.1	38.5	24.9	**10.0**	13.1	23.0
NATIONAL BK OF MIDDLEBURY	MIDDLEBURY	VT	**C+**	B-	B-	273	-0.78	4.4	0.6	33.0	20.3	**6.1**	8.1	13.1
NATIONAL BK OF NEW YORK C	FLUSHING	NY	**C-**	B+	A	265	0.33	1.7	0.0	0.2	9.0	**10.0**	14.0	18.9
NATIONAL BK OF OAK	OAK HARBOR	OH	**C-**	C-	C	198	7.92	5.7	6.3	17.3	19.9	**6.2**	8.2	13.6
NATIONAL BK OF	PETERSBURG	IL	**B+**	B+	B+	137	3.11	2.9	5.5	21.5	31.8	**10.0**	11.1	20.3
▲ NATIONAL BK OF SALLISAW	SALLISAW	OK	**B**	B	B	107	3.21	7.0	5.9	10.0	33.4	**10.0**	12.0	19.1
NATIONAL BK OF ST ANNE	SAINT ANNE	IL	**C-**	C-	C	46	3.28	2.6	10.9	18.4	1.1	**6.0**	8.0	13.9
NATIONAL BK OF TENNESSEE	NEWPORT	TN	**D**	D-	C+	170	-8.62	5.2	4.6	21.6	18.8	**7.2**	9.2	15.0
▼ NATIONAL BK OF TEXAS FT W	FORT WORTH	TX	**C+**	B-	B-	139	8.46	8.5	8.4	1.3	52.9	**9.5**	10.6	25.4
NATIONAL BK OF WAUPUN	WAUPUN	WI	**D-**	D-	C+	125	-3.99	10.5	4.5	15.5	18.6	**6.1**	8.1	12.2
NATIONAL CAPITAL BANK OF	WASHINGTON	DC	**A**	A+	A+	334	12.04	10.8	1.9	47.3	17.6	**10.0**	11.0	18.8
NATIONAL EXCHANGE BANK &	FOND DU LAC	WI	**A-**	A	A+	1,373	9.01	10.7	2.3	10.5	22.1	**10.0**	13.8	21.4
NATIONAL GRAND BK	MARBLEHEAD	MA	**A-**	A-	A-	249	0.27	3.2	3.1	42.9	19.8	**9.1**	10.4	18.7
NATIONAL INDEPENDENT	RUSTON	LA	**U**	U	U	6	10.07	0.0	0.0	0.0	3.8	**10.0**	92.5	122.4
▼ NATIONAL IRON BANK	SALISBURY	CT	**C**	C	C-	99	0.54	2.5	1.3	24.6	54.3	**5.9**	7.9	21.2
NATIONAL PENN BANK	BOYERTOWN	PA	**C**	C-	B	8,811	-4.19	9.1	2.7	16.2	24.5	**6.9**	8.9	14.7
NATIONAL PENN WEALTH	WILMINGTON	DE	**U**	U	U	12	-2.03	0.0	0.0	0.0	43.9	**10.0**	84.1	261.3
▼ NATIONAL REPUBLIC BK CHIC	CHICAGO	IL	**D+**	C-	C	1,279	1.51	2.6	0.1	3.4	13.1	**7.9**	9.6	13.4
NATIONAL UNION BANK KINDE	KINDERHOOK	NY	**B-**	B-	B-	248	4.14	8.6	0.9	22.5	27.4	**6.1**	8.1	14.0
NATIONWIDE BANK	COLUMBUS	OH	**A-**	A-	A-	3,933	22.98	4.2	5.5	15.0	70.2	**6.0**	8.0	19.7
▲ NATIVE AMERICAN BANK NA	DENVER	CO	**E+**	E-	D+	83	-16.29	45.8	6.5	3.2	14.7	**4.8**	6.8	17.5
NATURE COAST BANK	HERNANDO	FL	**D-**	D	D-	56	-4.66	3.5	0.8	7.4	10.5	**7.1**	9.1	12.6
NAUGATUCK SB	NAUGATUCK	CT	**C+**	C-	B-	852	-2.78	5.4	0.4	33.7	11.9	**9.0**	10.3	15.1
NAUGATUCK VALLEY SAVINGS	NAUGATUCK	CT	**C-**	C-	C-	567	2.09	6.1	0.2	40.7	8.1	**6.0**	8.0	11.8
▼ NBC OKLAHOMA	OKLAHOMA CITY	OK	**D+**	C	C+	439	-4.28	20.0	2.1	15.3	6.4	**5.5**	8.1	11.4
NBRS FINANCIAL BANK	RISING SUN	MD	**E-**	D-	D+	264	-3.75	18.1	1.1	20.7	6.2	**1.9**	6.1	8.9
NBT BANK NA	NORWICH	NY	**B-**	B-	B-	5,303	-2.25	10.4	16.4	16.8	23.0	**6.7**	8.7	13.0
NCB FSB	HILLSBORO	OH	**D**	D	B-	1,451	-8.73	17.7	0.9	19.9	2.0	**10.0**	11.5	15.6
NEBRASKA BANK OF	LINCOLN	NE	**D-**	D	C	56	-7.50	13.5	3.3	21.9	0.0	**10.0**	12.7	19.2
NEBRASKA BANKERS BANK	LINCOLN	NE	**D**	D	D-	37	43.64	1.6	0.8	0.0	0.0	**10.0**	12.2	16.1
NEBRASKA NATIONAL BK	KEARNEY	NE	**C+**	C	C	152	6.56	11.9	3.8	7.8	31.7	**6.6**	8.7	13.0
NEBRASKA STATE BK	BRISTOW	NE	**B-**	C+	B-	14	5.34	11.1	4.3	5.9	0.0	**10.0**	15.2	24.5
NEBRASKA STATE BK	LYNCH	NE	**C+**	C-	C+	12	-1.91	4.4	3.1	3.9	0.0	**10.0**	15.3	30.3
▲ NEBRASKA STATE BK	OSHKOSH	NE	**B**	B-	B-	45	4.50	3.1	0.2	0.2	19.1	**7.7**	9.5	14.4
NEBRASKA STATE BK &	BROKEN BOW	NE	**A-**	A-	A-	151	11.64	7.9	4.0	6.5	6.3	**7.5**	10.9	12.9
NEBRASKALAND NATIONAL BK	NORTH PLATTE	NE	**B**	B	C+	328	14.73	20.3	0.6	5.8	23.4	**7.4**	9.2	13.1
NECEDAH BANK	NECEDAH	WI	**D+**	D-	D	40	-8.38	4.6	1.7	17.2	27.2	**8.8**	10.2	16.6
NEEDHAM BANK	NEEDHAM	MA	**B**	C+	B+	1,160	5.86	1.9	1.5	46.6	12.0	**10.0**	16.1	25.0
NEFFS NATIONAL BK	NEFFS	PA	**A**	A	A	278	7.86	0.7	2.9	23.2	50.5	**10.0**	16.6	31.6
NEHAWKA BANK	NEHAWKA	NE	**B-**	B-	B-	17	12.35	3.4	6.5	51.4	1.0	**10.0**	14.3	23.8
NEIGHBORHOOD NATIONAL	SAN DIEGO	CA	**D-**	D-	D	131	-1.87	12.9	0.4	11.7	1.6	**5.6**	7.6	12.2
NEIGHBORHOOD NATIONAL	ALEXANDRIA	MN	**E-**	D	C-	49	-10.37	11.1	2.6	12.2	13.6	**5.1**	7.2	11.0
NEKOMA STATE BK	LA CROSSE	KS	**C+**	C	C	34	11.89	5.0	2.2	6.5	52.6	**6.7**	8.7	17.4
NEKOOSA PORT EDWARDS	NEKOOSA	WI	**B+**	B+	B+	211	0.66	4.1	1.6	35.1	21.0	**10.0**	11.0	20.8
NELSONVILLE HOME & SAVING	NELSONVILLE	OH	**C+**	C+	C+	20	22.37	0.0	1.7	66.6	11.3	**10.0**	11.6	25.3
▼ NEUBERGER BERMAN TRUST	WILMINGTON	DE	**U**	NR	NR	5	N/A	0.0	0.0	0.0	66.7	**10.0**	69.1	112.7
▼ NEUBERGER BERMAN TRUST	NEW YORK	NY	**U**	NR	NR	20	N/A	0.0	0.0	0.0	67.4	**10.0**	56.3	101.1
▲ NEVADA BANK & TRUST CO	CALIENTE	NV	**D+**	D+	D-	89	-5.94	2.4	6.6	16.4	29.1	**9.7**	10.8	23.3
NEVADA COMMERCE BANK	LAS VEGAS	NV	**E-**	E-	D-	145	-32.51	10.9	0.3	3.5	7.7	**0.0**	2.3	4.5
NEVADA NATIONAL BK	LAS VEGAS	NV	**D-**	C-	C-	35	-17.65	1.0	0.4	3.0	39.8	**10.0**	12.8	22.0
NEVADA STATE BK	LAS VEGAS	NV	**D**	D	C-	4,072	-3.89	8.6	1.7	8.0	13.6	**10.0**	12.7	22.5
NEW ALBIN SB	NEW ALBIN	IA	**A**	A	B+	186	5.54	2.8	0.9	7.7	67.6	**10.0**	13.1	35.2
NEW BUFFALO SAVINGS BANK	NEW BUFFALO	MI	**D**	D	D	96	-4.90	1.2	0.9	34.1	0.0	**10.0**	13.8	18.6
NEW CARLISLE FSB	NEW CARLISLE	OH	**D**	D	B-	94	-11.15	6.9	1.6	30.0	3.7	**7.5**	9.6	12.9
NEW CENTURY BANK	DUNN	NC	**D-**	D+	C-	625	-0.70	7.2	1.2	9.7	14.4	**7.1**	9.1	12.7
NEW CENTURY BANK NA	BELLEVILLE	KS	**B-**	B-	B-	22	5.35	8.4	8.4	23.7	3.9	**8.4**	9.9	14.9
NEW CITY BANK	CHICAGO	IL	**D-**	D	C+	92	-7.21	7.9	1.5	19.0	28.5	**5.8**	7.8	12.8
NEW COVENANT TRUST CO	JEFFERSONVILLE	IN	**U**	U	U	6	10.74	0.0	0.0	0.0	32.5	**10.0**	74.4	213.2
NEW ENGLAND BANK	ENFIELD	CT	**D+**	D+	C	677	0.80	9.6	1.6	28.0	8.7	**5.8**	7.8	12.1
NEW ERA BANK	FREDERICKTOWN	MO	**A**	A+	A+	283	-3.49	3.8	1.5	35.4	18.7	**9.8**	10.8	16.7

Asset Quality Index	Non-Performing Loans as a % of Total Loans	Non-Performing Loans as a % of Capital	Net Charge-offs Avg Loans	Profitability Index	Net Income ($Mil)	Return on Assets (R.O.A.)	Return on Equity (R.O.E.)	Net Interest Spread	Overhead Efficiency Ratio	Liquidity Index	Liquidity Ratio	Hot Money Ratio	Stability Index
4.1	3.60	16.4	0.47	**3.7**	0.8	0.60	4.64	4.00	75.1	**3.3**	30.1	15.2	**7.6**
5.6	0.91	6.9	0.29	**3.4**	1.7	0.62	7.32	4.12	80.8	**3.8**	23.3	10.6	**5.4**
1.0	6.28	32.6	0.02	**4.1**	1.9	0.75	5.49	2.77	67.3	**0.8**	23.3	57.2	**9.0**
2.5	1.90	14.6	0.31	**4.4**	1.4	0.72	8.49	4.03	70.8	**1.7**	13.3	21.4	**4.7**
8.6	0.38	1.7	-0.03	**4.4**	1.0	0.75	6.59	3.37	72.2	**4.8**	39.3	10.5	**7.4**
7.3	0.00	0.0	0.45	**6.3**	1.3	1.28	10.27	4.61	59.9	**2.8**	38.5	22.1	**6.3**
5.2	0.00	0.0	1.86	**1.5**	-0.1	-0.15	-1.14	3.96	67.9	**1.8**	32.0	30.8	**6.7**
1.2	5.51	34.9	1.23	**0.7**	-1.1	-0.64	-7.99	3.98	98.3	**2.5**	12.3	16.3	**3.6**
7.0	0.71	2.3	1.21	**3.0**	0.9	0.67	6.10	3.63	83.3	**3.9**	65.4	23.7	**5.9**
0.3	5.60	42.1	4.72	**0.0**	-1.1	-0.87	-8.95	4.17	77.4	**2.5**	22.4	17.4	**3.3**
9.1	0.00	0.0	0.03	**7.8**	3.8	1.21	10.26	4.01	51.1	**2.7**	4.6	14.5	**7.8**
5.3	3.37	13.3	0.65	**6.5**	13.8	1.07	7.57	3.77	51.9	**4.1**	27.9	13.5	**9.5**
8.0	0.40	2.5	0.04	**6.6**	3.0	1.19	11.37	3.98	58.6	**4.0**	29.9	11.7	**6.8**
10.0	0.00	0.0	0.00	**8.5**	0.6	10.27	11.53	1.94	87.7	**5.0**	310.3	101.0	**5.7**
10.0	0.00	0.0	0.00	**2.7**	-1.7	-1.63	-19.40	3.55	86.6	**3.5**	63.9	23.7	**4.8**
4.2	1.52	8.8	1.53	**3.1**	48.0	0.53	4.37	3.68	59.1	**3.9**	13.0	9.5	**6.5**
10.0	0.00	0.0	0.00	**10.0**	2.3	21.52	24.97	2.00	75.0	**5.0**	459.7	101.0	**5.0**
0.0	2.06	16.3	0.65	**9.5**	31.3	2.46	26.58	4.15	26.1	**0.4**	11.9	82.5	**8.7**
6.0	0.94	7.1	0.02	**3.7**	1.5	0.63	7.35	4.15	78.2	**3.9**	6.2	8.4	**5.2**
7.9	0.41	1.3	0.79	**6.1**	51.4	1.43	15.17	2.80	75.6	**4.3**	77.3	25.1	**9.6**
0.5	3.71	28.7	0.22	**4.0**	1.3	1.46	20.82	4.25	95.4	**0.5**	11.2	58.5	**3.6**
0.7	0.75	5.3	1.42	**0.1**	-0.3	-0.44	-3.69	3.51	95.1	**0.7**	14.9	48.6	**4.7**
3.2	2.23	15.8	0.51	**3.2**	3.7	0.42	4.41	3.78	78.6	**3.8**	13.1	9.8	**5.8**
1.6	3.76	35.1	0.16	**2.9**	2.3	0.40	5.15	3.41	69.4	**1.5**	11.6	22.7	**5.2**
0.9	3.33	29.0	0.16	**5.0**	5.0	1.12	13.77	4.20	67.4	**2.5**	11.3	16.3	**4.3**
0.3	3.14	32.2	1.73	**0.2**	-5.5	-2.03	-26.81	4.04	91.4	**1.7**	11.4	19.9	**0.0**
4.3	1.17	7.9	0.69	**5.7**	56.3	1.04	10.18	4.25	60.0	**3.9**	4.8	7.9	**8.5**
0.9	5.09	30.3	0.67	**3.4**	10.1	0.67	6.20	3.11	71.9	**1.2**	24.2	64.2	**6.2**
2.2	4.55	22.9	0.11	**0.0**	-2.6	-4.65	-47.95	2.37	164.8	**3.8**	28.7	12.0	**0.0**
1.1	5.87	26.9	1.66	**2.0**	0.1	0.17	1.41	3.78	90.2	**2.8**	55.1	30.8	**3.0**
3.1	2.39	14.8	0.31	**5.5**	1.7	1.11	13.13	4.45	50.2	**2.8**	29.4	17.7	**4.9**
8.2	0.01	0.1	-0.19	**3.2**	0.1	0.39	2.44	4.41	90.9	**1.9**	46.5	33.6	**7.5**
8.6	0.00	0.0	-0.39	**2.2**	0.0	0.34	2.09	3.74	92.0	**5.0**	64.0	12.6	**6.0**
7.1	0.05	0.3	-0.03	**9.6**	1.0	2.26	24.99	3.56	56.3	**1.4**	19.3	28.0	**7.0**
5.8	0.38	2.8	-0.03	**6.7**	2.3	1.60	13.32	4.21	61.6	**1.3**	14.3	26.8	**8.7**
7.1	0.00	0.0	0.01	**5.4**	3.3	1.04	11.07	4.09	62.6	**0.8**	12.0	34.7	**5.7**
2.7	2.00	10.3	1.12	**2.0**	0.1	0.28	2.73	3.35	81.8	**4.2**	24.8	8.5	**3.7**
3.5	4.12	19.4	0.18	**4.3**	6.4	0.56	3.42	3.76	49.8	**1.2**	14.0	30.4	**7.9**
7.7	2.08	5.4	0.07	**7.5**	3.5	1.31	7.70	3.88	38.2	**3.9**	60.1	21.7	**9.1**
8.2	0.04	0.2	0.23	**4.4**	0.1	0.67	4.50	5.54	79.3	**4.3**	14.9	6.2	**7.3**
0.3	4.61	31.0	1.79	**0.0**	-1.2	-0.81	-12.36	3.54	83.9	**0.7**	22.7	61.9	**3.3**
0.3	9.14	67.8	1.54	**0.1**	-1.3	-2.53	-28.71	3.54	106.0	**2.5**	24.3	17.5	**3.4**
9.1	0.00	0.0	-0.13	**3.5**	0.2	0.64	6.75	4.31	82.7	**6.4**	56.5	4.6	**5.3**
5.4	1.59	8.6	0.13	**5.0**	2.6	1.24	11.31	3.03	48.9	**2.0**	37.7	33.2	**7.6**
9.8	0.00	0.0	0.00	**2.4**	0.0	0.24	1.91	2.95	89.8	**1.3**	26.2	28.9	**6.9**
10.0	0.00	0.0	0.00	**3.7**	0.3	5.24	8.82	N/,	84.4	**5.0**	216.3	101.0	**4.8**
10.0	0.00	0.0	0.00	**3.7**	1.2	5.75	10.93	N/,	86.4	**4.3**	163.1	101.0	**5.7**
1.7	0.83	3.3	-0.91	**2.4**	0.6	0.61	5.83	4.36	93.0	**5.7**	38.4	4.4	**3.5**
0.3	10.40	118.4	3.50	**0.0**	-5.4	-2.90	-78.56	2.26	191.0	**0.6**	15.2	58.9	**0.8**
0.0	15.62	50.7	6.07	**0.0**	-4.0	-10.07	-53.13	4.32	740.4	**3.0**	48.4	23.9	**1.1**
1.0	8.71	28.7	7.47	**0.0**	-70.3	-1.72	-11.42	3.61	84.1	**5.8**	42.3	8.5	**5.1**
9.6	0.63	1.4	-0.06	**8.3**	3.2	1.75	12.27	3.63	27.3	**3.9**	65.7	23.6	**8.6**
1.4	3.76	19.0	0.39	**0.0**	-3.0	-3.10	-19.83	3.59	104.8	**0.9**	6.4	31.0	**5.7**
3.9	1.36	10.2	0.51	**0.8**	-0.6	-0.58	-6.12	3.68	83.0	**2.3**	11.1	17.1	**3.7**
1.8	2.25	15.6	3.30	**0.1**	-4.7	-0.73	-7.39	3.99	70.1	**1.0**	15.5	31.8	**4.7**
5.2	1.29	9.2	0.11	**5.8**	0.3	1.23	12.22	5.75	83.1	**3.0**	15.0	13.6	**5.0**
0.3	10.68	64.3	4.99	**0.6**	-2.7	-2.70	-30.49	5.08	71.3	**0.9**	27.1	65.9	**4.3**
10.0	0.00	0.0	0.00	**7.0**	0.5	8.06	10.90	2.03	91.4	**5.0**	349.0	101.0	**5.3**
1.5	2.34	21.4	0.30	**3.1**	3.3	0.49	4.88	3.56	71.1	**1.9**	12.2	19.2	**6.0**
7.0	0.43	2.9	0.09	**9.9**	6.8	2.46	20.98	3.84	39.1	**3.9**	9.5	8.7	**8.9**

Name	City	State	Rating	2008 Rating	2007 Rating	Total Assets ($Mil)	One Year Asset Growth	Asset Mix (As a % of Total Assets) Comm-ercial Loans	Cons-umer Loans	Home Mort-gages	Secur-ities	Capital-ization Index	Leverage Ratio	Risk-based Capital Ratio
▼ NEW FOUNDATION SAVINGS	CINCINNATI	OH	**D-**	D	C-	18	14.27	1.9	0.1	65.9	1.4	**7.6**	9.4	16.8
▼ NEW FRONTIER BANK	SAINT CHARLES	MO	**C-**	C-	D+	137	-6.66	9.8	0.5	15.0	10.7	**8.2**	9.8	14.1
▼ NEW HORIZON BANK NA	POWHATAN	VA	**D**	C	NR	24	128.60	27.1	2.1	9.6	26.8	**10.0**	30.0	37.0
NEW HORIZONS BANK	EAST ELLIJAY	GA	**E-**	E-	D	111	-11.68	3.2	2.1	15.4	9.4	**0.0**	0.3	0.8
NEW JERSEY COMMUNITY	FREEHOLD	NJ	**C-**	C	C	111	26.26	12.4	0.2	2.2	11.3	**10.0**	12.3	15.3
NEW MARKET BANK	NEW MARKET	MN	**D-**	C-	C	87	1.41	5.0	1.4	9.7	2.9	**6.9**	8.9	14.2
NEW MEXICO BANK & TRUST	ALBUQUERQUE	NM	**C-**	C-	C+	914	5.24	11.0	0.6	4.8	35.0	**6.0**	8.0	12.9
▼ NEW MILLENNIUM BANK	NEW BRUNSWICK	NJ	**E+**	D-	D-	219	-12.16	5.6	9.8	0.1	17.2	**3.2**	5.7	10.1
NEW PEOPLES BANK INC	HONAKER	VA	**D-**	D+	C+	857	-0.13	5.9	6.5	30.9	0.5	**4.8**	6.9	10.9
NEW REPUBLIC SAVINGS	ROANOKE RAPIDS	NC	**C**	C-	C	53	-0.01	1.3	0.5	52.8	0.0	**8.5**	10.0	15.6
NEW RESOURCE BANK	SAN FRANCISCO	CA	**D**	D	D	155	-2.88	16.2	0.3	2.4	16.7	**10.0**	12.1	17.4
▼ NEW TRADITIONS NATIONAL B	ORLANDO	FL	**D+**	C	C	351	29.66	5.7	0.5	1.6	51.2	**8.5**	10.0	20.3
NEW TRIPOLI BANK	NEW TRIPOLI	PA	**A-**	B+	A-	305	6.63	4.6	1.5	36.4	29.2	**10.0**	11.2	18.2
NEW WASHINGTON STATE BK	NEW WASHINGTON	IN	**B**	B	B-	222	0.53	6.7	6.9	22.7	11.4	**9.2**	10.4	14.6
NEW WEST BANK	GREELEY	CO	**C+**	C	C-	152	-0.36	7.6	0.6	7.7	39.5	**6.3**	8.3	14.0
▼ NEW WINDSOR STATE BK	NEW WINDSOR	MD	**D-**	D-	D+	249	6.43	9.0	3.5	27.5	5.3	**7.9**	9.7	13.2
NEW YORK COMMERCIAL	WESTBURY	NY	**C-**	B-	B	2,531	0.76	18.7	0.2	1.0	23.3	**10.0**	12.7	17.3
NEW YORK COMMUNITY BANK	WESTBURY	NY	**C-**	C-	B-	38,865	-3.20	0.6	0.1	13.3	10.8	**6.8**	8.8	14.0
NEWALLIANCE BANK	NEW HAVEN	CT	**B-**	B-	B-	9,021	7.07	5.1	0.1	32.2	31.7	**6.8**	8.8	17.1
NEWBANK	FLUSHING	NY	**C-**	C-	C+	132	8.26	35.0	0.0	0.0	4.3	**8.0**	9.7	13.8
NEWBRIDGE BANK	GREENSBORO	NC	**D**	D-	D	1,805	-7.16	7.3	3.0	18.0	17.4	**7.2**	9.3	12.7
NEWBURYPORT FIVE CENTS	NEWBURYPORT	MA	**B+**	B	B-	620	1.80	1.9	0.4	47.6	18.0	**10.0**	14.7	22.1
▼ NEWDOMINION BANK	CHARLOTTE	NC	**E-**	D-	C-	506	-6.19	6.5	0.1	5.4	17.9	**0.0**	2.4	7.5
NEWFIELD NATIONAL BK	NEWFIELD	NJ	**B-**	C+	C+	480	-7.35	9.3	1.4	19.6	24.2	**7.0**	9.0	14.1
NEWFIRST NATIONAL BK	EL CAMPO	TX	**C**	B	B	410	4.32	12.9	2.8	12.1	11.0	**7.0**	9.0	14.2
▲ NEWPORT FEDERAL BANK	NEWPORT	TN	**C**	C+	B	167	12.63	0.2	2.2	51.1	25.9	**6.7**	8.7	18.0
NEWPORT FSB	NEWPORT	RI	**C-**	C-	C-	447	-2.30	0.4	0.1	47.7	10.6	**7.5**	9.3	15.2
▼ NEWTON COUNTY BANK	NEWTON	MS	**C+**	B	A	152	-4.54	4.2	8.0	17.6	14.0	**9.8**	12.2	14.8
NEWTON COUNTY LOAN &	GOODLAND	IN	**D**	C	E	22	56.09	0.0	0.0	2.7	82.6	**10.0**	67.0	278.0
NEWTON FEDERAL BANK	COVINGTON	GA	**C-**	C-	C	252	-5.33	0.0	1.2	65.0	2.5	**10.0**	17.9	27.8
NEWTOWN SB	NEWTOWN	CT	**D+**	D+	C-	943	3.22	6.6	2.2	40.6	9.5	**5.6**	7.6	12.0
NEXBANK SSB	DALLAS	TX	**C-**	C-	C	591	-3.53	16.3	0.1	15.6	14.8	**10.0**	11.9	19.9
NEXITY BANK	BIRMINGHAM	AL	**E-**	E-	D-	794	-17.82	0.7	0.1	1.5	30.4	**0.0**	0.7	2.5
NEXTIER BANK NA	BUTLER	PA	**D-**	D-	C-	525	-9.14	7.3	0.9	10.4	14.6	**4.2**	6.2	10.6
NICOLET NATIONAL BK	GREEN BAY	WI	**C-**	C-	C+	656	-0.21	21.6	1.9	12.2	7.8	**7.2**	9.2	13.0
NICOLLET COUNTY BK OF ST	SAINT PETER	MN	**B-**	B-	B-	147	-3.77	9.2	4.1	8.5	24.0	**5.7**	7.7	13.9
NIXON STATE BK	NIXON	TX	**C-**	C	C	69	1.26	8.8	7.2	6.5	25.2	**6.1**	8.1	18.6
NJM BANK FSB	WEST TRENTON	NJ	**C**	C	C	585	2.49	0.5	0.3	44.6	35.8	**6.1**	8.1	21.7
▼ NOA BANK	DULUTH	GA	**D+**	C	C	81	46.96	4.5	0.1	2.1	22.7	**10.0**	17.0	22.3
NOBLE BANK & TRUST NA	ANNISTON	AL	**C-**	C-	C	170	2.08	8.3	2.1	13.5	28.8	**6.5**	8.5	15.4
NODAWAY VALLEY BANK	MARYVILLE	MO	**B**	B	B+	705	2.57	6.7	2.3	12.0	12.1	**7.2**	9.1	12.9
NOKOMIS SB	NOKOMIS	IL	**C**	C	C-	28	1.62	18.4	1.0	3.3	49.6	**10.0**	13.1	74.5
NORDSTROM FSB	SCOTTSDALE	AZ	**A-**	A-	A-	228	6.28	0.0	67.9	0.0	0.0	**10.0**	51.6	67.3
NORMANGEE STATE BK	NORMANGEE	TX	**A-**	A-	A-	84	4.63	0.5	17.6	15.9	50.6	**10.0**	11.4	27.1
NORSTATES BANK	WAUKEGAN	IL	**D-**	D-	D-	532	-14.53	3.0	0.3	7.8	17.3	**6.3**	8.3	13.1
NORTH ADAMS STATE BK	URSA	IL	**C**	C+	C	33	4.15	14.6	4.0	10.0	21.4	**8.6**	10.1	18.2
NORTH AKRON SB	AKRON	OH	**D+**	D+	D+	161	3.27	0.5	0.4	56.1	23.2	**7.1**	9.0	20.0
NORTH ALABAMA BANK	HAZEL GREEN	AL	**D-**	D-	C-	125	-20.33	5.7	2.7	12.1	7.4	**6.0**	8.0	12.2
NORTH AMERICAN BANKING	ROSEVILLE	MN	**D**	D	D-	268	10.72	13.4	1.8	8.6	11.2	**8.1**	9.7	14.0
NORTH AMERICAN SAVINGS	GRANDVIEW	MO	**B-**	B-	C+	1,315	-12.55	6.9	0.2	35.6	5.1	**9.5**	12.9	14.6
NORTH AMERICAN STATE BK	BELGRADE	MN	**D**	D	D	107	-8.53	7.2	1.6	9.5	15.1	**7.5**	9.3	13.8
NORTH ARUNDEL SAVINGS	PASADENA	MD	**C+**	C+	C+	34	5.68	0.0	1.0	64.0	21.1	**10.0**	12.0	24.5
NORTH BANK	CHICAGO	IL	**D+**	C-	C-	116	6.07	5.8	0.6	14.2	32.8	**6.4**	8.4	14.8
NORTH BROOKFIELD SB	NORTH BROOKFIELD	MA	**B**	B-	B	192	1.63	0.8	1.6	45.1	30.9	**10.0**	13.4	30.2
NORTH CAMBRIDGE CO-OP	CAMBRIDGE	MA	**C+**	C+	C+	91	2.16	0.0	0.1	47.8	35.1	**10.0**	18.7	35.1
▼ NORTH CASCADES NATIONAL	CHELAN	WA	**C-**	C-	B-	326	-2.57	6.8	0.8	9.9	15.8	**7.4**	9.3	14.3
▲ NORTH CENTRAL BANK	HENNEPIN	IL	**B-**	C	B-	115	-0.58	6.5	5.0	21.1	33.0	**7.9**	9.6	17.7
NORTH COMMUNITY BANK	CHICAGO	IL	**D-**	D	C-	499	-7.94	2.8	0.1	20.4	4.1	**8.0**	9.7	14.7
NORTH COUNTRY BANK NA	MCCLUSKY	ND	**B+**	B	B+	59	13.79	7.0	4.3	1.4	25.3	**9.5**	10.7	18.0
NORTH COUNTRY SB	CANTON	NY	**C+**	C+	C+	238	0.17	0.5	2.2	75.3	2.3	**10.0**	13.8	24.8

Asset Quality Index	Non-Performing Loans as a % of Total Loans	Non-Performing Loans as a % of Capital	Net Charge-offs Avg Loans	Profitability Index	Net Income ($Mil)	Return on Assets (R.O.A.)	Return on Equity (R.O.E.)	Net Interest Spread	Overhead Efficiency Ratio	Liquidity Index	Liquidity Ratio	Hot Money Ratio	Stability Index
3.6	1.13	9.0	0.26	**1.2**	0.0	-0.06	-0.59	2.68	101.8	**1.5**	17.6	24.0	**2.9**
1.7	6.66	40.4	0.53	**2.5**	0.5	0.34	3.39	4.05	75.3	**2.5**	14.1	16.5	**5.1**
8.9	0.00	0.0	0.00	**0.0**	-0.9	-5.21	-12.73	4.12	210.7	**1.5**	37.7	33.4	**1.5**
0.3	10.13	187.6	5.30	**0.0**	-6.9	-5.66	-131.90	2.69	148.7	**1.3**	16.2	27.4	**0.4**
7.4	0.00	0.0	0.22	**0.7**	0.2	0.14	1.12	3.42	83.7	**0.8**	18.9	42.0	**2.2**
1.7	4.82	29.8	1.22	**0.1**	-1.0	-1.18	-11.91	3.87	102.9	**4.5**	29.1	8.5	**3.9**
1.2	4.04	25.8	1.03	**5.8**	10.2	1.16	12.81	4.17	56.5	**1.8**	15.2	19.8	**5.5**
0.0	12.44	100.3	1.16	**0.0**	-7.9	-3.24	-40.27	4.22	105.1	**1.3**	11.7	26.4	**4.3**
0.2	5.76	50.9	1.64	**0.9**	-3.4	-0.40	-5.15	4.49	75.5	**1.4**	10.9	25.5	**5.0**
3.2	1.94	16.5	0.01	**3.7**	0.4	0.70	7.04	5.33	80.4	**0.5**	4.9	45.5	**4.7**
4.7	0.99	4.8	1.13	**0.0**	-2.1	-1.23	-9.96	4.33	111.4	**4.6**	35.2	10.3	**2.0**
9.6	0.00	0.0	0.00	**1.3**	1.0	0.33	3.11	2.19	69.6	**5.1**	51.7	12.5	**2.1**
5.5	2.44	12.8	0.18	**6.9**	4.7	1.59	14.17	4.18	46.7	**2.5**	18.5	16.9	**7.6**
4.6	0.92	6.1	0.30	**6.5**	3.3	1.48	14.08	5.25	69.6	**3.9**	20.0	9.9	**7.9**
4.4	2.67	15.6	0.80	**3.3**	1.1	0.76	9.25	3.79	75.1	**2.6**	41.7	26.6	**3.2**
0.3	2.99	23.6	0.32	**2.1**	0.3	0.14	1.56	4.18	84.6	**1.6**	10.7	22.2	**4.3**
2.3	3.69	17.9	0.60	**2.6**	5.1	0.20	0.97	4.38	80.2	**3.7**	11.0	10.3	**3.9**
0.1	2.11	17.5	0.18	**7.9**	556.5	1.41	10.49	3.56	34.5	**2.4**	6.4	16.4	**8.3**
4.5	1.46	9.4	0.29	**4.4**	69.1	0.80	5.14	3.08	57.3	**4.4**	24.6	10.3	**9.3**
2.2	3.60	22.2	2.16	**4.5**	1.0	0.80	8.24	3.58	53.3	**1.8**	31.8	30.5	**3.6**
2.1	3.22	21.8	2.01	**0.9**	4.1	0.22	2.25	4.10	74.9	**2.9**	15.1	15.1	**4.7**
6.7	1.18	5.9	0.06	**5.1**	6.5	1.07	7.18	3.59	58.8	**1.2**	22.5	31.5	**8.1**
0.0	9.64	106.6	3.61	**0.0**	-23.6	-4.33	-77.22	2.24	115.0	**1.3**	32.3	53.5	**2.0**
5.3	1.30	9.0	0.31	**3.9**	3.7	0.74	8.53	4.47	69.7	**3.8**	25.8	11.4	**4.9**
3.3	0.88	6.1	0.19	**7.9**	7.5	1.82	20.23	5.28	63.0	**2.7**	27.9	17.5	**6.6**
3.4	1.73	11.8	0.24	**4.2**	1.4	0.89	10.10	4.08	54.5	**1.4**	31.3	36.8	**5.0**
7.7	0.03	0.2	0.21	**2.5**	1.6	0.36	4.06	3.61	78.4	**4.0**	14.0	8.5	**5.2**
4.9	0.39	2.0	0.33	**3.1**	0.5	0.29	2.53	4.01	90.1	**2.1**	19.3	19.0	**7.7**
5.1	12.92	1.2	4.24	**0.0**	-0.7	-4.25	-6.83	2.14	-1,434.9	**6.3**	255.5	23.1	**3.3**
4.8	2.91	12.6	1.42	**0.8**	-1.2	-0.47	-2.65	3.73	70.4	**1.2**	16.5	29.7	**5.3**
1.7	3.40	31.3	0.62	**1.7**	1.2	0.12	1.76	3.29	78.5	**3.0**	12.5	13.5	**3.7**
2.3	5.44	22.7	1.44	**1.6**	2.0	0.32	2.99	1.92	87.6	**2.2**	45.7	46.9	**7.1**
0.2	16.85	351.3	5.03	**0.0**	-22.5	-2.45	-98.62	0.96	253.2	**0.8**	23.1	55.1	**0.0**
1.4	4.37	34.5	1.89	**0.1**	-2.7	-0.47	-7.07	3.68	98.5	**4.4**	13.8	5.8	**3.2**
3.5	2.09	15.9	1.24	**2.3**	1.7	0.26	2.59	3.75	63.8	**1.2**	15.8	29.0	**5.1**
5.1	0.81	5.1	0.03	**3.7**	1.3	0.89	10.88	3.20	74.6	**4.4**	29.2	9.5	**5.0**
4.0	3.42	15.0	1.18	**2.3**	0.1	0.17	1.79	4.20	87.0	**5.3**	57.5	11.5	**4.3**
7.0	0.89	5.4	0.00	**3.0**	2.3	0.39	4.86	1.87	68.1	**3.4**	52.4	23.4	**4.8**
5.3	0.00	0.0	0.00	**0.8**	0.2	0.24	1.12	4.01	93.1	**1.4**	33.9	54.5	**2.3**
5.3	0.80	4.7	1.06	**1.9**	0.5	0.26	3.14	3.49	81.9	**3.7**	32.6	13.9	**2.7**
4.8	0.52	3.9	0.37	**7.2**	12.1	1.73	15.38	4.31	55.4	**3.1**	12.2	13.1	**9.0**
8.9	0.00	0.0	0.00	**2.3**	0.1	0.36	2.60	2.79	84.4	**4.6**	52.3	14.2	**6.8**
5.3	1.94	2.2	9.98	**10.0**	75.2	37.19	68.82	10.99	43.7	**3.2**	51.8	26.3	**8.5**
7.9	0.69	2.4	0.42	**7.8**	1.2	1.47	11.66	4.63	52.3	**3.3**	56.8	23.2	**7.3**
0.0	7.09	42.4	2.29	**0.0**	-5.6	-0.98	-11.17	3.69	88.1	**1.2**	13.0	28.8	**4.1**
2.9	1.02	5.4	0.05	**5.4**	0.3	0.91	8.50	4.83	71.8	**5.0**	39.9	9.7	**5.4**
4.1	2.00	14.4	0.76	**1.7**	0.5	0.29	3.21	3.24	82.7	**3.5**	31.2	14.8	**4.5**
1.7	4.12	25.5	5.15	**0.0**	-2.9	-2.02	-25.03	4.24	113.6	**0.8**	14.9	37.0	**3.9**
2.8	1.13	6.9	0.56	**1.1**	0.8	0.30	2.90	3.18	92.7	**0.9**	23.4	39.9	**2.6**
3.7	3.04	18.6	1.71	**3.6**	8.1	0.57	4.81	4.07	62.7	**1.3**	6.8	24.9	**9.1**
0.3	10.23	56.1	0.72	**0.7**	-0.8	-0.36	-3.54	4.12	102.5	**3.9**	29.7	12.0	**4.0**
5.0	2.51	15.1	0.00	**3.0**	0.2	0.48	4.02	3.39	74.8	**2.0**	27.1	22.3	**6.2**
1.7	2.83	16.8	0.87	**2.4**	0.5	0.48	5.53	4.10	77.8	**2.9**	47.4	27.8	**3.9**
7.7	1.13	4.4	0.15	**4.4**	1.7	0.88	6.80	3.83	72.2	**4.6**	45.5	13.5	**7.3**
10.0	0.00	0.0	0.00	**3.0**	0.1	0.09	0.44	3.36	70.7	**3.1**	57.0	27.0	**7.4**
2.2	3.14	19.9	0.84	**3.3**	1.1	0.36	3.28	4.57	80.7	**3.3**	25.9	14.0	**5.7**
4.4	0.70	3.7	0.82	**4.3**	1.3	1.09	9.10	3.45	59.1	**2.7**	28.8	17.7	**7.7**
0.0	3.16	21.4	1.96	**5.3**	1.7	0.35	3.67	5.16	58.1	**2.5**	22.6	17.3	**4.7**
6.9	0.11	0.5	-0.05	**6.3**	0.7	1.33	11.67	4.53	65.5	**5.1**	41.8	9.7	**7.9**
7.3	1.05	6.2	0.08	**2.9**	0.8	0.32	2.50	4.08	86.7	**4.0**	11.0	8.3	**6.5**

Name	City	State	Rating	2008 Rating	2007 Rating	Total Assets ($Mil)	One Year Asset Growth	Asset Mix (As a % of Total Assets) Commercial Loans	Consumer Loans	Home Mortgages	Securities	Capitalization Index	Leverage Ratio	Risk-based Capital Ratio
NORTH COUNTY SB	RED BUD	IL	**C**	C-	C-	38	9.70	0.7	4.5	51.2	10.4	**6.1**	8.1	17.1
NORTH DALLAS BANK &	DALLAS	TX	**C+**	C+	B	1,117	3.95	6.0	1.0	8.8	43.3	**9.2**	10.4	35.5
NORTH EASTON SB	SOUTH EASTON	MA	**C-**	C-	C-	446	3.11	0.7	1.3	52.1	19.7	**6.5**	8.6	15.9
▼NORTH GEORGIA NATIONAL	CALHOUN	GA	**D+**	D	B-	126	-16.25	5.0	1.7	20.4	20.4	**9.0**	10.3	16.9
▲NORTH JERSEY COMMUNITY	ENGLEWOOD CLIFFS	NJ	**C+**	C	C	602	16.98	7.0	0.1	17.9	7.4	**5.5**	8.2	11.4
▼NORTH LOUP VALLEY BANK	NORTH LOUP	NE	**D**	C-	C-	20	6.51	5.8	5.4	3.1	13.8	**5.5**	9.2	11.4
NORTH MIDDLESEX SB	AYER	MA	**D**	C-	C-	337	-1.93	8.3	0.4	29.6	17.7	**5.7**	7.7	12.0
NORTH MILWAUKEE STATE BK	MILWAUKEE	WI	**D-**	D-	D-	89	-5.05	2.1	1.6	15.0	12.5	**6.8**	8.8	13.1
NORTH PENN BANK	SCRANTON	PA	**C+**	C	B-	163	4.84	1.9	1.3	20.7	9.0	**9.5**	10.7	14.8
NORTH SALEM STATE BK	NORTH SALEM	IN	**C**	C-	D+	158	13.26	9.4	5.0	12.4	21.0	**6.1**	8.1	12.5
NORTH SHORE BANK A CO-OP	PEABODY	MA	**C+**	C	C-	448	-1.53	9.3	0.1	20.2	15.8	**7.4**	9.3	14.7
▼NORTH SHORE BANK FSB	BROOKFIELD	WI	**D+**	C	B-	1,834	2.79	7.0	13.1	23.9	11.7	**9.3**	10.5	15.8
▲NORTH SHORE BANK OF	DULUTH	MN	**C-**	C	C	211	-2.16	5.1	1.0	44.8	7.5	**4.5**	6.5	10.9
▲NORTH SHORE COMMUNITY	WILMETTE	IL	**D+**	D	C-	1,487	11.50	24.8	11.0	6.2	11.6	**5.9**	7.9	13.1
NORTH SHORE TRUST &	WAUKEGAN	IL	**C+**	C+	C-	263	4.04	0.1	0.2	49.2	25.5	**10.0**	16.1	42.9
NORTH SIDE BANK & TRUST C	CINCINNATI	OH	**B-**	B-	B+	501	-1.50	30.1	2.1	10.0	20.7	**10.0**	12.3	18.9
NORTH SIDE FS&LA OF CHICA	CHICAGO	IL	**D+**	C-	C-	40	8.29	0.3	0.1	57.9	5.6	**10.0**	12.4	23.0
NORTH STAR BANK	ROSEVILLE	MN	**D-**	D-	D+	243	-8.62	11.1	1.8	9.5	26.9	**5.4**	7.5	11.3
NORTH STATE BK	RALEIGH	NC	**D-**	D+	C+	633	-6.79	6.8	0.5	18.6	1.5	**6.0**	8.0	13.0
▲NORTH TEXAS BANK NA	DECATUR	TX	**C**	C-	C+	120	13.35	15.4	3.2	18.1	6.2	**6.7**	8.7	14.1
NORTH VALLEY BANK	REDDING	CA	**D**	D-	C-	881	-0.17	6.1	1.7	6.0	30.2	**10.0**	12.1	18.1
NORTH VALLEY BANK	THORNTON	CO	**C-**	B-	C	130	-2.14	7.9	0.5	22.8	2.6	**9.4**	10.6	14.5
NORTH VALLEY BANK	ZANESVILLE	OH	**D-**	D-	D+	150	6.62	7.4	3.4	21.3	21.5	**5.2**	7.2	12.8
NORTHAMPTON CO-OP BANK	NORTHAMPTON	MA	**B-**	B-	B-	155	1.65	0.4	0.1	41.0	26.4	**10.0**	13.2	26.3
▲NORTHBROOK BANK & TRUST	NORTHBROOK	IL	**C-**	C-	C+	1,190	32.43	10.7	5.3	9.1	14.9	**5.1**	7.1	12.3
NORTHEAST BANK	LEWISTON	ME	**C-**	C-	C-	639	4.82	3.8	9.3	20.6	23.9	**8.0**	9.7	17.0
▲NORTHEAST BANK	MINNEAPOLIS	MN	**D**	D	D+	366	-6.46	24.8	0.5	2.1	15.4	**6.6**	9.1	12.2
▼NORTHEAST COMMUNITY	WHITE PLAINS	NY	**D+**	C	B	446	-11.86	2.7	0.0	0.1	4.7	**10.0**	18.4	29.8
▲NORTHEAST GEORGIA BANK	LAVONIA	GA	**C**	C	B-	437	2.42	4.6	2.3	8.3	17.6	**7.2**	9.2	14.5
NORTHEAST MISSOURI STATE	KIRKSVILLE	MO	**A**	A	A-	89	11.59	1.0	5.3	12.1	51.6	**9.9**	10.9	21.9
NORTHEAST SECURITY BANK	SUMNER	IA	**B-**	C-	C	111	-1.56	10.6	1.1	9.0	31.3	**6.6**	8.6	13.1
NORTHERN BANK & TRUST CO	WOBURN	MA	**C+**	C	B	670	16.80	18.1	0.2	9.1	6.1	**5.5**	9.3	11.4
NORTHERN CALIFORNIA NATL	CHICO	CA	**C+**	C	C	102	0.41	11.1	0.7	7.2	18.8	**10.0**	13.5	36.4
▼NORTHERN HANCOCK BANK &	NEWELL	WV	**C-**	C-	D+	31	2.10	4.9	14.1	41.3	8.2	**8.5**	10.0	15.1
▲NORTHERN MICHIGAN BANK &	ESCANABA	MI	**C-**	C	C+	214	-4.14	14.8	3.9	8.6	21.8	**6.4**	8.6	12.1
NORTHERN ST BK THIEF RVR	THIEF RIVER FALLS	MN	**B**	B	B+	242	6.48	8.4	5.0	13.4	8.7	**10.0**	11.5	28.9
NORTHERN STAR BANK	MANKATO	MN	**E-**	E	E	38	-17.19	13.5	2.2	23.4	10.5	**0.9**	5.1	7.8
▲NORTHERN STATE BK	CLOSTER	NJ	**D**	D	D+	78	27.92	9.7	0.3	7.9	12.4	**10.0**	32.1	37.9
NORTHERN STATE BK	ASHLAND	WI	**B**	B+	B+	223	23.97	8.5	2.3	26.8	31.7	**5.9**	7.9	13.9
▲NORTHERN STATE BK OF	GONVICK	MN	**B-**	B-	B+	33	-3.13	2.0	4.6	4.7	22.9	**10.0**	19.6	76.3
NORTHERN STATE BK OF	VIRGINIA	MN	**C-**	C	C	54	3.95	10.0	4.6	35.9	7.8	**5.5**	7.5	12.3
▼NORTHERN TRUST BANK FSB	BLOOMFIELD HILLS	MI	**C+**	B-	C+	1,443	5.54	5.0	28.5	29.8	0.2	**7.1**	10.1	12.6
NORTHERN TRUST CO	CHICAGO	IL	**B**	B	B-	70,374	2.27	7.9	2.2	4.2	27.4	**6.0**	8.0	16.2
NORTHERN TRUST CO OF	NEW YORK	NY	**U**	U	U	9	10.08	0.0	0.0	0.0	58.6	**10.0**	86.6	79.3
▲NORTHERN TRUST NA	MIAMI	FL	**B+**	B	B	12,432	-1.72	11.2	7.2	39.0	0.5	**8.7**	10.8	13.9
NORTHFIELD BANK	STATEN ISLAND	NY	**B-**	B	A-	2,192	13.38	2.8	0.0	4.3	55.2	**10.0**	13.4	27.4
NORTHFIELD SB	NORTHFIELD	VT	**B-**	B-	B-	630	3.52	2.6	0.3	37.7	24.2	**10.0**	12.4	21.5
NORTHLAND FINANCIAL	STEELE	ND	**C**	C-	D-	161	3.49	10.7	3.6	6.4	14.8	**5.4**	7.9	11.3
NORTHLAND NATIONAL BK	GLADSTONE	MO	**D-**	D-	D-	50	-17.52	12.6	0.4	9.3	31.8	**7.0**	9.0	18.0
NORTHMARK BANK	NORTH ANDOVER	MA	**B**	B	B+	304	6.12	6.6	0.4	41.4	10.1	**9.9**	10.9	18.8
NORTHPOINTE BANK	GRAND RAPIDS	MI	**E-**	E-	D	275	4.24	0.5	0.0	52.5	3.0	**1.6**	4.6	8.6
▲NORTHRIM BANK	ANCHORAGE	AK	**B**	C-	C+	1,050	5.12	16.3	0.6	4.7	21.0	**9.2**	11.3	14.4
NORTHSIDE BANK	ADAIRSVILLE	GA	**E-**	E-	E+	129	-1.94	4.5	1.3	12.6	17.4	**0.0**	3.6	6.0
NORTHSIDE COMMUNITY	GURNEE	IL	**D**	D-	D	435	-11.88	9.9	0.3	12.6	1.1	**10.0**	13.2	16.0
▼NORTHSTAR BANK	TAMPA	FL	**D+**	C-	C-	148	66.79	4.9	1.1	4.9	55.5	**6.7**	8.7	21.8
▲NORTHSTAR BANK	ESTHERVILLE	IA	**B**	C+	C+	81	-11.31	7.2	2.4	21.9	4.8	**7.8**	10.1	13.2
NORTHSTAR BANK	BAD AXE	MI	**D**	C-	C-	238	-1.84	6.4	3.6	23.1	8.9	**7.7**	9.4	13.7
▲NORTHSTAR BANK OF TEXAS	DENTON	TX	**D**	D	C	834	6.40	13.1	2.6	11.4	3.4	**6.9**	8.9	12.5
NORTHUMBERLAND	NORTHUMBERLAND	PA	**B-**	C+	C+	417	7.35	10.3	1.4	41.1	34.1	**6.2**	8.2	18.5
NORTHVIEW BANK	FINLAYSON	MN	**C**	C-	C-	161	-2.11	6.9	3.5	25.7	9.4	**6.9**	9.5	12.4

Asset Quality Index	Non-Performing Loans as a % of Total Loans	Non-Performing Loans as a % of Capital	Net Charge-offs Avg Loans	Profitability Index	Net Income ($Mil)	Return on Assets (R.O.A.)	Return on Equity (R.O.E.)	Net Interest Spread	Overhead Efficiency Ratio	Liquidity Index	Liquidity Ratio	Hot Money Ratio	Stability Index
9.3	0.08	0.6	0.00	**3.4**	0.2	0.60	7.34	3.02	71.9	**2.1**	34.0	28.2	**4.1**
8.8	1.44	4.1	0.01	**3.4**	6.0	0.54	5.08	2.55	66.8	**4.8**	67.0	17.9	**8.2**
4.8	1.80	13.8	0.12	**2.1**	1.4	0.31	3.68	3.13	86.3	**3.4**	25.9	13.1	**4.5**
1.7	9.13	47.0	1.52	**1.6**	0.4	0.31	3.14	3.21	76.6	**0.9**	14.8	33.3	**3.8**
4.3	0.96	8.5	0.06	**5.0**	4.7	0.84	11.06	4.30	54.3	**2.5**	14.3	16.4	**4.7**
4.0	2.60	13.5	0.77	**2.7**	0.1	0.38	4.04	3.20	72.6	**1.9**	42.7	31.1	**2.3**
2.6	2.38	19.2	1.31	**0.6**	-0.9	-0.27	-3.44	3.18	85.7	**2.4**	22.0	17.7	**4.1**
0.0	8.65	61.3	0.13	**3.3**	0.5	0.50	5.66	4.32	74.9	**0.8**	18.4	46.4	**3.9**
4.0	1.04	6.7	0.28	**3.5**	0.9	0.58	5.32	3.68	72.8	**3.1**	13.4	13.4	**6.6**
2.6	0.75	5.8	0.79	**3.1**	0.9	0.64	7.71	3.85	75.6	**1.4**	25.6	29.5	**3.3**
7.0	0.30	2.1	0.09	**3.9**	3.1	0.66	7.29	3.79	72.2	**2.7**	19.9	15.8	**5.2**
1.6	3.28	21.7	1.81	**1.4**	-2.7	-0.15	-1.25	3.78	72.2	**4.1**	19.6	9.4	**7.7**
4.2	1.20	13.4	0.09	**4.6**	2.3	1.09	16.82	4.46	80.6	**4.1**	13.0	7.8	**3.8**
4.5	0.36	3.2	1.30	**1.1**	3.0	0.22	2.83	3.06	80.7	**1.3**	11.5	27.4	**3.7**
8.2	1.75	6.0	0.24	**2.4**	0.5	0.18	1.13	2.78	84.7	**3.3**	48.0	21.7	**7.2**
2.9	1.59	8.2	1.43	**3.3**	2.3	0.46	3.70	3.76	52.4	**1.5**	12.9	23.5	**6.3**
2.7	5.73	32.4	0.00	**0.4**	-0.3	-0.68	-5.34	4.47	98.3	**3.3**	21.6	13.4	**6.0**
0.3	6.51	40.3	2.30	**0.0**	-2.6	-1.02	-13.21	3.81	86.4	**3.8**	31.9	13.5	**2.6**
0.0	2.11	19.1	1.04	**2.6**	1.5	0.23	2.94	3.82	62.5	**1.5**	8.7	21.9	**3.9**
8.4	0.00	0.0	0.39	**3.0**	0.6	0.48	5.56	4.28	78.7	**1.3**	23.6	29.7	**4.7**
2.7	3.91	16.3	2.06	**0.6**	-3.8	-0.42	-3.65	3.99	87.1	**3.0**	4.5	12.9	**5.7**
2.7	3.46	23.9	0.38	**4.8**	1.4	1.01	9.63	5.20	71.0	**3.7**	8.1	9.6	**7.3**
0.3	4.88	35.6	2.06	**1.1**	0.2	0.16	1.87	3.38	91.0	**3.3**	30.6	15.2	**3.4**
9.6	0.00	0.0	0.04	**3.3**	0.7	0.49	3.55	3.16	80.2	**3.3**	46.1	20.4	**7.1**
3.1	2.53	21.2	0.64	**6.2**	13.9	1.31	16.27	3.89	46.4	**1.1**	17.6	33.1	**4.4**
2.4	2.20	12.6	0.47	**3.8**	4.0	0.65	6.04	3.30	75.9	**1.6**	13.5	23.2	**6.8**
1.3	3.38	22.0	1.04	**1.1**	1.0	0.26	2.48	4.51	85.1	**4.2**	8.3	6.6	**5.0**
0.7	5.43	22.8	0.32	**1.8**	1.8	0.36	2.06	3.47	68.2	**1.3**	13.6	26.6	**6.5**
3.4	2.64	13.4	1.38	**3.4**	2.2	0.56	6.07	3.53	62.8	**2.7**	23.0	16.1	**5.6**
7.3	0.62	2.2	0.00	**7.3**	1.5	1.68	11.84	3.94	53.3	**3.3**	50.8	21.5	**9.1**
4.7	0.40	2.6	1.22	**3.6**	0.5	0.44	4.18	4.41	63.9	**3.3**	24.8	13.7	**5.1**
3.0	1.23	10.0	0.01	**6.5**	6.7	1.07	11.52	4.53	52.8	**2.2**	3.0	17.0	**6.3**
9.5	0.00	0.0	0.00	**2.7**	0.5	0.54	3.93	2.82	73.6	**2.6**	53.5	41.1	**4.7**
1.8	1.72	11.8	0.72	**7.0**	0.5	1.66	15.91	7.86	68.0	**0.9**	19.3	38.8	**6.9**
2.0	1.89	13.4	0.13	**4.6**	2.3	1.07	11.83	4.27	75.8	**1.4**	22.7	28.5	**5.6**
4.6	3.25	11.8	1.79	**3.8**	1.0	0.41	3.24	2.59	63.1	**6.4**	56.3	5.8	**9.6**
1.6	2.74	28.7	4.34	**0.0**	-1.8	-4.31	-59.88	3.93	126.6	**1.8**	14.2	20.4	**1.7**
6.4	1.99	4.9	1.24	**0.0**	-1.4	-2.18	-18.05	3.51	131.7	**2.3**	38.9	30.1	**1.5**
6.3	0.63	4.8	0.13	**5.5**	5.1	1.18	15.04	3.58	64.7	**3.4**	25.6	13.4	**6.0**
9.4	1.66	1.4	0.08	**2.7**	0.1	0.40	2.03	1.84	82.0	**6.8**	95.9	9.3	**8.4**
4.9	1.21	10.4	0.63	**2.1**	0.0	-0.05	-0.69	4.51	82.6	**3.2**	17.2	13.1	**4.0**
3.2	1.52	12.5	0.27	**2.5**	6.1	0.44	4.02	2.59	77.2	**2.9**	4.1	13.8	**6.3**
8.9	0.87	2.5	0.35	**5.5**	530.8	0.85	10.44	1.07	70.2	**4.2**	58.3	20.4	**6.6**
10.0	0.00	0.0	0.00	**9.5**	0.3	3.40	3.96	0.64	86.0	**5.0**	314.8	101.0	**6.3**
4.4	1.58	12.6	0.78	**5.3**	101.5	0.83	9.08	2.87	52.9	**3.4**	7.7	11.3	**7.6**
3.1	7.51	19.3	0.48	**3.9**	14.3	0.68	4.55	3.01	53.8	**4.4**	66.9	20.3	**4.1**
7.9	0.96	4.9	0.06	**3.6**	4.2	0.68	5.34	3.63	75.4	**2.0**	21.0	19.8	**8.0**
4.2	0.93	7.9	0.47	**4.1**	1.4	0.88	10.78	4.51	69.9	**1.7**	19.3	22.3	**3.6**
0.3	6.04	27.3	3.58	**0.0**	-2.3	-4.08	-38.41	1.35	284.4	**2.6**	47.5	30.4	**3.7**
9.3	0.00	0.0	0.00	**4.2**	2.1	0.70	6.41	3.30	63.8	**0.8**	17.3	37.4	**6.6**
0.3	5.48	60.3	3.07	**0.8**	0.1	0.02	0.36	4.32	70.4	**0.6**	13.3	53.5	**0.0**
4.9	1.64	8.6	0.66	**5.7**	10.3	1.06	8.63	5.19	64.7	**4.9**	28.2	9.4	**8.8**
0.3	7.92	113.2	1.37	**0.0**	-1.1	-0.81	-19.98	2.69	139.9	**0.8**	17.0	40.3	**0.0**
0.0	7.56	40.8	1.17	**1.9**	1.6	0.35	2.75	4.08	56.3	**0.9**	5.1	31.1	**5.3**
3.7	3.92	17.5	0.41	**1.1**	0.7	0.53	4.56	3.51	86.7	**2.0**	43.0	55.3	**2.0**
7.0	0.00	0.0	0.44	**5.4**	1.0	1.25	12.69	3.94	63.6	**1.7**	16.1	21.2	**5.9**
1.4	1.98	13.8	0.49	**4.6**	2.6	1.08	10.41	4.55	61.5	**1.5**	16.3	24.8	**4.6**
0.7	1.70	13.5	0.50	**4.7**	8.2	1.02	11.79	4.30	64.7	**1.5**	18.2	25.9	**6.3**
6.7	0.77	5.3	0.21	**4.0**	3.2	0.79	9.48	3.07	64.4	**2.7**	22.2	16.2	**4.7**
2.4	1.57	11.5	0.68	**5.6**	1.4	0.90	8.67	4.69	66.0	**1.2**	11.2	28.0	**5.4**

Name	City	State	Rating	2008 Rating	2007 Rating	Total Assets ($Mil)	One Year Asset Growth	Asset Mix (As a % of Total Assets) Comm-ercial Loans	Cons-umer Loans	Home Mort-gages	Secur-ities	Capital-ization Index	Leverage Ratio	Risk-based Capital Ratio
NORTHWAY BANK	BERLIN	NH	**D+**	C-	C	827	3.10	6.2	0.8	19.2	19.0	**5.6**	7.6	14.3
NORTHWEST BANK	SPENCER	IA	**C**	C	C	813	3.12	22.6	3.0	22.1	8.7	**6.2**	8.2	12.3
▼NORTHWEST BANK	LAKE OSWEGO	OR	**E**	D-	D-	126	2.96	26.9	0.4	0.8	7.3	**4.0**	7.2	10.5
NORTHWEST BANK & TRUST	DAVENPORT	IA	**C-**	D+	D+	207	4.51	16.6	3.5	15.9	8.3	**5.8**	7.8	12.6
NORTHWEST BANK OF	ROCKFORD	IL	**C**	C-	C	234	2.73	20.7	0.6	14.9	18.9	**6.4**	8.4	12.5
▼NORTHWEST COMMERCIAL	LAKEWOOD	WA	**C-**	C-	C-	79	5.77	24.5	3.4	9.0	4.6	**9.9**	11.6	14.9
▼NORTHWEST COMMUNITY	WINSTED	CT	**C**	C+	C	304	4.49	2.9	1.2	34.1	31.4	**9.8**	10.9	21.3
NORTHWEST COMMUNITY	ROLLING MEADOWS	IL	**D-**	C-	C	64	-20.46	7.2	0.1	11.3	16.5	**10.0**	12.4	18.5
NORTHWEST GEORGIA BANK	RINGGOLD	GA	**E-**	E	D-	557	-10.47	6.3	0.7	8.3	36.3	**4.8**	6.8	13.8
NORTHWEST SB	WARREN	PA	**B**	B-	B-	8,175	1.23	4.8	3.0	39.2	16.0	**10.0**	12.2	21.1
▼NORTHWESTERN BANK	ORANGE CITY	IA	**C+**	B	B	175	3.83	9.3	2.0	8.5	3.6	**6.3**	9.5	12.0
NORTHWESTERN BANK	TRAVERSE CITY	MI	**C-**	C-	C-	913	-0.25	9.4	0.9	19.7	5.1	**5.6**	8.0	11.4
NORTHWESTERN BANK	CHIPPEWA FALLS	WI	**D+**	D	D-	355	3.22	8.6	0.9	9.9	32.9	**7.0**	9.0	13.6
NORTHWESTERN BANK NA	DILWORTH	MN	**D+**	D+	C+	137	-0.47	12.4	4.3	11.2	27.8	**6.4**	8.5	14.5
NORTHWESTERN MUTUAL	MILWAUKEE	WI	**B+**	B+	B+	53	10.95	0.0	0.0	0.0	95.9	**10.0**	90.4	365.7
NORTHWOODS BANK OF	PARK RAPIDS	MN	**C-**	C	C-	118	-1.73	3.6	2.2	20.7	25.2	**7.5**	9.3	15.4
▲NORTHWOODS STATE BK	MASON CITY	IA	**C+**	C+	B	134	0.83	18.1	3.6	10.5	23.7	**6.1**	8.1	11.8
NORWAY SB	NORWAY	ME	**C+**	C+	B-	948	1.27	5.6	4.2	29.9	4.6	**8.1**	10.1	13.4
▼NORWOOD CO-OP BANK	NORWOOD	MA	**C-**	C-	D+	393	-1.67	1.5	0.1	28.4	14.3	**10.0**	14.3	19.5
NOVA BANK	BERWYN	PA	**E-**	E-	D-	625	3.91	11.9	0.4	15.5	24.1	**0.0**	2.5	5.0
NUVO BANK & TRUST CO	SPRINGFIELD	MA	**D-**	C	C	65	57.22	22.4	0.7	26.0	4.6	**6.6**	8.9	12.2
NVE BANK	ENGLEWOOD	NJ	**C-**	C-	C+	681	5.11	0.3	0.0	23.4	37.5	**10.0**	11.3	24.9
OAK BANK	CHICAGO	IL	**B+**	A-	A-	206	3.45	5.5	0.3	15.7	0.2	**10.0**	15.2	19.4
▼OAK BANK	FITCHBURG	WI	**C**	B-	C+	220	4.98	11.6	0.6	14.4	10.6	**8.1**	9.9	13.4
OAK CREEK VALLEY BANK	VALPARAISO	NE	**B+**	B	B-	60	10.20	2.7	1.3	9.2	31.8	**8.5**	10.0	15.7
OAK VALLEY COMMUNITY	OAKDALE	CA	**C-**	C-	C-	553	5.39	5.2	0.3	3.2	9.6	**9.9**	11.5	14.9
▼OAK VIEW NATIONAL BK	WARRENTON	VA	**D**	C	NR	93	53.52	8.1	2.7	30.2	4.8	**8.0**	9.7	15.1
OAKDALE STATE BK	OAKDALE	IL	**D+**	C-	C-	18	2.04	9.0	4.9	28.2	21.6	**6.1**	8.1	12.2
▲OAKSTAR BANK NA	SPRINGFIELD	MO	**C-**	D+	D	167	6.46	17.6	2.1	20.3	0.0	**10.0**	11.2	15.7
OAKWOOD STATE BK	OAKWOOD	TX	**B-**	B-	C+	3	2.63	0.5	4.9	0.2	63.1	**10.0**	27.0	205.9
▲OAKWORTH CAPITAL BANK	BIRMINGHAM	AL	**C**	C	C	181	39.25	14.7	3.3	4.0	18.4	**10.0**	21.0	26.6
OASIS BANK SSB	HOUSTON	TX	**D**	C-	D	76	13.33	1.6	1.1	50.4	3.7	**10.0**	11.1	22.0
OBA BANK	GERMANTOWN	MD	**C-**	C-	C+	354	-22.31	8.5	0.0	34.7	7.8	**10.0**	16.4	24.5
OBANNON BANKING CO	BUFFALO	MO	**C-**	C-	C-	147	3.62	6.7	3.6	26.1	15.0	**6.7**	8.7	13.6
▼OCEAN BANK	MIAMI	FL	**E**	E	E	3,649	-7.20	8.3	0.6	13.3	19.7	**2.8**	5.6	9.8
OCEAN CITY HOME BANK	OCEAN CITY	NJ	**B-**	B-	B	830	9.09	0.6	0.1	66.6	2.0	**9.1**	10.4	20.2
OCEANFIRST BANK	TOMS RIVER	NJ	**B-**	B-	B-	2,253	10.88	3.4	0.0	47.3	19.3	**7.2**	9.1	15.3
OCEANIC BANK	SAN FRANCISCO	CA	**B**	B-	B	190	-0.45	2.3	0.1	6.6	9.1	**10.0**	16.6	22.7
OCONEE FS&LA	SENECA	SC	**B**	B	B+	371	15.39	0.0	0.3	67.2	2.8	**10.0**	16.5	37.1
OCONEE STATE BK	WATKINSVILLE	GA	**D-**	D-	E	279	-2.20	3.5	2.1	10.3	26.5	**6.1**	8.2	14.2
OCULINA BANK	FORT PIERCE	FL	**D**	D	D	132	7.89	9.2	1.2	19.2	9.8	**6.5**	8.6	12.9
ODIN STATE BK	ODIN	MN	**B-**	C+	D+	35	1.33	13.2	3.7	4.1	24.9	**10.0**	11.9	18.2
▲OGLESBY STATE BK	OGLESBY	TX	**D+**	D	D-	14	-2.19	7.5	25.1	32.4	2.2	**6.7**	8.7	13.0
OHANA PACIFIC BANK	HONOLULU	HI	**D**	D-	D+	92	26.07	14.9	2.7	0.9	0.0	**10.0**	11.9	16.2
OHIO COMMERCE BANK	BEACHWOOD	OH	**C-**	NR	NR	80	N/A	28.5	0.1	8.3	0.0	**10.0**	11.9	18.9
▲OHIO HERITAGE BANK	COSHOCTON	OH	**D+**	C-	C+	288	4.02	3.6	4.6	42.8	9.7	**5.6**	7.6	14.7
OHIO RIVER BANK	IRONTON	OH	**C-**	C-	B-	95	3.17	6.6	3.4	28.1	30.7	**6.4**	8.4	15.6
OHIO STATE BK	MARION	OH	**E-**	E-	E-	116	-15.75	6.2	5.8	25.0	12.2	**3.2**	6.0	10.1
▼OHIO VALLEY BANK CO	GALLIPOLIS	OH	**C-**	C-	B-	841	4.86	5.4	11.2	27.4	12.7	**6.5**	8.6	13.4
OHIO VALLEY FINANCIAL GRO	HENDERSON	KY	**B**	B-	B-	248	9.44	17.5	3.2	18.8	15.1	**6.6**	8.6	12.6
OHNWARD BANK & TRUST	CASCADE	IA	**B-**	B+	B+	175	3.66	8.5	4.4	13.4	19.0	**8.4**	10.0	13.7
▼OJAI COMMUNITY BANK	OJAI	CA	**D-**	D-	C-	124	10.20	5.3	1.0	15.3	2.6	**6.6**	8.6	13.0
OKEMAH NATIONAL BK	OKEMAH	OK	**A-**	A-	A-	74	9.78	0.4	8.3	25.6	34.5	**10.0**	13.8	25.9
OKEY-VERNON FIRST	CORNING	IA	**B+**	B	B	57	26.63	3.3	1.4	4.2	43.3	**10.0**	13.7	25.9
OKLAHOMA BANK & TRUST CO	CLINTON	OK	**A+**	A+	A+	144	4.79	1.9	2.1	8.2	64.1	**10.0**	13.4	32.8
OKLAHOMA HERITAGE BANK	STRATFORD	OK	**C-**	C	C-	56	1.62	14.8	20.7	30.8	13.2	**4.9**	8.0	11.0
OKLAHOMA STATE BK	BUFFALO	OK	**B-**	B-	C+	48	14.26	4.3	9.3	7.0	32.2	**5.4**	7.4	12.9
OKLAHOMA STATE BK	GUTHRIE	OK	**C+**	C	C-	46	5.42	8.3	7.9	22.1	10.8	**8.2**	9.8	15.7
OKLAHOMA STATE BK	VINITA	OK	**C**	C-	C	100	19.43	31.3	4.5	10.3	9.2	**5.1**	9.4	11.1
OLD DOMINION NATIONAL BK	NORTH GARDEN	VA	**D-**	D-	C-	51	-5.18	11.0	4.7	24.9	16.9	**6.9**	8.9	12.6

Asset Quality Index	Non-Performing Loans as a % of Total Loans	Non-Performing Loans as a % of Capital	Net Charge-offs Avg Loans	Profitability Index	Net Income ($Mil)	Return on Assets (R.O.A.)	Return on Equity (R.O.E.)	Net Interest Spread	Overhead Efficiency Ratio	Liquidity Index	Liquidity Ratio	Hot Money Ratio	Stability Index
1.5	3.08	23.2	0.48	3.8	5.2	0.64	7.65	3.61	71.8	4.0	16.8	9.1	5.7
2.8	1.45	12.7	-0.03	5.4	10.2	1.31	15.58	3.99	63.0	2.3	15.4	17.8	5.5
1.0	5.57	38.9	1.65	0.0	-1.9	-1.47	-18.20	3.68	115.4	1.3	28.0	33.3	0.8
2.5	2.00	12.5	0.94	4.9	2.0	0.98	12.65	3.97	73.2	4.3	34.7	11.6	4.0
0.6	5.91	41.8	2.71	0.8	-0.5	-0.20	-2.43	4.36	64.7	1.3	10.6	25.6	4.9
1.7	5.06	32.5	0.83	1.6	-0.1	0.25	2.05	4.86	79.3	0.8	15.9	37.6	4.4
6.3	0.67	3.3	0.03	3.1	1.2	0.42	3.51	3.53	84.7	3.4	36.5	17.0	5.6
0.7	2.88	15.7	1.99	4.7	0.6	0.79	6.89	4.79	38.2	1.2	20.1	30.7	2.4
0.3	10.76	68.8	1.58	0.1	0.8	0.15	2.22	2.67	103.9	1.6	11.0	21.3	1.4
4.3	2.70	14.3	0.63	4.3	59.4	0.73	5.30	3.67	62.2	3.9	18.4	10.1	9.0
2.7	1.16	9.1	0.37	7.3	1.9	1.12	9.65	4.33	44.5	2.3	3.3	16.5	7.7
1.6	2.85	23.7	0.60	3.7	5.2	0.55	6.86	3.76	72.8	3.1	14.0	13.4	5.4
1.7	3.87	23.0	0.30	3.0	2.9	0.85	8.08	4.31	67.3	4.4	27.8	8.7	5.4
1.3	3.50	21.3	0.91	1.7	0.3	0.20	2.08	4.42	83.0	2.8	27.9	17.2	4.4
8.7	0.00	0.0	0.00	10.0	12.9	26.82	29.32	3.66	86.0	5.0	970.3	100.0	3.7
1.7	7.25	41.4	0.53	4.6	1.2	1.00	10.70	3.98	67.6	3.2	37.9	18.5	4.9
3.5	1.87	14.9	0.92	5.7	1.8	1.32	16.36	4.03	55.1	4.5	14.9	5.3	5.4
3.9	1.43	10.8	0.20	4.4	7.9	0.83	8.31	3.92	72.7	2.8	10.5	14.3	7.0
1.7	6.45	30.5	0.26	1.8	0.0	0.01	0.07	3.21	79.9	1.7	10.9	20.7	7.0
0.3	5.50	80.5	3.42	0.0	-15.2	-2.40	-63.80	2.98	87.2	0.9	15.4	33.7	1.1
4.5	1.29	11.7	1.15	0.0	-1.3	-2.51	-21.98	3.23	148.1	1.0	8.2	30.7	0.8
3.1	7.75	29.1	0.30	1.2	0.2	0.04	0.30	2.29	95.3	5.6	45.7	7.8	7.3
7.7	0.17	0.8	0.11	4.3	1.2	0.58	3.61	4.12	65.0	0.7	15.4	52.6	7.9
1.8	3.67	24.6	0.77	5.6	1.9	0.91	9.47	3.59	50.4	1.8	24.9	22.3	4.8
6.1	0.00	0.0	0.00	7.9	1.1	1.87	17.02	4.73	54.2	3.0	23.7	14.7	6.9
1.6	2.84	16.1	0.68	4.9	4.7	0.90	7.56	5.22	59.2	3.9	15.5	9.5	6.6
8.9	0.00	0.0	0.00	0.0	-1.6	-2.02	-16.68	2.67	154.5	1.9	23.7	21.1	0.8
6.7	0.27	2.2	0.00	3.7	0.1	0.69	8.27	4.14	79.1	1.5	12.6	23.1	3.0
2.5	1.79	11.3	0.56	2.0	0.7	0.45	4.04	3.54	81.9	1.3	14.4	27.3	3.5
10.0	0.00	0.0	1.57	3.7	0.0	0.50	1.75	3.10	91.6	7.7	88.8	0.0	7.8
8.6	0.00	0.0	0.00	2.6	1.9	1.31	5.65	3.48	79.4	4.9	37.6	9.9	4.1
9.1	0.15	0.9	0.19	0.0	-0.6	-0.81	-6.97	4.45	110.1	0.7	23.5	65.9	1.7
8.0	0.16	0.8	0.20	1.4	-0.4	-0.10	-0.69	3.26	92.3	3.2	16.1	13.2	5.9
3.7	1.16	8.6	0.79	3.0	0.5	0.35	3.95	4.05	76.5	2.9	11.4	14.3	4.2
0.3	11.58	110.8	4.80	0.0	-116.5	-3.01	-45.34	3.46	99.7	1.4	24.3	37.6	3.4
6.4	0.79	5.8	0.00	4.0	5.9	0.74	6.89	3.25	62.6	3.1	17.2	13.8	6.9
4.1	2.24	17.1	0.18	4.5	21.5	0.98	11.43	3.80	56.7	5.2	22.7	3.5	6.6
5.1	1.86	7.0	0.00	4.2	0.8	0.74	4.50	3.27	60.0	1.4	34.6	63.9	7.4
7.4	1.34	5.8	0.05	4.1	2.8	0.83	4.70	2.93	46.8	2.3	31.6	22.0	7.7
0.3	10.43	63.8	1.91	0.0	-1.0	-0.37	-4.23	3.68	90.8	1.9	21.2	20.6	3.0
0.4	6.27	42.2	3.96	0.0	-2.8	-2.20	-22.30	3.93	91.2	2.8	22.4	15.8	2.9
4.0	2.69	13.9	0.64	4.7	0.4	1.13	9.02	4.03	66.4	2.1	28.2	21.6	7.1
4.4	0.32	2.9	0.45	4.1	0.1	0.81	9.73	5.86	77.7	0.7	10.4	36.8	3.0
2.5	1.18	6.4	0.82	0.3	-0.2	-0.22	-1.88	3.93	88.3	1.4	31.8	35.9	1.8
4.8	1.35	7.7	0.00	1.5	0.6	0.72	5.55	N/,	66.2	0.9	22.9	38.6	3.5
2.8	1.79	14.2	0.76	1.4	0.2	0.05	0.71	2.59	79.7	2.1	20.5	19.2	3.4
5.5	0.28	2.0	0.08	8.4	1.3	1.44	16.67	4.35	53.1	2.5	16.9	16.5	4.3
0.3	9.39	94.7	1.82	0.5	-0.3	-0.34	-4.81	4.80	82.7	2.6	16.5	16.3	0.0
2.2	0.77	6.0	0.71	4.0	5.2	0.62	6.95	4.02	66.1	1.6	10.1	21.9	5.9
5.6	0.39	3.0	0.25	6.1	3.6	1.54	17.00	4.41	67.8	3.4	13.6	11.7	5.8
4.5	0.95	6.5	0.58	4.3	1.1	0.64	5.82	3.88	68.0	2.7	20.6	15.9	7.0
0.3	4.02	27.4	1.39	0.5	-0.2	-0.21	-1.94	4.35	70.8	2.2	29.4	21.9	5.0
6.8	1.16	3.8	0.00	4.1	0.0	0.05	0.38	N/,	62.4	3.1	37.4	18.4	8.3
9.5	0.00	0.0	0.00	4.5	0.5	0.99	6.74	4.09	70.3	5.5	58.6	10.6	7.4
9.5	0.26	0.6	0.11	6.5	2.0	1.48	10.03	3.28	57.5	3.4	57.4	27.4	10.0
4.9	0.41	3.4	0.32	4.8	0.5	0.78	9.85	4.57	67.3	0.7	11.9	44.9	3.7
7.8	0.23	1.6	0.00	9.2	1.0	2.11	28.66	4.49	59.5	1.7	23.2	24.2	5.0
3.4	1.50	10.6	0.18	5.7	0.6	1.34	11.50	5.21	72.3	2.1	18.1	18.6	6.3
3.0	1.42	11.6	0.24	5.1	1.0	1.09	11.11	5.33	74.3	0.8	7.5	32.4	5.0
3.6	0.90	6.3	0.73	0.0	-0.5	-0.92	-10.57	3.73	111.2	2.2	20.9	18.6	1.0

Name	City	State	Rating	2008 Rating	2007 Rating	Total Assets ($Mil)	One Year Asset Growth	Asset Mix (As a % of Total Assets) Comm-ercial Loans	Cons-umer Loans	Home Mort-gages	Secur-ities	Capital-ization Index	Leverage Ratio	Risk-based Capital Ratio
OLD EXCHANGE NB OF	OKAWVILLE	IL	**C+**	C+	C+	55	7.16	1.3	1.7	7.4	45.5	**7.1**	9.1	18.5
OLD FLORIDA NATIONAL BK	ORLANDO	FL	**D+**	D	C-	446	33.53	19.6	0.2	3.3	6.1	**10.0**	13.2	16.2
OLD FORT BANKING CO	OLD FORT	OH	**D+**	D	D+	370	-5.57	9.2	4.9	12.2	19.5	**6.4**	8.4	13.0
OLD HARBOR BANK	CLEARWATER	FL	**E-**	E-	D-	227	-10.87	10.5	0.4	5.7	15.2	**0.0**	2.6	4.7
OLD LINE BANK	BOWIE	MD	**C+**	B-	B	394	12.85	12.3	3.4	8.6	14.0	**6.4**	8.9	12.0
▲ OLD MISSION BANK	SAULT SAINTE MARIE	MI	**C**	C-	B-	96	-0.69	8.8	3.6	13.6	34.3	**8.9**	10.3	16.5
OLD MISSOURI BANK	SPRINGFIELD	MO	**C+**	C	C-	122	7.22	10.9	2.3	16.1	9.5	**6.1**	8.4	11.9
OLD NATIONAL BK	EVANSVILLE	IN	**C**	C+	B-	7,122	-9.23	10.0	7.5	12.4	36.0	**5.4**	7.4	12.4
▲ OLD PLANK TRAIL	NEW LENOX	IL	**C-**	D+	C-	297	-1.29	19.6	15.7	3.8	10.9	**7.7**	9.4	13.9
OLD POINT NATIONAL BK PHO	HAMPTON	VA	**C-**	C	B	882	-3.80	4.1	2.8	12.0	23.2	**6.6**	8.6	13.2
OLD POINT TRUST & FINANCI	NEWPORT NEWS	VA	**U**	U	U	5	2.81	0.0	0.0	0.0	70.0	**10.0**	99.1	448.5
OLD SECOND NATIONAL BK	AURORA	IL	**D-**	D-	C	2,126	-16.58	7.5	0.3	12.8	6.9	**5.8**	8.1	11.6
OLDTOWN BANK	WAYNESVILLE	NC	**D**	C-	C-	84	41.68	5.1	0.2	11.4	33.8	**10.0**	11.2	18.4
▼ OLMSTED NATIONAL BK	ROCHESTER	MN	**D-**	D-	D-	54	-12.37	12.9	1.8	15.6	5.3	**6.5**	8.6	12.2
OLPE STATE BK	OLPE	KS	**B+**	B+	B+	35	0.69	8.7	4.0	15.1	39.3	**10.0**	13.2	23.2
OLYMPIA FS&LA	OLYMPIA	WA	**B-**	B	B	548	7.63	0.0	0.1	58.8	9.8	**10.0**	13.7	26.2
OMAHA STATE BK	OMAHA	NE	**D**	C	B-	274	2.99	11.4	1.1	4.7	1.3	**7.9**	10.4	13.2
OMNI BANK	METAIRIE	LA	**D-**	D-	D	735	-1.61	5.6	1.3	21.5	11.9	**5.4**	7.4	11.3
OMNI BANK NA	ALHAMBRA	CA	**C-**	C-	B-	159	2.76	1.5	3.6	2.6	13.2	**10.0**	15.8	28.0
OMNIAMERICAN BANK	FORT WORTH	TX	**C-**	C-	C-	1,108	-2.28	4.2	18.3	26.5	28.8	**10.0**	14.9	24.0
OMNIBANK	JACKSON	MS	**D-**	D-	D	86	11.40	18.6	8.5	22.1	4.9	**6.7**	8.7	13.3
OMNIBANK NA	HOUSTON	TX	**D-**	D	C	381	-4.88	12.1	0.7	10.2	0.3	**7.4**	9.3	14.2
ONB BANK & TRUST CO	TULSA	OK	**C**	C	C+	613	-2.81	17.1	1.1	9.2	2.4	**9.1**	11.3	14.3
ONE BANK & TRUST NA	LITTLE ROCK	AR	**D**	C-	C-	448	8.63	20.9	3.9	24.4	0.0	**7.8**	9.7	13.2
ONE GEORGIA BANK	ATLANTA	GA	**E-**	D-	D-	193	-17.83	14.3	1.0	3.4	10.0	**0.0**	2.5	4.5
ONE SOUTH BANK	CHIPLEY	FL	**D+**	C	C	22	61.89	12.9	0.9	11.1	7.7	**10.0**	26.3	46.0
ONE WORLD BANK	DALLAS	TX	**D-**	C-	C-	93	-13.96	11.2	1.7	0.3	6.8	**10.0**	12.6	16.6
ONECALIFORNIA BANK FSB	OAKLAND	CA	**D-**	C-	C	292	196.93	16.1	0.7	3.5	23.7	**8.6**	10.1	16.7
▲ ONEIDA SB	ONEIDA	NY	**C+**	C	D+	660	11.54	5.7	5.5	16.0	38.0	**7.3**	9.2	15.2
ONEUNITED BANK	BOSTON	MA	**E-**	D-	D-	523	-2.54	0.3	0.1	10.6	28.7	**1.1**	4.7	8.1
ONEWEST BANK FSB	PASADENA	CA	**C-**	C+	NR	26,974	16.61	0.2	0.0	36.9	3.4	**10.0**	14.7	42.6
▼ OOSTBURG STATE BK	OOSTBURG	WI	**B**	B+	A-	168	9.19	15.8	3.6	15.6	16.0	**9.8**	12.7	14.8
OPEN BANK	LOS ANGELES	CA	**D-**	D-	D	118	-1.46	17.2	4.1	0.0	6.7	**9.9**	11.0	15.1
OPPORTUNITY BANK NA	RICHARDSON	TX	**D**	D	C-	61	-0.08	20.3	0.3	1.7	10.5	**10.0**	14.1	25.0
OPTIMA BANK & TRUST CO	PORTSMOUTH	NH	**C-**	C	C	157	71.96	5.7	0.2	28.0	14.9	**9.3**	10.6	17.9
OPTIMUMBANK	FORT LAUDERDALE	FL	**E-**	D-	B-	190	-29.53	0.1	0.1	21.2	26.2	**0.4**	4.0	6.7
OPTUMHEALTH BANK INC	SALT LAKE CITY	UT	**A+**	A+	A	1,501	25.63	1.8	0.0	0.0	81.0	**9.6**	10.7	16.1
OPUS BANK	REDONDO BEACH	CA	**D+**	E+	C	694	146.53	1.6	0.1	1.7	7.0	**10.0**	55.8	358.1
▼ ORANGE BANK OF FLORIDA	ORLANDO	FL	**E**	D-	D-	303	0.79	6.7	0.6	3.5	14.9	**4.1**	7.1	10.6
▲ ORANGE COMMUNITY BANK	ORANGE	CA	**C**	C+	B	224	9.48	12.6	0.3	1.2	13.8	**8.0**	9.7	14.6
ORANGE COUNTY BUSINESS	NEWPORT BEACH	CA	**D**	C-	B-	211	-17.58	9.0	0.9	2.5	14.0	**10.0**	22.1	28.9
ORANGE COUNTY TRUST CO	MIDDLETOWN	NY	**A**	A	A	566	5.80	11.1	0.1	11.7	41.6	**10.0**	14.8	26.1
ORANGE SB SSB	ORANGE	TX	**C**	C	D-	382	10.49	6.7	7.1	27.2	30.5	**8.1**	9.8	17.1
OREGON COAST BANK	NEWPORT	OR	**C-**	D+	B-	146	7.77	3.5	3.1	13.6	42.5	**6.4**	8.4	14.0
OREGON COMMUNITY BANK &	OREGON	WI	**D+**	D-	D+	188	-5.72	6.4	0.5	17.3	8.9	**10.0**	12.8	16.7
▼ OREGON PACIFIC BANKING	FLORENCE	OR	**D-**	C-	C+	164	-0.52	5.3	0.7	10.6	7.2	**6.4**	8.4	12.3
OREGON TRAIL BANK	GUERNSEY	WY	**D**	D+	D	30	-0.98	6.8	2.2	7.9	19.8	**5.9**	7.9	13.8
ORIENTAL BANK & TRUST	SAN JUAN	PR	**C**	C-	D+	7,168	11.79	1.8	0.6	14.5	60.7	**7.5**	9.3	26.8
ORITANI BANK	TOWNSHIP OF	NJ	**C+**	C-	B-	2,532	28.15	0.9	0.0	9.3	31.1	**10.0**	16.3	23.6
ORMSBY STATE BK	ORMSBY	MN	**B**	B	B	23	3.33	7.6	3.3	4.6	39.3	**10.0**	13.7	20.5
ORRSTOWN BANK	SHIPPENSBURG	PA	**B-**	B	B	1,492	24.92	4.1	0.5	21.1	27.6	**6.0**	8.0	12.7
OSAGE FEDERAL BANK	PAWHUSKA	OK	**B-**	C	C	153	-4.41	2.6	5.0	36.6	26.2	**10.0**	14.1	24.1
OSB COMMUNITY BANK	BROOKLYN	MI	**D-**	D	D	74	11.44	14.0	1.2	14.8	1.9	**5.8**	7.8	12.1
OSGOOD STATE BK	OSGOOD	OH	**D+**	B-	B-	128	3.51	8.3	3.4	15.7	34.0	**6.6**	8.6	15.4
▲ OSSIAN STATE BK	OSSIAN	IN	**C**	D+	D-	81	1.19	6.9	1.6	13.0	17.8	**7.2**	9.1	14.5
OSWEGO COMMUNITY BANK	OSWEGO	IL	**D**	C-	C-	187	-5.57	3.4	1.7	16.6	28.3	**3.2**	5.2	14.1
OTTAWA SAVINGS BANK	OTTAWA	IL	**D+**	C-	C-	195	-2.71	7.7	2.9	42.3	16.7	**7.5**	9.3	16.7
OTTOVILLE BANK CO	OTTOVILLE	OH	**A-**	A-	A-	73	7.03	3.8	1.1	10.6	43.8	**10.0**	18.1	36.7
OUACHITA INDEPENDENT	MONROE	LA	**B**	B-	C+	481	8.22	9.8	2.1	11.2	21.2	**6.0**	8.0	11.9
OWEN COMMUNITY BANK SB	SPENCER	IN	**C-**	C-	D+	74	4.06	0.3	3.9	65.2	4.7	**8.3**	9.9	18.1

Asset Quality Index	Non-Performing Loans as a % of Total Loans	Non-Performing Loans as a % of Capital	Net Charge-offs Avg Loans	Profitability Index	Net Income ($Mil)	Return on Assets (R.O.A.)	Return on Equity (R.O.E.)	Net Interest Spread	Overhead Efficiency Ratio	Liquidity Index	Liquidity Ratio	Hot Money Ratio	Stability Index
6.2	0.87	4.6	0.03	**3.5**	0.4	0.80	8.00	3.18	76.4	**3.4**	43.7	18.5	**6.0**
2.9	1.98	10.7	2.16	**1.1**	2.1	0.56	3.93	3.78	93.3	**3.5**	19.3	11.9	**4.4**
2.4	1.33	9.1	0.60	**2.5**	1.9	0.49	5.79	4.00	73.4	**1.7**	17.0	22.4	**3.1**
0.0	11.53	176.4	3.96	**0.0**	-6.9	-2.89	-79.38	3.29	88.1	**1.8**	18.9	21.0	**0.9**
4.0	0.90	7.1	0.38	**3.8**	2.0	0.52	5.66	3.89	72.2	**0.9**	19.4	35.5	**5.7**
2.9	2.49	13.1	0.13	**5.2**	1.0	1.07	10.66	4.03	69.2	**3.4**	39.4	17.7	**6.2**
3.8	0.14	1.2	0.33	**4.4**	1.0	0.84	10.15	4.22	62.2	**0.8**	11.2	34.6	**5.0**
4.2	1.86	11.8	0.75	**3.6**	47.8	0.64	7.05	3.57	76.6	**4.3**	21.0	8.9	**5.4**
5.3	0.34	2.3	0.48	**2.0**	0.9	0.30	3.36	3.23	73.5	**1.5**	15.1	23.8	**4.8**
2.7	3.57	22.9	0.55	**2.3**	1.5	0.16	1.96	3.67	74.2	**1.7**	12.1	20.5	**4.8**
10.0	0.00	0.0	0.00	**10.0**	0.4	7.40	7.59	1.09	83.7	**5.0**	78,866.7	101.0	**4.3**
0.0	12.51	81.7	4.07	**0.3**	-95.2	-3.95	-38.63	3.88	74.1	**2.5**	9.3	16.0	**5.9**
3.7	5.49	23.7	2.48	**0.0**	-1.6	-2.12	-15.32	3.03	102.0	**1.7**	36.7	51.0	**1.5**
1.1	3.71	28.4	-0.16	**0.2**	-0.2	-0.27	-2.27	4.20	129.5	**1.5**	17.1	25.5	**4.9**
7.4	0.12	0.5	0.90	**4.3**	0.3	0.91	6.37	3.42	67.5	**3.4**	36.3	16.9	**8.3**
5.8	1.72	9.0	0.00	**3.7**	3.5	0.66	4.77	3.39	63.8	**1.8**	25.4	24.2	**8.5**
0.0	3.81	29.5	0.03	**8.8**	4.2	1.50	14.18	5.74	66.4	**4.8**	6.5	2.0	**8.5**
0.3	6.46	54.3	1.30	**1.1**	0.2	0.02	0.28	4.85	92.0	**1.6**	14.6	22.2	**3.2**
4.1	4.33	16.2	-0.31	**1.4**	0.1	0.09	0.54	4.01	97.2	**1.3**	23.5	30.8	**6.6**
4.5	1.28	5.0	0.34	**1.9**	2.3	0.21	1.45	3.80	81.3	**4.0**	36.6	16.8	**3.2**
0.3	3.28	25.3	0.74	**0.2**	-0.6	-0.71	-7.49	5.03	111.8	**1.7**	20.4	23.1	**3.4**
0.0	8.83	58.1	1.23	**0.0**	-3.9	-1.02	-10.06	3.79	109.4	**3.5**	22.8	12.4	**5.3**
0.0	5.41	35.5	1.29	**1.3**	1.2	0.19	0.98	4.02	67.0	**0.7**	8.5	36.5	**5.6**
0.6	3.77	30.0	0.50	**2.4**	1.3	0.29	2.95	4.21	80.5	**0.6**	7.6	35.4	**4.7**
0.0	13.80	189.5	7.63	**0.0**	-17.9	-8.21	-108.40	2.71	156.0	**0.6**	11.5	52.1	**0.0**
8.7	0.00	0.0	0.01	**0.0**	-0.6	-2.95	-8.86	3.43	184.6	**1.7**	45.9	43.6	**0.4**
0.0	9.78	46.5	2.45	**0.0**	-1.5	-1.39	-12.66	3.45	61.6	**1.1**	14.1	30.5	**1.2**
1.7	8.43	42.4	0.82	**0.0**	-2.2	-1.68	-15.09	2.86	121.7	**2.6**	47.4	31.7	**0.0**
5.0	1.38	6.4	0.09	**3.6**	3.9	0.65	6.25	3.52	81.2	**4.1**	26.2	10.1	**6.7**
0.0	4.89	57.7	0.46	**1.1**	0.7	0.14	1.96	2.45	111.8	**1.5**	12.0	22.8	**2.9**
0.0	17.79	73.7	-0.13	**10.0**	781.5	2.90	19.40	4.07	36.2	**1.0**	19.2	35.0	**1.7**
4.6	1.51	8.2	0.75	**4.5**	1.4	0.86	6.72	4.09	63.3	**3.3**	21.2	13.3	**7.3**
0.0	2.11	12.2	4.67	**0.0**	-3.3	-2.64	-28.59	3.48	99.7	**1.4**	17.1	27.3	**1.3**
3.4	4.35	14.7	2.94	**0.0**	-2.3	-3.58	-22.00	3.78	160.7	**2.5**	38.9	26.9	**2.0**
4.9	1.13	8.2	0.00	**2.3**	0.5	0.44	4.09	3.77	75.2	**0.9**	23.2	37.7	**3.1**
0.0	30.00	305.4	7.16	**0.0**	-8.2	-3.76	-72.51	1.97	256.4	**1.2**	28.3	35.0	**1.5**
10.0	0.19	0.0	0.00	**9.5**	39.1	2.86	22.89	2.91	44.6	**8.8**	110.1	0.0	**9.8**
6.9	0.23	0.1	-0.04	**0.9**	-32.3	-32.86	-76.33	2.27	1,483.4	**6.7**	199.5	19.1	**6.7**
0.0	3.79	28.7	2.84	**0.0**	-6.2	-2.00	-24.36	3.01	112.5	**1.4**	19.0	27.0	**0.8**
3.1	2.30	13.2	-0.14	**3.7**	1.0	0.47	4.92	4.84	84.6	**2.5**	35.8	22.8	**5.3**
0.0	16.18	47.9	1.49	**0.0**	-5.4	-2.50	-10.93	3.39	127.6	**2.7**	32.1	19.0	**6.1**
6.0	2.14	6.8	0.15	**6.3**	7.2	1.27	8.47	4.11	56.6	**2.5**	9.5	16.0	**9.4**
6.9	0.19	1.2	0.03	**4.5**	2.6	0.70	6.74	4.43	65.2	**1.4**	15.7	25.7	**3.0**
2.3	4.27	22.6	0.36	**5.1**	1.8	1.26	14.21	4.76	71.2	**3.5**	35.9	16.0	**4.8**
1.0	1.24	6.9	3.54	**1.3**	0.3	0.13	1.05	3.95	85.9	**0.9**	11.3	31.9	**5.0**
0.0	4.68	32.1	0.24	**1.9**	0.2	0.12	1.32	4.67	85.0	**1.5**	15.1	24.5	**5.0**
2.9	1.61	9.2	0.55	**2.1**	0.1	0.22	2.55	3.86	93.6	**1.3**	23.8	30.8	**4.7**
3.5	8.86	22.3	0.43	**2.6**	10.0	0.14	1.68	2.08	74.8	**0.9**	13.5	33.4	**4.0**
3.1	2.11	8.1	0.51	**3.7**	13.6	0.60	4.23	3.32	56.8	**2.0**	20.8	20.5	**8.3**
3.7	0.00	0.0	-0.06	**6.9**	0.4	1.67	11.47	3.90	57.8	**3.2**	59.1	21.5	**9.3**
4.7	1.67	12.1	0.44	**6.4**	17.2	1.26	12.97	3.78	55.1	**0.8**	12.0	38.3	**8.7**
7.2	1.00	4.2	-0.01	**3.8**	1.3	0.84	6.11	3.46	61.8	**1.9**	39.4	39.2	**7.3**
2.7	1.18	9.7	0.68	**0.5**	-0.1	-0.20	-2.42	4.49	94.4	**3.1**	19.8	14.1	**2.4**
3.1	1.72	9.1	1.37	**1.8**	0.1	0.10	1.01	4.40	71.3	**4.5**	36.0	11.2	**6.1**
5.0	0.98	6.0	0.05	**2.7**	0.4	0.43	4.19	3.50	82.2	**3.5**	27.6	13.5	**4.5**
2.3	3.16	19.3	0.59	**0.7**	-12.3	-6.27	-47.47	4.20	245.1	**2.3**	37.8	28.4	**5.1**
1.4	3.84	23.2	1.45	**1.3**	-0.5	-0.24	-2.25	3.39	60.9	**1.2**	24.0	31.6	**0.6**
8.9	0.34	0.7	0.09	**6.4**	1.0	1.38	6.97	4.68	61.0	**2.3**	34.6	25.4	**9.1**
8.4	0.15	1.1	0.05	**7.9**	8.5	1.81	21.40	4.68	65.3	**1.8**	15.8	20.0	**6.0**
1.7	4.10	30.3	0.47	**4.2**	0.6	0.78	7.26	4.75	65.7	**1.8**	14.8	20.1	**5.2**

Name	City	State	Rating	2008 Rating	2007 Rating	Total Assets ($Mil)	One Year Asset Growth	Asset Mix (As a % of Total Assets) Comm-ercial Loans	Cons-umer Loans	Home Mort-gages	Secur-ities	Capital-ization Index	Leverage Ratio	Risk-based Capital Ratio
▼OWEN COUNTY STATE BK	SPENCER	IN	**C**	B-	B-	185	1.59	3.5	6.8	29.0	18.4	**6.7**	8.7	15.5
▼OWINGSVILLE BANKING CO	OWINGSVILLE	KY	**C-**	C	C	67	2.78	0.0	17.6	38.4	23.3	**8.9**	10.3	18.0
OXFORD BANK	OXFORD	MI	**E-**	E-	E-	285	-12.84	4.6	2.8	19.5	9.8	**0.0**	2.9	5.4
▼OXFORD BANK & TRUST	OAK BROOK	IL	**E**	D-	D	574	-10.46	3.0	9.6	3.7	4.8	**4.3**	6.8	10.7
OXFORD UNIVERSITY BANK	OXFORD	MS	**C+**	C-	C-	91	-3.19	7.7	7.8	26.1	14.8	**9.3**	11.0	14.4
OZARK BANK	OZARK	MO	**C-**	C	C+	217	-0.65	2.5	0.9	16.5	28.7	**10.0**	11.2	20.8
▲OZARK HERITAGE BANK NA	MOUNTAIN VIEW	AR	**D**	D-	C-	62	9.86	22.6	7.4	33.9	13.3	**7.2**	9.1	14.2
OZARK MOUNTAIN BANK	BRANSON	MO	**C+**	B-	B-	312	5.84	4.1	3.4	17.5	21.4	**5.8**	7.8	12.1
OZARKS FS&LA	FARMINGTON	MO	**B-**	B-	B	230	2.12	0.0	1.6	62.1	4.7	**10.0**	12.2	20.9
OZONA NATIONAL BK	OZONA	TX	**C**	B	A	194	6.10	7.3	2.2	3.6	27.8	**10.0**	11.1	18.8
PACESETTER BANK	HARTFORD CITY	IN	**C+**	B-	B+	109	2.69	9.3	7.4	37.8	17.8	**10.0**	12.0	19.8
PACIFIC ALLIANCE BANK	ROSEMEAD	CA	**D+**	C-	C	101	13.06	5.9	0.0	2.6	14.4	**10.0**	12.6	20.3
PACIFIC CAPITAL BANK NA	SANTA BARBARA	CA	**D-**	D	C-	6,084	-19.21	4.2	1.0	15.0	21.0	**7.3**	9.2	14.6
PACIFIC CITY BANK	LOS ANGELES	CA	**D-**	D	C-	538	0.21	22.3	5.9	3.2	0.8	**9.0**	10.3	14.3
▲PACIFIC COAST BANKERS BAN	SAN FRANCISCO	CA	**C-**	D+	B-	526	-14.58	1.6	0.0	1.7	26.6	**7.6**	9.4	27.8
PACIFIC COMMERCE BANK	LOS ANGELES	CA	**D-**	D-	D+	194	-3.29	13.4	0.2	11.9	16.4	**7.2**	9.1	13.0
▲PACIFIC CONTINENTAL BANK	EUGENE	OR	**C+**	C-	B	1,212	1.02	19.7	0.5	5.5	21.0	**10.0**	12.6	16.2
▲PACIFIC CREST SB	LYNNWOOD	WA	**D**	D-	D-	158	0.82	0.0	0.3	29.6	7.6	**7.0**	9.0	14.8
PACIFIC ENTERPRISE BANK	IRVINE	CA	**C**	C-	C-	179	28.97	44.4	0.2	4.8	8.7	**10.0**	12.3	21.4
PACIFIC GLOBAL BANK	CHICAGO	IL	**D-**	D+	B	170	1.06	0.3	0.1	44.9	7.5	**7.2**	9.1	16.0
PACIFIC INTERNATIONAL BK	SEATTLE	WA	**C-**	C-	C	285	-3.37	8.9	0.4	0.4	6.9	**10.0**	11.2	15.1
PACIFIC MERCANTILE BANK	COSTA MESA	CA	**D-**	D-	D+	1,015	-15.33	21.5	1.8	8.8	17.6	**4.9**	7.4	10.9
▲PACIFIC NATIONAL BK	MIAMI	FL	**D**	D-	B-	358	-10.05	3.4	0.1	5.4	42.1	**10.0**	13.9	30.5
PACIFIC PREMIER BANK	COSTA MESA	CA	**C+**	C-	C+	822	2.44	5.1	0.3	1.6	18.9	**8.9**	10.3	15.3
PACIFIC RIM BANK	HONOLULU	HI	**D-**	E	C-	137	0.76	22.4	1.1	8.7	0.0	**4.5**	6.5	12.1
▲PACIFIC TRUST BANK FSB	CHULA VISTA	CA	**D+**	D+	D+	861	-3.66	0.1	0.2	41.2	7.6	**10.0**	11.1	16.2
PACIFIC VALLEY BANK	SALINAS	CA	**D-**	D-	D-	172	-4.74	10.0	0.7	5.9	6.4	**9.0**	10.3	14.2
PACIFIC WEST BANK	WEST LINN	OR	**E-**	D	C	63	-18.81	22.3	1.0	14.4	0.0	**0.3**	4.1	6.5
PACIFIC WESTERN BANK	LOS ANGELES	CA	**D-**	D-	C	5,519	3.83	11.7	0.4	3.6	15.8	**6.5**	8.5	14.0
PADUCAH BANK & TRUST CO	PADUCAH	KY	**B+**	A-	B+	520	5.22	7.1	2.6	23.8	26.3	**7.7**	9.5	16.1
PAGE COUNTY FEDERAL	CLARINDA	IA	**C+**	C+	C+	38	12.69	2.9	4.3	46.7	11.8	**10.0**	13.2	27.1
PAGE COUNTY STATE BK	CLARINDA	IA	**B+**	B+	B+	78	26.76	15.4	6.1	4.8	42.6	**10.0**	13.3	18.9
PAGE VALLEY BANK	LURAY	VA	**C+**	C	C	150	14.47	3.0	1.5	42.2	14.5	**5.4**	7.4	12.4
▲PALISADES NATIONAL BK	PALISADE	CO	**D+**	D-	C	53	2.26	2.7	2.1	7.4	9.4	**6.9**	8.9	22.7
PALM BANK	TAMPA	FL	**D-**	E+	D-	143	-12.21	13.8	2.8	8.2	33.5	**5.4**	7.4	13.3
PALM BEACH COMMUNITY	BOYNTON BEACH	FL	**B**	C	C	153	16.52	20.0	0.5	20.9	18.9	**10.0**	15.8	29.8
PALM DESERT NATIONAL BK	PALM DESERT	CA	**E-**	E	D-	225	-23.47	3.4	0.3	4.1	15.5	**0.0**	2.7	7.3
▲PALMER BANK	TAYLORVILLE	IL	**D+**	C+	B-	93	21.26	11.8	4.3	7.8	36.7	**4.2**	6.2	10.8
▲PALMETTO BANK	GREENVILLE	SC	**D-**	D-	C-	1,357	-5.58	3.5	3.9	9.1	16.1	**6.1**	8.1	14.3
PALMETTO HERITAGE BANK &	PAWLEYS ISLAND	SC	**D**	D-	C-	139	17.10	3.4	3.5	27.9	5.9	**6.7**	9.1	12.3
PALMETTO STATE BK	HAMPTON	SC	**A-**	B+	A	495	6.68	3.4	3.4	7.7	40.3	**10.0**	11.6	23.4
PALMYRA STATE BK	PALMYRA	MO	**B-**	B-	B	143	8.64	6.0	2.2	12.0	12.7	**5.3**	9.2	11.2
PALMYRA STATE BK	PALMYRA	WI	**A**	A	A	38	4.85	12.6	2.2	12.3	31.2	**10.0**	17.8	27.6
PALO SB	PALO	IA	**A-**	B+	B	30	-4.05	2.3	3.1	28.5	33.2	**10.0**	12.1	26.9
PAN AMERICAN BANK	LOS ANGELES	CA	**D-**	D+	C-	42	3.51	4.8	2.9	61.8	0.0	**6.3**	8.3	14.5
PAN AMERICAN BANK	CHICAGO	IL	**C+**	B-	C+	206	41.90	4.9	0.9	14.7	30.3	**4.8**	6.8	11.5
PAN PACIFIC BANK	FREMONT	CA	**D-**	D-	C-	94	13.90	22.7	0.1	9.7	1.4	**5.6**	8.8	11.5
PANHANDLE STATE BK	SANDPOINT	ID	**D-**	D	C+	1,004	-6.96	11.6	1.4	6.7	20.4	**5.3**	7.3	11.9
PANOLA NATIONAL BK	CARTHAGE	TX	**B**	B	B	121	9.50	3.9	10.6	23.4	18.0	**6.3**	8.3	14.2
PANORA STATE BK	PANORA	IA	**A-**	B	B-	57	-1.24	2.6	3.0	24.6	44.0	**7.5**	9.3	16.9
PAPER CITY SAVINGS ASSN	WISCONSIN RAPIDS	WI	**C-**	C-	C+	156	1.30	0.0	2.0	61.1	4.3	**6.9**	8.9	16.4
▼PARADISE BANK	BOCA RATON	FL	**E**	D-	C-	305	-6.64	9.8	0.4	9.6	10.6	**4.0**	6.1	10.6
PARAGON BANK	WELLS	MN	**D-**	D	E-	31	-3.02	15.4	14.4	13.3	6.5	**5.8**	7.8	11.9
▼PARAGON COMMERCIAL BANK	RALEIGH	NC	**E+**	D+	C+	1,173	-10.24	7.9	0.9	6.6	17.3	**4.6**	6.6	11.4
PARAGON NATIONAL BK	MEMPHIS	TN	**D-**	D-	D-	247	-15.93	15.8	3.2	18.6	19.1	**8.0**	9.6	14.4
▲PARIS NATIONAL BK	PARIS	MO	**C**	C+	D+	77	-1.58	6.1	1.2	7.7	36.0	**10.0**	11.5	19.5
PARK AVENUE BANK	VALDOSTA	GA	**E-**	E-	D+	953	-22.59	7.2	1.7	11.4	15.5	**0.0**	1.7	4.1
PARK BANK	HOLMEN	WI	**B-**	C+	B-	43	2.84	23.6	4.9	28.3	15.1	**10.0**	14.6	21.2
PARK BANK	MADISON	WI	**D-**	C-	C	829	0.70	11.3	1.1	12.5	8.3	**7.0**	9.4	12.5
PARK BANK	MILWAUKEE	WI	**D**	D+	B-	772	-3.30	32.0	0.5	5.5	11.1	**6.7**	9.7	12.3

Asset Quality Index	Non-Performing Loans as a % of Total Loans	Non-Performing Loans as a % of Capital	Net Charge-offs Avg Loans	Profitability Index	Net Income ($Mil)	Return on Assets (R.O.A.)	Return on Equity (R.O.E.)	Net Interest Spread	Overhead Efficiency Ratio	Liquidity Index	Liquidity Ratio	Hot Money Ratio	Stability Index
5.3	1.00	6.7	0.42	**3.2**	0.7	0.39	4.29	3.68	80.2	**2.1**	26.0	20.2	**5.3**
2.3	3.29	20.1	0.79	**4.8**	0.6	0.88	8.64	5.18	69.8	**1.9**	23.3	21.7	**4.7**
0.3	5.31	57.3	2.87	**0.2**	-1.2	-0.37	-13.31	4.07	88.7	**3.6**	19.6	11.3	**0.4**
0.3	7.66	62.7	0.77	**0.0**	-7.3	-1.17	-15.53	3.47	125.2	**2.7**	23.5	16.2	**2.5**
6.7	0.30	1.8	0.09	**3.1**	0.2	0.23	2.49	3.82	76.7	**0.9**	22.5	40.4	**4.8**
5.9	2.21	10.0	1.20	**1.7**	0.0	0.01	0.04	3.74	80.9	**2.5**	26.1	17.6	**6.2**
3.6	1.88	13.6	0.21	**0.4**	0.0	0.01	0.06	3.61	87.2	**0.5**	12.8	66.5	**4.5**
4.2	0.77	5.3	0.39	**6.7**	3.5	1.13	13.85	4.12	60.4	**2.8**	14.2	14.9	**5.7**
5.3	1.56	8.9	0.15	**3.4**	1.2	0.54	4.75	3.38	69.0	**2.0**	23.0	20.0	**6.7**
3.6	0.72	3.3	0.69	**2.6**	0.2	0.12	0.99	3.96	87.2	**3.6**	43.5	18.0	**6.5**
6.6	0.93	4.8	0.12	**3.4**	0.5	0.46	3.77	4.05	81.7	**4.2**	29.9	10.8	**5.5**
5.2	0.27	1.4	0.60	**0.4**	0.1	0.09	0.72	3.31	100.1	**1.5**	27.9	30.4	**2.1**
0.0	27.80	186.5	0.00	**1.9**	27.2	1.17	18.14	3.42	70.1	**1.5**	20.2	28.5	**4.3**
0.0	4.31	27.1	5.41	**0.2**	-17.1	-3.11	-32.24	3.76	58.6	**0.9**	18.4	35.9	**4.4**
2.0	9.43	24.2	1.55	**1.3**	1.3	0.17	1.98	2.21	84.7	**5.8**	38.2	4.2	**5.0**
0.3	3.79	27.8	1.98	**1.0**	0.3	0.16	1.63	4.14	77.5	**0.6**	4.7	35.0	**4.1**
2.7	3.72	19.5	1.30	**4.0**	5.9	0.50	3.52	4.71	57.2	**3.8**	24.5	13.0	**7.9**
0.3	7.21	56.6	1.86	**1.5**	0.4	0.22	2.55	3.44	59.2	**3.8**	20.2	10.4	**3.8**
4.9	1.86	10.6	0.26	**2.5**	1.2	0.73	5.44	3.92	78.7	**0.8**	16.4	39.3	**4.0**
0.3	7.17	46.0	2.63	**1.1**	-2.2	-1.24	-12.30	3.92	55.3	**1.9**	15.5	19.6	**5.2**
0.0	6.19	35.5	1.04	**2.8**	1.0	0.33	3.06	3.40	68.7	**1.1**	18.4	32.1	**5.8**
1.9	2.94	22.3	1.31	**0.0**	-11.2	-0.96	-13.55	3.01	90.1	**0.8**	16.9	48.5	**3.6**
1.7	10.43	23.9	2.59	**0.4**	-0.3	-0.08	-0.71	3.80	103.7	**1.1**	27.3	42.1	**4.4**
4.7	0.44	2.7	0.39	**3.9**	4.7	0.59	5.83	3.99	64.5	**1.1**	23.3	32.4	**5.9**
1.6	3.10	26.2	0.73	**1.1**	0.1	0.10	1.45	4.23	85.7	**2.4**	34.4	22.7	**2.0**
1.4	4.20	27.0	0.97	**1.8**	1.2	0.13	1.31	3.64	65.2	**1.1**	16.3	31.3	**5.0**
0.0	6.87	39.7	1.90	**0.0**	-1.3	-0.77	-7.20	4.46	76.3	**1.5**	23.6	26.3	**3.9**
0.3	7.92	89.8	5.81	**0.0**	-4.5	-6.23	-104.54	3.33	145.5	**1.3**	15.1	26.9	**4.0**
0.2	2.33	15.6	5.44	**0.1**	-53.3	-0.98	-9.29	5.17	57.2	**2.4**	17.0	17.8	**6.3**
5.4	0.17	1.0	0.21	**9.6**	11.2	2.20	21.27	4.62	56.7	**2.6**	20.0	16.3	**8.4**
3.0	4.03	17.5	0.64	**3.2**	0.2	0.46	3.41	3.56	81.7	**2.2**	37.5	30.0	**5.3**
5.5	4.41	16.3	0.07	**6.0**	1.0	1.40	10.13	4.50	68.3	**5.7**	49.6	7.6	**7.2**
5.3	0.60	6.0	0.10	**4.4**	1.1	0.73	10.25	3.73	67.3	**2.1**	10.4	17.9	**4.1**
0.3	8.60	34.8	1.70	**1.2**	-0.3	-0.52	-3.63	3.96	109.9	**6.4**	46.8	2.3	**8.7**
0.8	6.66	40.7	1.55	**0.0**	-0.9	-0.54	-7.41	3.18	109.4	**2.1**	20.5	18.9	**1.6**
8.8	0.00	0.0	-0.10	**4.7**	2.1	1.43	8.90	4.36	62.7	**2.3**	24.0	18.2	**6.0**
0.0	20.62	172.3	3.28	**1.0**	-6.5	-2.42	-72.60	2.87	126.5	**1.1**	25.3	34.6	**0.9**
3.6	2.79	20.3	0.22	**4.8**	0.6	0.71	8.55	3.79	57.8	**2.3**	39.4	29.3	**5.2**
0.3	10.58	62.7	4.52	**0.5**	-59.4	-4.24	-85.57	3.19	135.3	**2.6**	26.2	21.0	**4.5**
0.9	5.29	39.6	0.44	**0.9**	0.1	0.05	0.51	2.95	79.0	**0.7**	13.7	47.0	**4.4**
7.0	1.26	4.1	1.21	**5.9**	5.1	1.04	9.22	3.82	48.1	**3.0**	40.3	20.4	**6.0**
4.6	0.50	3.8	0.13	**6.4**	2.0	1.52	16.38	4.17	65.9	**3.3**	20.1	12.9	**6.9**
8.8	0.00	0.0	-0.01	**5.7**	0.4	1.03	5.83	3.68	61.3	**4.1**	46.4	15.4	**8.6**
9.1	0.08	0.3	0.00	**8.0**	0.6	1.81	13.87	4.46	54.6	**3.8**	48.6	17.3	**8.0**
0.3	1.64	13.4	1.97	**0.8**	-0.1	-0.20	-1.99	5.10	103.3	**1.1**	10.7	29.2	**4.1**
5.2	0.54	4.5	0.02	**3.6**	1.5	0.83	13.37	2.99	75.2	**1.2**	28.6	44.9	**6.0**
2.0	1.50	11.4	0.93	**0.1**	-0.7	-0.74	-7.72	3.96	94.6	**1.7**	17.8	21.8	**1.1**
4.0	1.79	12.3	4.35	**0.1**	-30.3	-2.91	-31.86	4.05	113.8	**2.8**	24.2	18.0	**4.0**
7.5	0.44	2.4	0.02	**4.3**	1.0	0.86	9.25	3.77	78.4	**3.1**	46.4	23.4	**5.5**
8.3	0.00	0.0	0.00	**6.4**	0.6	1.80	14.87	3.98	43.4	**4.4**	48.3	14.6	**8.0**
4.6	1.10	9.4	0.03	**2.3**	0.6	0.37	4.23	2.97	74.5	**2.4**	19.0	17.7	**3.3**
0.4	3.96	35.7	1.76	**0.0**	-4.0	-1.21	-17.98	3.26	78.0	**3.1**	18.2	14.0	**0.5**
1.9	2.26	16.7	1.16	**2.6**	0.1	0.44	5.58	4.64	80.6	**4.2**	22.1	8.3	**1.7**
0.0	2.49	21.5	2.36	**0.0**	-7.1	-0.55	-7.62	2.65	83.1	**0.5**	6.5	50.4	**4.5**
1.3	4.50	30.0	1.06	**0.0**	-1.2	-0.45	-4.68	3.34	99.9	**1.2**	14.1	29.1	**3.7**
3.7	6.39	26.9	0.56	**3.4**	0.6	0.78	6.72	4.06	68.1	**2.9**	26.8	16.3	**5.0**
0.0	19.29	213.5	3.50	**0.0**	-43.7	-3.85	-104.34	1.89	241.1	**0.8**	18.2	38.2	**1.8**
5.9	0.87	4.1	0.91	**4.2**	0.3	0.68	4.66	6.44	82.4	**4.5**	4.2	3.9	**6.2**
0.0	3.59	27.4	1.37	**1.9**	0.7	0.09	0.90	3.58	76.9	**0.9**	13.0	32.3	**5.1**
0.8	3.57	24.2	2.06	**2.4**	0.9	0.11	1.13	3.90	58.6	**1.8**	20.5	21.8	**6.7**

Name	City	State	Rating	2008 Rating	2007 Rating	Total Assets ($Mil)	One Year Asset Growth	Asset Mix (As a % of Total Assets): Commercial Loans	Consumer Loans	Home Mortgages	Securities	Capitalization Index	Leverage Ratio	Risk-based Capital Ratio
▼ PARK CITIES BANK	DALLAS	TX	**E**	D-	C-	878	-0.44	17.7	0.3	3.7	7.9	**1.4**	4.5	8.4
PARK FSB	CHICAGO	IL	**D-**	D	D+	213	-2.50	0.2	0.1	46.6	14.1	**6.4**	8.4	15.7
▲ PARK MIDWAY BANK NA	SAINT PAUL	MN	**D+**	C-	B-	261	-4.03	18.9	0.6	5.0	9.3	**8.9**	10.3	14.8
▼ PARK NATIONAL BK	NEWARK	OH	**D+**	C	C	6,496	4.98	8.1	9.6	17.4	28.8	**4.7**	6.7	11.4
PARK RIDGE COMMUNITY	PARK RIDGE	IL	**A-**	B+	A	262	10.63	0.6	0.0	18.1	14.7	**9.5**	10.7	18.0
PARK STATE BK	DULUTH	MN	**E-**	E+	E	31	-4.83	11.1	3.6	27.1	12.0	**0.8**	4.3	7.6
PARK STATE BK & TRUST	WOODLAND PARK	CO	**D-**	D-	D-	90	-4.69	3.9	1.6	20.4	22.7	**5.3**	7.3	12.4
PARK STERLING BANK	CHARLOTTE	NC	**D**	C	C	616	30.22	7.9	1.2	6.9	22.8	**10.0**	27.4	43.1
PARK VIEW FSB	SOLON	OH	**D-**	E+	D-	841	-3.36	3.3	0.0	17.5	7.2	**6.8**	8.8	13.4
▼ PARKE BANK	SEWELL	NJ	**D-**	D	B	758	16.13	2.6	2.3	17.9	3.9	**9.0**	11.2	14.2
▲ PARKSIDE FINANCIAL BANK &	CLAYTON	MO	**C-**	C	C	186	21.40	38.4	1.1	4.6	1.2	**7.0**	9.5	12.5
PARKVALE SB	MONROEVILLE	PA	**C**	C+	C+	1,788	-6.64	2.2	2.2	40.0	28.2	**4.5**	6.5	11.2
▼ PARKWAY BANK	ROGERS	AR	**D-**	D-	D-	112	-2.18	5.7	2.7	12.5	18.3	**8.1**	9.7	13.9
PARKWAY BANK	LENOIR	NC	**E-**	D-	D	118	1.13	12.3	0.8	10.1	12.9	**1.1**	5.3	8.1
PARKWAY BANK & TRUST CO	HARWOOD HEIGHTS	IL	**D-**	D-	C	2,589	4.62	1.5	0.1	2.2	11.9	**5.9**	7.9	12.0
PARTNERS BANK OF	MISSION VIEJO	CA	**D-**	C	C	98	13.94	54.1	0.0	0.1	9.1	**5.9**	8.1	11.7
▲ PASCACK COMMUNITY BANK	WESTWOOD	NJ	**D**	D	D+	298	7.39	9.5	0.5	11.4	9.4	**5.0**	8.3	11.0
PASSUMPSIC SB	SAINT JOHNSBURY	VT	**C**	C-	D+	578	4.43	5.5	8.0	33.6	7.7	**5.4**	7.4	12.1
PATAPSCO BANK	DUNDALK	MD	**D-**	D-	D+	274	5.16	14.0	3.2	27.9	13.4	**5.7**	7.7	13.2
PATASKALA BANKING CO	PATASKALA	OH	**E+**	D-	D	34	3.55	2.9	2.5	39.9	14.7	**5.8**	7.8	16.7
PATHFINDER BANK	OSWEGO	NY	**C+**	C+	C	407	9.87	7.7	1.2	37.6	20.8	**6.1**	8.1	13.5
PATHFINDER COMMERCIAL	OSWEGO	NY	**B+**	B+	C+	49	12.84	0.0	0.0	0.0	92.7	**8.9**	10.2	48.2
PATHWAY BANK	CAIRO	NE	**D**	D-	D+	144	-7.48	10.8	3.1	5.2	19.0	**5.6**	7.7	11.4
▲ PATRIOT BANK	TRINITY	FL	**D-**	E-	D-	135	2.91	8.9	2.8	7.7	6.5	**4.6**	6.7	11.8
PATRIOT BANK	BROOKLYN	IA	**E-**	E-	E-	62	-34.85	7.7	5.0	14.4	16.4	**4.5**	6.5	11.4
PATRIOT BANK	BROKEN ARROW	OK	**D**	D	D-	64	20.81	19.0	1.8	15.2	5.1	**10.0**	11.9	18.5
PATRIOT BANK	MILLINGTON	TN	**B**	B	B+	226	7.03	9.4	2.4	17.9	19.5	**5.9**	7.9	12.5
▼ PATRIOT BANK	HOUSTON	TX	**D**	C	C-	1,262	0.65	19.7	0.4	9.7	17.1	**7.0**	9.0	12.7
▼ PATRIOT BANK MINNESOTA	FOREST LAKE	MN	**E-**	D-	D+	121	-12.62	21.1	1.6	1.3	9.9	**0.8**	5.5	7.7
PATRIOT BANK OF GEORGIA	CUMMING	GA	**E-**	E-	D-	162	-7.99	7.6	0.3	16.9	3.7	**0.0**	3.2	5.2
▲ PATRIOT COMMUNITY BANK	WOBURN	MA	**B-**	C	C	99	31.97	10.8	0.1	25.6	18.1	**8.1**	10.2	13.4
PATRIOT FEDERAL BANK	CANAJOHARIE	NY	**C**	C	C	86	13.42	6.7	1.6	42.5	24.3	**7.4**	9.2	17.1
▲ PATRIOT NATIONAL BK	STAMFORD	CT	**D-**	E-	D-	784	-9.52	0.9	0.2	34.8	5.7	**6.8**	8.8	16.5
PATRIOT STATE BK	FUQUAY-VARINA	NC	**D+**	D	D+	139	1.37	4.1	0.9	17.6	11.7	**10.0**	11.2	16.1
▲ PATRIOTS BANK	GARNETT	KS	**D+**	D	C-	90	-4.87	6.9	2.5	20.5	20.9	**6.9**	8.9	13.9
PATRIOTS BANK	LIBERTY	MO	**D-**	D+	D+	101	-3.44	8.9	1.4	11.4	4.0	**7.0**	9.2	12.5
PATTERSON BANK	PATTERSON	GA	**E-**	D	C-	149	-9.67	9.0	2.3	13.4	7.4	**0.4**	4.4	6.9
PATTERSON STATE BK	PATTERSON	LA	**D+**	D	D+	213	-5.40	10.8	2.9	40.0	25.9	**7.1**	9.1	16.9
PAULS VALLEY NATIONAL BK	PAULS VALLEY	OK	**B+**	B+	B	167	4.38	14.4	14.8	10.5	37.0	**9.7**	10.8	17.4
PAVILLION BANK	RICHARDSON	TX	**B-**	B-	C+	84	-3.88	7.4	1.9	17.7	1.9	**10.0**	11.2	17.6
PAYNE COUNTY BANK	PERKINS	OK	**A**	A	A	118	6.15	15.6	12.9	19.5	24.5	**10.0**	16.4	26.5
PBI BANK	LOUISVILLE	KY	**D**	D-	C-	1,720	-5.80	5.3	1.9	18.8	6.1	**8.3**	9.9	14.7
PBK BANK INC	STANFORD	KY	**D+**	D	B-	114	-3.24	2.8	2.0	16.9	21.7	**6.5**	8.5	15.6
PCSB COMMERCIAL BANK	BREWSTER	NY	**C+**	B	B+	30	3.47	0.0	0.0	0.0	83.1	**10.0**	20.1	124.3
▼ PEABODY STATE BK	PEABODY	KS	**D-**	C-	C-	40	-0.02	10.8	3.2	12.9	28.3	**6.5**	8.5	15.5
PEACH STATE BANK & TRUST	GAINESVILLE	GA	**E-**	D+	C-	154	-10.93	9.3	0.8	10.1	8.8	**1.6**	5.3	8.6
▼ PEACHTREE BANK	MAPLESVILLE	AL	**D**	C-	B-	58	-12.50	2.8	5.1	10.0	17.2	**6.7**	8.7	16.5
PEAPACK-GLADSTONE BANK	BEDMINSTER	NJ	**C+**	C+	C-	1,503	-0.31	1.9	0.4	29.6	27.4	**5.6**	7.6	13.3
PEARLAND STATE BK	PEARLAND	TX	**A+**	A+	A+	150	3.22	3.0	1.2	3.7	65.1	**10.0**	13.3	31.8
PECOS COUNTY STATE BK	FORT STOCKTON	TX	**B-**	B-	B	135	1.83	10.7	7.9	10.1	40.3	**6.5**	8.5	16.5
PEE DEE FSB	MARION	SC	**C+**	C+	C+	39	1.30	7.9	12.6	26.1	0.0	**10.0**	24.3	31.0
PEGASUS BANK	DALLAS	TX	**C-**	C-	C-	196	27.86	15.6	6.1	14.3	8.3	**6.8**	8.8	12.6
PEKIN NATIONAL BK	PEKIN	IL	**D**	D	D+	23	1.64	11.1	0.8	18.2	47.2	**10.0**	13.4	24.4
PELHAM BANKING CO	PELHAM	GA	**A**	A	A	60	2.89	7.8	7.5	10.5	31.7	**10.0**	15.2	26.3
PENDER STATE BK	PENDER	NE	**C+**	C+	C	130	7.09	3.9	1.2	1.7	2.1	**3.7**	9.4	10.3
PENDLETON COMMUNITY	FRANKLIN	WV	**C**	B	A	249	2.83	4.2	5.0	28.1	11.5	**9.1**	10.4	16.0
PENINSULA BANK OF ISHPEMI	ISHPEMING	MI	**B+**	A-	B+	136	0.06	4.4	4.5	23.7	8.1	**10.0**	11.8	17.6
PENN LIBERTY BANK	WAYNE	PA	**D**	D-	D+	471	11.31	15.9	0.1	14.0	2.0	**5.6**	8.7	11.5
PENN SECURITY BANK &	SCRANTON	PA	**B+**	B+	A	912	3.72	4.0	6.1	27.0	23.8	**8.7**	10.2	15.8
PENNSVILLE NATIONAL BK	PENNSVILLE	NJ	**C+**	C+	C+	197	0.10	0.5	0.7	22.0	61.1	**5.4**	7.4	18.8

Asset Quality Index	Non-Performing Loans as a % of Total Loans	Non-Performing Loans as a % of Capital	Net Charge-offs Avg Loans	Profitability Index	Net Income ($Mil)	Return on Assets (R.O.A.)	Return on Equity (R.O.E.)	Net Interest Spread	Overhead Efficiency Ratio	Liquidity Index	Liquidity Ratio	Hot Money Ratio	Stability Index
0.1	18.48	152.5	3.70	**0.0**	-42.1	-4.38	-61.50	1.81	115.1	**1.7**	36.7	47.1	**4.6**
0.3	7.46	52.1	0.57	**0.0**	-4.1	-1.90	-19.54	3.08	113.7	**1.8**	25.3	23.9	**3.3**
0.9	2.47	17.8	1.01	**4.6**	2.5	0.94	9.25	4.64	65.9	**1.6**	12.7	22.4	**5.9**
1.8	2.92	24.6	0.55	**9.7**	103.0	1.74	25.34	4.25	46.4	**2.2**	10.5	17.9	**6.3**
6.0	1.98	9.9	0.09	**6.8**	3.7	1.50	13.87	4.11	49.9	**4.4**	38.0	12.1	**8.3**
1.5	2.61	31.6	1.37	**0.0**	-0.7	-2.09	-36.56	5.00	109.5	**3.2**	18.7	13.2	**0.0**
1.3	6.07	40.5	1.35	**0.0**	-1.6	-1.70	-21.04	3.67	141.3	**2.7**	8.4	14.7	**2.3**
2.9	10.23	22.0	3.00	**0.0**	-7.9	-1.46	-8.09	2.96	72.4	**2.1**	46.0	54.4	**2.2**
0.3	10.16	65.1	0.00	**0.1**	-12.1	-1.39	-16.39	2.68	89.1	**1.8**	25.8	24.5	**3.9**
0.0	4.63	29.9	1.06	**7.7**	8.0	1.16	10.15	4.59	34.0	**1.1**	9.6	29.5	**7.9**
8.1	0.00	0.0	0.00	**2.4**	0.8	0.46	4.58	3.94	79.5	**1.1**	19.3	31.9	**3.2**
3.4	2.63	20.9	0.55	**2.6**	-14.9	-0.79	-9.75	2.28	65.1	**3.5**	20.8	13.1	**4.9**
0.3	3.28	17.7	1.60	**1.0**	0.3	0.29	2.56	3.89	98.5	**1.8**	14.6	20.1	**4.2**
0.1	11.04	99.0	1.87	**0.0**	-1.9	-1.57	-25.37	3.29	111.5	**1.1**	22.8	32.7	**2.7**
0.0	11.15	79.9	1.47	**1.0**	-0.8	-0.03	-0.36	2.77	55.7	**0.9**	18.2	41.8	**6.6**
7.7	0.23	1.7	1.55	**0.0**	-2.4	-2.45	-22.95	4.72	99.6	**0.9**	22.2	35.4	**1.0**
3.8	0.00	0.0	0.54	**1.7**	2.0	0.67	9.23	3.82	74.7	**4.1**	5.7	6.5	**2.9**
2.6	1.00	9.5	0.27	**3.9**	3.9	0.69	6.73	4.33	76.3	**2.0**	7.3	18.0	**6.5**
0.3	6.15	48.0	1.54	**0.0**	-2.5	-0.94	-11.87	3.50	100.8	**3.7**	23.4	11.5	**2.5**
1.7	7.40	47.7	0.17	**0.2**	-0.1	-0.40	-4.84	4.03	110.2	**6.3**	43.1	2.1	**2.3**
3.2	2.00	15.8	0.18	**4.0**	2.7	0.70	7.95	3.75	70.9	**2.2**	13.0	17.6	**4.5**
10.0	0.00	0.0	0.00	**5.5**	0.6	1.07	9.83	1.81	22.2	**3.6**	22.4	11.5	**6.5**
1.4	3.12	23.7	1.76	**0.8**	0.1	0.07	0.80	3.28	90.6	**1.4**	23.2	27.9	**3.0**
0.0	8.17	75.8	0.91	**0.0**	-0.5	-0.39	-3.34	3.84	102.4	**2.6**	13.7	15.6	**4.5**
1.6	2.94	21.1	4.79	**0.0**	-1.3	-1.95	-26.35	4.29	101.7	**2.9**	16.9	14.8	**1.3**
1.8	4.98	24.5	0.03	**0.0**	-0.9	-1.63	-9.28	3.09	113.1	**1.7**	33.0	32.7	**4.3**
5.7	0.59	4.2	0.45	**4.9**	1.9	0.87	10.19	3.84	68.1	**1.2**	14.2	28.6	**5.5**
2.2	3.91	28.1	0.67	**0.5**	-3.9	-0.30	-3.14	2.82	80.0	**1.9**	21.6	23.8	**6.5**
0.0	12.16	101.5	2.73	**0.0**	-7.3	-5.45	-56.57	3.21	165.6	**0.6**	4.3	35.9	**3.2**
0.0	20.97	322.9	2.65	**0.0**	-4.6	-2.70	-57.45	1.69	185.8	**0.7**	12.0	46.4	**0.0**
9.1	0.00	0.0	0.00	**4.6**	1.0	1.15	10.39	2.93	62.1	**1.2**	28.5	41.8	**5.4**
5.4	1.57	10.7	0.11	**3.9**	0.8	0.94	9.50	4.30	65.1	**1.1**	28.6	51.4	**2.0**
0.3	16.76	106.5	1.32	**0.0**	-14.8	-1.82	-34.32	2.97	129.2	**1.5**	24.9	27.4	**3.8**
1.7	3.97	24.1	1.16	**1.0**	0.4	0.26	2.22	3.22	86.6	**0.9**	22.5	39.4	**3.0**
1.9	1.28	8.8	0.00	**3.7**	0.8	0.86	9.87	4.29	80.8	**2.6**	17.6	16.2	**4.9**
1.2	0.85	5.8	4.13	**0.0**	-2.8	-2.70	-15.21	4.06	110.8	**2.5**	13.5	16.2	**4.6**
0.2	13.22	150.0	2.81	**0.2**	-2.7	-1.69	-31.35	3.56	97.8	**1.4**	15.1	25.8	**0.0**
3.4	2.27	15.2	0.75	**1.9**	1.0	0.43	4.82	3.95	77.4	**1.7**	21.7	23.4	**2.6**
4.8	1.26	5.8	0.79	**5.3**	1.5	0.93	8.14	5.01	65.8	**3.3**	48.2	21.9	**6.3**
4.5	2.35	12.6	0.65	**0.6**	-1.0	-1.09	-9.10	3.84	129.7	**2.1**	27.5	21.0	**5.6**
6.8	0.62	2.3	0.30	**9.2**	2.5	2.19	12.47	5.21	57.8	**3.2**	32.9	16.5	**9.3**
0.9	4.59	30.0	1.64	**2.0**	-3.3	-0.19	-1.74	3.62	69.2	**0.8**	14.2	40.2	**8.1**
4.7	1.15	7.0	0.13	**1.7**	0.2	0.15	1.77	3.47	84.2	**2.5**	28.6	18.6	**4.0**
10.0	0.00	0.0	0.00	**2.3**	0.1	0.14	0.83	0.47	51.2	**5.4**	21.8	0.0	**3.9**
3.7	4.78	27.2	1.40	**0.6**	0.0	-0.08	-0.80	4.16	87.7	**3.9**	32.2	12.8	**5.0**
0.3	5.27	50.5	2.79	**0.0**	-3.6	-2.14	-31.15	2.82	83.5	**1.3**	20.0	29.0	**0.0**
0.3	10.29	45.1	2.72	**0.0**	-0.5	-0.80	-8.55	3.85	86.8	**4.7**	44.3	12.3	**3.3**
3.7	2.01	14.7	0.93	**3.9**	7.8	0.53	7.12	3.63	66.6	**5.7**	32.0	5.9	**5.1**
7.9	2.71	4.8	0.23	**9.4**	3.1	2.09	14.30	4.20	49.1	**3.8**	79.6	30.2	**9.4**
5.4	0.63	3.4	0.20	**5.1**	1.8	1.34	15.34	4.11	73.6	**1.8**	20.8	22.1	**5.1**
4.9	3.07	8.7	0.23	**2.2**	-0.1	-0.37	-1.54	4.78	96.2	**3.4**	31.8	15.1	**6.0**
8.6	0.00	0.0	0.00	**2.2**	0.9	0.51	5.51	2.73	72.2	**6.3**	48.8	4.1	**3.1**
2.9	6.54	20.5	-0.46	**0.5**	0.0	0.08	0.61	3.77	110.3	**2.7**	45.3	21.5	**5.0**
8.4	0.32	1.0	0.17	**7.1**	0.9	1.53	9.49	4.71	64.1	**3.4**	47.8	19.2	**9.8**
3.4	0.43	3.9	0.00	**8.7**	2.7	2.13	15.10	4.08	46.4	**0.5**	4.1	41.0	**7.4**
2.6	2.52	16.8	0.32	**5.6**	2.4	0.95	8.36	4.42	57.1	**1.5**	10.1	22.4	**7.7**
7.0	0.64	3.7	0.19	**4.8**	1.0	0.69	5.87	4.58	71.6	**2.9**	19.1	15.1	**6.8**
3.6	1.26	10.9	0.28	**1.1**	1.3	0.29	3.24	3.38	81.9	**2.9**	11.5	14.1	**3.2**
4.7	0.92	6.0	0.30	**6.3**	11.2	1.27	9.58	4.46	63.3	**1.8**	12.3	19.7	**8.5**
6.1	2.31	9.8	0.06	**4.3**	1.6	0.80	9.87	3.19	69.6	**5.6**	62.4	12.2	**3.8**

	Name	City	State	Rating	2008 Rating	2007 Rating	Total Assets ($Mil)	One Year Asset Growth	Asset Mix (As a % of Total Assets) Commercial Loans	Consumer Loans	Home Mortgages	Securities	Capitalization Index	Leverage Ratio	Risk-based Capital Ratio
	PENTUCKET BANK	HAVERHILL	MA	**C**	C	C-	620	2.38	6.7	0.1	37.8	15.4	**8.4**	9.9	14.8
	PEOPLEFIRST BANK	JOLIET	IL	**C**	C	C	104	1.83	4.1	0.1	6.5	27.9	**10.0**	12.8	18.8
	PEOPLES B&TC OF CLINTON C	ALBANY	KY	**D-**	D-	D+	32	-2.36	12.4	16.7	31.4	2.0	**7.3**	9.2	13.0
	PEOPLES B&TC OF HAZARD	HAZARD	KY	**D**	D	D+	285	-0.24	23.2	9.5	23.9	6.9	**6.5**	8.5	12.2
▼	PEOPLES B&TC OF MADISON	BEREA	KY	**C+**	B-	B	421	0.82	1.9	2.1	25.0	25.4	**6.8**	8.9	15.8
	PEOPLES B&TC OF PICKETT C	BYRDSTOWN	TN	**D-**	D-	D+	130	4.71	13.3	14.0	18.5	6.1	**7.2**	9.1	12.6
▼	PEOPLES B&TC OF POINTE CO	NEW ROADS	LA	**B-**	B	B+	161	25.21	12.7	3.9	20.0	4.5	**7.7**	9.5	13.5
	PEOPLES BANK	MAGNOLIA	AR	**C+**	C+	C+	148	13.42	1.0	5.1	19.1	19.5	**5.9**	7.9	20.6
	PEOPLES BANK	SHERIDAN	AR	**A**	A	A-	112	12.90	13.0	6.4	7.8	39.2	**10.0**	11.7	20.4
	PEOPLES BANK	CONYERS	GA	**E-**	E-	D-	140	-12.90	1.6	1.2	14.4	15.7	**2.0**	5.3	9.0
	PEOPLES BANK	EATONTON	GA	**D-**	C-	C-	144	-7.96	2.2	3.8	26.0	6.8	**6.4**	8.4	14.0
	PEOPLES BANK	LYONS	GA	**D-**	D+	C+	56	-7.73	4.2	4.4	7.0	11.1	**6.6**	8.6	15.2
	PEOPLES BANK	WILLACOOCHEE	GA	**B-**	B	A-	63	3.22	2.1	5.2	14.8	24.9	**10.0**	11.5	21.1
	PEOPLES BANK	ROCK VALLEY	IA	**C+**	C+	B-	346	6.61	9.8	2.1	5.5	6.8	**7.3**	9.3	12.7
	PEOPLES BANK	BROWNSTOWN	IN	**B**	B	B	133	10.87	2.6	8.8	19.8	28.7	**9.4**	10.6	20.7
	PEOPLES BANK	COLDWATER	KS	**B**	B	B	40	2.63	8.2	5.2	5.7	28.7	**10.0**	11.0	18.1
	PEOPLES BANK	LAWRENCE	KS	**D-**	D	D+	374	8.85	8.3	0.8	29.1	6.5	**6.2**	8.2	12.9
▲	PEOPLES BANK	PRATT	KS	**C+**	B	A-	327	0.72	16.2	2.4	6.7	34.1	**10.0**	11.3	20.2
	PEOPLES BANK	LEBANON	KY	**D-**	D-	D-	46	-12.62	5.9	4.7	9.1	20.4	**6.3**	8.3	12.7
	PEOPLES BANK	MARION	KY	**D-**	D-	C-	37	12.60	17.7	10.5	23.3	12.5	**5.7**	7.7	11.8
▼	PEOPLES BANK	MOUNT WASHINGTON	KY	**C**	B+	A-	86	1.34	1.9	0.9	7.6	12.2	**10.0**	13.0	17.7
	PEOPLES BANK	TAYLORSVILLE	KY	**C+**	A-	A	104	2.00	5.0	4.0	22.7	15.8	**10.0**	11.4	18.0
	PEOPLES BANK	CHATHAM	LA	**B-**	B-	C+	20	0.70	4.4	16.0	30.1	5.9	**10.0**	17.1	30.0
▼	PEOPLES BANK	CHESTERTOWN	MD	**D-**	D+	C	245	-3.75	9.6	2.3	28.6	4.7	**9.1**	10.5	14.3
	PEOPLES BANK	CUBA	MO	**A-**	B+	B+	173	-3.92	3.1	4.1	32.7	22.0	**8.0**	9.6	15.4
▼	PEOPLES BANK	MENDENHALL	MS	**D**	C	B	214	8.13	7.8	6.5	14.0	14.5	**7.0**	9.0	14.2
	PEOPLES BANK	RIPLEY	MS	**B**	B	B	360	5.34	15.6	10.0	13.6	44.6	**7.3**	9.2	18.3
▲	PEOPLES BANK	NEWTON	NC	**D**	C	B-	1,065	1.81	5.7	1.1	18.0	25.4	**6.9**	8.9	13.2
	PEOPLES BANK	GAMBIER	OH	**C**	C	C	48	0.81	2.1	8.3	29.9	40.3	**6.9**	8.9	18.2
	PEOPLES BANK	TULSA	OK	**D**	D+	C	95	-8.47	26.4	6.6	16.5	2.3	**5.7**	8.7	11.5
	PEOPLES BANK	WESTVILLE	OK	**A-**	A-	A	53	-1.48	5.8	5.4	13.3	29.4	**9.5**	10.7	17.0
	PEOPLES BANK	IVA	SC	**D+**	D+	B	244	4.86	3.5	3.9	17.8	22.6	**6.7**	8.7	14.1
	PEOPLES BANK	CLIFTON	TN	**C-**	C-	C+	129	0.85	9.4	11.5	19.3	5.5	**6.8**	8.8	12.8
	PEOPLES BANK	SARDIS	TN	**D**	C-	B+	77	4.30	3.3	6.7	20.8	33.0	**4.2**	6.2	12.1
	PEOPLES BANK	COLLEYVILLE	TX	**D**	C-	C-	73	-11.34	7.7	1.2	16.0	16.3	**7.6**	9.4	16.5
	PEOPLES BANK	LUBBOCK	TX	**B-**	B-	B-	263	10.48	10.6	4.9	6.3	14.4	**6.5**	8.8	12.1
	PEOPLES BANK	PARIS	TX	**A-**	B+	B+	111	-4.46	9.2	5.5	33.1	27.9	**6.9**	8.9	17.1
	PEOPLES BANK	EWING	VA	**D-**	E	D	93	-7.07	11.0	1.9	25.1	15.3	**6.1**	8.1	13.3
	PEOPLES BANK	LYNDEN	WA	**C**	C+	C	1,177	3.61	5.2	7.1	13.1	1.9	**9.0**	10.3	14.5
	PEOPLES BANK	ELKHORN	WI	**D+**	D+	C+	189	-3.12	1.4	0.7	27.0	1.5	**8.6**	10.1	13.8
	PEOPLES BANK & TRUST	BUFORD	GA	**E-**	E-	D-	341	-13.38	1.6	1.8	18.9	16.2	**0.1**	3.5	6.1
	PEOPLES BANK & TRUST	PANA	IL	**C+**	C	C	278	25.91	20.6	1.2	6.9	25.9	**5.1**	7.4	11.1
	PEOPLES BANK & TRUST CO	MCPHERSON	KS	**B+**	B+	A-	332	14.81	16.7	3.2	4.8	40.5	**9.9**	11.0	18.4
	PEOPLES BANK & TRUST CO	OWENTON	KY	**A-**	A	A-	73	-13.32	1.7	3.4	20.6	32.6	**10.0**	13.9	19.7
	PEOPLES BANK & TRUST CO	TROY	MO	**E**	D+	C-	406	-3.88	7.9	0.9	8.3	20.8	**2.5**	6.6	9.5
	PEOPLES BANK & TRUST CO	NORTH CARROLLTON	MS	**A-**	A-	B+	53	3.34	0.4	6.3	13.7	67.5	**10.0**	13.8	38.6
▲	PEOPLES BANK & TRUST CO	RYAN	OK	**B-**	B-	B-	25	11.38	9.1	8.8	25.4	2.2	**10.0**	12.1	17.7
	PEOPLES BANK & TRUST CO	MANCHESTER	TN	**C**	C+	B	79	1.26	8.4	6.5	14.4	22.6	**8.9**	10.3	15.8
	PEOPLES BANK CO	COLDWATER	OH	**A-**	A-	A-	352	7.54	5.7	2.7	18.0	30.9	**7.4**	9.3	18.3
	PEOPLES BANK KANKAKEE	BOURBONNAIS	IL	**C+**	B-	B-	201	9.79	4.2	0.9	19.8	23.8	**5.3**	7.3	12.5
▼	PEOPLES BANK MONITEAU	JAMESTOWN	MO	**D+**	C-	C-	49	9.31	4.4	5.1	19.8	28.3	**6.4**	8.4	14.1
	PEOPLES BANK NA	MARIETTA	OH	**C**	C-	C	1,830	-8.31	8.2	4.6	12.1	33.5	**7.1**	9.0	15.6
	PEOPLES BANK OF ALABAMA	CULLMAN	AL	**D**	D+	C-	499	0.52	9.1	2.9	15.7	11.9	**5.2**	8.7	11.1
	PEOPLES BANK OF	ALTENBURG	MO	**D**	C	C-	48	-4.53	5.4	3.8	25.2	19.6	**6.9**	8.9	14.0
▲	PEOPLES BANK OF BEDFORD	SHELBYVILLE	TN	**B**	C+	B	102	4.07	5.3	7.6	20.7	24.6	**8.2**	9.8	15.8
▼	PEOPLES BANK OF BULLITT C	SHEPHERDSVILLE	KY	**B-**	A-	A-	219	12.41	0.0	3.2	24.3	45.5	**10.0**	13.0	26.1
	PEOPLES BANK OF	CAMBRIDGE	MN	**D**	D	C	311	-10.93	15.6	0.8	8.8	14.3	**9.6**	10.7	15.0
▲	PEOPLES BANK OF	MEDFORD	OR	**C-**	D+	B-	106	4.12	19.7	1.4	12.1	8.6	**10.0**	11.7	15.6
	PEOPLES BANK OF DEER	DEER LODGE	MT	**D-**	C-	C-	32	0.99	4.1	2.0	11.1	37.3	**6.7**	8.7	19.0
▼	PEOPLES BANK OF EAST	MADISONVILLE	TN	**D-**	D	C-	222	29.55	4.2	5.1	29.6	8.8	**6.1**	8.1	14.0

Arrows denote recent upgrades ▲ or downgrades ▼

Asset Quality Index	Non-Performing Loans as a % of Total Loans	Non-Performing Loans as a % of Capital	Net Charge-offs Avg Loans	Profitability Index	Net Income ($Mil)	Return on Assets (R.O.A.)	Return on Equity (R.O.E.)	Net Interest Spread	Overhead Efficiency Ratio	Liquidity Index	Liquidity Ratio	Hot Money Ratio	Stability Index
8.4	0.28	2.0	0.06	**3.0**	3.3	0.53	5.46	3.19	74.7	**0.9**	20.3	34.9	**6.2**
8.4	0.69	3.2	0.06	**2.3**	0.5	0.51	3.73	3.86	82.3	**1.2**	29.2	39.4	**4.3**
0.0	5.25	39.7	0.86	**0.2**	-0.2	-0.49	-5.24	4.63	88.8	**0.6**	8.8	49.8	**1.3**
0.6	2.01	16.8	0.50	**3.7**	2.8	0.98	11.11	4.03	68.5	**1.2**	19.4	29.9	**3.8**
2.8	2.55	16.6	0.35	**4.4**	3.4	0.81	7.15	3.98	67.1	**1.1**	14.6	30.1	**6.5**
0.0	7.56	55.9	1.19	**4.8**	0.7	0.58	6.44	4.67	54.2	**0.7**	12.4	38.8	**4.7**
3.3	0.61	4.8	-0.01	**6.8**	1.6	1.15	11.67	3.82	60.0	**1.2**	17.5	29.4	**7.0**
6.0	0.91	4.1	0.30	**4.6**	1.5	1.10	14.27	2.69	61.4	**5.4**	65.1	13.6	**4.5**
8.4	0.43	1.7	0.10	**8.2**	1.4	1.32	10.73	4.55	51.1	**2.2**	31.5	23.9	**7.7**
0.3	9.30	77.9	2.50	**0.0**	-2.4	-1.53	-28.53	2.92	135.0	**1.9**	20.5	20.1	**0.9**
0.3	7.63	52.7	0.77	**0.8**	-0.6	-0.42	-4.81	3.81	94.3	**2.6**	23.4	16.7	**3.6**
0.3	15.43	89.7	3.60	**0.0**	-0.9	-1.39	-14.54	3.23	97.4	**4.3**	28.7	9.8	**3.9**
8.9	0.26	1.0	0.03	**3.4**	0.3	0.57	4.69	3.68	81.8	**2.1**	35.1	29.0	**7.9**
3.3	0.82	6.5	0.07	**8.2**	6.3	1.88	17.37	4.61	52.7	**2.7**	10.5	15.0	**7.1**
4.0	2.89	13.0	0.25	**4.7**	1.1	0.86	7.64	4.55	72.2	**5.0**	51.7	12.8	**6.1**
5.8	1.52	6.9	0.17	**3.6**	0.2	0.61	4.69	3.89	79.0	**3.4**	34.6	16.1	**6.4**
0.3	3.63	27.7	0.86	**3.4**	1.9	0.53	6.51	5.01	87.1	**4.4**	13.5	5.6	**3.8**
0.8	5.93	27.9	1.31	**7.8**	4.0	1.23	8.90	4.83	56.6	**1.1**	20.5	32.9	**9.2**
4.1	0.58	3.9	2.81	**0.0**	-0.7	-1.44	-15.58	2.78	133.5	**1.9**	24.8	20.7	**2.9**
1.7	1.37	11.8	0.92	**2.5**	0.2	0.43	5.52	4.11	81.9	**1.4**	12.7	24.7	**3.4**
0.3	2.46	12.0	0.23	**3.8**	0.5	0.60	4.41	4.08	80.9	**3.3**	18.2	12.9	**9.2**
2.3	4.46	25.0	0.06	**8.3**	1.9	1.88	16.39	4.19	54.6	**2.8**	22.0	15.8	**8.8**
4.4	3.10	10.7	0.01	**4.4**	0.2	0.74	4.39	5.07	77.4	**2.5**	35.4	18.8	**7.9**
0.3	5.49	36.8	1.00	**1.9**	-0.5	-0.21	-1.98	4.05	61.9	**2.0**	9.0	18.5	**6.6**
6.1	0.08	0.6	0.08	**7.8**	3.3	1.91	18.38	4.80	59.6	**1.3**	3.6	23.7	**7.5**
0.8	3.96	32.5	0.50	**8.1**	3.5	1.68	18.78	4.98	57.4	**1.1**	8.3	28.3	**6.7**
6.9	0.27	1.3	0.55	**4.7**	3.4	0.97	10.02	3.21	60.1	**2.4**	39.6	28.1	**5.7**
1.6	5.52	35.9	2.16	**1.8**	2.2	0.20	2.18	3.50	65.2	**2.0**	22.8	24.7	**6.6**
6.2	0.80	4.4	0.18	**3.2**	0.3	0.58	6.09	3.89	81.1	**2.6**	34.1	19.8	**5.2**
0.8	3.93	33.4	1.11	**3.2**	0.3	0.34	3.79	4.41	78.3	**2.2**	9.0	17.3	**4.6**
6.6	0.62	3.4	0.06	**7.1**	1.0	1.87	17.33	3.79	69.0	**1.9**	32.1	29.1	**8.1**
2.0	3.22	20.9	1.06	**2.8**	1.2	0.50	5.38	3.66	67.5	**1.5**	22.0	25.9	**4.3**
2.7	0.92	6.9	0.85	**2.4**	0.4	0.29	3.32	4.11	74.7	**0.8**	16.3	37.3	**3.2**
3.4	1.27	9.1	0.66	**2.1**	0.3	0.43	5.98	4.06	83.3	**2.5**	42.4	29.4	**2.8**
2.4	0.37	2.2	0.81	**0.6**	-1.8	-2.25	-23.62	4.05	103.2	**2.2**	34.2	25.7	**4.6**
6.6	0.21	1.6	0.11	**5.2**	2.2	0.87	9.45	4.67	67.1	**1.4**	20.2	27.2	**5.5**
6.1	1.18	7.4	0.35	**9.2**	2.7	2.32	25.94	4.58	65.2	**3.5**	33.0	15.0	**7.1**
0.3	8.26	59.5	3.43	**1.7**	0.1	0.09	1.37	3.81	65.5	**2.1**	22.0	19.3	**2.9**
2.9	2.83	19.8	0.51	**4.5**	8.6	0.76	7.61	4.21	69.8	**1.4**	18.3	28.8	**7.0**
1.7	3.57	26.1	0.38	**3.5**	0.8	0.42	4.36	3.60	74.5	**2.2**	16.6	18.4	**5.5**
0.3	1.56	20.7	1.50	**0.0**	-4.6	-1.25	-28.27	2.71	135.1	**0.8**	13.0	35.1	**0.0**
5.1	0.55	4.6	0.34	**4.5**	2.6	1.08	13.09	4.08	71.6	**2.4**	9.0	16.3	**4.3**
7.6	0.31	1.3	0.08	**5.3**	3.3	1.04	8.72	3.77	65.8	**4.4**	36.6	11.8	**7.4**
5.3	2.23	8.3	0.26	**7.1**	0.1	0.11	1.22	4.35	59.2	**0.9**	23.7	41.0	**7.9**
0.3	6.15	49.2	1.29	**0.5**	-3.7	-0.90	-13.36	3.57	72.7	**2.5**	8.3	15.7	**3.1**
9.4	0.00	0.0	-0.01	**5.9**	0.6	1.12	8.43	2.99	49.7	**3.1**	59.9	29.2	**7.9**
3.9	1.79	10.6	1.05	**5.8**	0.3	1.29	11.74	4.82	65.5	**0.7**	17.1	46.8	**7.9**
3.1	1.21	6.5	0.20	**2.7**	0.2	0.25	2.38	4.11	77.9	**2.3**	24.6	18.5	**5.3**
6.4	0.36	2.0	0.05	**7.8**	4.7	1.39	13.48	3.57	48.9	**4.0**	33.7	12.8	**7.1**
2.9	2.07	17.3	0.77	**4.2**	1.9	0.99	12.56	3.36	58.9	**2.1**	19.0	19.2	**5.5**
2.7	2.82	20.0	0.55	**3.4**	0.4	0.90	10.42	4.28	72.0	**3.6**	32.9	14.6	**4.0**
2.7	4.19	21.3	2.66	**2.4**	7.9	0.41	3.77	3.58	65.9	**1.8**	16.5	21.6	**6.4**
0.5	3.53	26.3	1.22	**3.7**	2.3	0.46	5.70	3.84	73.8	**1.8**	8.1	19.4	**4.4**
3.7	2.22	15.3	-0.06	**2.4**	0.2	0.32	3.65	4.42	77.2	**4.0**	17.8	8.8	**2.3**
6.0	0.28	1.7	0.22	**5.1**	0.8	0.81	8.41	4.24	65.4	**1.1**	26.5	40.4	**5.2**
2.7	10.17	33.3	0.10	**4.8**	1.7	0.82	5.81	3.88	70.7	**4.5**	32.2	9.8	**7.7**
0.3	6.97	42.2	1.69	**2.2**	0.6	0.18	1.67	4.68	72.9	**3.4**	10.8	11.6	**5.2**
3.7	1.53	9.2	0.13	**2.5**	0.4	0.35	3.24	4.59	87.9	**1.7**	15.8	21.7	**5.9**
0.3	4.91	24.3	0.27	**1.9**	0.0	0.01	0.15	4.15	86.5	**5.2**	37.3	7.5	**4.0**
0.3	5.91	43.9	1.16	**4.4**	2.3	1.26	14.57	4.00	57.4	**1.5**	20.3	25.6	**2.1**

Name	City	State	Rating	2008 Rating	2007 Rating	Total Assets ($Mil)	One Year Asset Growth	Comm-ercial Loans	Cons-umer Loans	Home Mort-gages	Secur-ities	Capital-ization Index	Leverage Ratio	Risk-based Capital Ratio
								Asset Mix (As a % of Total Assets)						
▼ PEOPLES BANK OF	GRACEVILLE	FL	**A-**	A	A	75	0.77	1.8	3.2	17.1	56.2	**10.0**	13.7	38.9
▲ PEOPLES BANK OF	GREENSBORO	AL	**C+**	C	C-	83	7.86	6.4	9.0	12.5	35.4	**7.5**	9.4	16.3
PEOPLES BANK OF	FLEMINGSBURG	KY	**B-**	B-	B-	185	-2.62	6.4	11.4	19.6	10.9	**10.0**	13.1	18.2
PEOPLES BANK OF MACON	MACON	IL	**B-**	B-	B-	17	-5.99	8.9	4.4	20.1	46.3	**10.0**	14.9	34.2
PEOPLES BANK OF RED	RED LEVEL	AL	**C-**	B-	B-	15	5.98	2.0	13.6	10.1	54.0	**10.0**	11.9	25.7
PEOPLES BANK OF SENECA	SENECA	MO	**C+**	C	C-	86	-4.95	7.3	4.8	34.0	27.7	**6.0**	8.1	13.7
PEOPLES BANK OF	TALBOTTON	GA	**D+**	C-	B-	29	5.58	1.8	5.5	13.2	33.1	**9.6**	10.7	17.8
PEOPLES BANK OF THE	NIXA	MO	**D**	D	B-	309	-9.12	6.9	1.9	24.1	8.7	**7.0**	9.0	12.9
PEOPLES BANK OF THE	BUDE	MS	**D-**	D	C-	80	-7.68	3.5	17.2	26.6	13.7	**6.2**	8.2	12.9
▼ PEOPLES BANK OF THE	LAFOLLETTE	TN	**C**	B+	A	152	2.04	2.3	3.8	31.8	5.6	**10.0**	12.2	17.3
PEOPLES BANK OF VIRGINIA	RICHMOND	VA	**B-**	B+	A-	289	2.56	5.6	0.7	9.0	9.0	**10.0**	12.6	19.4
PEOPLES BANK OF	HAYWARD	WI	**D+**	C-	C+	293	-11.82	7.3	0.7	9.5	19.1	**10.0**	13.0	18.1
PEOPLES BANK OF	KAHOKA	MO	**B**	B-	B	70	7.99	3.0	3.4	11.3	36.5	**7.2**	9.1	16.9
PEOPLES BANK SB	MUNSTER	IN	**D+**	D+	B-	632	-4.70	9.8	0.1	21.2	25.5	**6.5**	8.5	12.8
▼ PEOPLES BK BILOXI MISSISS	BILOXI	MS	**C-**	C	B+	782	-9.53	5.5	1.0	9.2	36.9	**10.0**	12.3	20.0
▲ PEOPLES BK OF ARLINGTON H	ARLINGTON HEIGHTS	IL	**C-**	D-	C-	121	2.61	14.1	0.4	7.4	29.4	**6.5**	8.5	13.2
PEOPLES COMMUNITY BANK	GREENVILLE	MO	**A**	A	A	99	8.34	5.2	7.5	34.1	15.8	**10.0**	18.5	24.4
PEOPLES COMMUNITY BANK	MONTROSS	VA	**D+**	B-	B+	130	1.47	1.2	1.6	42.2	18.7	**6.9**	8.9	15.1
▲ PEOPLES COMMUNITY BANK	MAZOMANIE	WI	**C+**	C+	C+	244	0.15	10.1	3.7	9.2	12.4	**7.7**	10.0	13.1
▼ PEOPLES COMMUNITY	BREMEN	GA	**D-**	D-	D-	65	-7.39	4.6	1.3	11.8	22.0	**8.3**	9.9	17.6
PEOPLES COMMUNITY STATE	DONIPHAN	MO	**A**	A+	A	128	5.06	4.1	4.5	37.9	14.2	**10.0**	13.2	20.4
PEOPLES EXCH BK OF	BEATRICE	AL	**C**	B-	B	63	8.51	11.7	5.7	16.3	20.0	**10.0**	12.7	18.5
PEOPLES EXCHANGE BANK	BELLEVILLE	KS	**B-**	B-	B-	73	2.08	4.0	1.9	8.5	18.9	**7.8**	10.5	13.2
PEOPLES EXCHANGE BANK	STANTON	KY	**C-**	C-	C+	318	1.52	6.9	3.6	32.7	2.0	**4.1**	7.1	10.6
PEOPLES FIRST SAVINGS BAN	MASON	OH	**B-**	C+	C+	51	6.65	0.0	0.5	74.0	1.6	**10.0**	11.3	22.9
PEOPLES FS&LA	SIDNEY	OH	**D+**	D+	C+	136	-1.38	7.3	2.6	57.7	1.6	**10.0**	11.1	18.0
PEOPLES FSB	BRIGHTON	MA	**C**	B-	B+	530	9.80	0.9	0.4	44.1	4.8	**10.0**	14.8	24.0
PEOPLES FSB OF DEKALB	AUBURN	IN	**B-**	B-	B	462	-4.32	2.4	0.7	35.3	39.3	**10.0**	11.5	24.1
PEOPLES INDEPENDENT	BOAZ	AL	**C-**	D+	C-	169	-0.20	4.5	2.7	9.0	38.4	**7.5**	9.3	15.6
PEOPLES NATIONAL BK	COLORADO SPRINGS	CO	**D-**	D-	D+	175	-0.93	1.9	0.3	18.2	12.0	**6.5**	8.5	14.5
PEOPLES NATIONAL BK	NICEVILLE	FL	**D-**	D	C-	120	-9.62	5.3	2.7	16.6	26.7	**6.4**	8.4	15.8
PEOPLES NATIONAL BK	EASLEY	SC	**D**	D	D	321	-8.41	8.6	1.6	13.5	18.7	**6.9**	8.9	13.3
PEOPLES NATIONAL BK NA	MOUNT VERNON	IL	**C**	C	C+	855	8.93	15.0	1.0	6.3	13.3	**6.7**	9.2	12.3
PEOPLES NATIONAL BK	CHECOTAH	OK	**A**	A	A	117	1.36	3.5	14.3	12.1	40.7	**10.0**	16.3	30.8
PEOPLES NATIONAL BK	LEADVILLE	CO	**D-**	D	C-	45	3.28	0.5	0.6	13.8	38.1	**6.4**	8.5	31.1
PEOPLES NATIONAL BK OF KE	KEWANEE	IL	**B**	C+	B+	248	3.64	6.7	5.3	10.5	32.3	**10.0**	14.5	19.8
PEOPLES NATIONAL BK OF	MORA	MN	**D**	D-	C-	165	-4.83	8.9	2.9	13.5	31.7	**9.8**	10.9	16.9
PEOPLES NB OF MOUNT	MOUNT PLEASANT	OH	**B**	B-	C+	52	8.23	0.2	59.3	19.7	1.0	**10.0**	12.4	17.3
PEOPLES NB OF NEW	NEW LEXINGTON	OH	**C+**	B-	C+	105	2.55	3.4	10.0	39.6	13.7	**7.0**	9.0	15.0
PEOPLES NEIGHBORHOOD	HALLSTEAD	PA	**B-**	B	B	557	8.32	13.1	3.9	20.3	21.6	**6.1**	8.4	11.9
PEOPLES S&LA OF	MONTICELLO	IN	**B-**	B-	B-	37	3.33	0.0	0.3	77.3	0.0	**10.0**	33.9	73.5
PEOPLES SAVINGS & LOAN	BUCYRUS	OH	**C+**	C	C	135	3.86	0.0	0.8	49.0	19.0	**10.0**	16.5	38.2
PEOPLES SAVINGS & LOAN	WEST LIBERTY	OH	**B-**	B-	B-	44	0.56	1.6	2.9	55.4	0.0	**10.0**	12.1	21.5
PEOPLES SB	CRAWFORDSVILLE	IA	**B**	B	B	29	7.34	14.1	4.3	18.2	37.1	**8.7**	10.2	14.5
PEOPLES SB	ELMA	IA	**C-**	C-	C-	60	0.87	11.2	1.9	8.4	4.6	**6.0**	8.6	11.8
PEOPLES SB	INDIANOLA	IA	**C-**	C-	B-	130	2.72	8.1	1.1	15.8	33.0	**6.3**	8.3	14.8
PEOPLES SB	MONTEZUMA	IA	**D**	C-	B-	33	1.25	10.7	3.9	5.3	33.3	**9.2**	10.5	20.7
PEOPLES SB	WELLSBURG	IA	**C+**	C	B-	98	18.10	6.5	3.2	7.6	42.0	**5.3**	7.3	11.3
PEOPLES SB	NEW MATAMORAS	OH	**B-**	B	B+	43	3.90	16.0	4.8	38.3	26.5	**10.0**	12.2	20.7
▼ PEOPLES SB	URBANA	OH	**D+**	C	C-	87	4.45	0.0	4.2	59.3	1.3	**10.0**	12.2	19.9
PEOPLES SB OF RHINELAND	RHINELAND	MO	**C+**	C	C+	168	2.32	3.3	2.5	33.7	17.1	**6.9**	8.9	13.8
PEOPLES SECURITY BANK	LOUISA	KY	**B-**	B+	B+	50	1.40	2.9	6.4	22.8	33.0	**10.0**	13.3	26.1
▼ PEOPLES SOUTHERN BANK	CLANTON	AL	**B+**	A-	A	144	2.26	2.5	3.8	9.8	41.4	**10.0**	14.9	29.8
▼ PEOPLES STATE BK	LAKE CITY	FL	**D**	C-	C	79	-1.43	6.5	2.6	17.2	10.0	**7.7**	9.4	13.4
PEOPLES STATE BK	ALBIA	IA	**B+**	B	B	82	-0.19	17.4	3.1	12.8	41.3	**10.0**	11.5	19.4
▼ PEOPLES STATE BK	WINFIELD	IA	**D**	C-	C	24	-7.72	2.2	5.4	19.2	45.9	**7.4**	9.2	20.6
PEOPLES STATE BK	ELLETTSVILLE	IN	**D**	D	D	174	-19.31	12.5	2.3	8.0	30.5	**7.2**	9.1	13.0
PEOPLES STATE BK	CHERRYVALE	KS	**B**	B	B+	18	5.29	15.4	12.9	19.7	6.2	**10.0**	23.0	29.0
PEOPLES STATE BK	MCDONALD	KS	**C+**	C	C	106	4.82	13.4	2.4	4.4	7.7	**6.4**	8.7	12.0
PEOPLES STATE BK	MANY	LA	**C+**	C	C-	468	7.87	6.6	2.9	6.4	40.2	**7.6**	9.4	15.4

Arrows denote recent upgrades ▲ or downgrades ▼

Asset Quality Index	Non-Performing Loans as a % of Total Loans	Non-Performing Loans as a % of Capital	Net Charge-offs / Avg Loans	Profitability Index	Net Income ($Mil)	Return on Assets (R.O.A.)	Return on Equity (R.O.E.)	Net Interest Spread	Overhead Efficiency Ratio	Liquidity Index	Liquidity Ratio	Hot Money Ratio	Stability Index
6.6	5.77	13.0	2.06	**5.3**	1.0	1.26	7.93	3.09	51.9	**4.2**	76.0	19.6	**9.7**
4.6	1.03	5.5	0.15	**6.9**	1.3	1.60	15.27	3.93	58.8	**2.7**	44.5	26.7	**6.8**
3.6	2.29	12.6	0.79	**5.5**	2.0	1.04	8.11	4.55	59.4	**1.5**	8.9	23.1	**7.3**
9.4	0.00	0.0	0.00	**3.7**	0.1	0.60	3.84	4.09	79.0	**5.2**	62.7	11.2	**7.4**
4.3	5.31	14.1	2.70	**2.2**	0.0	0.05	0.39	4.75	79.5	**5.8**	71.4	9.1	**5.3**
5.2	1.36	9.7	0.71	**7.1**	1.1	1.28	16.52	4.60	52.6	**2.3**	19.9	18.2	**4.3**
3.6	2.86	11.8	2.73	**1.3**	0.0	0.06	0.52	4.69	91.6	**3.7**	48.1	18.0	**5.6**
1.7	1.54	11.7	1.86	**1.3**	0.1	0.02	0.26	3.66	70.5	**1.5**	9.1	22.9	**3.8**
3.1	0.78	6.0	1.14	**0.7**	-0.3	-0.36	-4.32	5.01	106.8	**1.2**	21.4	31.0	**2.0**
1.9	2.84	17.4	0.27	**5.1**	1.5	1.01	7.98	4.79	68.7	**1.1**	9.7	29.3	**7.9**
4.5	1.39	6.8	0.76	**3.0**	0.9	0.32	2.56	3.09	51.0	**0.9**	23.9	38.6	**7.2**
1.2	3.26	16.0	0.85	**7.0**	5.4	1.71	13.32	4.33	43.2	**0.7**	15.4	42.7	**7.6**
8.6	0.01	0.0	0.06	**5.1**	0.6	0.90	9.55	3.18	53.7	**2.3**	27.4	19.4	**5.9**
1.1	5.76	37.5	0.57	**4.0**	5.3	0.79	9.60	4.29	63.7	**2.8**	25.5	16.0	**4.6**
3.5	4.27	16.7	1.84	**1.4**	1.6	0.19	1.59	3.44	81.6	**1.0**	4.2	29.1	**6.0**
6.7	0.41	2.6	0.14	**2.2**	0.5	0.43	5.03	3.10	73.4	**2.4**	28.3	19.3	**4.0**
7.3	1.19	4.7	0.04	**10.0**	3.0	3.17	17.14	5.88	47.4	**1.7**	13.4	21.7	**9.0**
3.7	1.99	13.5	1.07	**1.4**	-0.4	-0.30	-3.09	4.32	83.2	**3.3**	21.2	12.9	**5.2**
3.8	0.64	4.6	0.89	**5.4**	2.0	0.83	7.55	4.25	54.6	**1.3**	6.5	24.9	**6.9**
1.0	8.99	41.0	5.52	**0.0**	-5.7	-7.86	-57.65	2.77	1,294.6	**1.7**	30.4	29.6	**3.5**
6.4	1.22	6.4	0.01	**10.0**	3.5	2.70	20.54	5.17	47.4	**3.3**	18.0	13.0	**9.4**
2.7	3.41	15.5	0.27	**3.7**	0.5	0.72	5.62	5.15	79.3	**2.8**	28.2	17.3	**6.2**
4.5	2.34	13.0	0.02	**5.2**	0.7	0.96	7.08	4.21	72.1	**2.8**	17.0	15.2	**5.9**
2.4	1.46	15.3	0.46	**3.3**	1.3	0.40	5.36	4.09	80.5	**1.6**	8.5	21.4	**3.8**
5.7	1.77	12.5	0.00	**2.9**	0.2	0.46	4.00	3.73	79.3	**3.1**	15.0	13.3	**7.1**
1.0	5.63	42.3	0.33	**3.2**	0.6	0.43	3.91	3.57	68.2	**3.8**	9.5	9.4	**6.2**
6.2	0.57	2.8	0.07	**2.2**	0.2	0.04	0.35	3.09	97.9	**3.4**	23.4	12.7	**8.4**
6.9	0.81	3.5	0.18	**3.9**	3.4	0.72	6.13	3.04	69.4	**5.2**	48.2	11.2	**6.8**
2.5	1.43	6.9	0.85	**4.0**	1.2	0.70	10.05	4.02	71.6	**3.4**	37.9	17.5	**3.3**
0.3	7.65	44.9	2.00	**0.0**	-0.8	-0.43	-4.52	3.51	102.3	**4.7**	18.5	4.8	**3.4**
0.3	6.28	36.7	3.35	**0.0**	-1.5	-1.19	-12.86	4.26	82.3	**1.5**	25.4	28.2	**3.1**
0.9	5.56	36.2	1.90	**0.5**	-0.4	-0.13	-1.34	4.12	76.2	**1.1**	15.3	30.8	**4.1**
2.4	2.01	15.1	0.80	**4.5**	8.4	1.04	11.03	3.98	67.0	**1.4**	7.3	24.0	**6.0**
7.3	0.56	1.4	0.11	**7.7**	2.1	1.78	10.62	4.11	62.8	**4.2**	50.7	16.9	**9.9**
3.7	3.40	11.2	0.84	**0.5**	0.0	-0.01	-0.07	2.16	103.2	**5.5**	57.4	10.4	**4.7**
4.9	3.13	9.8	0.24	**5.2**	1.7	0.70	4.37	5.07	63.3	**5.1**	46.1	11.1	**5.9**
1.3	7.19	33.5	-0.01	**2.1**	0.8	0.46	4.23	4.11	87.9	**2.9**	21.8	15.3	**4.9**
4.3	0.57	3.5	0.29	**5.3**	0.4	0.86	6.70	4.86	69.1	**2.0**	22.1	19.6	**6.7**
3.3	1.80	14.1	0.26	**4.5**	0.7	0.71	7.03	4.58	75.7	**2.9**	16.1	14.6	**5.5**
3.5	1.77	13.6	0.40	**6.0**	6.6	1.20	16.50	4.06	57.2	**4.3**	10.8	6.2	**5.2**
6.8	3.77	8.7	0.00	**3.2**	0.2	0.47	1.40	3.61	75.8	**3.2**	28.3	15.3	**7.1**
7.3	1.46	4.9	0.08	**2.7**	0.5	0.38	2.27	3.16	80.1	**4.5**	46.0	14.2	**7.6**
8.0	0.34	2.0	-0.01	**3.8**	0.3	0.65	5.69	3.92	73.9	**2.8**	14.3	14.8	**6.6**
6.1	0.90	4.3	0.00	**6.7**	0.4	1.32	12.73	4.86	64.0	**4.9**	51.8	12.5	**5.7**
2.5	1.38	12.7	0.47	**6.8**	0.9	1.57	16.98	4.06	49.4	**1.4**	9.9	24.2	**6.9**
2.7	2.35	13.9	1.32	**3.3**	0.7	0.49	5.72	3.60	68.5	**3.8**	24.7	11.0	**4.2**
4.0	4.27	14.9	0.78	**1.3**	0.0	0.04	0.34	4.27	88.2	**5.4**	66.4	12.2	**3.8**
4.8	1.39	9.7	0.08	**4.8**	0.9	0.98	13.54	3.54	64.1	**1.3**	24.1	30.0	**3.6**
3.0	2.73	14.2	0.83	**3.8**	0.3	0.59	4.83	4.83	82.3	**4.6**	25.3	6.4	**7.1**
3.2	3.03	19.2	0.31	**0.6**	-0.4	-0.46	-3.69	4.17	85.1	**1.0**	10.7	30.3	**6.4**
4.9	1.38	9.9	0.24	**3.6**	1.0	0.64	7.01	3.93	76.5	**2.8**	18.1	15.4	**4.3**
4.6	5.39	18.5	0.34	**3.9**	0.3	0.57	4.20	5.40	85.0	**4.1**	45.2	15.5	**7.1**
7.0	1.41	3.4	0.32	**4.9**	1.4	1.01	6.47	3.68	68.4	**4.3**	57.8	17.8	**8.8**
1.9	2.54	17.9	1.59	**2.2**	0.2	0.26	2.78	4.23	73.4	**1.7**	21.3	22.8	**4.1**
6.8	0.74	3.1	0.30	**4.8**	0.9	1.07	8.91	3.99	67.5	**3.0**	48.5	23.9	**6.8**
4.2	2.54	10.7	2.18	**1.4**	-0.1	-0.20	-2.06	4.04	87.2	**4.9**	58.9	12.2	**3.2**
3.4	1.41	7.7	2.55	**0.6**	-1.0	-0.51	-6.84	4.16	92.2	**2.9**	30.8	17.5	**2.8**
3.2	1.85	6.6	0.23	**10.0**	0.8	4.43	18.82	6.81	40.0	**1.9**	4.6	18.6	**7.7**
5.7	0.07	0.5	0.52	**7.6**	1.7	1.64	19.42	5.58	59.1	**1.4**	14.4	25.3	**4.4**
5.6	0.81	3.9	0.47	**3.0**	3.0	0.65	6.59	3.77	83.4	**3.1**	24.8	14.4	**4.3**

Name	City	State	Rating	2008 Rating	2007 Rating	Total Assets ($Mil)	One Year Asset Growth	Asset Mix (As a % of Total Assets) Comm-ercial Loans	Cons-umer Loans	Home Mort-gages	Secur-ities	Capital-ization Index	Leverage Ratio	Risk-based Capital Ratio
PEOPLES STATE BK	WESTHOPE	ND	**B**	B	B	64	6.96	5.7	2.8	4.1	37.9	**7.5**	9.3	15.9
PEOPLES STATE BK	BLAIR	OK	**B**	B+	B+	16	4.50	16.9	20.2	7.6	2.2	**7.4**	10.0	12.9
▲ PEOPLES STATE BK	DE SMET	SD	**B**	C-	C+	62	3.14	14.4	5.3	7.7	21.9	**10.0**	11.0	17.7
▲ PEOPLES STATE BK	SUMMIT	SD	**C+**	B-	C+	48	1.63	13.8	4.2	6.0	22.6	**8.2**	10.1	13.5
PEOPLES STATE BK	ROCKSPRINGS	TX	**A**	A	A-	58	5.23	4.9	3.7	7.4	46.2	**10.0**	12.0	22.2
PEOPLES STATE BK	SHEPHERD	TX	**B-**	B-	C+	92	1.14	4.2	7.7	12.6	26.5	**6.3**	8.3	13.5
PEOPLES STATE BK	PRAIRIE DU CHIEN	WI	**B-**	C	B-	404	12.56	10.3	1.4	12.7	16.8	**8.4**	9.9	13.8
PEOPLES STATE BK	WAUSAU	WI	**C**	C	C-	621	2.34	10.1	0.6	18.2	17.2	**7.6**	9.4	13.9
PEOPLES STATE BK & TRUST	BAXLEY	GA	**C-**	C-	B	72	-8.30	3.5	3.2	7.1	8.3	**10.0**	11.9	16.0
▼ PEOPLES STATE BK	FAIRMOUNT	ND	**D-**	C-	D+	20	14.98	6.9	4.7	10.6	30.3	**5.2**	7.2	14.7
PEOPLES STATE BK	HALLETTSVILLE	TX	**B**	B	B	215	17.10	1.7	2.4	5.4	53.7	**10.0**	11.4	56.1
PEOPLES STATE BK MADISON	MADISON LAKE	MN	**E+**	D	C-	29	20.38	12.3	12.7	8.1	9.0	**4.8**	6.9	12.5
PEOPLES STATE BK OF	BLOOMER	WI	**B+**	B-	B-	109	0.19	6.4	1.2	18.2	36.8	**10.0**	11.9	21.7
PEOPLES STATE BK OF	COLFAX	IL	**B+**	B	B	29	2.92	4.0	7.0	16.8	20.8	**9.4**	10.6	19.5
▼ PEOPLES STATE BK OF	NOLENSVILLE	TN	**D-**	D	C	256	-11.95	22.5	9.0	12.2	13.1	**5.7**	7.7	11.8
PEOPLES STATE BK OF MUNIS	MUNISING	MI	**B-**	C+	C+	115	2.90	4.0	6.4	26.4	26.4	**10.0**	11.8	18.8
PEOPLES STATE BK OF	NEWTON	IL	**B-**	B	B-	310	13.80	6.7	2.6	10.8	32.7	**5.7**	7.7	11.7
▲ PEOPLES STATE BK OF PLAIN	PLAINVIEW	MN	**B-**	B-	B	165	3.12	8.0	3.3	14.8	25.8	**7.2**	9.2	14.6
▼ PEOPLES STATE BK OF VELVA	VELVA	ND	**C-**	B	B+	57	35.52	7.1	4.1	4.0	20.4	**7.1**	9.1	14.0
PEOPLES STATE BK OF	WELLS	MN	**B-**	B-	B-	27	17.95	6.3	4.0	10.3	5.3	**9.4**	10.6	15.3
PEOPLES STATE BK OF	WYALUSING	PA	**D+**	D+	D+	235	10.62	10.2	2.2	34.4	16.3	**5.5**	7.5	12.1
PEOPLES TRUST & SB	CLIVE	IA	**D+**	D+	D	263	-2.00	4.9	2.6	17.2	14.2	**6.2**	8.3	13.1
PEOPLES TRUST & SB	RIVERSIDE	IA	**B**	B	B	24	13.08	2.4	3.6	8.8	52.2	**4.2**	6.2	16.2
PEOPLES TRUST & SB	BOONVILLE	IN	**B-**	B	B-	127	-3.50	5.0	2.4	35.5	21.7	**10.0**	18.6	29.2
▼ PEOPLES TRUST CO OF ST AL	SAINT ALBANS	VT	**C**	B	B	228	2.27	2.5	1.4	31.5	18.0	**10.0**	13.2	22.6
▼ PEOPLES UNITED BANK	BRIDGEPORT	CT	**C-**	B-	B	22,088	15.61	21.7	0.9	12.3	10.5	**9.5**	11.4	14.5
PEOPLES-WEBSTER COUNTY	RED CLOUD	NE	**A**	A	A	63	6.24	8.3	2.0	5.9	33.8	**10.0**	28.7	37.5
PEOPLESBANK	HOLYOKE	MA	**C+**	C+	C	1,589	4.51	2.6	0.1	23.9	26.5	**6.9**	8.9	14.3
▼ PEOPLESBANK A CODORUS	YORK	PA	**C-**	C-	C-	955	7.47	5.9	0.9	10.8	23.3	**6.5**	8.5	13.3
PEOPLESSOUTH BANK	COLQUITT	GA	**D**	D	C+	560	7.74	2.8	3.8	9.4	22.2	**6.3**	8.3	13.2
PEOPLESTRUST BANK	HAMILTON	AL	**D**	C-	B-	71	10.95	11.9	6.9	16.3	24.0	**7.4**	9.3	13.7
PERKINS STATE BK	WILLISTON	FL	**D+**	B	C+	185	-5.17	3.3	4.0	25.7	17.6	**7.1**	9.1	13.0
PERPETUAL FSB	URBANA	OH	**B-**	B-	B-	360	1.78	3.3	1.2	26.3	0.0	**10.0**	15.5	22.0
PERRYTON NATIONAL BK	PERRYTON	TX	**A**	A	A	122	2.62	8.3	6.7	1.8	54.2	**10.0**	11.1	27.2
PERU FSB	PERU	IL	**C-**	C-	C-	133	3.35	0.6	1.8	39.7	30.7	**9.2**	10.4	21.0
PESHTIGO NATIONAL BK	PESHTIGO	WI	**C+**	C+	C+	158	2.07	6.7	2.9	23.4	13.2	**7.0**	9.0	15.5
PETEFISH SKILES & CO	VIRGINIA	IL	**C-**	C+	C	174	3.53	4.9	7.3	14.8	35.2	**6.9**	8.9	14.7
▼ PETERSBURG STATE BK	PETERSBURG	NE	**C-**	C+	C+	33	9.76	10.1	5.1	0.3	9.9	**5.2**	7.5	11.2
PETIT JEAN STATE BK	MORRILTON	AR	**C**	C-	C-	147	4.82	6.7	7.1	19.5	30.2	**7.7**	9.5	18.9
PHELPS COUNTY BANK	ROLLA	MO	**B**	B	B-	263	5.08	3.5	1.8	37.1	35.7	**5.0**	7.0	14.6
▲ PHENIX-GIRARD BANK	PHENIX CITY	AL	**B+**	B+	A	148	4.03	3.8	1.0	14.3	31.2	**10.0**	16.0	25.4
PHILADELPHIA TRUST CO	PHILADELPHIA	PA	**B-**	B+	A-	16	-21.52	1.7	7.0	15.6	4.0	**10.0**	43.3	89.9
PHILO EXCHANGE BANK	PHILO	IL	**B**	B	A-	75	2.92	2.3	1.7	12.4	43.1	**7.3**	9.2	18.9
PHOENIXVILLE FEDERAL BANK	PHOENIXVILLE	PA	**C**	C	C	407	4.18	12.8	0.5	32.5	11.0	**7.8**	9.5	15.4
PICKENS SAVINGS & LOAN AS	PICKENS	SC	**C**	C	C+	105	-0.41	6.5	1.9	39.9	12.2	**5.9**	7.9	12.2
PIEDMONT BANK	LAWRENCEVILLE	GA	**E+**	D-	D-	359	33.31	10.6	1.1	2.3	9.1	**4.3**	9.2	10.7
PIEDMONT COMMUNITY BANK	GRAY	GA	**E-**	E-	E+	219	-12.04	2.7	0.9	9.0	14.0	**0.3**	4.2	6.5
PIEDMONT FSB	WINSTON-SALEM	NC	**B-**	B-	B+	920	1.48	0.0	0.0	55.3	21.3	**10.0**	22.4	63.0
▲ PIGEON FALLS STATE BK	PIGEON FALLS	WI	**C+**	C-	C-	66	10.96	3.8	1.4	11.9	13.9	**7.7**	10.3	13.1
PIGGOTT STATE BK	PIGGOTT	AR	**B+**	B	B	75	1.79	5.5	3.6	16.1	46.3	**7.5**	9.3	26.0
PIKE NATIONAL BK	MCCOMB	MS	**B-**	B	B+	200	-7.23	7.6	9.2	15.1	24.0	**10.0**	11.8	18.3
PIKES PEAK NATIONAL BK	COLORADO SPRINGS	CO	**D-**	D-	D	77	-9.58	5.2	3.2	10.8	0.0	**9.2**	10.5	19.6
▲ PILGRIM BANK	COHASSET	MA	**D+**	D-	D+	164	2.35	0.3	1.3	45.5	10.0	**4.8**	6.8	12.9
PILGRIM BANK	PITTSBURG	TX	**B-**	B-	C+	372	6.27	5.9	1.8	10.5	40.8	**6.4**	8.4	16.2
PILOT BANK	TAMPA	FL	**D-**	D-	D-	223	-5.58	13.1	12.7	11.3	10.6	**5.5**	8.2	11.4
PILOT GROVE SB	PILOT GROVE	IA	**B**	B	B	324	12.37	5.6	4.0	28.4	9.6	**6.4**	8.4	12.3
▼ PILSEN ST BK LINCOLNVILLE	LINCOLNVILLE	KS	**D-**	E-	C-	12	-12.44	13.3	10.0	7.3	3.9	**9.2**	10.5	14.9
▲ PINE BLUFF NATIONAL BK	PINE BLUFF	AR	**B-**	C+	C	376	4.35	5.5	3.9	7.1	22.8	**10.0**	11.4	16.0
PINE COUNTRY BANK	LITTLE FALLS	MN	**D**	C-	D+	144	13.21	7.9	1.7	8.0	35.7	**4.6**	6.7	11.1
▼ PINE ISLAND BANK	PINE ISLAND	MN	**D+**	C+	B-	67	8.72	2.8	1.4	11.9	22.2	**6.1**	8.1	12.4

Asset Quality Index	Non-Performing Loans as a % of Total Loans	Non-Performing Loans as a % of Capital	Net Charge-offs Avg Loans	Profitability Index	Net Income ($Mil)	Return on Assets (R.O.A.)	Return on Equity (R.O.E.)	Net Interest Spread	Overhead Efficiency Ratio	Liquidity Index	Liquidity Ratio	Hot Money Ratio	Stability Index
6.5	0.00	0.0	0.40	6.7	1.0	1.66	16.48	3.95	56.2	3.0	42.7	22.1	6.3
6.5	0.11	0.8	0.00	9.8	0.4	2.44	23.09	5.92	64.6	3.1	13.9	13.0	6.3
5.1	1.29	6.8	0.05	5.1	0.9	1.50	12.89	4.70	64.7	5.0	30.7	6.2	7.0
4.3	1.19	7.2	0.65	9.8	1.0	2.16	21.96	4.60	46.7	1.4	20.9	28.3	6.7
9.1	0.21	0.7	0.01	9.8	1.5	2.71	19.88	4.39	36.9	3.2	51.5	22.7	9.0
4.7	1.18	7.7	0.12	4.4	0.6	0.66	7.92	4.52	79.6	1.5	16.5	24.7	4.5
4.9	0.68	4.7	0.12	6.0	5.3	1.42	14.23	3.69	51.7	1.0	18.5	33.8	6.7
2.8	2.02	13.7	0.33	5.0	5.4	0.90	9.33	3.84	62.3	1.5	16.3	25.5	6.3
8.3	0.27	1.5	0.02	8.5	1.0	1.37	11.50	4.85	61.8	1.6	14.8	22.6	3.7
6.3	0.78	4.9	0.22	2.4	0.0	0.23	2.81	4.00	85.6	5.3	42.4	5.3	1.7
9.7	0.51	0.8	0.30	3.6	1.3	0.65	4.84	2.42	64.7	3.4	76.1	37.5	7.0
0.3	4.10	28.9	1.14	0.8	-0.1	-0.26	-2.45	3.82	96.0	4.6	42.0	12.5	3.9
5.2	3.14	13.7	0.10	5.7	1.3	1.21	10.19	4.63	62.0	4.4	43.6	14.0	5.8
7.0	0.41	1.9	0.05	6.6	0.3	1.17	10.54	4.56	63.3	5.2	44.4	9.4	6.3
3.1	0.91	6.3	0.32	0.1	-2.7	-0.94	-8.36	4.34	102.3	1.6	11.7	21.6	4.2
3.9	3.00	15.1	0.51	4.8	1.1	0.96	7.82	4.88	67.6	2.0	27.1	22.0	6.4
5.5	1.06	7.9	-0.08	5.1	2.8	0.95	10.88	3.38	61.2	2.8	15.4	15.0	4.9
4.4	1.82	11.5	0.31	5.1	1.9	1.15	11.89	4.02	65.4	3.0	17.6	14.1	6.4
8.3	0.00	0.0	0.00	1.5	-0.1	-0.18	-1.67	3.58	104.2	2.6	35.0	20.8	6.6
7.8	0.12	0.7	-0.01	4.8	0.3	1.13	9.93	4.13	70.6	5.4	33.3	4.4	6.9
2.0	4.45	31.7	2.15	3.2	1.2	0.51	6.96	4.60	75.2	2.6	24.1	16.8	2.6
2.1	3.71	27.9	1.04	1.5	0.1	0.02	0.21	4.03	83.6	1.5	20.4	25.4	3.8
9.5	0.00	0.0	0.00	5.0	0.3	1.07	14.27	3.10	60.4	6.7	79.4	5.3	4.9
5.8	1.45	5.1	0.19	3.3	0.8	0.59	3.11	4.03	80.9	2.4	23.3	18.0	7.4
1.7	6.01	28.6	0.21	3.8	1.3	0.58	4.36	4.78	82.1	3.7	27.4	12.4	7.5
1.9	3.50	22.7	0.39	3.4	98.3	0.47	2.52	3.98	79.4	3.9	17.5	10.3	2.2
8.6	1.04	2.0	0.03	9.0	0.9	1.50	5.13	4.32	47.9	5.7	45.4	6.7	9.6
5.6	0.83	5.5	0.07	3.1	8.7	0.55	6.16	2.94	75.5	3.4	18.2	12.8	6.8
2.0	2.89	21.1	0.39	4.2	6.7	0.73	8.15	3.79	70.5	1.7	16.1	21.9	5.4
1.5	4.43	28.9	1.35	3.9	3.3	0.61	7.20	3.26	52.5	1.2	23.8	32.1	5.3
0.9	4.53	27.5	0.24	3.2	0.2	0.31	2.92	3.68	78.3	1.9	30.5	26.6	5.8
1.7	5.99	38.3	2.10	1.6	-2.4	-1.28	-14.46	4.96	80.5	1.7	18.7	22.5	5.9
3.6	2.31	11.6	0.00	3.6	2.5	0.68	4.41	3.08	33.6	1.1	15.6	30.6	7.4
8.8	0.09	0.2	0.04	6.8	1.9	1.60	12.43	3.58	54.0	3.5	67.8	30.9	8.8
3.4	2.97	14.9	0.85	2.6	0.5	0.37	3.54	2.39	75.3	4.2	46.6	15.8	5.3
4.1	1.45	9.3	0.33	3.9	1.3	0.84	9.54	4.31	69.1	2.2	29.6	21.8	4.2
2.0	3.35	19.7	0.57	4.8	1.8	1.08	10.23	4.16	68.7	3.6	33.6	15.1	6.3
4.4	0.40	3.9	0.03	5.7	0.4	1.34	16.80	3.98	64.2	1.2	8.6	26.9	4.3
2.9	3.24	14.2	2.77	3.5	0.6	0.40	4.19	4.26	51.4	2.2	35.2	27.1	4.9
6.8	0.33	2.6	0.37	7.0	4.4	1.69	21.42	3.87	62.0	4.1	15.0	8.0	6.0
5.1	2.74	8.6	1.31	7.2	2.3	1.54	9.28	5.01	67.0	4.6	15.5	5.0	9.3
8.7	0.00	0.0	0.00	2.5	-0.8	-4.18	-8.43	2.28	115.6	3.3	99.1	60.1	9.6
4.7	1.80	8.9	-0.05	4.9	0.9	1.23	10.69	3.09	62.3	5.0	38.4	9.3	8.3
4.1	1.40	9.8	0.01	2.7	1.5	0.38	3.89	3.98	68.9	1.9	24.8	21.7	5.0
5.2	0.71	6.5	0.04	3.2	0.5	0.42	5.51	3.28	77.1	1.3	19.2	28.1	4.5
0.0	5.26	42.7	0.32	2.4	1.9	0.60	4.94	3.41	67.1	1.7	18.7	23.0	0.8
0.0	19.78	196.4	1.77	0.0	-6.3	-2.70	-48.68	1.92	153.6	1.6	6.2	20.8	1.7
9.9	0.46	1.2	0.05	3.4	5.1	0.56	2.49	2.59	67.0	3.2	53.4	27.6	8.3
6.1	0.00	0.0	0.67	4.1	0.4	0.63	5.64	4.76	73.2	1.5	17.0	24.7	4.6
9.3	0.00	0.0	-0.09	6.8	1.1	1.46	13.96	4.28	56.9	3.5	60.1	22.2	7.0
3.3	3.40	16.0	1.02	5.0	1.9	0.90	7.79	5.69	74.6	1.9	19.2	19.8	5.6
0.3	21.15	94.7	0.67	3.2	0.3	0.34	3.41	4.52	83.6	4.3	41.6	14.0	6.4
1.7	3.67	34.6	0.00	3.4	1.0	0.60	8.87	3.46	67.2	1.7	26.5	26.1	3.4
6.2	0.77	4.7	0.40	3.4	3.0	0.86	8.07	3.46	74.6	1.7	34.6	33.4	5.3
0.9	3.88	27.7	1.15	0.5	-0.1	-0.05	-0.56	4.00	86.3	3.1	13.1	13.5	3.1
5.9	0.44	3.7	0.40	5.8	4.1	1.35	13.49	4.03	54.5	4.1	19.5	8.8	6.3
0.0	12.91	85.4	0.00	6.1	0.8	6.71	73.40	2.78	36.4	1.8	25.7	21.3	3.1
5.2	1.17	6.1	0.36	7.6	5.0	1.31	11.80	4.63	60.0	1.0	13.4	31.1	7.3
2.6	2.22	16.5	0.37	2.8	0.4	0.31	4.56	3.85	76.5	1.8	25.4	22.8	2.7
1.4	6.37	41.4	0.67	3.0	0.3	0.48	4.20	4.11	76.3	3.3	29.8	15.1	4.4

Name	City	State	Rating	2008 Rating	2007 Rating	Total Assets ($Mil)	One Year Asset Growth	Asset Mix (As a % of Total Assets) Comm-ercial Loans	Cons-umer Loans	Home Mort-gages	Secur-ities	Capital-ization Index	Leverage Ratio	Risk-based Capital Ratio
PINE RIVER STATE BK	PINE RIVER	MN	**C**	C	C+	87	3.94	5.4	2.8	15.4	15.0	**7.2**	9.1	14.8
▼PINE RIVER VALLEY BANK	BAYFIELD	CO	**D**	D+	C+	175	-6.67	3.4	2.1	22.6	26.8	**5.9**	7.9	13.6
▲PINELAND STATE BK	METTER	GA	**D+**	C-	B	61	-0.74	7.8	5.9	15.8	6.2	**7.5**	9.3	14.8
▲PINERIES BANK	STEVENS POINT	WI	**B-**	C+	C+	59	3.31	2.5	2.4	43.4	5.1	**7.3**	9.2	16.5
PINNACLE BANK	JASPER	AL	**C**	C	B-	201	-7.21	10.0	2.7	12.6	31.4	**8.6**	10.1	17.0
PINNACLE BANK	ROGERS	AR	**D-**	D-	C	96	-14.17	0.7	0.2	10.9	21.3	**8.2**	9.8	16.9
▲PINNACLE BANK	SCOTTSDALE	AZ	**C-**	D-	C-	83	29.18	2.2	0.9	17.4	8.2	**10.0**	18.4	31.9
PINNACLE BANK	MORGAN HILL	CA	**D-**	D-	D	146	1.05	18.7	0.2	7.6	6.3	**7.3**	10.3	12.7
PINNACLE BANK	ORANGE CITY	FL	**E**	D-	C-	199	-9.39	5.8	3.8	5.1	21.3	**2.8**	6.1	9.8
PINNACLE BANK	ELBERTON	GA	**D-**	D	C-	588	-1.31	7.5	2.2	10.3	21.7	**3.2**	6.5	10.1
▲PINNACLE BANK	MARSHALLTOWN	IA	**C**	C-	D+	84	39.25	3.8	1.6	13.5	42.7	**10.0**	11.0	19.2
PINNACLE BANK	LINCOLN	NE	**B-**	B	B	2,952	16.27	9.1	2.7	10.5	23.2	**6.5**	8.9	12.1
PINNACLE BANK	KEENE	TX	**B**	B+	B+	522	4.60	6.6	3.8	9.4	33.1	**6.5**	8.5	14.6
PINNACLE BANK - WYOMING	TORRINGTON	WY	**B-**	B-	B	577	7.86	5.0	2.6	13.0	28.9	**6.3**	8.3	12.9
PINNACLE BANK SIOUX CITY	SIOUX CITY	IA	**B+**	A-	B+	64	17.37	4.9	3.6	28.5	17.7	**10.0**	11.0	17.2
PINNACLE BK OF SOUTH	GREENVILLE	SC	**C**	C	C-	128	4.54	5.8	1.8	12.9	13.2	**10.0**	12.8	17.9
PINNACLE NATIONAL BK	NASHVILLE	TN	**D**	C-	B	4,903	-4.55	20.2	1.0	8.0	20.7	**7.3**	9.2	13.4
PIONEER BANK	SERGEANT BLUFF	IA	**B**	B-	B-	130	10.43	13.9	1.8	19.4	24.8	**6.2**	9.6	11.9
PIONEER BANK	SAINT JAMES	MN	**D**	D+	D	266	11.35	6.8	1.2	12.3	0.7	**7.1**	9.1	13.4
▲PIONEER BANK	ROSWELL	NM	**B+**	B	B-	579	1.83	2.3	1.0	34.7	40.6	**7.8**	9.6	21.2
PIONEER BANK	STANLEY	VA	**C-**	C	B-	165	5.32	2.9	10.5	32.0	5.8	**7.9**	9.6	14.0
PIONEER BANK	AUBURNDALE	WI	**B-**	B-	B-	108	2.97	8.3	1.8	15.7	19.7	**10.0**	12.4	17.6
PIONEER BANK & TRUST	BELLE FOURCHE	SD	**A-**	B+	A	419	7.36	7.7	2.8	5.8	28.1	**8.0**	9.7	19.8
PIONEER BANK OF	LADYSMITH	WI	**C-**	C-	B-	59	3.38	4.4	1.4	3.2	56.0	**6.6**	8.6	18.1
PIONEER BANK SSB	DRIPPING SPRINGS	TX	**C**	C	C-	101	38.92	6.8	0.9	19.1	12.0	**10.0**	11.7	20.2
▲PIONEER COMMERCIAL BANK	TROY	NY	**C-**	C	C	41	14.91	0.0	0.0	0.0	85.8	**10.0**	11.1	67.0
PIONEER COMMUNITY BANK	IAEGER	WV	**C**	B-	B-	118	2.33	12.9	7.3	42.7	14.9	**6.5**	8.5	14.2
PIONEER FS&LA	DILLON	MT	**C**	C	B+	87	2.98	0.0	3.1	75.7	10.5	**10.0**	14.3	29.0
PIONEER NATIONAL BK OF DU	DULUTH	MN	**B+**	B	B	81	-0.94	23.7	1.1	22.8	6.2	**7.9**	9.6	13.7
▲PIONEER SB	TROY	NY	**C+**	C	B-	763	2.54	4.7	3.3	29.4	8.3	**9.8**	10.9	15.9
PIONEER SB	CLEVELAND	OH	**C**	C	C	26	-1.96	0.0	0.5	51.0	31.0	**10.0**	22.9	54.5
PIONEER TRUST BANK NA	SALEM	OR	**B+**	A-	A	284	3.93	16.8	1.1	11.2	18.2	**10.0**	15.0	22.2
PIQUA STATE BK	PIQUA	KS	**D+**	C-	D	26	-2.03	6.5	6.8	8.0	47.2	**7.0**	9.0	19.2
PISCATAQUA SB	PORTSMOUTH	NH	**B-**	B-	B-	223	6.89	0.0	0.9	60.2	25.1	**10.0**	15.8	31.1
PISGAH COMMUNITY BANK	ASHEVILLE	NC	**E-**	C	C	43	-31.30	8.0	0.3	2.0	0.0	**0.0**	2.0	4.8
PITNEY BOWES BANK INC	SALT LAKE CITY	UT	**C-**	C-	C-	688	-1.91	58.8	0.0	0.0	36.3	**4.9**	6.9	11.7
▲PITTSFIELD CO-OP BANK	PITTSFIELD	MA	**C**	C+	B-	226	-3.99	4.2	0.6	42.6	18.4	**10.0**	16.4	28.0
PLAINS COMMERCE BANK	HOVEN	SD	**C-**	C-	A-	401	0.11	7.5	1.9	9.1	17.2	**10.0**	11.7	15.4
PLAINS STATE BK	PLAINS	KS	**C+**	B-	B+	108	-0.03	9.6	4.4	2.2	46.3	**5.5**	7.5	13.6
PLAINS STATE BK	HUMBLE	TX	**C+**	C+	B-	180	42.09	10.7	0.9	7.1	8.3	**6.5**	8.5	14.2
PLAINSCAPITAL BANK	LUBBOCK	TX	**C+**	B-	B-	5,286	16.36	20.1	0.7	13.0	16.0	**7.6**	9.4	14.0
PLANTATION FEDERAL BANK	PAWLEYS ISLAND	SC	**E-**	E+	D+	629	-6.82	6.4	0.5	17.3	6.4	**0.6**	4.0	7.2
PLANTERS & CITIZENS BANK	CAMILLA	GA	**B-**	B-	B+	94	7.84	5.9	2.8	5.1	18.4	**9.2**	10.5	20.1
PLANTERS BANK	HOPKINSVILLE	KY	**B**	B	B-	609	22.98	13.8	1.9	13.8	22.2	**5.5**	7.5	11.6
PLANTERS BANK & TRUST CO	INDIANOLA	MS	**B-**	B-	B	622	9.54	7.3	5.2	16.3	33.8	**6.4**	8.4	14.3
PLANTERSFIRST	CORDELE	GA	**E-**	E-	D-	316	-8.76	5.2	3.9	14.9	10.0	**0.1**	3.6	6.1
PLAQUEMINE BANK & TRUST	PLAQUEMINE	LA	**B**	B	B+	130	-2.63	6.4	5.2	18.2	23.6	**10.0**	11.1	19.2
▼PLATINUM BANK	BRANDON	FL	**D**	C-	C-	387	0.51	13.6	0.8	5.9	13.7	**6.0**	8.0	12.6
PLATINUM BANK	OAKDALE	MN	**C**	C	C	103	24.32	19.9	5.6	10.0	14.7	**6.5**	9.2	12.2
▼PLATINUM BANK	LUBBOCK	TX	**D+**	C	D+	120	3.32	15.6	2.3	16.5	6.5	**9.7**	11.6	14.8
PLATTE VALLEY BANK	NORTH BEND	NE	**B+**	B+	A-	57	4.13	13.6	2.9	5.8	19.3	**10.0**	15.2	20.4
PLATTE VALLEY BANK	SCOTTSBLUFF	NE	**C**	C+	B-	381	5.78	13.4	2.8	24.5	10.1	**6.8**	8.8	12.9
▲PLATTE VALLEY BANK	TORRINGTON	WY	**C**	C+	B-	199	6.12	23.2	5.6	14.4	5.5	**6.7**	9.4	12.2
▼PLATTE VALLEY BANK OF MIS	PLATTE CITY	MO	**C+**	B-	B	349	7.29	4.5	1.5	17.9	27.7	**6.1**	8.1	12.6
▲PLATTE VALLEY STATE BK &	KEARNEY	NE	**C**	C-	C	388	-8.29	11.7	3.7	9.5	18.9	**6.7**	8.7	14.1
▲PLATTSMOUTH STATE BK	PLATTSMOUTH	NE	**C-**	C+	B-	81	-6.67	5.9	9.6	7.7	33.6	**7.0**	9.0	15.3
PLAZA BANK	IRVINE	CA	**C**	D+	E-	314	97.83	10.5	2.9	2.7	5.6	**10.0**	11.8	20.0
PLAZA BANK	NORRIDGE	IL	**D-**	D-	D	378	-4.10	2.7	0.2	14.9	2.7	**7.1**	9.1	14.2
PLAZA BANK	SEATTLE	WA	**D**	D-	C-	112	-9.94	17.0	0.4	2.4	12.3	**8.6**	10.0	14.3
▲PLAZA PARK STATE BK	WAITE PARK	MN	**C-**	D	C+	160	3.15	7.2	3.0	22.7	7.2	**6.9**	9.0	12.5

Asset Quality Index	Non-Performing Loans as a % of Total Loans	Non-Performing Loans as a % of Capital	Net Charge-offs / Avg Loans	Profitability Index	Net Income ($Mil)	Return on Assets (R.O.A.)	Return on Equity (R.O.E.)	Net Interest Spread	Overhead Efficiency Ratio	Liquidity Index	Liquidity Ratio	Hot Money Ratio	Stability Index
2.8	1.59	10.1	0.29	**3.2**	0.5	0.54	5.94	4.27	82.1	**4.1**	28.7	10.8	**5.2**
0.3	9.06	56.9	0.17	**2.7**	0.9	0.49	6.21	4.01	82.1	**1.9**	24.2	21.3	**3.4**
0.3	6.40	37.2	0.53	**2.8**	0.3	0.54	5.95	3.95	82.4	**1.9**	26.7	23.6	**3.7**
4.1	1.16	8.2	0.30	**7.0**	1.0	1.68	17.86	4.35	56.0	**2.4**	27.0	18.5	**7.0**
4.6	1.31	6.5	3.00	**3.1**	0.9	0.41	3.77	4.29	66.5	**2.2**	30.6	22.1	**4.8**
0.0	3.54	17.9	2.55	**0.0**	-1.5	-1.48	-14.58	2.28	145.5	**0.9**	18.6	36.3	**3.9**
3.0	3.11	9.4	0.11	**1.3**	0.3	0.45	2.72	3.54	88.7	**5.1**	45.9	10.2	**2.8**
0.0	5.20	34.2	1.52	**0.0**	-1.3	-0.88	-8.22	4.27	96.9	**0.8**	14.3	37.3	**1.3**
0.0	6.49	48.8	2.12	**0.0**	-4.0	-1.91	-24.58	2.94	117.2	**1.5**	26.8	28.9	**3.4**
0.2	5.92	40.3	3.12	**0.7**	-15.5	-2.59	-24.44	4.76	73.6	**2.2**	15.1	18.0	**7.7**
4.5	1.05	3.9	0.27	**3.1**	0.4	0.62	3.28	3.66	71.5	**5.8**	48.1	6.7	**6.1**
4.2	1.37	10.3	0.44	**8.4**	51.6	1.94	20.02	4.15	52.7	**2.4**	13.3	16.9	**7.9**
6.8	0.14	0.9	0.09	**6.6**	7.5	1.46	9.64	4.60	66.3	**2.8**	35.0	19.2	**6.3**
2.1	3.45	23.1	0.15	**7.8**	10.0	1.77	20.30	4.09	55.5	**1.7**	16.7	22.4	**7.3**
5.5	1.96	13.1	0.00	**9.3**	1.4	2.40	21.14	4.69	46.7	**1.5**	19.4	26.0	**7.9**
2.5	2.69	14.0	0.54	**2.4**	0.4	0.29	2.21	4.09	78.8	**0.8**	16.1	37.8	**4.4**
1.8	2.50	15.8	1.86	**0.7**	-20.8	-0.42	-3.02	3.33	78.9	**2.1**	9.8	18.4	**7.1**
5.0	1.18	8.0	0.01	**6.2**	1.8	1.48	15.47	4.38	63.3	**1.5**	19.1	25.1	**5.2**
1.3	2.64	21.1	0.67	**4.5**	2.6	1.03	9.12	4.29	61.1	**1.7**	15.6	20.9	**6.2**
7.8	0.09	0.4	0.07	**6.6**	9.1	1.54	16.36	3.10	66.0	**4.1**	48.0	16.7	**6.2**
2.5	2.00	14.9	0.31	**6.7**	2.0	1.24	13.13	5.01	58.6	**1.8**	17.0	20.7	**5.6**
8.1	0.26	1.4	0.15	**3.4**	0.4	0.41	3.29	4.37	85.2	**5.0**	32.2	6.6	**6.2**
8.3	0.20	0.9	0.04	**8.2**	7.9	1.97	19.16	3.49	55.3	**4.1**	40.4	14.5	**7.9**
4.6	3.12	11.2	1.92	**2.9**	0.2	0.34	3.33	3.77	80.5	**6.2**	70.3	8.7	**4.1**
8.3	0.64	3.2	0.03	**2.7**	0.4	0.41	3.22	4.15	84.7	**3.0**	34.7	18.2	**4.2**
10.0	0.00	0.0	0.00	**1.2**	0.0	0.02	0.22	0.56	154.2	**5.3**	25.1	1.1	**2.9**
2.4	2.39	19.3	0.19	**6.8**	1.4	1.20	12.94	5.29	66.4	**3.9**	20.4	10.0	**5.8**
7.5	0.47	2.5	0.13	**2.7**	0.3	0.31	2.27	3.77	76.2	**1.4**	15.3	26.4	**6.4**
7.9	0.13	1.0	0.04	**6.9**	1.3	1.51	15.29	5.40	68.4	**2.3**	15.5	17.6	**7.4**
6.2	0.48	2.8	0.05	**3.5**	3.0	0.40	3.97	3.51	81.2	**4.1**	24.3	9.2	**6.9**
4.5	6.39	16.5	0.28	**3.0**	0.1	0.39	1.66	4.89	76.3	**4.9**	49.6	12.2	**6.7**
4.0	3.77	17.1	0.46	**10.0**	6.8	2.43	16.27	4.97	34.9	**4.5**	26.2	7.0	**9.7**
2.7	5.88	24.5	-0.03	**1.3**	0.0	0.04	0.46	3.71	95.6	**5.9**	53.8	7.3	**4.7**
9.7	0.64	2.7	0.00	**3.6**	1.4	0.63	3.88	2.84	71.9	**2.3**	33.7	24.3	**7.8**
0.0	28.38	317.0	22.59	**0.0**	-9.6	-16.90	-488.96	1.48	229.2	**2.2**	34.5	27.1	**1.2**
2.2	3.14	19.1	4.41	**10.0**	82.4	11.58	154.89	14.90	1.7	**6.6**	41.7	0.0	**7.2**
8.0	1.26	4.8	0.44	**2.2**	0.4	0.19	1.18	3.28	79.5	**1.9**	30.1	26.7	**7.3**
0.9	5.09	30.0	0.60	**6.2**	5.0	1.24	9.23	5.34	60.5	**1.6**	15.6	23.5	**8.1**
5.6	0.94	4.8	0.57	**2.9**	0.4	0.31	3.73	3.06	70.0	**1.5**	33.1	43.8	**5.4**
6.8	0.01	0.1	0.02	**3.5**	0.9	0.61	5.58	4.81	71.7	**0.7**	15.6	46.8	**5.9**
3.2	2.01	13.2	2.00	**6.1**	50.9	1.04	9.93	4.22	74.4	**0.9**	15.4	34.5	**8.3**
0.0	10.21	138.9	1.01	**0.0**	-17.9	-2.69	-53.59	2.03	131.2	**0.9**	22.9	36.2	**0.2**
4.6	2.03	6.9	0.54	**3.8**	0.6	0.67	6.11	4.32	75.7	**4.4**	54.0	15.3	**5.2**
5.0	0.88	7.1	0.04	**6.6**	8.7	1.56	19.75	3.64	54.9	**0.7**	15.1	46.4	**5.5**
4.7	1.11	6.8	0.23	**7.1**	8.1	1.35	14.63	4.22	56.6	**1.7**	22.7	23.8	**6.6**
0.0	12.38	152.6	6.77	**0.0**	-5.6	-1.72	-46.08	3.71	90.2	**1.6**	24.9	25.3	**0.8**
5.5	2.59	12.4	0.28	**4.6**	1.0	0.80	7.37	4.37	68.3	**2.3**	32.0	22.1	**6.5**
2.0	2.24	16.2	1.22	**0.6**	-1.0	-0.25	-2.92	3.48	73.6	**1.4**	25.7	30.3	**4.7**
6.9	0.15	1.2	0.02	**2.6**	0.4	0.42	4.45	4.55	84.1	**1.8**	19.1	21.0	**3.5**
1.6	2.53	16.7	0.37	**2.6**	0.5	0.40	2.54	4.14	83.6	**0.7**	17.5	48.8	**2.9**
7.1	1.15	4.9	0.54	**4.8**	0.5	0.86	5.01	4.15	71.2	**4.5**	26.5	7.2	**8.0**
3.9	1.13	9.3	1.04	**4.5**	2.8	0.75	8.70	4.07	60.5	**1.6**	11.9	22.6	**5.2**
2.6	1.12	8.9	1.23	**3.9**	0.8	0.39	4.07	4.96	64.9	**0.8**	10.5	33.4	**4.9**
3.8	1.93	13.2	0.47	**4.2**	3.4	0.96	11.57	4.29	75.7	**2.9**	13.6	14.3	**5.2**
3.3	1.60	12.0	0.34	**5.7**	4.9	1.21	12.44	4.10	62.9	**1.8**	9.6	19.5	**4.9**
3.0	1.97	10.9	0.78	**3.8**	0.9	0.99	11.50	4.01	72.2	**3.4**	22.5	12.6	**5.2**
3.1	1.35	7.7	0.00	**3.3**	3.9	1.57	12.43	3.74	80.5	**0.7**	12.4	44.4	**5.3**
0.0	7.45	53.8	2.84	**1.4**	-1.1	-0.29	-3.21	4.78	56.4	**1.5**	16.8	25.2	**4.2**
1.8	1.72	10.4	1.25	**1.3**	0.4	0.30	3.52	3.93	96.7	**0.7**	22.2	63.6	**2.3**
3.0	1.69	13.7	0.36	**7.3**	2.4	1.55	17.71	4.94	61.0	**3.1**	13.0	13.2	**6.4**

							One	Asset Mix (As a % of Total Assets)						
Name	City	State	Rating	2008 Rating	2007 Rating	Total Assets ($Mil)	Year Asset Growth	Comm-ercial Loans	Cons-umer Loans	Home Mort-gages	Secur-ities	Capital-ization Index	Leverage Ratio	Risk-based Capital Ratio
PLEASANT HILL BANK	PLEASANT HILL	MO	**C+**	C+	B-	68	-0.45	6.8	5.9	27.4	26.9	**10.0**	12.0	21.2
PLEASANTS COUNTY BANK	SAINT MARYS	WV	**B**	B	B	59	6.47	12.0	13.5	23.8	22.9	**10.0**	11.4	19.2
PLEASANTVILLE STATE BK	PLEASANTVILLE	IA	**B+**	B+	B+	37	11.94	5.0	3.7	9.7	56.3	**10.0**	14.5	33.1
PLUMAS BANK	QUINCY	CA	**D-**	D	D-	483	-8.39	6.5	2.4	8.9	13.0	**6.9**	8.9	14.0
PLUS INTERNATIONAL BK	MIAMI	FL	**C+**	D+	D	96	-7.22	38.1	0.0	2.9	32.3	**10.0**	12.9	28.4
PNA BANK	DOWNERS GROVE	IL	**D-**	D-	C	186	-8.67	0.0	0.0	36.4	5.1	**6.1**	8.1	14.3
PNC BANK NA	WILMINGTON	DE	**C-**	C-	C-	256,639	-1.41	16.0	7.9	11.2	25.1	**8.6**	10.1	15.2
▲ POCA VALLEY BANK INC	WALTON	WV	**C**	D+	C	286	-3.83	11.6	9.1	27.4	15.7	**7.2**	9.1	15.1
POCAHONTAS STATE BK	POCAHONTAS	IA	**A**	A	A	77	2.51	4.3	0.9	4.7	48.1	**10.0**	14.0	24.1
POINTBANK	PILOT POINT	TX	**D**	D	B-	319	-4.61	3.0	2.8	9.8	23.1	**6.8**	8.8	13.9
POINTS WEST COMMUNITY	JULESBURG	CO	**C**	C	C-	128	8.81	7.5	1.9	6.3	28.4	**6.4**	8.4	14.3
POINTS WEST COMMUNITY	SIDNEY	NE	**C**	C	C-	313	7.83	5.2	3.1	4.8	41.1	**6.6**	8.6	16.6
POINTWEST BANK	WEST	TX	**B-**	B-	B+	70	11.94	0.9	11.1	13.3	39.1	**7.5**	9.3	22.3
POLK COUNTY BANK	JOHNSTON	IA	**E-**	E-	D-	102	-16.00	11.1	1.4	18.7	8.0	**0.1**	3.5	6.3
POLONIA BANK	HUNTINGDON VALLEY	PA	**C-**	C-	D+	296	35.43	7.0	1.1	41.4	18.1	**6.0**	8.0	16.8
▼ PONCE DE LEON FEDERAL	BRONX	NY	**D**	D	C-	739	2.87	4.6	0.3	41.4	2.6	**9.4**	10.6	16.2
PONY EXPRESS BANK	LIBERTY	MO	**B+**	B+	C-	131	-6.72	14.4	2.7	16.3	9.2	**9.9**	11.2	14.9
▲ PONY EXPRESS COMMUNITY	SAINT JOSEPH	MO	**B-**	C+	C-	68	85.44	7.2	2.6	17.3	10.2	**8.0**	9.7	17.6
POPLAR GROVE STATE BK	POPLAR GROVE	IL	**A-**	A-	A-	75	7.99	9.4	1.2	12.8	42.1	**10.0**	19.3	35.7
PORT AUSTIN STATE BK	PORT AUSTIN	MI	**B**	B	B	44	5.44	3.5	6.0	38.4	3.6	**10.0**	16.7	28.3
PORT BYRON STATE BK	PORT BYRON	IL	**D**	C	C	94	-0.15	10.9	2.6	7.3	12.8	**6.8**	8.8	12.9
▼ PORT RICHMOND SAVINGS	PHILADELPHIA	PA	**B+**	B+	B+	62	2.49	0.0	0.0	79.4	0.0	**10.0**	14.6	26.7
PORT WASHINGTON STATE	PORT WASHINGTON	WI	**D-**	D-	D+	391	3.01	16.4	1.4	18.0	19.8	**6.9**	8.9	13.1
PORTAGE COMMUNITY BANK	RAVENNA	OH	**C**	C-	C-	246	7.95	19.8	1.4	27.0	16.4	**6.6**	8.6	13.0
PORTAGE COUNTY BANK	ALMOND	WI	**C+**	C-	D+	98	-2.69	13.7	0.7	19.0	5.7	**8.2**	9.9	13.5
POST OAK BANK NA	HOUSTON	TX	**B-**	C+	C+	466	14.17	18.8	2.3	16.9	2.7	**10.0**	11.3	15.6
POTTER STATE BK OF	POTTER	NE	**B**	B	B-	27	8.89	10.7	5.7	1.6	26.1	**10.0**	12.7	19.6
POWELL STATE BK	POWELL	TX	**C-**	C-	C+	31	10.78	6.6	17.2	10.4	37.0	**6.9**	8.9	16.9
POWELL VALLEY NATIONAL	JONESVILLE	VA	**B-**	B+	A-	235	-2.19	5.9	5.7	31.7	17.2	**10.0**	14.4	21.4
PRAIRIE COMMUNITY BANK	MARENGO	IL	**D-**	C-	C-	142	-1.62	13.1	1.4	21.2	9.5	**7.0**	9.0	13.2
PRAIRIE MOUNTAIN BANK	GREAT FALLS	MT	**D+**	C+	C+	67	2.22	19.5	5.7	7.0	5.9	**6.7**	8.8	12.3
▼ PRAIRIE NATIONAL BK	STEWARDSON	IL	**C-**	C-	C-	55	4.66	9.5	4.5	15.7	30.1	**6.8**	8.8	15.0
PRAIRIE STATE BK & TRUST	MOUNT ZION	IL	**A-**	A-	A-	553	13.36	8.0	1.3	17.8	20.5	**6.9**	8.9	13.6
▼ PRAIRIE SUN BANK	MILAN	MN	**C**	C	C	27	-6.70	6.3	4.9	6.0	10.2	**5.4**	8.7	11.3
PREFERRED BANK	LOS ANGELES	CA	**D**	D-	D	1,257	-3.84	20.1	0.0	2.7	14.6	**10.0**	11.2	15.1
PREFERRED BANK	CASEY	IL	**D**	D-	D	52	-2.44	12.1	4.6	18.6	21.0	**6.3**	8.3	12.8
PREFERRED BANK	ROTHVILLE	MO	**B**	B+	B	71	65.16	6.9	3.3	13.7	33.1	**6.9**	8.9	16.4
▲ PREFERRED BANK	HOUSTON	TX	**B**	C-	B	215	9.87	4.6	1.0	12.9	27.4	**10.0**	13.8	29.6
▼ PREFERRED COMMUNITY	FORT MYERS	FL	**D-**	C-	C-	69	20.00	4.6	0.0	12.4	17.9	**8.4**	9.9	14.3
PREMIER AMERICAN BANK NA	MIAMI	FL	**B+**	NR	NR	2,460	N/A	2.3	0.2	2.2	65.7	**10.0**	13.9	61.9
PREMIER BANK	DENVER	CO	**E-**	E-	D-	66	-9.94	4.9	0.3	1.2	13.3	**1.9**	5.8	8.9
PREMIER BANK	TALLAHASSEE	FL	**E-**	E	D-	357	-15.35	10.0	0.6	9.7	7.3	**1.8**	5.2	8.8
PREMIER BANK	DUBUQUE	IA	**C-**	D-	C	289	-7.58	10.6	0.6	12.1	26.4	**6.8**	8.8	12.4
PREMIER BANK	ROCK VALLEY	IA	**B+**	B	B	221	13.13	13.3	2.9	5.3	8.8	**5.4**	9.5	11.3
▼ PREMIER BANK	WILMETTE	IL	**E-**	D	D	290	-17.18	19.4	0.1	4.4	11.0	**0.8**	4.1	7.5
PREMIER BANK	LENEXA	KS	**B-**	C	B-	180	-21.74	7.2	0.3	4.2	39.3	**10.0**	11.1	22.3
PREMIER BANK	MAPLEWOOD	MN	**D-**	D-	D-	596	-3.18	7.1	0.3	5.6	9.2	**3.0**	7.1	10.0
▲ PREMIER BANK & TRUST NA	NORTH CANTON	OH	**D-**	E-	E-	171	4.57	8.9	0.4	19.3	16.5	**8.0**	9.6	17.1
▲ PREMIER BANK MINNESOTA	FARMINGTON	MN	**D-**	E+	D-	196	1.90	5.1	0.3	3.8	20.9	**4.3**	6.9	10.7
PREMIER BANK OF	JACKSONVILLE	IL	**C**	C-	D+	158	15.70	4.1	16.8	15.2	23.9	**4.6**	7.2	10.8
PREMIER BANK OF THE	CULLMAN	AL	**B**	B	B+	135	-4.75	10.8	10.5	22.5	3.9	**8.1**	9.7	13.9
PREMIER BANK ROCHESTER	ROCHESTER	MN	**D-**	E+	D-	151	-2.79	6.6	0.2	4.8	13.0	**5.4**	7.8	11.3
PREMIER BUSINESS BANK	LOS ANGELES	CA	**C-**	C-	C-	95	-4.36	9.3	2.3	0.4	0.0	**10.0**	13.2	16.9
▼ PREMIER CMNTY BK EMERALD	CRESTVIEW	FL	**E-**	D	C-	152	-4.89	5.1	1.5	12.2	11.6	**2.9**	6.7	9.9
PREMIER COMMERCIAL BANK	GREENSBORO	NC	**C-**	C	C	101	28.26	11.3	0.5	6.0	21.3	**10.0**	15.5	20.5
▼ PREMIER COMMERCIAL BANK	ANAHEIM	CA	**C-**	C	C+	431	17.79	9.7	0.2	0.8	9.6	**6.7**	8.7	13.2
▲ PREMIER COMMUNITY BANK	MARION	WI	**C+**	C-	B-	197	-9.69	7.5	2.2	14.1	13.5	**9.5**	10.7	14.8
PREMIER SERVICE BANK	RIVERSIDE	CA	**D-**	D-	D+	156	-4.74	10.0	0.2	6.4	5.5	**5.9**	8.1	11.6
▼ PREMIER VALLEY BANK	FRESNO	CA	**D**	D-	D+	472	-0.50	12.9	1.8	12.0	14.1	**8.6**	10.2	13.9
PREMIERBANK	FORT ATKINSON	WI	**B-**	C-	A	282	-1.46	11.0	1.7	13.1	20.3	**10.0**	12.1	17.7

Asset Quality Index	Non-Performing Loans as a % of Total Loans	Non-Performing Loans as a % of Capital	Net Charge-offs Avg Loans	Profitability Index	Net Income ($Mil)	Return on Assets (R.O.A.)	Return on Equity (R.O.E.)	Net Interest Spread	Overhead Efficiency Ratio	Liquidity Index	Liquidity Ratio	Hot Money Ratio	Stability Index
4.8	3.04	14.1	0.42	**1.7**	0.0	0.02	0.14	3.57	95.2	**4.7**	24.0	5.4	**5.2**
5.7	0.79	3.8	0.21	**4.8**	0.4	0.66	5.71	4.57	71.4	**3.1**	38.6	19.1	**6.1**
9.2	0.01	0.0	0.13	**5.1**	0.4	1.02	6.45	3.52	60.0	**4.9**	76.9	16.5	**7.9**
0.3	7.77	48.3	2.39	**1.5**	1.3	0.26	2.74	4.35	74.9	**3.5**	20.8	12.2	**3.6**
2.6	4.62	22.5	0.66	**3.5**	0.5	0.53	4.28	4.83	77.0	**1.2**	34.3	83.5	**5.2**
0.3	9.61	79.1	0.50	**0.8**	-1.3	-0.65	-6.43	3.18	77.1	**1.5**	19.4	25.2	**3.9**
0.5	4.45	23.1	1.87	**5.0**	2,521.7	0.99	8.31	4.32	58.6	**4.3**	21.1	8.5	**8.0**
2.7	1.03	6.9	0.42	**3.5**	2.1	0.72	8.26	4.64	72.7	**2.0**	25.5	21.2	**2.8**
8.0	0.58	1.7	0.03	**10.0**	2.1	2.70	15.39	5.94	26.1	**3.7**	60.6	20.1	**9.1**
1.0	2.91	19.3	0.32	**4.9**	3.9	1.20	14.11	5.22	78.1	**2.9**	10.4	14.2	**5.4**
3.9	0.58	3.7	0.16	**5.5**	1.6	1.28	12.96	4.34	60.6	**1.6**	14.9	23.0	**5.8**
2.6	0.30	1.6	0.02	**7.6**	5.4	1.81	17.17	4.03	58.5	**1.8**	19.6	20.8	**5.8**
8.6	0.00	0.0	0.18	**3.5**	0.6	0.88	8.36	3.95	84.5	**5.2**	61.2	12.4	**5.1**
0.3	11.04	133.0	2.22	**0.0**	-2.9	-2.59	-55.12	3.91	181.8	**3.7**	14.4	10.3	**0.6**
4.1	1.47	10.4	0.11	**2.0**	0.3	0.12	1.25	2.93	98.7	**5.3**	39.7	8.0	**3.3**
0.5	6.59	49.1	0.29	**3.8**	5.4	0.75	7.24	5.02	66.8	**0.8**	9.6	33.2	**6.5**
4.8	1.22	8.5	1.32	**8.1**	2.8	2.02	15.30	5.14	46.7	**1.4**	6.6	23.4	**8.0**
6.7	0.48	2.7	-0.13	**6.9**	0.7	1.20	12.13	5.69	66.3	**4.5**	37.5	11.5	**4.7**
5.6	3.39	7.5	0.84	**6.6**	1.1	1.57	7.51	4.43	46.7	**4.3**	44.2	14.1	**9.0**
5.9	0.82	3.4	0.03	**5.1**	0.6	1.31	7.80	3.58	59.7	**1.7**	28.0	26.8	**8.3**
2.4	1.32	9.5	1.59	**1.4**	0.1	0.05	0.56	4.30	76.1	**2.7**	15.8	15.6	**4.7**
6.5	1.08	6.3	0.08	**4.7**	0.4	0.67	4.51	4.67	71.0	**1.1**	3.2	27.7	**7.9**
0.3	3.57	23.7	1.30	**3.0**	1.5	0.41	4.57	3.81	67.7	**3.1**	16.9	13.6	**3.9**
3.1	1.80	14.1	0.67	**4.0**	1.5	0.64	7.44	3.66	65.3	**3.1**	14.7	13.6	**4.8**
3.7	2.21	16.0	0.34	**3.5**	0.8	0.87	8.73	4.31	68.3	**0.9**	19.3	36.5	**4.8**
5.6	0.94	6.0	0.09	**3.6**	2.4	0.55	4.60	4.38	73.9	**0.8**	19.2	39.0	**6.0**
8.2	0.20	0.8	0.00	**4.4**	0.2	0.75	5.61	4.93	79.0	**3.1**	43.2	20.9	**7.9**
2.5	2.14	11.1	0.42	**4.8**	0.2	0.73	7.39	5.03	70.6	**2.4**	39.0	28.2	**5.3**
3.2	2.90	12.9	1.03	**4.9**	1.9	0.82	5.43	4.85	56.2	**1.2**	26.4	33.9	**7.4**
0.3	11.82	79.1	1.71	**0.0**	-1.3	-0.89	-9.16	3.46	82.2	**1.5**	21.2	27.0	**4.2**
1.7	5.88	44.4	0.30	**4.4**	0.4	0.52	5.56	4.94	73.2	**1.8**	17.6	20.7	**5.4**
3.7	2.58	15.2	0.54	**2.7**	0.3	0.52	5.45	3.31	79.7	**2.7**	36.3	21.1	**5.2**
6.2	0.44	3.1	0.25	**8.4**	10.7	2.07	23.29	3.87	52.4	**3.0**	16.9	14.0	**7.5**
3.9	1.86	14.1	0.20	**5.0**	0.3	1.13	13.26	5.11	77.9	**3.4**	12.7	11.7	**6.4**
0.0	11.13	56.2	2.71	**0.0**	-15.9	-1.17	-12.06	3.20	98.4	**0.8**	11.9	39.7	**6.0**
4.3	1.31	8.9	0.69	**1.4**	0.2	0.35	4.23	3.14	82.7	**3.3**	25.5	13.6	**2.6**
5.4	1.25	7.2	0.35	**6.1**	0.9	1.54	14.67	4.29	62.5	**4.8**	32.9	8.4	**7.5**
5.4	1.25	4.2	0.02	**6.2**	4.5	2.07	16.08	3.50	76.6	**5.1**	54.0	13.2	**4.7**
0.3	7.61	40.0	1.57	**0.0**	-1.2	-1.92	-12.69	3.34	134.3	**1.2**	28.2	37.6	**1.0**
6.1	5.26	8.1	0.00	**7.5**	31.7	1.79	11.01	2.26	65.1	**3.9**	60.5	26.2	**7.0**
0.0	5.82	55.1	0.18	**0.0**	-1.5	-2.13	-37.46	3.63	154.9	**0.9**	20.7	34.5	**1.8**
0.0	11.71	100.1	2.48	**0.0**	-11.0	-2.71	-38.44	3.29	104.7	**1.4**	19.0	27.2	**1.6**
5.4	0.00	0.0	0.71	**2.7**	1.2	0.41	5.01	3.38	77.7	**1.3**	9.7	26.6	**3.0**
6.8	0.02	0.1	0.04	**9.9**	5.5	2.65	26.03	4.31	34.2	**0.9**	9.1	31.6	**7.9**
0.3	11.61	110.1	5.51	**0.0**	-12.7	-3.79	-55.51	2.53	94.5	**0.9**	26.6	55.7	**0.8**
3.3	4.76	17.5	0.78	**5.6**	3.9	1.89	17.01	3.35	73.7	**5.7**	47.8	7.7	**6.8**
0.0	8.68	66.9	3.20	**0.0**	-5.5	-0.91	-11.08	3.42	72.1	**2.4**	10.6	16.6	**5.2**
2.5	3.30	18.0	0.92	**0.0**	-2.7	-1.56	-17.07	2.90	149.3	**2.9**	24.5	15.4	**2.1**
0.0	8.62	62.6	3.40	**0.0**	-4.8	-2.42	-34.27	3.01	101.1	**3.2**	15.7	13.3	**3.5**
3.8	0.55	4.9	0.72	**5.7**	1.6	1.03	14.38	4.24	50.6	**1.3**	8.5	25.5	**3.7**
5.5	0.29	2.1	0.71	**5.0**	1.6	1.11	11.69	4.97	68.2	**1.9**	13.3	19.5	**5.9**
0.0	7.56	55.1	3.20	**0.0**	-2.9	-1.88	-24.21	3.22	85.9	**2.9**	17.0	14.8	**4.3**
7.1	0.03	0.2	-0.07	**2.2**	0.6	0.65	5.40	4.41	84.7	**1.0**	23.4	34.8	**4.2**
0.0	10.24	83.2	4.78	**0.0**	-5.7	-3.62	-33.80	2.44	97.3	**4.7**	7.4	2.8	**0.2**
8.7	0.00	0.0	0.49	**0.0**	-1.2	-1.30	-7.25	3.01	124.7	**1.3**	29.9	37.1	**1.5**
2.3	2.58	16.0	0.39	**2.6**	1.1	0.26	2.59	3.31	75.2	**2.6**	28.6	18.0	**5.2**
3.9	1.84	10.8	0.31	**3.8**	1.4	0.67	6.57	4.29	72.0	**1.5**	21.7	27.0	**5.3**
0.0	6.99	53.5	2.70	**0.0**	-3.3	-2.05	-22.29	4.91	83.7	**4.7**	17.8	4.3	**3.9**
1.0	3.27	20.3	0.30	**4.2**	3.4	0.70	5.50	4.68	64.7	**3.3**	14.9	12.4	**6.1**
4.0	2.03	9.8	0.33	**7.8**	3.9	1.42	9.50	4.18	48.9	**4.1**	28.2	10.5	**7.8**

Name	City	State	Rating	2008 Rating	2007 Rating	Total Assets ($Mil)	One Year Asset Growth	Asset Mix (As a % of Total Assets) Comm-ercial Loans	Cons-umer Loans	Home Mort-gages	Secur-ities	Capital-ization Index	Leverage Ratio	Risk-based Capital Ratio
PREMIERWEST BANK	MEDFORD	OR	**D-**	D-	D	1,412	-7.93	10.7	3.0	3.2	15.2	**6.8**	8.9	12.6
PRESCOTT STATE BK	PRESCOTT	KS	**C-**	C	C-	15	3.88	10.9	5.5	16.8	24.9	**9.6**	10.8	20.5
PRESIDENTIAL BANK FSB	BETHESDA	MD	**D**	D	D-	609	0.77	12.1	0.6	28.0	0.4	**5.5**	7.5	13.4
PRESIDIO BANK	SAN FRANCISCO	CA	**C-**	C	C	292	19.39	26.5	2.6	0.7	0.2	**10.0**	13.8	15.3
▼ PRESTON NATIONAL BK	DALLAS	TX	**B+**	B+	B+	54	-12.64	19.1	3.9	26.3	0.0	**10.0**	14.0	18.6
▲ PRESTON STATE BANK	DALLAS	TX	**D**	D-	C+	150	-21.96	16.1	1.6	14.2	4.3	**10.0**	14.4	21.2
PRIME ALLIANCE BANK	WOODS CROSS	UT	**D-**	D-	D	105	-21.86	2.8	0.3	5.1	16.1	**10.0**	11.0	15.7
PRIME BANK	ORANGE	CT	**B**	B	B+	52	8.16	34.8	0.9	0.7	38.1	**10.0**	15.0	26.3
▲ PRIME BANK	EDMOND	OK	**B-**	C-	C	98	53.28	10.3	1.6	28.0	1.1	**5.6**	9.4	11.4
▼ PRIME MERIDIAN BANK	TALLAHASSEE	FL	**D+**	C	C	103	33.37	19.5	0.9	4.9	24.6	**10.0**	13.7	20.1
▼ PRIME PACIFIC BANK NA	LYNNWOOD	WA	**E-**	D-	D	151	-11.05	11.2	0.7	20.3	7.5	**0.6**	4.1	7.2
PRIME SECURITY BANK	KARLSTAD	MN	**E-**	E	D-	84	-11.66	5.5	1.9	10.8	2.1	**2.3**	6.0	9.3
▼ PRIMEBANK	LE MARS	IA	**C-**	B-	B-	321	-11.71	11.6	1.3	11.3	17.7	**9.0**	10.4	16.2
PRIMESOUTH BANK	TALLASSEE	AL	**C+**	C	B+	157	0.84	12.0	4.3	17.6	12.9	**7.7**	9.4	14.3
▼ PRIMESOUTH BANK	BLACKSHEAR	GA	**E-**	D	D-	422	-3.07	4.7	3.0	18.5	8.7	**2.8**	6.0	9.9
PRINCE GEORGES FSB	UPPER MARLBORO	MD	**B-**	B	A-	95	-3.87	0.2	0.9	74.5	0.0	**10.0**	12.9	22.1
▲ PRINCEVILLE STATE BK	PRINCEVILLE	IL	**D**	E+	E	68	-8.27	5.8	12.5	10.9	30.8	**7.2**	9.1	14.4
PRINCIPAL BANK	DES MOINES	IA	**D**	C-	C+	2,409	1.36	0.4	0.1	19.1	38.3	**5.3**	7.3	13.5
▲ PRINSBANK	PRINSBURG	MN	**C-**	B+	A-	107	87.70	8.7	0.7	6.9	4.3	**3.3**	9.0	10.1
▼ PRIOR LAKE STATE BK	PRIOR LAKE	MN	**B+**	A-	A	189	0.50	12.4	1.0	6.7	27.5	**10.0**	12.0	19.3
PRIORITY BANK	OZARK	AR	**B-**	B-	C	81	31.68	0.2	1.1	84.9	0.0	**6.2**	8.2	14.7
▼ PRIORITYONE BANK	MAGEE	MS	**C+**	B-	B+	492	0.51	5.2	6.6	19.1	17.5	**8.7**	10.2	14.1
PRIVATE BANK MINNESOTA	MINNEAPOLIS	MN	**D-**	C-	C+	162	-1.14	21.4	6.2	11.1	3.4	**5.2**	10.2	11.2
▲ PRIVATE BANK OF BUCKHEAD	ATLANTA	GA	**C+**	C-	D+	159	10.87	7.5	1.1	14.0	9.0	**7.1**	9.1	13.2
▼ PRIVATE BANK OF CALIFORNI	LOS ANGELES	CA	**D**	C-	C-	436	54.17	19.9	0.3	3.7	45.5	**7.8**	9.5	18.8
PRIVATE BANK OF THE PENIN	PALO ALTO	CA	**C-**	D+	D	317	2.86	16.7	0.6	2.7	18.7	**7.3**	9.2	12.9
PRIVATE TRUST CO NA	CLEVELAND	OH	**U**	U	U	16	3.09	0.0	0.0	0.0	78.4	**10.0**	96.4	400.3
PRIVATEBANK & TRUST CO	CHICAGO	IL	**D**	D+	C-	12,440	4.52	26.7	2.1	4.5	15.1	**6.8**	9.1	12.3
PROBANK	TALLAHASSEE	FL	**D-**	D	C-	90	14.98	9.0	2.0	4.5	16.6	**4.6**	7.1	10.8
PRODUCE STATE BK	HOLLANDALE	MN	**C-**	C+	B+	39	7.92	17.3	5.6	12.7	1.7	**10.0**	11.4	17.8
▼ PROFESSIONAL BANK	CORAL GABLES	FL	**D+**	C	C	115	42.53	12.4	1.2	5.1	26.9	**10.0**	12.1	18.9
PROFESSIONAL BUSINESS	PASADENA	CA	**C**	C	NR	317	590.88	15.6	0.9	1.4	4.3	**10.0**	51.0	15.7
PROFICIO BANK	SALT LAKE CITY	UT	**D**	D-	C-	152	-45.20	28.7	0.0	15.8	9.0	**10.0**	12.1	18.8
PROFILE BANK FSB	ROCHESTER	NH	**B-**	B-	B-	158	1.54	1.7	0.7	52.3	6.6	**10.0**	14.0	21.9
PROFINIUM FINANCIAL INC	TRUMAN	MN	**D**	D-	D	305	-6.74	8.3	4.0	5.0	23.9	**6.0**	8.0	12.4
PROGRESS BANK & TRUST	HUNTSVILLE	AL	**C**	C	C	321	34.30	9.8	1.6	11.7	21.9	**10.0**	11.6	15.1
PROGRESSIVE BANK	MONROE	LA	**B-**	C+	B-	498	33.93	10.6	1.5	14.1	5.9	**7.9**	10.0	13.3
PROGRESSIVE BANK NA	WHEELING	WV	**C+**	B-	B-	277	2.43	2.5	3.7	11.2	47.9	**8.9**	10.2	19.7
PROGRESSIVE NB DESOTO	MANSFIELD	LA	**C-**	C	C-	32	6.41	2.9	8.5	16.8	44.6	**6.1**	8.1	17.8
PROGRESSIVE OZARK BANK	SALEM	MO	**B+**	B	B-	109	-2.70	3.7	8.1	51.8	3.5	**7.7**	9.4	15.5
PROGRESSIVE SB	JAMESTOWN	TN	**D**	NR	NR	245	N/A	1.5	5.3	32.1	9.9	**5.6**	8.2	11.4
PROGRESSIVE-HOME FS&LA	PITTSBURGH	PA	**C-**	C-	D	51	2.78	0.0	0.6	44.6	44.3	**9.4**	10.6	23.9
PROGROWTH BANK	NICOLLET	MN	**D-**	E	D	147	-11.58	6.0	1.6	12.9	17.8	**4.5**	6.5	11.5
PROMARK TRUST BANK NA	NEW YORK	NY	**U**	U	U	59	-10.16	0.0	0.0	0.0	0.0	**10.0**	19.3	25.7
PROMERICA BANK	LOS ANGELES	CA	**D**	C-	C	117	22.44	8.1	0.0	0.4	0.0	**10.0**	15.8	22.3
PROSPECT FSB	WORTH	IL	**C**	C	C+	294	-0.41	0.0	0.0	15.9	47.1	**10.0**	13.7	43.4
PROSPER BANK	PROSPER	TX	**E-**	E-	D-	69	-9.00	18.2	0.9	8.9	6.9	**0.0**	3.2	5.8
▼ PROSPERITY BANK	SAINT AUGUSTINE	FL	**E-**	E+	E+	837	-9.81	3.0	1.4	22.3	16.0	**3.3**	5.8	10.2
PROSPERITY BANK	EL CAMPO	TX	**B-**	C+	B	9,473	7.09	3.6	0.9	9.6	50.0	**4.7**	6.7	14.6
PROVIDENCE BANK	ALPHARETTA	GA	**E-**	E-	D-	125	0.12	0.9	1.2	9.5	5.3	**2.6**	7.1	9.7
PROVIDENCE BANK	COLUMBIA	MO	**C-**	C	D+	803	506.46	2.6	0.4	7.5	10.9	**10.0**	11.8	28.3
▼ PROVIDENCE BANK	ROCKY MOUNT	NC	**C-**	C	C	167	14.12	9.4	0.3	16.4	1.5	**9.8**	11.4	14.8
PROVIDENCE BANK LLC	SOUTH HOLLAND	IL	**C**	D+	C-	307	16.26	17.1	0.3	9.3	27.3	**8.5**	10.0	14.3
▲ PROVIDENCE BANK OF TEXAS	SOUTHLAKE	TX	**D+**	C	C-	100	6.29	4.4	0.6	18.5	0.0	**6.7**	8.7	13.3
PROVIDENT BANK	AMESBURY	MA	**C+**	C+	C+	498	0.59	4.5	0.2	22.1	24.4	**6.1**	8.1	13.7
PROVIDENT BANK	JERSEY CITY	NJ	**C**	C-	C+	6,825	-0.08	4.1	1.2	24.8	25.4	**5.2**	7.2	12.2
▼ PROVIDENT BANK	MONTEBELLO	NY	**C+**	B-	B+	2,774	0.75	8.0	0.4	15.2	30.7	**6.9**	8.9	13.9
▼ PROVIDENT COMMUNITY	ROCK HILL	SC	**E-**	D-	D+	409	-10.54	4.4	1.2	9.6	36.3	**3.7**	5.7	11.0
PROVIDENT MUNICIPAL BANK	MONTEBELLO	NY	**B+**	A-	B+	338	0.79	0.0	0.0	0.0	43.0	**10.0**	11.6	36.0
PROVIDENT SAVINGS BANK	RIVERSIDE	CA	**D**	D-	D+	1,358	-3.99	0.4	0.1	49.3	2.3	**8.2**	9.8	15.2

Asset Quality Index	Non-Performing Loans as a % of Total Loans	Non-Performing Loans as a % of Capital	Net Charge-offs Avg Loans	Profitability Index	Net Income ($Mil)	Return on Assets (R.O.A.)	Return on Equity (R.O.E.)	Net Interest Spread	Overhead Efficiency Ratio	Liquidity Index	Liquidity Ratio	Hot Money Ratio	Stability Index
0.0	13.26	80.2	1.88	**0.3**	-3.1	-0.21	-2.48	4.17	90.1	**2.3**	11.4	17.4	**5.6**
8.6	0.00	0.0	0.29	**2.9**	0.1	0.39	3.69	3.72	81.4	**1.5**	28.4	27.7	**5.1**
0.3	4.87	40.3	0.00	**2.3**	1.2	0.20	2.73	4.17	77.6	**4.6**	22.7	5.8	**3.7**
5.7	0.93	5.4	0.40	**1.4**	0.9	0.33	2.32	4.28	84.4	**2.7**	12.7	15.2	**3.0**
5.0	1.50	8.8	0.13	**7.6**	0.9	1.57	11.50	5.92	71.8	**2.3**	1.8	16.3	**9.4**
0.6	10.75	48.2	2.90	**1.3**	0.4	0.21	1.73	3.34	78.1	**2.0**	28.1	22.7	**4.3**
0.3	5.89	30.2	3.39	**0.0**	-3.6	-2.95	-25.08	4.41	90.1	**0.6**	11.0	44.0	**4.7**
5.8	3.50	11.9	0.17	**3.5**	0.3	0.67	4.29	4.13	74.6	**2.6**	53.0	32.7	**7.9**
7.3	0.00	0.0	0.02	**7.3**	1.5	1.94	21.35	4.83	51.6	**0.5**	4.3	48.2	**5.2**
8.5	0.00	0.0	0.52	**0.7**	0.2	0.22	1.61	3.48	84.8	**2.9**	32.4	17.9	**2.2**
0.0	14.21	129.5	4.45	**0.0**	-5.8	-3.63	-43.79	3.93	140.4	**0.7**	17.3	52.6	**3.2**
0.3	4.81	46.4	2.96	**0.0**	-2.0	-2.25	-30.43	3.59	116.8	**3.8**	19.6	10.5	**2.1**
2.2	2.63	16.3	0.41	**5.2**	4.4	1.27	12.61	3.21	54.2	**3.5**	26.6	12.8	**5.2**
4.3	0.82	5.2	1.77	**3.1**	0.7	0.43	4.51	4.11	51.7	**1.2**	11.5	28.0	**5.8**
0.3	7.00	69.8	4.57	**0.0**	-6.8	-1.59	-20.14	3.96	64.8	**0.8**	18.3	37.9	**2.8**
2.8	4.41	28.9	0.00	**3.2**	0.4	0.37	2.96	3.91	55.3	**0.6**	8.7	38.9	**6.6**
1.9	3.74	19.3	0.52	**1.9**	0.3	0.48	5.53	3.87	86.8	**2.9**	28.4	16.8	**2.7**
3.6	1.97	12.2	5.78	**0.9**	-14.3	-0.59	-7.61	2.76	29.6	**3.1**	46.4	31.4	**4.7**
3.7	1.16	9.8	0.00	**6.5**	1.0	1.26	13.98	4.93	73.4	**3.1**	20.5	13.9	**7.3**
3.7	2.49	10.8	2.47	**5.5**	2.1	1.09	8.92	3.90	48.2	**5.0**	36.1	7.9	**8.7**
6.2	0.58	5.7	0.07	**10.0**	1.9	2.60	30.66	5.20	51.5	**0.6**	6.4	41.4	**6.3**
2.4	0.96	6.3	0.56	**5.6**	4.9	0.99	10.37	4.14	62.1	**1.7**	12.7	21.1	**6.0**
2.8	2.58	20.0	3.03	**0.0**	-2.1	-1.24	-11.12	4.10	66.1	**0.8**	3.0	31.2	**5.0**
5.3	0.09	0.8	0.34	**3.8**	1.7	1.10	12.44	4.11	69.5	**0.7**	15.3	49.1	**4.8**
5.8	0.63	3.1	0.66	**0.7**	0.1	0.03	0.25	3.17	97.6	**3.4**	10.1	11.5	**1.6**
4.0	2.40	14.4	0.35	**2.8**	2.2	0.67	7.27	4.02	74.2	**2.6**	33.9	20.6	**3.5**
6.7	0.00	0.0	0.00	**10.0**	0.9	6.03	6.30	1.77	72.9	**5.0**	2,155.9	101.0	**6.4**
1.1	3.91	27.0	2.06	**1.7**	31.7	0.26	2.63	3.55	52.9	**1.5**	17.7	25.9	**6.0**
4.7	0.00	0.0	3.68	**0.0**	-1.2	-1.39	-14.28	3.71	115.2	**0.7**	14.8	47.4	**1.0**
1.8	4.55	24.0	1.31	**4.5**	0.3	0.85	7.03	3.71	56.9	**4.8**	38.1	10.6	**8.1**
8.3	0.66	3.3	0.06	**0.0**	-2.1	-2.12	-15.32	3.25	140.8	**1.8**	26.9	24.9	**1.5**
1.7	6.22	36.7	-0.07	**5.3**	1.0	1.59	5.85	2.92	43.6	**1.6**	33.8	38.5	**4.8**
0.7	9.52	46.8	3.74	**0.0**	-6.3	-2.90	-24.28	3.17	101.6	**0.2**	6.3	97.6	**4.7**
4.8	1.99	10.5	0.04	**3.3**	0.9	0.60	4.28	4.26	76.7	**2.3**	15.0	17.5	**7.4**
0.8	3.64	24.9	0.82	**2.4**	3.1	0.96	10.98	3.46	82.1	**2.5**	18.0	16.9	**3.5**
8.5	0.02	0.1	0.07	**2.9**	3.8	1.32	11.44	3.54	81.8	**0.8**	6.5	32.5	**4.4**
6.4	0.41	2.8	0.32	**4.5**	2.6	0.69	6.64	4.74	75.5	**4.1**	32.8	12.2	**4.3**
3.7	3.94	15.8	0.04	**4.1**	2.4	0.87	7.54	3.91	75.1	**5.2**	45.0	10.2	**6.7**
6.0	0.88	4.2	0.05	**3.8**	0.2	0.65	8.15	4.59	86.6	**2.5**	39.0	26.2	**4.5**
6.6	0.47	3.9	0.02	**8.6**	2.3	2.10	22.72	5.43	66.3	**4.1**	12.2	7.7	**6.4**
2.8	2.05	16.3	0.00	**1.0**	0.9	0.38	4.36	N/,	86.9	**1.4**	18.8	27.9	**2.3**
4.6	1.65	7.1	0.11	**2.0**	0.1	0.18	1.38	3.05	89.5	**4.9**	54.8	12.8	**4.9**
2.4	3.33	22.7	0.80	**1.7**	0.3	0.19	3.20	3.54	84.5	**4.2**	29.0	10.4	**1.3**
10.0	0.00	0.0	0.00	**2.9**	0.2	0.30	1.46	0.10	99.8	**0.5**	23.4	101.0	**4.5**
3.2	1.48	5.9	0.05	**0.1**	-0.5	-0.47	-2.74	4.27	109.2	**1.8**	36.2	34.7	**1.6**
8.6	2.54	4.5	0.08	**1.7**	0.1	0.02	0.11	1.58	95.6	**4.5**	85.5	22.4	**7.0**
0.7	2.35	31.6	1.45	**0.0**	-0.7	-0.96	-26.12	3.52	122.9	**1.1**	21.2	32.6	**2.1**
0.3	3.70	32.3	2.07	**0.0**	-5.6	-0.63	-9.16	3.54	92.4	**4.0**	11.9	8.4	**2.3**
6.8	0.13	0.8	0.41	**8.4**	132.0	1.42	8.94	4.07	43.4	**4.0**	29.1	14.5	**10.0**
0.0	16.89	136.2	1.07	**0.0**	-0.8	-0.67	-7.51	2.03	113.3	**1.3**	18.7	28.9	**0.0**
0.0	9.25	50.4	0.46	**0.8**	-1.8	-0.61	-7.13	2.61	93.9	**2.3**	36.7	27.2	**7.0**
1.5	3.21	21.9	0.09	**3.7**	1.1	0.71	6.02	3.56	59.1	**0.7**	13.4	42.9	**2.5**
4.8	1.00	5.9	0.27	**3.3**	2.4	0.86	9.60	4.00	70.1	**1.9**	30.9	28.1	**4.1**
6.7	0.86	6.1	0.16	**2.2**	0.5	0.47	5.43	3.17	72.5	**1.6**	28.6	30.0	**3.5**
5.5	0.68	5.1	0.06	**3.4**	2.6	0.51	6.01	3.73	81.8	**3.3**	8.2	12.0	**6.3**
3.0	2.10	17.3	0.63	**3.3**	49.2	0.73	6.04	3.50	58.2	**4.2**	18.1	8.4	**7.8**
3.4	2.16	13.0	0.50	**4.2**	21.4	0.73	5.35	3.55	67.6	**5.7**	37.0	7.4	**9.2**
0.3	9.18	60.5	3.12	**0.0**	-13.5	-3.10	-39.65	2.28	100.8	**2.0**	24.6	20.2	**1.4**
10.0	0.00	0.0	0.00	**4.1**	3.1	0.76	6.29	1.67	46.0	**7.1**	65.1	3.4	**9.0**
1.2	4.60	32.4	1.21	**3.4**	12.8	0.91	10.19	3.02	61.7	**1.6**	15.1	24.1	**5.1**

Name	City	State	Rating	2008 Rating	2007 Rating	Total Assets ($Mil)	One Year Asset Growth	Asset Mix (As a % of Total Assets) Comm-ercial Loans	Cons-umer Loans	Home Mort-gages	Secur-ities	Capital-ization Index	Leverage Ratio	Risk-based Capital Ratio
PROVIDENT STATE BK	PRESTON	MD	**C**	C+	C+	258	2.61	8.5	1.7	11.2	18.8	**4.9**	8.0	10.9
▲ PROVINCE BANK FSB	MARIETTA	PA	**B**	C+	C	98	-0.27	2.6	0.4	17.7	31.7	**10.0**	18.3	32.8
▲ PROVINCIAL BANK	LAKEVILLE	MN	**D+**	D	D-	82	-1.67	10.3	7.2	26.3	3.9	**6.9**	8.9	12.8
PRUDENTIAL BANK & TRUST F	HARTFORD	CT	**B+**	B+	B+	2,034	13.98	0.0	0.0	0.0	94.9	**8.4**	9.9	27.0
PRUDENTIAL SB	PHILADELPHIA	PA	**C+**	C	C+	524	3.44	0.2	0.1	35.4	38.4	**7.7**	9.5	22.4
PUBLIC SB	HUNTINGDON VALLEY	PA	**E-**	D-	D-	48	-9.71	4.1	11.7	26.8	3.9	**0.0**	3.0	5.2
▼ PUEBLO BANK & TRUST CO	PUEBLO	CO	**D-**	D	D-	333	-5.78	5.1	0.5	6.0	19.9	**9.1**	10.4	16.0
PUGET SOUND BANK	BELLEVUE	WA	**C+**	C-	C-	222	12.56	25.3	1.8	3.0	12.5	**9.8**	11.7	14.9
▼ PULASKI BANK	CREVE COEUR	MO	**D-**	D	C-	1,462	2.38	9.6	0.2	38.3	3.5	**6.8**	9.1	12.4
PULASKI SB	CHICAGO	IL	**C-**	C	C-	48	9.34	0.0	0.9	59.4	24.9	**10.0**	13.3	36.6
▲ PURDUM STATE BK	PURDUM	NE	**C+**	C-	D	20	5.03	5.3	1.7	2.3	0.5	**10.0**	13.8	18.9
▼ PUTNAM 1ST MERCANTILE	COOKEVILLE	TN	**C-**	D	D	87	8.53	13.5	3.7	17.8	18.6	**10.0**	11.4	16.1
PUTNAM BANK	PUTNAM	CT	**D+**	D	C-	472	0.11	1.4	0.2	39.9	37.2	**5.3**	7.3	14.4
PUTNAM COUNTY BANK	HURRICANE	WV	**B+**	B	A-	561	8.79	4.3	1.0	28.0	19.0	**10.0**	12.8	24.3
PUTNAM COUNTY NB OF	CARMEL	NY	**C+**	B-	B	165	3.73	7.1	0.4	20.8	16.9	**10.0**	24.4	45.6
PUTNAM COUNTY SB	BREWSTER	NY	**C**	C+	B-	953	1.02	7.1	0.2	15.2	31.7	**10.0**	11.4	22.1
PUTNAM COUNTY STATE BK	UNIONVILLE	MO	**C+**	C+	C	136	7.32	11.2	3.1	9.4	6.6	**7.5**	9.4	12.9
PUTNAM STATE BK	PALATKA	FL	**E-**	E-	D-	176	-10.59	14.0	1.4	2.9	14.5	**0.4**	4.4	6.8
PYRAMAX BANK FSB	GREENFIELD	WI	**D-**	D	D+	463	-10.42	5.5	0.8	27.0	21.5	**5.8**	8.6	11.6
PYRAMIS GLOBAL ADVISORS T	SMITHFIELD	RI	**C-**	C	C	77	-30.22	0.0	0.0	0.0	0.9	**10.0**	66.2	80.2
QNB BANK	QUAKERTOWN	PA	**C+**	C+	B-	805	6.17	12.2	0.3	12.4	36.0	**5.0**	7.0	11.2
▲ QUAD CITY BANK & TRUST CO	BETTENDORF	IA	**C**	C	C	1,026	5.16	14.1	1.7	5.7	26.8	**6.5**	8.5	13.1
QUAIL CREEK BANK NA	OKLAHOMA CITY	OK	**B-**	B-	C+	459	4.98	5.8	2.2	10.1	6.9	**6.8**	8.9	12.4
▲ QUAINT OAK BANK	SOUTHAMPTON	PA	**B**	B-	B	100	12.05	0.0	0.1	45.8	9.9	**10.0**	13.6	22.8
▲ QUALITY BANK	PAGE	ND	**D-**	D-	D+	25	-0.52	4.1	5.6	3.0	25.7	**6.8**	8.9	12.5
▲ QUANTUM NATIONAL BK	SUWANEE	GA	**D**	D-	C-	346	-11.32	11.7	0.3	8.9	5.7	**7.2**	9.8	12.6
▲ QUARRY CITY SAVINGS & LOA	WARRENSBURG	MO	**C**	C-	C	42	18.62	11.6	2.7	35.0	0.0	**7.4**	9.3	13.5
QUEEN CITY FSB	VIRGINIA	MN	**D+**	C-	C	230	0.30	5.1	2.4	22.3	26.8	**7.1**	9.1	15.9
QUEENSBOROUGH NATIONAL	LOUISVILLE	GA	**D**	D+	C+	930	-0.27	6.3	3.0	15.5	17.3	**5.7**	7.7	13.1
▲ QUEENSTOWN BANK OF	QUEENSTOWN	MD	**D+**	C-	B-	447	2.67	5.0	3.1	20.5	3.9	**6.6**	9.4	12.2
▼ QUINNIPIAC BANK & TRUST C	HAMDEN	CT	**D**	C	C	57	35.88	28.9	3.3	16.8	3.4	**10.0**	12.6	17.9
QUOIN FINANCIAL BANK	MILLER	SD	**D**	D-	D+	126	1.95	15.4	3.3	2.5	17.4	**6.4**	9.4	12.1
QUONTIC BANK	GREAT NECK	NY	**D**	D-	D	56	70.90	1.7	0.5	38.2	10.2	**10.0**	13.8	32.7
R BANK	ROUND ROCK	TX	**D**	C	NR	92	108.22	9.5	1.0	10.3	33.3	**10.0**	13.1	19.3
RABOBANK NA	ROSEVILLE	CA	**C-**	C	C	11,023	16.84	4.3	0.4	5.5	14.5	**10.0**	11.7	15.2
RABUN COUNTY BANK	CLAYTON	GA	**D-**	D	D	265	-0.71	0.7	2.1	26.1	4.8	**6.8**	8.8	14.8
RACCOON VALLEY BANK	PERRY	IA	**C+**	C-	C+	175	3.28	9.9	2.4	6.1	25.7	**6.0**	8.7	11.7
RAMSEY NATIONAL BK & TRUS	DEVILS LAKE	ND	**C-**	C-	B	217	6.54	11.9	1.2	7.6	14.0	**8.2**	9.8	14.1
▲ RANCHO SANTA FE THRIFT &	SAN MARCOS	CA	**B**	C	B	51	9.05	0.0	54.1	0.0	48.0	**10.0**	52.7	81.5
RANDALL STATE BK	RANDALL	MN	**B-**	B-	C+	35	6.23	5.1	1.5	23.3	15.6	**10.0**	13.3	23.2
RANDALL-STORY STATE BK	STORY CITY	IA	**B+**	B+	B+	85	7.00	2.3	1.1	12.3	32.9	**9.5**	10.7	14.6
▼ RANDOLPH BANK & TRUST CO	ASHEBORO	NC	**D**	D	C-	292	0.66	5.7	1.8	23.3	11.9	**6.5**	8.5	12.7
▼ RANDOLPH NATIONAL BK	RANDOLPH	VT	**D+**	C	B-	157	-1.34	5.0	3.4	44.6	3.6	**6.0**	8.0	13.5
▼ RANDOLPH SB	RANDOLPH	MA	**D**	C-	C-	381	-4.64	0.8	0.2	25.0	34.5	**6.8**	8.8	17.3
▼ RANGE BANK NA	NEGAUNEE	MI	**B-**	B	B-	254	4.81	6.6	1.6	12.0	23.1	**6.9**	8.9	13.4
RARITAN STATE BK	RARITAN	IL	**D+**	C	C+	158	7.35	7.2	6.0	19.5	27.4	**5.4**	7.4	12.9
RAVALLI COUNTY BANK	HAMILTON	MT	**C-**	C+	B-	184	-3.67	6.8	1.2	29.4	15.3	**9.1**	10.4	17.9
▼ RAWLINS NATIONAL BK	RAWLINS	WY	**D**	D+	B	146	-3.32	13.3	3.3	4.3	18.0	**7.6**	9.4	14.1
RAYMOND FEDERAL BANK	RAYMOND	WA	**C-**	C-	C	58	-6.06	0.0	1.0	72.3	6.5	**7.2**	9.1	19.4
RAYMOND JAMES BANK FSB	SAINT PETERSBURG	FL	**C+**	C	C+	7,575	-4.06	8.9	0.1	25.3	5.1	**7.9**	11.1	13.2
RAYMOND JAMES TRUST NA	SAINT PETERSBURG	FL	**U**	U	U	12	27.04	0.0	0.0	0.0	8.9	**10.0**	74.0	147.0
RAYNE BUILDING & LOAN ASS	RAYNE	LA	**B**	B-	B-	63	13.05	0.0	1.8	38.4	37.6	**10.0**	15.7	36.5
RAYNE STATE BK & TRUST CO	RAYNE	LA	**B+**	B+	A-	250	12.20	16.7	2.0	10.3	19.0	**7.1**	9.1	13.0
RBC BANK (GEORGIA) NA	ATLANTA	GA	**D+**	C	C	252	15.29	0.0	85.0	0.0	1.6	**10.0**	17.8	20.7
RBC BANK (USA)	RALEIGH	NC	**D**	D-	D-	27,597	0.45	9.8	0.7	11.9	20.1	**10.0**	11.1	15.4
RBS CITIZENS NA	PROVIDENCE	RI	**D-**	D	C-	107,836	-7.77	11.0	13.0	17.7	12.8	**6.2**	8.2	12.7
RCB BANK	CLAREMORE	OK	**B-**	B	B+	1,909	35.16	5.1	3.8	8.8	42.3	**4.9**	6.9	14.4
▲ RCSBANK	NEW LONDON	MO	**E**	D-	D-	60	-2.61	9.5	2.1	10.3	29.8	**5.4**	7.4	12.6
READING CO-OP BANK	READING	MA	**B-**	C+	C+	331	7.62	2.5	0.3	38.7	24.2	**6.5**	8.5	15.2
READLYN SB	READLYN	IA	**A**	B+	B+	53	11.92	9.5	1.5	20.7	28.4	**10.0**	12.1	17.2

Asset Quality Index	Non-Performing Loans as a % of Total Loans	Non-Performing Loans as a % of Capital	Net Charge-offs Avg Loans	Profitability Index	Net Income ($Mil)	Return on Assets (R.O.A.)	Return on Equity (R.O.E.)	Net Interest Spread	Overhead Efficiency Ratio	Liquidity Index	Liquidity Ratio	Hot Money Ratio	Stability Index
5.9	0.48	3.9	0.14	**3.8**	1.8	0.68	8.70	3.92	72.8	**2.7**	20.9	16.3	**4.2**
6.7	1.86	6.1	0.00	**4.2**	0.9	0.89	5.06	3.92	64.0	**5.6**	44.0	7.1	**7.7**
2.6	0.74	5.8	0.60	**1.8**	0.3	0.32	3.81	3.71	84.4	**1.6**	12.4	21.9	**3.4**
9.2	0.00	0.0	0.00	**6.8**	28.9	1.48	12.82	2.78	23.8	**5.1**	112.0	22.8	**5.8**
5.3	2.90	13.8	0.27	**3.3**	2.7	0.51	5.19	3.04	65.2	**3.4**	52.9	24.4	**6.3**
0.1	7.96	130.2	1.12	**0.0**	-2.3	-4.46	-56.78	4.41	129.1	**1.4**	10.4	24.2	**3.5**
0.0	15.45	73.1	4.42	**0.0**	-11.0	-3.16	-24.64	4.42	116.8	**4.4**	20.9	6.9	**6.7**
5.6	1.49	8.5	0.30	**3.3**	1.4	0.62	5.16	3.66	70.3	**0.7**	11.1	34.8	**4.1**
0.0	4.31	36.9	0.65	**2.9**	5.1	0.36	3.85	3.75	51.0	**1.3**	5.1	24.3	**5.7**
7.2	1.48	6.8	0.39	**0.7**	-0.1	-0.11	-0.82	3.44	103.9	**2.3**	35.6	26.2	**6.7**
3.4	1.43	6.9	-2.04	**8.3**	0.4	2.21	17.21	5.04	72.4	**2.3**	24.1	18.0	**6.8**
4.3	1.49	8.6	1.01	**1.4**	0.3	0.36	3.07	3.98	72.2	**0.7**	14.1	42.6	**2.9**
2.2	2.47	17.0	0.19	**1.6**	1.0	0.21	2.53	2.62	83.5	**3.1**	42.5	20.3	**3.6**
4.9	0.83	3.7	0.96	**4.3**	3.4	0.63	4.71	3.31	49.5	**1.5**	33.0	40.9	**7.6**
2.7	8.63	20.4	0.14	**3.5**	0.8	0.45	1.84	3.29	72.9	**4.2**	32.6	11.3	**6.6**
6.8	1.11	5.0	0.62	**2.8**	3.3	0.34	3.15	2.88	71.5	**5.4**	47.4	9.8	**6.8**
3.5	1.24	9.6	0.17	**7.7**	1.7	1.29	13.83	3.88	42.9	**0.8**	17.0	36.2	**6.7**
0.0	15.65	133.2	2.78	**0.0**	-4.8	-2.48	-72.05	3.05	154.2	**0.8**	16.1	36.3	**1.2**
0.0	7.05	48.6	-0.07	**0.4**	-8.4	-1.67	-18.02	2.66	91.5	**1.9**	26.1	22.7	**3.9**
10.0	0.00	0.0	0.00	**0.0**	-38.2	-41.57	-99.24	-5.72	115.4	**2.1**	59.4	101.0	**1.7**
4.0	1.54	11.5	0.23	**5.0**	7.2	0.93	12.74	3.74	57.0	**3.0**	22.8	14.9	**4.9**
3.7	3.07	19.3	0.79	**4.0**	6.8	0.69	7.82	3.09	66.9	**2.1**	12.2	18.5	**6.1**
3.9	0.25	2.1	0.18	**9.6**	9.3	2.05	23.54	4.87	44.4	**1.6**	15.8	22.7	**7.4**
5.6	1.99	10.3	0.10	**4.7**	0.7	0.75	5.35	3.81	66.4	**1.4**	25.9	30.4	**7.5**
0.3	6.74	35.8	0.82	**0.3**	-0.1	-0.52	-5.39	4.63	103.4	**2.4**	15.6	16.8	**4.1**
1.6	2.12	15.1	0.91	**0.9**	0.6	0.16	1.66	3.51	82.7	**1.1**	8.9	29.0	**3.1**
8.3	0.15	1.3	0.01	**4.2**	0.4	1.04	11.31	3.78	61.6	**2.7**	12.1	15.0	**4.3**
2.9	1.72	10.6	0.79	**3.0**	0.8	0.30	2.19	3.77	72.1	**4.5**	34.7	10.5	**6.2**
1.5	4.49	30.4	2.20	**0.9**	-5.7	-0.61	-7.33	3.58	70.8	**1.0**	22.5	33.6	**4.7**
1.8	2.79	23.0	1.57	**4.0**	1.9	0.42	4.45	3.91	56.4	**0.8**	6.1	32.3	**6.0**
6.6	0.91	5.5	0.29	**0.0**	-0.7	-1.33	-9.42	3.47	115.3	**1.3**	21.7	30.0	**1.5**
1.0	4.63	32.8	2.25	**0.6**	0.3	0.23	2.21	4.48	80.5	**1.5**	13.1	23.7	**3.7**
4.8	2.61	11.2	1.14	**0.0**	-1.7	-3.69	-16.40	2.60	169.0	**2.6**	42.4	28.0	**0.0**
9.3	0.00	0.0	0.00	**0.0**	-0.7	-1.04	-6.34	2.45	121.9	**2.7**	52.2	30.9	**1.5**
0.8	4.28	25.3	1.49	**1.6**	6.2	0.06	0.29	3.70	64.0	**1.6**	3.0	20.3	**7.9**
0.3	12.17	83.8	0.79	**1.1**	-0.2	-0.06	-0.74	3.10	80.1	**1.6**	25.8	26.9	**4.4**
4.1	1.02	5.7	0.58	**4.6**	1.8	1.05	11.58	3.51	68.3	**5.4**	42.4	7.9	**5.9**
1.9	3.09	22.2	0.53	**5.1**	2.2	1.04	9.72	3.86	62.0	**3.2**	11.6	12.5	**6.2**
5.6	0.33	0.3	3.60	**6.7**	2.5	5.88	9.86	11.90	52.3	**6.0**	96.8	13.2	**6.3**
3.4	3.40	14.7	0.78	**5.8**	0.5	1.44	10.51	4.18	57.2	**3.7**	37.8	15.9	**9.2**
8.7	0.20	1.1	-0.01	**8.5**	1.1	1.47	13.06	3.84	44.1	**3.8**	40.2	16.2	**7.8**
3.2	3.85	28.0	0.87	**1.0**	-0.8	-0.27	-2.86	3.73	82.0	**2.0**	26.3	21.8	**3.0**
1.7	2.55	24.0	0.07	**3.1**	0.5	0.32	3.64	4.71	90.4	**3.5**	9.2	10.8	**5.3**
0.3	2.71	14.2	0.53	**2.8**	1.8	0.48	5.39	3.85	83.1	**4.6**	44.8	13.0	**3.9**
5.4	0.63	3.9	0.36	**4.5**	2.2	0.86	9.02	4.34	69.8	**4.1**	37.6	13.6	**6.1**
2.8	2.46	19.2	2.99	**1.7**	0.0	0.01	0.15	3.90	56.9	**1.8**	33.0	31.8	**4.0**
2.1	4.73	25.3	1.39	**2.8**	0.5	0.27	2.57	3.93	74.7	**3.5**	15.8	11.7	**5.6**
1.2	5.94	34.0	1.45	**0.5**	-1.1	-0.72	-7.12	4.02	98.1	**1.8**	20.9	21.6	**5.5**
7.1	0.28	2.3	0.56	**2.4**	0.1	0.17	1.98	3.84	76.8	**1.5**	17.2	25.5	**3.3**
3.0	2.23	14.1	1.13	**4.7**	84.2	1.00	10.17	3.15	21.8	**4.9**	16.5	3.2	**5.3**
10.0	0.00	0.0	0.00	**5.9**	0.5	5.32	6.70	0.54	94.4	**4.4**	169.5	101.0	**5.9**
5.1	3.22	8.7	0.00	**4.1**	0.6	1.01	6.03	3.54	59.0	**2.5**	61.8	59.6	**7.3**
8.5	0.05	0.4	-0.01	**7.2**	3.3	1.38	14.30	5.01	64.9	**2.4**	22.7	18.0	**6.3**
3.4	1.52	5.7	5.50	**5.7**	3.4	1.58	7.08	9.97	49.5	**0.4**	21.7	99.7	**3.0**
0.2	7.64	39.0	2.57	**0.0**	-392.6	-1.48	-9.76	3.09	109.8	**3.3**	11.5	12.3	**7.0**
2.0	2.45	19.0	2.12	**0.3**	-39.2	-0.03	-0.23	2.82	72.6	**4.0**	12.2	9.0	**2.8**
4.6	1.47	8.9	0.42	**7.7**	31.0	1.86	18.47	3.73	57.7	**2.8**	25.1	18.7	**8.7**
1.7	5.54	34.9	2.60	**0.1**	0.0	0.04	0.61	3.29	101.4	**4.7**	21.1	4.6	**2.3**
5.6	1.19	8.6	0.17	**4.3**	2.5	0.76	8.99	3.58	67.7	**2.8**	32.7	18.5	**4.9**
7.7	0.00	0.0	0.00	**7.3**	0.9	1.68	13.40	3.84	45.6	**2.6**	34.7	21.0	**8.3**

	Name	City	State	Rating	2008 Rating	2007 Rating	Total Assets ($Mil)	One Year Asset Growth	Asset Mix (As a % of Total Assets) Comm-ercial Loans	Cons-umer Loans	Home Mort-gages	Secur-ities	Capital-ization Index	Leverage Ratio	Risk-based Capital Ratio
	RECONTRUST CO NA	SIMI VALLEY	CA	**U**	U	U	334	23.12	0.0	0.0	0.0	0.0	**10.0**	86.8	351.0
	RED RIVER BANK	ALEXANDRIA	LA	**B**	B	B	884	11.00	12.7	2.2	15.4	22.4	**6.5**	8.5	14.0
	RED RIVER STATE BK	HALSTAD	MN	**C+**	C+	C+	49	16.07	29.9	29.3	5.0	0.0	**6.1**	9.5	11.9
	REDDING BANK OF	REDDING	CA	**C**	C	D	924	14.44	14.4	0.7	14.6	20.5	**9.5**	11.6	14.6
▼	REDSTONE BANK	CENTENNIAL	CO	**D**	C	C	39	62.54	18.4	1.1	8.4	6.7	**10.0**	21.2	28.5
	REDWOOD CAPITAL BANK	EUREKA	CA	**C+**	C-	C	212	14.02	7.9	1.3	13.5	9.8	**6.1**	8.1	13.0
	REELFOOT BANK	UNION CITY	TN	**C**	C	C-	147	2.23	12.9	7.1	18.3	27.2	**6.5**	8.5	15.5
▲	REGAL BANK	LIVINGSTON	NJ	**D+**	C	C	167	38.11	1.5	0.1	1.7	3.2	**5.2**	8.8	11.1
	REGAL BANK & TRUST	OWINGS MILLS	MD	**D-**	D-	D-	176	0.01	3.7	0.1	10.7	23.6	**6.2**	8.3	13.5
	REGAL FINANCIAL BANK	SEATTLE	WA	**E-**	E-	D	120	-20.26	19.3	0.1	0.4	2.0	**1.1**	5.1	8.1
	REGENT BANK	DAVIE	FL	**D-**	D-	C	475	4.39	10.0	0.3	18.8	7.0	**5.2**	8.2	11.2
	REGENT BANK	NOWATA	OK	**D**	D	D	155	4.16	20.3	2.4	14.4	7.3	**6.8**	8.8	13.2
	REGENT BANK	GREENVILLE	SC	**D-**	C	NR	45	96.33	8.7	1.6	24.6	0.0	**10.0**	16.7	20.9
▲	REGENTS BANK NA	LA JOLLA	CA	**C**	D	C+	322	-6.13	14.1	1.1	3.6	5.9	**10.0**	11.0	18.0
	REGIONAL MISSOURI BANK	MARCELINE	MO	**B**	B	B	122	10.53	6.7	3.8	23.9	17.5	**4.7**	7.5	10.8
	REGIONS BANK	BIRMINGHAM	AL	**D-**	D	C-	128,373	-6.98	11.7	2.1	13.9	17.4	**6.8**	8.9	14.9
	RELIABANK DAKOTA	ESTELLINE	SD	**B**	B	B	202	23.79	15.2	3.1	7.0	8.8	**5.3**	9.0	11.2
	RELIANCE BANK	ATHENS	AL	**D-**	D-	D+	150	3.75	8.9	1.7	11.6	28.1	**8.9**	10.3	19.1
	RELIANCE BANK	FARIBAULT	MN	**D**	D	C-	60	0.75	13.7	0.5	9.5	14.1	**10.0**	12.3	15.9
▼	RELIANCE BANK	FRONTENAC	MO	**E+**	D-	D	1,214	-15.32	6.2	0.2	3.0	18.1	**3.1**	7.3	10.0
▼	RELIANCE BANK FSB	FORT MYERS	FL	**E+**	D	D	88	-16.01	6.0	0.1	18.9	25.2	**5.1**	7.1	12.2
	RELIANCE SB	ALTOONA	PA	**B-**	C+	C+	363	4.93	5.3	2.9	28.5	21.0	**7.2**	9.4	12.7
▼	RELIANT BANK	BRENTWOOD	TN	**E+**	C-	C-	379	-0.74	15.8	2.2	13.0	7.8	**3.9**	7.9	10.4
	RELIANZBANK	WICHITA	KS	**C+**	C-	C-	39	5.64	19.7	1.1	11.4	0.0	**9.5**	10.6	15.6
	RENASANT BANK	TUPELO	MS	**D+**	C-	B-	4,292	18.08	5.9	1.5	13.8	19.0	**6.4**	8.4	14.0
	REPUBLIC BANK	PORT RICHEY	FL	**B-**	B-	B	114	0.52	2.7	0.3	18.2	10.5	**10.0**	13.4	22.7
	REPUBLIC BANK	PHILADELPHIA	PA	**D-**	D	D+	874	-13.18	6.9	0.1	7.6	16.4	**8.2**	9.9	13.5
	REPUBLIC BANK	BOUNTIFUL	UT	**C+**	C	D+	698	11.54	6.8	0.0	0.0	6.1	**9.1**	12.7	14.3
	REPUBLIC BANK & TRUST	NORMAN	OK	**C+**	C+	B-	341	3.31	13.0	2.1	19.1	12.0	**7.1**	9.1	12.6
	REPUBLIC BANK & TRUST CO	LOUISVILLE	KY	**B**	B-	B	3,524	-7.69	2.9	0.6	29.4	15.1	**9.6**	10.8	21.2
▲	REPUBLIC BANK INC	DULUTH	MN	**D**	C-	C+	311	10.76	19.3	1.2	10.7	2.8	**5.9**	8.7	11.7
	REPUBLIC BANK OF CHICAGO	OAK BROOK	IL	**D-**	D-	D-	1,463	9.17	26.5	0.1	4.4	8.5	**5.3**	8.9	11.2
	REPUBLIC BANKING CO	REPUBLIC	OH	**C+**	B	B	38	4.44	4.2	5.1	33.2	11.2	**10.0**	13.3	20.6
	REPUBLICBANKAZ NA	PHOENIX	AZ	**D-**	C	C	56	7.96	14.6	0.9	4.9	0.2	**7.5**	9.3	13.1
▲	RESOURCE BANK	COVINGTON	LA	**B**	C+	C-	379	3.80	5.2	1.7	15.3	8.3	**6.7**	10.0	12.3
▲	RESOURCE BANK NA	DEKALB	IL	**D+**	D+	B+	316	6.70	10.1	0.4	5.4	30.6	**8.0**	9.7	15.2
	RESURGENS BANK	ATLANTA	GA	**C-**	C	C	80	10.31	15.9	2.7	3.9	23.9	**10.0**	12.3	17.9
▼	REUNION BANK OF FLORIDA	TAVARES	FL	**D-**	C	C	125	36.30	12.2	2.0	2.3	22.3	**8.8**	11.0	14.0
▼	REVERE BANK	LAUREL	MD	**D-**	C	C	173	53.87	11.8	0.3	13.7	20.0	**6.0**	8.9	11.7
	REYNOLDS STATE BK	REYNOLDS	IL	**A**	A-	A-	92	3.01	0.6	0.3	0.4	89.4	**10.0**	17.5	34.5
▼	RHINEBECK SB	POUGHKEEPSIE	NY	**D-**	C-	B-	526	7.57	7.2	20.3	11.1	13.8	**8.0**	9.8	13.4
	RICHARDSON COUNTY BANK	FALLS CITY	NE	**A**	A-	A-	95	-3.17	10.1	4.7	10.2	30.8	**10.0**	13.6	24.3
	RICHLAND COUNTY BANK	RICHLAND CENTER	WI	**B**	B+	A-	106	-2.46	4.5	6.1	17.7	42.9	**10.0**	19.8	40.9
▲	RICHLAND STATE BK	RAYVILLE	LA	**A-**	B+	B+	211	1.50	10.8	4.1	10.1	33.8	**8.7**	10.1	17.2
	RICHLAND STATE BK	BRUCE	SD	**A-**	A-	A-	32	0.70	1.2	4.0	3.4	48.7	**10.0**	23.9	54.2
	RICHTON BANK & TRUST CO	RICHTON	MS	**B-**	C+	C+	80	6.03	3.5	5.9	18.5	33.6	**9.0**	10.4	18.2
	RICHWOOD BANKING CO	RICHWOOD	OH	**C+**	B-	B-	325	14.60	2.7	1.1	11.3	45.0	**5.8**	7.8	13.2
	RIDDELL NATIONAL BK	BRAZIL	IN	**C-**	C+	B-	168	3.76	9.6	8.2	35.4	16.4	**5.7**	7.7	12.0
	RIDGESTONE BANK	BROOKFIELD	WI	**D-**	D	D+	464	-0.65	19.8	0.0	1.1	6.7	**7.2**	9.2	12.6
	RIDGEWOOD SB	RIDGEWOOD	NY	**C+**	C-	B-	4,561	3.97	0.1	0.1	36.2	37.2	**10.0**	12.3	22.0
▼	RILEY STATE BK OF RILEY K	RILEY	KS	**C+**	B	B	70	55.61	12.2	5.8	10.1	22.4	**7.2**	9.2	13.8
▼	RIO BANK	MCALLEN	TX	**D-**	C+	C+	204	4.07	17.2	2.4	7.0	19.8	**7.1**	9.1	14.1
	RIO GRANDE SAVINGS & LOAN	MONTE VISTA	CO	**C-**	C	C+	97	4.80	0.8	3.1	65.3	0.0	**8.7**	10.1	18.5
	RIPLEY FSB	RIPLEY	OH	**D-**	D-	D-	76	-12.73	2.7	1.3	43.8	0.4	**7.7**	9.5	14.3
	RIVER BANK	STODDARD	WI	**C+**	B	B	391	8.97	8.4	1.2	14.0	8.3	**7.8**	10.0	13.2
▲	RIVER BANK & TRUST	PRATTVILLE	AL	**C**	C-	C-	361	18.96	13.3	2.9	7.1	17.7	**7.9**	9.6	15.4
	RIVER CITIES BANK	WISCONSIN RAPIDS	WI	**C-**	C-	C	188	0.45	5.9	0.4	9.3	18.7	**9.8**	10.9	15.3
▲	RIVER CITY BANK	SACRAMENTO	CA	**C-**	D	C-	1,026	-0.56	5.9	0.9	11.2	35.3	**8.5**	10.0	17.4
	RIVER CITY BANK	ROME	GA	**D-**	D-	C-	220	-3.41	6.4	0.9	11.3	11.2	**10.0**	11.2	16.5
	RIVER CITY BANK INC	LOUISVILLE	KY	**A-**	B+	A-	262	7.82	1.7	1.0	43.1	25.5	**10.0**	16.0	36.6

Asset Quality Index	Non-Performing Loans as a % of Total Loans	Non-Performing Loans as a % of Capital	Net Charge-offs Avg Loans	Profitability Index	Net Income ($Mil)	Return on Assets (R.O.A.)	Return on Equity (R.O.E.)	Net Interest Spread	Overhead Efficiency Ratio	Liquidity Index	Liquidity Ratio	Hot Money Ratio	Stability Index
10.0	0.00	0.0	0.00	**9.5**	53.1	16.63	20.58	0.26	55.9	**5.0**	610.1	101.0	**3.0**
7.9	0.05	0.4	0.12	**5.3**	8.6	1.02	11.94	3.85	64.6	**1.9**	27.3	24.4	**5.9**
5.2	0.28	2.2	0.56	**7.0**	0.7	1.58	15.72	4.58	57.1	**0.8**	19.8	42.3	**5.0**
2.4	3.23	17.2	1.78	**3.7**	6.5	0.75	6.41	4.13	45.8	**0.9**	18.5	36.1	**6.3**
8.9	0.00	0.0	0.00	**0.0**	-1.0	-3.35	-11.48	3.71	183.5	**1.8**	27.7	26.0	**1.5**
6.0	0.45	3.3	0.10	**4.9**	2.3	1.13	13.89	4.28	62.1	**2.0**	27.4	22.8	**4.0**
4.3	0.54	3.3	0.11	**3.1**	0.6	0.39	4.34	4.30	82.9	**3.2**	34.9	17.3	**4.1**
7.4	0.03	0.3	0.00	**2.2**	1.9	1.36	15.58	3.56	80.7	**1.8**	20.7	22.3	**3.0**
0.0	9.91	65.5	2.82	**0.0**	-2.4	-1.34	-13.89	3.93	86.6	**1.2**	17.8	29.8	**3.4**
0.0	10.86	105.3	2.58	**0.0**	-6.0	-4.33	-86.14	3.03	312.0	**1.1**	21.6	33.1	**1.5**
0.0	5.76	49.0	3.40	**0.9**	-2.2	-0.48	-5.13	4.14	74.7	**0.6**	9.6	45.8	**4.6**
2.5	1.62	13.1	0.62	**1.5**	0.3	0.19	1.74	3.94	81.5	**0.9**	15.7	33.4	**3.8**
8.2	0.00	0.0	0.00	**0.0**	-0.7	-2.04	-8.41	3.43	167.1	**0.9**	20.0	37.2	**0.0**
3.4	1.54	7.8	0.71	**2.9**	0.6	0.17	1.69	4.10	69.1	**4.4**	34.8	11.3	**4.8**
6.2	0.18	1.7	0.10	**6.3**	1.6	1.34	15.78	3.90	61.9	**1.3**	9.0	25.4	**6.1**
0.0	4.77	28.5	3.17	**0.0**	-251.7	-0.18	-1.47	3.10	63.6	**3.6**	12.8	11.1	**6.7**
5.4	1.04	8.3	0.10	**6.1**	2.1	1.21	14.17	4.36	62.1	**3.2**	17.9	13.2	**6.3**
5.3	1.02	4.3	0.57	**0.0**	-1.2	-0.79	-7.65	2.62	116.4	**2.0**	38.5	33.8	**3.5**
2.9	3.64	18.8	1.95	**0.0**	-0.6	-1.04	-7.72	3.91	72.3	**1.6**	20.6	25.1	**2.0**
0.0	15.33	115.5	2.89	**0.0**	-31.6	-2.38	-26.92	3.09	67.0	**2.2**	8.8	17.6	**3.9**
0.0	19.67	93.9	11.23	**0.0**	-12.0	-12.69	-73.06	2.96	454.1	**2.8**	34.2	19.2	**0.2**
4.2	0.76	5.3	0.05	**4.0**	2.5	0.70	6.71	3.60	77.2	**2.1**	12.9	18.3	**5.7**
1.7	5.42	43.0	1.00	**0.0**	-2.6	-0.68	-7.35	3.62	86.3	**1.5**	7.9	22.3	**1.3**
7.3	0.00	0.0	0.01	**3.9**	0.4	0.94	8.74	4.50	70.7	**0.8**	20.5	44.1	**4.7**
1.5	2.76	18.1	1.00	**4.6**	33.7	0.86	6.82	3.34	60.8	**1.8**	20.2	22.6	**8.1**
2.1	3.37	13.5	1.87	**2.5**	-3.1	-2.53	-11.40	3.04	151.3	**2.8**	38.0	20.3	**7.5**
0.0	6.45	40.0	2.73	**0.0**	-9.4	-1.00	-10.50	3.69	99.3	**2.4**	17.4	17.4	**4.6**
3.0	1.34	9.0	0.84	**9.3**	17.9	2.76	24.10	4.93	24.6	**0.2**	8.0	95.4	**8.0**
4.6	1.61	11.5	0.22	**6.4**	5.3	1.62	17.50	4.96	73.8	**1.8**	24.7	23.2	**5.0**
5.3	1.24	7.3	0.75	**9.8**	68.6	2.02	20.55	4.76	50.0	**1.8**	27.8	36.9	**6.5**
0.7	2.12	17.8	0.35	**3.8**	2.4	0.81	9.07	4.38	62.7	**1.1**	16.7	31.8	**3.8**
0.0	8.65	68.1	1.77	**4.1**	4.0	0.28	2.87	3.99	63.2	**1.3**	11.4	26.9	**8.2**
2.4	5.00	27.9	0.12	**4.8**	0.3	0.89	6.78	4.06	60.0	**1.4**	11.4	24.5	**7.3**
7.0	0.19	1.3	0.00	**0.2**	-0.4	-0.69	-6.88	4.54	98.4	**0.8**	18.8	38.1	**1.5**
5.9	0.00	0.0	0.07	**5.5**	3.8	1.00	10.28	4.96	67.6	**1.6**	6.5	20.8	**5.9**
1.7	4.54	24.4	1.09	**2.5**	1.6	0.51	4.96	3.74	86.2	**2.4**	21.0	17.7	**5.9**
8.3	0.00	0.0	-0.01	**2.0**	0.3	0.43	3.50	3.50	82.2	**3.8**	34.9	14.3	**3.7**
6.0	0.00	0.0	0.00	**0.0**	-0.4	-0.38	-2.75	3.29	116.5	**2.1**	31.6	25.5	**0.8**
8.1	0.23	1.8	0.22	**0.0**	-1.2	-0.79	-7.52	3.29	104.5	**1.2**	18.6	29.5	**0.8**
9.6	8.02	2.8	1.58	**8.3**	2.2	2.34	13.10	4.42	25.0	**6.6**	101.0	10.8	**9.0**
0.0	3.52	24.3	0.34	**4.5**	3.6	0.71	7.40	4.98	71.0	**2.6**	11.9	15.9	**6.3**
8.7	0.40	1.4	0.40	**7.7**	1.3	1.39	10.05	3.87	48.8	**3.9**	46.5	16.5	**8.9**
8.3	0.90	2.1	0.16	**4.5**	0.7	0.63	3.09	3.55	62.1	**5.9**	62.0	10.7	**8.0**
7.8	0.57	2.6	-0.24	**6.0**	2.9	1.42	13.58	5.08	71.0	**2.9**	38.6	20.1	**6.4**
9.0	0.00	0.0	-0.02	**4.3**	0.3	0.86	3.52	3.39	80.2	**4.1**	80.3	22.1	**9.2**
7.6	0.11	0.4	0.98	**4.5**	0.6	0.72	8.04	4.10	84.2	**3.7**	27.6	12.2	**5.1**
7.0	0.22	1.2	0.21	**4.4**	2.9	0.92	12.43	3.86	67.8	**1.5**	18.7	25.7	**3.5**
2.0	2.64	22.6	0.12	**4.2**	1.3	0.75	9.55	3.71	68.7	**2.1**	12.1	18.3	**4.2**
0.0	9.78	69.0	3.44	**2.0**	0.2	0.05	0.47	3.47	49.5	**0.6**	9.7	42.8	**5.8**
5.4	1.88	8.3	0.23	**2.8**	14.3	0.32	2.49	2.92	76.5	**4.7**	44.5	14.9	**8.3**
7.8	0.06	0.4	0.06	**4.4**	0.5	0.86	8.66	4.08	75.2	**1.6**	8.4	21.3	**5.5**
0.3	8.60	54.6	0.27	**3.8**	1.2	0.59	6.66	4.79	76.1	**4.3**	25.0	8.1	**4.3**
7.3	0.33	2.5	0.02	**2.6**	0.3	0.27	2.61	4.01	85.4	**1.1**	17.3	30.5	**5.7**
0.0	9.18	64.2	0.67	**0.5**	-0.2	-0.28	-3.35	3.00	109.8	**1.7**	12.0	20.2	**3.4**
3.3	0.85	6.6	-0.04	**8.2**	7.3	1.97	17.44	4.12	44.8	**1.1**	10.8	29.4	**7.6**
6.7	0.42	2.4	0.89	**3.0**	1.2	0.38	4.09	4.00	67.7	**2.0**	33.3	27.7	**4.0**
1.7	1.91	10.2	0.44	**4.8**	1.7	0.91	8.46	3.86	53.0	**1.5**	25.8	28.0	**6.0**
4.2	0.50	2.1	1.29	**2.2**	5.2	0.51	5.26	4.11	66.3	**4.8**	30.2	10.9	**6.6**
1.1	3.63	20.8	1.91	**0.2**	0.1	0.02	0.22	3.19	78.0	**1.5**	21.5	26.4	**2.2**
5.8	1.66	5.6	0.40	**6.6**	3.4	1.32	8.47	4.68	61.2	**5.9**	46.6	6.2	**7.1**

Name	City	State	Rating	2008 Rating	2007 Rating	Total Assets ($Mil)	One Year Asset Growth	Comm-ercial Loans	Cons-umer Loans	Home Mort-gages	Secur-ities	Capital-ization Index	Leverage Ratio	Risk-based Capital Ratio
								Asset Mix (As a % of Total Assets)						
RIVER COMMUNITY BANK NA	MARTINSVILLE	VA	**D+**	D-	C-	97	3.48	23.4	2.6	21.0	6.1	**6.7**	8.7	13.1
RIVER FALLS STATE BK	RIVER FALLS	WI	**B**	B+	B+	84	4.97	1.3	2.3	24.8	38.8	**10.0**	15.5	29.2
RIVER TOWN BANK	DARDANELLE	AR	**C+**	C+	B	176	2.02	3.8	7.4	27.6	3.3	**8.6**	10.1	15.0
▲ RIVER VALLEY BANK	WAUSAU	WI	**C-**	C+	C+	956	0.42	15.3	0.5	16.8	10.5	**7.0**	9.1	12.5
RIVER VALLEY COMMUNITY	YUBA CITY	CA	**B**	C+	C	136	24.40	3.5	0.2	3.4	47.6	**10.0**	12.5	22.8
RIVER VALLEY FINANCIAL BA	MADISON	IN	**C-**	C+	B-	386	-2.39	4.0	1.0	27.0	19.6	**8.1**	9.7	14.9
RIVERBANK	WYOMING	MN	**E-**	E-	D-	432	-10.05	9.3	2.3	13.3	7.2	**0.5**	4.7	7.0
▼ RIVERBANK	SPOKANE	WA	**D**	C-	D+	140	-8.52	12.4	1.4	13.1	3.4	**5.6**	8.5	11.5
RIVERBEND BANK	FORT WORTH	TX	**C-**	C-	A-	41	-7.92	12.0	4.4	8.3	0.1	**7.9**	9.6	15.2
RIVERHILLS BANK	PORT GIBSON	MS	**B+**	B	B	236	7.74	9.8	2.5	18.1	17.9	**6.6**	8.6	13.7
▼ RIVERHILLS BANK	MILFORD	OH	**D**	C-	C-	129	1.63	9.2	19.2	11.9	7.1	**4.4**	7.6	10.7
RIVERLAND BANK	JORDAN	MN	**E-**	E	D	35	-22.30	13.6	2.8	8.7	8.2	**0.5**	4.2	7.1
RIVERSIDE BANK	SPARKMAN	AR	**C+**	C+	B-	57	3.31	15.1	4.9	52.5	4.0	**5.4**	7.7	11.3
RIVERSIDE BANK	POUGHKEEPSIE	NY	**B-**	B-	B	185	7.97	41.8	0.4	0.3	4.6	**8.8**	10.5	14.0
RIVERSIDE COMMUNITY BANK	ROCKFORD	IL	**C-**	C-	C	290	2.39	11.5	1.4	8.0	37.1	**6.1**	8.1	13.8
RIVERVIEW COMMUNITY BANK	VANCOUVER	WA	**D-**	D-	C-	799	-3.52	5.9	0.3	12.2	1.1	**9.3**	11.4	14.4
▼ RIVERVIEW NATIONAL BK	MARYSVILLE	PA	**C-**	C	C-	275	8.87	3.9	0.8	26.5	17.7	**6.4**	8.4	15.1
RIVERWOOD BANK	BAXTER	MN	**D-**	D-	C-	164	-7.70	14.3	10.2	15.4	1.6	**6.0**	9.0	11.8
RIVERWOOD BANK	BEMIDJI	MN	**D-**	D+	C	169	0.82	5.6	6.8	19.5	5.3	**6.3**	8.3	13.7
▲ ROANOKE RAPIDS SB SSB	ROANOKE RAPIDS	NC	**C+**	C-	C-	56	-2.07	0.0	7.6	34.9	9.2	**10.0**	14.1	20.5
ROANOKE VALLEY SB SSB	ROANOKE RAPIDS	NC	**C-**	C	C	43	1.49	0.0	0.7	36.9	4.1	**10.0**	22.1	46.3
ROBERT LEE STATE BK	ROBERT LEE	TX	**C**	C	C	47	-4.45	3.8	8.8	12.4	41.1	**9.3**	10.5	21.4
ROBERTS COUNTY NB OF	SISSETON	SD	**A-**	A-	A-	49	-8.23	1.7	1.2	2.9	65.4	**10.0**	17.1	43.3
ROBERTSON BANKING CO	DEMOPOLIS	AL	**B-**	B+	B	234	-0.87	6.3	3.6	21.0	13.9	**8.4**	9.9	14.7
ROCHELLE STATE BK	ROCHELLE	GA	**C+**	C	C+	23	7.33	4.4	6.9	6.0	40.8	**10.0**	16.4	35.9
▼ ROCHESTER STATE BK	ROCHESTER	IL	**B**	B+	A-	68	13.00	4.9	5.2	11.6	49.7	**10.0**	14.1	26.0
▼ ROCK BRANCH COMMUNITY	NITRO	WV	**C**	C	C	72	10.67	8.7	7.6	36.6	15.9	**6.5**	8.6	16.0
▲ ROCK SPRINGS NATIONAL BK	ROCK SPRINGS	WY	**C+**	B-	B+	337	4.73	5.5	2.2	11.5	55.8	**6.5**	8.5	22.2
ROCKEFELLER TRUST CO NA	NEW YORK	NY	**U**	U	NR	9	5.66	0.0	0.0	0.0	86.0	**10.0**	85.5	520.3
ROCKFORD BANK & TRUST	ROCKFORD	IL	**C**	C-	C-	271	1.72	19.9	1.0	10.6	16.0	**10.0**	11.3	15.8
ROCKHOLD BROWN & CO	BAINBRIDGE	OH	**D-**	D-	D+	40	-5.40	4.6	2.3	35.7	8.0	**6.3**	8.3	14.4
ROCKLAND SAVINGS BANK	ROCKLAND	ME	**B-**	C+	B-	80	10.47	3.4	5.8	49.6	1.0	**10.0**	13.6	18.8
ROCKLAND TRUST CO	ROCKLAND	MA	**B-**	B-	B	4,702	4.83	11.8	1.4	17.5	12.3	**5.8**	7.8	11.9
ROCKPORT NATIONAL BK	ROCKPORT	MA	**C+**	C+	C+	166	5.00	5.5	1.5	34.2	11.6	**5.3**	7.3	12.6
ROCKVILLE BANK	SOUTH WINDSOR	CT	**B-**	C+	C	1,677	6.81	7.2	0.4	35.3	8.4	**7.1**	9.1	12.7
▼ ROCKWOOD BANK	EUREKA	MO	**D**	D	B	295	-6.68	4.2	1.3	16.4	4.4	**9.3**	10.8	14.4
ROCKY MOUNTAIN BANK	BILLINGS	MT	**C-**	D+	C	418	-11.06	6.7	1.1	8.8	30.9	**8.5**	10.0	15.7
▼ ROCKY MOUNTAIN BANK	WILSON	WY	**E**	D-	D	287	-15.32	6.1	1.9	12.7	3.5	**2.4**	5.3	9.4
ROCKY MOUNTAIN BANK &	FLORENCE	CO	**E-**	D-	D+	138	-20.42	2.7	0.1	7.4	56.2	**2.0**	6.8	9.0
▲ ROEBLING BANK	ROEBLING	NJ	**D+**	D	C	165	-2.79	0.4	0.2	48.3	25.3	**6.4**	8.4	15.1
ROLETTE STATE BK	ROLETTE	ND	**C**	C+	C+	32	-12.54	14.7	6.1	5.2	12.0	**7.1**	9.1	12.8
ROLFE STATE BK	ROLFE	IA	**B**	B-	B-	39	5.72	10.0	2.3	6.4	32.6	**9.3**	10.5	16.4
ROLLING HILLS BANK & TRUS	ATLANTIC	IA	**C+**	C+	B	189	3.26	11.8	1.5	4.7	1.5	**6.5**	9.1	12.1
ROLLSTONE BANK & TRUST	FITCHBURG	MA	**C+**	C+	C+	516	6.96	5.0	0.5	34.3	31.6	**7.1**	9.0	14.8
ROMA BANK	ROBBINSVILLE	NJ	**C+**	B-	B	1,680	38.03	2.1	3.1	27.9	40.3	**8.5**	10.0	18.4
ROMASIA BANK	MONMOUTH JUNCTION	NJ	**D**	C	C+	125	37.54	1.3	0.0	10.4	56.8	**7.7**	9.4	19.5
ROME SAVINGS BANK	ROME	NY	**B+**	B+	A-	328	-0.76	9.3	6.5	44.2	4.3	**10.0**	17.6	25.4
RONDOUT SB	KINGSTON	NY	**B-**	B-	B-	230	-0.69	6.6	0.5	36.2	19.3	**10.0**	11.8	17.1
ROOT RIVER STATE BK	CHATFIELD	MN	**B**	B-	C	60	0.34	7.6	1.2	17.0	17.7	**10.0**	11.8	19.0
ROSCOE STATE BK	ROSCOE	TX	**B**	B	B-	113	4.21	5.0	4.0	4.0	61.5	**6.6**	8.7	20.9
ROSE HILL BANK	ROSE HILL	KS	**B+**	B+	A-	242	9.02	4.0	8.4	24.3	29.7	**8.0**	9.7	16.3
ROSEDALE FS&LA	BALTIMORE	MD	**A-**	A+	A+	734	12.99	0.0	0.1	47.1	21.8	**10.0**	21.2	39.4
ROSELLE SB	ROSELLE	NJ	**C+**	C+	C+	411	1.35	0.0	0.1	19.6	66.5	**10.0**	14.6	55.7
ROSEMOUNT NATIONAL BK	ROSEMOUNT	MN	**E-**	E-	D-	38	-5.17	9.9	2.3	4.6	9.0	**0.0**	1.9	4.2
ROUND TOP STATE BK	ROUND TOP	TX	**B+**	B+	B+	318	6.33	3.6	3.3	14.7	44.9	**6.9**	8.9	19.5
▼ ROUNDBANK	WASECA	MN	**D+**	B-	B-	313	37.02	12.1	2.0	19.4	15.8	**7.0**	9.3	12.5
▼ ROWLEY SB	ROWLEY	IA	**D+**	C-	C-	13	3.29	9.4	7.2	21.3	0.3	**6.6**	8.6	19.2
ROXBORO SB SSB	ROXBORO	NC	**B-**	C-	B	183	0.26	0.9	1.0	35.1	36.6	**10.0**	15.6	30.1
▲ ROXBURY BANK	ROXBURY	KS	**D-**	E-	C+	16	-14.20	9.1	2.0	17.7	18.6	**7.2**	9.1	14.5
ROYAL ASIAN BANK	PHILADELPHIA	PA	**D-**	D	D+	88	-14.05	11.0	1.0	2.3	15.4	**9.8**	11.0	14.8

Asset Quality Index	Non-Performing Loans as a % of Total Loans	Non-Performing Loans as a % of Capital	Net Charge-offs / Avg Loans	Profitability Index	Net Income ($Mil)	Return on Assets (R.O.A.)	Return on Equity (R.O.E.)	Net Interest Spread	Overhead Efficiency Ratio	Liquidity Index	Liquidity Ratio	Hot Money Ratio	Stability Index
2.9	1.37	11.8	1.31	**3.8**	0.9	0.98	10.62	4.62	65.5	**0.7**	8.7	34.9	**3.9**
6.4	1.91	5.9	0.83	**4.3**	0.7	0.87	5.46	3.60	70.1	**4.8**	52.0	13.0	**7.9**
3.5	1.49	10.3	0.29	**5.6**	1.6	0.95	9.24	4.68	63.7	**1.5**	16.6	24.8	**6.3**
2.0	2.33	17.4	1.07	**4.4**	7.7	0.79	7.27	4.68	64.4	**2.3**	11.0	16.9	**7.6**
7.3	0.01	0.0	0.71	**4.5**	1.0	0.87	6.47	4.02	56.7	**5.6**	67.0	12.8	**5.8**
1.8	3.48	23.3	0.53	**3.7**	2.6	0.66	6.95	3.20	60.8	**2.1**	26.7	20.8	**4.7**
0.0	11.44	119.5	3.07	**0.0**	-7.8	-1.69	-30.57	3.14	93.6	**1.4**	5.2	23.3	**1.3**
1.1	3.86	29.2	1.28	**0.5**	-1.0	-0.70	-7.64	4.36	70.7	**0.7**	14.4	41.2	**1.5**
7.3	0.00	0.0	0.05	**0.3**	-0.5	-1.23	-11.72	4.46	110.3	**3.7**	27.7	12.5	**6.9**
7.2	0.48	3.4	0.21	**6.2**	3.3	1.41	15.96	3.67	55.2	**1.1**	15.7	31.1	**6.2**
1.1	1.02	9.4	1.28	**3.1**	0.5	0.38	4.94	3.95	71.1	**1.2**	10.7	27.8	**3.7**
0.3	3.14	25.7	2.12	**0.0**	-1.8	-4.17	-64.46	2.94	177.0	**0.9**	25.2	49.5	**0.0**
3.2	1.78	17.9	0.30	**10.0**	1.6	2.80	35.28	5.20	47.6	**0.5**	2.5	42.6	**6.5**
4.7	1.09	7.1	0.48	**4.5**	1.2	0.67	6.30	4.52	64.5	**1.6**	20.1	24.4	**5.5**
1.9	4.27	25.1	1.11	**2.1**	1.0	0.34	3.94	4.17	68.6	**4.2**	23.0	8.2	**4.3**
0.4	2.26	14.2	1.58	**1.6**	-0.4	-0.04	-0.35	4.89	77.9	**1.3**	7.0	25.0	**6.6**
2.5	2.42	16.6	0.61	**3.2**	1.4	0.51	5.33	3.70	68.6	**2.9**	20.7	15.0	**5.1**
0.0	6.34	46.1	0.51	**0.2**	-2.5	-1.42	-11.96	3.91	103.9	**1.7**	10.4	20.5	**5.0**
0.0	4.71	35.6	0.03	**1.4**	-0.4	-0.24	-2.09	2.89	82.4	**1.7**	27.7	27.8	**5.2**
8.0	0.38	2.1	0.44	**2.8**	0.2	0.32	2.30	4.01	78.3	**2.6**	17.1	16.4	**6.5**
9.1	1.61	3.6	0.00	**1.3**	0.1	0.16	0.72	2.14	99.3	**2.4**	53.1	35.9	**7.7**
8.8	0.17	0.6	-0.12	**2.6**	0.2	0.34	3.33	3.69	90.9	**2.0**	30.6	26.4	**4.9**
9.6	0.00	0.0	0.00	**6.9**	0.8	1.55	8.30	3.60	55.2	**6.6**	78.0	7.3	**9.1**
4.5	1.48	9.9	0.73	**5.5**	2.9	1.22	12.07	4.30	58.4	**1.3**	17.3	27.8	**6.9**
8.8	0.17	0.3	0.21	**3.2**	0.2	0.67	3.96	3.67	86.6	**3.1**	63.3	25.0	**7.9**
8.9	1.24	2.5	0.11	**3.9**	0.4	0.67	4.53	3.53	76.7	**6.2**	70.4	9.1	**7.4**
2.5	2.31	17.7	0.06	**5.0**	0.7	1.02	11.54	4.42	66.8	**1.0**	27.2	49.1	**4.8**
3.8	3.25	12.2	1.39	**4.6**	3.6	1.09	12.46	4.22	59.5	**3.1**	32.6	16.8	**5.9**
10.0	0.00	0.0	0.00	**9.5**	0.4	3.97	4.59	0.23	90.7	**5.0**	556.1	101.0	**6.2**
3.3	2.97	17.6	0.62	**1.7**	0.8	0.29	2.64	3.15	78.9	**1.1**	9.0	29.0	**4.5**
0.3	5.53	41.8	0.55	**1.2**	0.0	-0.10	-1.20	4.18	90.6	**4.1**	19.7	8.6	**4.3**
5.5	0.77	4.5	0.82	**3.2**	0.4	0.51	3.68	4.16	69.6	**1.1**	9.6	28.9	**6.3**
4.3	0.63	5.7	0.43	**4.9**	42.6	0.93	9.03	4.10	66.5	**4.3**	9.8	6.4	**7.8**
4.4	1.12	10.0	0.11	**5.3**	1.4	0.82	11.72	5.03	70.0	**4.5**	21.8	6.4	**4.5**
6.1	0.79	6.7	0.17	**4.6**	12.6	0.78	8.27	3.55	62.8	**2.4**	12.9	17.2	**7.5**
0.7	3.50	19.7	1.94	**1.1**	0.3	0.09	0.78	3.93	59.1	**2.4**	12.9	17.0	**4.7**
0.3	8.69	46.0	2.53	**1.9**	1.3	0.29	2.71	3.93	66.9	**3.4**	29.1	14.4	**5.0**
0.0	16.52	114.2	5.05	**0.0**	-22.2	-6.89	-84.80	2.96	141.2	**0.9**	26.4	55.9	**4.0**
0.3	22.56	85.8	3.75	**2.9**	0.5	0.31	8.34	3.64	86.6	**1.3**	32.2	63.5	**0.0**
1.9	3.09	23.2	0.01	**1.4**	0.0	-0.01	-0.08	3.41	88.7	**4.2**	29.7	10.7	**2.8**
7.9	0.14	1.0	0.01	**3.5**	0.2	0.61	6.99	3.74	85.6	**2.2**	13.6	17.8	**4.6**
4.0	0.68	3.7	0.71	**6.6**	0.5	1.37	13.12	4.74	65.3	**5.5**	42.0	7.2	**6.9**
3.3	0.10	0.7	-0.10	**3.9**	1.3	0.71	5.60	4.05	69.3	**4.4**	21.2	7.0	**5.6**
4.7	1.07	6.7	0.07	**3.4**	2.9	0.57	6.12	3.10	71.2	**2.3**	35.8	26.0	**5.9**
3.1	4.75	23.5	0.00	**2.8**	3.9	0.27	2.11	3.20	74.3	**5.0**	48.3	14.6	**7.6**
9.2	0.00	0.0	0.00	**0.9**	-0.1	-0.11	-0.95	2.73	98.9	**3.7**	67.9	28.2	**0.0**
5.4	1.13	5.0	0.51	**4.3**	3.4	1.03	6.18	4.50	62.3	**4.0**	12.2	8.4	**8.3**
5.3	2.19	11.8	0.18	**3.4**	1.1	0.46	3.85	4.08	77.7	**2.8**	13.8	14.9	**6.9**
6.4	0.86	4.5	0.31	**3.6**	0.3	0.51	4.17	4.65	78.5	**4.7**	32.4	8.6	**6.4**
9.0	0.00	0.0	0.05	**4.5**	1.3	1.16	10.79	4.28	80.0	**3.0**	38.9	19.9	**6.5**
5.9	0.51	3.2	0.19	**6.2**	2.7	1.13	11.49	4.77	60.9	**1.4**	26.4	31.0	**6.1**
8.8	1.05	3.4	0.00	**5.2**	8.4	1.20	5.53	3.62	41.5	**4.1**	38.0	13.9	**9.0**
9.3	2.00	2.8	0.00	**2.8**	1.3	0.32	2.06	2.12	71.1	**4.5**	81.8	20.9	**7.5**
0.2	9.36	150.4	4.70	**0.0**	-1.8	-4.80	-90.18	3.37	202.1	**5.6**	37.3	4.9	**1.5**
9.1	0.06	0.3	0.25	**7.1**	4.1	1.34	14.26	3.55	49.6	**2.9**	50.0	29.2	**6.1**
0.3	7.60	53.4	0.82	**7.8**	8.9	3.34	34.53	4.39	39.0	**1.4**	11.9	24.8	**5.7**
6.0	1.66	8.1	0.00	**3.4**	0.1	0.62	7.47	3.78	83.9	**6.2**	56.3	3.4	**3.0**
7.4	1.35	4.4	0.32	**4.0**	1.9	1.02	6.61	3.34	58.1	**2.8**	47.2	28.6	**7.1**
1.2	5.56	30.9	2.32	**0.8**	-0.5	-2.49	-31.10	3.79	152.6	**3.1**	13.2	13.2	**4.5**
0.1	4.44	26.9	0.00	**0.0**	-0.7	-0.69	-5.46	N/,	4,790.5	**1.6**	34.5	41.1	**2.3**

	Name	City	State	Rating	2008 Rating	2007 Rating	Total Assets ($Mil)	One Year Asset Growth	Asset Mix (As a % of Total Assets) Comm-ercial Loans	Cons-umer Loans	Home Mort-gages	Secur-ities	Capital-ization Index	Leverage Ratio	Risk-based Capital Ratio
	ROYAL BANK	ELROY	WI	**B-**	B-	C+	231	2.64	12.2	4.7	17.5	22.8	**6.5**	8.5	12.5
	ROYAL BANK AMERICA	NARBERTH	PA	**D-**	D-	D-	988	-18.10	8.0	0.1	3.0	31.5	**9.3**	10.5	17.2
▲	ROYAL BANKS OF MISSOURI	UNIVERSITY CITY	MO	**C+**	C-	C-	460	0.37	5.9	1.5	8.2	12.7	**7.3**	9.4	12.8
▼	ROYAL BUSINESS BANK	LOS ANGELES	CA	**D+**	C	C	301	67.58	18.3	0.0	4.1	17.9	**10.0**	21.0	29.2
▼	ROYAL PALM BANK OF FLORID	NAPLES	FL	**E-**	D+	D	119	-21.23	7.3	0.4	16.3	6.8	**0.5**	3.7	6.9
	ROYAL SB	CHICAGO	IL	**D**	D	D	89	-1.22	4.4	0.1	30.6	20.1	**10.0**	15.3	25.1
	RSI BANK	RAHWAY	NJ	**B-**	C	C	479	1.18	1.3	0.2	37.8	42.7	**10.0**	14.7	31.8
	RUBY VALLEY NATIONAL BK	TWIN BRIDGES	MT	**B-**	B-	B+	75	2.95	16.0	3.6	12.1	9.8	**10.0**	13.6	18.7
	RUMSON-FAIR HAVEN BANK &	RUMSON	NJ	**D+**	C-	C-	198	17.60	6.0	0.1	5.1	47.2	**6.1**	8.2	12.6
	RURAL AMERICAN BANK	BRAHAM	MN	**D+**	C-	C	109	4.65	6.0	3.0	23.1	37.6	**7.4**	9.3	17.2
▲	RURAL AMERICAN BANK-LUCK	LUCK	WI	**D+**	D+	C	55	-1.66	4.4	2.3	24.0	30.8	**5.2**	7.2	12.6
	RUSHFORD STATE BK	RUSHFORD	MN	**D+**	C-	D+	47	3.44	6.4	6.8	17.5	15.0	**5.0**	7.4	11.0
	RUSHVILLE STATE BK	RUSHVILLE	IL	**A-**	A	A	82	3.17	5.8	3.9	5.8	60.4	**10.0**	14.0	33.3
	RUSHVILLE STATE BK	RUSHVILLE	MO	**D-**	D	D+	29	3.63	8.4	4.0	30.4	21.6	**5.6**	7.6	16.1
▼	RUTH STATE BK	RUTH	MI	**D+**	C	B	32	0.46	5.9	1.2	11.3	39.8	**7.6**	9.4	21.8
	S&T BANK	INDIANA	PA	**D+**	D+	B-	4,098	-1.19	14.5	1.8	16.2	6.8	**5.6**	7.6	12.5
	S-BANK	WEYMOUTH	MA	**C**	C-	C	216	0.77	11.1	0.3	41.2	16.6	**5.4**	7.4	12.7
	SABADELL UNITED BANK NA	MIAMI	FL	**C-**	D-	C	2,357	28.97	8.1	1.0	5.6	31.4	**4.2**	6.2	12.3
	SABAL PALM BANK	SARASOTA	FL	**D-**	D-	D	87	-7.40	7.1	0.4	4.2	33.0	**6.3**	8.3	15.1
	SABINE STATE BK & TRUST C	MANY	LA	**C+**	C+	C+	686	5.42	7.7	4.2	7.6	22.8	**3.6**	6.6	10.3
▼	SACO & BIDDEFORD SAVINGS	SACO	ME	**D+**	C	C	752	0.83	1.2	0.8	50.1	15.5	**8.3**	9.9	16.9
	SACRAMENTO DEPOSIT BANK	SACRAMENTO	KY	**B+**	B+	B+	62	1.36	4.4	9.0	19.6	32.5	**10.0**	12.0	20.4
▲	SADDLE RIVER VALLEY BANK	SADDLE RIVER	NJ	**D**	D+	C	82	1.96	6.1	0.1	7.8	28.7	**10.0**	20.2	31.7
▲	SAEHAN BANK	LOS ANGELES	CA	**D-**	E-	D	590	-11.63	14.6	1.3	1.5	7.9	**8.8**	10.2	14.5
	SAFRA NATIONAL BK OF NEW	NEW YORK	NY	**B-**	B-	B-	4,134	9.73	27.2	2.9	1.1	9.9	**10.0**	12.9	26.4
	SAGE CAPITAL BANK NA	GONZALES	TX	**B-**	B-	B	251	2.95	6.7	2.2	6.9	24.1	**7.0**	9.0	15.2
▲	SAIGON NATIONAL BK	WESTMINSTER	CA	**D**	E-	D-	62	-4.01	4.4	0.0	4.4	7.3	**10.0**	12.3	18.9
	SAINT CASIMIRS SB	BALTIMORE	MD	**C-**	C+	C+	105	-2.43	0.0	0.1	15.0	57.6	**10.0**	20.9	73.1
▼	SAINT JOHN NATIONAL BK	SAINT JOHN	KS	**B+**	A-	A-	64	9.46	12.0	3.2	4.5	26.4	**10.0**	11.2	16.2
	SAINTE MARIE STATE BK	SAINTE MARIE	IL	**C-**	C	B-	19	-0.48	2.9	1.1	4.1	35.0	**10.0**	23.4	39.4
	SALEM CO-OPERATIVE BANK	SALEM	NH	**C+**	C-	C-	375	18.22	1.6	0.1	54.2	29.7	**10.0**	13.3	26.6
	SALEM FIVE CENTS SB	SALEM	MA	**C+**	C+	C	2,780	1.86	10.7	1.5	26.5	25.7	**7.3**	9.2	14.0
	SALIN BANK & TRUST CO	INDIANAPOLIS	IN	**D**	D+	D+	784	-0.85	15.5	2.3	4.9	21.6	**7.8**	9.6	13.2
	SALISBURY BANK & TRUST CO	LAKEVILLE	CT	**D+**	C-	B-	574	2.72	4.5	0.8	30.2	25.5	**4.7**	6.7	11.3
	SALLIE MAE BANK	MURRAY	UT	**B+**	B+	B+	7,582	-0.47	0.0	62.0	0.0	8.2	**10.0**	12.1	19.7
▲	SALT LICK DEPOSIT BANK	SALT LICK	KY	**D+**	C-	C+	78	-6.01	7.9	8.9	22.3	11.2	**6.6**	8.6	12.9
	SALYERSVILLE NATIONAL BK	SALYERSVILLE	KY	**B+**	B+	B+	103	3.02	6.2	4.5	21.8	40.2	**10.0**	13.1	27.4
	SAMSON BANKING CO INC	SAMSON	AL	**B+**	A-	A-	56	4.62	3.0	3.5	11.2	54.3	**10.0**	14.3	36.1
	SAN ANTONIO NATIONAL BK	SAN ANTONIO	TX	**D-**	D-	D-	218	-15.27	12.8	1.9	9.5	19.4	**5.8**	7.8	12.9
	SAN DIEGO PRIVATE BANK	LA JOLLA	CA	**D-**	C-	D	125	-3.86	13.6	2.9	22.2	13.6	**5.5**	7.5	15.3
	SAN DIEGO TRUST BANK	SAN DIEGO	CA	**C**	C+	B+	203	33.65	3.2	0.4	2.5	59.5	**6.7**	8.7	22.5
	SAN LUIS VALLEY FEDERAL B	ALAMOSA	CO	**B**	B	B+	207	6.49	2.5	1.4	49.3	7.6	**10.0**	14.9	24.3
	SANBORN SB	SANBORN	IA	**C**	C	C	60	7.68	4.3	2.7	7.4	24.8	**6.6**	8.8	12.2
	SANDHILLS BANK	NORTH MYRTLE BEACH	SC	**D-**	D-	E-	60	-15.06	2.8	0.5	6.7	34.0	**6.3**	8.3	17.7
▼	SANDHILLS STATE BK	BASSETT	NE	**D**	D	E+	60	102.95	4.5	1.5	0.7	10.6	**9.4**	11.1	14.5
	SANDY SPRING BANK	OLNEY	MD	**D+**	D+	C	3,518	-3.13	5.1	1.0	12.9	28.8	**6.9**	8.9	14.9
	SANFORD INSTITUTION FOR S	SANFORD	ME	**C**	C	C	428	-1.24	4.6	1.5	38.5	9.8	**8.0**	9.7	14.4
	SANGER BANK	SANGER	TX	**A-**	B+	B+	99	5.27	7.0	3.9	17.8	20.6	**10.0**	11.6	19.9
	SANIBEL CAPTIVA	SANIBEL	FL	**D-**	D-	D	240	1.14	3.4	0.5	34.9	4.1	**6.6**	8.6	12.7
	SANTA ANNA NATIONAL BK	SANTA ANNA	TX	**A-**	A-	B+	42	13.94	9.7	5.9	4.6	55.4	**10.0**	13.6	27.6
	SANTA CLARA VALLEY BANK N	SANTA PAULA	CA	**D-**	D-	C+	137	-2.23	11.2	0.5	3.9	22.3	**7.2**	9.2	15.7
▲	SANTA CRUZ COUNTY BANK	SANTA CRUZ	CA	**C+**	C	C	285	7.47	10.4	0.6	3.6	9.2	**6.3**	8.3	13.5
	SANTA LUCIA BANK	ATASCADERO	CA	**E-**	C-	B	250	-7.40	13.7	0.7	3.9	13.0	**1.2**	4.8	8.2
	SARATOGA NATIONAL BK & TR	SARATOGA SPRINGS	NY	**A-**	A-	B+	295	5.51	2.5	21.7	25.9	20.0	**6.9**	8.9	15.5
	SARGENT COUNTY BANK	FORMAN	ND	**A**	A	A	87	5.48	4.7	2.6	0.7	35.2	**10.0**	12.7	18.2
	SAUGUSBANK A CO-OP BANK	SAUGUS	MA	**D+**	D+	D+	196	-3.23	5.9	0.3	31.6	23.1	**6.0**	8.0	13.2
▲	SAUK VALLEY BANK & TRUST	STERLING	IL	**C-**	D+	D	227	7.59	14.0	1.6	8.4	21.6	**6.4**	8.4	13.4
	SAVANNA-THOMSON STATE	SAVANNA	IL	**D-**	E-	D-	76	-18.02	36.6	0.9	17.3	8.7	**6.4**	8.4	12.3
	SAVANNAH BANK NA	SAVANNAH	GA	**D**	D+	D	789	2.71	7.0	1.5	20.7	14.4	**6.0**	8.0	12.4
	SAVANNAH BANK NA	SAVANNAH	NY	**C+**	C	C	102	3.07	13.0	4.0	15.2	43.2	**6.2**	8.2	15.6

Arrows denote recent upgrades ▲ or downgrades ▼

Asset Quality Index	Non-Performing Loans as a % of Total Loans	as a % of Capital	Net Charge-offs Avg Loans	Profitability Index	Net Income ($Mil)	Return on Assets (R.O.A.)	Return on Equity (R.O.E.)	Net Interest Spread	Overhead Efficiency Ratio	Liquidity Index	Liquidity Ratio	Hot Money Ratio	Stability Index
4.1	1.21	8.8	0.26	**6.0**	2.5	1.14	11.82	4.83	65.3	**3.5**	23.6	12.4	**5.5**
0.3	13.46	55.6	2.96	**0.0**	-8.5	-0.72	-9.97	2.82	93.9	**1.4**	19.9	27.9	**3.7**
3.6	1.00	7.1	0.47	**4.1**	2.9	0.65	7.23	3.52	55.7	**1.4**	13.1	25.7	**4.8**
8.6	0.00	0.0	0.81	**0.0**	-3.7	-1.52	-5.89	3.36	106.1	**0.7**	21.3	61.3	**1.5**
0.0	18.91	137.8	6.76	**0.0**	-10.6	-7.97	-99.73	2.41	234.2	**0.9**	20.9	35.4	**3.0**
0.8	10.61	38.7	2.91	**0.0**	-0.9	-0.99	-6.39	4.17	89.9	**3.8**	22.5	10.8	**5.0**
6.5	3.59	11.1	0.16	**3.7**	2.9	0.61	4.23	3.21	63.1	**4.3**	51.5	16.4	**7.6**
2.2	5.19	26.3	0.06	**10.0**	2.2	3.04	23.15	6.23	47.0	**1.9**	23.8	21.2	**9.1**
6.0	0.66	3.2	0.64	**1.8**	0.8	0.40	4.85	2.93	83.2	**2.6**	36.5	22.0	**4.3**
1.9	3.95	20.5	0.30	**4.8**	1.3	1.18	9.41	4.05	65.1	**3.6**	29.5	13.7	**6.9**
2.0	3.57	25.0	0.14	**6.3**	0.8	1.44	19.11	4.08	64.8	**4.5**	34.7	10.7	**5.8**
5.7	0.67	5.9	0.06	**4.1**	0.4	0.80	10.32	4.94	80.1	**3.0**	12.9	13.6	**3.7**
6.8	3.91	8.0	2.66	**4.6**	1.0	1.19	7.84	3.43	59.4	**4.3**	56.6	16.4	**9.2**
1.6	6.00	38.7	0.73	**0.3**	-0.1	-0.39	-4.93	2.89	87.5	**4.0**	28.8	11.3	**4.5**
7.0	2.55	7.4	-0.64	**1.0**	-0.1	-0.46	-4.68	2.17	114.9	**4.2**	73.5	19.4	**4.8**
1.8	1.75	17.0	1.02	**6.0**	47.8	1.17	10.69	4.09	54.1	**2.9**	3.4	13.6	**7.8**
5.2	2.35	19.8	0.09	**3.3**	0.9	0.42	6.09	3.48	76.3	**1.8**	19.1	21.7	**3.8**
5.9	1.47	9.1	0.57	**2.6**	7.4	0.36	4.26	4.76	65.9	**4.8**	43.2	14.1	**5.4**
0.3	10.63	69.5	2.75	**0.0**	-0.7	-0.82	-6.82	3.14	118.5	**1.4**	25.0	29.0	**1.0**
6.0	0.49	4.4	-0.37	**7.2**	13.3	1.97	26.26	4.22	65.9	**1.7**	10.6	19.9	**4.5**
1.7	2.81	20.8	0.18	**3.1**	4.0	0.54	6.03	3.06	73.1	**1.3**	17.1	27.4	**5.7**
4.7	3.04	12.8	0.34	**7.1**	1.1	1.73	13.78	4.31	53.1	**2.6**	46.0	29.5	**8.8**
6.2	3.06	8.3	0.01	**0.2**	-0.6	-0.78	-8.35	3.56	97.0	**4.1**	52.6	16.4	**0.1**
0.0	8.68	45.7	5.29	**0.0**	-20.8	-3.19	-30.84	2.65	150.2	**1.0**	22.1	34.7	**4.5**
8.9	0.07	0.2	0.01	**3.6**	26.6	0.70	5.32	1.82	63.9	**3.0**	59.0	63.4	**8.7**
8.0	0.04	0.2	-0.01	**4.1**	1.5	0.63	5.91	4.03	80.2	**2.1**	35.9	29.7	**5.3**
0.0	12.31	49.4	5.00	**0.0**	-2.9	-4.37	-40.23	3.42	127.4	**1.2**	29.5	53.7	**1.5**
10.0	1.04	0.8	0.11	**1.3**	0.0	0.02	0.10	2.32	100.7	**6.9**	100.6	10.4	**7.4**
7.9	0.68	3.4	-0.02	**7.8**	0.9	1.41	12.63	4.85	60.6	**1.1**	13.6	29.5	**7.0**
8.9	0.79	1.7	0.00	**1.5**	0.0	0.07	0.29	2.21	97.0	**4.7**	59.8	13.1	**7.2**
7.7	0.00	0.0	0.03	**3.3**	2.9	0.83	5.61	3.13	61.6	**2.2**	35.6	27.3	**6.7**
4.8	1.52	10.6	0.19	**3.6**	17.6	0.65	6.83	2.86	67.2	**1.6**	10.3	22.5	**7.0**
0.9	3.69	24.2	0.78	**3.5**	5.0	0.64	6.65	4.23	70.8	**3.7**	15.8	10.7	**5.6**
1.6	2.86	24.3	0.16	**3.3**	3.7	0.64	8.13	3.43	76.1	**3.1**	21.8	14.3	**4.9**
5.7	0.04	0.2	0.00	**9.2**	130.2	1.71	10.38	3.82	11.6	**1.7**	30.3	78.8	**7.0**
2.5	1.50	11.9	0.96	**1.3**	0.1	0.16	1.73	2.46	82.3	**0.7**	13.0	38.6	**4.1**
7.9	0.03	0.1	-0.02	**5.1**	1.3	1.27	9.11	4.26	67.9	**2.5**	50.0	37.8	**7.9**
6.2	2.86	7.0	0.16	**3.5**	0.4	0.72	4.89	3.20	71.3	**5.2**	58.7	12.1	**7.9**
0.0	5.26	35.9	1.64	**0.0**	-9.6	-3.80	-41.12	2.89	220.0	**1.3**	10.7	26.5	**3.0**
5.2	2.49	15.2	3.88	**0.0**	-3.7	-2.74	-36.64	3.85	98.9	**3.4**	31.5	15.4	**1.3**
5.7	2.30	6.0	0.17	**3.1**	1.0	0.54	5.32	4.00	83.2	**6.5**	66.4	7.5	**5.3**
6.6	0.73	3.5	0.00	**4.0**	1.5	0.72	4.82	4.83	63.5	**2.6**	20.2	16.5	**7.6**
3.8	1.33	9.6	0.57	**3.7**	0.4	0.65	6.89	3.50	68.4	**4.0**	37.9	14.5	**5.6**
1.8	6.76	26.5	-0.06	**0.0**	-5.8	-8.73	-56.33	3.37	391.0	**3.2**	51.1	22.4	**3.1**
3.6	0.26	1.5	-0.02	**0.4**	-0.5	-1.78	-11.10	3.11	148.5	**1.7**	31.4	31.5	**4.5**
2.1	3.56	20.6	1.27	**3.2**	24.0	0.66	6.23	3.59	63.1	**4.1**	23.6	11.2	**6.9**
3.7	1.87	13.2	0.77	**3.5**	2.5	0.58	6.28	3.73	70.0	**3.1**	18.8	14.1	**5.7**
6.2	0.85	4.3	-0.01	**7.4**	1.3	1.43	12.55	4.89	63.3	**2.2**	29.7	22.4	**6.6**
0.3	4.61	37.9	0.95	**2.1**	0.5	0.23	2.73	3.89	63.0	**0.7**	11.3	38.6	**3.2**
8.7	0.25	0.7	-0.01	**7.2**	0.5	1.38	9.28	4.43	59.8	**3.6**	61.8	22.3	**8.6**
0.3	4.36	24.3	1.75	**0.7**	-0.4	-0.26	-2.88	4.13	91.6	**2.8**	37.6	21.0	**3.2**
5.4	2.26	15.0	0.33	**3.6**	1.8	0.66	8.79	4.51	74.0	**2.2**	27.6	20.2	**3.7**
0.0	12.63	100.6	3.74	**0.0**	-14.3	-5.32	-82.99	4.15	92.1	**1.6**	10.0	21.8	**3.5**
6.7	0.22	1.5	0.05	**7.7**	3.6	1.27	13.62	3.64	46.8	**3.8**	21.3	10.4	**7.3**
8.6	0.00	0.0	0.00	**9.5**	1.8	2.07	15.52	4.86	46.8	**3.4**	27.8	14.0	**9.9**
1.7	2.72	18.9	0.17	**2.4**	0.7	0.32	4.18	3.32	78.3	**3.8**	32.0	13.3	**4.0**
2.4	1.46	10.1	0.53	**4.4**	2.0	0.90	10.69	4.48	66.3	**3.2**	13.4	12.9	**3.7**
0.5	3.12	26.7	2.10	**0.0**	-0.3	-0.32	-2.86	3.47	72.9	**4.2**	14.3	7.0	**3.7**
1.2	3.57	28.1	1.68	**1.4**	-0.5	-0.06	-0.80	3.27	62.5	**1.5**	13.7	24.5	**5.1**
6.3	1.49	7.9	0.28	**4.1**	1.0	0.94	10.97	3.91	77.8	**1.9**	19.4	20.3	**4.5**

Name	City	State	Rating	2008 Rating	2007 Rating	Total Assets ($Mil)	One Year Asset Growth	Asset Mix (As a % of Total Assets) Comm-ercial Loans	Cons-umer Loans	Home Mort-gages	Secur-ities	Capital-ization Index	Leverage Ratio	Risk-based Capital Ratio
SAVANNAH RIVER BANKING	AUGUSTA	GA	**C-**	C	C	144	26.85	7.2	0.8	12.1	14.7	**10.0**	13.0	16.3
SAVERS CO-OP BANK	SOUTHBRIDGE	MA	**C**	C	C	401	5.68	1.6	8.0	44.8	19.2	**9.1**	10.4	19.0
SAVINGS BANK	PRIMGHAR	IA	**C+**	C	C+	114	11.49	7.8	6.3	12.8	17.1	**5.7**	8.3	11.5
SAVINGS BANK	WAKEFIELD	MA	**C**	C-	D+	424	1.66	2.3	0.3	32.5	26.5	**10.0**	11.7	21.0
SAVINGS BANK	CIRCLEVILLE	OH	**B+**	B+	B+	265	8.23	8.2	5.8	30.8	41.6	**10.0**	11.4	25.1
SAVINGS BANK OF DANBURY	DANBURY	CT	**D+**	C	C-	759	3.66	5.6	0.1	40.4	12.7	**7.9**	9.6	15.4
SAVINGS BANK OF MAINE	GARDINER	ME	**D**	E	D+	855	-3.76	4.5	2.3	21.0	4.7	**10.0**	13.0	19.5
▼ SAVINGS BANK OF	UKIAH	CA	**C+**	B	B+	885	15.49	3.3	2.5	9.1	48.2	**10.0**	15.3	21.6
SAVINGS BANK OF WALPOLE	WALPOLE	NH	**C**	C	C	296	3.54	3.8	0.7	37.7	17.8	**6.3**	8.3	17.3
SAVINGS INSTITUTE BANK &	WILLIMANTIC	CT	**C-**	C-	C-	911	5.85	4.5	0.4	32.3	19.0	**5.8**	7.8	15.3
SAVOY BANK	NEW YORK	NY	**D**	C	C	79	28.92	12.9	0.0	8.3	5.4	**10.0**	12.2	16.0
SAWYER SB	SAUGERTIES	NY	**C-**	C	C	189	6.71	4.3	0.3	41.9	32.4	**7.6**	9.4	19.8
SCANDIA AMERICAN BANK & T	STANLEY	ND	**B**	B-	C+	170	85.44	5.6	3.4	4.4	36.0	**5.5**	7.5	13.2
SCB BANK	SHELBYVILLE	IN	**D-**	D+	D	256	-3.27	16.2	0.9	11.7	26.3	**4.9**	7.5	10.9
SCBT NA	ORANGEBURG	SC	**C**	C	B	3,593	33.07	5.6	2.3	16.1	6.0	**6.4**	8.4	14.4
SCHERTZ BANK & TRUST	SCHERTZ	TX	**C+**	B+	A-	184	5.69	4.6	1.2	4.4	35.8	**10.0**	11.3	19.2
SCHUYLER SB	KEARNY	NJ	**C+**	C+	C+	120	0.64	0.0	0.2	49.3	26.2	**10.0**	14.1	38.5
SCHUYLER STATE BK	RUSHVILLE	IL	**C+**	C+	C-	52	0.48	3.2	5.8	17.4	8.5	**7.6**	9.4	14.9
▼ SCHWERTNER STATE BK	SCHWERTNER	TX	**C+**	B+	B+	38	12.99	4.3	2.0	0.8	41.3	**10.0**	11.9	28.6
SCITUATE FSB	SCITUATE	MA	**C**	C-	C	263	0.63	0.0	1.4	46.8	24.6	**5.6**	7.6	15.6
SCOTIABANK DE PUERTO	HATO REY	PR	**D-**	D-	D-	6,920	289.84	4.5	7.9	39.1	3.9	**4.7**	6.7	16.8
SCOTT COUNTY STATE BK	SCOTTSBURG	IN	**C-**	D	C	138	3.36	6.3	4.7	30.2	16.1	**8.0**	9.7	16.6
SCOTT STATE BK	BETHANY	IL	**B+**	B	B-	74	3.38	7.6	5.2	17.4	37.1	**10.0**	14.3	23.8
▲ SCOTT VALLEY BANK	YREKA	CA	**B-**	C	C-	482	7.15	11.5	2.3	0.7	27.7	**10.0**	11.1	16.6
SCOTTDALE BANK & TRUST	SCOTTDALE	PA	**B**	B	B	222	13.57	1.6	4.1	11.3	56.5	**10.0**	17.5	34.4
SCOTTRADE BANK	DES PERES	MO	**B**	B	B-	7,756	23.03	0.0	0.0	0.0	97.1	**6.1**	8.1	32.8
SCOTTSBURG BUILDING &	SCOTTSBURG	IN	**C+**	C	C+	91	-0.67	3.6	0.1	42.8	40.9	**10.0**	12.1	28.1
SCRIBNER BANK	SCRIBNER	NE	**A-**	A-	A-	62	-0.33	6.5	1.2	5.8	20.5	**9.8**	10.8	17.2
SEACOAST COMMERCE BANK	CHULA VISTA	CA	**D-**	D-	D	130	24.62	6.0	0.8	1.5	6.7	**9.3**	10.5	17.9
SEACOAST NATIONAL BK	STUART	FL	**D-**	D-	D-	2,015	-6.27	1.8	2.6	23.4	22.9	**7.4**	9.3	16.3
SEAMENS BANK	PROVINCETOWN	MA	**C-**	C+	C+	294	0.53	2.0	0.3	29.1	24.1	**9.2**	10.4	16.0
SEASIDE NATIONAL BK & TRU	ORLANDO	FL	**D-**	E+	C-	766	-8.32	27.3	0.7	8.1	29.0	**6.6**	8.6	13.3
SEATTLE BANK	SEATTLE	WA	**E-**	E-	E	468	-20.74	2.6	0.0	3.1	0.7	**0.0**	1.5	3.7
SEAWAY BANK & TRUST CO	CHICAGO	IL	**D+**	D	D-	517	33.93	8.7	0.8	17.2	37.6	**5.7**	7.7	17.9
SEAWAY COMMUNITY BANK	SAINT CLAIR	MI	**D-**	D+	D+	169	8.05	7.6	0.9	25.7	14.3	**7.3**	9.2	14.1
SEBREE DEPOSIT BANK	SEBREE	KY	**C-**	C+	C+	20	-10.55	7.4	10.2	27.4	17.2	**10.0**	11.2	23.5
SECOND FS&LA OF CHICAGO	CHICAGO	IL	**E-**	E+	D	211	-10.45	0.0	0.0	65.9	7.0	**2.5**	5.1	9.5
▲ SECOND FS&LA OF	PHILADELPHIA	PA	**C+**	C-	C-	15	2.42	0.0	0.0	40.5	46.7	**10.0**	42.5	70.5
SECURANT BANK & TRUST	MILWAUKEE	WI	**D-**	E+	D+	237	-6.61	24.0	0.5	22.4	9.2	**5.7**	8.0	11.5
SECURIAN TRUST CO NA	SAINT PAUL	MN	**U**	U	U	12	9.79	0.0	0.0	0.0	89.7	**10.0**	95.4	112.6
▼ SECURITY BANK	STEPHENS	AR	**D+**	C	C	45	7.35	12.3	7.4	33.0	13.7	**5.1**	7.1	11.8
▲ SECURITY BANK	RICH HILL	MO	**D+**	C-	D	65	0.47	8.0	11.4	24.8	14.6	**5.3**	7.3	14.1
SECURITY BANK	TULSA	OK	**C+**	C+	C	358	1.02	19.0	1.6	9.2	8.2	**9.7**	10.8	15.1
SECURITY BANK	NEWBERN	TN	**B**	B+	A-	162	2.32	6.2	3.0	9.8	42.4	**9.0**	10.4	17.6
SECURITY BANK	ODESSA	TX	**B-**	B-	C+	461	9.54	25.1	2.5	11.1	8.6	**7.8**	9.9	13.1
▲ SECURITY BANK	NEW AUBURN	WI	**D-**	D-	D	69	-10.66	5.2	2.0	19.4	16.0	**4.9**	8.7	10.9
SECURITY BANK & TRUST CO	MAYSVILLE	KY	**A-**	A-	A-	46	-1.92	4.0	4.1	31.8	18.5	**10.0**	22.3	22.8
▼ SECURITY BANK & TRUST CO	GLENCOE	MN	**D+**	C	B-	230	-6.43	7.4	1.1	5.9	31.4	**5.5**	7.5	11.8
SECURITY BANK & TRUST CO	SCOTT CITY	MO	**C-**	D	C-	70	-4.87	2.0	5.6	28.2	27.1	**6.6**	8.6	15.5
▼ SECURITY BANK & TRUST CO	MIAMI	OK	**C**	C-	D+	76	-5.66	16.3	4.0	13.6	39.3	**9.2**	10.4	19.0
SECURITY BANK & TRUST CO	PARIS	TN	**A-**	A-	A-	161	-2.51	10.7	3.9	27.8	7.3	**6.9**	8.9	16.4
▼ SECURITY BANK MINNESOTA	ALBERT LEA	MN	**C**	C-	B-	88	7.81	38.5	10.5	5.7	28.1	**8.2**	9.8	14.4
▼ SECURITY BANK NA	NORTH LAUDERDALE	FL	**E**	E	D-	124	-28.42	3.4	0.2	34.0	6.6	**4.3**	6.3	11.0
SECURITY BANK OF CALIFORN	RIVERSIDE	CA	**C**	C-	C	339	7.55	34.9	1.8	1.6	8.8	**10.0**	13.8	16.6
SECURITY BANK OF KANSAS C	KANSAS CITY	KS	**D+**	C-	C+	859	-3.34	16.0	1.5	2.5	16.9	**6.8**	8.8	13.2
▼ SECURITY BANK OF PULASKI	WAYNESVILLE	MO	**D-**	D+	C-	105	-0.99	6.1	5.2	21.4	13.6	**6.3**	8.3	12.3
SECURITY BANK OF	CASSVILLE	MO	**B-**	B-	C	68	1.72	7.7	4.7	23.3	23.0	**8.7**	10.1	16.1
SECURITY BANK OF THE OZAR	EMINENCE	MO	**D+**	C-	C-	47	-5.64	3.4	11.0	17.6	22.1	**4.9**	6.9	10.9
▲ SECURITY BANK OF	ROXTON	TX	**D+**	C	C+	105	2.51	2.8	6.0	33.7	7.4	**4.9**	6.9	13.6
SECURITY BANK SB	SPRINGFIELD	IL	**D-**	D-	D+	171	1.82	3.3	12.5	27.9	9.1	**6.5**	8.5	14.2

Asset Quality Index	Non-Performing Loans as a % of Total Loans	Non-Performing Loans as a % of Capital	Net Charge-offs Avg Loans	Profitability Index	Net Income ($Mil)	Return on Assets (R.O.A.)	Return on Equity (R.O.E.)	Net Interest Spread	Overhead Efficiency Ratio	Liquidity Index	Liquidity Ratio	Hot Money Ratio	Stability Index
8.2	0.01	0.1	0.05	**1.4**	0.2	0.16	1.08	3.34	85.5	**2.1**	31.0	24.1	**0.9**
4.9	0.88	5.4	0.09	**3.3**	2.2	0.56	5.47	3.34	75.2	**2.6**	28.3	18.1	**6.3**
3.9	0.46	4.0	0.09	**6.6**	1.7	1.62	19.81	3.73	47.5	**1.7**	10.5	20.1	**5.5**
6.9	1.10	5.0	0.03	**2.6**	1.4	0.35	2.65	3.61	88.1	**4.5**	45.0	13.6	**6.5**
5.6	2.16	9.3	0.21	**4.6**	2.4	0.92	7.61	3.76	68.6	**4.9**	48.3	12.4	**7.4**
2.5	3.86	29.9	1.14	**1.9**	1.1	0.15	1.57	3.29	72.5	**1.4**	4.7	23.2	**6.3**
0.3	12.82	55.2	1.35	**1.6**	3.3	0.37	3.21	3.27	94.7	**3.1**	28.5	15.9	**5.4**
2.2	12.79	33.7	0.68	**4.2**	6.0	0.73	4.71	4.54	64.2	**4.5**	54.6	16.0	**7.6**
5.3	1.80	12.2	0.42	**2.8**	1.2	0.41	4.71	3.25	80.8	**4.7**	35.1	9.5	**5.1**
5.4	0.78	6.4	0.10	**2.3**	3.0	0.34	4.01	3.16	85.0	**3.2**	29.8	15.7	**4.8**
0.7	6.62	36.1	0.35	**0.0**	-2.1	-3.11	-22.88	4.28	145.6	**1.1**	21.2	32.3	**1.5**
5.3	1.25	7.5	0.32	**2.3**	0.7	0.40	4.05	3.53	82.2	**0.9**	24.8	42.8	**5.7**
6.7	0.34	2.0	0.01	**5.5**	1.6	0.99	11.03	4.17	59.0	**4.7**	34.9	10.0	**6.0**
0.3	6.55	52.6	0.46	**0.4**	-1.4	-0.54	-6.61	2.73	83.4	**1.4**	32.0	49.0	**2.5**
3.1	2.60	19.9	1.69	**7.7**	53.5	1.48	14.55	4.16	46.2	**2.2**	9.9	17.7	**7.1**
2.8	5.41	23.4	0.10	**2.7**	0.4	0.22	1.82	3.96	87.5	**1.4**	18.1	26.3	**7.2**
7.2	2.13	7.5	0.16	**2.6**	0.3	0.22	1.57	2.82	77.8	**3.4**	52.4	23.7	**7.5**
5.5	1.64	10.9	0.13	**4.0**	0.5	0.97	10.39	3.58	72.7	**1.9**	24.2	21.8	**5.1**
9.6	0.17	0.3	0.50	**2.3**	0.0	0.11	0.87	2.78	91.9	**5.0**	81.6	16.3	**6.1**
5.1	1.16	9.0	0.06	**3.2**	1.4	0.51	7.02	3.31	73.1	**2.3**	30.9	21.7	**3.8**
0.0	4.24	43.6	0.59	**4.6**	85.5	1.58	18.23	4.97	55.7	**0.9**	9.0	32.9	**4.3**
2.3	1.95	12.5	1.31	**3.6**	1.1	0.80	7.88	4.48	66.3	**2.8**	30.8	18.0	**5.3**
5.9	2.10	6.3	0.38	**6.0**	1.1	1.43	9.47	4.09	64.5	**5.1**	39.0	9.2	**7.6**
4.7	1.47	7.0	0.26	**3.6**	2.4	0.54	4.49	4.27	77.0	**2.8**	29.3	17.3	**5.8**
9.3	1.66	2.8	0.01	**3.5**	1.4	0.68	3.49	3.69	78.9	**7.7**	78.7	2.0	**7.4**
9.7	0.00	0.0	0.00	**5.6**	84.0	1.20	12.72	1.41	17.8	**4.2**	109.3	42.9	**4.8**
6.5	0.77	3.1	0.00	**2.9**	0.4	0.40	3.37	2.44	74.0	**2.4**	48.2	32.7	**7.2**
6.7	0.82	3.9	0.08	**8.0**	0.7	1.23	11.20	4.09	74.0	**5.9**	40.1	3.8	**8.1**
0.6	0.87	5.9	3.13	**1.2**	0.3	0.27	2.86	3.62	74.0	**1.5**	14.6	23.8	**4.5**
0.3	5.45	30.5	2.95	**0.0**	-31.2	-1.50	-15.22	3.45	104.3	**2.9**	18.6	15.3	**5.2**
1.6	6.59	36.7	0.17	**3.0**	1.6	0.53	5.04	3.41	76.6	**4.3**	35.9	12.3	**6.5**
2.6	2.21	14.1	1.12	**0.0**	-5.5	-0.70	-7.33	2.55	113.5	**0.7**	19.9	57.7	**1.7**
0.3	5.55	109.0	3.75	**0.0**	-24.5	-4.84	-125.85	0.98	187.2	**0.7**	13.5	47.0	**4.1**
1.7	6.77	40.5	1.62	**4.5**	5.5	1.23	15.01	3.15	68.7	**0.8**	15.0	39.5	**3.5**
0.3	5.02	25.6	2.12	**0.0**	-3.3	-2.00	-21.34	3.70	82.7	**1.6**	24.2	25.9	**3.4**
8.0	0.84	3.2	0.08	**1.8**	0.0	0.08	0.72	3.93	97.9	**2.7**	35.9	18.0	**7.0**
0.3	9.64	105.3	0.00	**0.0**	-6.6	-3.00	-48.87	3.55	123.0	**2.0**	13.5	18.8	**0.3**
9.8	0.10	0.1	0.00	**4.0**	0.1	0.97	2.21	4.54	69.3	**4.9**	99.2	17.9	**6.5**
0.7	5.74	45.0	0.40	**1.0**	0.8	0.31	4.06	3.68	80.2	**1.1**	4.2	27.1	**3.0**
10.0	0.00	0.0	0.00	**0.3**	-0.1	-0.39	-0.40	5.09	102.8	**5.0**	937.4	101.0	**2.3**
4.1	1.20	10.5	0.68	**2.0**	0.1	0.12	1.57	4.66	82.9	**0.8**	15.4	37.4	**2.9**
2.5	1.13	8.2	0.80	**3.9**	0.4	0.66	6.68	4.70	73.4	**3.5**	35.3	16.0	**5.1**
2.9	1.16	7.6	0.91	**5.7**	5.0	1.39	13.34	3.75	36.6	**0.8**	20.3	45.8	**6.7**
4.5	1.18	4.6	0.11	**5.1**	1.6	0.97	8.51	3.97	72.2	**2.9**	39.2	20.1	**7.3**
4.1	0.52	3.7	0.17	**7.8**	7.1	1.67	10.94	5.99	66.1	**2.4**	8.6	16.3	**7.0**
1.0	4.01	28.4	1.89	**0.4**	0.0	0.03	0.24	4.16	79.2	**2.5**	21.3	17.2	**3.2**
7.2	1.39	4.1	0.22	**8.4**	0.9	1.92	8.70	4.60	57.3	**4.3**	31.5	10.9	**9.9**
4.7	1.52	10.2	0.76	**3.2**	1.2	0.51	5.87	3.59	68.4	**3.1**	19.4	13.8	**4.2**
5.0	0.35	2.4	0.76	**3.5**	0.6	0.75	8.97	4.17	75.6	**4.5**	28.5	8.4	**3.6**
5.8	1.22	5.7	0.07	**2.6**	0.6	0.75	7.11	3.76	89.1	**3.1**	30.7	16.6	**5.0**
8.5	0.22	1.6	0.01	**9.4**	3.7	2.16	23.74	4.16	48.6	**1.7**	23.9	23.7	**7.5**
2.2	1.19	7.5	0.98	**4.1**	0.7	0.81	8.49	4.72	67.6	**1.8**	18.6	20.8	**4.5**
0.0	25.23	182.4	8.27	**0.0**	-10.3	-6.82	-62.50	2.98	247.8	**1.0**	8.2	30.6	**4.3**
4.5	2.07	11.0	0.58	**2.5**	1.2	0.37	2.91	3.95	74.6	**1.6**	18.5	24.8	**4.0**
0.0	7.86	48.1	0.68	**2.1**	2.5	0.28	2.37	3.29	74.8	**2.0**	18.4	19.4	**6.0**
2.1	4.50	34.4	2.12	**0.3**	-0.3	-0.30	-3.34	4.38	78.8	**0.7**	14.2	41.0	**4.0**
4.3	2.01	12.5	0.10	**8.6**	1.4	2.09	20.35	4.67	60.1	**2.9**	29.1	16.8	**6.2**
6.1	0.66	5.2	0.07	**3.9**	0.3	0.71	8.95	5.06	83.5	**1.6**	15.2	23.1	**3.0**
3.7	1.32	10.5	1.02	**2.7**	0.4	0.40	5.67	3.30	86.3	**2.3**	33.4	23.2	**4.1**
0.2	4.38	33.9	1.60	**0.0**	-1.7	-1.01	-10.82	3.59	88.6	**3.5**	19.9	12.1	**2.9**

Name	City	State	Rating	2008 Rating	2007 Rating	Total Assets ($Mil)	One Year Asset Growth	Asset Mix (As a % of Total Assets)				Capital-ization Index	Leverage Ratio	Risk-based Capital Ratio
								Comm-ercial Loans	Cons-umer Loans	Home Mort-gages	Secur-ities			
▲ SECURITY BANK USA	BEMIDJI	MN	**D+**	C-	D+	104	1.74	16.2	5.1	21.9	0.2	**5.8**	8.6	11.6
▼ SECURITY BANK WACONIA	WACONIA	MN	**D+**	C+	B	173	-0.07	5.5	0.7	6.4	21.4	**6.2**	8.3	11.9
▼ SECURITY BUSINESS BK SAN	SAN DIEGO	CA	**D+**	B-	B-	225	14.24	10.9	2.5	6.2	10.4	**9.6**	10.8	14.8
SECURITY EXCHANGE BANK	MARIETTA	GA	**E-**	E-	D-	169	-2.98	5.8	0.4	4.9	18.3	**0.1**	3.7	6.3
▲ SECURITY FED SB MCMINNVIL	MCMINNVILLE	TN	**B-**	C	NR	152	3.60	10.6	8.5	29.3	11.0	**7.4**	9.3	13.5
SECURITY FEDERAL BANK	AIKEN	SC	**D+**	C-	C	929	-5.02	1.7	1.1	16.3	36.0	**6.2**	8.2	15.6
SECURITY FEDERAL BANK	ELIZABETHTON	TN	**B**	B+	A-	58	-1.93	5.5	3.3	49.7	4.7	**10.0**	21.0	38.0
▼ SECURITY FINANCIAL BANK	DURAND	WI	**D-**	D+	C+	291	-5.65	4.2	0.9	9.7	34.2	**5.5**	7.5	13.5
SECURITY FIRST BANK	FRESNO	CA	**D-**	C	C	117	8.30	22.7	0.1	3.5	20.9	**7.7**	9.7	13.1
▲ SECURITY FIRST BANK	LINCOLN	NE	**C+**	C	B-	816	16.41	8.5	2.5	6.0	40.8	**6.7**	8.7	15.2
SECURITY FIRST BANK	CHEYENNE	WY	**B-**	C+	C+	67	9.25	7.5	2.1	10.7	4.1	**8.7**	10.1	15.0
▲ SECURITY FIRST BANK OF ND	NEW SALEM	ND	**B+**	B	B	130	2.37	19.6	4.9	6.2	4.7	**7.0**	9.8	12.5
SECURITY FIRST NB OF HUGO	HUGO	OK	**B-**	B-	B	105	1.35	2.5	4.3	22.1	10.8	**5.2**	7.2	12.7
SECURITY FSB	JASPER	AL	**C-**	C-	C-	38	-1.19	8.2	15.1	12.8	10.4	**8.3**	9.8	24.7
SECURITY FSB	LOGANSPORT	IN	**B-**	C+	B-	194	6.13	3.8	2.8	49.5	12.4	**10.0**	11.3	19.1
SECURITY HOME BANK	MALMO	NE	**C+**	C+	C	31	8.77	4.6	3.9	25.8	11.3	**7.1**	9.2	12.6
SECURITY NATIONAL BK	WITT	IL	**C+**	B-	B-	62	-0.40	6.2	7.7	23.8	32.5	**10.0**	11.9	19.8
SECURITY NATIONAL BK	LAUREL	NE	**C**	C-	C	141	4.00	14.5	4.0	4.8	19.0	**9.4**	10.8	14.5
SECURITY NATIONAL BK OF E	ENID	OK	**B**	B	B	307	-4.58	6.8	1.8	12.1	49.0	**6.1**	8.1	13.2
▲ SECURITY NATIONAL BK OF O	OMAHA	NE	**A-**	A-	A-	642	4.33	15.1	4.0	8.7	28.3	**7.3**	9.2	14.8
SECURITY NATIONAL BK OF S	DAKOTA DUNES	SD	**B-**	B	B	130	-0.57	7.8	1.5	4.4	33.2	**5.1**	7.1	16.4
SECURITY NATIONAL TRUST C	WHEELING	WV	**U**	U	U	4	4.79	0.0	0.0	0.0	85.4	**10.0**	89.1	128.5
SECURITY NB OF SIOUX CITY	SIOUX CITY	IA	**B**	B	B+	698	5.88	10.3	1.7	13.4	22.5	**6.4**	8.4	16.1
SECURITY SB	EAGLE GROVE	IA	**B-**	B-	B-	112	3.85	28.9	0.9	4.9	24.9	**4.9**	6.9	11.2
SECURITY SB	GOWRIE	IA	**C**	C+	C	94	5.72	4.0	3.2	11.4	43.9	**5.4**	7.4	13.3
SECURITY SB	LARCHWOOD	IA	**B**	B	B	146	7.33	7.0	1.7	7.5	3.0	**6.4**	9.0	12.1
SECURITY SB	MONMOUTH	IL	**C-**	D+	C-	162	3.72	3.1	4.7	16.0	14.3	**7.1**	9.0	14.8
▼ SECURITY SB SSB	SOUTHPORT	NC	**E-**	D-	C-	358	-16.65	1.2	0.9	34.7	1.8	**1.8**	5.3	8.8
▼ SECURITY STATE BK	MCRAE	GA	**B**	A-	A-	40	4.11	5.3	7.6	13.1	29.4	**10.0**	13.3	22.4
SECURITY STATE BK	ALGONA	IA	**B+**	B+	B+	73	12.66	17.3	3.7	7.1	13.7	**9.1**	10.9	14.3
SECURITY STATE BK	ANAMOSA	IA	**C+**	B-	B-	129	4.70	8.8	3.0	19.6	15.8	**6.4**	8.4	13.2
▲ SECURITY STATE BK	GUTTENBERG	IA	**B**	C+	B+	90	4.62	7.7	4.0	17.8	34.7	**6.3**	8.3	14.6
▲ SECURITY STATE BK	HUBBARD	IA	**D-**	D	C-	58	3.88	5.8	4.1	31.5	2.3	**6.7**	8.7	13.8
▲ SECURITY STATE BK	INDEPENDENCE	IA	**B**	C	B-	84	-3.29	5.7	1.4	10.5	36.4	**8.2**	9.8	15.8
SECURITY STATE BK	NEW HAMPTON	IA	**C-**	D+	D	173	0.96	3.7	2.8	18.0	35.1	**6.2**	8.2	13.3
SECURITY STATE BK	RADCLIFFE	IA	**E+**	D+	D+	45	0.25	10.4	2.2	3.9	39.7	**5.1**	7.1	12.4
SECURITY STATE BK	SUTHERLAND	IA	**B-**	B-	B-	75	6.83	13.4	4.8	8.7	3.0	**3.7**	8.1	10.4
SECURITY STATE BK	WAVERLY	IA	**A-**	A-	A-	75	8.50	1.9	3.7	11.5	44.5	**7.3**	9.2	16.7
SECURITY STATE BK	SCOTT CITY	KS	**C-**	D	C-	139	-4.21	14.3	1.9	1.0	12.4	**8.4**	11.3	13.7
SECURITY STATE BK	WELLINGTON	KS	**B**	B	B+	49	7.52	10.5	9.3	5.4	48.3	**10.0**	13.5	24.7
SECURITY STATE BK	DUNSEITH	ND	**C**	C	B-	62	8.97	3.0	13.1	12.1	14.3	**5.3**	7.3	12.5
SECURITY STATE BK	ANSLEY	NE	**D**	D	D-	95	24.89	17.3	2.0	20.0	5.7	**4.0**	8.1	10.5
SECURITY STATE BK	CHEYENNE	OK	**A-**	A	A-	142	26.28	4.2	4.8	11.5	48.7	**6.6**	8.6	16.1
SECURITY STATE BK	ALEXANDRIA	SD	**B+**	B+	B+	66	3.38	5.3	4.9	5.6	36.8	**9.2**	10.5	17.7
▼ SECURITY STATE BK	EMERY	SD	**C+**	B-	B-	35	-3.08	9.0	5.4	2.9	14.7	**10.0**	14.3	15.2
SECURITY STATE BK	TYNDALL	SD	**B+**	B+	B+	31	1.03	13.7	4.0	1.7	7.3	**9.9**	11.0	15.2
▼ SECURITY STATE BK	ANAHUAC	TX	**D+**	C+	B-	117	69.62	6.0	3.9	9.1	52.1	**5.5**	7.5	17.7
SECURITY STATE BK	FARWELL	TX	**A**	A	A	118	1.72	4.2	0.8	5.9	60.5	**10.0**	11.9	25.1
SECURITY STATE BK	LITTLEFIELD	TX	**D**	C-	D+	104	-6.16	8.4	4.9	12.2	24.7	**6.7**	8.7	13.9
SECURITY STATE BK	PEARSALL	TX	**B-**	B	B	453	23.14	5.0	2.0	2.0	51.2	**4.8**	6.8	14.1
SECURITY STATE BK	WINTERS	TX	**C+**	C	C	35	-1.07	10.1	9.9	11.5	24.6	**6.9**	8.9	18.0
▲ SECURITY STATE BK	CENTRALIA	WA	**D+**	D-	D+	338	-4.39	12.8	2.7	10.2	5.3	**9.4**	10.6	17.3
▲ SECURITY STATE BK	IRON RIVER	WI	**D-**	D-	D+	92	-19.64	14.8	1.9	11.2	15.1	**10.0**	12.0	16.6
SECURITY STATE BK	BASIN	WY	**B-**	B-	C+	287	8.90	9.4	3.5	12.4	28.4	**6.8**	8.8	16.0
▲ SECURITY STATE BK & TRUST	FREDERICKSBURG	TX	**B-**	B-	B	628	2.10	8.1	5.5	13.2	23.2	**10.0**	15.7	22.6
▲ SECURITY STATE BK FERGUS	FERGUS FALLS	MN	**C+**	B-	C+	139	10.59	15.4	1.4	9.6	28.6	**6.2**	8.3	11.9
▲ SECURITY STATE BK	HOWARD LAKE	MN	**C+**	C-	C	77	-3.59	10.9	1.3	16.9	18.3	**7.2**	9.2	15.4
SECURITY STATE BK NA	ORE CITY	TX	**B-**	B-	B-	42	-9.88	8.7	11.9	15.4	27.2	**10.0**	15.0	24.7
▼ SECURITY STATE BK OF AITK	AITKIN	MN	**C+**	B+	B	86	-6.17	11.2	2.0	11.7	15.6	**8.2**	9.8	13.7
SECURITY STATE BK OF HIBB	HIBBING	MN	**D+**	D	D-	95	-3.46	18.6	2.3	10.6	21.1	**8.4**	9.9	15.1

Asset Quality Index	Non-Performing Loans as a % of Total Loans	Non-Performing Loans as a % of Capital	Net Charge-offs / Avg Loans	Profitability Index	Net Income ($Mil)	Return on Assets (R.O.A.)	Return on Equity (R.O.E.)	Net Interest Spread	Overhead Efficiency Ratio	Liquidity Index	Liquidity Ratio	Hot Money Ratio	Stability Index
1.7	2.63	21.7	0.85	2.1	0.2	0.20	2.27	3.27	80.1	4.2	11.1	7.1	6.0
0.3	4.79	31.9	0.23	5.0	1.9	1.14	13.05	4.03	47.6	2.7	20.6	15.9	5.3
0.5	4.32	26.4	1.18	1.1	-0.4	-0.20	-1.66	4.33	79.6	4.8	13.7	2.9	5.6
0.3	9.78	88.5	2.79	0.0	-3.1	-1.73	-35.78	1.91	223.1	0.8	17.2	45.5	0.8
4.3	0.45	3.4	0.08	4.1	0.9	0.61	6.71	3.29	73.1	1.3	12.1	26.9	5.4
1.5	4.33	25.7	0.75	2.5	1.9	0.20	2.37	3.09	64.8	2.3	40.6	31.0	4.0
8.6	0.30	1.1	0.76	4.1	0.5	0.76	3.70	4.79	57.1	0.9	22.1	37.5	7.8
1.2	3.98	24.1	2.39	0.1	-6.4	-2.06	-27.58	2.97	71.5	1.5	8.0	22.5	3.2
0.3	9.90	61.1	4.73	0.0	-4.4	-3.77	-30.32	4.15	78.5	1.1	15.1	29.8	1.3
3.5	1.81	9.5	0.74	4.6	7.2	0.93	8.34	3.75	69.0	2.5	28.5	18.7	7.0
5.1	1.16	6.6	0.76	2.0	0.1	0.24	2.32	3.53	81.2	2.0	34.0	28.9	4.9
6.3	0.12	0.9	-0.02	8.1	2.3	1.78	18.81	5.09	59.7	2.5	14.5	16.4	7.5
4.6	0.75	6.3	0.11	10.0	1.9	1.84	23.21	5.88	51.0	1.0	19.8	32.8	6.2
6.4	1.14	4.0	0.75	2.2	0.1	0.15	1.57	3.70	85.0	3.5	69.2	26.9	3.2
3.9	2.06	11.0	0.14	4.0	1.4	0.71	6.14	4.00	72.3	4.9	30.1	6.3	6.0
7.8	0.00	0.0	0.30	4.3	0.2	0.65	6.97	4.02	71.8	2.6	12.0	15.5	5.8
7.6	0.49	2.4	0.43	6.0	0.7	1.08	8.63	4.52	60.1	3.5	32.0	14.8	5.0
3.6	2.04	11.7	0.84	4.6	1.7	1.23	10.56	4.58	68.3	3.6	27.0	12.6	5.2
5.3	1.58	9.0	0.66	9.4	6.9	2.21	23.82	4.30	42.2	2.6	34.8	20.6	6.7
7.3	0.42	2.4	0.80	6.9	10.0	1.52	15.30	4.06	59.1	4.2	29.1	10.4	8.9
7.8	0.00	0.0	0.00	3.0	1.0	0.79	11.51	2.07	67.5	4.9	58.3	15.0	4.6
10.0	0.00	0.0	0.00	10.0	0.4	10.17	10.64	3.72	85.2	5.0	1,719.3	101.0	6.4
5.8	1.05	6.0	0.34	6.8	9.1	1.28	14.73	3.38	58.4	4.3	22.4	7.7	7.3
8.3	0.00	0.0	0.00	6.4	1.6	1.45	17.99	4.27	59.5	2.3	33.0	23.1	5.1
5.5	0.71	4.5	0.93	3.0	0.4	0.44	5.56	3.96	76.5	3.7	47.0	17.6	3.8
5.2	0.47	3.8	0.23	7.1	2.3	1.66	14.26	4.37	48.9	2.5	17.7	16.8	7.0
4.7	1.06	7.3	0.14	2.7	0.9	0.54	6.05	3.14	75.7	1.7	23.3	24.5	3.1
0.3	11.70	106.5	4.90	0.0	-16.0	-3.86	-51.23	2.57	101.2	1.0	17.3	33.3	2.4
7.7	0.95	3.9	1.35	4.8	0.3	0.74	5.29	4.96	71.9	2.9	38.9	20.2	7.6
6.9	0.33	1.9	0.00	6.0	0.8	1.08	9.57	3.99	54.8	1.9	27.3	24.4	7.3
3.7	0.14	1.1	0.09	5.5	1.2	0.96	11.63	3.89	56.3	2.3	19.9	18.2	5.4
5.2	0.77	4.5	0.44	6.2	1.3	1.46	10.65	3.68	48.1	3.3	47.9	19.9	7.4
1.0	4.26	34.1	2.71	0.7	-0.9	-1.53	-19.91	3.27	90.1	4.2	20.3	8.1	5.2
5.6	0.34	1.8	0.05	5.7	0.9	1.09	10.45	4.90	66.0	4.8	35.0	9.0	5.5
2.4	2.43	15.4	1.94	3.0	0.8	0.48	4.83	3.63	59.2	5.5	40.6	7.0	5.7
4.3	1.96	12.2	0.69	1.8	0.2	0.33	4.66	2.64	81.5	4.1	50.9	16.4	1.7
6.7	0.00	0.0	0.01	9.8	1.8	2.49	30.47	4.62	44.2	2.2	1.6	16.9	7.7
8.9	0.10	0.5	0.05	6.2	0.9	1.31	13.44	3.51	59.9	5.6	49.1	8.2	6.2
0.3	9.22	46.9	0.42	2.6	0.8	0.55	4.33	4.12	77.7	1.8	20.3	22.3	5.3
5.4	2.38	7.5	0.17	3.7	0.4	0.77	5.38	4.36	80.1	5.2	51.7	10.8	7.0
7.2	0.11	0.8	-0.09	3.3	0.3	0.55	7.27	4.18	83.9	2.9	25.3	15.8	4.7
1.0	3.68	34.5	0.67	9.1	1.9	2.21	26.19	4.93	65.4	0.7	10.3	39.9	4.9
8.5	0.23	1.2	0.10	7.8	2.4	1.78	17.33	3.83	55.6	1.4	23.3	28.2	7.1
8.1	0.17	0.9	0.21	5.1	0.8	1.16	10.48	3.82	64.3	2.4	33.6	21.9	7.0
8.7	0.01	0.0	0.08	2.3	0.1	0.34	2.41	2.98	87.8	6.1	63.3	8.1	7.3
5.6	1.14	5.8	-0.01	4.6	0.2	0.67	5.98	4.86	79.5	5.3	28.2	2.6	8.5
8.5	0.31	1.1	0.68	1.3	0.3	0.29	2.47	3.35	104.4	2.7	43.1	26.5	5.1
9.9	0.06	0.2	-0.03	6.7	1.6	1.59	11.32	3.13	53.1	2.8	56.1	38.6	8.7
8.4	0.03	0.2	0.88	1.5	0.1	0.06	0.72	4.47	85.8	2.6	16.6	16.3	4.8
7.0	0.04	0.2	0.33	5.9	5.1	1.23	14.53	3.37	49.4	1.0	16.0	31.6	5.2
8.5	0.19	0.9	0.41	4.4	0.3	0.90	9.74	4.04	78.3	2.6	34.3	20.8	5.1
1.4	4.62	22.2	2.25	1.7	0.3	0.09	0.80	5.01	70.5	3.5	30.1	14.2	6.2
0.3	15.39	72.1	0.73	2.9	0.9	0.89	8.53	3.70	64.9	0.9	13.1	33.5	3.7
6.1	0.60	3.4	0.35	4.5	2.2	0.80	8.83	3.47	65.0	1.5	20.1	26.7	4.4
3.4	4.29	17.7	0.37	6.9	7.1	1.16	7.32	4.82	66.0	2.5	13.4	16.2	10.0
4.6	0.96	7.0	0.53	5.1	1.6	1.22	14.69	3.37	57.9	1.6	24.5	25.5	5.4
3.0	3.61	20.7	1.37	5.1	1.2	1.52	15.38	3.78	62.0	2.3	23.2	18.2	5.5
6.8	0.63	1.9	0.66	3.6	0.3	0.66	3.56	4.41	81.0	2.0	22.0	19.8	5.5
1.7	7.33	46.5	0.50	6.3	1.2	1.32	13.19	4.94	62.4	4.4	13.8	6.2	7.7
1.5	4.33	20.7	1.73	3.1	0.5	0.51	5.69	4.58	84.3	2.8	24.7	16.1	4.1

Name	City	State	Rating	2008 Rating	2007 Rating	Total Assets ($Mil)	One Year Asset Growth	Asset Mix (As a % of Total Assets) Comm-ercial Loans	Cons-umer Loans	Home Mort-gages	Secur-ities	Capital-ization Index	Leverage Ratio	Risk-based Capital Ratio
SECURITY STATE BK OF KENY	KENYON	MN	**D-**	E	D-	53	-12.46	7.8	1.8	14.0	5.2	**6.0**	8.1	12.0
▲ SECURITY STATE BK OF LEWI	LEWISTON	MN	**D-**	D-	D+	68	-8.18	6.9	2.5	10.0	19.8	**5.9**	7.9	12.6
SECURITY STATE BK OF MARI	MARINE ON SAINT CROI	MN	**B+**	B+	A-	105	3.60	5.1	2.6	39.1	6.3	**10.0**	11.0	19.3
SECURITY STATE BK OF OKLE	OKLEE	MN	**B+**	A-	A-	30	-0.74	1.3	3.1	4.4	20.1	**10.0**	16.6	56.7
SECURITY STATE BK OF	WANAMINGO	MN	**B-**	B-	B	69	2.30	5.1	2.2	7.4	16.1	**7.4**	9.3	12.8
SECURITY STATE BK OF	WARROAD	MN	**B**	B	B	79	3.64	13.6	14.0	10.5	30.6	**10.0**	20.5	29.8
SECURITY STATE BK OF	WEWOKA	OK	**B**	C+	C-	91	17.65	7.9	13.9	19.8	20.1	**10.0**	12.0	19.8
SECURITY STATE BK WISHEK	WISHEK	ND	**B**	B+	B+	60	1.92	4.0	3.9	2.7	41.9	**10.0**	11.4	19.4
SECURITY TRUST & SB	STORM LAKE	IA	**A-**	B+	B	141	5.62	4.2	2.1	11.0	57.5	**9.3**	10.6	24.5
SEI PRIVATE TRUST CO	OAKS	PA	**B+**	B+	B+	114	14.60	0.0	0.0	0.0	70.6	**10.0**	91.5	318.2
SELECT BANK	GRAND RAPIDS	MI	**D-**	D-	D-	82	-15.33	8.9	0.5	15.5	5.4	**6.1**	8.7	11.8
SELECT BANK	EGG HARBOR CITY	NJ	**C**	D-	D	136	2.02	1.1	0.2	41.8	5.7	**5.7**	7.7	13.5
SELECT BANK	FOREST	VA	**D-**	C-	C-	101	11.11	4.8	1.7	24.6	0.5	**6.1**	9.1	11.8
SELECT BANK & TRUST CO	GREENVILLE	NC	**C+**	C+	B	194	1.65	10.8	0.7	18.2	13.6	**7.0**	9.0	12.6
SENATH STATE BK	SENATH	MO	**A**	A	A-	62	3.93	10.0	11.0	36.0	0.7	**10.0**	14.2	27.5
SENECA FALLS SAVINGS	SENECA FALLS	NY	**C**	C-	C-	239	8.96	3.9	13.8	48.7	9.9	**5.7**	7.7	12.1
SENECA FS&LA	BALDWINSVILLE	NY	**C-**	C	C+	151	2.55	6.0	1.4	48.7	22.2	**6.2**	8.2	18.6
SENECA NATIONAL BK	SENECA	SC	**D**	D	D+	76	2.10	5.6	2.3	8.6	29.9	**6.8**	8.8	13.7
SENTRY BANK	SAINT JOSEPH	MN	**B**	B+	A-	154	16.20	10.2	2.0	12.6	20.8	**6.8**	8.8	16.3
▲ SERVICE1ST BANK OF	LAS VEGAS	NV	**D**	D-	D	205	-3.14	17.6	0.1	4.4	3.5	**10.0**	18.1	30.0
SERVISFIRST BANK	BIRMINGHAM	AL	**B-**	C	C+	1,935	23.04	26.4	1.9	5.2	14.6	**5.8**	7.8	11.8
▼ SETTLERS BANK	MARIETTA	OH	**B**	B+	B	101	7.30	6.9	4.9	36.5	3.6	**8.9**	10.3	15.1
SETTLERS BANK	DE FOREST	WI	**C-**	C	C	89	21.10	12.1	0.3	3.1	0.9	**10.0**	11.8	15.7
SEVERN SAVINGS BANK FSB	ANNAPOLIS	MD	**C-**	D+	C+	958	-0.40	1.3	0.1	33.3	2.9	**10.0**	12.3	16.8
SEVIER COUNTY BANK	SEVIERVILLE	TN	**D-**	D-	D	368	-7.16	3.1	1.2	6.8	12.7	**9.1**	10.7	14.2
SEWICKLEY SB	SEWICKLEY	PA	**B**	B	B+	298	6.15	1.5	0.1	8.5	49.4	**10.0**	24.5	71.1
SEYMOUR BANK	SEYMOUR	MO	**B+**	B	B+	137	3.93	2.9	5.8	20.0	27.7	**10.0**	11.8	18.7
SHAMROCK BANK NA	COALGATE	OK	**A-**	B+	B	244	2.55	8.2	8.0	13.4	39.5	**8.7**	10.1	17.5
SHAMROCK BANK OF FLORIDA	NAPLES	FL	**D**	D	C-	81	10.56	4.0	1.0	18.8	13.0	**10.0**	16.6	29.1
▲ SHARE PLUS FEDERAL BANK	PLANO	TX	**C**	C-	C-	239	14.79	1.0	4.3	62.2	9.7	**10.0**	11.8	18.5
▲ SHARON SB	DARBY	PA	**C+**	D+	C-	224	0.39	0.2	1.5	39.6	33.6	**7.4**	9.2	15.4
▼ SHATTUCK NATIONAL BK	SHATTUCK	OK	**D**	C-	B-	51	1.21	37.1	1.9	4.8	22.2	**6.1**	8.1	21.1
▲ SHELBY COUNTY STATE BK	HARLAN	IA	**C**	C-	C	228	2.47	6.4	2.8	6.9	22.9	**6.0**	8.1	12.0
SHELBY COUNTY STATE BK	SHELBYVILLE	IL	**B**	B-	B+	186	7.66	6.4	4.1	13.9	36.8	**8.3**	9.8	17.3
SHELBY SB SSB	CENTER	TX	**A-**	B+	B	226	4.83	15.3	9.8	21.0	10.9	**8.7**	10.2	15.7
SHELBY STATE BK	SHELBY	MI	**B-**	C	B-	200	9.91	3.9	1.7	15.6	26.4	**7.0**	9.0	15.6
SHELL LAKE STATE BK	SHELL LAKE	WI	**A+**	A	A+	133	3.08	5.8	2.3	25.1	43.6	**10.0**	17.8	34.5
SHELTER FINANCIAL BANK	COLUMBIA	MO	**C+**	C+	C+	181	-8.27	2.8	29.1	37.4	0.0	**7.4**	9.2	13.5
▼ SHERBURNE STATE BK	BECKER	MN	**E**	D-	D	74	-6.03	2.2	1.4	18.4	8.8	**3.1**	6.2	10.1
▲ SHERIDAN STATE BK	SHERIDAN	IL	**C+**	C	C-	25	6.02	4.6	7.4	35.7	14.1	**9.0**	10.3	19.6
SHERWOOD COMMUNITY	CREIGHTON	MO	**C+**	C+	B-	32	-0.08	1.6	2.5	17.3	38.0	**8.6**	10.5	13.9
SHERWOOD STATE BK	SHERWOOD	OH	**C-**	D+	D-	47	4.10	9.9	6.8	20.4	26.1	**7.6**	9.4	14.7
SHINHAN BANK AMERICA	NEW YORK	NY	**D-**	D-	D+	940	-4.96	15.7	0.8	5.4	8.9	**7.4**	9.3	14.0
SHORE BANK	ONLEY	VA	**D-**	C-	B-	330	7.88	3.1	0.7	30.3	5.6	**4.6**	6.6	13.4
SHORE COMMUNITY BANK	TOMS RIVER	NJ	**D+**	D-	D	208	-2.89	2.0	0.1	12.1	31.4	**6.8**	8.8	16.4
SIBLEY STATE BK	SIBLEY	IA	**B-**	C+	C	81	-3.95	4.0	1.8	5.4	20.2	**5.7**	8.4	11.5
SICILY ISLAND STATE BK	SICILY ISLAND	LA	**B**	B	B-	35	9.53	12.1	15.5	17.2	11.1	**10.0**	12.5	19.8
SIDELL STATE BK	SIDELL	IL	**C-**	C	C	22	-5.41	2.5	5.0	2.0	38.7	**8.9**	10.3	24.6
SIDNEY FS&LA	SIDNEY	NE	**C-**	C-	C-	28	11.52	0.0	3.2	24.5	64.0	**7.4**	9.3	26.6
SIDNEY STATE BK	SIDNEY	MI	**D+**	D-	C+	53	0.03	3.6	5.8	56.8	6.7	**9.1**	10.4	17.7
SIERRA VISTA BANK	FOLSOM	CA	**D-**	D	C-	89	-15.58	25.1	0.7	4.8	10.9	**6.2**	8.2	12.6
SIGNATURE BANK	WINDSOR	CO	**E-**	E-	D+	73	-7.55	19.7	3.0	13.9	3.6	**0.4**	4.5	6.9
▲ SIGNATURE BANK	CHICAGO	IL	**C**	C-	D	288	17.12	35.7	0.6	5.8	0.0	**8.0**	11.3	13.3
SIGNATURE BANK	BAD AXE	MI	**D-**	D	D+	254	-7.00	7.7	1.6	25.3	5.9	**6.3**	8.3	12.2
▼ SIGNATURE BANK	MINNETONKA	MN	**D-**	D+	D+	171	-7.01	34.9	2.7	10.8	2.6	**7.8**	10.4	13.1
SIGNATURE BANK	NEW YORK	NY	**B**	B-	B-	11,673	27.63	10.9	1.6	2.3	48.1	**6.6**	8.6	15.2
SIGNATURE BANK	DALLAS	TX	**C**	C	C	126	10.97	5.0	3.1	18.6	11.2	**6.1**	8.1	17.8
▼ SIGNATURE BANK KC	HADDAM	KS	**C-**	C	C	5	14.07	22.1	0.8	13.2	12.3	**8.2**	11.2	13.5
SIGNATURE BANK NA	TOLEDO	OH	**B-**	C+	C+	508	12.31	17.7	2.1	10.2	4.8	**6.9**	8.9	12.5
SIGNATURE BANK OF	FAYETTEVILLE	AR	**D**	D+	D+	514	-28.06	15.2	2.8	25.2	10.6	**7.2**	9.1	14.0

Asset Quality Index	Non-Performing Loans as a % of Total Loans	Non-Performing Loans as a % of Capital	Net Charge-offs Avg Loans	Profitability Index	Net Income ($Mil)	Return on Assets (R.O.A.)	Return on Equity (R.O.E.)	Net Interest Spread	Overhead Efficiency Ratio	Liquidity Index	Liquidity Ratio	Hot Money Ratio	Stability Index
0.3	7.45	52.1	1.21	**0.7**	-0.5	-0.81	-9.74	4.51	90.7	**3.2**	17.4	13.1	**3.7**
3.3	0.64	4.2	3.96	**0.0**	-2.5	-3.56	-47.68	4.08	165.0	**4.0**	16.1	9.0	**2.3**
5.0	0.03	0.2	0.38	**5.1**	0.8	0.74	7.00	4.18	64.8	**2.2**	28.8	20.9	**6.8**
9.6	0.00	0.0	0.00	**3.9**	0.2	0.66	4.04	1.53	69.4	**6.0**	73.7	10.4	**8.9**
5.2	0.35	2.5	0.05	**6.1**	1.0	1.44	14.96	4.07	60.6	**2.9**	22.1	15.0	**7.0**
3.7	5.10	13.9	0.53	**5.5**	0.8	0.99	4.90	4.34	67.5	**4.3**	34.8	11.9	**7.2**
4.7	1.40	7.1	0.16	**8.4**	1.2	1.51	11.96	5.15	61.1	**1.6**	25.4	26.4	**6.4**
5.7	1.02	3.5	-0.19	**4.2**	0.5	0.84	7.09	3.39	70.7	**5.5**	45.8	7.8	**7.2**
8.3	0.67	2.3	0.11	**6.0**	1.8	1.27	11.30	3.96	53.2	**3.4**	51.3	22.3	**6.5**
6.5	0.00	0.0	0.00	**10.0**	13.7	12.98	14.20	4.15	83.9	**5.0**	835.9	100.0	**4.7**
0.0	5.80	40.8	2.02	**0.0**	-2.1	-2.43	-28.89	3.35	123.4	**0.7**	10.7	41.7	**2.5**
4.7	0.93	7.2	0.00	**3.8**	1.2	0.91	12.28	3.68	55.8	**2.3**	34.7	25.9	**3.9**
1.7	4.72	39.6	0.99	**0.1**	-0.4	-0.40	-3.60	3.72	89.6	**0.6**	7.5	43.5	**1.1**
6.1	0.05	0.4	0.33	**3.7**	1.0	0.55	5.58	3.47	61.4	**0.8**	18.5	44.7	**5.4**
6.8	0.83	3.3	0.05	**10.0**	1.5	2.53	16.55	4.74	52.7	**5.5**	41.6	7.0	**9.7**
4.2	0.61	5.8	0.04	**3.2**	1.2	0.50	6.89	3.59	77.2	**3.4**	15.1	12.1	**2.0**
8.1	0.50	3.6	0.00	**2.4**	0.4	0.27	3.83	2.78	87.4	**2.6**	40.8	25.9	**3.3**
2.3	1.83	11.2	1.24	**2.4**	0.6	0.72	7.92	3.45	77.1	**1.8**	35.8	33.5	**4.1**
4.9	0.59	3.7	0.02	**9.1**	4.8	3.11	24.10	4.09	36.1	**3.5**	26.5	13.1	**9.5**
0.5	9.93	29.6	0.00	**1.1**	0.1	0.38	3.32	3.94	87.7	**2.5**	49.4	34.2	**2.5**
4.9	1.02	8.9	0.54	**5.9**	18.9	1.13	13.88	4.08	43.7	**3.7**	22.5	12.7	**6.4**
4.6	0.25	1.8	0.06	**4.9**	0.9	0.87	8.44	3.65	60.6	**1.2**	12.3	28.5	**6.3**
7.3	0.00	0.0	0.28	**1.9**	0.3	0.37	3.11	3.45	77.4	**1.3**	29.6	35.4	**3.4**
1.6	4.43	26.6	0.00	**1.8**	2.0	0.20	1.67	3.52	72.3	**1.4**	11.8	25.3	**6.5**
0.0	13.96	71.4	0.28	**1.0**	0.2	0.05	0.46	3.06	88.0	**0.7**	12.0	44.6	**4.2**
9.9	2.72	2.2	0.00	**3.9**	1.7	0.60	2.41	2.06	56.8	**4.6**	98.0	25.5	**7.9**
7.9	0.70	3.5	0.32	**4.5**	1.3	0.93	7.41	4.00	66.9	**2.3**	31.2	21.2	**7.4**
6.1	0.89	4.1	0.34	**6.2**	3.3	1.37	12.04	4.66	68.8	**3.5**	51.2	20.9	**7.2**
1.7	4.28	14.2	5.14	**0.0**	-3.9	-4.94	-24.78	3.06	113.4	**2.0**	41.0	40.2	**1.7**
5.4	2.28	15.2	0.15	**2.4**	0.5	0.24	2.89	3.86	79.2	**2.4**	16.7	17.2	**4.8**
8.6	0.67	3.5	0.00	**3.6**	2.6	1.16	12.85	3.61	64.7	**3.0**	41.2	20.5	**4.3**
3.1	1.88	12.0	0.05	**5.0**	0.5	1.04	12.11	3.75	74.5	**1.7**	24.9	24.9	**3.0**
4.7	0.36	2.7	0.47	**6.3**	2.5	1.14	11.54	4.27	57.8	**4.4**	29.4	9.3	**5.5**
8.6	0.07	0.4	0.20	**4.7**	1.9	1.08	9.88	3.75	69.2	**4.5**	28.6	8.6	**6.3**
7.6	0.09	0.6	0.12	**7.7**	4.4	1.92	18.93	4.28	56.0	**1.6**	17.7	23.7	**6.6**
4.3	0.60	3.6	0.34	**4.3**	1.6	0.86	8.66	4.27	74.7	**3.7**	31.0	13.3	**6.0**
7.6	1.79	5.0	0.20	**9.0**	2.7	2.02	10.93	4.89	50.7	**3.2**	44.8	20.4	**9.5**
4.1	0.70	6.1	0.14	**3.2**	0.9	0.46	5.32	2.69	62.8	**0.6**	7.9	49.1	**4.6**
0.3	6.90	43.1	1.24	**0.2**	-2.2	-2.74	-33.23	4.74	96.0	**4.0**	15.7	8.7	**5.1**
5.2	0.73	4.2	0.00	**4.7**	0.2	0.77	5.86	3.98	66.4	**5.4**	33.7	4.8	**6.5**
4.3	0.35	1.6	0.14	**3.6**	0.2	0.56	5.02	4.65	87.4	**3.9**	30.5	12.1	**6.3**
3.8	2.15	13.6	0.86	**3.1**	0.2	0.52	5.41	4.81	76.7	**3.0**	21.6	14.5	**4.4**
0.0	3.59	21.5	2.06	**0.0**	-26.4	-2.72	-29.22	4.18	89.3	**1.5**	17.8	25.8	**4.7**
1.5	4.78	37.2	1.19	**1.1**	-0.1	-0.01	-0.19	2.91	71.6	**2.5**	32.2	20.4	**3.6**
1.6	6.78	37.5	0.58	**2.2**	0.7	0.31	3.52	3.47	72.6	**1.9**	30.6	26.9	**3.9**
6.6	0.02	0.2	0.25	**6.3**	0.9	1.10	12.92	4.00	54.5	**1.7**	12.1	20.6	**4.4**
5.9	0.10	0.5	1.37	**7.2**	0.5	1.63	13.00	5.49	66.6	**1.4**	28.3	32.0	**6.7**
8.6	0.00	0.0	-0.01	**2.2**	0.1	0.44	4.50	3.14	94.5	**5.1**	45.1	7.4	**5.8**
5.2	3.85	11.5	0.00	**2.5**	0.1	0.23	2.20	2.63	96.7	**4.0**	74.4	21.2	**4.6**
1.5	5.53	36.9	1.85	**3.0**	0.2	0.35	3.41	4.72	70.1	**4.2**	19.1	8.0	**5.7**
1.4	2.81	20.3	5.13	**0.0**	-3.5	-3.36	-38.59	4.81	88.5	**0.6**	7.8	36.5	**1.0**
0.3	4.94	47.6	4.47	**0.0**	-0.8	-1.02	-19.51	3.42	94.7	**0.7**	13.4	41.9	**3.1**
2.8	2.34	15.9	0.55	**3.3**	2.5	0.97	8.60	3.81	57.4	**0.9**	19.6	39.1	**3.8**
0.3	4.70	37.3	1.17	**0.8**	0.2	0.06	0.66	4.43	73.2	**2.1**	13.3	18.2	**3.2**
0.3	2.45	16.9	0.49	**2.3**	1.1	0.64	6.44	4.50	67.2	**0.9**	9.4	31.4	**3.9**
6.5	0.89	4.8	0.68	**5.3**	102.1	0.99	11.61	3.49	44.5	**4.2**	19.0	8.4	**5.6**
8.9	0.00	0.0	0.79	**3.2**	0.9	0.76	9.45	3.43	74.6	**3.8**	53.2	19.2	**2.8**
6.9	0.00	0.0	-0.03	**4.4**	0.0	0.74	4.55	5.18	70.8	**1.2**	12.2	26.9	**6.2**
4.7	0.41	3.2	0.28	**4.9**	4.1	0.88	9.70	3.66	55.7	**1.5**	23.8	27.3	**4.7**
0.3	7.57	52.7	3.58	**0.3**	-15.7	-2.46	-22.61	3.82	103.6	**1.1**	13.4	30.3	**1.4**

Name	City	State	Rating	2008 Rating	2007 Rating	Total Assets ($Mil)	One Year Asset Growth	Asset Mix (As a % of Total Assets) Commercial Loans	Consumer Loans	Home Mortgages	Securities	Capitalization Index	Leverage Ratio	Risk-based Capital Ratio
SIGNATURE BANK OF	SANDY SPRINGS	GA	**E-**	E	D-	194	-13.02	5.7	0.2	8.3	27.3	**2.0**	5.1	9.0
SILEX BANKING CO	SILEX	MO	**B**	B-	B	61	3.15	1.4	1.2	11.9	47.8	**10.0**	15.2	29.6
▼ SILICON VALLEY BANK	SANTA CLARA	CA	**B-**	B+	A-	16,332	33.96	24.0	1.0	1.6	48.4	**4.8**	6.8	15.5
SILVER LAKE BANK	TOPEKA	KS	**C**	A-	A	216	4.34	18.8	1.4	14.3	21.2	**10.0**	11.0	17.3
SILVERGATE BANK	LA JOLLA	CA	**C**	C	C-	371	2.15	1.3	0.0	16.8	17.4	**8.6**	10.0	16.0
SIMMESPORT STATE BK	SIMMESPORT	LA	**C-**	C-	B-	60	2.71	11.1	20.6	33.1	8.3	**10.0**	13.2	21.4
SIMMONS FIRST BANK OF NE	JONESBORO	AR	**B**	B	B	329	5.00	7.5	6.1	27.2	7.7	**7.1**	9.1	12.9
SIMMONS FIRST BANK OF NW	ROGERS	AR	**C+**	B-	B-	270	-1.02	4.6	1.5	13.5	21.2	**10.0**	12.4	19.6
SIMMONS FIRST BANK OF SEA	SEARCY	AR	**B**	B	B	152	1.43	8.2	3.3	20.4	13.7	**8.8**	10.2	15.1
SIMMONS FIRST BANK OF SOU	LAKE VILLAGE	AR	**B**	B	B	177	6.62	6.4	4.3	8.0	25.2	**7.1**	9.1	16.4
SIMMONS FIRST BK HOT SPRI	HOT SPRINGS	AR	**C+**	B-	B-	169	-1.94	3.2	1.7	21.1	32.4	**6.7**	8.7	18.7
SIMMONS FIRST BK OF EL DO	EL DORADO	AR	**B**	B	B	244	-15.55	7.8	3.5	12.0	41.9	**6.7**	8.7	18.9
SIMMONS FIRST BK RUSSELLV	RUSSELLVILLE	AR	**B**	B	B	182	-5.72	7.2	3.5	13.0	20.6	**10.0**	14.8	23.0
SIMMONS FIRST NATIONAL BK	PINE BLUFF	AR	**B-**	B	B	1,939	20.92	3.7	16.3	7.2	13.0	**6.3**	8.3	18.6
▲ SIMMONS FIRST TRUST CO NA	PINE BLUFF	AR	**B-**	U	B	2	-4.68	0.0	0.0	0.0	0.0	**10.0**	68.6	218.0
SIMSBURY BANK & TRUST CO	SIMSBURY	CT	**C**	C	C-	296	8.00	4.6	1.5	43.6	18.5	**5.0**	7.0	12.7
SIOUXLAND NATIONAL BK	SOUTH SIOUX CITY	NE	**D+**	C-	C	48	9.84	11.6	4.0	20.7	0.0	**6.3**	8.3	15.5
SIUSLAW BANK	FLORENCE	OR	**D**	D+	B-	300	5.35	7.4	2.4	7.3	5.2	**10.0**	13.2	17.6
SKAGIT STATE BK	BURLINGTON	WA	**C+**	C+	B+	693	6.94	8.0	2.4	5.0	31.7	**7.4**	9.3	15.8
SKOWHEGAN SB	SKOWHEGAN	ME	**B-**	C+	C	447	5.79	7.1	3.8	40.9	24.6	**10.0**	12.3	21.4
SKYLANDS COMMUNITY BANK	CHESTER	NJ	**D+**	C	B-	1,410	6.50	9.0	1.1	9.0	21.2	**5.3**	7.3	12.0
SLAVIE FSB	BEL AIR	MD	**C-**	C-	D+	203	1.55	1.0	0.1	52.0	2.8	**6.2**	8.2	15.4
SLOAN STATE BK	SLOAN	IA	**B+**	B+	B+	44	0.28	3.0	3.1	14.9	36.4	**9.8**	10.8	24.6
SLOCOMB NATIONAL BK	SLOCOMB	AL	**C+**	B-	C+	78	3.12	3.8	2.7	30.1	12.2	**7.2**	9.1	17.5
▼ SLOVAK SB	PITTSBURGH	PA	**C**	B-	B	84	9.03	1.3	0.5	60.3	5.8	**8.2**	9.8	20.3
SLOVENIAN S&LA OF	STRABANE	PA	**B**	B	B	261	9.14	0.0	0.2	45.2	37.2	**10.0**	12.2	28.3
SLOVENIAN S&LA OF FRANKLI	CONEMAUGH	PA	**C**	C+	C+	130	1.85	0.8	1.5	55.6	17.7	**7.3**	9.2	22.6
SMACKOVER STATE BK	SMACKOVER	AR	**B+**	B+	B	177	6.19	2.0	7.1	19.7	49.2	**8.4**	9.9	22.4
▼ SMALL TOWN BANK	WEDOWEE	AL	**D**	C+	A-	238	-0.64	4.2	6.2	14.9	29.6	**9.2**	10.5	17.6
SMARTBANK	PIGEON FORGE	TN	**C-**	C	C	304	7.98	9.8	0.8	17.4	13.3	**8.9**	10.2	14.2
▼ SOLERA NATIONAL BK	LAKEWOOD	CO	**D**	C-	C-	140	5.49	6.2	0.0	2.5	54.5	**10.0**	11.2	18.7
SOLOMON STATE BK	SOLOMON	KS	**A**	A	A	181	7.04	5.2	3.1	55.1	4.7	**10.0**	11.3	19.1
▲ SOLON STATE BK	SOLON	IA	**C**	C-	C+	86	-0.16	15.7	2.1	11.5	19.9	**10.0**	19.6	24.0
SOLVAY BANK	SOLVAY	NY	**B**	B	B+	588	6.36	11.2	3.8	33.7	32.4	**7.0**	9.0	18.7
SOMERSET HILLS BANK	BERNARDSVILLE	NJ	**B-**	C+	B-	328	-0.37	3.5	0.4	15.0	14.2	**9.2**	10.4	15.5
SOMERSET SAVINGS BANK	BOUND BROOK	NJ	**B-**	B-	B+	588	-4.42	0.0	0.0	44.9	35.3	**10.0**	16.8	43.9
SOMERSET TRUST CO	SOMERSET	PA	**B-**	C+	B-	643	15.96	13.1	2.9	12.9	35.0	**6.6**	8.6	12.9
SOMERVILLE BANK & TRUST C	SOMERVILLE	TN	**C**	C	C+	195	4.14	2.3	3.8	35.1	0.0	**7.2**	9.1	20.3
▼ SOMERVILLE NATIONAL BK	SOMERVILLE	OH	**C+**	B	B	148	5.30	3.5	3.1	28.3	28.1	**8.8**	10.2	19.7
SONABANK	MCLEAN	VA	**B+**	B-	C+	591	-3.20	13.1	0.4	15.0	9.3	**10.0**	14.7	21.1
SONORAN BANK NA	PHOENIX	AZ	**D-**	D+	B-	36	7.13	1.9	2.5	0.4	35.5	**6.6**	8.6	14.3
▼ SOONER STATE BK	TUTTLE	OK	**A-**	A	A	146	5.01	3.5	3.4	8.5	40.8	**10.0**	11.2	20.2
SOUND BANKING CO	MOREHEAD CITY	NC	**D+**	D	C-	124	-3.01	5.3	3.7	19.7	14.8	**6.5**	8.6	14.7
▼ SOUND BANKING CO	TACOMA	WA	**D+**	C+	C	47	-4.11	17.4	0.2	38.3	0.2	**5.1**	7.1	11.4
▲ SOUND COMMUNITY BANK	SEATTLE	WA	**D+**	C-	C-	334	-0.91	4.3	8.8	34.6	1.4	**5.9**	7.9	11.7
SOUTH ADAMS SB	ADAMS	MA	**B-**	C+	C	208	4.09	3.9	2.4	58.3	7.1	**10.0**	12.3	22.0
▼ SOUTH ATLANTIC BANK	MYRTLE BEACH	SC	**D-**	C	C	205	24.92	9.8	0.8	13.3	10.7	**7.3**	10.4	12.8
▲ SOUTH CAROLINA	COLUMBIA	SC	**E**	E-	D-	81	-12.72	4.0	1.5	18.1	6.7	**4.2**	7.1	10.6
SOUTH CENTRAL BANK INC	GLASGOW	KY	**C-**	C-	C+	278	-6.31	8.9	4.4	18.9	6.7	**9.8**	10.9	15.5
SOUTH CENTRAL BANK NA	CHICAGO	IL	**D+**	C-	C+	241	1.41	18.9	4.5	26.9	23.5	**5.6**	7.6	12.4
▼ SOUTH CENTRAL BK	BOWLING GREEN	KY	**C-**	C	B-	225	-3.06	1.9	3.7	27.8	10.5	**9.9**	10.9	17.0
SOUTH CENTRAL BK HARDIN	ELIZABETHTOWN	KY	**C-**	C	C+	78	4.98	2.7	1.8	25.8	18.5	**10.0**	11.0	18.1
▼ SOUTH CENTRAL BK MONROE	TOMPKINSVILLE	KY	**C-**	C-	B-	118	0.72	4.0	6.6	14.2	19.4	**10.0**	11.6	19.2
SOUTH CENTRAL BK OF DAVIE	OWENSBORO	KY	**C-**	C+	B-	195	0.66	6.4	6.8	17.4	23.0	**6.8**	8.8	16.3
SOUTH CENTRAL STATE BK	CAMPBELL	NE	**C+**	C+	C	96	5.00	5.6	12.3	3.4	5.7	**5.2**	8.5	11.1
▲ SOUTH COASTAL BANK	ROCKLAND	MA	**D+**	D+	D+	258	0.50	8.3	0.4	28.8	15.9	**5.2**	7.2	12.6
▼ SOUTH COUNTY BANK NA	IRVINE	CA	**E-**	D-	D-	179	-6.18	24.8	0.8	1.4	29.7	**3.6**	5.6	10.3
SOUTH END SAVINGS SB	HOMEWOOD	IL	**C**	C-	C-	36	0.27	0.0	0.0	49.8	33.8	**10.0**	15.4	40.3
SOUTH GEORGIA BANK	GLENNVILLE	GA	**D-**	D-	D-	138	2.17	6.5	7.9	19.8	10.2	**6.0**	8.0	12.4
▼ SOUTH GEORGIA BANKING CO	TIFTON	GA	**C-**	B-	B+	341	13.83	6.2	5.7	15.0	14.7	**8.6**	10.1	16.7

Asset Quality Index	Non-Performing Loans as a % of Total Loans	Non-Performing Loans as a % of Capital	Net Charge-offs Avg Loans	Profitability Index	Net Income ($Mil)	Return on Assets (R.O.A.)	Return on Equity (R.O.E.)	Net Interest Spread	Overhead Efficiency Ratio	Liquidity Index	Liquidity Ratio	Hot Money Ratio	Stability Index
0.0	6.32	60.3	5.24	**0.0**	-7.5	-3.42	-54.80	2.96	148.2	**2.7**	29.5	18.2	**0.0**
9.2	0.00	0.0	-0.05	**4.2**	0.6	0.90	5.84	3.43	61.9	**5.3**	60.3	12.1	**7.4**
7.5	0.72	3.5	0.78	**5.9**	129.0	0.92	12.70	3.25	58.4	**7.4**	62.2	2.9	**5.2**
6.9	0.13	0.8	1.80	**2.2**	-0.1	-0.03	-0.31	3.74	56.0	**1.8**	17.2	20.4	**6.5**
2.5	2.33	15.1	0.34	**4.6**	3.1	0.85	8.64	4.42	61.0	**2.0**	24.4	20.0	**5.6**
1.9	3.53	18.8	1.39	**5.7**	0.5	0.89	6.94	4.60	64.1	**1.0**	25.1	37.9	**6.5**
5.6	0.25	2.1	0.19	**9.6**	5.5	1.72	19.06	4.35	42.3	**1.3**	9.4	25.7	**6.6**
2.8	1.66	7.0	1.29	**1.0**	0.1	0.05	0.35	3.45	83.3	**1.5**	22.0	26.9	**5.8**
5.0	0.66	4.2	0.23	**8.9**	2.4	1.59	13.35	4.52	51.4	**1.4**	17.3	26.9	**7.5**
7.7	0.11	0.5	0.12	**9.8**	2.8	1.72	17.41	4.10	46.1	**2.8**	31.7	18.0	**5.7**
3.3	0.99	4.8	0.49	**4.7**	1.6	0.91	5.37	3.57	64.3	**4.3**	28.6	9.9	**7.5**
5.6	1.41	5.9	0.89	**6.8**	3.4	1.28	16.31	3.56	47.6	**3.5**	21.1	12.0	**5.7**
4.8	0.58	2.1	-0.15	**6.2**	2.1	1.11	5.81	4.30	60.2	**4.0**	32.7	12.5	**7.5**
2.9	1.59	9.4	0.87	**7.8**	24.8	1.48	18.25	3.62	59.7	**4.2**	27.2	12.7	**6.2**
10.0	0.00	0.0	0.00	**9.5**	0.3	21.44	28.58	N/,	89.9	**10.0**	248.1	0.0	**5.0**
4.9	1.13	10.0	0.32	**2.8**	1.2	0.41	5.48	3.92	80.7	**3.5**	24.3	12.5	**4.1**
4.2	1.71	11.0	0.05	**2.6**	0.2	0.38	4.59	2.89	84.9	**2.0**	32.4	27.9	**3.6**
0.0	4.37	21.5	0.27	**7.9**	3.8	1.29	9.81	5.35	66.9	**3.9**	22.9	10.0	**7.9**
3.3	3.51	18.0	0.39	**4.1**	5.7	0.84	8.66	3.49	66.4	**2.6**	34.2	19.9	**6.4**
5.4	2.05	10.2	0.17	**3.2**	2.3	0.52	3.84	3.48	73.8	**4.2**	31.2	10.8	**6.9**
1.1	2.74	21.7	0.75	**5.1**	13.6	0.96	7.95	3.97	55.4	**3.2**	13.2	13.1	**6.5**
2.8	3.84	31.3	0.01	**2.0**	0.5	0.27	3.25	2.93	78.1	**1.1**	23.2	32.5	**4.2**
7.6	0.57	2.2	-0.08	**7.0**	0.7	1.58	13.53	4.30	57.8	**5.4**	56.9	10.6	**8.2**
4.7	1.83	11.1	0.76	**2.9**	0.3	0.32	3.43	4.27	73.7	**1.7**	22.1	24.2	**5.6**
2.6	2.98	21.7	0.11	**3.1**	0.5	0.65	6.44	2.77	66.2	**0.9**	23.2	46.3	**6.2**
6.7	2.17	9.3	0.07	**4.1**	2.2	0.86	7.07	2.74	41.4	**2.4**	49.6	41.0	**7.4**
6.1	0.91	6.0	0.00	**3.1**	0.5	0.42	4.69	2.94	75.6	**4.3**	39.4	13.5	**4.7**
6.2	1.26	4.8	0.15	**6.3**	2.0	1.15	10.95	3.56	53.3	**2.3**	45.2	34.4	**6.6**
0.9	3.52	17.6	0.59	**7.8**	3.7	1.56	14.91	4.98	45.8	**1.4**	27.1	30.6	**8.0**
3.9	0.99	6.7	0.22	**2.0**	1.2	0.42	3.93	3.28	77.7	**0.6**	7.2	41.4	**3.3**
6.6	3.03	10.7	1.35	**0.2**	0.4	0.29	2.37	3.20	96.1	**2.7**	44.1	27.3	**2.2**
8.5	0.09	0.6	0.29	**7.9**	2.3	1.27	11.10	4.14	35.5	**1.4**	6.7	23.0	**7.5**
1.9	6.04	22.6	0.95	**10.0**	2.2	2.57	13.29	5.55	43.8	**4.3**	27.0	8.9	**10.0**
5.2	0.96	5.9	0.14	**5.2**	5.7	0.98	10.80	3.72	64.1	**2.4**	23.8	18.0	**6.6**
8.1	0.12	0.7	0.17	**4.8**	2.6	0.82	7.68	3.94	70.8	**4.8**	31.6	7.3	**6.0**
9.9	0.41	1.1	0.00	**3.7**	3.9	0.66	4.09	2.92	63.4	**5.6**	62.4	12.2	**8.7**
4.6	0.80	4.9	0.59	**4.6**	5.6	0.95	11.65	4.65	74.4	**3.4**	30.5	14.8	**4.3**
5.0	1.44	7.9	0.16	**5.5**	1.8	0.97	8.54	3.50	63.5	**3.5**	49.4	19.9	**5.0**
3.2	1.95	10.8	0.31	**4.0**	1.4	0.93	8.90	3.26	70.1	**3.9**	41.3	15.9	**6.4**
4.0	1.88	9.3	1.76	**4.9**	2.2	0.36	2.30	4.54	55.0	**0.7**	4.1	33.8	**6.2**
3.2	4.64	22.2	-0.02	**0.0**	-1.1	-2.94	-21.98	3.95	207.3	**4.4**	42.6	13.3	**1.3**
8.2	0.69	2.7	0.03	**6.2**	2.1	1.46	11.85	3.98	66.1	**3.2**	46.1	20.9	**9.0**
3.1	1.21	8.6	1.17	**2.3**	0.7	0.52	6.17	4.35	70.0	**0.9**	21.9	35.6	**3.0**
1.7	4.32	40.1	0.59	**5.7**	0.5	0.96	12.73	4.59	62.9	**0.7**	9.3	37.9	**6.5**
2.8	1.19	11.6	1.17	**2.9**	1.5	0.43	5.85	4.86	63.0	**1.3**	4.4	25.0	**2.6**
8.0	0.13	0.9	0.10	**3.3**	0.9	0.45	3.63	3.72	77.3	**1.8**	14.4	19.8	**6.6**
7.7	0.38	2.7	0.45	**0.0**	-0.7	-0.36	-3.27	3.09	95.1	**1.3**	9.4	25.3	**0.8**
0.0	9.27	75.5	1.52	**0.5**	-0.2	-0.23	-3.36	4.97	85.7	**0.6**	10.8	46.3	**2.7**
1.0	5.15	34.4	1.79	**3.1**	1.1	0.38	3.51	3.94	64.7	**1.5**	11.7	23.8	**5.1**
1.5	3.41	24.3	0.34	**3.2**	1.3	0.52	6.77	4.33	83.8	**1.2**	18.7	30.0	**4.8**
2.5	3.66	21.9	0.58	**3.8**	1.3	0.56	4.97	3.68	68.0	**2.1**	21.2	19.3	**5.9**
0.9	6.52	37.5	1.04	**2.4**	0.3	0.33	2.99	3.69	71.5	**3.1**	31.4	16.7	**4.1**
3.2	4.46	22.5	0.06	**5.6**	1.2	1.03	8.77	3.99	67.2	**2.0**	23.5	19.7	**5.6**
2.3	3.97	25.2	0.66	**3.5**	0.9	0.50	5.27	3.95	75.9	**2.0**	20.1	19.4	**4.3**
4.4	0.12	1.0	-0.05	**5.3**	0.9	0.92	10.03	3.75	60.3	**3.5**	18.2	11.8	**5.1**
1.7	3.86	35.7	0.03	**2.5**	0.9	0.36	4.91	3.36	84.3	**1.8**	17.9	20.4	**4.0**
0.3	12.08	85.2	3.39	**0.0**	-5.9	-3.05	-45.15	3.49	95.7	**1.4**	25.3	29.2	**1.9**
9.6	0.94	3.2	0.02	**2.7**	0.1	0.35	2.28	3.09	84.1	**3.4**	53.3	21.3	**7.1**
0.0	10.04	79.4	2.94	**1.2**	-0.3	-0.19	-2.34	5.10	55.9	**0.8**	21.5	49.5	**3.4**
1.9	3.33	17.9	0.62	**5.9**	3.2	1.05	7.60	5.00	67.3	**3.6**	40.2	17.0	**7.3**

Name	City	State	Rating	2008 Rating	2007 Rating	Total Assets ($Mil)	One Year Asset Growth	Asset Mix (As a % of Total Assets) Comm-ercial Loans	Cons-umer Loans	Home Mort-gages	Secur-ities	Capital-ization Index	Leverage Ratio	Risk-based Capital Ratio
SOUTH LAFOURCHE BANK &	LAROSE	LA	**C**	B-	C	167	12.20	17.5	6.3	41.5	4.1	**5.5**	7.5	14.2
SOUTH LOUISIANA BANK	HOUMA	LA	**B**	B	B	381	7.17	16.8	3.7	12.4	11.9	**10.0**	11.0	16.6
▼ SOUTH LOUISIANA BUSINESS	PRAIRIEVILLE	LA	**D+**	C	C	46	10.17	7.3	0.2	10.1	6.2	**10.0**	25.2	37.9
SOUTH OTTUMWA SB	OTTUMWA	IA	**C+**	D+	C+	244	2.75	2.2	0.5	13.8	50.1	**7.5**	9.3	18.7
SOUTH PADRE BANK NA	SOUTH PADRE ISLAND	TX	**B**	B	A-	39	0.48	9.4	1.4	32.3	6.4	**10.0**	17.8	30.0
▼ SOUTH SHORE SB	SOUTH WEYMOUTH	MA	**D+**	D+	C-	944	-0.21	3.4	0.4	28.8	26.2	**7.2**	9.1	13.7
SOUTH SIDE TRUST & SB PEO	PEORIA	IL	**B+**	A-	A-	634	6.40	4.7	3.7	25.4	32.6	**9.1**	10.4	18.3
SOUTH SOUND BANK	OLYMPIA	WA	**B+**	C+	A	172	10.83	19.2	1.5	5.6	11.1	**10.0**	13.2	18.5
SOUTH STORY BANK & TRUST	SLATER	IA	**B**	B+	B+	69	20.17	10.7	3.4	19.3	10.0	**5.8**	7.9	11.6
SOUTH VALLEY BANK &	KLAMATH FALLS	OR	**C-**	C+	B+	843	39.53	10.2	2.0	11.4	6.0	**6.1**	8.1	12.8
SOUTHBANK A FSB	HUNTSVILLE	AL	**D-**	D-	D+	263	0.82	1.8	1.5	14.7	21.0	**6.8**	8.8	14.3
SOUTHBANK A FSB	PALM BEACH GARDENS	FL	**E-**	E-	C-	24	-22.56	0.1	0.0	1.4	45.9	**3.9**	5.9	13.9
SOUTHBRIDGE SB	SOUTHBRIDGE	MA	**C**	D	D	409	-7.22	2.8	1.5	50.4	4.5	**7.3**	9.2	14.8
SOUTHCITY BANK	VESTAVIA HILLS	AL	**C+**	C	C	147	15.29	27.4	3.0	2.6	8.3	**6.1**	9.3	11.8
SOUTHCOAST COMMUNITY	MOUNT PLEASANT	SC	**D**	D	C+	472	-6.09	5.6	0.5	30.5	15.4	**9.1**	10.4	15.1
▲ SOUTHEAST BANK & TRUST	ATHENS	TN	**C**	D+	C+	272	1.67	10.0	3.6	22.7	10.3	**6.2**	8.2	12.7
▼ SOUTHEAST FIRST NATIONAL	SUMMERVILLE	GA	**D+**	C+	B-	67	-4.40	1.0	3.5	11.0	61.1	**6.5**	8.5	25.6
SOUTHEAST NATIONAL BK	MOLINE	IL	**C+**	C+	C+	135	-0.13	6.9	3.5	9.1	49.0	**10.0**	11.5	22.8
SOUTHEASTERN BANK	DARIEN	GA	**D-**	C	A	431	2.74	4.0	2.7	7.7	17.1	**9.2**	10.5	17.2
▲ SOUTHERN ARIZONA	TUCSON	AZ	**D**	C-	C-	108	14.31	6.1	1.2	5.0	0.0	**10.0**	22.2	27.4
SOUTHERN BANCORP BANK	ARKADELPHIA	AR	**C+**	C+	B-	1,079	51.98	6.1	4.3	13.3	25.1	**5.2**	7.2	11.9
SOUTHERN BANK	SARDIS	GA	**D**	D	C-	92	-4.68	1.1	8.9	21.1	14.2	**6.4**	8.4	13.0
SOUTHERN BANK	POPLAR BLUFF	MO	**B**	B	B-	690	30.28	10.9	2.5	26.6	10.0	**5.7**	9.4	11.5
SOUTHERN BANK & TRUST	CLARKESVILLE	GA	**D+**	C-	C-	90	20.19	3.5	2.5	15.8	25.9	**9.9**	10.9	17.0
SOUTHERN BANK & TRUST	AIKEN	SC	**D+**	NR	NR	185	N/A	5.9	0.8	12.6	19.9	**5.8**	7.8	13.1
SOUTHERN BANK & TRUST CO	MOUNT OLIVE	NC	**B-**	C+	B	1,339	4.88	5.1	1.7	9.5	25.1	**6.2**	8.2	15.7
SOUTHERN BANK CO	GADSDEN	AL	**C-**	C	C-	98	2.10	2.1	1.9	14.2	58.0	**10.0**	15.5	39.7
▲ SOUTHERN COMMERCE BANK	TAMPA	FL	**E+**	D-	D+	125	-45.08	12.5	0.5	4.4	5.4	**10.0**	12.9	27.1
▼ SOUTHERN COMMERCIAL	SAINT LOUIS	MO	**D-**	C	B-	514	-2.04	9.2	0.7	12.1	26.7	**7.6**	9.4	13.9
SOUTHERN COMMUNITY BANK	WINSTON-SALEM	NC	**D-**	D	C+	1,658	-3.86	8.7	1.1	14.6	21.1	**6.0**	8.3	11.7
SOUTHERN FIRST BANK NA	GREENVILLE	SC	**D+**	C	C+	736	2.42	11.6	1.0	15.4	8.7	**7.8**	9.6	13.2
SOUTHERN HERITAGE BANK	JONESVILLE	LA	**C+**	B-	B-	255	-3.29	6.4	7.2	24.7	26.9	**9.6**	10.8	19.6
▲ SOUTHERN HERITAGE BANK	CLEVELAND	TN	**C+**	D+	D+	206	-5.32	12.0	1.3	7.5	20.2	**10.0**	12.0	17.3
SOUTHERN ILLINOIS BANK	JOHNSTON CITY	IL	**C**	C-	C	81	25.19	3.3	3.6	18.3	48.8	**5.3**	7.3	13.8
SOUTHERN INDEPENDENT	OPP	AL	**C**	D+	D+	152	25.05	11.2	2.8	14.8	37.7	**6.5**	8.5	13.1
SOUTHERN MICHIGAN BANK &	COLDWATER	MI	**C-**	C	C-	493	6.85	8.7	2.1	15.8	12.0	**6.4**	8.4	14.0
▼ SOUTHERN MO BK OF	MARSHFIELD	MO	**C+**	C	C	105	3.98	7.6	3.3	26.3	7.4	**6.4**	8.7	12.1
▲ SOUTHERN STATES BANK	ANNISTON	AL	**C-**	C-	C-	192	13.11	10.6	2.8	7.3	9.9	**10.0**	14.7	19.0
▲ SOUTHERNTRUST BANK	GOREVILLE	IL	**D+**	C-	C-	51	10.94	8.3	5.9	28.8	17.2	**6.2**	8.2	12.8
SOUTHFIRST BANK	SYLACAUGA	AL	**D-**	D	D	131	0.39	3.0	2.4	36.7	8.9	**5.9**	7.9	11.9
▼ SOUTHPOINT BANK	BIRMINGHAM	AL	**E-**	E	D+	292	13.94	11.3	2.0	8.5	19.2	**2.5**	6.1	9.5
SOUTHPORT BANK	KENOSHA	WI	**E-**	E-	D	352	-14.95	4.8	0.5	14.6	11.8	**1.4**	5.7	8.4
SOUTHSHORE COMMUNITY	APOLLO BEACH	FL	**E-**	E-	D+	49	0.64	2.9	0.7	6.2	5.1	**0.0**	3.9	6.1
SOUTHSIDE BANK	TYLER	TX	**B**	B	B	2,994	-0.85	4.2	6.6	7.5	55.9	**6.1**	8.1	20.3
SOUTHWEST BANK	FORT WORTH	TX	**C-**	C-	D+	826	6.76	13.3	1.5	21.5	12.2	**7.4**	9.3	13.5
▼ SOUTHWEST BANK	ODESSA	TX	**B-**	B+	B	195	13.67	32.3	5.7	9.0	23.9	**6.4**	8.4	12.7
SOUTHWEST CAPITAL BANK	FORT MYERS	FL	**D-**	D	D+	115	8.98	8.4	0.8	15.9	7.7	**9.6**	10.7	15.8
SOUTHWEST GEORGIA BANK	MOULTRIE	GA	**C+**	C+	C+	296	1.94	3.3	1.7	16.8	34.3	**6.5**	8.5	16.8
SOUTHWEST MISSOURI BANK	CARTHAGE	MO	**B-**	C+	B-	548	-1.61	8.8	10.1	26.7	14.9	**7.0**	9.0	13.6
SOUTHWEST NATIONAL BK	WICHITA	KS	**B**	B-	C+	357	0.11	6.3	55.7	2.0	7.0	**5.3**	9.1	11.2
▲ SOUTHWEST NATIONAL BK	WEATHERFORD	OK	**B+**	B	B+	55	20.69	6.8	7.9	11.0	37.0	**10.0**	12.0	19.5
SOUTHWEST SECURITIES FSB	DALLAS	TX	**D**	C-	C-	1,532	-6.19	13.4	0.3	18.8	2.8	**7.7**	9.4	14.0
SOUTHWEST STATE BK	SENTINEL	OK	**B-**	B-	B-	107	-0.68	8.7	3.0	4.1	43.2	**5.7**	8.3	11.6
SOUTHWEST TRUST CO NA	OKLAHOMA CITY	OK	**U**	U	U	54	0.63	0.0	0.0	0.0	3.7	**10.0**	100.1	526.3
SOUTHWESTERN NATIONAL	HOUSTON	TX	**D-**	C-	C-	319	-4.69	6.8	0.2	3.1	15.6	**6.0**	8.0	11.8
SOVEREIGN BANK	BOSTON	MA	**D+**	D	D-	68,692	-2.15	14.2	3.1	18.4	18.0	**10.0**	11.4	15.9
▲ SOVEREIGN BANK	DALLAS	TX	**C+**	C-	C-	739	-2.99	19.7	0.5	3.5	34.7	**10.0**	12.1	19.1
SOY CAPITAL BANK & TRUST	DECATUR	IL	**A-**	B+	B	382	2.23	15.6	6.1	3.0	16.7	**9.0**	10.6	14.2
SPENCER COUNTY BANK	SANTA CLAUS	IN	**C-**	D+	C-	99	5.90	4.1	4.1	23.4	41.9	**6.7**	8.7	17.7
SPENCER SAVINGS BANK SLA	ELMWOOD PARK	NJ	**C+**	B-	B	1,809	-4.01	1.1	0.1	34.5	25.3	**10.0**	13.7	16.0

Asset Quality Index	Non-Performing Loans as a % of Total Loans	Non-Performing Loans as a % of Capital	Net Charge-offs / Avg Loans	Profitability Index	Net Income ($Mil)	Return on Assets (R.O.A.)	Return on Equity (R.O.E.)	Net Interest Spread	Overhead Efficiency Ratio	Liquidity Index	Liquidity Ratio	Hot Money Ratio	Stability Index
3.6	1.77	15.1	0.11	**7.0**	2.3	1.49	18.64	4.44	58.0	**0.9**	16.9	34.2	**6.7**
4.7	1.78	9.4	0.25	**7.1**	4.1	1.12	9.83	4.78	63.3	**1.7**	24.1	24.3	**7.5**
9.0	0.00	0.0	0.00	**0.0**	-0.4	-0.93	-3.38	2.58	144.6	**3.1**	46.4	21.5	**1.7**
4.6	1.35	5.8	3.45	**3.1**	1.8	0.73	7.63	3.82	56.0	**3.0**	48.5	25.8	**3.8**
8.8	0.05	0.2	0.04	**4.6**	0.3	0.77	4.59	3.92	67.3	**1.6**	29.1	30.1	**7.9**
1.3	4.35	29.0	0.24	**2.9**	5.8	0.63	6.53	3.05	77.7	**3.6**	26.9	12.6	**5.0**
4.5	0.59	3.0	0.23	**5.9**	6.3	1.02	9.62	3.52	59.0	**2.2**	26.4	19.3	**7.7**
6.2	0.92	4.2	1.21	**4.5**	1.0	0.60	4.39	3.89	63.9	**3.0**	28.2	16.0	**7.5**
5.8	0.18	1.5	0.00	**5.5**	0.8	1.29	8.86	4.49	65.5	**4.1**	19.5	8.5	**7.4**
1.7	2.86	23.3	0.78	**3.2**	2.8	0.38	4.10	4.76	69.4	**1.5**	8.7	22.3	**4.6**
1.9	6.05	32.1	0.19	**0.0**	-4.3	-1.60	-17.65	3.09	144.3	**2.9**	42.4	22.8	**3.1**
2.3	12.65	30.9	0.00	**0.1**	-0.3	-0.93	-14.36	1.76	155.3	**3.7**	81.4	25.3	**0.3**
4.0	1.42	12.0	0.70	**3.1**	2.2	0.50	5.83	3.69	73.1	**2.7**	9.2	14.9	**4.0**
6.3	0.13	1.0	0.16	**4.3**	1.6	1.25	13.45	4.68	62.0	**1.6**	17.7	24.3	**5.2**
1.0	5.83	33.7	1.26	**0.7**	0.6	0.13	1.28	2.92	85.6	**1.0**	13.9	32.4	**4.0**
3.1	1.10	8.6	0.56	**3.0**	1.0	0.37	4.67	4.15	74.6	**1.6**	16.2	24.1	**3.5**
4.2	5.67	14.5	0.85	**1.3**	-0.2	-0.31	-3.19	3.44	109.8	**5.4**	61.3	11.3	**4.4**
7.7	1.22	4.2	0.40	**2.3**	0.7	0.48	3.80	3.48	88.6	**5.4**	52.2	10.9	**6.4**
0.3	11.66	51.9	4.50	**0.3**	-7.7	-1.78	-15.44	3.42	88.9	**2.3**	23.2	18.4	**6.4**
3.2	1.88	6.8	0.33	**1.0**	-0.7	-0.66	-5.14	N/,	449.5	**2.4**	34.2	22.6	**5.7**
3.3	2.31	17.3	0.62	**5.7**	9.1	0.93	9.56	4.67	68.0	**1.3**	16.3	28.9	**8.0**
1.0	6.35	43.3	0.61	**1.4**	-0.2	-0.25	-2.96	4.04	93.9	**1.6**	19.6	24.7	**4.1**
7.1	0.13	1.3	0.08	**8.1**	9.5	1.70	19.46	3.47	45.8	**1.4**	5.6	23.5	**5.0**
4.7	1.09	6.1	0.43	**2.0**	0.8	0.98	8.92	4.08	80.9	**1.7**	26.2	25.8	**2.8**
3.7	1.85	12.9	0.00	**0.7**	0.4	0.22	2.82	N/,	66.0	**2.2**	35.7	28.2	**3.5**
5.6	0.47	2.9	0.43	**3.7**	7.1	0.56	5.92	3.58	75.5	**3.9**	31.4	16.1	**7.0**
9.7	0.07	0.1	0.03	**1.4**	0.1	0.14	0.83	2.67	96.1	**3.7**	60.8	20.3	**3.4**
0.3	33.50	87.7	4.72	**0.0**	-9.1	-4.33	-75.03	0.32	488.8	**2.4**	44.9	32.3	**4.2**
0.3	3.82	23.4	0.62	**3.7**	2.7	0.53	5.63	4.08	67.1	**3.4**	23.9	12.8	**5.9**
0.3	8.08	54.2	3.25	**0.4**	-11.9	-0.71	-8.03	3.71	68.5	**0.9**	11.5	32.7	**5.1**
4.0	1.63	11.7	0.86	**1.8**	1.3	0.18	1.90	3.07	71.5	**0.9**	13.7	33.4	**5.0**
4.0	2.25	12.2	0.79	**5.2**	2.4	0.93	9.01	4.56	64.5	**2.0**	21.3	19.8	**5.6**
4.9	1.61	8.1	0.62	**3.7**	1.6	0.78	6.80	3.93	68.5	**1.5**	24.6	27.2	**4.9**
6.7	0.62	3.6	0.13	**4.6**	0.8	1.07	14.12	3.97	64.6	**5.3**	30.8	4.3	**3.2**
2.7	3.07	17.6	-0.24	**3.8**	1.4	1.04	11.58	3.48	58.9	**1.5**	32.7	37.1	**3.6**
2.1	1.70	11.5	0.55	**4.0**	3.4	0.70	6.23	4.03	76.6	**3.4**	25.1	13.2	**5.1**
3.8	2.05	16.9	0.41	**5.6**	1.1	1.04	12.75	4.58	66.1	**0.5**	6.4	45.7	**5.3**
4.6	1.58	7.8	0.65	**1.4**	1.7	0.91	5.98	3.72	80.1	**1.7**	17.3	22.1	**3.0**
3.5	2.10	16.7	0.11	**1.6**	0.1	0.11	1.29	3.93	86.6	**1.7**	16.6	22.0	**2.5**
2.9	1.70	14.3	0.55	**0.1**	-1.3	-0.97	-11.72	3.25	95.7	**1.4**	14.7	25.7	**2.5**
0.9	2.70	25.3	0.43	**0.9**	0.3	0.12	1.82	3.25	91.5	**1.8**	29.2	26.9	**0.0**
0.0	14.93	105.0	4.52	**0.0**	-12.5	-3.16	-58.25	3.10	118.9	**1.3**	9.9	26.4	**3.1**
0.0	3.29	42.9	4.62	**0.0**	-0.9	-1.94	-40.60	3.43	102.4	**1.0**	25.4	35.0	**0.0**
6.2	1.31	5.3	1.25	**5.3**	42.7	1.46	16.62	3.57	60.5	**2.1**	28.0	30.9	**7.1**
4.7	0.08	0.6	0.33	**1.3**	1.2	0.15	0.99	4.83	93.1	**1.5**	7.0	22.0	**6.7**
4.5	0.17	1.2	0.08	**6.6**	2.8	1.56	16.20	5.03	70.5	**3.6**	30.8	13.8	**6.2**
2.0	4.60	26.7	2.60	**0.0**	-3.3	-2.77	-24.37	3.76	134.4	**0.9**	22.7	38.4	**1.3**
7.3	0.12	0.7	0.24	**3.5**	1.8	0.61	7.26	3.91	82.9	**3.3**	24.9	13.5	**5.1**
4.7	0.71	5.3	0.94	**4.4**	3.6	0.65	7.46	4.88	70.7	**2.5**	6.8	15.9	**5.3**
4.6	0.22	1.9	0.31	**9.9**	8.2	2.31	25.83	5.35	52.6	**1.5**	11.1	22.7	**7.1**
5.3	0.99	3.9	0.21	**8.0**	0.7	1.30	9.71	5.06	64.5	**3.1**	43.6	20.6	**7.4**
1.7	5.23	31.7	3.58	**0.7**	-46.3	-2.72	-30.19	4.49	81.3	**5.2**	20.4	2.0	**6.3**
3.7	5.05	31.1	1.44	**4.3**	0.9	0.89	10.18	3.82	59.7	**1.7**	20.7	23.9	**5.5**
10.0	0.00	0.0	0.00	**4.7**	0.3	0.64	0.64	1.09	48.6	**4.0**	N/A	101.0	**7.0**
0.0	10.38	66.6	0.74	**1.1**	-7.0	-2.04	-20.45	4.16	87.2	**1.8**	25.7	23.4	**5.6**
1.3	3.61	20.0	1.60	**3.8**	720.5	0.99	6.88	2.86	40.2	**5.1**	24.7	5.8	**6.8**
8.0	0.04	0.2	0.16	**3.0**	4.7	0.64	5.34	3.68	83.5	**2.0**	39.1	33.7	**6.2**
6.9	0.13	0.7	0.18	**6.5**	4.4	1.18	8.99	3.95	73.2	**2.6**	7.2	15.3	**7.3**
3.8	2.16	11.9	0.64	**3.1**	0.5	0.48	5.23	3.58	72.2	**2.8**	45.1	25.1	**3.1**
3.9	3.09	14.1	-0.02	**3.2**	9.7	0.51	4.46	2.97	60.4	**4.4**	31.7	13.6	**8.5**

Name	City	State	Rating	2008 Rating	2007 Rating	Total Assets ($Mil)	One Year Asset Growth	Asset Mix (As a % of Total Assets) Comm-ercial Loans	Cons-umer Loans	Home Mort-gages	Secur-ities	Capital-ization Index	Leverage Ratio	Risk-based Capital Ratio
SPENCER SB	SPENCER	MA	**C**	C-	B	393	-1.91	3.2	1.8	43.0	18.0	**10.0**	12.0	21.3
SPENCER STATE BK	SPENCER	NE	**C-**	C-	D	17	-0.17	2.0	5.8	3.4	7.2	**10.0**	12.2	25.3
SPIRIT BANK	BELMONT	MS	**C**	C	C+	24	2.32	10.5	6.7	12.0	23.7	**7.3**	9.2	15.5
SPIRIT OF TEXAS BANK SSB	COLLEGE STATION	TX	**D+**	D+	D	201	39.28	21.9	2.7	12.5	3.6	**10.0**	13.8	20.5
SPIRITBANK	TULSA	OK	**D+**	D+	C-	1,335	-2.31	17.9	1.2	23.5	5.2	**6.0**	8.0	12.7
SPIRO STATE BK	SPIRO	OK	**B-**	B-	B	51	5.79	2.0	5.9	12.8	38.0	**10.0**	12.0	30.6
SPIVEY STATE BK	SWAINSBORO	GA	**E**	D-	C-	89	-0.89	6.1	13.0	14.2	9.6	**5.9**	7.9	12.5
▲SPRATT SAVINGS & LOAN ASS	CHESTER	SC	**B-**	B-	A-	97	4.07	2.0	0.4	11.2	42.3	**10.0**	26.8	64.5
SPRING BANK	BROOKFIELD	WI	**C**	C	C	114	64.70	15.8	0.2	15.8	8.1	**9.7**	10.8	16.3
SPRING HILL STATE BK	LONGVIEW	TX	**C**	C	C-	162	0.39	10.3	8.4	39.6	2.5	**5.5**	7.5	13.8
▼SPRING VALLEY BANK	WYOMING	OH	**B+**	B+	B+	68	4.53	3.5	0.1	23.8	6.7	**10.0**	36.6	46.3
SPRING VALLEY CITY BANK	SPRING VALLEY	IL	**B+**	B+	B+	192	9.62	3.9	6.6	26.8	36.6	**10.0**	12.0	23.5
SPRINGFIELD FIRST COMMUNI	SPRINGFIELD	MO	**C-**	C	C	198	23.11	21.2	0.7	18.0	0.2	**8.1**	9.9	13.4
SPRINGFIELD STATE BK	SPRINGFIELD	KY	**A-**	A-	A	240	7.19	3.6	2.2	24.3	39.5	**10.0**	12.6	21.0
▼SPRINGFIELD STATE BK	SPRINGFIELD	NE	**C**	C+	C+	36	13.88	5.1	6.0	15.9	27.7	**6.8**	8.8	14.3
SPRINGS VALLEY BANK & TRU	FRENCH LICK	IN	**D-**	D-	D+	236	-6.87	4.5	4.0	31.5	19.1	**7.3**	9.2	14.9
SPUR SECURITY BANK	SPUR	TX	**B-**	B-	C	39	10.56	2.2	6.6	6.9	39.6	**8.6**	10.1	22.2
SQUARE 1 BANK	DURHAM	NC	**C+**	C+	C+	1,583	44.07	27.3	0.0	0.0	52.9	**6.7**	8.7	16.3
SSBBANK	STOCKBRIDGE	MI	**D-**	D-	D+	77	-4.35	6.0	5.9	34.0	22.5	**6.1**	8.1	16.3
ST ANSGAR STATE BK	SAINT ANSGAR	IA	**B**	C	C+	101	3.34	13.1	1.9	10.0	9.2	**10.0**	13.1	17.2
▲ST CHARLES BANK & TRUST C	SAINT CHARLES	IL	**C-**	D	C-	334	39.70	30.6	10.0	3.7	6.1	**8.1**	10.3	13.4
ST CLAIR COUNTY STATE BK	OSCEOLA	MO	**B**	B	B+	118	3.59	7.5	4.0	24.6	14.4	**9.7**	10.8	17.7
ST CLAIR STATE BK (INC)	SAINT CLAIR	MN	**A-**	B+	A-	68	2.01	8.5	7.2	14.3	0.7	**10.0**	12.2	18.6
ST EDMONDS FSB	PHILADELPHIA	PA	**D+**	C-	C-	313	0.46	0.0	0.1	43.4	24.3	**5.8**	7.8	16.1
ST HENRY BANK	SAINT HENRY	OH	**A+**	A+	A+	220	11.21	4.0	1.3	20.9	33.8	**10.0**	15.9	29.3
ST JAMES FS&LA	SAINT JAMES	MN	**D**	C-	C-	25	-1.52	20.7	5.4	34.2	3.3	**7.1**	9.1	14.2
ST JOHNS BANK & TRUST CO	SAINT JOHN	MO	**D-**	D-	D-	304	-8.06	4.7	1.2	9.1	16.5	**7.7**	9.5	13.1
▼ST LANDRY BANK & TRUST CO	OPELOUSAS	LA	**B-**	B	A-	239	-3.24	4.9	1.9	3.0	51.9	**10.0**	12.5	29.7
ST LANDRY HOMESTEAD FSB	OPELOUSAS	LA	**B-**	B	A-	265	-3.38	0.8	2.1	57.1	6.5	**10.0**	14.6	24.4
▲ST LOUIS BANK	TOWN AND COUNTRY	MO	**E+**	D-	D	507	-11.84	10.0	0.3	15.5	17.6	**4.7**	6.7	10.9
▼ST MARTIN BANK & TRUST CO	SAINT MARTINVILLE	LA	**C+**	B	B-	324	3.60	7.4	7.6	19.8	13.2	**7.8**	9.6	14.8
ST MARTIN NATIONAL BK	SAINT MARTIN	MN	**B+**	B+	B+	18	0.80	7.6	4.4	19.8	19.4	**10.0**	12.8	23.8
ST MARYS STATE BK	SAINT MARYS	KS	**C**	C	B-	77	-1.01	10.9	3.4	18.1	18.7	**7.6**	9.4	14.5
▲ST TAMMANY HOMESTEAD	COVINGTON	LA	**D**	C-	D+	104	-3.32	0.0	0.3	44.9	14.5	**7.7**	9.4	17.5
STAFFORD SB	STAFFORD SPRINGS	CT	**B**	B-	B-	213	2.91	0.0	0.4	35.3	43.7	**10.0**	26.2	43.6
STANDARD BANK & TRUST CO	HICKORY HILLS	IL	**D-**	D-	D	2,247	-5.66	6.7	0.8	6.1	6.4	**5.9**	8.3	11.7
STANDARD BANK PASB	MONROEVILLE	PA	**C+**	C+	C+	431	9.82	2.7	0.7	47.0	23.1	**10.0**	11.8	20.7
STANDING STONE NATIONAL	LANCASTER	OH	**D**	D	D	76	2.72	6.1	5.0	17.2	28.3	**6.0**	8.0	13.7
▼STANLEY BANK	OVERLAND PARK	KS	**C-**	B	A-	126	-6.97	33.2	3.0	9.3	4.1	**10.0**	13.9	24.3
STANTON STATE BK	STANTON	NE	**C**	C	C	36	-0.07	9.4	5.9	23.8	15.8	**7.8**	9.6	15.9
STAR BANK	BERTHA	MN	**C+**	C-	B	137	11.10	27.8	6.5	12.7	3.9	**4.7**	7.6	10.8
STAR BANK OF TEXAS	LAKE WORTH	TX	**B+**	NR	NR	108	17.58	3.8	2.6	28.1	29.3	**7.5**	9.4	16.5
STAR FINANCIAL BANK	FORT WAYNE	IN	**D+**	C+	C+	1,606	-3.28	16.7	9.1	14.0	14.9	**6.5**	8.9	12.1
▲STARION FINANCIAL	BISMARCK	ND	**B-**	C	B-	775	8.80	10.9	2.8	10.5	24.1	**6.5**	8.5	12.2
START COMMUNITY BANK	NEW HAVEN	CT	**C-**	NR	NR	13	N/A	0.0	0.0	0.0	0.0	**10.0**	605.1	326.9
STATE BK	LA JUNTA	CO	**D+**	D+	B-	93	4.70	6.9	4.0	12.1	8.0	**10.0**	12.6	17.6
STATE BK	SPENCER	IA	**C-**	C	C	65	16.25	8.9	4.3	20.6	12.7	**3.8**	6.8	10.4
STATE BK	SPIRIT LAKE	IA	**B-**	B	B	61	-4.79	10.5	1.6	14.5	24.4	**10.0**	11.2	17.4
STATE BK	FREEPORT	IL	**C+**	C+	C+	205	7.02	25.9	0.7	6.9	25.8	**6.2**	8.4	11.9
STATE BK	WONDER LAKE	IL	**C-**	C-	C	180	0.31	1.2	1.1	40.4	16.0	**10.0**	11.4	20.2
STATE BK	HOXIE	KS	**B+**	B+	A-	118	7.60	9.3	2.3	0.7	5.9	**8.3**	9.9	13.8
STATE BK	FENTON	MI	**E-**	E-	D-	300	-10.49	10.7	3.2	9.7	15.0	**3.0**	6.5	10.0
STATE BK	RICHMOND	MO	**B-**	B+	B+	27	-0.22	3.8	5.6	33.7	29.7	**6.3**	8.3	17.2
STATE BK	GRESHAM	WI	**B+**	B+	B+	23	5.41	2.8	1.4	10.6	6.8	**10.0**	28.1	59.5
STATE BK	GREEN RIVER	WY	**C-**	C-	D+	40	-4.69	14.4	6.0	10.1	10.4	**10.0**	11.0	15.6
STATE BK & TRUST	WINFIELD	AL	**B**	A	A-	185	2.40	2.3	8.4	13.5	42.2	**10.0**	14.2	30.7
STATE BK & TRUST	FARGO	ND	**C+**	C+	C+	2,072	5.27	18.1	3.0	11.4	2.1	**6.4**	9.4	12.1
STATE BK & TRUST CO	MACON	GA	**C**	C	C	2,811	12.55	4.6	0.7	6.7	14.4	**10.0**	12.6	42.1
▲STATE BK & TRUST CO	NEVADA	IA	**A-**	B+	B+	136	0.55	10.2	1.1	10.6	31.0	**8.4**	9.9	15.3
▼STATE BK & TRUST CO	WAVERLY	IA	**C+**	A-	A	148	4.62	5.2	0.7	7.9	50.5	**6.9**	8.9	16.7

Asset Quality Index	Non-Performing Loans as a % of Total Loans	Non-Performing Loans as a % of Capital	Net Charge-offs Avg Loans	Profitability Index	Net Income ($Mil)	Return on Assets (R.O.A.)	Return on Equity (R.O.E.)	Net Interest Spread	Overhead Efficiency Ratio	Liquidity Index	Liquidity Ratio	Hot Money Ratio	Stability Index
2.5	4.56	24.0	1.53	**2.0**	0.9	0.23	1.91	3.55	74.1	**2.6**	29.9	18.6	**6.0**
4.4	3.37	9.8	0.06	**1.6**	0.0	0.24	1.99	4.25	93.9	**5.8**	57.8	6.3	**5.1**
6.9	0.00	0.0	1.05	**1.6**	0.0	0.02	0.18	3.81	87.4	**1.8**	34.1	26.8	**3.6**
7.9	0.15	0.8	0.05	**1.4**	0.5	0.30	2.30	3.97	89.5	**1.5**	29.0	32.2	**4.9**
3.5	1.02	8.4	1.89	**1.0**	-3.0	-0.22	-2.60	4.36	77.2	**0.5**	4.4	53.0	**5.6**
9.3	0.34	0.8	-0.02	**2.8**	0.2	0.41	3.41	4.19	93.4	**5.9**	56.5	7.7	**6.4**
0.0	4.84	40.0	0.63	**3.4**	0.6	0.66	8.83	3.58	78.8	**1.8**	15.6	20.3	**2.5**
9.5	0.17	0.2	0.01	**3.2**	0.6	0.68	2.52	2.82	68.7	**5.9**	90.9	13.2	**8.1**
3.6	1.08	6.8	0.00	**3.0**	1.2	1.27	11.01	3.54	60.5	**1.9**	30.3	26.9	**3.8**
3.2	1.50	13.2	0.32	**5.1**	1.4	0.87	12.02	3.97	63.0	**2.0**	19.9	19.5	**3.9**
3.1	7.89	16.1	1.00	**10.0**	2.1	3.11	8.56	5.81	34.1	**4.1**	24.2	9.3	**9.1**
5.2	2.15	9.3	0.69	**4.5**	1.6	0.86	6.67	3.47	55.1	**3.4**	43.0	18.7	**7.6**
8.6	0.00	0.0	0.00	**2.2**	1.2	0.70	6.50	3.06	70.1	**2.9**	17.0	14.7	**3.0**
7.2	1.18	5.0	0.43	**5.6**	2.7	1.17	9.55	3.86	54.9	**2.2**	33.4	25.0	**7.7**
4.7	0.34	2.3	0.09	**5.5**	0.5	1.38	15.43	4.10	65.8	**4.4**	17.9	6.5	**5.9**
0.3	8.67	53.7	1.13	**2.0**	0.9	0.36	3.73	4.01	64.7	**2.6**	23.9	16.7	**4.5**
7.4	0.91	2.8	0.37	**3.9**	0.4	1.05	9.07	4.34	79.5	**2.7**	52.8	31.4	**6.1**
7.0	1.15	4.2	1.14	**3.4**	-10.9	-0.85	-11.22	4.17	70.9	**7.3**	53.3	1.9	**5.6**
1.2	4.17	27.0	1.40	**0.0**	-1.0	-1.29	-13.91	3.92	94.3	**4.4**	35.3	11.6	**2.6**
4.7	1.44	8.2	0.21	**6.5**	2.0	2.11	16.61	4.15	46.7	**4.0**	20.0	9.2	**5.5**
3.1	1.17	7.8	0.61	**0.4**	-0.1	-0.02	-0.17	3.24	77.6	**1.6**	22.7	24.5	**4.9**
6.7	0.38	2.5	0.02	**5.0**	1.0	0.87	8.10	3.34	60.2	**1.9**	18.2	19.9	**7.0**
8.1	0.40	2.1	0.00	**5.1**	0.6	0.84	6.79	3.57	58.2	**3.8**	35.1	14.5	**7.6**
2.4	3.10	23.0	0.24	**2.2**	0.4	0.14	1.91	2.96	75.4	**5.1**	33.3	6.6	**2.8**
9.2	0.03	0.1	0.00	**8.6**	3.4	1.62	9.43	4.32	48.6	**4.5**	45.5	13.7	**9.3**
4.5	0.95	7.2	0.13	**3.1**	0.1	0.45	5.01	4.25	75.0	**2.6**	24.8	16.9	**2.3**
0.0	8.79	53.9	-0.16	**1.6**	0.6	0.19	1.96	4.02	77.5	**4.0**	11.9	8.0	**3.4**
8.1	1.25	3.2	0.75	**3.4**	1.6	0.64	5.01	2.45	73.9	**5.9**	54.1	9.0	**6.7**
2.8	4.91	26.0	-0.03	**3.8**	1.5	0.57	4.07	3.30	61.8	**0.7**	15.7	46.1	**7.7**
0.3	11.91	88.1	2.45	**0.0**	-3.4	-0.62	-9.11	2.59	77.6	**0.8**	18.8	49.2	**1.2**
3.0	2.35	15.6	0.25	**9.1**	6.2	1.96	16.33	5.71	61.7	**3.6**	18.7	11.4	**8.6**
8.5	0.00	0.0	-0.01	**6.9**	0.3	1.50	11.18	4.30	68.8	**4.5**	41.6	10.2	**9.7**
4.9	1.37	8.4	0.68	**2.6**	0.2	0.28	2.95	3.71	73.5	**2.7**	16.8	15.9	**5.0**
1.9	4.55	29.9	0.00	**2.3**	0.4	0.38	4.12	3.44	78.4	**1.5**	27.2	30.3	**4.0**
10.0	1.27	1.9	0.00	**4.0**	1.8	0.88	3.33	3.12	69.4	**6.0**	79.1	12.5	**8.3**
0.0	4.80	35.5	4.38	**0.3**	-24.8	-1.06	-9.98	3.86	65.1	**1.4**	11.9	25.3	**7.0**
6.9	1.25	6.7	0.13	**3.3**	2.1	0.52	4.62	3.41	70.2	**3.8**	25.9	11.0	**7.2**
7.0	0.43	2.8	0.15	**1.3**	0.2	0.24	2.87	3.48	92.1	**2.3**	21.7	17.9	**3.8**
4.4	3.44	13.4	8.30	**0.4**	-4.8	-3.54	-19.52	3.20	53.6	**5.0**	35.2	7.9	**8.0**
8.4	0.00	0.0	0.00	**2.9**	0.1	0.34	3.62	4.14	87.6	**3.8**	18.5	10.2	**5.5**
6.1	0.26	2.3	0.02	**5.2**	1.4	1.09	12.58	4.95	76.2	**3.0**	19.9	14.7	**5.5**
9.0	0.00	0.0	0.08	**7.5**	1.7	1.72	18.34	5.32	64.0	**2.6**	38.3	24.9	**5.2**
1.8	2.59	18.0	0.98	**3.2**	8.0	0.49	5.63	3.92	71.5	**3.6**	17.6	11.8	**5.9**
4.4	0.72	5.1	0.84	**5.2**	9.0	1.21	13.56	4.22	56.4	**1.6**	12.8	21.6	**6.2**
10.0	0.00	0.0	0.00	**0.0**	-4.1	-30.49	-32.32	N/,	12,497.0	**10.0**	1,478.0	0.0	**2.0**
1.5	6.33	28.7	0.72	**3.0**	0.5	0.55	4.13	4.75	78.2	**1.8**	20.1	22.1	**6.6**
6.2	0.39	3.7	0.18	**5.0**	0.7	1.11	15.05	4.15	75.0	**1.9**	19.1	20.4	**3.5**
5.4	1.56	8.0	2.04	**3.1**	0.2	0.35	3.14	4.55	58.6	**1.5**	25.7	27.9	**6.7**
5.8	0.04	0.3	0.22	**7.5**	2.7	1.35	15.59	3.95	40.8	**2.1**	16.0	18.8	**5.0**
2.4	4.83	25.3	1.33	**1.5**	0.0	0.00	-0.04	4.16	74.1	**1.9**	21.9	20.7	**5.0**
4.3	0.01	0.1	0.07	**8.5**	2.2	1.93	19.10	4.17	53.9	**2.5**	24.1	17.6	**8.6**
0.3	6.00	42.2	2.41	**0.0**	-3.0	-0.95	-14.66	3.88	80.7	**2.7**	24.8	16.4	**1.7**
5.5	0.67	4.4	0.04	**5.7**	0.4	1.32	15.39	4.10	67.7	**2.6**	27.3	17.7	**6.0**
9.0	0.91	1.5	-0.04	**7.1**	0.3	1.50	5.39	4.08	60.4	**4.1**	76.1	18.9	**7.0**
4.8	0.26	1.6	0.70	**2.3**	0.1	0.11	1.01	4.46	85.3	**3.3**	23.7	13.3	**6.3**
5.1	5.83	13.3	0.97	**4.6**	2.0	1.06	7.10	4.41	57.4	**3.2**	68.2	37.3	**9.1**
4.0	1.13	9.6	0.63	**5.0**	17.6	0.90	9.27	4.36	57.0	**3.0**	10.6	13.7	**7.0**
2.5	6.04	22.9	0.10	**8.3**	42.2	1.61	12.62	6.91	52.0	**4.4**	26.2	11.1	**5.3**
7.0	0.06	0.3	0.38	**9.1**	2.5	1.80	17.90	4.12	39.9	**2.2**	23.5	18.8	**7.5**
7.3	0.00	0.0	0.00	**2.3**	0.0	0.00	0.00	N/,	86.7	**5.9**	62.7	10.7	**6.6**

Name	City	State	Rating	2008 Rating	2007 Rating	Total Assets ($Mil)	One Year Asset Growth	Asset Mix (As a % of Total Assets) Commercial Loans	Consumer Loans	Home Mortgages	Securities	Capitalization Index	Leverage Ratio	Risk-based Capital Ratio
STATE BK & TRUST CO	GOLDEN MEADOW	LA	**B-**	B-	B-	117	16.37	17.1	5.0	21.9	15.5	**5.1**	7.1	13.9
STATE BK & TRUST CO	GREENWOOD	MS	**C**	C-	B-	917	1.17	5.2	1.8	16.8	14.7	**6.8**	8.9	12.3
STATE BK & TRUST CO	DILLON	MT	**C-**	C-	C	94	-2.49	7.4	3.7	6.9	17.8	**7.9**	9.6	15.5
STATE BK & TRUST CO	DEFIANCE	OH	**D**	D+	B-	656	0.45	10.8	1.6	16.1	20.2	**4.9**	6.9	11.7
▼STATE BK & TRUST CO DALLA	CARROLLTON	TX	**C-**	C	D+	196	-5.11	17.7	0.6	17.9	1.1	**8.0**	9.8	13.3
STATE BK & TRUST OF KENMA	KENMARE	ND	**C+**	C+	C	94	-0.47	22.1	3.6	11.9	18.7	**5.5**	7.8	11.4
STATE BK FINANCIAL	LA CROSSE	WI	**D+**	C-	C-	317	0.77	9.4	0.4	5.8	23.7	**7.3**	9.2	15.5
STATE BK IN EDEN VALLEY	EDEN VALLEY	MN	**D**	D	C-	29	-6.84	5.0	4.2	9.2	27.1	**6.5**	8.5	14.0
STATE BK NORTHWEST	SPOKANE VALLEY	WA	**D+**	D	D+	99	-11.08	15.6	1.0	11.4	11.7	**7.5**	9.3	13.9
STATE BK OF ALCESTER	ALCESTER	SD	**B-**	B-	B-	102	7.84	4.6	7.9	13.5	21.2	**6.0**	8.0	12.2
STATE BK OF ARCADIA	ARCADIA	WI	**B-**	B-	B-	113	1.70	3.6	2.8	18.0	20.0	**6.4**	8.4	16.4
STATE BK OF ARTHUR	ARTHUR	IL	**B+**	B+	A-	92	3.12	16.8	10.3	9.5	29.9	**10.0**	14.6	25.7
▼STATE BK OF BARTLEY	BARTLEY	NE	**B-**	A-	A-	68	9.71	21.5	0.9	15.1	1.5	**6.9**	8.9	18.2
▼STATE BK OF BELLE PLAINE	BELLE PLAINE	MN	**C+**	B	B	95	3.09	2.1	1.6	8.3	47.6	**10.0**	12.0	24.2
STATE BK OF BELLINGHAM	BELLINGHAM	MN	**C+**	C+	C	32	7.54	3.0	2.0	0.3	4.4	**5.8**	7.8	12.1
STATE BK OF BEMENT	BEMENT	IL	**B-**	B-	B	62	1.43	16.4	4.4	13.0	15.4	**10.0**	14.7	20.3
STATE BK OF BERN	BERN	KS	**B+**	B+	B+	66	14.09	4.9	3.1	4.9	39.7	**10.0**	11.4	18.0
▼STATE BK OF BIRD ISLAND	BIRD ISLAND	MN	**C**	B-	B-	38	-10.86	11.8	2.1	1.2	32.9	**7.7**	9.5	15.2
STATE BK OF BLUE MOUND	BLUE MOUND	IL	**D**	C+	C+	34	20.48	23.8	6.2	10.2	10.7	**4.6**	7.1	10.8
STATE BK OF BLUE RAPIDS	BLUE RAPIDS	KS	**D+**	C	B-	50	17.81	13.3	8.0	17.0	45.3	**5.8**	7.8	15.7
STATE BK OF BOTTINEAU	BOTTINEAU	ND	**D-**	D	D+	50	-5.24	6.6	5.4	13.1	7.1	**6.3**	8.3	12.9
▼STATE BK OF BRICELYN	BRICELYN	MN	**B-**	B-	B	26	4.81	3.8	4.6	10.9	3.7	**9.1**	11.3	14.3
STATE BK OF BROOKS	CORNING	IA	**C+**	C+	C+	13	1.35	5.0	6.8	8.2	40.0	**10.0**	13.0	32.3
STATE BK OF BURNETTSVILLE	BURNETTSVILLE	IN	**C**	C-	C-	40	1.02	8.4	12.0	20.5	24.9	**7.7**	9.4	15.5
STATE BK OF BURRTON	BURRTON	KS	**D+**	D+	C-	9	4.17	3.0	2.6	24.8	2.6	**10.0**	11.3	18.9
STATE BK OF BUSSEY	BUSSEY	IA	**D**	C-	D	55	5.98	12.4	7.1	14.7	15.3	**6.0**	8.0	12.5
STATE BK OF CANTON	CANTON	KS	**B**	B	B+	29	1.62	8.5	2.8	3.5	56.9	**10.0**	17.0	37.9
▼STATE BK OF CARBONDALE	CARBONDALE	KS	**D**	C	C-	18	-1.14	11.7	8.0	22.2	28.8	**6.4**	8.4	15.0
STATE BK OF CAZENOVIA	CAZENOVIA	WI	**B**	B+	B+	35	-0.53	2.7	4.1	21.8	14.5	**10.0**	17.6	28.8
STATE BK OF CERRO GORDO	CERRO GORDO	IL	**B-**	B-	B-	24	-1.05	5.7	5.6	17.0	23.9	**10.0**	13.2	30.8
STATE BK OF CEYLON	CEYLON	MN	**C-**	C-	C-	11	-1.46	9.3	7.4	2.7	15.4	**9.3**	10.5	19.3
STATE BK OF CHANDLER	CHANDLER	MN	**B**	B	B	40	12.21	4.5	3.5	1.4	29.6	**9.5**	10.6	17.4
STATE BK OF CHERRY	CHERRY	IL	**B**	B	B	86	3.12	2.0	3.8	18.1	58.5	**8.8**	10.2	27.0
STATE BK OF CHESTER	CHESTER	NE	**C+**	C+	C	24	0.79	7.1	3.2	4.4	2.2	**9.3**	10.6	15.4
STATE BK OF CHILTON	CHILTON	WI	**D**	D	D	157	-1.33	9.1	1.9	7.9	5.4	**10.0**	12.9	17.7
STATE BK OF CHITTENANGO	CHITTENANGO	NY	**B**	B+	B	142	28.40	0.0	0.0	0.0	99.1	**5.0**	7.0	37.1
▼STATE BK OF CHRISMAN	CHRISMAN	IL	**C-**	C+	C	68	2.95	16.5	3.3	12.2	17.1	**6.0**	8.0	12.0
STATE BK OF CLARKS GROVE	ALBERT LEA	MN	**C**	C	C	18	6.14	20.3	1.9	3.5	5.6	**10.0**	12.6	22.5
▼STATE BK OF COCHRAN	COCHRAN	GA	**C-**	D+	C-	224	3.63	5.6	6.7	23.1	8.3	**9.1**	10.4	17.0
STATE BK OF COKATO	COKATO	MN	**E-**	E-	E-	57	-1.88	10.2	2.9	10.7	8.5	**1.7**	5.4	8.7
STATE BK OF COLD SPRING	COLD SPRING	MN	**D+**	D+	C	52	1.33	8.2	6.8	26.3	8.3	**5.8**	7.8	13.3
STATE BK OF COLON	COLON	NE	**C**	C-	C-	17	7.55	3.8	1.6	7.3	18.5	**10.0**	11.9	16.8
STATE BK OF CONWAY	CONWAY SPRINGS	KS	**C**	C-	D+	22	2.19	2.5	3.7	14.0	12.8	**8.3**	9.9	16.2
STATE BK OF COUNTRYSIDE	COUNTRYSIDE	IL	**D-**	D-	D-	810	-11.31	5.9	0.0	7.7	28.3	**7.2**	9.1	13.2
STATE BK OF CROSS PLAINS	CROSS PLAINS	WI	**D-**	D+	C+	798	10.54	10.0	2.1	19.0	11.6	**5.5**	8.2	11.3
STATE BK OF DANVERS	DANVERS	MN	**B**	B	B	40	3.20	7.4	2.0	1.5	27.7	**10.0**	11.3	16.6
STATE BK OF DAVIS	DAVIS	IL	**C**	C	C+	130	8.73	23.7	1.0	16.2	26.5	**6.7**	8.7	13.4
STATE BK OF DE KALB	DE KALB	TX	**B+**	A	A	119	-0.12	10.3	3.5	9.8	13.8	**10.0**	14.4	19.6
STATE BK OF DELANO	DELANO	MN	**E-**	D-	E	87	-9.35	11.0	1.5	10.6	12.3	**3.1**	6.5	10.1
STATE BK OF DELPHOS	DELPHOS	KS	**C+**	C+	C+	40	8.43	12.1	3.3	17.4	18.4	**7.0**	9.0	13.3
▼STATE BK OF DOWNS	DOWNS	KS	**C**	C-	B	59	1.42	19.0	1.7	14.6	2.2	**10.0**	12.8	15.4
STATE BK OF DRUMMOND	DRUMMOND	WI	**B**	B	B	42	1.12	6.4	2.9	31.4	23.6	**10.0**	13.1	20.5
STATE BK OF EAGLE BUTTE	EAGLE BUTTE	SD	**B**	B	B	35	7.29	6.9	31.2	4.9	29.6	**10.0**	12.9	19.4
STATE BK OF EASTON	EASTON	MN	**D+**	D+	C-	19	3.59	11.4	4.0	9.6	13.5	**10.0**	13.0	18.6
STATE BK OF EWEN	EWEN	MI	**B**	B	B+	48	3.89	5.9	7.8	26.8	40.4	**10.0**	16.9	35.3
STATE BK OF FAIRMONT	FAIRMONT	MN	**C**	C-	B-	91	0.05	19.7	6.8	6.7	20.4	**9.3**	10.5	14.9
STATE BK OF FARIBAULT	FARIBAULT	MN	**C**	C+	B-	179	-0.36	6.2	1.5	9.1	33.7	**8.8**	10.2	15.6
STATE BK OF FLORENCE	FLORENCE	WI	**D**	C-	C-	76	7.79	6.8	7.4	28.2	16.7	**6.9**	9.2	12.5
▼STATE BK OF GENEVA	GENEVA	IL	**D-**	B-	B-	97	9.72	2.9	1.4	7.6	35.4	**6.4**	8.4	14.2
▲STATE BK OF GEORGIA	FAYETTEVILLE	GA	**D+**	D+	C	103	2.65	16.1	1.3	11.9	16.8	**8.9**	10.3	16.6

Arrows denote recent upgrades ▲ or downgrades ▼

Asset Quality Index	Non-Performing Loans as a % of Total Loans	Non-Performing Loans as a % of Capital	Net Charge-offs Avg Loans	Profitability Index	Net Income ($Mil)	Return on Assets (R.O.A.)	Return on Equity (R.O.E.)	Net Interest Spread	Overhead Efficiency Ratio	Liquidity Index	Liquidity Ratio	Hot Money Ratio	Stability Index
4.5	1.51	11.3	0.06	**5.1**	1.3	1.14	14.87	4.21	73.3	**2.1**	28.8	22.6	**5.8**
3.1	1.00	7.4	0.90	**3.3**	5.0	0.55	4.54	4.28	72.9	**1.8**	17.2	21.3	**6.0**
2.3	1.24	7.1	0.09	**4.7**	1.0	1.07	10.96	4.89	77.5	**3.4**	35.9	16.4	**6.1**
1.1	2.75	23.1	1.77	**1.7**	0.1	0.02	0.19	3.85	80.3	**2.3**	12.6	17.4	**5.8**
1.6	0.73	5.5	0.15	**5.3**	2.5	1.31	9.99	4.63	67.1	**1.0**	11.5	31.1	**7.4**
8.1	0.06	0.6	-0.17	**4.2**	0.8	0.91	11.92	3.60	69.2	**2.6**	13.2	15.8	**3.9**
1.6	3.71	21.2	1.33	**3.7**	2.9	0.95	9.17	4.17	76.4	**2.4**	19.2	17.6	**4.8**
1.1	4.58	28.8	3.32	**0.4**	-0.3	-0.89	-10.60	4.26	99.5	**3.4**	29.6	14.8	**3.4**
1.7	3.06	20.4	0.43	**1.3**	0.0	0.04	0.39	4.07	91.4	**0.9**	17.4	34.7	**3.7**
7.7	0.18	1.5	0.05	**4.2**	0.9	0.88	10.09	3.63	71.4	**2.7**	22.0	16.1	**5.5**
6.7	0.40	2.7	0.13	**3.9**	1.0	0.90	10.75	3.09	66.2	**4.3**	33.9	11.7	**5.2**
4.5	3.45	11.0	0.71	**4.6**	0.8	0.90	5.68	4.32	66.3	**5.5**	51.0	8.9	**7.4**
6.4	0.73	5.6	0.58	**5.1**	0.6	0.90	9.58	4.02	62.9	**1.2**	20.1	30.8	**8.2**
2.3	9.29	27.9	1.67	**4.3**	0.7	0.76	5.81	4.26	75.9	**5.4**	48.0	9.1	**7.3**
7.0	0.01	0.1	0.00	**8.0**	0.4	1.16	14.90	4.45	51.1	**1.0**	1.9	28.8	**5.0**
5.8	2.13	9.4	0.13	**3.7**	0.4	0.64	4.32	4.47	77.5	**2.4**	24.6	17.8	**7.1**
8.3	0.05	0.2	-0.02	**5.8**	0.8	1.33	10.81	4.37	59.0	**3.9**	46.3	16.6	**6.8**
7.1	0.58	2.8	-0.01	**6.5**	0.8	1.99	16.31	N/,	8.2	**6.8**	49.0	0.3	**3.0**
5.2	0.88	7.5	0.10	**2.5**	0.0	0.03	0.38	3.92	78.4	**1.4**	17.4	26.3	**2.3**
4.0	1.62	9.8	1.02	**1.4**	-0.2	-0.40	-4.53	2.58	77.6	**2.7**	45.5	27.4	**4.8**
1.6	3.09	23.3	0.77	**1.4**	-0.1	-0.11	-1.24	4.40	81.8	**2.9**	17.5	15.0	**3.5**
6.8	0.11	0.8	0.23	**4.7**	0.3	1.00	8.55	4.70	73.2	**4.2**	7.6	6.4	**6.4**
2.9	12.29	24.6	0.26	**2.3**	0.0	0.24	1.81	2.90	86.7	**6.8**	82.1	5.4	**6.5**
5.6	0.09	0.5	2.32	**3.3**	0.3	0.66	6.77	4.75	66.5	**2.4**	37.3	26.8	**5.0**
3.6	1.34	6.5	-0.02	**0.7**	0.0	-0.28	-2.43	4.50	106.4	**5.3**	29.2	1.3	**5.4**
1.7	0.87	6.8	0.45	**3.9**	0.5	0.92	11.96	4.18	67.8	**2.0**	29.2	24.2	**2.5**
9.0	0.78	1.5	0.00	**3.4**	0.1	0.46	2.56	3.13	79.7	**6.9**	76.3	5.4	**7.7**
5.7	1.44	9.4	0.01	**2.7**	0.1	0.30	3.55	4.12	92.1	**4.0**	23.0	9.2	**5.2**
8.8	0.00	0.0	-0.02	**3.8**	0.2	0.59	3.46	4.20	77.7	**5.3**	43.5	8.8	**8.1**
8.3	0.49	1.4	-0.01	**2.7**	0.1	0.32	2.08	3.82	92.0	**3.0**	47.6	19.3	**6.8**
1.9	3.84	18.9	1.75	**2.1**	0.0	0.01	0.08	4.22	81.5	**1.1**	32.2	34.9	**6.6**
5.6	0.41	2.1	0.02	**5.0**	0.3	0.89	7.89	4.17	65.3	**4.5**	36.9	11.7	**5.9**
8.6	0.58	2.1	0.06	**4.9**	1.1	1.24	11.49	3.34	56.6	**3.7**	65.9	22.2	**7.2**
4.6	1.44	8.5	0.04	**5.7**	0.3	1.36	12.99	3.65	62.4	**2.0**	32.3	22.4	**7.0**
1.0	2.77	15.3	1.77	**0.0**	-1.6	-1.07	-8.03	3.82	79.5	**1.5**	14.8	24.6	**5.5**
10.0	0.00	0.0	0.00	**9.2**	2.4	1.87	25.26	2.58	8.0	**3.7**	4.7	9.1	**5.8**
1.7	3.60	29.2	0.14	**4.9**	0.5	0.80	10.01	4.26	64.2	**2.4**	19.1	17.5	**4.0**
5.2	2.96	10.3	0.25	**2.2**	0.0	0.19	1.48	3.94	91.9	**5.8**	45.7	3.3	**6.1**
1.5	3.27	18.3	1.42	**3.4**	0.9	0.41	4.00	3.97	65.7	**1.5**	21.1	26.4	**6.7**
0.3	3.95	37.6	0.95	**0.4**	-1.0	-1.73	-29.11	4.60	146.7	**2.6**	18.3	16.1	**0.0**
3.0	1.66	12.1	1.62	**2.4**	0.0	0.01	0.14	4.32	66.3	**4.0**	25.3	10.0	**5.3**
4.0	1.13	6.5	0.05	**4.0**	0.1	0.62	5.39	4.06	77.0	**2.7**	31.9	17.0	**6.7**
5.8	1.56	8.7	-0.08	**4.9**	0.3	1.32	12.97	4.39	71.0	**1.5**	29.9	26.8	**4.3**
0.0	15.83	87.6	3.49	**0.0**	-15.5	-1.79	-19.79	3.23	87.8	**4.1**	22.1	9.1	**6.5**
0.3	5.87	48.2	0.59	**3.7**	4.6	0.60	6.72	4.21	63.3	**2.4**	11.7	16.5	**5.4**
6.7	0.02	0.1	1.01	**4.8**	0.4	1.08	8.73	5.10	74.5	**2.8**	26.5	16.4	**6.8**
2.6	2.47	17.4	0.04	**5.9**	1.4	1.17	12.65	3.72	41.6	**1.6**	14.7	22.6	**5.8**
3.7	4.74	21.7	0.16	**7.4**	2.2	1.85	12.74	4.20	53.7	**2.2**	30.1	22.8	**9.7**
0.3	8.55	59.7	4.03	**0.0**	-3.0	-3.26	-41.71	4.03	118.5	**4.1**	24.4	9.2	**2.2**
4.8	1.17	8.7	0.14	**7.0**	0.7	1.62	18.19	4.11	63.0	**3.9**	5.3	8.2	**6.8**
1.8	5.69	31.7	0.91	**2.2**	0.2	0.26	2.01	4.68	74.1	**3.7**	19.2	10.7	**6.7**
4.8	2.15	9.4	0.91	**3.8**	0.3	0.58	4.35	5.20	72.7	**2.9**	34.3	18.6	**7.7**
6.8	0.09	0.4	1.16	**5.2**	0.3	0.90	6.65	7.49	74.0	**2.4**	9.1	16.4	**6.9**
1.0	7.77	35.0	0.94	**2.6**	0.1	0.28	2.07	3.71	82.1	**1.9**	31.0	22.9	**7.5**
4.4	5.43	13.2	0.65	**6.5**	0.6	1.28	7.22	4.89	59.2	**3.7**	64.3	21.6	**7.6**
2.3	2.82	16.4	0.24	**5.6**	1.3	1.36	12.77	4.14	60.2	**3.6**	31.6	14.0	**6.4**
4.4	1.25	5.3	1.50	**2.6**	0.4	0.20	1.91	3.75	75.4	**3.2**	26.0	14.1	**6.5**
1.0	6.89	46.9	0.41	**3.8**	0.3	0.39	4.16	4.98	76.5	**1.0**	25.5	39.0	**4.0**
0.3	0.57	3.2	0.83	**2.9**	0.6	0.63	7.25	3.69	77.6	**2.2**	37.1	28.7	**5.5**
1.7	3.32	20.6	0.95	**1.5**	0.5	0.46	4.40	3.52	83.9	**1.3**	14.1	27.0	**2.8**

Name	City	State	Rating	2008 Rating	2007 Rating	Total Assets ($Mil)	One Year Asset Growth	Asset Mix (As a % of Total Assets) Comm-ercial Loans	Cons-umer Loans	Home Mort-gages	Secur-ities	Capital-ization Index	Leverage Ratio	Risk-based Capital Ratio
STATE BK OF GIBBON	GIBBON	MN	**C-**	C	C-	25	12.58	3.4	1.4	5.0	0.7	**7.1**	9.1	12.7
STATE BK OF GRAYMONT	GRAYMONT	IL	**B-**	B-	B-	162	11.95	6.8	3.4	7.6	34.4	**5.8**	7.8	13.1
STATE BK OF HAMBURG	HAMBURG	MN	**D-**	D-	D	20	3.47	5.1	2.2	14.0	17.3	**5.8**	7.8	14.7
STATE BK OF HAWLEY	HAWLEY	MN	**B**	B-	B-	85	3.79	12.5	6.0	15.2	26.3	**7.0**	9.0	13.7
STATE BK OF HERSCHER	HERSCHER	IL	**D+**	C-	C+	195	4.58	18.4	2.1	19.3	17.6	**6.8**	8.8	13.2
STATE BK OF HILDRETH	HILDRETH	NE	**B-**	C+	C+	25	2.89	4.7	0.8	2.0	6.1	**10.0**	12.1	16.5
▼STATE BK OF ILLINOIS	WEST CHICAGO	IL	**C-**	B-	A-	206	4.75	0.9	0.4	22.2	28.3	**7.0**	9.0	15.9
▼STATE BK OF INDIA (CALIFO	LOS ANGELES	CA	**D+**	C	A-	781	-8.28	21.0	0.0	0.0	9.4	**10.0**	14.8	20.6
STATE BK OF INDUSTRY	INDUSTRY	IL	**B**	B	B	40	4.32	13.8	13.3	16.6	23.0	**10.0**	12.9	19.5
STATE BK OF JEFFERS	JEFFERS	MN	**B-**	B-	B-	20	9.67	5.8	3.7	5.5	25.9	**10.0**	13.6	24.4
STATE BK OF KANSAS	FREDONIA	KS	**A-**	A-	A-	74	-0.63	4.6	1.2	8.1	6.8	**10.0**	12.0	17.5
STATE BK OF KIMBALL	KIMBALL	MN	**B**	C+	C+	76	6.95	8.2	2.9	20.9	15.4	**7.0**	9.0	13.9
STATE BK OF LAKE PARK	LAKE PARK	MN	**C**	C	C	30	6.15	12.5	10.2	25.4	20.7	**6.0**	8.0	14.4
▼STATE BK OF LAKOTA	LAKOTA	ND	**B-**	B	B	41	-2.73	6.3	6.2	7.2	35.7	**8.1**	9.7	19.1
STATE BK OF LEDYARD	LEDYARD	IA	**B**	B-	B+	37	21.04	6.6	3.4	5.1	14.1	**10.0**	13.7	18.5
▼STATE BK OF LEON	LEON	KS	**D+**	C-	D+	10	14.82	20.3	7.9	14.1	25.5	**8.8**	10.2	16.2
STATE BK OF LIMA	LIMA	IL	**C+**	C+	C+	30	4.79	18.5	1.5	3.6	33.3	**8.0**	9.6	14.5
▼STATE BK OF LINCOLN	LINCOLN	IL	**B**	A-	A-	325	13.27	12.5	0.8	7.1	41.2	**5.4**	7.4	15.1
▼STATE BK OF LISMORE	LISMORE	MN	**C**	C+	C+	38	2.28	14.9	3.3	0.8	1.2	**5.7**	10.5	11.5
STATE BK OF LIZTON	LIZTON	IN	**C+**	B-	B+	371	1.94	5.9	1.5	7.7	29.5	**7.5**	9.3	15.0
STATE BK OF LONG ISLAND	JERICHO	NY	**C**	C-	B-	1,590	-1.05	21.5	0.3	1.7	24.1	**7.8**	9.5	13.5
STATE BK OF LUCAN	LUCAN	MN	**B-**	B-	B	38	5.85	5.6	2.1	2.1	27.4	**9.2**	10.5	16.8
▲STATE BK OF MARIETTA	MARIETTA	MN	**C-**	B	C-	11	6.16	6.7	2.9	4.5	3.7	**6.2**	8.2	14.0
STATE BK OF MEDORA	MEDORA	IN	**B**	B	B	60	4.83	2.8	9.8	29.8	33.4	**10.0**	15.7	28.9
▼STATE BK OF MISSOURI	CONCORDIA	MO	**B-**	B	A-	72	-0.98	4.1	2.9	36.0	25.8	**6.8**	8.8	17.2
STATE BK OF NAUVOO	NAUVOO	IL	**C-**	C-	C-	29	-4.58	6.2	9.2	45.8	6.9	**8.0**	9.6	15.3
STATE BK OF NEW PRAGUE	NEW PRAGUE	MN	**D**	D	C-	121	-5.71	3.6	0.6	12.9	42.1	**10.0**	11.4	18.7
STATE BK OF NEW RICHLAND	NEW RICHLAND	MN	**C-**	B-	C+	89	1.89	4.0	2.6	16.9	20.2	**5.9**	8.1	11.7
STATE BK OF NEWBURG	NEWBURG	WI	**C**	C-	C-	155	5.69	1.4	1.0	29.2	11.1	**10.0**	13.4	18.1
STATE BK OF NIANTIC	NIANTIC	IL	**B**	B-	B-	59	-0.28	4.2	8.6	29.0	17.4	**10.0**	13.2	23.3
STATE BK OF ODELL	ODELL	NE	**E**	D-	C	25	1.51	4.3	9.7	8.8	20.0	**6.3**	8.4	15.6
STATE BK OF OSKALOOSA	OSKALOOSA	KS	**C-**	C	C	31	8.41	1.5	3.5	18.5	29.0	**6.0**	8.0	28.7
STATE BK OF PARK RAPIDS	PARK RAPIDS	MN	**D-**	D-	D	90	-6.83	6.2	2.6	15.7	31.0	**5.8**	7.8	13.8
STATE BK OF PAW PAW ILLIN	PAW PAW	IL	**C-**	C-	A-	32	-19.29	6.9	1.2	29.0	15.1	**10.0**	15.9	23.7
STATE BK OF PEARL CITY	PEARL CITY	IL	**D+**	C-	C-	43	-5.60	4.1	19.7	10.3	41.4	**8.4**	10.0	18.1
STATE BK OF PRAIRIE DU RO	PRAIRIE DU ROCHER	IL	**C+**	C	C	53	12.40	2.0	9.6	33.9	24.3	**6.0**	8.0	13.7
STATE BK OF REESEVILLE	REESEVILLE	WI	**C+**	C	B	50	2.84	5.6	1.4	19.1	21.2	**10.0**	12.9	19.8
STATE BK OF RICHMOND	RICHMOND	MN	**A-**	A-	A-	86	8.40	1.9	1.8	17.1	45.0	**10.0**	12.5	24.3
STATE BK OF RIVERDALE	RIVERDALE	NE	**B-**	A-	A-	57	3.22	10.5	2.8	2.7	4.5	**4.3**	8.2	10.6
STATE BK OF SAUNEMIN	SAUNEMIN	IL	**C+**	B-	C+	29	8.57	9.7	3.0	12.2	41.7	**6.6**	8.6	16.3
STATE BK OF SCHALLER	SCHALLER	IA	**B-**	B-	B	23	3.17	6.0	2.4	2.7	55.1	**7.9**	9.6	22.3
▼STATE BK OF SCOTIA	SCOTIA	NE	**C**	B+	B+	28	4.26	6.6	4.2	7.3	11.4	**10.0**	27.5	33.1
STATE BK OF SLATER	SLATER	MO	**B+**	B+	B+	41	5.31	16.4	6.0	14.7	11.0	**10.0**	11.9	15.9
STATE BK OF SOUTHERN	CEDAR CITY	UT	**C-**	B-	A-	672	0.00	5.3	3.1	3.4	28.2	**10.0**	11.4	16.2
STATE BK OF SOUTHWEST	SPRINGFIELD	MO	**C+**	C	D+	90	5.87	1.9	3.7	39.2	7.7	**5.4**	7.5	11.3
STATE BK OF SPEER	SPEER	IL	**C**	C	C-	146	2.01	7.5	1.4	12.1	39.3	**5.0**	7.0	11.9
STATE BK OF SPRING HILL	SPRING HILL	KS	**C-**	C+	B-	41	2.09	4.7	2.8	10.3	63.2	**8.3**	13.1	13.6
STATE BK OF ST JACOB	SAINT JACOB	IL	**A-**	A-	A-	47	1.23	7.5	7.7	24.0	24.8	**10.0**	14.1	24.9
▲STATE BK OF TABLE ROCK	TABLE ROCK	NE	**D+**	D+	D-	50	-3.65	9.7	5.7	16.3	0.0	**5.8**	7.8	12.0
STATE BK OF TAUNTON	TAUNTON	MN	**B-**	B-	C+	52	25.59	11.2	7.6	10.3	19.5	**8.6**	10.0	14.4
▲STATE BK OF TEXAS	DALLAS	TX	**C-**	D+	D	663	5.00	3.0	0.2	0.6	14.4	**10.0**	14.1	17.3
STATE BK OF TEXAS	HOUSTON	TX	**D+**	C	C-	152	-16.35	6.4	13.6	10.2	28.8	**6.7**	8.7	18.4
STATE BK OF THE LAKES	ANTIOCH	IL	**C-**	C-	C+	733	3.61	15.1	16.8	5.1	17.2	**5.8**	8.3	11.6
STATE BK OF TOLEDO	TOLEDO	IA	**C+**	C	C	103	-1.20	8.3	3.9	25.7	17.4	**5.2**	7.2	12.3
▼STATE BK OF TOULON	TOULON	IL	**C+**	B-	C+	172	3.70	5.7	2.4	4.9	37.4	**5.1**	7.1	12.3
STATE BK OF TOWNSEND	TOWNSEND	MT	**C-**	C	C	45	11.61	5.5	3.3	8.7	11.5	**8.0**	9.6	17.5
STATE BK OF WAPELLO	WAPELLO	IA	**B**	B	B+	33	-4.22	4.0	5.2	14.6	30.2	**10.0**	16.4	29.4
▲STATE BK OF WATERLOO	WATERLOO	IL	**C-**	D+	B-	127	4.58	2.3	1.6	30.6	20.9	**6.8**	8.8	13.0
▲STATE BK OF WHEATON	WHEATON	MN	**C+**	C-	A-	66	-2.35	7.3	1.5	8.9	10.8	**10.0**	21.0	30.3
STATE BK OF WHITTINGTON	BENTON	IL	**C+**	C	C+	102	3.93	2.7	16.3	22.0	25.4	**6.2**	8.2	15.4

Asset Quality Index	Non-Performing Loans as a % of Total Loans	Non-Performing Loans as a % of Capital	Net Charge-offs Avg Loans	Profitability Index	Net Income ($Mil)	Return on Assets (R.O.A.)	Return on Equity (R.O.E.)	Net Interest Spread	Overhead Efficiency Ratio	Liquidity Index	Liquidity Ratio	Hot Money Ratio	Stability Index
4.0	1.23	9.0	0.04	**5.3**	0.3	1.22	13.16	3.91	69.0	**4.4**	35.5	11.7	**3.7**
5.2	1.10	6.8	0.19	**4.0**	1.2	0.82	9.03	3.33	67.6	**3.3**	39.8	18.3	**4.5**
4.2	2.25	12.8	-0.14	**0.8**	0.0	0.06	0.77	3.44	98.7	**4.0**	41.7	12.9	**4.1**
7.0	0.26	1.7	-0.22	**6.9**	1.4	1.75	19.28	4.48	62.5	**5.0**	31.1	6.0	**6.3**
1.0	3.02	22.8	0.85	**6.5**	2.6	1.38	15.26	4.78	52.5	**1.6**	21.9	25.5	**6.0**
5.1	1.32	6.8	-0.02	**3.9**	0.2	0.79	6.45	3.97	77.8	**4.0**	23.6	9.1	**7.9**
1.7	5.61	34.6	1.94	**1.3**	-0.8	-0.39	-3.90	4.18	90.0	**2.8**	20.3	15.7	**5.9**
0.0	5.69	24.3	1.09	**4.1**	5.4	0.63	5.35	4.02	34.9	**0.7**	14.5	41.7	**6.9**
7.0	0.81	4.0	0.70	**6.4**	0.6	1.46	11.06	3.86	52.8	**1.7**	29.3	28.9	**7.4**
8.2	0.10	0.4	-0.10	**3.2**	0.1	0.38	2.67	3.93	84.9	**5.3**	43.1	5.4	**7.9**
8.1	0.00	0.0	0.00	**7.9**	1.3	1.75	13.79	3.61	48.5	**2.6**	24.9	17.1	**9.1**
5.7	0.70	4.7	0.00	**7.6**	1.3	1.80	19.84	4.48	58.9	**4.5**	24.6	6.9	**6.9**
5.8	0.87	6.0	0.29	**4.7**	0.3	1.12	13.83	4.45	73.4	**2.8**	29.9	17.6	**4.3**
5.9	0.84	4.0	0.12	**4.7**	0.5	1.11	10.22	3.81	68.0	**5.1**	43.1	9.9	**6.3**
4.7	0.77	3.8	0.36	**6.2**	0.5	1.35	9.46	3.64	56.2	**1.4**	31.0	38.3	**8.7**
4.2	1.87	9.7	0.71	**1.8**	0.0	0.15	1.48	3.60	95.0	**4.1**	23.7	8.5	**4.8**
8.4	0.03	0.2	0.51	**6.1**	0.5	1.69	17.21	4.15	62.7	**2.9**	33.3	18.5	**5.0**
4.3	2.56	13.9	0.66	**9.3**	6.2	2.05	23.71	3.65	62.7	**3.6**	39.0	16.7	**7.0**
6.7	0.03	0.2	0.01	**5.1**	0.4	1.13	10.88	4.58	73.0	**2.6**	3.4	14.8	**5.0**
3.7	3.08	16.9	0.91	**2.9**	1.8	0.49	4.96	4.14	73.2	**3.7**	38.3	15.8	**5.8**
4.7	1.31	8.0	0.77	**3.2**	12.0	0.74	7.04	4.31	59.8	**2.6**	8.8	15.8	**5.8**
5.8	0.18	0.9	0.16	**4.0**	0.3	0.80	7.31	3.55	76.9	**4.3**	41.9	13.9	**6.9**
7.8	0.00	0.0	0.44	**5.0**	0.1	1.07	9.78	3.88	65.9	**4.2**	53.2	14.7	**4.3**
5.2	2.69	9.2	0.56	**4.9**	0.5	0.90	5.73	4.04	61.5	**3.2**	44.0	19.5	**7.3**
3.7	1.06	6.4	0.14	**5.3**	0.8	1.19	12.72	3.98	65.0	**2.1**	20.3	19.0	**6.1**
4.6	1.05	7.8	0.56	**2.1**	0.0	0.14	1.41	4.39	90.5	**3.0**	8.9	13.6	**5.0**
1.7	6.54	23.4	1.56	**3.8**	1.3	1.05	8.51	4.46	65.4	**2.1**	33.6	27.8	**5.1**
2.7	1.53	13.0	0.00	**9.3**	1.9	2.26	25.96	4.34	46.7	**2.8**	3.5	13.9	**6.2**
2.3	4.38	23.9	0.56	**9.0**	2.1	1.48	10.98	4.31	33.0	**1.8**	23.0	22.4	**8.3**
2.5	5.65	22.3	3.86	**2.5**	-1.1	-1.84	-12.24	4.26	70.0	**1.7**	32.2	31.0	**7.2**
2.1	3.05	17.3	0.39	**1.9**	0.1	0.35	4.14	3.57	82.2	**5.2**	46.1	10.1	**0.7**
9.7	0.00	0.0	0.23	**1.8**	0.0	0.01	0.16	2.06	97.5	**3.7**	45.8	17.3	**4.5**
1.1	5.76	32.7	1.62	**1.7**	0.6	0.68	8.58	3.67	83.2	**2.4**	22.5	17.7	**2.4**
0.1	13.66	50.5	1.90	**9.1**	0.5	2.91	18.48	4.53	78.5	**3.4**	21.3	12.4	**5.8**
4.9	0.88	4.3	1.05	**1.6**	0.1	0.18	1.91	3.91	85.4	**3.6**	40.7	17.0	**3.3**
8.2	0.08	0.6	0.02	**4.9**	0.6	1.23	15.30	3.71	69.7	**2.6**	26.1	17.2	**5.0**
6.5	0.58	2.7	1.62	**3.2**	0.3	0.54	4.11	4.33	75.1	**3.1**	43.3	20.4	**5.7**
8.6	1.32	4.2	0.32	**6.0**	0.8	0.92	6.61	3.62	52.9	**5.9**	59.5	8.3	**8.2**
6.7	0.13	1.1	0.03	**6.8**	0.6	1.04	8.99	4.42	63.7	**3.3**	19.7	12.9	**9.0**
7.7	0.59	3.1	0.43	**4.2**	0.3	0.96	10.21	3.47	69.7	**4.4**	42.6	13.7	**6.1**
4.6	2.05	6.9	1.44	**9.5**	0.5	1.79	18.08	4.18	57.0	**5.7**	61.6	8.1	**9.1**
0.7	10.74	29.8	-0.01	**7.9**	0.5	1.90	7.01	4.68	56.3	**4.3**	22.0	7.4	**8.1**
8.1	0.01	0.1	0.09	**5.9**	0.4	0.97	8.33	4.36	64.8	**2.3**	14.7	17.5	**7.5**
2.1	4.48	21.8	3.18	**1.9**	0.2	0.03	0.22	3.89	55.4	**1.8**	21.3	22.0	**8.0**
6.3	0.85	8.4	0.06	**5.2**	1.2	1.41	18.95	4.22	71.4	**1.4**	11.6	24.7	**4.7**
6.1	0.85	5.9	0.11	**3.7**	1.2	0.87	10.74	3.30	65.8	**2.1**	26.6	19.9	**3.8**
7.6	1.06	2.1	0.28	**1.8**	0.1	0.13	0.99	2.98	94.6	**6.0**	57.5	7.3	**7.1**
8.5	0.47	1.7	0.05	**7.4**	0.8	1.72	11.65	4.20	52.9	**4.0**	38.6	14.7	**9.7**
4.6	0.45	4.3	0.71	**2.1**	0.1	0.22	2.88	3.86	76.4	**3.6**	11.8	10.6	**3.5**
6.2	0.46	2.9	0.22	**3.5**	0.3	0.70	6.18	3.97	72.2	**1.2**	17.2	29.0	**5.2**
0.0	7.91	41.7	0.63	**10.0**	20.0	3.17	22.35	5.39	24.4	**5.0**	19.7	2.9	**8.6**
3.6	0.27	1.6	0.16	**1.8**	0.2	0.09	1.16	3.03	92.0	**2.0**	44.0	59.0	**2.5**
2.1	1.09	7.9	0.59	**5.5**	7.6	1.06	7.00	3.91	55.1	**1.0**	21.6	34.6	**6.6**
3.2	1.86	15.4	0.08	**5.2**	1.2	1.20	15.22	3.88	68.4	**3.5**	27.5	13.3	**4.6**
5.2	1.68	11.6	1.44	**3.3**	1.3	0.76	7.69	3.89	63.2	**1.9**	21.2	20.7	**5.7**
2.9	1.81	11.3	0.15	**5.2**	0.5	1.20	11.74	5.90	75.6	**2.3**	30.3	20.5	**6.6**
6.5	1.65	4.4	0.30	**4.3**	0.3	0.89	5.21	4.17	73.3	**6.9**	55.8	0.8	**7.5**
2.0	4.03	27.2	0.21	**2.9**	0.8	0.61	7.38	3.06	72.6	**2.7**	21.8	16.1	**4.0**
3.4	2.66	8.4	2.90	**3.0**	0.0	0.04	0.20	4.65	54.1	**2.1**	22.3	19.1	**8.2**
3.4	2.02	12.1	0.46	**4.8**	1.1	1.09	13.16	4.45	70.6	**3.5**	32.7	15.3	**5.4**

Name	City	State	Rating	2008 Rating	2007 Rating	Total Assets ($Mil)	One Year Asset Growth	Asset Mix (As a % of Total Assets) Comm-ercial Loans	Cons-umer Loans	Home Mort-gages	Secur-ities	Capital-ization Index	Leverage Ratio	Risk-based Capital Ratio
STATE BK OF WYNNEWOOD	WYNNEWOOD	OK	**A-**	A-	B+	64	0.89	10.1	4.8	12.2	33.9	**10.0**	12.4	18.9
STATE CENTRAL BANK	KEOKUK	IA	**E-**	D-	D-	242	-4.41	18.4	4.1	14.1	9.5	**0.1**	3.4	6.2
STATE EXCHANGE BANK	MANKATO	KS	**D**	D	C	34	3.28	6.8	6.1	6.1	39.8	**6.3**	8.3	14.0
STATE EXCHANGE BANK	LAMONT	OK	**D-**	D-	D	64	3.05	11.5	2.3	7.0	4.6	**6.1**	8.1	15.0
▲STATE FARM BANK FSB	BLOOMINGTON	IL	**D**	D-	D-	15,067	-6.44	0.7	37.6	16.2	23.6	**7.8**	9.6	13.4
STATE GUARANTY BANK	OKEENE	OK	**B**	B	B	37	4.98	6.9	3.1	2.2	59.9	**10.0**	11.2	21.0
STATE NATIONAL BK & TRUST	WAYNE	NE	**B+**	B+	A-	107	12.73	6.9	1.7	6.6	29.9	**10.0**	13.7	20.7
▼STATE NATIONAL BK BIG SPR	BIG SPRING	TX	**B**	A-	A-	268	18.14	5.5	1.5	0.4	60.3	**8.6**	10.0	34.5
▼STATE NATIONAL BK IN WEST	WEST	TX	**C**	B-	B-	59	5.31	7.6	4.6	2.2	67.9	**7.4**	9.2	27.7
STATE NATIONAL BK OF	GROOM	TX	**D**	D+	D	35	1.09	13.3	2.0	1.3	9.7	**5.3**	7.6	11.2
STATE NATIONAL BK OF TEXA	IOWA PARK	TX	**B**	B	B+	186	0.93	4.4	5.7	17.8	38.1	**7.0**	9.0	16.6
▲STATE SB	CRESTON	IA	**B-**	C+	C+	51	7.26	12.7	5.1	17.6	0.4	**6.7**	8.7	13.2
STATE SB	RAKE	IA	**D+**	C	C	53	2.10	8.1	2.3	2.4	9.3	**3.6**	8.2	10.3
▲STATE SB	WEST DES MOINES	IA	**B-**	B-	C+	91	-1.69	6.4	1.6	26.8	5.5	**8.7**	10.2	14.3
STATE SB	FRANKFORT	MI	**B+**	A-	A-	81	-6.78	1.8	2.1	22.9	8.4	**10.0**	15.7	25.1
STATE SB OF MANISTIQUE	MANISTIQUE	MI	**C+**	B-	C	117	1.70	8.8	4.6	16.9	35.5	**8.8**	10.2	16.6
STATE STREET B&TC CALIFOR	LOS ANGELES	CA	**U**	U	U	15	0.19	0.0	0.0	0.0	0.0	**10.0**	93.7	386.2
STATE STREET BANK &	QUINCY	IL	**B**	B	B+	149	5.22	5.6	24.2	13.9	25.8	**8.7**	10.1	16.5
STATE STREET BANK &	BOSTON	MA	**B+**	B+	B	155,529	1.16	0.0	0.1	0.0	60.4	**5.1**	7.1	19.9
STATE STREET BANK &	NEW YORK	NY	**U**	U	U	25	7.24	0.0	0.0	0.0	0.0	**10.0**	97.1	171.7
STATE-INVESTORS BANK	METAIRIE	LA	**C+**	C+	B-	209	-0.31	0.0	0.7	63.3	4.6	**8.8**	10.2	17.6
▲STC CAPITAL BANK	SAINT CHARLES	IL	**C+**	C+	C	160	-1.74	11.8	0.7	8.8	7.3	**10.0**	14.9	18.2
STEARNS BANK	HOLDINGFORD	MN	**B**	C+	B-	83	-3.68	0.5	0.3	0.8	2.3	**10.0**	11.9	20.3
▲STEARNS BANK NA	SAINT CLOUD	MN	**B**	C+	B-	1,231	-7.08	12.1	1.2	6.4	6.4	**10.0**	18.5	31.9
▲STEARNS BANK UPSALA NA	UPSALA	MN	**B**	C+	B-	66	-2.28	0.8	0.4	0.5	1.7	**10.0**	11.8	21.5
STEELE STREET BANK &	DENVER	CO	**B**	C+	C	370	16.00	10.0	1.2	17.4	11.9	**8.5**	10.0	14.9
▼STELLAR BUSINESS BANK	COVINA	CA	**D+**	C-	C-	98	2.72	2.0	0.1	1.4	33.9	**10.0**	17.7	30.9
▲STELLARONE BANK	CHRISTIANSBURG	VA	**C+**	C-	B+	2,923	-3.05	6.0	1.0	19.0	13.0	**9.6**	11.2	14.6
STEPHENS FEDERAL BANK	TOCCOA	GA	**D**	D	D+	207	-8.71	2.6	2.3	40.0	2.3	**6.1**	8.1	12.1
STEPHENSON NATIONAL BK &	MARINETTE	WI	**C+**	C+	B-	282	4.18	14.8	2.4	12.5	19.8	**7.9**	9.6	14.6
▼STERLING BANK	POPLAR BLUFF	MO	**B+**	B+	B+	257	40.63	19.4	1.4	9.0	1.6	**8.2**	11.1	13.5
STERLING BANK	HOUSTON	TX	**D**	D+	C-	5,191	5.14	11.4	0.8	5.1	30.0	**7.8**	9.5	16.9
STERLING BANK	BARRON	WI	**B+**	B+	B	182	10.41	6.5	1.3	16.7	25.3	**6.3**	8.4	12.6
STERLING BANK & TRUST FSB	SOUTHFIELD	MI	**D**	D	D-	724	-3.20	2.4	0.1	43.4	4.5	**7.8**	9.6	14.2
STERLING FEDERAL BANK	STERLING	IL	**D**	C	C	488	0.26	0.2	1.8	28.8	40.9	**6.1**	10.0	11.8
STERLING NATIONAL BK	NEW YORK	NY	**C+**	C+	B-	2,319	9.01	33.0	0.5	5.2	33.8	**6.4**	8.4	12.3
STERLING SB	SPOKANE	WA	**D-**	E-	D-	9,501	-7.76	4.9	1.7	15.2	29.7	**8.1**	9.8	17.0
STERLING STATE BK	AUSTIN	MN	**D**	C-	D+	287	3.60	9.8	0.7	9.9	9.4	**6.0**	8.0	12.2
STEUBEN TRUST CO	HORNELL	NY	**B+**	B	B-	341	0.58	5.9	6.6	18.8	30.7	**8.6**	10.1	17.3
▲STIFEL BANK & TRUST	SAINT LOUIS	MO	**B**	C+	B-	1,778	53.37	6.2	11.7	7.7	59.9	**5.8**	7.8	14.4
STILLMAN BANCCORP NA	STILLMAN VALLEY	IL	**C+**	B-	C+	394	10.25	3.9	1.1	6.9	40.5	**7.8**	9.6	19.5
STILLWATER NATIONAL BK &	STILLWATER	OK	**D**	D	C-	2,467	-10.16	15.8	1.2	2.2	9.2	**10.0**	13.8	17.2
▼STOCK EXCHANGE BANK	CALDWELL	KS	**D+**	C-	C+	38	19.22	2.5	4.2	6.0	35.5	**6.4**	8.4	19.9
STOCK EXCHANGE BANK	WOODWARD	OK	**B+**	A-	A	188	16.19	7.7	4.0	6.8	46.1	**10.0**	12.4	23.9
STOCK GROWERS BANK	NAPOLEON	ND	**A-**	A-	B+	54	7.21	1.9	2.2	3.4	22.6	**10.0**	11.0	17.1
STOCK YARDS BANK & TRUST	LOUISVILLE	KY	**B**	B	B+	1,892	6.92	15.7	1.9	10.1	12.7	**5.5**	8.1	11.4
STOCKGROWERS STATE BK	ASHLAND	KS	**B**	B	B	115	0.37	13.7	1.1	2.6	28.7	**10.0**	12.1	17.1
STOCKGROWERS STATE BK	MAPLE HILL	KS	**B**	B	B-	73	-1.01	9.9	1.3	10.1	46.6	**9.3**	10.6	20.3
▲STOCKMAN BANK OF	MILES CITY	MT	**B**	B-	B-	2,009	12.37	6.3	1.5	4.6	31.4	**6.8**	8.8	13.7
▲STOCKMANS BANK	ALTUS	OK	**D+**	E	E	120	-0.35	10.8	3.9	10.0	4.4	**5.0**	8.2	11.0
STOCKMENS BANK	CASCADE	MT	**B-**	B-	C+	29	9.25	3.2	4.3	9.4	17.8	**10.0**	12.6	20.3
STOCKMENS NATIONAL BK	COTULLA	TX	**B**	B	B+	64	13.01	10.4	4.4	2.9	47.7	**6.1**	8.1	16.3
STOCKTON NATIONAL BK	STOCKTON	KS	**B-**	B+	B+	67	-0.13	6.7	1.8	3.5	16.6	**10.0**	11.8	19.4
▼STONE COUNTY NATIONAL BK	CRANE	MO	**D**	C-	B-	85	-0.02	2.8	3.8	19.0	40.5	**8.2**	10.2	13.5
STONEBRIDGE BANK	MINNEAPOLIS	MN	**D+**	C-	C	100	24.61	16.4	7.0	11.7	7.0	**4.0**	8.1	10.5
STONEBRIDGE BANK	WEST CHESTER	PA	**D-**	D-	E+	386	-13.18	6.2	0.2	23.4	17.3	**4.7**	7.0	10.9
STONEGATE BANK	FORT LAUDERDALE	FL	**B-**	C+	C	637	15.53	6.9	0.6	10.3	21.8	**10.0**	15.5	22.1
STONEHAM SB	STONEHAM	MA	**E-**	E-	D+	380	-10.01	0.8	0.1	32.0	10.9	**0.6**	4.0	7.2
STONEHAMBANK	STONEHAM	MA	**C**	C-	C	407	-1.29	6.8	0.4	48.8	6.7	**6.4**	8.4	13.3
STOUGHTON CO-OP BANK	STOUGHTON	MA	**C-**	D+	C-	93	-11.90	0.0	3.1	59.5	21.5	**6.4**	8.4	18.0

Asset Quality Index	Non-Performing Loans as a % of Total Loans	Non-Performing Loans as a % of Capital	Net Charge-offs Avg Loans	Profitability Index	Net Income ($Mil)	Return on Assets (R.O.A.)	Return on Equity (R.O.E.)	Net Interest Spread	Overhead Efficiency Ratio	Liquidity Index	Liquidity Ratio	Hot Money Ratio	Stability Index
8.5	0.02	0.1	0.18	**7.9**	1.3	2.08	16.00	4.97	62.0	**2.4**	34.8	24.5	**9.0**
0.0	15.76	165.8	4.26	**0.2**	-12.0	-4.87	-101.70	3.73	89.1	**0.9**	16.9	33.7	**2.5**
4.4	0.54	3.1	3.12	**2.3**	0.2	0.65	7.38	3.78	70.7	**4.7**	26.7	6.2	**2.6**
0.3	10.72	63.5	2.08	**2.6**	-0.2	-0.31	-4.02	4.21	57.1	**2.3**	35.1	26.3	**4.4**
3.3	1.82	11.6	2.74	**0.5**	-38.0	-0.24	-2.59	3.34	64.7	**1.5**	26.9	55.6	**5.0**
8.4	0.71	2.2	0.22	**3.6**	0.2	0.67	5.35	2.95	77.6	**2.8**	61.0	33.2	**6.9**
8.4	0.60	2.5	0.03	**4.7**	0.8	0.77	5.20	3.74	66.3	**3.0**	18.6	14.4	**7.9**
9.7	0.03	0.1	-0.33	**3.8**	2.0	0.87	7.46	2.67	74.6	**6.0**	77.8	12.0	**6.3**
8.8	0.41	0.9	-0.13	**2.6**	0.1	0.24	2.54	3.18	89.6	**6.3**	68.6	7.6	**5.1**
6.6	0.00	0.0	1.65	**1.8**	-0.1	-0.18	-2.34	4.84	77.0	**2.4**	13.7	16.9	**4.8**
7.9	0.37	2.0	0.13	**5.2**	2.1	1.16	11.50	4.39	74.1	**3.4**	30.7	15.1	**7.0**
6.1	0.00	0.0	0.56	**8.4**	0.9	1.87	21.90	4.72	51.9	**3.7**	22.6	11.2	**6.8**
3.0	1.38	12.7	0.25	**4.9**	0.5	0.94	11.45	3.10	45.7	**0.9**	17.5	34.6	**5.3**
6.0	0.11	0.8	0.43	**4.8**	1.0	1.14	11.35	3.87	63.9	**1.6**	18.2	23.8	**6.3**
5.9	2.19	8.7	0.07	**6.4**	0.9	1.15	7.44	4.11	60.1	**4.1**	36.6	13.5	**7.7**
2.8	3.80	18.2	0.54	**4.6**	1.1	0.94	8.68	4.40	60.4	**4.9**	40.5	10.7	**6.5**
10.0	0.00	0.0	0.00	**9.5**	0.9	5.83	6.19	0.14	76.7	**5.0**	1,567.4	101.0	**7.0**
7.2	0.12	0.7	0.16	**6.1**	1.9	1.34	12.43	4.60	69.2	**4.8**	41.9	11.4	**6.8**
7.5	1.11	1.3	0.04	**7.1**	1,884.0	1.27	11.53	2.30	68.4	**3.7**	59.4	27.9	**7.7**
10.0	0.00	0.0	0.00	**10.0**	2.4	10.20	10.52	0.16	88.8	**5.0**	1,052.9	101.0	**7.0**
5.4	0.81	6.5	0.00	**3.2**	1.0	0.46	4.67	3.62	77.2	**1.2**	8.9	27.3	**5.7**
2.9	3.98	18.9	0.23	**3.2**	0.7	0.46	3.15	4.56	72.5	**1.2**	16.3	29.3	**4.9**
5.6	1.28	5.8	1.02	**6.5**	1.4	1.69	15.34	3.44	38.3	**2.1**	45.3	40.6	**7.4**
4.2	3.41	11.9	2.72	**9.1**	25.8	2.09	11.87	7.36	42.9	**0.6**	7.0	43.6	**8.9**
7.2	0.14	0.6	0.12	**7.2**	1.1	1.72	16.09	3.05	40.9	**2.3**	53.1	49.4	**7.0**
8.7	0.16	1.1	0.17	**5.4**	4.4	1.36	13.12	4.67	63.1	**1.6**	30.9	31.5	**5.3**
8.0	0.00	0.0	0.91	**0.0**	-0.5	-0.51	-2.79	3.88	111.2	**5.0**	32.9	7.1	**2.0**
2.4	2.11	12.9	1.17	**2.8**	11.3	0.38	2.74	3.68	72.0	**3.5**	14.5	11.6	**7.0**
1.7	5.07	44.3	0.22	**0.5**	-1.3	-0.60	-7.44	3.44	94.9	**0.7**	8.5	35.4	**2.9**
3.7	1.82	12.4	0.35	**5.3**	3.3	1.21	11.82	3.87	64.9	**2.4**	14.0	16.8	**6.6**
6.6	0.31	2.0	0.16	**5.0**	2.6	1.34	12.43	4.23	59.3	**0.9**	24.5	41.8	**6.0**
1.0	4.85	24.5	1.48	**1.9**	4.8	0.10	0.75	3.81	75.1	**4.1**	33.2	15.3	**7.6**
8.9	0.03	0.2	0.01	**7.4**	3.1	1.78	21.14	4.25	59.8	**2.1**	30.9	24.1	**6.5**
0.7	3.04	24.8	0.78	**1.9**	2.8	0.38	3.56	4.61	61.2	**1.5**	6.8	22.0	**5.3**
4.8	1.62	6.2	0.00	**1.3**	-1.1	-0.22	-2.33	3.15	120.1	**3.6**	55.4	23.3	**4.7**
5.9	0.52	3.3	2.42	**3.7**	10.7	0.49	6.21	4.23	69.5	**2.0**	25.4	27.9	**4.2**
0.3	10.65	51.3	5.16	**0.0**	-206.8	-2.09	-32.15	3.13	95.3	**1.1**	11.3	29.8	**2.3**
1.7	4.07	30.4	1.47	**0.5**	-2.7	-0.98	-11.06	4.19	92.0	**3.2**	28.4	15.1	**4.7**
5.7	0.75	4.1	0.12	**6.5**	4.1	1.17	11.81	4.65	69.8	**2.7**	7.5	14.9	**6.0**
8.0	0.15	0.6	-0.04	**4.4**	11.0	0.82	9.49	2.41	54.0	**8.0**	69.7	0.2	**7.4**
5.3	1.60	6.5	0.58	**3.8**	3.2	0.85	8.32	3.10	74.2	**2.4**	35.7	24.8	**5.4**
0.0	4.69	24.8	1.31	**4.3**	18.9	0.72	5.61	3.82	48.9	**0.8**	3.3	32.4	**6.8**
7.1	0.18	0.8	0.63	**1.4**	0.1	0.32	3.39	3.33	92.4	**3.7**	58.7	19.8	**3.4**
6.0	3.44	10.0	1.67	**4.1**	1.1	0.66	4.93	3.82	63.3	**4.5**	36.9	11.7	**6.2**
8.6	0.00	0.0	0.00	**7.4**	0.8	1.57	13.51	4.58	57.0	**3.7**	39.0	16.1	**8.4**
4.9	1.24	10.5	0.40	**7.8**	25.1	1.38	17.33	4.12	55.0	**3.6**	11.2	11.0	**8.0**
4.3	0.43	2.2	0.58	**3.8**	0.8	0.71	5.51	3.69	72.4	**1.7**	24.0	24.2	**6.6**
5.3	1.12	4.6	0.30	**6.9**	1.1	1.58	13.54	4.17	52.8	**3.6**	29.2	13.4	**7.7**
4.9	1.31	8.3	0.14	**7.2**	32.1	1.70	17.51	3.48	54.3	**1.6**	19.1	25.3	**9.6**
3.2	0.27	2.7	0.59	**3.9**	1.2	1.01	12.48	5.07	74.1	**1.4**	3.7	23.1	**2.2**
6.2	2.06	6.3	0.21	**3.2**	0.2	0.61	4.56	4.16	78.3	**4.5**	65.9	17.0	**7.5**
9.1	0.00	0.0	0.43	**7.0**	1.0	1.61	19.02	3.00	52.8	**2.5**	40.8	27.3	**5.7**
4.4	2.13	9.2	1.30	**2.4**	0.2	0.22	1.84	3.43	73.9	**3.5**	28.4	13.5	**6.2**
5.4	1.44	5.7	1.18	**0.6**	-0.6	-0.64	-6.06	4.39	100.1	**4.2**	27.2	9.4	**4.2**
8.4	0.04	0.4	0.00	**2.2**	0.4	0.42	4.89	3.42	86.4	**2.3**	34.1	24.4	**2.7**
0.3	9.36	73.5	3.82	**0.0**	-4.1	-0.98	-11.16	3.02	79.1	**0.9**	10.8	32.2	**2.7**
3.7	1.34	5.3	0.65	**3.2**	3.5	0.60	3.89	4.24	63.7	**1.2**	25.8	33.5	**6.6**
0.3	3.15	44.8	3.97	**0.0**	-5.0	-1.27	-18.82	2.97	131.1	**1.8**	26.1	24.4	**1.3**
5.1	0.96	8.8	0.05	**3.2**	1.9	0.47	5.77	3.44	80.2	**2.4**	10.6	16.4	**4.3**
4.6	2.10	16.4	0.09	**2.6**	0.4	0.41	5.07	3.31	77.4	**2.2**	27.7	20.1	**3.2**

Name	City	State	Rating	2008 Rating	2007 Rating	Total Assets ($Mil)	One Year Asset Growth	Asset Mix (As a % of Total Assets) Comm-ercial Loans	Cons-umer Loans	Home Mort-gages	Secur-ities	Capital-ization Index	Leverage Ratio	Risk-based Capital Ratio
▼ STRASBURG SB	STRASBURG	OH	**C-**	B	B+	41	-1.96	0.0	1.9	68.2	0.0	**10.0**	14.1	28.4
STRASBURG STATE BK	STRASBURG	ND	**C+**	C+	C+	52	8.91	3.2	1.0	0.1	24.4	**6.1**	8.9	11.8
▲ STRATFORD STATE BK	STRATFORD	WI	**D+**	D-	C-	104	-2.83	7.8	1.6	7.3	36.1	**7.1**	9.1	14.8
▼ STREATOR HOME BUILDING &	STREATOR	IL	**B+**	A	A	150	2.73	0.0	1.7	34.2	57.8	**10.0**	21.3	70.9
▼ STROUD NATIONAL BK	STROUD	OK	**C-**	C+	C+	81	0.41	13.9	6.3	24.1	19.5	**7.0**	9.0	14.2
STURDY SB	CAPE MAY COURT	NJ	**B**	B	B-	520	5.02	1.2	0.2	26.8	23.0	**10.0**	11.3	19.1
STURGIS BANK & TRUST CO	STURGIS	MI	**D**	C-	C-	370	0.00	6.4	1.4	26.3	9.3	**4.7**	6.7	12.2
SUBURBAN BANK & TRUST CO	ELMHURST	IL	**D-**	D-	D+	623	-5.99	4.2	0.1	4.7	15.0	**6.1**	8.1	12.0
SUCCESS BANK	BLOOMFIELD	IA	**A-**	B+	B-	112	14.75	3.6	2.4	7.8	6.2	**9.8**	11.4	14.8
SUFFOLK COUNTY NATIONAL	RIVERHEAD	NY	**C-**	B-	B-	1,618	-4.50	14.7	4.2	12.1	25.2	**6.6**	8.6	13.0
SUGAR RIVER BANK	NEWPORT	NH	**C+**	C+	B-	256	0.82	0.5	1.2	42.7	33.4	**10.0**	12.4	19.2
SUMITOMO TRUST & BANKING	HOBOKEN	NJ	**A-**	A+	A	1,255	3.06	0.0	0.0	0.0	0.4	**7.1**	9.0	75.3
SUMMIT BANK	ARKADELPHIA	AR	**B**	B	B	1,107	1.69	7.0	2.3	15.0	22.7	**6.4**	8.4	13.9
SUMMIT BANK	PRESCOTT	AZ	**E-**	E	C	81	-6.88	6.2	0.3	2.0	9.5	**0.0**	3.1	5.3
▼ SUMMIT BANK	OAKLAND	CA	**C-**	D+	B	185	3.45	24.1	1.6	2.0	0.4	**7.8**	9.6	13.8
SUMMIT BANK	TULSA	OK	**C-**	D	C	204	-0.80	32.9	0.8	10.3	3.0	**7.2**	9.5	12.7
SUMMIT BANK	EUGENE	OR	**D-**	D+	C+	118	-6.47	16.1	2.5	3.5	10.0	**6.5**	8.5	12.4
▼ SUMMIT BANK	BURLINGTON	WA	**E-**	C-	C+	147	-2.80	17.6	2.1	21.7	2.8	**0.0**	3.9	6.0
SUMMIT BANK & TRUST	BROOMFIELD	CO	**C-**	C-	C+	95	-1.66	7.2	0.4	12.1	35.1	**10.0**	12.1	19.6
SUMMIT BANK NA	PANAMA CITY	FL	**C-**	C	C	102	32.89	13.6	3.5	6.6	23.1	**10.0**	20.1	27.6
SUMMIT BANK OF KANSAS CIT	LEE'S SUMMIT	MO	**E+**	D	C-	56	-8.59	22.1	0.8	18.4	0.0	**7.1**	9.0	14.6
▲ SUMMIT COMMUNITY BANK	EAST LANSING	MI	**C-**	D+	D+	155	-2.23	11.6	0.4	36.7	9.5	**6.2**	8.2	12.9
SUMMIT COMMUNITY BANK	MAPLEWOOD	MN	**C-**	C-	C+	75	4.06	15.4	0.1	10.6	8.0	**9.8**	10.8	18.6
SUMMIT COMMUNITY BANK	MOOREFIELD	WV	**D**	D-	D+	1,470	-6.40	6.1	1.7	20.5	18.4	**6.5**	8.5	12.6
SUMMIT NATIONAL BK	HULETT	WY	**C-**	C	C-	74	0.30	6.7	3.3	4.6	23.0	**5.6**	7.6	13.5
SUMMIT STATE BK	SANTA ROSA	CA	**C-**	B-	B	348	2.21	12.3	0.2	16.7	9.7	**10.0**	14.6	19.8
SUMNER BANK & TRUST	GALLATIN	TN	**D**	D+	C	136	11.77	9.1	1.7	15.8	24.8	**5.9**	7.9	13.7
SUMNER NATIONAL BK OF	SHELDON	IL	**D+**	C-	C-	16	-3.56	4.3	7.8	37.5	19.7	**7.1**	9.1	19.0
SUN NATIONAL BK	VINELAND	NJ	**D-**	D	C-	3,413	-4.52	13.7	1.3	5.5	14.0	**6.6**	8.6	12.3
SUN SECURITY BANK	ELLINGTON	MO	**E-**	E-	E	381	-3.60	9.7	1.4	20.2	13.4	**1.3**	5.7	8.3
▲ SUNBANK NA	KANSAS CITY	MO	**D-**	D-	D+	74	44.94	4.4	0.2	0.0	4.2	**10.0**	11.4	46.2
▼ SUNCREST BANK	VISALIA	CA	**D**	C	C	76	8.35	8.9	0.2	4.3	16.5	**10.0**	16.6	21.7
SUNDANCE STATE BK	SUNDANCE	WY	**C+**	C+	C+	130	3.57	12.8	9.4	7.4	34.9	**5.8**	7.8	12.7
▲ SUNDOWN STATE BK	SUNDOWN	TX	**B-**	C+	C+	105	-10.69	14.8	2.7	7.1	19.5	**5.9**	7.9	12.3
▼ SUNFIRST BANK	SAINT GEORGE	UT	**E+**	D-	D-	225	-5.76	10.3	0.9	12.6	10.4	**3.8**	6.8	10.4
▲ SUNFLOWER BANK NA	SALINA	KS	**B-**	B-	B	1,694	-6.40	8.4	2.3	17.2	36.0	**5.5**	7.5	14.2
SUNMARK COMMUNITY BANK	HAWKINSVILLE	GA	**D**	D	C+	187	-4.62	7.1	5.2	21.9	7.2	**9.1**	10.4	14.8
▼ SUNNYSIDE FS&LA OF IRVING	IRVINGTON	NY	**D**	D	C-	95	-6.65	0.0	0.2	39.6	32.5	**4.9**	6.9	19.1
SUNRISE BANK	SAN DIEGO	CA	**E+**	NR	NR	232	247.58	18.6	0.4	4.8	0.9	**5.0**	7.0	11.2
SUNRISE BANK	COCOA BEACH	FL	**E-**	E-	D	119	-8.89	6.0	0.2	3.0	16.3	**0.0**	2.7	4.9
SUNRISE BANK	VALDOSTA	GA	**E-**	D-	C-	113	104.63	6.8	2.1	21.3	0.6	**0.0**	2.1	4.6
SUNRISE BANK DAKOTA	ONIDA	SD	**C+**	B-	B-	42	6.73	7.1	3.4	3.4	23.0	**9.3**	10.6	18.2
SUNRISE BANK OF	ALBUQUERQUE	NM	**E-**	D-	C-	74	-6.79	9.8	0.1	7.6	0.0	**0.0**	2.4	4.7
SUNRISE BANK OF ARIZONA	PHOENIX	AZ	**E-**	NR	NR	353	-28.90	7.9	0.3	6.9	0.1	**0.0**	0.7	1.8
SUNSET BANK & SAVINGS	WAUKESHA	WI	**D-**	D-	D-	140	-2.43	8.9	0.4	32.1	15.5	**6.5**	8.5	13.1
SUNSHINE SAVINGS BANK	TALLAHASSEE	FL	**D**	D	C-	149	-4.58	0.0	9.9	56.0	2.0	**6.9**	8.9	14.4
SUNSHINE STATE FS&LA	PLANT CITY	FL	**C-**	C+	B+	198	0.81	9.7	1.1	37.3	10.7	**10.0**	13.2	22.6
SUNSOUTH BANK	DOTHAN	AL	**D-**	D-	D+	208	-16.87	9.1	1.9	21.2	7.2	**6.8**	8.8	12.5
SUNSTATE BK	MIAMI	FL	**D-**	D-	C-	172	1.58	7.6	0.7	13.8	33.0	**10.0**	11.4	16.4
SUNTRUST BANK	ATLANTA	GA	**D-**	D-	D+	162,510	-1.11	15.4	10.1	20.6	12.2	**6.3**	8.3	12.6
▲ SUNWEST BANK	TUSTIN	CA	**B-**	C+	B	617	-5.48	13.1	1.2	7.1	22.3	**10.0**	11.1	17.5
SUPERIOR BANK	BIRMINGHAM	AL	**E-**	D-	D	3,028	-5.59	5.4	1.7	21.2	7.6	**0.0**	1.4	3.5
SUPERIOR BANK	HAZELWOOD	MO	**E-**	D-	D+	52	-8.63	3.4	0.0	15.1	0.0	**1.6**	5.9	8.6
SUPERIOR BANK	SUPERIOR	WI	**C+**	C+	B	33	-1.39	1.9	2.0	46.7	29.8	**10.0**	12.2	26.8
SUPERIOR NATIONAL BK & TR	HANCOCK	MI	**B**	A-	A-	452	7.88	8.9	7.6	28.6	30.1	**9.9**	10.9	19.1
SUPERIOR SB	SUPERIOR	WI	**C+**	B-	C	64	-4.64	1.8	4.1	55.7	5.4	**10.0**	15.6	25.8
SURETY BANK	DELAND	FL	**D-**	D-	D	122	-8.42	0.4	1.0	10.1	15.2	**7.9**	9.6	13.5
SURREY BANK & TRUST	MOUNT AIRY	NC	**B**	B+	B+	214	-1.52	30.0	3.2	13.2	0.9	**10.0**	11.7	17.0
SUSQUEHANNA BANK	LITITZ	PA	**C-**	C-	C+	13,823	2.43	11.1	4.4	11.4	16.5	**7.5**	9.3	12.9
SUSSEX BANK	FRANKLIN	NJ	**D-**	D-	D-	472	4.28	3.1	0.2	17.4	19.1	**7.1**	9.0	13.6

Asset Quality Index	Non-Performing Loans as a % of Total Loans	Non-Performing Loans as a % of Capital	Net Charge-offs Avg Loans	Profitability Index	Net Income ($Mil)	Return on Assets (R.O.A.)	Return on Equity (R.O.E.)	Net Interest Spread	Overhead Efficiency Ratio	Liquidity Index	Liquidity Ratio	Hot Money Ratio	Stability Index
1.7	1.86	10.1	0.06	**6.1**	0.6	1.53	10.70	4.25	64.6	**1.6**	18.0	23.7	**9.1**
7.8	0.00	0.0	0.00	**4.9**	0.5	1.00	11.01	3.29	63.7	**4.4**	41.7	13.4	**5.9**
4.2	2.14	11.4	0.57	**1.6**	0.3	0.24	2.25	3.54	85.6	**1.7**	35.9	37.5	**4.1**
9.9	0.18	0.3	0.01	**4.7**	1.5	1.01	4.82	2.83	50.7	**5.4**	78.3	15.4	**8.5**
1.9	3.88	26.0	0.16	**5.6**	1.0	1.15	12.79	5.14	71.8	**1.8**	21.7	22.3	**6.3**
5.8	2.33	11.5	0.07	**4.4**	4.7	0.92	7.71	3.89	73.3	**4.0**	21.5	9.7	**7.5**
0.9	2.38	19.9	0.96	**0.7**	-0.4	-0.10	-1.31	3.10	78.1	**2.3**	10.9	17.0	**4.1**
0.0	11.48	81.0	4.17	**0.0**	-14.8	-2.25	-26.26	3.34	77.4	**1.5**	14.0	24.6	**3.4**
6.0	0.51	3.2	-0.02	**8.0**	1.9	1.81	15.40	4.87	58.0	**2.7**	17.8	15.8	**7.0**
2.0	3.12	21.1	0.70	**6.2**	15.2	0.89	10.65	5.01	58.6	**2.6**	5.8	15.0	**8.9**
6.4	2.23	9.6	0.34	**2.3**	1.1	0.44	3.41	3.58	93.6	**3.2**	38.8	18.7	**7.1**
10.0	0.00	0.0	0.00	**5.2**	6.5	0.54	5.69	0.09	85.2	**8.7**	107.5	0.0	**10.0**
4.5	1.02	6.8	0.43	**5.1**	12.5	1.12	12.51	3.69	59.8	**1.2**	18.9	31.7	**8.3**
0.0	6.25	65.0	2.63	**0.0**	-3.3	-3.68	-69.00	3.95	115.8	**0.9**	19.3	36.4	**2.6**
2.0	1.03	6.0	0.82	**4.4**	1.1	0.58	5.94	4.81	62.7	**2.2**	29.6	20.9	**5.3**
2.2	2.46	17.9	0.26	**3.4**	2.1	1.08	11.82	4.06	72.0	**2.7**	22.0	16.0	**3.9**
0.2	3.63	26.5	0.50	**2.9**	0.3	0.27	3.15	3.91	79.7	**1.9**	15.7	19.5	**3.9**
0.3	8.35	100.9	5.05	**0.3**	-8.7	-5.60	-76.63	4.53	110.9	**0.8**	15.5	40.6	**3.2**
1.1	12.34	46.1	0.76	**1.1**	0.3	0.28	2.16	3.68	82.5	**2.5**	44.0	30.2	**5.1**
8.5	0.70	2.0	0.00	**1.2**	0.1	0.09	0.39	3.75	89.5	**2.3**	42.3	31.6	**2.7**
3.3	1.07	7.4	0.95	**0.0**	-0.3	-0.55	-5.47	3.43	78.8	**0.9**	21.8	35.9	**1.1**
2.7	1.65	13.5	1.02	**2.0**	0.4	0.24	2.84	3.50	77.2	**1.2**	15.8	28.5	**3.8**
5.3	1.49	7.0	0.30	**2.0**	0.3	0.35	3.26	2.49	80.5	**4.5**	41.5	12.7	**3.2**
2.0	2.14	15.3	1.94	**0.9**	-0.8	-0.06	-0.67	3.14	60.5	**0.7**	10.8	40.1	**4.3**
4.0	1.78	11.6	0.38	**3.3**	0.3	0.43	4.83	4.50	77.0	**3.8**	31.1	13.1	**4.2**
1.3	4.32	21.6	0.87	**4.3**	1.8	0.51	3.24	4.57	56.6	**0.5**	6.2	52.3	**7.1**
4.7	0.33	2.4	0.63	**0.7**	0.2	0.16	1.90	3.30	92.4	**1.2**	20.6	30.8	**1.5**
4.6	1.34	7.9	0.33	**3.2**	0.1	0.44	4.78	4.05	84.8	**2.7**	33.9	17.3	**5.6**
0.0	6.85	45.2	2.95	**0.0**	-182.9	-5.13	-47.72	3.64	158.2	**3.6**	10.0	10.8	**7.4**
0.1	12.61	112.3	1.41	**0.7**	0.6	0.16	2.69	3.19	81.3	**2.3**	6.7	16.4	**0.0**
0.3	56.47	69.8	15.57	**0.0**	-2.5	-3.21	-53.96	-0.55	183.2	**3.5**	85.9	33.8	**2.4**
7.0	0.46	1.8	0.09	**0.0**	-1.2	-1.55	-8.82	4.35	124.6	**1.6**	23.8	25.3	**2.0**
3.0	2.11	13.9	0.36	**5.0**	1.1	0.92	11.18	3.56	57.6	**2.7**	32.8	19.3	**4.1**
5.0	1.51	11.4	0.13	**5.9**	1.3	1.19	14.51	5.53	70.1	**1.6**	7.0	20.3	**4.6**
0.0	12.37	87.7	5.53	**0.0**	-6.0	-2.56	-26.39	2.96	144.4	**0.7**	16.8	56.5	**3.3**
4.3	1.25	8.1	1.24	**4.7**	16.9	0.99	10.87	3.49	68.2	**3.3**	21.4	14.1	**8.0**
1.4	3.44	21.9	2.28	**0.9**	-1.0	-0.50	-4.68	4.31	72.9	**1.8**	15.2	20.0	**5.5**
8.3	0.00	0.0	0.01	**1.7**	0.2	0.20	3.16	2.92	90.1	**3.9**	51.4	17.3	**1.7**
0.0	4.64	33.5	2.32	**0.0**	-10.4	-3.83	-43.91	4.44	143.1	**1.9**	22.3	20.6	**3.6**
0.0	7.84	95.4	5.36	**0.0**	-5.9	-4.59	-149.20	2.94	148.4	**3.5**	19.3	12.1	**0.0**
0.3	11.10	129.1	6.38	**0.0**	-8.5	-9.81	-244.89	3.64	304.9	**1.4**	24.1	28.7	**1.1**
3.1	1.45	7.8	0.41	**7.3**	0.7	1.72	15.03	4.97	58.8	**2.2**	32.3	23.8	**7.6**
0.0	9.01	109.4	2.58	**0.0**	-4.2	-5.28	-120.17	3.12	190.1	**0.9**	25.3	53.7	**2.0**
0.0	11.31	154.8	5.46	**0.0**	-41.5	-9.64	-411.91	2.97	-652.3	**0.9**	19.1	35.8	**0.9**
0.3	3.81	26.4	1.00	**1.2**	0.4	0.26	2.70	3.73	81.2	**2.8**	24.9	16.0	**2.6**
1.0	3.58	30.3	0.66	**1.6**	0.4	0.25	2.54	4.33	80.6	**3.1**	16.4	13.7	**0.3**
4.8	1.60	8.0	0.24	**1.8**	0.0	0.00	0.03	3.65	87.3	**3.9**	26.2	11.0	**5.9**
0.2	8.17	61.2	2.08	**2.0**	1.5	0.64	7.87	4.14	56.9	**0.5**	4.3	40.7	**4.1**
0.3	12.52	52.6	3.98	**0.0**	-0.7	-0.38	-3.47	2.99	84.9	**1.5**	25.6	28.8	**4.8**
0.3	3.49	25.9	2.44	**0.5**	33.4	0.03	0.23	3.49	69.0	**3.6**	14.6	11.6	**7.5**
4.7	2.58	10.9	0.64	**8.2**	8.9	1.36	12.73	6.41	59.8	**6.1**	47.4	5.5	**7.4**
0.0	11.84	259.2	2.92	**0.0**	-232.2	-7.15	-123.60	3.37	100.2	**1.1**	17.0	32.1	**0.0**
0.0	7.34	71.5	4.19	**0.0**	-1.7	-2.98	-37.46	3.44	90.8	**2.2**	9.8	17.4	**3.2**
3.7	2.57	11.4	0.83	**3.8**	0.3	0.75	6.20	4.17	72.6	**2.8**	35.5	19.7	**6.4**
4.0	2.81	15.1	0.58	**6.2**	5.0	1.13	9.90	3.90	56.7	**2.5**	33.0	20.2	**7.5**
6.5	0.91	4.0	0.61	**2.6**	0.2	0.29	1.82	4.34	63.0	**3.1**	19.8	13.9	**6.4**
0.0	8.90	52.3	2.29	**0.0**	-2.1	-1.59	-19.33	3.41	67.7	**1.0**	23.1	35.1	**6.2**
3.7	1.67	9.9	1.94	**4.0**	1.3	0.57	4.52	4.15	56.4	**1.5**	14.2	24.9	**8.1**
1.7	2.23	15.4	1.47	**3.6**	66.4	0.48	3.20	3.90	59.1	**3.0**	8.3	13.7	**7.5**
0.0	6.64	45.1	0.72	**3.3**	2.5	0.53	5.51	3.87	69.7	**4.3**	22.6	7.8	**5.1**

Name	City	State	Rating	2008 Rating	2007 Rating	Total Assets ($Mil)	One Year Asset Growth	Asset Mix (As a % of Total Assets) Comm-ercial Loans	Cons-umer Loans	Home Mort-gages	Secur-ities	Capital-ization Index	Leverage Ratio	Risk-based Capital Ratio
▲ SUTTER COMMUNITY BANK	YUBA CITY	CA	**C**	C-	D+	65	4.22	13.8	1.5	4.8	0.0	**10.0**	11.4	17.6
▲ SUTTON BANK	ATTICA	OH	**C-**	C-	C-	345	-3.99	9.9	3.5	8.0	27.2	**6.1**	8.1	13.0
SWEDISH-AMERICAN STATE	COURTLAND	KS	**C-**	C	D+	36	9.16	8.4	5.2	9.2	25.9	**6.8**	8.8	13.7
SWEET WATER STATE BK	SWEET WATER	AL	**B-**	B	B+	82	22.87	9.6	8.3	14.8	8.2	**6.9**	10.0	12.4
▼ SWINEFORD NATIONAL BK	MIDDLEBURG	PA	**C-**	C+	B-	309	-1.64	9.2	6.2	17.4	23.1	**6.0**	8.0	12.5
▼ SWISHER TRUST & SB	SWISHER	IA	**B-**	B	B	42	0.29	3.0	4.4	21.7	51.7	**10.0**	11.3	19.5
▼ SYCAMORE BANK	SENATOBIA	MS	**D+**	C-	D+	171	-2.29	6.5	5.4	18.4	17.2	**8.8**	10.2	15.8
SYNERGY BANK	HOUMA	LA	**B**	B+	B+	328	13.81	15.5	4.1	14.9	8.4	**6.6**	8.6	14.0
SYNERGY BANK SSB	MCKINNEY	TX	**D-**	D-	D-	130	-11.11	7.5	0.8	19.5	0.4	**8.2**	9.8	16.0
▲ SYNOVUS BANK	COLUMBUS	GA	**D**	D+	B	29,509	309.73	12.4	1.8	9.7	11.5	**7.9**	9.6	14.3
SYNOVUS TRUST CO NA	COLUMBUS	GA	**U**	U	U	41	15.51	0.0	0.0	0.0	3.4	**10.0**	91.7	94.1
SYRINGA BANK	BOISE	ID	**E-**	E-	D-	229	-18.10	18.6	2.2	6.7	5.2	**1.5**	5.7	8.5
SYSTEMATIC SAVINGS & LOAN	SPRINGFIELD	MO	**C-**	C-	C+	52	-0.03	0.0	0.8	66.9	0.0	**10.0**	15.3	29.8
T BANK NA	DALLAS	TX	**D-**	D-	D+	115	-17.42	55.9	0.9	2.8	4.1	**6.6**	9.4	12.2
T ROWE PRICE SAVINGS	BALTIMORE	MD	**C+**	C	C-	186	0.06	0.0	0.0	0.0	99.2	**10.0**	11.8	37.8
TABLE GROVE STATE BK	TABLE GROVE	IL	**C**	C-	C+	51	-2.37	1.7	4.9	7.5	39.9	**5.9**	7.9	15.4
TABLE ROCK COMMUNITY	KIMBERLING CITY	MO	**D+**	D+	C	40	21.32	6.1	5.8	38.7	9.7	**6.0**	8.0	13.4
▼ TALBOT BANK OF EASTON	EASTON	MD	**D**	C+	B	688	-3.91	8.2	1.6	19.0	5.7	**6.9**	9.6	12.4
TALBOT STATE BK	FAYETTEVILLE	GA	**D-**	D-	D+	72	-7.82	3.2	1.2	66.7	17.2	**6.0**	8.0	16.7
TALBOTS CLASSICS NATIONAL	LINCOLN	RI	**B+**	B+	B+	11	4.19	0.0	0.0	0.0	2.2	**10.0**	34.8	92.0
TALLAHATCHIE COUNTY BANK	CHARLESTON	MS	**C**	C+	C+	51	6.16	3.2	8.2	13.3	27.0	**7.4**	9.3	18.0
▼ TAMPA STATE BK	TAMPA	KS	**C-**	C-	B	44	-2.24	5.9	5.5	24.0	14.9	**9.7**	10.8	17.7
TARBORO SB SSB	TARBORO	NC	**C-**	C	C-	37	6.29	0.0	0.1	63.9	0.0	**10.0**	13.3	30.4
TARGET BANK	SALT LAKE CITY	UT	**B+**	B-	D-	68	-38.81	4.8	0.0	0.0	19.8	**10.0**	31.7	65.0
TARGET NATIONAL BK	SIOUX FALLS	SD	**A**	A	A	131	18.09	0.0	20.7	0.0	35.3	**10.0**	42.7	59.1
TAYLOR COUNTY BANK	CAMPBELLSVILLE	KY	**B**	B	B-	147	7.00	6.8	4.4	26.1	23.0	**7.2**	9.1	14.8
TAYLORSVILLE SB SSB	TAYLORSVILLE	NC	**D-**	D-	C-	88	1.23	1.8	2.0	39.2	13.9	**7.8**	9.5	15.4
TCF NATIONAL BK	SIOUX FALLS	SD	**D+**	D+	B-	18,481	3.12	11.0	0.1	29.3	10.5	**6.2**	8.2	13.3
TCM BANK NA	TAMPA	FL	**C+**	C-	C+	170	6.28	0.7	89.1	0.0	3.8	**10.0**	16.9	19.2
TD BANK NA	WILMINGTON	DE	**C**	C	C+	168,749	20.50	6.9	3.1	8.2	40.5	**5.6**	7.6	15.6
▼ TD BANK USA NA	PORTLAND	ME	**B**	C	C+	11,148	10.78	0.0	0.0	0.1	66.8	**10.0**	11.9	146.7
TEAM CAPITAL BANK	BETHLEHEM	PA	**D+**	NR	NR	708	N/A	9.8	0.1	12.9	37.7	**5.9**	7.9	12.5
TECHE BANK & TRUST CO	SAINT MARTINVILLE	LA	**A-**	A-	A	79	4.86	5.8	4.2	13.8	51.0	**7.2**	9.1	20.6
TECHE FEDERAL BANK	NEW IBERIA	LA	**C-**	B-	B-	748	-0.46	3.3	8.0	42.4	5.4	**6.7**	8.8	13.8
TECUMSEH FEDERAL BANK	TECUMSEH	NE	**C+**	C+	C+	56	1.48	1.1	0.5	50.5	23.9	**10.0**	13.4	32.3
▲ TEJAS BANK	IRAAN	TX	**C**	C	C-	67	138.03	14.0	8.4	8.3	29.6	**10.0**	11.6	18.7
TEMPLETON SB	TEMPLETON	IA	**A-**	A-	B+	88	2.97	8.6	4.2	13.4	25.9	**9.9**	11.0	16.7
TEMPO BANK A FSB	TRENTON	IL	**C-**	C-	C	95	9.21	0.0	2.3	67.1	0.0	**7.8**	9.6	21.0
TENNESSEE COMMERCE	FRANKLIN	TN	**D+**	C-	C	1,445	5.22	44.0	0.3	2.4	8.8	**5.4**	8.8	11.3
TENNESSEE STATE BK	PIGEON FORGE	TN	**D-**	D-	C-	763	0.05	1.1	0.9	15.7	21.6	**4.9**	7.3	11.0
TENSAS STATE BK	NEWELLTON	LA	**B**	B	B	121	4.85	25.4	4.3	12.7	21.1	**8.7**	10.1	14.0
TERRABANK NA	MIAMI	FL	**D-**	D-	D	260	-2.05	1.2	0.3	5.1	34.7	**7.3**	9.2	16.3
TERRE HAUTE SB	TERRE HAUTE	IN	**C**	C-	C-	297	1.12	7.8	1.1	38.4	15.7	**6.6**	8.6	14.6
TERRITORIAL SAVINGS BANK	HONOLULU	HI	**B**	B-	B	1,443	3.76	0.3	0.1	42.4	37.9	**10.0**	14.0	43.1
TEUTOPOLIS STATE BK	TEUTOPOLIS	IL	**A-**	A-	A	180	11.96	5.5	3.0	13.1	31.8	**10.0**	12.2	25.2
TEXANA BANK NA	LINDEN	TX	**C-**	C+	C-	120	-0.75	23.1	6.0	26.2	17.0	**6.6**	8.6	13.5
TEXAS ADVANTAGE	ALVIN	TX	**D+**	C	C	78	28.63	43.8	5.2	9.2	0.0	**5.8**	7.8	17.9
▼ TEXAS BANK	BROWNWOOD	TX	**B+**	A-	A-	292	5.02	4.6	2.5	24.9	25.7	**10.0**	11.5	18.8
▼ TEXAS BANK	HENDERSON	TX	**C-**	B-	B-	255	14.58	7.8	9.2	13.9	45.7	**4.7**	6.8	12.8
TEXAS BANK & TRUST CO	LONGVIEW	TX	**B+**	B+	B+	1,291	9.91	19.0	5.7	29.7	5.7	**6.5**	8.5	12.5
TEXAS BRAND BANK	GARLAND	TX	**C**	D	C-	85	-6.01	10.2	3.2	18.2	8.9	**7.5**	9.4	15.4
TEXAS CAPITAL BANK NA	DALLAS	TX	**C-**	C+	B-	6,438	13.05	30.9	0.3	21.3	2.9	**3.4**	7.9	10.2
▲ TEXAS CHAMPION BANK	CORPUS CHRISTI	TX	**C-**	D+	D+	346	2.71	18.7	5.0	7.6	3.4	**6.3**	8.3	12.0
TEXAS CITIZENS BANK NA	PASADENA	TX	**D-**	D-	C-	280	35.80	19.1	4.2	8.2	17.1	**6.7**	8.8	12.5
▼ TEXAS COASTAL BANK	PASADENA	TX	**E+**	D-	C+	34	-10.24	8.4	5.6	9.1	14.1	**5.3**	7.3	12.0
TEXAS COMMUNITY BANK NA	LAREDO	TX	**C+**	C+	C+	951	13.56	13.8	3.2	9.3	31.0	**6.2**	8.2	17.1
TEXAS COMMUNITY BANK NA	THE WOODLANDS	TX	**D-**	C	C-	375	-26.99	23.5	2.2	13.5	2.1	**7.1**	9.1	15.9
▼ TEXAS EXCHANGE BANK SSB	CROWLEY	TX	**C-**	C	C	84	26.80	12.4	1.6	4.2	24.6	**10.0**	16.3	30.8
TEXAS FINANCIAL BANK	EDEN	TX	**A-**	B+	B	71	1.30	1.2	2.2	1.2	43.4	**9.5**	10.7	27.7
TEXAS FIRST BANK	SANTA FE	TX	**C+**	B-	B	240	-1.85	4.9	3.5	4.2	21.4	**6.5**	8.5	12.6

Asset Quality Index	Non-Performing Loans as a % of Total Loans	Non-Performing Loans as a % of Capital	Net Charge-offs Avg Loans	Profitability Index	Net Income ($Mil)	Return on Assets (R.O.A.)	Return on Equity (R.O.E.)	Net Interest Spread	Overhead Efficiency Ratio	Liquidity Index	Liquidity Ratio	Hot Money Ratio	Stability Index
5.9	0.55	3.5	0.12	**3.0**	0.3	0.52	4.68	5.52	83.9	**1.2**	20.2	30.0	**5.0**
2.5	2.18	14.0	1.12	**3.2**	2.1	0.58	6.82	3.69	68.5	**2.7**	12.8	15.3	**4.4**
5.0	0.69	5.1	0.05	**5.3**	0.4	1.01	11.49	4.70	69.1	**1.4**	9.2	24.0	**4.1**
5.5	0.67	5.1	0.24	**5.8**	0.9	1.24	12.42	5.74	72.9	**0.9**	12.2	33.0	**5.8**
4.9	0.50	3.5	0.05	**8.3**	4.7	1.53	18.33	3.83	54.3	**3.9**	22.5	10.4	**4.3**
8.0	0.75	2.4	0.52	**3.2**	0.2	0.45	3.83	3.44	80.0	**6.6**	69.5	5.8	**7.0**
4.0	1.08	6.1	1.52	**0.6**	-0.3	-0.16	-1.52	4.44	79.1	**2.9**	7.7	13.6	**4.9**
5.5	0.67	4.8	0.12	**7.4**	3.9	1.26	15.18	3.99	54.9	**1.5**	23.0	26.5	**6.1**
0.0	10.83	60.9	0.08	**0.0**	-0.6	-0.46	-3.67	3.60	93.9	**2.0**	24.2	20.4	**5.1**
1.4	3.88	23.4	7.24	**0.0**	-1,038.8	-4.26	-50.16	4.10	74.6	**1.4**	17.0	27.7	**9.3**
6.7	0.00	0.0	0.00	**9.5**	3.5	9.35	10.10	0.26	83.9	**5.0**	721.0	101.0	**1.7**
1.0	4.80	49.5	2.53	**0.0**	-1.9	-0.75	-12.27	4.17	104.3	**1.4**	14.6	26.6	**2.4**
5.9	2.50	13.0	0.00	**1.8**	0.0	-0.01	-0.08	3.38	81.3	**1.2**	16.0	29.3	**6.3**
1.0	1.91	14.4	0.73	**0.4**	-0.3	-0.27	-3.18	4.23	96.1	**0.6**	9.8	44.2	**3.1**
9.8	0.00	0.0	0.00	**3.2**	1.1	0.56	4.47	1.61	41.4	**4.1**	114.1	44.9	**3.2**
6.4	0.32	2.0	0.50	**3.7**	0.5	0.89	10.61	3.55	77.5	**2.4**	31.5	20.1	**5.0**
3.7	1.51	12.7	0.41	**2.8**	0.3	0.76	9.28	4.47	68.4	**1.4**	24.3	29.1	**2.3**
0.3	4.68	36.5	2.62	**3.3**	-1.4	-0.20	-2.14	3.97	44.2	**0.6**	8.6	38.1	**6.0**
0.3	6.25	51.2	0.90	**0.7**	-0.3	-0.43	-5.78	4.44	94.3	**0.6**	13.3	53.9	**2.2**
10.0	0.00	0.0	0.00	**9.5**	0.4	3.81	10.35	2.49	86.0	**8.5**	122.2	0.0	**7.0**
5.1	1.32	6.2	0.55	**3.6**	0.4	0.75	7.92	3.45	69.1	**3.3**	41.4	18.5	**5.3**
3.2	1.93	10.4	1.47	**1.4**	-0.1	-0.18	-1.59	4.74	77.8	**1.3**	17.3	28.7	**5.4**
10.0	0.00	0.0	0.11	**1.8**	0.1	0.22	1.64	2.60	85.2	**1.6**	32.9	34.0	**7.3**
9.1	0.66	0.2	0.38	**8.3**	3.0	3.72	22.08	3.55	47.1	**8.4**	112.5	0.7	**4.7**
7.8	0.00	0.0	0.00	**9.8**	18.0	15.90	31.64	4.02	92.1	**2.5**	61.2	100.0	**8.3**
5.6	0.81	5.5	0.29	**7.8**	2.6	1.80	18.47	4.31	59.0	**2.6**	22.6	16.8	**6.4**
2.0	2.69	18.1	0.37	**0.6**	0.2	0.19	2.12	2.99	100.5	**1.8**	21.2	22.0	**3.8**
1.5	2.73	22.6	1.46	**5.0**	159.5	0.90	10.59	4.34	61.9	**4.7**	4.9	2.8	**6.2**
2.9	1.59	6.5	5.30	**6.4**	5.4	3.32	22.03	11.86	47.7	**0.3**	12.5	99.3	**5.6**
3.1	2.73	14.6	0.92	**3.1**	633.9	0.43	2.77	3.11	71.5	**6.6**	50.6	5.8	**7.3**
9.8	0.09	0.1	-0.01	**3.6**	-9.2	-0.09	-0.68	3.73	100.0	**7.8**	89.0	4.8	**6.4**
4.7	1.27	8.4	0.00	**1.1**	3.2	0.45	5.62	N/,	76.0	**3.3**	36.0	17.1	**3.1**
5.2	1.74	7.1	0.05	**7.0**	1.2	1.52	13.68	4.04	65.6	**2.5**	42.7	28.3	**7.9**
2.5	2.15	17.4	0.17	**4.5**	7.5	0.99	11.17	4.24	65.3	**3.9**	16.0	9.8	**5.9**
5.1	2.48	10.2	0.04	**2.7**	0.2	0.27	1.91	2.49	87.1	**4.4**	44.9	14.0	**7.1**
7.1	0.00	0.0	0.01	**1.9**	0.1	0.14	1.00	3.74	88.1	**1.7**	27.8	26.6	**6.6**
7.5	0.19	1.1	-0.01	**7.5**	1.2	1.35	10.61	4.16	50.3	**3.0**	16.7	14.1	**7.7**
4.9	1.94	15.2	0.08	**2.4**	0.2	0.19	1.93	2.75	83.3	**2.5**	20.7	17.0	**4.8**
1.6	4.55	37.2	1.53	**3.3**	6.0	0.43	4.91	4.11	49.4	**0.9**	6.1	31.1	**5.0**
0.0	8.17	60.0	1.02	**1.7**	1.2	0.15	1.97	3.37	72.9	**0.7**	9.8	35.6	**4.9**
4.1	1.98	12.3	0.11	**8.5**	2.3	2.03	19.08	4.85	56.5	**1.3**	25.7	31.8	**7.6**
1.3	3.60	20.5	0.18	**0.0**	0.1	0.04	0.41	3.14	118.6	**1.8**	37.6	45.4	**3.3**
4.6	1.63	12.8	0.39	**2.9**	1.1	0.38	4.39	3.23	73.6	**2.2**	25.7	19.5	**4.3**
8.9	0.12	0.4	-0.02	**4.0**	11.4	0.80	5.90	3.38	63.8	**5.9**	59.7	11.8	**9.0**
9.0	0.00	0.0	0.00	**5.3**	1.6	0.96	7.14	2.89	52.8	**6.0**	50.5	6.7	**8.2**
2.9	1.58	12.9	0.17	**1.6**	-0.5	-0.47	-5.16	4.17	102.1	**0.8**	17.9	35.8	**4.8**
5.1	0.64	6.2	0.03	**1.7**	0.3	0.35	4.27	3.87	89.8	**0.7**	13.0	37.1	**2.5**
3.7	0.16	0.9	0.08	**10.0**	9.8	3.56	29.68	5.59	50.2	**3.8**	21.8	10.5	**8.7**
7.1	0.35	2.3	0.33	**5.2**	2.5	1.06	15.54	4.65	73.8	**2.4**	39.5	29.0	**2.7**
6.5	0.80	6.7	0.16	**6.3**	13.7	1.12	12.61	3.81	57.2	**2.9**	12.7	14.8	**7.9**
5.5	0.54	3.7	0.43	**3.0**	0.5	0.56	6.20	4.19	79.2	**1.3**	25.6	30.8	**3.7**
3.4	1.95	19.3	0.95	**4.4**	41.0	0.70	7.96	4.30	56.2	**2.6**	5.5	15.4	**6.6**
2.3	2.22	17.3	0.77	**3.3**	1.3	0.38	4.15	5.05	77.2	**0.9**	21.4	35.4	**5.1**
4.6	0.48	3.6	0.14	**0.0**	-4.6	-1.81	-21.13	3.65	139.6	**1.0**	18.5	32.6	**0.8**
1.4	3.00	22.1	2.42	**0.6**	-0.2	-0.51	-6.68	3.57	104.9	**1.9**	37.4	33.7	**2.9**
5.1	0.97	6.0	0.51	**3.6**	5.0	0.56	6.62	3.14	63.6	**1.7**	38.1	50.7	**4.2**
0.0	7.25	52.6	1.33	**0.1**	-5.2	-1.19	-13.45	3.39	103.9	**1.4**	7.1	23.7	**4.1**
8.1	0.07	0.1	0.96	**1.0**	0.1	0.09	0.44	2.65	113.5	**3.0**	76.4	61.7	**4.9**
9.5	0.00	0.0	-0.09	**7.2**	0.9	1.22	10.91	3.75	67.1	**2.5**	51.7	32.7	**7.1**
0.6	3.44	23.2	1.47	**3.7**	0.7	0.32	3.55	5.06	72.9	**1.8**	14.9	20.0	**5.6**

Name	City	State	Rating	2008 Rating	2007 Rating	Total Assets ($Mil)	One Year Asset Growth	Asset Mix (As a % of Total Assets) Comm-ercial Loans	Cons-umer Loans	Home Mort-gages	Secur-ities	Capital-ization Index	Leverage Ratio	Risk-based Capital Ratio
TEXAS FIRST BANK	TEXAS CITY	TX	**B**	B	B	469	7.83	4.2	3.3	5.7	41.8	**7.3**	9.2	19.2
TEXAS FIRST STATE BK	RIESEL	TX	**C+**	C+	C-	288	7.94	7.5	5.4	11.1	55.7	**5.3**	7.3	17.1
TEXAS GULF BANK NA	FREEPORT	TX	**B+**	B+	A-	343	19.91	8.3	2.0	14.1	46.8	**9.4**	10.6	20.5
▲ TEXAS HERITAGE BANK	BOERNE	TX	**C+**	C	C+	90	2.13	6.5	6.3	19.3	5.2	**6.2**	8.2	13.1
TEXAS HERITAGE NATIONAL B	DAINGERFIELD	TX	**D**	D	C-	115	2.11	8.2	5.4	13.1	9.8	**6.0**	8.0	13.2
TEXAS LEADERSHIP BANK	ROYSE CITY	TX	**D**	C	C	53	-2.12	8.7	3.8	7.6	15.4	**10.0**	13.8	22.7
▲ TEXAS NATIONAL BK	MERCEDES	TX	**D+**	D-	E	75	5.75	5.8	3.1	32.8	10.0	**10.0**	11.8	18.8
TEXAS NATIONAL BK	SWEETWATER	TX	**A**	A	A-	80	4.39	8.2	3.4	5.9	52.6	**10.0**	12.3	23.9
TEXAS NATIONAL BK	JACKSONVILLE	TX	**C+**	C	C-	273	10.14	15.3	5.0	22.2	3.5	**5.5**	8.4	11.4
TEXAS REGIONAL BANK	HARLINGEN	TX	**C-**	C	C-	55	196.47	11.9	4.3	0.9	0.0	**10.0**	38.1	75.9
TEXAS REPUBLIC BANK NA	FRISCO	TX	**D-**	E+	D-	24	-23.35	14.8	8.0	7.4	0.0	**7.8**	9.5	15.3
TEXAS SB	SNYDER	TX	**D**	C-	B-	130	2.09	11.8	9.1	30.7	0.0	**6.3**	8.3	12.2
▼ TEXAS SECURITY BANK	DALLAS	TX	**D**	C	C	124	8.03	18.0	2.9	18.7	15.6	**10.0**	17.6	27.4
TEXAS STAR BANK	VAN ALSTYNE	TX	**C+**	C+	C+	262	5.86	16.1	9.1	14.0	2.1	**6.3**	8.3	12.4
TEXAS STAR BANK SSB	LOTT	TX	**B-**	C+	C+	68	-1.35	1.8	2.0	58.5	7.8	**6.2**	8.2	15.6
TEXAS STATE BK	JOAQUIN	TX	**C**	C+	B-	114	5.22	13.9	10.5	18.8	4.6	**4.6**	6.8	10.8
TEXAS STATE BK	SAN ANGELO	TX	**A-**	A-	A	195	2.08	4.5	2.5	15.1	25.4	**10.0**	11.5	22.9
▼ TEXICO STATE BK	TEXICO	IL	**D+**	C-	E+	9	8.72	0.2	2.2	17.5	51.7	**8.8**	10.2	22.8
TEXSTAR NATIONAL BK	UNIVERSAL CITY	TX	**C**	C	C	169	2.07	14.5	2.8	8.8	7.4	**9.2**	10.5	14.8
THAYER COUNTY BANK	HEBRON	NE	**D**	D	D	61	-4.13	7.2	2.8	14.2	25.7	**6.4**	8.4	13.3
THE BANK	OBERLIN	KS	**A-**	A-	A-	185	4.63	6.7	0.7	1.6	20.4	**6.7**	8.7	16.1
THE BANK	JENNINGS	LA	**B+**	B+	B	138	4.53	19.0	13.6	22.2	13.0	**7.9**	9.6	15.9
THE BANK	MOUNT LAUREL	NJ	**D**	D+	C	2,106	0.65	11.9	2.1	11.5	15.2	**6.8**	8.8	13.4
THE BANK	WEATHERFORD	TX	**D-**	D-	E	66	-2.68	4.1	0.7	24.4	29.3	**7.8**	9.5	20.8
THE FIRST NA	DAMARISCOTTA	ME	**B-**	B-	B-	1,362	4.80	6.3	1.3	25.0	29.6	**7.1**	9.0	16.1
THE NATIONAL BK	MOLINE	IL	**D-**	D	B-	1,178	-6.38	11.5	2.7	6.7	25.1	**6.0**	8.0	12.8
THE TRUST CO	SAN ANTONIO	TX	**D+**	C-	C-	79	14.98	11.6	2.2	5.0	3.5	**8.3**	9.9	17.1
THINK MUTUAL BANK	ROCHESTER	MN	**C+**	B-	B-	1,420	3.56	0.1	14.0	47.2	28.0	**10.0**	13.6	26.1
THIRD COAST BANK SSB	HUMBLE	TX	**D-**	C	C	193	25.94	30.8	1.0	3.3	4.2	**8.2**	11.0	13.5
THIRD FEDERAL BANK	NEWTOWN	PA	**C-**	B-	B-	688	-3.10	0.8	0.4	45.6	18.5	**7.8**	9.6	17.5
THIRD FS&LA OF CLEVELAND	CLEVELAND	OH	**C+**	C+	B-	11,016	3.23	0.0	0.1	65.4	5.1	**10.0**	13.5	21.3
THIRD NATIONAL BK OF SEDA	SEDALIA	MO	**C-**	C+	C+	317	3.30	4.4	10.8	11.3	30.2	**5.4**	7.4	12.9
▼ THOMAS COUNTY FS&LA	THOMASVILLE	GA	**C-**	B-	A-	294	-7.01	4.1	2.1	37.7	7.3	**10.0**	16.6	25.2
THOMASTON SB	THOMASTON	CT	**B**	B	B	652	6.00	2.1	0.5	43.1	26.9	**10.0**	13.3	23.6
▼ THOMASVILLE NATIONAL BK	THOMASVILLE	GA	**B+**	A-	B+	433	12.89	14.8	2.4	29.5	9.7	**6.7**	8.7	13.2
THREE RIVERS BANK OF	KALISPELL	MT	**B**	B+	B+	108	0.31	13.4	3.5	8.0	29.8	**10.0**	11.1	18.3
THRIVENT FINANCIAL BANK	APPLETON	WI	**C**	C	B-	550	1.10	0.9	2.3	48.6	13.7	**8.2**	9.9	13.5
THUMB NATIONAL BK & TRUST	PIGEON	MI	**C-**	C-	C-	218	1.59	9.4	1.8	14.6	14.3	**5.5**	7.6	11.4
THURSTON FIRST BANK	OLYMPIA	WA	**D-**	D	D-	114	2.15	31.7	8.0	5.8	5.3	**6.1**	8.1	14.5
▲ TIAA-CREF TRUST CO FSB	SAINT LOUIS	MO	**A-**	B-	C+	306	1274.77	0.0	0.0	0.0	58.1	**10.0**	13.6	106.4
TIB BANK	NAPLES	FL	**D-**	E-	D	1,757	3.21	3.0	2.1	15.3	23.8	**6.1**	8.1	13.1
TIB-INDEPENDENT	IRVING	TX	**C+**	C+	C+	2,286	14.98	3.4	3.6	2.2	15.1	**5.6**	7.6	20.5
▼ TIDELANDS BANK	MOUNT PLEASANT	SC	**E-**	D-	D+	573	-26.04	4.1	0.7	19.2	10.1	**3.5**	7.0	10.2
TIGHTWAD BANK	READING	KS	**D**	D+	C-	20	-5.58	10.2	1.0	22.8	5.1	**6.5**	8.5	13.0
TILDEN BANK	TILDEN	NE	**D+**	C-	D	67	14.57	14.2	7.0	4.6	8.1	**4.5**	8.2	10.8
TIMBERLAND BANK	HOQUIAM	WA	**D-**	D-	C-	718	1.52	2.4	1.2	20.5	1.8	**9.1**	10.4	15.2
▼ TIMBERLINE BANK	GRAND JUNCTION	CO	**D-**	C-	C+	184	-10.71	4.8	1.6	18.6	7.6	**6.8**	9.1	12.3
TIMBERWOOD BANK	TOMAH	WI	**D+**	D	D+	172	-5.07	14.4	0.9	15.8	13.8	**7.8**	9.8	13.2
TIME FSB	MEDFORD	WI	**A-**	B+	B+	588	4.00	0.2	0.3	59.1	36.2	**10.0**	16.1	42.6
TIOGA FRANKLIN SB	PHILADELPHIA	PA	**C-**	C+	C	32	6.17	0.0	0.0	71.0	14.8	**9.3**	10.6	21.0
TIOGA STATE BK	SPENCER	NY	**B**	B-	B-	377	7.19	12.3	2.1	27.6	33.4	**7.1**	9.1	15.9
TIPPINS BANK	CLAXTON	GA	**C+**	B-	B	67	7.45	7.1	1.4	15.2	30.3	**8.7**	10.1	19.2
TIPTON LATHAM BANK NA	TIPTON	MO	**B+**	B-	B-	91	11.88	12.1	5.7	20.9	31.3	**9.5**	10.7	16.3
▼ TITAN BANK NA	MINERAL WELLS	TX	**C-**	B-	C	47	6.38	3.1	3.8	18.5	8.5	**9.6**	10.8	22.5
▲ TITONKA SB	TITONKA	IA	**C+**	C-	B-	146	7.51	2.5	2.2	8.0	48.6	**7.9**	9.6	18.6
TNBANK	OAK RIDGE	TN	**D-**	D	D	174	-12.05	3.7	1.5	20.3	16.8	**7.0**	9.0	14.2
▼ TOLLESON PRIVATE BANK	DALLAS	TX	**B-**	B	B	352	13.92	20.2	2.2	29.3	13.5	**7.4**	9.2	14.3
TOMAHAWK COMMUNITY	TOMAHAWK	WI	**D-**	D-	C	79	-0.34	2.0	2.1	27.6	21.0	**5.7**	10.7	11.5
TOMATOBANK NA	DIAMOND BAR	CA	**D**	D-	C+	433	-0.77	9.9	0.0	0.9	0.9	**10.0**	14.5	17.7
TOMPKINS STATE BK	AVON	IL	**B-**	B-	C+	175	-1.51	6.6	4.4	17.3	29.0	**6.5**	8.5	14.3

Asset Quality Index	Non-Performing Loans as a % of Total Loans	Non-Performing Loans as a % of Capital	Net Charge-offs Avg Loans	Profitability Index	Net Income ($Mil)	Return on Assets (R.O.A.)	Return on Equity (R.O.E.)	Net Interest Spread	Overhead Efficiency Ratio	Liquidity Index	Liquidity Ratio	Hot Money Ratio	Stability Index
7.0	0.37	1.4	0.50	**6.3**	4.3	0.95	8.74	3.87	62.8	**3.7**	50.8	19.2	**6.3**
9.0	0.12	0.6	0.07	**4.1**	2.3	0.81	11.00	3.33	66.7	**3.2**	49.6	23.5	**3.5**
8.8	0.12	0.5	0.02	**4.5**	3.0	0.95	7.61	4.29	73.5	**4.8**	46.0	12.6	**7.1**
3.4	1.41	11.4	0.06	**6.0**	1.3	1.41	17.12	4.86	71.4	**3.4**	20.8	12.7	**5.8**
1.2	3.93	29.0	0.01	**2.7**	0.5	0.42	5.97	3.67	79.0	**1.0**	26.1	43.2	**3.4**
3.7	7.62	27.3	1.54	**0.0**	-2.1	-3.94	-22.51	3.68	117.3	**1.8**	29.8	28.4	**2.0**
1.6	3.79	22.1	0.56	**1.4**	0.2	0.21	1.76	6.41	97.5	**0.5**	5.6	45.2	**4.4**
9.0	0.15	0.4	-0.17	**7.5**	1.5	1.77	12.75	4.45	65.3	**3.1**	40.4	19.4	**9.0**
5.4	0.30	2.9	0.16	**7.2**	3.7	1.42	17.22	4.57	45.9	**0.5**	3.8	46.6	**4.0**
7.0	0.15	0.1	0.00	**0.9**	-0.7	-2.83	-6.96	2.30	229.0	**3.8**	94.1	31.4	**7.8**
0.6	5.31	29.7	0.77	**0.0**	-0.6	-2.19	-21.06	4.92	141.2	**2.0**	32.1	21.1	**3.6**
0.9	5.71	46.9	1.10	**3.3**	0.4	0.31	3.58	4.17	53.3	**1.1**	10.5	29.7	**6.5**
8.6	0.00	0.0	0.00	**0.3**	0.4	0.29	1.57	3.12	107.2	**2.0**	16.3	19.4	**2.3**
4.0	0.89	7.3	0.58	**6.0**	2.5	0.97	11.86	4.57	66.3	**1.4**	15.8	26.3	**5.2**
7.4	0.43	4.0	0.02	**4.9**	0.7	1.00	12.93	4.66	74.0	**0.6**	4.1	36.6	**4.8**
5.7	0.20	2.1	0.20	**3.9**	0.7	0.62	8.49	4.52	87.0	**1.7**	18.1	22.5	**4.5**
9.2	0.30	1.1	-0.01	**4.7**	1.8	0.98	7.65	3.65	76.6	**4.7**	44.6	12.8	**8.4**
5.9	3.00	10.2	0.00	**4.4**	0.1	1.09	10.20	5.67	80.6	**6.8**	58.5	0.0	**3.0**
4.2	0.98	6.7	0.27	**3.0**	0.9	0.52	5.28	3.96	77.2	**0.7**	15.6	49.8	**5.9**
2.3	1.53	10.2	0.40	**1.0**	-0.1	-0.21	-2.45	3.76	86.6	**0.9**	5.2	30.1	**3.7**
7.1	0.07	0.5	-0.30	**10.0**	5.3	2.88	28.78	4.58	39.2	**2.8**	15.7	14.9	**8.5**
7.6	0.15	0.9	0.20	**7.8**	1.9	1.37	13.93	5.13	61.2	**2.7**	21.2	16.3	**5.9**
0.5	4.40	28.7	2.09	**1.3**	-7.5	-0.36	-2.79	4.06	61.0	**2.9**	14.0	14.7	**6.0**
2.9	3.20	14.4	-0.02	**0.7**	0.0	0.05	0.65	3.35	98.9	**2.6**	53.4	32.9	**3.9**
4.5	2.50	16.5	0.94	**5.1**	12.2	0.92	10.04	3.46	50.1	**1.3**	24.2	45.5	**7.6**
0.3	6.18	38.9	3.00	**0.6**	-2.7	-0.23	-1.83	3.53	73.4	**2.7**	14.9	15.9	**6.0**
5.5	2.07	11.4	0.00	**1.1**	0.1	0.20	1.91	3.67	96.0	**5.8**	41.9	4.9	**2.1**
8.0	0.39	1.9	0.36	**3.2**	7.0	0.50	3.56	3.34	71.5	**6.2**	36.3	4.3	**4.6**
3.3	1.92	12.6	0.08	**0.7**	0.0	0.01	0.12	3.83	90.7	**0.9**	22.5	37.7	**1.5**
1.7	3.33	23.5	0.19	**3.6**	3.7	0.52	5.35	3.56	65.8	**4.0**	21.8	9.6	**6.4**
4.4	2.34	14.4	0.79	**1.9**	-4.3	-0.04	-0.32	2.17	56.8	**1.5**	9.4	23.1	**7.9**
1.7	2.64	18.2	0.26	**8.6**	4.2	1.33	16.99	4.01	52.8	**2.9**	11.1	14.1	**5.9**
3.1	4.89	20.3	0.80	**1.1**	-2.6	-0.83	-5.13	3.30	110.7	**1.7**	24.8	24.8	**7.0**
3.7	2.72	12.4	0.40	**3.7**	3.4	0.53	4.19	3.77	73.0	**2.5**	32.4	20.0	**8.5**
5.5	0.58	4.8	0.45	**5.9**	4.2	1.03	10.63	3.33	52.9	**2.7**	10.0	15.1	**6.3**
5.0	1.93	9.8	0.51	**4.9**	1.0	0.91	8.27	5.16	66.6	**1.5**	32.2	35.1	**5.8**
5.7	0.70	5.2	0.16	**2.9**	2.5	0.45	4.27	3.93	73.0	**1.1**	19.8	32.0	**6.2**
1.6	3.70	30.0	0.55	**2.7**	0.6	0.30	3.81	4.26	77.1	**2.0**	25.8	21.1	**4.0**
0.3	2.53	21.1	1.08	**2.5**	0.4	0.34	4.01	3.81	63.5	**0.8**	16.3	38.7	**3.1**
8.4	0.00	0.0	0.00	**10.0**	2.1	3.13	7.25	2.22	90.2	**8.7**	113.4	0.2	**4.0**
0.3	5.61	41.4	0.00	**0.7**	1.0	0.22	3.08	3.26	88.0	**2.5**	29.6	27.5	**3.6**
5.5	2.46	8.7	1.40	**3.3**	13.4	0.58	7.29	1.87	79.9	**4.4**	57.2	19.1	**5.3**
0.0	7.44	66.9	3.17	**0.0**	-10.6	-1.59	-23.68	2.97	98.3	**0.7**	10.5	37.3	**1.9**
1.7	6.02	50.0	0.17	**3.7**	0.2	0.86	9.53	3.58	77.0	**0.7**	17.5	42.7	**4.5**
2.3	1.39	12.6	0.15	**5.1**	0.5	0.86	9.76	4.78	66.8	**3.7**	8.3	9.8	**3.8**
0.0	4.94	30.8	2.19	**2.0**	-0.9	-0.13	-1.21	3.90	73.5	**2.7**	18.1	16.0	**6.3**
0.7	6.02	43.2	1.19	**0.0**	-3.3	-1.65	-16.46	3.95	86.3	**1.6**	9.4	21.5	**3.8**
1.9	1.72	10.4	-0.06	**3.0**	1.3	0.75	6.29	3.26	65.9	**1.2**	14.7	28.2	**4.2**
10.0	0.26	1.0	0.02	**6.1**	9.7	1.67	10.70	3.41	30.3	**2.7**	44.9	28.4	**8.9**
1.7	4.28	29.3	0.32	**3.7**	0.1	0.44	4.12	3.65	58.7	**0.9**	20.0	37.8	**6.5**
7.6	0.31	1.9	0.00	**4.8**	3.6	0.95	10.70	3.83	68.4	**3.5**	20.5	12.1	**5.4**
3.6	2.65	12.9	0.55	**5.0**	0.5	0.76	6.09	3.85	68.0	**1.5**	22.8	26.9	**5.8**
5.6	0.63	3.3	0.50	**6.8**	1.5	1.75	15.83	4.61	58.6	**2.3**	36.3	26.1	**6.9**
5.6	1.39	5.5	0.24	**1.9**	0.1	0.23	1.98	3.94	93.6	**2.5**	43.0	29.6	**5.4**
4.7	0.63	2.6	0.57	**3.5**	1.3	0.89	9.25	3.92	74.4	**3.1**	44.5	21.5	**4.0**
0.9	6.27	42.0	0.68	**0.1**	-0.6	-0.30	-3.07	3.31	106.0	**1.1**	16.3	31.5	**3.3**
5.9	0.03	0.3	0.00	**5.3**	4.5	1.36	15.78	2.87	50.4	**3.8**	29.0	12.4	**5.2**
1.5	5.93	26.7	2.63	**0.0**	-1.7	-2.30	-20.50	4.35	111.0	**5.5**	36.2	4.7	**4.6**
0.0	6.95	36.3	1.21	**0.9**	0.6	0.12	0.87	3.64	75.5	**0.6**	13.0	53.3	**5.4**
4.8	0.84	5.4	0.16	**3.9**	1.3	0.76	6.73	4.56	81.3	**1.9**	27.1	23.2	**5.6**

Name	City	State	Rating	2008 Rating	2007 Rating	Total Assets ($Mil)	One Year Asset Growth	Asset Mix (As a % of Total Assets) Comm-ercial Loans	Cons-umer Loans	Home Mort-gages	Secur-ities	Capital-ization Index	Leverage Ratio	Risk-based Capital Ratio
TOMPKINS TRUST CO	ITHACA	NY	**B**	B	B	1,526	1.46	7.3	4.0	17.6	39.4	**5.5**	7.5	13.7
TORREY PINES BANK	SAN DIEGO	CA	**D+**	C-	C-	1,452	25.00	13.7	3.4	4.6	19.5	**7.5**	9.3	14.0
TORRINGTON SB	TORRINGTON	CT	**B+**	B+	B+	789	-2.58	0.0	0.1	47.3	33.2	**10.0**	16.0	49.8
TOTALBANK	CORAL GABLES	FL	**D-**	D-	D+	2,047	6.74	8.6	0.1	8.3	31.9	**9.0**	10.4	17.4
TOUCHMARK NATIONAL BK	ALPHARETTA	GA	**D**	D	C	140	12.98	5.5	0.3	3.7	34.8	**10.0**	13.2	20.2
TOWANDA STATE BK	TOWANDA	KS	**D**	C-	D	9	-2.18	1.0	7.9	55.5	12.7	**7.5**	9.3	18.2
TOWER BANK & TRUST CO	FORT WAYNE	IN	**D+**	D-	D+	662	-2.90	19.5	2.4	14.5	16.6	**8.5**	10.1	13.7
TOWN & COUNTRY BANK	SPRINGFIELD	IL	**B-**	C	C+	269	-3.17	8.1	1.7	16.9	19.6	**8.9**	11.0	14.1
TOWN & COUNTRY BANK	SALEM	MO	**A-**	A-	A-	503	3.09	2.2	3.3	44.5	15.3	**7.3**	9.2	16.7
TOWN & COUNTRY BANK	RAVENNA	NE	**A**	A	A-	115	12.82	9.4	2.4	2.8	25.6	**9.2**	10.5	14.3
TOWN & COUNTRY BANK	LAS VEGAS	NV	**D+**	C-	B-	212	2.11	6.1	0.3	7.2	11.2	**6.8**	8.8	13.2
TOWN & COUNTRY BANK	STEPHENVILLE	TX	**B**	B+	B+	181	12.52	4.0	4.6	13.6	38.2	**7.2**	9.2	20.0
TOWN & COUNTRY BANK	SAINT GEORGE	UT	**D**	C-	C	68	20.53	14.6	2.7	8.3	0.0	**10.0**	11.1	15.9
TOWN & COUNTRY BANK	WATERTOWN	WI	**D-**	D-	D	47	-11.67	5.8	1.4	31.0	7.4	**6.6**	8.6	13.2
TOWN & COUNTRY BANK &	BARDSTOWN	KY	**D-**	C-	B+	432	-8.22	4.9	2.9	25.8	12.9	**5.9**	7.9	11.9
▲ TOWN & COUNTRY BANK	LA BELLE	MO	**B**	B	C+	22	-5.27	16.6	4.6	3.6	4.4	**8.1**	9.7	13.5
▲ TOWN & COUNTRY BANK OF	QUINCY	IL	**B**	B	C	114	-0.70	25.3	2.1	13.8	3.4	**8.7**	10.6	13.9
▲ TOWN & COUNTRY BK OF	LA GRANGE	MO	**B+**	B	C	27	-0.31	15.3	4.5	14.1	8.8	**8.1**	9.9	13.4
TOWN BANK	HARTLAND	WI	**D+**	D+	C	731	3.66	19.2	10.2	5.3	6.3	**6.3**	9.8	12.0
TOWN CENTER BANK	NEW LENOX	IL	**D-**	D	D	142	-4.90	8.9	8.7	9.0	27.5	**7.0**	9.0	13.5
TOWN NORTH BANK NA	DALLAS	TX	**D-**	E-	D+	861	-2.53	2.1	1.0	17.5	38.5	**6.7**	8.8	15.8
▲ TOWN NORTH BANK NEVADA	HENDERSON	NV	**E+**	C-	C-	11	-83.72	0.0	60.9	0.0	15.7	**10.0**	93.7	165.1
▼ TOWN SQUARE BANK INC	ASHLAND	KY	**C**	B-	B-	169	5.97	11.9	3.3	30.0	12.1	**7.1**	9.1	13.6
▲ TOWN-COUNTRY NATIONAL	CAMDEN	AL	**B**	C+	C	93	6.31	11.2	16.4	14.4	20.9	**10.0**	12.6	19.8
▼ TOWNEBANK	PORTSMOUTH	VA	**C+**	B-	B	3,871	7.34	8.0	1.1	12.6	14.7	**8.4**	10.6	13.7
TOYOTA FINANCIAL SB	HENDERSON	NV	**C-**	E	C-	818	-4.44	0.0	34.6	44.6	2.1	**10.0**	14.7	21.9
TRADERS & FARMERS BANK	HALEYVILLE	AL	**A-**	B+	B+	356	0.54	2.4	5.7	24.8	36.0	**10.0**	12.4	21.7
TRADERS BANK INC	RAVENSWOOD	WV	**D+**	D+	C+	158	-0.11	8.5	5.0	24.8	21.3	**9.5**	10.7	18.4
TRADERS NATIONAL BK	TULLAHOMA	TN	**C**	C	B+	155	8.25	12.5	2.8	29.4	16.2	**5.5**	7.5	12.0
TRADITION BANK	HOUSTON	TX	**C**	C-	D+	422	2.98	4.6	1.2	7.0	31.2	**6.7**	8.7	14.1
TRADITION CAPITAL BANK	EDINA	MN	**C+**	D+	C+	176	6.43	20.4	2.2	18.7	5.0	**7.0**	9.7	12.5
TRADITIONAL BANK INC	MOUNT STERLING	KY	**C+**	C+	B-	1,064	9.66	4.9	0.9	21.8	25.9	**6.0**	8.0	11.8
TRADITIONS BANK	CULLMAN	AL	**B-**	B-	C+	216	4.47	7.4	7.3	32.2	5.6	**7.2**	9.2	13.4
TRADITIONS FIRST BANK	ERIN	TN	**B-**	C+	B-	98	7.56	12.7	4.2	25.0	15.3	**8.7**	10.1	13.9
▲ TRANS PACIFIC NATIONAL BK	SAN FRANCISCO	CA	**D-**	D-	D+	126	-27.50	9.3	0.0	6.9	17.5	**6.4**	8.4	13.5
TRANSCAPITAL BANK	SUNRISE	FL	**D-**	D	D	255	3.17	5.2	0.2	23.1	0.3	**6.9**	8.9	13.9
TRANSPECOS BANKS	PECOS	TX	**D+**	C	C-	157	5.70	23.1	4.8	7.9	13.0	**6.2**	8.2	12.5
▲ TRANSPORTATION ALLIANCE	OGDEN	UT	**B+**	B	B+	488	1.95	69.2	0.3	0.3	0.9	**10.0**	15.2	17.7
▲ TRAVERSE CITY STATE BK	TRAVERSE CITY	MI	**D-**	E-	E+	179	-1.79	15.6	3.2	12.4	11.4	**5.2**	7.2	13.4
▼ TREASURE STATE BK	MISSOULA	MT	**E-**	D-	D	80	-11.83	13.4	0.9	9.7	4.7	**2.6**	6.1	9.6
TREATY OAK BANK	AUSTIN	TX	**E-**	D-	D+	110	-25.44	13.4	4.9	10.4	5.7	**0.3**	3.4	6.6
TREGO-WAKEENEY STATE BK	WAKEENEY	KS	**B**	B+	B+	60	0.05	2.3	1.2	9.8	25.4	**7.8**	9.5	16.7
TREYNOR STATE BK	TREYNOR	IA	**B-**	C+	C-	199	6.03	3.5	1.2	4.8	52.2	**6.4**	8.4	14.3
TRI CITY NATIONAL BK	OAK CREEK	WI	**C+**	B	A	1,140	1.45	2.2	1.6	23.0	19.9	**8.5**	10.0	15.2
TRI COUNTIES BANK	CHICO	CA	**C-**	C+	B+	2,189	0.89	4.4	1.8	7.0	12.7	**8.5**	10.0	14.2
▼ TRI PARISH BANK	EUNICE	LA	**C+**	B+	A-	176	8.07	6.8	2.6	5.6	64.2	**9.9**	10.9	24.4
▲ TRI STATE BK OF MEMPHIS	MEMPHIS	TN	**C-**	D	D	117	-3.68	3.1	1.3	14.6	19.0	**10.0**	14.7	21.1
▼ TRI VALLEY BANK	TALMAGE	NE	**E**	C	C-	29	87.67	9.4	0.9	6.5	3.8	**3.6**	6.8	10.3
TRI-COUNTY BANK	BROWN CITY	MI	**C-**	C-	C+	192	1.20	4.4	1.4	14.6	22.8	**7.4**	9.2	15.1
TRI-COUNTY BANK	STUART	NE	**C+**	C+	C+	76	7.97	7.0	2.8	6.4	19.3	**6.0**	8.0	13.2
TRI-COUNTY BANK	CHEYENNE	WY	**C**	C+	B-	54	1.94	7.7	1.2	23.3	9.3	**9.5**	10.6	15.5
TRI-COUNTY BANK & TRUST C	ROACHDALE	IN	**B+**	B+	B+	157	8.20	6.4	3.2	12.3	35.0	**10.0**	12.3	24.4
TRI-COUNTY TRUST CO	GLASGOW	MO	**D+**	D-	C+	49	2.84	9.2	7.5	26.5	12.8	**6.0**	8.1	12.6
TRI-STATE BK & TRUST	HAUGHTON	LA	**A**	A-	A-	34	-0.44	3.1	1.6	0.1	78.1	**10.0**	14.2	16.0
▼ TRI-VALLEY BANK	SAN RAMON	CA	**E-**	D-	D-	71	-18.82	21.0	2.0	2.5	7.8	**3.1**	7.3	10.0
TRI-VALLEY BANK	RANDOLPH	IA	**D+**	C-	C-	67	13.50	7.3	3.1	9.7	36.3	**6.9**	8.9	14.4
▼ TRIAD BANK	FRONTENAC	MO	**D+**	C	D-	173	8.87	11.7	0.3	10.3	10.4	**7.7**	10.0	13.1
▲ TRIAD BANK NA	TULSA	OK	**B-**	C	B-	142	5.09	22.0	3.3	31.1	2.3	**7.2**	9.2	13.9
TRICENTURY BANK	SIMPSON	KS	**D+**	C	C+	5	1.12	6.8	4.3	2.9	13.7	**9.3**	10.5	18.2
▼ TRINITY BANK	DOTHAN	AL	**D**	D	D	67	0.37	28.2	2.0	18.6	6.1	**10.0**	12.0	15.6

Asset Quality Index	Non-Performing Loans as a % of Total Loans	Non-Performing Loans as a % of Capital	Net Charge-offs Avg Loans	Profitability Index	Net Income ($Mil)	Return on Assets (R.O.A.)	Return on Equity (R.O.E.)	Net Interest Spread	Overhead Efficiency Ratio	Liquidity Index	Liquidity Ratio	Hot Money Ratio	Stability Index
4.8	2.35	14.9	0.18	**8.7**	20.3	1.37	18.49	3.70	59.5	**4.2**	16.9	8.4	**6.5**
2.6	1.28	9.0	0.88	**4.0**	7.3	0.88	9.61	5.60	58.3	**2.6**	16.9	16.5	**4.0**
9.7	0.65	2.0	0.03	**4.1**	5.9	0.74	4.72	2.27	52.4	**4.7**	56.3	15.4	**8.8**
1.3	2.35	11.9	2.18	**0.1**	-12.4	-0.62	-3.51	3.24	89.7	**1.0**	13.7	33.2	**6.0**
0.0	9.39	35.8	3.93	**0.0**	-4.0	-2.80	-18.11	3.38	95.4	**1.7**	36.7	44.2	**1.7**
5.2	2.57	17.6	-0.06	**2.5**	0.0	0.36	3.91	5.27	93.2	**4.6**	16.9	4.4	**2.3**
1.1	3.25	20.2	0.76	**2.9**	3.8	0.56	5.46	3.92	68.5	**1.6**	19.1	24.0	**4.6**
6.4	0.22	1.3	0.19	**4.4**	2.1	0.77	7.31	4.23	73.8	**2.2**	16.8	18.0	**5.8**
6.3	0.48	3.5	0.17	**7.4**	8.2	1.66	15.39	4.18	57.9	**2.2**	10.6	17.5	**8.5**
7.1	0.06	0.4	-0.07	**7.1**	1.4	1.27	11.77	4.20	55.7	**1.9**	20.9	20.3	**7.7**
0.0	7.56	37.1	0.44	**0.1**	-6.3	-2.89	-26.04	3.13	124.6	**0.8**	19.6	40.6	**4.4**
8.6	0.28	1.3	0.02	**5.5**	2.4	1.36	14.00	4.20	72.7	**4.9**	53.7	14.0	**6.8**
3.7	5.06	28.3	1.11	**0.0**	-0.7	-1.15	-9.90	4.42	102.0	**1.4**	32.4	42.1	**1.5**
0.3	2.77	20.4	0.87	**0.0**	-0.2	-0.40	-4.61	3.62	97.2	**1.4**	22.1	27.6	**3.1**
0.3	8.43	62.5	1.91	**0.0**	-3.4	-0.73	-8.92	3.54	90.2	**2.2**	11.4	17.4	**4.9**
7.7	0.24	1.5	0.01	**6.8**	0.3	1.43	15.23	4.77	65.6	**2.4**	18.9	17.2	**7.6**
5.3	1.28	8.8	0.54	**7.8**	2.1	1.78	17.63	4.68	52.6	**1.5**	12.8	23.2	**7.4**
6.1	0.00	0.0	0.39	**4.4**	0.3	0.96	10.33	4.36	66.7	**1.8**	12.9	20.0	**6.9**
1.6	1.47	11.3	1.53	**1.8**	0.8	0.12	0.97	3.51	59.9	**1.3**	8.5	25.2	**5.3**
1.1	5.71	33.6	6.26	**0.0**	-4.2	-2.84	-25.15	2.74	85.8	**1.4**	14.3	26.3	**1.3**
2.7	5.18	20.3	2.33	**0.0**	30.0	-0.42	-11.03	0.79	224.8	**0.8**	24.4	60.1	**1.2**
6.1	4.51	2.6	13.97	**0.0**	-0.4	-0.70	-0.79	3.42	75.6	**5.0**	977.9	100.0	**1.7**
3.3	2.82	21.8	0.21	**4.0**	1.3	0.75	8.34	3.97	72.1	**1.3**	15.3	27.1	**5.4**
4.4	1.18	5.4	0.65	**5.7**	1.1	1.25	9.97	5.12	59.8	**1.6**	31.8	32.9	**6.7**
3.0	2.09	13.6	0.65	**4.4**	30.3	0.83	6.44	3.74	71.6	**1.9**	15.4	20.0	**9.2**
2.1	2.60	12.2	3.91	**6.0**	16.3	1.92	14.75	4.40	18.8	**0.5**	9.5	61.0	**5.2**
5.6	4.29	17.2	0.78	**5.1**	3.7	1.02	8.46	4.51	60.9	**2.1**	35.7	29.6	**6.7**
0.0	2.53	13.7	0.31	**3.8**	1.6	1.03	6.46	4.32	67.3	**4.2**	30.5	10.8	**5.2**
4.3	0.40	3.5	2.34	**2.7**	0.1	0.07	0.94	4.26	71.8	**1.1**	15.3	31.0	**5.2**
6.5	0.33	2.0	0.30	**3.1**	2.7	0.63	7.23	4.22	80.6	**2.7**	33.0	19.0	**4.6**
2.8	1.36	10.9	0.93	**3.5**	1.4	0.84	8.45	4.65	62.1	**0.8**	8.8	32.6	**3.7**
3.7	1.94	14.7	0.54	**4.1**	9.6	0.95	11.23	3.47	54.2	**1.0**	20.1	35.0	**7.4**
6.8	0.49	3.6	0.62	**4.2**	1.1	0.55	6.06	5.56	71.8	**1.3**	12.4	27.1	**4.1**
7.3	0.01	0.0	0.48	**4.1**	0.8	0.86	8.70	4.44	68.8	**1.0**	14.5	32.5	**5.6**
0.4	5.73	33.7	1.40	**0.0**	-2.5	-1.56	-20.06	3.10	129.5	**1.5**	20.2	26.5	**3.5**
0.0	25.53	168.6	2.68	**0.0**	-6.1	-2.44	-23.72	3.28	76.2	**1.0**	21.5	33.8	**6.9**
1.6	3.94	27.0	1.25	**1.4**	-2.4	-1.54	-15.16	4.75	85.0	**1.6**	20.3	25.1	**6.3**
6.0	0.89	4.1	1.93	**6.8**	10.9	2.27	15.98	6.89	65.9	**0.6**	16.0	69.8	**6.3**
0.3	5.94	48.7	1.38	**0.6**	0.0	0.01	0.12	3.63	79.6	**1.4**	11.1	24.1	**3.1**
0.3	7.59	54.8	5.85	**0.0**	-4.5	-5.09	-52.09	3.45	92.4	**3.3**	17.5	12.7	**0.0**
0.0	11.70	80.1	3.96	**0.0**	-5.8	-4.64	-75.02	3.20	130.1	**2.5**	30.1	19.3	**2.1**
6.7	0.00	0.0	0.56	**5.2**	0.7	1.15	12.02	3.41	59.3	**4.3**	28.0	9.1	**6.5**
5.4	1.18	5.2	0.78	**7.0**	3.7	1.98	23.75	5.58	66.2	**1.7**	36.5	44.5	**3.6**
1.3	5.12	32.5	0.44	**8.6**	14.5	1.33	12.36	5.62	59.4	**4.2**	19.9	8.6	**8.8**
1.9	5.06	27.2	2.07	**3.6**	7.1	0.32	2.96	4.55	61.5	**4.0**	26.1	12.9	**7.8**
2.9	6.59	17.3	0.18	**6.3**	2.8	1.69	13.35	3.89	68.4	**3.5**	52.9	21.4	**8.1**
0.0	16.41	72.2	0.42	**3.0**	0.4	0.32	2.25	4.91	83.7	**1.3**	13.1	26.8	**6.3**
8.8	0.00	0.0	0.00	**0.8**	0.0	-0.02	-0.22	3.14	81.3	**2.4**	36.1	24.7	**0.7**
4.3	0.89	5.6	1.23	**2.0**	1.0	0.52	5.41	4.37	75.9	**3.8**	28.9	12.5	**3.9**
5.3	1.76	11.1	0.20	**3.4**	0.4	0.51	6.02	4.00	81.9	**4.2**	39.0	13.4	**4.9**
5.4	1.28	8.3	0.37	**2.9**	0.2	0.44	4.18	3.84	78.5	**0.9**	17.2	34.9	**5.6**
5.3	2.50	8.7	0.14	**4.4**	1.2	0.81	6.12	3.69	68.0	**5.8**	59.5	10.7	**7.5**
3.0	1.57	11.9	1.78	**3.4**	0.4	0.73	9.17	4.88	63.9	**1.4**	20.1	28.3	**4.0**
9.6	0.00	0.0	0.00	**10.0**	1.4	4.08	27.96	5.84	36.7	**5.0**	96.7	18.3	**9.0**
0.0	10.60	76.1	1.60	**0.0**	-2.5	-3.01	-35.41	3.94	131.4	**1.7**	11.5	20.0	**0.0**
5.3	0.89	5.3	0.75	**1.5**	0.1	0.21	2.19	4.02	89.4	**3.3**	41.6	18.9	**3.2**
1.5	3.53	25.2	0.30	**2.0**	0.4	0.23	2.20	3.44	65.1	**1.2**	10.0	27.0	**2.4**
6.4	0.08	0.6	0.07	**4.5**	1.5	1.04	10.92	3.80	68.0	**0.6**	9.1	48.3	**6.3**
6.0	0.00	0.0	3.94	**4.0**	0.0	0.53	5.09	5.09	92.6	**4.8**	71.5	14.6	**3.7**
1.7	7.39	46.8	0.84	**0.5**	-0.2	-0.26	-2.35	3.52	84.6	**1.3**	14.1	27.8	**2.5**

Name	City	State	Rating	2008 Rating	2007 Rating	Total Assets ($Mil)	One Year Asset Growth	Asset Mix (As a % of Total Assets) Comm-ercial Loans	Cons-umer Loans	Home Mort-gages	Secur-ities	Capital-ization Index	Leverage Ratio	Risk-based Capital Ratio
▲ TRINITY BANK NA	FORT WORTH	TX	**A-**	B+	B	154	1.82	22.8	1.2	5.8	38.7	**9.1**	10.4	17.2
▼ TRISTAR BANK	DICKSON	TN	**B-**	B	B	150	4.38	5.1	4.4	25.6	31.1	**7.5**	9.3	14.9
TRISTATE CAPITAL BANK	PITTSBURGH	PA	**D+**	D	C-	1,661	11.66	35.9	5.2	3.3	8.7	**7.1**	9.9	12.6
TRISUMMIT BANK	KINGSPORT	TN	**D**	C-	C-	273	11.53	5.7	0.9	13.3	41.8	**8.7**	10.2	19.0
TRIUMPH BANK	MEMPHIS	TN	**C-**	C-	C-	245	21.39	18.6	1.0	14.5	13.1	**3.9**	9.0	10.5
▲ TRIUMPH SB SSB	DALLAS	TX	**D+**	D-	D-	254	5.25	2.3	0.4	3.2	11.6	**10.0**	16.0	24.0
TRIUMPH STATE BK	TRIMONT	MN	**C+**	C+	C+	57	10.54	14.0	3.9	3.6	15.0	**6.7**	8.7	12.3
▼ TROY BANK & TRUST CO	TROY	AL	**C-**	C	B-	827	4.51	11.0	3.7	13.0	27.8	**6.9**	8.9	13.7
TROY STATE BK	TROY	KS	**C-**	C	C-	26	-1.53	4.1	5.2	13.1	38.0	**8.1**	9.7	19.5
TRUMAN BANK	SAINT LOUIS	MO	**E**	E-	D-	393	-15.52	6.5	1.5	18.1	4.4	**3.6**	6.6	10.3
TRUPOINT BANK	GRUNDY	VA	**D-**	D-	C-	493	0.35	4.0	5.8	17.3	22.6	**6.3**	8.4	15.8
TRUST BANK	LENOX	GA	**E-**	E+	E-	28	-18.23	12.4	9.5	9.2	19.0	**6.9**	8.9	14.3
▼ TRUST CO BANK	MASON	TN	**D**	C-	C-	32	52.37	12.9	20.0	9.5	5.9	**9.1**	10.4	15.9
TRUST CO OF AMERICA	CENTENNIAL	CO	**C+**	C+	B-	519	4.29	0.0	0.0	0.0	94.2	**3.6**	5.6	16.5
TRUST CO OF TOLEDO NA	HOLLAND	OH	**U**	U	U	4	0.52	0.0	0.0	0.0	85.8	**10.0**	74.3	159.3
▲ TRUST CO OF VIRGINIA	RICHMOND	VA	**B-**	C+	C+	6	9.48	0.0	0.0	0.0	76.4	**10.0**	78.4	253.5
▼ TRUSTATLANTIC BANK	RALEIGH	NC	**D**	D	D+	351	-1.45	8.1	0.3	10.1	15.4	**7.5**	9.5	12.9
TRUSTBANK	OLNEY	IL	**C**	D	B	167	4.23	3.4	4.5	12.7	29.8	**8.0**	9.6	15.7
TRUSTCO BANK	SCHENECTADY	NY	**C+**	B-	B	3,960	7.10	0.8	0.1	45.4	27.2	**4.3**	6.3	13.4
▲ TRUSTMARK NATIONAL BK	JACKSON	MS	**C**	C-	C	9,426	0.31	11.3	4.2	15.6	24.6	**8.4**	9.9	15.4
TRUSTTEXAS BANK SSB	CUERO	TX	**C-**	C+	C+	185	15.74	6.0	5.4	21.9	31.4	**10.0**	14.3	27.4
TSB BANK	LOMIRA	WI	**D+**	D	D	89	0.15	9.6	4.1	22.2	15.3	**5.5**	8.0	11.4
TUCUMCARI FS&LA	TUCUMCARI	NM	**C-**	C	C-	41	0.62	0.0	0.8	53.6	18.0	**8.2**	9.8	22.1
TULSA NATIONAL BK	TULSA	OK	**D+**	D	D+	176	-0.60	11.7	1.5	15.1	15.9	**8.4**	9.9	15.5
TURBOTVILLE NATIONAL BK	TURBOTVILLE	PA	**A-**	B+	B+	116	8.24	5.5	3.5	26.3	38.5	**10.0**	12.9	24.9
▼ TURTLE MOUNTAIN STATE BK	BELCOURT	ND	**D-**	C	C	19	37.34	27.1	4.8	3.8	14.1	**7.5**	9.3	21.1
TUSCOLA NATIONAL BK	TUSCOLA	IL	**C**	C	C	82	4.02	11.5	1.9	7.7	40.2	**10.0**	13.4	27.0
▲ TUSTIN COMMUNITY BANK	TUSTIN	CA	**B+**	C+	D+	61	4.32	2.1	32.4	0.6	0.1	**10.0**	13.0	16.2
TWIN CITY BANK	LONGVIEW	WA	**D**	D	D	43	2.70	16.1	0.6	9.3	13.6	**8.8**	10.2	14.1
▼ TWIN LAKES COMMUNITY	FLIPPIN	AR	**D+**	D+	C-	81	20.66	37.5	5.0	14.5	7.6	**10.0**	14.0	18.4
TWIN OAKS SB	MARSEILLES	IL	**C**	C	C	74	2.41	1.5	2.4	31.9	34.9	**6.6**	8.6	18.5
TWIN RIVER NATIONAL BK	CLARKSTON	WA	**B-**	B-	B	65	10.64	15.7	4.6	19.2	3.9	**7.0**	9.0	16.0
TWIN VALLEY BANK	WEST ALEXANDRIA	OH	**B**	B	B	47	9.14	7.0	6.5	20.0	16.3	**10.0**	12.2	17.9
▲ TWO RIVER COMMUNITY	MIDDLETOWN	NJ	**D**	D+	C	637	-1.14	13.2	0.1	13.0	7.2	**6.7**	9.7	12.3
TWO RIVERS BANK	BLAIR	NE	**D+**	C-	C+	132	0.68	9.4	2.5	9.5	32.0	**7.8**	9.6	14.6
TWO RIVERS BANK & TRUST	BURLINGTON	IA	**C+**	B-	D	684	26.16	15.6	0.9	10.9	16.0	**7.6**	9.4	14.3
UBS BANK USA	SALT LAKE CITY	UT	**B**	B	B	30,853	2.67	12.0	41.4	2.6	39.6	**7.3**	9.2	15.4
UBS TRUST CO NA	WILMINGTON	DE	**U**	U	U	55	-49.03	0.0	0.0	0.0	12.3	**10.0**	95.1	465.0
UINTA BANK	MOUNTAIN VIEW	WY	**C-**	C-	C-	89	22.32	7.1	1.5	5.4	54.8	**6.4**	8.5	23.2
ULSTER SB	KINGSTON	NY	**D+**	D	D+	723	2.57	1.3	0.3	46.3	7.7	**10.0**	11.0	15.6
ULTIMA BANK MINNESOTA	WINGER	MN	**D**	C-	C-	100	7.57	19.4	2.2	6.6	0.1	**8.6**	10.1	13.9
UMB BANK & TRUST NA	KANSAS CITY	MO	**U**	U	U	3	0.13	0.0	0.0	0.0	0.0	**10.0**	100.0	103.1
▼ UMB BANK ARIZONA NA	SCOTTSDALE	AZ	**C**	B-	B	110	25.88	48.9	0.2	3.9	8.4	**5.2**	10.2	11.2
UMB BANK COLORADO NA	DENVER	CO	**B**	B	B+	1,373	27.38	10.9	0.8	2.3	49.6	**5.2**	7.2	12.9
▼ UMB BANK NA	KANSAS CITY	MO	**C+**	B-	B	10,694	4.65	15.4	4.0	1.4	43.2	**4.1**	6.2	12.0
UMB NATIONAL BK OF AMERIC	SALINA	KS	**B**	B	B+	839	-2.83	5.1	0.6	2.9	42.2	**5.9**	7.9	16.6
UMPQUA BANK	ROSEBURG	OR	**D+**	C-	D+	11,666	24.40	8.7	0.4	3.8	25.1	**7.1**	9.0	15.3
UNIBANK	LYNNWOOD	WA	**B-**	C	C+	145	12.63	6.7	0.1	0.0	9.5	**10.0**	15.4	21.7
UNIBANK FOR SAVINGS	WHITINSVILLE	MA	**C+**	C	C	1,057	15.45	4.8	13.2	15.7	26.6	**6.1**	8.1	14.5
▼ UNICO BANK	MINERAL POINT	MO	**B-**	B-	B-	225	12.16	3.7	2.9	24.6	34.6	**6.9**	8.9	13.5
UNIFIED TRUST CO NA	LEXINGTON	KY	**U**	U	U	8	3.76	0.0	0.0	0.0	18.8	**10.0**	77.9	98.6
▲ UNION BANK	MARKSVILLE	LA	**E+**	E+	D-	236	-2.66	0.8	9.7	15.3	13.8	**5.0**	7.0	11.9
▼ UNION BANK	LAKE ODESSA	MI	**D-**	D	D	176	-3.19	6.7	0.8	13.3	6.0	**5.9**	8.0	11.7
UNION BANK	KANSAS CITY	MO	**E-**	D-	D	543	-14.95	9.8	0.5	8.4	1.6	**2.4**	6.9	9.4
UNION BANK	HALLIDAY	ND	**C-**	D+	C-	70	5.89	9.6	12.3	12.7	8.3	**3.8**	7.5	10.4
UNION BANK	JAMESTOWN	TN	**B**	B+	A-	181	9.75	5.9	13.8	21.8	18.9	**10.0**	11.1	16.9
UNION BANK	JELLICO	TN	**A-**	A-	A-	59	-2.13	5.2	11.1	26.8	23.7	**10.0**	12.2	19.3
UNION BANK	MORRISVILLE	VT	**B-**	B	B	453	1.43	4.3	1.3	28.9	5.3	**8.1**	9.7	15.1
UNION BANK & TRUST CO	MONTICELLO	AR	**C**	C	C	184	-2.02	10.3	3.2	15.2	20.5	**8.0**	9.7	14.7
▼ UNION BANK & TRUST CO	MINNEAPOLIS	MN	**B+**	A	A	85	12.48	6.4	0.2	0.6	33.2	**10.0**	12.8	29.0

Arrows denote recent upgrades ▲ or downgrades ▼

Asset Quality Index	Non-Performing Loans as a % of Total Loans	Non-Performing Loans as a % of Capital	Net Charge-offs Avg Loans	Profitability Index	Net Income ($Mil)	Return on Assets (R.O.A.)	Return on Equity (R.O.E.)	Net Interest Spread	Overhead Efficiency Ratio	Liquidity Index	Liquidity Ratio	Hot Money Ratio	Stability Index
7.3	1.15	4.7	0.00	**6.0**	2.0	1.31	11.64	3.36	47.8	**4.1**	51.6	17.3	**6.7**
3.7	1.35	7.8	0.49	**4.9**	1.4	0.92	9.73	4.20	67.8	**1.3**	28.7	34.9	**5.8**
5.1	1.15	7.6	0.32	**2.2**	16.2	0.97	10.31	2.70	72.2	**1.1**	23.2	58.1	**4.5**
6.2	2.54	11.4	0.25	**0.4**	0.4	0.14	1.26	2.86	97.2	**1.8**	38.4	40.8	**1.4**
5.4	0.69	5.6	0.18	**2.6**	1.4	0.60	6.92	3.64	73.4	**0.8**	17.3	40.7	**2.8**
0.0	16.20	60.5	-0.01	**4.1**	3.5	9.00	87.48	3.47	24.0	**2.3**	40.5	30.2	**4.0**
5.4	0.97	7.2	1.19	**4.7**	0.4	0.70	7.64	4.75	62.4	**2.7**	24.7	16.3	**5.2**
1.9	4.05	26.6	1.84	**3.2**	4.4	0.54	5.70	3.62	51.9	**1.5**	17.7	25.4	**4.3**
4.1	2.76	13.9	0.93	**2.9**	0.1	0.35	3.37	3.75	78.2	**3.6**	33.3	14.8	**4.7**
0.0	17.76	131.1	3.14	**0.0**	-3.4	-0.78	-9.76	2.49	88.6	**1.4**	12.9	26.0	**3.3**
0.1	8.22	53.4	2.51	**1.0**	-0.9	-0.18	-1.97	3.72	77.9	**2.3**	14.1	17.3	**3.3**
2.0	6.29	34.3	0.20	**1.0**	0.0	0.09	1.14	4.86	92.0	**2.0**	17.9	19.1	**0.7**
3.7	1.40	8.1	0.27	**0.0**	-0.4	-1.35	-7.49	4.22	152.5	**1.1**	27.8	40.0	**5.6**
10.0	0.00	0.0	0.00	**7.0**	10.2	2.00	29.46	3.17	75.2	**6.8**	46.5	0.0	**4.6**
10.0	0.00	0.0	0.00	**9.5**	0.7	17.23	20.93	2.45	84.8	**5.0**	552.7	101.0	**6.2**
6.7	0.00	0.0	0.00	**10.0**	0.7	12.33	15.15	3.11	85.0	**10.0**	388.1	0.0	**1.4**
0.7	2.60	18.1	0.69	**1.8**	0.4	0.10	0.98	3.78	60.8	**0.8**	20.0	47.7	**5.5**
2.6	2.37	13.8	0.81	**4.4**	2.4	1.49	12.99	3.56	67.4	**4.0**	26.4	10.3	**4.5**
4.8	2.09	16.6	0.81	**4.2**	29.9	0.78	12.23	3.45	51.6	**5.0**	41.1	12.9	**5.1**
2.8	2.27	14.2	0.96	**5.8**	100.1	1.09	8.60	4.36	61.6	**2.7**	9.1	15.0	**9.1**
7.2	1.30	4.2	0.17	**1.8**	0.4	0.21	1.43	4.02	97.4	**3.4**	36.7	17.1	**7.1**
2.2	2.62	21.9	0.94	**1.9**	0.3	0.36	4.66	3.78	80.9	**3.3**	20.1	12.8	**4.2**
4.6	2.03	13.8	0.06	**2.3**	0.1	0.14	1.38	3.30	72.8	**1.3**	30.5	43.6	**4.7**
1.7	4.01	25.1	0.68	**3.2**	0.9	0.51	5.08	3.88	69.9	**1.4**	26.3	30.3	**6.1**
5.4	1.34	5.2	-0.28	**5.5**	1.3	1.12	8.27	3.64	56.4	**4.2**	47.2	15.9	**7.9**
8.2	0.00	0.0	0.23	**0.0**	-0.1	-0.80	-6.35	3.55	111.9	**1.9**	31.0	22.1	**0.8**
6.7	2.36	7.1	0.60	**1.9**	0.2	0.28	2.00	3.34	88.9	**3.6**	50.9	18.6	**6.4**
6.8	0.22	1.1	0.80	**6.6**	1.1	1.86	14.40	7.47	59.7	**1.2**	18.9	30.1	**6.6**
1.8	1.08	7.3	0.55	**0.7**	0.0	0.08	0.82	4.09	94.1	**0.5**	6.0	45.8	**4.5**
0.4	4.97	25.0	0.23	**2.4**	0.4	0.53	3.51	3.98	80.6	**1.1**	21.1	32.3	**2.1**
7.9	0.38	2.1	-0.10	**3.1**	0.4	0.56	6.47	2.85	77.3	**3.5**	48.0	18.9	**4.9**
6.8	0.22	1.4	0.10	**3.6**	0.5	0.72	7.66	3.92	81.9	**5.0**	38.3	9.1	**5.3**
7.1	0.97	5.1	0.11	**4.6**	0.4	0.80	6.39	4.32	72.9	**4.2**	15.2	7.3	**7.6**
1.0	1.10	8.4	0.59	**3.0**	3.7	0.57	4.73	4.20	67.8	**3.7**	11.3	10.2	**5.9**
1.5	6.74	35.8	1.55	**1.5**	0.1	0.10	0.97	3.63	71.6	**1.5**	22.0	26.5	**4.1**
3.6	1.96	12.6	0.59	**3.4**	3.2	0.53	4.85	3.30	65.2	**1.9**	24.2	21.8	**4.9**
6.9	0.02	0.1	0.00	**4.8**	240.8	0.81	9.00	1.68	18.9	**6.9**	39.3	0.4	**7.3**
10.0	0.00	0.0	0.00	**0.0**	-1.2	-2.01	-1.90	0.51	149.9	**5.0**	3,049.4	101.0	**7.0**
7.3	0.38	1.5	0.05	**2.5**	0.4	0.49	5.62	3.35	74.8	**2.4**	53.6	40.8	**3.7**
1.2	6.59	45.1	0.21	**3.3**	3.1	0.44	3.84	4.08	84.3	**2.8**	10.7	14.7	**7.2**
1.2	2.14	17.4	0.61	**8.1**	2.1	2.02	20.51	5.26	51.6	**1.0**	2.5	28.4	**6.3**
10.0	0.00	0.0	0.00	**1.5**	0.0	0.10	0.10	N/,	99.9	**0.0**	0.0	101.0	**6.4**
6.1	0.27	2.1	0.84	**3.6**	0.6	0.57	5.07	4.57	58.9	**0.5**	2.6	37.8	**5.9**
7.6	0.32	1.9	0.16	**5.2**	10.8	0.96	7.10	3.34	66.1	**3.2**	4.0	12.1	**7.4**
7.3	0.71	4.0	0.54	**4.3**	69.6	0.74	10.50	3.14	75.9	**4.4**	24.8	10.4	**4.9**
7.0	0.59	2.4	0.23	**6.1**	7.0	1.03	11.43	2.51	48.3	**2.1**	35.3	28.1	**5.7**
2.1	2.19	13.0	1.83	**1.8**	31.6	0.29	1.89	4.32	65.6	**2.1**	24.7	26.1	**6.4**
4.1	3.54	16.0	0.78	**4.2**	1.2	0.87	5.38	3.93	60.7	**1.3**	23.3	29.8	**5.8**
4.9	1.08	6.7	0.24	**3.5**	6.0	0.64	8.44	3.15	72.5	**6.2**	49.2	8.6	**5.8**
5.2	1.88	10.3	0.47	**6.6**	3.3	1.52	16.78	4.24	61.0	**1.4**	26.5	31.2	**5.2**
10.0	0.00	0.0	0.00	**9.5**	0.6	7.86	10.16	0.69	94.6	**3.3**	111.7	101.0	**6.2**
0.3	8.58	69.4	2.34	**2.3**	1.7	0.69	10.48	3.93	64.1	**1.8**	16.6	21.1	**1.5**
0.8	3.12	22.6	2.30	**0.0**	-2.3	-1.29	-14.35	4.26	74.5	**3.2**	17.5	13.1	**3.6**
0.0	9.73	69.5	1.50	**0.0**	-18.0	-2.98	-37.93	3.20	82.4	**3.8**	9.8	9.3	**2.9**
7.3	0.17	1.5	0.02	**5.5**	0.7	0.98	13.34	4.47	60.9	**3.8**	14.6	9.8	**4.4**
4.3	2.17	11.6	0.65	**3.6**	0.9	0.52	4.44	4.27	73.5	**0.9**	24.1	39.5	**6.8**
5.3	2.37	11.8	0.35	**8.8**	1.1	1.84	14.72	5.49	59.0	**1.3**	24.4	30.2	**8.6**
4.6	0.91	7.3	0.07	**6.8**	5.9	1.32	14.01	4.64	67.1	**2.4**	12.4	16.8	**6.7**
2.6	0.93	5.7	0.59	**3.7**	1.1	0.58	6.01	4.26	74.4	**1.3**	16.1	28.1	**4.2**
8.1	3.25	6.9	1.08	**4.0**	0.3	0.33	2.39	3.05	86.2	**5.2**	81.3	15.6	**7.6**

Name	City	State	Rating	2008 Rating	2007 Rating	Total Assets ($Mil)	One Year Asset Growth	Asset Mix (As a % of Total Assets) Comm-ercial Loans	Cons-umer Loans	Home Mort-gages	Secur-ities	Capital-ization Index	Leverage Ratio	Risk-based Capital Ratio
UNION BANK & TRUST CO	OXFORD	NC	**B-**	C	C	189	6.54	11.9	3.2	31.3	13.0	**9.8**	10.9	15.8
UNION BANK & TRUST CO	LINCOLN	NE	**C+**	B	B	2,451	-4.80	7.0	27.6	4.6	10.1	**6.8**	8.8	14.0
UNION BANK & TRUST CO	POTTSVILLE	PA	**D**	D-	D+	123	-0.75	12.3	0.9	24.5	27.5	**7.0**	9.0	12.8
▼UNION BANK & TRUST CO	LIVINGSTON	TN	**C+**	B-	B+	81	1.18	3.3	6.4	27.3	31.1	**6.9**	8.9	16.9
UNION BANK & TRUST CO	EVANSVILLE	WI	**C-**	C-	C+	192	5.36	8.4	3.3	16.3	26.4	**6.2**	8.2	13.7
UNION BANK CO	COLUMBUS GROVE	OH	**D**	C-	B-	612	-0.56	9.6	1.3	12.2	22.9	**6.6**	8.6	12.9
UNION BANK INC	MIDDLEBOURNE	WV	**B-**	C+	C	180	3.42	3.4	5.4	20.8	40.6	**4.6**	6.6	14.9
UNION BANK NA	SAN FRANCISCO	CA	**C**	D+	B-	78,675	-7.65	16.7	0.2	22.7	28.4	**7.8**	9.6	13.9
UNION BANK OF BLAIR	BLAIR	WI	**C-**	C-	C-	74	15.83	21.7	6.7	16.1	6.1	**7.7**	9.5	13.7
UNION BANK OF MENA	MENA	AR	**B**	B	B	169	4.28	4.5	14.9	40.8	4.8	**6.8**	8.8	14.9
▲UNION BANKING CO	WEST MANSFIELD	OH	**C+**	C-	C-	58	-16.20	0.3	0.7	12.3	75.2	**7.9**	9.6	26.3
UNION BUILDING & LOAN SB	WEST BRIDGEWATER	PA	**B-**	C+	B-	41	2.00	0.0	0.0	68.5	0.5	**10.0**	16.1	31.2
UNION CENTER NATIONAL BK	UNION	NJ	**C+**	C-	C+	1,207	1.01	9.7	0.0	10.9	31.3	**7.8**	9.6	13.8
▲UNION COUNTY SB	ELIZABETH	NJ	**B**	C	C	1,353	11.86	0.0	0.1	6.9	70.3	**10.0**	13.8	46.8
▲UNION CREDIT BANK	MIAMI	FL	**D**	E	D	172	11.60	8.3	0.3	8.4	41.9	**10.0**	12.5	18.1
▼UNION FIRST MARKET BANK	RICHMOND	VA	**D+**	NR	NR	3,804	86.70	4.8	7.8	15.0	14.0	**7.3**	9.2	13.0
UNION FS&LA	KEWANEE	IL	**D+**	D+	C-	125	0.35	0.0	0.4	61.6	10.2	**5.9**	7.9	16.2
UNION FSB	NORTH PROVIDENCE	RI	**D**	D+	C+	71	-62.79	0.0	0.0	10.4	35.3	**10.0**	17.5	101.5
UNION NATIONAL BK	ELGIN	IL	**D-**	D	B-	468	1.13	11.0	0.1	3.9	6.3	**6.8**	8.9	12.4
▲UNION NATIONAL BK & TRUST	SPARTA	WI	**B**	B+	A-	93	11.37	6.0	4.0	14.8	28.3	**10.0**	15.5	21.6
UNION NATIONAL BK MOUNT C	MOUNT CARMEL	PA	**C+**	C+	C+	130	4.10	1.8	2.4	47.7	32.7	**6.7**	8.7	17.5
▼UNION NATIONAL COMMUNITY	LANCASTER	PA	**D**	D+	C	446	-8.67	7.9	1.1	15.1	8.0	**6.7**	8.7	13.5
UNION SAVINGS & LOAN ASSN	CONNERSVILLE	IN	**C-**	C-	C+	128	0.96	1.6	9.4	52.3	0.8	**6.9**	8.9	15.3
UNION SAVINGS & LOAN ASSN	NEW ORLEANS	LA	**B-**	B	B+	86	5.58	0.0	0.2	38.2	52.6	**10.0**	35.0	107.5
▼UNION SAVINGS BANK	ALBUQUERQUE	NM	**D**	C	C	67	-10.32	1.6	2.3	17.0	31.2	**9.4**	10.6	18.8
UNION SAVINGS BANK	CINCINNATI	OH	**B-**	B-	B-	2,125	9.20	0.0	0.0	70.3	0.0	**5.4**	7.4	13.3
▼UNION SB	DANBURY	CT	**D+**	C+	C+	2,411	25.61	3.9	0.4	44.8	13.7	**4.9**	6.9	11.4
UNION SB	FREEPORT	IL	**D-**	C-	C-	158	-2.08	8.7	4.8	30.8	25.0	**6.6**	8.6	14.4
UNION SB	SEDALIA	MO	**C-**	C-	B-	96	-9.98	10.5	2.1	8.1	42.7	**10.0**	11.5	23.0
UNION STATE BK	PELL CITY	AL	**D-**	D-	C-	281	-5.62	3.6	2.9	7.4	24.6	**6.3**	8.3	14.5
▲UNION STATE BK	GREENFIELD	IA	**C**	C	B-	61	6.44	3.3	3.8	19.5	21.4	**6.2**	8.2	12.7
UNION STATE BK	ROCKWELL CITY	IA	**A-**	A-	A-	36	-0.89	8.7	5.2	5.8	36.4	**10.0**	13.8	23.6
UNION STATE BK	WINTERSET	IA	**C-**	D+	D	72	1.67	5.6	2.0	18.2	31.0	**6.7**	8.7	14.4
▲UNION STATE BK	ARKANSAS CITY	KS	**B-**	C-	B-	218	5.97	7.3	2.4	16.5	40.4	**6.5**	8.5	14.5
UNION STATE BK	CLAY CENTER	KS	**D**	C	D+	137	-0.67	4.8	1.5	6.8	58.0	**8.4**	10.0	21.1
▼UNION STATE BK	OLSBURG	KS	**B+**	A-	B	28	2.84	7.9	6.0	9.5	45.5	**10.0**	13.8	27.9
▲UNION STATE BK	UNIONTOWN	KS	**C-**	D+	C-	34	-3.11	10.2	4.1	25.0	22.6	**6.5**	8.5	13.9
UNION STATE BK	FLORENCE	TX	**B-**	B	B	374	0.33	4.8	1.7	5.4	48.7	**7.1**	9.1	17.1
▲UNION STATE BK	KERRVILLE	TX	**D+**	D	D	36	9.00	14.6	25.4	8.1	6.7	**5.9**	7.9	12.9
UNION STATE BK	KEWAUNEE	WI	**C**	C-	C+	83	4.43	7.5	4.8	26.8	22.4	**8.1**	9.7	16.0
UNION STATE BK BROWNS	BROWNS VALLEY	MN	**B**	B	B	22	4.42	8.2	3.3	2.0	27.9	**10.0**	11.7	24.9
UNION STATE BK OF EVEREST	EVEREST	KS	**B-**	C+	C-	168	6.70	9.0	4.0	20.7	18.4	**6.3**	8.3	12.3
▲UNION STATE BK OF FARGO	FARGO	ND	**D+**	D	D+	71	16.89	24.2	8.1	28.7	1.4	**6.4**	8.4	13.3
UNION STATE BK OF HAZEN	HAZEN	ND	**D-**	D+	B-	92	4.24	6.8	8.5	14.9	17.0	**7.4**	9.3	13.7
UNION STATE BK OF WEST SA	WEST SALEM	WI	**B**	B-	B	57	0.51	5.9	5.2	30.9	14.6	**10.0**	13.8	20.3
▲UNISON BANK	JAMESTOWN	ND	**D**	D+	C	219	4.07	6.6	5.9	9.1	34.6	**6.5**	8.5	13.8
▼UNITED AMERICAN BANK	SAN MATEO	CA	**E**	D-	D+	320	-20.37	30.4	1.3	3.4	0.7	**1.4**	5.4	8.4
UNITED BANK	ATMORE	AL	**D-**	D-	C-	467	2.28	6.3	2.9	9.4	18.4	**6.7**	8.7	15.1
UNITED BANK	SPRINGDALE	AR	**D-**	C-	C-	186	8.77	7.5	0.9	26.4	0.0	**6.7**	8.8	13.5
UNITED BANK	ZEBULON	GA	**C-**	C+	B-	1,050	17.14	3.4	2.2	17.1	20.8	**7.3**	9.2	17.5
UNITED BANK	WEST SPRINGFIELD	MA	**B-**	B	B	1,574	2.97	7.7	1.3	24.3	21.5	**10.0**	11.5	16.3
UNITED BANK	VIENNA	VA	**B-**	B-	B-	3,667	-9.33	9.0	0.3	12.5	9.9	**7.8**	10.3	13.2
▼UNITED BANK	OSSEO	WI	**C-**	C	C	207	-7.54	7.9	2.1	17.5	9.8	**7.7**	9.5	13.1
UNITED BANK	PARKERSBURG	WV	**B-**	B-	B-	3,465	-7.30	15.5	7.0	22.1	9.9	**7.1**	9.1	13.5
UNITED BANK & TRUST	MARYSVILLE	KS	**C**	C-	C+	498	6.79	9.3	2.0	9.1	21.2	**7.9**	9.6	14.6
▲UNITED BANK & TRUST	ANN ARBOR	MI	**D**	D-	D	862	68.19	10.0	2.9	16.7	14.4	**7.5**	9.4	14.9
▲UNITED BANK & TRUST CO	HAMPTON	IA	**A**	A-	B+	123	1.26	5.4	4.0	15.5	36.0	**10.0**	11.9	18.1
UNITED BANK & TRUST CO	VERSAILLES	KY	**D**	D	C	614	-16.54	1.6	1.1	17.3	23.6	**6.6**	8.6	14.7
UNITED BANK & TRUST NA	MARSHALLTOWN	IA	**B+**	B	B+	107	-5.00	7.1	2.7	20.7	44.5	**7.8**	9.5	17.5
UNITED BANK NA	ABSAROKEE	MT	**D+**	C-	C-	71	5.76	5.5	3.5	7.1	36.0	**8.0**	9.7	16.9

Arrows denote recent upgrades ▲ or downgrades ▼

Asset Quality Index	Non-Performing Loans as a % of Total Loans	Non-Performing Loans as a % of Capital	Net Charge-offs / Avg Loans	Profitability Index	Net Income ($Mil)	Return on Assets (R.O.A.)	Return on Equity (R.O.E.)	Net Interest Spread	Overhead Efficiency Ratio	Liquidity Index	Liquidity Ratio	Hot Money Ratio	Stability Index
7.2	0.21	1.4	0.08	4.5	2.5	1.37	12.81	4.01	62.5	0.7	14.3	40.1	5.8
3.5	0.60	4.9	0.59	4.6	19.8	0.80	9.11	3.24	66.2	1.5	13.6	25.1	7.1
3.1	2.16	12.7	1.17	1.3	0.4	0.34	4.12	4.26	92.0	4.8	33.1	8.4	3.0
3.0	2.40	15.0	0.55	10.0	1.8	2.24	22.09	5.40	50.4	3.7	35.1	14.6	6.9
2.0	1.80	12.0	0.70	3.5	1.1	0.58	6.65	4.22	70.2	2.8	14.5	14.8	5.1
0.7	4.33	27.7	0.84	3.4	3.2	0.52	5.16	3.91	60.5	2.3	17.5	17.7	5.8
5.1	0.50	3.2	0.10	5.2	2.4	1.30	10.87	4.08	67.0	4.2	31.1	11.1	7.0
4.2	1.77	9.9	0.77	3.1	550.3	0.64	5.53	3.23	73.7	3.5	27.4	16.2	8.0
2.5	1.07	8.7	0.38	7.0	1.1	1.63	16.39	4.56	56.5	1.5	13.0	24.1	6.9
4.5	0.77	6.1	0.25	9.1	3.5	2.12	23.26	5.39	59.6	3.2	16.8	13.4	7.1
5.6	7.18	11.8	0.00	4.3	0.8	1.25	10.55	3.10	57.8	0.9	21.0	39.1	4.5
3.7	4.61	21.6	0.08	4.1	0.3	0.65	4.12	3.60	63.3	1.2	20.6	30.0	7.7
4.6	1.68	9.8	0.69	3.5	7.4	0.63	6.55	3.10	62.1	3.8	26.7	14.6	7.5
10.0	0.94	0.6	0.11	4.5	20.1	1.58	13.20	1.62	35.6	4.1	102.7	49.2	8.0
3.1	3.26	13.4	2.53	0.0	-2.3	-1.38	-10.32	3.14	114.7	2.0	42.0	45.6	4.0
0.3	3.40	26.0	0.64	4.6	25.1	0.75	6.89	5.03	69.6	1.8	12.2	20.2	7.7
5.0	0.35	3.5	0.19	1.7	0.1	0.10	1.35	3.53	89.0	2.8	13.4	14.8	3.2
4.9	16.94	10.9	0.00	0.0	-2.3	-1.56	-5.62	-0.21	972.2	5.3	103.9	17.6	6.0
0.0	10.73	83.0	0.96	3.1	4.1	0.83	9.74	2.66	49.6	0.6	15.1	55.6	6.3
6.6	0.55	2.3	0.20	4.5	0.7	0.85	5.11	4.44	72.9	3.1	39.1	19.4	6.9
8.0	0.65	4.3	0.07	3.2	0.8	0.63	7.07	3.36	78.3	2.3	27.2	19.2	5.0
3.6	1.80	12.7	0.52	0.7	-1.3	-0.27	-3.17	3.36	94.7	2.3	11.4	17.1	3.8
3.1	1.26	10.8	0.52	2.3	0.3	0.23	2.58	3.46	77.1	2.6	11.7	15.5	4.3
9.6	0.30	0.3	0.00	3.4	0.4	0.49	1.37	2.75	71.5	4.2	90.0	24.9	7.9
3.1	1.78	8.7	0.05	1.0	-1.0	-1.37	-12.68	3.75	163.7	2.8	41.5	24.4	4.8
4.2	1.24	13.2	0.00	8.6	46.2	2.25	32.00	2.19	44.6	1.5	6.0	21.5	7.0
1.7	2.52	25.9	0.24	2.4	5.2	0.23	2.91	3.48	83.1	2.0	5.6	18.3	5.9
0.3	4.36	29.7	0.27	1.8	0.3	0.21	2.49	3.41	87.8	3.7	26.2	11.9	3.6
8.9	0.09	0.3	-0.02	1.8	0.2	0.16	1.47	3.12	93.7	5.9	54.0	6.9	6.7
0.3	12.67	60.3	3.74	0.0	-6.0	-2.11	-25.51	2.97	112.8	2.7	33.6	19.6	2.5
2.7	1.08	8.4	0.67	6.8	0.9	1.51	9.12	4.96	53.8	2.1	20.5	18.9	7.7
8.1	0.04	0.1	0.06	7.4	0.6	1.61	11.23	3.87	57.5	4.4	40.6	12.9	8.9
3.1	1.63	9.6	0.66	2.5	0.3	0.41	4.57	4.11	83.4	4.2	41.4	14.4	3.9
5.9	0.18	0.9	0.38	3.2	1.5	0.68	4.95	3.93	73.6	3.0	36.0	18.4	5.2
3.1	1.38	5.0	4.34	0.6	-0.4	-0.31	-2.79	3.44	62.1	1.3	10.8	26.0	4.8
8.6	0.30	0.9	0.12	4.8	0.3	0.94	6.72	3.58	68.4	5.3	53.3	10.6	9.3
4.2	0.78	5.4	0.18	3.7	0.3	0.81	9.03	4.50	83.6	1.9	23.0	20.6	3.7
5.6	0.27	1.2	-0.04	4.3	4.0	1.05	11.05	3.76	72.3	1.4	12.4	24.5	5.3
3.4	0.81	5.9	0.14	3.0	0.2	0.48	5.78	5.38	88.9	2.6	36.7	22.9	3.0
2.7	2.78	16.8	0.37	2.4	0.4	0.28	2.68	4.19	89.0	4.1	32.8	11.9	5.2
8.8	0.00	0.0	-0.13	4.6	0.2	1.11	8.90	2.94	57.3	5.4	62.7	10.3	7.6
3.6	1.64	12.8	0.07	7.4	2.6	1.59	15.10	4.79	60.2	2.9	12.9	14.2	6.7
4.1	0.32	2.6	0.44	3.1	0.2	0.24	3.15	4.85	72.9	2.7	23.3	16.1	4.1
0.3	2.62	16.2	2.10	1.3	-0.3	-0.32	-3.57	4.68	70.3	2.7	14.1	15.5	5.2
3.9	3.22	16.4	0.13	4.9	0.5	0.99	6.91	4.62	67.8	4.1	19.2	8.4	7.0
0.3	2.16	12.7	0.70	2.7	0.8	0.39	3.73	3.85	64.3	2.6	26.2	17.4	3.9
0.3	13.77	149.9	4.85	0.0	-13.2	-3.59	-45.92	3.63	98.2	3.3	18.4	12.9	3.0
1.4	6.90	39.8	2.42	0.5	-0.6	-0.13	-1.29	3.56	90.4	2.8	30.5	17.7	3.7
0.3	13.72	81.8	2.18	0.5	-5.5	-3.12	-31.10	3.25	74.6	0.9	26.1	52.9	5.0
2.4	3.40	18.5	2.07	7.6	16.2	1.71	16.78	4.40	50.1	1.9	19.6	21.9	8.5
5.4	0.80	4.5	0.13	3.8	11.2	0.73	5.74	3.71	69.0	3.0	30.5	21.1	8.5
3.5	1.57	10.4	-0.07	5.8	37.5	0.99	6.19	3.90	56.5	1.9	9.7	19.0	7.4
2.3	3.08	22.7	0.09	4.4	1.6	0.78	8.38	4.17	77.8	1.5	14.1	24.1	4.8
5.3	0.98	7.0	0.38	6.6	40.1	1.07	14.50	3.56	55.9	2.4	9.3	16.8	6.6
3.5	0.71	4.4	0.29	3.3	3.0	0.65	5.54	3.60	63.7	2.3	10.9	17.2	6.0
1.2	4.50	26.0	2.96	0.2	-2.3	-0.30	-3.69	4.33	66.6	2.9	29.0	17.0	4.3
8.1	0.79	3.6	0.03	6.4	1.8	1.48	11.79	4.05	58.5	5.5	45.5	8.4	7.7
0.3	6.14	36.2	1.33	0.5	-2.8	-0.41	-4.61	2.83	91.0	1.8	14.3	19.8	3.3
4.6	2.43	11.4	0.73	4.6	1.2	1.10	11.83	3.55	57.3	3.8	17.0	10.4	5.9
2.0	5.77	26.3	1.09	1.3	0.1	0.15	1.53	3.88	90.2	3.1	35.1	17.8	4.1

Name	City	State	Rating	2008 Rating	2007 Rating	Total Assets ($Mil)	One Year Asset Growth	Asset Mix (As a % of Total Assets) Comm-ercial Loans	Cons-umer Loans	Home Mort-gages	Secur-ities	Capital-ization Index	Leverage Ratio	Risk-based Capital Ratio
UNITED BANK OF EL PASO DE	EL PASO	TX	**B-**	B-	B-	154	9.68	21.6	1.6	2.7	37.6	**6.4**	8.4	16.3
UNITED BANK OF IOWA	IDA GROVE	IA	**C+**	C+	C+	1,112	33.63	9.5	3.1	9.8	5.2	**6.3**	8.7	12.0
▼UNITED BANK OF KANSAS	LENEXA	KS	**C-**	C-	C-	100	-10.75	22.7	0.9	12.5	5.7	**5.2**	8.1	11.1
UNITED BANK OF MICHIGAN	GRAND RAPIDS	MI	**C+**	C	C	434	-0.23	8.8	2.0	18.9	1.2	**6.7**	9.2	12.3
UNITED BANK OF PHILADELPH	PHILADELPHIA	PA	**D-**	D-	D	74	8.54	7.8	3.0	16.2	22.4	**5.8**	7.8	13.5
UNITED BANK OF UNION	UNION	MO	**C+**	C+	B	270	-1.63	11.4	1.8	21.5	22.3	**8.9**	10.3	14.8
UNITED BANKERS BANK	BLOOMINGTON	MN	**C-**	C	C+	644	19.29	5.0	0.0	1.1	40.0	**5.1**	7.1	15.0
UNITED CENTRAL BANK	GARLAND	TX	**D**	C	B-	2,502	-4.87	2.9	0.1	0.9	7.3	**9.0**	10.4	19.9
▼UNITED CITIZENS BANK & TR	CAMPBELLSBURG	KY	**B+**	A-	A	85	1.22	1.9	2.2	18.1	18.6	**10.0**	12.7	20.9
UNITED CITIZENS BANK OF S	COLUMBIA	KY	**C+**	D+	C-	133	-6.99	9.5	5.7	25.8	9.7	**7.2**	9.2	13.6
UNITED COMMERCE BANK	BLOOMINGTON	IN	**D+**	C	C+	181	-5.26	16.9	1.4	31.3	5.5	**5.8**	7.8	12.1
UNITED COMMUNITY BANK	BLAIRSVILLE	GA	**D-**	D-	C-	7,426	-6.99	5.3	1.8	13.3	26.0	**5.5**	7.5	12.5
UNITED COMMUNITY BANK	MILFORD	IA	**B**	C+	B-	176	-3.63	8.3	1.7	14.2	3.8	**5.8**	9.3	11.6
UNITED COMMUNITY BANK	CHATHAM	IL	**B**	B+	B	843	-0.55	8.9	2.0	17.2	30.9	**5.7**	7.7	14.0
▼UNITED COMMUNITY BANK	OAKWOOD	IL	**D+**	D	D+	39	9.71	7.7	3.8	19.0	5.1	**8.5**	10.0	16.4
UNITED COMMUNITY BANK	LAWRENCEBURG	IN	**C-**	C	C-	484	23.64	1.4	1.3	27.8	29.1	**7.9**	9.6	16.8
▼UNITED COMMUNITY BANK	GONZALES	LA	**D+**	C+	B-	201	0.59	7.3	3.4	18.1	2.4	**6.5**	8.5	12.6
UNITED COMMUNITY BANK	PERHAM	MN	**D+**	D+	C+	196	-0.59	8.9	3.7	12.2	27.9	**6.8**	8.8	13.4
▲UNITED COMMUNITY BANK NA	HIGHLAND VILLAGE	TX	**D-**	E-	D	107	-4.34	23.5	0.9	10.2	10.6	**6.0**	8.0	14.5
UNITED COMMUNITY BANK OF	LEEDS	ND	**B-**	B-	C+	203	4.88	14.9	4.1	7.9	19.5	**5.5**	7.9	11.4
UNITED COMMUNITY BK WEST	MORGANFIELD	KY	**A-**	A-	B+	154	12.73	22.0	9.0	24.5	19.6	**7.7**	9.5	14.7
▼UNITED FARMERS & MERCH	MORRIS	MN	**D+**	C-	C-	36	9.33	4.7	2.5	5.5	27.1	**4.9**	6.9	12.4
UNITED FIDELITY BANK FSB	EVANSVILLE	IN	**C-**	C-	C-	206	-3.24	8.0	0.4	16.5	37.8	**8.6**	10.0	22.6
▲UNITED INTERNATIONAL BK	FLUSHING	NY	**D**	D-	D-	184	5.14	10.8	2.6	0.9	12.0	**9.8**	10.8	15.5
UNITED KY BK OF PENDLETON	FALMOUTH	KY	**C-**	C-	D+	30	-0.63	11.8	7.2	11.5	26.3	**9.6**	10.8	19.0
UNITED LABOR BANK FSB	OAKLAND	CA	**C**	C-	C-	256	-5.59	10.5	0.0	1.5	12.4	**6.4**	8.4	15.5
UNITED LEGACY BANK	WINTER PARK	FL	**D-**	E-	E+	183	31.97	3.2	6.2	10.2	24.1	**5.5**	7.5	12.8
UNITED MIDWEST SAVINGS	DE GRAFF	OH	**D-**	D-	D-	238	-10.74	0.3	11.5	44.9	0.2	**6.2**	8.2	12.7
▼UNITED MINNESOTA BANK	NEW LONDON	MN	**E+**	E+	D-	26	-1.29	15.4	8.3	16.5	6.0	**4.9**	6.9	11.0
▼UNITED MISSISSIPPI BANK	NATCHEZ	MS	**B+**	B+	A	246	13.40	15.1	6.1	15.1	8.0	**8.8**	10.7	14.0
UNITED NATIONAL BK	CAIRO	GA	**C+**	B	A-	179	10.60	11.0	4.1	12.6	5.4	**10.0**	11.6	15.3
UNITED NATIONAL BK	NATOMA	KS	**C+**	C+	C	93	7.13	5.8	4.1	7.8	35.4	**6.4**	8.4	17.4
UNITED ORIENT BANK	NEW YORK	NY	**C**	C-	C	90	-15.14	1.8	0.1	18.6	2.3	**9.6**	10.8	14.7
UNITED PACIFIC BANK	CITY OF INDUSTRY	CA	**D-**	D	C-	154	-6.76	0.7	0.0	3.1	3.0	**9.4**	10.6	14.9
UNITED PRAIRIE BANK	MOUNTAIN LAKE	MN	**B-**	B-	B-	525	-0.37	14.5	2.1	10.1	13.6	**5.8**	8.9	11.6
▲UNITED REPUBLIC BANK	OMAHA	NE	**C**	C	C	56	26.54	17.3	5.1	13.2	6.8	**10.0**	17.8	20.1
UNITED ROOSEVELT SB	CARTERET	NJ	**C+**	C	C	99	1.21	0.0	0.0	20.2	65.3	**10.0**	15.3	54.8
UNITED SB	PHILADELPHIA	PA	**B**	B	B	306	1.74	0.6	0.2	36.6	12.2	**10.0**	15.1	28.7
UNITED SECURITY BANK	FRESNO	CA	**D**	D-	D-	682	-1.77	14.9	1.4	8.4	7.6	**10.0**	11.4	16.0
UNITED SECURITY BANK	FULTON	MO	**A-**	A-	A-	47	15.51	1.9	6.8	38.0	29.0	**10.0**	12.9	23.9
UNITED SOUTHERN BANK	UMATILLA	FL	**C-**	C-	C+	393	-5.60	3.5	1.1	23.3	10.1	**7.3**	9.2	13.8
▼UNITED SOUTHERN BANK	HOPKINSVILLE	KY	**C-**	C+	C+	244	7.82	6.7	3.7	24.3	15.4	**6.9**	8.9	13.1
UNITED SOUTHWEST BANK	COTTONWOOD	MN	**D-**	D-	D-	40	-1.09	2.1	3.2	4.6	33.9	**5.1**	7.1	12.1
▼UNITED STATE BK	LEWISTOWN	MO	**B-**	B-	B-	102	10.42	5.7	4.4	9.4	17.0	**6.9**	8.9	12.6
▲UNITED TEXAS BANK	DALLAS	TX	**C-**	D+	C-	122	1.46	10.1	0.9	3.4	24.4	**6.8**	8.8	14.2
UNITED TRUST BANK	BRIDGEVIEW	IL	**D**	D	D-	42	26.46	0.0	0.4	19.9	5.9	**10.0**	12.2	19.5
UNITED VALLEY BANK	CAVALIER	ND	**C+**	C	C+	207	35.33	12.3	3.7	6.0	23.4	**6.1**	8.1	12.7
▲UNITED-AMERICAN SB	PITTSBURGH	PA	**C-**	D	E+	63	5.75	3.2	0.6	54.7	16.0	**7.8**	9.6	18.9
UNITI BANK	BUENA PARK	CA	**D-**	D-	B-	210	-7.97	11.0	0.0	1.3	15.5	**6.7**	8.7	14.8
UNITY BANK	RUSH CITY	MN	**C-**	C-	B-	188	-0.48	8.7	5.1	20.2	13.9	**5.1**	7.1	11.3
UNITY BANK	CLINTON	NJ	**D-**	D-	D+	818	-12.04	2.5	0.1	18.1	15.7	**6.5**	8.5	13.7
UNITY BANK	AUGUSTA	WI	**B**	B	B+	72	3.74	6.6	3.5	14.8	12.0	**9.2**	10.5	15.2
▼UNITY BANK NORTH	RED LAKE FALLS	MN	**B-**	B+	A-	71	5.12	11.5	13.1	21.1	12.9	**9.2**	10.5	16.7
UNITY NATIONAL BK OF HOUS	HOUSTON	TX	**D-**	D-	D-	65	5.55	22.6	1.3	12.1	10.5	**10.0**	11.4	16.9
UNIVERSAL BANK	WEST COVINA	CA	**D-**	D	B-	465	-12.42	6.9	0.2	4.9	0.2	**7.5**	9.4	13.0
▲UNIVERSITY BANK	PITTSBURG	KS	**C**	C-	C	105	-0.05	11.2	3.0	31.7	10.8	**9.8**	10.8	17.3
▲UNIVERSITY BANK	ANN ARBOR	MI	**D+**	C-	D	114	-14.89	3.1	0.3	51.4	2.6	**7.8**	9.6	19.5
▲UNIVERSITY NATIONAL BK	SAINT PAUL	MN	**C+**	C	C+	195	10.59	4.8	0.2	17.1	9.6	**10.0**	13.2	23.4
UNIVERSITY NB OF	LAWRENCE	KS	**D-**	D-	B	88	-9.82	7.1	1.6	28.0	0.0	**7.2**	9.1	17.1
▼UNIVEST NATIONAL BK & TRU	SOUDERTON	PA	**C+**	B	B+	2,104	2.46	19.4	2.1	9.5	21.7	**9.7**	10.9	14.7

Asset Quality Index	Non-Performing Loans as a % of Total Loans	Non-Performing Loans as a % of Capital	Net Charge-offs / Avg Loans	Profitability Index	Net Income ($Mil)	Return on Assets (R.O.A.)	Return on Equity (R.O.E.)	Net Interest Spread	Overhead Efficiency Ratio	Liquidity Index	Liquidity Ratio	Hot Money Ratio	Stability Index
5.4	0.28	1.7	0.28	**3.6**	0.9	0.60	6.71	4.12	72.8	**2.5**	43.5	29.9	**4.8**
3.7	1.26	10.7	0.26	**9.3**	17.3	1.88	21.54	4.54	46.6	**1.3**	9.9	26.3	**8.2**
3.7	0.11	1.0	0.51	**3.5**	0.7	0.67	7.06	3.42	69.2	**2.7**	8.5	15.0	**4.6**
3.6	0.75	6.2	0.37	**4.0**	3.2	0.73	8.10	4.42	70.2	**2.6**	6.8	15.4	**4.7**
1.2	5.46	36.7	1.17	**0.0**	-1.0	-1.36	-14.42	4.58	105.9	**1.3**	13.2	26.7	**3.4**
2.8	1.14	6.9	0.55	**6.0**	4.2	1.49	14.68	3.88	57.9	**1.9**	8.7	18.8	**7.1**
2.3	3.31	15.7	2.55	**3.3**	1.9	0.29	4.18	4.15	64.5	**7.3**	56.8	0.0	**3.7**
1.2	4.52	22.3	1.07	**4.6**	8.6	0.32	3.25	4.42	62.5	**0.6**	7.0	38.8	**8.7**
8.9	0.23	1.0	0.00	**5.1**	0.8	0.94	7.23	3.71	69.5	**4.3**	33.2	11.4	**8.2**
3.5	1.10	8.0	0.11	**3.6**	1.0	0.73	8.28	3.91	68.0	**1.2**	12.0	27.9	**4.4**
1.6	3.26	29.0	1.50	**2.3**	0.5	0.27	3.58	3.34	63.6	**1.3**	12.8	26.5	**4.6**
1.5	3.11	20.7	4.09	**0.0**	-336.9	-4.44	-37.01	3.78	180.3	**1.4**	10.4	25.9	**5.7**
7.7	0.00	0.0	0.00	**5.6**	2.3	1.31	11.64	4.84	72.1	**2.5**	8.4	16.0	**6.6**
5.7	0.52	3.6	0.17	**8.5**	19.0	2.24	27.25	3.79	49.8	**1.6**	22.1	25.0	**7.7**
4.9	0.96	5.6	0.06	**1.6**	0.1	0.26	2.56	3.91	90.1	**3.8**	38.2	15.5	**3.7**
1.7	6.67	40.5	0.20	**2.5**	1.2	0.26	2.46	3.03	72.9	**1.7**	36.4	47.2	**4.7**
1.4	2.37	19.2	0.61	**4.0**	1.3	0.64	7.82	3.96	66.3	**1.9**	17.2	19.9	**4.9**
1.7	4.15	24.9	1.18	**3.5**	1.5	0.78	8.57	4.07	67.1	**1.9**	31.8	29.0	**4.6**
1.2	7.76	46.3	1.05	**0.1**	-0.7	-0.63	-8.88	4.17	123.7	**2.8**	37.6	20.5	**2.3**
5.1	0.34	2.8	1.28	**7.6**	3.5	1.73	21.73	5.12	49.0	**1.6**	9.3	22.0	**5.4**
7.4	0.06	0.4	0.19	**8.7**	2.2	1.49	15.54	4.76	55.4	**3.0**	12.7	13.6	**6.7**
4.9	0.41	2.6	-0.01	**3.7**	0.2	0.60	7.06	3.94	85.0	**5.6**	46.6	7.8	**3.0**
2.0	5.28	21.7	0.94	**2.2**	0.6	0.26	2.46	3.41	74.7	**3.0**	44.0	23.3	**4.5**
0.0	8.99	54.7	0.49	**3.6**	2.5	1.42	14.65	3.71	73.3	**1.0**	21.3	33.3	**1.3**
4.3	1.33	5.9	0.15	**2.0**	0.1	0.32	2.94	3.82	83.3	**2.6**	16.9	16.2	**3.9**
3.4	0.87	5.1	0.50	**3.3**	1.3	0.49	5.99	4.42	74.5	**3.8**	42.2	16.4	**4.0**
1.5	4.36	25.2	4.19	**0.0**	-7.2	-3.91	-35.44	1.61	260.3	**2.1**	29.3	22.5	**2.5**
0.0	12.54	106.4	3.77	**0.1**	-9.5	-3.65	-41.31	4.11	85.5	**1.3**	8.1	25.5	**3.0**
2.5	0.35	3.2	0.10	**0.6**	0.0	-0.06	-0.80	4.55	122.3	**3.1**	23.6	14.2	**0.0**
7.3	0.32	2.2	0.35	**5.2**	3.0	1.27	11.15	4.50	76.2	**1.5**	16.9	24.4	**7.2**
3.7	0.41	2.5	0.57	**5.5**	1.3	0.76	6.52	4.86	53.8	**0.7**	13.4	40.9	**7.3**
5.0	2.30	9.7	-0.25	**4.0**	0.7	0.79	8.68	3.55	74.2	**4.5**	52.7	14.7	**4.8**
3.2	0.75	5.3	0.22	**3.3**	0.4	0.36	3.66	4.64	84.4	**1.5**	11.3	22.7	**5.9**
0.7	5.33	33.3	1.33	**1.6**	0.3	0.19	2.20	3.50	63.2	**1.0**	24.2	35.0	**4.7**
3.8	1.15	9.1	0.37	**3.5**	2.5	0.49	4.52	4.72	81.9	**2.8**	11.0	14.6	**6.6**
8.3	0.00	0.0	0.91	**0.3**	-0.1	-0.28	-1.44	4.00	90.2	**1.6**	10.6	22.0	**4.2**
9.0	2.62	3.5	0.05	**2.9**	0.4	0.38	2.48	2.94	78.1	**5.4**	90.3	15.4	**7.5**
10.0	0.01	0.1	0.00	**4.4**	2.4	0.79	5.40	3.00	59.4	**2.7**	37.9	22.7	**8.1**
0.2	7.95	37.8	2.24	**1.0**	-2.6	-0.37	-2.94	4.58	78.7	**1.3**	18.0	28.5	**6.8**
8.7	0.00	0.0	0.00	**6.3**	0.7	1.44	10.19	5.00	67.9	**3.4**	18.2	12.5	**8.5**
2.0	2.23	14.8	1.09	**2.8**	1.0	0.25	2.59	4.27	72.5	**1.9**	16.9	19.7	**5.1**
2.7	1.07	8.3	0.44	**2.1**	0.5	0.20	2.19	3.31	74.1	**0.8**	10.7	34.5	**5.1**
6.4	0.37	2.4	0.98	**0.5**	-0.2	-0.46	-5.97	4.67	113.3	**6.1**	42.4	3.1	**2.0**
4.4	1.31	9.6	0.58	**4.7**	1.0	1.09	11.41	4.15	63.0	**2.7**	15.9	15.4	**5.5**
5.2	4.40	17.1	0.39	**2.2**	0.8	0.54	6.27	3.75	87.1	**4.2**	53.0	17.4	**4.9**
1.6	8.08	36.3	0.00	**0.0**	-0.5	-1.39	-9.41	4.07	128.9	**1.6**	34.9	38.1	**3.9**
4.6	0.61	4.7	0.26	**4.1**	1.4	0.72	7.62	4.30	72.3	**2.7**	21.9	16.4	**4.0**
5.3	1.41	10.6	0.18	**3.7**	0.4	0.71	10.18	3.69	70.6	**1.8**	23.9	23.1	**2.5**
0.3	9.12	42.5	6.47	**0.0**	-4.7	-2.17	-19.11	3.13	86.2	**2.4**	46.2	33.8	**4.6**
4.4	0.73	6.7	0.73	**2.1**	0.7	0.37	5.06	4.18	79.9	**2.3**	7.2	16.8	**3.7**
0.0	3.14	22.6	1.05	**2.3**	2.3	0.27	3.24	3.71	70.5	**3.6**	14.6	11.0	**4.3**
4.5	1.02	6.4	0.14	**5.7**	0.9	1.22	10.47	4.57	70.4	**4.0**	17.5	9.0	**7.6**
4.0	1.30	8.0	0.19	**4.8**	0.7	0.99	9.12	4.51	74.2	**1.7**	17.1	21.8	**7.4**
5.1	1.55	6.9	1.77	**0.0**	-0.6	-0.96	-10.39	4.67	101.3	**1.9**	38.5	38.0	**4.6**
0.0	4.09	31.5	0.11	**0.7**	-1.7	-0.33	-3.84	3.20	90.3	**1.4**	7.3	23.9	**5.7**
3.3	2.19	13.8	0.95	**3.3**	0.7	0.68	7.07	3.77	68.9	**1.9**	21.6	20.4	**4.0**
2.1	2.32	14.6	0.82	**3.3**	0.0	0.39	7.14	3.78	92.7	**4.1**	20.5	8.8	**1.8**
4.5	4.00	16.9	1.21	**5.9**	2.3	1.33	13.12	5.21	51.5	**2.5**	39.7	27.5	**6.5**
0.9	8.42	47.4	4.70	**0.1**	-2.6	-2.73	-26.72	3.41	113.0	**1.9**	28.5	25.6	**5.7**
3.3	3.04	17.7	1.07	**4.4**	15.5	0.75	5.79	4.20	63.2	**3.9**	9.0	9.0	**8.5**

Name	City	State	Rating	2008 Rating	2007 Rating	Total Assets ($Mil)	One Year Asset Growth	Asset Mix (As a % of Total Assets) Commercial Loans	Consumer Loans	Home Mortgages	Securities	Capitalization Index	Leverage Ratio	Risk-based Capital Ratio
UPPER PENINSULA STATE BK	ESCANABA	MI	**A-**	A	A	192	12.32	3.9	3.8	14.3	30.1	**10.0**	13.9	22.9
UPSTATE NATIONAL BK	ROCHESTER	NY	**D-**	D-	D-	80	-13.63	19.3	0.7	1.2	12.7	**10.0**	14.3	22.8
▼URBAN PARTNERSHIP BANK	CHICAGO	IL	**D-**	NR	NR	1,383	N/A	14.5	0.1	13.7	2.4	**7.4**	9.2	29.1
URBAN TRUST BANK	ORLANDO	FL	**C+**	C+	D+	566	-18.79	0.3	0.3	73.3	14.7	**10.0**	12.8	21.6
▲US BANK NA	CINCINNATI	OH	**D+**	C	C-	302,260	9.37	11.1	13.3	15.2	17.0	**5.7**	7.7	12.4
US BANK NA ND	FARGO	ND	**C-**	C-	C+	5,533	8.00	38.5	30.3	16.7	0.0	**10.0**	13.7	17.2
▼US BANK TRUST CO NA	PORTLAND	OR	**U**	U	U	14	3.81	0.0	0.0	0.0	0.0	**10.0**	100.9	475.0
US BANK TRUST NA	WILMINGTON	DE	**U**	U	U	612	0.81	0.0	0.0	0.0	0.0	**10.0**	93.4	462.8
US BANK TRUST NA SD	SIOUX FALLS	SD	**U**	U	U	54	6.34	0.0	0.0	0.0	0.0	**10.0**	93.6	261.2
US CENTURY BANK	DORAL	FL	**D-**	D-	C-	1,681	-16.94	11.4	0.2	8.0	2.2	**3.0**	8.2	10.0
US METRO BANK	GARDEN GROVE	CA	**D**	D	D	102	-12.89	22.8	0.0	0.0	0.0	**10.0**	14.8	19.7
USAA FSB	SAN ANTONIO	TX	**B-**	B-	B-	44,642	17.93	0.0	52.5	9.5	15.6	**6.4**	8.6	12.0
USAA SB	LAS VEGAS	NV	**B+**	B	B	14,445	37.35	0.0	100.7	0.0	1.2	**10.0**	21.2	21.9
USAMERIBANK	CLEARWATER	FL	**D**	C+	C-	960	18.91	16.2	0.6	7.7	9.7	**4.3**	7.5	10.7
▲USNY BANK	GENEVA	NY	**B-**	C-	C-	86	33.47	12.7	0.9	9.5	0.0	**9.8**	11.8	14.8
UTAH COMMUNITY BANK	SANDY	UT	**D**	D	D	32	-16.69	6.4	2.0	23.7	3.4	**10.0**	15.1	24.2
▼UTAH INDEPENDENT BANK	SALINA	UT	**C+**	B-	A-	58	-1.27	14.9	7.2	12.3	13.9	**10.0**	12.4	19.2
▼UVALDE NATIONAL BK	UVALDE	TX	**C+**	B-	B-	34	-14.28	4.2	7.4	19.6	11.9	**9.1**	10.4	17.5
VALLEY BANK	FORT LAUDERDALE	FL	**D**	D	D	132	-3.31	13.6	0.4	9.0	22.2	**6.2**	8.2	12.8
VALLEY BANK	MOLINE	IL	**D+**	D+	D	636	0.41	15.5	0.6	13.8	21.3	**6.6**	8.6	13.0
▲VALLEY BANK	ROANOKE	VA	**C-**	D	D+	765	7.66	12.0	0.6	12.6	20.1	**6.3**	8.3	12.3
VALLEY BANK	PUYALLUP	WA	**A-**	A-	A	228	4.34	10.4	0.2	5.0	24.6	**10.0**	11.5	19.8
▲VALLEY BANK & TRUST	BRIGHTON	CO	**C**	D-	E-	233	-0.27	9.1	2.2	6.6	13.6	**7.4**	9.3	13.6
VALLEY BANK & TRUST	CHEROKEE	IA	**C**	C	C-	31	5.48	11.2	10.1	23.5	1.4	**6.7**	8.7	12.7
VALLEY BANK & TRUST	MAPLETON	IA	**B**	B-	B+	60	4.15	1.8	3.7	3.9	16.1	**8.7**	10.1	14.4
VALLEY BANK & TRUST CO	GERING	NE	**D**	D+	C	329	-0.80	14.2	3.7	10.2	13.9	**7.6**	9.4	13.0
VALLEY BANK OF COMMERCE	ROSWELL	NM	**B+**	B+	B	123	6.66	23.2	1.8	2.3	11.4	**5.1**	7.1	13.4
VALLEY BANK OF GLASGOW	GLASGOW	MT	**C-**	C-	C-	33	-1.55	6.2	4.7	8.5	16.5	**6.4**	8.4	13.9
VALLEY BANK OF HELENA	HELENA	MT	**C+**	B	A-	394	12.24	4.6	2.3	15.2	41.6	**6.0**	8.1	15.1
▼VALLEY BANK OF KALISPELL	KALISPELL	MT	**D**	C	B	104	7.77	12.0	3.4	12.0	34.8	**8.7**	10.2	18.5
▼VALLEY BANK OF RONAN	RONAN	MT	**C**	C	B-	66	6.56	13.5	7.9	14.7	4.7	**9.9**	10.9	15.2
VALLEY BUSINESS BANK	VISALIA	CA	**C+**	C-	B	341	0.37	11.6	0.6	3.7	14.9	**10.0**	12.0	17.4
VALLEY CENTRAL SB	READING	OH	**C+**	C+	B+	86	4.66	0.0	0.2	39.9	16.9	**10.0**	30.0	62.6
VALLEY COMMUNITY BANK	PLEASANTON	CA	**D-**	C	B-	207	-6.27	10.7	0.1	6.6	8.1	**9.4**	11.1	14.5
VALLEY EXCHANGE BANK	LENNOX	SD	**C+**	B-	B+	60	1.54	10.3	4.6	3.7	31.1	**10.0**	12.3	24.2
▲VALLEY GREEN BANK	PHILADELPHIA	PA	**D**	D	D+	174	70.88	11.9	0.1	23.7	0.0	**7.4**	9.2	13.0
VALLEY NATIONAL BK	WAYNE	NJ	**B-**	B-	B-	14,122	-0.98	12.0	6.6	14.9	20.8	**5.9**	7.9	12.4
VALLEY NATIONAL BK	ESPANOLA	NM	**D-**	D+	C	318	-4.82	5.8	1.8	8.6	38.5	**9.2**	10.5	19.9
▲VALLEY NATIONAL BK	TULSA	OK	**C**	C-	C+	218	-0.71	13.6	0.7	8.3	2.4	**7.1**	9.1	13.5
VALLEY REPUBLIC BANK	BAKERSFIELD	CA	**C-**	C	NR	205	46.48	11.7	0.3	1.9	56.2	**10.0**	15.6	39.0
VALLEY SB	CUYAHOGA FALLS	OH	**B-**	C+	C-	106	-2.71	2.9	4.7	45.6	0.0	**7.1**	9.0	13.2
VALLEY STATE BK	RUSSELLVILLE	AL	**C+**	C	B	109	4.41	5.9	3.1	16.0	43.0	**10.0**	14.6	30.0
VALLEY STATE BK	BELLE PLAINE	KS	**B-**	B-	B	118	1.80	6.5	6.9	14.6	45.2	**10.0**	11.0	23.7
▲VALLEY STATE BK	SYRACUSE	KS	**C**	C+	B-	71	0.04	5.6	2.6	2.9	32.9	**6.8**	8.8	16.3
▼VALLEY VIEW STATE BK	OVERLAND PARK	KS	**C-**	C	B	827	1.97	9.5	1.1	3.0	30.2	**10.0**	12.6	19.8
VALLIANCE BANK	OKLAHOMA CITY	OK	**D+**	C-	C-	182	-12.52	10.2	0.9	10.7	10.8	**7.0**	9.0	14.5
VALLIANCE BANK	MCKINNEY	TX	**D-**	D-	D+	116	-9.15	22.7	0.2	11.3	3.4	**8.1**	9.8	17.3
▲VALRICO STATE BK	VALRICO	FL	**C-**	D+	B-	196	-2.68	2.0	0.8	6.6	9.1	**10.0**	12.7	15.2
▼VALUEBANK TEXAS	CORPUS CHRISTI	TX	**B+**	A-	A-	158	2.19	8.7	2.1	11.3	12.9	**8.8**	10.2	16.5
VAN WERT FSB	VAN WERT	OH	**B-**	B-	B+	128	2.16	0.0	0.7	56.2	16.1	**10.0**	16.4	31.9
VANGUARD NATIONAL TRUST	MALVERN	PA	**U**	U	U	53	38.42	0.0	0.0	0.0	67.1	**10.0**	80.4	227.9
VANTAGE BANK OF ALABAMA	ALBERTVILLE	AL	**B-**	C-	C-	74	19.08	9.0	4.7	11.5	27.2	**10.0**	15.3	24.6
VANTAGE POINT BANK	FORT WASHINGTON	PA	**D-**	C	C	73	2.40	6.0	1.3	12.4	26.8	**6.3**	9.0	12.0
VANTAGESOUTH BANK	BURLINGTON	NC	**D-**	D-	D	81	-14.37	8.0	1.5	25.1	13.3	**9.2**	10.5	14.7
VECTRA BANK COLORADO NA	DENVER	CO	**D**	D	C-	2,299	-5.79	16.2	0.5	7.3	11.4	**8.6**	12.1	13.8
▼VENTURA COUNTY BUSINESS	OXNARD	CA	**E**	E-	D-	79	-14.72	9.2	0.3	0.0	15.9	**4.4**	6.5	10.7
VENTURE BANK	BLOOMINGTON	MN	**C+**	C	B	256	6.42	28.8	1.7	7.5	14.2	**6.5**	8.5	13.1
VERGAS STATE BK	VERGAS	MN	**B**	B-	C+	43	5.60	9.4	2.8	11.1	32.5	**10.0**	13.8	27.2
▼VERITEX COMMUNITY BANK	DALLAS	TX	**D**	C	D-	198	50.71	14.4	2.0	13.2	35.1	**6.1**	8.2	13.3
▼VERITY BANK	WINDER	GA	**D**	C	C	123	67.21	2.9	0.7	11.2	19.2	**10.0**	12.3	20.1

Asset Quality Index	Non-Performing Loans as a % of Total Loans	Non-Performing Loans as a % of Capital	Net Charge-offs Avg Loans	Profitability Index	Net Income ($Mil)	Return on Assets (R.O.A.)	Return on Equity (R.O.E.)	Net Interest Spread	Overhead Efficiency Ratio	Liquidity Index	Liquidity Ratio	Hot Money Ratio	Stability Index
5.1	4.46	15.9	0.30	**6.1**	2.1	1.15	8.09	4.17	54.9	**3.8**	43.3	16.7	**8.0**
1.4	5.65	24.0	0.87	**0.0**	-1.1	-1.35	-14.27	3.72	118.1	**4.0**	29.0	11.2	**5.3**
0.3	4.22	29.8	0.00	**1.3**	7.9	0.58	5.45	N/,	66.9	**0.7**	14.8	50.9	**3.0**
3.2	4.60	24.9	0.05	**2.8**	2.0	0.32	2.72	5.17	74.2	**1.0**	25.5	39.1	**5.5**
0.4	2.09	15.6	2.13	**6.2**	3,127.7	1.10	11.65	4.02	51.8	**4.3**	18.1	7.5	**8.6**
2.3	1.63	9.0	2.76	**8.7**	95.8	1.78	13.12	4.48	54.1	**0.4**	0.8	48.9	**6.6**
10.0	0.00	0.0	0.00	**9.5**	0.5	3.57	3.57	N/,	22.3	**5.0**	13,927.7	101.0	**2.3**
6.9	0.00	0.0	0.00	**5.7**	4.4	0.69	0.74	0.40	59.6	**5.0**	2,994.6	101.0	**2.3**
10.0	0.00	0.0	0.00	**9.5**	3.1	5.99	6.46	0.28	39.1	**5.0**	1,134.6	101.0	**2.3**
0.0	11.65	95.3	1.59	**0.2**	-43.2	-2.30	-23.19	3.52	94.6	**1.2**	4.2	26.2	**5.7**
2.2	2.16	10.3	2.31	**0.3**	-0.2	-0.17	-1.21	3.93	77.3	**1.0**	18.8	32.5	**2.0**
3.8	0.66	4.8	2.10	**5.0**	486.4	1.16	13.48	4.18	55.8	**2.2**	22.6	20.9	**6.7**
4.2	0.95	3.9	3.33	**9.4**	426.4	3.09	15.28	7.46	31.0	**0.1**	1.7	95.0	**9.3**
2.4	0.78	7.2	0.52	**4.1**	5.7	0.66	7.77	3.76	54.0	**1.0**	9.9	31.0	**2.3**
8.2	0.05	0.4	0.00	**4.5**	1.7	2.44	26.02	4.35	62.4	**0.7**	10.2	37.8	**5.3**
1.7	7.28	28.4	3.00	**0.0**	-1.0	-2.82	-17.30	4.15	141.1	**1.1**	27.1	36.2	**4.8**
3.2	2.16	9.7	2.92	**2.4**	-0.5	-0.76	-5.72	4.99	69.1	**4.2**	35.4	12.6	**8.6**
4.3	1.27	6.0	1.15	**0.6**	-0.2	-0.59	-4.92	4.93	93.1	**1.7**	36.8	45.1	**4.8**
0.9	4.24	29.2	1.94	**0.0**	-0.8	-0.60	-5.83	2.77	108.3	**0.7**	12.0	40.0	**3.6**
2.0	4.20	28.4	1.19	**2.2**	2.4	0.38	4.37	3.64	73.9	**1.2**	3.9	25.3	**4.0**
2.4	2.40	17.2	0.50	**2.6**	3.9	0.52	6.14	3.06	72.6	**1.7**	15.9	21.2	**3.8**
5.6	1.56	7.3	0.37	**5.5**	2.1	0.94	7.80	4.59	68.1	**3.8**	45.2	17.2	**7.3**
3.3	2.49	14.5	0.50	**3.5**	1.7	0.71	7.70	6.28	83.4	**2.9**	22.6	15.2	**4.2**
3.5	1.32	11.0	0.96	**3.6**	0.1	0.50	5.78	4.75	66.0	**2.6**	20.2	16.7	**6.3**
4.0	0.00	0.0	0.65	**6.1**	0.8	1.36	8.76	4.11	66.2	**4.1**	40.3	14.4	**7.7**
1.0	1.19	8.6	0.54	**3.7**	1.6	0.48	4.69	3.99	74.8	**1.2**	11.8	27.8	**4.4**
6.5	0.00	0.0	0.27	**8.5**	2.1	1.90	22.65	3.95	52.8	**5.9**	50.1	7.4	**6.1**
7.4	0.01	0.0	0.28	**2.5**	0.1	0.44	5.36	4.77	85.1	**3.6**	36.6	16.0	**2.8**
7.4	0.54	2.8	0.11	**10.0**	7.5	2.13	23.78	4.61	47.4	**3.1**	44.5	22.3	**5.0**
1.2	7.75	33.3	1.39	**2.6**	0.2	0.16	1.41	4.45	78.2	**3.8**	49.1	18.5	**6.0**
2.6	3.01	16.5	1.22	**3.8**	0.3	0.40	3.49	4.99	73.5	**3.0**	31.5	17.3	**6.9**
2.9	2.83	14.1	0.65	**3.7**	2.5	0.73	6.22	4.47	61.8	**1.7**	14.0	20.7	**6.0**
5.5	4.14	8.0	1.22	**2.3**	0.2	0.19	0.61	3.69	73.6	**3.7**	55.6	18.9	**6.6**
0.0	6.59	40.5	2.02	**2.5**	0.5	0.24	2.15	4.60	66.7	**1.3**	17.9	29.0	**4.9**
7.0	0.11	0.5	0.90	**0.2**	-0.5	-0.81	-5.83	2.51	108.4	**5.1**	38.5	8.7	**6.6**
3.9	1.25	10.5	0.03	**1.1**	0.3	0.24	2.73	4.70	94.5	**1.0**	19.3	32.6	**2.0**
3.4	1.08	8.4	0.28	**5.5**	144.8	1.03	10.59	3.77	55.7	**3.4**	15.0	12.5	**8.2**
0.2	21.27	80.7	1.91	**1.6**	0.6	0.19	1.84	3.71	73.1	**0.8**	16.4	39.1	**4.9**
3.1	0.55	3.9	0.42	**4.2**	1.5	0.66	7.76	3.13	67.1	**0.9**	22.7	36.6	**5.6**
9.6	0.00	0.0	0.00	**0.2**	-0.1	-0.04	-0.26	2.46	94.5	**7.8**	85.2	2.1	**1.7**
6.2	0.40	3.7	0.04	**5.1**	1.0	0.95	11.28	4.68	69.4	**3.7**	2.8	9.1	**4.8**
7.2	0.11	0.3	0.28	**3.0**	0.5	0.47	3.09	3.11	71.6	**2.7**	43.5	27.0	**6.6**
6.9	1.13	4.8	0.42	**3.4**	1.0	0.85	7.53	3.48	72.7	**2.2**	32.9	25.1	**6.3**
3.1	2.17	10.8	0.92	**3.7**	0.5	0.66	6.81	3.79	70.8	**2.2**	37.5	30.1	**5.2**
1.7	8.42	32.5	0.94	**2.8**	2.9	0.35	2.72	3.11	72.2	**3.7**	38.4	16.0	**6.6**
4.3	1.06	8.4	0.22	**1.6**	0.5	0.23	2.65	3.40	84.6	**0.7**	13.8	39.9	**3.2**
0.3	2.28	14.3	1.73	**0.0**	-2.8	-2.22	-23.33	2.47	148.2	**2.4**	18.0	17.4	**1.0**
0.0	7.94	34.7	0.81	**3.5**	1.0	0.51	2.38	4.54	66.6	**2.2**	22.4	18.8	**6.9**
7.4	0.72	3.7	0.06	**5.1**	1.3	0.83	7.98	5.02	81.2	**3.7**	30.2	13.5	**6.3**
8.7	0.72	2.8	-0.03	**3.1**	0.5	0.41	2.47	2.61	73.3	**2.8**	39.0	21.9	**7.6**
10.0	0.00	0.0	0.00	**10.0**	11.6	26.18	35.63	0.17	71.8	**5.0**	264.3	101.0	**6.5**
8.5	0.35	1.3	0.34	**4.1**	0.9	1.29	8.52	3.94	66.9	**2.1**	39.0	32.5	**5.8**
4.5	1.91	13.4	0.92	**0.0**	-0.3	-0.33	-3.30	3.46	108.8	**1.0**	17.5	33.4	**1.3**
4.2	0.71	4.3	4.77	**0.0**	-4.8	-5.39	-42.95	3.78	196.2	**1.5**	15.4	23.9	**1.0**
1.7	4.56	24.1	1.71	**2.4**	6.6	0.28	2.48	4.97	66.1	**4.1**	10.4	8.0	**5.1**
0.0	9.16	58.9	5.19	**0.0**	-5.6	-6.51	-114.17	3.60	238.4	**1.7**	29.7	28.9	**2.5**
3.9	0.95	6.7	1.10	**5.3**	3.6	1.37	15.84	4.91	57.7	**1.7**	22.0	23.7	**5.7**
8.9	0.46	1.5	0.07	**3.9**	0.3	0.66	4.62	3.33	69.9	**3.5**	55.5	20.1	**6.6**
5.3	0.36	2.4	0.05	**0.5**	-0.4	-0.84	-7.77	4.30	106.9	**3.6**	41.1	17.2	**4.9**
8.2	0.00	0.0	0.22	**0.0**	-1.4	-1.44	-9.31	2.47	135.2	**2.4**	32.9	22.6	**1.5**

Name	City	State	Rating	2008 Rating	2007 Rating	Total Assets ($Mil)	One Year Asset Growth	Asset Mix (As a % of Total Assets) Comm-ercial Loans	Cons-umer Loans	Home Mort-gages	Secur-ities	Capital-ization Index	Leverage Ratio	Risk-based Capital Ratio
VERMILION BANK & TRUST CO	KAPLAN	LA	**B**	B	B	110	1.78	25.5	6.9	15.6	31.8	**6.9**	8.9	15.1
VERMILION VALLEY BANK	PIPER CITY	IL	**A-**	B	C+	106	3.27	3.5	3.1	14.0	25.5	**9.4**	10.6	15.1
VERMILLION STATE BK	VERMILLION	MN	**A**	A	A	479	7.03	16.4	1.0	8.0	35.3	**10.0**	12.1	18.9
▼ VERMONT STATE BK	VERMONT	IL	**D**	D	C-	14	-4.71	3.1	35.0	31.5	16.3	**6.7**	8.7	14.5
VERNON BANK	LEESVILLE	LA	**C**	C	C	68	6.68	5.2	11.0	26.4	10.9	**6.3**	8.3	14.7
VERSAILLES SAVINGS & LOAN	VERSAILLES	OH	**B-**	B-	B	43	-3.50	0.9	2.5	63.7	3.4	**10.0**	22.0	37.5
VERUS BANK NA	DERBY	KS	**B**	B	B	109	6.49	2.9	4.6	19.1	21.6	**7.2**	9.1	14.2
▲ VERUS BANK OF COMMERCE	FORT COLLINS	CO	**C**	C-	C-	107	13.78	10.7	0.1	8.2	0.0	**7.3**	9.5	12.7
VIBRA BANK	CHULA VISTA	CA	**D**	C	C	74	43.56	18.9	0.8	6.5	8.8	**10.0**	15.2	21.1
VICTOR STATE BK	VICTOR	IA	**A**	A	A	39	0.97	13.3	2.5	11.6	49.3	**10.0**	19.5	33.3
VICTORY BANK	LIMERICK	PA	**D-**	C	C	84	50.55	33.0	10.1	11.4	8.0	**6.2**	9.7	11.9
▲ VICTORY COMMUNITY BANK	LAKESIDE PARK	KY	**B+**	B+	B+	143	-1.02	0.1	0.2	53.7	8.5	**10.0**	11.3	18.5
▼ VICTORY STATE BK	STATEN ISLAND	NY	**C**	B+	B	237	-0.59	6.1	0.2	5.5	51.3	**8.4**	10.0	25.9
VIDALIA FSB	VIDALIA	GA	**C+**	C+	C+	214	4.33	0.1	2.0	36.8	32.9	**10.0**	11.8	30.5
VIEWPOINT BANK	PLANO	TX	**C**	C-	C+	2,941	23.63	1.3	2.3	33.1	39.2	**8.1**	9.7	18.4
▲ VIGILANT FSB	BALTIMORE	MD	**D-**	D-	D-	54	-4.71	0.8	0.1	53.3	14.4	**4.8**	6.8	17.5
VIKING BANK	SEATTLE	WA	**E-**	E-	D	436	-26.47	17.0	0.4	11.8	0.7	**1.3**	5.3	8.3
VIKING SAVINGS BANK	ALEXANDRIA	MN	**C+**	C+	C+	149	2.75	10.0	1.7	30.1	12.6	**7.5**	9.3	13.4
VIKING STATE BK & TRUST	DECORAH	IA	**B**	B	B+	105	3.50	11.8	3.2	14.2	5.9	**8.6**	10.5	13.9
VILLA GROVE STATE BK	VILLA GROVE	IL	**C+**	C+	C+	69	6.75	5.8	4.1	35.1	11.8	**6.3**	8.3	13.0
VILLAGE BANK	SAINT LIBORY	IL	**C+**	C	C	73	7.85	3.8	9.1	27.1	3.7	**7.7**	9.4	16.0
VILLAGE BANK	AUBURNDALE	MA	**B-**	B+	B+	683	1.95	1.8	0.5	41.9	16.0	**10.0**	11.6	19.5
VILLAGE BANK	SAINT FRANCIS	MN	**D-**	D-	D+	251	-8.43	20.6	0.9	6.5	7.4	**4.9**	7.8	11.0
VILLAGE BANK	SPRINGFIELD	MO	**E-**	E+	E+	86	-5.68	18.2	1.3	9.0	15.0	**2.6**	5.9	9.6
VILLAGE BANK	SAINT GEORGE	UT	**E-**	D-	C	209	-15.79	10.5	1.3	5.7	14.1	**0.2**	4.0	6.4
VILLAGE BANK	MIDLOTHIAN	VA	**D-**	D-	D-	589	0.78	6.3	0.9	22.3	9.1	**6.5**	8.8	12.1
▲ VILLAGE BANK & TRUST	ARLINGTON HEIGHTS	IL	**D+**	D	C-	789	-0.27	27.2	8.6	2.0	12.9	**7.7**	9.5	13.3
VININGS BANK	SMYRNA	GA	**D-**	D-	C-	197	-0.88	9.4	0.3	2.2	42.5	**6.8**	8.8	14.1
▲ VINTAGE BANK	WAXAHACHIE	TX	**C-**	B-	B-	143	-2.47	14.2	3.0	19.5	0.0	**6.4**	8.4	12.7
VINTON COUNTY NB OF	MCARTHUR	OH	**C-**	C-	B-	701	0.31	2.3	12.2	30.2	25.2	**8.4**	9.9	15.3
VIRGINIA BANK & TRUST CO	DANVILLE	VA	**A**	A+	A+	158	4.15	6.1	12.1	21.3	8.9	**10.0**	16.0	22.5
VIRGINIA BUSINESS BANK	RICHMOND	VA	**E-**	D-	D-	107	-29.47	8.1	1.5	12.3	0.0	**0.0**	2.8	6.1
VIRGINIA COMMERCE BANK	ARLINGTON	VA	**D**	D-	C	2,739	0.67	8.0	0.5	10.2	15.1	**9.2**	10.8	14.3
▼ VIRGINIA COMMONWEALTH	PETERSBURG	VA	**D-**	C-	B	322	1.20	1.7	1.8	23.9	25.6	**10.0**	11.0	19.7
▼ VIRGINIA COMMUNITY BANK	LOUISA	VA	**D**	D+	C+	223	7.02	7.4	3.5	14.6	22.7	**6.3**	8.3	12.1
▼ VIRGINIA COMPANY BANK	NEWPORT NEWS	VA	**D+**	C-	D+	117	9.40	12.8	2.2	11.6	10.6	**8.9**	12.0	14.1
VIRGINIA HERITAGE BANK	FAIRFAX	VA	**C**	C	C	453	32.69	8.7	13.5	9.6	8.9	**6.7**	9.1	12.3
▲ VIRGINIA NATIONAL BK	CHARLOTTESVILLE	VA	**C+**	C	C	458	3.85	8.9	2.9	12.7	13.6	**8.9**	10.3	14.2
▼ VIRGINIA PARTNERS BANK	FREDERICKSBURG	VA	**D+**	C	C	141	31.65	5.1	1.0	24.8	21.4	**10.0**	11.7	17.7
▲ VIRGINIA SAVINGS BANK FSB	FRONT ROYAL	VA	**C-**	D+	D+	127	-0.02	2.1	3.2	35.2	12.0	**6.3**	8.3	14.6
VISALIA COMMUNITY BANK	VISALIA	CA	**D+**	C-	B	194	-0.36	15.0	3.5	4.0	1.3	**7.2**	9.1	13.2
▼ VISION BANK	PANAMA CITY	FL	**D+**	D	D+	809	-9.90	7.7	0.7	20.8	13.7	**10.0**	14.1	19.6
▼ VISION BANK - TEXAS	RICHARDSON	TX	**D+**	C-	C-	107	40.78	9.1	1.3	15.3	38.7	**10.0**	11.4	20.8
VISION BANK NA	ADA	OK	**C+**	B-	B-	574	11.78	8.0	3.1	17.4	17.8	**6.3**	8.3	13.2
VISIONBANK	TOPEKA	KS	**D+**	D+	D-	83	16.94	12.1	4.1	12.8	9.9	**6.7**	8.7	12.3
▲ VISIONBANK	SAINT LOUIS PARK	MN	**E+**	D-	D	36	-7.16	11.2	3.6	6.6	6.0	**7.1**	9.0	12.9
VISIONBANK	FARGO	ND	**D+**	D	C-	138	0.23	33.2	3.0	16.0	0.0	**6.6**	8.6	12.4
VIST BANK	WYOMISSING	PA	**D**	D+	C+	1,406	9.12	7.1	0.2	13.0	19.9	**4.1**	6.8	10.5
▲ VISTA BANK	RALLS	TX	**C-**	C	B-	207	24.31	11.2	4.6	5.3	17.2	**4.8**	7.1	10.9
▲ VISTA BANK TEXAS	HOUSTON	TX	**C+**	C-	D+	456	16.77	21.8	2.0	3.9	8.6	**9.4**	10.6	15.8
VISTABANK	AIKEN	SC	**D-**	C	C	116	-11.48	8.0	2.1	9.8	3.5	**5.6**	8.1	11.5
VNBTRUST NA	CHARLOTTESVILLE	VA	**U**	U	U	8	48.64	0.0	0.0	0.0	0.0	**10.0**	142.4	130.1
VOLUNTEER FS&LA OF	MADISONVILLE	TN	**B**	B-	B	170	1.79	1.9	5.9	53.5	0.0	**10.0**	11.7	17.4
▲ VOLUNTEER STATE BK	PORTLAND	TN	**C**	C-	C+	383	23.11	6.7	1.6	35.7	6.9	**5.9**	7.9	11.7
▼ VOYAGER BANK	EDEN PRAIRIE	MN	**D**	D-	D	415	-12.13	30.0	1.8	6.6	1.7	**4.9**	9.7	10.9
WABASH SB	MOUNT CARMEL	IL	**C-**	C-	C-	11	5.89	4.9	6.6	32.0	28.5	**10.0**	14.1	31.4
▲ WACCAMAW BANK	WHITEVILLE	NC	**E+**	D-	C-	561	5.41	4.7	2.3	10.3	12.0	**5.2**	7.5	11.1
WADENA STATE BK	WADENA	MN	**B-**	C	C+	116	3.86	11.1	2.7	19.5	22.0	**8.8**	10.2	16.2
WAGGONER NATIONAL BK OF	VERNON	TX	**A**	A	A	227	-1.84	5.3	10.1	10.5	24.6	**10.0**	13.7	21.0
WAHOO STATE BK	WAHOO	NE	**C-**	C	D+	62	5.04	6.2	3.7	31.7	8.1	**5.0**	7.0	13.5

Asset Quality Index	Non-Performing Loans as a % of Total Loans	Non-Performing Loans as a % of Capital	Net Charge-offs / Avg Loans	Profitability Index	Net Income ($Mil)	Return on Assets (R.O.A.)	Return on Equity (R.O.E.)	Net Interest Spread	Overhead Efficiency Ratio	Liquidity Index	Liquidity Ratio	Hot Money Ratio	Stability Index
5.3	0.63	3.9	0.03	**8.4**	1.7	1.79	19.96	4.70	62.3	**2.4**	15.6	17.2	**6.6**
5.9	0.56	3.5	0.39	**6.2**	1.4	1.44	11.79	4.66	59.5	**3.7**	22.6	11.2	**7.5**
6.6	0.72	3.4	0.86	**9.6**	10.3	2.26	18.34	4.08	28.8	**3.4**	43.0	19.0	**8.6**
0.9	4.29	29.9	2.10	**3.1**	0.1	0.48	5.17	5.58	55.8	**1.1**	16.2	30.0	**5.2**
6.2	0.46	3.3	0.70	**4.0**	0.4	0.67	8.12	4.66	78.5	**3.3**	23.0	13.4	**4.2**
7.9	0.24	0.9	0.04	**3.5**	0.2	0.53	2.68	3.35	73.2	**3.9**	13.3	9.1	**6.6**
6.7	0.41	2.6	0.01	**5.4**	1.3	1.22	12.90	4.63	78.6	**4.6**	24.4	6.2	**5.6**
4.0	0.49	3.9	1.02	**3.9**	0.6	0.58	6.00	3.78	52.5	**3.9**	12.0	8.9	**4.7**
8.7	0.00	0.0	0.00	**0.1**	-0.5	-0.88	-4.86	4.83	97.1	**0.9**	24.7	45.4	**1.6**
9.1	1.37	3.0	0.00	**10.0**	1.2	3.05	14.92	5.74	30.0	**3.6**	65.9	24.2	**9.0**
6.1	0.29	2.4	0.00	**0.0**	-0.5	-0.70	-7.14	3.72	109.9	**1.6**	9.3	20.7	**0.8**
5.1	2.35	16.6	0.05	**8.9**	3.2	2.17	21.44	3.25	46.2	**1.7**	16.8	21.9	**7.7**
1.7	7.81	25.2	-0.09	**5.9**	2.0	0.83	7.89	3.99	67.3	**2.7**	40.4	25.1	**6.1**
7.3	1.81	7.0	0.00	**2.7**	0.7	0.31	2.58	2.11	78.6	**2.9**	59.2	39.8	**6.5**
6.2	1.06	5.6	0.07	**3.5**	18.4	0.68	7.90	2.78	69.1	**3.4**	46.2	26.5	**3.6**
3.2	2.01	16.6	0.00	**1.7**	0.0	0.01	0.19	3.42	81.5	**4.7**	33.5	9.0	**1.7**
0.3	10.14	104.8	3.26	**0.0**	-9.6	-1.85	-29.78	3.59	97.6	**3.0**	15.5	13.9	**1.5**
3.0	1.48	11.9	0.69	**4.8**	1.5	0.96	5.94	4.00	52.3	**1.5**	17.9	24.8	**7.9**
4.3	0.77	5.1	0.10	**9.6**	2.1	2.17	21.12	4.74	42.8	**3.3**	24.2	13.3	**7.1**
5.2	0.54	4.8	0.00	**5.4**	0.9	1.24	15.60	3.59	63.9	**1.4**	10.2	24.9	**5.0**
5.9	0.28	1.9	0.15	**4.0**	0.6	0.87	9.18	3.92	75.5	**3.6**	26.5	12.5	**5.8**
3.7	4.55	26.0	0.54	**3.1**	2.5	0.36	3.17	3.38	64.9	**2.4**	27.2	18.8	**7.6**
0.0	7.96	58.0	1.57	**0.4**	-3.4	-1.28	-14.71	4.60	79.1	**1.6**	14.4	22.4	**4.8**
1.4	4.72	31.4	-1.08	**0.0**	-0.8	-0.85	-13.92	1.96	154.7	**0.9**	16.6	34.0	**2.0**
0.1	9.02	84.9	6.91	**0.0**	-5.1	-2.25	-29.62	4.16	108.1	**2.0**	16.9	19.3	**3.2**
0.3	4.36	35.6	1.68	**1.8**	1.9	0.33	3.84	3.73	76.7	**1.2**	11.3	28.0	**3.3**
0.9	0.97	6.5	1.84	**1.4**	0.9	0.11	0.97	3.99	66.1	**1.0**	18.9	32.7	**5.1**
2.5	2.37	10.9	3.04	**0.3**	-0.3	-0.12	-1.43	3.50	63.1	**2.1**	26.9	20.7	**1.6**
2.6	0.97	8.0	1.72	**4.6**	1.3	0.89	10.75	4.83	59.7	**3.0**	16.7	14.4	**5.5**
2.1	2.77	17.2	0.79	**4.4**	5.9	0.83	7.95	4.38	62.5	**2.1**	22.4	19.0	**6.4**
6.7	1.03	4.9	0.10	**7.6**	1.8	1.14	7.32	4.76	67.7	**3.9**	18.7	10.1	**9.2**
0.0	13.72	148.7	5.16	**0.0**	-6.0	-4.20	-97.00	2.80	106.1	**0.7**	24.5	67.0	**0.0**
0.7	2.58	15.7	1.03	**4.0**	26.2	0.93	8.94	4.12	47.9	**1.7**	6.2	19.7	**6.5**
0.3	9.21	43.9	1.07	**0.4**	0.0	0.01	0.05	3.03	80.3	**3.3**	38.6	18.2	**1.7**
0.9	5.09	31.9	0.78	**1.1**	-0.3	-0.11	-1.35	4.42	77.1	**3.2**	21.6	13.5	**4.8**
5.6	0.35	2.3	0.03	**1.4**	0.2	0.19	1.50	3.73	90.8	**0.9**	11.5	32.7	**2.2**
3.2	0.95	7.8	0.21	**4.2**	5.2	1.29	14.70	3.88	69.3	**0.6**	14.3	57.9	**4.1**
3.8	1.59	9.8	0.10	**4.8**	4.0	0.94	9.49	4.21	73.5	**1.8**	30.8	29.5	**6.0**
8.6	0.49	2.9	0.01	**0.0**	-0.9	-0.73	-5.35	3.04	102.0	**1.8**	21.9	22.0	**1.5**
2.9	2.11	16.9	0.07	**2.1**	0.5	0.37	4.26	4.01	83.0	**3.0**	21.9	14.5	**3.7**
1.4	3.15	19.9	0.52	**1.8**	0.3	0.16	1.82	4.18	84.4	**3.6**	26.7	12.5	**4.3**
0.2	26.82	106.6	5.49	**0.0**	-29.3	-3.41	-25.07	3.55	129.3	**1.2**	2.1	25.6	**4.5**
8.8	0.37	1.5	0.01	**0.6**	0.1	0.15	1.17	3.02	101.2	**5.6**	53.4	10.3	**2.1**
2.8	1.39	9.8	1.48	**4.6**	4.2	0.77	9.08	4.36	69.9	**1.1**	18.0	32.1	**5.9**
3.0	1.97	15.2	0.35	**1.9**	0.2	0.21	2.15	3.73	82.4	**1.7**	13.4	21.6	**2.8**
0.0	4.81	30.5	0.43	**0.0**	-0.7	-1.57	-16.52	3.53	134.2	**0.8**	15.9	41.9	**0.5**
1.3	2.01	17.2	0.93	**2.0**	0.3	0.23	2.52	3.65	79.6	**1.6**	15.1	22.7	**3.5**
0.8	2.52	24.2	0.75	**2.2**	3.7	0.28	3.14	3.57	71.4	**1.3**	5.5	25.5	**5.7**
7.7	0.22	1.7	0.17	**2.1**	0.5	0.28	3.50	4.11	96.2	**2.3**	32.2	22.1	**4.1**
7.3	0.07	0.4	0.01	**3.6**	3.7	0.89	7.47	4.06	70.7	**1.7**	23.6	24.3	**6.5**
2.7	3.96	34.4	1.09	**0.0**	-3.1	-2.45	-25.36	3.25	98.8	**1.7**	14.4	21.5	**1.0**
10.0	0.00	0.0	0.00	**8.0**	2.1	47.42	48.75	0.23	43.0	**5.0**	222.6	101.0	**5.4**
4.8	1.60	11.0	0.07	**4.0**	1.3	0.77	6.79	4.07	67.2	**1.6**	11.6	22.2	**6.6**
3.0	1.11	10.4	0.94	**8.1**	6.6	1.93	23.00	4.35	71.1	**0.5**	5.2	44.0	**5.8**
1.7	3.05	23.6	0.95	**2.7**	1.5	0.34	3.99	4.18	70.1	**1.5**	10.4	22.8	**2.5**
6.1	0.11	0.4	0.88	**1.3**	0.0	0.13	0.96	3.54	93.5	**3.7**	51.3	16.7	**6.7**
0.3	10.38	80.5	1.88	**0.0**	-7.7	-1.37	-23.89	2.31	98.5	**0.7**	11.2	41.1	**3.0**
4.6	0.89	4.7	0.46	**6.2**	1.5	1.26	11.75	4.76	63.4	**4.9**	39.4	10.3	**5.6**
7.3	0.22	0.9	0.18	**8.6**	4.9	2.18	15.35	4.71	49.5	**1.8**	15.8	20.6	**9.5**
5.6	1.01	8.4	0.30	**4.8**	0.7	1.15	16.57	4.43	70.7	**4.3**	22.1	7.8	**4.3**

Name	City	State	Rating	2008 Rating	2007 Rating	Total Assets ($Mil)	One Year Asset Growth	Asset Mix (As a % of Total Assets) Comm-ercial Loans	Cons-umer Loans	Home Mort-gages	Secur-ities	Capital-ization Index	Leverage Ratio	Risk-based Capital Ratio
WAINWRIGHT BANK & TRUST	BOSTON	MA	C	NR	NR	1,106	9.06	16.8	0.1	34.6	0.5	5.1	7.5	11.1
WAKE FOREST FS&LA	WAKE FOREST	NC	C+	C+	A	114	1.65	0.0	0.2	26.3	2.0	10.0	18.2	32.0
WAKEFIELD CO-OP BANK	WAKEFIELD	MA	C	C-	C	141	0.07	0.1	0.1	48.1	37.2	5.8	7.8	18.1
WALCOTT TRUST & SB	WALCOTT	IA	A-	A	A	90	6.59	15.3	0.8	15.7	11.9	10.0	19.7	27.8
WALDEN FS&LA	WALDEN	NY	D	D+	B-	155	-0.55	7.6	0.4	48.2	0.2	9.2	10.5	14.4
WALDEN SAVINGS BANK	MONTGOMERY	NY	D+	C	C	398	2.17	6.8	0.5	35.5	8.8	6.2	8.2	12.7
WALDO STATE BK	WALDO	WI	C+	B-	B-	50	15.57	8.4	2.7	34.5	17.8	10.0	12.4	20.5
WALKER STATE BK	WALKER	IA	B	B	B	33	4.06	8.0	3.4	12.3	22.9	6.3	8.4	12.0
WALLIS STATE BK	WALLIS	TX	C	B-	B	325	0.88	10.8	1.2	5.1	4.5	7.6	9.6	13.0
WALLKILL VALLEY FS&LA	WALLKILL	NY	C-	B-	B	126	3.39	0.8	0.4	50.2	8.1	10.0	19.6	32.5
WALPOLE CO-OP BANK	WALPOLE	MA	C+	C	B+	344	0.29	7.1	0.1	14.2	13.6	10.0	20.2	25.1
WALTERS BANK & TRUST CO	WALTERS	OK	B+	B+	A-	55	4.02	7.3	7.5	14.8	40.0	10.0	21.9	59.6
WALTON STATE BK	WALTON	KS	E+	D-	E+	7	-8.29	2.8	8.1	20.6	43.5	5.5	7.5	16.9
WALWORTH STATE BK	WALWORTH	WI	D+	D+	D+	243	1.83	14.0	1.7	30.4	6.2	7.3	9.2	13.6
▼WANDA STATE BK	WANDA	MN	B-	B	B	108	7.83	1.8	0.9	5.5	28.2	10.0	15.6	20.7
WAREHOUSE TRUST CO LLC	NEW YORK	NY	U	NR	NR	21	N/A	0.0	0.0	0.0	0.0	10.0	52.3	260.3
WARREN BANK & TRUST CO	WARREN	AR	C	B	B+	129	3.21	2.2	5.8	14.5	48.4	10.0	13.8	22.2
WARREN-BOYNTON STATE BK	NEW BERLIN	IL	A-	A-	A-	116	7.58	8.5	3.2	16.3	17.6	10.0	12.1	16.2
WARRINGTON BANK	PENSACOLA	FL	C+	C+	B-	71	15.44	0.2	1.0	1.7	45.3	10.0	20.0	39.4
WARSAW FS&LA	CINCINNATI	OH	D+	C-	C-	71	1.85	0.0	0.3	56.0	5.2	10.0	13.7	28.9
WASHINGTON BUSINESS	OLYMPIA	WA	D	D-	D	73	-4.17	28.1	0.8	3.1	4.4	5.5	8.5	11.4
WASHINGTON COUNTY BANK	BLAIR	NE	C	C	C	282	2.22	9.4	2.0	6.8	21.4	6.3	8.4	12.0
WASHINGTON FEDERAL BANK	CHICAGO	IL	B-	B-	B-	97	12.77	0.0	0.1	80.8	0.0	7.4	9.3	18.1
WASHINGTON FINANCIAL	WASHINGTON	PA	C	C	NR	819	8.09	4.3	11.5	28.6	16.1	9.6	10.7	17.5
WASHINGTON FS&LA	SEATTLE	WA	B-	C+	B+	13,174	6.06	1.1	0.7	46.7	21.5	10.0	11.7	23.8
WASHINGTON SAVINGS BANK	PHILADELPHIA	PA	C-	C-	C-	185	-1.10	0.3	1.6	58.3	5.8	4.7	6.8	13.4
WASHINGTON SAVINGS BANK	BOWIE	MD	D	D-	C	394	-8.43	0.9	0.1	26.5	20.1	10.0	12.2	20.4
WASHINGTON SB	EFFINGHAM	IL	C+	B-	C+	238	12.41	3.9	3.9	30.9	38.2	9.2	10.5	19.0
WASHINGTON SB	LOWELL	MA	C-	C-	C-	172	4.62	2.2	0.3	37.8	24.8	7.7	9.5	18.9
WASHINGTON STATE BK	WASHINGTON	IA	A-	A-	A-	217	0.33	9.2	2.4	26.4	21.8	10.0	12.8	22.4
WASHINGTON STATE BK	WASHINGTON	IL	C+	C+	B	52	0.98	4.1	5.6	24.6	53.9	6.9	8.9	22.6
▼WASHINGTON STATE BK	HOUMA	LA	D	C-	B+	128	1.11	13.8	2.5	9.6	14.6	8.3	9.9	14.4
WASHINGTON TRUST BANK	SPOKANE	WA	C	C-	C+	3,972	-3.08	15.9	2.3	8.3	24.3	9.7	10.8	15.7
WASHINGTON TRUST CO	WESTERLY	RI	B-	B-	B	2,906	0.81	4.1	1.9	24.1	20.7	6.1	8.1	12.6
▼WASHINGTONFIRST BANK	RESTON	VA	D+	C-	D+	435	22.31	17.4	0.8	3.8	10.5	5.6	8.8	11.4
▲WASHITA STATE BK	BURNS FLAT	OK	B	C-	B-	167	-14.25	16.0	0.5	1.3	55.8	9.1	10.4	16.7
WASHITA VALLEY BANK	FORT COBB	OK	A-	B+	B+	36	5.68	2.5	9.8	1.3	43.1	10.0	16.0	22.7
WATERFORD BANK NA	TOLEDO	OH	C+	C-	C-	314	47.91	16.2	1.2	6.3	23.0	9.7	10.8	16.5
WATERFORD COMMERCIAL &	WATERFORD	OH	B-	B	B	42	11.20	1.3	8.6	33.4	12.2	8.9	10.3	22.4
▼WATERMAN STATE BK	WATERMAN	IL	D+	C-	C	44	0.14	11.5	1.2	14.2	34.9	5.8	7.8	13.4
WATERSTONE BANK SSB	WAUWATOSA	WI	D-	D-	D-	1,805	-2.84	1.7	0.0	37.9	11.1	6.8	8.8	14.2
WATERTOWN SB	WATERTOWN	MA	B-	C+	C-	1,041	-2.16	0.5	0.4	43.6	34.7	5.9	7.9	16.4
WATERTOWN SB	WATERTOWN	NY	C-	C-	B-	434	6.82	5.9	1.8	13.9	23.6	8.6	10.1	13.8
WATKINS SB	WATKINS	IA	A-	A-	B+	58	0.37	1.8	1.6	8.7	41.8	10.0	13.3	21.8
WAUCHULA STATE BK	WAUCHULA	FL	D+	C-	B-	562	-2.98	4.3	1.6	20.9	22.0	6.5	8.5	13.0
WAUKEGAN SB	WAUKEGAN	IL	E-	E	D-	94	-8.54	6.7	1.0	47.9	11.5	1.6	4.6	8.6
WAUKESHA STATE BK	WAUKESHA	WI	B+	A-	A	782	-0.63	5.1	2.6	9.6	15.4	10.0	12.6	17.5
WAUKON STATE BK	WAUKON	IA	B	B-	B+	114	-0.60	11.1	1.8	14.8	13.0	10.0	11.2	15.7
▲WAUMANDEE STATE BK	WAUMANDEE	WI	C+	C-	C+	153	4.95	13.9	4.2	14.1	14.8	5.8	7.8	11.9
▼WAWEL SAVINGS BANK	WALLINGTON	NJ	C-	C	C	94	-2.57	1.8	0.5	40.6	16.2	10.0	18.7	30.3
WAYCROSS BANK & TRUST	WAYCROSS	GA	C+	B	B+	135	10.85	7.0	1.9	10.2	35.1	7.5	9.3	14.9
WAYLAND STATE BK	MOUNT PLEASANT	IA	A	A-	A-	71	-4.94	10.2	2.6	14.9	31.7	10.0	17.1	27.9
▼WAYNE BANK	HONESDALE	PA	A-	A	A	537	1.46	2.6	2.1	23.3	27.2	10.0	12.1	19.2
▼WAYNE BANK & TRUST CO	CAMBRIDGE CITY	IN	D+	C-	D+	156	1.46	5.6	2.6	18.5	6.0	9.0	10.4	14.6
WAYNE COUNTY BANK	WAYNESBORO	TN	D	D	B-	264	3.52	10.6	14.5	21.5	3.2	9.2	11.1	14.4
WAYNE SAVINGS COMMUNITY	WOOSTER	OH	C+	C	C+	407	1.52	1.9	0.4	35.1	32.5	6.3	8.3	15.2
▲WEBBANK	SALT LAKE CITY	UT	C	D	C+	85	29.53	10.3	12.4	0.0	0.6	10.0	24.1	68.6
▲WEBSTER BANK NA	WATERBURY	CT	D+	D	C-	17,983	1.60	14.3	0.2	22.8	30.9	6.6	8.6	14.3
WEBSTER CITY FSB	WEBSTER CITY	IA	B-	C+	C-	89	-4.86	0.8	2.4	57.4	13.5	10.0	12.7	26.2
WEBSTER FIVE CENTS SB	WEBSTER	MA	C-	C+	B-	555	-0.84	6.9	6.6	25.4	24.1	10.0	11.6	17.6

Asset Quality Index	Non-Performing Loans as a % of Total Loans	Non-Performing Loans as a % of Capital	Net Charge-offs / Avg Loans	Profitability Index	Net Income ($Mil)	Return on Assets (R.O.A.)	Return on Equity (R.O.E.)	Net Interest Spread	Overhead Efficiency Ratio	Liquidity Index	Liquidity Ratio	Hot Money Ratio	Stability Index
4.6	0.48	5.1	0.02	**0.8**	-6.8	-5.34	-63.78	4.04	71.7	**1.7**	11.7	21.2	**6.8**
6.3	0.98	3.0	0.00	**2.5**	0.2	0.21	1.16	2.35	68.1	**2.2**	43.6	38.5	**7.0**
4.1	2.04	14.6	0.10	**3.1**	0.7	0.53	6.76	3.00	74.4	**4.3**	42.2	14.1	**3.7**
6.2	2.53	8.9	0.09	**7.4**	1.1	1.29	6.51	4.44	56.5	**3.9**	32.4	12.7	**9.0**
0.8	4.45	35.7	0.27	**3.1**	0.6	0.40	3.92	4.52	77.7	**1.4**	3.5	23.0	**5.6**
1.8	2.49	21.7	0.34	**4.0**	2.8	0.73	8.88	4.30	66.9	**4.2**	16.0	7.6	**1.2**
2.4	5.75	30.4	0.22	**5.0**	0.4	0.87	6.50	4.17	61.1	**3.1**	30.9	16.3	**7.6**
8.5	0.00	0.0	0.00	**7.1**	0.4	1.25	14.65	4.86	55.3	**4.6**	34.0	10.1	**5.9**
5.9	0.00	0.0	0.82	**3.7**	2.6	0.81	8.32	4.32	69.0	**1.5**	18.0	25.3	**5.6**
2.9	5.40	20.8	0.24	**1.9**	-0.1	-0.04	-0.23	3.95	85.4	**1.5**	14.8	23.8	**7.4**
2.0	4.07	15.7	0.22	**5.9**	3.1	0.93	4.71	4.06	60.0	**2.1**	17.3	18.9	**8.1**
8.7	0.43	0.8	-0.22	**4.0**	0.5	0.82	3.50	4.04	80.6	**4.9**	58.2	13.5	**8.3**
2.8	3.03	17.2	0.65	**1.9**	0.0	0.08	1.00	3.58	92.8	**4.3**	38.5	10.7	**1.0**
1.9	3.06	23.8	0.95	**5.8**	3.1	1.25	14.16	4.37	48.2	**1.5**	18.4	26.1	**5.9**
7.2	1.03	3.4	0.00	**4.0**	0.8	0.80	4.96	3.33	62.8	**4.6**	48.4	14.2	**7.4**
10.0	0.00	0.0	0.00	**9.5**	7.8	70.66	106.22	0.00	74.5	**4.8**	188.2	101.0	**7.0**
2.9	5.00	15.0	0.01	**6.7**	2.2	1.70	12.01	3.75	58.6	**3.2**	45.4	20.9	**7.3**
8.2	0.00	0.0	0.23	**6.4**	1.3	1.17	9.28	4.37	55.0	**1.3**	8.9	25.9	**6.9**
10.0	0.00	0.0	0.00	**3.8**	0.4	0.58	2.80	3.27	73.9	**6.4**	71.7	7.4	**6.3**
8.7	0.60	2.7	0.00	**1.2**	-0.1	-0.12	-0.86	2.65	95.0	**5.1**	39.5	8.9	**5.9**
0.5	1.67	13.8	1.66	**0.9**	-0.1	-0.08	-0.92	4.57	75.0	**1.5**	14.9	24.1	**3.4**
5.1	0.53	4.2	0.34	**5.5**	2.8	0.98	12.20	3.42	60.2	**2.7**	10.2	14.8	**5.4**
9.1	0.00	0.0	0.00	**4.6**	0.9	1.01	11.01	4.64	58.0	**0.6**	6.2	41.1	**5.4**
5.2	0.85	5.1	0.25	**3.2**	3.8	0.48	4.27	3.19	73.3	**2.6**	20.5	16.5	**5.2**
3.5	3.21	17.1	0.16	**4.4**	135.9	1.01	7.50	3.24	33.8	**2.6**	32.2	28.3	**8.3**
8.5	0.12	1.2	0.04	**1.9**	0.1	0.08	1.04	2.77	93.7	**2.7**	25.9	16.7	**3.4**
0.4	8.69	41.4	0.53	**0.3**	-3.7	-0.89	-7.92	3.31	125.1	**1.6**	29.9	31.4	**4.3**
6.5	1.06	5.3	0.02	**3.0**	1.2	0.54	4.81	2.78	77.4	**3.8**	39.5	15.9	**6.3**
2.9	3.85	22.3	0.59	**2.0**	0.6	0.36	3.65	3.23	81.4	**2.8**	39.6	22.3	**5.3**
5.7	1.97	8.9	0.53	**5.7**	2.4	1.09	8.10	3.77	46.2	**3.1**	35.6	18.0	**7.8**
4.0	3.38	14.8	0.31	**3.2**	0.3	0.48	5.01	2.91	74.7	**3.1**	47.2	22.2	**5.7**
0.0	7.90	49.8	0.86	**3.5**	0.3	0.23	2.17	4.32	58.9	**1.3**	14.4	27.6	**7.8**
3.8	2.46	13.3	1.63	**3.1**	9.1	0.23	2.14	4.03	59.9	**2.9**	22.6	16.8	**6.7**
4.4	0.89	6.9	0.24	**4.7**	25.4	0.88	8.66	3.04	66.6	**1.1**	5.9	28.6	**7.9**
2.0	1.07	8.7	0.40	**3.0**	1.5	0.38	3.61	3.74	72.7	**0.9**	16.8	34.0	**4.6**
8.5	0.67	1.5	0.65	**6.5**	-0.3	-0.14	-1.35	2.92	36.6	**1.9**	45.3	82.3	**5.9**
7.2	1.89	4.8	0.22	**9.2**	0.6	1.77	11.09	6.44	55.7	**4.2**	56.8	16.8	**9.0**
8.5	0.00	0.0	0.00	**3.6**	2.0	0.76	6.28	3.83	67.6	**1.6**	35.0	39.4	**4.4**
6.8	0.73	3.8	0.05	**3.6**	0.2	0.47	4.26	4.01	81.3	**2.7**	35.4	20.2	**4.9**
2.8	2.61	16.3	0.74	**2.2**	0.1	0.22	2.59	4.04	77.3	**1.5**	15.8	24.9	**5.4**
0.3	5.99	43.4	1.73	**0.3**	-2.6	-0.14	-1.53	2.90	73.8	**1.6**	10.5	22.8	**5.3**
6.5	1.31	9.1	0.08	**4.4**	0.5	0.04	0.54	3.64	59.9	**3.6**	39.4	19.2	**5.2**
1.5	4.15	21.7	0.03	**3.5**	2.7	0.63	4.92	3.48	76.1	**5.2**	33.2	5.9	**7.9**
9.1	0.23	0.8	0.00	**6.4**	0.8	1.40	10.21	3.94	49.8	**5.1**	55.8	12.1	**8.4**
2.4	2.92	21.7	1.46	**6.5**	8.5	1.49	17.49	4.62	51.6	**1.1**	18.7	31.9	**6.1**
0.3	4.58	61.6	1.36	**0.0**	-1.5	-1.51	-30.03	3.09	119.2	**1.7**	19.4	22.5	**0.9**
3.7	4.50	20.6	1.67	**4.3**	5.6	0.73	5.56	4.29	63.1	**4.4**	24.4	7.3	**9.3**
4.9	1.33	7.7	0.85	**7.8**	2.1	1.90	16.33	4.36	48.4	**4.3**	29.2	9.7	**7.1**
4.0	0.88	7.4	0.38	**3.9**	1.0	0.68	7.12	4.24	67.3	**1.5**	23.4	26.8	**5.2**
1.5	7.62	27.1	0.65	**2.9**	0.3	0.32	1.71	4.88	78.5	**1.7**	22.8	23.2	**7.1**
8.8	0.10	0.6	0.11	**3.1**	0.7	0.49	5.11	3.53	84.9	**1.9**	30.4	27.1	**5.4**
8.8	0.01	0.0	0.36	**7.5**	1.0	1.38	8.02	3.93	50.1	**5.6**	51.1	8.7	**8.8**
4.7	1.14	5.8	0.24	**7.5**	7.5	1.41	11.47	4.07	53.5	**2.8**	19.3	15.2	**8.8**
0.9	5.17	34.0	0.56	**4.6**	1.0	0.63	5.96	4.37	62.4	**4.4**	19.5	6.8	**7.8**
1.2	3.36	21.3	1.99	**5.3**	2.4	0.91	8.29	4.94	52.3	**0.5**	8.5	51.4	**6.4**
4.0	1.65	10.9	0.08	**3.5**	2.3	0.57	6.30	3.39	73.3	**3.6**	38.9	16.5	**4.6**
3.0	5.10	7.4	0.65	**6.0**	4.3	6.14	27.67	10.42	60.2	**2.9**	82.3	88.2	**4.5**
1.4	2.46	15.3	1.23	**2.1**	81.1	0.46	4.16	3.45	70.9	**4.3**	19.7	7.6	**6.3**
7.7	0.57	2.8	-0.01	**2.9**	0.5	0.50	4.07	3.46	72.3	**3.6**	37.0	16.1	**7.0**
2.2	5.09	26.9	0.93	**3.9**	3.3	0.59	5.23	4.18	74.3	**1.3**	25.7	31.4	**7.4**

Name	City	State	Rating	2008 Rating	2007 Rating	Total Assets ($Mil)	One Year Asset Growth	Asset Mix (As a % of Total Assets) Comm-ercial Loans	Cons-umer Loans	Home Mort-gages	Secur-ities	Capital-ization Index	Leverage Ratio	Risk-based Capital Ratio
WEDBUSH BANK	LOS ANGELES	CA	**C**	B-	C	197	41.89	3.3	0.2	7.1	46.8	**9.5**	10.7	24.4
WELCH STATE BK OF WELCH	WELCH	OK	**B**	B	B	193	-3.98	4.4	4.3	16.2	23.6	**8.8**	10.2	18.9
▼WELCOME STATE BK	WELCOME	MN	**C+**	B-	C+	24	13.84	11.2	7.5	5.0	7.9	**6.3**	9.8	12.0
▼WELLESLEY BANK	WELLESLEY	MA	**C**	C	C+	262	6.59	5.7	0.2	27.8	9.8	**5.7**	7.7	11.9
WELLINGTON STATE BK	WELLINGTON	TX	**C+**	C+	C+	173	7.40	12.4	6.6	7.3	28.7	**6.3**	8.3	13.5
WELLINGTON TRUST CO NA	BOSTON	MA	**U**	U	U	88	15.57	0.0	0.0	0.0	0.0	**10.0**	29.6	25.4
▼WELLS BANK OF PLATTE CITY	PLATTE CITY	MO	**C-**	B	B	87	11.70	4.0	1.1	22.9	37.1	**5.8**	7.8	12.5
WELLS FARGO BANK LTD	LOS ANGELES	CA	**C-**	C	C-	394	53.08	0.0	0.0	0.0	0.0	**10.0**	46.8	90.4
▲WELLS FARGO BANK NA	SIOUX FALLS	SD	**C-**	C-	D+	1,102,278	81.06	10.7	8.0	20.3	13.7	**6.5**	8.5	13.1
▲WELLS FARGO BANK	OGDEN	UT	**C**	C-	C-	16,582	14.33	11.6	56.8	0.9	7.8	**6.6**	8.6	15.3
WELLS FARGO BANK SOUTH	HOUSTON	TX	**D+**	D	D	31,826	-21.54	0.0	0.1	94.0	0.0	**6.7**	8.8	23.3
▲WELLS FARGO CENTRAL	CALABASAS	CA	**C-**	C-	C-	6	-77.78	0.0	0.0	0.0	0.0	**10.0**	85.1	437.3
▲WELLS FARGO DELAWARE TR	WILMINGTON	DE	**C+**	B	B+	503	1.68	0.0	0.0	0.0	0.0	**10.0**	94.8	481.7
WELLS FARGO FINANCIAL NAT	LAS VEGAS	NV	**C-**	C	C-	3,663	-5.43	0.0	94.1	0.0	9.6	**10.0**	13.7	15.7
WELLS FEDERAL BANK FSB	WELLS	MN	**C**	D+	D+	239	-9.97	4.3	8.4	17.5	6.1	**9.1**	10.4	14.3
▼WELLS RIVER SB	WELLS RIVER	VT	**C+**	C+	C	152	4.48	9.1	3.6	42.9	18.4	**9.8**	10.9	18.0
WELLSVILLE BANK	WELLSVILLE	KS	**C**	C	C	32	6.28	8.4	5.1	25.3	41.4	**6.4**	8.4	15.0
WEMPLE STATE BK	WAVERLY	IL	**C**	C+	C+	62	2.03	20.8	2.7	15.7	15.5	**4.6**	7.9	10.8
▲WENONA STATE BK	WENONA	IL	**C+**	C+	B-	35	21.46	10.0	3.7	8.0	44.9	**10.0**	13.1	25.0
▼WESBANCO BANK INC	WHEELING	WV	**C-**	C	B	5,348	-0.56	5.9	4.5	14.6	26.5	**5.8**	7.8	12.4
WEST ALABAMA BANK &	REFORM	AL	**D+**	C	B	577	1.25	5.7	2.2	11.2	32.3	**7.6**	9.4	14.7
▲WEST BANK	WEST DES MOINES	IA	**B-**	C-	B-	1,290	-17.80	23.1	0.4	5.0	19.7	**9.5**	10.7	16.6
▼WEST CARROLL COMMUNITY	OAK GROVE	LA	**C+**	C+	B-	21	2.30	8.3	4.7	3.9	35.8	**10.0**	12.2	25.6
WEST CENTRAL BANK	ASHLAND	IL	**B-**	B+	B+	131	3.30	9.4	7.1	27.2	18.5	**8.7**	10.1	15.4
WEST CENTRAL GEORGIA	THOMASTON	GA	**A**	A	A	108	5.45	2.5	8.5	22.5	31.1	**10.0**	21.0	35.2
▲WEST CHESTER SB	WASHINGTON	IA	**C-**	C	B+	48	-0.36	10.8	5.1	21.9	27.7	**6.7**	8.7	13.7
▲WEST COAST BANK	LAKE OSWEGO	OR	**D+**	D-	D	2,456	-10.01	9.3	0.6	4.1	26.2	**10.0**	12.5	18.1
WEST END BANK SB	RICHMOND	IN	**C-**	C-	C-	216	13.61	1.2	24.6	28.0	19.1	**6.0**	8.0	13.2
WEST GATE BANK	LINCOLN	NE	**D+**	C	C	294	3.88	8.0	1.1	8.2	4.1	**5.3**	9.3	11.3
▼WEST IOWA BANK	WEST BEND	IA	**B**	B	B	87	0.13	8.1	1.8	9.5	22.8	**8.0**	10.1	13.4
WEST LIBERTY STATE BK	WEST LIBERTY	IA	**C+**	D+	C+	78	-6.94	2.9	1.6	8.8	52.0	**8.6**	10.1	21.6
WEST MICHIGAN BANK &	FRANKFORT	MI	**B-**	B	B	39	5.22	1.4	0.5	8.0	73.7	**10.0**	19.6	64.5
▲WEST MICHIGAN COMMUNITY	HUDSONVILLE	MI	**E+**	E-	D-	123	-17.02	14.3	3.4	12.2	12.3	**5.0**	7.5	11.0
WEST MICHIGAN SB	BANGOR	MI	**C-**	C+	B-	38	11.85	3.6	2.0	23.3	35.1	**9.3**	10.5	24.8
WEST MILTON STATE BK	WEST MILTON	PA	**C+**	C+	C+	311	4.91	3.3	3.9	9.9	56.2	**5.0**	7.0	14.2
▼WEST ONE BANK	KALISPELL	MT	**C-**	C+	B-	49	-16.79	8.1	9.2	15.3	0.0	**10.0**	12.4	16.9
WEST PLAINS BANK	AINSWORTH	NE	**B+**	B	B+	83	0.94	14.5	1.8	0.7	32.8	**10.0**	11.9	17.1
WEST PLAINS BANK & TRUST	WEST PLAINS	MO	**B+**	B+	B+	286	1.99	7.5	2.5	15.5	27.1	**6.8**	8.8	13.9
WEST PLAINS SAVINGS & LOA	WEST PLAINS	MO	**B**	B	B+	85	5.80	0.0	1.3	63.0	26.7	**10.0**	14.4	34.1
▲WEST POINT BANK	RADCLIFF	KY	**A-**	B+	A-	129	11.44	1.0	1.5	37.4	31.1	**9.4**	10.6	26.5
WEST POINTE BANK	OSHKOSH	WI	**C**	D+	B-	409	-11.46	20.6	0.6	22.6	7.9	**6.7**	8.7	12.6
WEST SHORE BANK	LUDINGTON	MI	**C**	C	C+	335	-0.07	3.0	5.6	29.2	24.3	**6.6**	8.7	15.2
WEST SIDE BANK & TRUST	FORT WORTH	TX	**D+**	D+	C+	50	-0.21	13.0	1.1	11.4	0.0	**10.0**	11.2	16.6
▼WEST SUBURBAN BANK	LOMBARD	IL	**D**	C-	B-	1,961	1.45	9.0	0.7	11.7	37.8	**5.9**	7.9	12.9
WEST TEXAS NATIONAL BK	MIDLAND	TX	**C-**	C+	B-	586	6.13	19.1	4.7	4.3	13.6	**8.1**	9.7	15.9
WEST TEXAS STATE BK	ODESSA	TX	**A-**	A-	B+	271	-0.71	36.5	3.5	5.8	25.5	**10.0**	11.3	15.4
WEST TEXAS STATE BK	SNYDER	TX	**B-**	B+	B	134	1.73	11.0	7.6	11.2	23.7	**7.9**	9.6	13.3
▲WEST TOWN SB	CICERO	IL	**D+**	D-	E+	111	26.20	3.2	2.2	56.8	5.4	**6.7**	8.7	13.9
WEST UNION BANK	WEST UNION	WV	**B-**	B-	B	109	6.15	9.0	10.6	22.0	23.9	**9.7**	10.8	17.1
WEST VALLEY NATIONAL BK	AVONDALE	AZ	**D**	D	D	35	-7.01	14.0	0.3	8.0	7.8	**10.0**	34.1	45.4
WEST VIEW SB	PITTSBURGH	PA	**C-**	C	C	273	-30.32	1.2	0.1	6.8	72.3	**8.2**	9.8	16.0
WESTAMERICA BANK	SAN RAFAEL	CA	**B-**	B	B-	4,893	-0.96	7.7	10.0	6.9	25.8	**6.2**	8.2	15.3
WESTBOUND BANK	KATY	TX	**D+**	C-	C	157	-1.22	10.3	1.3	3.6	10.2	**10.0**	13.3	17.1
WESTBURY BANK	WEST BEND	WI	**D**	D	C-	625	-2.80	9.1	1.5	27.6	11.3	**6.1**	8.1	12.4
WESTCHESTER BANK	YONKERS	NY	**D**	C	C	206	53.09	24.6	1.1	3.3	25.2	**6.8**	8.8	14.2
WESTERN BANK	SAINT PAUL	MN	**B-**	B-	B-	358	3.24	15.9	0.5	7.7	10.8	**10.0**	12.7	16.8
WESTERN BANK	ALAMOGORDO	NM	**B**	B+	B+	72	-8.37	2.7	2.4	20.2	26.8	**10.0**	12.9	27.0
WESTERN BANK	LORDSBURG	NM	**A**	A-	B+	129	7.44	6.2	5.2	7.7	27.9	**10.0**	12.8	21.6
WESTERN BANK	COAHOMA	TX	**C-**	C	C-	192	-2.78	13.1	6.1	15.6	10.1	**6.7**	8.9	12.3
WESTERN BANK OF CLOVIS	CLOVIS	NM	**B**	B	B	53	15.60	11.6	2.8	7.9	17.8	**10.0**	11.8	15.6

Asset Quality Index	Non-Performing Loans as a % of Total Loans	Non-Performing Loans as a % of Capital	Net Charge-offs Avg Loans	Profitability Index	Net Income ($Mil)	Return on Assets (R.O.A.)	Return on Equity (R.O.E.)	Net Interest Spread	Overhead Efficiency Ratio	Liquidity Index	Liquidity Ratio	Hot Money Ratio	Stability Index
8.7	0.00	0.0	0.00	**2.9**	0.6	0.33	2.63	3.24	75.2	**4.0**	71.6	24.5	**1.7**
4.9	1.24	7.3	0.42	**8.2**	3.4	1.68	18.02	5.25	60.7	**0.8**	18.4	40.8	**8.0**
4.8	2.25	13.6	0.88	**8.3**	0.4	1.72	16.56	4.84	60.5	**4.1**	28.4	9.1	**4.3**
5.2	0.97	8.8	0.24	**4.9**	2.2	0.85	11.10	4.27	57.4	**1.0**	16.1	32.5	**4.6**
7.5	0.22	1.4	0.28	**4.3**	1.7	1.06	11.77	4.14	73.7	**2.9**	23.1	15.3	**3.5**
10.0	0.00	0.0	0.00	**8.9**	3.7	5.19	17.58	-1,468.00	97.4	**0.0**	0.2	101.0	**6.7**
6.1	1.59	10.6	0.05	**9.6**	2.0	2.46	32.87	4.32	49.1	**2.0**	20.6	19.8	**5.5**
6.5	0.00	0.0	0.00	**6.7**	18.8	6.89	8.20	0.25	84.8	**3.9**	119.5	85.5	**2.3**
0.3	4.81	31.9	2.06	**6.2**	10,712.0	1.02	9.53	4.28	55.8	**4.6**	18.9	5.5	**8.7**
3.1	1.07	6.1	5.31	**6.3**	355.0	1.95	25.65	5.17	15.9	**6.1**	29.0	2.2	**5.9**
0.3	4.92	34.9	1.64	**8.8**	569.0	1.41	16.63	4.05	9.1	**4.3**	0.1	4.5	**5.3**
7.6	0.00	0.0	0.00	**1.2**	0.0	0.04	0.15	0.16	63.9	**5.2**	749.3	78.9	**3.4**
7.8	0.00	0.0	0.00	**7.6**	7.1	1.43	1.51	0.34	24.1	**5.0**	279.0	101.0	**2.3**
2.5	1.63	7.8	5.66	**10.0**	123.1	3.37	27.45	12.95	21.5	**5.0**	0.3	0.0	**6.5**
3.2	1.26	9.0	0.15	**4.2**	2.2	0.86	8.74	3.94	65.6	**3.3**	16.6	12.7	**5.4**
5.2	1.28	7.6	0.21	**3.2**	0.7	0.46	4.23	4.73	86.3	**2.8**	26.2	16.4	**6.3**
5.4	0.70	3.9	0.16	**4.9**	0.4	1.13	12.70	4.56	74.8	**4.7**	36.0	10.1	**4.3**
4.0	1.12	9.8	0.69	**4.9**	0.7	1.09	13.08	4.56	65.2	**3.1**	17.5	13.8	**4.6**
6.5	2.82	9.1	1.84	**3.0**	0.2	0.51	3.75	3.85	84.1	**5.9**	49.6	6.5	**6.3**
1.7	1.57	11.3	1.28	**3.8**	38.4	0.71	5.63	3.72	62.2	**2.0**	18.5	19.8	**7.7**
2.1	3.15	17.8	1.18	**2.3**	3.0	0.52	4.93	3.35	72.8	**1.1**	17.7	30.7	**5.7**
5.6	0.91	4.8	0.63	**3.8**	13.5	0.87	9.28	3.12	48.5	**1.7**	15.3	22.6	**6.5**
8.9	0.00	0.0	-0.03	**2.8**	0.1	0.26	2.04	4.13	92.7	**2.9**	50.0	21.5	**5.5**
5.3	0.46	3.0	0.17	**3.7**	0.8	0.66	5.59	3.68	84.4	**2.3**	22.3	18.2	**8.0**
8.5	0.26	0.7	0.13	**8.0**	1.6	1.53	7.46	4.96	57.5	**2.6**	27.8	17.9	**9.1**
3.7	1.66	10.3	2.18	**1.4**	-0.1	-0.17	-1.77	4.18	72.0	**3.6**	31.6	14.1	**5.3**
2.8	3.80	16.7	1.05	**1.3**	4.2	0.17	1.39	3.61	77.3	**4.5**	14.8	6.1	**5.7**
2.3	1.69	13.7	0.48	**2.3**	0.5	0.25	2.96	3.59	76.7	**2.1**	24.9	19.6	**3.2**
2.0	1.61	11.7	0.71	**4.2**	2.6	0.98	10.44	3.90	66.7	**2.1**	17.9	18.7	**5.7**
4.0	1.33	8.2	0.19	**7.3**	1.2	1.35	12.36	4.37	49.0	**2.0**	24.2	20.3	**6.8**
3.7	3.33	10.8	1.49	**2.8**	0.7	0.90	6.47	3.34	83.3	**3.8**	47.8	17.4	**4.5**
9.1	3.89	3.5	0.42	**2.9**	0.2	0.48	2.36	2.95	86.3	**5.5**	86.0	14.6	**8.0**
1.3	3.71	25.8	0.54	**0.0**	-0.9	-0.63	-9.06	3.62	90.4	**1.8**	19.3	21.7	**1.9**
3.9	3.99	14.8	0.51	**1.6**	0.0	-0.08	-0.72	4.69	98.7	**5.2**	65.8	13.2	**6.2**
8.0	0.22	1.0	0.07	**5.6**	2.9	0.95	13.05	3.50	52.5	**4.9**	44.6	11.8	**3.8**
3.6	4.31	22.1	2.41	**1.3**	-0.4	-0.69	-6.20	3.90	73.1	**1.3**	18.0	28.2	**5.6**
6.7	0.71	3.2	-0.67	**5.8**	1.0	1.27	10.29	4.23	65.0	**3.9**	28.7	11.7	**6.4**
7.1	0.74	4.8	0.14	**6.3**	3.9	1.45	15.96	3.80	59.3	**2.0**	12.1	18.5	**6.6**
7.1	1.35	6.1	0.03	**3.9**	0.6	0.74	5.12	3.01	52.2	**1.9**	34.7	31.6	**7.8**
5.4	1.87	8.7	0.76	**5.0**	1.1	0.87	7.96	4.04	56.2	**4.4**	17.9	6.2	**6.8**
4.7	0.48	3.5	0.49	**3.2**	1.7	0.38	4.55	3.87	31.9	**0.4**	12.2	78.4	**4.1**
2.9	2.13	14.2	0.71	**3.7**	2.3	0.69	7.87	3.70	69.5	**1.4**	10.6	25.1	**4.7**
0.3	6.80	39.8	0.31	**0.7**	-0.1	-0.15	-0.87	3.81	100.8	**0.9**	20.7	40.5	**4.4**
0.3	7.77	44.4	1.44	**2.1**	3.4	0.17	2.25	3.44	71.3	**5.9**	39.3	7.3	**5.5**
2.8	1.39	7.1	0.75	**4.6**	-6.5	-1.20	-11.87	4.46	63.7	**5.0**	46.5	11.5	**7.0**
5.0	1.25	6.4	0.06	**7.0**	5.3	1.98	17.21	3.93	62.4	**3.4**	36.2	16.7	**8.1**
4.1	1.79	10.3	0.22	**7.3**	2.4	1.89	19.16	4.38	57.6	**3.2**	25.8	14.1	**7.2**
1.6	4.04	35.8	0.34	**5.6**	2.2	2.17	24.28	3.86	82.6	**0.9**	10.0	32.5	**2.6**
4.1	1.71	9.9	0.09	**3.6**	0.7	0.61	5.39	4.39	84.2	**3.9**	18.0	9.7	**6.6**
2.0	9.10	18.1	3.82	**0.0**	-2.1	-5.76	-15.88	4.73	183.5	**3.2**	22.9	13.9	**1.7**
6.4	4.33	8.2	0.00	**2.3**	0.4	0.12	1.59	1.18	83.7	**3.8**	65.8	25.7	**4.1**
3.4	2.07	14.0	0.56	**10.0**	96.7	2.01	18.18	5.29	46.5	**3.1**	15.9	14.0	**10.0**
0.6	8.08	39.0	0.47	**1.6**	0.6	0.37	2.85	3.62	83.8	**1.1**	18.0	30.8	**2.6**
0.7	4.33	35.2	0.27	**1.0**	-1.3	-0.21	-2.41	3.39	99.0	**4.4**	21.2	7.1	**4.5**
8.8	0.04	0.2	0.06	**1.4**	1.1	0.66	7.24	3.91	81.5	**5.4**	37.7	6.4	**2.2**
4.0	2.00	11.1	0.33	**6.5**	5.4	1.52	11.81	5.40	62.0	**3.8**	18.1	10.1	**8.2**
7.4	0.15	0.6	-0.27	**4.1**	0.4	0.49	3.94	5.11	84.5	**2.4**	31.4	20.4	**6.2**
7.6	0.85	3.4	0.06	**6.8**	1.9	1.41	10.83	5.44	68.5	**3.5**	35.8	16.0	**8.9**
4.3	0.67	5.1	0.29	**2.6**	0.6	0.33	3.55	4.48	90.8	**1.3**	13.0	26.8	**3.5**
5.7	0.00	0.0	-0.02	**5.3**	0.4	0.86	7.13	4.80	71.1	**1.9**	30.2	27.0	**7.3**

Name	City	State	Rating	2008 Rating	2007 Rating	Total Assets ($Mil)	One Year Asset Growth	Asset Mix (As a % of Total Assets) Commercial Loans	Consumer Loans	Home Mortgages	Securities	Capitalization Index	Leverage Ratio	Risk-based Capital Ratio
WESTERN BANK OF WOLF	WOLF POINT	MT	C+	C	C+	68	1.78	3.3	3.8	4.9	37.7	7.5	9.3	17.4
▼ WESTERN BK ARTESIA NEW	ARTESIA	NM	C+	B-	A-	165	14.76	21.5	4.5	2.4	30.3	6.9	8.9	13.4
▼ WESTERN CAPITAL BANK	BOISE	ID	D	C	C	96	22.40	23.4	0.1	0.2	18.9	10.0	36.2	41.1
WESTERN COMMERCE BANK	CARLSBAD	NM	A	A	A	332	5.55	10.0	0.9	11.2	29.5	8.6	10.1	18.3
WESTERN COMMUNITY BANK	OREM	UT	D-	E-	D-	110	-2.92	3.6	1.8	11.3	0.1	9.0	10.4	15.1
▼ WESTERN DAKOTA BANK	TIMBER LAKE	SD	D+	C-	C-	30	11.73	6.1	3.5	1.6	6.0	5.2	7.2	15.9
WESTERN HERITAGE BANK	LAS CRUCES	NM	D	D-	D-	59	39.09	19.7	4.1	9.0	8.6	8.8	10.2	15.4
WESTERN NATIONAL BK	PHOENIX	AZ	E-	D-	C-	201	-14.98	3.5	0.2	13.4	2.7	0.0	3.6	5.6
▲ WESTERN NATIONAL BK	SUMMERFIELD	KS	D+	D+	D-	23	43.77	5.2	1.5	16.3	0.7	10.0	11.1	15.5
WESTERN NATIONAL BK	CASS LAKE	MN	C	C	C+	34	-15.21	16.6	9.6	29.2	23.3	5.3	7.3	12.8
WESTERN NATIONAL BK	DULUTH	MN	C	C	C+	121	-2.63	9.5	4.2	22.2	9.5	5.1	7.8	11.1
▲ WESTERN NATIONAL BK	ODESSA	TX	C	C-	B-	1,090	10.73	28.9	0.7	2.5	36.6	6.5	8.5	14.0
WESTERN NATIONAL TRUST	SALT LAKE CITY	UT	U	U	U	14	-0.66	0.0	0.0	0.0	0.0	10.0	97.8	390.6
WESTERN RESERVE BANK	MEDINA	OH	D-	D+	C-	191	-5.15	10.3	2.3	8.0	6.8	5.4	8.0	11.3
WESTERN SECURITY BANK	BILLINGS	MT	C+	B-	B+	767	22.74	8.2	1.7	5.5	44.9	7.3	9.2	16.6
WESTERN SPRINGS NB&T	WESTERN SPRINGS	IL	E-	D-	D-	187	-19.75	4.4	1.4	16.2	2.2	0.0	1.7	3.5
WESTERN STATE BK	GARDEN CITY	KS	B+	B-	B-	425	7.76	9.1	0.9	5.1	19.9	8.6	10.1	17.6
▲ WESTERN STATE BK	DEVILS LAKE	ND	C	D+	B-	420	0.83	23.8	3.5	7.4	8.1	7.5	9.7	12.9
WESTFIELD BANK	WESTFIELD	MA	B-	B	B	1,232	4.87	11.0	0.2	10.9	52.1	10.0	17.4	32.7
WESTFIELD BANK FSB	WESTFIELD CENTER	OH	C	C+	C+	540	11.84	17.9	9.3	15.3	28.7	6.1	8.1	13.2
WESTMORELAND FS&LA	LATROBE	PA	B	B	A-	169	3.95	0.0	0.0	53.7	8.6	10.0	22.0	65.1
▼ WESTSIDE BANK	HIRAM	GA	E-	D-	D	139	-7.93	2.3	0.5	6.6	11.7	1.8	5.8	8.8
WESTSIDE COMMUNITY BANK	UNIVERSITY PLACE	WA	E-	D-	D	148	-8.27	16.3	1.1	8.6	2.3	3.2	7.5	10.1
WESTSIDE STATE BK	WESTSIDE	IA	B-	B-	C+	69	7.82	9.3	2.8	18.7	17.0	6.0	8.0	13.8
▲ WEYMOUTH BANK	EAST WEYMOUTH	MA	C	C-	C+	196	11.53	3.9	0.8	34.5	16.8	6.1	8.1	14.4
▼ WHEATLAND BANK	SPOKANE	WA	C	B-	B-	262	8.82	8.3	0.8	4.5	9.2	8.4	10.0	14.8
▲ WHEATON BANK & TRUST CO	WHEATON	IL	D+	C-	C-	735	64.51	14.2	6.3	4.1	9.7	6.1	8.1	13.8
WHEATON COLLEGE TRUST	WHEATON	IL	U	U	U	3	-0.22	0.0	0.0	0.0	95.3	10.0	96.2	2,094.6
WHEELER COUNTY STATE BK	ALAMO	GA	C+	C	C+	108	0.90	18.8	10.4	18.0	7.3	10.0	11.4	18.7
▼ WHIDBEY ISLAND BANK	OAK HARBOR	WA	B-	A-	B+	1,704	63.19	5.9	6.7	6.9	11.6	10.0	11.3	20.8
▼ WHITAKER BANK	LEXINGTON	KY	C+	B-	B-	1,588	4.78	4.3	3.3	20.3	36.1	6.4	8.4	15.9
▼ WHITE HALL BANK	WHITE HALL	IL	C-	C+	C	48	3.96	13.7	2.3	18.0	27.0	3.8	8.1	10.4
WHITE OAK STATE BK	WHITE OAK	TX	C	C	D+	78	2.75	11.4	9.3	31.8	0.0	4.6	6.6	12.0
▲ WHITE ROCK BANK	CANNON FALLS	MN	D+	E+	D-	144	-4.05	8.8	3.0	8.0	8.0	4.4	7.5	10.7
WHITE STATE BK	SOUTH ENGLISH	IA	B	B	B	29	-2.93	12.3	2.5	11.8	25.2	10.0	12.3	20.9
▼ WHITESVILLE STATE BK	WHITESVILLE	WV	C+	B-	B+	72	6.22	1.8	9.0	19.0	45.8	8.3	9.9	17.0
WHITNEY NATIONAL BK	NEW ORLEANS	LA	D-	D-	D+	11,781	-0.81	22.2	1.9	8.6	21.7	6.2	8.2	13.3
WILBER NATIONAL BK	ONEONTA	NY	D+	C+	B-	869	-4.14	6.7	6.3	12.8	30.9	6.4	8.5	14.5
WILBURTON STATE BK	WILBURTON	OK	B-	C+	C+	61	0.16	8.7	9.3	17.0	32.5	4.9	6.9	13.3
WILCOX COUNTY STATE BK	ABBEVILLE	GA	B-	B-	C+	68	26.75	5.4	6.8	36.3	17.5	6.9	9.0	15.1
WILKINSON COUNTY BANK	IRWINTON	GA	B+	B+	B+	52	7.22	12.8	5.2	20.4	29.9	10.0	12.8	24.9
WILLAMETTE COMMUNITY	ALBANY	OR	C	C	C	85	16.98	12.6	0.8	6.6	14.9	6.2	8.2	12.2
▲ WILLAMETTE VALLEY BANK	SALEM	OR	C	C-	C+	144	3.22	3.1	0.3	18.5	2.0	10.0	11.0	16.8
WILLIAM PENN BANK FSB	LEVITTOWN	PA	B	B	B	319	0.27	0.7	0.2	47.8	14.7	10.0	15.0	25.5
WILLIAMSTOWN BANK INC	WILLIAMSTOWN	WV	B+	B	B	125	11.23	4.2	8.9	38.0	10.4	9.1	10.4	15.4
WILLIAMSTOWN SB	WILLIAMSTOWN	MA	C-	C	C-	228	-5.87	3.3	0.3	30.8	34.0	5.5	7.5	12.5
▼ WILLIAMSVILLE STATE BK &	WILLIAMSVILLE	IL	C-	C	C	110	5.45	7.4	3.1	26.0	46.8	9.4	10.6	24.7
WILMINGTON SAVINGS FUND	WILMINGTON	DE	C	C-	B	3,921	5.55	15.6	0.7	15.1	19.5	7.7	9.5	13.6
WILMINGTON SB	WILMINGTON	OH	D+	C-	C	214	3.12	6.7	4.0	45.9	0.0	10.0	16.1	23.7
WILMINGTON TRUST CO	WILMINGTON	DE	D-	D	C+	9,285	-3.38	13.1	6.5	6.3	5.6	4.2	7.6	10.6
WILMINGTON TRUST FSB	BALTIMORE	MD	D-	D	C-	1,874	-14.80	14.4	9.9	8.7	3.5	5.3	7.3	13.3
WILSHIRE STATE BK	LOS ANGELES	CA	D	C	B+	2,976	-13.30	11.1	0.5	2.2	10.6	7.7	9.5	14.3
▼ WILSON & MUIR BANK & TRUS	BARDSTOWN	KY	B-	B+	B-	404	2.06	11.6	3.3	19.4	17.2	6.6	8.6	13.4
WILSON BANK & TRUST	LEBANON	TN	C	B-	B	1,484	2.31	3.9	3.2	25.2	19.6	7.5	9.4	12.9
WILSON STATE BK	WILSON	KS	B	B-	C	65	65.93	18.9	4.7	19.5	16.1	7.4	9.3	13.1
WILTON BANK	WILTON	CT	D	D	D	84	-11.61	5.5	0.7	3.5	9.6	10.0	14.1	20.8
WINCHESTER CO-OP BANK	WINCHESTER	MA	B-	B	B	488	10.71	0.0	0.5	57.3	18.2	9.7	10.8	25.2
WINCHESTER FEDERAL BANK	WINCHESTER	KY	C+	B-	B-	171	-0.52	0.6	0.1	55.2	1.3	7.3	9.2	17.4
WINCHESTER SB	WINCHESTER	MA	C	C	C+	531	3.31	0.8	0.2	40.3	25.5	9.0	10.4	20.5
▼ WINDSOR FS&LA	WINDSOR	CT	C+	B-	B	370	3.41	5.8	0.3	33.7	28.1	8.3	9.9	17.9

Asset Quality Index	Non-Performing Loans as a % of Total Loans	Non-Performing Loans as a % of Capital	Net Charge-offs Avg Loans	Profitability Index	Net Income ($Mil)	Return on Assets (R.O.A.)	Return on Equity (R.O.E.)	Net Interest Spread	Overhead Efficiency Ratio	Liquidity Index	Liquidity Ratio	Hot Money Ratio	Stability Index
3.9	2.94	12.3	0.27	**5.9**	0.9	1.43	13.97	4.37	62.7	**2.9**	32.9	18.2	**5.5**
3.1	2.81	14.4	0.14	**8.8**	2.9	2.01	19.49	4.36	50.3	**4.7**	55.9	15.4	**5.9**
7.6	0.07	0.1	-0.12	**0.6**	-0.1	-0.06	-0.17	4.20	99.0	**4.3**	60.2	16.6	**2.1**
7.8	0.02	0.1	0.13	**9.9**	7.1	2.26	23.09	4.90	56.9	**2.5**	33.7	21.0	**8.1**
0.0	11.93	60.7	4.72	**0.0**	-5.1	-4.52	-46.35	4.32	213.5	**1.7**	22.5	23.3	**4.3**
8.5	0.22	0.9	0.10	**1.9**	0.1	0.20	2.33	5.26	93.9	**5.7**	69.9	11.5	**3.3**
8.5	0.00	0.0	0.01	**1.2**	0.1	0.16	1.74	4.74	91.2	**3.7**	38.9	15.9	**2.6**
0.0	8.64	91.3	4.77	**0.0**	-11.7	-5.17	-90.93	3.56	116.4	**0.5**	8.9	54.1	**2.7**
6.2	0.00	0.0	0.04	**0.9**	0.0	0.17	1.03	3.30	83.0	**1.4**	19.3	26.5	**5.9**
2.6	1.54	12.6	0.06	**6.0**	0.5	1.27	15.91	5.37	65.3	**1.4**	10.5	24.7	**5.6**
4.5	1.03	8.6	0.46	**3.6**	0.8	0.66	6.74	4.07	66.7	**0.9**	19.1	36.4	**5.6**
2.9	2.66	15.7	0.16	**7.2**	18.4	1.92	22.54	3.77	51.8	**3.3**	35.9	20.1	**7.0**
10.0	0.00	0.0	0.00	**1.0**	-0.1	-0.90	-0.92	0.68	105.5	**5.0**	2,508.2	101.0	**4.2**
0.0	4.73	36.7	1.63	**0.4**	-1.9	-0.93	-10.59	3.51	73.9	**1.3**	12.0	26.5	**4.3**
3.8	2.03	8.7	0.67	**6.9**	8.5	1.30	9.81	3.89	57.3	**2.8**	51.7	31.3	**7.2**
0.0	19.25	300.7	5.66	**0.0**	-12.2	-5.75	-129.78	3.13	115.4	**1.5**	13.4	23.8	**2.9**
5.3	0.99	4.7	0.53	**5.4**	4.4	1.08	9.83	3.81	61.9	**2.6**	33.3	19.8	**8.0**
3.0	1.30	9.6	1.02	**4.1**	4.1	1.01	10.66	5.32	61.0	**2.8**	11.6	14.8	**4.7**
7.8	0.63	1.4	2.01	**3.3**	5.9	0.49	2.60	2.57	59.2	**5.0**	63.9	16.6	**8.4**
2.8	1.22	8.3	0.11	**3.5**	2.3	0.46	5.38	2.95	67.2	**2.5**	37.4	24.4	**4.9**
7.4	2.94	7.1	0.00	**4.1**	1.3	0.81	3.65	2.87	47.2	**6.5**	58.0	5.7	**8.2**
0.0	19.16	177.4	1.86	**0.0**	-4.1	-2.75	-37.00	2.09	166.9	**0.7**	16.5	50.7	**0.0**
0.0	20.93	168.6	2.02	**0.0**	-1.1	-0.71	-9.21	3.19	79.4	**1.7**	13.7	21.8	**2.8**
7.8	0.21	1.6	0.05	**7.9**	1.1	1.66	18.25	4.76	55.4	**2.6**	25.7	17.2	**7.5**
2.9	1.35	10.8	0.29	**3.6**	0.9	0.50	6.05	3.67	75.3	**2.2**	28.6	20.9	**3.4**
1.7	2.51	14.5	0.37	**3.4**	1.1	0.44	4.51	4.41	82.0	**5.2**	34.3	6.3	**5.4**
0.6	3.75	29.1	0.65	**6.2**	16.9	2.44	23.70	3.10	26.7	**1.5**	11.1	24.0	**5.4**
10.0	0.00	0.0	0.00	**2.0**	0.0	0.00	0.00	0.41	100.0	**5.0**	3,069.3	101.0	**4.0**
2.9	3.55	19.7	1.24	**3.1**	0.5	0.43	3.82	3.91	63.6	**1.3**	30.0	39.2	**5.5**
2.5	3.70	20.8	0.89	**8.4**	26.1	1.73	13.73	5.05	48.1	**1.8**	12.5	20.3	**8.2**
4.7	1.84	11.0	0.65	**2.9**	6.5	0.41	4.34	3.67	77.6	**1.8**	22.1	26.5	**6.5**
2.9	2.46	17.6	1.20	**3.8**	0.5	0.95	11.08	3.92	65.8	**2.9**	31.3	17.6	**4.1**
8.1	0.07	0.7	0.15	**5.8**	0.7	0.95	14.13	4.64	70.6	**1.2**	24.7	32.4	**3.7**
1.5	4.07	33.8	0.00	**4.5**	0.7	3.97	75.10	7.15	38.4	**2.2**	23.6	18.8	**4.3**
7.6	0.00	0.0	0.00	**9.5**	0.5	1.58	10.33	4.23	44.0	**5.1**	46.6	10.7	**6.3**
7.9	0.83	2.9	0.53	**3.3**	0.4	0.50	4.81	3.64	90.1	**3.4**	54.2	20.5	**5.2**
0.7	4.18	27.4	4.04	**0.0**	-135.3	-1.17	-9.30	4.13	83.3	**4.0**	17.5	9.5	**7.3**
1.9	3.74	23.2	0.50	**3.7**	7.3	0.79	9.69	3.66	74.7	**2.6**	14.5	15.7	**5.7**
8.2	0.14	0.9	0.22	**9.3**	1.3	2.15	25.74	4.66	56.0	**2.6**	44.1	27.5	**6.6**
4.4	0.90	6.0	-0.03	**5.6**	0.6	1.02	10.42	4.66	72.5	**1.0**	20.0	33.5	**5.3**
6.0	2.79	11.1	0.05	**4.4**	0.3	0.56	4.28	4.17	65.5	**1.9**	33.2	29.8	**7.4**
7.2	0.08	0.6	0.12	**2.5**	0.2	0.24	2.73	4.02	85.2	**2.4**	32.8	21.0	**4.8**
3.6	1.75	9.8	0.74	**2.9**	0.5	0.33	2.98	4.13	86.4	**2.2**	29.8	22.1	**5.0**
7.6	1.23	5.9	0.09	**4.7**	3.3	1.04	7.13	3.01	44.2	**1.9**	24.9	21.8	**8.1**
6.9	0.07	0.5	0.12	**5.4**	1.2	1.01	9.83	4.77	65.8	**3.8**	21.9	10.5	**5.0**
1.7	3.13	20.3	0.30	**2.4**	0.3	0.13	1.65	2.28	88.0	**4.3**	21.0	7.6	**3.5**
5.5	2.09	8.1	0.27	**2.2**	0.3	0.30	2.76	3.23	87.5	**4.1**	54.8	18.0	**6.0**
3.5	2.56	15.8	0.97	**2.7**	13.4	0.35	3.78	3.63	64.1	**3.1**	32.4	20.3	**6.3**
0.8	6.45	29.7	3.35	**0.9**	-3.4	-1.61	-9.21	3.98	51.0	**0.6**	10.0	51.3	**7.0**
0.0	15.64	94.1	6.45	**1.0**	-655.2	-7.14	-73.77	3.17	86.8	**1.7**	24.5	30.6	**5.6**
0.0	8.49	43.2	1.47	**0.0**	-32.3	-1.65	-12.56	2.30	90.0	**7.3**	48.2	0.9	**4.4**
0.9	2.31	14.2	3.60	**1.9**	-22.4	-0.67	-6.77	3.71	45.0	**1.0**	2.9	28.3	**8.0**
3.2	1.96	14.1	0.38	**8.1**	6.9	1.80	19.83	4.55	60.0	**3.1**	18.2	14.1	**7.3**
3.5	2.24	15.3	0.84	**4.3**	9.3	0.62	6.60	3.67	54.4	**1.6**	13.3	24.0	**8.1**
7.6	0.08	0.6	0.04	**6.5**	0.8	1.35	10.41	4.84	66.8	**3.8**	21.4	10.8	**6.3**
0.0	39.15	142.4	2.29	**0.8**	-1.5	-1.66	-10.83	2.72	159.5	**3.4**	26.2	13.3	**5.9**
3.5	3.29	19.3	0.01	**4.9**	4.2	0.88	8.16	2.92	49.3	**1.7**	37.0	41.8	**6.4**
5.5	0.75	6.1	0.44	**3.6**	0.8	0.48	5.14	2.48	55.5	**1.0**	18.0	33.4	**5.0**
8.0	0.86	4.8	-0.01	**2.8**	1.9	0.36	3.57	2.82	78.5	**3.7**	39.5	16.4	**6.7**
3.9	1.54	8.6	0.60	**3.9**	2.4	0.67	6.57	3.37	64.1	**3.9**	40.0	15.7	**6.3**

Name	City	State	Rating	2008 Rating	2007 Rating	Total Assets ($Mil)	One Year Asset Growth	Asset Mix (As a % of Total Assets) Comm-ercial Loans	Cons-umer Loans	Home Mort-gages	Secur-ities	Capital-ization Index	Leverage Ratio	Risk-based Capital Ratio
▼ WINFIELD COMMUNITY BANK	WINFIELD	IL	**E-**	D-	D+	68	-4.23	6.1	0.4	8.2	7.8	**1.8**	5.1	8.8
WINNSBORO STATE BK &	WINNSBORO	LA	**B+**	B+	B	120	8.89	4.9	9.0	7.7	36.7	**7.7**	9.5	18.4
WINONA NATIONAL BK	WINONA	MN	**D**	C-	C	322	-6.06	11.6	1.9	6.7	41.8	**6.8**	8.8	14.4
WINSIDE STATE BK	WINSIDE	NE	**B**	B	B	21	-0.04	2.0	4.0	3.7	33.7	**10.0**	20.6	27.4
WINTER HILL BANK FSB	SOMERVILLE	MA	**C**	C	NR	262	0.39	0.0	0.6	28.6	17.3	**7.6**	9.4	18.1
▲ WINTHROP STATE BK	WINTHROP	MN	**B-**	B-	C+	19	-0.39	2.3	5.2	9.2	39.8	**10.0**	11.9	33.9
WISCONSIN COMMUNITY	MADISON	WI	**C-**	C-	C	474	5.86	21.9	0.5	6.7	20.8	**7.8**	9.6	13.5
WOLF RIVER COMMUNITY	HORTONVILLE	WI	**C+**	C	C+	119	2.28	8.3	3.6	31.6	16.2	**9.2**	10.9	14.3
WOLVERINE BANK FSB	MIDLAND	MI	**D+**	C+	NR	314	3.16	3.3	0.4	36.0	0.1	**10.0**	13.3	20.2
▲ WOOD & HUSTON BANK	MARSHALL	MO	**C**	B-	B	479	-3.25	9.7	2.3	23.0	7.7	**8.0**	9.7	13.8
WOOD COUNTY NATIONAL BK	QUITMAN	TX	**B-**	B-	B-	65	0.52	2.6	11.1	32.1	9.7	**8.9**	10.3	18.3
▼ WOODBURY BANKING CO	WOODBURY	GA	**D-**	D	C-	29	-10.00	1.8	8.4	22.8	27.9	**5.5**	7.5	13.7
WOODFORD STATE BK	WOODFORD	WI	**C-**	C-	C+	190	-9.20	10.7	3.5	21.0	12.5	**6.4**	8.4	12.5
WOODFOREST BANK	REFUGIO	TX	**B+**	A	NR	133	57.17	0.3	0.1	49.2	2.1	**9.2**	10.5	16.4
WOODFOREST NATIONAL BK	THE WOODLANDS	TX	**A-**	A	A-	3,218	0.78	4.4	0.4	10.0	12.2	**9.8**	10.9	20.2
WOODHAVEN NATIONAL BK	FORT WORTH	TX	**B-**	C+	B-	390	4.22	11.7	2.3	15.5	9.2	**6.2**	8.2	12.6
WOODLAND BANK	REMER	MN	**D**	D	D	109	5.61	8.7	5.9	27.9	6.4	**5.2**	7.2	11.6
WOODLANDS BANK	WILLIAMSPORT	PA	**C**	C-	D+	289	1.17	10.8	0.5	27.1	20.4	**5.5**	7.5	12.0
WOODLANDS COMMERCIAL	SALT LAKE CITY	UT	**B+**	B-	E-	2,558	-25.76	23.2	0.0	0.0	7.3	**10.0**	31.5	62.9
WOODLANDS NATIONAL BK	HINCKLEY	MN	**B-**	B	B	125	6.15	11.4	5.8	16.5	14.4	**10.0**	12.7	18.4
WOODRUFF FS&LA	WOODRUFF	SC	**C+**	C+	NR	95	7.33	0.0	0.0	48.2	7.9	**10.0**	30.8	65.0
▼ WOODSBORO BANK	WOODSBORO	MD	**D+**	C-	C	218	5.98	6.0	1.0	16.9	14.2	**6.2**	8.2	13.8
WOODSFIELD SB	WOODSFIELD	OH	**C-**	D+	C-	35	3.32	0.0	1.5	36.6	24.5	**7.6**	9.4	22.8
WOODSVILLE GUARANTY SB	WOODSVILLE	NH	**C**	C	C-	387	4.19	9.1	2.8	38.4	7.1	**6.4**	8.4	13.1
WOODTRUST BANK NA	WISCONSIN RAPIDS	WI	**B-**	C+	B+	323	-5.17	9.5	1.2	6.0	30.2	**8.0**	9.7	15.5
▲ WOORI AMERICA BANK	NEW YORK	NY	**D+**	D	C	1,039	-3.49	8.5	0.3	13.1	9.2	**9.3**	10.5	18.1
WORLD FINANCIAL CAPITAL B	SALT LAKE CITY	UT	**C-**	C-	B	539	28.66	1.2	88.5	0.0	0.9	**7.8**	14.6	13.1
WORLD FINANCIAL NETWORK	WILMINGTON	DE	**B-**	A	A	5,054	140.61	0.0	96.0	0.0	2.0	**10.0**	11.9	19.4
WORLDS FOREMOST BANK	LINCOLN	NE	**B**	A	A	2,918	259.94	0.0	96.7	0.0	0.1	**6.5**	10.2	12.2
WORTHINGTON FEDERAL	HUNTSVILLE	AL	**D**	D-	NR	170	-0.25	7.5	1.3	28.7	1.9	**6.9**	8.9	14.2
WORTHINGTON FSB FSB	WORTHINGTON	MN	**B**	B	NR	59	2.02	0.2	1.8	61.3	15.4	**10.0**	14.0	32.0
▼ WORTHINGTON NATIONAL BK	ARLINGTON	TX	**D**	C-	D-	176	-1.15	19.6	1.7	13.8	0.0	**9.3**	10.6	14.7
WPS COMMUNITY BANK FSB	MONONA	WI	**D**	C	NR	34	24.47	8.1	0.7	14.9	27.4	**10.0**	25.4	43.1
WRAY STATE BK	WRAY	CO	**C-**	C-	C+	78	11.42	8.8	6.4	4.9	15.2	**5.8**	8.1	11.6
WRENTHAM CO-OP BANK	WRENTHAM	MA	**B-**	B-	B-	107	3.10	0.2	0.4	39.3	12.8	**10.0**	12.2	34.3
WRIGHT EXPRESS FINANCIAL	MIDVALE	UT	**B**	B	B+	993	19.08	95.6	0.0	0.0	0.9	**8.6**	13.0	13.8
WSB MUNICIPAL BANK	WATERTOWN	NY	**C+**	C+	C	32	32.21	0.0	0.0	0.0	76.2	**10.0**	11.4	57.7
▼ WYOMING BANK & TRUST	CHEYENNE	WY	**C-**	B+	B+	121	24.40	8.9	1.4	8.1	11.1	**6.2**	8.2	14.1
WYOMING NATIONAL BK	RIVERTON	WY	**C-**	C-	C	109	13.85	11.2	5.4	9.4	24.3	**5.1**	7.1	11.5
WYOMING STATE BK	LARAMIE	WY	**C-**	C	C-	124	-2.49	4.2	1.7	10.2	5.3	**7.5**	9.3	15.3
▲ XENITH BANK	RICHMOND	VA	**C-**	D	C-	251	24.61	15.1	1.3	10.1	23.4	**10.0**	14.8	21.4
YADKIN VALLEY BANK & TRUS	STATESVILLE	NC	**D**	D+	B-	2,298	8.89	8.7	1.9	9.8	13.0	**4.0**	7.0	10.5
YAKIMA FS&LA	YAKIMA	WA	**A-**	B	NR	1,686	4.06	0.0	0.1	38.7	48.5	**10.0**	17.9	43.1
YAKIMA NATIONAL BK NA	YAKIMA	WA	**B-**	B-	B-	115	7.09	20.2	1.8	6.2	1.3	**6.9**	8.9	13.2
YAMPA VALLEY BANK	STEAMBOAT SPRINGS	CO	**C+**	B-	C+	167	0.83	12.7	3.7	15.6	22.2	**6.4**	8.4	12.6
YELLOWSTONE BANK	LAUREL	MT	**A**	A	A	428	0.39	17.3	1.6	8.3	14.3	**10.0**	18.0	25.9
YOAKUM NATIONAL BK	YOAKUM	TX	**A**	A	A-	164	16.54	3.1	6.3	15.9	57.6	**10.0**	11.2	27.7
▲ YORK STATE BK & TRUST CO	YORK	NE	**C**	C-	C	127	-0.37	10.2	3.4	4.0	16.2	**6.5**	8.5	12.4
YORK TRADITIONS BANK	YORK	PA	**C-**	C-	C-	239	4.42	17.4	0.3	18.6	16.8	**8.3**	10.2	13.5
▲ YOUNG AMERICANS BANK	DENVER	CO	**D-**	D-	D-	14	3.16	0.0	0.2	0.0	21.2	**5.1**	7.1	87.5
▲ YOUR COMMUNITY BANK	NEW ALBANY	IN	**C-**	D+	C-	665	-3.76	13.7	0.6	11.8	27.4	**8.0**	9.6	15.0
YUKON NATIONAL BK	YUKON	OK	**C+**	C+	C	209	3.03	6.6	3.6	22.7	36.5	**5.8**	7.8	13.6
ZAPATA NATIONAL BK	ZAPATA	TX	**A-**	B+	B+	109	-5.69	2.4	4.5	17.9	42.6	**6.9**	9.0	23.1
ZAVALA COUNTY BANK	CRYSTAL CITY	TX	**B+**	B+	B+	58	2.86	2.9	6.9	2.9	62.2	**9.9**	10.9	25.7
▲ ZIONS FIRST NATIONAL BK	SALT LAKE CITY	UT	**D+**	D	C+	16,168	-9.47	13.7	1.4	5.9	10.1	**7.5**	10.4	12.9

Asset Quality Index	Non-Performing Loans as a % of Total Loans	Non-Performing Loans as a % of Capital	Net Charge-offs Avg Loans	Profitability Index	Net Income ($Mil)	Return on Assets (R.O.A.)	Return on Equity (R.O.E.)	Net Interest Spread	Overhead Efficiency Ratio	Liquidity Index	Liquidity Ratio	Hot Money Ratio	Stability Index
1.5	3.03	30.2	1.48	**0.0**	-2.4	-3.40	-45.62	3.01	183.1	**1.8**	30.3	27.7	**2.0**
5.5	1.40	5.8	0.32	**8.3**	2.0	1.74	16.87	5.15	63.5	**3.2**	40.2	19.0	**6.5**
1.0	7.41	34.2	1.90	**2.2**	-0.4	-0.12	-2.21	3.48	78.4	**1.8**	30.2	28.9	**2.4**
7.1	0.00	0.0	-0.52	**5.6**	0.3	1.37	6.64	3.44	68.1	**3.6**	34.1	13.3	**8.6**
6.1	1.36	8.1	0.00	**3.0**	1.5	0.58	6.21	3.82	78.4	**4.1**	39.4	14.3	**5.5**
7.6	0.08	0.2	0.64	**2.5**	0.1	0.26	2.05	4.20	91.3	**6.8**	68.7	1.9	**7.2**
1.5	3.28	21.7	0.83	**7.5**	7.4	1.60	14.68	4.28	51.6	**4.4**	20.1	7.0	**6.0**
3.4	2.46	15.2	0.49	**5.2**	1.3	1.08	9.85	4.28	56.8	**1.9**	20.2	20.0	**6.9**
4.6	2.28	11.0	-0.07	**0.7**	-3.6	-1.16	-8.37	2.66	111.1	**1.6**	23.6	26.0	**6.9**
3.6	1.16	8.5	1.18	**5.1**	5.4	1.13	11.28	4.43	60.5	**3.5**	13.5	11.4	**6.4**
4.7	0.77	4.4	0.23	**3.8**	0.4	0.59	4.68	4.51	84.2	**3.9**	29.7	11.9	**5.2**
1.6	4.14	29.8	1.99	**0.8**	-0.2	-0.50	-5.98	3.97	84.1	**0.9**	22.1	45.2	**3.4**
2.2	2.87	21.7	1.18	**3.4**	0.4	0.21	2.54	4.21	59.5	**3.5**	18.1	11.6	**4.3**
7.4	0.03	0.1	0.00	**0.8**	-17.3	-13.45	-121.78	3.57	128.0	**5.6**	38.1	5.0	**5.9**
6.2	2.39	9.3	1.73	**9.8**	86.5	2.70	28.05	3.83	76.0	**6.2**	42.3	6.3	**9.1**
4.2	1.26	10.4	0.21	**5.8**	5.2	1.35	16.14	4.81	66.5	**2.1**	18.9	19.0	**5.1**
0.9	3.19	28.3	0.27	**2.9**	0.4	0.37	5.22	4.32	84.6	**1.8**	14.5	20.0	**2.9**
3.4	1.70	13.4	0.17	**5.1**	3.0	1.06	14.23	3.94	67.5	**2.5**	13.3	16.1	**4.7**
7.2	0.12	0.1	0.00	**8.4**	161.2	5.23	21.65	-1.28	-31.3	**3.6**	94.6	98.8	**7.0**
3.0	3.66	18.6	1.34	**3.5**	0.5	0.39	2.67	4.98	71.8	**3.4**	15.7	11.9	**6.6**
5.2	2.68	5.1	0.11	**3.0**	0.5	0.58	1.85	2.94	71.9	**2.5**	45.9	30.1	**7.2**
1.7	4.88	33.1	0.39	**2.0**	0.6	0.27	3.20	3.92	86.4	**3.0**	33.2	17.9	**4.6**
4.2	3.32	14.2	0.04	**2.6**	0.2	0.42	4.50	3.30	81.8	**4.4**	58.2	16.1	**3.7**
2.7	0.81	7.3	0.43	**3.5**	1.9	0.52	6.01	3.64	78.1	**2.8**	12.9	14.6	**4.6**
3.2	1.75	8.4	0.09	**8.0**	7.0	2.16	20.11	3.24	58.7	**5.7**	42.0	6.0	**7.3**
2.2	2.14	11.1	6.26	**0.1**	-76.1	-7.07	-72.32	3.61	145.8	**4.4**	35.4	14.5	**7.8**
1.3	2.53	10.8	7.85	**10.0**	11.2	2.64	18.98	19.13	31.9	**0.1**	7.1	99.2	**8.0**
2.4	3.46	16.1	8.90	**10.0**	209.0	4.20	37.43	21.49	40.4	**0.1**	1.7	97.0	**9.3**
5.4	0.60	4.2	3.72	**7.6**	32.0	1.07	13.98	6.38	72.9	**0.1**	4.0	98.9	**9.3**
1.1	3.48	27.4	0.07	**1.4**	0.4	0.22	2.14	3.29	78.5	**1.3**	19.9	28.5	**4.0**
9.6	0.10	0.5	0.00	**3.9**	0.4	0.71	5.19	3.22	64.1	**5.2**	34.8	6.3	**7.1**
1.7	2.22	14.2	0.78	**0.2**	-1.6	-0.87	-7.46	4.76	101.1	**1.3**	13.4	27.3	**6.5**
8.8	0.00	0.0	0.00	**0.0**	-0.5	-1.54	-5.36	2.97	148.5	**2.1**	38.2	31.7	**0.0**
3.6	0.82	6.0	0.46	**2.7**	0.4	0.51	4.25	4.00	71.6	**1.0**	16.8	32.6	**5.4**
10.0	0.01	0.1	0.00	**3.2**	0.6	0.51	4.19	3.07	75.7	**4.7**	56.5	15.8	**7.0**
4.8	0.50	3.5	2.04	**10.0**	77.5	8.49	64.60	25.81	52.8	**0.3**	2.4	68.8	**8.4**
10.0	0.00	0.0	0.00	**2.8**	0.1	0.43	3.59	1.20	31.3	**5.2**	40.0	8.6	**4.3**
1.7	1.76	10.9	0.53	**5.5**	1.4	1.26	12.95	3.87	84.1	**3.2**	33.9	17.1	**6.2**
2.4	1.88	15.1	0.31	**4.1**	0.8	0.79	10.48	4.76	76.3	**2.1**	26.9	20.2	**3.8**
2.6	1.52	9.5	0.06	**1.9**	0.2	0.13	1.02	4.18	87.7	**2.8**	29.5	17.4	**3.3**
3.9	1.81	7.7	0.19	**0.0**	-5.9	-2.62	-11.41	4.42	145.0	**1.5**	21.9	27.1	**4.8**
1.7	3.96	32.8	2.08	**0.9**	1.4	0.06	0.75	3.20	73.4	**1.7**	19.6	24.1	**4.7**
8.2	0.20	0.5	0.00	**6.0**	24.2	1.46	8.17	3.43	35.6	**3.5**	65.3	32.9	**10.0**
4.5	1.39	9.6	0.40	**3.8**	0.6	0.50	5.44	3.90	83.7	**1.8**	30.0	27.8	**5.1**
3.2	2.21	15.6	0.36	**5.9**	2.4	1.48	16.85	4.88	65.2	**1.5**	18.4	26.0	**5.6**
7.4	1.10	3.9	0.44	**9.7**	10.1	2.38	13.74	5.00	41.6	**4.1**	28.7	10.9	**9.1**
8.8	0.43	1.4	-0.02	**5.9**	1.6	1.08	8.30	3.62	58.3	**2.9**	54.1	31.7	**7.8**
4.9	0.15	1.1	0.05	**4.9**	1.1	0.89	7.34	4.10	68.1	**3.5**	18.0	12.0	**6.4**
5.5	0.59	4.3	0.25	**2.8**	1.1	0.48	4.55	3.11	78.4	**2.5**	3.7	15.6	**5.5**
10.0	4.17	0.1	0.00	**0.0**	-0.7	-4.81	-56.03	2.27	294.0	**7.9**	99.5	0.8	**1.7**
1.9	3.14	17.4	1.62	**3.4**	7.1	1.06	10.76	3.93	61.1	**3.1**	23.3	14.4	**4.1**
4.3	2.05	13.2	0.16	**2.8**	0.1	0.04	0.46	3.88	86.8	**1.4**	20.0	27.8	**3.9**
9.4	0.09	0.3	0.00	**8.7**	2.0	1.90	19.26	3.89	50.1	**1.5**	33.6	48.7	**7.1**
8.9	0.00	0.0	-0.02	**4.8**	0.7	1.12	8.51	4.25	75.3	**2.7**	56.2	32.2	**6.2**
0.8	3.61	21.6	2.38	**1.5**	-48.4	-0.26	-2.76	4.25	62.1	**4.8**	14.1	3.4	**4.4**

Section II

Weiss Recommended Companies

A compilation of those

U.S. Commercial Banks, Savings Banks,

and Savings and Loans

receiving a Weiss Financial Strength Rating
of A+, A, A-, or B+.

Institutions are ranked by Financial Strength Rating
in each state where they have a branch location.

Section II Contents

This section provides a list of Weiss Recommended companies and contains all financial institutions receiving a Financial Strength Rating of A+, A, A-, or B+. Recommended institutions are listed in each state in which they currently operate one or more branches. If a company is not on this list, it should not be automatically assumed that the firm is weak. Indeed, there are many firms that have not achieved a B+ or better rating but are in good condition with adequate resources to weather an average recession. Not being included in this list should not be construed as a recommendation to immediately withdraw deposits or cancel existing financial arrangements.

Institutions are ranked within each state by their Weiss Financial Strength Rating, and then listed alphabetically by city. Companies with the same rating should be viewed as having the same relative safety regardless of their ranking in this table.

1. **Institution Name** The name under which the institution was chartered. A company's name can be very similar to, or the same as, the name of other companies which may not be on our Recommended List, so make sure you note the exact name, city, and state of the main branch listed here before acting on this recommendation.

2. **City** The city in which the institution's headquarters or main office is located. With the adoption of intrastate and interstate branching laws, many institutions operating in your area may actually be headquartered elsewhere. So, don't be surprised if the location cited is not in your particular city.

3. **State** The state in which the institution's headquarters or main office is located. With the adoption of interstate branching laws, some institutions operating in your area may actually be headquartered in another state. Even so, there are no restrictions on your ability to do business with an out-of-state institution.

4. **Telephone** The telephone number for the institution's headquarters, or main office. If the number listed is not in your area, or a local phone call, consult your local phone directory for the number of a location near you.

5. **Financial Strength Rating** Weiss rating assigned to the institution at the time of publication. Our ratings are designed to distinguish levels of insolvency risk and are measured on a scale from A to F based upon a wide range of factors. Highly rated companies are, in our opinion, less likely to experience financial difficulties than lower rated firms. See *About Weiss Financial Strength Ratings* on page 7 for more information and a description of what each rating means.

Weiss Financial Strength Ratings are not deemed to be a recommendation concerning the purchase or sale of the securities of any bank or thrift that is publicly owned.

Alabama

Rating: A

City	Name	Telephone
BOAZ	FIRST BANK OF BOAZ	(256) 593-8670
GENEVA	CITIZENS BANK	(334) 684-2222

Rating: A-

City	Name	Telephone
GERALDINE	LIBERTY BANK	(256) 659-2175
GREENSBORO	CITIZENS BANK	(334) 624-8888
HALEYVILLE	TRADERS & FARMERS BANK	(205) 486-5263
HAMILTON	FIRST NATIONAL BK	(205) 921-7435
LAFAYETTE	FARMERS & MERCHANTS BANK	(334) 864-9941
MUSCLE SHOALS	FIRST METRO BANK	(256) 386-0600
TALLADEGA	FIRST NATIONAL BK OF TALLADEGA	(256) 362-2334
WATERLOO	FARMERS & MERCHANTS BANK	(256) 766-2579
WINFIELD	CITIZENS BANK OF WINFIELD	(205) 487-4277

Rating: B+

City	Name	Telephone
CALERA	CENTRAL STATE BK	(205) 668-0711
CLANTON	PEOPLES SOUTHERN BANK	(205) 755-2240
PHENIX CITY	PHENIX-GIRARD BANK	(334) 298-0691
SAMSON	SAMSON BANKING CO INC	(334) 898-7107

Alaska

City	Name	Telephone
Rating: A		
FAIRBANKS	MOUNT MCKINLEY BANK	(907) 452-1751
Rating: A-		
ANCHORAGE	FIRST NATIONAL BK ALASKA	(907) 777-4362

Arizona

City	Name	Telephone
Rating: A-		
SCOTTSDALE	NORDSTROM FSB	(480) 596-3459

Arkansas

City	Name	Telephone
Rating: A		
AUGUSTA	BANK OF AUGUSTA	(870) 347-2511
CALICO ROCK	FIRST NATIONAL BK IZARD COUNTY	(870) 297-3711
DELIGHT	BANK OF DELIGHT	(870) 379-2293
MCGEHEE	MCGEHEE BANK	(870) 222-3151
MOUNTAIN HOME	FIRST NATIONAL BK & TRUST CO	(870) 425-2101
PARAGOULD	FIRST NATIONAL BK	(870) 239-8521
SHERIDAN	PEOPLES BANK	(870) 942-5707
Rating: A-		
BEARDEN	BANK OF BEARDEN	(870) 687-2233
LITTLE ROCK	BANK OF THE OZARKS	(501) 978-2265
RISON	BANK OF RISON	(870) 325-6251
SCRANTON	LOGAN COUNTY BANK	(479) 938-2511
WALNUT RIDGE	FIRST NATIONAL BK LAWRENCE CTY	(870) 886-5959
Rating: B+		
GREENWOOD	FARMERS BANK	(479) 996-4171
HEBER SPRINGS	HEBER SPRINGS STATE BK	(501) 362-5821
HOT SPRINGS	FIRST NATIONAL BK	(501) 525-7999
PIGGOTT	PIGGOTT STATE BK	(870) 598-3802
PRESCOTT	BANK OF PRESCOTT	(870) 887-2688
SMACKOVER	SMACKOVER STATE BK	(870) 725-3051
STAR CITY	BANK OF STAR CITY	(870) 628-4286
WARREN	FIRST STATE BK OF WARREN	(870) 226-2601

California

Rating: A

City	Name	Telephone
IRVINE	CALIFORNIA FIRST NATIONAL BK	(949) 255-5300

Rating: A-

City	Name	Telephone
BAKERSFIELD	MISSION BANK	(661) 859-2500

Rating: B+

City	Name	Telephone
IRVINE	CAPITAL BANK & TRUST CO FSB	(949) 975-5000
LODI	FARMERS & MERCH BK CENTRAL CA	(209) 367-2300
LONG BEACH	FARMERS & MERCH BK LONG BEACH	(562) 437-0011
LOS ANGELES	BANK OF NY MELLON TRUST NA	(213) 630-6400
PALOS VERDES	MALAGA BANK FSB	(310) 375-9000
PLEASANTON	FIRESIDE BANK	(925) 460-9020
TUSTIN	TUSTIN COMMUNITY BANK	(714) 730-5662

Colorado

City	Name	Telephone
Rating: A		
DOLORES	DOLORES STATE BK	(970) 882-7600
ESTES PARK	FIRST NATIONAL BK ESTES PARK	(970) 586-4485
Rating: A-		
ALAMOSA	ALAMOSA STATE BK	(719) 589-2564
ENGLEWOOD	AMG NATIONAL TRUST BANK	(303) 694-2190
LAMAR	FRONTIER BANK	(719) 336-4351
Rating: B+		
BRUSH	FARMERS STATE BK OF BRUSH	(970) 842-5101
CALHAN	FARMERS STATE BK OF CALHAN	(719) 347-2727
WALSH	COLORADO STATE BK OF WALSH	(719) 324-5206

Connecticut

Rating: B+

City	Name	Telephone
ESSEX	ESSEX SB	(860) 767-4414
HARTFORD	PRUDENTIAL BANK & TRUST FSB	(888) 244-6295
SUFFIELD	FIRST NATIONAL BK OF SUFFIELD	(860) 668-3950
TORRINGTON	TORRINGTON SB	(860) 496-2152

Delaware

City	Name	Telephone
Rating: A+		
WILMINGTON	APPLIED BANK	(302) 326-4200
Rating: A-		
WILMINGTON	FIRST BANK OF DELAWARE	(302) 529-5984
Rating: B+		
WILMINGTON	DEUTSCHE BK TRUST CO	

District Of Columbia

City	Name	Telephone
Rating: A		
WASHINGTON	NATIONAL CAPITAL BANK OF WA	(202) 546-8000

Florida

City	Name	Telephone
Rating: A		
CHIEFLAND	DRUMMOND COMMUNITY BANK	(352) 493-2277
Rating: A-		
GRACEVILLE	PEOPLES BANK OF GRACEVILLE	(850) 263-3267
Rating: B+		
MIAMI	NORTHERN TRUST NA	(305) 372-1000
MIAMI	PREMIER AMERICAN BANK NA	(305) 740-6000

Georgia

Rating: A

City	Name	Telephone
PELHAM	PELHAM BANKING CO	(229) 294-2341
THOMASTON	WEST CENTRAL GEORGIA BANK	(706) 647-8951

Rating: A-

City	Name	Telephone
WAYNESBORO	FIRST NATIONAL BK WAYNESBORO	(706) 554-8100

Rating: B+

City	Name	Telephone
ATLANTA	INVESCO NATIONAL TRUST CO	(404) 892-0896
BLAKELY	FIRST STATE BK OF BLAKELY	(229) 723-3711
CARROLLTON	COMMUNITY & SOUTHERN BANK	(770) 832-3557
DAWSON	BANK OF DAWSON	(229) 995-2141
DUBLIN	FARMERS STATE BK	(478) 275-3223
IRWINTON	WILKINSON COUNTY BANK	(478) 946-5531
THOMASVILLE	THOMASVILLE NATIONAL BK	(229) 226-3300

Illinois

City	Name	Telephone
Rating: A+		
BREESE	GERMANTOWN TRUST & SB	(618) 526-4202
Rating: A		
ALBION	CITIZENS NB OF ALBION	(618) 445-2344
CHESTER	BUENA VISTA NATIONAL BK	(618) 826-2331
DWIGHT	FIRST NATIONAL BK OF DWIGHT	(815) 584-1212
EFFINGHAM	CROSSROADS BANK	(217) 347-7751
REYNOLDS	REYNOLDS STATE BK	(309) 372-4242
WATSEKA	FIRST TRUST & SB OF WATSEKA IL	(815) 432-2494
Rating: A-		
ALBANY	FIRST TRUST & SB OF ALBANY IL	(309) 887-4335
ALLENDALE	FIRST NATIONAL BK OF ALLENDALE	(618) 299-4411
ALPHA	FARMERS STATE BK OF WESTERN IL	(309) 629-4361
ATHENS	ATHENS STATE BK	(217) 636-8214
AVA	FIRST NATIONAL BK OF AVA	(618) 426-3303
BEARDSTOWN	FIRST NATIONAL BK BEARDSTOWN	(217) 323-4105
DECATUR	SOY CAPITAL BANK & TRUST CO	(217) 428-7781
FARMINGTON	BANK OF FARMINGTON	(309) 245-2441
HENRY	HENRY STATE BK	(309) 364-2302
HOFFMAN	FARMERS STATE BK OF HOFFMAN	(618) 495-2225
KAMPSVILLE	BANK OF KAMPSVILLE	(618) 653-4311
LEWISTOWN	FARMERS STATE BK FULTON CNTY	(309) 547-3006
MARION	BANK OF MARION	(618) 997-4341
METROPOLIS	CITY NATIONAL BK OF METROPOLIS	(618) 524-2161
MOUNT ZION	PRAIRIE STATE BK & TRUST	(217) 864-2353
NEW BERLIN	WARREN-BOYNTON STATE BK	(217) 488-6091
NOKOMIS	FIRST NATIONAL BK OF NOKOMIS	(217) 563-8311
OGLESBY	ILLINI STATE BK	(815) 883-8400
PARK RIDGE	PARK RIDGE COMMUNITY BANK	(847) 384-9200
PINCKNEYVILLE	FIRST NB IN PINCKNEYVILLE	(618) 357-9393
PIPER CITY	VERMILION VALLEY BANK	(815) 686-2258
POPLAR GROVE	POPLAR GROVE STATE BK	(815) 765-3333
RUSHVILLE	RUSHVILLE STATE BK	(217) 322-3323
SAINT JACOB	STATE BK OF ST JACOB	(618) 644-5555
SAINT PETER	FIRST STATE BK OF ST PETER	(618) 349-8343
TAYLORVILLE	FIRST NATIONAL BK TAYLORVILLE	(217) 824-2241
TEUTOPOLIS	TEUTOPOLIS STATE BK	(217) 857-3166
Rating: B+		
ANDALUSIA	ANDALUSIA COMMUNITY BANK	(309) 798-2800
ANNA	ANNA STATE BK	(618) 833-2151
ARTHUR	STATE BK OF ARTHUR	(217) 543-2111
BETHANY	SCOTT STATE BK	(217) 665-3321
BLOOMINGTON	COUNTRY TRUST BANK	(309) 821-4600
CANTON	MIDAMERICA NATIONAL BK	(309) 647-5000
CARLYLE	FIRST NATIONAL BK IN CARLYLE	(618) 594-2491
CHICAGO	OAK BANK	(312) 440-4000
COLFAX	PEOPLES STATE BK OF COLFAX	(309) 723-2111
EASTON	COMMUNITY BANK OF EASTON	(309) 562-7420
FRANKLIN	FRANKLIN BANK	(217) 675-2311
FRANKLIN GROVE	FRANKLIN GROVE BANK	(815) 456-2311
GALVA	COMMUNITY STATE BK	(309) 932-8181
GOODFIELD	GOODFIELD STATE BK	(309) 965-2221
MASON CITY	MASON CITY NATIONAL BK	(217) 482-3246
MONMOUTH	COMMUNITY NATIONAL BK	(309) 734-5131
O'FALLON	BANK OF OFALLON	(618) 632-3595
PANA	FIRST NATIONAL BK OF PANA	(217) 562-3961
PEORIA	SOUTH SIDE TRUST & SB PEORIA	(309) 676-0521
PETERSBURG	NATIONAL BK OF PETERSBURG	(217) 632-3241
PROPHETSTOWN	FARMERS NB OF PROPHETSTOWN	(815) 537-2348
QUINCY	BANK OF QUINCY	(217) 223-7100
RANTOUL	BANK OF RANTOUL	(217) 892-2143
SPRING VALLEY	SPRING VALLEY CITY BANK	(815) 663-2211
STREATOR	STREATOR HOME BUILDING & LOAN	(815) 673-5566

Indiana

City	Name	Telephone
Rating: A		
GENEVA	BANK OF GENEVA	(260) 368-7288
Rating: A-		
LYNN	MERCHANTS BANK OF INDIANA	(765) 874-2511
Rating: B+		
BERNE	FIRST BANK OF BERNE	(260) 589-2151
JASPER	GERMAN AMERICAN BANCORP	(812) 482-1314
KENTLAND	KENTLAND BANK	(219) 474-5155
ROACHDALE	TRI-COUNTY BANK & TRUST CO	(765) 522-1000
TERRE HAUTE	FIRST FINANCIAL BANK NA	(812) 238-6000

Iowa

City	Name	Telephone
Rating: A		
ATLANTIC	FIRST WHITNEY BANK & TRUST	(712) 243-3195
BRITT	FIRST STATE BK	(641) 843-4411
CENTERVILLE	IOWA TRUST & SB	(641) 437-4500
COLFAX	FIRST STATE BK OF COLFAX	(515) 674-3533
CORYDON	CORYDON STATE BK	(641) 872-2212
DES MOINES	IOWA STATE BK	(515) 288-0111
DURANT	LIBERTY TRUST & SB	(563) 785-4441
GRINNELL	GRINNELL STATE BK	(641) 236-3174
HAMPTON	UNITED BANK & TRUST CO	(641) 456-5587
MAXWELL	MAXWELL STATE BK	(515) 387-1175
MAYNARD	MAYNARD SB	(563) 637-2289
MOUNT PLEASANT	WAYLAND STATE BK	(319) 385-8189
NEW ALBIN	NEW ALBIN SB	(563) 544-4214
POCAHONTAS	POCAHONTAS STATE BK	(712) 335-3567
READLYN	READLYN SB	(319) 279-3321
SOMERS	HEARTLAND BANK	(515) 467-5561
STORM LAKE	CITIZENS FIRST NATIONAL BK	(712) 732-5440
VICTOR	VICTOR STATE BK	(319) 647-2231
WILLIAMSBURG	FARMERS TRUST & SB	(319) 668-2525
WYOMING	CITIZENS STATE BK	(563) 488-2211
Rating: A-		
BLAIRSTOWN	BENTON COUNTY STATE BK	(319) 454-6230
BLOOMFIELD	SUCCESS BANK	(641) 664-2006
BOONE	BOONE BANK & TRUST CO	(515) 432-6200
HAMPTON	FIRST NATIONAL BK OF HAMPTON	(641) 456-4793
HAMPTON	HAMPTON STATE BK	(641) 456-2559
HAWKEYE	CITIZENS SB	(563) 427-3255
JEFFERSON	HOME STATE BK	(515) 386-2131
KINGSLEY	KINGSLEY STATE BK	(712) 378-2341
LAURENS	LAURENS STATE BK	(712) 845-2627
MANNING	FIRST NATIONAL BK OF MANNING	(712) 655-3557
MASON CITY	FIRST CITIZENS NATIONAL BK	(641) 423-1600
MOUNT VERNON	MOUNT VERNON BANK & TRUST CO	(319) 895-8835
NEVADA	STATE BK & TRUST CO	(515) 382-2191
NEW LONDON	DANVILLE STATE SB	(319) 392-4261
PALO	PALO SB	(319) 851-2241
PANORA	PANORA STATE BK	(641) 755-2141
ROCKWELL CITY	UNION STATE BK	(712) 297-7556
ROYAL	HOME STATE BK	(712) 933-5511
SPILLVILLE	CITIZENS SB	(563) 562-3674
STORM LAKE	SECURITY TRUST & SB	(712) 732-3022
TEMPLETON	TEMPLETON SB	(712) 669-3322
TRIPOLI	AMERICAN SB	(319) 882-4279
VICTOR	FARMERS SB	(319) 647-3141
WALCOTT	WALCOTT TRUST & SB	(563) 284-6202
WASHINGTON	WASHINGTON STATE BK	(319) 653-2151
WATKINS	WATKINS SB	(319) 227-7773
WAVERLY	SECURITY STATE BK	(319) 352-3500
Rating: B+		
ALBIA	PEOPLES STATE BK	(641) 932-7887
ALGONA	SECURITY STATE BK	(515) 295-9501
AMES	FIRST NATIONAL BK AMES IOWA	(515) 232-5561
ASHTON	ASHTON STATE BK	(712) 724-6326
BELLE PLAINE	CHELSEA SB	(319) 444-3144
CHEROKEE	CHEROKEE STATE BK	(712) 225-3000
CLARINDA	PAGE COUNTY STATE BK	(712) 542-5661
CORNING	OKEY-VERNON FIRST NATIONAL BK	(641) 322-3101
COUNCIL BLUFFS	MIDSTATES BANK NA	(712) 388-0505
CRESCO	C US BANK	(563) 547-2040
FOSTORIA	FARMERS SB	(712) 262-2708
FREDERIKA	FARMERS SB	(319) 275-4301
IOWA FALLS	IOWA FALLS STATE BK	(641) 648-5171
MAQUOKETA	MAQUOKETA STATE BK	(563) 652-2491
MARCUS	FARMERS STATE BK	(712) 376-4154
MARION	FARMERS STATE BK	(319) 377-4891
MARSHALLTOWN	UNITED BANK & TRUST NA	(641) 753-5900
MELVIN	MELVIN SB	(712) 736-2420
MONTICELLO	CITIZENS STATE BK	(319) 465-5921
NEWELL	FIRST COMMUNITY BANK	(712) 272-3321
PATON	COMMUNITY STATE BK	(515) 968-4131
PELLA	MARION COUNTY STATE BK	(641) 628-2191
PLEASANTVILLE	PLEASANTVILLE STATE BK	(515) 848-5741
REMBRANDT	FIRST NATIONAL BK OF REMBRANDT	(712) 286-5491
ROCK VALLEY	PREMIER BANK	(712) 476-9100
SHELDON	CITIZENS STATE BK	(712) 324-2519
SIOUX CITY	PINNACLE BANK SIOUX CITY	(712) 276-5333
SIOUX RAPIDS	FIRST STATE BK	(712) 283-2593
SLOAN	SLOAN STATE BK	(712) 428-3344
STORY CITY	RANDALL-STORY STATE BK	(515) 733-4396
WINTERSET	FARMERS & MERCHANTS STATE BK	(515) 462-4242

Kansas

City	Name	Telephone
Rating: A+		
COUNCIL GROVE	FARMERS & DROVERS BANK	(620) 767-5138
Rating: A		
DODGE CITY	FIDELITY STATE BK & TRUST CO	(620) 227-8586
GREENSBURG	GREENSBURG STATE BK	(620) 723-2131
LOUISBURG	FIRST NATIONAL BK OF LOUISBURG	(913) 837-5191
PARSONS	COMMERCIAL BANK	(620) 421-1000
SOLOMON	SOLOMON STATE BK	(785) 655-2941
Rating: A-		
CENTRALIA	FIRST NATIONAL BK OF CENTRALIA	(785) 857-3341
CHENEY	CITIZENS STATE BK OF CHENEY KS	(316) 542-3142
ESKRIDGE	FLINT HILLS BANK OF ESKRIDGE	(785) 449-2266
FREDONIA	FIRST NATIONAL BK IN FREDONIA	(620) 378-2151
FREDONIA	STATE BK OF KANSAS	(620) 378-2114
HIAWATHA	CITIZENS STATE BK & TRUST CO	(785) 742-2101
HUGOTON	CITIZENS STATE BK	(620) 544-4331
LAKIN	KEARNY COUNTY BANK	(620) 355-6222
MARYSVILLE	FIRST COMMERCE BANK	(785) 562-5558
NESS CITY	FIRST STATE BK	(785) 798-3347
OBERLIN	THE BANK	(785) 475-3817
PHILLIPSBURG	FARMERS NATIONAL BK	(785) 543-6541
PHILLIPSBURG	FIRST NATIONAL BK & TRUST	(785) 543-6511
RANSOM	FIRST STATE BK OF RANSOM	(785) 731-2261
STERLING	FIRST BANK	(620) 278-2161
WASHINGTON	FIRST NATIONAL BK WASHINGTON	(785) 325-2221
Rating: B+		
ATCHISON	EXCHANGE NATIONAL BK & TRUST	(913) 367-6000
BELOIT	FIRST NATIONAL BK OF BELOIT	(785) 738-2251
BERN	STATE BK OF BERN	(785) 336-6121
ELLSWORTH	CITIZENS STATE BK & TRUST CO	(785) 472-3141
GARDEN CITY	WESTERN STATE BK	(620) 275-4128
HAVILAND	HAVILAND STATE BK	(620) 862-5222
HOLCOMB	FIRST NATIONAL BK OF HOLCOMB	(620) 277-0077
HOLTON	DENISON STATE BK	(785) 364-3131
HOXIE	STATE BK	(785) 675-3261
LARNED	FIRST STATE B&TC OF LARNED	(620) 285-6931
LEAVENWORTH	FIRST NATIONAL BK & TRUST CO	(913) 682-2265
MCPHERSON	PEOPLES BANK & TRUST CO	(620) 241-2100
MOUNDRIDGE	CITIZENS STATE BK	(620) 345-6317
OLPE	OLPE STATE BK	(620) 475-3213
OLSBURG	UNION STATE BK	(785) 468-3341
ROSE HILL	ROSE HILL BANK	(316) 776-2131
SAINT JOHN	SAINT JOHN NATIONAL BK	(620) 549-3225
SALINA	BENNINGTON STATE BK	(785) 827-5522
SCANDIA	ASTRA BANK	(785) 335-2243
TESCOTT	BANK OF TESCOTT	(785) 283-4217
TOPEKA	FIDELITY STATE BK & TRUST CO	(785) 295-2100
WAMEGO	KAW VALLEY STATE BK & TRUST CO	(785) 456-2021

Kentucky

City	Name	Telephone
Rating: A+		
ASHLAND	KENTUCKY FARMERS BANK CORP	(606) 929-5000
Rating: A		
CAMPBELLSVILLE	CITIZENS BANK & TRUST CO	(270) 465-8193
EDMONTON	EDMONTON STATE BK	(270) 432-3231
HARDINSBURG	FARMERS BANK	(270) 756-2166
LEITCHFIELD	LEITCHFIELD DEPOSIT BANK & TR	(270) 259-5611
MCKEE	JACKSON COUNTY BANK	(606) 287-8484
PRINCETON	FARMERS BANK & TRUST CO	(270) 365-5526
Rating: A-		
ARLINGTON	CITIZENS DEPOSIT BK ARLINGTON	(270) 655-6921
BEAVER DAM	BANK OF OHIO COUNTY INC	(270) 274-5678
BRANDENBURG	MEADE COUNTY BANK	(270) 422-4141
CLARKSON	BANK OF CLARKSON	(270) 242-2111
CLINTON	FIRST COMMUNITY BK OF W KY	(270) 653-4301
DIXON	DIXON BANK	(270) 639-5815
ELKTON	ELKTON BANK & TRUST CO	(270) 265-9841
HODGENVILLE	LINCOLN NB OF HODGENVILLE	(270) 358-4116
IRVINGTON	FIRST STATE BK	(270) 547-2271
LEWISBURG	LEWISBURG BANKING CO	(270) 755-4818
LOUISVILLE	RIVER CITY BANK INC	(502) 585-4600
MARTIN	FIRST GUARANTY BANK	(606) 285-3294
MAYSVILLE	BANK OF MAYSVILLE	(606) 564-4001
MAYSVILLE	SECURITY BANK & TRUST CO	(606) 564-3304
MILTON	FARMERS BANK OF MILTON	(502) 268-5256
MORGANFIELD	UNITED COMMUNITY BK WEST KY	(270) 389-3232
OWENTON	PEOPLES BANK & TRUST CO	(502) 484-3466
PRESTONSBURG	FIRST CMNWLTH BK	(606) 886-2321
RADCLIFF	WEST POINT BANK	(270) 351-1414
RUSSELL SPRINGS	FIRST NB OF RUSSELL SPRINGS	(270) 866-4343
SOMERSET	CITIZENS NB OF SOMERSET	(606) 679-6341
SPRINGFIELD	SPRINGFIELD STATE BK	(859) 336-3939
Rating: B+		
BOWLING GREEN	FARMERS NB OF SCOTTSVILLE	(270) 783-8300
CAMPBELLSBURG	UNITED CITIZENS BANK & TRUST	(502) 532-7392
CARROLLTON	FIRST NATIONAL BK CARROLLTON	(502) 732-4406
CLINTON	CLINTON BANK	(270) 653-4001
CYNTHIANA	HARRISON DEPOSIT BANK & TRUST	(859) 234-3150
FREDONIA	FREDONIA VALLEY BANK	(270) 545-3301
GRAYSON	COMMERCIAL BANK OF GRAYSON	(606) 474-7811
LAKESIDE PARK	VICTORY COMMUNITY BANK	(859) 341-2265
LIBERTY	CASEY COUNTY BANK	(606) 787-8394
PADUCAH	PADUCAH BANK & TRUST CO	(270) 575-5700
SACRAMENTO	SACRAMENTO DEPOSIT BANK	(270) 736-2212
SALYERSVILLE	SALYERSVILLE NATIONAL BK	(606) 349-3131

Louisiana

Rating: A

City	Name	Telephone
HAUGHTON	TRI-STATE BK & TRUST	(318) 949-4173

Rating: A-

City	Name	Telephone
ABBEVILLE	GULF COAST BANK	(337) 893-7733
BELLE CHASSE	MISSISSIPPI RIVER BANK	(504) 392-1111
DE RIDDER	CITY SB & TRUST CO	(337) 463-8661
DE RIDDER	FIRST NATIONAL BK IN DE RIDDER	(337) 463-6231
DELHI	COMMERCIAL CAPITAL BANK	(318) 878-2274
DELHI	GUARANTY BANK & TRUST CO DELHI	(318) 878-3703
ERATH	BANK OF ERATH	(337) 937-5816
JENNINGS	JEFF DAVIS BANK & TRUST CO	(337) 824-1422
KAPLAN	KAPLAN STATE BK	(337) 643-7110
MARINGOUIN	BANK OF MARINGOUIN	(225) 625-2377
MORGAN CITY	M C BANK & TRUST CO	(985) 384-2100
NATCHITOCHES	EXCHANGE B&TC NATCHITOCHES	(318) 352-8141
PLAQUEMINE	FIRST FINANCIAL BANK & TRUST CO	(225) 687-6337
RAYVILLE	RICHLAND STATE BK	(318) 728-2024
SAINT	TECHE BANK & TRUST CO	(337) 394-9726
VIDALIA	CONCORDIA BANK & TRUST CO	(318) 336-5258

Rating: B+

City	Name	Telephone
ABBEVILLE	ABBEVILLE B&L ST CHARTERED	(337) 893-1170
BREAUX BRIDGE	FIRST LOUISIANA NATIONAL BK	(337) 332-5960
CROWLEY	FIRST NATIONAL BK OF LOUISIANA	(337) 783-4014
DERIDDER	BEAUREGARD FSB	(337) 463-4493
GUEYDAN	BANK OF GUEYDAN	(337) 536-9203
HODGE	HODGE BANK & TRUST CO	(318) 259-7362
JACKSON	HIGHLANDS BANK	(225) 634-7741
JENNINGS	THE BANK	(337) 824-0033
JONESBORO	JONESBORO STATE BK	(318) 259-4411
LAKE CHARLES	CAMERON STATE BK	(337) 310-2265
LEESVILLE	MERCHANTS & FARMERS BANK & TR	(337) 239-6504
MANSFIELD	COMMUNITY BANK OF LOUISIANA	(318) 872-3831
NATCHITOCHES	CITY BANK & TRUST CO	(318) 352-4416
OPELOUSAS	AMERICAN BANK & TRUST CO	(337) 948-3056
RAYNE	RAYNE STATE BK & TRUST CO	(337) 334-3191
SUNSET	BANK OF SUNSET & TRUST CO	(337) 662-5222
WINNFIELD	BANK OF WINNFIELD & TRUST CO	(318) 628-4677
WINNSBORO	FRANKLIN STATE BK & TRUST CO	(318) 435-3711
WINNSBORO	WINNSBORO STATE BK & TRUST CO	(318) 435-7535

Maine

City	Name	Telephone
Rating: A-		
FARMINGTON	FRANKLIN SB	(207) 778-3339
Rating: B+		
BAR HARBOR	BAR HARBOR BANK & TRUST	(207) 288-3314

Maryland

City	Name	Telephone
Rating: A		
BERLIN	CALVIN B TAYLOR BANKING CO	(410) 641-1700
Rating: A-		
BALTIMORE	ROSEDALE FS&LA	(410) 668-4400
JARRETTSVILLE	JARRETTSVILLE FS&LA	(410) 692-5151
MIDDLETOWN	MIDDLETOWN VALLEY BANK	(301) 371-6700
Rating: B+		
CHESTERTOWN	CHESAPEAKE BANK & TRUST CO	(410) 778-1600
OCEAN CITY	BANK OF OCEAN CITY	(410) 213-0173

Massachusetts

City	Name	Telephone
Rating:	**A-**	
ARLINGTON	LEADER BANK NA	(781) 646-3900
BOSTON	BOSTON TRUST & INVESTMENT	(617) 726-7250
BOSTON	FIDELITY MANAGEMENT TRUST CO	(617) 563-7000
EDGARTOWN	MARTHAS VINEYARD SB	(508) 627-4266
FRAMINGHAM	FRAMINGHAM CO-OP BANK	(508) 820-4000
MARBLEHEAD	NATIONAL GRAND BK MARBLEHEAD	(781) 631-6000
Rating:	**B+**	
BOSTON	FIDELITY PERSONAL TRUST CO FSB	(617) 392-0491
BOSTON	MERCANTILE BANK & TRUST CO	(617) 247-2800
BOSTON	STATE STREET BANK & TRUST CO	(617) 786-3000
CAMBRIDGE	CAMBRIDGE TRUST CO	(617) 876-5500
EASTHAMPTON	EASTHAMPTON SB	(413) 527-4111
NEWBURYPORT	NEWBURYPORT FIVE CENTS SB	(978) 462-3136

City	Name	Telephone

Michigan

Rating: A-

City	Name	Telephone
ESCANABA	UPPER PENINSULA STATE BK	(906) 789-7000

Rating: B+

City	Name	Telephone
FRANKFORT	STATE SB	(231) 352-9691
ISHPEMING	PENINSULA BANK OF ISHPEMING	(906) 485-6333
NORWAY	FIRST NATIONAL BK OF NORWAY	(906) 563-9233

Minnesota

City	Name	Telephone
Rating: A		
GLENWOOD	EAGLE BANK	(320) 634-4545
SAINT CLOUD	LIBERTY SAVINGS BANK FSB	(320) 252-2841
VERMILLION	VERMILLION STATE BK	(651) 437-4433
Rating: A-		
ADAMS	FARMERS STATE BK OF ADAMS MN	(507) 582-3448
ALTURA	ALTURA STATE BK	(507) 796-6761
BEMIDJI	FIRST NATIONAL BK OF BEMIDJI	(218) 751-2430
CASTLE ROCK	CASTLE ROCK BANK	(651) 463-7590
CLINTON	CLINTON STATE BK	(320) 325-5401
FAIRFAX	FIRST NATIONAL BK OF FAIRFAX	(507) 426-7242
JANESVILLE	JANESVILLE STATE BK	(507) 234-5108
RICHMOND	STATE BK OF RICHMOND	(320) 597-2145
ROSEAU	CITIZENS STATE BK OF ROSEAU	(218) 463-2135
SAINT CLAIR	ST CLAIR STATE BK (INC)	(507) 245-3636
WINNEBAGO	FIRST FINANCIAL BANK IN WINNEB	(507) 893-3155
Rating: B+		
BATTLE LAKE	FIRST NATIONAL BK BATTLE LAKE	(218) 864-5275
DULUTH	PIONEER NATIONAL BK OF DULUTH	(218) 624-3676
EDINA	FIDELITY BANK	(952) 831-6600
FAIRMONT	FIRST FARMERS & MERCHANTS NB	(507) 235-5556
LUVERNE	FIRST FARMERS & MERCHANTS NB	(507) 283-4463
MARINE ON SAINT	SECURITY STATE BK OF MARINE	(651) 433-2424
MINNEAPOLIS	UNION BANK & TRUST CO	(612) 379-3222
MORA	KANABEC STATE BK	(320) 679-3131
NEW ULM	CITIZENS BANK MINNESOTA	(507) 354-3165
NEWFOLDEN	MARSHALL COUNTY STATE BK	(218) 874-7265
OKLEE	SECURITY STATE BK OF OKLEE	(218) 796-5157
PIPESTONE	FIRST STATE BK SOUTHWEST	(507) 825-0055
PRIOR LAKE	PRIOR LAKE STATE BK	(952) 447-2101
SAINT MARTIN	ST MARTIN NATIONAL BK	(320) 548-3555
SAUK CENTRE	FIRST STATE BK OF SAUK CENTRE	(320) 352-5771
TRIMONT	FARMERS STATE BK OF TRIMONT	(507) 639-9921
WATKINS	FARMERS STATE BK OF WATKINS	(320) 764-2600

Mississippi

City	Name	Telephone
Rating:	**A**	
CORINTH	COMMERCE NATIONAL BK	(662) 286-5577
Rating:	**A-**	
BALDWYN	FARMERS & MERCHANTS BANK	(662) 365-1200
LAUREL	BANK OF JONES COUNTY	(601) 649-4700
MCCOMB	FIRST BANK	(601) 684-2231
MERIDIAN	GREAT SOUTHERN NATIONAL BK	(601) 693-5141
MORTON	BANK OF MORTON	(601) 732-8944
NEW ALBANY	BNA BANK	(662) 534-8171
NORTH	PEOPLES BANK & TRUST CO	(662) 237-9272
WIGGINS	BANK OF WIGGINS	(601) 928-5233
Rating:	**B+**	
BROOKHAVEN	BANK OF BROOKHAVEN	(601) 835-3033
CLARKSDALE	FIRST NATIONAL BK CLARKSDALE	(662) 627-3261
CLEVELAND	CLEVELAND STATE BK	(662) 843-9461
NATCHEZ	UNITED MISSISSIPPI BANK	(601) 445-7000
PORT GIBSON	RIVERHILLS BANK	(601) 437-4271
WALNUT GROVE	BANK OF WALNUT GROVE	(601) 253-2411

Missouri

Rating: A

City	Name	Telephone
ADVANCE	BANK OF ADVANCE	(573) 722-3517
DONIPHAN	PEOPLES COMMUNITY STATE BK	(573) 996-2114
FREDERICKTOWN	NEW ERA BANK	(573) 783-3336
GREENVILLE	PEOPLES COMMUNITY BANK	(573) 224-3267
KANSAS CITY	BANK OF GRAIN VALLEY	(816) 373-1905
KIRKSVILLE	NORTHEAST MISSOURI STATE BK	(660) 665-6161
LINN	LEGENDS BANK	(573) 897-2204
MOBERLY	BANK OF CAIRO & MOBERLY	(660) 263-2280
SENATH	SENATH STATE BK	(573) 738-2646

Rating: A-

City	Name	Telephone
ALTON	ALTON BANK	(314) 842-5290
CUBA	PEOPLES BANK	(573) 885-2511
FULTON	UNITED SECURITY BANK	(573) 592-0100
JOPLIN	FIRST STATE BK OF JOPLIN	(417) 623-8860
LAMAR	LAMAR BANK & TRUST CO	(417) 682-3348
MARSHALL	COMMUNITY BANK OF MARSHALL	(660) 886-9621
MEXICO	MARTINSBURG BANK & TRUST	(573) 581-6566
SAINT LOUIS	TIAA-CREF TRUST CO FSB	(314) 244-5000
SALEM	TOWN & COUNTRY BANK	(573) 729-3155
STANBERRY	FARMERS STATE BK STANBERRY	(660) 783-2820
URBANA	BANK OF URBANA	(417) 993-4242

Rating: B+

City	Name	Telephone
BOWLING GREEN	COMMUNITY STATE BK OF MISSOURI	(573) 324-2233
BROOKFIELD	BANK OF BROOKFIELD-PURDIN NA	(660) 258-3394
CARROLLTON	CARROLL COUNTY TC CARROLLTON	(660) 542-2050
COLE CAMP	CITIZENS-FARMERS BK COLE CAMP	(660) 668-4416
EL DORADO	COMMUNITY BK EL DORADO	(417) 876-6811
ELDON	CITIZENS BANK OF ELDON	(573) 392-3381
GRANDIN	BANK OF GRANDIN	(573) 593-4211
KENNETT	KENNETT NATIONAL BK	(573) 888-9051
LA GRANGE	TOWN & COUNTRY BK OF MISSOURI	(573) 655-2297
LIBERTY	PONY EXPRESS BANK	(816) 781-9200
LOUISIANA	MERCANTILE BK OF LOUISIANA MO	(573) 754-6221
MACON	MACON-ATLANTA STATE BK	(660) 385-3161
MANSFIELD	BANK OF MANSFIELD	(417) 924-3211
MONTROSE	MONTROSE SB	(660) 693-4424
NEOSHO	COMMUNITY BANK & TRUST	(417) 451-1040
POPLAR BLUFF	STERLING BANK	(573) 778-3333
SALEM	PROGRESSIVE OZARK BANK FSB	(573) 729-4146
SEYMOUR	SEYMOUR BANK	(417) 935-2293
SLATER	STATE BK OF SLATER	(660) 529-2222
SPRINGFIELD	LIBERTY BANK	(417) 888-3000
TIPTON	TIPTON LATHAM BANK NA	(660) 433-2004
UNIONVILLE	FARMERS BANK OF NORTHERN MO	(660) 947-2474
WEST PLAINS	WEST PLAINS BANK & TRUST CO	(417) 256-2147

Montana

City	Name	Telephone
Rating: A		
FAIRFIELD	CITIZENS STATE BK OF CHOTEAU	(406) 467-2531
LAUREL	YELLOWSTONE BANK	(406) 628-7951
SHELBY	FIRST STATE BK OF SHELBY	(406) 434-5567
Rating: A-		
BAKER	BANK OF BAKER	(406) 778-3382
MALTA	FIRST STATE BK OF MALTA	(406) 654-2340
SIDNEY	1ST BANK	(406) 433-3212
STANFORD	BASIN STATE BK	(406) 566-2238
Rating: B+		
HAVRE	INDEPENDENCE BANK	(406) 265-1241
ROUNDUP	FIRST SECURITY BANK OF ROUNDUP	(406) 323-1100

Nebraska

City	Name	Telephone
Rating: A		
CHADRON	FIRST NATIONAL BK OF CHADRON	(308) 432-5552
FALLS CITY	RICHARDSON COUNTY BANK &	(402) 245-2486
RAVENNA	TOWN & COUNTRY BANK	(308) 452-3225
RED CLOUD	PEOPLES-WEBSTER COUNTY BANK	(402) 746-2251
REPUBLICAN CITY	COMMERCIAL STATE BK	(308) 799-2885
SAINT PAUL	CITIZENS BANK & TRUST ST PAUL	(308) 754-4426
Rating: A-		
AUBURN	AUBURN STATE BK	(402) 274-4342
BROKEN BOW	NEBRASKA STATE BK & TRUST CO	(308) 872-2466
CLARKSON	CLARKSON BANK	(402) 892-3411
COZAD	HOMESTEAD BANK	(308) 784-2000
EWING	FARMERS STATE BK	(402) 626-7272
FAIRBURY	FIRST NATIONAL BK OF FAIRBURY	(402) 729-3344
GORDON	FIRST NATIONAL BK OF GORDON	(308) 282-0050
GOTHENBURG	GOTHENBURG STATE BK	(308) 537-7181
GRAND ISLAND	FIVE POINTS BANK	(308) 384-5350
HERSHEY	HERSHEY STATE BK	(308) 368-5555
LOUISVILLE	HOME STATE BK	(402) 234-2155
MADISON	MADISON COUNTY BANK	(402) 454-6511
MARQUETTE	BANK OF MARQUETTE	(402) 854-2221
MINDEN	MINDEN EXCHANGE BANK & TRUST	(308) 832-1600
OMAHA	SECURITY NATIONAL BK OF OMAHA	(402) 344-7300
RANDOLPH	FIRST STATE BK	(402) 337-0323
SCRIBNER	SCRIBNER BANK	(402) 664-2561
WAVERLY	HORIZON BANK	(402) 786-2555
WOOD RIVER	HERITAGE BANK	(308) 583-2262
Rating: B+		
ADAMS	ADAMS STATE BK	(402) 988-2255
AINSWORTH	WEST PLAINS BANK	(402) 387-2381
CERESCO	CERESCOBANK	(402) 665-3431
CHAMBERS	CHAMBERS STATE BK	(402) 482-5222
FULLERTON	FIRST BANK & TRUST FULLERTON	(308) 536-2492
HASTINGS	FIVE POINTS BANK OF HASTINGS	(402) 462-2228
HUMPHREY	FARMERS STATE BK	(402) 923-1717
MURRAY	MURRAY STATE BK	(402) 235-2351
NORTH BEND	PLATTE VALLEY BANK	(402) 652-3221
PRAGUE	BANK OF PRAGUE	(402) 663-4317
UNADILLA	COUNTRYSIDE BANK	(402) 828-3210
VALPARAISO	OAK CREEK VALLEY BANK	(402) 784-2200
WAYNE	STATE NATIONAL BK & TRUST CO	(402) 375-1130

Nevada

City	Name	Telephone
Rating: A		
LAS VEGAS	CREDIT ONE BANK NA	(702) 269-1100
Rating: A-		
CARSON CITY	EAGLEMARK SB	(775) 886-3000
Rating: B+		
LAS VEGAS	USAA SB	(702) 862-8891

New Jersey

City	Name	Telephone
Rating: A-		
HOBOKEN	SUMITOMO TRUST & BANKING CO	(201) 595-8969
Rating: B+		
EDISON	FIRST INVESTORS FSB	(732) 855-3041
NEWARK	LUSITANIA SAVINGS BANK FSB	(973) 344-5125

New Mexico

Rating: A

City	Name	Telephone
CARLSBAD	WESTERN COMMERCE BANK	(575) 887-6686
CLOVIS	CITIZENS BANK OF CLOVIS	(575) 769-1911
DEMING	FIRST NEW MEXICO BANK	(575) 546-2691
LAS CRUCES	FIRST NEW MEXICO BK LAS CRUCES	(575) 556-3000
LORDSBURG	WESTERN BANK	(575) 542-3521
SILVER CITY	FIRST NM BANK OF SILVER CITY	(575) 388-3121

Rating: A-

City	Name	Telephone
ALAMOGORDO	FIRST NATIONAL BK ALAMOGORDO	(575) 437-4880
CARLSBAD	CARLSBAD NATIONAL BK	(575) 234-2500
FARMINGTON	CITIZENS BANK	(505) 599-0100
RUIDOSO	FIRST NATIONAL BK OF RUIDOSO	(575) 257-4033

Rating: B+

City	Name	Telephone
ROSWELL	PIONEER BANK	(575) 624-5200
ROSWELL	BANK OF THE SOUTHWEST	(575) 625-1122
ROSWELL	VALLEY BANK OF COMMERCE	(575) 623-2265
TAOS	CENTINEL BANK OF TAOS	(575) 758-6700

New York

City	Name	Telephone
Rating:	**A**	
GROTON	FIRST NATIONAL BK OF GROTON	(607) 898-5871
MIDDLETOWN	ORANGE COUNTY TRUST CO	(845) 341-5000
UTICA	BANK OF UTICA	(315) 797-2700
Rating:	**A-**	
COXSACKIE	NATIONAL BK OF COXSACKIE	(518) 731-6161
DRYDEN	FIRST NATIONAL BK OF DRYDEN	(607) 844-8141
FLUSHING	ASIA BANK NA	(718) 961-9700
FULTON	FULTON SB	(315) 592-4201
GLENS FALLS	GLENS FALLS NATIONAL BK & TR	(518) 793-4121
NEW YORK	GOLDMAN SACHS BANK USA	(212) 902-1000
SARATOGA	SARATOGA NATIONAL BK & TRUST	(518) 583-3114
UNION SPRINGS	CAYUGA LAKE NATIONAL BK	(315) 889-7358
Rating:	**B+**	
ALDEN	ALDEN STATE BK	(716) 937-3381
CATSKILL	GREENE COUNTY COMMERCIAL	(518) 943-2600
COBLESKILL	BANK OF RICHMONDVILLE	(518) 234-4397
GLEN HEAD	FIRST NATIONAL BK LONG ISLAND	(516) 671-4900
GOUVERNEUR	GOUVERNEUR SAVINGS & LOAN	(315) 287-2600
HORNELL	STEUBEN TRUST CO	(607) 324-5010
MASPETH	MASPETH FS&LA	(718) 335-1300
MILLBROOK	BANK OF MILLBROOK	(845) 677-4266
MONTEBELLO	PROVIDENT MUNICIPAL BANK	(845) 369-8040
NEW YORK	ABACUS FSB	(212) 285-4770
NEW YORK	ALPINE CAPITAL BANK	(212) 328-2555
NEW YORK	DEUTSCHE BK TRUST CO AMERICAS	(212) 250-2500
OSWEGO	PATHFINDER COMMERCIAL BANK	(315) 343-0057
ROME	ROME SAVINGS BANK	(315) 336-7300

North Carolina

City	Name	Telephone
Rating: A-		
CHARLOTTE	CEDAR HILL NATIONAL BK	(704) 554-8510

North Dakota

City	Name	Telephone
Rating: A		
FORMAN	SARGENT COUNTY BANK	(701) 724-3216
Rating: A-		
MILNOR	FIRST NATIONAL BK	(701) 427-5212
NAPOLEON	STOCK GROWERS BANK	(701) 754-2226
Rating: B+		
CROSBY	FARMERS STATE BK OF CROSBY ND	(701) 965-6333
DRAYTON	KODABANK	(701) 454-3317
FARGO	GATE CITY BANK	(701) 293-2485
LANGDON	FARMERS & MERCHANTS STATE BK	(701) 256-5431
MCCLUSKY	NORTH COUNTRY BANK NA	(701) 363-2265
NEW SALEM	SECURITY FIRST BANK OF ND	(701) 843-7521
WILTON	FIRST STATE BK OF WILTON	(701) 734-6316

Ohio

City	Name	Telephone
Rating: A+		
SAINT HENRY	ST HENRY BANK	(419) 678-2358
Rating: A		
MASON	FDS BANK	(513) 573-2265
TIFFIN	FIRST BANK OF OHIO	(419) 448-9740
Rating: A-		
COLDWATER	PEOPLES BANK CO	(419) 678-2385
COLUMBUS	NATIONWIDE BANK	(614) 249-7111
DESHLER	CORN CITY STATE BK	(419) 278-0015
OTTOVILLE	OTTOVILLE BANK CO	(419) 453-3313
SPENCER	FARMERS SB	(330) 648-2441
Rating: B+		
BEVERLY	CITIZENS BANK CO	(740) 984-2381
BLANCHESTER	FIRST NATIONAL BK BLANCHESTER	(937) 783-2451
BROOK PARK	CREDIT FIRST NA	(216) 362-5000
CIRCLEVILLE	SAVINGS BANK	(740) 474-3191
CUTLER	BARTLETT FARMERS BANK	(740) 551-2271
EDON	EDON STATE BK CO OF EDON OHIO	(419) 272-2521
HAMLER	HAMLER STATE BK	(419) 274-3955
KENTON	HOME SAVINGS & LOAN CO OF	(419) 673-1117
KILLBUCK	KILLBUCK SB CO	(330) 276-4881
KINGSTON	KINGSTON NATIONAL BK	(740) 642-2191
NEW BREMEN	FIRST NATIONAL BK NEW BREMEN	(419) 629-2761
WYOMING	SPRING VALLEY BANK	(513) 761-6688

Oklahoma

Rating: A+

City	Name	Telephone
CLINTON	OKLAHOMA BANK & TRUST CO	(580) 323-2345

Rating: A

City	Name	Telephone
ANADARKO	FIRST STATE BK	(405) 247-2471
CHECOTAH	PEOPLES NATIONAL BK CHECOTAH	(918) 473-2237
CLEO SPRINGS	CLEO STATE BK	(580) 438-2223
FAIRVIEW	FARMERS & MERCH NB OF FAIRVIEW	(580) 227-3773
FORT SILL	FORT SILL NATIONAL BK	(580) 357-9880
OKARCHE	COMMUNITY NATIONAL BK OKARCHE	(405) 263-7491
PERKINS	PAYNE COUNTY BANK	(405) 547-2436
PERRY	FIRST BANK & TRUST CO	(580) 336-5562

Rating: A-

City	Name	Telephone
CHEYENNE	SECURITY STATE BK	(580) 497-3354
COALGATE	SHAMROCK BANK NA	(580) 927-2311
CUSHING	BANK OF CUSHING & TRUST CO	(918) 225-2010
FORT COBB	WASHITA VALLEY BANK	(405) 643-2305
HOOKER	FIRST NATIONAL BK OF HOOKER	(580) 652-2448
LAWTON	CITY NB&TC OF LAWTON	(580) 355-3580
OKARCHE	FIRST BANK OF OKARCHE	(405) 263-7215
OKEMAH	OKEMAH NATIONAL BK	(918) 623-1211
OKLAHOMA CITY	BANK 2	(405) 946-2265
PORTER	FIRST STATE BK OF PORTER	(918) 483-2241
SAPULPA	AMERICAN HERITAGE BANK	(918) 224-3210
STILWELL	BANK OF COMMERCE	(918) 696-7745
TUTTLE	SOONER STATE BK	(405) 381-2326
WAURIKA	FIRST FARMERS NB OF WAURIKA	(580) 228-2326
WEATHERFORD	FIRST NATIONAL BK & TRUST CO	(580) 772-5574
WESTVILLE	PEOPLES BANK	(918) 723-5453
WILBURTON	LATIMER STATE BK	(918) 465-2327
WYNNEWOOD	STATE BK OF WYNNEWOOD	(405) 665-2001

Rating: B+

City	Name	Telephone
ADA	CITIZENS BANK OF ADA	(580) 332-6100
ANTLERS	FIRSTBANK	(580) 298-3368
ARDMORE	AMERICAN NATIONAL BK	(580) 226-6222
ARNETT	FARMERS & MERCHANTS BANK	(580) 885-7515
BROKEN BOW	1ST BANK & TRUST	(580) 584-9123
CHICKASHA	FIRST NATIONAL BK & TRUST CO	(405) 224-2200
GUYMON	BANK OF THE PANHANDLE	(580) 338-2593
IDABEL	FIRST NATIONAL BK	(580) 286-3357
IDABEL	IDABEL NATIONAL BK	(580) 286-7656
LAVERNE	BANK OF LAVERNE	(580) 921-3321
MARLOW	FIRST NATIONAL BK IN MARLOW	(580) 658-5457
MCALESTER	FIRST NATIONAL BK & TRUST CO	(918) 426-0211
MIDWEST CITY	FIRST NATIONAL BK	(405) 732-4571
OKLAHOMA CITY	BANCFIRST	(405) 270-1086
OKLAHOMA CITY	BANKERS BANK	(405) 848-8877
PAULS VALLEY	PAULS VALLEY NATIONAL BK	(405) 238-9321
PAWNEE	FIRST NATIONAL BK OF PAWNEE	(918) 762-2503
POTEAU	CENTRAL NATIONAL BK OF POTEAU	(918) 647-2233
SALLISAW	FIRST NATIONAL BK SALLISAW	(918) 775-9136
SEILING	FIRST NATIONAL BK OF SEILING	(580) 922-4211
TEXHOMA	FIRST NATIONAL BK OF TEXHOMA	(580) 423-7541
THOMAS	FIRST NATIONAL BK OF THOMAS	(580) 661-3515
WALTERS	WALTERS BANK & TRUST CO	(580) 875-3396
WEATHERFORD	SOUTHWEST NATIONAL BK	(580) 774-0900
WOODWARD	STOCK EXCHANGE BANK	(580) 256-3314

Oregon

City	Name	Telephone
Rating: B+		
SALEM	PIONEER TRUST BANK NA	(503) 363-3136

Pennsylvania

City	Name	Telephone
Rating: A		
GRATZ	GRATZ NATIONAL BK	(717) 365-3181
LATROBE	COMMERCIAL BANK & TRUST OF PA	(724) 539-3501
NEFFS	NEFFS NATIONAL BK	(610) 767-3875
SMETHPORT	HAMLIN BANK & TRUST CO	(814) 887-5555
Rating: A-		
ALBION	COMMUNITY NATIONAL BK OF NW	(814) 756-4138
ERIE	MARQUETTE SB	(814) 455-4481
HONESDALE	HONESDALE NATIONAL BK	(570) 253-3355
HONESDALE	WAYNE BANK	(570) 253-1455
LANDISBURG	BANK OF LANDISBURG	(717) 789-3213
MIFFLINBURG	MIFFLINBURG BANK & TRUST CO	(570) 966-1041
NEW TRIPOLI	NEW TRIPOLI BANK	(610) 298-8811
TURBOTVILLE	TURBOTVILLE NATIONAL BK	(570) 649-5118
Rating: B+		
LIVERPOOL	FIRST NATIONAL BK OF LIVERPOOL	(717) 444-3714
MILTON	MILTON SAVINGS BANK	(570) 742-8541
NEWTOWN	FIRST NATIONAL BK & TRUST CO	(215) 860-9100
OAKS	SEI PRIVATE TRUST CO	(610) 676-1000
PHILADELPHIA	PORT RICHMOND SAVINGS	(215) 634-7000
RADNOR	HAVERFORD TRUST CO	(610) 995-8700
ROCHESTER	FARMERS BUILDING & SB	(724) 774-4970
SCRANTON	PENN SECURITY BANK & TRUST CO	(570) 346-7741
WELLSBORO	CITIZENS & NORTHERN BANK	(570) 724-3411

Rhode Island

City	Name	Telephone
Rating: B+		
LINCOLN	TALBOTS CLASSICS NATIONAL BK	(401) 335-5750

South Carolina

City	Name	Telephone
Rating: A		
GAFFNEY	FIRST PIEDMONT FS&LA OF	(864) 489-6046
HONEA PATH	COMMERCIAL BANK	(864) 369-7326
Rating: A-		
HAMPTON	PALMETTO STATE BK	(803) 943-2671
HOLLY HILL	FARMERS & MERCH BANK OF SC	(803) 496-3430
MANNING	BANK OF CLARENDON	(803) 433-4451
Rating: B+		
CHARLESTON	BANK OF SOUTH CAROLINA	(843) 724-1500
DARLINGTON	CAROLINA BANK & TRUST CO	(843) 398-8000
YORK	BANK OF YORK	(803) 684-4249

South Dakota

City	Name	Telephone
Rating: A		
BURKE	FIRST FIDELITY BANK	(605) 775-2641
PARKSTON	FARMERS STATE BK	(605) 928-7991
PIERRE	AMERICAN STATE BK OF PIERRE	(605) 224-9233
SIOUX FALLS	FIRST PREMIER BANK	(605) 357-3000
SIOUX FALLS	TARGET NATIONAL BK	(605) 362-4400
Rating: A-		
BELLE FOURCHE	PIONEER BANK & TRUST	(605) 892-2536
BRUCE	RICHLAND STATE BK	(605) 627-5671
DAKOTA DUNES	1ST FINANCIAL BANK USA	(605) 365-5191
PHILIP	FIRST NATIONAL BK IN PHILIP	(605) 859-2525
SISSETON	ROBERTS COUNTY NB OF SISSETON	(605) 698-7621
Rating: B+		
ALEXANDRIA	SECURITY STATE BK	(605) 239-4306
ARLINGTON	CITIZENS STATE BK OF ARLINGTON	(605) 983-5594
FORT PIERRE	FIRST NATIONAL BK	(605) 223-2521
GROTON	FIRST STATE BK OF CLAREMONT	(605) 397-2711
HERREID	CAMPBELL COUNTY BANK	(605) 437-2294
IPSWICH	IPSWICH STATE BK	(605) 426-6031
RAPID CITY	FIRST WESTERN FSB	(605) 341-1203
TYNDALL	SECURITY STATE BK	(605) 589-3313

Tennessee

City	Name	Telephone
Rating: A		
CARTHAGE	CITIZENS BANK	(615) 735-1490
RUTLEDGE	CITIZENS B&TC GRAINGER COUNTY	(865) 828-5237
Rating: A-		
JELLICO	UNION BANK	(423) 784-9446
PARIS	SECURITY BANK & TRUST CO	(731) 642-6644
SHELBYVILLE	FIRST COMMUNITY BK OF BEDFORD	(931) 684-5800
WAYNESBORO	BANK OF WAYNESBORO	(931) 722-2265
Rating: B+		
DICKSON	BANK OF DICKSON	(615) 446-3732
ELIZABETHTON	ELIZABETHTON FSB	(423) 543-5050
LIVINGSTON	FIRST NATIONAL BK OF TENNESSEE	(931) 823-1261
MANCHESTER	FIRST NATIONAL BK MANCHESTER	(931) 728-3518
MEMPHIS	FINANCIAL FSB	(901) 756-2848

Texas

City	Name	Telephone
Rating:	**A+**	
ALVIN	FIRST NATIONAL BK OF ALVIN	(281) 331-3151
BRADY	COMMERCIAL NATIONAL BK BRADY	(325) 597-2961
BURNET	FIRST STATE BK OF BURNET	(512) 756-2191
LIVINGSTON	FIRST NATIONAL BK LIVINGSTON	(936) 327-1234
MUENSTER	MUENSTER STATE BK	(940) 759-2257
PEARLAND	PEARLAND STATE BK	(281) 485-3211
TYLER	CITIZENS 1ST BANK	(903) 581-1900
Rating:	**A**	
AMARILLO	FIRSTBANK SOUTHWEST	(806) 355-9661
CARTHAGE	FIRST STATE BK & TRUST CO	(903) 693-6606
COLUMBUS	FIRST STATE BK	(979) 732-2332
COMANCHE	COMANCHE NATIONAL BK	(325) 356-2577
CORSICANA	COMMUNITY NATIONAL BK & TRUST	(903) 654-4500
DALLAS	INWOOD NATIONAL BK	(214) 358-5281
FARWELL	SECURITY STATE BK	(806) 481-3327
MARFA	BIG BEND BANKS NA	(432) 729-4344
PARIS	LAMAR NATIONAL BK	(903) 785-0701
PERRYTON	PERRYTON NATIONAL BK	(806) 435-9641
ROCKSPRINGS	PEOPLES STATE BK	(830) 683-2119
SWEETWATER	TEXAS NATIONAL BK	(325) 235-4997
VERNON	WAGGONER NATIONAL BK OF	(940) 552-2511
WILLS POINT	CITIZENS NB OF WILLS POINT	(903) 873-4157
YOAKUM	FIRST STATE BK	(361) 293-3572
YOAKUM	YOAKUM NATIONAL BK	(361) 293-5225
Rating:	**A-**	
ABILENE	FIRST FINANCIAL BANK NA	(325) 627-7200
ALBANY	FIRST NATIONAL BK OF ALBANY	(325) 762-2222
ANDREWS	NATIONAL BK OF ANDREWS	(432) 523-6800
ASPERMONT	FIRST NATIONAL BK OF ASPERMONT	(940) 989-3505
BROWNSVILLE	INTERNATIONAL BK OF COMMERCE	(956) 547-1000
BROWNWOOD	CITIZENS NB AT BROWNWOOD	(325) 643-3545
BUCKHOLTS	BUCKHOLTS STATE BK	(254) 593-3661
CENTER	SHELBY SB SSB	(936) 598-5688
COLORADO CITY	CITY NATIONAL BK COLORADO CITY	(325) 728-5221
CROSBYTON	CITIZENS NB OF CROSBYTON	(806) 675-2376
DEL RIO	AMISTAD BANK	(830) 775-0295
DESOTO	BANK OF DESOTO NA	(972) 780-7777
DILLEY	DILLEY STATE BK	(830) 965-1511
EASTLAND	FIRST FINANCIAL BANK NA	(254) 629-6100
EDEN	TEXAS FINANCIAL BANK	(325) 869-5511
FLOYDADA	FIRST NATIONAL BK OF FLOYDADA	(806) 983-3717
FORT WORTH	TRINITY BANK NA	(817) 763-9966
GROESBECK	FARMERS STATE BK	(254) 729-3272
GRUVER	GRUVER STATE BK	(806) 733-5061
HEBBRONVILLE	FIRST NATIONAL BK HEBBRONVILLE	(361) 527-3221
HENDERSON	HENDERSON FSB	(903) 657-2577
HUGHES SPRINGS	FIRST NB OF HUGHES SPRINGS	(903) 639-2521
JACKSONVILLE	AUSTIN BANK TEXAS NA	(903) 586-1526
JOHNSON CITY	JOHNSON CITY BANK	(830) 868-7131
JUNCTION	JUNCTION NATIONAL BK	(325) 446-2531
KILLEEN	FIRST TEXAS BANK	(254) 634-2132
LAMPASAS	FIRST TEXAS BANK	(512) 556-3691
LAREDO	COMMERCE BANK	(956) 724-1616
LAREDO	INTERNATIONAL BK OF COMMERCE	(956) 722-7611
LIBERTY	FIRST LIBERTY NATIONAL BK	(936) 336-6471
LIVINGSTON	FIRST STATE BK OF LIVINGSTON	(936) 327-5211
LUBBOCK	AMERICAN STATE BK	(806) 767-7000
MARION	MARION STATE BK	(830) 420-2331
MASON	MASON NATIONAL BK	(325) 347-5911
MINERAL WELLS	FIRST STATE BK MINERAL WELLS	(940) 325-7821
MOUNT VERNON	FIRST NATIONAL BK MOUNT	(903) 537-2201
MULESHOE	FIRST BANK OF MULESHOE	(806) 272-4515
NORMANGEE	NORMANGEE STATE BK	(936) 396-3611
ODESSA	WEST TEXAS STATE BK	(432) 337-2851
PARIS	LIBERTY NATIONAL BK IN PARIS	(903) 785-5555
PARIS	PEOPLES BANK	(903) 783-3800
SAN ANGELO	FIRST FINANCIAL BANK NA	(325) 659-5900
SAN ANGELO	TEXAS STATE BK	(325) 949-3721
SANGER	SANGER BANK	(940) 458-4600
SANTA ANNA	SANTA ANNA NATIONAL BK	(325) 348-3108
STRATFORD	FIRST STATE BK	(806) 396-5521
THE WOODLANDS	WOODFOREST NATIONAL BK	(832) 375-2000
THREE RIVERS	FIRST STATE BK	(361) 786-2525
ZAPATA	INTERNATIONAL BK OF COMMERCE	(956) 765-8361
ZAPATA	ZAPATA NATIONAL BK	(956) 765-4302
Rating:	**B+**	
ATHENS	FIRST STATE BK	(903) 676-1900
AUSTIN	HORIZON BANK SSB	(512) 637-5730
BANDERA	BANDERA BANK	(830) 796-3711
BELLVILLE	FIRST NATIONAL BK OF BELLVILLE	(979) 865-3181
BROWNWOOD	TEXAS BANK	(325) 649-9200
BUFFALO	CITIZENS STATE BK	(903) 322-4256
BURTON	BURTON STATE BK	(979) 289-3151
CARMINE	CARMINE STATE BK	(979) 278-3244
CENTER	FARMERS STATE BK	(936) 598-3311
CLAUDE	CITIZENS BANK	(806) 226-2661
CLEBURNE	FIRST FINANCIAL BANK NA	(817) 556-5000
COLDSPRING	BANK OF SAN JACINTO COUNTY	(936) 653-4395
CORPUS CHRISTI	VALUEBANK TEXAS	(361) 888-4451
CRYSTAL CITY	ZAVALA COUNTY BANK	(830) 374-5866
DALLAS	FIRST ASSOCIATIONS BANK	(972) 701-1100
DALLAS	PRESTON NATIONAL BK	(972) 960-6000
DE KALB	STATE BK OF DE KALB	(903) 667-2553
DE LEON	FARMERS & MERCHANTS BANK	(254) 893-2031
ELDORADO	FIRST NATIONAL BK OF ELDORADO	(325) 853-2561
EMORY	FIRST NATIONAL BK OF EMORY	(903) 473-2611
FALFURRIAS	FIRST NATIONAL BK FALFURRIAS	(361) 325-2565
FAYETTEVILLE	FAYETTEVILLE BANK	(979) 378-4261
FORT WORTH	FIRST COMMAND BANK	(888) 763-7600
FREEPORT	TEXAS GULF BANK NA	(979) 297-7211
GEORGETOWN	FIRST TEXAS BANK	(512) 863-2567
GRAHAM	GRAHAM SAVINGS & LOAN ASSN FA	(940) 549-2066
GRANBURY	FIRST NATIONAL BK OF GRANBURY	(817) 573-2655
HENDERSON	CITIZENS NATIONAL BK	(903) 657-8521
HEREFORD	FIRST FINANCIAL BANK	(806) 363-8200
HICO	FIRST NATIONAL BK OF HICO	(254) 796-4221
HOUSTON	HOUSTON COMMUNITY BANK NA	(281) 537-7200
HUNTSVILLE	FIRST FINANCIAL BANK	(936) 295-2224
INDUSTRY	INDUSTRY STATE BK	(979) 357-4437
JACKSBORO	JACKSBORO NATIONAL BK	(940) 567-5551
JASPER	FIRST NATIONAL BK OF JASPER	(409) 384-3486
JOURDANTON	JOURDANTON STATE BK	(830) 769-3557
KRESS	KRESS NATIONAL BK	(806) 684-2231
LAKE WORTH	STAR BANK OF TEXAS	(817) 238-7827
LOCKHART	FIRST-LOCKHART NATIONAL BK	(512) 398-3416

Texas (Continued)

Rating: B+ (Continued)

City	Name	Telephone
LONGVIEW	TEXAS BANK & TRUST CO	(903) 237-5500
LYTLE	LYTLE STATE BK OF LYTLE TEXAS	(830) 709-3601
MINERAL WELLS	FIRST FINANCIAL BANK NA	(940) 327-5400
MOODY	FIRST NATIONAL BK OF MOODY	(254) 853-2115
OVERTON	FIRST STATE BK	(903) 834-3161
REFUGIO	WOODFOREST BANK	(361) 526-2318
ROMA	CITIZENS STATE BK	(956) 849-2311
ROUND ROCK	FIRST TEXAS BANK	(512) 255-2501
ROUND TOP	ROUND TOP STATE BK	(979) 249-3151
SAN ANTONIO	BROADWAY NATIONAL BK	(210) 283-6500
SAN SABA	CITY NATIONAL BK OF SAN SABA	(325) 372-5721
SEALY	CITIZENS STATE BK	(979) 885-3571
SHALLOWATER	FIRST STATE BK	(806) 832-4525
SWEETWATER	FIRST FINANCIAL BANK NA	(325) 235-6600
TEMPLE	EXTRACO BANKS NA	(254) 774-5500
TEXAS CITY	MAINLAND BANK	(409) 948-1625
VAN	FIRST STATE BK	(903) 963-8651

Utah

Rating: A+

City	Name	Telephone
SALT LAKE CITY	OPTUMHEALTH BANK INC	(866) 234-8913

Rating: A

City	Name	Telephone
SALT LAKE CITY	GE CAPITAL FINANCIAL INC	(801) 733-2820

Rating: A-

City	Name	Telephone
LOGAN	CACHE VALLEY BANK	(435) 753-3020
SALT LAKE CITY	MEDALLION BANK	(801) 284-7065

Rating: B+

City	Name	Telephone
MURRAY	SALLIE MAE BANK	(801) 281-1423
OGDEN	TRANSPORTATION ALLIANCE BANK	(801) 624-4800
PARK CITY	LCA BANK CORP	(435) 658-4824
SAINT GEORGE	HERITAGE BANK	(435) 628-0433
SALT LAKE CITY	CIT BANK	(801) 412-6800
SALT LAKE CITY	CONTINENTAL BANK	(801) 595-7000
SALT LAKE CITY	MARLIN BUSINESS BANK	(888) 479-9111
SALT LAKE CITY	TARGET BANK	
SALT LAKE CITY	WOODLANDS COMMERCIAL BANK	(801) 264-6900

Virginia

City	Name	Telephone
Rating: A		
CARSON	BANK OF SOUTHSIDE VIRGINIA	(434) 246-5211
DANVILLE	VIRGINIA BANK & TRUST CO	(434) 793-6411
Rating: A-		
ALEXANDRIA	BURKE & HERBERT BK & TRUST CO	(703) 549-6600
BLACKSBURG	NATIONAL BK OF BLACKSBURG	(540) 951-6228
DANVILLE	AMERICAN NATIONAL BK & TRUST	(434) 792-5111
GRUNDY	GRUNDY NATIONAL BK	(276) 935-8111
NEW CASTLE	FARMERS & MERCH BK CRAIG CTY	(540) 864-5156
PHENIX	BANK OF CHARLOTTE COUNTY	(434) 542-5111
Rating: B+		
APPOMATTOX	FARMERS BANK OF APPOMATTOX	(434) 352-7171
MCLEAN	CARDINAL BANK	(703) 584-3400
MCLEAN	SONABANK	(703) 893-7400

City Name Telephone

Washington

City	Name	Telephone
Rating: A-		
KENNEWICK	COMMUNITY FIRST BANK	(509) 783-3435
PUYALLUP	VALLEY BANK	(253) 848-2316
YAKIMA	YAKIMA FS&LA	(509) 248-2634
Rating: B+		
OLYMPIA	SOUTH SOUND BANK	(360) 705-4200

West Virginia

Rating: A-

City	Name	Telephone
CLAY	CLAY COUNTY BANK INC	(304) 587-4221
CROSS LANES	CITY NATIONAL BK OF WV	(304) 769-1100
MOUNT HOPE	BANK OF MOUNT HOPE INC	(304) 877-5551
PARKERSBURG	COMMUNITY BANK OF	(304) 485-7991
UNION	BANK OF MONROE	(304) 772-3034
WESTON	CITIZENS BANK OF WESTON	(304) 269-2862

Rating: B+

City	Name	Telephone
FAYETTEVILLE	FAYETTE COUNTY NB	(304) 574-1212
HURRICANE	PUTNAM COUNTY BANK	(304) 562-9931
LOGAN	LOGAN BANK & TRUST CO	(304) 752-1166
THOMAS	MINERS & MERCHANTS BANK	(304) 463-4155
WILLIAMSON	FIRST NATIONAL BK WILLIAMSON	(304) 235-5300
WILLIAMSTOWN	WILLIAMSTOWN BANK INC	(304) 375-6262

Wisconsin

City	Name	Telephone
Rating:	**A+**	
SHELL LAKE	SHELL LAKE STATE BK	(715) 468-7858
Rating:	**A**	
FOND DU LAC	AMERICAN BANK	(920) 922-9292
GRAND MARSH	GRAND MARSH STATE BK	(608) 339-3351
HILLSBORO	FARMERS STATE BK HILLSBORO	(608) 489-2621
PALMYRA	PALMYRA STATE BK	(262) 495-2101
WHITEWATER	FIRST CITIZENS STATE BK	(262) 473-2112
Rating:	**A-**	
BONDUEL	BONDUEL STATE BK	(715) 758-2141
FOND DU LAC	NATIONAL EXCHANGE BANK &	(920) 921-7700
MADISON	FPC FINANCIAL FSB	(608) 821-2000
MEDFORD	TIME FSB	(715) 748-2231
PRAIRIE DU SAC	BANK OF PRAIRIE DU SAC	(608) 643-3393
WAUPACA	FARMERS STATE BK OF WAUPACA	(715) 258-1400
Rating:	**B+**	
AMHERST	INTERNATIONAL BK OF AMHERST	(715) 824-3325
BARRON	STERLING BANK	(715) 537-3141
BLACK RIVER	BLACK RIVER COUNTRY BANK	(715) 284-9448
BLOOMER	PEOPLES STATE BK OF BLOOMER	(715) 568-1100
GRESHAM	STATE BK	(715) 787-3201
HUSTISFORD	HUSTISFORD STATE BK	(920) 349-3241
LAND O'LAKES	HEADWATERS STATE BK	(715) 547-3383
MILWAUKEE	NORTHWESTERN MUTUAL WEALTH	(414) 665-5599
NEKOOSA	NEKOOSA PORT EDWARDS STATE	(715) 886-3104
PARK FALLS	FIRST NATIONAL BK PARK FALLS	(715) 762-2411
PLATTEVILLE	CLARE BANK NA	(608) 348-2727
WAUKESHA	WAUKESHA STATE BK	(262) 549-8500

City	Name	Telephone

Wyoming

City	Name	Telephone
Rating: A+		
NEWCASTLE	FIRST STATE BK OF NEWCASTLE	(307) 746-4411
Rating: A-		
CASPER	HILLTOP NATIONAL BK	(307) 265-2740
DOUGLAS	CONVERSE COUNTY BANK	(307) 358-5300

Section III

Rating Upgrades and Downgrades

A list of all

U.S. Commercial Banks, Savings Banks,

and Savings and Loans

receiving a rating upgrade or downgrade
during the current quarter.

Section III Contents

This section identifies those institutions receiving a rating change since the previous edition of this publication, whether it be a rating upgrade, rating downgrade, newly-rated company or the withdrawal of a rating. A rating upgrade or downgrade may entail a change from one letter grade to another, or it may mean the addition or deletion of a plus or minus sign within the same letter grade previously assigned to the company. Ratings are normally updated once each quarter of the year. In some instances, however, an institution's rating may be downgraded outside of the normal updates due to overriding circumstances.

1. **Institution Name** The name under which the institution was chartered. A company's name can be very similar to, or the same as, that of another, so verify the company's exact name, city, and state to make sure you are looking at the correct company.

2. **New Financial Strength Rating** Weiss rating assigned to the institution at the time of publication. Our ratings are designed to distinguish levels of insolvency risk and are measured on a scale from A to F based upon a wide range of factors. Highly rated companies are, in our opinion, less likely to experience financial difficulties than lower rated firms. See *About Weiss Financial Strength Ratings* on page 7 for more information and a description of what each rating means.

3. **State** The state in which the institution's headquarters or main office is located.

4. **Date of Change** Date that rating was finalized.

New Ratings

BANK NAME	STATE	DATE OF CHANGE
Rating: C		
WAINWRIGHT BANK & TRUST CO	MA	09/30/10
Rating: C-		
BANK MIDWEST NA	MO	09/30/10
FARMERS STATE BK	SD	09/30/10
HILLCREST BANK NA	KS	09/30/10
START COMMUNITY BANK	CT	09/30/10
Rating: D+		
SOUTHERN BANK & TRUST	SC	09/30/10
TEAM CAPITAL BANK	PA	09/30/10
Rating: D		
PROGRESSIVE SB	TN	09/30/10

Rating Upgrades

Rating: A

BANK NAME	STATE	PREVIOUS RATING	DATE OF CHANGE
BANK OF AUGUSTA	AR	A-	09/30/10
CITIZENS BANK & TRUST ST PAUL	NE	A-	09/30/10
FIRST NATIONAL BK ESTES PARK	CO	A-	09/30/10
FIRST TRUST & SB OF WATSEKA IL	IL	A-	09/30/10
GRINNELL STATE BK	IA	A-	09/30/10
IOWA TRUST & SB	IA	A-	09/30/10
MCGEHEE BANK	AR	A-	09/30/10
UNITED BANK & TRUST CO	IA	A-	09/30/10

Rating: A-

BANK NAME	STATE	PREVIOUS RATING	DATE OF CHANGE
BANK 2	OK	B+	09/30/10
BANK OF BAKER	MT	B+	09/30/10
BOONE BANK & TRUST CO	IA	B+	09/30/10
CITIZENS NB OF SOMERSET	KY	B+	09/30/10
COMMERCIAL CAPITAL BANK	LA	B+	09/30/10
FIRST BANK	MS	B+	09/30/10
FIRST NATIONAL BK OF NOKOMIS	IL	B+	09/30/10
FIRST STATE BK	TX	B+	09/30/10
FPC FINANCIAL FSB	WI	B	09/30/10
FRONTIER BANK	CO	B+	09/30/10
HENDERSON FSB	TX	B+	09/30/10
HENRY STATE BK	IL	B+	09/30/10
HERITAGE BANK	NE	B+	09/30/10
HOME STATE BK	IA	B+	09/30/10
HOME STATE BK	NE	B+	09/30/10
HONESDALE NATIONAL BK	PA	B+	09/30/10
JARRETTSVILLE FS&LA	MD	B+	09/30/10
LEADER BANK NA	MA	B+	09/30/10
MASON NATIONAL BK	TX	B+	09/30/10
RICHLAND STATE BK	LA	B+	09/30/10
SECURITY NATIONAL BK OF OMAHA	NE	B+	09/30/10
STATE BK & TRUST CO	IA	B+	09/30/10
TIAA-CREF TRUST CO FSB	MO	B	09/30/10
TRINITY BANK NA	TX	B+	09/30/10
WEST POINT BANK	KY	B+	09/30/10

Rating: B+

BANK NAME	STATE	PREVIOUS RATING	DATE OF CHANGE
ASTRA BANK	KS	B	09/30/10
BANK OF QUINCY	IL	B	09/30/10
BANKERS BANK	OK	B	09/30/10
BLACK RIVER COUNTRY BANK	WI	B	09/30/10
CARDINAL BANK	VA	B	09/30/10
CHESAPEAKE BANK & TRUST CO	MD	B	09/30/10
CITIZENS STATE BK	IA	B	09/30/10
COMMUNITY & SOUTHERN BANK	GA	B	09/30/10
CONTINENTAL BANK	UT	B	09/30/10
FARMERS SB	IA	B	09/30/10
FARMERS STATE BK	IA	B	09/30/10
FIRESIDE BANK	CA	B	09/30/10
FIRST NATIONAL BK BLANCHESTER	OH	B	09/30/10
FIRST NATIONAL BK CARROLLTON	KY	B	09/30/10
FIRST NATIONAL BK OF EMORY	TX	B	09/30/10
FIRST NATIONAL BK OF HICO	TX	B	09/30/10
FIRST NATIONAL BK OF PANA	IL	B	09/30/10
GOODFIELD STATE BK	IL	B	09/30/10
HEADWATERS STATE BK	WI	B	09/30/10
MERCANTILE BANK & TRUST CO	MA	B	09/30/10
MIDSTATES BANK NA	IA	B	09/30/10
NORTHERN TRUST NA	FL	B	09/30/10
PHENIX-GIRARD BANK	AL	B	09/30/10
PIONEER BANK	NM	B	09/30/10
SECURITY FIRST BANK OF ND	ND	B	09/30/10
SOUTHWEST NATIONAL BK	OK	B	09/30/10
TOWN & COUNTRY BK OF MISSOURI	MO	B-	09/30/10
TRANSPORTATION ALLIANCE BANK	UT	B	09/30/10
TUSTIN COMMUNITY BANK	CA	B	09/30/10
VICTORY COMMUNITY BANK	KY	B-	09/30/10

Rating: B

BANK NAME	STATE	PREVIOUS RATING	DATE OF CHANGE
5 STAR BANK	CO	B-	09/30/10
AMERICAN BANK	PA	B-	09/30/10
AMERICAN NATIONAL BK OF SIDNEY	NE	B-	09/30/10
BANK OF ENGLAND	AR	B-	09/30/10
BANK OF MCCRORY	AR	B-	09/30/10
BANK OF THE RIO GRANDE NA	NM	B-	09/30/10
BANNER COUNTY BANK INC	NE	B-	09/30/10
BEAL BANK NEVADA	NV	B-	09/30/10
BROWN COUNTY STATE BK	IL	B-	09/30/10
CALIFORNIA PACIFIC BANK	CA	B-	09/30/10
CAPITOL FSB	KS	B-	09/30/10
CITIZENS BANK OF EDINA	MO	B-	09/30/10
COMMERCE BANK NA	MO	B-	09/30/10
COMMUNITY FIRST BANK	IA	B-	09/30/10
CULLMAN SAVINGS BANK	AL	B-	09/30/10
DE WITT BANK & TRUST CO	AR	B-	09/30/10
DECORAH BANK & TRUST CO	IA	B-	09/30/10
FARMERS BANK OF LOHMAN MO	MO	B-	09/30/10
FARMERS STATE BK	KS	B-	09/30/10
FARMERS STATE BK OF CAMP POINT	IL	B-	09/30/10
FARMERS TRUST & SB	IA	B-	09/30/10
FIDELITY BANK OF TEXAS	TX	B-	09/30/10
FIDELITY FS&LA	OH	B-	09/30/10
FIRST BANK	AK	B-	09/30/10
FIRST BANK	TX	B-	09/30/10
FIRST BANK OF OWASSO	OK	B-	09/30/10
FIRST FS&LA OF MCMINNVILLE	OR	B-	09/30/10
FIRST NATIONAL B&T ELK CITY	OK	C+	09/30/10
FIRST NATIONAL BK INDEPENDENCE	KS	B-	09/30/10
FIRST NATIONAL BK LAKE JACKSON	TX	B-	09/30/10
FIRST NATIONAL BK OF HEREFORD	TX	B-	09/30/10
FIRST NATIONAL BK OF HUGO	CO	B-	09/30/10
FIRST SECURITY BANK	AR	B-	09/30/10
FIRST STATE BK OF MUNICH	ND	B-	09/30/10
FIRST UNITED BANK	TX	B-	09/30/10
FOUNDATION BANK	OH	B-	09/30/10
GREAT SOUTHERN BANK	MO	B-	09/30/10
HOMETOWN BANK	WI	B-	09/30/10
HSBC BANK NEVADA NA	NV	B-	09/30/10
IBERIABANK	LA	B-	09/30/10
ILLINI BANK	IL	B-	09/30/10
JEFFERSON BANK	MS	B-	09/30/10
JUSTIN STATE BK	TX	B-	09/30/10
LAMESA NATIONAL BK	TX	B-	09/30/10
MAGNOLIA BANK INC	KY	B-	09/30/10
MONTROSEBANK	CO	B-	09/30/10
NATIONAL BK OF SALLISAW	OK	B-	09/30/10
NEBRASKA STATE BK	NE	B-	09/30/10
NORTHRIM BANK	AK	B-	09/30/10
NORTHSTAR BANK	IA	B-	09/30/10
PEOPLES BANK OF BEDFORD COUNTY	TN	B-	09/30/10
PEOPLES STATE BK	SD	B-	09/30/10
PREFERRED BANK	TX	B-	09/30/10
PROVINCE BANK FSB	PA	B-	09/30/10
QUAINT OAK BANK	PA	B-	09/30/10
RANCHO SANTA FE THRIFT & LOAN	CA	B-	09/30/10
RESOURCE BANK	LA	B-	09/30/10
SECURITY STATE BK	IA	B-	09/30/10
SECURITY STATE BK	IA	B-	09/30/10
STEARNS BANK NA	MN	B-	09/30/10

Rating Upgrades (Continued)

Rating: B (Continued)

BANK NAME	STATE	PREVIOUS RATING	DATE OF CHANGE
STEARNS BANK UPSALA NA	MN	B-	09/30/10
STIFEL BANK & TRUST	MO	B-	09/30/10
STOCKMAN BANK OF MONTANA	MT	B-	09/30/10
TOWN & COUNTRY BANK MIDWEST	MO	B-	09/30/10
TOWN & COUNTRY BANK OF QUINCY	IL	B-	09/30/10
TOWN-COUNTRY NATIONAL BK	AL	B-	09/30/10
UNION COUNTY SB	NJ	B-	09/30/10
UNION NATIONAL BK & TRUST CO	WI	B-	09/30/10
WASHITA STATE BK	OK	B-	09/30/10

Rating: B-

BANK NAME	STATE	PREVIOUS RATING	DATE OF CHANGE
ALLY BANK	UT	C+	09/30/10
ALTAPACIFIC BANK	CA	C+	09/30/10
AMERICAN NATIONAL BK	NE	C+	09/30/10
ANNANDALE STATE BK	MN	C	09/30/10
ARKANSAS COUNTY BANK	AR	C+	09/30/10
AUSTIN COUNTY STATE BK	TX	C+	09/30/10
BANK IOWA	IA	C+	09/30/10
BANK IOWA	IA	C+	09/30/10
BANK NORTHWEST	MO	C+	09/30/10
BANK OF GALESVILLE	WI	C+	09/30/10
BANK OF LAKE VILLAGE	AR	C+	09/30/10
BANK OF LUXEMBURG	WI	C+	09/30/10
BANK OF MILTON	WI	C+	09/30/10
BANK OF RIVER OAKS	TX	C+	09/30/10
BANK TOKYO-MITSUBISHI UFJ TC	NY	C	09/30/10
BANKERS BANK NORTHEAST	CT	C+	09/30/10
CAPITAL BANK	MN	C+	09/30/10
CITIZENS BANK & TRUST CO	AR	C+	09/30/10
CITIZENS STATE BK	KS	C+	09/30/10
CITIZENS STATE BK OF CLAYTON	WI	C+	09/30/10
CITY FIRST BANK OF DC NA	DC	C	09/30/10
COLORADO FSB	CO	C+	09/30/10
COLUMBUS FIRST BANK	OH	C+	09/30/10
COMMUNITY BK OF THE ARBUCKLES	OK	C+	09/30/10
COMMUNITY BKG CO OF FITZGERALD	GA	C+	09/30/10
COTTAGE SB	OH	C+	09/30/10
COTTONPORT BANK	LA	C+	09/30/10
DAKOTA HERITAGE STATE BK	SD	C+	09/30/10
EAGLE BANK & TRUST CO	AR	C+	09/30/10
ELMIRA SAVINGS BANK FSB	NY	C+	09/30/10
EVERETT CO-OP BANK	MA	C+	09/30/10
FARMERS NATIONAL BK OF KANSAS	KS	C+	09/30/10
FARMINGTON STATE BK	WA	C	09/30/10
FIDELITY NATIONAL BK	AR	C+	09/30/10
FIRST CITIZENS BANK & TRUST CO	SC	C+	09/30/10
FIRST FEDERAL BANK LITTLEFIELD	TX	C+	09/30/10
FIRST LIBERTY BANK	OK	C+	09/30/10
FIRST NATIONAL BK	TX	C+	09/30/10
FIRST NATIONAL BK & TRUST CO	KS	C+	09/30/10
FIRST NATIONAL BK OF BARRY	IL	C+	09/30/10
FIRST NATIONAL BK OF ELMER	NJ	C+	09/30/10
FIRST SECURITY BANK CANBY	MN	C+	09/30/10
FIRST SECURITY BANK-SLEEPY EYE	MN	C+	09/30/10
FIRST SECURITY BK-LAKE BENTON	MN	C+	09/30/10
FIRST STATE BK OF BEECHER CITY	IL	C+	09/30/10
FIRST TRUST & SB	IA	C+	09/30/10
FREESTAR BANK NA	IL	C+	09/30/10
GARFIELD COUNTY BANK	MT	C	09/30/10
GATEWAY BANK	MN	C+	09/30/10
GE MONEY BANK	UT	C+	09/30/10
GOLD COAST BANK	IL	C+	09/30/10
GOLDEN VALLEY BANK	CA	C+	09/30/10
GRAND MARAIS STATE BK	MN	C+	09/30/10
GREATER HUDSON BANK NA	NY	C	09/30/10
HILL-DODGE BANKING CO	IL	C+	09/30/10
HINGHAM INSTITUTION FOR SAVING	MA	C+	09/30/10
INTERBANK	OK	C-	09/30/10
LEVEL ONE BANK	MI	C	09/30/10
LIBERTY BANK OF ARKANSAS	AR	C+	09/30/10
LITTLE BANK INC	NC	C+	09/30/10
MAPLE CITY SAVINGS BANK FSB	NY	C-	09/30/10
MILLENNIUM BANK	KS	C+	09/30/10
NORTH CENTRAL BANK	IL	C+	09/30/10
NORTHERN STATE BK OF GONVICK	MN	C+	09/30/10
PATRIOT COMMUNITY BANK	MA	C+	09/30/10
PEOPLES BANK & TRUST CO	OK	C+	09/30/10
PEOPLES STATE BK OF PLAINVIEW	MN	C+	09/30/10
PINE BLUFF NATIONAL BK	AR	C+	09/30/10
PINERIES BANK	WI	C+	09/30/10
PONY EXPRESS COMMUNITY BANK	MO	C+	09/30/10
PRIME BANK	OK	C+	09/30/10
SCOTT VALLEY BANK	CA	C+	09/30/10
SECURITY FED SB MCMINNVILLE	TN	C+	09/30/10
SECURITY STATE BK & TRUST	TX	C+	09/30/10
SIMMONS FIRST TRUST CO NA	AR	U	09/30/10
SPRATT SAVINGS & LOAN ASSN	SC	C+	09/30/10
STARION FINANCIAL	ND	C+	09/30/10
STATE SB	IA	C+	09/30/10
STATE SB	IA	C+	09/30/10
SUNDOWN STATE BK	TX	C+	09/30/10
SUNFLOWER BANK NA	KS	C+	09/30/10
SUNWEST BANK	CA	C	09/30/10
TRIAD BANK NA	OK	C+	09/30/10
TRUST CO OF VIRGINIA	VA	C+	09/30/10
UNION STATE BK	KS	C+	09/30/10
USNY BANK	NY	C+	09/30/10
WEST BANK	IA	C+	09/30/10
WINTHROP STATE BK	MN	C+	09/30/10

Rating: C+

BANK NAME	STATE	PREVIOUS RATING	DATE OF CHANGE
AMERICAN EXCHANGE BANK	NE	C-	09/30/10
AMERICAN STATE BK	IA	C	09/30/10
ANTWERP EXCHANGE BANK CO	OH	C	09/30/10
BANK IOWA	IA	C	09/30/10
BANK OF ALMA	WI	C	09/30/10
BANK OF ANGUILLA	MS	C	09/30/10
BANK OF CAMDEN	TN	C	09/30/10
BANK OF DENVER	CO	C	09/30/10
BANK OF DONIPHAN	NE	C	09/30/10
BANK OF HILLSBORO	MO	C	09/30/10
BANK OF LEXINGTON INC	KY	C	09/30/10
BANKFIRST	NE	C	09/30/10
BANKFIVE	MA	C	09/30/10
BANNER BANKS	WI	C	09/30/10
BURLING BANK	IL	C	09/30/10
CAMDEN NATIONAL BK	AL	C	09/30/10
CITIZENS ALLIANCE BANK	MN	C	09/30/10
CITIZENS NB OF PARK RAPIDS	MN	C	09/30/10
CITY NATIONAL BK	CA	C	09/30/10
COMERICA BANK & TRUST NA	MI	C-	09/30/10
COMMUNITY BANK	NE	C	09/30/10
COMMUNITY STATE BK	IA	C	09/30/10
COMMUNITY STATE BK	OK	C	09/30/10
COUNTRY BANK FOR SAVINGS	MA	C	09/30/10
CRAWFORD COUNTY TRUST & SB	IA	C	09/30/10
CUMBERLAND BANK & TRUST	TN	C	09/30/10
CUSTODIAL TRUST CO	NJ	U	09/30/10
DESOTO COUNTY BANK	MS	C	09/30/10
DURDEN BANKING CO INC	GA	C	09/30/10

Rating Upgrades (Continued)

Rating: C+ (Continued)

BANK NAME	STATE	PREVIOUS RATING	DATE OF CHANGE
EQUITY BANK A NA	KS	C	09/30/10
EXCHANGE STATE BK	IA	C	09/30/10
EXCHANGE STATE BK	MI	C	09/30/10
F&M BANK	NE	C	09/30/10
FARMERS & MERCH STATE BK	MN	C	09/30/10
FARMERS BANK & TRUST CO	KY	C	09/30/10
FARMERS STATE BK	KS	C	09/30/10
FIDELITY BANK	TX	C	09/30/10
FIRST AMERICAN TRUST FSB	CA	C	09/30/10
FIRST BANK OF CONROE NA	TX	C	09/30/10
FIRST ELECTRONIC BANK	UT	C-	09/30/10
FIRST FSB	TN	C	09/30/10
FIRST FSB OF LINCOLNTON	NC	C	09/30/10
FIRST FSB OF MASCOUTAH	IL	C	09/30/10
FIRST NATIONAL BK IN CRESTON	IA	C	09/30/10
FIRST NATIONAL BK IN MUNDAY	TX	C	09/30/10
FIRST NATIONAL BK OF BORGER	TX	C-	09/30/10
FIRST NATIONAL BK OF FRIEND	NE	C	09/30/10
FIRST NATIONAL BK OF LOGAN	IA	C-	09/30/10
FIRST NATIONAL BK OF OMAHA	NE	C-	09/30/10
FIRST NATIONAL BK OF PANDORA	OH	C	09/30/10
FIRST NATIONAL BK OF PICAYUNE	MS	C	09/30/10
FIRST NB OF THE MID-CITIES	TX	C	09/30/10
FIRST SOUTH BANK	TN	C	09/30/10
FIRST SOUTHERN BANK	AL	C	09/30/10
FIRST VALLEY BANK	MT	C	09/30/10
GEORGETOWN SAVINGS BANK	MA	C	09/30/10
GIBRALTAR BANK	NJ	C	09/30/10
GLENNVILLE BANK	GA	C	09/30/10
GRAND BANK	OK	C-	09/30/10
HEARTLAND STATE BK	SD	C	09/30/10
HERITAGE BANK	WA	C-	09/30/10
HOME FS&LA OF NILES	OH	C-	09/30/10
HOME STATE BK	MN	C	09/30/10
INDEPENDENT BANK	TX	C	09/30/10
JACKSONVILLE SB	IL	C	09/30/10
KCB BANK	MO	C	09/30/10
KEARNEY TRUST CO	MO	C	09/30/10
KENTLAND FS&LA	IN	C-	09/30/10
LA FARGE STATE BK	WI	C	09/30/10
LANDMANDS BANK	IA	C-	09/30/10
LINCOLN FSB OF NEBRASKA	NE	C	09/30/10
LUTHER BURBANK SAVINGS	CA	C-	09/30/10
MALVERN NATIONAL BK	AR	C	09/30/10
MEDINA SAVINGS & LOAN ASSN	NY	C	09/30/10
MERCHANTS BANK NA	MN	C	09/30/10
MERRIMACK COUNTY SB	NH	C	09/30/10
MID AMERICA BANK	MO	C	09/30/10
MIDSOUTH BANK NA	LA	C-	09/30/10
MILLEDGEVILLE STATE BK	IL	C	09/30/10
MONSON SB	MA	C	09/30/10
MOODY NATIONAL BK	TX	C	09/30/10
MORRIS COUNTY NATIONAL BK	TX	C	09/30/10
MVB BANK INC	WV	C	09/30/10
NORTH JERSEY COMMUNITY BANK	NJ	C	09/30/10
NORTHWOODS STATE BK	IA	C	09/30/10
ONEIDA SB	NY	C	09/30/10
PACIFIC CONTINENTAL BANK	OR	C-	09/30/10
PEOPLES BANK	KS	C	09/30/10
PEOPLES BANK OF GREENSBORO	AL	C	09/30/10
PEOPLES COMMUNITY BANK	WI	C	09/30/10
PEOPLES STATE BK	SD	C	09/30/10
PIGEON FALLS STATE BK	WI	C	09/30/10
PIONEER SB	NY	C	09/30/10
PREMIER COMMUNITY BANK	WI	C	09/30/10
PRIVATE BANK OF BUCKHEAD	GA	C	09/30/10
PURDUM STATE BK	NE	C	09/30/10
ROANOKE RAPIDS SB SSB	NC	C	09/30/10
ROCK SPRINGS NATIONAL BK	WY	C	09/30/10
ROYAL BANKS OF MISSOURI	MO	C	09/30/10
SANTA CRUZ COUNTY BANK	CA	C	09/30/10
SECOND FS&LA OF PHILADELPHIA	PA	C	09/30/10
SECURITY FIRST BANK	NE	C	09/30/10
SECURITY STATE BK FERGUS FALLS	MN	C	09/30/10
SECURITY STATE BK HOWARD LAKE	MN	C	09/30/10
SHARON SB	PA	C	09/30/10
SHERIDAN STATE BK	IL	C	09/30/10
SOUTHERN HERITAGE BANK	TN	C	09/30/10
SOVEREIGN BANK	TX	C	09/30/10
STATE BK OF WHEATON	MN	C	09/30/10
STC CAPITAL BANK	IL	C	09/30/10
STELLARONE BANK	VA	C-	09/30/10
TEXAS HERITAGE BANK	TX	C	09/30/10
TITONKA SB	IA	C	09/30/10
UNION BANKING CO	OH	C	09/30/10
UNIVERSITY NATIONAL BK	MN	C-	09/30/10
VIRGINIA NATIONAL BK	VA	C	09/30/10
VISTA BANK TEXAS	TX	C	09/30/10
WAUMANDEE STATE BK	WI	C	09/30/10
WELLS FARGO DELAWARE TR CO NA	DE	U	09/30/10
WENONA STATE BK	IL	C	09/30/10

Rating: C

BANK NAME	STATE	PREVIOUS RATING	DATE OF CHANGE
1ST CAPITAL BANK	CA	C-	09/30/10
ACCESS BANK	NE	C-	09/30/10
AFFILIATED BANK	TX	C-	09/30/10
ALLEGHENY VALLEY BK PITTSBURGH	PA	C-	09/30/10
ALMA BANK	NY	C-	09/30/10
AMERICAN EXCHANGE BANK LINDSAY	OK	C-	09/30/10
AMERICAN MOMENTUM BANK	FL	C-	09/30/10
AMERICAN NATIONAL BK OF TEXAS	TX	C-	09/30/10
ANCHOR BANK NA	MN	C-	09/30/10
ARMED FORCES BANK OF CA NA	KS	C-	09/30/10
ARMSTRONG BANK	OK	C-	09/30/10
BANK NORTH	WI	C-	09/30/10
BANK OF BELLEVILLE	IL	C-	09/30/10
BANK OF DADE	GA	C-	09/30/10
BANK OF HEMET	CA	C-	09/30/10
BANK OF JACKSON HOLE	WY	D+	09/30/10
BANK OF MINDEN	MO	C-	09/30/10
BANK OF MONTGOMERY	IL	C-	09/30/10
BANK OF SAN FRANCISCO	CA	C-	09/30/10
BANK OF THE WEST	CA	C-	09/30/10
BANK OF WEDOWEE	AL	C-	09/30/10
BANKFIRST FINANCIAL SERVICES	MS	C-	09/30/10
BENCHMARK COMMUNITY BANK	VA	C-	09/30/10
BERKSHIRE BANK	MA	C-	09/30/10
BIG SKY WESTERN BANK	MT	C-	09/30/10
BK & TRUST BRYAN/COLLEGE STATN	TX	D+	09/30/10
BLUESTEM NATIONAL BK	IL	C-	09/30/10
CARROLLTON BANK	IL	C-	09/30/10
CENTRAL VALLEY BANK	WA	C-	09/30/10
CENTURY BANK OF OKLAHOMA	OK	C-	09/30/10
CITIZENS B&TC OF JACKSON	KY	C-	09/30/10
CITIZENS BANK	KY	C-	09/30/10
CITIZENS FIRST BANK	KY	C-	09/30/10
CITIZENS STATE BK	NE	C-	09/30/10
CLAREMONT SB	NH	C-	09/30/10
COLONIAL SAVINGS FA	TX	D	09/30/10
COMERICA BANK	TX	C-	09/30/10

Rating Upgrades (Continued)

Rating: C (Continued)

BANK NAME	STATE	PREVIOUS RATING	DATE OF CHANGE
COMMERCIAL BANK & TRUST CO	AR	C-	09/30/10
COMMERCIAL SB	OH	C-	09/30/10
COMMERCIAL STATE BK	TX	C-	09/30/10
COMMUNITY BANK	IA	C-	09/30/10
COMMUNITY BANK	KS	C-	09/30/10
COMMUNITY BANK	LA	C-	09/30/10
COMMUNITY BANK OF MISSISSIPPI	MS	C-	09/30/10
COMMUNITY NATIONAL BK	KS	C-	09/30/10
COPPERMARK BANK	OK	D+	09/30/10
COUNTY BANK	MO	C-	09/30/10
CREST SAVINGS BANK	NJ	C-	09/30/10
CROGHAN COLONIAL BANK	OH	C-	09/30/10
CROSS COUNTY BANK	AR	C-	09/30/10
DISCOVER BANK	DE	C-	09/30/10
DNB FIRST NA	PA	C-	09/30/10
DOUGLAS NATIONAL BK	GA	C-	09/30/10
EITZEN STATE BK	MN	C-	09/30/10
EMBARCADERO BANK	CA	C-	09/30/10
ENCORE NATIONAL BK	FL	C-	09/30/10
ENNIS STATE BK	TX	C-	09/30/10
ENTERPRISE BANK & TRUST	MO	C-	09/30/10
F & M BANK NA OKLAHOMA CITY OK	OK	C-	09/30/10
FARMERS & MERCH BK ST CLAIR	MO	C-	09/30/10
FARMERS & MERCHANTS BANK	TN	C-	09/30/10
FARMERS & TRADERS BK CAMPTON	KY	C-	09/30/10
FARMERS BANK FRANKFORT INDIANA	IN	C-	09/30/10
FARMERS DEPOSIT BANK	KY	C-	09/30/10
FARMERS EXCHANGE BANK	OK	C-	09/30/10
FARMERS STATE BK	KY	C-	09/30/10
FIA CARD SERVICES NA	DE	C-	09/30/10
FIDELITY S&LA OF BUCKS COUNTY	PA	C-	09/30/10
FIFTH THIRD BANK	OH	C-	09/30/10
FIRST BANK & TRUST CO	OK	D+	09/30/10
FIRST BANK FINANCIAL CENTRE	WI	C-	09/30/10
FIRST CENTRAL BANK	NE	C-	09/30/10
FIRST CENTRAL BANK MCCOOK	NE	C-	09/30/10
FIRST CHOICE BANK	NJ	C-	09/30/10
FIRST COMMUNITY BK SILVER LAKE	MN	C-	09/30/10
FIRST FS&LA OF LAKEWOOD	OH	C-	09/30/10
FIRST MISSOURI NATIONAL BK	MO	C-	09/30/10
FIRST NATIONAL BK	NE	C-	09/30/10
FIRST NATIONAL BK & TRUST CO	NE	C-	09/30/10
FIRST NATIONAL BK OF FLETCHER	OK	C-	09/30/10
FIRST NATIONAL BK OF PIKEVILLE	TN	C-	09/30/10
FIRST NATIONAL BK PENNSYLVANIA	PA	C-	09/30/10
FIRST NATIONAL BK SIOUX FALLS	SD	C-	09/30/10
FIRST RESOURCE BANK	PA	C-	09/30/10
FIRST SECURITY BANK OF HELENA	MT	C-	09/30/10
FIRST SOUTHERN STATE BK	AL	C-	09/30/10
FIRST STATE BK	NE	C-	09/30/10
FIRST STATE BK CENTRAL TEXAS	TX	C-	09/30/10
FIRST STATE BK OF BIGFORK	MN	C-	09/30/10
FIRST STATE BK OF WYOMING	MN	C-	09/30/10
FIRSTATLANTIC BANK	FL	C-	09/30/10
FNB BANK	AL	C-	09/30/10
FRANKLIN SB	NH	C-	09/30/10
FREEDOM BANK OF VIRGINIA	VA	C-	09/30/10
FREMONT NATIONAL BK & TRUST CO	NE	C-	09/30/10
FRONTIER STATE BK	OK	C-	09/30/10
GATEWAY BANK OF PENNSYLVANIA	PA	C-	09/30/10
GLEN ROCK SB	NJ	C-	09/30/10
GRANT COUNTY BANK	KS	C-	09/30/10
HARRIS CENTRAL NA	IL	U	09/30/10
HARTSBURG STATE BK	IL	C-	09/30/10
HOLCOMB STATE BK	IL	C-	09/30/10
HOLMES COUNTY BANK & TRUST CO	MS	C-	09/30/10
HOME LOAN SB	OH	C-	09/30/10
HOME SB OF ALBEMARLE SSB	NC	C-	09/30/10
HOOSAC BANK	MA	C-	09/30/10
HUDSON VALLEY BANK NA	NY	C-	09/30/10
HYDEN CITIZENS BANK	KY	C-	09/30/10
INTEGRITY BANK SSB	TX	C-	09/30/10
IOWA STATE BK & TRUST CO	IA	C-	09/30/10
IRELAND BANK	ID	C-	09/30/10
JIM THORPE NATIONAL BK	PA	C-	09/30/10
KENNEBUNK SB	ME	C-	09/30/10
KEYSTONE BANK	AL	C-	09/30/10
LAKESIDE NATIONAL BK	TX	C-	09/30/10
LONE STAR STATE BK OF WEST TX	TX	C-	09/30/10
MANSON STATE BK	IA	C-	09/30/10
MANUFACTURERS BANK & TRUST CO	IA	C-	09/30/10
MID-CENTRAL FSB	MN	C-	09/30/10
MIDWEST BANK	MN	C-	09/30/10
MIDWESTONE BANK	IA	C-	09/30/10
MILESTONE BANK	PA	C-	09/30/10
MINERS BANK	PA	C-	09/30/10
NEWPORT FEDERAL BANK	TN	C-	09/30/10
NORTH TEXAS BANK NA	TX	C-	09/30/10
NORTHEAST GEORGIA BANK	GA	C-	09/30/10
OAKWORTH CAPITAL BANK	AL	C-	09/30/10
OLD MISSION BANK	MI	C-	09/30/10
ORANGE COMMUNITY BANK	CA	D+	09/30/10
OSSIAN STATE BK	IN	C-	09/30/10
PARIS NATIONAL BK	MO	C-	09/30/10
PINNACLE BANK	IA	C-	09/30/10
PITTSFIELD CO-OP BANK	MA	C-	09/30/10
PLATTE VALLEY BANK	WY	C-	09/30/10
PLATTE VALLEY STATE BK & TRUST	NE	C-	09/30/10
POCA VALLEY BANK INC	WV	C-	09/30/10
QUAD CITY BANK & TRUST CO	IA	C-	09/30/10
QUARRY CITY SAVINGS & LOAN ASSN	MO	C-	09/30/10
REGENTS BANK NA	CA	C-	09/30/10
RIVER BANK & TRUST	AL	C-	09/30/10
SHARE PLUS FEDERAL BANK	TX	D+	09/30/10
SHELBY COUNTY STATE BK	IA	C-	09/30/10
SIGNATURE BANK	IL	C-	09/30/10
SOLON STATE BK	IA	C-	09/30/10
SOUTHEAST BANK & TRUST	TN	C-	09/30/10
SUTTER COMMUNITY BANK	CA	C-	09/30/10
TEJAS BANK	TX	D+	09/30/10
TRUSTMARK NATIONAL BK	MS	C-	09/30/10
UNION STATE BK	IA	C-	09/30/10
UNITED REPUBLIC BANK	NE	C-	09/30/10
UNIVERSITY BANK	KS	C-	09/30/10
VALLEY BANK & TRUST	CO	C-	09/30/10
VALLEY NATIONAL BK	OK	C-	09/30/10
VALLEY STATE BK	KS	C-	09/30/10
VERUS BANK OF COMMERCE	CO	C-	09/30/10
VOLUNTEER STATE BK	TN	C-	09/30/10
WEBBANK	UT	D+	09/30/10
WELLS FARGO BANK NORTHWEST NA	UT	C-	09/30/10
WESTERN NATIONAL BK	TX	C-	09/30/10
WESTERN STATE BK	ND	C-	09/30/10
WEYMOUTH BANK	MA	C-	09/30/10
WILLAMETTE VALLEY BANK	OR	C-	09/30/10
WOOD & HUSTON BANK	MO	C-	09/30/10
YORK STATE BK & TRUST CO	NE	C-	09/30/10

Rating: C-

BANK NAME	STATE	PREVIOUS RATING	DATE OF CHANGE
ALASKA PACIFIC BANK	AK	D	09/30/10

Rating Upgrades (Continued)

Rating: C- (Continued)

BANK NAME	STATE	PREVIOUS RATING	DATE OF CHANGE
AMERICAN BANK OF OKLAHOMA	OK	D+	09/30/10
AMERICAN BANK OF TEXAS NA	TX	D+	09/30/10
AMERICAN COMMUNITY BANK	NY	D-	09/30/10
ATLANTIC CENTRAL BANKERS BANK	PA	D+	09/30/10
BANK OF BEAVER CITY	OK	D+	09/30/10
BANK OF CADIZ & TRUST CO	KY	D+	09/30/10
BANK OF CAPE COD	MA	D+	09/30/10
BANK OF FRANKLIN	MS	D+	09/30/10
BANK OF IBERIA	MO	D+	09/30/10
BANK OF INDIANA NA	IN	D+	09/30/10
BANK OF LITTLE ROCK	AR	D+	09/30/10
BANK OF WALTERBORO	SC	D+	09/30/10
BANKANNAPOLIS	MD	D+	09/30/10
BARCLAYS BANK DELAWARE	DE	D+	09/30/10
BARRINGTON BANK & TRUST CO NA	IL	D+	09/30/10
BATH STATE BK	IN	D+	09/30/10
BELMONT BANK & TRUST CO	IL	D+	09/30/10
BUSEY BANK	IL	D+	09/30/10
CAPAHA BANK SB	MO	D+	09/30/10
CASS COUNTY BANK INC	NE	D+	09/30/10
CENTRAL BANK	UT	D+	09/30/10
CIRCLE BANK	CA	D+	09/30/10
CITIZENS FIRST BANK	FL	D+	09/30/10
CITIZENS STATE BK & TRUST CO	KS	D+	09/30/10
COMMERCIAL BANK OF MINNESOTA	MN	D+	09/30/10
COMMERCIAL ST BK OF EL CAMPO	TX	D+	09/30/10
COMMONWEALTH BUSINESS BANK	CA	D+	09/30/10
COMMUNITY BANK COAST	MS	D+	09/30/10
COMMUNITY BANK OF NORTHERN WI	WI	D+	09/30/10
COMMUNITY BUSINESS BANK	CA	D+	09/30/10
CONSOLIDATED BANK & TRUST CO	VA	D+	09/30/10
CRYSTAL LAKE BK & TRUST CO NA	IL	D+	09/30/10
DE WITT BANK & TRUST CO	IA	D+	09/30/10
DHANIS STATE BK	TX	D+	09/30/10
EAGLE NATIONAL BK	PA	D+	09/30/10
EASTWOOD BANK	MN	D+	09/30/10
EMIGRANT MERCANTILE BANK	NY	U	09/30/10
EXCHANGE STATE BK	IL	D+	09/30/10
FAIRFAX STATE SB	IA	D+	09/30/10
FARMERS & MERCH BANK & TRUST	WI	D+	09/30/10
FARMERS & MERCH STATE BK	MN	D+	09/30/10
FARMERS & MERCH STATE BK ALPHA	MN	D+	09/30/10
FARMERS STATE BK OF HARTLAND	MN	D+	09/30/10
FARMERS TRUST & SB	IA	D	09/30/10
FIELDPOINT PRIVATE BANK & TRUST	CT	D	09/30/10
FIRST CAPITAL BANK OF KENTUCKY	KY	D+	09/30/10
FIRST COMMONWEALTH BANK	PA	D+	09/30/10
FIRST CREDIT BANK	CA	D	09/30/10
FIRST INDEPENDENT BANK	MO	D+	09/30/10
FIRST NATIONAL BK OF BUFFALO	WY	D+	09/30/10
FIRST SENTINEL BANK	VA	D+	09/30/10
FIRST STATE BK	TN	D+	09/30/10
FIRST STATE BK OF MURDOCK	MN	D	09/30/10
FIRST STATE BK OF SWANVILLE	MN	D+	09/30/10
FIRST TENNESSEE BANK NA	TN	D+	09/30/10
FISHER NATIONAL BK	IL	D+	09/30/10
FRANKLIN FSB	VA	D	09/30/10
GARDNER BANK	KS	D+	09/30/10
GRANT COUNTY DEPOSIT BANK	KY	D+	09/30/10
GREAT PLAINS BANK	SD	D+	09/30/10
GUADALUPE NATIONAL BK	TX	D+	09/30/10
HARDIN COUNTY SB	IA	D+	09/30/10
HARFORD BANK	MD	D+	09/30/10
HERITAGE BANK OF THE SOUTH	GA	D+	09/30/10
HERITAGE COMMUNITY BANK	SC	D+	09/30/10
HERRIN SECURITY BANK	IL	D+	09/30/10
HOME BANK & TRUST CO	KS	D+	09/30/10
HOME FEDERAL BANK	ID	D+	09/30/10
HOME SAVINGS BANK	KS	D+	09/30/10
HOMETOWN BANK OF CORBIN INC	KY	D+	09/30/10
ING BANK FSB	DE	D+	09/30/10
INTERNATIONAL CITY BANK NA	CA	D+	09/30/10
KEYBANK NA	OH	D+	09/30/10
KITSAP BANK	WA	D+	09/30/10
LEWISTON STATE BK	UT	D	09/30/10
LIBERTAD BANK SSB	TX	D+	09/30/10
LOWRY STATE BK	MN	D+	09/30/10
MEGA BANK	CA	D+	09/30/10
MID AMERICA BANK	WI	D+	09/30/10
MID AMERICA BANK & TRUST CO	MO	D+	09/30/10
MISSION VALLEY BANK	CA	D	09/30/10
NORTH SHORE BANK OF COMMERCE	MN	D+	09/30/10
NORTHBROOK BANK & TRUST CO	IL	D	09/30/10
NORTHERN MICHIGAN BANK & TRUST	MI	D+	09/30/10
OAKSTAR BANK NA	MO	D+	09/30/10
OLD PLANK TRAIL COMMUNITY BANK	IL	D+	09/30/10
PACIFIC COAST BANKERS BANK	CA	D+	09/30/10
PARKSIDE FINANCIAL BANK & TR	MO	D+	09/30/10
PEOPLES BANK OF COMMERCE	OR	D+	09/30/10
PEOPLES BK OF ARLINGTON HGHTS	IL	D+	09/30/10
PINNACLE BANK	AZ	D+	09/30/10
PIONEER COMMERCIAL BANK	NY	U	09/30/10
PLATTSMOUTH STATE BK	NE	D+	09/30/10
PLAZA PARK STATE BK	MN	D+	09/30/10
PRINSBANK	MN	D+	09/30/10
RIVER CITY BANK	CA	D+	09/30/10
RIVER VALLEY BANK	WI	D+	09/30/10
SAUK VALLEY BANK & TRUST CO	IL	D+	09/30/10
SOUTHERN STATES BANK	AL	D+	09/30/10
ST CHARLES BANK & TRUST CO	IL	D+	09/30/10
STATE BK OF MARIETTA	MN	D+	09/30/10
STATE BK OF TEXAS	TX	D	09/30/10
STATE BK OF WATERLOO	IL	D+	09/30/10
SUMMIT COMMUNITY BANK	MI	D+	09/30/10
SUTTON BANK	OH	D+	09/30/10
TEXAS CHAMPION BANK	TX	D+	09/30/10
TRI STATE BK OF MEMPHIS	TN	D	09/30/10
UNION STATE BK	KS	D+	09/30/10
UNITED TEXAS BANK	TX	D+	09/30/10
UNITED-AMERICAN SB	PA	D+	09/30/10
VALLEY BANK	VA	D+	09/30/10
VALRICO STATE BK	FL	D+	09/30/10
VINTAGE BANK	TX	D+	09/30/10
VIRGINIA SAVINGS BANK FSB	VA	D+	09/30/10
VISTA BANK	TX	D+	09/30/10
WELLS FARGO BANK NA	SD	D	09/30/10
WELLS FARGO CENTRAL BANK	CA	U	09/30/10
WEST CHESTER SB	IA	D+	09/30/10
XENITH BANK	VA	D+	09/30/10
YOUR COMMUNITY BANK	IN	D+	09/30/10

Rating: D+

BANK NAME	STATE	PREVIOUS RATING	DATE OF CHANGE
ADAMS NATIONAL BK	DC	D	09/30/10
ALDEN STATE BK	MI	D	09/30/10
ALLIANCE BANK OF ARIZONA	AZ	D	09/30/10
AMEGY BANK NA	TX	D	09/30/10
AMERICAN BANK & TRUST CUMBERLD	TN	D	09/30/10
AMERICAN BANK OF TEXAS	TX	D	09/30/10
AMERICAN COMMUNITY BANK & TR	IL	D	09/30/10
ARLINGTON STATE BK	MN	D	09/30/10

Rating Upgrades (Continued)

Rating: D+ (Continued)

BANK NAME	STATE	PREVIOUS RATING	DATE OF CHANGE
ASTORIA FS&LA	NY	D-	09/30/10
ATLANTIC STEWARDSHIP BANK	NJ	D	09/30/10
AURORA BANK FSB	DE	D	09/30/10
BANK OF AMERICA CALIFORNIA NA	CA	D	09/30/10
BANK OF COMMERCE	OK	D	09/30/10
BANK OF COMMERCE	OK	D	09/30/10
BANKUNITED	FL	D	09/30/10
BANKVISTA	MN	D	09/30/10
BCBANK INC	WV	D	09/30/10
BEDFORD FSB	IN	D	09/30/10
BONANZA VALLEY STATE BK	MN	D	09/30/10
BORDER CAPITAL BANK NA	TX	D	09/30/10
BRANNEN BANK	FL	D	09/30/10
BRYANT BANK	AL	D	09/30/10
CALIFORNIA BANK & TRUST	CA	D	09/30/10
CALIFORNIA BANK OF COMMERCE	CA	D	09/30/10
CALLAWAY BANK	MO	D	09/30/10
CAPITALSOURCE BANK	CA	D	09/30/10
CARLINVILLE NATIONAL BK	IL	D	09/30/10
CATHAY BANK	CA	D	09/30/10
CBW BANK	KS	D	09/30/10
CENTERPOINTE COMMUNITY BANK	OR	D	09/30/10
CENTRAL BANK & TRUST CO	KY	D	09/30/10
CENTRAL NATIONAL BK & TRUST CO	OK	D	09/30/10
CHOICE FINANCIAL GROUP	ND	D	09/30/10
CHOICE FINANCIAL SAVINGS BANK	MN	D	09/30/10
CINCINNATI FS&LA	OH	D	09/30/10
CITICORP TRUST BANK FSB	DE	D	09/30/10
CITIZENS BANKING CO	OH	D	09/30/10
CITIZENS FIRST BANK	TN	D	09/30/10
CITIZENS NB GREATER ST LOUIS	MO	D	09/30/10
CITIZENS STATE BK	GA	D	09/30/10
CITIZENS STATE BK OF SHAKOPEE	MN	D	09/30/10
CITIZENS STATE BK OF SHIPMAN	IL	D	09/30/10
COMMONWEALTH BANK FSB	KY	D	09/30/10
COMMUNITY BANK DELAWARE	DE	D	09/30/10
COMMUNITY BK NORTH MISSISSIPPI	MS	D	09/30/10
COMMUNITY BK OF THE CUMBERLAND	TN	D	09/30/10
COMMUNITY BUSINESS BANK	WI	D	09/30/10
COMMUNITY DEVELOPMENT BANK	MN	D-	09/30/10
CORNERSTONE COMMUNITY BANK	WI	D	09/30/10
CROSSFIRST BANK LEAWOOD	KS	D	09/30/10
CROWN BANK	NJ	D-	09/30/10
CUSTER FS&LA	NE	D	09/30/10
CUSTOMERS BANK	PA	D	09/30/10
DELANCO FSB	NJ	D	09/30/10
DRAKE BANK	MN	D	09/30/10
EAST CAROLINA BANK	NC	D	09/30/10
EASTERN FEDERAL BANK	CT	D	09/30/10
EMIGRANT BANK	NY	D-	09/30/10
EMIGRANT SB - MANHATTAN	NY	D	09/30/10
FARMERS NATIONAL BK OF BUHL	ID	D	09/30/10
FARMERS STATE BK	KS	D	09/30/10
FIRST AMERICAN BANK	IL	D	09/30/10
FIRST COMMUNITY BANK	MI	D-	09/30/10
FIRST COMMUNITY BK OF EAST TN	TN	D	09/30/10
FIRST FEDERAL BANK A FSB	AL	D	09/30/10
FIRST NATIONAL BK CHILLICOTHE	IL	D	09/30/10
FIRST NATIONAL BK COFFEE CTY	GA	D	09/30/10
FIRST NATIONAL BK OF CHISHOLM	MN	D	09/30/10
FIRST NATIONAL BK OF IPSWICH	MA	D	09/30/10
FIRST NATIONAL BK OF WAKEFIELD	MI	D	09/30/10
FIRST NATIONAL BK SCOTTSDALE	AZ	D-	09/30/10
FIRST NORTHERN BANK OF DIXON	CA	D	09/30/10
FIRST SECURITY BANK	MN	D	09/30/10
FIRST STATE BK	AR	D	09/30/10
FIRST STATE BK	ND	D	09/30/10
FIRST STATE BK OF DIX	IL	D	09/30/10
FIRST STATE BK OF NORTH DAKOTA	ND	D	09/30/10
FLORIDA SHORES BANK-SOUTHWEST	FL	D	09/30/10
FORT DAVIS STATE BK	TX	D	09/30/10
FRANDSEN BANK & TRUST	MN	D	09/30/10
GATEWAY BUSINESS BANK	CA	D	09/30/10
GCF BANK	NJ	D	09/30/10
GILMORE BANK	CA	D	09/30/10
GREAT WESTERN BANK	SD	D	09/30/10
HIGH PLAINS BANK	OK	D	09/30/10
HOME BANK OF CALIFORNIA	CA	D	09/30/10
HOME STATE BK NA	IL	D	09/30/10
HOWARD BANK	MD	D-	09/30/10
HURON VALLEY STATE BK	MI	D	09/30/10
HYPERION BANK	PA	D	09/30/10
ILLINOIS-SERVICE FS&LA	IL	D	09/30/10
INTERVEST NATIONAL BK	NY	D	09/30/10
KAISER FEDERAL BANK	CA	D	09/30/10
LAGRANGE BANKING CO	GA	D	09/30/10
LANDMARK COMMUNITY BANK NA	MN	E+	09/30/10
LEGG MASON INVESTMENT COUNSEL	MD	U	09/30/10
LEWIS & CLARK BANK	OR	D	09/30/10
LIBERTY FS&LA	MD	D	09/30/10
MCVILLE STATE BK	ND	D	09/30/10
NATIONAL BK OF COMMERCE	AL	D	09/30/10
NATIONAL BK OF COMMERCE	WI	D	09/30/10
NEVADA BANK & TRUST CO	NV	D	09/30/10
NORTH SHORE COMMUNITY BK & TR	IL	D	09/30/10
OGLESBY STATE BK	TX	D	09/30/10
OHIO HERITAGE BANK	OH	D	09/30/10
PACIFIC TRUST BANK FSB	CA	D	09/30/10
PALISADES NATIONAL BK	CO	D-	09/30/10
PALMER BANK	IL	D	09/30/10
PARK MIDWAY BANK NA	MN	D	09/30/10
PATRIOTS BANK	KS	D	09/30/10
PILGRIM BANK	MA	D	09/30/10
PINELAND STATE BK	GA	D	09/30/10
PROVIDENCE BANK OF TEXAS	TX	D	09/30/10
PROVINCIAL BANK	MN	D	09/30/10
QUEENSTOWN BANK OF MARYLAND	MD	D	09/30/10
REGAL BANK	NJ	D-	09/30/10
RESOURCE BANK NA	IL	D	09/30/10
ROEBLING BANK	NJ	D	09/30/10
RURAL AMERICAN BANK-LUCK	WI	D	09/30/10
SALT LICK DEPOSIT BANK	KY	D	09/30/10
SECURITY BANK	MO	D	09/30/10
SECURITY BANK OF WHITESBORO	TX	D-	09/30/10
SECURITY BANK USA	MN	D	09/30/10
SECURITY STATE BK	WA	D	09/30/10
SOUND COMMUNITY BANK	WA	D	09/30/10
SOUTH COASTAL BANK	MA	D	09/30/10
SOUTHERNTRUST BANK	IL	D	09/30/10
STATE BK OF GEORGIA	GA	D	09/30/10
STATE BK OF TABLE ROCK	NE	D	09/30/10
STOCKMANS BANK	OK	D	09/30/10
STRATFORD STATE BK	WI	D	09/30/10
TEXAS NATIONAL BK	TX	D	09/30/10
TRIUMPH SB SSB	TX	D-	09/30/10
UNION STATE BK	TX	D	09/30/10
UNION STATE BK OF FARGO	ND	D	09/30/10
UNIVERSITY BANK	MI	D	09/30/10
US BANK NA	OH	D	09/30/10
VILLAGE BANK & TRUST	IL	D	09/30/10

Rating Upgrades (Continued)

Rating: D+ (Continued)

BANK NAME	STATE	PREVIOUS RATING	DATE OF CHANGE
WEBSTER BANK NA	CT	D	09/30/10
WEST COAST BANK	OR	D	09/30/10
WEST TOWN SB	IL	D	09/30/10
WESTERN NATIONAL BK	KS	D	09/30/10
WHEATON BANK & TRUST CO	IL	D	09/30/10
WHITE ROCK BANK	MN	E	09/30/10
WOORI AMERICA BANK	NY	D-	09/30/10
ZIONS FIRST NATIONAL BK	UT	D	09/30/10

Rating: D

BANK NAME	STATE	PREVIOUS RATING	DATE OF CHANGE
ALLIANCE BANK CORP	VA	D-	09/30/10
ALMENA STATE BK	KS	D-	09/30/10
AMERICAN EAGLE BANK	IL	D-	09/30/10
AMERICAN EAGLE BANK OF CHICAGO	IL	D-	09/30/10
AMERICANWEST BANK	WA	E-	09/30/10
ASSOCIATED BANK NA	WI	D-	09/30/10
BANK OF ALAMEDA	CA	D-	09/30/10
BANK OF CANTON	MA	D-	09/30/10
BANK OF LINCOLN COUNTY	TN	D-	09/30/10
BANKCDA	ID	D-	09/30/10
BARABOO NATIONAL BK	WI	D-	09/30/10
BILTMORE BANK OF ARIZONA	AZ	D-	09/30/10
BUSINESS BANK	WI	D-	09/30/10
CAPITAL PACIFIC BANK	OR	D-	09/30/10
CASTLE ROCK BANK	CO	D-	09/30/10
CITIZENS BANK	TN	D-	09/30/10
COLORADO EAST BANK & TRUST	CO	D-	09/30/10
COMMERCE NATIONAL BK & TRUST	FL	D-	09/30/10
COMMERCIAL BANK	MS	D-	09/30/10
COMMUNITY FIRST BANK	WI	D-	09/30/10
COMMUNITY NATIONAL BK	IA	D-	09/30/10
E*TRADE BANK	VA	D-	09/30/10
E*TRADE SAVINGS BANK	VA	D-	09/30/10
EAST RIVER BANK	PA	D-	09/30/10
ECLIPSE BANK INC	KY	D-	09/30/10
EMIGRANT SB - LONG ISLAND	NY	D-	09/30/10
EMIGRANT SB-BRONX/WESTCHESTER	NY	D-	09/30/10
EMIGRANT SB-BROOKLYN/QUEENS	NY	D-	09/30/10
ENTERPRISE BANK	TX	D-	09/30/10
ENTERPRISE NATIONAL BK NJ	NJ	D-	09/30/10
EVERBANK	FL	D-	09/30/10
FAR EAST NATIONAL BK	CA	D-	09/30/10
FARMERS BANK & TRUST CO	AR	D-	09/30/10
FARMERS TRUST & SB	IA	D-	09/30/10
FIRST BANK OF THE SOUTH	AL	D-	09/30/10
FIRST COUNTY BANK	CT	D-	09/30/10
FIRST NATIONAL BK OF FARRAGUT	IA	D-	09/30/10
FIRST PEOPLES BANK OF TENNESSEE	TN	D-	09/30/10
FIRST RESOURCE BANK	MN	E-	09/30/10
FIRST SECURITY BANK	IL	D-	09/30/10
FIRST SECURITY TRUST & SB	IL	D-	09/30/10
FIRST STATE BK OF EAST DETROIT	MI	D-	09/30/10
FIRST STATE BK OF KANSAS CITY	KS	D-	09/30/10
FIRSTBANK - WEST MICHIGAN	MI	D-	09/30/10
GULF COAST BANK & TRUST CO	LA	D-	09/30/10
HOME LOAN INVESTMENT BANK FSB	RI	D-	09/30/10
HOME LOAN STATE BK	CO	D-	09/30/10
HOME SB	UT	D-	09/30/10
HOME STATE BK	CO	D-	09/30/10
INDEPENDENT BANKERS BANK OF FL	FL	D-	09/30/10
KEYSTONE COMMUNITY BANK	MI	D-	09/30/10
LAKE CITY FEDERAL BANK	MN	D-	09/30/10
LAKESIDE BANK	IL	D-	09/30/10
LAPEER COUNTY BANK & TRUST CO	MI	D-	09/30/10
MADISON COUNTY COMMUNITY BANK	FL	D-	09/30/10
MANHATTAN BANK	MT	D-	09/30/10
MOUNTAIN PACIFIC BANK	WA	D-	09/30/10
NORTHEAST BANK	MN	D-	09/30/10
NORTHERN STATE BK	NJ	D-	09/30/10
NORTHSTAR BANK OF TEXAS	TX	D-	09/30/10
OZARK HERITAGE BANK NA	AR	D-	09/30/10
PACIFIC CREST SB	WA	D-	09/30/10
PACIFIC NATIONAL BK	FL	D-	09/30/10
PASCACK COMMUNITY BANK	NJ	D-	09/30/10
PEOPLES BANK	NC	D-	09/30/10
PRESTON STATE BANK	TX	D-	09/30/10
PRINCEVILLE STATE BK	IL	D-	09/30/10
QUANTUM NATIONAL BK	GA	D-	09/30/10
REPUBLIC BANK INC	MN	D-	09/30/10
SADDLE RIVER VALLEY BANK	NJ	D-	09/30/10
SAIGON NATIONAL BK	CA	D-	09/30/10
SERVICE1ST BANK OF NEVADA	NV	D-	09/30/10
SOUTHERN ARIZONA COMMUNITY BK	AZ	E+	09/30/10
ST TAMMANY HOMESTEAD S&LA	LA	D-	09/30/10
STATE FARM BANK FSB	IL	D-	09/30/10
SYNOVUS BANK	GA	D-	09/30/10
TWO RIVER COMMUNITY BANK	NJ	D-	09/30/10
UNION CREDIT BANK	FL	D-	09/30/10
UNISON BANK	ND	D-	09/30/10
UNITED BANK & TRUST	MI	D-	09/30/10
UNITED INTERNATIONAL BK	NY	D-	09/30/10
VALLEY GREEN BANK	PA	D-	09/30/10

Rating: D-

BANK NAME	STATE	PREVIOUS RATING	DATE OF CHANGE
ALLIED FIRST BANK SB	IL	E+	09/30/10
AMERICAN BANK OF BAXTER SPRING	KS	E-	09/30/10
ATHOL-CLINTON CO-OP BANK	MA	E	09/30/10
BANK OF ATLANTA	GA	E+	09/30/10
BANK OF BOZEMAN	MT	E-	09/30/10
BANK OF IDAHO	ID	E+	09/30/10
BANK OF VIRGINIA	VA	E-	09/30/10
CARVER STATE BK	GA	E+	09/30/10
CORNERSTONE BANK	KS	E+	09/30/10
CORNERSTONE BANK	ND	E-	09/30/10
DICKINSON COUNTY BANK	KS	E-	09/30/10
EAST DUBUQUE SB	IA	E+	09/30/10
ERICSON STATE BK	NE	E+	09/30/10
FIRST STATE BK OF WARNER SOUTH	SD	E-	09/30/10
GREENCHOICE BANK FSB	IL	E+	09/30/10
GUNNISON VALLEY BANK	UT	E-	09/30/10
INDEPENDENCE STATE BK	WI	E+	09/30/10
LOWELL CO-OP BANK	MA	E-	09/30/10
MONTGOMERY BANK & TRUST	GA	E-	09/30/10
PALMETTO BANK	SC	E-	09/30/10
PATRIOT BANK	FL	E+	09/30/10
PATRIOT NATIONAL BK	CT	E-	09/30/10
PREMIER BANK & TRUST NA	OH	E+	09/30/10
PREMIER BANK MINNESOTA	MN	E+	09/30/10
QUALITY BANK	ND	E+	09/30/10
ROXBURY BANK	KS	E	09/30/10
SAEHAN BANK	CA	E+	09/30/10
SECURITY BANK	WI	E	09/30/10
SECURITY STATE BK	IA	E+	09/30/10
SECURITY STATE BK	WI	E+	09/30/10
SECURITY STATE BK OF LEWISTON	MN	E+	09/30/10
SUNBANK NA	MO	E-	09/30/10
TRANS PACIFIC NATIONAL BK	CA	E+	09/30/10
TRAVERSE CITY STATE BK	MI	E	09/30/10
UNITED COMMUNITY BANK NA	TX	E+	09/30/10
VIGILANT FSB	MD	E+	09/30/10

Rating Upgrades (Continued)

Rating: D- (Continued)

BANK NAME	STATE	PREVIOUS RATING	DATE OF CHANGE
YOUNG AMERICANS BANK	CO	E+	09/30/10

Rating: E+

BANK NAME	STATE	PREVIOUS RATING	DATE OF CHANGE
BORDER STATE BK	MN	E	09/30/10
BUILDERS BANK	IL	E	09/30/10
BUTTE STATE BK	NE	E	09/30/10
CFBANK	OH	E-	09/30/10
FARMERS STATE BK OF SUBLETTE	IL	E-	09/30/10
FIRST NATIONAL BK & TRUST	WI	E	09/30/10
FLORIDA CITIZENS BANK	FL	E	09/30/10
FOUNDATIONS BANK	WI	E-	09/30/10
FREEDOM BANK	MT	E-	09/30/10
HOME FEDERAL BANK OF	FL	E-	09/30/10
MILLENNIUM BANK	CO	E-	09/30/10
MISSION OAKS NATIONAL BK	CA	E	09/30/10
NATIVE AMERICAN BANK NA	CO	E-	09/30/10
SOUTHERN COMMERCE BANK NA	FL	E-	09/30/10
ST LOUIS BANK	MO	E-	09/30/10
TOWN NORTH BANK NEVADA NA	NV	E	09/30/10
UNION BANK	LA	E-	09/30/10
VISIONBANK	MN	E	09/30/10
WACCAMAW BANK	NC	E	09/30/10
WEST MICHIGAN COMMUNITY BANK	MI	E-	09/30/10

Rating: E

BANK NAME	STATE	PREVIOUS RATING	DATE OF CHANGE
CITIZENS STATE BK OF CORTEZ	CO	E-	09/30/10
CITY NATIONAL BK OF NEW JERSEY	NJ	E-	09/30/10
COVENANT BANK	IL	E-	09/30/10
FARMERS BANK	GA	E-	09/30/10
HERITAGE FIRST BANK	GA	E-	09/30/10
MAIN STREET BANK	MI	E-	09/30/10
MILTON SB	WI	E-	09/30/10
RCSBANK	MO	E-	09/30/10
SOUTH CAROLINA COMMUNITY BANK	SC	E-	09/30/10

Rating Downgrades

Rating: A

BANK NAME	STATE	PREVIOUS RATING	DATE OF CHANGE
COMMUNITY NATIONAL BK & TRUST	TX	A+	09/30/10

Rating: A-

BANK NAME	STATE	PREVIOUS RATING	DATE OF CHANGE
CITIZENS NB AT BROWNWOOD	TX	A	09/30/10
CITY NB&TC OF LAWTON OKLAHOMA	OK	A	09/30/10
FARMERS & MERCHANTS BANK	MS	A	09/30/10
FIRST NATIONAL BK & TRUST	KS	A	09/30/10
FIRST NATIONAL BK ALAMOGORDO	NM	A	09/30/10
FIRST NATIONAL BK OF DRYDEN	NY	A	09/30/10
FIRST NATIONAL BK OF RUIDOSO	NM	A	09/30/10
LIBERTY NATIONAL BK IN PARIS	TX	A	09/30/10
PEOPLES BANK OF GRACEVILLE	FL	A	09/30/10
SOONER STATE BK	OK	A	09/30/10
WAYNE BANK	PA	A	09/30/10

Rating: B+

BANK NAME	STATE	PREVIOUS RATING	DATE OF CHANGE
1ST BANK & TRUST	OK	A	09/30/10
ABACUS FSB	NY	A-	09/30/10
ALPINE CAPITAL BANK	NY	A-	09/30/10
ANNA STATE BK	IL	A-	09/30/10
BANK OF GUEYDAN	LA	A-	09/30/10
BANK OF MILLBROOK	NY	A-	09/30/10
BANK OF SOUTH CAROLINA	SC	A-	09/30/10
BANK OF THE PANHANDLE	OK	A	09/30/10
BURTON STATE BK	TX	A-	09/30/10
CAMERON STATE BK	LA	A-	09/30/10
CARROLL COUNTY TC CARROLLTON	MO	A-	09/30/10
CHELSEA SB	IA	A-	09/30/10
CITIZENS STATE BK	TX	A-	09/30/10
ELIZABETHTON FSB	TN	A-	09/30/10
FARMERS & MERCH BK CENTRAL CA	CA	A-	09/30/10
FARMERS & MERCHANTS BANK	OK	A-	09/30/10
FARMERS & MERCHANTS BANK	TX	A-	09/30/10
FARMERS BANK	AR	A-	09/30/10
FARMERS STATE BK	NE	A-	09/30/10
FARMERS STATE BK OF CROSBY ND	ND	A-	09/30/10
FIRST COMMAND BANK	TX	A-	09/30/10
FIRST FARMERS & MERCHANTS NB	MN	A-	09/30/10
FIRST FINANCIAL BANK	TX	A-	09/30/10
FIRST FINANCIAL BANK NA	TX	A-	09/30/10
FIRST INVESTORS FSB	NJ	A-	09/30/10
FIRST NATIONAL BK & TRUST CO	OK	A-	09/30/10
FIRST NATIONAL BK OF LIVERPOOL	PA	A-	09/30/10
FIRST SECURITY BANK OF ROUNDUP	MT	A-	09/30/10
FIRST STATE BK	TX	A-	09/30/10
FIRST TEXAS BANK	TX	A-	09/30/10
FRANKLIN BANK	IL	A-	09/30/10
HERITAGE BANK	UT	A-	09/30/10
HOME SAVINGS & LOAN CO OF	OH	A-	09/30/10
INDEPENDENCE BANK	MT	A-	09/30/10
JOURDANTON STATE BK	TX	A-	09/30/10
KANABEC STATE BK	MN	A-	09/30/10
LOGAN BANK & TRUST CO	WV	A-	09/30/10
PEOPLES SOUTHERN BANK	AL	A-	09/30/10
PORT RICHMOND SAVINGS	PA	A-	09/30/10
PRESTON NATIONAL BK	TX	A-	09/30/10
PRIOR LAKE STATE BK	MN	A-	09/30/10
SAINT JOHN NATIONAL BK	KS	A-	09/30/10
SPRING VALLEY BANK	OH	A-	09/30/10
STERLING BANK	MO	A-	09/30/10
STREATOR HOME BUILDING & LOAN	IL	A-	09/30/10
TEXAS BANK	TX	A	09/30/10
THOMASVILLE NATIONAL BK	GA	A-	09/30/10
UNION BANK & TRUST CO	MN	A-	09/30/10
UNION STATE BK	KS	A-	09/30/10
UNITED CITIZENS BANK & TRUST	KY	A-	09/30/10
UNITED MISSISSIPPI BANK	MS	A-	09/30/10
VALUEBANK TEXAS	TX	A-	09/30/10

Rating: B

BANK NAME	STATE	PREVIOUS RATING	DATE OF CHANGE
BANK OF BREWTON	AL	B+	09/30/10
BANK OF CROCKETT	TN	B+	09/30/10
BANK OF HALLS	TN	B+	09/30/10
BANK OF HANCOCK COUNTY	GA	B+	09/30/10
BANK OF OLD MONROE	MO	B+	09/30/10
BANKPLUS	MS	B+	09/30/10
BREDA SB	IA	B+	09/30/10
CATTLE NATIONAL BK & TRUST CO	NE	B+	09/30/10
CITIZENS STATE BK OF OURAY	CO	A-	09/30/10
DONLEY COUNTY STATE BK	TX	B+	09/30/10
FIRST COMMUNITY NATIONAL BK	MO	B+	09/30/10
FIRST FARMERS & MERCH STATE BK	MN	B+	09/30/10
FIRST FARMERS & MERCH STATE BK	MN	B+	09/30/10
FIRST FARMERS & MERCHANTS NB	MN	B+	09/30/10
FIRST NATIONAL BK BROOKSVILLE	KY	B+	09/30/10
FIRST NATIONAL BK CARROLLTON	MO	B+	09/30/10
FIRST NATIONAL BK MCMINNVILLE	TN	B+	09/30/10
FIRST NATIONAL BK OF BANGOR	WI	B+	09/30/10
FIRST STATE BK	IA	B+	09/30/10
FIRST STATE BK BOURBON INDIANA	IN	B+	09/30/10
FORDYCE BANK & TRUST CO	AR	B+	09/30/10
GATES BANKING & TRUST CO	TN	B+	09/30/10
JERSEY SHORE STATE BK	PA	B+	09/30/10
MENNO STATE BK	SD	B+	09/30/10
MISSOURI BANK	MO	A-	09/30/10
OOSTBURG STATE BK	WI	B+	09/30/10
ROCHESTER STATE BK	IL	B+	09/30/10
SECURITY STATE BK	GA	B+	09/30/10
SETTLERS BANK	OH	B+	09/30/10
STATE BK OF LINCOLN	IL	B+	09/30/10
STATE NATIONAL BK BIG SPRING	TX	A-	09/30/10
TD BANK USA NA	ME	B+	09/30/10
WEST IOWA BANK	IA	B+	09/30/10

Rating: B-

BANK NAME	STATE	PREVIOUS RATING	DATE OF CHANGE
AMERICAN BANK	OK	B	09/30/10
AMERICAN BANK NA	TX	B	09/30/10
BANK - OLDHAM COUNTY INC	KY	B	09/30/10
BANK FEDERATED ST MICRONESIA	FM	B	09/30/10
BANK NA	OK	B	09/30/10
BANK OF COMMERCE	TX	B	09/30/10
BANK OF INTERNET USA	CA	B	09/30/10
BANK OF MAGNOLIA CO	OH	B	09/30/10
BANK OF OAK RIDGE	LA	B	09/30/10
BANK OF TIOGA	ND	B+	09/30/10
BANK OF WOLCOTT	IN	B	09/30/10
BLENCOE STATE BK	IA	B	09/30/10
BLISSFIELD STATE BK	MI	B	09/30/10
CECILIAN BANK	KY	B	09/30/10
CEDAR SECURITY BANK	NE	B	09/30/10
CITIZENS & FARMERS BANK	VA	B	09/30/10
CITIZENS BANK	IA	B	09/30/10
CITIZENS BANK	MS	B	09/30/10
CITIZENS STATE BK OF GLENVILLE	MN	B	09/30/10
COMMUNITY BANK	IL	B	09/30/10
DEDICATED COMMUNITY BANK	SC	B	09/30/10
DELTA NATIONAL BK & TRUST CO	NY	B	09/30/10
ELKVILLE STATE BK	IL	B	09/30/10
FALLS CITY NATIONAL BK	TX	B+	09/30/10

Rating Downgrades (Continued)

Rating: B- (Continued)

BANK NAME	STATE	PREVIOUS RATING	DATE OF CHANGE
FARMERS & MERCH BANK	IN	B	09/30/10
FARMERS & MERCH BANK	MD	B	09/30/10
FARMERS & MERCHANTS BANK	WI	B	09/30/10
FARMERS & MERCHANTS STATE BK	ND	B	09/30/10
FARMERS STATE BK ASTORIA	IL	B	09/30/10
FARMERS STATE BK OF ELKTON	MN	B	09/30/10
FELICIANA BANK & TRUST CO	LA	B	09/30/10
FIRST ILLINOIS BANK	IL	B+	09/30/10
FIRST NATIONAL BK CHILLICOTHE	TX	B	09/30/10
FIRST NATIONAL BK IN WHITNEY	TX	B	09/30/10
FIRST NATIONAL BK OF CAMBRIDGE	NE	B	09/30/10
FIRST NATIONAL BK OF HARTFORD	AL	B	09/30/10
FIRST NATIONAL BK OF MERTZON	TX	B	09/30/10
FIRST NATIONAL BK OF PRIMGHAR	IA	B	09/30/10
FIRST NATIONAL BK OF SEDAN	KS	B	09/30/10
FIRST NATIONAL BK PORT LAVACA	TX	B	09/30/10
FIRST PIONEER NATIONAL BK	CO	B	09/30/10
FIRST SECURITY BUSINESS BANK	CA	B	09/30/10
FIRST STATE BK	TX	B	09/30/10
FIRST STATE BK OF ST ROBERT	MO	B	09/30/10
FIRST STATE COMMUNITY BANK	MO	B	09/30/10
GRANT COUNTY BANK	OK	B	09/30/10
GREEN BELT BANK & TRUST	IA	B+	09/30/10
H F GEHANT BANKING CO	IL	B	09/30/10
HAMILTON BANK	MO	B	09/30/10
HBANK TEXAS	TX	B	09/30/10
HERITAGE BANK NA	AR	B	09/30/10
HOME BANK	LA	B	09/30/10
JONES NATIONAL BK & TRUST CO	NE	B	09/30/10
LINDELL BANK & TRUST CO	MO	B+	09/30/10
MCKENZIE COUNTY BANK	ND	B	09/30/10
MENARD NATIONAL BK	TX	B	09/30/10
MUNICIPAL TRUST & SB	IL	B	09/30/10
PEOPLES B&TC OF POINTE COUPEE	LA	B	09/30/10
PEOPLES BANK OF BULLITT COUNTY	KY	B	09/30/10
RANGE BANK NA	MI	B	09/30/10
SILICON VALLEY BANK	CA	B	09/30/10
SOUTHWEST BANK	TX	B+	09/30/10
ST LANDRY BANK & TRUST CO	LA	B	09/30/10
STATE BK OF BARTLEY	NE	A-	09/30/10
STATE BK OF BRICELYN	MN	B	09/30/10
STATE BK OF LAKOTA	ND	B	09/30/10
STATE BK OF MISSOURI	MO	B	09/30/10
SWISHER TRUST & SB	IA	B	09/30/10
TOLLESON PRIVATE BANK	TX	B	09/30/10
TRISTAR BANK	TN	B	09/30/10
UNICO BANK	MO	B	09/30/10
UNITED STATE BK	MO	B	09/30/10
UNITY BANK NORTH	MN	B	09/30/10
WANDA STATE BK	MN	B	09/30/10
WHIDBEY ISLAND BANK	WA	B	09/30/10
WILSON & MUIR BANK & TRUST CO	KY	B	09/30/10

Rating: C+

BANK NAME	STATE	PREVIOUS RATING	DATE OF CHANGE
ALLIANCE BANK	IN	B-	09/30/10
AMERICAN NATIONAL BK	TX	B-	09/30/10
ANZ GUAM INC	GU	B-	09/30/10
BANK 7	OK	B-	09/30/10
BANK OF BELLE GLADE	FL	B	09/30/10
BANK OF BENNINGTON	VT	B-	09/30/10
BANK OF COMMERCE	WY	B-	09/30/10
BANK OF GREENE COUNTY	NY	B-	09/30/10
BANK OF HAMILTON	ND	B-	09/30/10
BANK OF HINDMAN	KY	B-	09/30/10
BANK OF LOUISIANA	LA	B-	09/30/10
BANK OF MAUSTON	WI	B-	09/30/10
BANK OF MCLOUTH	KS	B+	09/30/10
BANK OF WHITEWATER	KS	B-	09/30/10
BANK OF WINONA	MS	B-	09/30/10
BANKSOUTH	AL	B-	09/30/10
CARTER COUNTY BK ELIZABETHTON	TN	B-	09/30/10
CENTRAL STATE BK	IA	B-	09/30/10
CENTRAL STATE BK	IA	B-	09/30/10
CITIZENS BANK & TRUST CO	LA	B-	09/30/10
CITIZENS BANK NA	TX	B	09/30/10
CITIZENS BANK OF LAS CRUCES	NM	B-	09/30/10
CNB BANK INC	WV	B-	09/30/10
COMMUNITY BANK & TRUST	TN	B-	09/30/10
COMMUNITY BANK NA	MO	B-	09/30/10
COMMUNITY FIRST BANK	IL	B	09/30/10
COMMUNITY NATIONAL BK	TX	B-	09/30/10
CORNERSTONE BANK	OK	B-	09/30/10
COUNTY FIRST BANK	MD	B-	09/30/10
CROCKETT NATIONAL BK	TX	B-	09/30/10
DELAWARE NATIONAL BK OF DELHI	NY	B-	09/30/10
DEMOTTE STATE BK	IN	B-	09/30/10
DEPOSIT BANK OF CARLISLE	KY	B-	09/30/10
DIAMOND BANK	AR	B-	09/30/10
DUBLIN NATIONAL BK	TX	B-	09/30/10
FARMERS & MERCHANTS SB	IA	B-	09/30/10
FARMERS BANK & TRUST	KS	B-	09/30/10
FARMERS STATE BK	KS	B-	09/30/10
FARMERS STATE BK ALLEN OK	OK	B-	09/30/10
FIRST & CITIZENS BANK	VA	B-	09/30/10
FIRST BANK & TRUST	IL	B-	09/30/10
FIRST BANK & TRUST CO	VA	B	09/30/10
FIRST COLLINSVILLE BANK	IL	B-	09/30/10
FIRST COUNTY BANK	IL	B-	09/30/10
FIRST FS&LA	KY	B-	09/30/10
FIRST MINNETONKA CITY BANK	MN	B-	09/30/10
FIRST NATIONAL BK	IA	B-	09/30/10
FIRST NATIONAL BK & TRUST CO	MI	B-	09/30/10
FIRST NATIONAL BK BOSQUE CTY	TX	B-	09/30/10
FIRST NATIONAL BK IN CIMARRON	KS	B-	09/30/10
FIRST NATIONAL BK LITCHFIELD	IL	B-	09/30/10
FIRST NATIONAL BK OF ELY	NV	B-	09/30/10
FIRST NATIONAL BK OF HOPE	KS	B-	09/30/10
FIRST NATIONAL BK OF OSAKIS	MN	B-	09/30/10
FIRST NATIONAL BK OF WAHOO	NE	B-	09/30/10
FIRST NATIONAL BK OF WAUCHULA	FL	B-	09/30/10
FIRST NATIONAL BK S CAROLINA	SC	B-	09/30/10
FIRST NATIONAL BK THROCKMORTON	TX	B-	09/30/10
FOWLER STATE BK	KS	B	09/30/10
GATEWAY STATE BK	IA	B	09/30/10
HOMETOWN BANK A COOPERATIVE BK	MA	B-	09/30/10
KLEBERG FIRST NB OF KINGSVILLE	TX	B-	09/30/10
LINCOLN SB	IA	B-	09/30/10
LORRAINE STATE BK	KS	B-	09/30/10
LYNNVILLE NATIONAL BK	IN	B-	09/30/10
MANUFACTURERS & TRADERS TRUST	NY	B-	09/30/10
MARION COUNTY SB	IL	B-	09/30/10
MASSENA SAVINGS & LOAN	NY	B-	09/30/10
MASSMUTUAL TRUST CO FSB	CT	B-	09/30/10
MERCHANTS & PLANTERS BANK	AR	B-	09/30/10
MOJAVE DESERT BANK NA	CA	B-	09/30/10
MT VICTORY STATE BK	OH	B-	09/30/10
NATIONAL BK OF TEXAS FT WORTH	TX	B-	09/30/10
NEWTON COUNTY BANK	MS	B-	09/30/10
NORTHERN TRUST BANK FSB	MI	B-	09/30/10
NORTHWESTERN BANK	IA	B-	09/30/10

Rating Downgrades (Continued)

Rating: C+ (Continued)

BANK NAME	STATE	PREVIOUS RATING	DATE OF CHANGE
PEOPLES B&TC OF MADISON COUNTY	KY	B-	09/30/10
PLATTE VALLEY BANK OF MISSOURI	MO	B-	09/30/10
PRIORITYONE BANK	MS	B	09/30/10
PROVIDENT BANK	NY	B-	09/30/10
RILEY STATE BK OF RILEY KANSAS	KS	B-	09/30/10
SAVINGS BANK OF MENDOCINO CNTY	CA	B-	09/30/10
SCHWERTNER STATE BK	TX	B-	09/30/10
SECURITY STATE BK	SD	B-	09/30/10
SECURITY STATE BK OF AITKIN	MN	B+	09/30/10
SOMERVILLE NATIONAL BK	OH	B-	09/30/10
SOUTHERN MO BK OF MARSHFIELD	MO	B-	09/30/10
ST MARTIN BANK & TRUST CO	LA	B-	09/30/10
STATE BK & TRUST CO	IA	A-	09/30/10
STATE BK OF BELLE PLAINE	MN	B-	09/30/10
STATE BK OF TOULON	IL	B	09/30/10
TOWNEBANK	VA	B-	09/30/10
TRI PARISH BANK	LA	B-	09/30/10
UMB BANK NA	MO	B-	09/30/10
UNION BANK & TRUST CO	TN	B-	09/30/10
UNIVEST NATIONAL BK & TRUST CO	PA	B-	09/30/10
UTAH INDEPENDENT BANK	UT	B-	09/30/10
UVALDE NATIONAL BK	TX	B-	09/30/10
WELCOME STATE BK	MN	B-	09/30/10
WELLS RIVER SB	VT	B-	09/30/10
WEST CARROLL COMMUNITY BANK	LA	B-	09/30/10
WESTERN BK ARTESIA NEW MEXICO	NM	B-	09/30/10
WHITAKER BANK	KY	B-	09/30/10
WHITESVILLE STATE BK	WV	B-	09/30/10
WINDSOR FS&LA	CT	B-	09/30/10

Rating: C

BANK NAME	STATE	PREVIOUS RATING	DATE OF CHANGE
ADRIAN BANK	MO	B-	09/30/10
ATASCOSA NATIONAL BK	TX	C+	09/30/10
BANK OF EUFAULA	OK	B+	09/30/10
BANK OF KAUKAUNA	WI	B	09/30/10
BANK OF MILAN	TN	C+	09/30/10
BANK OF NORTH CAROLINA	NC	C+	09/30/10
BANK OF WHITTIER NA	CA	C+	09/30/10
BANKERS TRUST CO	IA	C+	09/30/10
BAXTER STATE BK	KS	C+	09/30/10
BLANCO NATIONAL BK	TX	B-	09/30/10
BRIGHTON BANK	UT	B-	09/30/10
CATTARAUGUS COUNTY BANK	NY	C+	09/30/10
CBANK	OH	C+	09/30/10
CENTRAL BANK OF MISSOURI	MO	B	09/30/10
CENTRAL STATE BK	IL	C+	09/30/10
CHARTER BANK EAU CLAIRE	WI	C+	09/30/10
CITIZENS FIRST BANK	WI	C+	09/30/10
CITIZENS ST BK OF TAYLOR CTY	GA	C+	09/30/10
CITIZENS STATE BK OF LOYAL	WI	B-	09/30/10
COMMERCIAL BANK OF MOTT	ND	C+	09/30/10
COMMERCIAL STATE BK OF WAGNER	SD	C+	09/30/10
COMMUNITY BANK	OR	C+	09/30/10
COMMUNITY BANK	TN	B-	09/30/10
COMMUNITY STATE BK	AR	C+	09/30/10
CORNERSTONE STATE BK	MN	C+	09/30/10
CORTLAND SAVINGS & BANKING CO	OH	C+	09/30/10
EASTERN BANK	MA	B-	09/30/10
F&M BANK	GA	C+	09/30/10
FARMERS & MERCHANTS BANK	AR	C+	09/30/10
FARMERS & MERCHANTS BANK	OK	C+	09/30/10
FARMERS STATE BK	KS	B-	09/30/10
FARMERS STATE BK	SD	B-	09/30/10
FARMERS STATE BK HIGHLAND KS	KS	C+	09/30/10
FIRST NATIONAL BK	AR	C+	09/30/10
FIRST NATIONAL BK & TRUST CO	OK	C+	09/30/10
FIRST NATIONAL BK IN EXETER	NE	B-	09/30/10
FIRST NATIONAL BK OF LA GRANGE	IL	C+	09/30/10
FIRST NATIONAL BK OF SONORA	TX	B-	09/30/10
FIRST NATIONAL BK OF WOODSBORO	TX	C+	09/30/10
FIRST NAVY BANK	FL	C+	09/30/10
FIRST PROGRESSIVE BANK	AL	C+	09/30/10
FIRST SHORE FS&LA	MD	C+	09/30/10
FIRST STATE BK	TX	C+	09/30/10
FIRST STATE BK OF NORTHWEST AR	AR	B-	09/30/10
GRAYSTONE TOWER BANK	PA	C+	09/30/10
HANCOCK BANK OF ALABAMA	AL	C+	09/30/10
HERITAGE BANK OF NEVADA	NV	C+	09/30/10
INDEPENDENCE BANK	OH	C+	09/30/10
JOHNSON COUNTY BANK	TN	B-	09/30/10
KING SOUTHERN BANK	KY	C+	09/30/10
KOSCIUSZKO FSB	MD	C+	09/30/10
LAKELAND BANK	NJ	C+	09/30/10
LAWSON BANK	MO	C+	09/30/10
LITCHFIELD NATIONAL BK	IL	C+	09/30/10
M&T BANK NA	NY	B	09/30/10
MANSFIELD STATE BK	SD	C+	09/30/10
MONROE STATE BK	IA	C+	09/30/10
MORGAN STANLEY PRIVATE BANK NA	NY	B-	09/30/10
NATIONAL IRON BANK	CT	C+	09/30/10
NORTHWEST COMMUNITY BANK	CT	C+	09/30/10
OAK BANK	WI	C+	09/30/10
OWEN COUNTY STATE BK	IN	C+	09/30/10
PEOPLES BANK	KY	B-	09/30/10
PEOPLES BANK OF THE SOUTH	TN	C+	09/30/10
PEOPLES TRUST CO OF ST ALBANS	VT	C+	09/30/10
PRAIRIE SUN BANK	MN	C+	09/30/10
ROCK BRANCH COMMUNITY BANK INC	WV	C+	09/30/10
SECURITY BANK & TRUST CO	OK	C+	09/30/10
SECURITY BANK MINNESOTA	MN	C+	09/30/10
SLOVAK SB	PA	C+	09/30/10
SPRINGFIELD STATE BK	NE	C+	09/30/10
STATE BK OF BIRD ISLAND	MN	B-	09/30/10
STATE BK OF DOWNS	KS	B-	09/30/10
STATE BK OF LISMORE	MN	C+	09/30/10
STATE BK OF SCOTIA	NE	C+	09/30/10
STATE NATIONAL BK IN WEST	TX	C+	09/30/10
TOWN SQUARE BANK INC	KY	B-	09/30/10
UMB BANK ARIZONA NA	AZ	B-	09/30/10
VALLEY BANK OF RONAN	MT	C+	09/30/10
VICTORY STATE BK	NY	B-	09/30/10
WELLESLEY BANK	MA	C+	09/30/10
WHEATLAND BANK	WA	C+	09/30/10

Rating: C-

BANK NAME	STATE	PREVIOUS RATING	DATE OF CHANGE
ALLIANCE NATIONAL BK	GA	C	09/30/10
AMERICAN NB OF MT PLEASANT	TX	C+	09/30/10
AMERICAN STATE BK	TX	C+	09/30/10
BANK OF GIBSON CITY	IL	C	09/30/10
BANK OF KILMICHAEL	MS	C	09/30/10
BANK OF LAS VEGAS	NM	B	09/30/10
BANK OF LEES SUMMIT	MO	C	09/30/10
BANK OF MCCREARY COUNTY	KY	C	09/30/10
BANK OF NEW CAMBRIA	MO	C	09/30/10
BANK OF SALEM	AR	C	09/30/10
BANK OF TURTLE LAKE	WI	C+	09/30/10
BANK OF ZUMBROTA	MN	C	09/30/10
BANKERS BANK	WI	B	09/30/10
BANKWEST OF KANSAS	KS	C	09/30/10
BITTERROOT VALLEY BANK	MT	C+	09/30/10

Rating Downgrades (Continued)

Rating: C- (Continued)

BANK NAME	STATE	PREVIOUS RATING	DATE OF CHANGE
BLUE GRASS VALLEY BANK	VA	C	09/30/10
BTC BANK	MO	C	09/30/10
CCB COMMUNITY BANK	AL	C+	09/30/10
CENTER BANK	CA	C	09/30/10
CENTURY BANK	OR	C+	09/30/10
CENTURY BANK & TRUST	GA	C	09/30/10
CITIZENS BANK OF BLOUNT COUNTY	TN	C	09/30/10
CITIZENS NB OF BLUFFTON	OH	C	09/30/10
CITY BANK OF HARTFORD	AL	C	09/30/10
COMMERCIAL BANK	WI	C	09/30/10
COMMONWEALTH BANK & TRUST CO	KY	C	09/30/10
COMMUNITY 1ST BANK	ID	C	09/30/10
COMMUNITY BANK OF OELWEIN	IA	C	09/30/10
COMMUNITY SAVINGS	OH	C+	09/30/10
COUNTYBANK	SC	C+	09/30/10
DAKOTA PRAIRIE BANK	SD	C+	09/30/10
DEARBORN FSB	MI	C+	09/30/10
EAGLE BANK & TRUST CO OF MO	MO	C+	09/30/10
EDGAR COUNTY BANK & TRUST CO	IL	C	09/30/10
EUDORA BANK	AR	C+	09/30/10
EVANS BANK NA	NY	C	09/30/10
FARMERS & MERCHANTS BANK	VA	C	09/30/10
FARMERS NATIONAL BK OF LEBANON	KY	C+	09/30/10
FARMERS SB	IA	B	09/30/10
FARMERS STATE BK	IA	C	09/30/10
FARMERS STATE BK OF JETMORE KS	KS	C	09/30/10
FARMINGTON BANK	CT	C	09/30/10
FIDELITY DEPOSIT & DISCOUNT BK	PA	C	09/30/10
FIRST AMERICAN BANK & TRUST	LA	C	09/30/10
FIRST BANK & TRUST SB	IL	C	09/30/10
FIRST BANK OF CHANDLER	OK	C+	09/30/10
FIRST BANK OF FAIRLAND	OK	C	09/30/10
FIRST FEDERAL BANK OF OHIO	OH	C+	09/30/10
FIRST FINANCIAL BANK	AR	C	09/30/10
FIRST FS&LA OF OLATHE	KS	C+	09/30/10
FIRST NATIONAL BK OF FREDERICK	SD	C	09/30/10
FIRST NATIONAL BK OF HOLDREGE	NE	C	09/30/10
FIRST NATIONAL BK OF KEMP	TX	C	09/30/10
FIRST NATIONAL BK OF MCGEHEE	AR	C+	09/30/10
FIRST NATIONAL BK OF MILACA	MN	C+	09/30/10
FIRST NATIONAL BK OF MINEOLA	TX	C	09/30/10
FIRST NATIONAL BK OF ODON	IN	C	09/30/10
FIRST NATIONAL BK OF PULASKI	TN	C	09/30/10
FIRST NB OF PORT ALLEGANY	PA	C+	09/30/10
FIRST STATE BK	TX	C	09/30/10
FIRST STATE BK OF DONGOLA	IL	C	09/30/10
FIRST STATE BK OF MOBEETIE	TX	C	09/30/10
FIRST UNITED SECURITY BANK	AL	C	09/30/10
FLANAGAN STATE BK	IL	C+	09/30/10
FREEDOM NATIONAL BK	RI	C	09/30/10
GOTHAM BANK OF NEW YORK	NY	C	09/30/10
GRAND RIDGE NATIONAL BK	IL	C+	09/30/10
GRAND TIMBER BANK	MN	C	09/30/10
HAMLIN NATIONAL BK	TX	C	09/30/10
HARRISON BUILDING & LOAN ASSN	OH	C	09/30/10
HARTWICK STATE BK	IA	C	09/30/10
HERITAGE BANK	WI	C	09/30/10
HIGH PLAINS BANK	CO	B-	09/30/10
HIGH POINT BANK & TRUST CO	NC	C	09/30/10
HOME SB	OH	C	09/30/10
INDEPENDENT BANK	TN	C	09/30/10
INTEGRITY BANK	PA	C	09/30/10
IOWA STATE BK	IA	C+	09/30/10
IOWA STATE BK	IA	C	09/30/10
LAKE FOREST BANK & TRUST CO	IL	C	09/30/10
LEE BANK	MA	C	09/30/10
LIBERTY SAVINGS ASSN FSA	KS	C	09/30/10
LITCHFIELD BANCORP	CT	C	09/30/10
M&I BANK OF MAYVILLE	WI	C	09/30/10
MEMBERS TRUST CO	FL	C+	09/30/10
MERCHANTS & FARMERS BANK	AL	C	09/30/10
MERCHANTS & FARMERS BANK	MS	C+	09/30/10
MERCHANTS & PLANTERS BANK	TN	C	09/30/10
MERCHANTS BK OF CALIFORNIA NA	CA	C	09/30/10
MIDLAND COMMUNITY BANK	IL	C	09/30/10
MILFORD BANK	CT	C	09/30/10
MINERS NATIONAL BK OF EVELETH	MN	C	09/30/10
NEW FRONTIER BANK	MO	C	09/30/10
NORTH CASCADES NATIONAL BK	WA	C	09/30/10
NORTHERN HANCOCK BANK & TRUST	WV	C	09/30/10
NORTHWEST COMMERCIAL BANK	WA	C	09/30/10
NORWOOD CO-OP BANK	MA	C+	09/30/10
OHIO VALLEY BANK CO	OH	C	09/30/10
OWINGSVILLE BANKING CO	KY	C	09/30/10
PEOPLES BK BILOXI MISSISSIPPI	MS	C	09/30/10
PEOPLES STATE BK OF VELVA	ND	C	09/30/10
PEOPLES UNITED BANK	CT	B-	09/30/10
PEOPLESBANK A CODORUS VLY CO	PA	C	09/30/10
PETERSBURG STATE BK	NE	C	09/30/10
PRAIRIE NATIONAL BK	IL	C	09/30/10
PREMIER COMMERCIAL BANK NA	CA	C	09/30/10
PRIMEBANK	IA	C	09/30/10
PROVIDENCE BANK	NC	B-	09/30/10
PUTNAM 1ST MERCANTILE BANK	TN	C	09/30/10
RIVERVIEW NATIONAL BK	PA	C	09/30/10
SIGNATURE BANK KC	KS	C	09/30/10
SOUTH CENTRAL BK BOWLING GREEN	KY	C	09/30/10
SOUTH CENTRAL BK MONROE CNTY	KY	C	09/30/10
SOUTH GEORGIA BANKING CO	GA	C+	09/30/10
STANLEY BANK	KS	B-	09/30/10
STATE BK & TRUST CO DALLAS	TX	C+	09/30/10
STATE BK OF CHRISMAN	IL	C	09/30/10
STATE BK OF COCHRAN	GA	C	09/30/10
STATE BK OF ILLINOIS	IL	C	09/30/10
STRASBURG SB	OH	B	09/30/10
STROUD NATIONAL BK	OK	C	09/30/10
SUMMIT BANK	CA	C+	09/30/10
SWINEFORD NATIONAL BK	PA	C	09/30/10
TAMPA STATE BK	KS	C	09/30/10
TEXAS BANK	TX	C+	09/30/10
TEXAS EXCHANGE BANK SSB	TX	C+	09/30/10
THOMAS COUNTY FS&LA	GA	B-	09/30/10
TITAN BANK NA	TX	C	09/30/10
TROY BANK & TRUST CO	AL	C	09/30/10
UNITED BANK	WI	C	09/30/10
UNITED BANK OF KANSAS	KS	C	09/30/10
UNITED SOUTHERN BANK	KY	C	09/30/10
VALLEY VIEW STATE BK	KS	C	09/30/10
WAWEL SAVINGS BANK	NJ	C	09/30/10
WELLS BANK OF PLATTE CITY	MO	B	09/30/10
WESBANCO BANK INC	WV	C	09/30/10
WEST ONE BANK	MT	C	09/30/10
WHITE HALL BANK	IL	C	09/30/10
WILLIAMSVILLE STATE BK & TRUST	IL	C	09/30/10
WYOMING BANK & TRUST	WY	B-	09/30/10

Rating: D+

BANK NAME	STATE	PREVIOUS RATING	DATE OF CHANGE
1ST BANK OF TROY	KS	C-	09/30/10
1ST BANK YUMA	AZ	C	09/30/10
1ST COLONIAL NATIONAL BK	NJ	C-	09/30/10

Rating Downgrades (Continued)

Rating: D+ (Continued)

BANK NAME	STATE	PREVIOUS RATING	DATE OF CHANGE
ADAMS COUNTY BUILDING & LOAN CO	OH	C-	09/30/10
ALLIANCE BANK CENTRAL TEXAS	TX	C	09/30/10
AMERICAN BANK OF MISSOURI	MO	C-	09/30/10
AMERICAN HOME BANK	IL	C-	09/30/10
AMERICAN RIVIERA BANK	CA	C-	09/30/10
AMERICAN SAVINGS BANK FSB	OH	C+	09/30/10
AMERIFIRST BANK	AL	C-	09/30/10
AMFIRST BANK NA	NE	C-	09/30/10
ANSON BANK & TRUST CO	NC	C-	09/30/10
AQUESTA BANK	NC	C-	09/30/10
BALLY SB	PA	C-	09/30/10
BANDERA FIRST STATE BK	TX	C-	09/30/10
BANK 21	MO	C-	09/30/10
BANK OF CATTARAUGUS	NY	C-	09/30/10
BANK OF LANCASTER	VA	C-	09/30/10
BANK OF STAPLETON	NE	C-	09/30/10
BANK OF STEINAUER	NE	C-	09/30/10
BANK OF TEXAS	TX	C-	09/30/10
BANK OF TEXAS	TX	C-	09/30/10
BANKFINANCIAL FSB	IL	C-	09/30/10
BANKGLOUCESTER	MA	C-	09/30/10
BENEFICIAL MUTUAL SB	PA	C-	09/30/10
BENEFIT BANK	AR	C-	09/30/10
BRIDGEWATER BANK	MN	C+	09/30/10
BROWARD BANK OF COMMERCE	FL	C-	09/30/10
CABARRUS BANK & TRUST CO	NC	C-	09/30/10
CAMBRIDGE STATE BK	WI	C-	09/30/10
CENTENNIAL BANK	CO	C-	09/30/10
CENTRAL FS&LA	IL	C-	09/30/10
CENTURY BANK	NM	C-	09/30/10
CHATTAHOOCHEE BANK OF GEORGIA	GA	C-	09/30/10
CHESTERFIELD STATE BK	IL	C	09/30/10
CHINO COMMERCIAL BANK NA	CA	C+	09/30/10
CHISHOLM TRAIL STATE BK	KS	C-	09/30/10
CITIZENS STATE BK OF FINLEY	ND	C	09/30/10
CNB	MD	C-	09/30/10
COASTAL BANK & TRUST	NC	C-	09/30/10
COLLINSVILLE SAVINGS SOCIETY	CT	C-	09/30/10
COMMERCE BANK OF ARIZONA	AZ	C	09/30/10
COMMERCE BANK OF OREGON	OR	C-	09/30/10
COMMERCE STATE BK	WI	C-	09/30/10
COMMERCIAL BANK	TN	C	09/30/10
COMMONWEALTH NATIONAL BK	AL	C-	09/30/10
COMMUNITY BANK CORP	MN	C	09/30/10
COMMUNITY BANK INC	MT	C-	09/30/10
COMMUNITY BANK MISSOULA	MT	C-	09/30/10
COMMUNITY BANK NA	AL	C-	09/30/10
COMMUNITY FINANCIAL BANK	WI	C-	09/30/10
COMMUNITY FIRST BANK	PA	C-	09/30/10
CORE BUSINESS BANK	WA	C-	09/30/10
COUNTRY BANK	IL	B-	09/30/10
DAIRY STATE BK	WI	C-	09/30/10
DAVIDSON TRUST CO	MT	C-	09/30/10
ELYSIAN BANK	MN	C-	09/30/10
ENTERPRISE BANK OF S CAROLINA	SC	C-	09/30/10
FAHEY BANKING CO	OH	C-	09/30/10
FARMERS & MERCH TRUST CO	PA	C-	09/30/10
FARMERS & MERCHANTS UNION BANK	WI	C-	09/30/10
FARMERS & TRADERS STATE BK	IL	C	09/30/10
FARMERS BANK & TRUST CO	AR	C-	09/30/10
FARMERS BANK OF GREEN CITY	MO	C-	09/30/10
FARMERS STATE BK	IL	C-	09/30/10
FARMERS STATE BK	NE	C-	09/30/10
FEDERATED BANK	IL	C-	09/30/10
FIRST BANK	VA	C-	09/30/10
FIRST BANK OF BALDWIN	WI	C-	09/30/10
FIRST BANK OF GEORGIA	GA	C-	09/30/10
FIRST CAHAWBA BANK	AL	C-	09/30/10
FIRST CENTURY BANK NA	WV	C-	09/30/10
FIRST CLOVER LEAF BANK FSB	IL	C-	09/30/10
FIRST COMMONS BANK NA	MA	C-	09/30/10
FIRST COMMUNITY BK OF CRAWFORD	AR	C-	09/30/10
FIRST FEDERAL BANK OF WISCONSIN	WI	C-	09/30/10
FIRST FREEDOM BANK	TN	C-	09/30/10
FIRST GUARANTY BANK	LA	C-	09/30/10
FIRST NATIONAL BK & TRUST	KY	C-	09/30/10
FIRST NATIONAL BK & TRUST CO	IL	C-	09/30/10
FIRST NATIONAL BK OF BAGLEY	MN	C-	09/30/10
FIRST NATIONAL BK OF LIPAN	TX	C-	09/30/10
FIRST NATIONAL BK OF OTTAWA	IL	C-	09/30/10
FIRST NATIONAL BK OF WYNNE	AR	C-	09/30/10
FIRST NATIONAL BK SOUTHERN KS	KS	C-	09/30/10
FIRST STATE BK	OK	C-	09/30/10
FIRST STATE BK	OK	C-	09/30/10
FIRST STATE BK	OK	C-	09/30/10
FIRST STATE BK	OK	C-	09/30/10
FIRST STATE BK	SD	C-	09/30/10
FIRST STATE BK	TX	C-	09/30/10
FIRST STATE BK & TRUST CO	NE	C-	09/30/10
FIRST TRI-COUNTY BANK	NE	C-	09/30/10
FIRSTSTATE BK	AL	C	09/30/10
FLATHEAD BANK OF BIGFORK MT	MT	C-	09/30/10
FOOTHILLS BANK & TRUST	TN	C-	09/30/10
FORREST CITY BANK NA	AR	C-	09/30/10
FOUNDATION FIRST BANK	NE	C-	09/30/10
GATEWAY BANK & TRUST	GA	C-	09/30/10
GATEWAY COMMERCIAL BANK	AZ	C-	09/30/10
GRAND BANK FOR SAVINGS FSB	MS	C-	09/30/10
GREAT STATE BK	NC	C-	09/30/10
HARRIS NA	IL	C-	09/30/10
HERITAGE BANK	NC	C	09/30/10
HOMEBANC NA	FL	C-	09/30/10
HOOSIER HEARTLAND STATE BK	IN	C-	09/30/10
HYDE PARK BANK & TRUST CO	IL	C-	09/30/10
JPMORGAN CHASE BANK DEARBORN	MI	C-	09/30/10
KAHOKA STATE BK	MO	C-	09/30/10
KANSASLAND BANK	KS	C-	09/30/10
KARNES COUNTY NATIONAL BK	TX	C	09/30/10
KENNEY BANK & TRUST	IL	C-	09/30/10
LEMONT NATIONAL BK	IL	C-	09/30/10
LIBERTYVILLE SB	IA	C-	09/30/10
LINCOLN COMMUNITY BANK	WI	C-	09/30/10
LIVE OAK BANKING CO	NC	C-	09/30/10
LOS ANGELES NATIONAL BK	CA	C-	09/30/10
LYONS STATE BK	KS	C-	09/30/10
MERIT BANK	KS	C-	09/30/10
MIDLAND STATES BANK	IL	C-	09/30/10
MIDWEST BANK OF WESTERN IL	IL	C-	09/30/10
MUTUAL FEDERAL BANK	IL	C-	09/30/10
MUTUAL SB	IN	C-	09/30/10
NAFH NATIONAL BK	FL	C	09/30/10
NARA BANK	CA	C-	09/30/10
NATIONAL REPUBLIC BK CHICAGO	IL	C-	09/30/10
NBC OKLAHOMA	OK	C-	09/30/10
NEW TRADITIONS NATIONAL BK	FL	C-	09/30/10
NOA BANK	GA	C-	09/30/10
NORTH GEORGIA NATIONAL BK	GA	C-	09/30/10
NORTH SHORE BANK FSB	WI	C-	09/30/10
NORTHEAST COMMUNITY BANK	NY	C	09/30/10
NORTHSTAR BANK	FL	C-	09/30/10

Rating Downgrades (Continued)

Rating: D+ (Continued)

BANK NAME	STATE	PREVIOUS RATING	DATE OF CHANGE
PARK NATIONAL BK	OH	C	09/30/10
PEOPLES BANK MONITEAU COUNTY	MO	C-	09/30/10
PEOPLES SB	OH	C	09/30/10
PINE ISLAND BANK	MN	C-	09/30/10
PLATINUM BANK	TX	C	09/30/10
PRIME MERIDIAN BANK	FL	C-	09/30/10
PROFESSIONAL BANK	FL	C-	09/30/10
RANDOLPH NATIONAL BK	VT	C	09/30/10
ROUNDBANK	MN	C-	09/30/10
ROWLEY SB	IA	C-	09/30/10
ROYAL BUSINESS BANK	CA	C-	09/30/10
RUTH STATE BK	MI	C-	09/30/10
SACO & BIDDEFORD SAVINGS INST	ME	C-	09/30/10
SECURITY BANK	AR	C-	09/30/10
SECURITY BANK & TRUST CO	MN	C-	09/30/10
SECURITY BANK WACONIA	MN	C-	09/30/10
SECURITY BUSINESS BK SAN DIEGO	CA	C-	09/30/10
SECURITY STATE BK	TX	C+	09/30/10
SOUND BANKING CO	WA	C	09/30/10
SOUTH LOUISIANA BUSINESS BANK	LA	C-	09/30/10
SOUTH SHORE SB	MA	C-	09/30/10
SOUTHEAST FIRST NATIONAL BK	GA	C	09/30/10
STATE BK OF INDIA (CALIFORNIA)	CA	C-	09/30/10
STATE BK OF LEON	KS	C-	09/30/10
STELLAR BUSINESS BANK	CA	C-	09/30/10
STOCK EXCHANGE BANK	KS	C-	09/30/10
SYCAMORE BANK	MS	C+	09/30/10
TEXICO STATE BK	IL	C-	09/30/10
TRIAD BANK	MO	C-	09/30/10
TWIN LAKES COMMUNITY BANK	AR	C-	09/30/10
UNION FIRST MARKET BANK	VA	C-	09/30/10
UNION SB	CT	C	09/30/10
UNITED COMMUNITY BANK	IL	C-	09/30/10
UNITED COMMUNITY BANK	LA	C	09/30/10
UNITED FARMERS & MERCH ST BK	MN	C-	09/30/10
VIRGINIA COMPANY BANK	VA	C-	09/30/10
VIRGINIA PARTNERS BANK	VA	C-	09/30/10
VISION BANK	FL	C-	09/30/10
VISION BANK - TEXAS	TX	C-	09/30/10
WASHINGTONFIRST BANK	VA	C-	09/30/10
WATERMAN STATE BK	IL	C-	09/30/10
WAYNE BANK & TRUST CO	IN	C-	09/30/10
WESTERN DAKOTA BANK	SD	C-	09/30/10
WOODSBORO BANK	MD	C-	09/30/10

Rating: D

BANK NAME	STATE	PREVIOUS RATING	DATE OF CHANGE
1ST CENTURY BANK NA	CA	D+	09/30/10
ADAMS DAIRY BANK	MO	D+	09/30/10
AMERICAN CONTINENTAL BANK	CA	D+	09/30/10
AMERICAN PRIDE BANK	GA	D+	09/30/10
AMERICAN TRUST & SB	IA	D+	09/30/10
AMERICAN TRUST BANK OF EAST TN	TN	D+	09/30/10
BANK @LANTEC	VA	C-	09/30/10
BANK MUTUAL	WI	C	09/30/10
BANK OF CHICKAMAUGA	GA	D+	09/30/10
BANK OF CORDELL	OK	D+	09/30/10
BANK OF CROCKER	MO	D+	09/30/10
BANK OF DOOLY	GA	D+	09/30/10
BANK OF DUDLEY	GA	C	09/30/10
BANK OF GUAM	GU	D+	09/30/10
BANK OF STANLY	NC	C-	09/30/10
BANK OF VICI	OK	D+	09/30/10
BLUEGRASS COMMUNITY BANK	KY	D+	09/30/10
BOONVILLE FSB	IN	D+	09/30/10
BRUNSWICK BANK & TRUST CO	NJ	D+	09/30/10
BUSINESS BANK OF SAINT LOUIS	MO	D+	09/30/10
CALIFORNIA UNITED BANK	CA	C-	09/30/10
CAROLINA ALLIANCE BANK	SC	D+	09/30/10
CEDAR RAPIDS STATE BK	NE	C-	09/30/10
CENTENNIAL BANK	NE	D+	09/30/10
CENTIER BANK	IN	D+	09/30/10
CENTRAL BANK	AR	C-	09/30/10
CHAMBERS BANK	AR	D+	09/30/10
CHARTERBANK	GA	D+	09/30/10
CHOICE BANK	WI	D+	09/30/10
CITIZENS BANK	GA	D+	09/30/10
CITIZENS BANK	MO	D+	09/30/10
CITIZENS BANK OF LOGAN	OH	C-	09/30/10
CITIZENS BANK OF WEST VIRGINIA	WV	C+	09/30/10
CITIZENS BK OF OREGON MISSOURI	MO	C-	09/30/10
CITIZENS NB OF HAMMOND	NY	D+	09/30/10
CITIZENS STATE BK	AR	C	09/30/10
CITIZENS STATE BK	TX	D+	09/30/10
COMMERCIAL STATE BK	NE	D+	09/30/10
COMMUNITY FIRST BANK	NJ	D+	09/30/10
CONWAY BANK NA	KS	D+	09/30/10
CRESCENT BANK & TRUST	LA	D+	09/30/10
DEAN CO-OP BANK	MA	D+	09/30/10
DESERT COMMERCIAL BANK	CA	D+	09/30/10
EMERALD BANK	KS	D+	09/30/10
ENTERPRISE BANK OF FLORIDA	FL	D+	09/30/10
ESQUIRE BANK	NY	D+	09/30/10
FAIRFIELD COUNTY BANK	CT	D+	09/30/10
FARMERS STATE BK	WY	C-	09/30/10
FIRST BANK OF UTICA	NE	C-	09/30/10
FIRST CAPITAL BANK	SC	D+	09/30/10
FIRST COMMUNITY BANK & TRUST	IL	D+	09/30/10
FIRST FEDERAL SB ELIZABETHTOWN	KY	D+	09/30/10
FIRST GREEN BANK	FL	D+	09/30/10
FIRST INDEPENDENCE BANK	MI	D+	09/30/10
FIRST INTERNET BANK OF INDIANA	IN	D+	09/30/10
FIRST NATIONAL BK OF CROSSETT	AR	D+	09/30/10
FIRST NATIONAL BK OF PADUCAH	TX	D+	09/30/10
FIRST NATIONAL BK OF SHELBY	NC	D+	09/30/10
FIRST STATE BK	OK	D+	09/30/10
FIRST STATE BK OF ROSEMOUNT	MN	D+	09/30/10
FORT WASHINGTON SAVINGS CO	OH	D+	09/30/10
FRANKLIN COUNTY UNITED BANK	TN	D+	09/30/10
GENERATIONS BANK	AL	D+	09/30/10
GEORGIA PRIMARY BANK	GA	D+	09/30/10
GLOBAL TRUST BANK	CA	D+	09/30/10
GOLD COAST BANK	NY	D+	09/30/10
GOOSE RIVER BANK	ND	D+	09/30/10
GRAND BANK OF TEXAS	TX	D+	09/30/10
GREATER ROME BANK	GA	D+	09/30/10
GREENEVILLE FEDERAL BANK FSB	TN	D+	09/30/10
HARRIS BANK NA	AZ	D+	09/30/10
HARWOOD STATE BK	ND	C-	09/30/10
HIGHLAND FALLS FS&LA	NY	D+	09/30/10
HOMETRUST BANK	NC	D+	09/30/10
ILLINOIS NATIONAL BK	IL	D+	09/30/10
INDEPENDENCE BANK OF GEORGIA	GA	D+	09/30/10
INLAND COMMUNITY BANK NA	CA	C-	09/30/10
JEFFERSON BANK OF FLORIDA	FL	D+	09/30/10
JPMORGAN BANK & TRUST CO NA	CA	C-	09/30/10
KEY COMMUNITY BANK	MN	C-	09/30/10
LAKESIDE BANK	LA	C-	09/30/10
LIBERTY BANK	TX	D+	09/30/10
LIBERTY BAY BANK	WA	D+	09/30/10
MARION NATIONAL BK	KS	D+	09/30/10

Rating Downgrades (Continued)

Rating: D (Continued)

BANK NAME	STATE	PREVIOUS RATING	DATE OF CHANGE
MINT NATIONAL BK	TX	D+	09/30/10
MONROE FS&LA	OH	D+	09/30/10
NEW HORIZON BANK NA	VA	D+	09/30/10
NORTH LOUP VALLEY BANK	NE	D+	09/30/10
OAK VIEW NATIONAL BK	VA	C-	09/30/10
PATRIOT BANK	TX	D+	09/30/10
PEACHTREE BANK	AL	D+	09/30/10
PEOPLES BANK	MS	D+	09/30/10
PEOPLES STATE BK	FL	D+	09/30/10
PEOPLES STATE BK	IA	C-	09/30/10
PINE RIVER VALLEY BANK	CO	C-	09/30/10
PLATINUM BANK	FL	D+	09/30/10
PONCE DE LEON FEDERAL BANK	NY	D+	09/30/10
PREMIER VALLEY BANK	CA	D+	09/30/10
PRIVATE BANK OF CALIFORNIA	CA	C-	09/30/10
QUINNIPIAC BANK & TRUST CO	CT	D+	09/30/10
RANDOLPH BANK & TRUST CO	NC	D+	09/30/10
RANDOLPH SB	MA	D+	09/30/10
RAWLINS NATIONAL BK	WY	D+	09/30/10
REDSTONE BANK	CO	D+	09/30/10
RIVERBANK	WA	C-	09/30/10
RIVERHILLS BANK	OH	D+	09/30/10
ROCKWOOD BANK	MO	D+	09/30/10
SANDHILLS STATE BK	NE	C-	09/30/10
SHATTUCK NATIONAL BK	OK	D+	09/30/10
SMALL TOWN BANK	AL	D+	09/30/10
SOLERA NATIONAL BK	CO	D+	09/30/10
STATE BK OF CARBONDALE	KS	D+	09/30/10
STONE COUNTY NATIONAL BK	MO	D+	09/30/10
SUNCREST BANK	CA	D+	09/30/10
SUNNYSIDE FS&LA OF IRVINGTON	NY	D+	09/30/10
TALBOT BANK OF EASTON MARYLAND	MD	D+	09/30/10
TEXAS SECURITY BANK	TX	D+	09/30/10
TRINITY BANK	AL	D+	09/30/10
TRUST CO BANK	TN	D+	09/30/10
TRUSTATLANTIC BANK	NC	D+	09/30/10
UNION NATIONAL COMMUNITY BANK	PA	D+	09/30/10
UNION SAVINGS BANK	NM	D+	09/30/10
VALLEY BANK OF KALISPELL	MT	D+	09/30/10
VERITEX COMMUNITY BANK NA	TX	C-	09/30/10
VERITY BANK	GA	D+	09/30/10
VERMONT STATE BK	IL	D+	09/30/10
VIRGINIA COMMUNITY BANK	VA	C-	09/30/10
VOYAGER BANK	MN	D+	09/30/10
WASHINGTON STATE BK	LA	C-	09/30/10
WEST SUBURBAN BANK	IL	D+	09/30/10
WESTERN CAPITAL BANK	ID	D+	09/30/10
WORTHINGTON NATIONAL BK	TX	D+	09/30/10

Rating: D-

BANK NAME	STATE	PREVIOUS RATING	DATE OF CHANGE
AFFINITY BANK OF PENNSYLVANIA	PA	D	09/30/10
ARBOR BANK	NE	D	09/30/10
BANK 1440	AZ	D	09/30/10
BANK OF BOTETOURT	VA	D	09/30/10
BANK OF COMMERCE	NC	D	09/30/10
BANK OF GREELEYVILLE	SC	D	09/30/10
BANK OF KANSAS	KS	D	09/30/10
BANK OF MONTICELLO	GA	D	09/30/10
BANK OF NEVADA	NV	D	09/30/10
BANK OF SOUTHERN CALIFORNIA NA	CA	D	09/30/10
BANK OF WYANDOTTE	OK	D	09/30/10
BARRE SB	MA	D+	09/30/10
BAY CITIES BANK	FL	D	09/30/10
BCB COMMUNITY BANK	NJ	D	09/30/10
BEN FRANKLIN BANK OF ILLINOIS	IL	D	09/30/10
BERKSHIRE BANK	PA	D	09/30/10
BLUERIDGE BANK	MD	D	09/30/10
BRAINERD S&LA A FEDERAL ASSN	MN	D	09/30/10
BRAZOS VALLEY BANK NA	TX	D	09/30/10
BRYAN BANK & TRUST	GA	D	09/30/10
BUCKS COUNTY BANK	PA	D	09/30/10
CAMBRIDGE STATE BK	MN	D+	09/30/10
CAPITALBANK	SC	D	09/30/10
CARNEY STATE BK	OK	D	09/30/10
CARROLLTON BANK	MD	D+	09/30/10
CITIZENS BANK	AL	D+	09/30/10
CITIZENS BANK & TRUST CO	GA	D	09/30/10
CITIZENS BANK & TRUST CO	MN	D	09/30/10
CITIZENS BANK INC	AL	D	09/30/10
CITIZENS SB & TRUST CO	TN	D	09/30/10
COLONIAL CO-OP BANK	MA	D	09/30/10
COMMERCEFIRST BANK	MD	D	09/30/10
COMMERCIAL BANK	GA	D	09/30/10
COMMUNITY BANK	VA	D	09/30/10
COMMUNITY FIRSTBANK CHARLESTON	SC	D	09/30/10
CONNECTICUT COMMUNITY BANK NA	CT	D	09/30/10
CORNER STONE BANK	MO	D	09/30/10
CRESCENT BANK	SC	D	09/30/10
DAMASCUS COMMUNITY BANK	MD	D+	09/30/10
DECATUR COUNTY BANK	TN	D	09/30/10
DESJARDINS BANK NA	FL	D	09/30/10
DIME BANK	PA	D	09/30/10
EMBASSY NATIONAL BK	GA	D	09/30/10
ENCORE BANK NA	TX	D	09/30/10
EXCHANGE BANK	GA	D	09/30/10
EXCHANGE NB COTTONWOOD FALLS	KS	D	09/30/10
F & M BANK & TRUST CO	GA	D+	09/30/10
FARMERS & MERCHANTS BANK	OH	D	09/30/10
FARMERS STATE BK OF W CONCORD	MN	D	09/30/10
FIDELITY BANK	GA	D	09/30/10
FIRST BANK OF DALTON	GA	D	09/30/10
FIRST BANK OF MIAMI	FL	D	09/30/10
FIRST BUSINESS BANK	WI	D	09/30/10
FIRST CENTURY BANK	TN	C-	09/30/10
FIRST COMMUNITY BANK	MO	D+	09/30/10
FIRST ENTERPRISE BANK	OK	D	09/30/10
FIRST FIDELITY BANK NA	OK	D	09/30/10
FIRST NATIONAL BK GRANT PARK	IL	D	09/30/10
FIRST NATIONAL BK GULF COAST	FL	D	09/30/10
FIRST NATIONAL BK OF LINDSAY	OK	D	09/30/10
FIRST NATIONAL BK OF THE LAKES	MN	D	09/30/10
FIRST NATIONAL BK POLK COUNTY	GA	D	09/30/10
FIRST OKLAHOMA BANK	OK	C-	09/30/10
FIRST SECURITY BANK	MO	D	09/30/10
FIRST SECURITY BANK	MT	D	09/30/10
FIRST SOUTH BANK	NC	D	09/30/10
FIRST SOUTHWEST BANK	CO	D	09/30/10
FIRST STATE BK	AR	D	09/30/10
FIRST STATE BK	NE	D	09/30/10
FIRSTCITY BANK OF COMMERCE	FL	D	09/30/10
FLATIRONS BANK	CO	D	09/30/10
FLORIDA BANK OF COMMERCE	FL	D	09/30/10
FLORIDA SHORES BANK-SOUTHEAST	FL	D	09/30/10
FOLSOM LAKE BANK	CA	D	09/30/10
GATEWAY BANK OF SOUTHWEST FL	FL	D	09/30/10
GOLD COUNTRY BANK NA	CA	D+	09/30/10
GREENBANK	TN	D	09/30/10
GULFSHORE BANK	FL	D+	09/30/10
HANOVER COMMUNITY BANK	NY	D+	09/30/10
HOME FS&LA OF COLLINSVILLE	IL	D	09/30/10

Rating Downgrades (Continued)

Rating: D- (Continued)

BANK NAME	STATE	PREVIOUS RATING	DATE OF CHANGE
HOME SB	WI	D	09/30/10
HOMETOWN BANK NA	MO	D	09/30/10
HOMETOWN COMMUNITY BANK	MN	D	09/30/10
INDEPENDENT BANK OF TEXAS	TX	D	09/30/10
INLAND BANK & TRUST	IL	D	09/30/10
KENTUCKY FS&LA	KY	D	09/30/10
LAKE BANK	MN	D	09/30/10
LAKEWOOD BANK NA	MN	D	09/30/10
MERCANTILE BANK	IL	D	09/30/10
MERCHANTS & SOUTHERN BANK	FL	D	09/30/10
MONROE COUNTY BANK	GA	D	09/30/10
NATIONAL BK OF CAMBRIDGE	MD	D	09/30/10
NEW FOUNDATION SAVINGS BANK	OH	D	09/30/10
NEW WINDSOR STATE BK	MD	D	09/30/10
OJAI COMMUNITY BANK	CA	C-	09/30/10
OLMSTED NATIONAL BK	MN	D	09/30/10
OREGON PACIFIC BANKING CO	OR	D	09/30/10
PARKE BANK	NJ	D	09/30/10
PARKWAY BANK	AR	D	09/30/10
PEABODY STATE BK	KS	D	09/30/10
PEOPLES BANK	MD	D	09/30/10
PEOPLES BANK OF EAST TENNESSEE	TN	D+	09/30/10
PEOPLES COMMUNITY NATIONAL BK	GA	D	09/30/10
PEOPLES STATE BK FAIRMOUNT ND	ND	D+	09/30/10
PEOPLES STATE BK OF COMMERCE	TN	D	09/30/10
PILSEN ST BK LINCOLNVILLE KS	KS	D	09/30/10
PREFERRED COMMUNITY BANK	FL	D	09/30/10
PUEBLO BANK & TRUST CO	CO	D	09/30/10
PULASKI BANK	MO	D	09/30/10
REUNION BANK OF FLORIDA	FL	D+	09/30/10
REVERE BANK	MD	D	09/30/10
RHINEBECK SB	NY	D	09/30/10
RIO BANK	TX	D	09/30/10
SECURITY BANK OF PULASKI COUNT	MO	D	09/30/10
SECURITY FINANCIAL BANK	WI	D+	09/30/10
SIGNATURE BANK	MN	D	09/30/10
SOUTH ATLANTIC BANK	SC	D	09/30/10
SOUTHERN COMMERCIAL BANK	MO	D	09/30/10
STATE BK OF GENEVA	IL	C-	09/30/10
TIMBERLINE BANK	CO	D	09/30/10
TURTLE MOUNTAIN STATE BK	ND	D+	09/30/10
UNION BANK	MI	D	09/30/10
URBAN PARTNERSHIP BANK	IL	D+	09/30/10
VIRGINIA COMMONWEALTH BANK	VA	C-	09/30/10
WOODBURY BANKING CO	GA	D	09/30/10

Rating: E+

BANK NAME	STATE	PREVIOUS RATING	DATE OF CHANGE
ATLANTIC COMMUNITY BANK	SC	D-	09/30/10
BANK OF CORAL GABLES	FL	D-	09/30/10
BANK OF LAS COLINAS	TX	D-	09/30/10
BANK OF PALATINE	IL	D-	09/30/10
BANK OF SOUTH TEXAS	TX	D-	09/30/10
BANK OF THE CAROLINAS	NC	D-	09/30/10
BANK OF THE COMMONWEALTH	VA	D-	09/30/10
BANK OF WESTMINSTER	SC	D-	09/30/10
BENCHMARK BANK	OH	D-	09/30/10
BISCAYNE BANK	FL	D-	09/30/10
BROOKLYN FSB	NY	D-	09/30/10
CAPITAL BANK	NC	D-	09/30/10
CENTRAL FLORIDA STATE BK	FL	D-	09/30/10
CITIZENS BANK OF CHATSWORTH	IL	D	09/30/10
CLOVER COMMUNITY BANK	SC	D-	09/30/10
CNLBANK	FL	D-	09/30/10
COCONUT GROVE BANK	FL	D-	09/30/10
COMMUNITY BANK OF SAN JOAQUIN	CA	D-	09/30/10
CONCORD BANK	MO	D	09/30/10
CURRIE STATE BK	MN	D-	09/30/10
DORAL BANK FSB	NY	D-	09/30/10
EXCEL BANK	MO	D-	09/30/10
FARMERS STATE BK OF DENT	MN	D-	09/30/10
FIRST ASIAN BANK	NV	D-	09/30/10
FIRST BANK	FL	D-	09/30/10
FIRST NATIONAL BK OF BUHL	MN	D-	09/30/10
FIRST NATIONAL COMMUNITY BANK	PA	D-	09/30/10
FLAGSHIP BANK WINSTED	MN	D-	09/30/10
FLORIDA BANK	FL	D-	09/30/10
FRIENDS BANK	FL	D-	09/30/10
GOLD CANYON BANK	AZ	D-	09/30/10
GULFSOUTH PRIVATE BANK	FL	D-	09/30/10
HARBOR BANK OF MARYLAND	MD	D-	09/30/10
HEARTLAND BANK	MO	D-	09/30/10
INDEPENDENCE NATIONAL BK	SC	D-	09/30/10
JASPER BANKING CO	GA	D-	09/30/10
LAKE REGION BANK	MN	D-	09/30/10
MCCLAVE STATE BK	CO	D-	09/30/10
NEW MILLENNIUM BANK	NJ	D-	09/30/10
PARAGON COMMERCIAL BANK	NC	D-	09/30/10
RELIANCE BANK	MO	D-	09/30/10
RELIANCE BANK FSB	FL	D-	09/30/10
RELIANT BANK	TN	D-	09/30/10
SUNFIRST BANK	UT	D-	09/30/10
TEXAS COASTAL BANK	TX	D-	09/30/10
UNITED MINNESOTA BANK	MN	D	09/30/10

Rating: E

BANK NAME	STATE	PREVIOUS RATING	DATE OF CHANGE
AMERICAN METRO BANK	IL	D-	09/30/10
ARTHUR STATE BK	SC	E+	09/30/10
BANK OF FORT BEND	TX	D-	09/30/10
BANK VI	KS	E+	09/30/10
BOUNDARY WATERS BANK	MN	D-	09/30/10
CASCADE BANK	WA	D-	09/30/10
COAST NATIONAL BK	CA	D-	09/30/10
FARMERS & MERCH NB OF HATTON	ND	E+	09/30/10
FARMERS BANK OF LYNCHBURG	TN	D-	09/30/10
FIRST COMMUNITY BK THE OZARKS	MO	D-	09/30/10
FIRST NATIONAL BK GERMANTOWN	OH	D-	09/30/10
FIRST NATIONAL BK OF WAYNE	NE	D-	09/30/10
FOUR OAKS BANK & TRUST CO	NC	D-	09/30/10
GLASGOW SB	MO	D-	09/30/10
GLOBAL COMMERCE BANK	GA	D-	09/30/10
GRAND RIVERS COMMUNITY BANK	IL	D-	09/30/10
INDUS AMERICAN BANK	NJ	D-	09/30/10
NORTHWEST BANK	OR	D-	09/30/10
OCEAN BANK	FL	E+	09/30/10
ORANGE BANK OF FLORIDA	FL	D-	09/30/10
OXFORD BANK & TRUST	IL	D-	09/30/10
PARADISE BANK	FL	D-	09/30/10
PARK CITIES BANK	TX	D-	09/30/10
ROCKY MOUNTAIN BANK	WY	D-	09/30/10
SECURITY BANK NA	FL	D-	09/30/10
SHERBURNE STATE BK	MN	D-	09/30/10
TRI VALLEY BANK	NE	D-	09/30/10
UNITED AMERICAN BANK	CA	D	09/30/10
VENTURA COUNTY BUSINESS BANK	CA	D-	09/30/10

Rating: E-

BANK NAME	STATE	PREVIOUS RATING	DATE OF CHANGE
ACCESS 1ST CAPITAL BANK	TX	E	09/30/10
ALABAMA TRUST BANK NA	AL	E	09/30/10
ALLEGIANCE COMMUNITY BANK	NJ	E	09/30/10
ANCHOR COMMERCIAL BANK	FL	E	09/30/10

Rating Downgrades (Continued)

Rating: E- (Continued)

BANK NAME	STATE	PREVIOUS RATING	DATE OF CHANGE
BAILEYVILLE STATE BK	KS	E	09/30/10
BANK 360	SD	E+	09/30/10
BANK OF CHOICE	CO	E	09/30/10
BANK OF ELK RIVER	MN	E+	09/30/10
BANK OF NEWINGTON	GA	E	09/30/10
BANK OF THE EASTERN SHORE	MD	E	09/30/10
BANK OF WAUSAU	WI	D-	09/30/10
BANKWEST	MN	E+	09/30/10
BARWICK BANKING CO	GA	E	09/30/10
BAYTREE NATIONAL BK & TRUST CO	IL	E+	09/30/10
BRIGHTON BANK	TN	D-	09/30/10
CENTRUST BANK NA	IL	D-	09/30/10
CHEROKEE BANK NA	GA	D-	09/30/10
CITIZENS BANK & TRUST	FL	D-	09/30/10
CITIZENS BANK OF EAST TENNESSE	TN	D-	09/30/10
CMMNTY BK-WHEATON/GLEN ELLYN	IL	E+	09/30/10
COASTAL BANK	FL	D-	09/30/10
COASTAL COMMUNITY BANK	WA	E+	09/30/10
COLONIAL AMERICAN BANK	PA	E	09/30/10
COLORADO CAPITAL BANK	CO	E	09/30/10
COMMUNITY SOUTH BANK	TN	D-	09/30/10
COMMUNITY STATE BK	TX	E	09/30/10
CORTEZ COMMUNITY BANK	FL	D-	09/30/10
CREDICARD NATIONAL BK	AZ	E	09/30/10
DUPAGE NATIONAL BK	IL	E	09/30/10
EXCHANGE BANK	OK	E	09/30/10
FARMERS STATE BK	GA	E+	09/30/10
FIRST CAROLINA STATE BK	NC	E+	09/30/10
FIRST CHICAGO BANK & TRUST	IL	E	09/30/10
FIRST FINANCIAL BANK	AL	D-	09/30/10
FIRST INTERNATIONAL BK	TX	E	09/30/10
FIRST NATIONAL BK	KS	E	09/30/10
FIRST NATIONAL BK OF CRESTVIEW	FL	E+	09/30/10
FIRST SOUTH BANK	SC	E+	09/30/10
FIRST SOUTHERN NATIONAL BK	GA	E+	09/30/10
FIRST STATE BK	NJ	D-	09/30/10
FLAGSHIP BANK MINNESOTA	MN	D-	09/30/10
FORT LEE FEDERAL SAVINGS BANK	NJ	D-	09/30/10
FREEDOM BANK OF AMERICA	FL	D-	09/30/10
FRONTENAC BANK	MO	E	09/30/10
FRONTIER BANK FSB	CA	E	09/30/10
GOLDEN SECURITY BANK	CA	E	09/30/10
GOLDEN STATE BK	CA	E	09/30/10
GRAND BANK & TRUST OF FLORIDA	FL	E+	09/30/10
GREAT FLORIDA BANK	FL	E+	09/30/10
GULF COAST COMMUNITY BANK	FL	E	09/30/10
HEARTLAND BANK	KS	D-	09/30/10
HERITAGE BANK	GA	E+	09/30/10
HOME SAVINGS OF AMERICA	MN	E	09/30/10
HORRY COUNTY STATE BK	SC	E+	09/30/10
INTEGRITY FIRST BANK	WI	E	09/30/10
LEAD BANK	MO	D-	09/30/10
LONE SUMMIT BANK	MO	E+	09/30/10
MID CITY BANK INC	NE	D-	09/30/10
MONROE BANK & TRUST	MI	E	09/30/10
NEWDOMINION BANK	NC	E+	09/30/10
PATRIOT BANK MINNESOTA	MN	E+	09/30/10
PREMIER BANK	IL	D-	09/30/10
PREMIER CMNTY BK EMERALD COAST	FL	D-	09/30/10
PRIME PACIFIC BANK NA	WA	D-	09/30/10
PRIMESOUTH BANK	GA	E	09/30/10
PROSPERITY BANK	FL	E	09/30/10
PROVIDENT COMMUNITY BANK NA	SC	D-	09/30/10
ROYAL PALM BANK OF FLORIDA	FL	D-	09/30/10
SECURITY SB SSB	NC	E	09/30/10
SOUTH COUNTY BANK NA	CA	E	09/30/10
SOUTHPOINT BANK	AL	E+	09/30/10
SUMMIT BANK	WA	E	09/30/10
TIDELANDS BANK	SC	E+	09/30/10
TREASURE STATE BK	MT	D-	09/30/10
TRI-VALLEY BANK	CA	D-	09/30/10
WESTSIDE BANK	GA	D-	09/30/10
WINFIELD COMMUNITY BANK	IL	E+	09/30/10

Rating: F

BANK NAME	STATE	PREVIOUS RATING	DATE OF CHANGE
FIRST NATIONAL BK OF DAVIS	OK	C	09/30/10
LEGACY BANK	WI	E-	09/30/10

Rating: U

BANK NAME	STATE	PREVIOUS RATING	DATE OF CHANGE
BARCLAYS WEALTH TRUSTEES (US)	DE	D	09/30/10
NEUBERGER BERMAN TRUST CO DE	DE	C	09/30/10
NEUBERGER BERMAN TRUST CO NA	NY	B-	09/30/10
US BANK TRUST CO NA	OR	D-	09/30/10

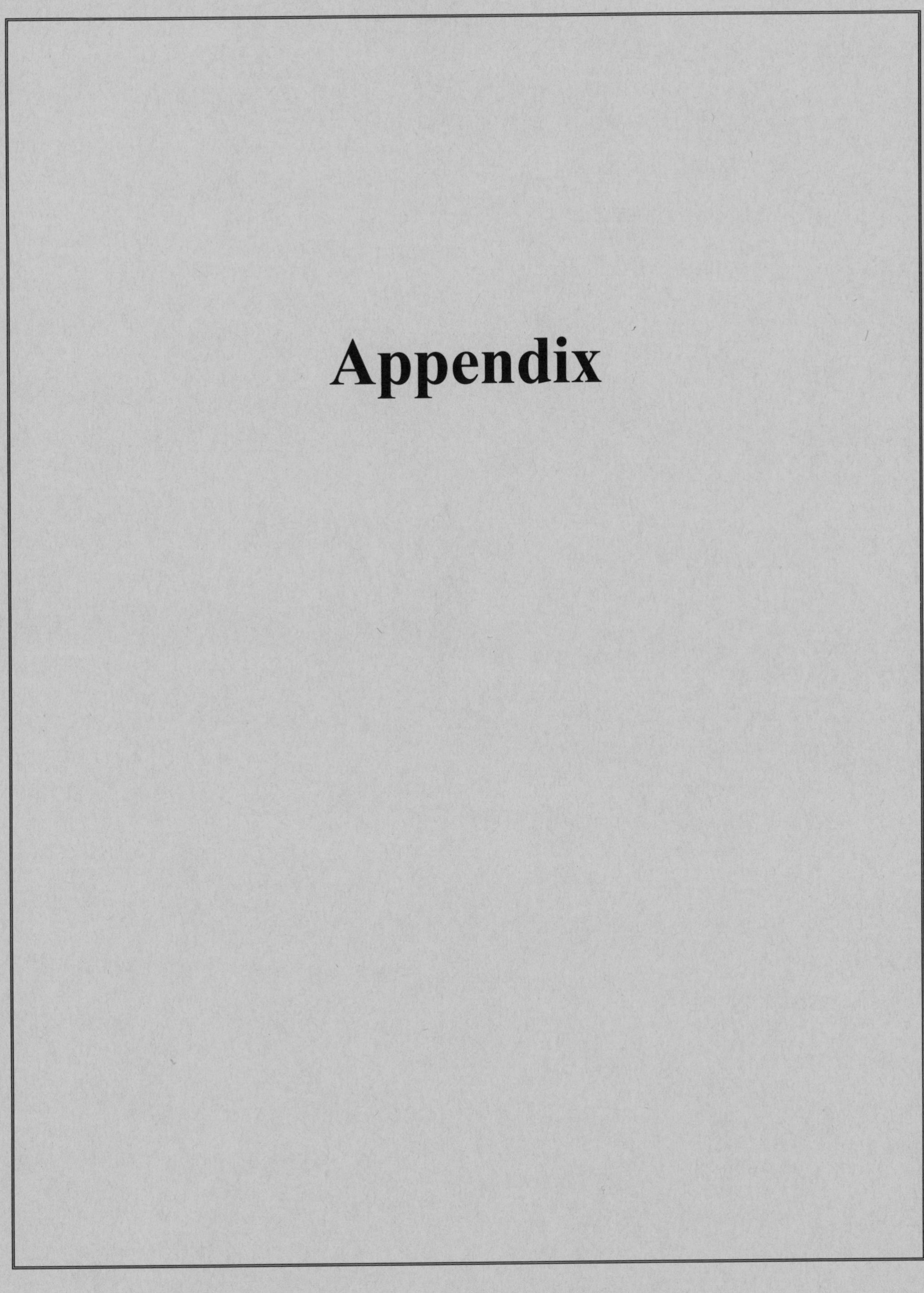

Appendix

RECENT BANK AND THRIFT FAILURES

2011

Institution	Headquarters	Date of Failure	At Date of Failure	
			Total Assets ($Mil)	Financial Strength Rating
First National Bank of Davis	Davis, OK	03/11/11	90.2	C (Fair)
Legacy Bank	Milwaukee, WI	03/11/11	190.4	E-(Very Weak)
Valley Community Bank	St. Charles, IL	02/25/11	123.8	E-(Very Weak)
Charter Oak Bank	Napa, CA	02/18/11	120.8	E-(Very Weak)
Citizens Bank of Effingham	Springfield, GA	02/18/11	214.3	E-(Very Weak)
Habersham Bank	Clarkesville, GA	02/18/11	387.6	E-(Very Weak)
San Luis Trust Bank FSB	San Luis Obispo, CA	02/18/11	332.6	E-(Very Weak)
Badger State Bank	Cassville, WI	02/11/11	83.8	E-(Very Weak)
Canyon National Bank	Palm Springs, CA	02/11/11	210.9	E-(Very Weak)
Peoples State Bank	Hamtramck, MI	02/11/11	390.5	E-(Very Weak)
Sunshine State Community Bank	Port Orange, FL	02/11/11	125.5	E-(Very Weak)
American Trust Bank	Roswell, GA	02/04/11	238.2	E-(Very Weak)
Community First Bank	Chicago, IL	02/04/11	51.1	E-(Very Weak)
North Georgia Bank	Watkinsville, GA	02/04/11	153.2	E-(Very Weak)
Evergreen State Bank	Stoughton, WI	01/28/11	246.5	E-(Very Weak)
First Community Bank	Taos, NM	01/28/11	2310.0	E-(Very Weak)
First State Bank	Camargo, OK	01/28/11	43.5	C- (Fair)
FirsTier Bank	Broomfield, CO	01/28/11	781.5	E-(Very Weak)
Bank of Asheville	Asheville, NC	01/21/11	195.1	E-(Very Weak)
CommunitySouth Bank & Trust	Easley, SC	01/21/11	440.6	E-(Very Weak)
Enterprise Banking Co	McDonough, GA	01/21/11	100.9	E-(Very Weak)
United Western bank	Denver, CO	01/21/11	1650.0	E-(Very Weak)
Oglethorpe Bank	Brunswick, GA	01/14/11	230.6	E- (Very Weak)

First Commercial Bank of Fl.	Orlando, FL	01/07/11	598.5	E- (Very Weak)
Legacy Bank	Scottsdale, AZ	01/07/11	150.6	E- (Very Weak)

2010

Institution	Headquarters	Date of Failure	At Date of Failure	
			Total Assets ($Mil)	Financial Strength Rating
Appalachian Comm. Bank FSB	McCaysville, GA	12/17/10	68.2	E- (Very Weak)
Bank of Miami	Coral Gables, FL	12/17/10	448.2	E- (Very Weak)
Chestatee State Bank	Dawsonville, GA	12/17/10	244.4	E- (Very Weak)
Community National Bank	Lino Lakes, MN	12/17/10	31.6	D- (Weak)
First Southern Bank	Batesville, AR	12/17/10	191.8	C- (Fair)
United Americas Bank NA	Atlanta, GA	12/17/10	242.3	E- (Very Weak)
Earthstar Bank	Southampton, PA	12/17/10	112.6	E- (Very Weak)
Paramount Bank	Farmington Hills, MI	12/10/10	252.7	E- (Very Weak)
Allegiance Bank of N. America	Bala Cynwyc, PA	11/19/10	106.6	E- (Very Weak)
First Banking Center	Burlington, WI	11/19/10	750.7	E- (Very Weak)
Gulf State Commercial Bank	Carrabelle, FL	11/19/10	112.1	E- (Very Weak)
Copper State Bank	Scottsdale, AZ	11/12/10	204.0	E- (Very Weak)
Darby Bank & Trust Co	Vidalia, GA	11/12/10	654.7	E- (Very Weak)
Tifton Banking Co	Tifton, GA	11/12/10	143.7	E- (Very Weak)
First Vietnamese American Bank	Westminster, CA	11/05/10	48.0	E- (Very Weak)
K Bank	Randallstown, MD	11/05/10	538.3	E- (Very Weak)
Pierce Commercial Bank	Tacoma, WA	11/05/10	221.1	E- (Very Weak)
Western Commercial Bank	Woodland Hills, CA	11/05/10	98.6	E- (Very Weak)
First Arizona Savings a FSB	Scottsdale, AZ	10/22/10	272.2	E- (Very Weak)
First Bank of Jacksonville	Jacksonville, FL	10/22/10	81.0	E- (Very Weak)
First Natinal Bank of Barnesville	Barnesville, GA	10/22/10	131.4	E- (Very Weak)
First Suburban National Bank	Maywood, IL	10/22/10	148.7	E- (Very Weak)

Gordon Bank	Gordon, GA	10/22/10	29.4	E- (Very Weak)
Hillcrest Bank	Overland Park, KS	10/22/10	15400.0	E- (Very Weak)
Progress Bank of Florida	Tampa, FL	10/22/10	110.7	E- (Very Weak)
Premier Bank	Jefferson City, MO	10/15/10	11800.0	E- (Very Weak)
Security Savings Bank FSB	Olathe, KS	10/15/10	508.4	E- (Very Weak)
WestBridge Bank & Trust Co	Chesterfield, MO	10/15/10	91.5	E- (Very Weak)
Shoreline Bank	Shoreline, WA	10/01/10	100.2	E- (Very Weak)
Wakulla Bank	Crawfordville, FL	10/01/10	386.3	E- (Very Weak)
Haven Trust Bank Florida	Point Vedra Beach, FL	09/24/10	133.6	E- (Very Weak)
North County Bank	Arlington, WA	09/24/10	276.1	E- (Very Weak)
Bank of Ellijay	Ellijay, GA	09/17/10	168.8	E- (Very Weak)
Bramble Savings Bank	Milford, OH	09/17/10	47.5	E- (Very Weak)
First Commerce Comm. Bank	Douglasville, GA	09/17/10	248.2	E- (Very Weak)
ISN Bank	Cherry Hill, NJ	09/17/10	81.6	E- (Very Weak)
Maritime Savings Bank	West Allis, WI	09/17/10	350.5	E- (Very Weak)
Peoples Bank	Winder GA	09/17/10	447.2	E- (Very Weak)
Horizon Bank	Bradenton, FL	09/10/10	164.6	E- (Very Weak)
Butte Community Bank	Chico, CA	08/20/10	498.8	E- (Very Weak)
Communiy Natil Bank at Bartow	Bartow, FL	08/20/10	67.9	E (Very Weak)
Imperial Savings & Loan Assoc	Martinsville, VA	08/20/10	9.4	E- (Very Weak)
Independent National Bank	Ocala, FL	08/20/10	156.2	E- (Very Weak)
Los Padres Bank	Solvang, CA	08/20/10	870.4	E- (Very Weak)
Pacific State Bank	Stockton, CA	08/20/10	312.1	E- (Very Weak)
ShoreBank	Chicago, IL	08/20/10	21600.0	E- (Very Weak)
Sonoma Valley Bank	Sonoma, CA	08/20/10	337.1	E- (Very Weak)
Palos Bank & Trust Co	Palos Height, IL	08/13/10	493.4	E- (Very Weak)
Ravenswood Bank	Chicago, IL	08/06/10	264.6	E- (Very Weak)
Bayside Savings Bank	Port St. Joe, FL	07/30/10	66.1	E- (Very Weak)

Coastal Community Bank	Panama City Bch, FL	07/30/10	372.9	E- (Very Weak)
Cowlitz Bank	Longview, WA	07/30/10	529.3	E- (Very Weak)
Liberty Bank	Eugene, OR	07/30/10	768.2	E- (Very Weak)
Northwest Bank & Trust	Acworth, GA	07/30/10	167.7	E- (Very Weak)
Southwest USA Bank	Las Vegas, NV	07/30/10	214.0	E- (Very Weak)
Community Security Bank	New Prague, MN	07/23/10	108.0	E- (Very Weak)
Crescent Bank & Trust Co	Jasper, GA	07/23/10	10100.0	E- (Very Weak)
Home Valley Bank	Cove Junction, OR	07/23/10	251.8	E- (Very Weak)
Sterling Bank	Lantana, FL	07/23/10	407.9	E- (Very Weak)
Thunder Bank	Sylvan Grove, KS	07/23/10	32.6	E- (Very Weak)
Willamsuburg First Natonal Bank	Kingstree, SC	07/23/10	139.3	E- (Very Weak)
First National Bank of the South	Spartanburg, SC	07/16/10	682.0	E- (Very Weak)
Mainstreet Savings Bank FSB	Hastings, MI	07/16/10	97.4	E- (Very Weak)
Metro Bank of Dade County	Miami, FL	07/16/10	442.3	E- (Very Weak)
Olde Cypress Community Bank	Clewiston, FL	07/16/10	168.7	E- (Very Weak)
Turnberry Bank	Aventura ,FL	07/16/10	263.9	E- (Very Weak)
Woodlands Bank	Bluffton,SD	07/16/10	376.2	E- (Very Weak)
Bay National Bank (Lutherville)	Baltimore,MD	07/09/10	282.2	E- (Very Weak)
Home Nat Bank (Arkansas City)	Blackwell,OK	07/09/10	644.5	D- (Weak)
Ideal Federal Savings Bank	Baltimore,MD	07/09/10	6.3	E+ (Very Weak)
USA Bank	Port Chester,NY	07/09/10	193.3	E- (Very Weak)
First National Bank	Savannah,GA	06/25/10	252.5	E- (Very Weak)
High Desert State Bank	Albuquerque,NM	06/25/10	80.3	E- (Very Weak)
Peninsula Bank	Englewood,FL	06/25/10	644.3	E- (Very Weak)
Nevada Security Bank	Reno,NV	06/18/10	480.3	E- (Very Weak)
Washington First Intl. Bank	Seattle,WA	06/11/10	520.9	E- (Very Weak)
Arcola Homestead Savings Bank	Arcola,IL	06/04/10	17.0	C (Fair)
First National Bank	Rosedale,MS	06/04/10	60.4	A- (Excellent)

TierOne Bank	Lincoln,NE	06/04/10	2800.0	E- (Very Weak)
Bank of Florida - Southeast	Ft. Lauderdale,FL	05/28/10	595.3	E- (Very Weak)
Bank of Florida - Southwest	Naples,FL	05/28/10	640.9	E- (Very Weak)
Bank of Florida - Tampa Bay	Tampa Bay,FL	05/28/10	245.2	E- (Very Weak)
Granite Community Bank, NA	Granite Bay,CA	05/28/10	102.9	E- (Very Weak)
Pinehurst Bank	St. Paul,MN	05/28/10	61.2	E- (Very Weak)
Sun West Bank	Las Vegas,NV	05/28/10	360.7	E- (Very Weak)
Midwest Bank & Trust Co	Elmwood Park,IL	05/14/10	31700.0	E- (Very Weak)
New Liberty Bank	Plymouth,MI	05/14/10	109.1	E- (Very Weak)
Satilla Community Bank	Saint Marys,GA	05/14/10	135.7	E- (Very Weak)
Southwest Community Bank	Springfield,MO	05/14/10	96.6	E- (Very Weak)
1st Pacific Bank of California	San Diego,CA	05/07/10	335.8	E- (Very Weak)
Access Bank	Champlin,MN	05/07/10	32.0	E- (Very Weak)
Bank of Bonifay	Bonifay,FL	05/07/10	242.9	E- (Very Weak)
Towne Bank of Arizona	Mesa,AZ	05/07/10	120.2	E- (Very Weak)
BC National Banks	Butler,MO	04/30/10	67.2	E- (Very Weak)
CF Bancorp	Port Huron,MI	04/30/10	16500.0	E- (Very Weak)
Champion Bank	Creve Coeur,MO	04/30/10	187.3	E- (Very Weak)
Eurobank	San Juan,PR	04/30/10	25600.0	E- (Very Weak)
Frontier Bank	Everett,WA	04/30/10	35000.0	E- (Very Weak)
R-G Premier Bank of Puerto Rico	Hato Rey,PR	04/30/10	59200.0	E- (Very Weak)
Westernbank Puerto Rico	Mayaguez,PR	04/30/10	11940.0	E+ (Very Weak)
Amcore Bank NA	Rockford,IL	04/23/10	3800.0	E- (Very Weak)
Broadway Bank	Chicago,IL	04/23/10	1200.0	E- (Very Weak)
Citizens BnkTrust Co of Chicago	Chicago,IL	04/23/10	77.3	E- (Very Weak)
Lincoln Park Savings Bank	Chicago,IL	04/23/10	199.9	E- (Very Weak)
New Century Bank	Chicago,IL	04/23/10	485.6	E- (Very Weak)
Peotone Bank & Trust Co	Peotone,IL	04/23/10	130.2	E- (Very Weak)

Wheatland Bank	Naperville,IL	04/23/10	437.2	E- (Very Weak)
AmericanFirst Bank	Clermont ,IL	04/16/10	90.5	E- (Very Weak)
Butler Bank	Lowell,MA	04/16/10	268.0	E- (Very Weak)
City Bank	Lynnwood,WA	04/16/10	11300.0	E- (Very Weak)
First Federal Bank of N. Florida	Palatka,FL	04/16/10	393.3	E- (Very Weak)
Innovative Bank	Oakland,CA	04/16/10	268.9	E- (Very Weak)
Lakeside Community Bank	Sterling Heights,MI	04/16/10	53.0	E- (Very Weak)
Riverside Natil Bank of Florida	Ft. Pierce,FL	04/16/10	34200.0	E- (Very Weak)
Tamalpais Bank	San Rafael,CA	04/16/10	628.9	E- (Very Weak)
Beach First National Bank	Myrtle Beach, SC	04/09/10	585.1	E- (Very Weak)
Desert Hills Bank	Phoenix, AZ	03/26/10	496.6	E- (Very Weak)
Key West Bank	Key West, FL	03/26/10	88.0	E- (Very Weak)
McIntosh Commercial Bank	Carrolton, GA	03/26/10	362.9	E- (Very Weak)
Unity National Bank	Cartersville, GA	03/26/10	292.2	E- (Very Weak)
Advanta Bank Corp	Draper, UT	03/19/10	1,600.0	E- (Very Weak)
American National Bank	Parma, OH	03/19/10	70.3	E- (Very Weak)
Appalachian Community Bank	Ellijay, GA	03/19/10	10,100.0	E- (Very Weak)
Bank of Hiawassee	Hiawassee, GA	03/19/10	377.8	E- (Very Weak)
Century Security Bank	Duluth, GA	03/19/10	96.5	E- (Very Weak)
First Lownders Bank	Fort Deposit, AL	03/19/10	137.2	E- (Very Weak)
State Bank of Aurora	Aurora, MN	03/19/10	28.2	E- (Very Weak)
Old Southern Bank	Orlando, FL	03/12/10	315.6	E- (Very Weak)
Park Avenue Bank	New York, NY	03/12/10	520.1	E- (Very Weak)
Statewide Bank	Covington, LA	03/12/10	243.2	E- (Very Weak)
LibertyPoint Bank	New York, NY	03/11/10	209.7	E- (Very Weak)
Bank of Illinois	Normal, IL	03/05/10	211.7	E- (Very Weak)
Centennial Bank	Ogden, UT	03/05/10	215.2	E- (Very Weak)
Sun American Bank	Boca Raton, FL	03/05/10	535.7	E- (Very Weak)

Waterfield Bank	Germantown, MD	03/05/10	155.6	E- (Very Weak)
Carson River Community Bank	Carson City, NV	02/26/10	51.1	E- (Very Weak)
Rainier Pacific Bank	Tacoma, WA	02/26/10	717.8	E- (Very Weak)
George Washington Savings Bk	Orland Park, IL	02/19/10	412.8	E- (Vey Weak)
La Coste National Bank	La Coste, TX	02/19/10	53.9	C+ (Fair)
La Jolla Bank FSB	La Jolla, CA	02/19/10	3,600.0	E+ (Very Weak)
Marco Community Bank	Marco Island, FL	02/19/10	119.6	E- (Very Weak)
1st American State Bank of MN	Hancock, MN	02/05/10	18.2	E- (Very Weak)
American Marine Bank	Bainbridge Island, WA	01/29/10	373.2	E- (Very Weak)
Community Bank & Trust	Cornelia, GA	01/29/10	121,000.0	E- (Very Weak)
First Nationl Bank of Georgia	Carrollton, GA	01/29/10	832.6	E- (Very Weak)
First Regional Bank	Los Angeles, CA	01/29/10	218,000.0	E- (Very Weak)
Florida Community Bank	Immokalee, FL	01/29/10	875.5	E- (Very Weak)
Marshall Bank NA	Hallock, MN	01/29/10	59.9	E- (Very Weak)
Bank of Leeton	Leeton, MO	01/22/10	20.1	E- (Very Weak)
Charter Bank	Santa Fe, NM	01/22/10	1,200.0	E- (Very Weak)
Columbia River Bank	The Dalles, OR	01/22/10	1,100.0	E- (Very Weak)
Evergreen Bank	Seattle, WA	01/22/10	488.5	E- (Very Weak)
Premier American Bank	Miami, FL	01/22/10	350.9	E- (Very Weak)
Barnes Banking Co	Kaysville, UT	01/15/10	827.8	E- (Very Weak)
St. Stephen State Bank	St. Stephen, MN	01/15/10	24.7	E- (Very Weak)
Town Community Bank & Trust	Antioch, IL	01/15/10	69.6	E- (Very Weak)
Horizon Bank	Bellingham, WA	01/08/10	1,300.0	E- (Very Weak)

2009

Institution	Headquarters	Date of Failure	At Date of Failure	
			Total Assets ($Mil)	Financial Strength Rating
Citizens State Bank	New Baltimore, MI	12/18/09	168.6	E- (Very Weak)
First Federal Bank of CA	Santa Monica, CA	12/18/09	6,100.0	E (Very Weak)
Imperial Capital Bank	La Jolla, CA	12/18/09	4,000.0	E- (Very Weak)
Independent Bankers Bank	Springfield, IL	12/18/09	585.5	D (Weak)
New South Federal Savings Bank	Irondale , AL	12/18/09	1,500.0	E- (Very Weak)
Peoples First Community Bank	Panama City, FL	12/18/09	1,800.0	E- (Very Weak)
Rockbridge Commercial Bank	Atlanta, GA	12/18/09	294.0	E- (Very Weak)
Republic Federal Bank NA	Miami, FL	12/11/09	433.0	E- (Very Weak)
SolutionsBank	Overland Park, KS	12/11/09	511.1	E- (Very Weak)
Valley Capital Bank NA	Mesa, AZ	12/11/09	40.3	E- (Very Weak)
AmTrust Bank	Cleveland, OH	12/04/09	12,000.0	E- (Very Weak)
Benchmark Bank	Aurora, IL	12/04/09	170.0	E- (Very Weak)
Buckhead Community Bank	Atlanta, GA	12/04/09	874.0	E- (Very Weak)
First Security National Bank	Norcross, GA	12/04/09	128.0	E- (Very Weak)
Greater Atlantic Bank	Reston, VA	12/04/09	203.0	E- (Very Weak)
Tattnall Bank	Reidsville, GA	12/04/09	49.6	E- (Very Weak)
Commerce Bank of SW Florida	Ft. Myers, FL	11/20/09	79.7	E- (Very Weak)
Gateway Bank of St Louis	St. Louis, MI	11/16/09	27.7	E- (Very Weak)
United Security Bank	Sparta, GA	11/16/09	157.0	E- (Very Weak)
Century Bank FSB	Sarasota, FL	11/13/09	728.0	E- (Very Weak)
Orion Bank	Naples, FL	11/13/09	2,700.0	E- (Very Weak)
Pacific Coast National Bank	San Clemente , CA	11/13/09	134.4	E- (Very Weak)
Home Federal Savings Bank	Detroit , MI	11/06/09	14.9	E- (Very Weak)
Prosperan Bank	Oakdale, MN	11/06/09	199.5	E- (Very Weak)

United Commercial Bank	San Francisco, CA	11/06/09	11,200.0	E (Very Weak)
Bank USA NA	Phoenix, AZ	10/30/09	185.0	E (Very Weak)
California National Bank	Los Angeles, CA	10/30/09	7,065.0	E- (Very Weak)
Citizens National Bank	Teague, TX	10/30/09	106.0	D+ (Weak)
Community Bank of Lemont	Lemont , IL	10/30/09	82.0	E- (Very Weak)
Madisonville State Bank	Madisonville, TX	10/30/09	230.0	D- (Weak)
North Houston Bank	Houston, TX	10/30/09	315.0	D- (Weak)
Pacific National Bank	San Francisco, CA	10/30/09	2,132.0	E- (Very Weak)
Park National Bank	Chicago, IL	10/30/09	4,821.0	E (Very Weak)
San Diego National Bank	San Diego, CA	10/30/09	3,396.0	E- (Very Weak)
American United Bank	Lawrenceville, GA	10/23/09	111.0	E- (Very Weak)
Bank of Emwood	Racine, WI	10/23/09	327.4	E- (Very Weak)
First DuPage Bank	Westmont, IL	10/23/09	279.0	E- (Very Weak)
Flagship National Bank	Bradenton, FL	10/23/09	190.0	E- (Very Weak)
Hillcrest Bank Florida	Naples, FL	10/23/09	83.0	E- (Very Weak)
Partners Bank	Naples, FL	10/23/09	65.5	E- (Very Weak)
Riverview Community Bank	Otsego, MN	10/23/09	108.0	E- (Very Weak)
San Joaquin Bank	Bakersfield, CA	10/16/09	775.0	E- (Very Weak)
Jennings State Bank	Spring Grove, MN	10/02/09	56.3	E- (Very Weak)
Southern Colorado Nat.Bank	Pueblo, CO	10/02/09	39.5	E- (Very Weak)
Warren Bank	Warren, MI	10/02/09	538.0	E- (Very Weak)
Georgian Bank	Atlanta, GA	09/25/09	2,000.0	D (Weak)
Irwin Union Bank & Trust	Columbus, IN	09/18/09	27,000.0	E (Very Weak)
Irwin Union FSB	Louisville, KY	09/18/09	493.0	D- (Weak)
Brickwell Community Bank	Woodbury, MN	09/11/09	72.0	E- (Very Weak)
Corus Bank NA	Chicago, IL	09/11/09	7,000.0	E- (Very Weak)
Venture Bank	Lacy, WA	09/11/09	970.0	E- (Very Weak)
First Bank of Kansas City	Kansas City, MO	09/04/09	16.0	E- (Very Weak)

First State Bank	Flagstaff, AZ	09/04/09	105.0	E- (Very Weak)
InBank	Oak Forest, IL	09/04/09	212.0	D- (Weak)
Platinum Community Bank	Rolling Meadows, IL	09/04/09	345.6	D- (Weak)
Affinity Bank	Ventura, CA	08/28/09	1,000.0	E- (Very Weak)
Bradford Bank	Baltimore, MD	08/28/09	452.0	E- (Very Weak)
Mainstreet Bank	Forest Lake, MN	08/28/09	459.0	E- (Very Weak)
CapitalSouth Bank	Birmingham, AL	08/21/09	617.0	E- (Very Weak)
Ebank	Atlanta, GA	08/21/09	143.0	E- (Very Weak)
First Coweta	Newman, GA	08/21/09	167.0	E- (Very Weak)
Guaranty Bank	Austin, TX	08/21/09	13,000.0	E- (Very Weak)
Colonial Bank	Montgomery, AL	08/14/09	2,500.0	D- (Weak)
Community Bank of Arizona	Phoenix, AZ	08/14/09	158.5	E+ (Very Weak)
Community Bank of Nevada	Las Vegas, NV	08/14/09	152,000.0	E- (Very Weak)
Dwelling Hse Svngs/Loan Assoc.	Pittsburgh, PA	08/14/09	13.4	E- (Very Weak)
Union Bank	Gilbert, AZ	08/14/09	124.0	E- (Very Weak)
Community First Bank	Prineville, OR	08/07/09	209.0	E- (Very Weak)
Comm. Nat.Bnk of Sarasota Cnty	Venice, FL	08/07/09	97.0	E- (Very Weak)
First State Bank	Sarasota, FL	08/07/09	463.0	E- (Very Weak)
First Bankamericano	Elizabeth, NJ	07/31/09	166.0	E- (Very Weak)
First State Bank of Altus	Altus, OK	07/31/09	103.4	E- (very Weak)
Integrity Bank	Jupiter, FL	07/31/09	119.0	E- (Very Weak)
Mutual Bank	Harvey, IL	07/31/09	1,600.0	E- (Very Weak)
Peoples Community Bank	West Chester, OH	07/31/09	705.8	E- (Very Weak)
Security Bank of Bibb County	Macon, Ga	07/24/09	1,200.0	E- (Very Weak)
Security Bnk of Gwinnett County	Suwanee, GA	07/24/09	322.0	E- (Very Weak)
Security Bnk of Houston County	Perry, GA	07/24/09	383.0	E- (Very Weak)
Security Bank of Jones County	Gray, GA	07/24/09	453.0	E+ (Very Weak)
Security Bank of North Fulton	Alpharetta, GA	07/24/09	209.0	E- (Very Weak)

Security Bank of North Metro	Woodstock, GA	07/24/09	224.0	E- (Very Weak)
Waterford Village Bank	Clarence, NY	07/24/09	61.4	E- (Very Weak)
Bankfirst	Sioux Falls, SD	07/17/09	275.0	E (Very Weak)
First Piedmont Bank	Winder, GA	07/17/09	115.0	E- (Very Weak)
Temecula Valley Bank	Temecula, CA	07/17/09	1,500.0	E (Very Weak)
Vineyard Bank, NA	Rancho Cucamonga, CA	07/17/09	1,900.0	E- (Very Weak)
Bank of Wyoming	Thermopolis, WY	07/10/09	70.0	E- (Very Weak)
Elizabeth State Bank	Elizabeth, IL	07/02/09	55.5	D+ (Weak)
First National Bank of Danville	Danville, IL	07/02/09	166.0	D+ (Weak)
First State Bank of Winchester	Winchester, IL	07/02/09	36.0	E (Very Weak)
Founders Bank	Worth, IL	07/02/09	962.5	D (Weak)
John Warner Bank	Clinton, IL	07/02/09	70.0	D (Weak)
Millenium State Bank of Texas	Dallas, TX	07/02/09	118.0	E- (Very Weak)
Rock River Bank	Oregon, IL	07/02/09	77.0	D (Weak)
Comm. Bank of West Georgia	Villa Rica, GA	06/26/09	199.4	E- (Very Weak
Horizon Bank	Pine City, MN	06/26/09	87.6	E (Very Weak)
Metro Pacific Bank	Irvine, CA	06/26/09	80.0	E (Very Weak)
Mirae Bank	Los Angeles, Ca	06/26/09	456.0	D- (Weak)
Neighborhood Community Bank	Newman, GA	06/26/09	221.6	E (Very Weak)
First National Bank of Anthony	Anthony, KS	06/19/09	156.9	E- (Very Weak)
Southern Community Bank	Fayetteville, GA	06/19/09	377.0	E- (Very Weak)
Cooperative Bank	Wilmington, NC	06/10/09	970.0	E (Very Weak)
Bank of Lincolnwood	Lincolnwood, IL	06/05/09	214.0	E (Very Weak)
Citizens National Bank	Macomb, IL	05/22/09	437.0	E- (Very Weak)
American Sterling Bank	Sugar Creek, MO	04/17/09	181.0	E- (Very Weak)
Great Basin Bank of Nevada	Elko, NV	04/17/09	270.9	E- (Very Weak)
Cape Fear Bank	Wilmington, NC	04/10/09	492.0	E- (Very Weak)
New Frontier Bank	Greely, CO	04/10/09	2,000.0	D- (Weak)

Omni National Bank	Atlanta, GA	03/27/09	956.0	E- (Very Weak)
Colorado National Bank	Colorado Springs, CO	03/20/09	123.5	D (Weak)
First City Bank	Stockbridge, CA	03/20/09	297.0	D- (Weak)
Team Bank NA	Paola	03/20/09	669.8	D- (Weak)
Freedom Bank of Georgia	Commerce, GA	03/06/09	173.0	E- (Very Weak)
Heritage Community Bank	Glenwood, IL	02/27/09	232.9	E (Very Weak)
Security Savings Bank	Henderson, NV	02/27/09	238.3	E (Very Weak)
Silver Falls Bank	Solverton, OR	02/20/09	131.4	D- (Weak)
Corn Belt Bank & Trust	Pittsfield, IL	02/13/09	271.8	E- (Very Weak)
Pinnacle Bank	Beaverton, OR	02/13/09	73.0	E- (Very Weak)
Riverside Bank of the Gulf Coast	Cape Coral, FL	02/13/09	539.0	E- (Very Weak)
Sherman County Bank	Loup City, NE	02/13/09	129.8	D+ (Weak)
Alliance Bank	Culver City, CA	02/06/09	1.1	E- (Very Weak)
County Bank	Merced, CA	02/06/09	1.7	E- (Very Weak)
First Bank Financial Services	McDonough, GA	02/06/09	337.0	E (Very Weak)
Magnet Bank	Salt Lake City, UT	01/30/09	292.9	E- (Very Weak)
Ocala National Bank	Ocala, FL	01/30/09	223.5	E- (Very Weak)
Suburban Federal Savings Bank	Crofton, MD	01/30/09	360.0	E- (Very Weak)
1st Centennial Bank	Redlands, CA	01/23/09	803.3	E (Very Weak)
Bank of Clark County	Vancouver, WA	01/16/09	446.5	D (Weak)
National Bank of Commerce	Berkeley, IL	01/16/09	430.9	E- (Very Weak)

2008

Institution	Headquarters	Date of Failure	At Date of Failure: Total Assets ($Mil)	At Date of Failure: Financial Strength Rating
Haven Trust Bank	Duluth, GA	12/12/08	572.0	D- (Weak)
Sanderson State Bank	Sanderson, TX	12/12/08	37.0	D+ (Weak)
First Georgia Community Bank	Jackson, GA	12/05/08	237.5	E- (Very Weak)
Community Bank	Loganville, GA	11/21/08	681.0	E- (Very Weak)
Downey Savings & Loan	Minneapolis, MN	11/21/08	3.7	E (Very Weak)
Franklin Bank SSB	Houston, TX	11/07/08	5.1	D- (Weak)
Security Pacific Bank	Los Angeles, CA	11/07/08	561.1	E- (Very Weak)
Freedom Bank	Bradenton, FL	10/31/08	287.0	E- (Very Weak)
Alpha Bank & Trust	Alpharetta, GA	10/24/08	354.1	E- (Very Weak)
Main Street Bank	Northville, MI	10/10/08	98.0	E- (Very Weak)
Meridian Bank	Eldred, IL	10/10/08	39.2	E- (Very Weak)
Washington Mutual Bank	Henderson, NV	09/25/08	299,417.0	D+ (Weak)
Ameribank, Inc.	Northfork, WV	09/19/08	115.0	E- (Very Weak)
Silver State Bank	Henderson, NV	09/05/08	2.0	D (Weak)
Integrity Bank	Alpharetta, GA	08/29/08	1.1	E- (Very Weak)
The Columbian Bank & Trust Co	Topeka, KS	08/22/08	735.0	D- (Weak)
First Priority Bank	Bradenton, FL	08/01/08	259.0	E- (Very Weak)
First Heritage Bank, N.A.	Newport Beach, CA	07/25/08	250.0	D+ (Weak)
First National Bank of Nevada	Reno, NV	07/25/08	3.4	D- (Weak)
IndyMac Bank, FSB	Pasadena, CA	07/11/08	32.0	E- (Very Weak)
First Integrity Bank, Nat. Assoc.	Staples, MN	05/30/08	54.7	C- (Fair)
ANB Financial, Nat. Assoc.	Bentonville, AR	05/09/08	1,929.0	E (Very Weak)
Hume Bank	Hume, MO	03/10/08	18.7	D (Weak)
Douglass National Bank	Kansas City, MO	01/25/08	61.0	E- (Very Weak)

2007

Institution	Headquarters	Date of Failure	At Date of Failure	
			Total Assets ($Mil)	Financial Strength Rating
Miami Valley Bank	Quincy, OH	10/04/07	86.7	E- (Very Weak)
NetBank	Alpharetta, GA	09/28/07	2,500.0	E- (Very Weak)
Metropolitan Savings Bank	Pittsburgh, PA	02/02/07	15.8	D- (Weak)

2006

Institution	Headquarters	Date of Failure	At Date of Failure	
			Total Assets ($Mil)	Financial Strength Rating
No banks or thrifts failed in 2006.				

How Do Banks and Credit Unions Differ?

Since credit unions first appeared in 1946, they have been touted as a low-cost, friendly alternative to banks. But with tightening margins, pressure to compete in technology, branch closures, and the introduction of a host of service fees — some even higher than those charged by banks — the distinction between banks and credit unions has been gradually narrowing. Following are the key differences between today's banks and credit unions.

	Banks	Credit Unions
Access	Practically anyone is free to open an account or request a loan from any bank or thrift. There are no membership requirements.	Credit unions are set up to serve the needs of a specific group who share a "common bond." In order to open an account or request a loan, you must demonstrate that you meet the credit union's common bond requirements.
Ownership	Banks are owned by one or more investors who determine the bank's policies and procedures. A bank's customers do not have direct input into how the bank is operated.	Although they may be sponsored by a corporation or other entity, credit unions are owned by their members through their funds on deposit. Therefore, each depositor has a voice in how the credit union is operated.
Dividends and Fees	Banks and thrifts are for-profit organizations where the profits are used to pay dividends to the bank's investors or are reinvested in an effort to increase the bank's value to investors. In an effort to generate more profits, bank services and fees are typically more costly.	Credit unions are not-for-profit organizations. Any profits generated are returned to the credit union's members in the form of higher interest rates on deposits, lower loan rates, and free or low-cost services.
Management and Staffing	A bank's management and other staff are employees of the bank, hired directly or indirectly by its investors.	Credit unions are frequently run using elected members, volunteer staff, and staff provided by the credit union's sponsor. This helps to hold down costs.
Insurance	Banks and thrifts are insured by the Federal Deposit Insurance Corporation, an agency of the federal government.	Credit unions are insured by the National Credit Union Share Insurance Fund, which is managed by the National Credit Union Administration, an agency of the federal government.

Glossary

This glossary contains the most important terms used in this publication.

ARM Adjustable-Rate Mortgage. This is a loan whose interest rate is tied to an index and is adjusted at a predetermined frequency. An ARM is subject to credit risk if interest rates rise and the borrower is unable to make the mortgage payment.

Average Recession A recession involving a decline in real GDP that is approximately equivalent to the average of the postwar recessions of 1957-58, 1960, 1970, 1974-75, 1980 and 1981-82. It is assumed, however, that in today's market, the financial losses suffered from a recession of that magnitude would be greater than those experienced in previous decades. (See also "Severe Recession.")

Bank Holding Company A company that holds stock in one or more banks and possibly other companies.

Brokered Deposits Deposits that are brought into an institution through a broker. They are relatively costly, volatile funds that are more readily withdrawn from the institution if there is a loss of confidence or intense interest rate competition. Reliance on brokered deposits is usually a sign that the institution is having difficulty attracting deposits from its local geographic markets and could be a warning signal if other institutions in the same areas are not experiencing similar difficulties.

Capital The cushion an institution has of its own resources to help withstand losses. The basic component of capital is stockholder's equity which consists of common and preferred stock and retained earnings. (See also "Core Capital")

Cash & Equivalents Cash plus highly liquid assets which can be readily converted to cash.

Core (Tier 1) Capital A measurement of capital defined by the federal regulatory agencies for evaluating an institution's degree of leverage. Core capital consists of the following: common stockholder's equity, preferred stockholder's equity up to certain limits, and retained earnings net of any intangible assets.

Critical Ranges Guidelines developed to help you evaluate the levels of each index contributing to a company's Weiss Financial Strength Rating. The sum or average of these grades does not necessarily have a one-to-one correspondence with the final rating for an institution because the rating is derived from a wider range of more complex calculations.

Equity Total assets minus total liabilities. This is the "capital cushion" the institution has to fall back on in times of trouble. (See also "Capital.")

FDIC Federal Deposit Insurance Corporation. The provider of insurance on deposits. This agency also plays an active role when banks and thrifts are found to be insolvent or in need of federal assistance. It is the governing body of both the Bank Insurance Fund (BIF) and the Savings Association Insurance Fund (SAIF).

Federal Home Loan Bank (FHLB) A quasi-governmental agency (reporting to the Federal Housing Finance Board) whose chartered purpose is to promote the issuance of mortgage loans by providing increased liquidity to lenders. This agency raises money by issuing notes and bonds and then lends the money to thrifts and other mortgage lenders.

Federal Reserve America's central bank, regulating all banks that offer transaction accounts. It works hand-in-hand with the FDIC, providing examination and regulation of its member banks.

Federal Savings and Loan Insurance Corporation (FSLIC) The now-defunct agency of the Federal Home Loan Bank Board that provided deposit insurance to savings and loans until it was replaced by the Savings Association Insurance Fund (SAIF) in 1989. The FSLIC was also responsible for examining thrifts and liquidating insolvent institutions. Savings and loans are now examined by the Office of Thrift Supervision and liquidated by the FDIC.

Financial Strength Rating Weiss Financial Strength Ratings, which grade institutions on a scale from A (Excellent) to F (Failed). Ratings are based on many factors, emphasizing capitalization, asset quality, profitability, liquidity, and stability.

FSB Federal Savings Bank. A thrift institution operating under a federal charter.

Goodwill The value of an institution as a going concern, meaning the value which exceeds book value on a balance sheet. It generally represents the value of a well-respected business name, good customer relations, high employee morale and other intangible factors which would be expected to translate into greater than normal earning power. In a bank or thrift acquisition, goodwill is the value paid by a buyer of the institution in excess of the value of the institution's equity because of these intangible factors.

Hot Money Individual deposits of $100,000 or more plus those deposits received through a broker. These types of deposits are considered "hot money" because they tend to chase whoever is offering the best interest rates at the time and are thus relatively costly and fairly volatile sources of funds.

Loan Loss Reserves The amount of capital an institution sets aside to cover any potential losses due to the nonrepayment of loans.

N.A. National Association. A commercial bank operating under a federal charter.

Net Charge-offs The amount of foreclosed loans written off the institution's books since the beginning of the year, less any previous write-offs that were recovered during the year.

Net Interest Spread The difference between the interest income earned on the institution's loans and investments and the interest expense paid on its interest-bearing deposits and borrowings. This "spread" is most commonly analyzed as a percentage of average earning assets to show the institution's net return on income-generating assets.

Since the margin between interest earned and interest paid is generally where the company generates the majority of its income, this figure provides insight into the company's ability to effectively manage interest spreads. A low Net Interest Spread can be the result of poor loan and deposit pricing, high levels of nonaccruing loans, or poor asset/liability management.

Net Profit or Loss The bottom line income or loss the institution has sustained in its most recent reporting period.

Nonaccruing Loans Loans for which payments are past due and full repayment is doubtful. Interest income on these loans is no longer recorded on the income statement. (See also "Past Due Loans.")

Nonperforming Loans The sum of loans past due 90 days or more and nonaccruing loans. These are loans the institution made where full repayment is now doubtful. (See also "Past Due Loans" and "Nonaccruing Loans.")

Past Due Loans Loans for which payments are at least 90 days in arears. The institution continues to record income on these loans, even though none is actually being received, because it is expected that the borrower will eventually repay the loan in full. It is likely, however, that at least a portion of these loans will move into nonaccruing status. (See also "Nonaccruing Loans.")

OCC Office of the Comptroller of the Currency. This agency of the U.S. Treasury Department is the primary regulator of national banks.

OTS Office of Thrift Supervision. This regulatory agency of the U.S. Treasury Department is responsible for chartering, examining, and supervising savings and loan institutions.

Overhead Expense Expenses of the institution other than interest expense, such as salaries and benefits of employees, rent and utility expenses, and data processing expenses. A certain amount of "fixed" overhead is required to operate a bank or thrift, so it is important that the institution leverage that overhead to the fullest extent in supporting its revenue-generating activities.

RBCR See "Risk-Based Capital Ratio."

Resolution Trust Corporation (RTC) The now-defunct federal agency that was formed to handle the liquidation of insolvent savings and loans.

Restructured Loans Loans whose terms have been modified in order to enable the borrower to make payments which he otherwise would be unable to make. Modifications could include a reduction in the interest rate or a lengthening of the time to maturity.

Risk-Based Capital Ratio A ratio originally developed by the International Committee on Banking as a means of assessing the adequacy of an institution's capital in relation to the amount of credit risk on and off its balance sheet. (See also "Risk-weighted Assets.")

Risk-Weighted Assets The sum of assets and certain off-balance sheet items after they have been individually adjusted for the level of credit risk they pose to the institution. Assets with close to no risk are weighted 0%; those with minor risk are weighted 20%; those with low risk, 50%; and those with normal or high risk, 100%.

R.O.A Return on Assets calculated as net profit or loss as a percentage of average assets. This is the most commonly used measure of bank profitability.

R.O.E.	Return on Equity calculated as net profit or loss as a percentage of average equity. This represents the rate of return on the shareholders' investment.
S.A.	Savings Association.
Savings and Loan (S&L)	A financial institution that traditionally offered primarily home mortgages to individuals and served small depositors. However, in 1980, savings and loans were given power to diversify into other areas of lending. Also known as a thrift.
Savings and Loan Holding Company	A company that holds stock in one or more savings and loans and possibly other companies.
Savings Association Insurance Fund (SAIF)	Fund created in 1989 by Congress to replace the FSLIC as the provider of deposit insurance to thrifts. This fund is administered by the Federal Deposit Insurance Corporation (FDIC). (See also "Bank Insurance Fund.")
Savings Bank	A financial institution created to serve primarily the small saver and to lend mortgage money to individuals. Though savings banks have expanded their services, they are still primarily engaged in providing consumer mortgages and accepting consumer deposits. Also known as a thrift.
Severe Recession	A drop in real GDP which is significantly greater than that of an average postwar recession. (See also "Average Recession.")
Stockholder's Equity	See "Equity."
Thrift	Generic term for an institution formed primarily as a depository for consumer savings and a lender for home mortgages, such as a savings and loan or a savings bank.
Total Assets	Total resources of an institution, primarily composed of cash, securities (such as municipal and treasury bonds), loans, and fixed assets (such as real estate, buildings, and equipment).
Total Equity	See "Equity."
Total Liabilities	All debts owed by an institution. Normally, the largest liability of a bank or thrift is its deposits.
Trust Company	A financial institution chartered to provide trust services (legal agreements to act for the benefit of another party), which may also be authorized to provide banking services.